CRITICAL SURVEY
OF
POETRY

CRITICAL SURVEY

OF

POETRY

Second Revised Edition

Volume 7

Robert Louis Stevenson - Stefan Zweig

Editor, Second Revised Edition
Philip K. Jason
United States Naval Academy

Editor, First Edition, English and Foreign Language Series
Frank N. Magill

SALEM PRESS, INC.
Pasadena, California   Hackensack, New Jersey

Editor in Chief: Dawn P. Dawson
Managing Editor: Christina J. Moose
Developmental Editor: Tracy Irons-Georges
Research Supervisor: Jeffry Jensen
Acquisitions Editor: Mark Rehn
Photograph Editor: Philip Bader
Manuscript Editors: Sarah Hilbert, Leslie Ellen Jones,
Melanie Watkins, Rowena Wildin
Assistant Editor: Andrea E. Miller
Research Assistant: Jeff Stephens
Production Editor: Cynthia Beres
Layout: Eddie Murillo

Library of Congress Cataloging-in-Publication Data

Critical survey of poetry / Philip K. Jason, editor.—2nd rev. ed.
    p. cm.
Combined ed. of: Critical survey of poetry: foreign language series, originally published 1984, Critical survey of poetry: supplement, originally published 1987, and Critical survey of poetry: English language series, rev. ed. published 1992. With new material. Includes bibliographical references and index.
    ISBN 1-58765-071-1 (set : alk. paper) — ISBN 1-58765-078-9 (v. 7 : alk. paper) —
    1. Poetry—History and criticism—Dictionaries. 2. Poetry—Bio-bibliography. 3. Poets—Biography—Dictionaries. I. Jason, Philip K., 1941 -   .

PN1021 .C7 2002
809.1'003—dc21   2002008536

Second Printing

3/05

CONTENTS

COMPLETE LIST OF CONTENTS

VOLUME 1

VOLUME 2

VOLUME 3

VOLUME 4

VOLUME 5

VOLUME 6

VOLUME 7

VOLUME 8

POETRY AROUND THE WORLD

RESEARCH TOOLS

INDEXES

CRITICAL SURVEY

OF

POETRY

ROBERT LOUIS STEVENSON

Born: Edinburgh, Scotland; November 13, 1850
Died: Vailima, near Apia, Samoa; December 3, 1894

PRINCIPAL POETRY

Moral Emblems, 1882
A Child's Garden of Verses, 1885
Underwoods, 1887
Ballads, 1890
Songs of Travel and Other Verses, 1896

OTHER LITERARY FORMS

Robert Louis Stevenson is primarily remembered for his prose fiction, although he was a notable essayist and enjoyed a small reputation as a poet. Stevenson also tried his hand at drama and collaborated with William Ernest Henley in the writing of four plays (*Deacon Brodie*, 1880; *Beau Austin*, 1884; *Admiral Guinea*, 1884; and *Macaire*, 1885), and with his wife, Fanny Van de Grift Osbourne Stevenson, on one (*The Hanging Judge*, 1887). His first published works were collections of essays, which he would continue to publish throughout his career. His short stories are collected in *The New Arabian Nights* (1882), *More New Arabian Nights* (1885), *The Merry Men and Other Tales and Fables* (1887), and *Island Nights' Entertainments* (1893). Of his novels, the four romances of adventure, *Treasure Island* (1881-1882), *Kidnapped* (1886), *The Black Arrow* (1888), and *Catriona* (1893; American title, *David Balfour*), along with his psychological work, *The Strange Case of Dr. Jekyll and Mr. Hyde* (1886), firmly established him as a master storyteller and assured him a place in popular culture for the several generations of readers (and viewers of film adaptations) whose imagination he captured. His lesser romances (*Prince Otto*, 1885), and especially those written in collaboration with his stepson, Lloyd Osbourne, are of a much lower order than his major novels, *The Master of Ballantrae* (1889) and the unfinished *Weir of Hermiston* (1896).

ACHIEVEMENTS

Robert Louis Stevenson's unquestionable literary achievements as a storyteller and as an accomplished es-

sayist in an age of prolific essayists overshadow his prominence as a poet who excelled in occasional verse and perfectly captured the impermanent and various moods of childhood and who, in *Underwoods*, exerted a profound and lasting influence on Scots poetry of the twentieth century. Tusitala, "the teller of tales," as the Samoans called him, achieved a measure of fame as an essayist, sometimes as a controversialist, but was most at home writing the tales of adventure and romance upon which his reputation justly rests.

His uncompleted masterpiece, *Weir of Hermiston*, and *The Master of Ballantrae* rank him as a serious novelist of the first order, who dealt with the complexities of human personality in its own depths and as it is subject to both inexorable fate and the buffets of history. His extraordinarily penetrating study of the divided self, "the war in the members," has made his creations Dr. Jekyll and Mr. Hyde household words. His tales of adventure, especially *Treasure Island*, *Kidnapped*, and *Catriona*, have become classics not only for youth but also for those who would recapture their youth. Enjoyment, in a word, characterizes the purpose and effect of much of Stevenson's fiction; it is also the principal object of much of his poetry.

One does not read—certainly one does not reread—Stevenson's poetry for its examination of adult life's complexities or its wrestling with the ultimate questions which each generation must ask for itself. These concerns are certainly present in some of the poetry but do not dominate it. Rather, in the bulk of Stevenson's verse, one reads to find an emotion crystallized, an occasion noted, a fleeting mood artfully captured and rendered. One reads the poetry primarily to enjoy a highly realized sense of childhood, a freshness and naïveté that is usually full of wonder, sometimes on the verge of joyous laughter, and often tinged with an almost inexpressible sadness. Stevenson is unmistakably a minor poet who has something in common with William Ernest Henley and Rudyard Kipling, other minor poets of the age, as well as with the early William Butler Yeats. A. E. Housman's poetry owes a clear debt to Stevenson's.

BIOGRAPHY

Robert Louis Stevenson was born to Thomas and Margaret Isabella (Balfour) Stevenson in Edinburgh on

Robert Louis Stevenson (Library of Congress)

November 13, 1850, the midpoint of the Victorian age. Thomas Stevenson, destined to be the last of a line of illustrious Scottish engineers, had hopes that his only child would take up that profession. His hopes proved to be unrealized when Stevenson switched from a sporadic study of engineering to a sporadic study of the law at Edinburgh University. Never a strong child, Stevenson spent much of his childhood and, indeed, much of his adulthood, either undergoing or convalescing from long and serious bouts of illness, chiefly respiratory disorders. His early life and education were overshadowed by illness, confinement, and frequent changes of climate. His youthful wanderings after health and sun led to later trips to France, Switzerland, and America, and, finally, to the South Seas in 1888 where he ultimately built a house, "Vailima," in Samoa. There he remained until his death from a cerebral hemorrhage in 1894. His recent biographers make much of his turbulent adolescence and hint of his several early love affairs, especially the

platonic affair with Fanny Sitwell whom he met in 1873 when she was newly separated from her husband. The more important woman in his life was the American, Fanny Van de Grift Osbourne, whom he met at Grez, France, in 1876, and married in California in 1880. From the time of his marriage (which drew him away from such friends as Charles Baxter, Sidney Colvin, and William Ernest Henley) until his death, Stevenson passed his time in constant writing, constant illness, and nearly constant travel. Periodically exiled from Scotland by its harsh climate and finally leaving it forever in 1888, Stevenson often returned there imaginatively to find sources for both his prose and his poetry. He was survived by his mother, his wife, and her children, Lloyd Osbourne, and Isobel Osbourne Strong Field. The latter two wrote reminiscences of him.

ANALYSIS

Robert Louis Stevenson himself, in a letter to his cousin R. A. M. Stevenson (September, 1868), wrote what is both a summary of his evaluation of Horace and Alexander Pope and a just index of his own intentions and later poetic achievement: "It is not so much the thing they say, as the way they say it. The dicta are often trivial and commonplace, or so undeniably true as to become part of orthodox boredom; but when you find an idea put in either of them, *it is put in its optimum form*." Stevenson's poetry is often about the commonplace—childhood, partings, reunions, homesickness, felicitations, greetings, friendship, the open road, the sea—but it is a crafting of common experience into heightened language and optimum form. His verse usually achieves its effects by a rigid application of meter and fixed rhyme scheme, although on occasion he breaks into a Whitmanesque style with a force far exceeding that of his more conventional poetry. Even in conventional poetic forms, however, he generally succeeds in lifting ordinary sentiment to a higher plane by the very simplicity, directness, and clarity of his language. This is one aspect, for example, of *A Child's Garden of Verses*, accounting for its appeal to adults as well as to children.

Stevenson's is a poetry of sentiment. At times, the sentiment appears to be artificial posturing that ranges from melancholy to high spirited. He does not make intellectual demands of his readers, but he does ask them to listen carefully; indeed, listening to his poems read aloud is the way most people first come to him. He also asks his readers to participate in the moment as he captures it, if only for that moment's sake. The quality of that moment is often twofold; it has the permanence that poetry can give it, and it vanishes as it is apprehended by the reader.

A CHILD'S GARDEN OF VERSES

One can find no better starting place for examining Stevenson's poetry than his envoy "To Any Reader" in *A Child's Garden of Verses*. Here, in eight rhymed couplets he encapsulates the sentiment of the volume. The reader is first carried back to childhood; Stevenson likens the reader's watchful care over the child in the verses to that which mothers exercise over their children as they play. Then, reminded of the commonplace event of a mother knocking at the window to get her child's attention, the reader is told that the child in the book will not respond in the familiar way. The child is there in the garden in one sense, but not there in another: "It is but a child of air." Stevenson suggests that, however much one might observe and watch over his child, he cannot successfully intervene in his child's life or break out of the historical confinement in which, as an adult, he finds himself. The moment one tries to do more than fix his attention upon the child, to have the child in the verses give ear to his concerns, warnings, admonitions, or summonses, the child vanishes; he becomes "grown up," and is "gone away."

The reader must proceed warily in *A Child's Garden of Verses* and not disturb the moments of the fifty-eight poems but, rather, enjoy them for what they are, privileged to observe and fleetingly share them before they dissolve, as they will when one tries to bring adult reflection to bear on them. Stevenson creates an ideal and somewhat idealized world of childhood—a special childhood, to be sure, but also a universal one. Although it is clear that the volume has for its background his own holiday visits to his maternal grandfather's house, Colinton Manse, near the Water of Leith, and is dedicated to Alison Cunningham ("Cummy"), his childhood nurse, to read the poems for the autobiography they contain would be to miss their point as poetry. Further, the child who narrates the poems is, above all, a persona

created by a man in his thirties, a persona that is sometimes the object of gentle irony (in "Looking Forward" and "Foreign Children," for example) and often (although children actually do this) speaks with a wisdom beyond his years (in "The Gardener" and "System").

Each poem, in the words of "From a Railway Carriage," "is a glimpse and gone for ever!" In those glimpses Stevenson renders portraits that are quite new in children's literature. Neither out to produce a didactic primer nor to condescend to children, he does provide childlike insights while retaining for his narrator a sense of wonder about the world. Just as, literarily speaking, the child was the invention of nineteenth century literature, so this child is a new invention who speaks in a language which the adult has outgrown. Where Charles Baudelaire, for example, had written of the philosophy of children's toys in "Morale du joujou," Stevenson goes to the heart of the matter in such poems as "The Dumb Soldier," "The Land of Story Books," and "The Land of Counterpane."

UNDERWOODS

Stevenson's *Underwoods*, best known for its Scottish dialect poems, also contains many occasional pieces in English that are of some interest, because in them is found a preeminent prose writer paying tribute, returning thanks, or commemorating a gift, a death, a visit, an illness. Much the same can be said of *Songs of Travel*. The Scots poems (Book II) are, by contrast, more interesting as poems in their own right. "A Lowden Sabbath Morn" and "Embro Hie Kirk" are perfect in their resonances of Robert Burns's language, style ("the Burns stanza"), treatment of common religious themes, and, in the latter, religious controversy. Full of humor and hominess, like his earlier "pieces in Lallan" addressed to Charles Baxter, the poems in Scots lack an overall seriousness of purpose that might raise them from the status they achieve as minor poetry.

BALLADS

His *Ballads* amply illustrate that Stevenson's forte was prose. The South Seas ballads "The Song of Rahero" and "The Feast of Famine" are, in his words, "great yarns" that suffer primarily because, as he wrote, they are "the verses of a Prosater." "Heather Ale" is a curious retelling of a Pictish legend, and "Christmas at Sea" is the story of a young man's first voyage in icy waters; it is not, except for the poignancy of the last two lines, remarkable. Stevenson is much more in his element in "Ticonderoga: A Legend of the West Highlands." Here his storytelling ability comes to the fore, as does his undoubted ability to catch the conversational tones of the Scots language. The ballad has all that one could wish for—a murder, a test of honor in the face of ghostly visitation, far-flung travel and military exploits, inevitable fate, and the eerie sense of supernatural forces at work. Yet, like the other ballads, "Ticonderoga" would be better suited to Stevenson's prose than to his mechanical verse.

Except for a very few poems (notably, "Requiem" and the poems in Scots), the master of prose succeeded best as a poet when he sought to recapture the evanescent moments of youth. Stevenson's poetry takes its place far below that of the greater Victorians. His poetry is not a reminder to man of his precarious place in the universe or of the tenuous grasp he has upon civilization. His poetry does, however, express the sheer delight, the cares, the rewards, and the experience itself of childhood. Like the child of *A Child's Garden of Verses* the reader looks to Stevenson the novelist and poet with a fondness for the magic of his "dear land of Storybooks."

OTHER MAJOR WORKS

LONG FICTION: *Treasure Island*, 1881-1882 (serial), 1883 (book); *Prince Otto*, 1885; *The Strange Case of Dr. Jekyll and Mr. Hyde*, 1886; *Kidnapped*, 1886; *The Black Arrow*, 1888; *The Master of Ballantrae*, 1889; *The Wrong Box*, 1889; *The Wrecker*, 1892 (with Lloyd Osbourne); *Catriona*, 1893; *The Ebb-Tide*, 1894 (with Osbourne); *Weir of Hermiston*, 1896 (unfinished); *St. Ives*, 1897 (completed by Arthur Quiller-Couch).

SHORT FICTION: *The New Arabian Nights*, 1882; *More New Arabian Nights*, 1885; *The Merry Men and Other Tales and Fables*, 1887; *Island Nights' Entertainments*, 1893.

PLAYS: *Deacon Brodie*, pb. 1880 (with William Ernest Henley); *Admiral Guinea*, pb. 1884 (with Henley); *Beau Austin*, pb. 1884 (with Henley); *Macaire*, pb. 1885 (with Henley); *The Hanging Judge*, pb. 1887 (with Fanny Van de Grift Stevenson).

NONFICTION: *An Inland Voyage*, 1878; *Edinburgh: Picturesque Notes*, 1879; *Travels with a Donkey in the Cévennes*, 1879; *Virginibus Puerisque*, 1881; *Familiar Studies of Men and Books*, 1882; *The Silverado Squatters, Sketches from a Californian Mountain*, 1883; *Memories and Portraits*, 1887; *Across the Plains*, 1892; *A Footnote to History*, 1892; *Vailima Letters*, 1895; *In the South Seas*, 1896; *The Letters of Robert Louis Stevenson to His Family and Friends*, 1899 (2 volumes), 1911 (4 volumes); *The Lantern-Bearers and Other Essays*, 1988.

BIBLIOGRAPHY

Bell, Ian. *Dreams of Exile: Robert Louis Stevenson*. New York: H. Holt, 1995. Bell's biography makes a case for Stevenson's genius as a writer and tries to counter the romanticized images that surround him.

Binding, Paul. *Robert Louis Stevenson*. London: Oxford University Press, 1974. A sensitive, well-written biography of the poet and author of *Treasure Island* and many favorite books and stories. Binding relates his strict religious upbringing in Scotland, his marriage to Fanny Van de Grift Osbourne, an American divorcée whom he met in Paris, and their travels in the Pacific from California to Australia. Ink drawings accompany each chapter.

Calder, Jenni. *Robert Louis Stevenson: A Life Study*. New York: Oxford University Press, 1980. A richly detailed, engaging biography of "Tusitala"—the teller of tales, as the Samoan natives called Stevenson. Calder concentrates on the personal history, leaving literary criticism to other writers. She sympathetically presents Fanny Van de Grift Osbourne, Stevenson's wife, who travelled on many journeys with her popular husband. Includes thirty-three photographs, notes, and an index.

Davies, Hunter. *The Teller of Tales: In Search of Robert Louis Stevenson*. New York: Interlink Books, 1996. Davies recounts Stevenson's life as well as the author's own visits to places where Stevenson lived. Neither conventional scholarly biography nor a book for the armchair traveler, this work is strictly for cultists and would be ideal for someone who, like Davies, wants to tread every corner of the earth, from England to California to Samoa, trod by Stevenson himself.

Eigner, Edwin M. *Robert Louis Stevenson and the Romantic Tradition*. Princeton N.J.: Princeton University Press, 1966. Eigner shows the influence of the nineteenth century prose romance on Stevenson's work. The poet and novelist freely admitted his debt to other writers (William Hazlitt, Charles Lamb, William Wordsworth, Nathaniel Hawthorne, and Michael Eyquem de Montaigne) in the development of his famous style. In eight chapters, Eigner discusses "serious romance" as a teacher of moral values and a source of Stevenson's ideas on mysticism, realism, law, and nature. Contains an index.

Hennessy, James Pope. *Robert Louis Stevenson*. London: Jonathan Cape, 1974. Out of the more than twenty-five hundred letters (often long ones) that Stevenson wrote in his forty-four years, Hennessy has created a fascinating life portrait. Stevenson's struggles with illness, his love for friends and good conversation, his gallant Scottish mother, and his American wife—all are here in brilliant detail. Supplemented by a select bibliography and an index.

Kiely, Robert. *Robert Louis Stevenson and the Fiction of Adventure*. Cambridge, Mass.: Harvard University Press, 1964. Well known and loved as a poet and writer of adventure stories, Stevenson appears to modern critics surprising for his pessimism, his maturity of thought, and his polished style. He foreshadowed Joseph Conrad in many ways. In five chapters, Kiely discusses the aesthetic belief "art is rational," and the use of fantasy, comedy, and symbolism in Stevenson's work. Includes a select bibliography, notes, and an index.

Soposnik, Irving S. *Robert Louis Stevenson*. New York: Twayne, 1974. This useful book treats the forms in which the versatile Stevenson wrote. Following a chapter of biography, Soposnik reviews the essays, poems, stories (with a separate chapter on Dr. Jekyll and Mr. Hyde), and novels. The poems reveal a personality that wants to soar to the heights but is condemned to a lonely journey in life. The child's voice of *A Child's Garden of Verses* expresses feelings of wonder and longing. Contains notes, a bibliography, and an index.

John J. Conlon;
bibliography updated by the editors

JAMES STILL

Born: Double Creek, Alabama; July 16, 1906
Died: Hindman, Kentucky; April 28, 2001

PRINCIPAL POETRY
Hounds on the Mountain, 1937
River of Earth, 1983
The Wolfpen Poems, 1986
From the Mountain, from the Valley: New and Collected Poems, 2001

OTHER LITERARY FORMS
James Still's highly acclaimed novel *River of Earth* first appeared in 1940. *Sporty Creek* (1977) continues the story of the family introduced in *River of Earth*. Still's short stories are collected in *On Troublesome Creek* (1941), *Pattern of a Man* (1976), and *The Run for the Elbertas* (1980). Like his novels, Still's short stories are admired for their deceptively simple narrative technique, skillful character delineation, and psychological insight. They have been compared to the stories of Anton Chekhov, Katherine Anne Porter, and Bernard Malamud.

The exact, colorful language of Still's novels, short stories, and poems is often achieved through the artful use of folk speech, examples of which are found in two collections of Appalachian riddles and rusties (playful, formulaic uses of language): *Way Down Yonder on Troublesome Creek* (1974) and *The Wolfpen Rusties* (1975). *Jack and the Wonder Beans* (1977) is a delightful retelling of "Jack and the Beanstalk" in the local idiom. Still has also prepared his version of the Mother Goose rhymes as *An Appalachian Mother Goose* (1998).

In *The Wolfpen Notebooks: A Record of Appalachian Life* (1991), Still drew from the notebooks which he has kept for more than fifty years, recording the distinctive expressions and customs of the Appalachian region.

Critical attention has been more often directed to Still's novels and short stories than to his poems. Still was rightly admired for his prose, however, because he was first of all a poet. After reading his novel *River of Earth* and the poems in *Hounds on the Mountain*, Katherine Anne Porter said in a letter that the two books should be read together. The novel was "an extension of the poems" while the poems were "further comment on the experience that made the novel." Still's poems, then, are doubly deserving of critical attention. Rewarding in themselves, they also belong to any assessment of his total achievement.

ACHIEVEMENTS

James Still's poems, short stories, and novels consistently received high critical acclaim. *Hounds on the Mountain* was reviewed favorably in *Poetry, The Atlantic Monthly, The New York Times Book Review*, and other newspapers and journals, while *The Wolfpen Poems* was praised by James Dickey in the *Los Angeles Times Book Review*. Still was the recipient of a number of awards, honors, and prizes. These include two Guggenheim Fellowships, the Southern Authors Award, the O. Henry Memorial Prize, and the Marjorie Peabody Waite Award of the American Academy and Institute of Arts and Letters for the "continuing achievement and integrity of his art." He received a number of honorary doctorates as well. Scholarships and fellowships have been established in his name, including fellowships funded by the Andrew W. Mellon Foundation for Advanced Study in the Humanities and Social Science and in Appalachian studies at the University of Kentucky. The James Still Room at Johnson-Camden Library, Morehead State University, was dedicated in 1961. In 1981, Still received the Milner Award, given by the Kentucky Arts Council, in recognition of outstanding leadership in the arts. In 1987 he was awarded a Book of the Year citation from the Appalachian Writers Association. He served as Kentucky's poet laureate in 1995-1996.

BIOGRAPHY

James Still was born in Double Creek, Alabama, in 1906. He attended Lincoln Memorial University and Vanderbilt University in Tennessee, and the University of Illinois, earning B.A. degrees in both arts and sciences, and the M.A. degree in English. Beginning in the early 1930's he lived in Knott County, Kentucky (except for time spent in travel and in military service in Africa and the Middle East in World War II). His home on Dead Mare Branch is a two-story log house built before 1840, given to him for life by a farmer and dulcimer maker named Jethro Amburgey. Still served as librarian for the Hindman Settlement School and taught at Morehead State University and a number of other institutions.

Still kept his private life and his life as a writer separate—in order to remain "intact." Those who knew him as a teacher and writer knew little about his day-to-day life among neighbors, for the most part farmers and coal miners, who knew next to nothing about him as a writer. To them he was a farmer, a gardener, and the librarian at the Hindman Settlement School. Still's success in keeping separate his private life and his life as a writer resulted in misunderstandings about both his life and his writing.

Because he lived an apparently isolated life and made no effort to advertise himself or promote his writing, or even to accept awards and honors, and because he published infrequently, Still was perceived as a hermit-writer. His failure to accept the award of the American Academy of Arts and Letters, and an invitation to be Phi Beta Kappa poet at Columbia University in the 1940's, contributed to his reputation as a recluse. This is a misperception. According to Still, he declined in both instances because he lacked bus fare and suitable clothing for the occasions.

While he appeared to be living an isolated life at the Hindman Settlement School, Still was a constant reader of *The Nation, The New Republic*, and *The New York Times*. He was publishing in *The Atlantic Monthly, The Yale Review, Poetry*, and many other magazines and journals. At this time he numbered among his friends Marjorie Kinnan Rawlings, Katherine Anne Porter, Elizabeth Madox Roberts, and Robert Frost. Still considered himself fortunate to have lived in Knott County, Kentucky, lucky to have been assigned post office box 13 at Hindman. "Hindman was surely the only place you could cash a check at four A.M. and call for your mail at midnight. The cashier was an early riser, the postmaster an insomniac."

The notion that Still was a recluse in flight from modernity is mistaken. Cosmopolitan in his tastes and habits, he read several hours per day for more than seventy years. His favorite writers were the Scandinavians and the Russians, especially Anton Chekhov, Nikolai Gogol, and Ivan Turgenev. He often traveled, spending ten winters in Mexico, Guatemala, Honduras, and El Salvador studying Mayan civilization. His advice to anyone wishing to write was to learn to type. When reminded that William Shakespeare did not type, his response was: "What might Shakespeare not have additionally accomplished with a Coronamatic 2000 [typewriter] with a pop-out ribbon!"

Because Appalachia has been the object of numerous sociological studies concerned with poverty and economic exploitation, there have been efforts to interpret Still's writing from both sociological and political perspectives. Still resisted these efforts, although he was not politically unaware. He helped distribute food and clothing to beleaguered strikers in Wilder, Tennessee, in 1930. He lived in east Kentucky during the time of the mine wars. He worked, as a temporary replacement, for the Emergency Relief Administration in the mid-1930's. "To live in that time and place . . . was to be politically aware," Still said. He cited the poems in *Hounds on the Mountain* as evidence of his awareness ". . . that at least in my area something was there that would not last much longer. . . . We were living in the nineteenth century, so to speak, and the twentieth would not long be denied."

Instead of a political consciousness, Still brought the temperament, habits, and, to some extent, the methods of the scientist to bear on his writing. In his notebooks he recorded every facet of the community in which he lived. He considered himself "something of a botanist" and experiments with the development by natural selection of the wild strawberry and wild violet. The grounds around his house on Dead Mare Branch he described as a "cross between a botanical garden and an experiment station." Where writing is concerned, however, he had no theories regarding artistic creation, recommended no methods or techniques. He could not imagine having been influenced by other writers, and he was not interested in grooming a protégé. When his advice was solicited, he stressed preparation and familiarity with tools of the trade. "A writer gets ready to enter the profession, just as a truck driver learns to operate a truck. I'm fairly certain Chopin didn't compose his works on the piano with one finger, or even two. The preparation is the point." Still advised against looking too closely "into the springs of creativity." The creative process—if it is a

process—remained a mystery to him, and he was content with that. When he talked about how he wrote, however, his imagery suggested the scientific approach. The writing does not begin until he touches the "quick" of the material, as with a scalpel.

In the last two decades of his life, he served as a member of the board of directors of the Kentucky Humanities Council, beginning in 1980; as a speaker at the Lilyan Cohen Lecture Series, Clinch Valley College in 1987; and as a commentator for National Public Radio's *All Things Considered* in the 1990's.

ANALYSIS

"I have gone softly," James Still wrote in *Hounds on the Mountain*. He compared himself to a child walking on "a ridge/ Of sleep . . . a slope hung on a nightjar's speech." He was a child "with hands like leaves" and eyes "like swifts that search the darkness in a perilous land" ("With Hands Like Leaves"). The similes define Still's unobtrusive approach to his material—the way that he blended in, to become invisible as a speaker in the poems, insisting upon objectivity and exactness of detail. In "Eyes in the Grass" the eyes are those of a speaker unnoticed by either bird or insect. The speaker is "lost to any wandering view"; he is "hill uncharted"; his breathing is the wind; he is "horizon . . . earth's far end."

SOUTHERN APPALACHIA

This approach to a people and a place, and Still's achievement as a poet, can be appreciated only in comparison with the way in which the southern Appalachian region of the United States has been typically depicted. The French critic Roland Barthes maintained (*Mythologies*, 1972) that there is an inherent difficulty in writing about mountains and mountain people, the result of a bourgeois alpine myth that causes writers and readers to take leave of their senses "anytime the ground is uneven."

Whatever the cause or causes, southern Appalachia appears in American writing as a veritable funhouse of distorted and contradictory images which have since the mid-nineteenth century suited the needs, motives, and perspectives of abolitionists, social workers, Protestant missionaries, industrialists, and entrepreneurs. Southern Appalachia was known through an either/or literature, either as a place of problems, poverty, and peculiar people, or as a preserve of fundamentally American virtues and values, sterling Anglo-Saxon and Anglo-Celtic qualities. The region entered the popular American mind during the 1880's by way of local colorists (chief among them Mary N. Murfree, who wrote under the pseudonym "Charles Egbert Craddock"), who noted the quaint and sensational aspects of an old-fashioned way of life. By the 1920's a careful student of southern Appalachia remarked that more was known about the region that was not true than about any other part of the country.

At a time when it was fashionable, indeed almost obligatory, for poetry about southern Appalachia to be either a witless romanticizing of mountains and mountain people, or proletarian verse, Still walked softly. He presented no diagnosis of economic ills, preached no social gospel, offered no program. He declined to participate in the either/or literature, ambitious to do no more—and no less—than to show people in their place and tell how it was with these people at a particular time.

As a consequence, Still's poems discover neither merely a landscape of beauty and wild freedom nor only visual blight, exploitation, and hard, unrelenting conditions. All these things are caught in a vision that is both local and universal. Still's poems embodied certain universal themes implicit in the experience of people in a particular place and time—the themes of endurance, perseverance, and self-preservation under harsh and perilous circumstances.

Details and images created an impression of a difficult life at subsistence level. In "Court Day," the hill folk rise and set out toward the county seat before dawn, when the day is still "dark as plowed earth." The road into town is a stony creek bed. The waters of Troublesome Creek are a "cold thin flowing." The fields of the county poor farm are "hungry" ("On Double Creek"). Descriptions of coal camps suggest unyielding, inhospitable conditions. Coal camp houses are "hung upon the hills" ("Mountain Coal Town"). Underground, the miners are "Breaking the hard, slow-yielding seams" of coal ("Earth-Bread"). Life is not only difficult and meagerly provided for, it is also somehow blighted. Chestnut trees are "cankered to the heart" ("On Red Bird Creek"). The ridges in "Journey Beyond the Hills" are "stricken and

unforested." Early morning hours are "gaunt," the mist "leprous," the day "lean" ("The Hill-Born").

Danger and death are ever-present. Death sits "quiet upon a nest" in "Year of the Pigeons." The furrows of the county poor farm are "crooked as an adder's track" ("On Double Creek"). Stars in the night sky over a mountain coal camp are "cool as the copperhead's eyes." The underground shift of the miners is an "eight-hour death," a "daily burial" ("Earth-Bread"). The quarry in "Fox Hunt" is "gaunt and anxious," his life imperiled by the hounds. In the title poem the fox turns at the head of a cove to confront the hounds. The fox's blood laves "the violent shadows" of that place, and even the dry roots "questing beneath the earth."

STARK CONTRASTS

Life under such conditions is characterized by stark contrasts—between the bitterness and sweetness of experience; between toughness and tenderness. Beauty and blight, untrammeled freedom and imprisonment coexist. The "starveling trees" in "The Hill-Born" bear sweet fruit. In "Horse Swapping on Troublesome Creek" the mare is spavined, while the foals have "untamed hearts" and "toss unbound heads/ With flash of hock and unsheared flowing manes." The stark contrasts of this life are implicit in the details of "Infare." The groom is "sunbronzed, resolute and free." His bride is "sweet apples from high green orchards." The old who have gathered for this wedding party have "ashy" faces and "rheumy" eyes. The wildness and freedom found in this place exist, paradoxically, in a setting that imprisons. Still refers to the "prisoned waters" of Troublesome Creek ("The Hill-Born") and to "men within their prisoning hills" ("Journey Beyond the Hills").

From birth to death the circumscribed life of man and beast is difficult, uncertain, constantly endangered. A foal is dropped "under the hard bead/ Of the crow's eyes" ("On Buckhorn Creek"). Life is vulnerable to powerful natural forces, as suggested by "Spring-tides surging to the naked root" ("The Hill-Born"). The forces of nature continue to work on people, plants, and animals even after death. In "Rain on the Cumberlands" the speaker passes "broken horns within the nettled grass/ . . . hoofs relinquished on the breathing stones/ Eaten with rain-strokes." Rain sweeps down the nests of pigeons that have succumbed to the depredations of men and animals, until "not a slate-blue feather blows on any hill" ("Year of the Pigeons"). The dead are not spared the unrelenting harshness of conditions; they lie "under the hard eyes of hill and tree" ("Graveyard"). The dead are "quartered with the roots/ That split firm stone and suck the marrow out,/ And finger yellowing bones" ("Death on the Mountain").

PERSEVERANCE

The characteristic response to these adverse and unrelenting conditions is to endure, to carry on, as suggested by "Horseback in the Rain." The speaker is wet, hungry, lonely. His horse's hooves clatter on stone. Yet he has little choice but to "Halt not. Stay not./ Ride the storm with no ending/ On a road unarriving." The poem "Heritage" expresses a determination to stay on in the "prisoning hills" even though "they topple their barren heads to level earth/ And the forests slide uprooted out of the sky."

The response is not only to persevere, but also to preserve something of one's self and one's experiences. "Child in the Hills" emphasizes the perseverance of the child in a man who has "drifted into years of growth and strange enmeshment." The music of the "Mountain Dulcimer" preserves not only the sounds of mountain life— the ringing anvil, the creak of saddlebags and oxen yokes—but also the stillness, "Bitter as salt drenching the tongue of pain."

The characteristic qualities of his style blend with Still's ever-present themes in the representative "Spring on Troublesome Creek." The restraint and understatement of the opening line is gently insisted upon by repetition that suggests conversation, or a ballad: "Not all of us were warm, not all of us." Subsequent lines illustrate Still's simple diction and objective reporting of concrete details: "We are winter-lean, our faces are sharp with cold/ And there is a smell of woodsmoke in our clothes;/ Not all of us were warm, though we hugged the fire/ Through the long chilled nights." The poem concentrates Still's themes of endurance, perseverance, and self-preservation: "We have come out/ Into the sun again, we have untied our knot/ Of flesh." Here too is Still's tendency to see people and place as parts of one subtly interdependent whole. In this poem the condition of the people resembles that of the animals and plants that have also endured the winter. "We are no thinner than a hound or mare,/ Or an unleaved poplar. We have come through/ To grass, to the cows calving in the lot."

SHARED IDENTITY OF PEOPLE AND PLACE

In a poem titled "Anecdote of Men by the Thousand," Wallace Stevens writes: "There are men of a province/ who are that province." Still's poems suggested a similar identity between people and place. People are like the hills; their physical features, characteristics, and qualities mirror their environment. In the poem "On Troublesome Creek," men wait "as mountains long have waited." Hills are like the people. In "Court Day," the hills are so near they seem like people crowding close at the open courthouse window. The ridges in "Journey Beyond the Hills" are "heavy-hipped." Still's human being is himself land walking, weathered by seasons, loving, aging, dying, and coming back in spring, and the land bears not only the spiritual but the physical imprint of the person who has lived a life on it, in it, and with it. In the life-landscape, even the wounds are duplicated; the land takes them on:

Uncle Ambrose, your hands are heavy with years,
Seamy with the ax's heft, the plow's hewn stock,
The thorn wound and the stump-dark bruise of time.
Your face is a map of Knott County
With hard ridges of flesh, the wrinkled creekbeds,
The traces and forks carved like wagon tracks on stone;
And there is Troublesome's valley struck violently
By a barlow's blade.

Like the dress of Stevens's woman of Lhassa, Still's poems were "an invisible element" of a place "made visible." Making himself almost invisible as a speaker in the poems, concentrating not on sensibility, or on social and economic views, Still allowed an elusive element of a place and people to come into sharp focus. This elusive element, the theme of endurance, perseverance, and self-preservation implicit in the life he wrote about, is rendered visible not only in the content of the poems but also through style and structure. The economy and concreteness of expression, the spareness of style, reflect not only the laconic quality of folk speech but also the conditions of the life from which the language comes. Structure and content, style and theme are blended in a genuine expression of a people and a place.

PORTRAYAL OF A SHARED EXPERIENCE

Fresh in his expression and point of view, Still avoided the superficiality and sensationalism of local colorists and propagandists. Local colorists give the impression of having looked at mountain people and noted the quainter aspects of their traditional life. Reformers emphasize the deplorable circumstances resulting from the inadequacies of that traditional life, or from its destruction through the incursion of mercantile interests. Still gave the impression not merely of having looked at a place and a people but of having lived with them. While the local colorists and proponents of social and economic points of view say "they," Still says "we."

At its best, according to the novelist Wilma Dykeman, the literature of the Appalachian region is "as unique as churning butter, as universal as getting born." Such a combination of uniqueness and universality, found in the best literature of any time and place, is present in Still's poems. They are poems in which abstractions consists of what particulars ultimately mean. Like all genuine poems, they are, as William Carlos Williams puts it, "a vision of the facts."

OTHER MAJOR WORKS

LONG FICTION: *River of Earth*, 1940, 1968, 1978; *Sporty Creek*, 1977.

SHORT FICTION: *On Troublesome Creek*, 1941; *The Wolfpen Rusties: Appalachian Riddles and Gee-Haw Whimmy-Diddles*, 1975; *Pattern of a Man*, 1976; *The Run for the Elbertas*, 1980.

NONFICTION: *The Man in the Bushes: The Notebooks of James Still, 1935-1987*, 1988; *The Wolfpen Notebooks: A Record of Appalachian Life*, 1991.

CHILDREN'S LITERATURE: *Way Down Yonder on Troublesome Creek*, 1974; *Jack and the Wonder Beans*, 1977; *An Appalachian Mother Goose*, 1998.

BIBLIOGRAPHY

Berry, Wendell. "A Master Language." *Sewanee Review* 105, no. 3 (Summer, 1997): 419-422. Berry discusses the works of James Still and their masterful use of dialect and language.

Cadle, Dean. "Pattern of a Writer: Attitudes of James Still." *Appalachian Journal* 15 (Winter, 1988): 104-143. Cadle presents notes from conversations he had with Still between December, 1958, and December, 1959. Includes Still's views on writing; also has photographs of Still, his house, and neighbors and friends.

Dickey, James. Review of *The Wolfpen Poems*, by James Still. *Los Angeles Times Book Review*, 1, (December 7, 1986): 19. Dickey states that these poems establish Still as the "truest and most remarkable poet of mountain culture." Notes his sincerity and modesty and commends him for the feel of the country in his poems. Sees the strength of *The Wolfpen Poems* collection in that it underscores the necessity of Appalachian culture and its values.

Fletcher, James Gould. "Camera in a Furrow." *The New Republic* 91 (July 28, 1937): 343. When this review of *Hounds on the Mountain* was written, Still was a young poet, and Fletcher alludes to this in his critique. Comments on the monotony and lack of fire in the poems but acknowledges his attention to details and background knowledge of his subject.

Foxfire 22 (Fall, 1988). This special issue on Still concentrates on *The Wolfpen Notebooks*; it contains an interview and selections from the book (not yet published at the time of the issue).

Harriss, R. P. "Granite Appalachian Poetry." *New York Herald Tribune Books* (July 4, 1937): 5. Harris compares Still to Robert Frost and states that it is not easy to align Still with other living Southern poets. In reviewing *Hounds on the Mountain*, Harris says the poems "hark back to archaic mountain farms"; a notable exception is "Court Day," which is a contemporary look at mining towns. Praises Still for being articulate but not in a glib way.

The Iron Mountain Review 2 (Summer, 1984). This issue devoted to Still contains an interview with Still as well as essays on his poetry ("James Still's Poetry: 'The Journey of a Worldly Wonder,'" by Jeff Daniel Marion) and short fiction and a Still bibliography.

Marowski, Daniel G., and Roger Matuz, eds. *Contemporary Literary Criticism. Vol. 49*. Detroit: Gale Research, 1988. The entry on Still mentions that he is highly regarded for his prose and verse, which document Appalachian life. Comments favorably on the "restrained and evocative qualities" of *The Wolfpen*

Poems. Contains excerpts from reviews of his work spanning fifty years.

Miller, Jim Wayne. "Jim Dandy: James Still at Eighty." *Appalachian Heritage* 14 (Fall, 1986): 8-20. A profile of Still emphasizing his views of life and literature and his achievement as a writer; contains biographical information and frequent humorous interjections of local sayings and quotations.

Turner, Martha Billips. "A Vision of Change: Appalachia in James Still's *River of Earth*." *Southern Literary Journal* 24, no. 2 (Spring, 1992): 11. James Still's writings have established his reputation as a serious, talented writer of the Appalachian region. Still's portrayal of Appalachia in *River of Earth* is discussed.

Jim Wayne Miller;
bibliography updated by the editors

MARK STRAND

Born: Summerside, Prince Edward Island, Canada; April 11, 1934

PRINCIPAL POETRY

Sleeping with One Eye Open, 1964
Reasons for Moving, 1968
Darker, 1970
The Story of Our Lives, 1973
The Sargeantville Notebook, 1973
Elegy for My Father, 1973
The Late Hour, 1978
Selected Poems, 1980
Prose: Four Poems, 1987
The Continuous Life, 1990
Dark Harbor, 1993
Blizzard of One, 1998
Chicken, Shadow, Moon, and More, 1999

OTHER LITERARY FORMS

Mr. and Mrs. Baby and Other Stories (1985) is a collection of short stories with a bent for fantasy; another work of fiction, *The Monument* (1978), is primarily prose but contains a few dozen poems integral to the discourse. Mark Strand has translated poetry into English, the most noteworthy volumes of which are *Eighteen Poems from the Quechua* (1971) and *The Owl's Insomnia: Poems by Rafael Alberti* (1973). He has edited or coedited several anthologies of poetry, the most important of which are *The Contemporary American Poets: American Poetry Since 1940* (1969) and *The Making of a Poem* (2000). His books on art include *Edward Hopper* (1993), *William Bailey* (1987), and *Art of the Real: Nine American Figurative Painters* (1983). In *The Weather of Words* (2000), Strand collects many of his magazine essays on poetry. His most successful book for children is *The Planet of Lost Things* (1982).

ACHIEVEMENTS

From early in his career, Mark Strand has been received with respect by critics. His poetry, while grounded in a reality that borders on the surreal, manages to evoke sensations and sensitivity, flavored with a taste for the abstract and bizarre, which convey the haunting, factual nature of the human psyche. Although his poetry is clearly unusual in this ability, and while he has been given a series of awards and other recognitions, his work has not received the final honor—that is, his poems have not been commonly anthologized. Strand has been awarded two Fulbright fellowships (1960 and 1965), followed by grants from the Ingram-Merrill Foundation, the National Endowment for the Arts, and the Rockefeller Foundation in 1966, 1967, and 1968, respectively. In 1974 he was honored with a Guggenheim Fellowship and won the Edgar Allan Poe Award for *The Story of Our Lives* from the Academy of American Poets. The National Institute of Arts and Letters made another award in 1975, as did the Academy of American Poets in 1980. Strand was honored with a MacArthur Fellowship in 1987, the Bobbitt Prize in 1992, and the Bollingen Prize in 1993. He served as Poet Laureate of the United States from 1990 to 1991, and his *Blizzard of One* was awarded the Pulitzer Prize.

BIOGRAPHY

Although a Canadian by birth, Mark Strand moved to the United States in 1938, when he was four years old, and has remained there most of the time since then.

He has consistently described his parents, Robert Joseph and Sonia Apter Strand, as "bookish," intellectual types who emphasized education and the humanities in his childhood. The youth at first fought his parents' influence in this regard and sought to become an athlete, although he was interested in art from an early age. He grew up in the country, spending much time without the companionship of other children. In 1954 he entered Antioch College in northern Ohio, where he immediately came under the influence of Nolan Miller, his freshman English teacher and a respected critic, editor, and writer. In his college years his attraction to and involvement with poetry became undeniable; he discovered that he liked reading it as well as writing it, and, whether consciously or unconsciously, set upon a career course that would eventually lead to the announcement that he had been appointed poet laureate of the United States by the Library of Congress.

The intervening years were characterized by a series of professional achievements not only in the classroom but also as a poet, translator, writer of fiction, editor, and art critic. Strand has been the recipient of numerous

Mark Strand (© Lilo Raymond)

awards and fellowships, most of which were made by national committees or organizations.

Specifically, he earned a bachelor's degree in fine arts from Yale University in 1959, where he also received the Cook Prize and the Bergin Prize. Upon graduation, he was appointed a Fulbright Fellow and spent a year at the University of Florence. In 1961 he was married to Antonia Ratensky, from whom he was divorced in 1973; the marriage saw the birth of one daughter, Jessica. While teaching at the University of Iowa, he earned his third degree, a master of arts, in 1962. He has taught at the University of Brazil, Mount Holyoke College, the University of Washington, Yale, Brooklyn College, Princeton University, Brandeis University, the University of Virginia, Wesleyan University, and Harvard University. From 1981 to 1993, he taught at the University of Utah. Later he taught at The Johns Hopkins University and at the University of Chicago.

In the early 1960's Strand's first poems were accepted for publication by East Coast literary establishment magazines, particularly *The New Yorker*. He has consistently published poetry since then, with his works (including translations) appearing in more than a dozen volumes. In 1976 he was married to Julia Rumsey Garretson, and with her he had a son, Thomas Summerfield. Ostensibly, Strand's children's books were written in part for his own children, after the fashion of Charles Dickens.

ANALYSIS

Mark Strand's poetry is entirely characteristic of the age in which he writes. Solipsism, alienation, and self-definition are the principal concerns. His work manifests a certain self-involvement that sometimes goes over the line into narcissism. Many of his poems are an inner dialogue that reaches into the realm of clinical schizophrenia. He is unable to define himself, finally, except as a sensitive soul searching for definition. He does not sound Whitmanesque "barbaric yawp" over the rooftops of the world so much as he makes a distinguishable Eliotian "whimper" from the closet of his bedroom. Overall, Strand's poetry fits clearly, quickly, and neatly into the packaged, near-formulaic modes of poetry manufactured in the second half of the twentieth century. Nevertheless, he has a voice, experience, and expression all quite his own, and certain identifiable attributes of his work do serve not only to separate it from the works of others but also to make it deserving of the attention it has received.

Strand's work depicts, to use his own word, the sourceless "darkness" that pervades human existence. In this depiction fear is present, to be sure, as are over-sensitivity, bifurcation of identity in the voice of the poet(s), spiritual nakedness, a strange combination of fantasy and the almost-surreal, and an elusive peace that never exists in the conscious and remains undiscoverable in both the subconscious and the unconscious. Strand's poetry, then, is not distinctive so much in its subject matter or the ideas it expresses as in the techniques it employs: He thus has a far different domain from those of other poets writing in this subgenre of late modernism and postexistentialism.

The poetry of Mark Strand is distinctive not so much in content as in approach. His contribution to twentieth century American poetry is the singularity in method and mode of expressing ideas common to other poets of his time. He stands apart from others, however, specifically through his estranged—though assuredly successful—mixture of the haunting darkness of reality with the fantastic and sexual, with self-alienation whose form is self-involvement, and with a recognition of the bifurcated personality, neither side of which can be subject functionally to the other. The mark of the superior quality of his works is that somehow he convinces the reader that life truly is this way and that the experiences he describes, however bizarre, are experiences that they share.

SLEEPING WITH ONE EYE OPEN

Two poems from Strand's first published collection, *Sleeping with One Eye Open*, demonstrate most of these qualities. In "The Tunnel," the speaker of the poem is aware of a second self lurking, perpetually lurking, in the front yard of his house, itself a metaphor for his body. The primary persona of the poem experiences angst in both his ability and his inability to confront the other persona of his own self. He shines a flashlight at it, opens the door for a direct confrontation (which turns out to be more of a peek), makes obscene gestures at the other, leaves it suicide notes, tears up his (their) living-room furniture, and, finally, decides to dig a tunnel to es-

cape to a neighbor's yard. The attempt fails; there can be no communication or contact with another until he has first set his own house in order. The poet finishes digging the tunnel to find himself immobilized. He does not enter this escape route, although it is fully prepared; the poem ends with him aware that he is still being watched by the other self, now not in immediate physical visibility, and knowing that he will not leave the other after all. The self will remain fractured, and the fear will not go away. Escape is not possible, because it would be at least a partial enactment of suicide, which is unacceptable, accomplishing nothing.

In "Poem," the primary persona is again visited by the secondary self, who sneaks into his house (again a metaphor for the poet's body), climbs the stairs to the bedroom, where the poet is not sleeping but waiting, and announces that he is going to kill him. In this companion poem to "The Tunnel," the situation is reversed and enhanced. In the first poem the primary consciousness of the poet's existence tries only to escape the second consciousness and chooses not to do so. In "Poem," the second self succeeds in confronting the first one to announce not escape, but murder. Both halves meet with failure. The would-be murder of self is to be carried out by mutilation: The second self starts cutting away at the body, beginning with the toenails and proceeding upward, to stop only when "nothing is left of me," at least emotionally. The mutilating self stops when he reaches the neck; that is, he leaves the head to go on thinking, and he departs. Predictably, the poem ends just as the first one did. Both selves are left only to go on in a dual existence of irresolution and terror.

REASONS FOR MOVING

Strand revisits the same motifs and existence in many of the poems that were collected in *Reasons for Moving*. These are particularly evident in "The Man in the Mirror," a longer poem of thirty quatrains in which the poet reveals his innermost thoughts while routinely confronting himself in a mirror. The reflection becomes first an image, then an embodiment with a personality of its own, as the poet tries to define himself and find meaning in his life. The voyeuristic narcissism and the fact of the fractured self struggling for union and self-comprehension provide the framework, context, and message of the poem. The poet views himself in the mirror on his living-room wall, contemplating the meaning of what he sees—his other self. The emergence of identities is evident early in the poem: "I remember how we used to stand/ wishing the glass/ would dissolve between us." Yet this wistful attempt at merging the two parts is incomplete, therefore unsuccessful. "But that was another life./ One day you turned away/ and left me here/ to founder in the stillness of your wake." The body of the poem is then a matter of recording a list of ways in which he had tried to cope with this wake. He watches and studies the other self; he tries to forget him; he is driven to walking around the house, performing strange actions. The other continues to be present, but pointlessly so. Finally, as in the case of the two poems already discussed, the poet gives up; he knows that "it will always be this way./ I stand here scared/ that you will disappear, scared that you will stay."

Strand published "The Dirty Hand" in the same collection. This poem is, for both the poet and the reader, an experience in the self-involvement of narcissism and masturbation. The poet bemoans the fact that his hand is dirty and cannot be cleaned, ostensibly for the reason that he will simply get it dirty again: The stain of the flesh cannot be removed, because the flesh itself is dirt. He is aware of no guilt, only uncleanness. Repeatedly, he washes his hand (notice that the poet never refers to the hand in the plural; only one hand is problematic), scrubbing and polishing yet unable to remove the stain. He tries to hide the hand from others, an endeavor that meets with little success, and he cannot hide the hand from himself either. The intensity of the problem increases, until finally he recognizes that he cannot live with it and proclaims that he will cut it off, chop it into pieces, and throw it into the ocean. This desire to rid himself of his nature, however, is not the main thrust of the poem, which ends with the wish for "another hand" to come to take its place, not at the end of his arm but by fastening itself to his arm. The poet wants someone else to assume the role of self-involvement, which leaves him unclean.

Darker

Darker, which was published in 1970, remains Strand's best collection of poetry. These poems focus on the fear and dread of the human conscious that occur because of the immobility he had recognized and written of in earlier poems. Aware that it is not enough to maintain that individuals are trapped in fear, the poet turns to the "darker" realization that there is no change, no hope, and no progress. In his earlier poems he had recognized as much, but he now turns to dealing with the consequences of such a realization. Previously, he had expressed himself as entrapped; in *Darker*, the poems worry with the meaning of that permanent and irreversible entrapment.

The third poem in *Darker* is called "Giving Myself Up." In it the poet lists a series of some dozen items that he "gives up," parts of his body as well as his "smell" and his "clothes." The poet gives up every matter of importance to his self-involvement, even the "ghost" that lives in his clothes. The poem concludes, "And you will have none of it because already I am beginning/ again without anything." His surrender to fear, the hopelessness of isolation, and the immobility caused by having two identities accomplishes nothing. He has finished without anything and will start again without anything. He knows that he is hopelessly trapped in a cycle from which there is no escape—only a minimal comprehension of the process. Along with the other side of his schizophrenic self, he will begin again only to reach the same purposeless point later. Giving up to the other self will not let him out of his present state. Thus one answer is given to the problem of existing in permanent entrapment: Self-abnegation will not work.

A second meaning of this fixated condition is similarly expressed in several other poems in *Darker*, particularly "Black Maps." Here, the poet maps out his existential life against a background of blackness. He begins the poem by recognizing that his birth (here called "arrival") is unacknowledged either by the "attendance of stones," an image representing the kinds of mental torture and persecution the poet later experiences, or an "applauding wind" thus he asserts that nature takes no joy from the appearance of the individual. "Nothing will tell you/ where you are" either at the time of birth or later in life. Individuals struggle and cope alone in a present that "is always dark." In this life all "maps are black," and life is a voyage only into the surrounding emptiness. By attempting to study these maps of the dark night of the soul, the poet learns only that "what you thought/ were concerns of yours/ do not exist." The cares and worries of this life are unimportant, because they have no physical or mental reality. In fact, the poet concludes, "Only you are there." Once again, the poet addresses his other self, the recognition of which entirely prevents him from any spiritual mobility. Only a dual loneliness pervades.

Also in *Darker* is a short poem that is in many ways Strand's bleakest expression of his condition. He writes "My Death" from the perspective of the other side of the grave. He asserts that sadness, confusion, and waste are commonplace, expected elements of the event, of which he is consciously aware. The poet seemingly enjoys the chaos he precipitates among his friends and relatives by telling them that he had tried to commit suicide several times. He shocks them into leaving: "Soon I was alone." The poet is now returned, by his own will and force and intention, to his original state: Nothing is gained from death, not even momentary relief from the condition he has had in life.

THE STORY OF OUR LIVES

In *The Story of Our Lives* Strand presents a new way of looking at his state. On the one hand he is given to the usual self-involvement; on the other there is a rather complete self-detachment. The title poem, the best in the collection, can be rightfully interpreted in a straightforward manner. The narrator of the poem is addressing someone, presumably a woman whom he loves and to whom he is probably married. He tells her that they have been reading "the story of our lives;" that is, the frame of this long poem is to explore the possibilities of what it would mean to be able to read their lives as though they were recorded in a book, here ostensibly a novel. They jointly read on, learning of themselves as their plots and plights unfold.

The poem, which is one of his better and more readable pieces, is written in seven stanzas of some twenty lines each. In the first one, Strand reports to readers (and undoubtedly to himself) that the "*we*" of the poem are trying to find meaning and direction in their "lives" by reading in a book where, at least, what happens is known. The "*we*" here garners two legitimate interpretations. First, it is clearly the poet himself and the lover whom he is addressing. At the same time, Strand has constructed the poem so as to legitimize it as another fractured-self conversation typical in his works. In either

case, the personas of the poem are sitting together on a couch in their living room, knowing that "the book of our lives is empty"; the furniture is never changed; even the rugs become "darker" through the years as "our shadows pass over them." The second stanza opens with "We are reading the story of our lives/ as though we were in it/ as though we had written it." Life is just as vacuous in the novel as in their other, daily existence. The poet recognizes early that if such a book did exist, it would be unable to reveal meaning for him; that, perhaps, would be somebody else's life (or lives). In all stanzas except the first one, a few random passages from the imagined book are interwoven into the poet's own lines so as to make evident the futility of the endeavor. Because the book offers nothing new, the poet records that "it wants to divide us."

In the third and fourth stanzas, the other self becomes both bored and tired and falls asleep, as it is written in the book. The primary narrator-self reads on to see what will happen; of course he learns that the answer is, more or less, nothing. People fall asleep and people wake up—their lives remain empty whether they be well rested or not. By the fifth stanza, the poet has given up on finding something in the book that would foretell purpose in his (their) existence; he wishes only for a "perfect moment," one in which he could have momentary relief from the dark. Were there such a moment, so he ponders, he could then perpetually live and relive it by always starting at the beginning of the book and reading to that point. Such a moment is not to be found; it does not exist in their lives and cannot be found in a record of their lives. The concluding stanzas of the poem reinforce such a stance. The poet and his companion are left with loneliness and despair. They grow tired of reading the book, of studying the "tired phantoms" that occupy the "copy" as well as inhabit their own bodies. Thus they determine to accept this truth, realizing that "they are the book and they are/ nothing else."

SELECTED POEMS

Selected Poems is a collection that, as would be expected, contains his best poems, and the volume does serve well to represent Strand's life's work to 1980. Five new poems appeared in this publication, the most important of which is the unusual "Shooting Whales." The poet recalls an event from his childhood in which he, his father, and other family members get in a boat to watch fishermen who have gone out to shoot whales in St. Margaret's Bay. They are out all day, and as they are returning, after dark, their boat's engine dies. The speaker's father takes the oars and rows all the way home, speechlessly. That night the young speaker lies in bed envisioning the whales moving in the ocean beneath him: "they were luring me/ downward and downward/ into the murmurous/ water of sleep." His existence, then, is made akin to that of the whales; they are like singing mermaids who would lure him into the depths of his later darkness, self-involvement, and loneliness.

THE CONTINUOUS LIFE

Strand did not publish another volume of poetry for ten years. *The Continuous Life* displays a variety in form and content. Many of the poems are ostensibly prose but qualify as poems, if at all, because each of their meanings is conveyed poetically, through a series of images. More noticeably, there is less focus on split personality and psychosis. Though the poet never gets out of himself to the extent that his subject matter is actually another person, he does focus on external people and conditions in some poems in this volume. A few of these poems are not even written in first person; some are recordings of conversations, almost in dramatic form; two or three of them are called "letters."

The majority of the thirty poems in *The Continuous Life* are composed in the same vein as those already discussed here, with little tampering with previous themes. In the poem "The Continuous Life," Strand gives advice about what parents should tell their children. First, he instructs, "confess/ To your little ones the night is a long way off"—that is, tell them of death but explain that it is far in the distant future. His second advice is to inform them of how "mundane" life is, and he then offers a list of household chores and implements. Parents should also explain that life is a period "between two great darks," birth and death. In the meantime, individuals conduct a great "search" for "something . . ., a piece of the dark that might have been yours." Finally, the poet recognizes the existence and reality of "small tremors of love through your brief,/ Undeniable selves, into your days, and beyond." It is unusual for Strand to acknowledge the existence of love, or even of "small tremors

of love," which here arguably counter the darkness upon which the bulk of his work focuses. The poet sees love, possibly, as an experience that can give partial and momentary relief in the present.

"The End," the short poem that concludes *The Continuous Life*, serves as a final comment about Strand's life, and therefore his poetry, "Not every man knows what he shall sing at the end," writes the poet in such a way as to suggest that he does. He then gives a short list of typical activities of life that come to an end when a man becomes eternally "motionless" and it is "clear that he'll never go back." The poem concludes, "Not every man knows what is waiting for him, or what he shall sing/ When the ship he is on slips into darkness, there at the end." The poet knows what awaits him at his end and what song he will then sing. Strand has explored his death sufficiently, he foresees, to know that he will comprehend and experience the darkness at that time just as he has lived his life. It will truly change nothing.

DARK HARBOR

In *Dark Harbor*, this darkness is made all the more visible. Strand has fashioned a book-length poetic sequence comprising forty-five numbered parts introduced by a "Proem." All but one of the individual units fit on a single page, and they are cast in loose, three-line stanzas, occasionally ending in couplets. Strand employs this muffled echo of Dante's terza rima to thread a graceful, somber meditation on loss, dislocation, and the general unease of a mind and spirit strangely alienated from all that they attend to and even accept. Either too decorous or too numb to celebrate or rebel, Strand's persona charts a quiet, restrained course in which a mood of seeming passivity or resignation manages to establish and build tension.

BLIZZARD OF ONE

Blizzard of One will strike many as a rather slight volume for a Pulitzer Prize winner. As ever, Strand's realm is a place caught in the oscillation of the ordinary and the extraordinary. Time's erasure of the many selves one puts on is mourned in various inventive ways. Strand's rich melancholic intonations carry a greater edge of wit here, perhaps the gift of the even greater distancing from tragedy that comes with age. Many of the poems, like "A Suite of Appearances" and "Five Dogs," are multipart sequences. Most striking is "The Delirium

Waltz," a poem that marks a celebratory occasion of some kind without ever pinning down its true nature or meaning. Alternating heavily patterned, pantoum-like quatrains with stretches of prose, the poem seems a gathering of the damned, old friends locked in repetitive patterns of social interaction, the motion everything as they lose whatever recognition they ever had of who they are and why they came. The hours of the waltz become years and then a season. The dancers, many of whom wish to stop, cannot.

OTHER MAJOR WORKS

LONG FICTION: *The Monument*, 1978.

SHORT FICTION: *Mr. and Mrs. Baby and Other Stories*, 1985.

NONFICTION: *Art of the Real: Nine American Figurative Painters*, 1983; *William Bailey*, 1987; *Edward Hopper*, 1993; *The Weather of Words*, 2000.

CHILDREN'S LITERATURE: *The Planet of Lost Things*, 1982; *The Night Book*, 1985; *Rembrandt Takes a Walk*, 1986.

TRANSLATIONS: *Eighteen Poems from the Quechua*, 1971; *The Owl's Insomnia: Poems by Rafael Alberti*, 1973; *Travelling in the Family: Poems by Carlos Drummond de Andrade*, 1986.

EDITED TEXTS: *The Contemporary American Poets: American Poetry Since 1940*, 1969; *New Poetry of Mexico*, 1970; *Another Republic*, 1976 (with Charles Simic); *The Golden Ecco Anthology*, 1994; *The Making of a Poem: A Norton Anthology of Poetic Forms*, 2000 (with Eavan Boland).

BIBLIOGRAPHY

Aaron, Jonathan. "About Mark Strand: A Profile." *Ploughshares* 21, no. 4 (Winter, 1995/1996): 202-205. This is an excellent short overview of Strand's career, accomplishments, and sense of himself as a writer. Strand is the guest editor of this issue of the magazine.

Bloom, Harold. "Dark and Radiant Peripheries: Mark Strand and A. R. Ammons." *Southern Review* 8 (Winter, 1972): 133-141. This article is formally divided into four main sections: The introduction and conclusion briefly compare the poetry of Strand and Ammons, while the second section is given to Strand and the third to Ammons. Critical commentary is provided for the title poems of Strand's first three volumes: *Sleeping with One Eye Open*, *Reasons for Moving*, and *Darker*. Bloom focuses upon the "dark" elements of Strand's work.

Cooper, Philip. "The Waiting Dark: Talking to Mark Strand." *The Hollins Critic* 22 (1984): 1-7. This article does not record line by line an interview with the poet; rather, Cooper makes use of an interview from which he quotes frequently and extensively in articulating his own understanding of Strand's poetry. Specifically, he finds it humorous, dreamlike, and haunting, while finding the central theme of Strand's work to be elusive.

French, Robert. "Eating Poetry: The Poetry of Mark Strand." *The Far Point* 5 (1970): 61-66. French interprets Strand's poetry in general in context of the opening poem in *Reasons for Moving*. "Eating Poetry" is seen not as a poem to be criticized singularly but as a springboard for understanding Strand's theory of poetry and poetic techniques. Several poems from *Reasons for Moving* and *Darker* are addressed. French also provides comments about the influence of Franz Kafka upon Strand.

Gregorson, Linda. "Negative Capability." *Parnassus: Poetry in Review* 9 (1981): 90-114. Gregorson discusses poems selected from Strand's *Selected Poems*. She focuses on the rhymes and meters of the poetry, as well as the imagery. Also included are some critical analyses of the poet's use of prosody. Her overall effort is to trace the developing forms and formats of the recognizably better poems.

Howard, Richard. "Mark Strand." In *Alone with America: Essays on the Art of Poetry in the United States Since 1950*. New York: Atheneum, 1980. Howard writes critically of Strand's first two collections of poems, *Sleeping with One Eye Open* and *Reasons for Moving*. He sees the second volume as an outgrowth and continuation of the first one. Howard focuses on the duality of Strand's nature and his inability to reconcile the different aspects of his personality.

Kirby, David. *Mark Strand and the Poet's Place in Contemporary American Culture*. Columbia: University of Missouri Press, 1990. A fascinating exploration of the public roles and stances of the poet, with Strand as the central case in point. More a study in the sociology of literature than a work of literary criticism, yet important because Strand's public persona and his writing have a strange symbiotic relationship.

Olsen, Lance. "Entry to the Unaccounted For: Mark Strand's Fantastic Autism." In *The Poetic Fantastic: Studies in an Evolving Genre*, edited by Patrick D. Murphy and Vernon Hyles. New York: Greenwood Press, 1989. In this short article of some ten pages, Olsen interprets much of Strand's work in terms of fantasy. He deals specifically with poems taken from *Sleeping with One Eye Open* and *Reasons for Moving*. The critic sees many elements of science fiction in Strand's poems, as well as metafiction.

Carl Singleton,
updated by Philip K. Jason

LUCIEN STRYK

Born: Kolo, Poland; April 7, 1924

PRINCIPAL POETRY
Taproot, 1953
The Trespasser, 1956
Notes for a Guidebook, 1965
The Pit and Other Poems, 1969
Awakening, 1973
Selected Poems, 1976
Collected Poems, 1953-1983, 1984
Bells of Lombardy, 1986
Of Pen and Ink and Paper Scraps, 1989
Where We Are: Selected Poems and Zen Translations, 1997
And Still Birds Sing: New and Collected Poems, 1998

OTHER LITERARY FORMS
Although Lucien Stryk is known for his significant work as a poet—A. Poulin, Jr. included Stryk's work in several editions of the influential anthology *Contempo-*

rary American Poetry—Stryk has also made innumerable contributions in his work as a translator, editor, and commentator on the importance of Zen philosophy and the art created by those who follow such a philosophy. As a translator, Stryk worked diligently, along with his frequent collaborator Takashi Ikemoto, to shed light on the work of important Zen masters such as Shinkichi Takahashi, Issa, and Basho. Some of his most significant work as a translator is found in *Zen: Poems, Prayers, Sermons, Anecdotes, Interviews* (1965); *Afterimages: Zen Poems of Shinkichi Takahashi* (1970); *Zen Poetry: Let the Spring Breeze Enter* (1977); *Traveler, My Name: Haiku of Basho* (1984); *Triumph of the Sparrow* (1986); and *The Dumpling Field: Haiku of Issa* (1991). As a Zen Buddhist commentator and practitioner as well as cultural historian, Stryk has created work that has proved to be vitally important in opening up a space first for the study of Zen and later for its celebration. Work relating to Zen Buddhist thought and art may be found in such volumes as *World of Buddha: An Introduction to Buddhist Literature* (1968) and *Encounter with Zen: Writings on Poetry and Zen* (1981). In his role as editor, Stryk is best known for his celebration of place, specifically the Midwest, in two collections that highlighted the work of emerging and established poets. *Heartland: Poets of the Midwest* (1967) and *Heartland II: Poets of the Midwest* (1975) continue to define the study of poetry in this region. Stryk also edited *The Gift of Great Poetry* (1992), demonstrating his range both as a poet and teacher.

ACHIEVEMENTS
Although Lucien Stryk has not won many major awards, he has received numerous grants, including a National Endowment for the Arts Poetry Fellowship, a Rockefeller Foundation Fellowship, a Ford Foundation Fellowship, a Fulbright grant and lectureship, and a National Institute of Arts and Letters award. For his work as a translator, Stryk received the Islands and Continents Translation Award for *The Penguin Book of Zen Poetry*.

BIOGRAPHY
Lucien Stryk was born in Kolo, Poland, to Emil and Celia (Meinstein) Stryk in early April of 1924. His family moved to the United States in 1928, settling in Chi-

cago and narrowly escaping the horrors that would ravage Poland during the 1930's and 1940's. Although
Stryk and his family were spared what undoubtedly
would have been an appalling and inevitable march toward death, they still felt the aftermath of the events as
members of their extended family remained in Poland,
only to meet their untimely deaths at the hands of Nazism.

During the turbulence of the depression and World
War II, Stryk came of age on the South Side of Chicago.
Many poems, including "A Sheaf for Chicago" and
"White City," chronicle Stryk's everyday life as a boy
growing up in an urban landscape that was teeming with
immigrants and the sons and daughters of immigrants.
Although many reviewers of Stryk's poetry note the influence of his study of Zen thought—a clear and strong
force throughout his poems and translations—too few
mention the impact of Stryk's early years as the son of
outsiders. As is common with young children and teen-
agers, the idea that one might be different from a given
peer group presents a dilemma that at the time seems
staggering, yet that may later offer a better vantage for
the creation of art. In "White City," Stryk describes the
act of climbing on an abandoned roller coaster track as
other children hurl stones at him. "This was no/ King-of-
the Mountain game," he tells us. Indeed, such a gauntlet
presented the very pressures of life and death, of acceptance or rejection based upon the foolish dares of those
who are members of groups we wish to join. Having to
stand at the margins of his community, however, established a perspective for Stryk that leads to many of the
quiet, modest, yet profoundly truthful, insights that he
reaches in the writing of poems later in his career. This
sense of difference—a sense of belonging to more than
just an American community—manifests itself in
Stryk's work in a variety of ways: in his connection to
Zen teachings and his translations of Zen texts and poems, in his Polish heritage and the many cities in Europe
and Asia that he has lived in or visited, in his understanding of place—moving from the particular to the
universal, and in his celebration of the many years he
lived in a small, rural Midwestern town.

Soon after graduation from high school, Stryk served
with the U.S. Army artillery in the South Pacific from
1943 to 1945. At the end of World War II, Stryk returned
to the United States and enrolled in the English program
at Indiana University where he received his B.A. in
1948. While studying at Indiana University, Stryk wrote
an essay, "The American Scene Versus the International
Scene," which establishes a part of the philosophical
framework that will continue to support the more universal vision of his poetry throughout his career. In this
essay—first published in *Folio*, the Indiana University
undergraduate review, in 1947—Stryk explains that the
isolationist thought he sees in so much American literature, with the exception of that of Ernest Hemingway,
"who identifies himself with the universal man," is
harmful and ill advised. Stryk asserts, "The nationalism
and regionalism—devotion to regional interests—that
so obviously manifest themselves in our literature, art,
and science can, with the social implications which follow, prove to be a detriment to international progress."
What Stryk calls for is an embrace of the variegated and
multifaceted collage that comprises the landscape of the
United States. "Men of all creeds, national origins, and
races—white, black, brown, yellow, and many intermediate hues—speaking in thousands of languages, strange
dialects, esoteric idioms, and fantastic variations of
American English," he contends, "are the mighty laboring forces that create the tremendous wealth, power, and
grandeur that is the United States of America."

Following his own call for a more cosmopolitan
embrace of the world and its riches, in 1948 Stryk studied literature and philosophy at the Sorbonne in Paris,
France, under the auspices of the University of Maryland program. During his stay in Paris, Stryk engaged
with philosophy under Gaston Bachelard and was particularly attracted to phenomenology. In Paris, he also
encountered other artists and intellectuals such as James
Baldwin, Roger Blin, and the French Resistance fighter
Jean-Paul Baudot, who appears in Stryk's poem, "Letter
to Jean-Paul Baudot, at Christmas." In 1950 he received a Master of Foreign Study degree from the University of Maryland and then traveled to England to
study comparative literature at Queen Mary College,
University of London. In 1951 he met and married
Helen Esterman, a native Londoner, and in that year
the couple bore their first child, a son named Dan.
The young family continued to reside in London from
1952 to 1954. In 1953, Stryk's first book of poems, *Tap-*

root, was published by Fantasy Press. In January of 1955, he returned to the United States with his family to study writing at the University of Iowa. In 1956, Stryk graduated with the Master of Fine Arts from Iowa and had his second collection of poetry, *The Trespasser*, published by Fantasy Press.

Stryk again left the United States from 1956 to 1958 to journey to Niigata University in Japan, where he held a lectureship. It was during this time that he became involved with the study of Zen Buddhism after a meeting with a Zen priest who happened to be a potter. In *Encounter with Zen*, Stryk explains that his visit with the priest "left an extraordinary impression. Home again, sipping tea from the superb bowl he made for me . . . I began making plans. Soon I was inquiring seriously into Zen. . . . I visited temples and monasteries, meeting masters and priests throughout the country and, most important of all, began to meditate."

This initial encounter with Zen thought and practice has continued to color and inform not only Stryk's poems but also his way of life. Following this revelatory two-year period, in 1958 Stryk accepted an appointment at Northern Illinois University in DeKalb as an assistant professor of English, teaching poetry, poetry writing, and Asian literature. His daughter Lydia was born the same year, and Stryk and his wife, Helen, stayed at the university until 2000, when they moved to a suburb of Chicago. Stryk continues to split his time between England and Chicago, and his travels often take him into Asia as well.

ANALYSIS

Stryk's devotion to place grows naturally out of his dedication to Zen principles, and as he suggests in the introduction to his second edited collection of Midwestern poetry, *Heartland II* (1976), if one is to find peace as a poet or philosopher or human, then one must, as the Zen master Qingyuan explains, see "mountains as mountains, waters as waters." For Stryk then, there can be no richer place on earth than the Midwest for the creation of poetry. There, he finds the vast sprawl of cities connected by rail and commerce, the dark, furrowed fields undulating with growth to the farthest horizon, and towns rising up out of nowhere, their quiet streets offering passage into what is most human and telling

about the human condition. As an editor of two landmark collections of Midwestern poetry—*Heartland* (1967) and *Heartland II*—and as the author of such poems as "Farmer," "Scarecrow," "Return to DeKalb," and "Fishing with My Daughter in Miller's Meadow," Stryk searches the Midwestern landscape, not for spectacle but for daily life. It is in daily living that Stryk moves, capturing in minimalist lines the wonder of a father holding his daughter's hand, walking through a meadow filled with fresh manure and grazing horses, or in "Farmer," first published in *Taproot*, magnifying the farmer's eyes that are "bound tight as wheat, packed/ hard as dirt." Stryk, in an essay titled "Making Poems," which is collected in *Encounter with Zen*, explains that the writing of poetry demands that one engage in "pure seeing," and from such seeing, he creates a poetry of simple Midwestern images that illustrate clearly the beauty, diversity, and breadth of life in the heartland.

AND STILL BIRDS SING

Although all of the works included in *And Still Birds Sing* are not set exclusively in the Midwest, the vision of life found in this collection is shaped by Stryk's long life as a resident of the Midwest. He explains in the introduction to *Heartland II*:

> As one who has worked for a number of years, in Asia and the United States on the translation and interpretation of Zen poetry, I am sometimes asked why in the face of such "exotic" pursuits I have an interest in the poetry of my region—or, worse, why my own poetry is set for the most part in small-town Illinois. To one involved in the study of a philosophy like Zen, the answer to such questions is not difficult: one writes of one's place because it is in every sense as wonderful as any other, whatever its topography and weathers, and because one cannot hope to discover oneself elsewhere.

The discovery of self is at the root of Stryk's poetry. Time and again the poet enters a moment, seemingly mundane in nature, and discovers how he is connected to all life. The search for self—an act of enlightenment—should not be misconstrued as indulgent or selfish in Stryk's poems, however. Far from indulging himself, Stryk's poetry exudes a humility born out of a desire to understand how people are all connected to one another, how any suffering or any joy people encounter must be seen as a shared suffering or joy—not as something that can be hoarded or cloistered away from the rest of the world. A fine example of such a moment occurs in "What Is Moving." Here the poet watches the sky above the water, but finds no birds flying there. As he munches a sweet potato, he asks "Do I still live?" The recognition that he does indeed still live comes to him in his understanding of how he relates to others: "The same thing / Runs through both of us," he declares. "My thought moves the world:/ I move, it moves." Similarly, in "Words," the poet explains that he does not "take" the words of another, that he cannot possess the other as he or she speaks. Instead, he acknowledges how such words connect the speaker and the listener: "I listen/ To what makes you talk—/ Whatever that is—/ And me listen." People's shared humanity compels them, Stryk suggests, to listen and to speak of the space they all must share as they live in this place and in this time.

AWAKENING

In an interview, Stryk speaks about the "curiosity and hunger . . . that will take a man very far across the earth looking for things." He contends that "This excitement about reality is part and parcel of the making of poems." Such an attitude about discovery—the act of coming into contact with places and people and animals and plants never before encountered—is the other powerful force and theme that drives Stryk's work. The path to such encounters, for Stryk, can only be found if one is aware or awake, however. In the title poem of *Awakening* (1973), the poet discovers and celebrates the act of wakefulness—the key to enlightenment within Zen thought. As he gathers shells with his daughter, he considers how perception shapes the universe: "I take them from her,/ make, at her command,/ the universe. Hands clasped,/ making the limits of/ a world, we watch till sundown/ planets whirling in the sand." Unlike some of his contemporaries, Stryk does not struggle with the idea of "limits"—nor does he fear the darkness of people's finite existence. Rather, he concludes "Awakening" with the image of the darkness that "takes" the trees outside his home one by one into the night and proclaims that "At this hour I am always happy,/ ready to be taken myself,/ fully aware." Perhaps this is what distinguishes

Stryk's vision and the poems that are created out of that vision: an acceptance of self and world that finds its root in a person who has made peace with the human condition.

OTHER MAJOR WORKS

NONFICTION: *Encounter with Zen: Writings on Poetry and Zen*, 1981.

TRANSLATIONS: *Zen: Poems, Prayers, Sermons, Anecdotes, Interviews*, 1965 (with Takashi Ikemoto); *Afterimages: Zen Poems of Shinkichi Takahashi*, 1970 (with Ikemoto); *The Crane's Bill: Zen Poems of China and Japan*, 1973 (with Ikemoto); *Zen Poetry: Let the Spring Breeze Enter*, 1977 (with Ikemoto); *The Penguin Book of Zen Poetry*, 1977 (with Ikemoto); *Traveler, My Name: Haiku of Basho*, 1984; *On Love and Barley: Haiku of Basho*, 1985; *Triumph of the Sparrow: Zen Poems of Shinkichi Takahashi*, 1986 (with Ikemoto); *The Dumpling Field: Haiku of Issa*, 1991 (Noboru Fujiwara); *Cage of Fireflies: Modern Japanese Haiku*, 1993.

EDITED TEXTS: *Heartland: Poets of the Midwest*, 1967; *World of Buddha: An Introduction to Buddhist Literature*, 1968; *Heartland II: Poets of the Midwest*, 1975; *The Gift of Great Poetry*, 1992.

BIBLIOGRAPHY

Abbot, Craig S., ed. "Lucien Stryk: A Bibliography." *Analytical and Enumerative Bibliography* 5, nos. 3/4 (1991). The most comprehensive bibliography to date. Abbot includes sections that chronicle Stryk's career as a poet, reviewer, and critic.

Krapf, Norbert. "Discovering Lucien Stryk's *Heartland*." *Eclectic Literary Forum* 5, no. 4 (Winter, 1995): 50-52. A close look at Stryk as an editor, particularly of *Heartland*, and his relevance to the Midwest.

Porterfield, Susan. "Portrait of a Poet as a Young Man: Lucien Stryk." *Midwestern Miscellany* 22 (1994): 36-45. An examination of Stryk as a young man, with emphasis on his Midwest upbringing.

_____, ed. *Zen, Poetry, the Art of Lucien Stryk*. Athens, Ga.: Swallow Press and Ohio University Press, 1993. An extensive collection of essays by Stryk on the making of poems and the study of poetry, Zen

Buddhist thought, and the act of translation. It also includes two interviews with Stryk and four critical essays originally published in academic journals. The volume concludes with a selection of Stryk's poetry.

Stryk, Lucien. "Finding the Way: An Interview with Lucien Stryk. Parts I and II." Interview by Richard A. Deming. *Eclectic Literary Forum* 7, nos. 2/3 (Summer/Fall, 1997): 6-10. Stryk discusses his poetry and thoughts about American literature in an interview with Richard A. Deming.

Todd F. Davis

SIR JOHN SUCKLING

Born: Whitton, Twickenham, England; February, 1609
Died: Paris, France; 1642

PRINCIPAL POETRY

Fragmenta Aurea, 1646
The Last Remains of Sir John Suckling, 1659

OTHER LITERARY FORMS

Between 1637 and 1641, Sir John Suckling completed three plays: *Aglaura* (1638), *The Goblins* (1638), and *Brennoralt* (1646). *The Sad One*, an unfinished fragment, was written sometime earlier. *Aglaura* was published in 1638 in folio format; none of the other plays was printed during the poet's lifetime. Most of Suckling's fifty-odd letters are personal in subject matter, but two of them—one to "A Gentleman in Norfolk" and one to Henry Jermyn—are essentially political tracts dealing with the Scottish Campaign of 1639 and the opening of the Long Parliament in 1640, respectively. Suckling was also the author of "An Account of Religion by Reason," a defense of Socinianism that attempts to reconcile biblical revelation with the mythologies of the ancients. Suckling's letters and "An Account of Religion by Reason" have been collected by Thomas Clayton in *The Works of Sir John Suckling: The Non-Dramatic Works* (1971).

ACHIEVEMENTS

During his lifetime, Sir John Suckling's reputation as courtier and rakehell overshadowed his literary endeavors. His attacks on the Neoplatonic amatory conventions of the 1630's led him into poetic skirmishes with Edmund Waller and a swarm of lesser poets; his much vaunted dislike of the aged and ailing Ben Jonson earned him the enmity of the Sons of Ben. In his satire "The Wits," Suckling took on the entire Caroline literary establishment, with a good word for no one but Lucius Cary, Viscount Falkland. Such combativeness, joined with the theatricality of his personal life, isolated Suckling from his fellow poets, and his work elicited few of the usual encomia from contemporaries. The raciness and adolescent flippancy that are the hallmarks of his style, moreover, constitute a reaction against the prevailing Caroline tastes that was little appreciated in his own day.

Suckling's style, however, was precisely suited to the poets of the succeeding generation, and the Restoration wits found in him a model for their own aspirations. In John Dryden's *Of Dramatic Poesie: An Essay* (1668), Eugenius argues that the ancients "can produce nothing so courtly writ, or which expresses so much the conversation of a gentleman, as Sir John Suckling"; William Congreve and John Wilmot, Earl of Rochester, both praised his ease and naturalness. Restoration poets eagerly imitated "The Wits," using it as the pattern for their own literary squibs; they also appropriated the ballad stanza that Suckling introduced into formal poetry.

Although enthusiasm for Suckling waned during the eighteenth century, he continued to command a firm place in the poetic pantheon. Samuel Johnson praised him for not falling into the metaphysical excesses of poets such as Abraham Cowley. Since that time the critical estimation of Suckling has remained relatively constant: Although a minor poet, he was a good one, and several of his lyrics are frequently anthologized.

John Dryden undoubtedly exaggerated Suckling's achievement, but his recognition of the part that Suckling played in transforming English poetic diction is valid. Suckling's ability to capture the rhythms of colloquial speech in rhymed verse represents a real innovation in seventeenth century poetry. Although his attitudes toward women and love are often cynical and occasionally grating, his earthy common sense usually comes across as a necessary antidote to the stylized Neoplatonism of so much amatory verse of the 1630's. In similar fashion, Suckling's embrace of native literary forms such as the ballad and the riddle serves as a corrective to the classicizing tendencies of Renaissance poetry. Suckling's œuvre is small, but the role he played in English poetry was a pivotal one: His experiments in diction and essays in satire furthered the shift from a Renaissance to a Restoration aesthetic.

BIOGRAPHY

Sir John Suckling was born in February, 1609, into a prominent gentry family. His father, also Sir John, was a longtime member of Parliament who held a number of minor positions at court; in 1622, he purchased the office of Comptroller of the King's Household, which he occupied until his death in 1627. The poet's mother, Martha, was the sister of Lionel Cranfield, later first Earl of Middlesex and, until his impeachment in 1624, Lord Treasurer of England. Although his mother died in

Sir John Suckling (Hulton Archive)

1613, Suckling maintained close ties with the Cranfield family; his uncle's disgrace, countenanced by the royal favorite the Duke of Buckingham, alienated Suckling from the inner circles of the court.

Suckling matriculated at Trinity College, Cambridge, between 1623 and 1628; he was admitted to Gray's Inn in 1627. He may have served in the English expedition against the French on the Ile de Ré in 1627 and definitely fought in Lord Wimbledon's regiment in the Dutch service in 1629-1630. In October, 1631, Suckling joined the embassy to Gustavus Adolphus led by Sir Henry Vane, who was negotiating with the Swedish monarch for the return of the Palatinate to Charles I's brother-in-law, the Elector Frederick. Vane sent Suckling to England in March, 1632, with dispatches for the King. His mission complete, Suckling remained in England and plunged into a course of gambling and womanizing that lasted for the rest of the decade. During this period, according to John Aubrey, Suckling invented the game of cribbage. In order to recoup the vast sums he lost at cards and bowling, Suckling entered into a prolonged courtship of the northern heiress Anne Willoughby. Although the King supported his suit, Suckling's prospective in-laws did not; after a series of challenges, threatened lawsuits, and pitched battles between the two families and their allies, Suckling ceased his attentions. Shortly after this abortive courtship, Suckling entered into a relationship with the woman he called "Aglaura," probably Mary Bulkeley of Beaumaris, Anglesey. Despite the intensity of feeling that Suckling expresses in his few surviving letters to Aglaura, the affair flickered out by 1639, when Mary married a local squire. During the remainder of his life Suckling's closest emotional ties were with his Cranfield relatives, his uncle and his cousin Martha, Lady Cary.

Suckling had begun writing poetry during adolescence, but the lyrics for which he is best known were composed during the mid-1630's. In 1637, he turned seriously to drama; his tragedy *Aglaura* was produced with great fanfare in February, 1638, by the King's Company at Blackfriars. Suckling provided *Aglaura* with a tragicomic ending for a performance before the King and Queen in April, 1638; the play was printed in a lavish folio edition later that year.

The outbreak of trouble in Scotland in 1639 put an end to Suckling's literary activities. Raising a troop of one hundred horsemen, whom he clad at his own expense in white doublets and scarlet breeches, Suckling joined King Charles in the north. Because of illness, perhaps dysentery, he saw little action and was later accused of cowardice in the campaign. With the Treaty of Berwick in June, 1639, Suckling returned to London and was elected to the Short Parliament as an MP for Bramber, Sussex, in a by-election. Suckling returned to the border country in August, 1640, for the Second Bishops' War. After the defeat of the King's forces at Newburn he participated in the general retreat, during which he reportedly lost his coach and a wardrobe worth £300 to the Scottish commander Leslie.

With the opening of the Long Parliament in November, 1640, Suckling began to assume a more active role in politics. He became involved in a conspiracy to stage a coup d'état which would have dissolved Parliament and returned effective political power to the king. The plans of the plotters were discovered; after a preliminary examination by the House of Commons, Suckling fled to France on May 5, 1641. A writ for his arrest was issued the same day. Suckling arrived in Paris on May 14, but nothing is known of his subsequent activities. Although the exact details of his death are unclear, the most plausible account is that he committed suicide by poison sometime in 1642.

ANALYSIS

Sir John Suckling was a poet of reaction. Assuming the role of roaring boy at the Caroline court, he assaulted with an almost adolescent glee the conventions, literary and amatory, that prevailed during the 1630's. Suckling challenged the fashionable cult of Platonic Love with a pose of libertinism. He rejected the sophisticated Continental models employed by Ben Jonson and Thomas Carew in their lyrics, introducing in their stead native, "subliterary" forms such as the ballad and the riddle. Finally, Suckling rejected the title "poet," vaunting his amateur status in a pursuit that he implied had become increasingly dominated by ungentlemanly professionals. For the greater part of his short poetic career, Suckling was an iconoclast rather than an innovator, more

certain of what he was attacking than what he proposed to offer in its place. In the final poems, however, he achieved a balance between the successive waves of idealism and cynicism that rocked his short life. This newfound confidence in his art manifests itself most clearly in the good humor and good sense of "A Ballad upon a Wedding."

Thomas Clayton divides Suckling's poetic career into four periods. The earliest poems, discovered by L. A. Beaurline in manuscript in the late 1950's, consist of a Christmas devotional sequence and two meditations upon faith and salvation written before or during 1626. These pieces are derivative and not of great literary value, but they do suggest the young Suckling's receptiveness to influences and stylistic options open to him. Two of the eleven poems are important inasmuch as they forecast the themes that will run through Suckling's best-known lyrics. In "Faith and Doubt," the speaker contemplates the Christian mysteries of the incarnation and redemption; suspended between a desire to believe and an inability to move beyond the rational, he prays for the experience vouchsafed the apostle Thomas—the confirmation of faith through the senses. The speaker's troubled doubt serves as a prologue to the pose of libertine skepticism that Suckling later adopted in his amatory verse. Even more central to Suckling's poetic vision, perhaps, is the exuberant description of rustic customs and superstitions in "Upon Christmas Eve." With a sensitivity reminiscent of Robert Herrick, Suckling testified to his rural upbringing and his obvious delight in country life. Beneath the elegant courtliness of later poems this theme will persist, eventually reemerging in "A Ballad upon a Wedding."

The poems that Clayton assigns to the years 1626 to 1632 are a mixed lot, suggesting that the young Suckling was still in search of a personal style. While a number of these pieces represent essays in popular, usually humorous, forms—the riddle, the character, the ballad—others are serious attempts at the type of lyric that flourished at court. A final group fuses the popular and courtly strains in parody or, more rarely, in a delicate mixture of humor and compliment. With only a few exceptions, the poems exhibit a preoccupation with love and sexuality.

"A CANDLE" AND OTHER BAWDY RHYMES

The short riddle "A Candle" is essentially an adolescent joke that allows the poet to talk bawdy but evade the consequences. In a series of double entendres, Suckling describes the "thing" used by "the Maiden Female crew" in the night; to the discomfiture of the reader, the answer to the riddle proves to be "a candle." The poet is obviously intensely interested in sex, but apparently too unsure of his poetic powers to deal with it directly. The same type of double entendre informs "A Barley-break" and three characters—"A Barber," "A Pedler of Small-Wares," and "A Soldier." In "A Soldier," the speaker offers his love to an audience of ladies, combining bluster with a winning naïveté. The assertion "I cannot speak, but I can doe," with its obvious pun on "doe," well describes Suckling's own position in the early 1630's— willing and eager to besiege the ladies, but unskilled in the language of amatory gallantry.

"THE MIRACLE": PETRARCHAN EXPERIMENTS

Suckling's attempts to write conventional love lyrics underscore the truth of the admission in "A Soldier." While technically correct, these pieces seem flat after the exuberance and leering smuttiness of the riddles and characters. "The Miracle," for example, is an uninspired rehash of the Petrarchan fire and ice paradox. "Upon the first sight of my Lady Seimor," an exercise in Caroline Neoplatonism, is a stillborn blazon. In "*Non est mortale quod opto:* Upon Mrs. A. L.," Suckling tackles the same theme that Carew treats so successfully in "A Divine Mistress," that of the woman who is so perfect that the poet can find no way to approach her. Whereas Carew wittily solves the dilemma by praying to the gods to grant his lady "some more humanitie," Suckling blunders badly with his closing couplet, "I love thee well, yet wish some bad in thee,/ For sure I am thou art too good for me." The acquisition of "some bad," unlike "humanitie," can only mar the lady's perfection. Carew effects an accommodation between poetic convention and amatory pragmatism without compromising either; Suckling, facing the same dilemma, is forced to choose between them.

What is interesting about these poems written in an unblinking Platonic vein is that they are contemporaneous with the characters and ballads. The disjunction between love and sexuality, moreover, assumes a literary form inasmuch as Suckling reserves his bawdiness for the "subliterary" genres. In Suckling's mature style, the gap is bridged: Courtly verse forms are employed to set off the very grossness of the "country matters" they discuss. In "The deformed Mistress," Suckling weds the high-flown diction and exotic imagery of the serious blazon to the most unattractive physical blemishes with striking effect:

> Her Nose I'de have a foot long, not above,
> With pimples embroder'd, for those I love;
> And at the end a comely Pearl of Snot,
> Considering whether it should fall or not.

"Upon T. C. having the P." reemploys the fire and water conceit of "The Miracle" in unexpected fashion: The subject of the poem is Carew's difficulties in urinating when he has the pox.

"UPON MY LADY CARLILES WALKING IN HAMPTON-COURT GARDEN"

The best of these pieces is "Upon my Lady Carliles walking in Hampton-Court garden," a dialogue between T. C., presumably Tom Carew, and J. S., Suckling himself. While T. C. deifies the countess and falls into raptures over her beauty, J. S. mentally strips her until she is as naked as Eve in her first state. The degradation of Lady Carlisle from goddess to mortal woman to whore becomes complete when J. S. suggests in the final lines that countless fools have enjoyed the favors of this leading court beauty; if he and T. C. are men, they will do likewise rather than contenting themselves with merely praising her charms.

The humor of the poem should not distract the reader from the serious problem it raises. J. S., claiming that he is not "born to the Bay," disavows the title of poet; instead, he assumes the role of the plain-dealer who refuses to acquiesce in the fictions purveyed by Caroline lyricists. The dialogue dramatizes the opposition between "speaking" and "doing" that first appears in "A Soldier"; it also represents the externalization of an internal conflict inasmuch as Suckling, with little success, had for several years been penning the same platonic sentiments that he here fobs off on T. C. The attack on poetic conventions seems as much designed to conceal Suckling's inability to conform to the prevailing mode as to herald a new epoch in English lyric.

LOVE AND SEXUALITY

Between 1632 and 1637, Suckling composed the lyrics for which he is best remembered. Although most of these poems trade upon the blunt, skeptical attitude toward love that he affects in "Upon my Lady Carliles walking in Hampton-Court garden," others deal with love seriously, often in terms of the amatory Platonism that he had seemingly rejected. In the mid-1630's, Suckling was still searching for a congenial lyric stance, one that would allow him to reconcile love and sexuality, innocence and experience. Both Platonism and libertinism prove in the end to be inadequate solutions to the problem, since Suckling is uneasy with the one and much too strident in the other.

"WHY SO PALE AND WAN, FOND LOVER?"

In the song "Honest Lover whosoever," the speaker gently prescribes the proper Platonic behavior for the youth who aspires to amatory correctness. The effect is one of humorous indulgence; Suckling treats the absurdities of young love with the same bemused tolerance that Geoffrey Chaucer displays in Book I of *Troilus and Criseyde* (1382). The two poems "To his Rival" display the same comic delicacy, but it is a delicacy that begins to cloy.

In "Why so pale and wan, fond Lover?," however, Suckling finds a formula that combines sympathy and humor in a winning way. After counseling a pining young lover in the arts of seduction, the long-suffering speaker finally loses patience: In the last line he dismisses the unyielding woman with the exclamation, "The Devill take her." The use of comic reversal for purposes of closure becomes a standard element in Suckling's lyrics; the formula provides the perfect means for the poet to indulge his platonic sentiments while protesting his superiority to them with a wink or a leer.

LIBERTINE LYRICS

Darker in tone are the libertine lyrics, those which insist that love is a mere physical act without moral or spiritual implications. Suckling employs an argumentative style that superficially recalls the elegies, songs, and sonnets of John Donne, but the argument is less metaphorical and logically innovative than that of the elder poet. The tendency of these poems is to reduce love to mere appetite. In "Sonnet II," love is described as a good meal. In "Womans Constancy" lovemaking is compared

to bees extracting pollen from a flower: "One lights, one tastes, gets in, gets out." Suckling reaches his nadir in "Loves Offence," in which he arrives at the conclusion that "love is the fart/ of every heart."

"AGAINST FRUITION"

The two "Against Fruition" poems present Suckling at his most cynical. In "Against Fruition I," the speaker argues against sexual consummation, not because of any moral or philosophical scruples, but because fruition compares unfavorably with the more exquisite delights of sexual anticipation. The speaker argues that "Women enjoy'd (what s'ere before th'ave been)/ Are like Romances read, or sights once seen." This mistress, reified rather than deified, reappears throughout Suckling's lyrics of the mid-1630's. "Against Fruition II," an address to a mistress, is disturbing in its violence. One wonders how the lady should deal with the paradox, "Shee's but an honest whore that yeelds, although/ She be as cold as ice, as pure as snow." Suckling provides no answer to the dilemma. The subversion of the platonic arguments to a libertine end renders the "Against Fruition" poems a fascinating intellectual exercise, but they prove to be a poetic dead end.

RECONCILING CONTRARIES

In the final years of his life, Suckling at last found a framework within which he could reconcile his own hateful contraries. In the prose "Letter to a Friend" and "An Answer," both undoubtedly written by Suckling, "Jack" attempts, with the usual libertine arguments, to dissuade his friend "Tom" from marriage. Tom, however, has the last word: Turning the libertine commonplaces upside down, he argues that the "ravishing *Realities*" of marriage far surpass the "pleasing *Dreames*" of the sort that Suckling champions in "Against Fruition I." The reconciliation of idealism and skepticism is here suggested rather than achieved; yet, the recognition that love and sexuality are not necessarily incompatible prefigures the high-spirited synthesis of "A Ballad upon a Wedding."

"A BALLAD UPON A WEDDING"

In both style and substance, "A Ballad upon a Wedding" returns to the poems of the late 1620's. Suckling revitalizes the tired tradition of the epithalamium by describing an aristocratic wedding through the eyes of a yokel. The poem, written in an eight-eight-six ballad stanza, is remarkable for its exquisite imagery; in employing the homely details of rural life—mice, Katherine pears, a young colt—to blazon the bride's beauty, Suckling rediscovers the themes and techniques of his early Christmas poems. Coupled with the freshness of the imagery is a relaxed, accepting attitude toward the problem of love and sexuality that had bedeviled Suckling throughout his career. The poem closes with a comic reversal: The naïve speaker demonstrates that he is not so naïve after all when he speculates on what takes place in the nuptial chamber once the ceremony is over:

> At length the candles out, and now
> All that they had not done, they do:
>   What that is, who can tell?
> But I beleeve it was no more
> Than thou and I have done before
>   With *Bridget*, and with *Nell*.

The speaker's sexual awareness does not vitiate his fundamental innocence, nor does the bride's sexuality vitiate the romantic idealism that she inspires in the early parts of the poem. The real and the ideal are integrated into a comprehensive vision of love.

"THE WITS"

Aside from "A Ballad upon a Wedding" and one other epithalamium, Suckling's final poems deal primarily with literary affairs. As with love, Suckling achieves a balanced, mature outlook toward his position as a poet only with a struggle. "The Wits," probably composed during the summer of 1637, describes the scramble for the laureateship touched off by the death of Jonson in August of that year. Employing the same ballad form he had used in "A Ballad upon a Wedding," Suckling lampoons all the chief Caroline pretenders to wit. Jonson and Carew come in for some especially hard knocks; only Lucius Cary, Viscount Falkland, escapes the general opprobrium, perhaps because by this time he had given over poetry for philosophy. Suckling alone is absent from the convocation: A bystander tells Apollo,

> He loved not the muses so well as his sport;
>   And
> Prized black eyes, or a lucky hit
> At bowls, above all the Trophies of wit.

Angered at this information, the deity promptly declares Suckling an outlaw in poetry. No role, perhaps, suited Suckling better. Falling back on the role of plain-dealer he had perfected in his lyrics, Suckling rejects the poetic establishment but at the same time betrays his anxiety that he does not quite measure up to its standards.

FINAL POEMS

In the last poems, however, Suckling demonstrates a growing willingness to accept his vocation. In "An Answer to some Verses made in his praise," he sheds his customary *sprezzatura* and, with convincing modesty, accepts the tribute of another poet. Suckling at long last takes his place among the wits he had feigned to scorn less than two years earlier.

The outbreak of civil war cut short Suckling's career. Before his death in 1642, however, he had achieved a poetic and personal maturity: His last poems, which suggest a new accommodation of the conflicting motives so evident in the earlier works, are also his best. Suckling's small œuvre of some eighty poems is erratic in quality. Those pieces that argue doctrinaire positions on love and life tend to be his worst: The poems taking the stock platonic line are insipid, the libertine exercises too often grating. Yet, Suckling displays throughout his work a sure sense for the comic and a sensitivity to rural life matched in this period only by Herrick. Suckling's poems record his progress, sometimes halting but always fascinating, toward a sure sense of himself and his art.

OTHER MAJOR WORKS

PLAYS: *Aglaura*, pr., pb. 1638; *The Goblins*, pr. 1638; *Brennoralt*, pr. 1646; *The Works of Sir John Suckling: The Plays*, pb. 1971 (L. A. Beaurline, editor).

MISCELLANEOUS: *The Works of Sir John Suckling: The Non-Dramatic Works*, 1971 (Thomas Clayton, editor).

BIBLIOGRAPHY

Beaurline, L. A. "'Why so Pale and Wan?': An Essay in Critical Method." In *Seventeenth-Century English Poetry: Modern Essays in Criticism*, edited by William R. Keast. Rev. ed. London: Oxford University Press, 1971. Beaurline sees the poem as a dramatic lyric with a "facetious" (in the sixteenth century sense) narrator whose wit reflects unity in situation, character, argument, and language. Beaurline also discusses the poem as a response to the more complex Metaphysical poetry.

Clayton, Thomas. "'At Bottom a Criticism of Life': Suckling and the Poetry of Low Seriousness." In *Classic and Cavalier: Essays on Jonson and the Sons of Ben*, edited by Claude J. Summers and Ted-Larry Pebworth. Pittsburgh, Pa: University of Pittsburgh Press, 1982. Clayton's essay provides an overview of Suckling criticism and proceeds to analyze four poems: the early "Upon St. Thomas's Unbelief," "An Answer to Some Verses Made in His Praise," "Why So Pale and Wan," and "Love's Clock." Places Suckling's work in its literary context.

Miner, Earl. *The Cavalier Mode from Jonson to Cotton.* Princeton, N.J.: Princeton University Press, 1971. Though he disapproves of Suckling the man, Miner often finds in him the poetic embodiment of Cavalier love poetry. In fact, Miner believes the "battle of the sexes" cliché was first given Cavalier expression in Suckling's "A Soldier" and "Loves Siege."

Skelton, Robin. *Cavalier Poets.* London: Longmans, Green, 1960. Skelton devotes one chapter of his monograph to Suckling's poetry, which he finds self-conscious and heavily influenced by John Donne. Much of the chapter is devoted to an appreciation of Suckling's "A Ballad upon a Wedding."

Squires, Charles L. *Sir John Suckling.* Boston: Twayne, 1978. Although Squires covers Suckling's life, plays, poems, prose, and literary reputation, he also provides careful readings of several poems, and his criticism of the four plays is detailed. Suckling emerges as the spokesman for the Cavalier era. Supplemented by a chronology and an annotated select bibliography.

Summer, Joseph H. *The Heirs of Donne and Jonson.* Oxford, England: Oxford University Press, 1970. Summers considers Suckling as an exemplar of the gentleman at court and finds in his verse debts to Ben Jonson and John Donne. Treating the narrative voice in poetry, Summers makes interesting distinctions between the Donne originals and the Suckling responses, particularly in the cases of "The Indifferent" and "Love's Deity," which are answered in Suckling's Sonnets II and III.

Van Strien, Kees. "Sir John Suckling in Holland." *English Studies* 76, no. 5 (September, 1995): 443. Suckling traveled in the Low Countries in the early 17th century, yet left no record of his journeys. A letter written by Suckling and additional material are pieced together to develop a picture of the writer during a little-known period of his life.

Michael P. Parker;
bibliography updated by the editors

HENRY HOWARD, EARL OF SURREY

Born: Hunsdon, Hertfordshire, England; 1517
Died: London, England; January 19, 1547

PRINCIPAL POETRY

An excellent Epitaffe of syr Thomas Wyat, 1542
Songes and Sonettes, 1557 (also known as *Tottel's Miscellany*)
The Poems of Henry Howard, Earl of Surrey, 1920, 1928 (Frederick Morgan Padelford, editor)

OTHER LITERARY FORMS

Henry Howard, earl of Surrey, did not contribute to English literature with any other form besides poetry. His poetic innovations, however, helped to refine and stabilize English poetry.

ACHIEVEMENTS

As a translator and original poet, Henry Howard, earl of Surrey prepared the way for a number of important developments in English poetry. His translations and paraphrases are not slavishly literal; they are re-creations of classical and continental works in terms meaningful to Englishmen. He naturalized several literary forms—the sonnet, elegy, epigram, and satire—and showed English poets what could be done with various stanzas, metrical patterns, and rhyme schemes, including terza rima, ottava rima, and poulter's measure. He invented the English or Shakespearean sonnet (three quatrains and a couplet) and set another precedent by using the form for subjects other than love. His poems exerted considerable influence, for they circulated in manuscript for some time before they were printed. Forty of them appear in *Songes and Sonettes* (better known as *Tottel's Miscellany*), a collection of more than 270 works which saw nine editions by 1587 and did much to establish iambic meter in English poetry. Surrey shares with Sir Thomas Wyatt the distinction of having introduced the Petrarchan mode of amatory verse in England.

His innovations in poetic diction and prosody have had more lasting significance. Surrey refined English poetry of aureate diction, the archaic and ornate language cultivated by fifteenth century writers. His elegant diction formed the basis of poetic expression until well into the eighteenth century.

His greatest achievement is his demonstration of the versatility and naturalness in English of the iambic pentameter line. Surrey invented blank verse, which later poets brought to maturity. The metrical regularity of much of his rhymed verse (a regularity perhaps enhanced by Tottel's editor) had a stabilizing effect on English prosody, which had long been in a chaotic state. In *The Arte of English Poesie* (1589), George Puttenham hailed Wyatt and Surrey as "the first reformers of our English meetre and stile," for they "pollished our rude & homely maner of vulgar poesie." Until the present century Surrey's smoothness was generally preferred to Wyatt's rougher versification.

Surrey's essential quality, a concern with style, informed his poetry, his life, and the Tudor court of which he was a brilliant representative. Consistently as a poet and frequently as a courtier he epitomized learning and grace; for his countrymen he was an exemplar of culture.

BIOGRAPHY

Henry Howard, earl of Surrey from 1524, was the eldest son of Thomas Howard, third Duke of Norfolk. The elder Howard, one of the most powerful leaders of the old nobility, saw to it that his heir received an excellent education. At the age of twelve, Surrey was translating Latin, French, Italian, and Spanish and practicing martial skills. He was selected as the companion of Henry Fitzroy, Henry VIII's illegitimate son who had been created Duke of Richmond. The youths, both proud, impetuous, and insecure, were settled at Windsor in the spring of 1530. Surrey was married in 1532 to Lady Frances de Vere; the couple began living together a few years later, and he was evidently devoted to her for the rest of his life.

Surrey and Richmond accompanied the King to France in the autumn of 1532. The young men resided with the French court, then dominated by Italian culture, for most of the following year. Surrey acquired courtly graces and probably became acquainted with the work of Luigi Alamanni, a Florentine writer of unrhymed verse. Shortly after Surrey and Richmond returned to the English court, the King's son married Surrey's sister Mary.

In 1540, Surrey was appointed steward of the University of Cambridge in recognition of his scholarship.

Henry Howard, earl of Surrey (Hulton Archive)

Having also distinguished himself in martial games, in 1541 he was made Knight of the Garter. His military education was completed when he was sent to observe the King's continental wars. The first English aristocrat to be a man of letters, statesman, and soldier, the handsome and spirited earl was esteemed as a model courtier. During his final seven years, he was occupied with courtly, military, and domestic matters, finding time to write only when he was out of favor with Henry VIII or otherwise in trouble.

Early in 1543, Surrey, Thomas Clere, Thomas Wyatt the Younger, and another young man indulged in disorderly behavior which led to the earl's brief imprisonment in the Fleet. Still in the king's good graces, he spent most of the next three years serving in France and building an elegant, costly house in the classical style. As Marshal of the Field and commander of Boulogne, he proved to be a competent officer who did not hesitate to risk his own life. He was wounded while leading a courageous assault on Montreuil. After a defeat in a minor skirmish, he was recalled in the spring of 1546.

By that time he had made enemies who were intent on destroying him. He was imprisoned for threatening a courtier who had called Norfolk morally unfit to be regent during the minority of the king's son, Edward. Making much of Surrey's pride in his Plantagenet ancestry, his enemies built a case that he intended to seize power. His request to be allowed to confront his chief accuser in single combat—characteristic of his effort to live by the chivalric code of a vanishing era—was denied. His sister Mary and certain supposed friends testified against him. Maintaining his innocence, Surrey forcefully defended himself and reviled his enemies during an eight-hour trial for treason; but, like many others whom the Tudors considered dangerous or expendable, he was condemned and beheaded on Tower Hill.

ANALYSIS

An aristocrat with a humanistic education, Henry Howard, earl of Surrey, considered literature a pleasant diversion. As a member of the Tudor court, he was encouraged to display his learning, wit, and eloquence by writing love poems and translating continental and classical works. The poet who cultivated an elegant style was admired and imitated by his peers. Poetry was not considered a medium for self-expression. In the production of literature, as in other polite activities, there were conventions to be observed. Even the works that seem to have grown out of Surrey's personal experience also have roots in classical, Christian, Italian, or native traditions. Surrey is classical in his concern for balance, decorum, fluency, and restraint. These attributes are evident throughout his work—the amatory lyrics, elegies, didactic verses, translations, and biblical paraphrases.

LOVE POEMS

He produced more than two dozen amatory poems. A number of these owe something to Petrarch and other continental poets. The Petrarchan qualities of his work, as well as those of his successors, should not be exaggerated, however, for Tudor and Elizabethan poets were also influenced by native tradition and by rhetorical treatises which encouraged the equating of elegance and excellence. Contemporaries admired the fluency and eloquence which made Surrey, like Petrarch, a worthy model. His sonnet beginning "From Tuscan cam my ladies worthi race," recognized in his own time as polite verse, engendered the romantic legend that he served the Fair Geraldine (Elizabeth Fitzgerald, b. 1528?), but his love poems are now recognized as literary exercises of a type common in Renaissance poetry.

Surrey's courtly lovers complain of wounds; they freeze and burn, sigh, weep, and despair—yet continue to serve Love. Representative of this mode is "Love that doth raine and live within my thought," one of his five translations or adaptations of sonnets by Petrarch. The poem develops from a military conceit: The speaker's mind and heart are held captive by Love, whose colors are often displayed in his face. When the desired lady frowns, Love retreats to the heart and hides there, leaving the unoffending servant alone, "with shamfast looke," to suffer for his lord's sake. Uninterested in the moral aspects of this situation, Surrey makes nothing of the paradox of Love as conqueror and coward. He does not suggest the lover's ambivalence or explore the lady's motives. Wyatt, whose translation of the same sonnet begins "The longe love, that in my thought doeth harbor," indicates (as Petrarch does) that the lady asks her admirer to become a better man. Surrey's speaker, taught only to "love and suffre paine," gallantly concludes, "Sweet is the death that taketh end by love."

The point is not that Surrey's sonnet should be more like Wyatt's but that in this poem and in many of his lyrics Surrey seems less concerned with the complexity of an experience than with his manner of presenting it. Most of the lines are smooth and regularly iambic, although there are five initial trochees. The poem's matter is carefully accommodated to its form. The first quatrain deals with Love, the second with the lady, and the third with the lover's plight. His resolve is summarized in the couplet: Despite his undeserved suffering, he will be loyal. The sonnet is balanced and graceful, pleasing by virtue of its musical qualities and intellectual conceit.

Some of the longer poems do portray the emotions of courtly lovers. The speaker in "When sommer toke in hand the winter to assail" observes (as several of Surrey's lovers do) that nature is renewed in spring, while he alone continues to be weak and hopeless. Casting off his despondency, he curses and defies Love. Then, realizing the gravity of his offense, he asks forgiveness and is told by the god that he can atone only by greater suffering. Now "undone for ever more," he offers himself as a "miror" for all lovers: "Strive not with love, for if ye do, it will ye thus befall." Lacking the discipline of the sonnet form, this poem in poulter's measure seems to sprawl. Surrey's amatory verse is generally most successful when he focuses on a relatively simple situation or emotion. "When sommer toke in hand the winter to assail," not his best work, is representative in showing his familiarity with native poetry: It echoes Geoffrey Chaucer's *Troilus and Criseyde* (1382) and describes nature in a manner characteristic of English poets. In seven other love poems, Surrey describes nature in sympathy with or in contrast to the lover's condition.

A WOMAN'S PERSPECTIVE

At a time when most amatory verse was written from the male perspective, Surrey assumed a woman's voice in three of his lyrics. The speaker in "Gyrtt in my giltlesse gowne" defends herself against a charge of craftiness pressed by a male courtier in a companion poem beginning "Wrapt in my carelesse cloke." Accused of encouraging men she does not care for, the lady compares herself to Susanna, who was slandered by corrupt elders. Remarking that her critic himself practices a crafty strategy—trying to ignite a woman's passion by feigning indifference—she asserts that she, like her pro-

totype, will be protected against lust and lies. This pair of poems, if disappointing because Surrey has chosen not to probe more deeply into the behavior and emotions generated by the game of courtly love, demonstrates the poet's skill in presenting a speaker in a clearly defined setting or situation. His finest lyrics may fairly be called dramatic.

Two other monologues, "O happy dames, that may embrace" and "Good ladies, ye that have your pleasure in exyle," are spoken by women lamenting the absence of their beloved lords. They may have been written for Surrey's wife while he was directing the siege of Boulogne. Long separations troubled him, but his requests to the Privy Council for permission to bring his family to France were denied. After an exordium urging her female audience to "mourne with [her] awhyle," the narrator of "Good ladies" describes tormenting dreams of her "sweete lorde" in danger and at play with "his lytle sonne" (Thomas Howard, oldest of the Surreys' five children, was born in 1536). The immediate occasion for this poem, however personal, is consciously literary: The lady, a sorrowful "wight," burns like a courtly lover when her lord is absent, comforted only by the expectation of his return and reflection that "I feele by sower, how sweete is felt the more" (the sweet-sour antithesis was a favorite with courtly poets). Despite the insistent iambic meter characteristic of poulter's measure, one can almost hear a voice delivering these lines. In the best of his love poetry, Surrey makes new wholes of traditional elements.

ELEGIAC POEMS

His elegiac poems reflect his background in rhetoric. Paying tribute to individuals, he would persuade his readers to become more virtuous men and women. "Wyatt resteth here, that quick could never rest," the first of his works to be published, devotes more attention to praise of Wyatt than to lament and consolation. Using the figure of *partitio* (division into parts), he anatomizes the physique of this complete man in order to display his virtues—prudence, integrity, eloquence, justice, courage. Having devoted eight quatrains to praise, Surrey proceeds to the lament—the dead man is "lost" to those he might have inspired—with a consolation at the thought that his spirit is now in heaven. He implies that God has removed "this jewel" in order to punish a nation blind to his worth. In so coupling praise and dispraise, Surrey follows a precedent set by classical rhetoricians. He again eulogized Wyatt in two sonnets, "Dyvers thy death do dyversely bemoan" and "In the rude age," both attacking Wyatt's enemies. The former devotes a quatrain to each of two kinds of mourners, hypocrites who only seem to grieve and malefactors who "Weape envyous teares heer [his] fame so good." In the sestet, he sets himself apart: *He* feels the loss of so admirable a man. Here, as in a number of his sonnets, Surrey achieves a harmony of form and content. There is no evidence that he knew Wyatt personally. His tributes to the older courtier are essentially public performances, but they convey admiration and regret and offer a stinging rebuke to courtiers who do not come up to Wyatt's standard.

Many sixteenth century poets wrote elegies for public figures; more than twenty appear in *Tottel's Miscellany*. Surrey, as indicated above, was familiar with the literary tribute. In "Norfolk sprang thee," an epitaph for his squire Thomas Clere (d. 1545), he uses some of the conventions of epideictic poetry to express esteem, as well as grief, for the dead. Developed according to the biographical method of praise (seen also in "From Tuscan cam my ladies worthi race"), the sonnet specifies Clere's origins and personal relationships; it traces his career from his birth in Norfolk to his mortal wound at Montreuil—incurred while saving Surrey's life—to his burial in the Howards's chapel at Lambeth. By "placing" Clere geographically and within the contexts of chivalric and human relationships, Surrey immortalizes a brave and noble person. He has succeeded in writing a fresh, even personal poem while observing literary and rhetorical conventions.

Personal feeling and experience certainly went into "So crewell prison," a lament for Richmond (d. 1536) and the poet's youthful fellowship with him at Windsor—ironically, the place of his confinement as a penalty for having struck Edward Seymour. Subtly alluding to the *ubi sunt* tradition, he mentions remembered places, events, and activities—green and graveled courts, dewy meadows, woods, brightly dressed ladies, dances, games, chivalric competition, shared laughter and confidences, promises made and kept—as he does so, conveying his sense of loss. He praises, and longs for, not only his friend but also the irrecoverable past. Of Richmond's soul he says nothing. His consolation, if so it may be called, is that the loss of his companion lessens the pain of his loss of freedom. "So crewell prison," perhaps Surrey's best poem, is at once conventional and personal.

DIDACTIC POEMS

Taught to regard the courtier as a counselor, he wrote a few explicitly didactic pieces. His sonnet about Sardanapalus, "Th' Assyryans king, in peas with fowle desyre," portrays a lustful, cowardly ruler. Such depravity, Surrey implies, endangers virtue itself. The poem may allude to King Henry VIII, who had executed two Howard queens. (Surrey witnessed Anne Boleyn's trial and Catherine Howard's execution.) The degenerate monarch in Surrey's sonnet, however, bears few resemblances to Henry VIII, who had often shown his regard for Norfolk's heir and Richmond's closest friend. John Gower, John Lydgate, and other poets had also told the story of Sardanapulus as a "mirror" for princes. Surrey's "Laid in my quyett bedd" draws upon Horace's *Ars Poetica* (13-8 B.C) and First Satire (35 B.C.). The aged narrator, after surveying the ages of man, remarks that people young and old always wish to change their estate; he concludes that boyhood is the happiest time, though youths will not realize this truth before they become decrepit. Like certain of the love poems, "Laid in my quyett bedd" illustrates Surrey's dramatic ability.

"LONDON, HAS THOU ACCUSED ME"

The mock-heroic "London, has thou accused me" was probably written while Surrey was imprisoned for harassing and brawling with some citizens and breaking windows with a stonebow. As C. W. Jentoft points out, the satirist, presenting himself as a God-sent "scourge for synn," seems to be delivering an oration. "Thy wyndowes had don me no spight," he explains; his purpose was to awaken Londoners secretly engaged in deadly sins to their peril. Appropriating the structure of the classical oration, he becomes, in effect, not the defendant but the prosecutor of a modern Babylon. The peroration, fortified with scriptural phrasings, warns of divine judgment.

POETRY TRANSLATIONS

Surrey's translations also reflect the young aristocrat's classical and humanistic education. He translated two poems advocating the golden mean—a Horatian ode and an epigram by Martial. In the former ("Of thy lyfe, Thomas") he imitates the terseness of the original. "Marshall, the thinges for to attayne," the first English translation of that work, is also remarkably concise. His intention to re-create in English the style of a Latin poet is evident in his translations of the second and fourth books of the *Aeneid*. He did not attempt to reproduce Vergil's unrhymed hexameters in English alexandrines (as Richard Stanyhurst was to do) or to translate them into rhymed couplets (as the Scottish poet Gawin Douglas had done). Familiar with the decasyllabic line of Chaucer and other native poets and the *verso sciolto* (unrhymed verse) of sixteenth century Italy, he devised blank verse, the form that was to be refined by Christopher Marlowe, William Shakespeare, and John Milton.

Textual scholars have encountered several problems in studying Surrey's translation of the *Aeneid*. His manuscripts are not extant, and all printed versions appeared after his death. The work may have been undertaken as early as 1538 or as late as 1544; in the light of his service at court and in France, it seems likely that the translation was done intermittently. Modern scholars now favor an early period of composition, which would make this translation earlier than many of Surrey's other works and help to account for their refined, decorous style.

Another issue is the relationship of Surrey's work to the *Eneados* of Gawin Douglas (1474?-1522), whose translation had circulated widely in manuscript during Surrey's youth. According to Florence Ridley, "In more than 40 percent of his lines Surrey's wording was noticeably influenced by that of Douglas" (*The "Aeneid" of Henry Howard, Earl of Surrey*, 1963). In Book Four, perhaps completed later than Book Two, Surrey borrowed from Douglas less frequently. There is other evidence that his style was maturing and becoming more flexible: more frequent run-ons, feminine endings, pauses within the line, and metrical variations.

The distinctive qualities of Surrey's translation are largely owing to his imitation of Vergil's style. A young humanist working in an immature language and using a new form, Surrey was trying, as Italian translators had done, to re-create in the vernacular his Latin master's compactness, restraint, and stateliness. He did not al-

ways succeed. Generally avoiding both prosaic and aureate vocabulary, he uses relatively formal diction. To a modern reader accustomed to the blank verse developed by later poets, the iambic meter is so regular as to be somewhat monotonous. By means of patterned assonance, consonance, and internal rhyme, as well as the placement of caesuras, he has achieved a flowing movement which approximates Vergilian verse paragraphs. Phonetic effects often pleasing in themselves heighten emotional intensity and help to establish the phrase, not the line, as the poetic unit. It is not surprising, then, that Thomas Warton called Surrey England's first classical poet. Imitation led to innovation, the creation of a form for English heroic poetry. Even though blank verse did not come into general use until late in the sixteenth century, Surrey's achievement remains monumental.

BIBLICAL PARAPHRASES

The paraphrases of Ecclesiastes 1-5 and Psalms 55, 73, and 88, Surrey's most nearly autobiographical works, portray the "slipper state" of life in the Tudor court. Probably written during his final imprisonment in late 1546, they speak of vanity and vexation of spirit and cry out against vicious enemies, treacherous friends, and a tyrant who drinks the blood of innocents. Like Wyatt, whose penitential psalms he admired, he used Joannes Campensis's Latin paraphrases which had been published in 1532. Surrey's translations are free, amplifying and at times departing from the Vulgate and Campensis, as in this line from his version of Ecclesiastes 2: "By princely acts [such as the pursuit of pleasure and building of fine houses] strave I still to make my fame indure." Although his background was Catholic, these poems express Protestant sentiments.

In his versions of Psalms 73 and 88 he speaks of God's "elect" and "chosen," apparently placing himself in that company. While praying for forgiveness in Psalm 73, he notes that his foes are going unscathed and asks why he is "scourged still, that no offence have doon." Psalm 55 calls for divine help as he faces death and exulting enemies; at the end of this unpolished, perhaps unfinished poem, Surrey completely departs from his printed sources to inveigh against wolfish adversaries. The time to live was almost past, but it was not yet the time to keep silence. Like the other biblical paraphrases, this work has chiefly biographical interest. Expecting imminent execution, Surrey was still experimenting with prosody: Psalm 55 is the one poem in this group to be written in unrhymed hexameters rather than poulter's measure. Even in his last works, the poet is generally detached and self-effacing. Surrey's greatest legacy to English poets is a concern for fluent, graceful expression.

OTHER MAJOR WORKS

TRANSLATIONS: *The Fourth Boke of Virgill*, 1554; *Certain Bokes of Virgiles Aenaeis*, 1557.

BIBLIOGRAPHY

Casady, Edwin. *Henry Howard, Earl of Surrey*. New York: Modern Language Association of America, 1938. While Casady's book is essentially a biography of Surrey, it contains a twenty-page appendix that evaluates Surrey's "contribution to English literature." Casady acknowledges Surrey's debt to Sir Thomas Wyatt but claims that Surrey created a fresh poetic diction and experimented with new metrical forms. Provides an overview of Surrey's verse but does not analyze any poem in depth.

Heale, Elizabeth. *Wyatt, Surrey, and Early Tudor Poetry*. New York: Longman, 1998. An indispensable resource that brings together critical analysis of the early Tudor poets. Those who would study Spenser and Shakespeare's sonnets will benefit from the reading of these wonderful authors.

Lever, J. W. *The Elizabethan Love Sonnet*. 1956. Reprint. London: Methuen, 1978. Through a comparison of Surrey's love poems with their Petrarchan originals, Lever demonstrates Surrey's experimentation and use of sensory images. For Lever, the experimental early love poems are inferior to the later poems addressed to a noble lady, Sir Thomas Wyatt, a comrade, and Henry VIII.

Mazzaro, Jerome. *Transformations in the Renaissance English Lyric*. Ithaca, N.Y.: Cornell University Press, 1970. Mazzaro regards Surrey's poetry as completing the process of humanizing the lyric, of preferring the literal to the metaphorical, and of describing a natural rather than a moral world. He finds "When Raging Love" modern in its logical framework and in its emphasis on linear development rather than repetition.

Sessions, William A. *Henry Howard, the Poet Earl of Surrey: A Life*. New York: Oxford University Press, 1999. Sessions's narrative combines historical scholarship with close readings of poetic texts and Tudor paintings to reveal the unique life of the first Renaissance courtier and a poet who wrote and created radically new forms.

Spearing, A. C. *Medieval to Renaissance in English Poetry*. Cambridge, England: Cambridge University Press, 1985. After discussing Renaissance classicism in Surrey's poetry, Spearing proceeds to extended analyses of three poems: two epitaphs on Sir Thomas Wyatt and "So crewell prison," the poem about Surrey's imprisonment at Windsor.

Thomson, Patricia. "Wyatt and Surrey." In *English Poetry and Prose, 1540-1674*, edited by Christopher Ricks. London: Barrie & Jenkins, 1970. Reprint. New York: Peter Bedrick Books, 1987. Thomson first compares Sir Thomas Wyatt and Surrey to John Skelton, whose poetry was primarily late medieval, then discusses Surrey and particularly Wyatt as inheritors of the Petrarchan tradition. Contains a fairly extensive discussion of Surrey's translation of the *Aeneid*.

*Mary De Jong;
bibliography updated by the editors*

———————————

MAY SWENSON

Born: Logan, Utah; May 28, 1919
Died: Ocean View, Delaware; December 4, 1989

PRINCIPAL POETRY

Another Animal: Poems, 1954
A Cage of Spines, 1958
To Mix with Time: New and Selected Poems, 1963
Half Sun Half Sleep, 1967
Iconographs, 1970
Windows and Stones: Selected Poems by Tomas Tranströmer, 1972 (translation; with Leif Sjöberg)

New and Selected Things Taking Place, 1978
In Other Words, 1987
The Love Poems of May Swenson, 1991
Nature: Poems Old and New, 1994
May Out West: Poems of May Swenson, 1996

OTHER LITERARY FORMS

May Swenson's forays away from poetry included short fiction, drama, and criticism. A number of her short stories have appeared in magazines and anthologies. A play, *The Floor*, was produced in New York in 1966 and published a year later. Her best-known critical essay, "The Experience of Poetry in a Scientific Age," appeared in *Poets on Poetry* (1966). She also wrote the introduction to the 1962 Collier edition of Edgar Lee Masters's *Spoon River Anthology*.

Several books for young people have expanded the audience for Swenson's poetry. *Poems to Solve* (1966), *More Poems to Solve* (1971), and *The Complete Poems to Solve* (1993) are selections of her riddle poems. For still younger children there is *The Guess and Spell Coloring Book* (1976). Many poets owe a heavy debt to their childhoods, and few have discharged that debt more gratefully or delightfully. As a child, Swenson learned from her immigrant parents the language that she would later render into English in *Windows and Stones: Selected Poems by Tomas Tranströmer* (1972), a translation (with Leif Sjöberg) for which she won the International Poetry Forum Translation Medal. She recorded her own poems on both the Folkways and the Caedmon labels.

ACHIEVEMENTS

As traditional as she was inventive, as alliteratively Anglo-Saxon as she was typographically contemporary, May Swenson was well respected among twentieth century American poets. Her thirty-five-year career was an ongoing celebration of language wed to life-as-it-is. Her sharp-eyed curiosity led her to address a broader and more diverse range of subjects than did many of her contemporaries; she was rural and urban, scientific and mythic, innocent and worldly, and, sometimes, even literary; and she could be any number of these within the same poem. Once she fixed her attention on something, she had a remarkable gift for letting that object of her

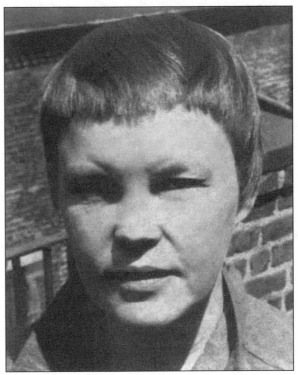

May Swenson (© Henry Carlisle)

curiosity find its voice and for allowing the poem to determine its own form. No poet wrote more perceptively or persuasively about birds—or about astronauts.

Swenson was a member of the National Institute of Arts and Letters and a chancellor of the Academy of American Poets. She was awarded grants and fellowships by a number of agencies and organizations, including the Ford, Rockefeller, and Guggenheim Foundations, and the National Endowment for the Arts. In 1968, she won the Shelley Memorial Award, and in 1981, she shared with fellow poet Howard Nemerov the prestigious Bollingen Prize in Poetry, in recognition of her collection *New and Selected Things Taking Place*. She has, as well, served as a judge for the Lamont Award of the Academy of American Poets and for the National Book Awards. Her frequent readings and visiting professorships at a number of colleges and universities enhanced her contribution to American letters.

BIOGRAPHY

The daughter of Swedish immigrants, May Swenson grew up in Logan, Utah, a small college town. Her parents had left behind both their native land and their Lutheran faith to follow the teachings of the Mormon Church, which Swenson came to reject in spite of (or perhaps because of) her strict upbringing among the Latter-day Saints. As the oldest daughter in a large family, she learned early to value solitude, and at the age of thirteen, alone with her father's typewriter, she pecked out with two fingers a short piece she had written. When she looked at the resultant shape of the words on the page, she said, "This is a poem"; her life's work had begun.

Swenson's father taught woodworking and carpentry at Utah State University, which at the time was known as Utah State Agricultural College. Swenson studied English and art there and received her B.A. degree in 1939. She then worked as a reporter for a Salt Lake City newspaper; but after about a year, she made her break with home and family and moved to New York's Greenwich Village. Before gaining recognition as a poet, she worked at a variety of office jobs and, after a few years, began publishing in various magazines, including *Poetry* and *The New Yorker*. In 1954, a selection of her poems was chosen to appear with the work of two other poets (Harry Duncan and Murray Noss) in the first volume of Scribner's *Poets of Today* series. Within the next few years, she began the round of fellowships, residencies, and visiting professorships that sustained her for the rest of her career. Among her more notable positions and appointments were the editorship of New Directions Press, 1959-1966; positions as poet in residence at Purdue University, 1966-1967, at the University of North Carolina at Greensboro, 1968-1969 and 1975, at Lethbridge University in the Canadian province of Alberta, 1970, and at the University of California at Riverside, 1973; she also held a position on the staff of the Bread Loaf Writers' Conference, 1976. In addition, she spent time at the Yaddo and MacDowell colonies, sojourned in Europe, and traveled widely in the United States, giving readings and teaching. From 1970 until her death in 1989, Swenson and her longtime friend and companion, Rozanne Knudson, made their home in what Swenson called an "Adirondack shack" in Sea Cliff, New York, on Long Island Sound.

Analysis

In his introduction to the first volume of the *Poets of Today* series, John Hall Wheelock assessed the task of the contemporary poet as one of rediscovery and revelation, and in which a world gone stale must be renewed: "A poem gives the world back to the maker of the poem, in all its original strangeness, the shock of its first surprise. It is capable of doing the same for the rest of us." That volume included May Swenson's first book-length collection of poems, *Another Animal*. In the thirty-five years to follow, no voice in contemporary poetry showed more commitment to that task of poetic revelation and renewal. Although she was often spoken of as a nature poet, Swenson was as adept at celebrating the skyline of Brooklyn as a quiet wood. She was equally at home with astronauts and angels, with swans and subways. If she could bring her senses to bear upon a subject, it was the stuff of poetry.

ANOTHER ANIMAL

Swenson's verse can be classified as poetry of the senses—especially of and for the eye. A good starting point for a consideration of her work is "Horses in Central Park," a celebration of light, color and texture: "Colors of horses like leaves or stones/ or wealthy textures/ liquors of light." A horse is not, at first glance, very much like a leaf or a stone, but Swenson always looks past that first glance to something more. The alliteration in the third line is only a mild example of her wordplay, which ranges from pure Anglo-Saxon to latter-day E. E. Cummings. Everything works together; the poem introduces a liquid tone, the sense suggests intoxication. What follows is no mere catalog of horses, but the play of light and words put through their paces. There is an autumnal truth, a lean horse the color of "sere October," fall cantering through fall. The procession continues, as "mole-gray back" and a "dappled haunch" pass by, along with "fox-red bay/ and buckskin blond as wheat." The reader takes in all the richness of the harvest and of October's light, distilled into the colors and liquid movements of horses. One need only witness the "Sober chestnut burnished/ by his sweat/ to veined and glowing oak" to let one's eyes at last convince the mind of what it may have shied away from at the poem's opening. Not only does this comparison work, of horse to oak leaf; it could not be better. This effortless rhetoric of the senses distinguishes Swenson's verse. One cannot believe everything one sees or hears, she seems to say, but one had better believe *in* it.

ICONOGRAPHS

Swenson's verse is variously described as fierce, fresh, inquisitive, innovative, and sensuous. Her frequent experimentation with the physical appearance of her poems, however, has caused such adjectives to alight in the wrong places. Though she had dealt from the start in unorthodox punctuation, spacing, and typographic arrangements, Swenson's experiments in this direction culminated in *Iconographs*. This collection of shaped poems—"image-writing," as she described them—is mistakenly referred to by some as concrete poetry. Swenson makes it clear in an afterword that the poems were all finished down to the last word before being arranged into shapes that would enhance the words. In visual terms, the poems are the paintings, the shapes only frames. Thus, a poem on a José de Rivera mobile twists and turns on the page. In a poem called "The Blue Bottle," the words outline the shape of a bottle; in "How Everything Happens," a poem written after close observation of how ocean waves gather, break, and recede, the lines of the poem gather, break, and recede in a visual variation on the poem's message. Such devices are certainly consistent with Swenson's belief that words are, among other things, objects, and that a poem is itself an object, to be encountered by the eye and its companion senses, not merely by the intellect. These shaped poems are innovative enough in their appearance before they are even read, but it is not in their shapes that they succeed as poetry. When these or any of Swenson's poems succeed it is because of an absolute sureness of touch and rightness of language.

Her images are at times startling, but they work upon the senses and emotions in such a way that readers cannot help giving in to their aptness and inevitability. In "The Garden at St. John's," a mother caresses her baby, whose hair is "as soft as soft/ as down as the down in the wingpits of angels." Any momentary hesitation over "wingpits" is lulled by the enchanting repetition of "soft" and "down," and the image rings, or rather, whispers, true. "Water Picture," the upside-down world reflected in the surface of a pond would seem to be a conventional enough idea for a poem, but Swenson is not so interested in *ideas* as in *things*, and it is, indeed, the *thing* that finds expression here. Everyone has gazed into still water and watched the reflections, but when, in this poem, "A flag/ wags like a fishhook/ down there in the sky," when a swan bends to the surface to "kiss herself," and the "tree-limbs tangle, the bridge/ folds like a fan," one is *there* with a powerful immediacy.

RIDDLING POEMS

Again and again Swenson affirmed that the wonders of the world are too good merely to be described or talked about. They must be shared as directly as possible. Her mode of sharing experience was to involve herself completely in an experience, to "live into" the experience in order to express it. Thus, there is much more to poetry than the mere recording or labeling of experience. Some of Swenson's most successful poems came out of the avoidance of simply giving a name to an object. Many of these are her "riddling" poems, in which the object shared is never named, but only hinted at. As one might expect, the images are heavily sensory, most often visual. One of her best known riddle poems is "By Morning":

> Some for everyone
> plenty
> and more coming
> Fresh   dainty   airily arriving
> everywhere at once.

As in most of Swenson's riddles, the clues reveal rather than obscure their answer. One need not read far into this particular poem to realize that it is about snow, but the real charm of the poem lies much deeper than the simple solution of the riddle. Systems of imagery are at work as "a gracious fleece" that spreads "like youth like wheat/ over the city." "Fleece" is picked up several lines down in the prediction that "Streets will be fields/ cars be fumbling sheep." "Youth" and "wheat" resolve themselves together at the poem's conclusion: "A deep bright harvest will be seeded/ in a night/ By morning we'll be children/ feeding on manna/ a new loaf on every doorsill." The avoidance of any explicit reference to snow is part of the poem's success, but the real strength of the piece is in the same rightness of expression that Swenson's work so consistently displays, right down to the use of extra space between certain words to vary the tempo, and, at times, the sense of a line.

SCIENCE

In her work of "living into" the world, Swenson explored one territory which many poets have avoided—

science. She wrote poems on electronic sound patterns and on the DNA molecule, as well as a number of poems on America's space program. To one who can derive so much wonder from the ordinary and familiar, the astronaut is a wonderful figure, though not solemnly so. In "August 19, Pad 19," the astronaut waits in his cramped capsule, "Positioned for either breech birth/ or urn burial," anticipating the liftoff that will drag him "backward through 121 sunsets." Just before the mission is aborted on account of weather, he puts himself into an unheroic perspective:

> Never so impotent, so important.
> So naked, wrapped, equipped, and immobile,
> cared for by 5000 nurses.
> Let them siphon my urine to the nearest star.

The treatment is more playful than disrespectful. The fun is not at the astronaut's expense; on the contrary, he knows to what extent he is to be admired, to what extent to be pitied, yet asks for neither admiration nor pity. He is no longer so distant from humanity as he might have seemed in space, umbilicaled, "belted and bolted in" ten stories above the pad. As he gazes through the capsule's tiny window seeing "innocent drops of rain" and "Lightning's golden sneer," the reader can sneer right back with him; the same things that ruin simple Sunday picnics ruin his splendid plans as well.

NEW AND SELECTED THINGS TAKING PLACE

To say Swenson strove for variety in her work would not be quite accurate. Her variety came naturally; more often than not it came from within a poem. Once a poem had found its form, discovered its voice, and appeared in print, she rarely revised it. An apparent exception to this rule is the selection of formerly shaped poems that appear in *New and Selected Things Taking Place*, minus their iconographic frames. Probably this indicates that, having done as much as she cared to do with the iconographic poem, she chose to second-guess herself and present some of these in more conventional configurations.

A thorough study of this comprehensive collection reveals something else. Beginning with her early work, Swenson moved toward more conventional form in her poems; certainly her punctuation grew less experimental. Behind her later verses is a mature poet, more aware than ever of her considerable strengths and less willing to divert the reader's attention in any way from what she does best. One of the finest poems of her later years is "October." It speaks in hard, clear images of growing older gracefully. In one of the poem's seven sections:

> I sit with braided fingers
> and closed eyes
> in a span of late sunlight.
> The spokes are closing.
> It is fall: warm milk of light,
> though from an aging breast.

Here, many years after the dappled light of "Horses in Central Park," light keeps its liquid quality but is less intoxicating, a more nourishing, comforting distillate. In this "warm milk" of a later, mellower light, the watcher is moved to something like prayer, in spite of herself.

Swenson was not an intensely literary poet, conscious of working in a particular tradition. Certainly any poet who addressed herself so fully to "the thing" could be expected to feel a special kinship with such writers as Marianne Moore and Elizabeth Bishop. Swenson acknowledged that kinship, as well as a special feeling for another master of wordplay, E. E. Cummings. There are, as well, poets whom she considered "healthy to read," and they are rather a mixed bag—Theodore Roethke, Gerard Manley Hopkins, Emily Dickinson, Walt Whitman, and among Swenson's contemporaries, Richard Wilbur, Anthony Hecht, Anne Sexton, and James Merrill, but this is no matter of influence or imitation. Swenson acknowledged as much affinity with such visual artists as Georgia O'Keeffe and Marcel Duchamp as with any literary artist.

The poetry of others rarely moved her to song, and "literary" poems are rare among her works. Typically, a poem on Robert Frost, "R. F. at Bread Loaf His Hand Against a Tree," avoids the temptation to indulge in literary assessment and instead addresses Frost as part of the literal scene: "Companions he and the cross/ grained bark. . . ." What might have been, in other hands, literary history in verse is rendered instead into an exuberant portrait in wordplay. For purposes of inspiration, Swenson was less likely to look to literature than to the newspaper, the zoo, *Scientific American*, a walk in the woods, or a ride on the subway.

IN OTHER WORDS

In this regard, Swenson's last volume of poems, *In Other Words*, is of a piece with her earlier work. Here are plenty of examples of Swenson's gift for discovering poetry taking place in unexpected places—a hospital blood test; the consignment of Charlie McCarthy, perhaps history's most famous ventriloquist's dummy, to the Smithsonian after the death of Edgar Bergen; a magazine ad for a digital watch. In Swenson's hands, all are the stuff of poetry.

A package received in the mail prompts "A Thank-You Letter." For the package? No, for "the wonderful cord 174" long" that bound the package. The poem ends with the narrator's cat entangled in the string, "having a wonderful puzzle-playtime." The narrator admits,

> . . . I haven't yet
>
> taken the sturdy paper off your package.
> I hardly feel I want to. The gift has been
> given! For which, thank you ever so much.

The process in this poem in many ways encapsulates Swenson's approach to poetry as a whole: Swenson's approach is eclectic in the very best sense, for "eclectic" means, at its root, not "to throw together" but "to pick out."

Because she picked and chose so well, because she was so much a part of the experiences that she made into poetry, and because her poems are so resistant to paraphrase and explication, her works are their own best commentary. "A Navajo Blanket" is a sort of guided tour of one of the "Eye-dazzlers the Indians weave." Having worked in from the edges over paths of brilliant colors,

> You can sleep at the center,
> attended by Sun that never fades, by Moon
> that cools. Then, slipping free of zigzag and
> hypnotic diamond, find your way out
> by the spirit trail, a faint Green thread that
> secretly crosses the border, where your mind
> is rinsed and returned to you like a white cup.

No matter what colors she worked in, what patterns she wove, Swenson was always careful to include that "faint Green thread" that was her perpetual wonder at things as they are. By following that thread, the reader can em-brace the world, a world clean and new, good to look upon, good to hold.

OTHER MAJOR WORKS

PLAY: *The Floor*, pr. 1966, pb. 1967.

NONFICTION: *The Contemporary Poet as Artist and Critic*, 1964; "The Experience of Poetry in a Scientific Age" in *Poets on Poetry*, 1966.

CHILDREN'S LITERATURE: *Poems to Solve*, 1966; *More Poems to Solve*, 1971; *The Guess and Spell Coloring Book*, 1976; *The Complete Poems to Solve*, 1993.

BIBLIOGRAPHY

Doty, Mark. "Queen Sweet Thrills: Reading May Swenson." *The Yale Review* 88, no. 1 (January, 2000): 86-110. Doty discusses Swenson's work. Over the course of her eleven books of poetry, Swenson developed a dramatic dialogue between revelation and concealment.

Gould, Jean. *Modern American Women Poets*. New York: Dodd, Mead, 1984. Gould's volume of literary biographies contains the single most complete account of Swenson's life. It includes details of her childhood, the influence—or lack of influence—of her parents' Mormon faith, and her associations with other writers, especially Robert Frost and Elizabeth Bishop. Gould also explores Swenson's longtime relationship with teacher and children's author Rozanne Knudson.

Hammond, Karla. "An Interview with May Swenson: July 14, 1978." *Parnassus: Poetry in Review* 7 (Fall/Winter, 1978): 60-75. In this piece, Swenson talks in some detail on a range of subjects, from her childhood and education to her writing habits, her approach to poetry, and her admiration for such poets as Elizabeth Bishop and E. E. Cummings. Throughout, she illustrates the discussion with examples from her work.

Howard, Richard. *Alone with America*. New York: Atheneum, 1969. This book-length study of modern American poets includes a chapter on Swenson, "Turned Back to the Wild by Love." Howard provides a fine, detailed study of Swenson's poetics and technique, illustrated by dozens of examples from her early poems.

SWIFT, JONATHAN

Critical Survey of Poetry

Salter, Mary Jo. "No Other Words." *The New Republic* 201 (March 7, 1988): 40-41. This review of Swenson's last volume of poems, *In Other Words*, offers a brief but perceptive discussion of Swenson's poetic strengths and limitations. Salter compares her work to that of poets as diverse as Elizabeth Bishop, Gerard Manley Hopkins, and George Herbert.

Stanford, Ann. "May Swenson: The Art of Perceiving." *The Southern Review* 5 (Winter, 1969): 58-75. This essay treats Swenson as a master of observation and perception. Through numerous examples—drawn mostly from the poet's nature poems—Stanford explores Swenson's ability to surprise and delight the reader by observing the world from unexpected angles, or by simply noticing and recording the all-too-easily overlooked detail.

Zona, Kirstin Hotelling. "A 'Dangerous Game of Change': Images of Desire in the Love Poems of May Swenson." *Twentieth Century Literature* 44, no. 2 (Summer, 1998): 219-241. Zona argues that Swenson's strategy of employing blatantly heterosexual or stereotypically gendered tropes is central to the relationship between sexuality and subjectivity that shapes her larger poetic.

Richard A. Eichwald;
bibliography updated by the editors

JONATHAN SWIFT

Born: Dublin, Ireland; November 30, 1667
Died: Dublin, Ireland; October 19, 1745

PRINCIPAL POETRY

"Verses wrote in a Lady's Ivory Table-Book," wr. 1698(?)
"Mrs. Harris' Petition," wr. 1701
"A Description of the Morning," wr. 1709
"A Description of a City Shower," wr. 1710
"Mary the Cook-Maid's Letter to Dr. Sheridan," wr. 1718
"Phillis: Or, The Progress of Love," wr. 1719
"The Progress of Beauty," wr. 1719-1720

"The Progress of Poetry," wr. 1720
"The Progress of Marriage," wr. 1721-1722
"A Satirical Elegy on the Death of a late Famous General," wr. 1722
Cadenus and Vanessa, pb. 1726
"Mad Mullinix and Timothy," wr. 1728
"The Lady's Dressing Room," wr. 1730, pb. 1732
Verses on the Death of Dr. Swift, D.S.P.D, wr. 1731, pb. 1739
"The Day of Judgement," wr. 1731
"A Beautiful Young Nymph Going to Bed," wr. 1731, pb. 1734
"Strephon and Chloe," wr. 1731, pb. 1734
"Cassinus and Peter," wr. 1731, pb. 1734
"A Love Song in the Modern Taste," wr. 1733
"An Epistle to a Lady," wr. 1733
On Poetry: A Rapsody, pb. 1733
"A Character, Panegyric, and Description of the Legion Club," wr. 1736
The Poems of Jonathan Swift, pb. 1937, 1958 (3 volumes; Harold Williams, editor)

OTHER LITERARY FORMS

Jonathan Swift's major satires in prose are *A Tale of a Tub* (1704) and *Gulliver's Travels* (originally titled *Travels into Several Remote Nations of the World, in Four Parts, by Lemuel Gulliver, First a Surgeon, and Then a Captain of Several Ships*, 1726); both are included in the most useful general collection, *The Prose Works of Jonathan Swift* (1939-1968; 14 volumes.; Herbert Davis, editor); but *"A Tale of a Tub" to Which Is Added "The Battle of the Books" and the "Mechanical Operation of the Spirit"* (1958, A. C. Guthkelch and D. Nichol Smith, editors) is also notable. Swift is also master of the short satiric treatise, as evidenced by *An Argument to Prove That the Abolishing of Christianity in England May, as Things Now Stand, Be Attended with Some Inconveniences and Perhaps Not Produce Those Many Good Effects Proposed Thereby* (1708) and *A Modest Proposal for Preventing the Children of Poor People of Ireland from Being a Burden to Their Parents or the Country, and for Making Them Beneficial to the Public* (1729). Noteworthy as well are his comical satires in prose, best exemplified by the "Bickerstaff" pamphlets against Partridge the Almanac-Maker (such as

Jonathan Swift (Library of Congress)

ire in the English language. The long pseudo-narrative of his later years, *Gulliver's Travels*, is acknowledged to be his masterpiece.

For this very mastery, Swift was in his time considerably dreaded and feared. In his case, the pen *was* mightier than the sword, and politicians trembled and dunces quavered at his power. In many instances, his satire could instantly shade into invective, and Swift wrote many powerful tirades against individuals whom he openly named, reducing them to impotence by powerful mockery and public scorn. At one time, he was the most important political writer for the ruling Tory party; his essays, projects, and analyses were a potent force in the halls of government.

Yet all was not terror, violence, and indecorum. In addition to his nasty side—his "serious air"—he could, as Alexander Pope acknowledged, praising him in *The Dunciad* (1728-1743), take his rightful place as a great comedian; he could "laugh and shake in Rab'lais' easy chair." Swift was terribly potent precisely because he could be so terribly funny. He was an absolute master at writing little idiotic mock-solemn invitations to dinner, in composing poetry in pig Latin, in donning masks and voices and assuming the roles of others. He will be remembered as the imitator of the voices of dunces: the perplexed but grandly complacent "Modern" hack writer of *A Tale of a Tub*; the utterly self-satisfied Isaac Bickerstaff (the Astrologer who could See Into and Predict the Future); the ceaselessly chattering poor female servant, Frances Harris; the quintessential public-defender M. B.; the "Patriot" Drapier; and the tautological and ever-to-be-befooled Lemuel Gulliver.

Finally, Swift was a poet of considerable skill. He deprecated his verse; he preferred throughout his career the jog-trot of the octosyllabic line, deliberately avoiding the heroic couplet that was in his day the reigning poetic form. He chose to treat "low" topics and paltry occasions in his verse, and he was ever fond of coarseness: Many of his poems take up nearly unmentionable topics—particularly excrement. For such reasons, Swift was for long not taken seriously as a poet; the staid Victorians, for example, found in him nothing of the Arnol-

Predictions for the Year 1708, 1708; *The Accomplishment of the First of Mr. Bickerstaff's Predictions*, 1708; and *A Vindication of Isaac Bickerstaff, Esq.*, 1709). Swift's major political diatribes are included in *The Drapier's Letters to the People of Ireland* (1935); other notable political writings include his contributions to *The Examiner* (1710-1711); and the treatise termed *The Conduct of the Allies* (1711). The letters are assembled in *The Correspondence of Jonathan Swift* (5 volumes.; 1963-1965, Harold Williams, editor). Equally interesting is his chatty and informal *Journal to Stella* (1766, 1768).

ACHIEVEMENTS

By common consent, Jonathan Swift is perhaps the greatest satirist who ever lived. His prose creation *A Tale of a Tub* is clearly one of the densest and richest satires ever composed. His terse mock-treatise *A Modest Proposal* is considered the most brilliant short prose sat-

dian "high seriousness" and grim cheerfulness that heralded and endorsed progress. Currently, however, there is a renewed interest in Swift's poetry; a flurry of studies is annually appearing; and in this realm too, Jonathan Swift is coming to occupy his rightful—and rightfully very high—place.

BIOGRAPHY

Jonathan Swift, as Louis Bredvold has observed, was the "greatest genius" among the Augustan wits, and even more clearly "one of the most absorbing and enigmatic personalities in literature." He was a man of brute talent with the pen, a man with remarkable intensity and drive, yet one who was frequently alienated and rebuffed. Of English parentage, Swift was born in 1667 in Dublin, seven months after his father's death. In straitened circumstances, Swift was reared in Ireland. His father had settled there at the time of the Restoration of Charles II (1660); his paternal grandfather had been an Anglican minister in England. Swift and his mother were dependent upon a relatively well-to-do uncle, who did see to young Jonathan's education at Kilkenny Grammar School (at that time, the best in the land). Swift's mother, Abigail, returned to England to live; Swift remained in Ireland, and subsequently, with the help of his uncle, attended Trinity College, Dublin.

Going to England in 1689, Swift obtained a secretaryship under Sir William Temple at Moor Park in Surrey, where he resided with few interruptions for some ten years. Temple had been a major diplomat, an ambassador to The Hague, and a wise conservative who had even arranged for the future King William's marriage. Twice refusing to become Secretary of State, he had at last retired with dignity and honor to a rural plot. At the least, Swift could anticipate great instruction and "connections," but he never did realize any actual preferment from this affiliation. It was also at Moor Park that Swift met "Stella" (Esther Johnson), the eight-year-old daughter of Sir William's housekeeper; a compelling and intimate relationship (still not fully fathomed or explained) developed over the years between the two, which led to Stella's following Swift to Ireland and living close to him for the remainder of her life. Neither ever married. In 1694 Swift became an Anglican priest in Dublin, with a remote parish in the isolated countryside at Kilroot.

Nevertheless, Swift stayed mostly at Moor Park in England until Temple's death in 1699, whereupon he accepted the chaplaincy to the Earl of Berkeley, who was settling in Ireland as Lord Justice. Still, preferment and advancement eluded the young man.

After several false starts in literature, Swift found his true voice—in prose and in verse—as a satirist. He wrote many short, incisive poems in the early years of the new century, and a prose masterpiece, *A Tale of a Tub*, appeared in 1704. The next decade was perhaps the most crucial in his career, for Swift helped the Tories gain office after a lengthy absence, and he became their chief spokesman, apologist, and potent political satirist (1710-1714). His power and success in London were inordinate; he did not lack glory. During this period Swift held court with the brightest of the Tory wits in the so-called Scriblerus Club (the most famous of its kind in literary history), which included such distinguished authors as Alexander Pope, Dr. John Arbuthnot, Matthew Prior, and John Gay.

Ireland, however, could not be avoided for long. Swift had held (though as an absentee) a post as minister to the parish of Laracor in Ireland, and the most he could extract from his political allies (he had every reason to expect more) was the Deanship of St. Patrick's in Dublin. Moreover, there were other reasons for disillusionment: The Tory leaders had taken to squabbling among themselves, and their authority became precarious. Unable to patch up this rift, Swift sadly withdrew from London. The Tories fell resoundingly from power in 1714, with the sudden death of Queen Anne. There were immediate political repercussions: A Whig government even went so far as to seek to imprison the Tory leadership. Swift had already retired—for safety and out of necessity—to Ireland. He would seldom be able to return.

After a period of quiet adjustment to the catastrophe which brought him to exile (1714-1720), Swift finally came to terms with his destiny and entered upon a great creative period. From 1719 on he wrote a great deal of poetry, and produced his prose masterpieces, *Gulliver's Travels* in 1726 and *A Modest Proposal* in 1729. His great period culminated with *Verses on the Death of Dr. Swift, D.S.P.D.* and *On Poetry: A Rapsody*.

In his old age, Swift was kept busy with cathedral affairs, with overseeing an extensive edition of his "Collected Works" being printed by George Faulkner in Dublin throughout the 1730's, and with polishing old works that he had not previously brought to fruition. His health—never too hardy—commenced rapidly to decline. After what is believed to have been a crippling stroke in 1742, Swift was declared incompetent, and others were assigned by a court to handle his affairs. He died in October, 1745, and was buried in St. Patrick's Cathedral. As a final touch of satiric bravado, Swift in his will left his little wealth for the establishment of a "hospital" or asylum for incurables—both fools and madmen. Jonathan Swift, if he had had the last word, would have implied that among humankind, there are fools and knaves—and little else.

ANALYSIS

In 1689 Jonathan Swift, at twenty-two, came to Moor Park to serve as secretary under Sir William Temple. It was to be Swift's brush with gentility, polite learning, and aristocracy, and it served him well. As a raw, aspiring man of letters, the youthful Swift hoped to make his name as a serious poet, and in this period he composed a series of rather maudlin and certainly pedestrian poems that sought to soar in the panegyric strain, Pindaric odes in the manner of Abraham Cowley (and of John Dryden in his youth): polite but plodding celebrations and praises—to King William after the Battle of the Boyne ("Ode to the King," 1690-1691), to a supposedly Learned Organization ("Ode to the Athenian Society," 1692), to Dr. William Sancroft, to the successful Irish playwright William Congreve, and two effusions to Sir William Temple himself (all in 1692 and 1693). Like many young beginners, he was rather excessively enamored of his own productions ("I am overfond of my own writings . . . and I find when I writt what pleases me I am Cowley to my self and can read it a hundred times over," he tells a relative in a letter of May 3, 1692), but by 1693 even Swift himself recognized the hopeless nature of this stiflingly formal and elevated gentlemanly verse, for he broke off rudely in the midst of his second Ode to Temple and renounced such a Muse forever.

Certainly, *politesse* and officious, gaudy, and Cavalier verse (already a mode passing out of date since the Restoration in 1660) were never to be Swift's *forte*, yet even in these formal pieces there are some sparks and

signs of the later Swift, for he could not restrain periodic outbursts of an inborn satiric temper as in "Ode to the Athenian Society":

> *She seems a Medly of all Ages*
> With a huge Fardingal to swell her Fustian Stuff,
> A new Comode, a *Top-knot*, and a Ruff,
> Her Face patch't o'er with *Modern Pedantry*,
>   With a long sweeping Train
> Of Comments and Disputes, ridiculous and vain,
>   *All of old Cut with a new Dye. . . .*

And in a rather strained posture—even for a satirist—he let himself boast of "*My hate, whose lash just heaven has long decreed/ Shall on a day make sin and folly bleed . . .*" ("To Mr. Congreve"). In his poem to Congreve, in fact, he had recommended that the writer should "*Beat not the dirty paths where vulgar feet have trod,/ But give the vigorous fancy room.*"

ANTIPOETIC PRACTICES

Within a year Swift would take his own advice and relinquish oppressive formal structures and grand studied compliments. Indeed, throughout the remainder of his career as a poet, Swift purposely eschewed all hints of genteel elegance, polite praise, or formal density. Thereafter, his verse was rough, chatty, and colloquial, deliberately informal, low in diction and in subject—scrupulously out of the beaten track of the faddish mode in verse, the heroic couplet. For the rest of his life, Swift's poetry took its measure instead from the witty, learned, and coyly antipoetic practices of Samuel Butler's *Hudibras* (1663-1678), making use of the almost sing-song, Mother Goose-like octosyllabic couplet, pedestrian subjects, far-fetched rhymes, and coarse mien. In addition, Swift never indulged in the longer epical modes so much in favor in his day; his poems remained prosaic and short.

"VERSES WROTE IN A LADY'S IVORY TABLE-BOOK"

Hence, in the next extant verse of Swift to appear ("Verses wrote in a Lady's Ivory Table-Book"), the new mode is almost fully formulated and matured. He mocks the typical empty-headed young lady whose hall guestbook is entirely scribbled over (by suitors and herself as well) with the muck of self-regard and of shallow tastes, flirtatious clichés, and torpid vanities; such "Brains Issue" the poet considers "Excrement"—and real gentlemen are warned to avoid such a tart:

> Whoe're expects to hold his part
> In such a Book and such a Heart,
> If he be Wealthy and a Fool
> Is in all Points the fittest Tool,
> Of whom it may be justly said,
> He's a Gold Pencil tipt with Lead.

A number of strategies in operation here are certainly worthy of note, for they remained Swift's hallmarks throughout his career. First, Swift owes many of his themes to the Restoration and its stage themes of fops, seducers, and fashionable lovers; a frequent topic of his art is the idle, frivolous, vacant, and flirtatious city maiden and her mindless, posturing fop or "gallant." Swift endows these conventional and even humdrum subjects with venomous sting: Such a woman is, in his imagery, no better than a whore, a prostitute of fashion, and her suitors are portrayed as perverse and impotent whoremasters: "tools" "tipt with Lead."

SAVAGE SATIRE

Swift's poetry transforms the polite inanities of social intercourse into monstrosities. His poetry gains all the more telling force precisely because of its seemingly innocuous outer clothing; bobbing along in quaint, informal four-footed lines, and immersed in chatty diction, the verse promises to be no more than light and witty. Yet the images soon transform such poetry into a species of savagery. Swift once mildly observed in one of his poems that "*Swift* had the Sin of Wit no venial Crime," and that "Humour, and Mirth, had Place in all he writ. . . ." It is true that Wit and Mirth are featured dramatically in virtually all Swift's creations, but let no reader be lulled into expectations of mild pleasure and repose, for the Dean's poetry often turns wit and humor deliberately sour.

"THE DESCRIPTION OF A SALAMANDER"

A good example of this transformation may be observed in an early lampoon, "The Description of a Salamander," a deliberate cold-blooded attack on Baron Cutts the warrior, who had been nicknamed the "Salamander." In the poem, Cutts is metamorphosized into a salamander and reptile. Swift savors setting up the analogy, and does so with painstaking nicety:

> . . . should some Nymph who ne'er was cruel,
> Like *Carleton* cheap or fam'd *Duruel*,
> Receive the Filth which he ejects,
> She soon would find, the same Effects,
> Her tainted Carcase to pursue,
> As from the *Salamander's* Spue;
> A dismal shedding of her Locks
> And, if no Leprosy, a Pox.

Although this is an early effort, there is no doubt that Swift is adept at being ruthlessly unkind: words such as *cheap, Filth, Spue*, and *Pox* are staccato-like Anglo-Saxon monosyllables, and only seemingly simplistic. What is more, they are amassed with furious delectation and vigor. Yet the poem remains tightly contained, purporting throughout to be a calm, disinterested argument, a scientific demonstration, a precise comparison. Swift's robustness arises precisely because he can interfuse the careful language of reasoning with the gross irrationality of nightmarish visions of infectious and loathsome vice and disease.

CLASSICAL INFLUENCES

Needless to say, a number of Swift's poems are less vicious, but there is always in them a certain flickering spark that implies imminent combustion. A number of his early poems are deliberate imitations or paraphrases of Horace, and others follow Ovid in telling a far-fetched story. Swift learns much from both of these classical authors about the manipulation of animal imagery, about the handling of diverse tones, and above all about sophistication: the juggling with diction, the juxtaposition of high and low styles, and the sly use of irony and indirection. Behind these deft usages is the potential adder and spike of the Swiftian assault.

CITY PASTORALS

Two companion pieces in this early period are almost universally admired: "A Description of the Morning" and "A Description of a City Shower." Both are studied presentations, ironic, quiet, and steady, while they also demonstrate another of Swift's strengths: parody. The two poems are species of City Pastoral, a mock-form that laughs at the fad of writing polite bucolic pieces about some never-never land of innocent shepherds and of the happy life in a pristine garden. Swift simply moves eclogues and idylls heavy-handedly indoors— and into the reeking, overcrowded, dirty London of the eighteenth century. The result (a frequent strategy in much of Swift's verse) is polite Vergilian verse that is overcome by gross content: thieving swains, whorish nymphs, and maids and apprentices too lazy to do any work.

EXPOSING AFFECTATION

Swift likes nothing better than to puncture civilization's postures, to divulge what Henry Fielding called *affectation*, and to blast holes in a nation's language of hypocrisy, concealment, euphemism, and deceit. Such uncovering can take the form of exposé: polite, tedious love-verse that is merely a tissue of clichés is rigorously parodied and exposed by hilarious ineptitudes of language ("A Love Song in the Modern Taste"), or a gross physical deformity is laid bare as a "modern nymph" disrobes and reveals herself to be in the last stages of disintegration from syphilis ("A Beautiful Young Nymph Going to Bed"). Swift would argue that false and impure language is exactly as viciously deceptive as ulcerous and pox-ridden physical reality. Both are instances of man-made corruption. With satiric glee, Jonathan Swift loves to paint a running sore in technicolor.

Swift is not always savage, cunning, or voracious. Some of his most pleasant verse remains Horatian, and plays quieter games. An early piece, "Mrs. Harris' Petition," reveals his mastery of mimicry; he assumes the voice and exact intonations of a middle-aged busybody servant who has lost her purse—and considers that event the greatest cataclysm since The Flood. (For a similar tone of voice, consult "Mary the Cook-Maid's Letter to Dr. Sheridan"). One of his longest poems in the early years, *Cadenus and Vanessa* is a masterpiece of coy indirection; one Esther Vanhomrigh had indiscreetly pursued the older Dr. Swift with some heat and passion: A polite and circuitous allegorical tale is used to cool her down and warn her off.

POEMS TO STELLA

Swift is at times at his most elegant (if such a term may be applied to his hobble-footed, four-stressed, grossly rhymed lines) in a number of poems over the years (1719-1727) to Stella. These are usually poems on slight topics, birthday celebrations, or graver reflections in the later years upon her growing illness. They are always light and bantering in style, polite yet quaintly backhanded with compliments, and sometimes almost insulting. Swift was a master not only of the direct attack but also of ironic indirection, and, following Vincent Voiture, he loved what he called *raillery*—a kind of bantering jest that paid compliments by seeming complaints and mock- or near-insults. A good example would be lines from "On Stella's Birth-day 1719":

> STELLA this Day is thirty four,
> (We shan't dispute a Year or more)
> However Stella, be not troubled,
> Although thy Size and Years are doubled,
> Since first I saw Thee at Sixteen
> The brightest Virgin on the Green,
> So little is thy Form declin'd
> Made up so largely in thy Mind.

The jesting continues until that last line, and so do the whimsical inaccuracies: Stella was *not* thirty-four (but older), and Swift had *not* first met her when she was sixteen (more likely at eight); she is obviously invited to wince at the trite phrases about *bright Virgins, lofty queens, village greens*, and *sweet sixteens*, for these are the pabulum of most pedestrian Muses (even today they thrive in popular lyrics and Hallmark cards). Finally, there is the innuendo about her girth—so paradoxically multiplied but nevertheless "So little . . . declin'd." Swift could not resist in some way speaking the truth. Much of his verse is of this seriocomic, semiprivate nature (and includes epigrams, puns, some pig Latin, invitations to dinner, verse epistles, windowpane scribblings, and merest notes), but all of it has a certain effervescence— and the Stella poems are surely the most accomplished in this vein.

POLITICAL INVECTIVE

Another body of poems, like the verse attacking Lord Cutts, consists of savage political invective, bred of the heat and animosity of factions, contentions, and parties. Some of the most acerb include a potent libel against Richard Tighe in "Mad Mullinix and Timothy," a most vicious portrayal of the Duke of Marlborough, the renowned Whig general ("A Satirical Elegy on the Death of a late Famous General"), and, in his strongest poem of this type, a savage libelous attack upon the Irish Parliament, in "A Character, Panegyric, and Description of the Legion Club," which indicts the group as a crowd of mad demoniacs. One of the most artful of these politically tinged poems incorporates themes about similar corruptions in the arts: *On Poetry: A Rapsody*. Like Pope's *Peri-Bathos: Or, The Art of Sinking in Poetry* (1727), this poem purports to be a manual of instruction, a how-to handbook guiding one who seeks to become a degenerate modern-day political hanger-on and hack writer. The final implication is that most men are already so degraded, abject, and profligate that there ought to be no one, really, who needs such "helpful" advice. That is exactly Swift's point: The so-called Age of Reason is in reality decimated and dissolute, the last, the Fifth or Iron Age of Vice (in Hesiod's terms): the final stage of creation's decline. Like Juvenal before him, Swift the satirist found it expedient to assume the worst about man's propensity for deterioration and debasement.

SCATOLOGICAL POEMS

Perhaps Swift's most renowned poems are his most shocking; they defame women, employ scatology, and have often been considered "obscene" and even "unprintable." They use the typical Swiftian ploy of jolting the reader into paying attention by using paradoxes and coarse language, and they include in their number some of Swift's best verse. On the borderline in this category are such fine poems as "The Progress of Marriage" and "Phillis: Or, The Progress of Love," poems that speak in the crassest terms of ill-matched marriages, and which frankly wage battle against the trifling romantic slogans that presume that "true-love" and "feelings" and "good intentions" and "high hopes" will win out against all practical odds. Rather grimly, Swift shows—in gruesome detail—the fate of such marriages.

The most blatantly offensive of the scatalogical poems include "The Lady's Dressing Room," "A Beautiful Young Nymph Going to Bed," "Strephon and Chloe," and "Cassinus and Peter." Every one of these poems mocks the "double standard" that allows men to be most coarse in their everyday affairs and yet somehow naïve about the single topic of women (whom they place upon pedestals in the tradition of courtly love). This self-deception leads inevitably to disillusionment, misery, and the destruction of lives, just as it has made for sheaves of tedious, lackluster love poetry. In Swift's poems, rather dirty modern urban swains are baldly confronted with nymphs who defecate and stink (as do all people) and who in extreme cases are coming apart with

syphilis and gonorrhea. The bane of Venus, in short, is that she is fetid and venereal. As a consequence of such a confrontation, the knavish and foolish men in these poems usually run mad—precisely as Gulliver does when he encounters man-as-Yahoo. The lesson applies as well to these dubious Lovers as it does to Gulliver: They are so easily unhinged because their minds never were screwed very well together; they have trained themselves—and society has trained them—to ignore or distort reality, to set up screens and shields and ideals—clouds of obfuscation that cut one off from everyday physical reality. Swift implies that if such men shut out actuality, they deserve the manure and laughter he heaps rather furiously upon them. These verses deserve more consideration than they usually receive.

VERSES ON THE DEATH OF DR. SWIFT, D.S.P.D.

Swift's most fruitful years span the period from 1730 to 1733, and special notice should be given to his masterpiece, the 484-line *Verses on the Death of Dr. Swift, D.S.P.D.* In it, the Dean chooses to defend a rather nasty maxim by François La Rouchefoucauld asserting that adversities befalling our friends do not necessarily displease us. Here is a sterling opportunity to expose human perversity, and Swift rises to the occasion. He points out amicably that all people like to get ahead of their acquaintances, and especially of their friends. Then he commences to use a marvelous example to "prove" his case: the occasion of his own demise. Sure enough, as Swift would have it, all of his friends in some way gloat over his passing. Even more curiously, enemies actually lament the Dean's death! Before the poem is through, it is paradoxically worked out that only men "indifferent," absolute strangers, can ever fairly assess one's merits or judge one's worth.

There is a further stickler that the reader should grasp in the thorny thicket of ironies infesting Swift's delightful poem: *All* men do in some way indulge in self-aggrandizement; a man naturally exalts his ego over others, and does not mind in the least treading upon toes (or heads) in the implacable urge to ascend. The last touch of irony includes even Dean Swift, who was so curiously "generous" in consenting hypothetically to "sacrifice" his own life so that he might win this argument. That is the very point: Swift, like the rest of humankind, will stop at nothing to salve his ego or to engineer a victory—even the most trifling triumph in a debate. Men will sacrifice friends, relatives, and even twist and convert enemies, so that they might, in Swift's fond phrase, "lie uppermost." Men are engendered in heaps; it is each one's voracious inclination to climb to the top. Thus stands one of Swift's most pleasing (and yet vexing) conundrums.

CRITICAL RESPONSE

For some two hundred years, Swift's poetry was seldom taken very seriously; it was, after all, not in the mainstream of the poetry of his own day, and much of it was crass and vulgar in the bargain. Swift himself had contributed to this downplaying of his talents, typically paying himself a left-handed compliment: His verse, he reports in a prose addendum to a poem ("A Left-handed Letter to Dr. Sheridan," 1718), is slight, for he composes with his "Left Hand, [when he] was in great Haste, and the other Hand was employed at the same Time in writing some Letters of Business." More and more often, however, recent criticism has been coming to take that self-deprecation with a grain of salt. The truth is that Swift's poetry is both dexterous *and* sinister—full of easy grace as well as of two-fisted power. His poems are disturbing yet pleasing, and growing numbers of readers are acknowledging that vexation and that pleasure. Perhaps the oppressive reality of warfare, terrorism, and recession has suggested that Swift and La Rochefoucauld came close to putting humanity in its place.

OTHER MAJOR WORKS

LONG FICTION: *A Tale of a Tub*, 1704; *Gulliver's Travels*, 1726 (originally titled *Travels into Several Remote Nations of the World, in Four Parts, by Lemuel Gulliver, First a Surgeon, and Then a Captain of Several Ships*).

NONFICTION: *A Discourse of the Contests and Dissensions Between the Nobles and the Commons in Athens and Rome*, 1701; *The Battle of the Books*, 1704; *The Accomplishment of the First of Mr. Bickerstaff's Predictions*, 1708; *An Argument to Prove That the Abolishing of Christianity in England May, as Things Now Stand, Be Attended with Some inconveniences and Perhaps Not Produce Those Many Good Effects Proposed Thereby*, 1708; *Predictions for the Year 1708*, 1708; *A Project for the Ad-*

vancement of Religion, and the Reformation of Manners By a Person of Quality, 1709; *A Vindication of Isaac Bickerstaff, Esq.*, 1709; *The Conduct of the Allies*, 1711; *A Proposal for Correcting, Improving and Ascertaining the English Tongue, in a Letter to the Most Honourable Robert Earl of Oxford and Mortimer, Lord High Treasurer of Great Britain*, 1712; *The Public Spirit of the Whigs, Set Forth in Their Generous Encouragement of the Author of the Crisis*, 1714; *A Letter to the Shop-Keepers*, 1724; *A Letter to Mr. Harding the Printer*, 1724; *A Letter to the Whole People of Ireland*, 1724; *A Letter to . . . Viscount Moleworth*, 1724; *Some Observations upon a Paper*, 1724; *A Modest Proposal for Preventing the Children of Poor People of Ireland from Being a Burden to Their Parents or the Country, and for Making Them Beneficial to the Public*, 1729; *Journal to Stella*, 1766, 1768; *Letters to a Very Young Lady on Her Marriage*, 1797; *The Drapier's Letters to the People of Ireland*, 1935; *The Correspondence of Jonathan Swift*, 1963-1965 (5 volumes; Harold Williams, editor).

MISCELLANEOUS: *Miscellanies in Prose and Verse*, 1711; *Miscellanies*, 1727-1733 (by Swift, Alexander Pope, and other members of the Scriblerus Club; 4 volumes); *A Complete Collection of Genteel and Ingenious Conversation*, 1738; *The Prose Works of Jonathan Swift*, 1939-1968 (14 volumes; Herbert Davis, editor); *Directions to Servants in General . . .*, 1745; *"A Tale of a Tub" to Which Is Added "The Battle of the Books" and the "Mechanical Operation of the Spirit,"* 1958 (A. C. Guthkelch and D. Nichol Smith, editors).

BIBLIOGRAPHY

Glendinning, Victoria. *Jonathan Swift*. New York: Henry Holt, 1999. Glendinning illuminates this proud and intractable man. She investigates the main events and relationships of Swift's life, providing a portrait set in a rich tapestry of controversy and paradox.

Hunting, Robert. *Jonathan Swift*. Boston: Twayne, 1989. While primarily useful as a source for biographical information, this volume does contain much insightful, if general, analysis of Swift's art. One chapter is devoted entirely to *Gulliver's Travels*.

Supplemented by a chronology, notes and references, a select bibliography, and an index.

Milic, Louis Tonko. *A Quantitative Approach to the Style of Jonathan Swift*. The Hague: Mouton, 1967. A detailed and quantitative analysis of the language Swift uses in his art, including analysis of such linguistic components as word patterns and frequency. Complemented by a list of tables and figures, a bibliography, an index, and an appendix.

Price, Martin. *Swift's Rhetorical Art: A Study in Structure and Meaning*. Hamden, Conn.: Archon Books, 1963. In this fascinating work, Price examines Swift's work in terms of rhetorical structures and especially in terms of persuasion. The author provides an introduction to the history of rhetoric as persuasion, then examines most of Swift's major novels. Supplemented by a general index.

Rembert, James A. W. *Swift and the Dialectical Tradition*. New York: St. Martin's Press, 1988. This scholarly work analyzes Swift in terms of the rhetorical tradition. After giving a brief history of the tradition, beginning with classical rhetoric, Rembert traces Swift's utilization of various rhetorical strategies. Includes a select bibliography and an index.

Rosenheim, Edward W. *Swift and the Satirist's Art*. Chicago: University of Chicago Press, 1963. In this useful study, Rosenheim first defines satire, then analyzes much of Swift's work in terms of that definition. Specific and comprehensive attention is given to *A Tale of a Tub*. Supplemented by an index.

Swift, Jonathan. *The Correspondence of Jonathan Swift*. Edited by David Woolley. New York: Peter Lang, 1999. A collection of letters by Swift that offer invaluable insight into his life and work. Includes bibliographical references.

John R. Clark;
bibliography updated by the editors

ALGERNON CHARLES SWINBURNE

Born: London, England; April 5, 1837
Died: Putney, England; April 10, 1909

PRINCIPAL POETRY
Poems and Ballads, 1866
A Song of Italy, 1867
Ode on the Proclamation of the French Republic, 1870
Songs Before Sunrise, 1871
Songs of Two Nations, 1875
Poems and Ballads: Second Series, 1878
Songs of the Springtides, 1880
The Heptalogia, 1880
Tristram of Lyonesse and Other Poems, 1882
A Century of Roundels, 1883
A Midsummer Holiday and Other Poems, 1884
Gathered Songs, 1887
Poems and Ballads: Third Series, 1889
Astrophel and Other Poems, 1894
The Tale of Balen, 1896
A Channel Passage and Other Poems, 1904
Posthumous Poems, 1917
Rondeaux Parisiens, 1917
Ballads of the English Border, 1925

OTHER LITERARY FORMS
The most learned and versatile of all the Victorian poets, Algernon Charles Swinburne tried his hand with varying degrees of success at virtually every literary form available to him. He sought to make his mark as a dramatist and novelist as well as a poet, and in the course of his career he published twelve complete plays excluding juvenilia and fragments. They are all tragedies written predominantly in blank verse. *Atalanta in Calydon* (1865) and *Erechtheus* (1876) are based on the Greek model. *Chastelard* (1865), *Bothwell* (1874), and *Mary Stuart* (1881) constitute a trilogy that harks back in spirit and style to Swinburne's beloved Elizabethan period. *The Sisters* (1892) is his only play with a nineteenth century English setting.

He wrote two semi-autobiographical novels, *Love's Cross-Currents* (1901; serialized as *A Year's Letters* in 1877) and the fragmentary *Lesbia Brandon* (1952), not published until many years after his death. The first makes use of the eighteenth century epistolary form, while the second adopts the omniscient point of view. Swinburne projected a collection of short prose tales on the model of Giovanni Boccaccio to which he gave the

Algernon Charles Swinburne (Library of Congress)

title *Triameron*. He left a list of nineteen titles, but only four tales have survived: "Dead Love," "The Portrait," "Queen Fredegond," and "The Marriage of Mona Lisa." In addition to numerous critical articles written for newspapers and periodicals, Swinburne left behind sixteen volumes of literary criticism, dating from 1866 when *Byron* was published to the posthumous *Contemporaries of Shakespeare*, which appeared in 1919. *William Blake: A Critical Essay* (1868), *Essays and Studies* (1875), *A Study of Shakespeare* (1880), and *Miscellanies* (1886) are the most significant of this body of material. He was also a voluminous letter writer. Cecil Lang has collected more than two thousand of Swinburne's letters in his six-volume edition.

ACHIEVEMENTS

Algernon Charles Swinburne comes closest of all the Victorians to being a Renaissance man. John Ruskin said that he could write as well in Greek, Latin, Italian, and French as he could in English. He wrote two

burlesques entirely in French, a novel titled *La Fille du Policeman* and a play, *La Soeur de la Reine*, of which only two acts are known to have survived. Swinburne was intimately familiar with five great literatures. Only John Milton among the English poets exceeded him in knowledge. Swinburne was a great parodist and translator, a prolific and fascinating letter writer, a novelist, and a voluminous dramatist and critic. His *The Heptalogia*, in addition to the well-known parody of Alfred, Lord Tennyson—"The Higher Pantheism in a Nut Shell"—contains a devastating parody of himself, the "Nephilidia," and fiendishly clever parodies of the Brownings, Coventry Patmore, "Owen Meredith," and Dante Gabriel Rossetti. Cecil Lang in his introduction to his edition of Swinburne's letters comments that Swinburne's ability to absorb the manner and reproduce the mannerisms of his targets constitutes "a miracle of 'negative capability.'" The same could be said of his border ballads, which seem more authentic than imitative or derivative. "Lord Scales," "Burd Margaret," and "The Worm of Spindlestonheugh" capture the form and essence of the early ballad as well as any modern poems.

According to Cecil Lang, Swinburne as a translator "could have ranked with the great masters." Passages from Greek and Latin poets appear in his works as well as selections from nineteenth century Italian and French writers. His only sustained translations are of François Villon, and some of them are masterpieces. His "Ballad of the Lords of Old Time" and "Ballad of the Women of Paris" capture the spirit of Villon's original poems as closely as it is possible for translations to do, and as English translations they are equaled only by Dante Gabriel Rossetti's "Ballad of Dead Ladies." Swinburne's failure to translate Villon's *The Great Testament* (1461), must be counted as a great loss to literature.

As a novelist Swinburne was the only certified aristocrat of the period to write fiction about the aristocracy. *Love's Cross-Currents* and *Lesbia Brandon*, in the words of Edmund Wilson, introduce us to "a world in which the eager enjoyment of a glorious out-of-door life of riding and swimming and boating is combined with adultery, incest, enthusiastic flagellations and quiet homosexuality" (*The Novels of A. C. Swinburne*). Wilson regards *Love's Cross-Currents* as almost a neglected masterpiece. *Lesbia Brandon* contains passages of superb description, strong characterization, and convincing dialogue. Both works suggest that Swinburne had at least the potential of being a significant novelist. Unfortunately, these novels are the most neglected of his major writings.

Although Swinburne's reputation is based primarily on his poetry, it was as the author of *Atalanta in Calydon* that he first gained fame. This little-read play is best remembered today for its choruses, which are often included in anthology collections of Swinburne, but it is a genuine *tour de force:* a treatment in English, on the model of Greek tragedy, of a famous myth which had not been used before as the subject of a play. It is widely regarded by critics as the finest Greek tragedy in English, although the concentration of Milton's *Samson Agonistes* (1671) is closer to the Greek tragedians than the diffuse blank verse of Swinburne's work. About *Erechtheus*, Swinburne's other experiment with Greek drama, David G. Riede writes in his *Swinburne: A Study of Romantic Mythmaking* that it "is a masterpiece in all respects—it is unrivaled as a re-creation of the Greek spirit and drama, nearly untouchable as a sustained lyric effusion, astounding in its metrical variety, dazzling in its metaphoric representation, and even remarkable in its philosophical import. . . ." Unfortunately, this play today is even less read than *Atalanta in Calydon*. Swinburne's trilogy on Mary Stuart was deeply researched and created over a period of many years, but it is entirely unsuited for the theater. *Bothwell* alone has well over fifty characters and the epic length of its five acts illustrates Swinburne's disregard for the contemporary stage. *Chastelard* is the easiest of the trilogy to read, but the extent of its preoccupation with sexual passion has prevented it from being as widely appreciated as its artistry warrants. *Mary Stuart* is given high marks by T. Earl Welby in his *A Study of Swinburne* for transforming prose matter into poetry, but Welby concludes that it "inspires respect rather than enthusiasm." Of Swinburne's other plays it should perhaps be said that *Marino Faliero* compares favorably with Byron's treatment of the same subject; *The Duke of Gandia* displays the powerful concentration of style of which Swinburne was capable, and *The Sisters* provides a fascinating insight into Swinburne's strange sexual proclivities.

As a critic, Swinburne's contributions are more substantial. At his best he is capable of judicious insights expressed in fine prose, while at his worst his strong feelings lead to idiosyncratic pronouncements and his prose style is baroque to the point of opacity. Swinburne left behind no innovations of critical approach and no permanent principles of judgment. Critical theory did not particularly interest him. Although he is the most cosmopolitan of the Victorian critics, his attentions are directed almost exclusively to literature or in some few cases to painting. Unlike Matthew Arnold, he does not travel in the broader ranges of society and religion. Swinburne's strength as a critic rests in his abiding love of literature and his genuine respect for those who made permanent contributions. This most aristocratic of English writers created in his mind an aristocracy of genius which included not only William Shakespeare and Victor Hugo, whom he revered to the point of idolatry, but also such writers as François Villon, William Blake, Robert Burns, and Charles Baudelaire. He had a special affinity for those writers who cut across the grain of convention. His *William Blake: A Critical Essay* is immensely original, charting new paths through the wilderness of the Prophetic Books and repairing years of neglect of this poet. If the insights now appear dated, certain passages have retained the freshness of great poetry.

It was as a poet that Swinburne made his most memorable and lasting contributions to literature. The seventeen volumes of poetry he published in his lifetime, exclusive of volumes printed only for private circulation, constitute a remarkable feat of creative exuberance even in an age as prolific as the Victorian. His early poetry is sometimes characterized by such rhetorical excess that the figures of speech call attention to themselves rather than enforce wider meanings. Such uncontrolled use of rhetoric is especially pronounced in the lengthy *A Song of Italy* and in the sadomasochistic poems of the first series of *Poems and Ballads*. As he matured as a poet, Swinburne came to exercise greater imaginative control over his materials, and his finest poems display a masterful command of the resources of language to create visions of striking beauty. "A Forsaken Garden" and "Ave Atque Vale," Swinburne's magnificent elegy on Baudelaire, clearly illustrate that rhetorical richness held in check by imaginative restraint which is characteristic of Swinburne at his best. A similar progressive mellowing of subject matter is evident in Swinburne's poetry. The violent denunciations of traditional Christianity and the preoccupation with various forms of sexual perversion that mark so much of Swinburne's early work disappear from the middle and later poetry, just as the melancholy hedonism of the early poems gives place to optimistic declarations about the triumph of freedom in the political poems and to a kind of quiet stoicism in the more personal ones. That said, it should be remembered that variety of subject matter and form remains the hallmark of Swinburne's huge body of poetry, and easy generalizations about it must be regarded with suspicion.

BIOGRAPHY

Algernon Charles Swinburne was born in London on April 5, 1837. His family on both sides was aristocratic, the Swinburnes being clearly traceable to the time of Charles I and the Ashburnhams dating back before the Norman Conquest. As the eldest of six children, Swinburne had an active childhood, spent mainly at the family seat on the Isle of Wight with regular visits to another family house in Northumberland. The contrasting beauty of these diverse parts of England left a lasting impression on Swinburne, who as a child displayed an almost Wordsworthian responsiveness to nature. He early developed a passion for the sea, which is reflected in much of his poetry.

From the beginning Swinburne was surrounded by books and fine paintings. His mother, Lady Jane, introduced him to a wide range of literature, including the Bible, William Shakespeare, Sir Walter Scott, Charles Dickens, Dante, and Molière. She also taught her son French and Italian, laying the foundation for his cosmopolitanism. In April of 1849 Swinburne entered Eton College. In the four years he spent there he received a thorough grounding in Greek and Latin poetry and some acquaintance with the French and Italian classics. He acquired independently a remarkable knowledge of English literature. He was especially attracted to the Elizabethan dramatists, an interest that would remain constant for the remainder of his life. *The Unhappy Revenge*, a blood-curdling fragment in the manner of Cyril Tourneur and John Webster, dates from about 1849. His

earliest poem to survive, "The Triumph of Gloriana," was a school exercise to commemorate a visit by Queen Victoria and Prince Albert to Eton on June 4, 1851. Its stiff heroic couplets give no clue of the direction Swinburne's genius was to take.

Although his academic record at Eton was good, it was decided in August of 1853 for reasons that are not entirely clear that he would not return, much to the surprise of his classmates. Instead, he would receive private tutoring for his entrance into Oxford, where his family expected him to pursue a degree leading to a legal or ecclesiastical career. Swinburne's patriotism was fired when he learned of Balaklava in the fall of 1854 and he wished to enter the army, but his father, Admiral Charles Henry Swinburne, would not permit it, perhaps because of his son's frailty. After a summer trip to Germany in the company of an uncle, Swinburne entered Balliol College, Oxford, on January 23, 1856.

At Oxford, Swinburne fell under the influence of John Nichol, the guiding spirit of Old Mortality, a small group of student intellectuals to which Swinburne belonged. Nichol, who was to remain a lifelong friend, undermined Swinburne's religious faith and confirmed him in political republicanism. It was under Nichol's influence that Swinburne wrote the "Ode to Mazzini" and became a devotee of the Italian patriot. Later, Swinburne was to be an outspoken advocate of Italian Unity. Most of Swinburne's future political poems were either to espouse Liberty and Freedom or castigate Tyranny in equally fervent language. Percy Bysshe Shelley may have become the main spiritual presence in Swinburne's political poetry, but it was Nichol who first directed Swinburne's thought along republican lines.

Another major influence on Swinburne at Oxford was the Pre-Raphaelite Brotherhood. In 1857 he met Dante Gabriel Rossetti, William Morris, and Edward Burne-Jones and immediately fell under their spell. Morris's poems, particularly "The Defence of Guenevere," influenced Swinburne profoundly. Shortly after meeting Morris he began *Queen Yseult*, and until 1860 his poems are, in the words of Georges Lafourcade, "a long self-imposed grind, a series of prosodic exercises" (*Swinburne: A Literary Biography*). One such exercise was *Laugh and Lie Down*, an Elizabethan pastiche written in 1858-1859, the sadomasochistic elements of which anticipate Swinburne's discovery of the writings of the Marquis de Sade in 1861. In 1860, because of his preoccupation with poetry and his irregular habits, which were cause for increasing concern, Swinburne encountered serious academic difficulties at Oxford, and he left without taking a degree.

In the spring of 1861, after a visit to France and Italy, Swinburne settled in London determined to make his mark as a poet. Shortly before, he had published *The Queen-Mother. Rosamond. Two Plays*, plays which did nothing to establish his reputation. His father had reluctantly agreed to a literary career for his son and settled upon him a small allowance. Swinburne quickly resumed his relations with the Pre-Raphaelites, developing a close friendship with Rossetti which was to last until 1872. He also made friends with such notable figures as Richard Burton, the explorer, and Simeon Solomon, the painter, and throughout the decade lived a bohemian life marked by increasingly severe alcoholic debauches from which he was repeatedly rescued by his father. In 1862 an affair with Jane Faulkner, the only serious love of his life, ended unhappily, causing him to write "The Triumph of Time," one of his finest poems. About this time he also wrote an autobiographical novel, *A Year's Letters*, which appeared under the pseudonym of "Mrs. Horace Manners" in 1877. Also to 1862 belongs "Laus Veneris," his first poem to crystallize many of the themes of the first series of *Poems and Ballads:* the apotheosis of female beauty, the celebration of eroticism, the wish for death, the defiance of God, and the damnation of Christianity as a religion of restraint.

Along with poetry, Swinburne wrote a number of critical reviews in the early 1860's including favorable articles on Charles Baudelaire's *Les Fleurs du Mal* (1857; *Flowers of Evil*) and George Meredith's *Modern Love* (1862). In spite of all these efforts, serious recognition continued to elude Swinburne until *Atalanta in Calydon* was published, at his father's expense, in 1865. The reviews were all but unanimously enthusiastic. Swinburne was at last established in the front ranks of Victorian poets. His triumph was marred only by the fact that Walter Savage Landor, whom he had visited in Florence the year before to dedicate the then unfinished work, had died. Also in 1865 appeared *Chastelard*, the first part of a dramatic trilogy on Mary Stuart. The next

year saw the publication of *Poems and Ballads* (first series), which scandalized the reading public. The volume was widely condemned by the reviewers as immoral, heretical, and insincere. Swinburne, never one to take criticism calmly, replied in kind with *Notes on Poems and Reviews*.

After *Poems and Ballads*, Swinburne's drinking grew worse and in 1867 he had an affair with the scandalous Adah Isaac Menkin, which was the talk of London society. Swinburne's image as the *enfant terrible* of the Victorian Period was firmly established. Yet throughout this period of storm and stress Swinburne was able to do some of his best work. After several years of writing and revising, *William Blake: A Critical Essay* made its appearance in 1868, as did "Ave Atque Vale," the serenely beautiful elegy on Baudelaire. According to Lafourcade, these two works bring an end to the Pre-Raphaelite and Art-for-Art's-Sake phases of Swinburne's poetic growth.

In London on March 20, 1867, Swinburne met Giuseppe Mazzini, whom he had idolized since his Oxford days, and his political consciousness was intensified. He gave up writing his erotic novel, *Lesbia Brandon*, and for the next three years devoted his efforts to writing poems on political and social themes. A visit to France in the summer of 1869 confirmed his hatred of Napoleon III, which he recorded in several scathing sonnets. Swinburne's renewed interest in world affairs came to a head in 1871 with the publication of *Songs Before Sunrise*. This volume makes a dramatic shift in the direction of Swinburne's poetry. The private eroticism of *Poems and Ballads* had given way to public denunciations of political and religious repression and Shelleyan prophecies of the triumph of freedom.

After the publication of *Songs Before Sunrise* Swinburne began to dissipate more than ever, and yet his output throughout the decade was prodigious. In the 1870's his poetry becomes quieter in tone and more melancholy and introspective. The second series of *Poems and Ballads* is tinged with a stoical acceptance of the impermanence of youth and love which is absent from the first. *Bothwell*, the most impressive work of his dramatic trilogy, appeared in 1874, followed by *Erechtheus* in 1876. In the 1870's Swinburne turned increasingly to criticism. His *Essays and Studies*, which contains discerning appreciations of several contemporaries, was published in 1875. From 1875 to 1880 he worked on *A Study of Shakespeare*. Always contentious, he became increasingly involved in quarrels of various kinds. His attack on Ralph Waldo Emerson in the form of a public letter was occasioned by an unfavorable remark that Emerson allegedly made about him to the press. He attacked George Eliot in his *A Note on Charlotte Brontë* (1877) and was involved in a protracted dispute with F. J. Furnival, the Shakespearean scholar, on ideological grounds. He wrote a brilliant parody of Tennyson and revised earlier ones on the Brownings, all published in *The Heptalogia* in 1880.

After his father's death in 1877 Swinburne's health broke. Through much of 1878 he was bedridden from dissipation, and the decade that began with his expulsion from the Arts Club ended with the poet prostrate in his disordered London chambers near death from alcoholism. His friend and legal adviser, Theodore Watts (later Watts-Dunton), rescued him, and for the last thirty years of his life Swinburne lived at Watts's home, "The Pines," in Putney. Watts severely restricted Swinburne's social contacts, but he did accompany him to Paris in 1882 for his meeting with Victor Hugo, whom Swinburne had revered for so long. This was to be his last visit to the Continent. During his years at "The Pines" Swinburne contributed well over two hundred articles to newspapers and periodicals and published more than twenty volumes. *Mary Stuart* was published in 1881, finally completing the dramatic trilogy conceived years before. Swinburne's early interest in Arthurian materials was revived and *Tristram of Lyonesse and Other Poems* appeared in 1882 and *The Tale of Balen* in 1896. He also continued to write political poems, directed largely against Russia abroad and William Gladstone and Charles Parnell at home. His aristocratic background never allowed him to regard the liberal prime minister as anything other than a dangerous radical. He opposed Home Rule as fiercely as earlier he had advocated the liberation of Italy. He ended as a republican who was opposed to democracy.

Having outlived most of his friends and all of his family except for one sister, Swinburne died at "The Pines" on April 10, 1909. He was buried in Bonchurch Churchyard on the Isle of Wight. Theodore Watts-

Dunton, true to the poet's request, would not permit the Burial of the Dead to be read over the grave.

ANALYSIS

The body of Algernon Charles Swinburne's poetry is so vast and varied that it is difficult to generalize about it. Swinburne wrote poetry for more than sixty years, and in that time he treated an enormous variety of subjects and employed many poetic forms and meters. He wrote English and Italian sonnets, elegies, odes, lyrics, dramatic monologues, ballads, and romances; and he experimented with the rondeau, the ballade, and the sestina. Much of this poetry is marked by a strong lyricism and a self-conscious, formal use of such rhetorical devices as alliteration, assonance, repetition, personification, and synecdoche. Swinburne's brilliant self-parody, "Nephilidia," hardly exaggerates the excessive rhetoric of some of his earlier poems. The early *A Song of Italy* would have more effectively conveyed its extreme republican sentiments had it been more restrained. As it is, content is too often lost in verbiage, leading a reviewer for *The Athenaeum* to remark that "hardly any literary bantling has been shrouded in a thicker veil of indefinite phrases." A favorite technique of Swinburne is to reiterate a poem's theme in a profusion of changing images until a clear line of development is lost. "The Triumph of Time" is an example. Here the stanzas can be rearranged without loss of effect. This poem does not so much develop as accrete. Clearly a large part of its greatness rests in its music. As much as any other poet, Swinburne needs to be read aloud. The diffuse lyricism of Swinburne is the opposite of the closely knit structures of John Donne and is akin to the poetry of Walt Whitman.

POEMS AND BALLADS

Nowhere is this diffuseness more clearly visible than in those poems of the first series of *Poems and Ballads* which proved so shocking to Victorian sensibilities: "Anactoria," "Laus Veneris," "Dolores," "Faustine," and "Felise." Although they all exhibit technical virtuosity, these poems are too long, and their compulsive repetition of sadomasochistic eroticism grows tiresome. Poems that celebrate the pleasures and pains of sexual love are most successful when the language is sufficiently sensuous to convey the immediacy of the experience—Ovid's

Amores comes to mind—and it is ironic that Swinburne's sensual poems in this early volume fall somewhat flat because they are not sensuous enough. Faustine and Dolores fail to come to life, just as the unnamed speakers, reveling in the pains of love, remain only voices. One feels that the dramatic form is ill-chosen. Swinburne tells us in his *Notes on Poems and Reviews* that in "Dolores" he strove "to express that transient state of spirit through which a man may be supposed to pass, foiled in love and weary of loving, but not yet in sight of rest; seeking refuge in those 'violent delights' which 'have violent ends,' in fierce and frank sensualities which at least profess to be no more than they are." This is a legitimate purpose for a poem, but it is not realized in these early works.

Still, this volume cannot be dismissed too lightly. Swinburne wrote it partly to shock and partly to accomplish what he attributed to Charles Baudelaire's *Flowers of Evil:* the transformation of ugliness into beauty, immorality into morality by the sheer power of the imagination. He certainly succeeded in shocking, and at times he was able to invest desperate and dark thoughts with a languorous beauty of sound, as in these lines from "The Garden of Proserpine":

> I am tired of tears and laughter,
> And men that laugh and weep;
> Of what may come hereafter
> For men that sow to reap:
> I am weary of days and hours,
> Blown buds of barren flowers,
> Desires and dreams and powers
> And everything but sleep.

This is quintessential early Swinburne. Nothing had been heard in English poetry quite like it. For all their defects, the longer dramatic poems in the first series of *Poems and Ballads* expanded the boundaries of the subject matter of English poetry in much the way that Whitman did for American poetry. In the shorter lyrics, such as "A Leave-taking," "Rococo," and "A Match," Swinburne created a note of elusive melancholy that had not been heard before. "Madonna Mia," one of the most exquisitely beautiful lyrics in the language, by itself compensates for the flawed longer poems and ends on a more hopeful note than the other poems of the volume.

SONGS BEFORE SUNRISE

In Swinburne's next volume of poems, *Songs Before Sunrise*, the Femme Fatale is replaced by the goddess Freedom; the earlier obsession with flagellation is sublimated into a more acceptable form of violence—namely, the overthrow of tyranny; and the desperate hedonism of the "Hymn to Proserpine" gives way to the militant humanism of the "Hymn of Man." "A little while and we die; shall life not thrive as it may?" is changed to "Men perish, but man shall endure; lives die, but the life is not dead." The doctrine of Art for Art's Sake evaporates in these poems of social concern as the influence of Victor Hugo and Giuseppe Mazzini replaces that of Charles Baudelaire and the Marquis de Sade. With the exception of "Before a Crucifix," a powerful attack on the Roman Catholic Church for self-aggrandizement in a suffering world, the poems of *Songs Before Sunrise* are aggressive, forward-looking accounts of the defeat of oppression and the triumph of liberty. "Hertha" affirms the immortality of man—"In the buds of your lives is the sap of my leaves; ye shall live and not die"—and asserts that "the morning of manhood is risen, and the shadowless soul is in sight." This philosophical poem ends, in words that echo Percy Bysshe Shelley's *Prometheus Unbound* (1820), with a revelation of the death of God and the birth of "love, the beloved Republic, that feeds upon freedom and lives." The other philosophical poems of *Songs Before Sunrise*, the "Hymn of Man," similarly asserts the immortality of the race and proclaims the demise of God, who in the figure of Christ is imaged as a tyrant: "By the spirit he ruled as his slave is he slain who was mighty to slay/ And the stone that is sealed on his grave he shall rise not and roll not away." The poem concludes with a striking perversion of Scripture, a characteristic technique of Swinburne:

> Thou art smitten, thou God, thou art smitten; thy death
>   is upon thee, O Lord.
> And the love-song of earth as thou diest resounds
>   through the wind of her wings—
> Glory to Man in the highest! for Man is the master of
>   things.

The other poems of this volume are more closely related to the events of the day. "Super Flumina Babylonis" celebrates the release of Italy from bondage in imagery that recalls the resurrection of Christ. The open tomb, the folded graveclothes, the "deathless face" all figure in this interesting poem that sings out, "Death only dies." In "Quia Multum Amavit," France, shackled by tyranny, is personified as a harlot who has been false to liberty. She has become "A ruin where satyrs dance/ A garden wasted for beasts to crawl and brawl in." The poem ends with France prostrate before the spirit of Freedom, who speaks to her as Christ spoke to the sinful woman in the Pharisee's house, in a tone of forgiveness.

A CHANNEL PASSAGE AND OTHER POEMS

Although Swinburne's later political poems continued to attack tyranny abroad, especially in Russia, the emphasis in them shifted to England. In *A Channel Passage and Other Poems*, Swinburne's last volume of poetry published in his lifetime, the poems having to do with political subjects tend to reflect Swinburne's insularity. Poems such as "The Centenary of the Battle of the Nile," "Trafalgar Day," and "Cromwell's Statue" celebrate glorious moments of England's past in language of chauvinistic hyperbole, while others such as "The Commonweal: A Song for Unionists," "The Question," and "The Transvaal" counsel the severest measures against England's enemies, who, be they Irish or Boers, are invariably depicted as the "cowardliest hounds that ever lapped/ blood" or "dogs, agape with jaws afoam." These poems lack the rhetorical richness of *Songs Before Sunrise*, suggesting that in the twilight of his career Swinburne's strength lay not in contention but in the peaceful lyricism that informs "The Lake of Gaube" and "In a Rosary," the finest of the poems in this volume.

POEMS AND BALLADS: SECOND SERIES

With the publication in 1878 of *Poems and Ballads: Second Series*, Swinburne reached the height of his powers as a poet. The unhealthy eroticism and hysterical denunciations of Christianity have disappeared. The language is altogether more restrained and there is a greater harmony of form and substance. The major themes are the impermanence of love and the inevitability of death. The predominant mood is elegiac, but the despair of "Hymn to Proserpine" has been replaced by the resignation of "At Parting," and a few of the poems hold out some hope of personal immortality, although on this subject Swinburne's private beliefs are never made clear.

In "A Forsaken Garden," one of the loveliest of Swinburne's poems, the landscape as dry as "the heart of a dead man" serves as an emblem for "lovers none ever will know/ Whose eyes went seaward a hundred sleeping/ Years ago." "Love deep as the sea as a rose must wither" and lovers now living must follow those who have gone before. The poem concludes that the forsaken garden is now beyond further change until the world itself ends, and there with the ghosts of bygone lovers "As a god self-slain on his own strange altar/ Death lies dead." This mood-piece manages to convey through the effective use of detail and tight control of rhetoric a landscape more vividly realized than is to be found in Swinburne's earlier poems. "A Vision of Spring in Winter" displays an equally rich texture of natural description brought into focus by a restrained imagination. In this lovely poem Swinburne bids farewell to youth. The poet tells the spirit of Spring, "I would not bid thee, though I might, give back/ One good thing youth has given and borne away." The loves and hopes of youth "Lie deeper than the sea" and Spring could not restore them even if the poet wished for their return. The poem ends on a wistful note: "But flowers thou may'st and winds, and hours of ease/ And all its April to the world thou may'st/ Give back, and half my April back to me."

Virtually all of the elegies in this remarkable volume merit special mention. In "Inferiae," a poem of simple and quiet beauty, Swinburne pays tribute to his father, who has just died; and in words whose marmoreal quality recalls Landor, the poet who earlier had proclaimed the death of God expresses hope of immortality. "In Memory of Barry Cornwall" opens with a marvelous picture of a kind of Socratic paradise "where the singers whose names are deathless/ One with another make music unheard of men." "To the beautiful veiled bright world where the glad ghosts meet" has gone "Barry Cornwall." Although Time has taken him and other poets from us, the poem affirms that he shall not take away "the flower of their souls," nor will "the lips lack song for ever that now lack breath." The elegy on Baudelaire, "Ave Atque Vale," was written soon after the publication of the first series of *Poems and Ballads*, but it is closer in language and tone to this volume, where it properly appears. Swinburne's deep affection for the dead French poet is felt throughout, and the resonant poignance created by the sibilance and dark vowels of the majestic stanzas and accentuated by the speaker's apostrophe of Baudelaire as *brother* helps make this one of the great elegies of English poetry. It conveys more sincerity than either "Lycidas" or "Adonais" and it is more tender than "Thyrsis." After paying tribute to Baudelaire's genius— "Thou sawest, in thine old singing season, brother/ Secrets and sorrows unbeheld of us"—the poem affirms that even though he is "far too far for wings of words to follow," his poetry lives on. Remembering that everyone will one day meet death as the poet has, the poem concludes with a profound serenity.

There is no such serenity in "Fragment on Death," one of Swinburne's masterful translations of François Villon. Here death is depicted in all its medieval horror. This and the other translations, particularly the "Ballad of the Women of Paris," provide a contrast to the poems already discussed, but not so shocking a one as the four sonnets attacking Russia, which appear completely out of place in this volume.

LATER WORKS

After the second series of *Poems and Ballads*, Swinburne continued to publish poems for twenty-six years in a continuing variety of subject matter and form. The Arthurian romances *Tristram of Lyonesse and Other Poems* and *The Tale of Balen*, while containing passages of undisputed power and beauty, suggest that Swinburne's forte as a poet was not in extended narration. The many poems about babies in *A Century of Roundels* reveal a mature tenderness that one would not have expected from the author of *Songs Before Sunrise*. There are beautiful passages in *Songs of the Springtides*. The second series of *Poems and Ballads*, however, remains the pinnacle of Swinburne's achievement as a poet, and if he had written no more poetry after 1878, his reputation would have been essentially unchanged.

OTHER MAJOR WORKS

LONG FICTION: *Love's Cross-Currents*, 1901 (serialized as *A Year's Letters* in 1877); *Lesbia Brandon*, 1952.

PLAYS: *The Queen-Mother*, pb. 1860; *Rosamond*, pb. 1860; *Atalanta in Calydon*, 1865; *Chastelard*, pb. 1865; *Bothwell*, pb. 1874; *Erechtheus*, pb. 1876; *Mary Stuart*, pb. 1881; *Marino Faliero*, pb. 1885; *Locrine*,

pb. 1887; *The Sisters*, pb. 1892; *Rosamund, Queen of the Lombards*, pb. 1899; *The Duke of Gandia*, pb. 1908.

NONFICTION: *Byron*, 1866; *Notes on Poems and Reviews*, 1866; *William Blake: A Critical Essay*, 1868; *Under the Microscope*, 1872; *George Chapman*, 1875; *Essays and Studies*, 1875; *A Note on Charlotte Brontë*, 1877; *A Study of Shakespeare*, 1880; *Miscellanies*, 1886; *A Study of Victor Hugo*, 1886; *A Study of Ben Jonson*, 1889; *Studies in Prose and Poetry*, 1894; *The Age of Shakespeare*, 1908; *Three Plays of Shakespeare*, 1909; *Shakespeare*, 1909; *Contemporaries of Shakespeare*, 1919.

MISCELLANEOUS: *The Complete Works of Algernon Charles Swinburne*, 1925-1927 (20 volumes; reprinted 1968).

BIBLIOGRAPHY

Harrison, Antony H. *Swinburne's Medievalism: A Study in Victorian Love Poetry*. Baton Rouge: Louisiana State University Press, 1988. Although most of this book deals with Swinburne's poetic dramas, the chapter on *Poems and Ballads*, "Historicity and Erotic Aestheticism," provides an illuminating discussion of the influence of "historicist, erotic, and formal concerns" on several of Swinburne's most famous medieval lyrics.

Hyder, Clyde K., ed. *Swinburne: The Critical Heritage*. New York: Barnes & Noble Books, 1970. This volume in the Critical Heritage series charts the reception and evolving evaluation of Swinburne's work to 1920. Authors from Henry Brooks Adams to Sir Max Beerbohm state their opinions, ranging from amusement to damnation. Notable omissions are T. S. Eliot and Ezra Pound. The controversy over *Poems and Ballads* is well represented. The introduction provides an excellent overview.

Louis, Margot Kathleen. *Swinburne and His Gods: The Roots and Growth of an Agnostic Poetry*. Montreal: McGill-Queen's University Press, 1990. An intelligent investigation of the importance of Swinburne's "religious polemics." The use of "demonic parody" and whore goddesses in the early works is compared to the biblical sources. The alternative mythologies of later works are also discussed and related, in an appendix, to the mythmaking of William Blake. Includes an extensive bibliography.

McGann, Jerome J. *Swinburne: An Experiment in Criticism*. Chicago: University of Chicago Press, 1972. This "experiment in criticism" uses historical, psychological, and textual approaches in the form of an imaginative dialogue among five people acquainted with Swinburne. While claiming to offer "nothing definitive" in the way of literary analysis, it nevertheless offers a wealth of insights. Its "earnest self-parody" suggests "the absurd limits of analytic knowledge."

Peters, Robert L. *The Crowns of Apollo: Swinburne's Principles of Literature and Art*. Detroit: Wayne State University Press, 1965. An examination of Swinburne's prose that discovers the foundations of Swinburne's poetry. In addition to Swinburne's reactions against the didactic and moral aims of art, Peters explores the importance of detail to Victorian aesthetics and the notion of "gathering form" in Swinburne's poetics. Numerous plates illustrate the relevance of Swinburne's theories to the visual arts.

Riede, David G. *Swinburne: A Study of Romantic Mythmaking*. Charlottesville: University Press of Virginia, 1978. A study in influence in the best sense, Riede's book sees Swinburne's poetry attempting to resolve certain conflicted projects of the Romantics, choosing William Blake's myth over his Christian mysticism, George Gordon, Lord Byron's heroic stance over his posing, William Wordsworth and Samuel Taylor Coleridge's humanism over their divinely informed pantheism, and Percy Bysshe Shelley's mythmaking over his skepticism.

Rooksby, Rikky. *A. C. Swinburne: A Poet's Life*. Brookfield, Vt.: Ashgate, 1997. Rooksby sets out to show that Swinburne's poetry is closely entangled with the particularities of his own life and memories. Rooksby is critical of what he sees as the unfair share of caricature which has been accorded to Swinburne.

Rooksby, Rikky, and Nicholas Shrimpton, eds. *The Whole Music of Passion: New Essays on Swinburne*. Brookfield, Vt.: Ashgate, 1993. A gathering of commissioned essays devoted to a poet whose neglect the editors and seven contributors are determined to redress. Includes bibliographical references and an index.

Thomas, Donald. *Swinburne: The Poet in His World*. New York: Oxford University Press, 1979. This biography takes Swinburne as a "child of his time," despite his reputation as "the figurehead of rebellion and modernity in literature." Thomas's coolheaded discussion of the poet's sadomasochism, alcoholism, and atheism allows him to discuss the relation between Swinburne's life and letters without hysteria and with great insight.

Robert G. Blake;
bibliography updated by the editors

WISŁAWA SZYMBORSKA

Born: Bnin (now Kórnik), Poland; July 2, 1923

PRINCIPAL POETRY
Dlatego żyjemy, 1952
Pytania zadawane sobie, 1954
Wołanie do Yeti, 1957
Sól, 1962
Sto pociech, 1967
Wszelki wypadek, 1972
Wielka liczba, 1976
Sounds, Feelings, and Thoughts: Seventy Poems, 1981
Ludzie na moście, 1986 (*People on a Bridge*, 1990)
Koniec i początek, 1993
View with a Grain of Sand: Selected Poems, 1995
Widok z ziarnkiem piasku, 1996
Nothing Twice: Selected Poems, 1997
Poems: New and Collected, 1957-1997, 1998
Miracle Fair: Selected Poems of Wisława Szymborska, 2001

OTHER LITERARY FORMS
Wisława Szymborska is primarily a poet, but she also published several collections of short articles written during her career as a columnist at the weekly

Życie Literackie in the years 1968-1981. *Lektury nadobowiązkowe* (1973; nonrequired reading) is a collection of witty, short essays inspired by a vast and eclectic selection of books ranging from the classics of literature to cooking and gardening manuals. Szymborska began publishing *Lektury nadobowiązkowe* in the daily *Gazeta Wyborcza* in the mid-1990's.

In *Życie Literackie*, Szymborska also hosted (anonymously) a column for aspiring writers. Her witty responses to hopeful writers have been collected in the volume *Poczta literacka* (literary mail, 2000).

Wisława Szymborska (AP/Wide World Photos)

ACHIEVEMENTS

Wisława Szymborska is known as the first lady of Polish poetry. Her poetry is elegant, witty, and delightfully intelligent. Szymborska is that rare phenomenon: a poet of universal appeal. Her poems—beloved by both demanding intellectuals and high school students—introduced humor, irony, and wit into the dreary reality of Communist Poland. Her work, however, is by no means of merely local consequence. Szymborska's poetry has been translated into nearly all European languages as well as into Hebrew, Chinese, Japanese, and Hindu.

Szymborska received numerous literary awards, including the City of Cracow Award, the Polish Pen Club Award, the Solidarność Award, the Jurzykowski Foundation Award, the Kallenbach Foundation Award, the Goethe and Herder Prizes, and the Nobel Prize in Literature for 1996. Szymborska is also known for her superb translations of French poetry, especially of the sixteenth and seventeenth centuries.

BIOGRAPHY

Wisława Szymborska was born in Bnin (now Kórnik), a small town situated near Poznań in the western part of Poland. When she was eight years old, her family moved to Cracow, the city that the poet made her home for life. There, Szymborska went to a prestigious school

for girls, run by nuns of the St. Ursula order. Her education was interrupted by the outbreak of World War II; she had to continue her schooling at clandestine classes, whereby she received her high school diploma. After the war, Szymborska studied sociology and Polish philology at the Jagiellonian University, but neither of those fields held enough interest for the young poet. She left the university in 1948 and embarked on a number of proofreading and editorial jobs.

In the years 1953-1981 Szymborska worked for the weekly *Życie Literackie*, where she was responsible for two extremely popular columns: *Poczta literacka*, featuring responses to aspiring writers and *Lektury nadobowiązkowe*, a series of playful commentaries on all sorts of reading matter.

In the early 1950's Szymborska became a member of Polska Zjednoczona Partia Robotnicza (PZPR), the official party of the Communist regime. She gave up her membership in 1966, disillusioned by the party's policies—a decision requiring considerable courage in the political climate of the time. Szymborska became part of the Cracow underground literary movement and cooperated with the monthly *Pismo*. She was one of the founding members of Stowarzyszenie Pisarzy Polskich (Polish Writers' Association), created in 1988 and legalized in the following year.

After she left *Życie Literackie*, Szymborska refused to form permanent professional ties with any institution. The poet became known for her reclusive ways; she shunned publicity, rarely appeared in the media, and would speak about herself only with the greatest reluctance. She very seldom left Cracow. When she received the Nobel Prize in Literature, she reacted with joy but also apprehension; she knew that this international honor would interfere with her fundamentally private lifestyle.

Annually, Szymborska has been known to write about four or five poems intended for publication—a slow pace fully rewarded by the quality of her poetry. The author of limericks, she has also created collages, which she produced out of newspaper scraps and mailed to her friends in the form of postcards. These pieces, reminiscent of Surrealist and Dada games, combine elements of the quotidian to give them unexpected (and often ironic) meanings—a method characteristic also of Szymborska's poetic technique.

ANALYSIS

The two key qualities of Wisława Szymborska's poetry are curiosity and a sense of wonder. She has the ability to look at things as if seeing them for the first time. In her curious eyes, nothing is ordinary; everything is part of the ongoing "Miracle Fair." Her poetry forces the reader to abandon schematic thinking and to distrust received wisdom. On the level of language, this distrust is expressed through a constant play with fixed phrases and clichés. Both language and thought are turned upside down, revealing new and surprising meanings. Such poetry is very humorous, but it also conveys a sense of profound philosophical discomfort, prompting the reader to probe deeper and to adapt new perspectives. Szymborska's poems skillfully combine seriousness and play, seemingly opposite categories that, in the eyes of the poet, are of equal value.

DLATEGO ŻYJEMY AND PYTANIA ZADAWANE SOBIE

The earliest poems of Wisława Szymborska, published in newspapers in the years following World War II, dealt with experiences common to the poet's generation:

the trauma of the war, the dead child-soldiers of the Warsaw Uprising, the hope for a new, peaceful future. None of these poems found its way into Szymborska's first two collections, *Dlatego żyjemy* (this is why we live) and *Pytania zadawane sobie* (the questions we ask ourselves). By the 1950's the political climate in Poland had changed considerably; poetry was to become an extension of state propaganda and a reinforcement of the official ideology. For a time, Szymborska naïvely subscribed to this agenda. Her first two collections give testimony to her youthful political beliefs. Later, the poet would disown her early work; however, the brief period of idealism and the subsequent disillusionment taught her to distrust totalizing ideologies of any kind.

Although the primary theme of Szymborska's earliest collections was the building of the perfect socialist state, some poems dealt with nonpolitical subjects such as love, intimacy, and relationships between people. Stylistically, these early poems bettered typical products of socialist propaganda and contained a promise of Szymborska's later achievements. Nevertheless, most critics (as well as the poet herself) prefer to begin discussions of Szymborska's oeuvre with her third collection.

WOŁANIE DO YETI

Wołanie do Yeti (calling out to Yeti) marks a turning point in the work of Szymborska and is considered her true literary debut. The poet cuts herself away from the earlier political creed; her former assurance is replaced by a profound distrust. This change of heart is expressed in the poem "Rehabilitacja" ("Rehabilitation") in which the speaker refers to her deluded head as "Poor Yorick." By 1957 Szymborska had become a poet of doubtful inquiry and profound uncertainty.

Wołanie do Yeti introduces a number of themes and devices that would become permanent features of Szymborska's poetics. The poem "Dwie malpy Brueghla" ("Brueghel's Two Monkeys") exemplifies both the poet's characteristic use of the anecdote and her growing interest in looking at the human world from a nonhuman perspective. The speaker in the poem is taking a final exam in "the History of Mankind" while the two monkeys look on:

One monkey stares and listens with mocking disdain,
The other seems to be dreaming away—

But when it's clear I don't know what to say
He prompts me with a gentle
Clinking of his chain.

Similarly, the poem "Z nieodbytej wyprawy w Himalaje" ("Notes from a Nonexistent Himalayan Expedition") portrays the achievements of humankind, as presented to a nonhuman listener. Characteristically, Szymborska creates a hypothetical, alternative world, thus making possible her imaginative investigations.

These poems mark the beginning of Szymborska's poetic anthropology: her study of the condition of human beings in the world, as observed and analyzed from various unexpected perspectives. *Wołanie do Yeti* reveals another seminal feature of Szymborska's poetics: her skillful use of irony as a cognitive and poetic category.

SÓL

The publication of *Sól* (salt) in 1962 was pronounced a major literary event. This collection gives a taste of Szymborska's mature style, with its brilliant paradoxes, its skillful intertextuality and allusions, and its mastery of puns, antitheses, and metonymy. The poet also develops her characteristic art of phraseological collage, playing with readers' linguistic expectations, as in the lines: "Oh, not to be a boxer but a poet,/ one sentenced to hard shelleying for life," or "written on waters of Babel."

Sól contains a number of very private, intimate poems, which is quite unusual in Szymborska's work. An important theme is communication between two people, or, rather, the impossibility or breakdown of communication, as in the poem "Wieża Babel" ("The Tower of Babel"). While this poem explores the failure of a dialogue between a man and a woman, the poem "Rozmowa z kamieniem" ("Conversation with a Stone") reveals the futility of human attempts at communicating with nature. The speaker "knocks at the stone's front door," but the stone remains inscrutable:

. . . You may get to know me, but you'll never know
  me through.
My whole surface is turned toward you,
all my insides turned away. . . .

Another important theme developed in *Sól* is the dichotomy of nature and culture, biology and art. This problem appears in poems such as "Woda" ("Water"),

"Muzeum" ("Museum"), and "Kobiety Rubensa" ("Rubens Women"), a playful poetic parody of the Baroque style:

Daughters of the Baroque. Dough
thickens in troughs, baths steam, wines blush
. . . .
O pumpkin plump!

The Baroque giantesses' "skinny sisters woke up earlier,/ before dawn broke" and "went single file/ along the canvas's unpainted side." This image reveals other key features of Szymborska's poetic imagination: her incessant search for the other side of the picture; her defense of those excluded and pushed to the margins; and her love of exceptions.

STO POCIECH

In "Mozaika bizantyjska" ("A Byzantine Mosaic"), from the next collection, *Sto pociech* (no end of fun), the Baroque situation is reversed—here slenderness is the norm, and everyone is offended by the sight of a fat baby. *Sto pociech* explores a number of other cultural myths, ancient and modern. This collection also shows Szymborska's fascination with discourses of biological sciences in general and the theory of evolution in particular. This fascination is linked to the poet's desire to extend the language of poetry to include discursive modes commonly labeled as nonpoetic.

Another major theme in *Sto pociech* is time, and art's ability to suspend it. While "Pejzaż" ("Landscape") deals with the art of painting, "Radość pisania" ("The Joy of Writing") is a hymn to "The joy of writing./ The power of preserving./ Revenge of a mortal hand."

WSZELKI WYPADEK

Szymborska's sixth collection, *Wszelki wypadek* (could have), confirms her reputation as a philosophical poet. Critics point out her affinities with existentialism, Positivism, and, most important, the French Enlightenment. Moreover, Szymborska's poetry has strong links with the rhetorical tradition. Many of her poems are structured around questions, dialogues, or theses with supporting examples. Moreover, in a typical rhetorical approach, the poet strives to make even the most difficult problems appear accessible: "Don't bear me ill will, speech, that I borrow weighty words,/ then labor heavily so that they may seem light."

The title poem of the 1972 collection, "Wszelki wypadek," ("Could Have"), introduces the weighty theme of necessity and coincidence: "It could have happened./ It had to happen." Similarly, "Pod jedna gwiazdka" ("Under one Small Star") begins: "My apologies to chance for calling it necessity./ My apologies to necessity if I'm mistaken, after all."

Wszelki wypadek confirms Szymborska's distrust of fundamentalism. The poet presents the world as relative. She speaks to us from shifting and surprising perspectives. "Wrażenia z teatru" ("Theater Impressions") describes her favorite act of a tragedy—the sixth, after the curtain has fallen. In "Prospect" ("Advertisement") the speaker is a tranquilizer:

> Sell me your soul.
> There's no other buyer likely to turn up.
>
> There's no other devil left.

WIELKA LICZBA

Szymborska's next collection, opened by "Wielka liczba" ("A Large Number") and closed by "Liczba pi" ("Pi") juxtaposes the amazing vastness and multiplicity of the world against the limitations of human perception and cognition. The world evokes a childish delight but also despair: There are "four billion people on this earth" but the poet's imagination is still "bad with large numbers/ . . . still taken by particularity." Faced with excess, the poet defends the particular. Confronted with the cosmos, she rehabilitates the quotidian: for example, the soup "without ulterior motives" described in the warmly ironic portrait of her sister, or the "silver bowl" which might have caused the biblical Lot's wife to look back, against the angel's orders. As always, Szymborska is fascinated with particularities and complexities, with human imperfections.

PEOPLE ON A BRIDGE

In *People on a Bridge*, Szymborska addresses political questions for the first time since *Wołanie do Yeti*. The problems of human history and civilization appear next to the themes of chance, necessity, abstraction, and particularity continued from the preceding collections. "Our twentieth century was going to improve on the others" begins "Schylek wieku" ("The Century's Decline"), while "Dzieci epoki" ("Children of Our Age") warns: "We are children of our age,/ it's a political age." Here, Szymborska's irony is at its most poignant and subtle. This collection also marks the beginning of the poet's effort to deal with death: "There's no life/ that couldn't be immortal/ if only for a moment."

KONIEC I POCZĄTEK

Koniec i początek (the end and the beginning) contains a number of very private poems, many elegiac in tone, dealing with memory and loss. In "Kot w pustym mieszkaniu" ("Cat in an Empty Apartment") the death of a human being is shown from the perspective of a cat. "Nic darowane" ("Nothing's a Gift") reminds the reader that: "Nothing's a gift, it's all on loan" and "I'll have to pay for myself/ with my self." In "Może być bez tytułu" ("No Title Required"), the poet poses the metaphysical questions: what is important and what is not? How can we be certain? In comparison with Szymborska's earlier work, the poems in this collection are more direct, less dependent on masks and role-playing. However, the poet retains her propensity for unusual perspectives. In "Wielkie to szczęście" ("We're Extremely Fortunate") she claims: "We're extremely fortunate/ not to know precisely/ the kind of world we live in." Such knowledge would require adopting a cosmic point of view, from which "the counting of weekdays" would seem "a senseless activity," and "the sign 'No Walking On The Grass'/ a symptom of lunacy." There is irony here, but also a great tenderness toward the counting of days and the grass—a human quotidian.

OTHER MAJOR WORKS

NONFICTION: *Lektury nadobowiązkowe*, 1973.

TRANSLATIONS: *Poezje wybrane*, 1964 (of Charles Baudelaire); *Poezje*, 1977 (of Alfred de Musset).

MISCELLANEOUS: *Poczta literacka*, 2000.

BIBLIOGRAPHY

Aaron, Jonathan. "In the Absence of Witnesses: The Poetry of Wisława Szymborska." *Parnassus: Poetry in Review* 11, no. 2 (1981/1982): 254-264. An insightful overview of the major themes in Szymborska's poetry based on the 1981 and 1982 English language collections of her poems.

Balbus, Stanisław, and Dorota Wojda, eds. *Radosc czytania Szymborskiej*. Cracow: Znak, 1996. A collection of seminal essays dealing with Szymborska's work, written by prominent Polish poets, critics and journalists. Available only in Polish.

Cavanagh, Clare. "Poetry and Ideology: The Example of Wisława Szymborska." *Literary Imagination* 2, no. 1 (1999): 174-190. An analysis of Szymborska's poetry written by its American translator. Cavanagh emphasizes the dialogical character of Szymborska's work, as well as its affinities with poststructuralist thought.

Czerniawski, Adam, ed. *The Mature Laurel: Essays on Modern Polish Poetry.* Chester Springs, Pa.: Seren Books, Dufour, 1991. A collection of essays dealing with twentieth century Polish poets, including Szymborska.

Legezynska, Anna. *Wisława Szymborska.* Poznań, Poland: Rebis, 1996. This extremely helpful work contains Szymborska's biography and a careful analysis of each poetry collection. In Polish.

Magdalena Mączyńska

T

Rabindranath Tagore

Born: Calcutta, India; May 7, 1861
Died: Calcutta, India; August 7, 1941

PRINCIPAL POETRY

Saisab sangit, 1881
Sandhya sangit, 1882
Prabhat sangit, 1883
Chabi o gan, 1884
Kari o komal, 1887
Mānashi, 1890
Sonār tari, 1893 (The Golden Boat, 1932)
Chitra, 1895
Chaitāli, 1896
Kanika, 1899
Kalpana, 1900
Katha o kahini, 1900
Kshanikā, 1900
Naivedya, 1901
Sisu, 1903 (The Crescent Moon, 1913)
Smaran, 1903
Utsarga, 1904
Kheya, 1905
Gitānjali, 1910 (Gitanjali (Song Offerings), 1912)
The Gardener, 1913
Gitali, 1914
Balāka, 1916 (A Flight of Swans, 1955, 1962)
Fruit-Gathering, 1916
Gan, 1916
Stray Birds, 1917
Love's Gift, and Crossing, 1918
Palataka, 1918 (The Fugitive, 1921)
Lipika, 1922
Poems, 1922
Sisu bholanath, 1922
The Curse at Farewell, 1924
Prabahini, 1925
Purabi, 1925

Fifteen Poems, 1928
Fireflies, 1928
Mahuya, 1929
Sheaves: Poems and Songs, 1929
Banabani, 1931
The Child, 1931
Parisesh, 1932
Punascha, 1932
Vicitrita, 1933
Bithika, 1935
Ses saptak, 1935
Patraput, 1936, 1938 (English translation, 1969)
Syamali, 1936 (English translation, 1955)
Khapchada, 1937
Prantik, 1938
Senjuti, 1938
Navajatak, 1940
Rogsajya, 1940
Sanai, 1940
Arogya, 1941
Janmadine, 1941
Poems, 1942
Sesh lekha, 1942
The Herald of Spring, 1957
Wings of Death: The Last Poems, 1960
Devouring Love, 1961
A Bunch of Poems, 1966
One Hundred and One, 1967
Last Poems, 1973
Later Poems, 1974

OTHER LITERARY FORMS

Besides more than fifty collections of poetry, Rabindranath Tagore wrote thirteen novels, ten collections of short stories, more than sixty plays, and numerous volumes of literary criticism, letters, translations, reminiscences, lectures, sermons, travel sketches, philosophy, religion, and politics. In addition, he translated a considerable amount of his own work from its original Bengali into English.

Tagore's drama, which generally tends to be more lyric than dramatic, is best represented by *Visarjan* (pb. 1890; *Sacrifice*, 1917), *Chitrāngadā* (pb. 1892; *Chitra*, 1913), *Prayaschitta* (pr. 1909; atonement), *Rājā* (pb. 1910; *The King of the Dark Chamber*, 1914), *Dākghar* (pb. 1912; *Post Office*, 1914), and *Raktakarabi* (pb. 1924; *Red Oleanders*, 1925). Examples of later plays—*Muktadhārā* (pb. 1922; English translation, 1950), *Natir Pujā* (pb. 1926; *Worship of the Dancing Girl*, 1950), and *Chandālikā* (pr., pb. 1933; English translation, 1938)—were translated by Marjorie Sykes in *Three Plays* (pb. 1950).

Tagore's fiction, which also reflects his lyric bent, sometimes seems to prefigure the "open form." Including some of his best work, his short stories have been compared to those of Guy de Maupassant. Some of his short stories have been translated in *The Hungry Stones and Other Stories* (1916), *Mashi and Other Stories* (1918), and *The Runaway and Other Stories* (1959). *Gora* (1910; English translation, 1924) is usually considered his best novel, but others of interest are *Chokher bāli* (1902; *Binodini*, 1959), *Ghare bāire* (1916; *Home and the World*, 1919), *Chaturanga* (1916; English trans-

lation, 1963), *Jogajog* (1929; cross currents), *Shesher kabita* (1929; the last poem), and *Dui bon* (1933; *Two Sisters*, 1945).

Tagore's nonfictional prose, some of which was originally written as lectures in English, is represented by *Jivansmriti* (1912; *My Reminiscences*, 1917), *Personality* (1917), *Nationalism* (1919), *Creative Unity* (1922), *The Religion of Man* (1931), and *Towards Universal Man* (1961).

ACHIEVEMENTS

Few writers have achieved such fame as came to Rabindranath Tagore when he was awarded the 1913 Nobel Prize for Literature. The first Asian to receive the award, he was viewed in the West as the embodiment of Eastern mystical wisdom. Indian critics at the time, however, often attacked his work, usually for political reasons, even though he did more than any other writer to establish Bengali as a flexible literary language (he was experimenting with it to the end of his life). Perhaps needing money for the school he had established at Santiniketan, Tagore took advantage of his fame to churn out English translations. Although he admitted his limited skill in English, he was shrewd enough to satisfy the sentimental streak in his English-speaking audiences. The combination of modest skill and banality was devastating for his poetry. His so-called "prose poems"—usually paraphrases, though they occasionally break into Whitmanesque free verse—are noteworthy examples of what is lost in the translation of poetry. Eventually, these translations caught up with his reputation, which began sinking in the West about the time that graduates of Santiniketan began producing books on their *Gurudev*. One of these former students, Aurobindo Bose, has produced the best English translations of Tagore's poetry now available.

As Jane Addams (of Hull House) noted, Tagore was "at once a poet, a philosopher, a humanitarian, an educator," and, as Hermann Hesse said, Tagore's reputation was built in part on "the rich heritage of ancient Indian philosophy." Similarly, Tagore's work reflects certain native literary traditions, such as Indian drama and the *Baul* folk songs, which are alien to the West. Finally, where his poetry is concerned, it should be borne in mind that Tagore was a songwriter (he composed about

Rabindranath Tagore, Nobel laureate in literature for 1913.
(© The Nobel Foundation)

two thousand songs), that he set some of his poems to music, and that in Bengali his poetry has rich musical qualities—rhythm, rhyme, alliteration, assonance—that accompany the words, images, and ideas. All these factors must be carefully weighed in evaluating Tagore's overall achievement.

Otherwise, each individual work must be considered separately. Tagore wrote too much, so there is repetition and wide variation in quality, especially in his poetry. (Apparently he needed a critical audience off which to bounce his poems, but he found it neither in his Indian milieu nor in the adulatory West.) For example, the same period that produced *Gitanjali* and *A Flight of Swans* also produced the soppy poems in *The Crescent Moon*. Besides *Gitanjali* and *A Flight of Swans*, perhaps his finest works are the short stories translated in *The Hungry Stones and Other Stories*. Readers of English would also do well to rediscover his lectures, wherein Tagore speaks for peace, internationalism, and understanding—themes prominent in his literary work.

BIOGRAPHY

Rabindranath Tagore was born into a wealthy, influential, and culturally active Brahmin family. The name Tagore is an English corruption of the title *Thakur* (that is, Brahmin), and the name Rabindranath means "lord of the sun" (*rabi* means "the sun"). Tagore's father was Maharishi (Great Sage) Devendranath Tagore, an important religious writer and leader of Brahmo Samaj (Society of God), a new monotheistic religion founded on a return to the *Upanishads* and progressive political ideas. A response both to orthodox Hinduism (characterized by idolatry, the caste system, suttee, and similar oppressive practices) and to Western culture (especially Christianity), the reformist Brahmo Samaj virtually defined the development of Tagore's own thought.

Despite his apparent advantages, Tagore, the youngest of fourteen children, had a difficult childhood. His father was involved with his activities as a Maharishi, and Tagore's mother was sickly (she died when he was thirteen). The infant Rabi was turned over to the care of servants, who simplified their duties by confining him within rooms and chalk circles. He did not last long in any of the several schools he attended, consequently receiving little formal education. He was saved by his father and family

activities. At the age of twelve, he accompanied his father, whom he idolized, on an extended journey to Santiniketan (his father's rural retreat, about one hundred miles west of Calcutta), Amritsar, and the Himalayas, where they lived in a mountain hut and where his father instructed him. On his return to Calcutta, the young Tagore gradually became involved in family activities.

The family was ostracized by orthodox Hindus, thus leaving the Tagores free to do as they pleased. As a result, the family home, Jorasanko Palace, was the cultural center of Calcutta, buzzing with more than a hundred inhabitants as well as a steady flow of distinguished visitors—reformist religious leaders, nationalist politicians, writers, artists, and musicians. The evenings were filled with musical performances, plays, readings, and discussions that lasted far into the night. Even the women were involved, further scandalizing the neighbors, who still practiced purdah (the formal seclusion of women from public view). The lively teenage Tagore plunged into this activity, contributing songs, readings, and critical observations. When, in 1877, the family started its own monthly magazine, *Bharati*, the sixteen-year-old Tagore helped edit it and was a main contributor. What better education could one find for Tagore the writer (not to mention Tagore the singer, songwriter, actor, critic, politician, philosopher, and artist)?

One more try at formal education occurred in 1878, when Tagore was sent to Great Britain to prepare to study law, first at a school in Brighton, then at University College, London. He continued to make contributions to *Bharati*, expressing his dislike for the British people and his love for British literature (especially William Shakespeare and the Romantics). After two years, Tagore returned home, and in 1883 a marriage was arranged for him with Mrinalini Devi (then only nine years old), whom he called Nalini. In 1891, they settled down in Shelidah, where Tagore's father assigned him to manage the family estates and where Tagore for the first time came into direct contact with the Indian countryside and peasant life. This period was an eye-opener for Tagore, providing him with some of his best material for short stories. (For example, he rescued a tenant's wife who was being swept down a flooding river, but did she thank him? No, she was trying to commit suicide.) Sympathy for the conditions of peasant life also deepened his involvement in the growing Indian Nationalist movement, for which he wrote and made speeches. When the Nationalist movement eventually became violent, however, he broke off his involvement and withdrew to Santiniketan (which, appropriately, means "abode of peace"). Later, he would come to believe that nationalism is one of the great evils of the modern world.

In 1901, Tagore began his career as an educator, starting a school at Santiniketan. It is ironic, but understandable, that the dropout should become the educator; some of his five children were of school age, and, recalling his school experience, he had his own ideas about how to teach them. These ideas he put into practice at Santiniketan. He was also responding to the conditions around him, seeking to uplift his countrymen in a way that did not involve violence. Besides, there was always something of the teacher in Tagore, as shown by his campaign to enlighten first his own countrymen and later the West. The teacher comes out frequently (through indirectly) in his poetry, in which he sometimes seems to adopt the stance of the Great Sage. Above all, Tagore was interested in seeing certain ideas prevail, as proclaimed by the motto of Santiniketan: "Santam, sivam, advaitam" (peace, good, union).

The early years at Santiniketan were marred for Tagore by great personal loss: In 1902 his wife died, in 1904 his eldest daughter, in 1905 his father, and in 1907 his youngest son. Yet the deepening process of meditating on these losses produced his best poetry, *Gitanjali* and *A Flight of Swans*. The school was also in constant need of money, which eventually required him to make several fund-raising and lecture trips to the United States, Great Britain, and the European Continent. These journeys established him as an ambassador to the West—a role he found much easier to fill after he won the 1913 Nobel Prize for Literature. Everywhere he went, he was received as the Great Sage, and he was awarded numerous honors (such as a British knighthood in 1915). He visited the Soviet Union and Japan, both of which he admired, but he criticized Communist suppression of individual rights and the militant nationalism of the Japanese. He was especially appalled by Japanese efforts to conquer China.

Tagore's last years were spent in traveling, in expanding the Santiniketan complex, in practicing a new art (painting), and in pointing the world toward peace. In 1922, he established Sriniketan (abode of grace), an institute for agriculture and rural reconstruction, and Visva-Bharati (universal voice), an international university for bringing the message of the East to the West. His paintings were exhibited in Europe to favorable reviews. He was disappointed in his work for peace, thinking that nations which had endured one world war would not want another. The 1930's were increasingly depressing for him, and he died in 1941, just as World War II was reaching its full incarnation.

ANALYSIS

The main theme of Rabindranath Tagore's poetry is the essential unity (or continuity) of all creation, which is also the main theme of the ancient Hindu *Upanishads*. Indeed, a brief summary of Hindu belief provides a useful introduction to Tagore's work. According to Hindu thought, the only absolute, unchanging, eternal thing is Brahman, the supreme being or world soul who forms the essence of everything. In living things, the essence of Brahman is known as Atman, or soul. Brahman operates through three aspects: Brahma, the creator; Siva, the destroyer; and Vishnu, the preserver or renewer. Brahma's work is finished, but Siva and Vishnu are necessary for change, and change is necessary so that living things may grow toward union with Brahman, a perfect, changeless state, Nirvana. Few, if any, achieve Nirvana in one lifetime, so reincarnation is necessary. In each successive incarnation, one improves one's status in the next through good Karma or deeds (broadly interpreted as actions, thoughts, or faith).

The questions raised by Hindu belief may be ignored here (for example, why would Brahman create something imperfect in the first place?); so also may certain negative social implications (such as the potential for inaction, the caste system, and unconcern for the individual human life). Instead, what should be noticed is the positive emphasis of Hinduism, in contrast to Western thought as characterized by the old Germanic notion that everything is moving toward *Götterdämmerung*; the Christian emphasis on Original Sin, evil, and hell; the masked versions of human sacrifice. It is the positive implications of Hindu belief that Tagore develops in his poetry. For example, his imagery—dwelling on sunrises and sunsets, flowers and their scents, songs and musical instruments, the beautiful deodar tree (*deodár* meaning "divine wood"), the majestic Himalayas—is a constant reminder that creation is charged with divinity: Beauty and majesty are concrete manifestations of Brahman. Change, natural disasters, and death are necessary for renewal, which will come. All people have divine souls, so they should tolerate, respect, and love one another. The advantaged should help the disadvantaged; thereby, they both rise toward Brahman. The individual should strive to live in such a way as to throw off impurities and achieve the essence of divinity within the self. The development of these and related themes can be traced throughout Tagore's œuvre.

GITANJALI

Published in 1910, *Gitanjali* is Tagore's most popular work. The English edition, published in 1912, includes translations not only from the original *Gitanjali* but also from other collections, particularly *Naivedya* (offerings). As light work to keep his mind occupied, Tagore did the translations himself while he was convalescing from an illness at Shelidah and on board a ship for Great Britain. He showed them to British friends who wanted to read his work. They in turn showed the translations to William Butler Yeats, and the result was English publication followed by the 1913 Nobel Prize for Literature. Aware of the undistinguished quality of his translations, Tagore himself could never understand why he was rash enough to do them or why they created such a sensation.

Sometimes compared to the Book of Psalms, *Gitanjali* (song offerings) explores the personal relationship between the poet and divinity. This divinity he calls *Jivandevata*, which he often translates as "Lord of my life" or "life of my life" but also refers to as "my God," "King," "Father," "Mother," "lover," "friend," and "innermost one." The range of terms here suggests the varied associations of *Jivandevata* and also the conventional metaphors Tagore generally uses to develop his relationship with *Jivandevata*. Perhaps the most numerous poems are those in which, like John Donne or St. Teresa of Ávila, Tagore speaks of the deity as a lover with whom he longs to be united. In Song 60 (numbers refer to the English edition), Tagore varies the formula somewhat. He describes a woman who dwells in purdah

within his heart. Many men have come asking for her, but none has seen her face, because she waits only for God. The woman represents the spark of divinity in Tagore which longs to be reunited with its source, and the purdah suggests its loneliness and purity. The divinity within inspires Tagore's songs and motivates him to lead a pure life, but he confesses that involvement in commonplace events sometimes creates a smoke screen which obscures the divinity within and without. The commonplace, however, also has its divinity. God is to be found not only in the temple but also with the workmen in the fields. Because divinity runs through everything, even the metaphors which Tagore uses to describe God have an element of literal truth.

The most interesting poems in *Gitanjali* are a group dealing with death. Songs 86 and 87 are about a family member—probably the poet's wife—whom death has taken. Although heartbroken by her death, Tagore welcomes the visit of God's "servant" and "messenger," and seeking her in the oneness of the universe has brought Tagore closer to God. Thus reconciled, Tagore welcomes his own death as "the fulfillment of life." His dying will be like a bride meeting her bridegroom on the wedding night or like a feeding babe switching from the right breast to the left breast of its mother. Meanwhile, his soul is like "a flock of homesick cranes," on the wing day and night to reach "their mountain nests."

A FLIGHT OF SWANS

Perhaps Tagore's best work, *A Flight of Swans*, takes its title from the image on which *Gitanjali* ends. Thematically, *A Flight of Swans* also takes up where *Gitanjali* ends. Although *A Flight of Swans* continues to develop the personal relationship between the poet and divinity, there is a new emphasis on the impersonal workings of divinity throughout creation. The dual emphasis can be seen in the opening poem of the English edition, the title poem, wherein the flight of swans breaking the silence of the evening symbolizes not only the aspiration of the human soul but also the yearning of inanimate nature for "the Beyond." Even the mountains and deodar trees long to spread their wings like the "homeless bird" inside the breast of Tagore and "countless others." The images of movement and yearning here also serve to introduce the theme of change so prominent in *A Flight of Swans*.

For Tagore, the abstract notion of change is embodied in the dance of Siva, the destroyer, who is featured in several poems. Sometimes called Rudra (the terrible one), Siva brings violence, destruction, and death. To scholars of Sigmund Freud, Tagore's worship of Siva might sound like an Eastern version of the death wish, and his reveling in "the sea of pain" and "the sport of death" might repel squeamish readers. Nevertheless, there is a reason for Tagore's embrace of resounding agony. The dance of Siva purges the cosmological systems. It prevents the flow of "gross Matter" from backing up and putrefying, "renews and purifies" creation in "the bath of death," and speeds souls onward toward Nirvana. The only thing which survives Siva's dance is immortal art, as represented by the Tāj Mahal. Becoming Siva's partner, Tagore aligns himself with the young rather than the old, with the unknown rather than the known, with wandering rather than home, with movement rather than stagnancy.

With its focus on movement and change, on the cyclic nature of things, *A Flight of Swans* breathes the same spirit as Percy Bysshe Shelley's "Ode to the West Wind": If Siva comes, can Vishnu be far behind? Indeed, Tagore hoped that Vishnu, the preserver and renewer, would come soon. Tagore wrote *A Flight of Swans* at the outset of World War I, and the poems reflect his awareness of the war's catastrophic violence. Once the war started, he hoped that it would at least bring about some good results—that it would clean out the evils of the old world system and bring about a new order of peace and brotherhood.

PATRAPUT

Patraput means "a cup of leaves." The poems in this collection are the leaves shed by the poet's tree of life during his old age. *Patraput* is also a reminder that Tagore wrote poetry on subjects other than religion. He was a love poet, especially in his early career, a nature poet (*Banabani*) concentrating on trees and plants, and he even wrote a collection of humorous poems that he called *Khapchada* (a little offbeat). *Patraput* represents not only the mellowness of Tagore's old age but also the variety of his subjects. There are even a few love poems from the seventy-five-year-old poet.

Many of the poems in *Patraput* celebrate subtle effects. With humor and sensitivity, two poems (2 and 7) explore the idleness of holidays. At home by himself in the countryside (probably Santiniketan), the poet has trouble adjusting to doing nothing but feels himself better off than vacationers scrambling through railway stations. In the surrounding scenes of nature that Tagore pauses to observe, God provides him with a "change of air" and a visit to "the eternal ocean" for free. Meanwhile, he knows his "return ticket" will soon expire and he will have to return to the workaday world, "to return here from here itself." These two poems and others contain some attractive descriptions of nature. Another excellent example is Poem 9, which traces the coming and passing of a storm. A number of the poems also trace shifts of mood, from one season to another, from one time of day to another, from one scene to another. In some of these small effects, there are suggestions of bigger themes. For example, there are intimations of the poet's coming death ("return ticket") in the description, as though he is sinking slowly into the placid Indian countryside. The epiphany in Poem 1, where the poet climbs a mountaintop to see the sun setting on one hand and the moon rising on the other, is reminiscent of William Wordsworth's topping of Mt. Snowdon in *The Prelude* (1850).

Another interesting group of poems in *Patraput* consists of those containing social commentary. In Poem 6, Tagore urges the reader ("O thou hospitable") to invite in the destitute pilgrim so that the poor fellow can rise above his mere struggle for existence. In Poem 15, Tagore, himself ostracized when a child, identifies with the untouchables who are prohibited from entering temples, and with the itinerant *Baul* singers, who sing that God is "the Man of my heart." Like them, Tagore has no caste, no temple, no religion except the religion of Man. Poem 16 is a lament for Africa, ransacked for slaves by the purveyors of Christian "civilization." Their phony belief in religion is duplicated in the modern era by the militarists who seek Buddha's blessings for their killing (apparently a slap at Japanese aggression in Manchuria).

CRITICISM OF FORMAL RELIGION

As the unflattering references to Hindus, Christians, and Buddhists indicate, Tagore had no more enthusiasm for formal religion than he had for formal education. Nevertheless, along with such figures as Gerard Manley

Hopkins and T. S. Eliot, Tagore is a leading religious poet of the modern era. The social commentary in *Patraput* marks the final stage of his spiritual journey. In *Gitanjali*, he is concerned with his personal fate, his individual relationship to God. In *A Flight of Swans*, he explores the impersonal workings of divinity through the terrible dance of Siva; and in *Patraput*, he shows that religious belief must ultimately be expressed through concern (and action) for one's fellow men. With his "religion of Man," Tagore ends up in a position very similar to Western Humanism, but it is a position that retains its ties to ancient religious belief, belief summed up in the teaching of the humble *Baul* singers that God is "the Man of my heart."

OTHER MAJOR WORKS

LONG FICTION: *Bau-Thakuranir Hat*, 1883; *Rajarshi*, 1887; *Chokher bāli*, 1902 (*Binodini*, 1959); *Naukadubi*, 1906 (*The Wreck*, 1921); *Gora*, 1910 (English translation, 1924); *Chaturanga*, 1916 (English translation, 1963); *Ghare bāire*, 1916 (*Home and the World*, 1919); *Jogajog*, 1929; *Shesher kabita*, 1929; *Dui bon*, 1933 (*Two Sisters*, 1945).

SHORT FICTION: *The Hungry Stones and Other Stories*, 1916; *Mashi and Other Stories*, 1918; *Stories from Tagore*, 1918; *Broken Ties and Other Stories*, 1925; *The Runaway and Other Stories*, 1959.

PLAYS: *Prakritir Pratishodh*, pb. 1884 (verse; *Sanyasi: Or, The Ascetic*, 1917); *Rājž o Rāni*, pb. 1889 (verse; *The King and the Queen*, 1918); *Visarjan*, pb. 1890 (verse; based on his novel *Rajarshi; Sacrifice*, 1917); *Chitrāngadā*, pb. 1892 (verse; *Chitra*, 1913); *Prayaschitta*, pr. 1909 (based on his novel *Bau-Thakuranir Hat*); *Rājā*, pb. 1910 (*The King of the Dark Chamber*, 1914); *Dākghar*, pb. 1912 (*The Post Office*, 1914); *Phālguni*, pb. 1916 (*The Cycle of Spring*, 1917); *Arupratan*, pb. 1920 (revision of his play *Rājā*); *Muktadhārā, pb. 1922 (English translation, 1950); Raktakarabi*, pb. 1924 (*Red Oleanders*, 1925); *Chirakumār Sabhā*, pb. 1926; *Natir Pujā*, pb. 1926 (*Worship of the Dancing Girl*, 1950); *Sesh Rakshā*, pb. 1928; *Paritrān*, pb. 1929 (revision of *Prayaschitta*); *Tapati*, pb. 1929 (revision of *Rājā o Rāni*); *Chandālikā*, pr., pb. 1933 (English translation, 1938); *Bānsari*, pb. 1933; *Nritya-natya Chitrangādā*, pb. 1936 (revision of his play *Chitrangādā*); *Nritya-natya Chandālikā*, pb. 1938 (revision of his play *Chandālikā*); *Three Plays*, pb. 1950.

NONFICTION: *Sadhana*, 1913; *Jivansmriti*, 1912 (*My Reminiscences*, 1917); *Personality*, 1917; *Nationalism*, 1919; *Greater India*, 1921; *Glimpses of Bengal*, 1921; *Creative Unity*, 1922; *Talks in China*, 1925; *Lectures and Addresses*, 1928; *Letters to a Friend*, 1928; *The Religion of Man*, 1931; *Mahatmaji and the Depressed Humanity*, 1932; *Man*, 1937; *Chhelebela*, 1940 (*My Boyhood Days*, 1940); *Sabhyatar Samkat*, 1941 (*Crisis in Civilization*, 1941); *Towards Universal Man*, 1961.

MISCELLANEOUS: *Collected Poems and Plays*, 1936; *A Tagore Reader*, 1961.

BIBLIOGRAPHY

Chakravorty, B. C. *Rabindranath Tagore: His Mind and Art*, New Delhi, India: Young India Publications, 1970. A biographical and critical study of Tagore's life and works. Includes a selected bibliography of Tagore's work.

Chatterjee, Bhabatosh. *Rabindranath Tagore and Modern Sensibility*. Delhi, India: Oxford University Press, 1996. A collection of essays that records a common reader's changing perceptions of the literary achievement of Rabindranath Tagore. It addresses certain central concerns of the writer's work and underlines aspects that have not, so far, received sufficient attention. It does not offer definitive explanations, but aims instead to confront the issues his work raises and to study them from different points of view.

Dutta, Krishna and Andrew Robinson. *Rabindranath Tagore: The Myriad-Minded Man*. New York: St. Martin's Press, 1996. Dutta and Robinson cover a tremendous amount of fresh biographical, cultural, and political terrain without losing their narrative thread. The authors excel at chronicling the particulars of Tagore's life, and portraying his personality.

Kripalani, Krishna. *Rabindranath Tagore*. 2d ed. Calcutta, India: Visva-Bharati, 1980. A narrative biography of Tagore's life. Includes bibliographic references.

Lesny, V. *Rabindranath Tagore: His Personality and Work*. London: George Allen & Unwin, 1939. A critical assessment of Tagore's work. Includes bibliographic references and an index.

Thompson, Edward. *Rabindranath Tagore: Poet and Dramatist*. Westport, Conn.: Greenwood Press, 1975. A biographical and critical study of Tagore's poetic and dramatic works. Includes bibliogrphic references.

Harold Branam;
bibliography updated by the editors

TAO QIAN

T'ao Ch'ien

Born: Xingyang, China; 365
Died: Xingyang, China; 427

PRINCIPAL POETRY

T'ao the Hermit: Sixty Poems, 1952 (William Acker, translator)

The Poems of T'ao Ch'ien, 1953 (Lily Baohu Zhang and Marjorie Sinclair, translators)

The Poetry of T'ao Ch'ien, 1970 (James Robert Hightower, translator)

Complete Works of Tao Yuanming, 1992 (Tan Shilin, translator)

OTHER LITERARY FORMS

Tao Qian is known primarily as a poet. Among his extant works are two *fu* rhyme-prose compositions (that is, rhythmic and occasionally rhymed prose); the renowned "Return" in *ci* form (another quasi-poetic genre); a letter to an acquaintance; prefaces; seven *can* collophons, or *envois*; a biographical note on an official colleague; several essays; obituaries; and the celebrated "Record of the Peach Grove."

ACHIEVEMENTS

Probably more has been written about Tao Qian, in whatever language, than about any other Chinese poet. Studies by Japanese scholars alone, to whom Tao Qian most strongly appealed, run into many hundreds of titles. Tao Qian is primarily associated with the foundations of the *tianyuan*, or "pastoral" (literally, "cultivated fields and orchards") school of poetry (as opposed to the rugged *shanshui* "mountains and waters" landscapes of his contemporary, the celebrated nobleman Xie Lingyun, 385-433). The unadorned directness of his poetic diction and the innocent, touching sentiment of his anchorite forbearance have perennially appealed to the oversophisticated Chinese bureaucrat-litterateur. Writing in the prevailing pentameter line of his day, Tao Qian was the first to exploit the *shi* lyric form extensively for such topics as wine (which he tirelessly celebrated) and the idiosyncrasies of his own children. These eventually became favorite themes in Tang and later poetry. As James Robert Hightower has observed in *The Poetry of T'ao Ch'ien*, "even the shortest and most selective list of famous Chinese poets would have to find a place for Tao Qian," and his poetry above that of all others appears the most frequently in anthologies of Chinese verse.

BIOGRAPHY

Biographies in the Chinese dynastic histories are principally concerned with their subject's official career and influence on national politics. Since Tao Qian's service career was minimal, and grudging at that, little contemporaneous record was kept, and the few remarks about him were included in the section on hermits, rather than in the "literati" category. His various sobriquets, too, reflect his preference for eremitic life. Later efforts to construct, or contrive, a respectable account befitting the life of a universally beloved poet relied largely upon anecdote and upon Tao Qian's autobiographical self-evaluations, such as "Biography of Mr. Five Willows" (a nom de plume describing his rustic environment). By his own account, Tao Qian was a quiet, unassuming man. He enjoyed scholarship but took no pleasure in pedantic obscurities. He would have his readers believe that he was a great drunkard, and indeed the greater part of the official record consists of stories illustrating his love of tippling, noting, for example, his insistence on cultivating brewing grain rather than food, however destitute his family. Even the memoir bringing him into friendly association with the then-ascendant court poet Yan Yazhi (384-456) focuses on wine, relating how Tao Qian had deposited a large sum of money given him by Yen in a local wine shop.

Tao Qian lived during the decline of the Eastern Jin regime (317-420) of the Sima clan on a small farm south of the Yangzi River. His forebears had once been eminent officials, but the family had fallen on hard times, and Tao Qian lacked the all-important connections at court that would have secured for him, at the outset, an entrée into higher echelons of the administration. He was assigned various minor provincial posts, but he became disgusted with the pervasive corruption of the regime and with the petty drudgery of local officers and resigned rather than "crook his back for a five-peck salary." Thus, for most of his life he was a sort of gentleman farmer, living in relative poverty but wryly content with his wife and children, wine, chrysanthemums, friends, stringless lute, and poetry.

ANALYSIS

Scholars of Chinese literature, and literati throughout the ages, have unanimously admired Tao Qian's poetry. Some eighty-eight of his poems survive. These are of varying length and in tetrasyllabic or pentasyllabic lines. Many are prefaced by an introduction explaining the circumstances under which they were composed. Tao Qian found no place for the artificial *yuefu* (music bureau) compositions popular in his time—lyrics written to ancient tunes and titles which dictated theme, mood, and style. He did, however, on his own terms produce a set of poems "imitating" or "in the style of" earlier compositions.

Typical rhetoric describes Tao Qian's moral sentiments as "far-reaching waves, and lofty soaring clouds." Other famous poet-critics were drawn to imitate Tao Qian's style, notably the eleventh century poet Su Tungp'o, who wrote a set of one hundred and twenty matching verses. A focus of controversy to this day is the dissenting judgment of the sixth century Chung Hung, who, in his *Shipin* (classification of poets), placed Tao Qian in the second of three categories of poets because, in an age of florid ornamentation, Tao Qian's work disdained empty embellishments.

In the development of Chinese literature, Tao Qian is most securely associated with the flourishing of the *dianyuan* (pastoral) genre, the embryonic origins of which stem from the tetrasyllabic odes of the great eleventh to seventh century B.C.E. canon. Poetry, thereafter,

particularly during the Tang (618-907) and the Song (960-1279) dynasties, was imbued with his influence.

Although unwilling to compromise his principles for a corrupt regime, Tao Qian was acutely aware of the Confucian moral obligation of the literate gentleman to make his abilities available to the state. A number of his poems recall this duty, and they laud members of his own clan and other eminent bureaucrats who contributed their energies to public administration: "In hearing lawsuits he is just/ A hundred miles enjoy his help." He had had no taste for office as a youth, he says, but he too had tried to be of service, "fallen by mischance into the dusty net/ And thirteen years away from home." Such occupation was intolerable for him "in a time of decadence, when one longs for the ancient kings." Far too long he had been a "caged prisoner." In the end, he was "not one to volunteer his services" and would "not be bound by love of rank," "scorning the role of opportunist." On the topic of posthumous fame, he was ambivalent. He asks, Daoist-like, what is the use of an honored name if it costs a lifetime of deprivation, yet he also suggests that fame may endure as an inspiration for a thousand years. Seeking solace for what he considered his own lifetime of failure, however, he stresses the transience of fame rather than its inspirational legacy.

DESTITUTION

In versifying the destitution to which he was reduced, Tao Qian indulged in no bleak self-pity. Virtually every one of his poems, and many of his famous prose works, mention his poverty, but he counts his blessings—and by Chinese standards, then and now, he must have been relatively self-sufficient. He owned a few acres of land and an ill-thatched cottage with "four or five" rooms (sometimes interpreted "as four plus five" rooms), shaded by elms and willows at the back, and with peaches and plums stretching out in front. He cultivated (or, more likely, oversaw the farming of) hemp, mulberry, and beans, and daily extended the area under his plow, delighting in the pleasures of the woods and fields.

Occasionally resorting to hyperbole, he claims in his poems that when his crops did badly, hunger drove him to begging, knocking on doors and fumbling for words. His house burned down several times, pests decimated his stock of grain, and even in winter, his family slept without covers, longing for the dawn. On a more cheerful note, his hut is repaired; plowing and spinning supply his needs; and if he is diligent in the fields, he will not be cheated. In fact, two poems specifically praise the farmer's lot, describing how new shoots enfold new life, and how labor, too, gives joy. Another dozen or so verses laud the "impoverished gentleman" along with other humble but principled men of ancient days. A long lament mourns "gentlemen born out of their times," who relinquished glory and took pleasure in poverty and low condition.

WINE

One consolation in Tao Qian's rustic plight was wine. A major part of his official biography and of his autobiographical comments focuses on his tippling, and some critics complain that his poetry revolves around little else. Certainly, no other poet before him had ever sung the praises of alcohol so prolifically and insistently, and in this, Tao Qian set a precedent for a subgenre that was to catch the imagination of later poets, notably Li Bo (701-762) and Dongpo (1036-1101). Like poverty, wine is mentioned in virtually every one of his poems: Twenty poems were written "after drinking wine"; another describes "drinking alone in the rainy season"; yet another long poem gives "an account of wine"; and there is a rather pathetic poem in which Tao Qian confides that he wishes he could stop drinking—though the pathos of this admission is attenuated by the form of the verse, a game wherein the word "stop" appears in each of the twenty lines.

However undesirable Tao Qian's apparent alcoholism may seem to the modern Western reader, no odium attached itself to the poet in his time. The Chinese heritage better appreciated the spiritual liberation achieved by mild inebriation and credited much of the innocent genius of Tao Qian's poetry to this condition. Later critics, too, have defended Tao Qian by arguing that such drunkenness was a timeworn ploy in China (the antics of the poet Ruan Ji, 210-263, constitute a formidable example), to a large extent feigned to avoid the jeopardy of involvement in political machinations.

CHRYSANTHEMUMS

Almost as much as with wine, Tao Qian was fascinated by the chrysanthemum, a flower which has come to be associated with his poetry. The chrysanthemum bloom survives the blight of autumn; as the last flower of the year, it represented for Tao Qian his own fortitude in adversity. So too appear in his lines the cypress and the pine—evergreens that symbolize Confucian moral steadfastness.

Tao Qian found great comfort in his family. He was the first Chinese poet to record his feelings about his children so freely, and in doing so he left to posterity some of the most appealing lines in the Chinese literary heritage. In "Finding Fault with My Sons," the poet complains about the laziness and self-indulgence of his five boys: The nine-year-old, for example, wants only pears and chestnuts, and the thirteen-year-olds cannot even count to their age. It is Tao Qian's ability to capture casual moments from childhood, however—the toddler peeking through a crack in the door, anticipating his father's return from the fields—that has given his poems on children a timeless appeal.

RURAL DELIGHTS

Tao Qian's pastoral poetry typified the *dianyuan* genre. Rather than tramping in climbing boots among the wooded peaks and precipices of a Jiangsu-Zhejiang estate, as did Xie Lingyun, Tao Qian would sit quietly at his casement window in his tumbledown thatched cottage and contemplate the passing scene, sip his wine, think of old and absent friends, and muse upon his approaching old age. Gentle delight in the rural community fills his verse, rather than the wonder of nature's vast power and magnificence that erupts from Hsieh Ling-yün's nature poetry. Noteworthy, too, is the absence from Tao Qian's diction of the color, glitter, mysticism, classical obscurantism, and pedantic reference and allusion of the overrefined, overembellished poetry then in vogue—in particular the unctuous congratulatory court verse of his friend, Yen Yen-chih.

In the most simple, natural language, Tao Qian writes about the dense, hovering clouds, and the fine rain at dusk that settles on the road, making it impassable. These, typically, are static images, reinforced by the absence of boat or carriage which might bring visiting friends. Movement lies more in the new blossoms springing forth, eliciting the emotions of a sensitive observer. Still-life landscapes depict new grains and the waters of a wide lake stretching endlessly into the distance. Herbs and flowers grow in rows, over which trees and bamboo cast their shade. "Interior" scenes show a cittern across a bench, and a jug half-filled with muddy wine.

Time passes in the pell-mell revolution of the seasons. Blossoms are dead by morning; the cicada's mournful chirp heralds the fading of summer's heat; plum and peach of springtime give way to autumn's chrysanthemum; one sees migrating geese and notes the morning cockcrow. Frosts wither the crops, and evening dew soaks the poet's gown. His years slip away, his hair turns gray, his children mature. As the sun sets, a torch serves in place of a costly candle, and if the company is congenial, dawn arrives too soon. Thousand-year cares may be forgotten; tomorrow need not concern man in his enjoyment of the moment.

Tao Qian's poems further adumbrate a kind of farmer's almanac, detailing the activities of his daily life. There is habitual drinking, but the poet also writes of hitching up his wagon at early dawn and starting along the road to his plowing and weeding. He discusses with the locals the prospects for the harvest of mulberry and hemp. Tired, staff in hand, he returns home by a path twisting through the bushes, pausing to bathe his feet in a mountain stream. He digs a well for water, and plucks a wild chrysanthemum by a bank. For leisure, there are books wherein to discover heroic models from the past who may inspire him in his adversity. As a series of thirteen poems reveals, he especially delights in the fantasies and adventures of the imaginative *Shan Hai Jing* (*Classic of the Mountains and Seas*) and the magic and marvels of the *Travels of King Mu*. Always he sings of his contentment, however poor: how neat his garden is, and how glad he is to have relinquished worldly affairs.

CLASSICAL PHILOSOPHICAL VIEWS

The philosophical views that Tao Qian espoused were entirely classical. Although he lived within the shadow of Mount Lu, the great monastic seat of Hui Yuan's (334-416) White Lotus sect of Buddhism, to which Xie Lingyun and other intellectual literati had been massively attracted, Tao Qian's ideas exhibit no interest in the newly introduced faith—celibacy and abstention were hardly characteristic of him. The popular Daoism of the time, too, with its mysticism and dilettante metaphysical speculation, and searches for elixirs

of immortality, seems to have touched him but little, and he both doubts and eschews the labors and regimens recommended for the attainment of transcendent sagehood.

DEATH

Nor did death itself threaten Tao Qian. He concludes his long discourse on "Substance, Shadow, and Spirit" with the simple attitude, "When it is time to go, then we shall simply go—there is nothing, after all, that we can do about it." Life, he explains, is nothing but a shadow play, which in the end reverts to nothingness: There is no immortality, no afterlife, no rebirth. Indeed, the primitive concepts he expresses smack most strongly of the early Daoism of Laozi (sixth century B.C.E.) and Zhuangzi (third century B.C.E.).

If frequency of citation is a criterion, then the Confucian *Analects*, a collection of aphorisms attributed to Confucius (551-479 B.C.E.) and compiled some two centuries after his death, were Tao Qian's favorite source of classical philosophical reference. He was especially observant of passages wherein the Master sanctioned retirement from officialdom during the administration of a corrupt and unworthy regime, doubtless to assuage his own pangs of conscience. The heroes who appear in his "Impoverished Gentlemen," drawn from philosophies and histories through the third century Han Dynasty, also exemplify the man of pure principle, who, like himself, would rather eke out his existence in humble obscurity than strive for empty glories in sycophantic court service.

One often anthologized verse exemplifies these various elements of Tao Qian's work and thought. The poem is dated in the ninth month of the year 410, after the rice harvest, and located in some "western field":

> Man's life may conform to the Way,
> But clothing and food are indeed fundamental.
> If no provision be made for them,
> How can one seek peace?
> At the opening of springtime, I took care of
> the ordinary jobs,
> And the harvest has turned out considerable.
> . . . .
> My four limbs in truth so weary,
> . . . .
> Far, far though the mind of Chü and Ni be,

A thousand years I still sense affinity with them.
Would that things be forever thus:
It is not plowing the fields that I complain of!

Tao Qian affirms that mortal life is bound by morality, but, echoing the Confucian rationalist, Mencius (327-289? B.C.E.), he realizes that the basis of ethical behavior is material sustenance. The life of the producer of these essential commodities is not an easy one, subject as it is to wearisome toil and the exigencies of the natural world. Well enough he appreciates the attitudes of the plowmen Zhangzhu and Jie, who rejected the overtures of Confucius and his disciple Zilu to engage them in discourse (a clever closure balancing the Confucian sentiments of the opening). Indeed, it is not the productive plowing of which Tao Qian complains. Rather, he implies, he grieves over the political situation, for the men of power and status have reneged on their mandate of moral leadership.

UTOPIA

Tao Qian left his vision of Utopia in his renowned "Peach Blossom Spring," the story of a fisherman who loses his way, enters a flowering peach grove, and comes upon a lost society—refugees from the rapacious Qin regime (221-206 B.C.E.). He remains there for several days, entertained by the inhabitants, and although enjoined to secrecy, upon his return home he reports his experience to the authorities. Searches, however, fail to rediscover the location of the peach grove.

As described in the narrative, Tao Qian's perfect society enjoys broad plains of rich fields and ponds, and substantial dwellings. Well-tended paths traverse the fields, whereabout grow mulberry and bamboo. Courtyards are stocked with domestic animals; the people dress unpretentiously and are happy and carefree. They till the soil in mutual contract, and at sunset cease from their toil. No taxes are extorted for imperial indulgences; roads remain untraveled by the king's officers. No calendar regulates the natural progression of the seasons; artful machines are not needed.

Such is the nature of Tao Qian's views as presented in his poetry. His wistful forbearance in the adversity of humble poverty—when riches and honor, however tainted by dishonorable service, could have been his—

his cheerful self-consolation, and his sincere attachment to the life of farmer and peasant which he intimately chronicled; his love of family, his high morality tempered by human failings, his doubts as to the rectitude of his retirement from admittedly evil times, and his refuge in quiet inebriation have endeared him and his work to Oriental and Occidental readers irrespective of era, class, or aspiration.

BIBLIOGRAPHY

Barnhart, Richard M. *Peach Blossom Spring: Gardens and Flowers in Chinese Paintings*. New York: Metropolitan Museum of Art, 1983. Treats of Peach Blossom Spring as a pastoral utopia in paintings.

Davis, A. R. *Tao Yuan-ming (A.D. 365-427): His Works and Their Meaning*. 2 vols. New York: Cambridge University Press, 1983. Insightful study of the complete poetic works of Tao Qian with a meticulous translation. Volume 2 contains the original of the Chinese text.

Field, Stephen L. "The Poetry of Tao Yuanming." In *Great Literature of the Eastern World*, edited by Ian P. McGreal. New York: HarperCollins, 1996. A brief teaching guide with an analysis of Tao Qian's three poems "A Returning to Live in the Country," "Return Home!" and "Peach Blossom Found."

Hightower, James Robert, trans. *The Poetry of Tao Ch'ien*. Oxford, England: Oxford University Press, 1970. A scholarly translation with a concise introduction about Chinese poetic tradition and Tao Qian's life. Contains elaborate annotations.

Kwong, Charles Yim-tze. *Tao Qian and the Chinese Poetic Tradition: The Quest for Cultural Identity*. Ann Arbor: Center for Chinese Studies, University of Michigan, 1994. A study of Tao Qian in the light of Chinese poetic and cultural traditions.

Yu, Pauline. "The Poetry of Retreat." *Masterworks of Asian Literature in Comparative Perspective*, edited by Barbara Stoler Miller. Armonk: M. E. Sharpe, 1994. A thoughtful discussion of Tao Yuanming in the Chinese poetic tradition of the recluse, along with other poets such as Ruan Ji and Xie Lingyun.

John Marney;
bibliography updated by Qingyun Wu

TORQUATO TASSO

Born: Sorrento, Italy; March 11, 1544
Died: Rome, Italy; April 25, 1595

PRINCIPAL POETRY

Rinaldo, 1562 (English translation, 1792)
Gerusalemme liberata, 1581 (*Jerusalem Delivered*, 1600)
Rime, 1581, 1591, 1593 (*From the Italian of Tasso's Sonnets*, 1867)
Gerusalemme conquistata, 1593 (*Jerusalem Conquered*, 1907)
Le sette giornate del mondo creato, 1607

OTHER LITERARY FORMS

Torquato Tasso's literary work begins and ends with his discussions of poetic theory. As early as 1561 but certainly before 1570, he had composed *Discorsi dell'arte poetica* (1587; discourses on the poetic art), and he published a much revised and expanded version of the same work, *Discorsi del poema eroico* (1594; *Discourses on the Heroic Poem*, 1973) the year before his death. The latter is both a defense of Tasso's own epics and an influential statement of Renaissance critical theory. Tasso's *Dialoghi* (1581) embraces a variety of subjects and often includes Tasso himself as one of the speakers; these dialogues are modeled after those of Plato. Tasso's *Lettere* (1587, 1588, 1616-1617), numbering as many as seventeen hundred, constitute a rich source of information about his life in elegantly crafted prose. Tasso's pastoral drama *Aminta* (pr. 1573; English translation, 1591), celebrates love and has been far more influential than his tragedy of mistaken identities and incest, *Il re Torrismondo* (pb. 1587; the King Torrismondo).

ACHIEVEMENTS

Torquato Tasso's importance in the history of letters is twofold: His own prodigious work has great merit, and he exerted enormous influence on artists who followed him. Tasso, the representative genius of the late Italian Renaissance, was the creator of Christian epic. In him the erudition of classical literature and Aristotelian poetic theory combined with the force of the Counter-Reformation and court life to produce *Jerusalem Delivered*. His reputation as a writer rests on this epic, his superb pastoral drama *Aminta*, some of his lyric poetry, and his synthesis of epic poetic theory.

Tasso enjoyed almost immediate renown both in and out of Italy. The romance *Rinaldo* showed promise, but *Aminta*, on the theme of innocent and natural love triumphing over various adversities of law and circumstance, established his reputation as a poet. *Jerusalem Delivered*, completed three years later, touched off a spirited controversy over poetic theory, with comparisons to Homer, Vergil, and Ludovico Ariosto that always recognized Tasso's stature, whether the commentary was hostile or admiring. Tasso's epic also excited interest in England. As early as 1584 a Latin translation of *Jerusalem Delivered* by Scipio Gentili was published in London. Edmund Spenser in his 1587 "Letter to Raleigh" mentioned Tasso as one of his models for *The Faerie Queene* (1590, 1596). In 1594, the second part of the British play *Godfrey of Bulloigne* was performed by

Torquato Tasso (Library of Congress)

the Admiral's Men. Also in 1594, Richard Carew published the Italian text and English translation of the first five cantos of *Jerusalem Delivered*. In the early seventeenth century, Tasso influenced Samuel Daniel, Michael Drayton, Abraham Cowley, and John Milton. Later Tasso's reputation suffered an eclipse, although John Hoole's 1763 translation of *Jerusalem Delivered* into heroic couplets was very popular. The nineteenth century saw as many as eight new translations of the epic, the most influential being Jeremiah Holmes Wiffen's 1824 version in Spenserian stanzas. Whether Tasso's epic was read for its own sake or used as a source, it was admired for its love stories. Leigh Hunt, for example, chose the romantic trials of Olindo and Sofronia, Tancred and Clorinda, and Rinaldo and Armida for his *Stories from the Italian Poets* (1846). Early in the twentieth century, however, many critics evinced little sympathy for Tasso's works or his reputation.

That reputation, the picture of a man driven to or feigning madness because of persecutions endured for love, was fostered by the biography *Vita di Torquato Tasso* (1621), published by the poet's friend G. B. Manso. As early as 1594, a now lost play, *Tasso's Melancholy*, was performed in London. The Romantic age saw in Tasso's writings his supposed love for Leonora d'Este and made Tasso a symbol of the suffering artist. The legend that grew up around his life inspired the drama *Torquato Tasso* (1790) by Johann Wolfgang von Goethe and the monologue *Lament of Tasso* (1817) by Lord Byron, in addition to numerous musical and pictorial works. Psychological interest in Tasso has not completely disappeared, but interest in his legend no longer overshadows the worth of his writing.

BIOGRAPHY

Torquato Tasso was born on March 11, 1544, in Sorrento, the son of the poet and courtier Bernardo Tasso and Porzia de' Rossi. He began his education in Naples with Jesuit teachers. His family life was disrupted first when young Tasso followed his father, exiled from the kingdom of Naples, to Rome in 1554, and again in 1556 when his mother died unexpectedly. Perhaps influenced in choice of genre by his father's recently completed epic *Amadigi* (1560) and in choice of a subject by his sister's escape from an Ottoman attack on Sorrento,

Tasso wrote 116 stanzas of what was to become later his epic *Jerusalem Delivered* but laid aside the story of Godfrey and the First Crusade when his father sent him to Padua to study law in 1560. In Padua, law was far less interesting than Sperone Speroni and the discussion of philosophy, rhetoric, and poetic theory. Tasso wrote and published the chivalric romance *Rinaldo* and began writing Petrarchan love lyrics. After a period of study interspersed with escapades at the University of Bologna, he returned to Padua, probably where he wrote *Discorsi dell'arte poetica*. In 1565, Tasso left school (without a degree) for Ferrara and the service of Cardinal Luigi d'Este.

In Ferrara, Tasso resumed work on his epic on the liberation of Jerusalem. He also wrote lyrics for the two sisters of Duke Alfonso II, Lucrezia and Leonora d'Este. Tasso suffered the death of his father in 1569; in 1570, he traveled to Paris, his only trip outside Italy.

Entering the service of Duke Alfonso in January, 1572, Tasso began a very productive period of his life. His pastoral masterpiece *Aminta* was performed in 1573; he began a tragedy based on classical models in 1574; and he completed *Jerusalem Delivered* in 1575 at the age of thirty-one. Although he was anxious to publish his epic, Tasso submitted it to the criticism of Scipione Gonzaga and others. Tasso wished nothing in his work to offend either poetic theory or Church doctrine, but he could not bear the criticism that resulted. He left Ferrara only to return; he felt spied upon and attacked a servant with a knife; he was placed under guard, but escaped to stay with his sister in Sorrento. Tasso returned to Ferrara, then soon left to wander through Mantua, Padua, Venice, Urbino, Pesaro, and Turin before returning again to Ferrara in 1579. This time his accusations and irrational behavior led Duke Alfonso to imprison him in Sant'Anna, where Tasso remained for seven years.

Biographers have variously attributed Alfonso's imprisonment of Tasso to the Duke's anger at Tasso's love for Alfonso's sister, pique at the suggestions that his poet wished to find a new patron, fear over what Tasso might reveal to the Inquisition, or the sincere concern of an exasperated ruler to save all concerned, including Tasso himself, from the effects of real madness. Regardless of the causes of Tasso's madness or melancholy, the conditions of his long imprisonment did not prevent him from writing, although it did prevent him from having any control over the many unauthorized editions of his works published in those years. During the years of his imprisonment, Tasso composed more than four hundred letters, many of his dialogues, considerable occasional poetry, and an *Apologia* (1586) for *Jerusalem Delivered*.

Released from prison in 1586, Tasso first went to Mantua, where he completed his tragedy, renaming it *Il re Torrismondo*. He traveled restlessly and published his earlier epic, *Jerusalem Conquered*. He also composed a number of religious poems, one of which was the religious epic *Le sette giornate del mondo creato* (the seven days of the creation of the world). The last of Tasso's many journeys was to Rome, where he was to be crowned poet laureate by the Pope. Tasso became ill, however, and died at the monastery of Sant' Onofrio on April 25, 1595.

Analysis

It is apparent that, from the first, Torquato Tasso set out to reconcile a number of seeming opposites in his work: lyric and heroic, myth and history, fantasy and religion, romance and epic, popular variety and Aristotelian principle. The tension of this attempt at synthesis caused Tasso to abandon his early draft of an epic poem for a series of less ambitious compositions. Many critics believe that the tension remains unresolved.

Tasso's lyric voice is amply represented in the almost two thousand short poems produced throughout his life. Many of them are imitative of Petrarch. In 1589, Tasso planned to publish his poems in separate volumes according to subject—amorous, encomiastic, and sacred. The love poems are among the earliest lyrics, sometimes linked to historical women such as Lucrezia Bendidio or Laura Peperara, but often general and diffuse in praise of beauty, love, and emotion. Rich in poetic devices the lyrics luxuriate in the suffering of the poet.

If the middle style characterizes Tasso's amorous verse, the grand style characterizes his encomiastic verse. Many of these poems in praise of influential men risk being sterile or self-serving, but they can also be poignant. Many of the lyrics written in Sant' Anna are pleas for help or pardon, addressed to Duke Alfonzo, the Ferrara princesses, or the Duke of Urbino. The Sant' Anna lyrics exhibit a remarkable variety in tone and mood, and include a famous and atypical sonnet addressed to the cats of the prison.

RELIGIOUS LYRICS

Tasso's religious lyrics reflect both personal experience and the general tenor of the Counter-Reformation. There are sonnets, canzones, madrigals, and ballads. They are concerned with both his personal fears and common religious themes such as "Le lagrime di Gesù Cristo" ("The Tears of Jesus Christ"), "Le lagrime di Maria Vergine" ("The Tears of the Virgin Mary"), and "Monte Oliveto" ("Mount Olivet"), a poem on the founding of the religious order that sheltered Tasso in Naples in 1588. The poems reflect the restlessness, melancholy, and personal suffering that are also present in so many of Tasso's other works. Just as Erminia in *Jerusalem Delivered* finds a temporary respite from her troubles in a pastoral sanctuary, so various people in the sonnets retire from the world to an idealized, cloistered life which Tasso envies but cannot join. Tasso's sacred verse is similar in language, style, and tone to his secular verse.

LE SETTE GIORNATE DEL MONDO CREATO

Also on a religious theme, *Le sette giornate del mondo creato* illustrates some of Tasso's characteristic strengths and weaknesses. Tasso wrote the poem between 1592 and 1594 after he had finished *Jerusalem Conquered*, a version of his great epic that he felt to be immune from any possible religious or stylistic criticism, and this new theme would allow him to expand his unimpeachable views. *Le sette giornate del mondo creato* is eight thousand lines of blank verse. It is derivative of pagan authors, the Bible, the Church fathers, and Renaissance writers including Guillaume du Bartas. It is neither original nor coherent, although it does attempt to reconcile Aristotle and the Neoplatonists. It is digressive; it succumbs to superfluous praise of noble contemporaries, such as the Pope; it subordinates art to moral lesson. Yet for all this, the poem also sees in nature a reflection of the poet's own circumstance. Even at the end of his life, Tasso reflects his person in his art: doubt, suffering, a love of the marvelous, and the lyric mood in epic expression.

RINALDO

Tasso seems always to have aspired to the writing of epic, and, like Vergil, trained for his magnum opus by writing less noble works. *Rinaldo* is just such an exercise. It is a romance in the tradition of Ariosto's *Orlando furioso* (1516-1532; English translation, 1591) or Bernardo Tasso's *Amadigi*. *Rinaldo* is composed of twelve cantos of ottava rima, preceded by an address, "A i lettori" ("To the Readers") which discusses his artistic choices. Tasso was influenced by the study of Aristotle which blossomed following new translations of and commentaries on Aristotle's *Poetics* (334-323 B.C.E.). Tasso claims to follow Aristotelian precedent and to improve upon Ariosto by limiting the action to the unity of a single hero and eliminating personalized prologues to each canto. Tasso, however, places the enjoyment of his readers above even Aristotle, and so the unity of action in Tasso's plays will admit considerable variety, along with love interest and marvels.

Both Tasso's method and his material are derivative. Commentators have found in *Rinaldo* echoes of Bernardo Tasso, Petrarch, Matteo Maria Boiardo, and Ariosto, as well as Homer, Theocritus, Vergil, Ovid, and others. The story tells of the trials endured by the protagonist in his search for glory and love. Rinaldo, Orlando's cousin, falls in love with Clorice, the sister of the king of Gascony, but must undergo many adventures on land and sea before at last rescuing Clorice from the infidels and marrying her. There are battles, magic, the glitter of the court, and the suffering of love. Just as Rinaldo in *Jerusalem Delivered* is seduced by Armida, but ultimately renounces passion in favor of duty, so is this Rinaldo temporarily wooed away from his true love by the alluring Floriana. When Rinaldo ultimately rejects Floriana, she, like Armida, attempts suicide but is saved. In another incident, Clizia is accidentally shot by her husband just as Clorinda is slain by the unsuspecting Tancred in *Jerusalem Delivered*. *Rinaldo* is the story of the education of a young knight who must prove himself both moral and brave in order to win his love. In theme, incident, style, and tone, this early romance prepares for the epic that follows. *Rinaldo* was written in ten months, and published in 1562 when Tasso was only eighteen years old. It was immediately popular, going through six editions during Tasso's lifetime.

JERUSALEM DELIVERED

Tasso then returned to the 116 stanzas of the *Jerusalem Delivered*, which he had begun in 1559. Manuscripts of that text, an intermediate version of about 1570, and the final version of 1575 all survive, and comparisons of the three show some of the poem's development. The original *Jerusalem Delivered* was militaristic and moralistic. It described the arrival of the Christian army, an unsuccessful negotiation, and the anticipation of strife. Almost half of these stanzas survive in the final version of *Jerusalem Delivered*, but there are no love adventures and no supernatural marvels. Tasso expanded his epic to six cantos by 1566, and by 1570 the whole poem had been written. In the 1570 version, Armida and the accompanying love interest were present, but the poem's protagonist was still Ubaldo, a forebear of the duke of Urbino. Significant changes and deletions occurred before the poem, first called *Il Goffredo*, was completed in 1575.

The twenty cantos of ottava rima, which now followed the exploits of an imaginary Rinaldo d'Este rather than Ubaldo, were submitted by Tasso to his friend Scipione Gonzaga and others for suggestions for further revision. The period of revision lasted for two years. Tasso did alter some things, but the most sweeping criticisms were followed only when Tasso rewrote the epic as *Jerusalem Conquered* in 1593. Tasso was imprisoned in Sant'Anna when the first unauthorized and incomplete version of his epic was published in 1580 under the title *Godfrey*. This was followed in 1581 by a complete but still unauthorized edition printed by Angelo Ingegneri, who was responsible for naming the epic *Jerusalem Delivered*. Tasso himself apparently collaborated with Febo Bonnà in preparing two corrected editions that followed in the same year.

Jerusalem Delivered is a conscious effort to exceed the accomplishments of Homer, Vergil, and Ariosto. Tasso wished to surpass his predecessors by reconciling the antithetical genres represented by those authors—classical epic and chivalric romance—all within the context of Christian history. He refused to admit that romance is a genre distinct from epic. Judith Kates, in her 1974 essay "Revaluation of the Classical Heroic in Tasso and Milton" persuasively argues that Tasso is the creator of Christian epic.

Jerusalem Delivered is the story of the First Crusade, in which Godfrey of Boulogne recaptures the Holy City from the Turks. As a subject it is neither too ancient nor too modern. In canto 1, the Archangel Gabriel tells Godfrey, who is discovered praying, that he has been elected commander of the army about to set out for Jerusalem. Pagan defenders reinforce the city and the fortunes of war sway back and forth, with each side aided by supernatural agents of good or evil. After a last terrible battle, the victorious and blood-stained Godfrey leads his men in prayer at the Sepulcher of Christ. C. M. Bowra, in *From Virgil to Milton* (1963), sees the three main heroes as representative of three different ideal virtues. The historical Godfrey is here the consummate Christian leader, renowned for wisdom and piety. He is a Christian Aeneas, subordinating even personal glory to divine plan. The non-historical Rinaldo, in comparison, comes close to exemplifying a Homeric ideal. He is an Achilles, with "a brave heart impatient of repose" and "a burning boundless thirst for fame." Tancred exemplifies the courtly virtues and suffers from the courtly malady, laid low by a doomed love "which feeds on grief and grows forevermore."

These Christian warriors are opposed by an array of pagan heroes, the mightiest of whom are Argante and Solyman, differentiated and noble as much as any mortal outside a state of grace can be. The most memorable pagans, however, are women, exhibiting and eliciting very different types of love. The three women, Clorinda, Erminia, and Armida, are very different manifestations of an ideal of feminine beauty and love. Clorinda is an Amazon, like Vergil's Camilla, but also capable of tears, when she is moved by the plight of the lovers Olindo and Sophronia (canto 2), and of forgiveness, when she experiences God's grace through baptism at the moment of her death (canto 12). She is loved by Tancred, who unwittingly kills her, as Achilles did Penthesilea. Erminia, in contrast, epitomizes shy and delicate tenderness. Her love for Tancred is revealed only at the end of the epic, but Tasso leaves its resolution ambiguous. Nevertheless, it allows the poet to include two famous episodes: Erminia's venture, dressed in Clorinda's armor, to look for Tancred (canto 6), and her sojourn among shepherds (canto 7), a pastoral idyll in which the evil life of a court suffers by comparison with the humble, tranquil life of shepherds. Armida, the third pagan woman, is a temptress who, like Circe, changes men into nonhuman forms and, like Dido, seduces heroes from their heaven-

appointed duty. Armida's garden (canto 16) is the pattern for Spenser's Bower of Bliss (*The Faerie Queene*, book 2, canto 12). Her enchantments based on sensual beauty are effective against all but direct heavenly intervention. Even when Tasso ends a love story happily, as here when Armida submits to Rinaldo and to Christianity with the words of the Virgin at the Annunciation, the lasting impression is one of tears and suffering.

The whole problem of justifying the love interests in the epic concerned Tasso very much. He set out to surpass Ariosto, and considered *Jerusalem Delivered* to be superior to Ariosto's *Orlando furioso* in many respects. Tasso's epic conforms to ancient poetic theory, as he proves in his *Discorsi dell'arte poetica*, and expands upon in *Discourses on the Heroic Poem*. It also expresses the true piety of a man of the Counter-Reformation. The classical and religious elements are as much a part of the epic as are the love episodes, although the latter are what readers of all ages have tended to remember.

Tasso writes in an elevated style, decorous and humorless, describing a single action and beginning in medias res. The scope of the action encompasses Heaven, Earth, and Hell. He uses supernatural elements, Homeric similes, and a Latinate vocabulary. In addition to the correspondences between Tasso's characters and characters from previous epics (such as Godfrey/Aeneas or Rinaldo/Achilles), specific actions are reminiscent of earlier epic scenes: God the Father ratifies his decrees with a nod similar to that of Homer's Zeus; a statue of the Virgin, rather than the Palladium of Troy, is stolen; there are night sorties, single combats, troop reviews, espionage missions, the burning of enemy strongholds, and a beautiful woman who stands on the battlements and names the enemy combatants on the field below.

Tasso never forgets, however, that he is writing a Christian epic. As much as he admires the classical tradition, he sees it as deficient in several respects. Tasso speaks of his epic as an allegory in a letter in which he calls Godfrey "the head" and Rinaldo "the right hand." Later, the Bonnà editions of *Jerusalem Delivered* include Tasso's *Allegoria del poema* (1581), in which Tasso claims that the entire plot of his epic ought to be read as a continuous allegory. Spenser seems to have believed this, but some modern critics dismiss the

Allegoria del poema as an afterthought, a ruse to placate the Inquisition and excuse the marvels and love interest. For example, C. P. Brand in *Torquato Tasso* admits that Armida's garden and the enchanted wood are both symbolic, but he concludes that even these episodes function essentially on a literal level. Andrew Fichter represents the opposite view when he reads the whole poem allegorically, saying that "the thematic subject . . . is the spiritual progress of the Christian man toward the other Jerusalem."

Despite their classical and romantic antecedents, Tasso's characters are always judged from a Christian perspective. Admitting the nobility of an Argante or the seductive power of an Armida does not alter this fact. Fichter sees the shape of Tasso's epic as reflecting the workings of Providence through history. All the diverse episodes are subordinated to this perspective and ranked by it. *Jerusalem Delivered* is divided into twenty cantos, not the usual twelve or twenty-four. The action divides these cantos in half, with the pagans in ascendance throughout the first half, the Christians throughout the second. The first half begins with the action of God, the second with that of Godfrey. The poem also divides into quarters, with Rinaldo present and active in the first and last sections, absent and enchanted in the middle two. Lastly, the poem exhibits a mirror-symmetry, in which each pair of cantos, starting with the first and last, deals with parallel or opposite material. For example, Argante enters the action in canto 3 and is killed in canto 19; the Crusaders first see Jerusalem in canto 3 and first breach its walls in canto 18.

JERUSALEM CONQUERED

Near the end of his life, Tasso himself completed a version of his epic so substantially revised that it deserved and was given a new name, *Jerusalem Conquered*. The new poem, in twenty-four books instead of twenty cantos, is increasingly allegorical and doctrinaire. It purges many of the most fondly remembered episodes (Sophronia and Olindo, Erminia among the shepherds, the trip to the Fortunate Islands) and the most magical or sentimental ones (Armida transforming the knights into fish, the reconciliation of Rinaldo and Armida). Diction is smoothed; Homeric elements are increased; and many characters are renamed (Rinaldo becomes Riccardo, for example). Tasso considered *Je-*

rusalem Conquered to be far superior to his earlier epic; critics have not agreed with him, however, and have either dismissed the poem or vilified it. Francesco De Sanctis is representative when he says that there is "hardly a change that is not unfortunate, second-hand, and done in cold blood."

This, however, does not negate Tasso's achievements. He is a consummate storyteller. He epitomizes the Renaissance in his veneration of classical learning and human worth. He redefines the meaning of "heroic" by transforming both the epic poem and its heroes to conform to religious ideals and his own emotional sensibility. No poet more effectively reflects the Renaissance spirit while anticipating the Romantic.

OTHER MAJOR WORKS

PLAYS: *Aminta*, pr. 1573 (verse play; English translation, 1591); *Il re Torrismondo*, pb. 1587 (verse play; *King Torrismondo*, 1997).

NONFICTION: *Allegoria del poema* 1581; *Dialoghi*, 1581; *Apologia*, 1586; *Discorsi dell'arte poetica*, 1587; *Lettere*, 1587, 1588, 1616-1617; *Discorsi del poema eroico*, 1594 (*Discourses on the Heroic Poem*, 1973).

BIBLIOGRAPHY

Boulting, William. *Tasso and His Times*. 1907. New York: G. P. Putnam's Sons, 1968. Reprint of a standard biography, stronger on the life than the works.

Brand, Charles Peter. *Torquato Tasso: A Study of the Poet and of His Contributions to English Literature*. Cambridge, England: Cambridge University Press, 1965. A fairly compact book that attempts a "comprehensive study of Tasso and his work." Treats his life briefly, lays out the major and minor works, and spends roughly one-third the book's length on England's reception of his major works.

Cody, Richard. *The Landscape of the Mind: Pastoralism and Platonic Theory in Tasso's "Aminta" and Shakespeare's Early Plays*. Oxford, England: Clarendon Press, 1969. A study of the esoteric and allegorical nature of pastoralism and characters in *Aminta*.

Finucci, Valeria, ed. *Renaissance Transactions: Ariosto and Tasso*. Durham, N.C.: Duke University Press,

1999. This collection of essays represents a cross-section of critical approaches to "foster a dialogue" among schools of thought on *Gerusalemme* and its relationship with Ariosto's work.

Günsberg, Maggie. *Epic Rhetoric of Tasso: Theory and Practice*. Oxford: Legenda, 1998. A study of *Jerusalem Delivered*.

Kates, Judith A. *Tasso and Milton: The Problem of the Christian Epic*. Lewisburg, Pa.: Bucknell University Press, 1983. A study of *Jerusalem Delivered* with an eye on its similarities, and those of its poet, to *Paradise Lost* and its poet, John Milton. A study of analogies, not influences.

Sellstrom, A. Donald. *Corneille, Tasso, and Modern Poetics*. Columbus: Ohio State University Press, 1986. An exploration of Tasso's influence on Pierre Corneille, which, though never acknowledged, seems clear to the author and advances understanding of both Corneille's work and Tasso's European influence.

Sherberg, Michael. *Rinaldo: Character and Intertext in Ariosto and Tasso*. Saratoga, Calif.: ANMA Libri, 1993. Part 2 examines Tasso's treatment of the Carolingian "knight," which downplays Rinaldo's rebellious nature and actions while expanding his character, especially through psychological depth.

Elizabeth A. Holtze;
bibliography updated by Joseph P. Byrne

ALLEN TATE

Born: Winchester, Kentucky; November 19, 1899
Died: Nashville, Tennessee; February 9, 1979

PRINCIPAL POETRY

The Golden Mean and Other Poems, 1923 (with Ridley Wills)
Mr. Pope and Other Poems, 1928
Poems, 1928-1931, 1932
The Mediterranean and Other Poems, 1936
Selected Poems, 1937
The Winter Sea, 1944
Poems, 1920-1945, 1947
Poems, 1922-1947, 1948
Poems, 1960
The Swimmers and Other Selected Poems, 1971
Collected Poems, 1919-1976, 1977

OTHER LITERARY FORMS

Although Allen Tate earned his literary reputation as a poet, the majority of his published works are prose. He is well known as an essayist, having published nine books of essays and contributed essays to a number of anthologies, including the Agrarian manifesto *I'll Take My Stand* (1930). His other nonfiction works include two biographies, *Stonewall Jackson: The Good Soldier* (1928) and *Jefferson Davis: His Rise and Fall* (1929). He also published a critically acclaimed novel, *The Fathers* (1938), set during the Civil War. Tate also worked as an editor and a translator, editing poetry anthologies and other literary works and translating some of the works of Charles Baudelaire and various classical poets. Each of these works demonstrates at least one of Tate's three major concerns: poetry, history, and the state of modern culture.

ACHIEVEMENTS

Much of Allen Tate's popular reputation as a poet rests on a single poem, "Ode to the Confederate Dead," written before he was twenty-six years old. It brought its author considerable fame both in America and abroad, but unfortunately it "typecast" him. Tate later wrote poems that were perhaps better and certainly ideologically different, but he was and still is so strongly identified with that work that his later poetry was for the most part neglected.

If the public saw him as a one-poem poet, however, he fared better at the hands of critics. He received a number of honors, including many honorary degrees; perhaps his most outstanding award was the National Medal for Literature in 1976. He also received the Bollingen Prize for Poetry in 1956, the Brandeis University Medal for Poetry in 1961, and the Gold Medal of the Dante Society of Florence in 1962. He was elected to both the American Academy of Arts and Letters in 1964 and the American Academy of Arts and Sciences in 1965. His *Collected Poems, 1919-1976* was awarded the Lenore Marshall Prize for Poetry in 1978.

Tate was one of the most widely known of the Agrarian/Fugitive poets. While some of his themes, techniques, and concerns were similar to those of his Southern colleagues, unlike some of them, he was not labeled (and subsequently dismissed as) a "regional" poet. Tate was as popular and as comfortable in the literary circles of New York and Europe as he was in that of his Vanderbilt associates, and his poetry demonstrates that Southern concerns are universal concerns as well.

BIOGRAPHY

John Orley Allen Tate was born in Winchester, Kentucky, the third son of John Orley and Eleanor Varnell Tate. His early life foreshadowed the gypsy-like wanderings of his later years; because of his father's various business interests, the family moved frequently. These moves resulted in Tate's rather sketchy education. As a teenager, he wrote a few poems, but his real love was music. He studied the violin under excellent teachers at the Cincinnati Conservatory of Music, but left when his teachers concluded that, while he had some talent, he had no exceptional gift for music.

Tate, his musical ambitions thwarted, was accepted at Vanderbilt University and entered in 1918. He had no particular interest in literature when his college career began. He was, however, strongly influenced by some of his teachers, especially Walter Clyde Curry. The medieval and Renaissance scholar lent him books, encouraged him to write poetry, and introduced him to John Crowe Ransom, with whom he later also studied. Under the influence of these two gifted teachers, Tate joined Vanderbilt's Calumet Club, a literary society whose membership also included Donald Davidson. Davidson invited Tate to participate in a discussion group which evolved into the Fugitives. Tate was an eager participant in this group of teachers and students and contributed many poems to its literary journal, *The Fugitive*. He was graduated from Vanderbilt in 1923 after having taken a year off from his studies because of poor health; his diploma was dated 1922, so that technically he was graduated "with his class." In his last year at Vanderbilt, he met Robert Penn Warren, a

sixteen-year-old sophomore, who became his lifelong friend.

Tate had envisioned New York as the literary mecca of the United States, and he visited the city in 1924. He met Hart Crane, whose work he admired, as well as other authors. Upon his return, he visited the Warrens and there he met Caroline Gordon, the first of his three wives. After their marriage, they moved to New York, where Tate worked as an editor and continued to contribute to *The Fugitive* until it ceased publication in 1925. The Tates remained in New York until 1930, except for two years spent abroad on a Guggenheim Fellowship; then they moved back to Tennessee.

In Tennessee, Tate was able to enjoy the company of almost all of his old friends again. From this "reunion" arose the Agrarian movement. In 1934, Tate, seriously in debt, turned to college teaching. He taught at a number of colleges, but not until 1951 was he offered a tenured position, at the University of Minnesota, where he taught until his retirement in 1968. After his retirement, he returned to Sewanee, Tennessee.

Tate was a Southern poet in every sense of the term, but he was not limited to regional issues and popularity. His circle of literary friends included T. S. Eliot, Ford Madox Ford, and John Peale Bishop; his fame was international.

ANALYSIS

Allen Tate's poetry has often been described as obscure, but although it is difficult and frequently misunderstood, it is not obscure. The difficulties in reading Tate's poems arise mainly from his allusions, many of which are classical.

A facet of Tate's poetry which is frequently misunderstood is his use of history as a theme. To Tate, a sense of history is no mere nostalgic longing for bygone glory. It is rather an understanding of those qualities of earlier cultures which made them human. In several poems, Tate expresses the belief that modern man has discarded too many of these qualities and thus has become less human. Tate does not suggest that man turn his back on modern culture and attempt to return to a more classical and simpler way of life, but he does seem to believe that modern technology and humanism are mutually exclusive. He is in favor of the creation of a new culture rather than the recreation of an older one.

Tate's techniques as well as his themes are worthy of study. He rejected at first, but later acknowledged, the truism that form and content should be inextricably related, and he described free verse as a failure. His poems show an experimentation with many different forms. Also typical of Tate's poems is the use of unusual adjectives. "Ambitious November" and "brute curiosity of an angel's stare" (both from "Ode to the Confederate Dead") may be cited. These adjectives have the effect of capturing the attention of readers and forcing them to explore the images in order to understand them. A similar technique is his play of word upon word, frequently by exact repetition. Tate's poetry is also characterized by the use of concrete details to modify highly abstract language. Such details, sometimes consisting of single words only, are somewhat jarring to the reader, as they are no doubt meant to be. Finally, Tate can move easily from a formal, "scholarly" style to the use of highly sensuous diction, often within the same poem. He seems to be acutely aware of the tension that is produced by the contrast between Latinate and Anglo-Saxon vocabulary. He chooses the diction suited to his subject, with the language illustrating changes in imagery or tone.

Much attention has been focused on the effect other poets have had on Tate's poetic techniques and themes. His early poetry has been compared with that of his teacher and friend, John Crowe Ransom, while his later work is often compared to that of T. S. Eliot, whom Tate greatly admired. Tate was, however, writing such poetry before he had even read Eliot. In any case, the issue of anyone's "influence" on Tate is nebulous; certainly his work is not derivative, whatever the generalized debt he may owe Ransom, Eliot, and other writers with whose work he was familiar.

Throughout his poetry, Tate's major concern is the state of modern culture and modern humankind. He is a sort of prophet, warning people of the consequences of his way of life. In some of his works he offers remedies for human dilemmas, although he does not hesitate to blame people for being the cause of their own problems. Tate's poems will no doubt be read in the future as a fairly accurate record of the concerns of

twentieth century humanity. Read in the chronological order in which they appear in *Collected Poems, 1919-1976*, they further serve as a record of the spiritual development of Tate himself, a poet of considerable talent and vision.

"THE MEDITERRANEAN"

A good introduction to Tate's poetry is "The Mediterranean," a poem which displays many of his techniques and concerns. In fact, this poem appears as the first item in each of his collections (except *Collected Poems, 1919-1976*, which is arranged in order of first publication); it is considered to be one of the best of his shorter pieces. The poem begins with a Latin motto, which, as usual, Tate neither identifies nor translates. The motto comes from the first book of the *Aeneid* (c. 29-19 B.C.E.) and in the original reads "Quem das finem, rex magne, laborum?" ("What limit, great king, do you place on their labors?") Tate changes "laborum" to "dolorum" (pain, either physical or mental, but here probably mental). This motto should indicate to the reader that a knowledge of the *Aeneid* is necessary to an understanding of the poem. Indeed, a reader without a great deal of knowledge of the *Aeneid* would probably overlook or not understand many of Tate's allusions to it. The poem is, first of all, dramatic; it can be read simply as a description of the dramatic setting. Beneath this surface, however, is the reference, maintained throughout the poem, to the events in the *Aeneid*, as well as a commentary on the modern human condition by contrast with the past.

The dramatic situation of the poem is simple: a group of people is on a boat trip, a sort of party. The speaker is a member of that group. The voyage of Aeneas is recalled by the speaker, setting up what seems to be an unlikely parallel, although many a weekend sailor may imagine himself to be a Columbus, a Magellan—or even an Aeneas.

In the first stanza, the setting is described. It is a long bay surrounded by a cliff, similar to the bay on which Aeneas landed in Italy. The cliff, called the "peaked margin of antiquity's delay," serves as a symbol of the border between the past and present. Time is an important element here, and the first image illustrates Tate's belief that a difficult barrier exists between the past and present. This idea is developed throughout the poem by means of a contrast between the mythical past, represented by the heroic Aeneas, and the monotonous present, represented by the modern sailors who are attempting to retreat into antiquity. They themselves, however, as symbols of modern man, have made that return impossible.

The third stanza contains an important allusion to the *Aeneid* which continues to develop the contrast between the past and present. The speaker says that the party "made feast and in our secret need/ Devoured the very plates Aeneas bore." The reference is to the third book of the *Aeneid*, in which the harpies place a curse on Aeneas and his men: Aeneas will not find the land he is searching for until he and his men have become desperate enough to eat the plates they are carrying. The terms of the curse are fulfilled when the men eat wheat cakes on which they have placed food, thus signaling that they have arrived at their destination. The modern sailors parody this fulfillment of the curse on Aeneas; they too are "cursed" and are seeking another land. The image is repeated in the fourth and fifth stanzas, emphasizing the idea of the removal of a curse.

The curse is explored in the last four stanzas; a question indicates what the curse is: "What prophecy of eaten plates could landless/ Wanderers fulfill by the ancient sea?" By sailing on the "ancient sea" and recalling Aeneas, the wanderers have established some contact with the past, but the contact is incomplete and ephemeral. Tate tells the reader why this is so in stanza 6: It is modern man's "lust for power" which has been his undoing. His final, strong image is that of a land of plenty in which what should be a bountiful harvest is left to "rot on the vine." This is the land, he reminds the reader, where he was born; one needs not seek a foreign land to regain the qualities of a great culture.

"ODE TO THE CONFEDERATE DEAD"

A somewhat similar theme is treated in Tate's best-known poem, "Ode to the Confederate Dead." The title of the poem is somewhat misleading, since the poem is not an ode, or public celebration, to the dead Confederate soldiers. The speaker is a modern man who must face the fact of his isolation, which becomes evident to him through his reflection on the various symbols in the poem, most significant of which is the cemetery where

he stands. The speaker is not characterized; in fact, his lack of individuality is an important element in the poem.

Like many of Tate's other poems, "Ode to the Confederate Dead" contains striking diction. He makes use of unusual adjectives, oxymorons, and other techniques and figures, letting the reader know immediately that the poem is not a conventional glorification of the men who fought and died for the Confederacy. Tate's vision is broader than that, and his theme is more universal.

The first section contains a great deal of nature imagery, the speaker personifying nature in an almost Romantic fashion. It is interesting to note, however, that he describes the wind as whirring, a sound associated with machinery rather than nature. This section also contains an extended image of piles of fallen leaves; the month is, as is made explicit in the next section, November. The deadness of the leaves is emphasized, drawing a parallel between the leaves and the soldiers.

In the second section, the speaker focuses his attention on the graves. The graves, like the men who lie in them, have been unable to withstand the effects of time. The stone angels on the graves have been stained, chipped, and even broken. This section also reveals that the speaker sees the dead soldiers as having lost their individual identities; they have become merely the "Confederate dead," a group of people from whom time has removed all sense of individuality. The speaker sympathizes with such a loss, for he feels that he has been similarly imposed on by modern culture.

The third and fourth sections emphasize this sense of loss. The speaker feels that modern man is ineffectual; he has "waited for the angry resolution/ Of those desires that should be yours tomorrow." Modern man has praise for the dead Confederate soldiers, he says, but does not see that the dead soldiers were "hurried beyond decision" to their deaths.

The last sections of the poem contain a question. How, the speaker asks, should people commemorate the dead soldiers? He refers again to their anonymity and uses the word "chivalry," an idea he has merely suggested before. "Chivalry" connotes high ideals and historical tradition, but the tradition died because its followers failed to put its ideals into practice. The speaker has no desire to recapture the past of the dead soldiers; it seems to him no better than the present, which, by the end of the poem, he has come to accept.

The speaker in "Ode to the Confederate Dead" is a philosopher, but he is also a solipsist, believing that the self is the only reality. This flaw, the belief only in self, is a failing that Tate seems to feel is typical of modern man. Thus the theme is similar to that of "The Mediterranean," as well as others of Tate's poems. The concerns of modern man, he suggests, are petty, somehow not human. There is, however, no resolution to the problem; the tone is despairing. Several critics have pointed out that "Ode to the Confederate Dead" is "dark," containing none of the images of light of which Tate was so fond. The speaker seems truly doomed by his inability to see beyond himself.

"SEASONS OF THE SOUL"

The problems and failings of modern man also dominate "Seasons of the Soul," considered by many critics to be the best of Tate's later poetry. The poem is dedicated to John Peale Bishop, Tate's friend and a poet for whom he had great respect. The two men occasionally wrote companion poems and frequently helped and criticized each other's work. Following the dedication in the poem, there is an epigraph, which, like the motto in "The Mediterranean," is neither identified nor translated (it is from Dante's *Inferno*). In the lines quoted, the speaker says that he reached up and broke a branch from a thorn tree, which cried out asking, "Why have you torn me apart?" Imprisoned inside the tree is the soul of a man, presumably a man who has died by suicide. The punishment fits the crime; the soul which denied its human form has been given a nonhuman exterior in which to spend eternity. The epigraph is significant in three ways. First, Dante in this part (Canto XIII) of the *Inferno* is describing the punishment of the violent, and Tate feels that violence is another of modern man's great flaws. Second, there is the suggestion that modern man, in denying his humanity, has damned himself to a fate similar to that of suicide. Finally, the epigraph alerts the reader to the presence of allusions to Dante in the poem.

"Seasons of the Soul" is divided into four sections named for each of the seasons, and critics disagree on their significance in the poem. Some have seen a correspondence between the seasons and the elements, while others argue that the seasons represent the recurring obsessions of man. The idea of the unending rotation of the seasons is emphasized in several places. Three of the sections, "Summer," "Winter," and "Spring," begin similarly with an invocation, a technique associated with the epic tradition. The epic poets asked in their invocations for help in treating their subjects adequately, for they wrote of great deeds far beyond their own capabilities. They sought to go beyond their own limitations through the aid of the muse, who represented the epic tradition. In "Seasons of the Soul," Tate's use of the invocation is ironic, since a major element in the poem is man's search for salvation through some source outside himself, a search which is futile. The one section which has no invocation is "Autumn." The most likely explanation for this omission, according to George Hemphill in *Allen Tate* (1964), is that this section is devoted to the obsessions of man as solipsist. Since solipsistic man is unable to accept anything but himself as reality (and, by extension, as significant), he would not feel the need to invoke the aid of any muse or god.

The seasons are presented in sequence, beginning with summer. By choosing thus to begin the poem, Tate indicates that he is not using the four seasons in the traditional manner to represent the four ages of man; using the seasons in that manner would necessitate beginning with spring. In fact, most critics have noticed a logical progression in the poem from season to season and have pointed out that much of its meaning is lost if the reader attempts to begin reading the sequence at some section other than "Summer." The sequence is representative of man's development; to return to Hemphill's interpretation of the poem's sections, "Summer" concerns man as activist or politician, "Autumn" concerns him as solipsist, "Winter" concerns him as a sexual being, and "Spring" concerns him as a religious being. These concerns are similar to the seasons in their unrelenting reoccurrence.

In "Summer," Tate is concerned with the effects of political activity, especially war, on man's humanity, and he once again denounces whatever leads to dehumanization. The poem refers to World War II and the occupation of "Green France," a basically agrarian culture, by the "caterpillar feet" of Germany's technical culture.

Here Tate's view of war is that of a true conscientious objector; he seems to feel that no war is justified, since the effect of violence on man's soul is so devastating as to render every victory Pyrrhic.

The season of the second part of the poem is autumn, the season of "Ode to the Confederate Dead." The speaker, often identified as the poet, relates a dream he had of falling down a well into a house. He tries to leave the house, but what appears to be the front door is a false door. His parents are in the house, but they do not recognize him. The speaker seems to have wandered (or, more accurately, fallen) into a hell especially designed for him since it fulfills his worst fear, that of the loss of his own identity. In losing his identity, the solipsist loses all. He has been damned by his inability to transcend himself, like the speaker in "Ode to the Confederate Dead." Once again Tate warns of the dangers of modern man's egocentricity.

While a logical link exists between the first and second sections of the poem, some critics have been unable to see such a transition between the second and third sections. Since the third is about sex, apparently that is the retreat of the speaker from his personal hell. He looks for comfort and perhaps even salvation in sex, for he begins with an invocation to Venus, goddess of love. He asks her to return to the sea, from which she came; this impossible act, the speaker feels, is preferable to modern religion in which God is seen as dried up, no longer bearing the wounds of Christ which represent man's salvation. God is as dead to modern man as the sea-gods such as Neptune, are. Unlike these gods, Venus is still alive as far as modern man is concerned. Tate, however, uses images of coldness and violence to describe modern man's sexual feelings. The shark is a symbol of man's sexual "perversion." This section ends with a return to the section of the *Inferno* from which the epigraph comes. The speaker breaks a branch from a tree and hears the blood of a suicide speak to him as it drips on him from the tree. The blood tells him that it is the blood of men who have killed themselves because of love's deceit. The reference to blood is reminiscent of all the water imagery used throughout this section. The blood imagery further reminds the reader that this section deals with the heart, whereas the previous section deals with the mind and the first section with the tension between the mind and heart. There clearly is no salvation through sex for modern man.

The final section deals with religion; man, having found no help elsewhere, turns to Christianity. The invocation is to spring, described as "irritable"—reminiscent of T. S. Eliot's description of April as "the cruelest month" in *The Waste Land* (1922). Spring is irritable because it is unable to stay and settle down. In the second stanza the speaker recalls his childhood innocence, which refused to acknowledge the reality of death but was amused, rather, by the "ancient pun" which equated death and orgasm.

In the fourth stanza Tate suggests that man can find peace only when he accepts the idea of death. Although this concept is Christian, the imagery is pagan, with references to Plato's cave and Sisyphus's rock. Tate moves from this thought into the specific mother imagery of the last two stanzas. The first mother has been identified as St. Monica, mother of St. Augustine of Hippo. According to legend, St. Monica was a difficult mother, insisting that her son become a Christian. The early images of death as a gentle, loving "mother of silences" are continued through the reference to St. Monica, a stern mother who led her son to the salvation of Christianity, and the nameless mother of the last stanza. In this final stanza Tate raises a question which he does not answer: Is death a "kindness"? Certainly the orthodox view of Christianity insists that man turn his eyes toward heaven where a "better life" awaits him. Tate, however, is a rather unorthodox Christian and in this poem is still trying to come to terms with religious questions.

OTHER MAJOR WORKS

LONG FICTION: *The Fathers*, 1938.

NONFICTION: *Stonewall Jackson: The Good Soldier*, 1928; *Jefferson Davis: His Rise and Fall*, 1929; *Reactionary Essays on Poetry and Ideas*, 1936; *Reason in Madness, Critical Essays*, 1941; *On the Limits of Poetry, Selected Essays 1928-1948*, 1948; *The Hovering Fly and Other Essays*, 1949; *The Forlorn Demon: Didactic and Critical Essays*, 1953; *The Man of Letters in the Modern World: Selected Essays, 1928-1955*, 1955; *Collected Essays*, 1959; *Essays of Four Decades*, 1968; *The Poetry Reviews of Allen Tate, 1924-1944*, 1983.

BIBLIOGRAPHY

Bishop, Ferman. *Allen Tate*. United States Authors series. New York: Twayne, 1967. Though composed while Tate was still writing, Bishop's book offers a good survey of his life and work up to that point; Tate's final years did not change much. Includes a chronology, detailed notes and references, and a select bibliography.

Brooks, Cleanth. *Cleanth Brooks and Allen Tate: Collected Letters, 1933-1976*. Edited by Alphonse Vinh. Columbia: University of Missouri Press, 1998. A selection of letters that constitute a feisty and enjoyable account of the history of two leading participants in the literary critical wars during an era when the way to read and to teach poetry in the English language was being profoundly recast.

Dupree, Robert S. *Allen Tate and the Augustinian Imagination: A Study of the Poetry*. Baton Rouge: Louisiana State University Press, 1983. Dupree has accomplished here the most thorough traversal of Tate's poetry to date, but he does confine his attention to the poetry. His approach is methodical and comprehensive, disclosing ingenious insights. Since poetry was Tate's central concern, what Dupree discovers here carries over to other aspects of his work. Includes an index, a bibliography, and notes.

Hammer, Langdon. *Hart Crane and Allen Tate*. Princeton, N.J.: Princeton University Press, 1993. Three chapters are devoted to Tate, the focus of the study being on the two poets' relationship within the framing context of literary modernism, beginning with T. S. Eliot in 1914 and ending with Robert Lowell's *Life Studies* (1959). Bibliography, index.

Huff, Peter A. *Allen Tate and the Catholic Revival: Trace of the Fugitive Gods*. Paulist Press, 1996. Examines Tate in the context of the Catholic Revival following the "lost generation" post-World War I years. Tate incorporated the revival's Christian humanism into his critique of secular industrial society.

Malvasi, Mark G. *The Unregenerate South: The Agrarian Thought of John Crowe Ransom, Allen Tate, and Donald Davidson*. Baton Rouge: Louisiana State University Press, 1997. Addresses these poets' approaches to social issues including rural poverty, religion, race relations, and the effects of the New Deal on the twentieth century South, tracing the influence that their literary views had on their social and political thought. Two chapters are devoted to Tate. Index.

Meiners, P. K. *Everything to Be Endured: An Essay on Robert Lowell and Modern Poetry*. Columbia: University of Missouri Press, 1970. Although not primarily concerned with Tate, this eighty-nine-page essay reveals much about him and his impact on mid-twentieth century poetry. Because it offers no bibliography, its usefulness is limited, but some of the insights into Tate remain unsurpassed.

Squires, Radcliffe. *Allen Tate: A Literary Biography*. New York: Bobbs-Merrill, 1971. Also written before Tate's death, this book is primarily a writing biography—that is, it considers the life of the writer with reference to his writings. The telling benefits from the personal acquaintance of Squires with Tate. Contains much anecdotal material, a bibliography, indexes, and notes.

_____, ed. *Allen Tate and His Work: Critical Evaluations*. Minneapolis: University of Minnesota Press, 1972. Squires here assembles essays on all phases of Tate's writing, editing, teaching, and life, including several by Tate's associates in the Agrarian movement, especially John Crowe Ransom and Donald Davidson. Cleanth Brooks, Howard Nemerov, and Louis D. Rubin, Jr. are also represented. Contains a complete bibliography.

Stewart, John Lincoln. *The Burden of Time: The Fugitives and the Agrarians*. Princeton, N.J.: Princeton University Press, 1965. This valuable study focuses more on the intellectual movements associated with Tate than on Tate himself. Since, however, these movements formed a large part of his life, they are revealing. Includes substantial comments on both poetry and criticism, and the coverage is thorough and deep. Complemented by footnotes and a bibliography.

Underwood, Thomas A. *Allen Tate: Orphan of the South*. Princeton, N.J.: Princeton University Press, 2000. A biographical study of Tate and his part in the Agrarian and Fugitive movements. Includes bibliographical references and index.

Claire Clements Morton;
bibliography updated by the editors

James Tate

Born: Kansas City, Missouri; December 8, 1943

Principal poetry

The Lost Pilot, 1967
The Oblivion Ha-Ha, 1970
Hints to Pilgrims, 1971, 1982
Absences: New Poems, 1972
Viper Jazz, 1976
Riven Doggeries, 1979
Constant Defender, 1983
Reckoner, 1986
Distance from Loved Ones, 1990
Selected Poems, 1991
Worshipful Company of Fletchers, 1994
Shroud of the Gnome, 1997
Police Story, 1999
Memoir of the Hawk, 2001

Other literary forms

James Tate is known primarily as a poet, although he has produced some fiction and nonfiction.

Achievements

James Tate came onto the literary scene at the age of twenty-three, when his first full-length manuscript of poems, *The Lost Pilot*, was published in the Yale Younger Poets Series, for which a prestigious competition is run by Yale University Press. Other works, long and short, followed, and Tate became editor of the *Dickinson Review* in 1967. He has also served as an associate editor at Pym-Randall Press and Barn Dream Press (small presses located in Cambridge, Massachusetts) and as a consultant to the Coordinating Council of Literary Magazines. For two years running, in 1968 and 1969, and again in 1980, he received writing fellowships from the National Endowment for the Arts. In 1972, he was the Phi Beta Kappa poet at Brown University. He won a National Institute of Arts and Letters Award in 1974, followed two years later by a Guggenheim Fellowship. He was awarded the Pulitzer Prize in 1992 for *Selected Poems*. In 1994 he was honored with a National Book Award for *Worshipful Company of Fletchers*, and in

1995 with a Tanning Prize from the American Academy of Poets.

Tate has established himself as a formidable exponent of literary surrealism of a peculiarly American kind. His work has garnered the praise of many academic critics and journal reviewers; his poetry has appeared across the gamut of magazines in North America and England and has influenced the style of many young writers.

Biography

James Tate was born in Kansas City, Missouri, in 1943. He began college study at the University of Missouri in Columbia and finished his B.A. at Kansas State College in Pittsburg, Kansas, in 1965. He entered the Writers Workshop at the University of Iowa and received an M.F.A. in poetry in 1967. In 1966, Tate began teaching creative writing and literature courses at the University of Iowa (1966-1967), the University of California at Berkeley (1967-1968), Columbia University (1969-1971), and Emerson College in Boston (poet in residence, 1970-1971). He joined the regular teaching faculty at the University of Massachusetts at Amherst in 1971, where he would remain except for short periods of residence in such places as Sweden, Ireland, and Spain.

Analysis

There are two kinds of poets in the world: those who grow with age and alter style, outlook, and argument over the years, and those who burst onto the scene fully fledged and polish what is in essence an unchanging perception of life throughout their careers. James Tate is of the second sort; his stunning appearance in his first major book, *The Lost Pilot*, set the pattern for all he would write over the succeeding decades. The poetry of *Distance from Loved Ones* is a richer, denser, more masterful execution of the style and themes he set for himself as a young man.

Variation for Tate is a subtle thing; beneath the variances of style and diction lies a core of subjects and emotions that are constant in his poetry: loss of relations, the quixotic world of appearances, a violent underworld of emotion waiting to erupt through the crevices of the mundane. The central theme running throughout Tate's canon is the desire to shatter superficial experience, to break through the sterility of suburban life and drown it in erotic passion. His characters languish from unfulfilled longings; the objects he contemplates are all prisoners of definition and stereotype; life is a desert of routine expectation waiting to blow up from the forces of liberated imagination, whimsy, outrage, and humor.

Tate joins a long line of midwestern writers who fought in their writing against the domestic tedium of their region. Theodore Dreiser set the pattern of the rebellious midwestern writer in his novels about youths trapped in the social coils of work, poverty, and loveless marriages; Sherwood Anderson paved the way of modernist writers through his depictions of the sterile sanity of small-town life in his novel *Winesburg, Ohio* (1947). F. Scott Fitzgerald and Ernest Hemingway explored the unrealizable dreams of their characters, who had escaped only partway from their families and bleak pasts. Poets of the Midwest, including T. S. Eliot, Ezra Pound, and Carl Sandburg, emphasized realistic detail in their unflinching reports of what had gone wrong in American society in their time.

James Tate (© Jill Krementz)

THE LOST PILOT

The Lost Pilot joins this tradition of harsh assessments of midwestern life; the argument itself is a rather somber account of a young man's loneliness, despair, and feelings of isolation. "The End of the Line," from the middle section of the book, is emblematic of the themes treated in the poems. "We plan our love's rejuvenation/ one last time," the speaker comments, but the jaunty tone of the piece breaks down as he admits that the relationship has gone sour for good. The poems acutely examine the meaning of relationships, the risk of loving someone, the desolation at losing a father or lover through unexplained accident or fatal whim. This instability lying at the heart of emotion makes everything else around him equally shimmering and unreal.

Tate's use of surrealist language, the dreamy, irrational figures and images that define his view of things, is derived from European and South American writing of the twentieth century. The original motives of surrealism sprang from the devastations of war and the corruption of the state. For Tate, though, the corruption lies somewhere else: in the incapacity of human beings to face their dilemmas honestly, to admit that the heart is wild, immoral, anarchic, or that life is essentially a reality beyond the grasp of moral principles. For Tate, the American situation is the opposite of war-torn Europe or politically corrupt South America. The American scene is *too* stable, too ordered and domesticated; underneath the neat appearances of reality lies a universe of chaotic energies waiting to spring back. To that degree, one may casually link Tate's vision to the horrific suspense of Stephen King's novels or to the wounded idealism of Tom Wolfe and Hunter Thompson. In each of these writers lives a certain purity of taste for the natural world, and for the lost values of a pastoral and Edenic past which modernity has outraged and insulted.

To love in Tate's poetry is to tap into this hidden volcano of impacted irrationality, to tease its powers awake. Most often, his lovers quake at the first sign of wilderness in their emotions and drift back to the safety of their homely, selfish worlds. To fall in love is to touch nature directly, and to break through to the other side of reality. This sentiment is expressed at the close of *The Lost Pilot* when Tate writes, "I am falling, falling/ falling in love, and desire to leave this place." The place he desires to leave is that parched desert of convention where all of his characters languish.

The poetry of this first collection generates a kind of philosophical earthquake in its brief descriptions, debunking the moral fictions of an ordered life through the riotous outpouring of illogical imagery. This is a poetry of emotional purgings, of discreet, Janovian primal screams into the bedroom mirror.

The Lost Pilot is grounded by its title poem, an elegy combining a son's wit, fantasy, and tears over the death of his father in World War II. The phrase itself is instructive; a pilot is one who finds his way through dark skies. The father as lost pilot compounds the son's forlornness; here is a father who has disappeared, a guide without compass who leaves his son behind in a dull, seemingly trackless void. The reader learns in the poem that the son keeps an annual vigil and looks up to see his father orbiting overhead—a curious, droll, and yet appropriate image for the son's grief. Another poem, written to his mother, commemorates Father's Day in an ironic reference to the missing father. A careful look at all the poems reveals the image of the missing father in each of them: He haunts the world as a peculiar absence of love, as when lovers leave the poet, or emotion goes rank and sour.

In the closing poem, "Today I Am Falling," even the title suggests something of Tate's humor in poetry: The falling has no object, but in the text the reader finds that the falling is toward love, which in turn leads only to the desire to escape. The place the speaker is trying to reach is a "sodium pentothal landscape," a place of lost memories aroused by the intravenous intake of a "truth serum" once used in psychotherapy. That landscape lies behind repression and emotional stagnation, its "bud about to break open." The trembling surface of Tate's language here and elsewhere is that effort to break through the false appearance of things, the dull veneer of human convention concealing passion and the energy of nature.

Yet for a poet trying to break through, the early poems are terse, carefully worked miniatures that technically belie their purpose. Tate prefers a short, three-line stanza as his measure, with a varying line of between five and six syllables, usually end-stopped—that is, punctuated with a comma-length pause, or ended with a period. The flow of speech often requires enjambment, the running through of one line to the next, but not in the free-verse fashion of breaking lines arbitrarily at prepositions, adjectives, and nouns after the manner of prose. Instead, Tate makes sure his phrases are well-defined rhythmically before cutting to the next line. If he carries the rhythm through to the next line, or allows it to leap over a stanza break, usually he has found some emphatic word to terminate the line before he does so.

The poems on the page look slightly cramped and compressed, as if the thinking were squeezed down to an essence of protest. The poetry written by Tate's contemporaries is expansive, even sprawling by comparison. Few poets took the medium to these limits of compression, and when they did, they were freer with the pattern of line and accent. One may speculate that Tate's statements are intended as whispers in tight places—quick, emergency pleas to the reader or to himself. However they are intended, the language is uniformly limpid, purified, the hesitation revised out of each smoothly cresting phrase. There is high finish in the wording and phrasing, which may at times work against the sense of emotional torment Tate wants to convey.

Thumbing through the pages of *The Lost Pilot*, one is struck by the contradiction between polished execution and troubled content. The move in poetry after 1945 was to incorporate into the linguistic and prosodic structure of the poem the *movement* of emotion tracked by the meaning of words. The poem should come apart in sympathy with, or in representation of, the emotional disarray of the speaker, and the language of the poem should involve the detritus of spent or erupting emotion in its configuration. Distillation of language down to an essence was in some ways a Christian aesthetic carried over into "closed" or traditional poetics—a sense of language as having a spiritual inner text which the poet pared down to achieve communication with the soul. The throwing up of verbal dross and trivia into the language stream of lyric after 1945 was an effort to join "soul music" with the blunt, earthy matter of nature; hence the languorous and wayward course of much lyric energy in the postmodern era. In Tate, however, and in a contingent of "Southern" male poets who came of age with him, one finds uniformly tidy and balanced typographical structures that avoid technical deformation.

Tate's aesthetic tradition, which includes Wallace Stevens, Robert Frost, the European Symbolists, and the Deep Image movement of Robert Bly and James Wright, rejected a "projective" aesthetic that would incorporate the turmoil of mind into the finished artwork. That distinction between content and execution may have proved over the years to be confining to the range of Tate's subject matter and stylistic virtuosity. There is the hint of a technical repression of feeling in this mode of terse lyric, of funneling into sparse and smoothly patterned verses the chaos of longing and rage intended by the poems. The risk one takes in keeping to this method of writing is that emotional diversity may be diluted by the repetition of lyric forms.

Through the succession of Tate's later books, the poem does not change its technical strategy except to grow in size: Stanza and line are fleshed out, articulation is fuller and more sonorous, and rhythm has greater sweep, but the poet set his stylistic signature in *The Lost Pilot*, and the rules he gave himself were essentially unalterable thereafter. The burden on readers is to pay keen attention to content against a background of similar, even uniform measures, to make out with sympathetic attention the varying inner world that has been systematized in repetitive lyrical patterns. The burden on Tate is to risk everything on the line itself, to dazzle, compel, and sweep away the reader on the force of an image, a powerful phrase, the stunning resolution of a whole poem on a single word.

THE OBLIVION HA-HA

In *The Oblivion Ha-Ha*, a three-stanza poem, "The Pet Deer," works on the principle of the single line holding the poem aloft. Stanza 1 is purely functional exposition, given in limpid phrases; stanza 2 sets up the conflict implied in the deer's realizing that it is a kind of centaur in love with a human girl; stanza 3 builds slowly toward the closing line, revealing that the girl is unaware of "what/ the deer dreams or desires." Here repression is located in an animal, a deft reversal of Tate's usual argument. The girl is placid, lovely, unaffected in her sexual allure; the deer is the captive soul unable to break out and satisfy desire.

The poem hangs by the thread of its final line along with the touches in several other phrases, but in sum, it works on the plainness of its exposition, its setup of an incident, which it transforms by a single lyric thrust of insight. This is Symbolist methodology given an American stamp by Tate's withholding the intellectual and ideological motives of the lyric act. In Symbolist poetry almost any incident will reveal the poet's own psyche, which he will have expressed referentially through an object, animal, or character.

The deer is, by the twists of psychic projection in this poem, the poet himself, the girl a combination of lovers longed for and lost. The art of the poem is to raise the ordinary theme of repression and longing to a degree of generality that turns experience into fable, myth, or even allegory. Too broad a stroke, and the delicate suggestibility of language collapses; too little said, and the poem remains a mere fragment of thought without affect.

"Here is my heart,/ I don't know what to do with it," Tate writes in another poem, "Plea Based on a Sentence from a Letter Received by the Indiana State Welfare Department." The line expresses succinctly the theme of *The Oblivion Ha-Ha*. The title has confused critics; it is usually taken to mean a kind of maniacal laughter in the face of a bitter world. But a secondary definition of "ha ha" is a garden enclosure, usually of hedge or earthwork, separating one small planting bed from surrounding ground. In early Roman gardens, a raised inner court often supported a small statue of Adonis, a chthonic god of fertility; in modern times, gazebos and small terraces take the same role as the Adonis mound. Curiously, the garden meaning of the word, derived from French, bears the same hyphen as the first meaning. Tate's conceit may be that one laughs helplessly at sight of the enclosed Eden, thus doubling the meanings into one trope.

That inner garden reserve, perhaps, is the point of the title, an inner garden that is shut in or inaccessibly remote and psychological, but rooted in the familiar world of human senses. The oblivion ha-ha is the soul, the secret inner self in its own mound of earth, which the poems try to capture.

In "The Salute," a man dreams about a black widow whom he loves; yet he "completely misunderstood" her "little language." The secret soul is located on one side or another of broken relationships; lovers who try to reach across the distance confront either the sorrows of the deer or the suicidal love of this dreamer, willing to mate with a spider who kills her lovers. "Nobody gets what he wants," Tate writes in a later poem, "Consumed," which closes on this characteristic remark about a lover, "You are the stranger/ who gets stranger by the hour." Another poem on parents, "Leaving Mother Waiting for Father," returns to the theme of loss, with the speaker leaving his doll-like, decrepit mother leaning against a hotel, as he goes off into the world an adult orphan.

ABSENCES

In every case, Tate creates a portrait of an isolated heart longing for relation and failing to achieve it. The world that denies love to his characters is superficially intact, but beneath appearance it festers with neurotic passion and chaos. Is it any wonder, therefore, that his next book would be called *Absences*? In it, Tate experiments with a looser style; prose poems appear in section 3, while long poems occupy section 2. The title poem and "Cycle of Dust" are sequential works that have more diffuse imagery and lack the point of surprise perfected in the short lyric.

The interesting turn in *Absences* is in the image making itself; it focuses on characters who dismantle themselves, or try to disappear, in their blind effort to cross over to the "other" side of reality. These figures do not quite make it; they practice escaping from the blind literalism of things but end up dismantling only their defined selves. They do not reach Paradise. The shift to decomposing this part of reality marks Tate's decision to alter the lyric path he was on. From here onward, Tate drops the Edenic or pastoral ideal altogether and concentrates instead on exploding the empirical world of sense and definition. Experience itself will be his target.

Put another way, in *Absences* and beyond, one half of the metaphoric principle of his poetry drops away, the ideal and hidden dimension of vision. What remains is the imploding and decaying half of reality, the objects metaphor dwells on to hint at possibilities in the dream world. There are only the objects themselves now, deformed, fragmentary, increasingly meaningless as the stuff of lyric. More and more, Tate will imply the end of such language: There is still the need to escape, to break out of reality into the other world, but references to the other world by image or suggestion are rare. His poems dwell on the disappearance of reality itself, its decomposition into fantasy and paradox. In "Harm Alarm," the second poem of *Absences*, a man fearfully examines his street, decides that all harm lies "in a cradle/ across the ocean," and resumes his walk after observing that his "other" self should "just about awake now" as the source of that harm. The divided self splits evenly between dream and waking, serene emptiness and conflictual, wounded life. Pain abounds as the defining attribute of consciousness; the pin functions as a motif in a number of these poems.

There is little or no plot, and no organization to narrate the flow of language. The poems accumulate around the thematic abstraction of reality's own breakup. That means that individual lines and sentences have the burden of forming the book. Reading Tate, one looks for lines, images, and stunning metaphors as the point of poetry. There is no structural principle embodying language or visionary argument. Tate's assumption is that reality is dead, and the surreal lyric depicts that through its own formlessness and its occasional glimpses into magic through a phrase or word. Another position would hold that the poem itself is an object of nature, an expression of creative principles. Tate's metaphysic, however, is still linked with the Christian view that meaning derives from a spiritual source outside of nature. These poems, strange and irrational as they are, are secularized forms of prayer, beseeching an "outside" for grace and succor.

These matters are summed up in "Wait for Me," when he writes, "A dream of life a dream of birth/ a dream of moving/ from one world into another// All night dismantling the synapses/ unplugging the veins and arteries." The rest of the poem is about the dissolving self, the fading consciousness, as the reader continues to watch, in this world, with him. The tone is not far removed from the self-abnegating fervor of the medieval martyr, whose longing to purify life and join God are merely the extreme of Tate's lyrics of self-abandonment. "I hear a laugh swim up/ from the part of myself/ I've killed," he writes in "Delicate Riders," in which the reader sees that it is the spiritual self that has died out in the contemporary desert of materialism. "I who have no home have no destination either," he writes in "The Boy." "One bone against another,/ I carve what I carve/ to be rid of myself by morning/ by deep dreams disintegrated."

Tate's feud with reality is that it has no soul; it is the broken world of modern, spiritless philosophy. What remains is the memory of soul in magical lyricism, which surveys the fallen world and discovers fading glimmers of spirit in paradox, accidental juxtaposition, chaotic series, and the like.

VIPER JAZZ

This mordant perspective on the world is the subject of his next major book, *Viper Jazz*, published in the Wesleyan Poetry Program series (Wesleyan University Press) in 1976. In it Tate reins in the experimentalism of *Absences* and writes in short, stanzaic lyrics and prose poems on the theme of "worlds refused by worlds." A man goes crazy with his obsessions in "Many Problems," his suffering soul dying on "the boneyard of vegetables/ the whole world is built on." In "Read the Great Poets," the couch allows "the spirit to leave/ the broken body and wander at will" through "this great dull life."

In "Blank-Stare Encounter," the speaker blurts out a new imperative, "I want to start a new religion," but the dead world's "blank stare drags me along." The point is, however, that no "new religion" is forthcoming from Tate. Midway through *Viper Jazz* one begins to feel a withdrawal from that premise and the setting in of a reductive new attitude that is partly resignation and partly a return to the chattier, amusing voice of early lyrics. There is a quality here of stand-up comedian, the one-liner gag writer who keeps his audience off balance by surrealist turns.

RIVEN DOGGERIES

From *Viper Jazz* to the following book, *Riven Doggeries*, one notes with misgivings a certain carelessness in the work; the language is flimsy, form is lazily sketched in, and poems turn on anecdote and coincidence, sometimes without the clinching phrase to energize them. The theme for much of *Riven Doggeries* is travel, both actual and mind-travel, the feverish transport into and out of reality as the locus of mere existence. By now it is obvious that there is no Paradise opening through the mist; instead, Tate's style hardens into a parody of the real world, a burlesque of the poet's daily life on which the shreds of a previous idealism still cling. "We are all members/ of Nature's alphabet. But we wanted more," he writes in "Nature Poem: Demanding Stiff Sentences," a pun-laced and well-crafted lyric tucked into the middle of the book. Yet such reminders of his romantic principles do not make up for his lax writing.

As a sign that the verse poem may be wearing out here, Tate turns increasingly to the prose poem as miniature short story and frame for the fantasized speech he is using. In "Missionwork," part 3 of *Riven Doggeries*, the language is dense and humorous again, and self-mocking. "It's a sickness, this desire to fly," he notes. Here too the ideal slips away in a dozen forms, from fireflies to dogs—the dog is an essential motif of the absconding spirit throughout the book, the "rivening" of the title.

The prose poem, used here with skill, crept into poetry and has become a standard form in the American repertoire. Beginning with the French poet Charles Baudelaire's *Petits Poèmes en prose* (1869; also known as *Le Spleen de Paris*; *Paris Spleen* 1869), an early experiment in the mode, poets have discovered its use as a form of fantasizing meditation, but without the rhythmic intimacy or precision required in verse. Prose is borderless, a more "submerged" form of writing in that line breaks and phrasings are no longer functions of intense feeling or ideation. A poet's prose makes the presumption of being literal, often somber self-analysis, just as fantasy and the absurd slowly decompose the argument. The trick is to construct an elaborate ruse of confidentiality that is undone the moment the next improbable detail is sprung on the reader's belief, crushing it. Some writers, including Tate and his friend Charles Simic, compound the irony by going past the point of disbelief to reestablish partial credibility.

CONSTANT DEFENDER

Both books show Tate trying to find ways to open the poem, to spread out its intricate patterns and create more space for rambling monologue and humorous asides. Tate's efforts are directed at colloquializing his verse speech, which begins to take effect in *Constant Defender*, published in 1983. Here a well-balanced fantasy mixes with verse compression, though the clinching phrase is often muted in the process. The dialectic between spiritual ideals and the morbidity of the real take subtler form, as in "Tall Trees by Still Waters," where "the actual world was pretending again,/ no, not pretending, imagining an episode/ of unbelievable cruelty, involving invalids."

The self of these poems is more harried, beaten down, and Kafkaesque than in previous books. One detects the wearing down of the idealist in such poetry, intimated in the title—the wearying vigilance of the "constant defender" of his beliefs. The theme running throughout is of abandoned houses to which the speaker returns forlornly, disillusioned once more at cruelty and indifference. In "Tell Them Was Here," the "I" being left blank, the poem ends, "Started to leave,// turned, scratched out my name—/ then wrote it back again." A darker look at self occurs in "Lousy in Center Field," a wonderful poem with dazzling imagery that remarks, "I'm frozen once again/ in an attitude of unfortunate/ interior crumbling mouseholes." He is the ball-player who has lost all interest in catching the ball, which flies over him in a cobwebbed sky.

The landscape is filling up with the dead souls of the modern city. This theme, though tentative and sketchy in *Constant Defender*, becomes pronounced in Tate's later books: *Reckoner*, published in 1986, and *Distance from Loved Ones*, which appeared in 1990. Both continue the breezier, conversational style that set in with *Constant Defender*. The poems work as accumulations of one-line observations, some pithy, some empty, with here and there a humorous turn or a startling image to enliven the pace of what is often tedious aggregates of lines. One poem flows into the next in these books, in which a manic speaker seems desperate to keep up his chatter against a growing sense of loss in his life.

RECKONER

Reckoner mixes prose poems and lyric or narrative verse; the tone shifts slightly from one to the other, but Tate has turned his attention away from the formality and finish of individual poems to the sense of words running together across boundaries to create a metatextual whole. The poems no longer hold up as unique, intricately structured maps of thought; their titles and shapes on the page maintain a certain ghost of formality over which the content leaps. The resulting flow of commentary creates the impression of a speaker's feverish avoidance of some impending tragedy. Even the humor is shrill, worn out, the emotions exhausted by frenetic articulation. The jokes and grotesque exaggeration have an almost menacing insistence; the reader has come upon their formulas many times before in Tate.

Many of the poems open on the same frenetic tempo, with fully punctuated sentences lined up as stanzas, as in "The Flithering Ignominy of Baba Ganoosh," which begins,

> He played the bongo drums and dated infant actresses.
> His signature still glitters in all the most exhausted
> hotels.
> He has positive contempt for rain, for chattering.
> His sofa was designed by a butcher.

This is the sort of shtick Henny Youngman made famous, the one-liner that waits for guffaws or the drummer's rim shot in the background. A pace of this kind wears out humor and begins arousing other emotions by its drugged repetition. Poem after poem renounces the minutiae of the waking world, as some other, darker voice hints that the underlying hidden world has sealed itself for good. The speaker is someone left behind, unable to imagine the possibility of regaining what he somewhere calls the "parallel world." "I've been feeling so cooped up in this hotel," begins a prose poem, "Magazines," where banter goes on for a page without resolution, without argument, without premise even, but for this dejection that pervades all of *Reckoner*.

DISTANCE FROM LOVED ONES

In *Distance from Loved Ones*, the pace does not slacken, but the theme of universal death gathers emphasis and becomes a central motif, with many references to death, the dying, the already deceased who are memories of the speakers. There are now "citizens of the deep," as the speaker remarks in the opening poem, "Quabbin Reservoir," while he alone kills time along the shore as the last of the living voices. Other ghosts are portrayed, as in "Peggy in the Twilight," who "spent half of each day trying to wake up, and/ the other half preparing for sleep."

Tate's characters in *Distance from Loved Ones* keep lonely vigils among the dead; their voices have turned to memory. Many of the poems are variations on the elegy, the very form with which *The Lost Pilot* began. The poems' characters, variations on that youthful speaker who awaited his father's orbital return each birthday, live futile, empty lives waiting to join the dead around them. They have no purpose in life; their only defense against remorse is their disjunctive humor, their ability to disconnect the tedious logic of their world and playfully deconstruct their own identities.

In "How Happy We Were," one of these loners notes that his vision of eternity included "a few of the little angels/ whose sole job it is to fake weeping for people like us." Crowds in America practice "dead mall worship," he writes in "Beaucoup Vets," and in "Anatomy," a beautiful girl studies anatomy and continually cries. The others "know she is dying inside." In "Taxidermy," "Everything is dead anyway." In a sense, the death of the father in Tate's first book has spread out over his many books to encompass the world; the memory of the dead father created a glimmering afterlife Tate never could bring into sharp focus or make the basis of a sustaining vision. His poetry began as elegy and has built a vast edifice of language to exhaust the content of that emotion.

WORSHIPFUL COMPANY OF FLETCHERS

The title of his next book, National Book Award winner *Worshipful Company of Fletchers*, refers to the ancient guild of arrow makers. The tone shifts to the sort of dark humor of Paul Auster's novels, particularly his dystopian fantasy *In the Country of Last Things* (1987). In that book and in Tate's later poetry, one finds a deepening sense of gloom over the future of cities, and something of the mordant tone of the poet Leonard Cohen's lyric, "the future is murder," and of Don DeLillo's wry assessment, "The future is crowds." For Tate, the city is fast becoming a barren landscape of parentless people, those without fathers who accept routine merely because it distracts them from desperate loneliness and a sense of futility.

In the title poem, a small boy, Tate's alter ego, is confronted by the older poet, who notes that he "lives at the edge of the woods" and that it is "still not clear to me where he really lives." The "really" underscores the ironic tone of the story: In Tate's world, no one appears to be living in reality; rather, one escapes from reality by means of fantasy and self-delusion. The speaker goes on to note that "he'd live with animals if they'd take him in," and thus withdraw altogether from an untrustworthy community of adults. The woods are still Robert Frost's place of retreat, where the mind may heal itself from the woes of this world, and William Wordsworth's woods, where innocence may live unviolated by the evils of city life. At the "edge" of the woods, however, one is neither

protected by the animals nor free of adult corruptions, and the boy's vaguely orphaned state permits Tate to expand on his identity as the picture of Everyman groping for relationships, loath to accept the meager terms of existence he might find in his suburban neighborhood.

The poems are still page-length lyrical narratives or commentaries, nearly all of which are composed in Tate's wry, drily surreal style, which derives part of its voice from the matter-of-fact tone of Frost, who depicts a life of drudging and narrow-mindedness from which he tries to escape by remembering his childhood and by proposing outrageous questions to his dowdy neighbors. Tate grows out of the same rebellious nature set against uneventful lives, whose language has leapt beyond mere representation of events to fracture common sense by shifting to different subjects without transition or logical connectives.

In this sense, Tate has moved all his strategies from his previous books into a single thrust of reasoning aimed at the disenchanted world of adulthood and its mundane circumstances. He is the confirmed orphan living without benefit of a father's counsel or affection, who finds others laboring without joy and merely using up their mortal span. His defense against this empty materialism is to bend logic by allowing dreams and the anarchy of the unconscious to erupt at will. Tate's definition of the orphan soul is that it is without membranes between a rational self and its fortified ego, on one hand, and the great swampy interiors of one's dream self and the night world of longings and unfulfilled love, on the other.

In page after page of this and succeeding books, the poems report events from a slightly cracked perspective. The company of fletchers who feather arrow shafts take their work seriously, though their product belongs mainly to the fantasy lives of boys who look for their roots in myth and folklore and wilderness landscapes, like the orphan in the title poem. By means of his fractured accounts of daily life, Tate creates a Norman Rockwell painting of ordinary America in which the certainties in the background—small houses and neat little roads—peel away from the surface to reveal some other landscape that the soul longs for and cannot reach. Tate's humor is laced with bitterness and disillusionment that he could not grow up normally after losing a father in the war when he was an infant.

Some other, more difficult motive is at play in this and the books to come: a desire to so muddle the usual progress of lyric argument as to make each word an unpredictable event, thus preventing the reader from feeling as if the language could be anticipated and thus ignored. The poem becomes resistant to being read, to being predicted or interrupted by the reader's own wandering thoughts. Average poems have about them what the poet Charles Bernstein calls "absorptiveness," or a kind of senseless spongy believability in which readers even forget that what they are reading is a poem or that there is any alternative reality to the thing being read. The "anti-absorptive" work of art is so fashioned as to make the reader aware of its every word as if it were a physical object, not a convenient screen of illusion in which to lose one's self. Tate's thinly veiled surrealism is enough to make the reader uncomfortable, slightly puzzled, and on guard against all the rug-pulling in the average Tate lyric. In the last poem of this volume, "Happy as the Day Is Long," the fallen world of mere reality is itemized:

> I take the long walk up the staircase to my secret room.
> Today's big news: they found Amelia Earhart's shoe,
> size 9.
> 1992: Charlie Christian is bebopping at Minton's in
> 1941.
> Today, the presidential primaries have failed us once
> again.
> We'll look for our excitement elsewhere, in the last
> snow
> that is falling, in tomorrow's Gospel Concert in
> Springfield.
> It's a good day to be a cat and just sleep.

SHROUD OF THE GNOME

Shroud of the Gnome, Tate's twelfth full-length collection, opens with the poem "Where Do Babies Come From?," the perennial question of growing youngsters to their parents, which receives this jaundiced report about hapless orphans forced into hard labor,

> Many are from the Maldives,
> southwest of India, and must begin
> collecting shells immediately.
> The larger ones may prefer coconuts.
> Survivors move from island to island

> hopping over one another and never
> looking back. After the typhoons
> have had their pick, and the birds of prey
> have finished with theirs, the remaining few
> must build boats.

Other poems move into Wallace Stevens's tropical landscape of cockatiels and sunny rooms, only to find reality equally dismembered in Tate's world. If reality is Tate's target, he snips at its ligaments with surgical scissors in this volume, keeping up the pretense that his form of chatter has rails under it when in fact it races off its track from line to line, silently mocking the flimsy laws of grammar and veracity on which most conversation is based. Tate is our metaphysical satirist, a comedian of the laws of verisimilitude, who finds everything floating on illusory foundations. Hence, his poems read like idle chitchat after dinner among half-educated well-meaning suburbanites, whose generalities and clichés allow us to glimpse the quicksand on which reality has built its world.

Shrouds are winding sheets of the dead, and gnomes are out of fairy tales; the title doubles the references to a world at the edge of consciousness, where gnomes have died but live on in some other dimension to haunt us. Reality has excluded them, but the mere act of juxtaposing items creates a nonsense argument in which things happen in spite of one's attempts to "make sense" of life. This "cut up" method, invented by the novelist William Burroughs, is used here with drier, but more telling, effect. Here is how the method works in the title poem,

> And what amazes me is that none of our modern
>   inventions
> surprise or interest him, even a little. I tell him
> it is time he got his booster shots, but then
> I realize I have no power over him whatsoever.
> He becomes increasingly light footed until I lose sight
> of him downtown between the federal building and
> the post office. A registered nurse is taking her
> coffee break. I myself needed a break, so I sat down
> next to her at the counter. "Don't mind me," I said,
> "I'm just a hungry little gnostic in need of a sandwich."

The "gnostic" may be a clue to the subversive logic of Tate's entire canon; for gnostic wisdom is based on intuitive glimpses into mysteries independent of the senses or the logic of empiricism. The gnostic believes in other worlds and their power to merge with our own sensory experience. Tate's speaker is often confronting those who have no alternative world to draw from, making his own "gnostic" processes seem disjointed and absurd, as in the poem, "Same As You":

> I put my pants on one day at a time.
> Then I hop around in circles hobbledehoy.
> A projectile of some sort pokes me,
> in the eye—I think it's a bird
> or a flying pyramid that resembles a bird.

MEMOIR OF THE HAWK

In *Memoir of the Hawk*, Tate covers a widening range of subjects that include a young woman's desire to see a "blue antelope," in the closing poem, and after removing her clothes in a park she begins to see them moving "like angels" toward her. The situation is a page torn from Eugène Ionesco's Surrealist one-act play *Rhinocéros* (pr., pb. 1959; *Rhinoceros*, 1959), those without the menacing suggestion of fascism's contagious spirit. This "antelope" is a creature of innocence longed for by a woman and a man who both lie naked as if to return to childhood and visionary experience. The poem, like so many others before it, is a testament to Tate's enduring ability to find new expressions for a lifelong antidote to the sorrows of aging and the burden of the merely material world, made orthodox long ago as the logical view of things. He has challenged this view by drawing on the literature of rebellion from Romanticism to Surrealism to make the case that other worlds are sandwiched between the objects of reality and signify a multitude of possibilities excluded by an official grammar of experience.

OTHER MAJOR WORKS

LONG FICTION: *Lucky Darryl*, 1977 (with Bill Knott).

SHORT FICTION: *Hottentot's Ossuary*, 1974.

NONFICTION: *The Route as Briefed*, 1999.

EDITED TEXT: *The Best American Poetry: 1997*, 1997.

BIBLIOGRAPHY

Levis, Larry. "Eden and My Generation." In *Conversant Essays: Contemporary Poets on Poetry*, edited by James McCorkle. Detroit: Wayne State University Press, 1990. A broad-ranging survey of the lines and forces of contemporary poetry, in which James Tate is located, and of its major theme in the loss of Eden.

Rosen, R. D. "James Tate and Sidney Goldfarb and the Inexhaustible Nature of the Murmur." In *American Poetry Since 1960: Some Critical Perspectives*, edited by Robert B. Shaw. Cheshire, England: Carcanet Press, 1973. Argues that both Tate and Goldfarb belong to a generation that uses poetry to escape from the postwar age; their writing, notes Rosen, is that of moral outlaws.

Tate, James. *The Route as Briefed*. Ann Arbor: University of Michigan Press, 1999. Collects Tate's interviews, essays, occasional writings together, where he comments on his composing method, or fields questions from various interviewers about the peculiar nature of his lyric arguments, his influences and the like.

Upton, Lee. *The Muse of Abandonment: Origin, Identity, Mastery in Five American Poets*. London: Associated University Presses, 1998. A critical study of the works of five twentieth century American poets, including Tate, and their points of view on alienation, power, and identity. Includes bibliographical references and index.

Paul Christensen, updated by Christensen

EDWARD TAYLOR

Born: Near Sketchley, Leicestershire, England; c. 1645
Died: Westfield, Massachusetts; June 24, 1729

PRINCIPAL POETRY

The Poetical Works of Edward Taylor, 1939 (Thomas H. Johnson, editor)

The Poems of Edward Taylor, 1960 (Donald E. Stanford, editor)

A Transcript of Edward Taylor's Metrical History of Christianity, 1962 (Stanford, editor)

Edward Taylor's Minor Poetry, 1981 (volume 3 of *The Unpublished Writings of Edward Taylor*; Thomas M. Davis and Virginia L. Davis, editors)

OTHER LITERARY FORMS

Edward Taylor is best known today for his poetry. To his congregation at Westfield, Massachusetts, however, he was far better known for his sermons. He did apparently write the moral sequence of thirty-five poems, "God's Determinations," as a guide for members of his congregation, who were unable to assure themselves that they had achieved the state of grace. Even so, the Westfield minister did not intend that his poems should ever be published. There is some indication, however, that he did plan to publish some of his sermons, particularly those gathered together by Norman S. Grabo as *Edward Taylor's Treatise Concerning the Lord's Supper* (1966); these eight sermons attack Solomon Stoddard's liberal position regarding the admission of persons to the Eucharist who were not always certain they possessed the gift of God's grace.

The fourteen sermons collected, again by Grabo, as Edward Taylor's *Christographia* (1962) deal with two major issues: First that the "blessed Theanthropie," God's son united with man in the body of Jesus of Nazareth, was a necessary condition created by God to redeem the elect among humankind; and, second, that this God-man constitutes the perfect model after whom each of the saints should construct his life. These fourteen sermons correspond precisely in subject matter to poems forty-two through fifty-six of the "Preparatory Meditations," Second Series. All of these published sermons are necessary reading for serious students of Taylor's poetry; they reveal his public attitudes toward many issues with which he grapples in his private poetry. In 1981, there appeared a three-volume set, *The Unpublished Writings of Edward Taylor* (Thomas M. Davis and Virginia L. Davis, editors), which includes Taylor's church records, minor poems, and additional sermons.

In 1977, an extensive holograph manuscript of thirty-six sermons, dating from 1693 to 1706, was recovered. These as yet unpublished sermons treat "types": events, persons, or things in the Old Testament which represent or shadow forth similar events, persons (particularly Je-

sus of Nazareth), or things in the New Testament. Taylor's *Diary* has been published (1964, F. Murphy, editor); he kept this record during his journey to New England and until he located, after graduation from Harvard in 1671, at Westfield. The style of the *Diary* is candid and immediate; one almost shares with Taylor his vividly described seasickness.

ACHIEVEMENTS

For today's readers, Edward Taylor's finest achievement is his poetry. Those of his own time, however, remembered Taylor for his accomplishments as minister and physician to the Westfield, Massachusetts, community. In his edition of Taylor's poems, Thomas H. Johnson lists an inventory of the poet's library that includes the titles of several now arcane books on surgery and alchemy. Appropriately enough, the vocabulary of Taylor's medical practice often makes its way into his poetry.

Perhaps it was this professional versatility that enabled Taylor to construct elaborate metaphysical conceits with such agility. His poems can bear comparison to the work of John Donne, George Herbert, and Andrew Marvell. Indeed, Taylor's best poems are among the finest composed by an American.

BIOGRAPHY

The details of Edward Taylor's life are not abundant. He was born in or near Sketchley, Leicestershire, England, probably in the year 1645. He may have attended the University of Cambridge or one of the dissenting academies, for when he was admitted to Harvard in 1668, he was given advanced standing. It is certain that he early began training for the ministry. He had been brought to New England by the Act of Uniformity of Charles II; passed in 1662, this law required all schoolmasters (Taylor may have served in that capacity at Bagworth, Leicestershire) and ministers to take an oath of allegiance to the Anglican church. Of course, Taylor's religious orthodoxy in the Puritan mode of worship prevented him, in good conscience, from taking the oath.

Taylor records his voyage across the Atlantic with vivid precision in his *Diary*. Even before his ship could get away from the British Isles, it was beset by a "violent storm" that filled the forecastle of the ship "ankle-deep" with water and so bathed the mate that "the water ran out of the waist of his breeches." Although the young man often found himself subdued by the constant rocking of the vessel, he was particularly taken with the life he discovered in the sea; he describes more than ten different types of fishes and several kinds of "sea fowl." On a few occasions he and the crew spotted different kinds of driftwood. One such event held a pleasant surprise for them. Upon finding "a piece of white fir-wood full of barnacles, which are things like dew-worm skins about two inches long hanging to the wood," they learned that the other end housed a species of shellfish, so "we had a dish of them." Toward the end of the journey as the vessel approached land, Taylor saw his first fireflies: "About eight I saw a flying creature like a spark of red fire (about the bigness of an bumble bee) fly by the side of the ship; and presently after, there flew another by. The men said they were fireflies." The poet's fascination with nature continued in later years, as poems such as "Upon a Spider Catching a Fly" and "Upon a Wasp Chilled with Cold" attest.

The *Diary* also records his admission to Harvard, some humorous incidents that occurred there, and his calling after graduation in 1671, to minister to the congregation at Westfield, Massachusetts. While he was at Harvard, he roomed with Samuel Sewall, author of the famous *Diary* (1878-1882) and the judge at the Salem witch trials. In later years, Sewall names Taylor some fourteen times in the *Diary* and records in a letter that it was Taylor who induced him to attend Harvard. During his student days, the future minister of Westfield served as college Butler, a position of responsibility which, however, did not prevent him from becoming involved in some youthful acts of relatively innocuous consequence. He took his calling to the ministry of the Westfield congregation, however, very seriously; in his *Diary* he records his doubts about his suitability as a minister. This sincere examination of his conscience before God establishes for the first time in Taylor's known writings the pattern that prevails in his private, poetic "Meditations," Series One and Two.

On November 5, 1674, after courting her through letters and verse, Taylor married Elizabeth Fitch of Norwich, Connecticut. The first Mrs. Taylor died some fifteen years later, having given birth to eight children.

Taylor recorded his grief in one of his most moving poems, "A Funerall Poem upon the Death of My Ever Endeared and Tender Wife." In 1692, at the age of about fifty, the Westfield minister was married again, to Ruth Wyllys of Hartford, who bore him six more children and who survived him by about six months. Taylor's ministry of almost sixty years was a fruitful one. While bearing the responsibility of meeting his congregation's medical as well as spiritual needs, Taylor wrote his "Preparatory Meditations," attacked Solomon Stoddard's "liberalism" (Stoddard, who attended Taylor's ordination on August 27, 1679, had served as Harvard's first librarian during Taylor's attendance at the college), received an M.A. degree from Harvard in 1720, and visited Samuel Sewall, whom he solicited on one occasion (in 1691) to supervise the apprenticeship of one of his sons to a shopkeeper at Ipswich. Taylor died on June 24, 1729, a much-loved and revered divine whose tombstone records that as a "Venerable, Learned, and Pious Pastor" he "had served God and his Generation Faithfully."

ANALYSIS

At the time when English poetry, following the lead of John Dryden, was moving into a century of neoclassicism, Edward Taylor was writing verse in the Metaphysical mode of John Donne, characterized by complex syntax, striking conceits, and intimate direct address: Most of Taylor's poems are addressed to God. In addition to his Metaphysical style, of primary interest to today's readers of Taylor's poetry are his propensity to employ the meditative technique, his practice of coordinating private poetic meditation with public sermon, his perhaps unexpected but nevertheless felicitous use of classical allusions, and his attention to the function of the fancy or the imagination in the poetic process.

"HUSWIFERY"

"Huswifery," perhaps Taylor's most famous poem, also displays one of his most eloquent conceits. As did most Puritans of his time, Taylor often found evidence of God's providence in the quotidian. In "Huswifery," he discovers God's purpose for the poet's public ministry in his wife's spinning wheel, perdurable symbol of America's pioneer struggle. The poem begins with this arresting plea, "Make me, O Lord, Thy spinning wheel complete." The poet then develops this conceit in a logical fashion, first according to ingenious analogies drawn between the various components of the spinning wheel and second by focusing on the machine's product, clothing. That which holds the fibers of wool to be spun, the distaff, becomes "Thy holy word"; the flyers that twist the fibers into thread (or yarn) represent the poet's religious emotions; and the spool that collects the thread embodies his soul. Extending the spinning wheel conceit a bit further, the poet next asserts that the loom on which the threads are woven into cloth serves, like a minister of God's message, as the instrument for delivering his message to those in need (his congregation). The clothes prepared in this fashion should then become the minister's apparel, displaying God's "shine" and revealing that he is "clothed in holy robes for glory."

"MEDITATION THIRTY-NINE"

Another poem that employs conceits with equal success is Taylor's "Meditation Thirty-nine" (First Series). This longer poem develops two conceits: sin as poison, and Jesus of Nazareth as "the sinner's advocate" or defense attorney before God. The inspiration for this meditation is I John 2:1 "If any man sin, we have an advocate with the Father, Jesus Christ the righteous." Taylor opens the poem with the exclamation: "My sin! My sin, My God, these cursed dregs,/ Green, yellow, blue streaked poison." These "Bubs [pustules] hatched in nature's nest on serpents' eggs" act in his soul like poisons in his stomach and "set his soul acramp." He alone cannot conquer then, "cannot them destroy." Alone and unassisted without God's help, these "Black imps . . . snap, bite, drag to bring/ And pitch me headlong hell's dread whirlpool in." By delaying the preposition "in" until the end of the line, Taylor startles his readers, thereby focusing attention on his wretched predicament as sinner. To be sure, Taylor's intention, since he wrote these poems as private meditations with God, in preparation for the administration of the Eucharist, was not to appeal to an audience schooled in the Metaphysical style. Such recognition does not, however, lessen the certainty that his intention is most definitely to appeal to an even more critical audience, his God, whose attention he does indeed want to capture and hold.

At this most critical point in his acknowledgment of his fallen state, the poet catches a glimpse of "a twin-

kling ray of hope," Christ as advocate; for him, then, "a door is ope." With this introduction of an advocate, Taylor begins to build his legal conceit. The sight of the advocate first engenders a promise of release from his pain. Temporary joy is replaced by a renewed sense of guilt, however, as he realizes that all his advocate has to work with is "the state/ The case is in." That is, if the case his advocate pleads before God, the final judge, is short of merit, then judgment may still go against him. As Taylor puts it, if the case is bad: "it's bad in plaint." He continues by observing, "My papers do contain no pleas that do/ Secure me from, but knock me down to, woe." Again the poet wrenches the syntax, but again for the same reason. Despite the "ray of hope," he fears that the gravity of his "Black imps" may yet doom him to hellfire. As before, his purpose is to focus on his apparently hopeless condition. His reason then begins to instruct him. Even though the biblical text causes him to recall his past sins while also promising him a defense attorney before God, he concludes, without benefit of understanding, "I have no plea mine advocate to give." He is forced to cry out, "What now?" His reason teaches him that his advocate is unique; as God's only Son, he has sacrificed his human body to provide the believing and worthy sinner the gift of redemption. These "dear bought arguments" are "good pleas" indeed. Following this grasp of his reason which informs him that the "ray of hope" is constant and true, the poet asks "What shall I do, my Lord?" How can he act or conduct his life so "that I/ May have Thee plead my case?" He exercises his will and decides to "fee" or pay his lawyer "With faith, repentence, and obediently" give the efforts of his ministry to fighting against the commission of "satanic sins" among his parishioners. This unique agreement between lawyer and client obliges the lawyer "My sins [to] make Thine," while at the same time it emboldens the client, the poet, "Thy pleas [to] make mine hereby."

The agreement is struck, then; "Thou wilt me save; I will thee celebrate." Taylor intends, however, not merely to celebrate his advocate through his works "'gainst satanic sins," but he desires intensely that "my rough feet shall Thy smooth praises sing." This intense desire to please God in return for God's love freely given, the eros-*agape* motif, pervades Taylor's meditative poetry. The *ababcc* rhyme scheme, which Taylor adopts for all of his meditations, serves a purpose beyond that ordinarily expected; the final words of each line are "I," "advocate" (the noun), "hereby," "celebrate," "within," and "Sing." With slight rearrangement, these words make this fitting statement: I hereby celebrate [my] advocate within song. Thus Taylor accomplishes his end both directly and implicitly. In doing so, he well fulfills John Calvin's dictum in *The Institutes of the Christian Religion* (1536) that "We recommend the voice and singing as a support of speech [in the worship service], where accompanying love [that is] pure of spirit."

The process that governs this poem's construction is that of the meditation, an intellectual exercise codified by St. Ignatius Loyola in his *Spiritual Exercises* (1548) and passed on to Taylor probably through the widely circulated and immensely popular (among Puritans) *The Saints' Everlasting Rest* (1650), written by one of the seventeenth century's foremost Puritan authorities on meditation, Richard Baxter. While this mental process or guide to philosophical contemplation was implicitly understood from pre-Christian days (see the entry, *meditation* in Charlton T. Lewis and Charles Short's *A Latin Dictionary*, 1879), Loyola's *Spiritual Exercises* did much to make commonplace this process which uses the mental faculties of memory, understanding, and will. As the poem itself illustrates, the memory of the one engaged in meditation is jogged or aroused, usually by some biblical text; the understanding or reason of the meditator then grapples with the significance of this memory recalled in conjunction with the biblical text; and, finally, the meditator's grasp of the significance of text and memory lead him to pledge to serve God with the new understanding he has acquired. The biblical text, "If any man sin, we have an advocate with the Father, Jesus Christ the righteous," causes the poet to remember his own poisonous sins, and to recall his redeemer, but also to fear that his sins may weigh too heavily against him in the balance of God's justice. His understanding then reassures him that Christ, having bought his sins in his human sacrifice, is a formidable advocate in his behalf and that the strength of his belief will give his advocate all the "surety" he will need. The knowledge of God's gift of his only Son so overwhelms the poet or meditator that he pledges to serve him in both deeds and poetry.

"MEDITATION EIGHT"

Taylor adopts this basic mode of construction in many of his meditations, as a brief examination of "Meditation Eight" (First Series) affirms. This poem derives its inspiration from another biblical text, John 6:51, part of which is "I am the living bread which came down from heaven." This text moves the poet to conjure up a vision in which he is looking up toward heaven, trying to discover how man can ever have "pecked the fruit forbad" and consequently have "lost . . . the golden days" and fallen into "celestial famine sore." What is man to do now? How can he regain paradise? His reason informs him that, alone and without God's help, this earth "cannot yield thee/ here the smallest crumb" of that living bread. According to the poem, the only way out of this barren mortality is by way of "The purest wheat in heaven, His dear—dear Son." The fallen sinner must "eat thy fill of this, thy God's white loaf." If one exercises his will and chooses to eat this "soul bread," then "thou shalt never die." Once again scripture provokes memory, which in turn stimulates the understanding, which finally brings about a resolve of the will.

One can easily see how this meditative process accords well with preparation and resolve to administer God's word with as much intensity and expression as a sincere and gifted pastor can muster. Investigation among those sermons with which scholars are able to align specific meditative poems proves rewarding indeed. All the fourteen sermons of the *Christographia*, for example, correspond exactly to the "Meditations" (Second Series), forty-two through fifty-six. The examination of but one such pair, sermon and poem, serves the present purpose. Both "Meditation Fifty-Six" and the fourteenth sermon of the *Christographia* collection are based on the same biblical text, John 15:24: "Had I not done amongst them the works, that none other man hath done, they had not had Sin." This final sermon of the series marks the culmination of Taylor's analysis of the "blessed Theanthropie," his explanation for the person of God's divine Son. In this concluding homily, the minister attempts to establish that no works of men or of nature (since God is the author of both) surpass the works of God or his Son; God, therefore, commands the devotion of his believers.

The sermon opens with the observation that the

white blossom of the clove tree, when "turned to be green, . . . yields the pleasentest [sic] Smell in the World." The minister uses this clove blossom imagery as a structural device by means of which, when he returns to it at the sermon's conclusion, he unifies his text, for the flower which exudes the most pleasant order predicts the closing corollary that the works of Christ are "the Sweetest Roses, and brightest flowers of his own Excellency." This flower imagery does not, however, play a significant structural role in the poem. The poet delays this sensuous appeal to smell until the thirteenth line. Preceding the poem's "White-green'd blossoms" are evocations of other senses, including the sight of his "Damask Web of Velvet Verse" that the poet offers in humility to God, and the taste of "Fruits so sweete that grow/ On the trees of righteousness." This explication of the senses follows rather closely Loyola's recommendation given in some of his *Spiritual Exercises* (see, for example, the First Week, Fifth Exercise); Taylor, therefore, here conforms, whether consciously or not, to Loyola's famous codification of the meditative process. The purpose of the sermon, however, is clearly not meditation but utilitarian and effective communication of the doctrine, which the minister articulates as follows: "That Christ's works were so excellent, that never any did the like thereto."

Throughout both sermon and poem, the author expands upon the Tree of Life metaphor, which appears first in Genesis. In the popular *The Figures or Types of the Old Testament* (1683), a copy of which Taylor owned and annotated, Samuel Mather, whose nephew was one of Taylor's classmates at Harvard, explains that "the Tree of Life in Paradise was a Type of Christ." This Old Testament Tree of Life, which was located in the center of Eden, "shadows forth" or prefigures Christ in the New Testament. When Adam and Eve were cast out of Paradise, they were denied the gift of God's grace available to them from the eating of the fruit of this tree; according to Christian understanding of the Adamic myth, it then became necessary for Christ to come into the world of men in order to restore this "fruit" of God's grace; that is, to redeem fallen men. Understandably, Taylor often refers to this myth in his poems and sermons, but he does so with particular intensity in this sermon and this poem. The minister tells his parishioners

that "his [Christ's] Works are his rich Ornaments," while the poet extolls Christ as "a Tree of Perfect nature trim" whose branches "doe out/ shine the sun."

This "Tree of Perfect nature" produces, in the poem, fruits of this perfection which he identifies as God's gift of grace. The minister is also, of course, much interested in the question of grace, but he does not regale his congregation with conceits spun about the Tree of Life; rather, with attention to practicality, he emphasizes "Christ's works mediatoriall" [sic] which translate "the Soule from a State of Sin, and a Sinfull life, into a State of holiness." Underscoring this distinction between the poem's richness of imagery and the sermon's concentration on the delivery of practical doctrine are their respective descriptions of Christ. While the sermon calls Christ "the brightness of his Fathers Glory," the poem more extravagantly describes him as one whose "fruits adorne/ Thyselfe, and Works, more shining than the morn" and as one whose "Flowers more sweet than spice/ Bende down to us."

The sweet flowers of Christ's works, says the minister, far exceed "Kingly Performances." Kings and rulers of the temporal world "ofttimes build their Palaces in oppression." The minister does not expand his case to include the naming of specific illustrations. The poet, however, provides rich examples of worldly power. Indeed, he names Psammetichos's huge labyrinth, supposed to have been built by Daedalus; the Roman emperor Titus (A.D. 40-81), and his Colosseum; Nero's Golden Palace; and other symbols of temporal power. Whereas the poet heaps up specific cases of earthly artifice and thereby poignantly contrasts God's works and man's most ambitious constructions, the minister, more simply concerned with the transience of earthy mortality, explains how man's buildings, no matter how magnificent, "are but of Clayy natures."

The minister is also disposed to contrast the egalitarian nature of the laws of God, which apply to all men equally, with the laws of kings that "are like Copwebs that catch little flies, but are Snapt in pieces by the greater." This web imagery occurs in the poem, but in a quite different context. As noted above, the poet sees his verse as "A Damask Web of Velvet," hardly as an ensnaring "copweb." It is possible, however, that the labyrinthine image of Psammetichos's maze conjured up in the mind of the minister the image of man's laws seen as oppressive "copwebs." It should be observed, nevertheless, that at this point as at others, poems and sermon are not always in exact agreement.

The conclusion of Taylor's sermon is the more interesting precisely because it does not appear to agree fully with the poem. In the poem, Taylor prays that his God will "Adorn my Life well with thy works" and will "make faire/ My Person with apparrell thou prepar'st." For, if he is so clothed, his "Boughs," extending the Tree of Life conceit to himself, "shall loaded bee with fruits that spring/ Up from thy Works." Such a prayer reveals the preparation of a sincere minister about to deliver God's word to his flock. The minister, however, appears to rebuke the poet for his extravagance. In the sermon's conclusion, the minister declares that all the most excellent works of man in this world "are but dull drudgeries and lifeless painted cloaths compared to Christs." Of especial significance at this crucial point in the sermon's concluding lines, however, is the comparison that Taylor draws between man's works and those of God.

He cites the example of the famous Alexandrian painter, Apelles, who rebuked one of his students for overlaying a painting of Venus with gold; Apelles told the student that he had not created a beautiful representation, but simply a rich one. Taylor the poet has done precisely the same thing in his poem; he has decorated God's word with elaborate images and drawn out conceits, but he has expressed the hope that God will adorn him in a similar fashion. The minister determinedly concludes that men's works are "of no worth." "Ours are Worth nothing," the minister says "without he puts . . . the Worthiness of his on them." To be sure, the poet is as devoted to God as the minister is, and has carefully sought God's assistance in the construction of his poem. Nevertheless, the minister, who has written a much less "adorned" sermon, appears to admonish the poet, as well as his congregation, not to forget that the "clothes" he would wear both in the poem and in the sermon are worn with God's benevolence. What appears to be reticence on the part of the poet here was full-blown trepidation at an earlier point in Taylor's poetic career. The twenty-first meditation of the First Series (1686) displays this fear in unmistakable candor: "Yet I feare/ To say a Syllable [as poet] lest at thy day [Judgment Day]/ I be presented for my Tattling here."

"MEDITATION FIFTY-SIX" AND "SERMON FOURTEEN"

In his introduction to his edition of *Christographia*, Norman S. Grabo concludes, as others have, that Taylor's "sermons seem to explicate the poems." This observation is no less true of "Meditation Fifty-six" and "Sermon Fourteen." More appears to be at work, however, in this pair. The medium of the poem, with its possibilities for elaborate tropes and figures, together with the poem's condition of privacy, allows Taylor to pursue his personal devotion to God with virtually limitless zeal; indeed, knowing that his heavenly audience, God, will hardly misconstrue his motives but that his earthly audience, the members of his congregation, very well may, Taylor the poet can, his earlier trepidation notwithstanding, express himself with more candor and fervor than Taylor the minister can. As a result, his meditations are always richer and more passionate than his often somber and always sober sermons. Two other factors that characterize his poetry corroborate this assumption: his use of classical allusions and the manner in which he describes the function of the imagination in the poetic process.

USE OF CLASSICAL ALLUSIONS

As is the case of the Apelles allusion, Taylor uses classical allusions in his sermons as exempla or as instructional illustrations for the benefit of his parishioners. In his poems, his application of them is quite predictably more figurative. Wholly unexpected, however, is the fact that Taylor applies references to classical paganism in contexts that are usually positive or favorable. For example, in the long series of thirty-five poems, "Gods Determinations," the poet seems to revel in drawing implied allusions to Greek mythology when describing God's creation of the world in the first poem of the sequence. The poet asks, "Who blew the Bellows of his Furnace Vast?"—doubtless a reference to Hephaestus, Greek god of the hearth and metalworking. Surely Atlas stands beneath the line: "Where stand the Pillars upon which it stands?"

This engaging use of classical references usually gives way to a more serious and often more complex application. In the seventy-ninth meditation of the Second Series, for example, Taylor, contrary to the expected and even prescribed convention, extends the practice of typology to classical mythology. The poet's practice here is of particular significance since it points toward the nineteenth century emphasis on symbolism to be found in the works of such American writers as Herman Melville and Nathaniel Hawthorne. The text for this meditation is Canticles 2:16; "My beloved is mine and I am his." Since the Puritans (and many others) interpreted this entire book, which contains some of the most sensuous and sensual poetry in the Bible, as an allegory of man's relation to God, one might conclude that the subject of this poem must be the analogy between sexual love (eros) and God's unconditional, unselfish love for man (*agape*).

With that expectation, one may find the first four lines of the poem somewhat puzzling: "Had I Promethius' filching Ferula [fennel]/ Filld with its sacred theft the stoln Fire:/ To animate my Fancy lodg'd in clay,/ Pandora's Box would peps [pelt] the theft with ire." Knowledge of the Greek myth of Prometheus, who stole fire from the gods and gave it to man, helps to explain what is happening in these lines. Prometheus was seen by the ancients as a truly heroic champion of humankind, as Aeschylus's tragedy *Prometheus Bound* illustrates. As a consequence of Prometheus's defiance, however, Zeus sent Pandora, whom he forced to bring to man the infamous box of woes and tribulations. Zeus forbade Pandora to open the box, but knowing her to be inveterately curious, he also knew that her opening of the box would merely be a matter of time. Now the typology may be made clear. Taylor has obviously rejected the Prometheus myth as insufficient to animate his "Fancy lodg'd in clay"; that is, to set his imagination into motion so that he can compose a meditation appropriate to his devotion to God. The stanza's final lines, however, do suggest to him the source suitable for the kind and degree of inspiration he requires: "But if thy Love, My Lord, shall animate/ My Clay with holy fire, 'twill flame in State."

The Prometheus myth fails to give him the necessary inspiration, not because it is pagan but because, in Taylor's conception here, it is typological of the Adamic myth (of man's fall from grace). Prometheus, like Satan, defies Zeus, or God, and Pandora, a type of Eve, manifests the unfortunate trait of curiosity that causes her to disobey Zeus, just as Eve's curiosity prompts her to disobey God and to yield to Satan's temptation to eat of the Tree of Knowledge (of good and evil). Although

Taylor's complex typology here is aesthetically pleasing, it is surprising, since Samuel Mather had cautioned against such a practice. In *The Figures or Types of the Old Testament*, which, it will be recalled, the poet owned and annotated, Mather unequivocally states, "It is not safe to make any thing a type meerly upon our own fansies and imaginations; it is *Gods* Perogative to make *Types*." Here Taylor clearly exceeds the limitations that his Puritan compatriots would impose upon him. Perhaps Taylor recognized this quality in his poetry and such recognition led to his request that his poems not be published.

THE IMAGINATION

At any rate, as the investigation of the Prometheus myth suggests, the drawing out of typologies that are not God's is not the only practice for which Taylor could have received censure had his poems appeared in print. As Taylor's lines and Mather's dictum suggest, the poet is here "guilty" of indulging himself with the making of inventions of his own imagination. Whereas his attitude toward the use of classical allusions is unguarded, particularly in his poetry—he simply uses such references when he feels moved by the demands of the verse to do so, often creating rich and satisfying lines—such is not the case with his management of the imagination. Toward this essentially aesthetic idea, Taylor sometimes appears to be ambivalent. Certainly Mather's injunction against its use offers a partial explanation of Taylor's ambivalence. Earlier in the seventeenth century, William Perkins, renowned patriarch of English Puritanism, wrote A Treatise of Mans Imaginations (1607) in which he calls the imagination a "corrupt fountaine." He arrives at this conclusion from Genesis 8:21, "the imaginacion of mans heart is evil even from his youth" (from the Geneva Bible). In one of his *Christographia* sermons, Taylor himself espouses a similar position when he admonishes his congregation not to be deluded by "Fictitious imaginations" which "indeed are the Efficacy of Errors."

Regarding his attitude toward the imagination, Taylor the poet contradicts Taylor the minister. Unlike the minister who refers to the imagination only twice in his published sermons (both times in a negative context), the poet cites "fancy," "Phansy," or some other form of this word (as verb or adjective) forty-six times in his published poetry. He never uses the synonym "imagination" in his poetry, probably preferring the disyllabic "fancy" to the pentasyllabic synonym for purposes of rhythm. When he cites "fancy" and its various spellings and forms, he does so in a manner that establishes a readily discernible pattern. When the word occurs at the beginning of a poem, always in a meditation, it is invariably used within the positive context of serving the poet as a necessary tool for setting poesies into motion. When "fancy" appears somewhere internally within a poem, however, as it does twice in the perhaps publicly recited "Gods Determinations," the concept usually identifies the imperfect human attempt to construe points of Puritan theology; these imperfect attempts to interpret theological or doctrinal matters without dependence upon the truly regenerate heart (informed by the gift of God's grace) always conclude incorrectly.

In the "Second Ranke Accused," from the "Gods Determinations" series, for example, the poet-minister threatens that those captured by God's justice, the so-called regenerate, may not be regenerate if their hearts are not filled with the "sweet perfume" of God's grace; if such is not the case, "Your Faith's a Phancy," and therefore untrue. In those poems that begin with the concept of the fancy, however, the poet applies it to the initiation of his meditative process. It is Taylor's recognition of the necessary role of the imagination in the writing of exalted verse (in his case, his most impassioned "talks" with God) that most interests today's readers. Of great significance, then, is the fact that the poet identifies the essential role of the imagination in the "Prologue" to the "Preparatory Meditations." Here he describes himself as but a "Crumb of Dust which is design'd/ To make my Pen unto thy Praise alone." Immediately following this exercise in self-deprecation, however, he writes: "And my dull Phancy I would gladly grinde/ Unto an Edge of Zion Precious Stone." At one point in the Second Series meditations, the poet asks God's angels to "Make me a pen thereof that best will write./ Lende me your fancy, and Angellick skill/ To treate this theme, more rich than Rubies bright." Another of the same series opens with this enthusiastic line: "I fain would have a rich, fine Phansy ripe." Finally, the discussion of the Prometheus typology that begins the seventy-ninth meditation of this series establishes that, although the subject of the entire poem is the eros-*agape* theme, the poem's first problem

is to discover the difference between man's myths, which served ancient poets such as Vergil, Catullus, and Ovid for poetic inspiration, and God's Word, which, finally, can alone animate the poetic process of this believer's "Fancy lodg'd in clay."

There can be little doubt, then, that, despite injunctions against the allegedly "evil" fruits of this mental faculty, Taylor the private poet found it a necessary tool for colloquies with his God. A possible explanation for this contradiction between private poet and public minister (who was also author of "Gods Determinations") may be offered by observing that Loyola had prescribed, in his *Spiritual Exercises*, the use of the imagination as requisite to begin the process of meditation. The exercitant must place himself in the proper frame of mind for meditation by picturing to himself events in the life of Christ or biblical history or occurrences in his own life that prompt him to recognize the need for spiritual colloquy. Later in his own century, Baxter appears somewhat to mollify Perkins's attitude toward this mental faculty when he advises, in *The Saints' Everlasting Rest*, that the person engaged in meditation should focus his mental attention on the joys of heaven by getting "the liveliest Picture of them in thy minde that thou canst." At the same time, nevertheless, it should be observed that, in *A Treatise Concerning Religious Affections* (1746), Jonathan Edwards, some seventeen years after Taylor's death, summarily condemns this faculty as that means by which the devil produces evil thoughts in the soul; as the Great Awakener puts it, "it must be only by the imagination that Satan has access to the soul, to tempt and delude it."

Taylor's consistent acknowledgment of the power of the imagination should make him appealing to contemporary students of American literature. At a time when attitudes toward the imagination were, for the most part, hostile (recall Alexander Pope's line from *An Essay on Man*, 1733-1734, "Imagination plies her dang'rous art," II, 143), Taylor identified the concept as a paramount significance to poesies, anticipating Samuel Taylor Coleridge's analysis of imagination in *Biographia Literaria* (1817).

OTHER MAJOR WORKS

NONFICTION: *Christographia*, 1962 (Norman S. Grabo, editor); *Diary*, 1964 (F. Murphy, editor); *Ed-*

ward Taylor's Treatise Concerning the Lord's Supper, 1966 (Grabo, editor).

MISCELLANEOUS: *The Unpublished Writings of Edward Taylor*, 1981 (3 volumes; Thomas M. Davis and Virginia L. Davis, editors).

BIBLIOGRAPHY

Gatta, John. *Gracious Laughter: The Meditative Wit of Edward Taylor*. Columbia: University of Missouri Press, 1989. Gatta is an insightful expositor of Taylor's poetry, citing his "peculiar blend of verbal wit, meditative earnestness, and comic exuberance" as an index of his "singularity as a sacred artist." Gatta has opened up a new avenue of inquiry into Taylor's acknowledged supremacy as a Colonial poet, positing his wit as the bridge between his theology and his poetics. In addition, Gatta's bibliography provides the most comprehensive source of primary and secondary sources available.

Grabo, Norman. *Edward Taylor*. Rev. ed. Boston: Twayne, 1988. This updated version of an earlier biocritical introduction to Taylor's life and work remains the single best source of explication of Taylor's aesthetic and theological influences. Grabo believes Taylor "operates within a mystical tradition without being a mystic," and thus explains how Taylor is able to marry his reasoned Calvinism to an aesthetic imagination to embrace the infinite in words.

Hammond, Jeffrey A. *Edward Taylor: Fifty Years of Scholarship and Criticism*. Columbia, S.C.: Camden House, 1993. Five chapters examine Taylor scholarship in chronological order, from its beginnings to the latter decades of the twentieth century. Bibliography, index.

Keller, Karl. *The Example of Edward Taylor*. Amherst: University of Massachusetts Press, 1975. A groundbreaking biocritical work of Taylor's poetry. Keller argues convincingly that Taylor must be viewed as a Christian humanist and calls for—and achieves—a reevaluation of Taylor as Colonial America's foremost poet and aesthetician.

Miller, David G. *The Word Made Flesh Made Word: The Failure and Redemption of Metaphor in Edward Taylor's "Christographia."* Selinsgrove, Pa.: Sus-

quehanna University Press, 1995. Provides a reading of Taylor's *Christographia* sermon material and a study of the use of metaphorical language in the sermons.

Rowe, Karen E. *Saint and Sinner: Edward Taylor's Typology and the Poetics of Meditation*. Cambridge, England: Cambridge University Press, 1986. Rowe notes, as no other Taylor scholar has previously, the relationship between Puritan typology—its use of Old Testament narratives as a guide to the meaning of the mundane devotional life of Colonial believers—and its role in Taylor's craftsmanship as a poet. Offers appendices that exhaustively examine the relationship between individual Taylor poems and their sources in sermons prepared for congregational consumption. According to Rowe, Taylor sought—and achieved—a transcendent language for expressing the infinite in the finite.

Scheick, William. *The Will and the Word: The Poetry of Edward Taylor*. Athens: University of Georgia Press, 1974. Scheick's primary focus here is on Taylor's "Preparatory Meditations," a close reading and explication of his Lord's Supper poems. His thesis is that Taylor derives his aesthetic vision and his theological virtue from the works of Saint Augustine.

Schuldiner, Michael, ed. *The Tayloring Shop: Essays on the Poetry of Edward Taylor*. Newark: University of Delaware Press, 1997. This collection of critical essays on Taylor's poems provides readers with insights into several traditions of the past that informed Taylor's poetry, from the Puritan concept of nature to Puritan casuistry. Includes bibliographical references and index.

Stanford, Donald. *Edward Taylor*. Minneapolis: University of Minnesota Press, 1965. This early pamphlet in the University of Minnesota series is still an incisive introduction to Taylor's poetics and, in particular, his personal version of Milton's *Paradise Lost*, "God's Determinations." Stanford hits his target consistently and elucidates Taylor's opposition to the heretical view of the Lord's Supper propounded by his Colonial adversary, Richard Henry Stoddard.

John C. Shields;
bibliography updated by the editors

HENRY TAYLOR

Born: Loudon County, Virginia; June 21, 1942

PRINCIPAL POETRY

The Horse Show at Midnight, 1966
Breakings, 1971
An Afternoon of Pocket Billiards, 1975
Desperado, 1979
The Flying Change: Poems, 1985
Understanding Fiction: Poems, 1986-1996, 1996
Brief Candles: 101 Clerihews, 2000

OTHER LITERARY FORMS

Although Henry Taylor is known primarily for his poetry collections, he has also published a number of significant works in other genres. His translations include Euripides' *The Children of Herakles* (1981; with Robert A. Brooks) and Bulgarian poet Vladimir Levchev's *Leaves from the Dry Tree* (1996). *Compulsory Figures: Essays on Recent American Poets*, a collection of critical essays on the works of seventeen twentieth century American poets, was published in 1992.

Taylor has also been active as a literary scholar and critic, having published the text *Poetry: Points of Departure* (1974) and contributed essays, poetry, and translations to various anthologies and journals, including *Contemporary Southern Poetry: An Anthology*, *The Morrow Anthology of Younger American Poets*, *Southern Review*, *Nation*, and *Virginia Quarterly Review*. From 1970 to 1977 he served as a contributing editor for *Hollins Critic* and was poetry editor of *New Virginia Review* in 1989.

ACHIEVEMENTS

Richard Dillard observed in *Hollins Critic* that Henry Taylor's poems have "all the ring and authority of an American Hardy, intensely aware of the darkness that moves around us and in us." Taylor's pronounced sense of irony, combined with a style that tends decidedly toward the formal, distinguishes his poetry from that of many of his contemporaries. His disciplined, introspective style has garnered recognition and praise from a wide array of sources. He was awarded the Witter Bynner Prize for Poetry in 1984 and one of poetry's

highest honors, the Pulitzer Prize, for his 1985 collection *The Flying Change*.

Taylor has also achieved a distinguished record as an academic. A lifelong writing teacher, he has been a member of the faculties of Roanoke College, the University of Utah, and American University, where he was made a professor of literature in 1976.

BIOGRAPHY

Henry Splawn Taylor was born in 1942 in Loudon County, Virginia. His father, Thomas Edward Taylor, was a high school principal and farmer. Henry attended the Loudon County public schools and the George School, then graduated with a B.A. in English from the University of Virginia in 1965. He spent the following year earning an M.A. in creative writing from Hollins College in Roanoke, Virginia.

In 1966 Taylor began an impressive career as an academic and teacher of writing. Between 1966 and 1968 he served as an instructor of English at Roanoke College. From 1968 through 1971 he was an assistant professor of English at the University of Utah, where he directed the University of Utah Writers' Conference. He accepted a position in 1971 as associate professor of literature at Washington D.C.'s American University, where he was promoted to professor in 1976. He has also served as director both of American University's M.F.A. program in creative writing and the university's American Studies program.

ANALYSIS

Two aspects of Taylor's background significantly influence his poetry—his upbringing as a rural farmer and as a Quaker. Born into a largely Quaker community that had already flourished in Loudon County for nearly two centuries, Taylor has infused his poetry with its strong reverence for tradition, charity, and sense of place. From his childhood as a Southern farmer, Taylor has retained a keen sense of the subtle and delicate workings of the natural world. In addition, his work with horses as a young boy has brought his poetry again and again to that animal, which is a totemic image in his work. Equine imagery permeates Taylor's first major books of poetry, *An Afternoon of Pocket Billiards* (1975) and *Desperado* (1979). A horse motif even emblazons the cover of

Henry Taylor (© Sandra Ehrenkranz)

1985's *The Flying Change*, which employs the animal as its central metaphor and has proven to be Taylor's most widely embraced collection, receiving the Pulitzer Prize for poetry in 1986.

Although Henry Taylor's poetry primarily chooses rural settings and themes for its subject matter, it cannot accurately be described as "pastoral." As critic Sharon Hall has observed, Taylor's poems instead expose "the horror and violence of country life as well as its beauty, describing rural life with humor and unflinching realism." This makes them a unique study in contrasts; while they embrace the redemptive qualities of rural living, they remind the reader at every turn that destruction, fatality, and absurdity are less common in country life than they are in urban environments. In this way, Taylor seeks to point out that darkness, mystery, and irony inhabit all corners of the human experience, even its most isolated and bucolic.

"RIDING A ONE-EYED HORSE"

From Taylor's earliest mature collection, *An Afternoon of Pocket Billiards* (1975), "Riding a One-Eyed Horse" epitomizes two of the poet's seminal traits:

equestrian themes and formal structural regularity. Taylor has observed of his own writing, particularly the poems in *An Afternoon of Pocket Billiards*, "I think in terms of analogies to equitation when I'm writing. Nerve and touch, and timing." In "Riding a One-Eyed Horse," the reader comes to know just what he means. A poem of four four-line stanzas, the poem reflects structurally the cadenced rhythm of a well-trained horse's gait, suggesting parallels to Taylor's own belief in the importance of regularity and discipline in poetry.

Thematically, the poem explores an idea common in Taylor's work—the need to impose a sense of order upon even the most chaotic situation. A sort of "how to" tutorial on the seemingly absurd act of training a visually impaired animal to function as a fully sighted one would, the poem suggests metaphorically that meaning may be extracted from, if not imposed upon, even the most absurd of circumstances. The speaker initially remarks of the horse, "One side of his world is always missing," but through an act of determined faith in human will, he is able to summon from the animal an extraordinary effort:

> . . . Do not forget
> to turn his head and let what comes come seen:
> he will jump the fences he has to if you swing
> toward them from the side that he can see

This "side" the animal "can see" represents that part of humans that continually beckons them to reconsider what they may have overlooked, to revisit what they have deemed lost. "Riding a One-Eyed Horse" expresses Taylor's optimism, albeit tinged with an almost rigid sobriety, in the desire to embrace all the possibilities people are routinely encouraged to dismiss.

"BERNARD AND SARAH"

In this poem, also from *An Afternoon of Pocket Billiards*, Taylor seeks to come to grips with an ancestral heritage that seems both vague and tangible at the same time. Even those people who have countless photos and artifacts that link them with their ancestors often have problems connecting with their humanness, with bridging the gap between their world and the past. In "Bernard and Sarah," the speaker is no exception. When presented with a photograph of his "great-great-great-grandparents," taken in an era "when photography was young, and they were not," the speaker and his father are at a loss with what to do with it. The father decides to stow the portrait in a closet, taking it out "only on such occasions as the marriage/ of one of his own children," when he tersely instructs each of them, "I think you ought/ to know the stock you're joining with."

Ironically, the speaker's father feels no stronger connection with this "stock" than his children do. However, gazing into the distant but curiously familiar faces of his progenitors, the speaker develops a relentless compulsion to see what the photograph has to show him. This drive leads to the poem's resolute, confident conclusion, in which the speaker finds himself turning repeatedly to the photograph, which reveals to him important insights into the deepest, most enduring mysteries of family. In his mind's eye, the speaker's ancestors "light up the closet of my brain/ to draw me toward the place I started from,/ and when I have come home, they take me in."

"LANDSCAPE WITH TRACTOR"

Perhaps Taylor's most widely discussed poem, "Landscape with Tractor," the opening poem of *The Flying Change*, has all the trappings of the quintessential Taylor lyric—a rural setting, a tightly regular and disciplined structure, a trained eye for the unexpectedly grotesque. In the poem, a middle-aged male narrator describes the experience of discovering a corpse while mowing a field on a remote part of his farm. Stirred from an otherwise routine, almost meditative chore by this unsettling encounter with mortality, he initially has a difficult time coming to terms with it. From the helm of his oversized "bushhog" mower, he thinks the body is "a clothing-store dummy, for God's sake," and that "People/ will toss all kinds of crap from their cars."

Gradually, however, he realizes that he must "contend with it," by acknowledging that it is the result of some horrifically violent act and notifying the authorities. Later he hears much local gossip and speculation "at the post office" as to how the body got there, but he never learns the real story. This draws the narrator into a round of deep introspection in which he realizes that regardless of how much or little he knows about the actualities of the corpse he has discovered, it has brought to him a more profound, universal message about the inevitability and certitude of his own death. He ominously muses that from this point on he will continue "putting gas in the tractor, keeping down thistles,// and seeing . . ./ . . . the bright yellow skirt,/ black shoes, the thing not quite like a face" and knowing that it will "stay in that field till you die."

"GREEN SPRINGS THE TREE"

Also from *The Flying Change*, "Green Springs the Tree" is one of those rare but poignant Taylor poems that concerns itself more with where family relationships are going rather than where they have been. One of the shortest, but metaphorically rich, poems in the collection, it examines a relationship between a father and his young son. Written from the father's point of view, it describes his fear of the awesome responsibility of ensuring his son's comfort, safety, and survival. The speaker explains that "Most of the time/ I am too far away to break the fall/ that seldom comes," expressing beautifully the exquisite and nearly overwhelming irony that even though humans are pathologically fallible, in many ways parenting demands an almost inhuman perfection. He laments that he prays "for skill in this," a "high wire [his son] will keep/ both of us on" until he one day steps into his own father's shoes.

BRIEF CANDLES: 101 CLERIHEWS

Taylor's 2000 collection *Brief Candles: 101 Clerihews* marks an unexpected and whimsical stylistic departure for Taylor. The slender volume attempts to resurrect a long-forgotten poetic form and explores its playfully sardonic possibilities in a contemporary context. The clerihew, a light verse quatrain written in lines of unspecified length in an *aabb* rhyme scheme, typically concerns the deeds or character of the person named in its opening line. It was invented by British poet Edmund Clerihew Bentley, who popularized it in the early decades of the twentieth century. The clerihew was taken up by some other notable poets, including W. H. Auden and Clifton Fadiman, but was dismissed by the subsequent generation as a limited, even anachronistic form.

However, *Brief Candles* suggests that the clerihew is hardly ready for retirement, particularly considering its possibilities as a vehicle for scathing but good-natured satire. Although never devoid of humor, Taylor's previous poetry was marked by a preoccupation with the ironic, disquieting aspects of human nature; this makes the bulk of his work brooding in tone. However, *Brief*

Candles shows a different side to Taylor, suggesting that he too can poke fun at poetry's often overly self-absorbed elitism. Poems like the following show that no figure is too revered, no poetic cliché too sacred, to elude comic scrutiny:

> Jerry Falwell
> may not think at all well
> but has done some sharp dealing
> with organized feeling.

OTHER MAJOR WORKS

NONFICTION: *Compulsory Figures: Essays on Recent American Poets*, 1992.

TRANSLATIONS: *The Children of Herakles*, 1981 (with Robert A. Brooks; of Euripides' *Hērakleidai*); *Leaves from the Dry Tree*, 1996 (of Vladimir Levchev).

EDITED TEXTS: *Poetry: Points of Departure*, 1974; *The Water of Light: A Miscellany in Honor of Brewster Ghiselin*, 1976.

BIBLIOGRAPHY

Dillard, R. H. W. Review of *The Flying Change*, by Henry Taylor. *Hollins Critic* 23, no. 2 (April, 1986). A close friend and mentor from Taylor's formative Hollins days, Dillard provides a particularly perceptive and personal reading of Taylor's most widely recognized collection, *The Flying Change*. The review focuses on the collection's preoccupation with irony, as well as its penchant for violence. Dillard receives the book enthusiastically, calling it "a coming of age for a poet who has foreseen this moment throughout his work."

Garrett, George. "Henry Taylor." In *Dictionary of Literary Biography: American Poets Since World War II*. Vol. 5, part 2. Edited by Donald J. Greiner. Detroit: Gale Research Company, 1980. An important overview of Taylor's early career. Provides detailed insight into Taylor's methods of composition, particularly in his early books of poetry, *The Horse Show at Midnight*, *Breakings*, and *An Afternoon of Pocket Billiards*. Explores the pronounced sense of formal discipline in these early poems.

Hall, Sharon K., ed. *Contemporary Literary Criticism 44*. Detroit: Gale Research Company, 1986. Pro-vides selections from the major critical responses to Taylor's most widely reviewed book of poetry, 1985's *The Flying Change*. Contains the reactions of several critics, including Daniel L. Guillory, Joseph Parisi, and Reed Whittemore.

Stitt, Peter. "Landscapes and Still Lives." *The New York Times Book Review*, May 4, 1986. Including some of the most poignant remarks made about *The Flying Change*, Stitt's review of the book praises Taylor's "traditional American feeling" and commends the collection as a "solidly written, hauntingly conceived volume."

Gregory D. Horn

SARA TEASDALE

Born: St. Louis, Missouri; August 8, 1884
Died: New York, New York; January 29, 1933

PRINCIPAL POETRY

Sonnets to Duse and Other Poems, 1907
Helen of Troy and Other Poems, 1911
Rivers to the Sea, 1915
Love Songs, 1917
Flame and Shadow, 1920
Dark of the Moon, 1926
Stars To-Night: Verses New and Old for Boys and Girls, 1930
Strange Victory, 1933
The Collected Poems of Sara Teasdale, 1937
Mirror of the Heart: Poems of Sara Teasdale, 1984

OTHER LITERARY FORMS

Sara Teasdale attempted drama in a one-act play, *On the Tower* (1911), which appeared in *Helen of Troy and Other Poems*. She began a biography of Christina Rossetti, her favorite woman poet, in 1931, but never completed it. Finally, Teasdale edited two anthologies: *The Answering Voice: One Hundred Love Lyrics by Women* (1917) and *Rainbow Gold: Poems Old and New Selected for Boys and Girls* (1922).

ACHIEVEMENTS

Sara Teasdale is remembered as a lyric poet. She was one of the most widely read poets in America in the years before her death in 1933. Her later collections, *Flame and Shadow, Dark of the Moon,* and *Strange Victory* are considered her best. Her collection *Love Songs* went through five editions in 1917, and she was awarded a five-hundred-dollar prize, the forerunner of the Pulitzer Prize, by Columbia University.

BIOGRAPHY

A line of Sara Teasdale's poetry aptly describes her early life: "I was the flower amid a toiling world." Teasdale grew up in a sheltered atmosphere of reading, painting, and music, and literary interests became a large part of her life at an early age. Because of her frail health, she had fewer activities than the average child and was doted upon by her middle-aged, wealthy parents. She was the youngest of four children of Mary Elizabeth Willard and John Warren Teasdale.

Teasdale's family, Puritanical and devout, embraced the ideals of a New England education brought to St. Louis, Missouri, by T. S. Eliot's grandfather, the Reverend William Greenleaf Eliot, who founded the Mary Institute for girls. Born in St. Louis, she attended the Mary Institute and later Hosman Hall, from 1898 to 1903, and the intellectual and social influence of these schools was strong. She did translations of Heinrich Heine, her first poetic influence, and she began writing poetry as a schoolgirl. Her contributions to the *Wheel*, a monthly magazine published by herself and her friends, the "Potters," 1904-1907, just after high school, revealed her early talent for lyrics, songs, and sonnets.

Teasdale had a gift for friendship. She formed strong and lasting friendships with some of the most interesting writers of her generation, many of them living in St. Louis, which in the late nineteenth and early twentieth centuries was an intellectual hub. Her friends among fellow-poets included John Myers O'Hara, John Wheelock, Orrick Johns, Amy Lowell, Joyce Kilmer, and Vachel Lindsay. Her friendships with women were strong and she remained close to some of the "Potters," including Grace and Willamina Parish, Caroline Risque, and Vine Colby, as well as having special friendships with Marion Cummings, Marguerite Wilkinson, and

Sara Teasdale (© Underwood and Underwood/Corbis)

Margaret Conklin. The latter was a young woman whom she met at the Connecticut College for Women who was a faithful companion at the end of her life.

Teasdale will be remembered as the woman who rebuffed Vachel Lindsay's offer of marriage. To Lindsay, Teasdale was a "jewel-girl" and he immortalized his love for her in his poem "The Chinese Nightingale." Teasdale, though fond of Lindsay and cherishing their friendship, had quite a different "angle" on life. Lindsay was usually penniless, full of vitality and energy, a man of the soil in life and in his poetry; Teasdale was used to a life of luxury, easily sapped of energy, and desirous of seclusion. She married a man of her own class and background who would take care of her; she and Ernst Filsinger, an expert on international trade, were married on December 14, 1914, and the early years of their marriage were happy. They lived in New York City, which Teasdale captured in several of her poems in *Helen of Troy and Other Poems* and *Rivers to the Sea.*

In the late 1920's, Teasdale decided to leave her husband because of his constant traveling and preoccupation with business. She took a painful trip to Reno and secured a divorce while Filsinger was in South America. After that, she became more and more reclusive and her health worsened. Like Alice James, she renounced full participation in life, using her ill-health as a weapon. She began a biography of Christina Rossetti in 1931 but was not able to complete it. Greatly affected by her friend Marguerite Wilkinson's drowning, her divorce from Filsinger, and Lindsay's suicide in 1931, and suffering from the aftereffects of an attack of pneumonia, Teasdale was found submerged in a bathtub, dead from an overdose of barbiturates, in New York City, in 1933.

ANALYSIS

Sara Teasdale is distinguished as a lyric poet who evokes moods related to romantic love, the beauty of nature, and death. The substance of much of her early poetry is longing and dreams, and the image of the fantasy lover is virtually omnipresent: a lover who is elusive and disembodied, like the male figures in the work of the lonely Emily Brontë.

RESTRAINT AND RENUNCIATION

A major theme, a concomitant of the fantasy lover image in Teasdale's poetry, is delight in restraint and renunciation, "the kiss ungiven and long desired." This delight in restraint has its origins in four strands of Teasdale's life and reading that interweave in her poetry: the Romantic tradition of John Keats, Percy Bysshe Shelley, A. C. Swinburne, and, later, Christina Rossetti; her devout Puritan background; her ill-health, which separated her from full participation in life and led her to imagine rather than to participate in experience; and the role of women in the early twentieth century. This delight in the unattainable is evident in her early poems, such as "The Look," one of her most widely reprinted poems: "Strephon's kiss was lost in jest,/ Robins's lost in play/ But the kiss in Colin's eyes/ Haunts me night and day." Though long an admirer of Eleonora Duse, it is said that when she had the opportunity actually to see Duse dance, she chose not to. It was very typical of Teasdale; the *idea* of Duse's art was enough for her.

This theme of renunciation in her life and poetry is related to her religious background. Though religious sentiment was never overtly expressed in her poetry, she followed a strict moral code all her life. Her official biographer, Margaret Haley Carpenter, notes that Teasdale was never tempted to enter the bohemian lifestyle of some of her contemporaries even though Teasdale herself noted that the Puritan and the pagan warred within her. She remained a sensitive, shy, orderly, restrained woman throughout her life, and this reticence is reflected in her poetry. Except for "kisses," "looks," and "voices," the physical body is not present in her poetry, even though much of it deals with romantic love.

In the experience of nature, unlike the experience of love, there is a sense of Teasdale's presence and participation. Her joy in the beauty of nature, particularly the sea and the stars, is embodied in many of her most successful poems. Her early poems reveal this delight—not quite the animal "appetite" found in William Wordsworth, but a direct and simple emotion that continues to charm the reader. Her nature poems are like gem-cut lockets holding precious snippets of experience; not surprisingly, they were intriguing to the Japanese, who have translated many of them. She, in turn, loved the *idea* of Japan and said of Japanese writing, "When I look at those vertical lines, they remind me of wisteria blooms."

THE LATER POETRY

In her later poetry, *Flame and Shadow*, *Dark of the Moon*, and *Strange Victory*, however, the beauty and simplicity of nature turn into a kind of terror related to death, as in "The Sea Wind":

> In the dead of night when the sky is deep
> The wind comes awaking me out of sleep—
> Why does it always bring to me
> The far-off, terrible call of the sea?

The death of Teasdale's mother and her older brother, George, in 1924, transformed her perspective and a new somberness and awareness of death entered her poetry. Her later verse expresses the attitude, ripened toward the end of her life, of one who is self-sufficient and possesses one's soul in silence, as in "The Solitary":

> My heart has grown rich with the passing of years,
>   I have less need now than when I was young
> To share myself with every comer
>   Or shape my thoughts into words with my tongue.

Teasdale's use of simple, unaffected language, easily accessible to readers, together with her interest in presenting the feminine experience of love, links her with her contemporaries. In her anthology *The Answering Voice: One Hundred Love Lyrics by Women*, she notes that sincere love poems by women are rare in England and America in the nineteenth century; in making her selections, she "avoided poems in which the poet dramatized a man's feelings rather than her own." Although the modern reader may feel that Teasdale's fantasy lovers, her denial of the body, and her frail romantic moods do not go far enough in representing the subtleties and complexities of women's relationships with men, she must be acknowledged to be a woman who found her voice.

OTHER MAJOR WORKS

PLAY: *On the Tower*, pb. 1911 (with *Helen of Troy*).

EDITED TEXTS: *The Answering Voice: One Hundred Love Lyrics by Women*, 1917; *Rainbow Gold: Poems Old and New Selected for Boys and Girls*, 1922.

BIBLIOGRAPHY

Carpenter, Margaret Haley. *Sara Teasdale: A Biography*. New York: Schulte, 1960. An excellent, lengthy, and detailed biographical source. Eleven chapters are devoted to Teasdale's life, one chapter to her ancestry and early influences, and another to her work. Supplemented by a select bibliography and an index.

Drake, William. *Sara Teasdale: Woman and Poet*. San Francisco: Harper & Row, 1979. The definitive biographical source on Teasdale. Drake has done meticulous research and makes many valuable insights into Teasdale's life and work. Complemented by notes and an index.

_____. "Sara Teasdale's Quiet Rebellion Against the Midwest." *The Bulletin—Missouri Historical Society Bulletin* 36 (July, 1980): 221-227. A very interesting discussion of selected poems in terms of a negative Midwest cultural influence. Thought-provoking, though limited in scope.

Larsen, Jeanne. "Lowell, Teasdale, Wylie, Millay, and Bogan." In *The Columbia History of American Po-*

etry, edited by Jay Parini and Brett C. Millier. New York: Columbia University Press, 1993. A biographical and critical study of Teasdale and her American contemporaries.

Monroe, Harriet. *A Poet's Life*. New York: Macmillan, 1938. A useful survey of Teasdale's life and work by a close friend. It contains many fascinating recollections and is easy to read. Monroe makes frequent perceptive comments on Teasdale's poetic achievements. The work is useful primarily for anecdotal and biographical information. Supplemented by an index and a bibliography.

Schoen, Carol B. *Sara Teasdale*. Boston: Twayne, 1986. A fine, detailed, concise analysis of much of Teasdale's poetry, focusing on important themes and topics. Contains much specific discussion of Teasdale's poetry and biographical material that supplements the analysis. Includes a chronology, notes and references, a select bibliography, and an index.

Patricia Ondek Laurence;
bibliography updated by the editors

ALFRED, LORD TENNYSON

Born: Somersby, England; August 6, 1809
Died: Near Haslemere, England; October 6, 1892

PRINCIPAL POETRY

Poems by Two Brothers, 1827 (with Charles Tennyson and Frederick Tennyson)
Poems, Chiefly Lyrical, 1830
Poems, 1832, imprinted 1833
Poems, 1842
The Princess, 1847
In Memoriam, 1850
Maud and Other Poems, 1855
Idylls of the King, 1859-1885
Enoch Arden and Other Poems, 1864
The Holy Grail and Other Poems, 1869, imprinted 1870
Gareth and Lynette, 1872
The Lover's Tale, 1879

Ballads and Other Poems, 1880
Tiresias and Other Poems, 1885
Locksley Hall Sixty Years After, Etc., 1886
Demeter and Other Poems, 1889
The Death of Œnone and Other Poems, 1892

OTHER LITERARY FORMS

Although Alfred, Lord Tennyson, is best known to-day for his poetry, he wrote several dramatic works that were popular in his own day. His first play, *Queen Mary*, was published in 1875. From that time until his death he continued writing verse dramas: *Harold* (1876), *The Falcon* (1879), *The Cup* (1881), *Becket* (wr. 1879, pb. 1884), and *The Foresters* (wr. 1881, pr., pb. 1892). Most of these were staged very successfully. The renowned producer and actor Henry Irving starred opposite Ellen Terry in *The Cup*, which ran for more than 130 nights. Irving also produced *Becket* several times after Tennyson's death, achieving success in both England and America. Generally speaking, however, his contemporaries' judgment that Tennyson was a greater poet than a dramatist has been confirmed by modern critics. Tennyson's only prose composition was also a play, *The Promise of May* (1882); it was not well received by theatergoers. Although he published no criticism in his lifetime, Tennyson, like most of his contemporaries, expressed his critical opinions of his own and others' works in his conversations and in numerous letters. Hallam Tennyson's two-volume *Alfred, Lord Tennyson: A Memoir* (1897) of his father prints many of these documents, and preserves as well many of Tennyson's conversations and remarks about literature.

ACHIEVEMENTS

During his lifetime Alfred, Lord Tennyson, attracted a popular following seldom achieved by any poet in any age. While his first four volumes received little favorable attention, the publication of *In Memoriam* in 1850 brought him overnight fame, and his subsequent works were all best-sellers. His Victorian contemporaries liked all forms of his poetry: More than sixty thousand copies of *In Memoriam* were sold in the first few months after publication; ten thousand copies of the Arthurian tales titled *Idylls of the King* sold in the first week after publication in 1859, and the remainder of the first edition

shortly thereafter; and the first edition, sixty thousand copies, of his volume of narrative poems and lyrics, *Enoch Arden and Other Poems* sold out shortly after it was published. His popularity continued until his death; twenty thousand copies of *Demeter and Other Poems* were sold before publication. Readers found in Tennyson's poetry excitement, sentiment, and moral solace; his works were a lighthouse in a stormy sea of social and moral uncertainty. Many turned to Tennyson as a teacher, seeing in his works a wisdom not available in churches, schools, or public institutions.

Perhaps because he was so popular in his own day, Tennyson became the primary target for scores of critics of the two generations that followed. Critics of the post-World War I era condemned Tennyson for pandering to public demands that poetry be "uplifting," that it contain a moral for public consumption, and that it avoid controversial subjects. During the years between the World Wars, it became fashionable to speak of "the two Tennysons"; critics condemned the public poet who

Alfred, Lord Tennyson (Library of Congress)

preached jingoism and offered moral platitudes in works such as *Maud and Other Poems* and *Idylls of the King*, yet found much of value in the private poet, a morbid, introverted person whose achievement lay in his lyrics, with their private symbolism developed to express personal anxieties and frustrations.

Critics writing since World War II have generally been more appreciative of the entire canon of Tennyson's poetry. Following the lead of Sir Charles Tennyson, whose sympathetic yet scholarly biography of his grandfather rekindled interest in Tennyson as a serious poet both in his public and private roles, scholars have reexamined *In Memoriam, Idylls of the King, The Princess*, and *Maud and Other Poems* and found them to be works of considerable artistic merit. "Ulysses" is regarded as a significant short poem; *Idylls of the King* has been called one of the truly great long poems of the language; and *In Memoriam* is considered one of the world's great elegies.

BIOGRAPHY

Alfred Tennyson was born at Somersby in the Lincolnshire district of England on August 6, 1809, the fourth of twelve children. His father, the Reverend George Tennyson, was a brooding, melancholic man, whose lifelong bitterness—inspired by his having been disinherited in favor of a younger brother—manifested itself in his behavior toward his family. Alfred was spared much of his father's wrath, however, because George Tennyson apparently recognized his fourth son's special brilliance and took pains to tutor him in history, science, and literature. Tennyson spent five years at Louth Grammar School (1815-1820), then returned home to continue his studies under his father's personal guidance.

Tennyson began writing poetry at an early age; at eight he was imitating James Thomson, at twelve he was writing romances in the manner of Sir Walter Scott. In 1827, the year he entered Trinity College, Cambridge, he and his brother Charles published *Poems by Two Brothers*.

At Cambridge, Tennyson was an undisciplined student. He was well received by his fellow students, however, and in 1829 he was elected a member of the Apostles, a club devoted to intellectual inquiry. Through this association he met Arthur Henry Hallam, who was to figure prominently in his life. In 1829, Tennyson won the Chancellor's medal for his poem "Timbuctoo," and in 1830 he published *Poems, Chiefly Lyrical*. In March 1831, George Tennyson died, and shortly afterward Tennyson left Cambridge without a degree.

Tennyson's 1832 volume, *Poems*, like his earlier one, was treated rather roughly by reviewers. Their comments, coupled with the death of Hallam in 1833, caused him to avoid publication for ten years. Hallam's death was an especially severe blow to Tennyson. Hallam had been engaged to Tennyson's sister, and the two men had become very close friends. The poet suffered prolonged fits of depression after receiving the news of Hallam's death. Eventually, however, he was able to transform his grief into a series of lyrics which he published in 1850, titling the elegy *In Memoriam A. H. H.*

During the years between Hallam's death and the publication of *In Memoriam*, Tennyson was far from inactive. He lived with his mother and other members of his family, assisting in their moves from Somersby to Tunbridge Wells, then to Boxley. During these years he spent time in London, Cornwall, Ireland, and Switzerland, gathering material for his poems. In 1834, he fell in love with Rosa Baring, and when that relationship cooled, he lighted upon Emily Sellwood, whose sister had married his brother Charles. Tennyson had no real means of supporting a family at that time, so he was forced to wait fourteen years to marry. He returned to publishing in 1842, issuing a two-volume set titled simply *Poems*; it contained both new materials and revisions of previously published poems. In 1847, he published *The Princess*, a long narrative exploring the roles of men and women in modern society.

Months after *In Memoriam* appeared in May 1850, Tennyson's fortunes rose meteorically. In June of that year he married Emily Sellwood. In November, he was named poet laureate, succeeding the recently deceased Wordsworth. During his forty-two years as laureate, he wrote numerous poems commemorating various public events, among them some of his more famous works, including "Ode on the Death of the Duke of Wellington" (1852) and "The Charge of the Light Brigade" (1854). He came to be lionized by the British public, and even the Royal Family made numerous personal requests for him to commemorate events of importance.

The decade of the 1850's was a productive and important one. In 1855 Tennyson published *Maud and Other Poems*; in 1859 he brought out a volume containing the first four Arthurian stories that would be joined by eight others during the next twenty-five years to form *Idylls of the King*.

The Tennysons' first child was stillborn, but in 1852 Hallam Tennyson was born. The family moved to Farringford on the Isle of Wight in 1853. The following year a second son, Lionel, was born.

The remainder of Tennyson's life can be characterized as personally stable but artistically tumultuous. During the 1860's, 1870's, and 1880's, several collections of his poems were issued. The poet added eight new volumes to his growing list of works. Beginning in the mid-1870's, Tennyson turned to drama, writing several successful plays and taking great interest in the details of their production. In 1886 his son Lionel died while returning from India. His elder son, Hallam, remained with the poet, serving as a kind of secretary and executor. In the early months of 1892, Tennyson's health began to fail, and he died in bed in October of that year, his hand resting on a volume of Shakespeare.

ANALYSIS

Always praised for his ability to create musical lyrics, Alfred, Lord Tennyson, is now recognized as a master of a number of verse forms and a thinker who brooded deeply over the problems of his age, attempting to capture these problems and deal with them in his poetry. He is also credited with being one of the few poets whose works demonstrate a real assimilation of the poetic tradition that preceded him. His poems reflect an insight into the crises of his own age, as well as an appreciation of problems that have faced all men, especially the problems of death, loss, and nostalgic yearning for a more stable world.

Early works such as "The Palace of Art" and "The Two Voices" are clear examples of the kind of poem for which Tennyson traditionally has been acclaimed. In each, the poet presents a sensitive person who faces a crisis and is forced to choose between radical alternatives. In "The Palace of Art," the speaker must choose

between self-indulgence in a world of artistic beauty and commitment to a life of service; in "The Two Voices," the speaker's choice is either to escape the harsh realities of an oppressive world through suicide, or to continue living with only the faintest glimmer of hope.

"THE LOTOS-EATERS"

Tennyson's highly regarded classical poem "The Lotos-Eaters" explores similar themes to "The Palace of Art" and "The Two Voices." For his subject, the poet drew on the incident in the *Odyssey* (c. 800 B.C.E.) in which Odysseus's men disembark in the paradisiacal land of the lotus-eaters and fall under the enchantment of the lotus fruit. The poem is also influenced by Edmund Spenser's *The Faerie Queene* (1590, 1596), where the figure of Despair argues for the same kind of languid repose that the mariners sing of in "The Lotos-Eaters." Tennyson uses all his powers of description and his special command of the language to select words and phrases whose tonal qualities and connotative meanings strongly suggest the sense of repose and stasis. The musical quality of the poem is enhanced by the meter, the effectiveness of caesura and enjambment, and the varying line lengths used throughout, especially the extensive use of long lines broken by numerous caesuras near the end of the lyric. "The Lotos-Eaters," a combination of narrative and choric song, describes the arrival of the mariners in a land that appears to be perpetually "afternoon," where "all things always seemed the same." Here the "wild-eyed melancholy Lotos-eaters" bring to the travelers the food that will dull their desire to continue on to Ithaca. Having partaken of the fruit of the lotus, the mariners begin to think of their homeland as merely a dream, too distant a goal, no longer worth striving for. As they lie on the beach, one suggests that they "return no more," and the others quickly take up the chant; their choric song, in eight sections, makes up the remainder of the poem. In the song, the mariners review the many hardships they have faced and the many more that await them if they continue their journey. About them they see that "all things have rest"; they ask "Why should we toil alone?" Rather than continue, they beg to be given "long rest or death, dark death, or dreamful ease." The poem's final statement is an exhortation to "rest, ye brother mariners, we will not wander more." It is unwise, however, to assume that the mariners' decision to opt for "dreamful ease" over a life of "toil" is Tennyson's own position. Rather, "The Lotos-Eaters" explores, from only one perspective, the dilemma of commitment versus retreat. The poet treats the same theme in many other poems in which the speaker takes a decidedly different view.

"ULYSSES"

Tennyson's complex treatment of this theme of commitment to ideals can be seen in one of his most famous shorter works, "Ulysses." This poem also exemplifies numerous other characteristics common to much of Tennyson's poetry, particularly his use of irony. Indeed, in "Ulysses" the reader can see the glimmerings of the essentially ironic poetic form that emerged during the nineteenth century, made popular by Robert Browning—the dramatic monologue. "Ulysses" is a poem inspired by Tennyson's personal experiences; yet in the poem Tennyson transforms his experiences into a work of art that speaks of an issue that concerns all people. In "Ulysses," Tennyson is both typically Victorian and still a poet for all times. The call to action at the end of the poem and the emphasis on each man's "work" was no doubt appealing to the poet's contemporaries. In the twentieth century, under the scrutiny of critics more aware of the subtleties of Tennyson's ironic vision, the poem provides pleasure for its refusal to yield to a simplistic reading.

In "Ulysses" the reader discovers how Tennyson uses the poetic tradition, especially the legacy of classical and Renaissance poets. Like "The Lotos-Eaters," "Ulysses" is based in part on Homer's *Odyssey*. The classical epic is not the only source, however, for by the poet's own admission the poem owes much to the portrait of Ulysses in Dante's *Inferno*. In Dante's poem, Ulysses is found in hell, condemned as a deceiver for having led his men away from Ithaca in search of vain glories. That Tennyson chose to draw his own hero from sources that present such radically different views of Ulysses suggests that he wanted to create an ironic tension in his own work. In the *Inferno*, Ulysses tells Dante that, unable to remain at home, he was compelled by wanderlust to set forth in search of new adventures. The spirit of Homer's unconquerable quester is captured in Tennyson's poem, but Dante's condemned spirit is always there to remind the reader that there may be dangers in pursuing the ideal at the expense of other considerations.

When one first reads "Ulysses" one can easily be swept along by the apparent vigor of the hero's argument. His description of life in his native Ithaca, where he is "matched with an aged wife," forced to "meet and dole/ Unequal laws" in a land whose people he regards as "savage," makes it easy for the reader to understand Ulysses' wish to return to a life of seafaring adventure. Among these people, Ulysses is not appreciated for the adventures that have caused him to "become a name" throughout the Mediterranean world. His experiences have become absorbed into the very fiber of his being; he reflects that "I am a part of all that I have met." Small wonder that the confines of his island home seem to imprison him! He realizes that his many exploits are only doorways to future experiences, an "arch" beyond which "gleams/ That untravelled world" he has yet to see. At home he finds himself becoming "dull," like a weapon left to "rust unburnished."

Realizing that he can no longer be happy as ruler in such a land, Ulysses declares that he will leave his "sceptre and the isle" to his son Telemachus, a man more capable and more patient than his father when operating in the "sphere/ Of common duties." Ulysses recognizes that he and his son are different—"He works his work, I mine"—and it is best for all if each man follow his own destiny. This difference is easy for the modern reader to accept, as it suggests a truism about human nature that those imbued with the Romantic desire for self-fulfillment find immediately palatable.

Having passed on his kingship to his son, Ulysses turns to the companions who have "toiled, and wrought, and thought" with him, and calls them to one last voyage. As night draws near, he urges them to embark once more in the ship that will carry them to lands where "some work of noble note, may yet be done." "'Tis not too late," he exhorts them, "to seek a newer world." His purpose is to "sail beyond the sunset" until he dies. The unextinguishable spirit of adventure, burning still in the heart of this old warrior, is summed up best in the closing lines, where he proclaims to those who accompany him that, although they are no longer young, they can still be men of "heroic hearts," "strong in will,/ To strive, to seek, to find, and not to yield."

Because the poem was composed shortly after the death of Tennyson's friend Arthur Henry Hallam, some critics have seen "Ulysses" as a statement of the poet's personal commitment to continue living and writing even after suffering a great personal tragedy that seemed to have robbed life of its meaning. Looking at himself as an old man who had been deprived of the spark of adventure and facing a fast-approaching death of his creative self, Tennyson chose to continue living and working. Only through an active commitment to life itself could he hope one day to see "the great Achilles," here meant to represent Hallam. Such a biographical interpretation is supported by Tennyson's comment, preserved in Hallam Tennyson's *Alfred, Lord Tennyson: A Memoir*, that "Ulysses" expressed his "feeling about the need of going forward, and braving the struggle of life" after Hallam's death.

The biographical interpretation can be supported in part by a close reading of the text. The resounding note of optimism, at least on the surface of the poem, is apparent. All of the images associated with life on the isle of Ithaca suggest dullness, a kind of death-in-life. Tennyson displays his mastery of the single line in his withering description of the people of Ithaca; ten monosyllables capture the essence of those whom Ulysses has come to despise: They "hoard, and sleep, and feed, and know not me." Here is avarice, indolence, a suggestion of animal satisfaction with physical ease, and, most important, a lack of appreciation for the man who has raised himself from the multitude and won fame through bravery, cleverness, and other distinctly human qualities. Similarly, Tennyson has Ulysses describe the life of wandering and the yearning for further adventures in most appealing terms, both sensual and intellectual. Ulysses is a "hungry heart"; he wishes to "drink/ Life to the less," having previously "drunk delight of battle with my peers." In a single phrase borrowed from Homer, Tennyson's Ulysses recalls the great struggle in which he first won fame, far away from home on the "ringing plains of windy Troy." The excitement of battle serves as a counterpoint to the dullness of life in Ithaca. The hero's excitement is captured in his final exhortation, in which the poet once again resorts to a line of monosyllables that bombard the reader in staccato fashion: "To strive, to seek, to find, and not to yield." Active verbs call the mariners to action and the reader to acceptance of the hero's decision.

Despite the stirring note of optimism in this final line, however, the poem cannot be accepted simply as another example of strident Victorian rhetoric aimed at encouraging one to have faith in oneself and one's God and press on in the face of uncertainties. In fact, when the uncertainties in the poem are considered carefully, the reader begins to see another side of the aged hero. Ulysses is certain of his boredom with having to govern the "savage race" and of the resentment he harbors toward them because they fail to honor him for his past exploits. What Ulysses will substitute for his present life, and what good he will accomplish in leaving Ithaca, is not at all clear. Some notable work "may yet be done," but he cannot be certain that his new wanderings will lead to anything but death: "It may be that the gulfs will wash us down," he cautions. Of course, he and his mariners may "touch the Happy Isles" where they will be reunited with "the great Achilles," but the chance of such a reunion is at best tenuous. In fact, such a desire implies a kind of death wish, since Achilles has departed this life for Elysium.

One may sympathize with Ulysses, seeing that his present life is unfulfilling, and agree that pursuing tenuous goals is better than stagnating. At this point, though, one must recall that the dreary condition on Ithaca is not related by the poet as factual, but rather is described by Ulysses himself. Since the poem is dramatic in nature, only the hero's own word provides a touchstone for judging things as they really are, and it is possible that Ulysses' view is jaundiced. One must consider, too, that Tennyson draws not only from Homer but also from Dante for his portrait of Ulysses; the Dantean quality of the hero cannot be overlooked, and in the *Inferno* Ulysses is found in hell, having led his mariners to their doom. In the version of the *Inferno* that Tennyson probably read, that by H. F. Cary (1805), Ulysses tells Dante that no familial feelings could overcome the "zeal" he had to explore the world, a feeling that he calls "man's evil and his virtue." Tennyson's Ulysses may also be a victim of this curse and blessing. Despite his pronounced enthusiasm for a life of heroic adventure, Ulysses may in fact merely be running away from his responsibilities. If the reader recalls from the *Odyssey* the hero's struggles to return to his wife and son, Ulysses' behavior in Tennyson's poem must appear a little suspect. The beloved and faithful Penelope is now scorned as an "aged wife." Telemachus, although praised for his sagacity and patience, is still not of the heroic mold.

A word of caution is in order here. In the past, critics have been quick to call Ulysses' description of his son a thinly disguised piece of sarcasm, but this reading smuggles twentieth century notions into a nineteenth century context. Words such as "blameless" and "decent" were not terms of disapprobation in the nineteenth century, nor would Tennyson have been denigrating Telemachus by pointing out that he worked best in the sphere of "common duties." In fact, in his other poetry and in the writings preserved in Hallam Tennyson's *Alfred, Lord Tennyson: A Memoir*, Tennyson clearly had great respect for men and women who served society at the expense of personal gratification. Precisely because the duties that Ulysses turns over to Telemachus are ones that Tennyson and his contemporaries considered important for the continuation of ordered society, Ulysses' decision to abdicate them makes his motives questionable. It is at least possible to see that behind the hero's rhetoric lies a clever scheme to convince his listeners, and the reader, that his actions are motivated by the highest intentions, when in fact he is abandoning a job he finds distasteful and difficult in order to pursue a lifestyle he finds more gratifying. Such a possibility makes it difficult to see Ulysses as a hero; rather, he appears to be an irresponsible villain for whom Tennyson and the critical reader can have little sympathy. That Tennyson would have held such a man in low regard is evident from his own remarks; as recorded in Hallam Tennyson's *Alfred, Lord Tennyson: A Memoir*, he once told a young aspirant to university life that a man "should embark on his career in the spirit of selfless and adventurous heroism and should develop his true self by not shirking responsibility."

In the light of this ambiguity, it is easy to construe Ulysses' real decision as an affirmation not of life but of death, and to see his desire to journey forth again as a kind of death-wish. Whether one adopts such a reading depends largely on the way one views the tone of the final segments of the poem, in which Ulysses states publicly his reasons for undertaking such a voyage. If this

public harangue is merely a rhetorical pose intended to win over skeptical followers so that they will man the hero's ship on this futile journey, then "Ulysses" is a poem of deceit and despair, a warning to the reader of the hypnotic power of such rhetoric to sway listeners into a mood of naïve optimism. On the other hand, if one is convinced of the hero's sincerity in his call to strive, seek, find, and not yield, one cannot help considering "Ulysses" another of the many poems in which Tennyson offers hope and support to his fellow Victorians, tempering such optimism with the notion that one can never be absolutely certain whether the journey through life will lead to paradise or merely to death, adrift on an angry sea.

The dilemma may never be solved satisfactorily, for in "Ulysses," Tennyson is experimenting with a relatively new poetic form, the dramatic monologue, in which ambiguity and ironic distance are characteristic. Although "Ulysses" does not possess all the formal qualities of the dramatic monologue, it does contain the essentials. Situation and action are inferred only from the speech of the main character, and the reader's assessment of motives rests on his estimation of the character of the speaker. The hero's exhortation is intended not only to be heard by his fellow mariners but also to be overheard by the reader; one feels compelled to judge the merits of the hero's philosophy. What one brings to the poem—knowledge of the *Odyssey* or *The Divine Comedy*, or of Tennyson's life—may help to determine whether one should accept or reject Ulysses' call. In any case, the act of choosing demanded by the poem forces one to make a moral commitment of some kind. The need for making such judgments, and the complexities involved in making them, are matters which concern Tennyson in all of his poetry. The ambiguity of the poem is intentional, reflecting the dilemmas faced in the real world by Tennyson and his readers.

THE PRINCESS

The same concerns that one finds in Tennyson's shorter compositions, such as "Ulysses," are also reflected in the poet's longer works. Tennyson wrote four long poems: *The Princess*, *In Memoriam*, *Maud*, and *Idylls of the King*. None of these is typical of traditional narrative poetry, and in several ways they anticipate the long poems of the twentieth century. All four are fragmented in some way; none tells a single story from a consistent perspective. *The Princess* is the most tightly constructed of Tennyson's long poems. In this medley a group of seven young men and women each create part of a tale about a princess who has removed herself from the world of men to establish a college for women. Princess Ida and the prince who comes to "rescue" her and win her love are the products not of a single creator but of seven, as each young person participating in the game adds to both story line and character development. As a result, the poem is actually two stories—that of the princess whose tale is created by the young people, and that of the young people who are themselves very like the characters they create. Throughout the poem songs are interspersed to serve as counterpoint to the narrative and to highlight major themes.

MAUD AND IDYLLS OF THE KING

Maud is also a medley. Here, however, the variation is in the verse form, and the fragmentary structure mirrors the nature of the hero, a man poised on the edge of disaster and dementia.

Idylls of the King, Tennyson's Arthurian poem, consists of twelve separate pieces tied together by the overarching structure provided by the legend itself—the rise and fall of Arthur and his Round Table. Within this framework, individual idylls remain relatively self-contained units. The poet's examination of the downfall of a society that abandons its ideals is carried forward through an intricate patterning of repeated images and parallel scenes.

IN MEMORIAM

Tennyson's most fragmented long poem is the one for which he is best remembered and most praised. *In Memoriam* is a collection of more than 130 lyrics, composed by the poet over seventeen years and finally pieced together to record his reaction to the death of his dearest friend. Rather than being a continuous narrative, *In Memoriam* is a loosely assembled collage that, when read as a whole, reflects the varied emotions that one man experiences when prompted by the death of a loved one to face the reality of death and change in the world and the possibilities for life after death. Like "Ulysses," the poem is inspired by Tennyson's personal grief, yet it uses this personal experience as a touchstone for examining an issue that plagued all men of his era: human-

ity's ability to cling to faith in God and an afterlife in the face of the challenges of the new science.

The "I" of *In Memoriam* is not always to be identified with the poet himself; rather, as Tennyson himself said, the speaker is sometimes "the voice of the human race speaking thro' him [that is, the poet]." Nine years before Darwin published *Origin of Species*, Tennyson was questioning the value of the individual human life in the light of scientific discoveries proving that whole species of animals that once roamed the earth had long ago become extinct. In the much-anthologized middle section of *In Memoriam*, Tennyson's narrator observes of nature, "So careful of the type she seems,/ So careless of the single life," only to cry despairingly in the next lyric,

> "So careful of the type?" but no.
> From scarpéd cliff and quarried stone
> She cries, "A thousand types are gone:
> I care for nothing, all shall go."

Here is the "Nature, red in tooth and claw" that men of Tennyson's age, nurtured on faith in a benevolent God, found impossible to comprehend.

Tennyson sees his personal dilemma over the loss of Hallam and the larger problem involving the conflict between the biblical account of creation and scientific discoveries as essentially similar. The speaker of *In Memoriam* passes through several emotional stages: from grief and despair over his loss; to doubt, which presumes that all is not lost in death; to hope, based not solely on blind trust but also on "intuition," man's sense that a higher person exists to guide his life and the life of nature itself; to, finally, faith, an acceptance of the notion of immortality and permanence even in the face of changes in nature that the speaker cannot deny. In the poem, Tennyson's friend Hallam becomes a symbol of a "higher Race," a harbinger of a better life, one sent to earth ahead of his time to offer hope to all men that the changes and impermanences of life exhibit not chaos but rather a divine pattern of progress, a movement toward God himself. In terms that anticipate the twentieth century theologian and mystic, Pierre Teilhard de Chardin, Tennyson concludes his elegy with a tribute to his friend who appeared on earth "ere the times were ripe," and who now lives with the beneficent God who guides this process of evolution, "who ever lives and loves,/ One

God, one law, one element,/ And one far-off divine event,/ To which the whole creation moves."

The note of optimism at the end of *In Memoriam* is achieved only after a great deal of agonizing doubt. In fact, T. S. Eliot believed that the strength of Tennyson's elegy lay not in its final affirmation of faith, but rather in the quality of its doubt. The fragmentary nature of the poem allows Tennyson to explore that doubt with much greater range and intensity than would a more typical narrative structure. For example, Section LX begins with two lines that refer directly to the speaker's grief over his lost friend: "He past; a soul of nobler tone:/ My spirit loved and loves him yet." The remaining fourteen lines, however, are an extended simile, in which the speaker compares his grief to the feelings of a young girl for a boy who is above her in social status. The girl's "heart is set/ On one whose rank exceeds her own." Seeing the young man "mixing with his proper sphere," and recognizing "the baseness of her lot," the girl experiences jealousy, without knowing what she should be jealous of, and envy of those who are fortunate enough to be near her beloved. She goes about her life in the "little village" that "looks forlorn" to her, feeling that her days are "narrow" as she performs her common household chores in "that dark house where she was born." From her friends she receives no pity (they "tease her" daily), and she is left alone at night to realize the impossibility of ever achieving the union she desires: "How vain am I," she weeps, "How should he love a thing so low?"

The link to the larger themes of the poem, the speaker's grief over the loss of his friend, is found most obviously in the lyric's opening lines. Once that link is established, the parallels between the feelings of the speaker and the young girl he describes in the remaining lines become apparent at numerous points. The different "spheres" in which the girl and her beloved live represent the difference the speaker sees between himself and his friend, whom he calls elsewhere the "herald of a higher race." The "little village" is the speaker's world, into which the dead friend will no longer come. The most important image used to link this lyric with the other sections of *In Memoriam* is the "dark house" in which the girl must pass her days. That image, first appearing in Section VII when the speaker stands before his friend's house in London shortly after learning that

his friend has died, recurs in several other sections and always suggests the loss the speaker feels at his friend's death.

Section LX, then, is typical of many lyrics that Tennyson pieced together to form *In Memoriam*. In it, the speaker's grief, inexpressible in its magnitude, is made realizable by comparison with feelings that immediately touch the reader. One develops a sense of the speaker's loss, and his friend's greatness, through the process of empathetic association with more familiar feelings of loss and pain experienced in the sphere of everyday life. Similarly, when the speaker begins to understand that the loss of his friend should not be cause for despair, but rather for joy, that joy is transmitted to the reader by associating the speaker's feelings with traditional symbols of happiness—the three Christmas seasons that form important structural links within *In Memoriam* and the wedding celebration that closes the poem. The celebration of the wedding is a most appropriate close for this poem: the union of two lives to form a single unit from which new life will spring mirrors man's ultimate union with God, "To which the whole creation moves."

OTHER MAJOR WORKS

PLAYS: *Queen Mary*, pb. 1875; *Harold*, pb. 1876; *Becket*, wr. 1879, pb. 1884; *The Falcon*, pr. 1879 (one act); *The Cup*, pr. 1881; *The Foresters*, wr. 1881, pr., pb. 1892; *The Promise of May*, pr. 1882; *The Devil and the Lady*, pb. 1930 (unfinished).

NONFICTION: *The Letters of Alfred Lord Tennyson: Volume 1, 1821-1850*, 1981 (Cecil Y. Lang and Edgar F. Shannon, editors); *The Letters of Alfred Lord Tennyson: Volume 2, 1851-1870*, 1987 (Lang and Shannon, editors); *The Letters of Alfred Lord Tennyson: Volume 3, 1871-1892*, 1990 (Lang and Shannon, editors).

MISCELLANEOUS: *The Works of Tennyson*, 1907-1908 (9 volumes; Hallam, Lord Tennyson, editor).

BIBLIOGRAPHY

Buckley, Jerome Hamilton. *Tennyson: The Growth of a Poet.* Cambridge, Mass.: Harvard University Press, 1961. The first major favorable treatment of the poet following decades of disparagement, organized as a critical biography. Buckley examines Tennyson's growing awareness of his vocation as a poet and provides a critical assessment of all the major poetry. This is the first study to make extensive use of unpublished manuscripts; it is especially valuable for its discussion of Tennyson's major Arthurian poem, *Idylls of the King*.

Culler, A. Dwight. *The Poetry of Tennyson*. New Haven, Conn.: Yale University Press, 1977. A comprehensive examination of Tennyson's poetic corpus, focusing on ways the poet exemplifies Victorian concerns, especially those dealing with the notion of apocalypse. Culler avoids biographical criticism, opting instead to show how the poet mirrors his age. The discussion of earlier poems and of some of those not normally given serious attention (such as the English idylls and the civic poems) is particularly valuable.

Hair, Donald S. *Domestic and Heroic in Tennyson's Poetry*. Toronto: University of Toronto Press, 1981. Hair explores a central concern of all Tennyson's poetry: the importance of the family as a center of values. In examining the major poems and several minor pieces, Hair shows how heroic qualities emerge from domestic situations and are linked to domestic values. The final section on *Idylls of the King* provides an extended discussion of Tennyson's method of elevating domestic values to heroic status.

Jordan, Elaine. *Alfred Tennyson*. Cambridge, England: Cambridge University Press, 1988. Jordan devotes individual chapters to the English idylls, the dramatic monologues, and the major poems (*The Princess*, *In Memoriam*, *Maud*, and *Idylls of the King*) to illustrate her thesis that Tennyson was intensely interested in gender issues and was ambivalent regarding the validity of patriarchal methods of governing society.

Martin, Robert Bernard. *Tennyson: The Unquiet Heart*. New York: Oxford University Press, 1980. This critical biography attempts to get behind the public mask created by the poet and his family in order to explore the psychological tensions out of which Tennyson's greatest poetry came. Includes important supplementary material on the Tennyson family and an excellent select bibliography.

Shaw, W. David. *Alfred Lord Tennyson: The Poet in an Age of Theory*. New York: Twayne, 1996. An intro-

ductory biography and critical study of selected works by Tennyson. Includes bibliographical references and index.

Tucker, Herbert F. *Tennyson and the Doom of Romanticism*. Cambridge, Mass.: Harvard University Press, 1988. Focusing on the poems written during the first half of the poet's career, Tucker traces the influence of the poetic tradition, especially the Romantic poets, on Tennyson before he became his country's laureate and in the years immediately following his rise to fame after the publication of *In Memoriam*. Contains an exceptionally good bibliography.

Tucker, Herbert F., ed. *Critical Essays on Alfred Lord Tennyson*. New York: G. K. Hall, 1993. A collection of critical essays dealing with Tennyson's life and work. Includes bibliographical references and index.

Laurence W. Mazzeno;
bibliography updated by the editors

THEOCRITUS

Born: Syracuse, Sicily; c. 308 B.C.E.
Died: Syracuse, Sicily; c. 260 B.C.E.

PRINCIPAL POETRY

The *Idylls* is the name customarily given to a collection of about thirty poems of various types by Theocritus, eight of which are no longer considered authentic. In addition to these, some twenty-six epigrams in the *Greek Anthology* (C.E. 980, printed 1606) appear under the name of Theocritus or are elsewhere attributed to him. Both are relatively modern groupings, the first dating from a 1566 collection, the second from the early tenth century. These are derived from unknown earlier collections. The *Idylls* was first published in English in 1684. It is not known whether Theocritus published his poems in collected form.

OTHER LITERARY FORMS

As an adherent to the Callimachean belief in short, polished poetic forms, Theocritus probably did not attempt epic, dramatic, or didactic poetry—though a late reference work, the *Suda* (tenth century), does mention two supposedly large works or collections, *The Heroines* and *The Daughters of Proetus*, known only by their titles.

ACHIEVEMENTS

Although Theocritus wrote in a variety of forms—pastorals, erotic lyrics, mimes, hymns, encomia, miniature epics, and epigrams—he is best known in the history of literature as the creator of pastoral poetry, which was to become, according to author Gilbert Lawall, "the most sophisticated and artificial literary tradition in Western Europe." It has been argued that Theocritus himself produced and published a collection of his rustic poems which established his identity and reputation as a pastoral poet, but there is no external evidence for such a collection. Rather than a fixed formula, the pastoral idyll was for Theocritus a loosely defined species of sketch set in the central or eastern Mediterranean countryside and peopled by herdsmen with a fondness for poetry and music. Love motifs are common in these rustic landscapes, as are recitations of poetry made up by herdsmen for some small occasion such as a casual singing match. It was for Vergil, writing nearly 250 years later, to add layers of sentiment and allegory to Theocritus's semirealistic and self-contained country scenes, and it was largely through Vergil that Theocritus made his mark on European letters. Elements of the pastoral appeared here and there in earlier Greek literature: musical or poetic herdsmen in Homer and Hesiod, a lament for Daphnis in Stesichorus, rustic settings in Euripides and even in Plato's *Phaedrus* (c. 370 B.C.E.), mime in the works of Sophron and Epicharmus in the fifth century B.C.E., and the prominence of erotic motifs in much late classical poetry, drama, and fiction. It is hard, in fact, to assess the originality of Theocritean pastoral because so much of what was written in the fourth century B.C.E. has been lost, but it was early claimed and has never been disproved that Theocritus was the one who brought the elements of the pastoral or bucolic idyll together in a definitive way.

Theocritus's pastoral poems share with the other idylls a distinctive, pungent realism that gives his vignettes a flavor of authenticity, as if the reader were witnessing actual scenes of Hellenistic country and city

Theocritus (Hulton Archive)

life. The effect is achieved in part by Theocritus's use of a Doric dialect like that of his native Sicily, chosen partly for its phonetic qualities, but also, no doubt, because it bypassed the literary Attic, Ionic, and Aeolian usages, which were associated in his readers' minds with earlier Greek poetry. The realistic effect is also the result of his preference for everyday characters belonging to the lower social and economic ranks. A mythical King Oedipus or Medea could be representative of the human condition to a classical (or neoclassical) theater audience, but neither could be as typical as the Alexandrian housewives in Idyll 15 or as real as the Coan peasant-poets in Idyll 7. Theocritus's achievement is therefore not confined to the creation of pastoral poetry. Of the twenty-two idylls attributable to him, only eight are pastoral, and no more than a half dozen of his twenty-six epigrams are rustic. The balance of his poems survived, one must suppose, because they are vivid and credible epiphanies of the Hellenistic world which Theocritus inhabited. Granted, Theocritus's realism is not as literal as it is made to seem: His Doric

Greek is an artificial patois drawn from a variety of dialects within the Dorian family, and his fictions are too artfully concocted to be real slices of rustic or urban life—this is the paradox of all literary realism. It is a more striking paradox that the creator of the genre which was to become the most artificial in European belles lettres should also have been one of the first great masters of literary realism.

BIOGRAPHY

Little is known with certainty about the life of Theocritus. Born in or near Syracuse not long before the beginning of the third century B.C.E., he traveled as a young man to the Aegean island of Cos. The reasons for this sojourn are unknown. Family connections may have provided an initial foothold there, but the existence of a kind of medical center and school outside the city of Cos, the Asclepieion, where his friend Nicias was a student, could have been the main attraction for him. A detailed knowledge of eastern Mediterranean plant life in the *Idylls* suggests that Theocritus made a special study of botany in that age when plants were the chief source of medication. Another possible motive was the community of poets around Philetas, a distinguished scholar and poet who had been the tutor of the Egyptian monarch Ptolemy Philadelphus. Idyll 7, "The Harvest Festival," is a lightly disguised tribute to this group, of which Theocritus counts himself a member under the alias Simichidas. The idea of a herdsman-poet may have evolved from a self-sufficient commune headed by Philetas, dedicated to the pursuit of writing in a setting which (like Epicurus's famous garden in Athens) insulated its members from the distractions of city life. From this perspective, the combination of goatherding and poetry would have been a sensible expedient rather than the affectation it became in later ages.

It was probably on Cos that Theocritus had his first success as the creator of a new style of poetry, the pastoral. He was noticed in Alexandria, and at some point, no doubt with the encouragement of his mentor Philetas, Theocritus sought the patronage of the royal court. Idyll 16 is evidence of an earlier unsuccessful bid for the patronage of Hiero II of Syracuse; with Ptolemy, Theocritus was apparently more successful, as his praises of the Egyptian monarch in Idylls 14 and 17 suggest. It was during the reign of Ptolemy II Philadelphus (285-246 B.C.E.) that Theocritus lived in Alexandria, some time between 278 B.C.E. and the summer of 270 B.C.E. The nature and extent of his contact with Callimachus and Apollonius Rhodius is uncertain, but it was fruitful, and together the three became the leading poets of the Hellenistic Age, placing an "Alexandrian" stamp on literary tastes for the two and a half centuries culminating with Vergil, Horace, and Ovid. Ptolemy himself promoted science and scholarship in Alexandria by establishing the museum and library in the royal quarter and gathering under his patronage one of the most remarkable assemblages of talent in history. In this most cosmopolitan of all settings, far from the fields of Cos, Theocritus was in the company not only of gifted literary contemporaries, but of Archimedes (a fellow Syracusan) and the geometer Euclid as well—and also enjoyed access to the largest library ever assembled to that date. Already famous for his pastoral poetry, Theocritus turned here to court poetry, *epyllia* (miniature epics), and mimes which dramatized the lives of ordinary city people. Nothing is known about the time or circumstances of Theocritus's death; if he died, as most authorities guess, some ten years after his latest datable poem, his lifetime spans approximately the four golden decades of Hellenistic poetry (300-260 B.C.E.), which he did as much as any other to shape.

ANALYSIS

From the range of poetic types which Theocritus essayed, this analysis will concentrate on the three most typical: the pastoral idylls (numbers 1, 3, 4, 5, 6, 7, 11), the mimes (numbers 2, 10, 14, 15), and the *epyllia* (numbers 13, 22, 24). Except for the epigrams, which are mostly in the elegiac couplets customary for fictive inscriptions in the Hellenistic Age, Theocritus's poems are set in the same dactylic hexameter that Homer used. In English, they are called "idylls," a somewhat misleading generic term suggesting peace, tranquillity, and an Arcadian pleasantness—associations relevant only to the pastoral idylls. Even the Greek *eidullion* was not Theocritus's word; a diminutive of *eidos* (form), it means something like "little form," or "short separate poem." It is sometimes explained as meaning "little picture"; although Theocritean poetry is not especially pictorial, the poet did excel in drawing vignettes, and vivid presentation is a special Theocritean talent.

The pastoral, or bucolic (from *boukolos*, "cowherder"), idylls arc not written in accordance with strict rules; consequently, idylls 4 and 10 may or may not be considered strictly pastoral, the former because it has no song recited within it, the latter because the singers are agricultural workers, not herdsmen. In any case, the herdsman-poet is the hallmark of the genre, and some kind of poetic recitation usually occurs in the course of the poem. Exceptions are sometimes called rustic mimes, in accordance with the convention that poetry set in the country is not pastoral without the herdsman-poet and the song within the song. An early ancestor of pastoral song may be the Linos song performed in the vineyard on the shield of Achilles in book 18 of the *Iliad* (c. 800 B.C.E.). Closer to the literary beginnings of pastoral is the legendary Sicilian cowherd-poet Daphnis, whose death on the slopes of Mt. Etna is the subject of Thyrsis's song in Idyll 1. Another source of pastoral is the singing matches observed in ancient and modern times in Sicily, southern Italy, and Greece. It is still sometimes said, on the weakest of evidence, that pastoral has ritual origins connected with a Sicilian cult of Daphnis, but such speculations have little to do with what Theocritus wrote.

The rustic setting on which pastoral depends has moral overtones even in Theocritus, although they were given more explicit emphasis by Vergil and his successors. Theocritean shepherds do not moralize on the superiority of country to city life, but they are creatures of instinct whose fluency in describing their restful surroundings gave rise to a literary topos: the *locus amoenus*, or pleasant spot, where a spreading tree provides shelter from the noonday sun, cicadas chirp in the background, cool waters babble nearby, and grasses offer a natural couch in the shade. The locale is otherwise left to the reader's imagination; Vergil placed his shepherds in Arcadia for its remoteness from Italy, but in Theocritus the *locus amoenus* could be anywhere in the eastern Mediterranean: Idylls 4 and 5 are in southern Italy, Idyll 7 on Cos, the rest unspecified. Unlike earlier Greek poetry, which was addressed to a particular *polis* and therefore specific as to location, Theocritean pasto-

ral is addressed to the *oikoumenē*, or civilized world in general, and downplays the specifics of place. Pastoral is an escape to any rustic spot where the sun shines, trees make shade, and shepherds sing. The timelessness of Theocritus's themes and situations also contributes to pastoral's escapism. Like the pleasant spots where they loaf, his shepherds belong to any generation or century; unlike their urban counterparts, they are in no hurry, having nowhere to go and nothing to do but watch their herds and sing about love.

Eros was a favorite Hellenistic topic, being both timeless and apolitical, and in Theocritus it is the chief disturber of the midsummer calm. Even love is toned down, however, to reduce its potential for tragedy or pathos. Daphnis dies because of love in Idyll 1 but, the reader is never told exactly how or why, and the whole business is only a shepherd's prize poem, not a first-hand narrative. The goatherd's serenade to Amaryllis in Idyll 3 paints the lover's country pathos in quaint rather than tragic colors, so that his threats of suicide are no more believable than his warning that the wolves will eat him. The one-eyed Polyphemus's love for the sea nymph Galatea in idylls 6 and 11 is comic for the same reasons. The carnality in idylls 4 and 5 is no more than a whiff of goatishness to liven up a scene. The love stories in Idyll 7 come naturally to the singers, who seem not at all involved in the tales they tell of unrequited love (pastoral love is always unrequited); it is only a song. Love ripples the serenity of pastoral life from time to time, but it never makes waves.

In Theocritean pastoral, therefore, very little happens and nothing of much consequence is discussed. Its characters are unreflective, its actions involve no crisis and little tension, nor does the larger world of change, cities, wars, or politics intrude. In fact, most of the concerns that may be said to lie at the core of literature seem to be excluded from the Theocritean version of pastoral. Its underlying mythos, as Charles Segal has noted, is "a return to origins, to childhood, to simplicity, and to clarity of feeling." Unlike (for example) much prose fiction of the American South in which a similar return is suggested, the Theocritean return contains few deep reverberations. Theocritus turns his back on the goings-on and the interests of his time: the passion for learning shared by his contemporaries Callimachus, Apollonius

Rhodius, Herondas, and others; the life of the great Hellenistic courts and the intrigues of their kings; the emotionalism of much Hellenistic poetry and art, the cosmopolitanism of the Hellenistic cities, and the expanding ethical horizons of the age in which he lived—all are forgotten in the quiet simplicity of the pastoral idylls. Recent scholarship has shown it to be a poetry of subtlety and some complexity, but it is a poetry which avoids depth of meaning. In one respect alone, it can be said that Theocritus brought his readers into contact with the serious thinking of his time. Both Stoic and Epicurean philosophies held that the highest truths lie in the rhythms of nature and the basic instincts common to men and animals. By leading the way to a pastoral life of nature and instincts, Theocritus dramatized a simpler and perhaps better world for his citified readers. Pastoral is therefore essentially an urban form, and Theocritus's initial success as a poet probably came from an urban audience's vicarious participation in that simpler world.

The line between pastoral and mime is not easy to draw, because all pastoral is also mime—that is, a dramatized scene with one or more characters, emphasizing character in a single situation rather than action in a plot. Pastoral mime typically brings two herdsmen together in a situation which elicits song. Sometimes—in the beginning of Idyll 1 and throughout Idyll 5—the speech is amoebean, with the second speaker trying to cap the verses of his rival. In idylls 6, 7, and 10, the singing contest takes the form of one song from each of two performers, a modification of the folk contests which must have influenced Theocritus in his creation of pastoral. In this perspective, both pastoral and mime are sketches from life, imaginary conversations done into verse and a made-up Doric dialect.

IDYLLS 2 AND 15

Idyll 2 is a dramatic monologue, but there is nothing pastoral about it, nothing of the male bucolic world in which women are mentioned only as objects of love's unhappy passion. Here, for the first and only time in Theocritus, a single woman is the speaker, and the reader sees through her eyes Theocritus's favorite theme: love's unhappiness. The comic stage had begun in the previous generation to present love stories with happy endings, but romantic love was not yet a cultural attitude, and when Hellenistic poets wrote of love, it was more often than not in the tradition of destructive passion; it was the same tradition which produced the tragedy of Dido in the *Aeneid* (29-19 B.C.E.). In Idyll 2, the woman in love is Simaetha, recently struck with a sudden passion for Delphis, a young playboy, as he was walking back from the gymnasium. In his careless way, he has made love to her and gone on to other conquests, leaving her the victim of an aroused passion. As Steven Walker has recently shown, however, Simaetha is not the victim of a male seducer. As her own account of the encounter with Delphis reveals, she is the one who suffered love at first sight and took all the initiative, to the point of pushing him down on her bed. Now she is given another traditionally male role to play—that of the forlorn lover—as she calls upon the feminine powers of darkness, Selene, Hecate, Aphrodite, and Artemis, to make her lover return or to hurt him if he refuses. For all this, she is a figure of pity; her nighttime monologue, punctuated by the refrains of her spells to bind a lost lover, could well be Theocritus's masterpiece. It is an evocative and realistic portrayal of a woman in a state of passionate obsession, representative of the interest which Hellenistic poets shared in this subject.

Another Theocritean masterpiece, Idyll 15, also looks to the life of women, but in a lighter vein. Gorgo and Praxinoa are two young matrons from Syracuse who are living in Alexandria. Here, Theocritus's interest is not in a woman's crisis, but in the ordinary life of lively but unsophisticated women. The occasion is the autumn festival of Adonis, the lover of Aphrodite whose death symbolized the annual withering of vegetation. Queen Arsinoe has opened the Ptolemaic palace for a public viewing of the artworks created for the occasion: the dead or dying Adonis represented in a tapestry, a couch with figures of Adonis and Aphrodite embracing, and an impressive array of surrounding adornments. The two ladies take this opportunity for time out from their domestic routine, and the reader overhears their conversation as they meet at Praxinoa's house, walk through the streets of Alexandria, and marvel at the display before them in the palace. The scenes of everyday life include a singer performing an "Adonis" song, which Walker calls "a deliberately parodistic example of Alexandrian kitsch." The whole is a tour de force of representation. The matrons are contemptuous of their husbands and sharp-tongued when jostled in the crowd, but Theocritus's intent is not entirely malicious, and the reader gets a persuasive view of a subject which other Greek poets chose to ignore: "a page torn fresh out of the book of human life," as Matthew Arnold called it.

IDYLLS 10 AND 14

Idylls 10 and 14 are skits of the male world, the first representing two hardworking reapers (not the idle herdsmen of the pastoral idylls) who exchange songs. The lovesick Bucaeus sings a clumsy ode to a skinny, sun-blackened girl named Bombyca (after the pipes she plays for the field hands), and the pragmatic Milon answers with a brace of Hesiodic couplets of advice to the farmer which sound as if they came from some ancient farmer's almanac. The characters who converse in Idyll 14 are also men, but through their conversation the reader gets a glimpse of a woman, Cynisca, who has left the lovesick Aeschinas for a gentler boyfriend after he has beaten her up in a jealous rage. Thyonichus advises his friend to enter the service of Ptolemy as a mercenary to forget his troubles. Both mimes are humorous commentaries, the one on a lover's blindness to his girl's plainness, the other on a quick-tempered lover's inability to treat decently a mistress he finds it so hard to do without.

IDYLLS 13, 22, AND 24

One important difference between Theocritus's pastoral and his mimes is that the latter present their subjects in low mimetic style, with a characteristic capacity for irony, humor, and parody, while the pastorals temper those features with a lyricism in the presentation of pastoral life. The *epyllion*, or "little epic," was a Hellenistic attempt to revive characters and stories of a high mimetic form in an age when the epic was becoming obsolete. Callimachus wrote a homey interlude in the exploits of Theseus in the *Hecale* (third century B.C.E.), of which some fragments still survive. Theocritus's "Hylas" (Idyll 13) shows Heracles distraught over the loss of his young companion, taken by the nymphs of a pool where he had come for water during the expedition of the Argonauts. The point of this short narrative, addressed to the poet's friend Nicias, is that although love can upset the stoutest heart, man—like Heracles in this story—must eventually return to his tasks. The episode

also appears in the *Argonautica* (third century B.C.E.) of Theocritus's contemporary Apollonius Rhodius, perhaps written before this version. Theocritus's poem has been much admired. It is the subject of a well-known Victorian painting by J. W. Waterhouse, *Hylas and the Nymphs*, and Alfred, Lord Tennyson, was so moved by Theocritus's poem that he is said to have exclaimed, "I should be content to die if I had written anything equal to this!" Idyll 22, "The Dioscuri," describes in its first part an episode in the *Argonautica* involving a boxing match between Polydeuces and Amycus; the second part, describing a duel between Castor and Lynceus, is a pastiche of Homeric formulae from the *Iliad* and does its author little credit. "Little Heracles" is the title of Idyll 24, apparently composed for a contest. It is a reworking of Pindar's first Nemean ode (fourth century B.C.E.), in which the story is told of how the infant Heracles killed the snakes sent by Hera to devour him. The poem's movement from the heroic to the domestic follows a Hellenistic tendency to domesticate epic themes, and Heracles' emergence as what anthologizer Anna Rist calls "a Hellenistic gentleman, complete with all proper accomplishments" is a reminder that the royal house of Ptolemy, Theocritus's patron, claimed descent from Heracles.

Theocritus was a major writer in a period that produced no great literature. It is of little use to disparage his work as lacking in profundity, because it was subtlety and polish rather than scope and depth that the poets of the age prized. He was Hellenism's keenest observer of men and women; he expanded the vision of the age with his choice of subjects, his lyric powers, and his detailed representations. Finally, his pastoral myth has provoked the imaginations of great poets for more than two millennia.

BIBLIOGRAPHY

Burton, Joan B. *Theocritus's Urban Mimes: Mobility, Gender, and Patronage*. Berkeley: University of California Press, 1995. Burton presents sophisticated readings of Theocritus's urban mimes. Unlike Theocritus's bucolic poems, which focus on the male experience, all of his urban mimes represent women in more central and powerful roles, reflecting the growing visibility of Greek women at the time.

Haber, Judith. *Pastoral and the Poetics of Self-Contradiction.* New York: Cambridge University Press, 1994. A review of the origins and development of the pastoral tradition, with an especially acute focus on the criticism and interpretations of Theocritus over the centuries.

Halperin, David. *Before Pastoral: Theocritus and Ancient Tradition of Bucolic Poetry.* New Haven: Yale University Press, 1983. A reexamination of Theocritus's place as the originator of the pastoral poetry genre in Western literature. Halperin credits him with far more originality and considerably greater influence than previous critics.

Hubbard, Thomas. *Pipes of Pan.* Ann Arbor: University of Michigan Press, 1998. A review of the pastoral tradition from ancient Greece to the European Renaissance, with special attention being paid to Theocritus as the originator and prime exponent of the genre.

Hunter, Richard. "Commentary." In *Theocritus: "Idylls," a Selection.* New York: Cambridge University Press, 1999. Provides both an excellent selection of Theocritus's verse and good background to his themes, including city and town life, pastoral poetry, and the artistic world of the ancient Mediterranean.

_____. *Theocritus and the Archaeology of Greek Poetry.* New York: Cambridge University Press, 1996. An interesting study of the historical and literary context of the Greek archaic age from which Theocritus's poems emerged. The focus is more on the hymns, mimes, and erotic poems of Theocritus rather than his more frequently studied pastorals.

Segal, Charles. *Poetry and Myth in Ancient Pastoral: Essays on Theocritus and Virgil.* Princeton, N.J.: Princeton University Press, 1981. A critical study of the works of Theocritus and Virgil. Includes bibliographical references and index.

Walker, Steven F. *Theocritus.* Boston: Twayne Publishers, 1980. A study providing a solid introduction and background to the author, his world, and his works.

Zimmerman, Clayton. *The Pastoral Narcissus: A Study of the First Idyll of Theocritus.* Lanham, Md.: Rowman and Littlefield, 1994. Uses information from the fields of linguistics, philosophy, history, and archaeology to link Theocritus's poem on Narcissus to the visual arts in the Hellenistic period. Sheds new light on the subject, especially in terms of what pastoral poetry meant for the period.

Daniel H. Garrison;
bibliography updated by Michael Witkoski

THEOGNIS

Born: Megara(?), Greece; c. seventh century B.C.E.
Died: Megara(?), Greece; c. sixth century B.C.E.

PRINCIPAL POETRY

Theognidea, seventh or sixth century B.C.E.
The Elegies of Theognis and Other Elegies Included in the Theognidean Sylloge, 1910

OTHER LITERARY FORMS

Theognis is remembered only for his poetry.

ACHIEVEMENTS

The words of Theognis the Megarian transcend their age, occasion, and audience. Although his images, assumptions, and advice were based on an archaic value system, much of what he wrote still has currency today. Theognis predicted the universal acceptance and immortality of his poetry. Time has proved him an accurate seer. After all, poverty is still painful; youth is still fleeting; ships of state are still capsized; true friends are few.

BIOGRAPHY

Verses 22 and 23 of the *Theognidea* assert that they are "the words of Theognis the Megarian, known by name among all men." This assertion provides most of the available information about him. No ancient biography survives, and perhaps none ever existed. The dates and even the place of his origin are disputed. Because Plato makes him a citizen of the Megara in Sicily, this view has had its adherents; most often, however, he is associated with Megara on the Isthmus of Corinth, near Athens.

The few historical allusions in the *Theognidea* span a period from the seventh to the fifth century B.C.E. Passages that seem to anticipate a tyranny at Megara were presumably composed before the actual tyranny of Theagenes, which perhaps began about 630; the threat from the Medes in verses 764 and 775 should be the invasion of Xerxes in 480. Some medieval sources place the floruit of Theognis between 552 and 541 B.C.E. The tenth century lexicon, the *Suda*, gives the fifty-ninth Olympiad, 544 to 541, as his floruit. The dates of 544 to 541 and the 630's have gained the most favor. Passages which seem earlier and later than the chosen floruit are explained as anonymous compositions included before about 300 B.C.E. among the genuine poems of Theognis.

Verses 19 to 23 of the passages cited above invite this kind of speculation. Theognis claims to put a *sphregis*, or seal, upon his words so that it would be obvious if they were stolen. This *sphregis* is commonly assumed to be the name of Kyrnos, a youth to whom these verses are addressed. Accordingly, the name Kyrnos or his patronymic, Polupaides, in a poem identifies it as genuinely by Theognis. Thus, of almost fourteen hundred verses attributed to Theognis, about one-fourth are usually considered genuine, with Theognis's name attached to the whole because of the predominance and prominence of the Kyrnos poems.

A radically different view sees the name of Theognis as generic, traditionally associated with Megarian gnomological elegiac poetry. From this perspective, the chronological range of the poetry has no significance; the poetry was composed over time. The *sphregis* becomes the message of the poetry, the traditional code of behavior for the aristocracy.

ANALYSIS

Named after Theognis, the *Theognidea* is a collection of elegiac poetry addressed to aristocratic audiences of archaic Greece. The poems are paraenetic and didactic; that is, they seek to give counsel and to teach. One ancient name for the collection is *Gnomology*, a compilation of gnomic statements or maxims. Theognis's favorite terms, "the good" and "the bad," originally had connotations relating to birth, status, and politics; nevertheless, they are not tied down by names, events, or places. Because his advice was adaptable to time and circumstances, he spoke to "the good" everywhere.

Many of Theognis's observations are now so familiar as to seem clichés. Most were traditional wisdom even for the poet: There is no place like home; youth is fleeting; poverty is painful. On the other hand, some seem fresh. For example, the increasingly widespread phenomenon of coined money made an impact on Theognis's poetry. Not found in Homer and Hesiod are such derivative images as Theognis's counterfeit friend and need for a touchstone to test purity of character, images which were developed by Plato and others.

Theognis is often cited for confirmation or quibbling in the works of ancient and medieval authors. The poems of the *Theognidea*, however, were transmitted through medieval manuscripts rather than from scattered citations, as was the case with most archaic elegiac, iambic, and melic poetry. The perceived usefulness of the counsel undoubtedly contributed to its survival.

STRUCTURE OF THE THEOGNIDEA

The *Theognidea* is divided into two books of unequal length. In *Studies in Greek Elegy and Iambus*, Martin L. West concludes that the division was made about 900 C.E. The second book contains fewer than two hundred verses, concerned with various aspects of pederasty. These verses had originally been scattered throughout the collection. The theme of pederasty is consonant with other preoccupations of the *Theognidea*: status and wealth, the faithfulness of friends, moderation and excess. The author of the elegies upholds the mores and privileges of the aristocracy against encroachment by an increasingly aggressive "middle class."

Most of the poems consist of one or two couplets. Two of the longer passages, 19 to 38 and 237 to 254, bound a core admitted by all to be genuine. The former begins with Kyrnos's name, identifies Theognis as author, and introduces the problem of the seal. Within the core passage, the poet declares his intentions:

> Being well-disposed to you, I shall advise you, Kurnos,
>   on such things as I myself learned
> from the good when I was a youth.
> Be wise; amass neither honors nor glories nor wealth at
>   a price of either shameful or
> unjust deeds.

Just know these things: do not associate with bad men,
   but keep yourself always with the
good.
Drink and eat beside them; sit with them and please
   them; their power is great.
For from the noble you will learn noble things, but if
   you mix with the bad, you will lose
even the sense you now have.
Learn these things and associate with the good; at some
   time you will say that I give good
counsel to my friends.

In verses 237 to 254, the poet claims to have given Kyrnos immortality. Kyrnos will be present at every banquet and feast, in poems sung to the accompaniment of an oboe. The immortality of Kyrnos assumes the immortality of Theognis's poetry through its being sung at banquets and feasts—that is, at symposia. As the symposium was an institution of the leisure class, so the poetry passes on the values of this class. The good and noble are the aristocrats; the bad are those with unimpressive pedigrees, whose wealth requires that they be noticed. The poet cannot deny this notice, but it is hostile and scornful.

THE SKOLIA

As Plato's *Symposium* (c. fourth century B.C.E.) suggests, after the consumption of food and along with the consumption of wine, demonstrations of cleverness contributed to the entertainment on such occasions. The poems of the *Theognidea* agree in tone and content with the drinking songs, or *skolia*, collected in the *Deipnosophists* (second century C.E.; learned men at dinner) of Athenaeus. Some are riddles; some make observations on the symposium itself: A man who chatters all the time is a nuisance and is invited only by necessity. A guest should not be forced to go home or forced to stay. One who drinks too much also talks too much and makes a fool of himself. He who has drunk very much but is still sensible is unsurpassed. A symposium is pleasant when everything is said in the open and there are no quarrels. When drunk, the wise and foolish are indistinguishable. Wine shows the mind of a man. At a banquet, it is good for one to sit beside a wise man and to go home having learned something. Drink when people drink; when sad, drink so no one will know. Many are friends over food and drink, but few can be relied on in a serious matter.

FRIENDSHIP

The task of distinguishing true friends from false requires the versatility of Odysseus. The poet adjures his heart to cultivate a changeful character, to be like his companion, to have the temperament of the octopus, which looks like the rock to which it clings. The poet frequently advises testing a friend before trusting him in a serious matter. The antitheses of tongue and deed and tongue and thought are marked; men love deceit. Kyrnos should, therefore, speak as if he were a friend to all but become involved with no one in anything serious. A man who says one thing and thinks another cannot be a good friend. Some friends are counterfeit; the poet longs for a touchstone. Blessed is he who dies before having to test his friends.

Theognis's apparent pessimism concerning friendship is part of a more general pessimism typical of archaic poetry. In the *Iliad* (c. 800 B.C.E.), a generation of men is like a generation of leaves. The best possibility for man is a mixture of good and evil. Theognis says that the best thing for those on Earth is not to be born; for one born, it is best to die as quickly as possible. Death is preferable to oppressive poverty, and poverty forces men into wickedness. Wealth confers honor; wealth and poverty should be distributed according to personal worth, but they are not. Divine favor gives money even to one completely worthless; few have virtue.

MODERATION

Since wealth does not belong only to the good, it cannot carry a completely positive valence. The wealth of wicked men who lack sound judgment and are unjust leads to excess, to hubris. Examination of the passages in which hubris appears reveals that in the diction of the *Theognidea*, the context of hubris is always, although not always overtly, political. The greatest danger of hubris is that it causes the destruction of cities. For private gain, the bad give unjust judgments and injure the people; from hubris comes factionalism, internecine killings, and tyrants. On the other hand, the gods give political moderation, *gnome*, as the best thing for mortals; all things are accomplished through moderation.

Theognis uses many other terms for political moderation. The most familiar, *sophrosune*, is explicitly opposed to hubris, but Theognis's most striking call to political moderation begins with the phrase *meden agan*.

The phrase *meden agan* (nothing in excess) was carved on the entrance to the temple of Apollo at Delphi and was associated with the wisdom of the Seven Sages. *Gnothi sauton* (know yourself) was inscribed with *meden agan*; the two warnings against hubris are important for interpreting much of classical Greek literature, especially tragedy and the *History* (c. 430 B.C.E.) of Herodotus.

The middle way is urged in several poems beginning with *meden agan*: Do not in any way strive too eagerly; the middles of all things are best. The opportune moment is best for all the deeds of men. Do not in any way too much glut your heart with difficulties or rejoice too much in good things, because it is the mark of a good man to bear everything. Comparison with other injunctions shows the pattern of the negative command followed by a reinforcing positive statement. These reinforcing statements are separable from the particular commands, and both are reusable. Since the diction of Solon, Hesiod, Homer, and others shows the same pattern, similarities of Theognis to other poetry can be attributed to the traditional nature of the language and the general importance of moderation in the archaic value system.

SEA AND SAILING IMAGERY

That the dominant metaphors in the *Theognidea* concern the sea and sailing is perhaps natural, because Greece is surrounded by water, and the major archaic city-states all founded colonies overseas. Not only was sailing vital to Greek economic life, but also, as the *Odyssey* (c. 800 B.C.E.) suggests, it was vital to the Greek psyche. On the wings of Theognis's poetry, Kyrnos will be universally known, borne easily over the boundless sea. The poet advises that doing a favor for a bad man is like sowing the sea. A bad man should be avoided like a bad harbor. Like a ship, the poet keeps his distance from one whom time has exposed as a counterfeit friend. A boy was rough but relented; after the storm, the poet rests at anchor with night coming.

The ship can also be the ship of state. The first extant examples of this image are found in two fragments of the Greek poet Alcaeus; the best known is in the Augustan poet Horace. Theognis is an important link in the transmission of the metaphor. It appears in verses 575 to 576 and verses 855 to 856, but it receives extended treatment in verses 667 to 682. The wealth of the poet is not equal to his character. The state is beset by difficulties that could have been foreseen but were not. The skilled helmsman has been displaced. There is no order, no concern for the common good. The bad rule over the good. The ship is in danger of being swallowed by the waves. The poet calls his extended metaphor a code to the good, but one comprehensible even to a bad man if he is wise.

PEDERASTIC POEMS

Pausanias's encomium of Eros in the *Symposium* of Plato sheds much light on the pederastic poems of the second book of the *Theognidea*. According to Pausanias, pederasty is acceptable in a context of moral improvement. The lover aims to make the young man better; the beloved gratifies his lover in the hope of becoming better. In Theognis, the situation is much the same. Through his association with the poet, the young Kurnos learns how to conduct himself, how to interact with his own kind, and what attitudes to adopt toward social inferiors. Because the role of beloved can be played for only a short time, he learns the part of the lover also, able to take his turn. As an institution, pederasty tightened the bonds of aristocratic solidarity.

Many of the pederastic poems are facetious, befitting their sympotic setting. A boy is advised to quit running away, since he will not be of an age for long. As long as the boy's cheek is smooth, the poet will fawn on him, even if the price is death. Love is bitter and sweet, hard and soft. The poet laments the public exposure of his love for a boy, but he will endure the attacks; the boy is not unseemly. Finally, in verses 1345 to 1350, the poet adduces a mythic exemplum:

> Loving a boy has been something pleasant since the son
>   of Kronos, the king of the
> immortals, was in love with Ganymede.
> He snatched him up and carried him off to Olympus and
> made him a divinity while he
> had the lovely flower of his boyhood.
> So do not marvel, Simonides, that I too was shown
>   conquered by love of a pretty boy.

BIBLIOGRAPHY

Bing, Peter, and Rip Cohen. *Games of Venus: An Anthology of Greek and Roman Erotic Verse from Sappho to Ovid*. New York: Routledge, 1991. A wide-ranging sample of verse that runs throughout Greek and Roman literature, but which provides valuable examples and critical insight into the works of Theognis.

Edmunds, Lowell. "The Seal of Theognis." In *Poet, Public, and Performance in Ancient Greece*, edited by Lowell Edmunds and Robert Wallace. Baltimore: The Johns Hopkins University Press, 1997. Traces the relationship of the poet and his work to his audience, who are seen as less readers and literary enthusiasts than fellow citizens in the polis and friends of the poet's tribal group. The fundamental effect sought in Theognis's work is therefore not aesthetic but political.

Figueire, Thomas, and Gregory Nagy, eds. *Theognis of Megara: Poetry and the Polis*. Baltimore: The Johns Hopkins University Press, 1985. This collection of essays examine a number of topics but focuses especially on the relationship between Theognis's work and his native city of Megara. The result is a combinaton of poetic, literary, social, and historical insights.

Hudson-Williams, T. Introduction to *The Elegies of Theognis*. New York: Arno Press, 1979. A reprint of the classic 1910 edition, this provides a still valuable overview of the history of the poet's works and is especially good in its review of Theognis's place in ancient literature and literary criticism.

Sacks, Richard. *The Traditional Phrase in Homer: Two Studies in Form, Meaning, and Interpretation*. New York: Brill, 1987. The first part of this work focuses on Theognis and the "Homeric phrase," that is the traditional oral element which is an essential part of Greek epic poetry but which is also key to shorter works including those of Theognis.

Carrie Cowherd;
bibliography updated by Michael Witkoski

DYLAN THOMAS

Born: Swansea, Wales; October 27, 1914
Died: New York, New York; November 9, 1953

PRINCIPAL POETRY
Eighteen Poems, 1934
Twenty-five Poems, 1936
The Map of Love, 1939
New Poems, 1943
Deaths and Entrances, 1946
Twenty-six Poems, 1950
In Country Sleep, 1952
Collected Poems, 1934-1952, 1952
The Poems of Dylan Thomas, 1971 (Daniel Jones, editor)

OTHER LITERARY FORMS

Dylan Thomas wrote one novel, *The Death of the King's Canary* (1976), in collaboration with John Davenport. His stories and collections of stories include the very popular, essentially autobiographical, *Portrait of the Artist as a Young Dog* (1940) and many posthumous publications. Scripts include the extremely popular *Under Milk Wood* (1953); *The Doctor and the Devils* (1953), which has been translated into German, Czech, and Spanish and was republished with four additional scripts in 1966; and *Quite Early One Morning* (1944), which has variant English and American versions. Thomas's letters are rich with biographical materials and critical insights. There are three important collections: *Letters to Vernon Watkins* (1957), written to, and edited by, Vernon Watkins, his friend and fellow poet; *Selected Letters of Dylan Thomas* (1966), edited by Constantine FitzGibbon, his "official" biographer; and *Twelve More Letters by Dylan Thomas* (1969), a limited edition supplemental to the FitzGibbon collection. Many other articles, poems, letters, scripts, and stories are widely scattered in manuscripts, anthologies, newspapers, and magazines. Whether a complete bibliography, much less an inclusive edition, of Thomas's work can ever be made is an open question. J. Alexander Rolph's *Dylan Thomas: A Bibliography* (1956) and Ralph Maud's *Dylan Thomas in Print: A Bibliographical History* (1970) are important efforts in this direction.

ACHIEVEMENTS

Whatever else may be said about Dylan Thomas's poetry, it had the qualities needed to bring its author to the attention of the English-speaking world by the time

Dylan Thomas (Library of Congress)

he was twenty-two years old. Whether it was simply his tone, his subject matter, or a bit of both, Thomas's poems elicited a marked response in readers caught in a fierce economic depression. In any immediate sense, the poems were not optimistic; they sang of no golden age in the offing. Instead, mildly outrageous in subject matter and language, defiant of the ugly processes of life and death, and apparently even more defiant of conventional poetic forms, they seemed to project a knowledge of the inner workings of the universe denied to other mortals but toughly shared.

Small wonder, then, that Thomas gained a hearing as poet and seer in the literary world and among general readers. While the first impact of *Eighteen Poems* was slight, *Twenty-five Poems* established Thomas as a writer to be reckoned with. The book generated several critical questions. Did the world have a new John Keats on its hands, a poet who came almost at once to literary maturity and whose works would be permanent; or was Thomas simply a minor poet who had struck a rich topical vein which would soon be exhausted; or was he, worst of all, as seemed to some most likely, a mere wordmonger whose obscure rantings would soon be-

come mere curiosities, interesting, if at all, only to literary historians? Nearly five decades after *Eighteen Poems*, Thomas has been firmly established as a true poet, but discussion of the ultimate value of his poetry continues. What is clear is that he had a strong hold on the public imagination for roughly two decades and, during that time, helped to shape the idea of what poetry is or can aspire to be.

BIOGRAPHY

Dylan Marlais Thomas is firmly identified in many minds as the Welsh poet par excellence, as the voice of modern Wales speaking in the bardic tradition of *The Mabinogion* (c. twelfth and thirteenth centuries) and in the Renaissance tradition of William Shakespeare's mystic, Owen Glendower. In fact, Thomas's poetry is scarcely Welsh at all. G. S. Fraser, in his excellent critical biography, *Dylan Thomas* (1965), points out that Thomas loved Wales without being especially Welsh. Jacob Korg remarked in his biography, *Dylan Thomas* (1965), that Thomas's life and times have only a limited relevance to his poetry, and what influence there is, is transformed into a personal inner world. "Fern Hill," "Over Sir John's Hill," and a few other poems are set in the countryside and seashore that Thomas knew, and "Hold Hand, These Ancient Minutes in the Cuckoo's Month" speaks accurately of the brutality of the Welsh winter and spring, but rarely does Thomas's poetry treat in any serious way either the real or mythical history and countryside of Wales, the realities of the depressed industrial Wales he knew as an adolescent, or the postwar Wales he returned to after the horrors of the London bombing or the triumph of the American tours. The rough and intimate life of the family and village he treats so graphically in other genres seems to lie outside his idea of poetic fitness.

Thomas was born and reared in Swansea, in southern Wales, east by a few miles from Carmarthen and its environs, Fern Hill and Laugharne, which were to play such an important part in his personal life. Swansea, urban and industrial, contrasts strongly with the idyllic Carmarthenshire. Thomas's immediate family consisted of his father, David John Thomas; his mother, Florence Thomas (née Williams); and an older sister, Nancy. He was liberally supplied with aunts, uncles, and cousins of all sorts, and shared the usual family closeness of the Welsh, though his wife, Caitlin, recorded in *Leftover Life to Kill* (1957) that he tried hard but unsuccessfully to free himself from its puritanical background.

Thomas's paternal grandfather was, among a number of other vocations, a poet, not especially distinguished, who took for himself the bardic name "Gwilym Marles." "Gwilym" is William and "Marles" was taken from the Welsh stream Marlais, which, in its proper spelling, later became Thomas's middle name. Thomas's father had poetic ambitions of his own and was determined that his son should have his chance to become a poet. Disappointed in his hope for a distinguished career in education, he had settled with some lasting bitterness for a schoolmastership in the south of Wales. Thomas's poem "Do Not Go Gentle into That Good Night" furnishes some measure of his bitterness at his father's lingering death from cancer, and of the son's reciprocation of the father's love.

Thomas's school days were unusual only in that he began to write poetry early. His close friend in grammar school was Daniel Jones, who was later to edit *The Poems of Dylan Thomas*. They wrote more than two hundred poems together, each contributing alternate lines—Jones odd, Thomas even.

Thomas left school in 1931 and worked until 1932 for the *South Wales Daily Post*. The period of his most intense activity as a poet had already begun in 1930 and was to extend to 1934. Daniel Jones calculated that during this period Thomas's output was four times greater than that of the last nineteen years of his life. Ralph Maud has edited the four so-called "Buffalo Notebooks," which contain working drafts of Thomas's poems from 1930 to August, 1933—except for the period of July, 1932, to January, 1933—publishing them, with other manuscript material, in *Poet in the Making: The Notebooks of Dylan Thomas* (1968). Maud has observed that Thomas came to think of these poems as a sort of mine of early drafts and drew upon them, generally with some revision, for a number of poems in *Twenty-five Poems*; he continued to do so until the notebooks were purchased in 1941 for what is now the Lockwood Memorial Library of the State University of New York at Buffalo.

Thomas's last two years in Swansea, 1932 to 1934, foreshadowed the importance of the theater in his life. Bill Read, in his too-lightly regarded biography, *The Days of Dylan Thomas* (1964), traces an active interest in acting and playwriting while Thomas was still in school, then details Thomas's journeyman experience in a community theater group, the Mumbles Stage Society. By all accounts, Thomas rapidly became a competent actor, but the bohemianism which was to mar his personal life had already become established and caused his expulsion from the group.

In 1933, Thomas began to place poems in British papers and magazines which had more than local circulation. In September, 1933, he began a correspondence with the future novelist Pamela Hanford Johnson, who eventually married another novelist, C. P. Snow. The correspondence ripened into a friendship, which in turn became a love affair after visits in 1934. In November, Thomas moved to London, the center of his activities until 1937.

Eighteen Poems appeared in December, 1934. Although the book caused hardly a ripple, when it was followed in 1936 by *Twenty-five Poems*, Thomas's reputation was established, helped not a little when the book was received by the prestigious poet Edith Sitwell.

Twenty-five Poems contains a rich trove of some of Thomas's best work. The sonnet sequence "Altarwise by Owl-Light," for example, has still not been exhausted by critical study. The sequence is generally viewed as containing the elements which make Thomas's poetry at once difficult and rewarding: religious, overtly Christian, motifs; packed metaphor and imagery, some of it traditional, some of it esoteric in various ways; high style mixed with colloquial phrasing; and the always-present theme of life-and-death as a process centered around, informed by, and powered through, sexuality.

Perhaps the central event of Thomas's personal life was his meeting with Caitlin Macnamara at a London pub party in April, 1936. The daughter of the eccentric Yvonne Majolier and Francis Macnamara, Caitlin was immediately drawn to Thomas and the affair quickly became serious. By all accounts, Caitlin's temperament was as mercurial as Thomas's own. After a trip together to Cornwall, they married on July 11, 1937, in Penzance, without any visible means of support or any moral support from Thomas's family. They lived at first in Hampshire, southwest of London, with Caitlin's mother. It was a relatively happy and carefree time.

In the fall of 1938, Thomas and his wife moved to Wales, living at first with Thomas's parents, then alone in Laugharne, where their first son, Llewelyn, was born in January, 1939. In August, *The Map of Love* was published, complete with Augustus John's portrait of Thomas. This book contains a number of more or less surrealistic stories plus sixteen poems. In spite of the celebrated episode of Thomas's participation in the Surrealist Exhibition of June 26, 1936, where he read poetry and passed around a cup of strong tea, the notion that Thomas was at any time a surrealist writer has been thoroughly exploded. G. S. Fraser argued that *The Map of Love* generated the New Apocalypse movement, later the New Romanticism, which was, in turn, superficially influenced by Surrealism and Dadaism. H. H. Kleinman, in *The Religious Sonnets of Dylan Thomas* (1963), argued that Thomas could not have been a Surrealist because he was essentially nonliterary as a reader. Earlier than either, Marshall Stearns, in "Unsex the Skeleton: Notes on the Poetry of Thomas" (1944), placed a high value on Thomas's poetry because of its originality and because of the influence it had on the Apocalypse group, specifically Henry Treese, G. S. Fraser, and J. F. Hendry. When Richard Church, a Dent publishing company official, objected to some of Thomas's poems as surrealistic, Thomas rejected the charge and described Surrealism as a "pernicious experiment" which was beneath him, adding that "every line of his poetry was to be understood by the reader thinking and feeling." In any case, the book was well received and contained at least two outstanding poems, the brittle elegy "After the Funeral (In Memory of Ann Jones)" and the splendid compact birthday piece, "Twenty-Four Years."

On September 3, 1939, Great Britain declared war against Nazi Germany, beginning a struggle from which the world as Thomas had known it would never reemerge. During the relatively quiet early stages, before the German drives in the spring of 1940 which led first to the evacuation of Dunkirk and then to the surrender of France, Thomas registered shock about the war and determined not to be involved in it. Called up for military service in April, just after *Portrait of the Artist as a Young Dog* was published, he was found unfit for service. In June, he moved to an artist's colony in the Cotswolds and thence to London in the fall. There began a long period of poverty and writing scenarios for war documentaries, an occupation which may have been emotionally damaging, but which also stood him in good stead as preparation for later participation in filmmaking. His personal life continued to be on the windy side of bohemianism, especially during the periods when Caitlin was in Wales. On March 3, 1943, his daughter Aeron was born while Caitlin was still in London. The Thomases were to have no more children until their second son, Colm, was born in Carmarthen on July 24, 1949, just over four years before his father's death.

The war years saw only a single slim volume of poetry produced, *New Poems*. Included in this book were several poems of first importance: "And Death Shall Have No Dominion," "The Marriage of a Virgin," "The Hunchback in the Park," the long and controversial "Ballad of the Long-Legged Bait," "Once Below a Time," "Deaths and Entrances," and one of his few war poems, "Among Those Killed in the Dawn Raid Was a Man Aged One Hundred." In spite of the title, the poems were not "new"; they were drawn from earlier publication in scattered periodicals.

In the spring of 1945, the European phase of the war was finished and the Thomases returned once more to Wales, settling this time in New Quay on the western coast and moving from there to Oxford in 1946, and finally, in the spring of 1949, to the Boat House in Laugharne, with which Thomas is, perhaps, most often associated. He produced one book of poetry during this period, *Deaths and Entrances*. Meanwhile, he was busy writing and acting for the British Broadcasting Corporation, writing filmscripts, and traveling abroad to Italy, Czechoslovakia, and, finally, America, on the first of four tours.

In August, 1950, after his return from America, *Twenty-six Poems* was published. This limited edition, printed by hand in Italy, signed by Thomas, and in all ways a pretentious production, signaled a new sort of arrival. Rather a large number of people were now willing to pay handsomely for the status conferred by owning a copy of a limited edition of his work.

The American tours were triumphs for Thomas. He appears to have basked in the adoration of American society and academic groups. From the detailed accounts of his mentor, John Malcolm Brinnin, recorded in his biographical *Dylan Thomas in America: An Intimate Journal* (1955), Thomas worked very hard while at the same time continuing to behave in off-hours in the feckless manner for which he was now notorious.

Even so, in February, 1952, a second handsome edition appeared, the six poems of *In Country Sleep*. This book was almost immediately eclipsed by the publication in November of Thomas's most important book, *Collected Poems, 1934-1952*. Again, the format was impressive and the edition included a number of specially bound copies. This volume includes nearly all of Thomas's poetry and forms the point of departure for any serious study of his work.

While the fourth American tour was under way, Thomas was taken ill in New York, lapsed into a coma, and died on November 9, 1953. He was buried on November 24 in St. Martin's Churchyard, Laugharne, Wales.

ANALYSIS

In placing Thomas as a poet, Howard Nemerov's conclusion, expressed in *The Kenyon Review* (1953), that "he has written a few beautiful poems" furnishes a good point of departure. In a way, that is the best that can be said for any poet, even the greatest. David Daiches, who denied a place of greatness to Thomas in his essay in *College English* (1954), said that "it is enough that he wrote some poems that the world will not willingly let die." Richard A. Werry, again in *College English* (1955), allowed Thomas's poetry greater depth than is generally granted, suggesting that at least a half dozen of his poems will last out the twentieth century. This is rather faint praise. Even if Thomas's poetry comes down to no more than that, a few lasting poems, still, to have caught the imagination and the spirit, if not fully the understanding, of the people who endured the Depression and World War II, to have embodied in his poetry a fearless, if bitter, search for reality and a limited hope in a world bereft of its traditional theological certainties, is no mean feat. This much, at least, Thomas achieved.

Three poems will serve to illustrate, provisionally, the range in theme and technique of Dylan Thomas's poetry: "And Death Shall Have No Dominion," "Altarwise by Owl-Light," and "Over Sir John's Hill." All three deal with the life-in-death theme which permeates Thomas's work. The first is a very early poem, rather clear and personal in its statement; the second, consisting of ten sonnets treated as a single entity, involves a great deal of Christian material, though it is not incontrovertibly a Christian poem and presents many problems of analysis and interpretation; the third is a "Welsh" poem inasmuch as it is set in Wales and may well spring from Welsh folk material. While the middle poem is considered to be difficult, the last is sequentially clear in its narrative progression, panorama of images, and vivid descriptions.

"AND DEATH SHALL HAVE NO DOMINION"

"And Death Shall Have No Dominion" appears in the "Buffalo Notebooks" dated April, 1933, and was published in *The New English Weekly* on May 18, 1933, and in *Collected Poems, 1934-1952*. It consists of three stanzas, each beginning and ending with the phrase "And death shall have no dominion." The rhythm is based on a four-stress count with enough variations to intrigue the serious prosodist. These may involve eccentric massing of stresses, as in the title line, or stressing or not stressing the same word in a single line, as in "When their bónes are picked cleán and the cleán bones góne." Aside from the title-refrain, the poem does not lend itself to simple syllable count, though lines two and six consistently have eight syllables and line five has nine. The other four lines are more or less irregular. For the most part, the lines tend to fall irregularly into the iambic and anapestic patterns common to English versification. Alliteration runs throughout the poem. End-rhyme, assonance, and consonance also play a part in the sound pattern. Lines two and three of the second stanza, for example, substitute alliteration for end rhyme with "windily" and "way," while "way" is assonant with "break" in line five. Moreover, "windily" is assonant with the first word of the following line, "twisting," which, in turn, is assonant with both words of the phrase "sinews give." More alliteration is found in line three in "lying long," and "lying" echoes "windings" in line two. Such intricacy of sound patterning is the rule in Thomas's poetry.

This rhythmical music contributes much to the readability and understanding of the poem. Prosed, the first stanza says little more than that human beings will die in many ways and places and their bodies will return to the elements and be scattered. The elements, however, will live again because love will continue its purpose of regeneration, and death will not rule life. Of course, prosing cannot indicate the cosmic triumph of "They shall have stars at elbow and foot." The second paragraph works with images of sea death and of torture, and plays on the paradox that the broken will remain whole. The third stanza picks up a minor theme of madness and couples it with a wasteland setting. In spite of madness, in spite of burial and dissolution, the poem insists that something will continue to hammer the elements into life until the sun itself breaks down. Again, the prosing gives little notion of the desolation evoked by "Where blew a flower may a flower no more/ Lift its head to the blows of the rain."

In an essay in the *Explicator* (1956), Thomas E. Connolly professed to see both Christian and Platonic elements in the poem and suggested the influence of Percy Bysshe Shelley's *Adonais* (1821) and John Milton's "Lycidas" (1645) as well. The Christian note is at best vague, while the breaking down of the sun and the persistence with which the elements return to the flesh instead of to the godhead seems clearly enough to refute Platonism. Whatever the merits of the *Adonais* identification may be, Thomas's resources would be poor indeed if he had to depend on "Lycidas" for sea-drowning imagery. On the other hand, Korg agrees with Connolly's identification of St. Paul's Epistle to the Romans as the source of the title-refrain and the language indicating that the dead in the sea will rise again. Korg rejects the idea that the lines Christianize the poem and sees them, instead, as part of a "more generalized mysticism."

"ALTARWISE BY OWL-LIGHT"

"Altarwise by Owl-Light" is a much more difficult and controversial poem. The first seven of its ten sonnets were published in *Life and Letters Today* (1935) and the last three were published at various times during 1936 in *Contemporary Poetry and Prose*. They were printed later as a sequence in *Twenty-five Poems*.

The poems comprising "Altarwise by Owl-Light" are traditional sonnets mainly inasmuch as they have fourteen lines each; they do not follow the rhyme scheme of either the English or the Italian form. In fact, their rhyme is of the incidental and varied pattern characteristic of so much of Thomas's poetry. Terminal sounds are patterned, but hardly enough so to be considered formalized. The rhythm is equally irregular. Most lines contain five stressed syllables, many of them iambic, but that the overall pattern is dominated by iambs is doubtful. Even so, the poems are recognizable as variants of the twentieth century sonnet.

Elder Olson, in *The Poetry of Dylan Thomas* (1954), developed what must be by far the most intricate analysis of the poems' symbolism. He assembled charts to demonstrate that the poems are based on astrology, basically Herculean in identity. Although Olson's interpretation has been rejected for the most part by other critics, it hardly merits Jones's curt dismissal as "ludicrously complex decipherment." On a different tack, Bernard Knieger, in an essay in the *Explicator* (1956), offered an interpretation to counter a rather muddled one by R. N. Maud earlier in the same periodical. Knieger defined the themes of "Altarwise by Owl-Light" as being simultaneously Christian and sexual. E. H. Essig, again in the *Explicator* (1958), built on Olson's and Knieger's interpretations to demonstrate a fully Christian poetry. In 1965, G. S. Fraser rejected Olson's position out of hand and joined David Daiches in the opinion, expressed in *College English* (1954), that, although splendid in parts, the sonnets are, as wholes, "oppressive and congested." At the same time, he declared that the sonnets "are important because they announce the current orthodox Christian feeling . . . which was henceforth increasingly to dominate Thomas's work in poetry." The opinion is interesting in the face of Thomas's remark, reported by J. M. Brinnin in an article in the *Atlantic Monthly* (1955), that he now intended to write "poems in praise of God's world by a man who doesn't believe in God." Daniel Jones, perhaps, deserves the last word. He argued that "Altarwise by Owl-Light" could be termed "absolute poetry," held together, not by ordinary logic, but by a pattern of words and images joined by a common relationship with such things as "sex, birth, death, Christian and pagan religion and ritual." He saw the poem as "sustained by a single metaphor" and as beyond translation into other words or thoughts. Like Fraser, he saw the poem marking a change in Thomas's poetry, but unlike Fraser, he saw it as moving away from the extravagant expression of the earlier work and toward economy.

It is clear that "Altarwise by Owl-Light" demonstrates Thomas's concern for the life-death paradox taken on the grandest scale and illuminated, at least in part, by the Christian mythos. Also helpful is the understanding that the persona of the poem is a universalized character who is at once himself and the Christ who dies, and who is also all the human beings who have ever died and who will ever die. With their insistence upon the mysteries of life in death, mercy in destruction, God in man, the sonnets are quintessentially Thomas.

"OVER SIR JOHN'S HILL"

"Over Sir John's Hill" first appeared in *Botteghe Oscure* in 1949 and was later included in the *Collected Poems, 1934-1952*. Daniel Jones pointed out that the poem was written during Thomas's residence at Laugharne. The area of "Sir John's Hill" borders an estuary east of the outlet of the River Towy, a semi-wilderness area supporting many wildfowl and birds of prey. The poem, then, reflects a setting which was intimately familiar to Thomas; even so, except for the place-names, the setting could be nearly any waste area in the world where land and a large body of water meet.

Jones's detailed study of the prosody of "Over Sir John's Hill" is interesting. He has noted the varied but exact patterning of the long and short lines based on a syllabic count, the longest line containing fifteen syllables, the shortest containing only one; lines of either thirteen and fourteen syllables, or four to six syllables are the most common line lengths. Jones also observed that the poem's four stanzas have a rhyme pattern of *aabbccbxdadxx*, *a*, *b*, *c*, and *d* being either full-rhymes or half-rhymes, and *x* indicating alliteration with first-syllable assonance. Jones considered the verse form to be representative of Thomas's work at its best and most mature. While he conceded that such intricacy is open to the charge of artificiality and that syllabic verse tends to be "easily overcome by the natural patterns of the English language, based upon combinations of weak and strong stresses," he argued that all artists must work within "self-imposed discipline."

While "Over Sir John's Hill" exists on many levels, it can be approached quite usefully from the point of view of allegory. Allegory works by having each actor's part function on several levels simultaneously in a linear story. The trick is to see that each actor functions differently, though interrelatedly, in several stories at once. Thus, an actor may be a bird, functioning as a bird, and a bird functioning as a mortal man, and a man functioning as an immortal soul, all at the same time. Put another way, one actor plays three parts in three stories, all fully coherent, in the telling of one tale. In "Over Sir John's Hill," there is a persona who narrates the action, observes it, and participates in it. The "young Aesop fabling" watches the drama of bird life and bird death on the estuary shortly before sunset. On the literal level, the persona watches while a hawk, during last light, is destroying sparrows. A fishing heron watches and grieves and the grief is echoed by the "tear" of the river. The bird life then settles down, an owl hoots, and the persona hears the sound of the river in the willows just before the plunge of night.

On the ethical level, "Over Sir John's Hill" is a grim sort of parody of the legal system and of institutionalized religion. The birds and the countryside echo human behavior. The hill itself represents a judge who has, on evidence which is never presented in the poem, reached a verdict of condemnation; thus, he is sitting with the symbol of the death sentence on his head, the "black cap of jackdaws." That the cap is formed of jackdaws is instructive. The jackdaw's habit of playing jokes on people is reflected in the term "gulled birds," which Thomas may have picked up from his interest in Jacobean tragedy. "Gulled," in that context, means "fooled" and here functions to undercut the quality of human justice. As jackdaws are also minor carrion birds, their use as a "black cap" heightens the grim note. The hawk represents the executioner, as is indicated by the adjective "tyburn," an allusion to the Tyburn Tree or Tyburn Elms, a thirteenth century place of execution on the River Tybourne and later the slang name for the gallows built near the site of London's Marble Arch. The identification is intensified by an immediate reference to "wrestle of elms" and the "noosed" hawk. The law, it would seem, chooses its victims at random, and the victims themselves are by nature young and silly, foredoomed and courting death. They sing "dilly dilly, come let us die," and are described by the persona and the heron as "led-astray birds." The saintly heron, at the ethical level, stands for the church, which observes the workings of human justice without protest, though it grieves for the victims. The heron, like the church, continues to carry on its own business in spite of the mundane horrors about it. On the ethical level, then, society is formal, filled with sorrow but not with mercy, and its conceptions of justice, death, and divinity are at once structured and casual.

The divine level is still more disquieting. The persona regards nature in an old-fashioned way, his words couched in fresh metaphor, as he describes nature as the Book in which divinity can be read. He opens "the leaves of water" and reads psalms there, and in a shell he reads "death." He and the heron-church ask for God's mercy, the God who, in silence, observes the sparrow's "hail," a term implying not only the sparrows' song of praise but also the numbers in which their dead bodies pelt the earth. If the God of the poem is more merciful than the indifferent hill-judge, the poem does not say so. Of salvation and an afterlife there is no affirmation; the "lunge of night" seems dreadfully final, not Thomas's more usual affirmation of a circular process in which death is the entrance to life, in which life is repeated rather than translated to a divine realm. It may be that, after the war, Thomas was no longer able to see the cycle of nature as an endlessly repeating pattern. If "Over Sir John's Hill" is in fact a celebration, it is an unusually dark one, even for Thomas.

OTHER MAJOR WORKS

LONG FICTION: *The Death of the King's Canary*, 1976 (with John Davenport).

SHORT FICTION: *Portrait of the Artist as a Young Dog*, 1940; *Selected Writings of Dylan Thomas*, 1946; *A Child's Christmas in Wales*, 1954; *Adventures in the Skin Trade and Other Stories*, 1955; *A Prospect of the Sea and Other Stories*, 1955; *Early Prose Writings*, 1971; *The Followers*, 1976; *The Collected Stories*, 1984.

PLAY: *Under Milk Wood*, pr. 1953 (public reading), pr. 1954 (radio play), pb. 1954, pr. 1956 (staged; musical settings by Daniel Jones).

SCREENPLAYS: *Three Weird Sisters*, 1948 (with Louise Birt and David Evans); *No Room at the Inn*, 1948 (with Ivan Foxwell); *The Doctor and the Devils*, 1953; *The Beach at Falesá*, 1963; *Twenty Years A'Growing*, 1964; *Rebecca's Daughters*, 1965; *Me and My Bike*, 1965.

RADIO PLAYS: *Quite Early One Morning*, 1944; *The Londoner*, 1946; *Return Journey*, 1947; *Quite Early One Morning*, 1954; (twenty-two radio plays).

NONFICTION: *Letters to Vernon Watkins*, 1957 (Vernon Watkins, editor); *Selected Letters of Dylan Thomas*, 1966 (Constantine FitzGibbon, editor); *Poet in the Making: The Notebooks of Dylan Thomas*, 1968 (Ralph Maud, editor) *Twelve More Letters by Dylan Thomas*, 1969 (Constantine FitzGibbon, editor).

MISCELLANEOUS: *"The Doctor and the Devils" and Other Scripts*, 1966 (two screenplays and one radio play).

BIBLIOGRAPHY

Davies, Walford. *Dylan Thomas*. Philadelphia: Open University Press, 1986. A biography and an introduction are followed by several chapters on the poems: poems on poetry, early poetry, comparisons of early and late poems, "Fern Hill," and the last poems. The final chapter attempts to put Thomas's work in context and to draw some conclusions regarding the poet in relationship to society, his style, and the way he uses language. Good notes contain bibliographical references.

_____. *A Reference Companion to Dylan Thomas*. Westport, Conn.: Greenwood Press, 1998. A valuable aid to understanding Thomas's troubled life and enduring body of work. Begins with an insightful biography that provides a useful context for studying his writings. The second section provides a systematic overview of his works, while the third section summarizes the critical and scholarly response to his writings. The volume concludes with a bibliography of the most helpful general studies.

Ferris, Paul. *Dylan Thomas: The Biography*. Washington, D.C.: Counterpoint, 2000. This excellent biography contains material found in American archives and also those of the British Broadcasting Corporation. Ferris interviewed more than two hundred people who either knew Thomas or worked with him.

He attempts to separate the facts from the legendary reputation of Thomas. This book elaborates on, and enhances, the "approved" biography by Constantine FitzGibbon (*The Life of Dylan Thomas*, 1965), the personal memoirs by Caitlin Thomas (*Leftover Life to Kill*, 1957), and John Malcolm Brinnin (*Dylan Thomas in America*, 1955).

Kleinman, Hyman H. *The Religious Sonnets of Dylan Thomas: A Study in Imagery and Meaning*. Berkeley: University of California Press, 1963. Analyzes the religious sonnets in sequence seeing them as a development from uncertainty to an affirmation of spiritual faith. Detailed explications give a close analysis of the imagery which is drawn from sources as varied as the medieval mystery plays, English poetry, myth, seventeenth century sermons, and movies. A short but fine study of the work, not the man.

Korg, Jacob. *Dylan Thomas*. New York: Twayne, 1965. A general discussion of Thomas and his work ("The Rhetoric of Mysticism") begins this study. Readings and analyses of two early collections, *Eighteen Poems* and *Twenty-five Poems*, are followed by discussions of the later poems, fiction, and the dramatic works. Thomas is characterized throughout as a mystic with a romantic and mythic disposition. Korg explores the dichotomy between Thomas's sophisticated style and his often "barbaric" subject matter. Includes a chronology, a biographical sketch, notes and references, and a somewhat dated select bibliography. An excellent survey for the student.

Olson, Elder. *The Poetry of Dylan Thomas*. Chicago: University of Chicago Press, 1954. This book examines Thomas's original use of language and proposes an interesting and provocative point of view: that he was basically a symbolist writer concerned with a "nightmare universe"—particularly up to his later poems. A bibliography by William H. Huff is appended.

Sinclair, Andrew. *Dylan Thomas: No Man More Magical*. New York: Holt, Rinehart and Winston, 1975. This study examines Thomas's Welsh heritage and characterizes "the finest lyric poet of his age" as essentially a Welsh bard and minstrel. The text describes the life and artistic development of this con-

tradictory poet and his quest for a "sweet final resolution of the soul." Published in England under the title *Dylan Thomas: Poet of His People*.

Tindall, William York. *A Reader's Guide to Dylan Thomas*. New York: Farrar, Straus & Giroux, 1963. This book is a poem-by-poem explication of Thomas's *Collected Poems, 1934-1952*. The author follows a development of themes and aesthetics from the dark early poems to the brighter poems later in the collection. An excellent guide for students, this survey includes an introductory essay examining Thomas's reputation and investigating the political, religious, Surrealistic, Freudian, and Welsh elements in his work.

B. G. Knepper;
bibliography updated by the editors

EDWARD THOMAS

Born: London, England; March 3, 1878
Died: Arras, France; April 9, 1917

PRINCIPAL POETRY
Six Poems, 1916
Poems, 1917
Last Poems, 1918
Collected Poems, 1920, enlarged 1928
The Poetry of Edward Thomas, 1978

OTHER LITERARY FORMS

Although Edward Thomas is remembered today as a poet, throughout his working life he supported himself and his family by writing various sorts of prose. He always considered himself to be a writer, and the lasting tragedy of his life was that he never seemed able, until the outbreak of World War I, to buy enough time to devote himself to the art of writing as he obviously wished to do.

Ironically, the war in which he died also provided him with the structured, organized environment and the freedom from financial anxiety which enabled him to produce the work which has secured his reputation.

His entire prose opus runs to nearly forty volumes, most of which were published during his lifetime. The titles cover a variety of subjects. It is also possible to see what a remarkable volume of work he produced in the years 1911 to 1912, a productivity which culminated, after nine published works, in a breakdown in 1912.

Although the prose work of Thomas is often dismissed as being unimportant, it is obvious from merely reading the titles where his main interests lay. Themes of nature and of the British countryside predominate, together with literary criticism.

In fact, Thomas was a remarkably perceptive literary critic. He was among the first reviewers to appreciate the work of Robert Frost, and he also recognized Ezra Pound's achievement in *Personae* (1909), which he reviewed in its first year of publication. When he began to write, he was heavily influenced by Walter Pater's code of aesthetics, his love of rhetoric, and his formality. He was later to have to work hard to rid his prose of those features, which he recognized as being alien to his own poetic voice.

ACHIEVEMENTS

In his poetry, Edward Thomas succeeded in realizing two ambitions, which another poet of nature set out as his aims more than a century earlier. In the preface to the *Lyrical Ballads* (1800), William Wordsworth stated that his intent in writing poetry was "to exalt and transfigure the natural and the common," and also to redefine the status of the poet so that he would become "a man speaking to men." Wordsworth's poetry received both acclaim and abuse when it first appeared, and formed an expectation of poetry which continued until the end of the nineteenth century. By that time, the aesthetic movement had come to the fore, and poetry was well on its way, at the outbreak of World War I, toward suffocating itself with overblown rhetoric.

Thomas is not generally regarded as a war poet, being discussed more often in conjunction with Thomas Hardy and Walter de la Mare than with Wilfred Owen, Siegfried Sassoon, and Isaac Rosenberg. By combining his acute perceptions of both nature and political events, however, Thomas produced poetry in which evocations of place and detailed descriptions of nature become a metaphor for man's spiritual state. F. R. Leavis, writing in *New Bearings in English Poetry* (1932) made this observation: "He was exquisitely sincere and sensitive, and he succeeded in expressing in poetry a representative modern sensibility. It was an achievement of a very rare order, and he has not yet had the recognition he deserves." Today, Thomas's poetry is widely known, and he has become almost an establishment figure in the literature of the early twentieth century. Yet it is a measure of his achievement that in returning to his slender *Collected Poems*, it is always possible to be stimulated and surprised by his work.

BIOGRAPHY

Edward Philip Thomas was born in London, the eldest of six boys. Both of his parents were Welsh, and Thomas always had an affinity with the principality, spending much time there during his childhood, although the landscapes of his poetry are predominantly those of the south of England. Thomas's father was a stern, unyielding man who had risen by his own efforts to a social position far above that which might be expected from his poor background. Having succeeded in elevating himself, he was naturally very ambitious for his eldest son, and Thomas received an excellent education, attending St. Paul's school, Hammersmith (as a contemporary of G. K. Chesterton and E. C. Bentley, among others), and going on from there to Jesus College, Oxford.

Shortly before going to Oxford, Thomas met Helen Noble; it was one of the momentous events in his life. Both he and Helen had very advanced ideas for their time; they were already lovers while Thomas was still an undergraduate. They discussed their future lives together, and how they would bring up their children in accordance with Richard Jeffries's theories of freedom and the open-air life. Helen herself said, "We hated the thought of a legal contract. We felt our love was all the bond there ought to be, and that if that failed it was immoral to be bound together. We wanted our union to be free and spontaneous." In the spring of 1899, Helen discovered that she was pregnant and was rather appalled to discover that Edward himself, as well as her friends in the bohemian community in which she lived, thought that they should be married. Helen's family were shocked to learn of Helen's pregnancy, insisting on a hurried marriage and refusing to help the young couple in any way. Thomas's family was more sympathetic, allowing Helen to live with them and helping Thomas while he worked toward his degree.

Once he was graduated, the need to earn money to support his family became pressing, and, determined not to become submerged in the drudgery of an office job, Thomas solicited work from publishers. Until the time that he joined the Artists' Rifles, Thomas was to support himself and his family by writing. They were always poor, and he often reproached himself bitterly because he had no regular source of income.

Writing became a chore to him, something to be done merely for the sake of the money. In 1912, he suffered a breakdown brought on by overwork. At about that time, also, he met Robert Frost and formed a close friendship with the American poet. Thomas was among the first to appreciate Frost's poetry, and Frost encouraged Thomas to try his hand at writing poetry himself; Thomas gradually gained confidence in his ability to say what he wanted in poetry. When he was killed by a bombshell in the spring of 1917, what might have become a considerable voice in English poetry was tragically silenced.

Analysis

Perhaps the most notable feature of Edward Thomas's poetry, which strikes the reader immediately, is its characteristic quietness of tone and its unassertive, gentle quality. He is primarily a poet of the country, but through his descriptions of the English landscape, impressionistic and minutely observed, he also attempts to delineate some of the features of his own inner landscape.

As may be seen from the titles of the many books of prose that he wrote before beginning to write poetry at the behest of Robert Frost, he was always deeply interested in nature and the land. Many of the fleeting observations in his poetry are drawn from his notebooks, in which he recorded such things as the first appearance of a spring blossom and the first sightings of various species of birds. In his prose, as opposed to the notebooks, his style was highly rhetorical, so that the keen observations which make his poetry so effective are lost in a plethora of adjectival excess. In one of his reviews he wrote that "The important thing is not that a thing

should be small, but that it should be intense and capable of unconsciously symbolic significance." In his poetry, by the acuity of his observation and the spareness and tautness of his language, he certainly achieves remarkable—if low-key—intensity. He also achieves, in his best work, an unforced symbolic resonance.

"As the Team's Head-Brass"

"As the Team's Head-Brass" is one of Thomas's most impressive achievements; at first reading, it may appear to be only an account of a rural dialogue between the poet and a man plowing a field. It begins with a reference to the plowman, and to some lovers who are seen disappearing into the wood behind the field being plowed. The lovers are not directly relevant to the substance of the poem, but they are an important detail. The poem begins and ends with a reference to them, and although they are in no sense representative of a Lawrentian "life-force," their presence in the poem does suggest the triumph of life and love over death and destruction. The very mention of the lovers reinforces the image of the plow horses "narrowing a yellow square of charlock"—that is, destroying the (living) weeds, that *better* life may grow.

"If we could see all all might seem good" says the plowman, and this seems to be Thomas's contention in this poem. The writing throughout is highly controlled, the structure of the poem reinforced with alliteration and internal rhyme—seeming to owe something to Gerard Manley Hopkins and ultimately even to the Welsh *cynghanedd* form, with the use of "fallen/fallow/plough/narrowing/yellow/charlock" all in four lines, and then later in the same opening section, "word/weather/war/scraping/share/screwed/furrow." Writing about Thomas in *New Bearings in English Poetry* (1932), F. R. Leavis observes that "we become aware of the inner life which the sensory impressions are notation for." This is particularly true of "As the Team's Head-Brass." The closing lines bring the whole poem together most succinctly—the lovers, forgotten since the opening lines, emerge from the wood; the horses begin to plow a new furrow; "for the last time I watched" says Thomas, and the reader must pause here to ask whether he means "for the last time on this particular occasion" or "for the last time ever." All the conversation in the poem has been about war, and in the last two lines come the words "crumble/

topple/stumble," which, although used ostensibly with reference to the horses and the soil, may equally be taken to refer back to the fallen tree upon which the poet is sitting, the plowman's workmate who has been killed in the war, the changing state of society, and the relentless passage of time.

"ADLESTROP"

This poem is not typical of Thomas's work, however, for it is longer and much more detailed and elaborate than most of his poems. More typical of his work are poems like "Tall Nettles" and "Adlestrop," which evoke the moment without attempting to do more than capture the unique quality of one particular place or one particular moment in time. "Adlestrop" is a poem much anthologized, and much appreciated by those who love the English countryside. It has been described as the most famous of modern "place" poems, and yet it also seems to conjure up an almost sexual tension (perhaps by the use of the words "lonely fair"?) of a kind which is often implicit in such hot summer days. This is a sense of the poem which the contemporary poet Dannie Abse has obviously found, for he has written a poem titled "Not Adlestrop," in which the unspecified lady actually makes an appearance in a train going in the opposite direction. Abse's poem is something of a literary joke, but it does pinpoint an element of unresolved sexual tension in several of Thomas's poems.

"NO ONE SO MUCH AS YOU"

For example, "Some Eyes Condemn," "Celandine," and "The Unknown" all seem to be worlds away in mood from "And You, Helen," a poem written for his wife. The poignant "No One So Much As You," a kind of apologia for an imperfectly reciprocated love, was written for Mary Elizabeth Thomas, the poet's mother, although it has often been mistaken for a love poem to his wife. In either case it would seem that familiarity did not necessarily increase Thomas's love for his family—in fact, it was obvious, both from his despairing reaction to the news of Helen's second pregnancy and from his well-documented impatience with domestic life—that distance and mystery were important elements of attraction for him. Perhaps fortunately for all concerned, Thomas's dissatisfactions and unfulfilled longings seem to have made up only a very small part of his nature. Having come to poetry late, he wastes little time in cataloging regrets for what he might have been and concentrates mainly on what he was able to do best—that is, to capture his own impressions of English rural life and country landscapes and combine them in poetry with various insights into his own personality.

AFFINITY FOR COUNTRY LIFE

It would not be possible to offer a succinct analysis of Edward Thomas's poetry without referring to his deeply felt patriotism. In her excellent book *Edward Thomas: A Poet for His Country* (1978), Jan Marsh describes an incident which occurred soon after Thomas enlisted in the British Army, although he was in fact over the usual age limit for enlistment. A friend asked the poet what he thought he was fighting for; Thomas bent down and picked up a pinch of earth and, letting it crumble through his fingers, answered, "Literally, for this."

This is the predominant impression which the reader carries away from an encounter with Thomas's poetry, for here is a sensitive, educated man who, despite his cultivation, is deeply attuned to the land. This affinity is particularly clear in the country people who inhabit Thomas's poetry, for they are always portrayed as being part of a long and noble tradition of rural life. Thomas does not romanticize his vision: He portrays the cruelties of nature as well as its beauties. A recurring image in his poetry is that of the gamekeeper's board, hung with trophies in an attempt to discourage other predators. Perhaps because he makes an honest attempt to describe the reality of country life without attempting to gloss over or soften its less attractive aspects, he succeeds superbly. Since his death, when his poetry was scarcely known, Thomas's work has become steadily more popular, so that today he is known as one of England's finest nature poets.

OTHER MAJOR WORKS

NONFICTION: *The Woodland Life*, 1897; *Horae Solitariae*, 1902; *Oxford*, 1903; *Rose Acre Papers*, 1904; *Beautiful Wales*, 1905; *The Heart of England*, 1906; *Richard Jeffries*, 1909; *The South Country*, 1909; *Rest and Unrest*, 1910; *Rose Acre Papers*, 1910; *Feminine Influence on the Poets*, 1910; *Windsor Castle*, 1910; *The Isle of Wight*, 1911; *Light and Twilight*, 1911; *Maurice Maeterlinck*, 1911; *Celtic Stories*, 1911; *The Tenth Muse*, 1911; *Algernon Charles*

Swinburne, 1912; *George Borrow: The Man and His Books*, 1912; *Lafcadio Hearn*, 1912; *Norse Tales*, 1912; *The Icknield Way*, 1913; *The Happy-Go-Lucky Morgans*, 1913; *The Country*, 1913; *Walter Pater*, 1913; *In Pursuit of Spring*, 1914; *The Life of the Duke of Marlborough*, 1915; *A Literary Pilgrim in England*, 1917; *Cloud Castle and Other Papers*, 1922; *Essays of Today and Yesterday*, 1926; *Chosen Essays*, 1926; *The Last Sheaf*, 1928; *The Childhood of Edward Thomas*, 1938; *The Prose of Edward Thomas*, 1948 (Roland Gant, editor); *Letters from Edward Thomas to Gordon Bottomley*, 1968; *Letters to America, 1914-1917*, 1978.

CHILDREN'S LITERATURE: *Four-and-Twenty-Blackbirds*, 1915.

BIBLIOGRAPHY

Farjeon, Eleanor. *Edward Thomas: The Last Four Years*. Foreword by P. J. Kavanagh. Introduction and editing of revised edition by Anne Harvey. Thrupp, Gloucestershire, England: Sutton, 1997. A double memoir that uses Thomas's letters and Farjeon's diaries to provide a candid account of their developing friendship. Offers a unique account of Thomas's development as a poet, including his meeting Robert Frost, whose encouragement led to Thomas's first poems. Thomas's letters describe his family, his friendships with other writers, and provides a detailed account of his experiences in World War I.

Gant, Roland, ed. *Edward Thomas on the Countryside*. London: Faber & Faber, 1977. Traces the evolution of both the prose and poetry of Thomas as he matured as a writer. An interesting introduction sets forth the background and pastoral influences on him as an individual and on his works categorized by groups.

Kirkham, Michael. *The Imagination of Edward Thomas*. Cambridge, England: Cambridge University Press, 1986. Kirkham ignores chronology as he explores Thomas's imagination by identifying the characteristic style that is evidenced in his poetry. Augmented with a solid bibliography and an index, this book is extremely helpful for an in-depth study of Thomas.

Marsh, Jan. *Edward Thomas: A Poet for His Country*. New York: Barnes & Noble Books, 1978. Marsh pursues the image of Thomas as a melancholic who used his poetry and prose to "paint" landscapes celebrating the English countryside. His natural and unobtrusive style illustrates the vital English life in which he fervently believed.

Motion, Andrew. *The Poetry of Edward Thomas*. London: Routledge & Kegan Paul, 1980. Motion approaches Thomas's poetry as drawing from the Georgian tradition while anticipating the arrival of the modernists in content and in form. Motion examines the subtle style of Thomas and introduces him as an evolutionary poet.

Smith, Stan. *Edward Thomas*. London: Faber & Faber, 1986. Thomas is considered in this book as the "quintessential English poet," whose devotion to the rural countryside is reflected in his poetry. Several critical approaches are presented, and the selected bibliography is helpful.

Thomas, Edward. *Selected Letters*. Edited by R. George Thomas. New York: Oxford University Press, 1995. A selection of letters from a lifetime of correspondence which offers invaluable biographical material and insight into the period and Thomas's work.

Thomas, R. George. *Edward Thomas: A Portrait*. Oxford, England: Clarendon Press, 1985. This book provides rare insight into the life and work of Edward Thomas by making use of letters, memoirs, and personal papers. Biographical in nature, and supported by an excellent bibliography, the book gives a solid foundation for the study of his prose and poetry.

*Vivien Stableford;
bibliography updated by the editors*

JAMES THOMSON

Born: Ednam, Roxburgh, Scotland; September 7, 1700
Died: Richmond, Surrey, England; August 27, 1748

PRINCIPAL POETRY
Winter, 1726
Summer, 1727

Spring, 1728

Autumn, 1730

The Seasons, 1730 (includes four previous titles; revised in 1744)

A Hymn, 1730

Liberty, 1735-1736

The Castle of Indolence: An Allegorical Poem, 1748

OTHER LITERARY FORMS

Although James Thomson's reputation is as a poet, he also wrote plays that were generally successful in their day. He wrote five plays and coauthored a sixth. *The Tragedy of Sophonisba*, a tragedy about the Carthaginian queen Sophonisba, was performed and published in 1730. Thomson's second tragedy, *Agamemnon*, appeared in 1738. His next two plays followed rapidly: *Edward and Eleonora* (1739) was prohibited by the censorship, and *Alfred* (1740) was coauthored with David Mallet. The play about King Alfred contains Thomson's famous ode "Rule, Britannia," still well known in England, especially the refrain: "Rule, Britannia, rule the waves;/ Britons never will be slaves." Thomson's most successful play, the tragedy *Tancred and Sigismunda* (1745), continued to be performed in the second half of the eighteenth century and was translated into French and German. His final play, the tragedy *Coriolanus* (1749), was not performed until after Thomson's death.

ACHIEVEMENTS

For more than a century, James Thomson's most famous work, *The Seasons* (1730, 1744), was among the most widely read poems in English. It went through over two hundred editions in the eighteenth century. Even though William Wordsworth replaced Thomson as the poet of nature for English readers beginning in the nineteenth century, *The Seasons* remained popular; there have been more than four hundred editions of the poem since the eighteenth century.

BIOGRAPHY

James Thomson was born in the village of Ednam, Roxburgh, in Scotland, close to the border with England. His father, Thomas Thomson, was a minister. The poet's mother, Beatrix Trotter Thomson, communicated enthusiasm for religious devotion to her children. James

James Thomson (Hulton Archive)

was the fourth of nine children. When he was an infant, Thomson's family moved to the nearby hamlet of Southdean. Here the future poet of nature roamed a varied landscape that included snow on the Cheviot Hills, the Jed Water, and a pastoral setting in which light and shade, cloud and horizon, wind and weather, and greens and browns produce an environment of remarkable variety and dramatic vividness.

Thomson was a student for almost ten years at Edinburgh University, beginning in 1715. He studied for the Presbyterian ministry, but poetry, which he began writing before college, became increasingly more important to him. By early 1725, Thomson had decided to go to London to attempt a literary career. His successes were quick by any standards. The first version of what would become his immensely popular *The Seasons* was the 406-line poem *Winter*, published in April, 1726. This was followed by a second edition just two months later. *Summer* appeared in 1727, *Spring* in 1728, and *Autumn* and *A Hymn* in 1730 as part of the first edition of the collected *Seasons*. During these first five years in England,

Thomson also wrote "Poem to the Memory of Sir Isaac Newton" (1727), "Britannia" (1729), and his first play, *The Tragedy of Sophonisba* (1730).

From 1730 to 1733 Thomson took a Grand Tour as traveling companion and tutor to Charles Richard Talbot, eldest son of the Solicitor-General Charles Talbot. Between his return from the Grand Tour and his death fifteen years later, Thomson wrote five plays and produced his imitation of the Spenserian stanza from *The Faerie Queene* (1590, 1596) of the Renaissance poet Edmund Spenser, in *The Castle of Indolence: An Allegorical Poem* (1748).

The poet moved to the village of Richmond, Surrey, in 1736, and spent the last twelve years of his life there. Richmond was about ten miles from London, with rural beauty and reasonable proximity to the capital. There Thomson enjoyed friendships with the writers Alexander Pope, John Dyer, Aaron Hill, David Mallet, Richard Savage, William Shenstone, and Tobias Smollett. Thomson courted Elizabeth Young, the sister-in-law of Thomson's old Scottish friend William Robertson. He wrote her tortured love letters, which became more desperate as her indifference continued. Thomson did not give up until she married someone else. Thomson never married. He died just two weeks before his forty-eighth birthday of a fever on August 27, 1748.

ANALYSIS

The plays of James Thomson are largely forgotten, as is the poem Thomson regarded as his finest work, *Liberty* (1735-1736). His reputation rests on *The Seasons* and, to a lesser extent, *The Castle of Indolence*. Thomson critics and scholars generally agree, as Richard Terry puts it, that there is no doubt that "Thomson is a major poet of his time . . . but there is still scope for the nature of his individual achievement to be redefined." Whatever redefinition future scholarship on Thomson attempts, *The Seasons* will remain his distinctive contribution to English poetry.

THE SEASONS

The main debate in Thomson scholarship about *The Seasons* concerns whether or how thoroughly this long poem is unified. David Anderson claims that the poem demonstrates a structural principle which gives an effective direction to the reader about how to comprehend the many topics that appear in Thomson's poem. Anderson describes the structure of the poem as leading readers from "landscape description, through emotional response to landscape, to enthusiastic praise of the landscape's Creator." He names this structure an "emotive theodicy." Since any theodicy attempts to justify the ways of God to human beings, Anderson is being logical when he argues that the central fact of *The Seasons* is contained in the following lines: ". . . tho' conceal'd, to every purer Eye/ Th' informing Author in his Works appears:/ Chief, lovely Spring, in thee, and thy soft Scenes,/ The SMILING GOD is seen. . . ."

The first collected edition of *The Seasons* was published in 1730. Its total length was 4,569 lines. Thomson produced a major revision of his most famous poem, which appeared in 1744; this edition is a quarter longer, adding about a thousand lines. These are certainly not two different poems, but much changed in the intervening fourteen years. The 1744 edition makes *Spring* and *Autumn* only about one hundred lines longer. About three hundred lines are added to *Winter*, and approximately six hundred to *Summer*. Sambrook notes that the later edition extends the historical and geographical material. He also notes that in *Winter* Thomson doubles the number of ancient heroes and makes the passage five times longer than in the 1730 text. Sambrook emphasizes that in *Summer*, the 1744 edition more evenly balances pleasures and pains as well as horrors and delights in nature. This attempt at a balancing act in the revisions of *The Seasons* serves both a religious and a political purpose.

If religion and praise of God are important to *The Seasons*, so is politics. Scholar Tim Fulford emphasizes that Thomson's landscapes in *The Seasons*, especially in the 1744 edition, are imagined by the poet as political spaces. Thomson sees wild landscapes as bastions of natural British freedom, and he presents cultivated landscapes as indexes of the virtues of the patrons whose political commitments Thomson shared. The poet perceives this wild native freedom and cultivated virtues of British landscapes as threatened by the spreading corruption of Prime Minister Robert Walpole's government of arbitrary and abusive power. This corruption is literally covering the landscape, attacking both natural freedom and the civil freedoms of a just society. In *Winter*, Thomson describes the arrogance and barbarism of corrupt power: "Ah little think the gay licentious Proud,/ Whom Pleasure, Power, and Affluence surround," while others "feel, this very Moment, Death/ And all the sad Variety of Pain." Thomson, in trying to marry religious and political commitments in his presentation of natural and cultivated landscapes, risks both the unity of his poem and the integrity of his poetic vision.

LIBERTY

Thomson's time in France and Italy inspired him to write what he regarded as his most important poem, *Liberty*. Thomson originally intended *Liberty* to be a "poetical landscape of countries, mixed with moral observations on their governments and people." This approach would have identified the poem as by the author of the highly successful *The Seasons*, but Thomson did not follow this plan. The poet who reestablished natural description in English poetry in *The Seasons* barely mentions nature in *Liberty*, which was an utter failure with the public. It was published in separate parts: Three thousand copies of part 1 were printed, two thousand copies of parts 2 and 3, and only one thousand copies of parts 4 and 5, indicating the failure of the poem. Yet Thomson considered it his most important and finest poem. Samuel Kliger feels that it is understandable that Thomson considered it his greatest poem; he said, *Liberty* "could be considered great because its theme—the increment of history turned back to enrich the lives of England's humblest citizens—was great."

Liberty argues against luxury and corruption as the causes of tyranny. This 3,378-line poem describes the cyclical rise and fall of freedom in various states, principally Greece and Rome. Thomson feared that Great Britain was beginning to decline because of indulgence in luxury and party faction by eminent Britons. The poem is a dissuasion against self-interest, attempting to show that freedom is a delicate condition which must be nurtured and maintained with great care. The poem deals with the necessity of harmonizing all aspects of the personality so that one will not be susceptible to corruption in any of its forms. *Liberty* is a fable about political virtue that embodies Thomson's conception of spiritual evolution and that holds up the ideal of "*boundless Good without the power of Ill*."

THE CASTLE OF INDOLENCE

In April, 1748, Thomson wrote a letter to his friend William Paterson about what would be Thomson's last major poem: "after fourteen or fifteen Years, the Castle of Indolence comes abroad in a Fortnight." Thomson's friend Patrick Murdoch described the genesis of the poem as a mockery of himself and some friends whom he thought indolent. This playful origin of the poem and a more serious application of the moral of the poem—to live an active life of public service—are both present in the tone of *The Castle of Indolence*. In the same letter about the poem, Murdoch added: "But he saw very soon, that the subject deserved to be treated more seriously, and in a form fitted to convey one of the most important moral lessons."

The Castle of Indolence consists of two cantos. It is a poem of 1,422 lines. The first canto is composed of 77 Spenserian stanzas, or 693 lines. The Spenserian stanza uses eight iambic lines of ten syllables and a ninth line of twelve syllables, and its rhyme scheme is *ababbcbcc*. Canto 1 describes a castle where imagination and romantic images create earthly paradises suggested by the Bower of Bliss in Spenser's *Faerie Queene*. This castle is ruled by the Wizard of Indolence, who uses Nepenthe, the drink from the *Faerie Queene*, to enchant people and draw them into the luxurious ease of the castle. The influence of the drink is to provide "sweet Oblivion of vile earthly Care;/ Fair gladsome waking Thoughts, and joyous Dreams more fair." The inhabitants of the castle, however, become ill and are left in a dungeon to languish.

The second canto is composed of 81 stanzas, or 729 lines. It presents the Knight of Arts and Industry destroying the romantic imagination and replacing it with moral responsibility and hard work. This commitment to hard work, public service, and progress leads to eternal activity: "Heirs of Eternity! yborn to rise/ Through endless States of Being, still more near/ To Bliss approaching, and Perfection clear, . . ."

The Castle of Indolence was praised by William Wordsworth. Another nineteenth century English poet, Percy Bysshe Shelley, said that "the Enchanter in the first canto was a true philanthropist, and the Knight in the second an oligarchical imposter, overthrowing truth by power." Scholar James Sambrook argues that the achievement of Thomson's poem "is to make us feel the power of romanticism and respond with delight to its appeal, while at the same time we judge it, and know the dangers of its rejection of responsibility and reality."

Other major works

PLAYS: *The Tragedy of Sophonisba*, pb. 1730; *Agamemnon*, pr., pb. 1738; *Edward and Eleonora*, pb. 1739; *Alfred*, pr., pb. 1740 (with David Mallet); *Tancred and Sigismunda*, pr., pb. 1745; *Coriolanus*, pr., pb. 1749.

Bibliography

Campbell, Hilbert H. *James Thomson, 1700-1748: An Annotated Bibliography of Selected Editions and the Important Criticism*. New York: Garland, 1976. What makes this book valuable for the study of Thomson are the terse, balanced, insightful, and interesting annotations to editions and criticism of James Thomson's writings. This bibliography is inclusive; it even lists theses and dissertations on Thomson from the United States and abroad.

McKillop, Alan Dugald, ed. *James Thomson (1700-1748): Letters and Documents*. Lawrence: University of Kansas Press, 1958. An important biographical and literary record for the study of Thomson, this book presents the seventy-four letters then known. McKillop discovered two additional letters in 1962, and three more letters were uncovered in 1972 by A. S. Bell. The book is also important for the documents it publishes, such as newspaper articles from the 1730's and 1740's about the poet, copyright documents, and documents connected to Thomson's death.

Sambrook, James. *James Thomson, 1700-1748: A Life*. New York: Clarendon Press, 1991. This is the first extensive biography of Thomson since Douglas Grant's in 1951. It places Thomson in his social and cultural context, explores his relationships with fellow writers such as Alexander Pope, and thoroughly examines Thomson's Whig politics and relationship with Frederick, Prince of Wales, leader of the opposition to Prime Minister Robert Walpole. Sambrook supplies biography, history, and literary criticism by producing a detailed analysis of the whole body of Thomson's writings.

Scott, Mary Jane W. *James Thomson, Anglo-Scot*. Athens: University of Georgia Press, 1988. This book argues for the importance of the Scottish dimensions of Thomson's writings. For example, although the third earl of Shaftesbury has always been considered a major influence on Thomson's ideas about benevolence and the poetry of sensibility, this book shows that the Scottish writer Francis Hutcheson, a follower of Shaftesbury, was the more important influence. Hutcheson had a Calvinist interpretation of benevolence, which moved Thomson to his frequent promotion in his poetry of sympathy as a universal social duty.

Terry, Richard, ed. *James Thomson: Essays for the Tercentenary*. Liverpool, England: Liverpool University Press, 2000. This is the first book of essays devoted to Thomson's works. Part 1 focuses on Thomson's poetry and drama, and part 2 examines Thomson's influences on later writers and his reputation. There is a useful introduction that gives a good overview of Thomson scholarship. This book offers a reappraisal of Thomson from the perspective of the early twenty-first century, to show how he transcends his own time, as well as being a barometer of the trends of his day.

Robert Eddy

James Thomson

Born: Port Glasgow, Scotland; November 23, 1834
Died: London, England; June 3, 1882

Principal poetry
The City of Dreadful Night and Other Poems, 1880
Vane's Story, Weddah and Om-el Bonain, and Other Poems, 1881
Shelley, a Poem: With Other Writings Relating to Shelley, 1884
A Voice from the Nile and Other Poems, 1884
The Poetical Works of James Thomson, 1895 (2 volumes; Bertram Dobell, editor)

OTHER LITERARY FORMS

James Thomson wrote criticism, journalism, essays, and imaginative prose works from the early 1860's through his last years, primarily for magazines dedicated to the Free Thought movement, including the *London Investigator* and *National Reformer*. His subjects were often literary, as in his essays on Walt Whitman and fellow atheist poet George Meredith. One selection of Thomson's essays, *Essays and Phantasies* (1881), appeared in book form in the poet's lifetime. Several posthumous volumes followed, including one volume of his translations.

ACHIEVEMENTS

James Thomson's long narrative poem "The City of Dreadful Night" established the poet's reputation, although many critics were slow to recognize its qualities. In its monumental depiction of a lone soul's journey through a city bathed in darkness, it communicated a melancholy yet beautiful vision of the human condition, a vision distinctively different from those offered by Thomson's contemporaries. The poem earned him the appellation "laureate of pessimism," given him by Bertram Dobell.

The poem's impact was acknowledged by such contemporaries as George Eliot and George Meredith, and by such later figures as Rudyard Kipling and T. S. Eliot, the latter whose *The Waste Land* (1922) is considered by some critics a direct literary descendent. In this and others of his works, in both subject and literary tone, Thomson expressed a sensibility more akin to that found in the poetry of the twentieth century than in that of the nineteenth.

BIOGRAPHY

James Thomson was born to Scottish parents whose chief characteristics became some of his own. His father, an officer of the merchant marine, was known for his geniality and love of the drink, while his mother was known for her melancholy.

Thomson's father was a chief officer in a ship out of Greenock, Scotland, when he was disabled by a paralytic stroke in 1840. He moved the family to London, where within two years the young Thomson was admitted to the Royal Caledonian Asylum, an institution for the children of indigent Scottish servicemen. His ailing mother died soon thereafter, in 1842.

Thomson's relatives determined his future as an army schoolmaster and in 1850 enrolled him in the military normal school of the Royal Military College at Chelsea. Successful in his studies, Thomson was posted in 1851 as assistant teacher in a regimental school in Ballincollig, near Cork, Ireland. His nearly year-and-a-half stay there proved pivotal. He made friends with a trooper in the dragoons, Charles Bradlaugh, who later would become an editor and leading proponent of the Free Thought movement in England. He also fell in love with the young Matilda Weller. To Thomson's great despair, she died soon after his duties took him back to Chelsea. To his dying day he kept a curl of her hair in a locket.

Made an army schoolmaster in 1854, for the next eight years he served in Devonshire, Dublin, Aldershot, Jersey, and Portsmouth. He also began his career as a poet. His works appeared in periodicals including the *Edinburgh Magazine* above the signature "B. V." The first initial represented "Bysshe," to invoke Percy Bysshe Shelley, while the second represented "Vanolis," an anagram on Novalis, pseudonym of German Romantic poet Friedrich von Hardenberg. Thomson's identification with the latter was strengthened by the fact that Hardenberg's one love had also died in childhood.

In 1862 Thomson was court-martialed and dismissed from the army along with several companions, ostensibly for a minor rules infraction. Thomson's dismissal also may have been due to his increasing suffering from melancholy and bouts of drunkenness.

Bradlaugh came to his aid, taking him in and helping him locate work, initially as a clerk and later as a journalist. Thomson wrote for the freethinker journal *London Investigator* and subsequently for *National Reformer*, which eventually came under Bradlaugh's sole editorship. In these journals Thomson, as "B.V.," enjoyed a growing, if still small, reputation as both poet and dedicated proponent of rationalism. Conversant in several languages, he also translated the works of Giacomo Leopardi, Heinrich Heine, and Novalis, among others.

Earning only a meager living through these writings, Thomson was forced to live in single-room apartments in the London slums. He briefly held two promising positions in the early 1870's. In 1872-1873 he served as secretary for London's Champion Gold and Silver Mines Company, which sent him to Central City, Colorado, for nine months to inspect its holdings. These being worthless, the company went into bankruptcy soon after Thomson's return.

Later in 1873, Bradlaugh helped Thomson obtain a post with the New York *World* to report on the Spanish civil conflict between Royalists and Republicans, a conflict that proved of such low intensity it provided inadequate material for coverage, leading to his recall after six weeks.

The following year brought Thomson new recognition, however. His masterwork, *The City of Dreadful Night, and Other Poems* (1880), appeared in serial form in the weekly *National Reformer*, in issues from March 22 through May 17, 1874. Among those taking notice was Bertram Dobell, who met the poet and arranged for the publication of Thomson's first book in 1880. By then, however, Thomson and Bradlaugh had broken off their friendship, in part due to the influence of Bradlaugh's new associate and future theosophist, Annie Besant. Thereafter Thomson's writings appeared in another Free Thought magazine, the *Secularist*, and a combination trade and literary journal, *Cope's Tobacco Plant*. Dobell helped secure publication of two more volumes of collected works.

Thomson, who had long struggled with insomnia, melancholy, and alcoholism, enjoyed some spells of happiness in 1881 and 1882 but suffered a hemorrhage after a drunken bout and died June 3, 1882, in University College Hospital, London. He was buried in Highgate Cemetery.

ANALYSIS

While Bertram Dobell dubbed James Thomson the "laureate of pessimism," a title that accurately captures the initial impression given by some of his works, the appellation has the unfortunate effect of leading readers to ignore one of Thomson's major concerns. The poet spoke of despair, undoubtedly. Yet he did so in order to seek a way past the pessimism that pure rationalism had a tendency to produce.

While "The City of Dreadful Night" seems outwardly about despair, it pointedly concerns itself with questions about the meaning and purpose of life in an in-

different universe. The narrator of the poem, along with many of its other shadowy characters, persist with their lives despite the prevailing despair, a fact in keeping with the conclusion stated in the poem's final lines: while the weak despair, the strong endure. Facing the mystery central to existence, "The strong . . . drink new strength of iron endurance,/ The weak new terrors."

Perceiving the oppositions at work within the human mind as well as within the larger universe, Thomson embraced rationalism without dismissing the simple joys possible in life. In both shorter and longer works he concerned himself with related topics born of rationalism, in terms that are deeply emotional. His attitude is most clearly summed up in "Philosophy" (1866).

Thomson's poetry is marked by a measured clarity of image and language, guided by a strong narrative instinct. The poems are largely stanzaic, often structured with repeating motifs or phrases to help emphasize their dramatic movement.

"THE DOOM OF A CITY"

Subtitled "A Fantasia," the early long poem "The Doom of a City" (1857) anticipated "The City of Dreadful Night" in its imagery and thematic elements. Divided into the three sections, "The Voyage," "The City," and "The Judgments," the poem offers a journey across a strange, storm-tossed sea to a darkness-shrouded city whose inhabitants have been frozen into stonelike stillness. The tragedy the traveler discovers, which the reader takes to be the source of the city's doom, is the motionless funeral procession for a beautiful young girl.

The traumatic experience of having a loved one die too young, and too soon, Thomson would later address directly in his short poem "Indeed You Set Me in a Happy Place" (1862), which ends with the lines, "Ah, ever since her eyes withdrew their light,/ I wander lost in blackest stormy night." In the earlier "The Doom of a City," the vision of the dead girl evokes the transitory nature of beauty and youth, and the fleeting pleasures of life. The early date of this poem's composition reveals the lifelong nature of Thomson's struggle to deal with the opposition between a relentlessly changing universe and the ephemeral possibility of personal joy.

"PHILOSOPHY"

The four-canto poem "Philosophy" (1866) presents in capsule form Thomson's concern with the implications of rational or scientific thought and embodies many of his major thematic concerns. The unidentified central character of the poem "Looked through and through the specious earth and skies," making him akin to the "City of Dreadful Night" inhabitants who see that "all is vanity and nothingness." The question he faces, "How could he vindicate himself?," parallels the struggle to find solace and meaning in the longer poem of 1874.

"Philosophy" presents an optimistic vision, even in its rationality, and makes an argument for the importance of human love, echoing his earlier poem "The Deliverer" (1859). It ends with one of the most charming moments in Thomson's works, a quatrain on an insect:

> If Midge will pine and curse its hours away
> Because Midge is not Everything For-aye,
> Poor Midge thus loses its one summer day;
> Loses its all—and winneth what, I pray?

"IN THE ROOM"

A subdued yet powerful poem, "In the Room" (1867-1868) is a tour de force in which the objects of a room speak to one another, as though animate beings equipped with speech and memory. The object of their conversation is their sense of a change having occurred in the room, which is revealed to be the death of the room's lone inhabitant, whose life had been quiet and unhappy. Remarkable not only for its conceit but for its execution, "In the Room" is a focused and unsentimental exploration of the theme of isolation, found in many other Thomson poems.

"THE CITY OF DREADFUL NIGHT"

A long poem of unusual emotional strength, thematic consistency, and intellectual rigor, "The City of Dreadful Night" (1874) offers the tale of a man consigned to existence in a "City of the Night," whose only dwellers are "melancholy Brothers." Divided into twenty-one cantos, the poem alternates between sections of a descriptive and reflective nature, and of a narrative nature.

The unfortunate main character travels through a series of telling situations and incidents, first overhearing conversations alongside a darkened river, unveiling the nature of the city. He discovers a palace lighted as for a festival and finds inside a bier with a dead young girl,

over whom a young man kneels in sorrow. He then approaches a cathedral, whose doorkeeper demands each entrant's story. Each of these brief stories ends with what amounts to an invocation: "I wake from daydreams to this real night."

Inside the cathedral, he listens to a "great sad voice" from the pulpit who raises the question of the search for meaning that propels the poem and speaks of the beckoning solace of oblivion, an idea introduced in the poem's first canto as the "One anodyne for torture and despair." The speaker at the pulpit leaves a message ringing in the ears of his listeners: "End it when you will," he says, perhaps referring to the river in canto 19.

The poem ends with a series of striking tableaus. Canto 19 speaks of the "River of Suicides" and describes the ways different suffering souls enter its waters. Canto 20 describes a silent confrontation between an armed angel and an impassive sphinx, in which the latter, whose "vision seemed of infinite void space," emerges the motionless victor. The final canto, 21, describes a great "bronze colossus of a winged Woman," named Melancolia. It is to her the strong turn their eyes, "to drink new strength of iron endurance," while the weak look to her for "new terrors."

Like the much shorter "Philosophy," "The City of Dreadful Night" both reaffirms and issues a challenge to the Deist rationalism and free thinking Thomson embraced in his own life. In the poem, God is a "dark delusion of a dream." Yet the poem warns both specifically and in its imagery against a way of thinking "most rational and yet insane" and embodies the search for meaning and solace in an indifferent universe found also in "Philosophy."

"A VOICE FROM THE NILE"

Written in Thomson's last years, "A Voice from the Nile" (1881) strikes a different chord from many of his other works, the central conceit being that the river Nile itself is the poem's speaker. The great river observes the various animal inhabitants on its shores and notes how they exist contentedly within their various spheres of existence. The river then observes the "children of an alien race," the people who built great structures along its shores. ". . . Man, this alien in my family,/ Is alien most in this, to cherish dreams/ And brood on visions of eternity, . . ." More than any other characteristic in humankind, the river Nile focuses on the "religions in his brooding brain" as the characteristic that estranges humankind from the rest of nature. "O admirable, pitiable Man," the river says. The poem has unusual rhetorical impact, establishing a nearly pastoral tone before developing its rationalist theme with increasing incisiveness.

OTHER MAJOR WORKS

NONFICTION: *Essays and Phantasies*, 1881; *Satires and Profanities*, 1884 (G. W. Foote, editor); *Biographical and Critical Studies*, 1896 (Bertram Dobell, editor); *Walt Whitman, the Man and the Poet*, 1910 (Dobell, editor).

TRANSLATION: *Essays, Dialogues and Thoughts*, 1905 (of Giacomo Leopardi; Bertram Dobell, editor).

BIBLIOGRAPHY

Gerould, Gordon Hall. *Poems of James Thomson "B. V."* New York: Henry Holt and Company, 1927. Gerould's early evaluation of Thomson's poetry remains valuable for its balanced defense and consideration of poems beyond the most frequently considered works. He observes that Thomson pursued his art for twenty-five years. Thomson's finest work, he also argues, was not the product of bursts of inspiration. "It was the work of a man whose capacity for steady effort was as marked as his imaginative power," a fact made more striking in that it "continued without the stimulus of an audience." Gerould notes the "austere but melodic dignity" found in Thomson's works.

Leonard, Tom. *Places of the Mind: The Life and Work of James Thomson ("B. V.")*. London: Cape, 1993. Leonard's carefully researched, documentary account gives factual depth to the story of Thomson and his times, shedding light on the poet's surroundings, friends, and writings. The book includes extensive writings and letters by both Thomson and his friends.

Morgan, Edwin. Introduction to *The City of Dreadful Night, and Other Poems*, by James Thomson. Reprint. Edinburgh: Canongate Classics #53, 1998. In a wide-ranging and insightful essay, Morgan explores the nature of Thomson's poetry, challenging the notion of Thomson as the "laureate of pessimism" and examining some of Thomson's legacy.

Ridler, A. *Poems and Some Letters of James Thomson*. London: Centaur Press, 1963. Provides a later complete selection of Thomson's poetry.

Salt, H. S. *The Life of James Thomson ("B. V.")*. London: Reeves & Turner & Dobell, 1889. One of the earliest accounts of Thomson's life, and the primary source of many subsequent biographies.

Mark Rich

HENRY DAVID THOREAU

Born: Concord, Massachusetts; July 12, 1817
Died: Concord, Massachusetts; May 6, 1862

PRINCIPAL POETRY

Poems of Nature, 1895
Collected Poems of Henry David Thoreau, 1943 (first critical edition)

OTHER LITERARY FORMS

Henry David Thoreau published two books during his lifetime: *A Week on the Concord and Merrimack Rivers* (1849) and *Walden: Or, Life in the Woods* (1854). Three additional books edited by his sister Sophia and his friend William Ellery Channing were published soon after his death: a collection of his travel essays titled *Excursions* (1863), *The Maine Woods* (1864), and *Cape Cod* (1864). During his lifetime Thoreau also published essays in various periodicals. They were generally of three kinds: travel essays such as "A Yankee in Canada," nature essays such as "Walking," and social and political essays such as "Life Without Principle" and "Civil Disobedience." Those essays are collected in the standard "Walden" edition of Thoreau's complete writings, and the best of them are generally available today in paperback collections. Thoreau also dabbled in translations and occasionally published in *The Dial* his translations of Greek and Roman poetry. Perhaps Thoreau's greatest literary work, however, is his journal, which he kept throughout most of his adult life and most of which is available in the last fourteen volumes of the "Walden" edition of his collected writings. A portion of the journal from 1840 to 1841 was omitted from the collected writings but was later edited and published by Perry Miller in *Consciousness in Concord* (1958). Also not included in the collected writings were portions of the journal dealing with Thoreau's first trip to Maine and portions which Thoreau himself cut out for use in his books. The Princeton University Press brought together Thoreau's journals in a more unified way in *Journal*, a five-volume edition published between 1981 and 1997.

ACHIEVEMENTS

During his own lifetime, Henry David Thoreau met with only modest literary success. His early poems and essays published in *The Dial* were well-known and appreciated in transcendentalist circles but were generally unknown to popular audiences. As a lecturer, his talks were appreciated by the most liberal of his audiences but were generally found to be obscure or even dangerous by more conservative listeners. Thus, he had brief spurts of popularity as a lecturer, particularly in 1859 to 1860, but was not generally popular on the lecture circuit. His first book, *A Week on the Concord and Merrimack Rivers*, was published in 1849 at his own expense in an edition of one thousand copies. It met with very little success; only 294 copies were sold or given away, while the remaining copies were finally shipped four years later to Thoreau himself, who sarcastically remarked in his journal, "I have now a library of nearly nine hundred volumes, over seven hundred of which I wrote myself: Is it not well that the author should behold the fruits of his labor?" Although *A Week on the Concord and Merrimack Rivers* carried an advertisement of the forthcoming publication of *Walden*, the failure of the first book prompted Thoreau to withhold publication of the later one until he could feel more certain of its success. After much revision, Thoreau published *Walden* in 1854. It met with generally favorable reviews and good sales, over seventeen hundred copies of an edition of two thousand being sold in the first year. By 1859 it was out of print, but it was reissued in a second edition shortly after Thoreau's death. *Walden* won Thoreau some fame with general audiences and created a small but devoted number of disciples who would occasionally visit Thoreau in

Concord or send him complimentary copies of books. After the success of *Walden*, Thoreau found it easier to publish his essays in the more popular periodicals, such as *Putnam's Magazine* and the *Atlantic Monthly*. In his last years he also acquired some notoriety as an abolitionist through his impassioned lectures and essays on John Brown.

Thoreau's literary reputation has risen steadily since his death, his writings appealing primarily to two very different kinds of readers: those who see him as an escapist nature writer and those who see him as a political radical. As Michael Meyer suggests, his advice to people to simplify their lives and return to an appreciation of nature has had especially strong appeal in times of economic difficulty such as the 1920's and 1930's, and it has also served to cushion criticism of Thoreau in times such as the 1940's, when his political views seemed unpatriotic. Today it is probably still his nature writing that appeals to most readers. His social and political views,

Henry David Thoreau (Library of Congress)

particularly his concept of passive resistance expressed in his essay "Civil Disobedience," have periodically made their influence felt in the actions of major social and political reformers such as Mahatma Gandhi and Martin Luther King. Thoreau's popularity peaked in the 1960's when his nature writing and his political views simultaneously found an audience of young American rebels advocating retreat from urban ugliness and materialism and passive resistance to an unpopular war. Since the 1960's his popularity has subsided somewhat, but he continues to be widely read, and his place among the great writers of American literature seems secure.

BIOGRAPHY

Henry David Thoreau (christened David Henry Thoreau) was born in Concord, Massachusetts, on July 12, 1817, the third of four children of John and Cynthia Thoreau. His father was a quiet man whose seeming lack of ambition had led to a series of unsuccessful attempts to establish himself as a shopkeeper prior to his finally establishing a very successful pencil factory in Concord. His mother was an outgoing, talkative woman who took in boarders to supplement the family's income. Both parents were fond of nature and could often be seen taking the children picnicking in the Concord woods.

Thoreau received a good grammar school education at the Concord Academy and seems to have had an essentially pleasant and typical boyhood. He attended Harvard College from 1833 to 1837, taking time out during his junior year to recuperate from a prolonged illness and to supplement his income by teaching for several months in Canton, Massachusetts. Upon being graduated near the top of his class, he took a teaching job in the Concord public schools, but after a few weeks he resigned in protest over the school board's insistence that he use corporal punishment to discipline his students. Unable to find another position, Thoreau opened a private school of his own and was eventually joined by his older brother John. John's cheerful disposition together with Henry's high academic standards made the school very successful until it was closed in 1841 because of John's prolonged illness.

During these years as a teacher, Thoreau traveled to Maine, took, with his brother, the famous excursion on the Concord and Merrimack rivers which eventually became the subject of his first book, delivered his first lecture, and published his first essay and his first poetry in *The Dial*. Through one of his students, Edmund Sewall (whom he praises in one of his best-known poems, "Lately, Alas, I Knew a Gentle Boy") he met Ellen Sewall, the only woman to whom he seems to have been romantically attracted in any serious way. Ellen seems to have been the subject or recipient of a number of Thoreau's poems of 1839 and 1840, but his brother John was the more forward of the two in courting Ellen, and it was after John's proposal to Ellen had failed that Henry also proposed, only to be rejected as John had been.

After the closing of the school, Thoreau was invited to live with Ralph Waldo Emerson's family as a handyman; he stayed two years, during which time he continued to contribute to, and occasionally help Emerson edit, *The Dial*. In 1842, his brother John died suddenly of a tetanus infection, leaving Thoreau so devastated that he himself briefly exhibited psychosomatic symptoms of the disease. The following year, a brief stint as a tutor to William Emerson's family on Staten Island confirmed his prejudice against cities, so he returned to Concord, where in 1844 he and a companion accidentally set fire to the Concord Woods, thus earning some rather long-lasting ill will from some of his neighbors and some long-lasting damage to his reputation as a woodsman.

For several years, Thoreau had contemplated buying a house and some land of his own, but in 1845 he settled for permission from Emerson to use some land near Walden Pond to build his own cabin. He built a one-room cabin and moved in on July 4, thus declaring his intention to be free to work on his writing and on a personal experiment in economic self-reliance. He continued to use the cabin as his main residence for two years, during which time he wrote *A Week on the Concord and Merrimack Rivers* and much of *Walden*, raised beans, took a trip to the Maine Woods, and spent his famous night in the Concord jail for nonpayment of taxes. An invitation from Emerson to spend another year as a resident handyman finally prompted him to leave the pond in the fall of 1847, but he left with little regret, because, as he says in *Walden*, "I had several more lives to live, and I could not spare any more time for that one." The fruits of his stay at the pond finally began to appear in

1849, when *A Week on the Concord and Merrimack Rivers* and his essay on "Resistance to Civil Government" (later renamed "Civil Disobedience") were both published.

Throughout the 1840's, Thoreau had become increasingly interested in the natural sciences, and he began to spend much time gathering and measuring specimens, often at the expense of his writing, so that by 1851 he had reason to complain in his journal, "I feel that the character of my knowledge is from year to year becoming more distinct and scientific; that, in exchange for views as wide as heaven's scope, I am being narrowed down to the field of the microscope." His scientific and mechanical abilities had benefits for the family's pencil-making business, however, because in 1843 he had developed a more effective means of securing the graphite in the pencils and was later to improve the quality of pencils still further. Throughout his life he maintained of necessity an interest in the family business, although he seldom enjoyed having to take active part in it. His aversion to the routine of regular employment also applied to his surveying talents, which were called on by his neighbors increasingly after 1850. Although by 1851 Thoreau seems to have felt that life was passing him by without his having been able to achieve his goals, the publication of *Walden* in 1854 revived his self-esteem when the book sold well and brought a small but devoted group of admirers.

Throughout the 1850's Thoreau made several excursions to Canada, the Maine Woods, and Cape Cod which culminated in travel essays in popular periodicals. He also traveled to New Jersey and to Brooklyn, where he met Walt Whitman, with whom he was favorably impressed. Thoreau's admiration for Whitman's raw genius was surpassed only by his admiration for John Brown, the abolitionist, whom he first met in 1857 and whose cause he vigorously supported in lectures and published essays.

In 1860, Thoreau caught a bad cold which eventually developed into tuberculosis. Advised to seek a different climate, Thoreau took a trip to Minnesota in 1861, a trip which provided him with some brief glimpses of "uncivilized" Indians but with no relief from his illness. After returning to Concord, his health continued to deteriorate, and he died at home on May 6, 1862.

ANALYSIS

For Henry David Thoreau, the value of poetry lay not primarily in the poem itself, but in the act of writing the poem and in that act's influence on the poet's life. The importance of poetry to the poet is, as he says in *A Week on the Concord and Merrimack Rivers*, in "what he has become through his work." Since for the Transcendentalists life was superior to art, Thoreau could assert that "My life has been the poem I would have writ,/ But I could not both live and utter it." No art form could surpass God's act of creating nature or man's act of shaping his own life. In his journal for 1840, Thoreau suggests that the best an artist can hope for is to equal nature, not to surpass her. The poet's job is to publish nature's truth accurately, and thus at times, verse seemed to him to be the best vehicle for publicizing nature because of its greater precision. By the mid-1840's, however, he had mostly abandoned verse and concluded that "Great prose, of equal elevation, commands our respect more than great verse, since it implies a more permanent and level height. . . . The poet often only makes an irruption . . . but the prose writer has conquered . . . and settled colonies." In 1851 he found it necessary to warn himself to beware "of youthful poetry, which is impotent." Another problem with poetry was that it was too artificial. One could not capture in words the rhythms of the wind or the birds. He found that "the music now runs before and then behind the sense, but is never coincident with it." One could make music, or one could make sense; Thoreau eventually preferred the latter.

Because of this ambiguous attitude toward the value of verse (he eventually came to speak of both good verse and good prose as "poetry"), Thoreau's poetry is seldom first-rate, and even at its best it does not rival that of such contemporaries as Emily Dickinson and Walt Whitman. Nevertheless, it is of significance to the modern reader, first, because it demonstrates vividly the problems that American poets faced in freeing themselves artistically from European influences, and second, because it provides some fresh insights, not available as fully in his prose, into some of the deepest problems of Thoreau's life, especially his attempts to cope with the problems of love and friendship and of his own role as an artist.

Thoreau could never quite free himself from imitating the great poets he admired to find a voice of his own. He mined his expert knowledge of Greek and Latin to write epigrams or odes (essentially Horatian in form) such as "Let Such Pure Hate Still Underprop," which is also reminiscent of the seventeenth century Metaphysical poets in its use of paradox. Indeed, it is the Metaphysicals to whom Thoreau seems to have turned most often as muses for his own poetry: the paradoxes, introspection, and elaborate conceits of John Donne or Andrew Marvell. At other times one can find in Thoreau's verse the loose rhythms of John Skelton's near-doggerel dimeter, as in "The Old Marlborough Road," or the more graceful tetrameter couplets, which are Thoreau's most frequently used form and which, as critic Henry Wells suggests, can also be traced to the Metaphysicals. Finally, Thoreau frequently employs the three-part structure and tight stanza form of George Herbert's meditations. The stanza form of "I Am a Parcel of Vain Strivings Tied," for example, is clearly modeled on Herbert, while a poem such as "The Poet's Delay" has, as H. Grant Sampson suggests, the three-part meditative structure which moves from a particular scene in nature to the poet's awareness of the scene's wider implications, and finally to the poet's recognition of the scene's specific spiritual meaning for him.

THE INFLUENCE OF THE ROMANTIC POETS

Although Thoreau most frequently looked to the past for poetic models, he did admire some of the Romantic poets of his own day, particularly William Wordsworth. Thoreau's "I Knew a Man by Sight," for example, portrays a typical Wordsworthian rustic wanderer, while in Thoreau's unfortunate attempt at rhyme in the lines "Late in a wilderness/ I shared his mess" readers also see the glaring difference in poetic skill between the two poets. In "My Books I'd Fain Cast Off, I Cannot Read," Thoreau expresses a view of the superiority of nature to books, very much like that in Wordsworth's "Expostulation and Reply." In several other poems he seems to echo Wordsworth's theories of human development. In "Manhood," for example, Thoreau presents the same view of the child as father of the man that Wordsworth presents in "Ode: Intimations of Immortality." In "Music," he also presents a view of man's loss of youthful faculties and of compensation for that loss with adult wisdom similar to that presented by Wordsworth in "Lines Composed a Few Miles Above Tintern Abbey" and in *The Prelude* (1850).

From this unlikely mixture of classical, Metaphysical, and Romantic influences, Thoreau apparently hoped to create a poetry which would express his own love of paradox, introspection, and nature, while creating a style both stately and rugged, at once elevated and natural. The task was, as Thoreau himself came to realize, impossible. It is also interesting to note, however, that Thoreau seems not to have looked to his own countrymen, except perhaps Ralph Waldo Emerson, for models. His diction and rhythms are most frequently traceable to European influence, and when he attempts to break free of that influence, he usually meets with only modest success or complete failure.

Because Thoreau's prose is generally more effective than his poetry, when he deals with a topic in both genres the poetry is generally valuable primarily as a gloss on the prose. In "Wait Not Till Slaves Pronounce the Word," for example, Thoreau reminds the reader that slavery is as much a state of mind as an external condition: "Think not the tyrant sits afar/ In your own breasts ye have/ The District of Columbia/ And power to free the Slave." His statement in *Walden*, however, makes the same point more powerfully: "It is hard to have a Southern overseer; it is worse to have a Northern one; but worst of all when you are the slave driver of yourself." Some of Thoreau's nature poems do present some fresh minor insights into Thoreau's view of nature, but those poems which are of most value and interest in their own right are those which shed autobiographical light on some of his personal dilemmas either unexpressed or not expressed as well in his prose, particularly his attempt to find an ideal friendship and his attempt to meet the artistic goals he set for himself.

THE IDEAL OF FRIENDSHIP

Thoreau's ideal of friendship, expressed most fully in the "Wednesday" chapter of *A Week on the Concord and Merrimack Rivers*, is typically Transcendentalist in its insistence on paradox in human relationships. To Thoreau, friends were to be united with one another and yet separate. They were to love one another's strengths while at the same time hating one another's weaknesses, to be committed to one another and yet be free, to express their love and yet remain silent. They were to be equal, and yet he insists that only a friendship contracted with one's superior is worthwhile. Friendship, as he suggests in a manuscript poem titled "Friendship," was to combine truth, beauty, and goodness in a platonic spiritual oneness, symbolized in the poem by two oak trees which barely touch above the ground but which are inseparably intertwined in their roots. Although he tends to over-intellectualize this concept of friendship, Thoreau was quite in earnest in seeking it in his friends, especially after his college years when he was trying to define his own identity through those he cared about. The person who perhaps came closest to being the soulmate whom Thoreau sought was his brother John. Unfortunately, as is often the case with affection for relatives, Thoreau found that he could seldom express his love for John adequately. When John died, his only outlet was to pour out his affection in his writings by dedicating his first book to him and by writing a gently moving poem, "Brother Where Dost Thou Dwell."

Others who for a time seemed to realize his ideal were Edmund Sewall (one of his students) and Edmund's sister, Ellen. To Edmund, Thoreau wrote one of his best poems, "Lately, Alas, I Knew a Gentle Boy." In this poem, Edmund Sewall is described as one who effortlessly wins the love of all around him by his quiet virtue. Mutual respect between the poet and the boy leads them both to keep their love unexpressed, however, and they paradoxically find themselves "less acquainted than when first we met." The friendship thus slips away without being overtly expressed, and the poet is left to cherish only "that virtue which he is." Although this poem certainly has androgynous qualities and is sometimes used to suggest a youthful homosexuality in Thoreau, it seems wiser to take it for what it more obviously is: one of the clearest and most moving of Thoreau's expressions of the joys and frustrations of platonic love. His poems to Edmund's sister, Ellen, are similarly platonic in tone. In one poem ("Love"), for example, he describes himself and Ellen as a "double star" revolving "about one center." In "The Breeze's Invitation," he adds a pastoral touch, describing himself and Ellen as a carefree king and queen of a "peaceful little green." In such poems, the reader sees a Thoreau who, beneath the platonic and pastoral conventions, is a young man

earnestly seeking affection—a young man much more vulnerable than the didactic prose philosophizer of *A Week on the Concord and Merrimack Rivers* or the self-confident chanticleer in *Walden*.

ARTISTIC HOPES

That same human vulnerability is also the most striking quality of those poems that deal with Thoreau's artistic goals. Aside from his journals, it is in his poems that Thoreau most fully reveals his artistic hopes and disappointments. Those hopes were a typically romantic mixture of active achievement and passive reception. On one hand, as he suggests in "The Hero," a man must contribute something new to his world; he must, as he says in *Walden*, "affect the quality of the day." On the other hand, he can achieve such results only if he is receptive to the inspiration of God through nature. Such inspiration at its most powerful culminates in the sort of mystical experience described by Thoreau in his poem "The Bluebirds," in which he describes his feelings as if "the heavens were all around,/ And the earth was all below" and as if he were a "waking thought-/ A something I hardly knew."

INSPIRATION

Such mystical experiences were the crucial source of the poet's action, whether in writing or in deeds; thus, as Paul O. Williams has demonstrated, much of Thoreau's poetry deals directly or indirectly with the subject of inspiration. The fullest and clearest treatment of the theme is in "Inspiration," a poem in which he describes having occasionally felt a godlike sensitivity to the world so powerful that he felt thoroughly reborn and ready to "fathom hell or climb to heaven." The poet's predicament, however, was that such pure inspiration could seldom be translated untainted into action, and it is this predicament which is at the heart of several of his best poems. In "Light-Winged Smoke, Icarian Bird," one of the most often reprinted and discussed of his poems, he cryptically describes himself as a flame and his poetry as the smoke which he sends heavenward to God. Unfortunately, as the smoke rises to God, it also blots out the truth of God's sun and negates the poet's purpose of clarifying that truth. Thoreau's point here, as Eberhard Alsen convincingly argues, is that even the "clear flame" of the poet is not pure enough to avoid misrepresenting God's truths. That sense of the human artist's limitations in a world of infinite wonder sometimes led Thoreau to feel that his life was being wasted, as in "The Poet's Delay," in which he expresses his fear that while nature's seasons progress into autumn and bear fruit, his own "spring does not begin." Elsewhere, however, as in "I Am a Parcel of Vain Strivings Tied," he consoles himself with a sacrificial satisfaction that his own failures will allow others to be more fruitful. If he is a parcel of picked flowers unable to produce further beauty, at least the other flowers can bloom more beautifully because his have been thinned out of the garden.

In such poems as these, one realizes that Thoreau sensed early what is quite clear when one surveys the body of his poetry: that verse was not the best vehicle for his thoughts but that it freed him to make his prose more powerful. He would have to wait until the publication of *Walden* to feel that the slow-paced seasons of his artistic life had truly begun to bear fruit. Nevertheless, his poetry served him both as a valuable testing ground for his ideas and as an outlet for some of his deepest private problems. It is also worth the modern reader's time because it provides an occasional peek behind the persona of his prose works and because it helps in understanding the dilemma of the Romantic artist, attempting to convey the ideal while being hindered by the very real limitations of human language—a problem which confronts many modern poets as well.

OTHER MAJOR WORKS

NONFICTION: *A Week on the Concord and Merrimack Rivers*, 1849; *Walden: Or, Life in the Woods*, 1854; *Excursions*, 1863; *The Maine Woods*, 1864; *Cape Cod*, 1865; *Letters to Various Persons*, 1865 (Ralph Waldo Emerson, editor); *A Yankee in Canada, with Anti-Slavery and Reform Papers*, 1866; *Early Spring in Massachusetts*, 1881; *Summer*, 1884; *Winter*, 1888; *Autumn*, 1892; *Familiar Letters of Henry David Thoreau*, 1894 (F. B. Sanborn, editor); *Journal*, 1981-1997 (5 volumes).

MISCELLANEOUS: *The Writings of Henry David Thoreau*, 1906; *Collected Essays and Poems*, 2001.

BIBLIOGRAPHY

Cain, William E. *A Historical Guide to Henry David Thoreau*. New York: Oxford University Press, 2000.

Historical and biographical context and treatment of Thoreau.

Hahn, Stephen. *On Thoreau*. Belmont, Calif.: Wadsworth, 2000. A concise study intended to assist a beginning student in understanding Thoreau's philosophy and thinking. Includes bibliographical references.

Harding, Walter. *The Days of Henry Thoreau*. New York: Alfred A. Knopf, 1965. This fine scholarly biography has not been surpassed and remains a model for readability. Harding places the poetry insightfully in the pattern of Thoreau's life. Complete with illustrations, a bibliographical note, and a thorough index.

Harding, Walter, and Michael Meyer. *The New Thoreau Handbook*. New York: New York University Press, 1980. This updated version of a standard basic reference on Thoreau is generally the first source to be consulted for help. Contains a considerable amount of factual information about the writings and the writer, arranged for easy access. Chronologies, indexes, and cross-references increase its usefulness.

Howarth, William. *The Book of Concord: Thoreau's Life as a Writer*. New York: Viking Press, 1982. Howarth presents a writer's biography, paying particular attention to the relationship between the life and the writings and showing exactly how the work evolved. Includes a list of sources, an index, notes, and a number of drawings.

Myerson, Joel, ed. *The Cambridge Companion to Henry David Thoreau*. Cambridge, England: Cambridge University Press, 1995. A guide to the works and to the biographical, historical, and literary contexts. Includes a chronology and further readings.

Richardson, Robert D. *Henry Thoreau: A Life of the Mind*. Berkeley: University of California Press, 1986. This outstanding study focuses primarily on the development of Thoreau's leading themes and the formulation of his working philosophy. Richardson offers unusually clear accounts of some of the writer's complex theories. Provides helpful notes, a bibliography, and an index.

Salt, Henry S. *Life of Henry David Thoreau*. Hamden, Conn.: Archon Books, 1968. Written by a former master of Eton who wrote the first biography of Thoreau in 1890, this is the 1908 (third) version, valuable for the insight it offers of both a late nineteenth century figure and some of his contemporaries, including anecdotes and facts gathered from Samuel Arthur Jones, F. B. Sanborn, Ernest W. Vickers, Raymond Adams, Fred Hosmer, and Mohandas K. Gandhi.

Schneider, Richard J., ed. *Thoreau's Sense of Place: Essays in American Environmental Writing.* Iowa City: University of Iowa Press, 2000. A collection of essays which address a central question in Thoreau studies: How immersed in a sense of place was Thoreau really, and how has this sense of place affected the tradition of nature writing in America?

Shugard, Alan. *American Poetry: The Puritans Through Walt Whitman.* Boston: Twayne, 1988. Contains both informative introductory sketches and a running account of the evolution of American poetry. Shugard's account of Thoreau is brief but just. Includes extensive notes, references, and a useful bibliography.

Tauber, Alfred I. *Henry David Thoreau and the Moral Agency of Knowing.* Berkeley: University of California Press, 2001. This portrait of Thoreau the moralist is written by a professor of philosophy of medicine. Tauber shows how Thoreau's metaphysics of self-knowing informed all that this multifaceted writer, thinker, and scientist did. A clear presentation of the man in the context of social and intellectual history.

Thoreau, Henry David. *Henry David Thoreau: Collected Poems.* Edited by Carl Bode. Enlarged. ed. Baltimore: Johns Hopkins University Press, 1964. Contains all the poetry Thoreau is known to have written. Provides an excellent thirteen-page introduction, sixty-eight pages of textual introduction and notes, forty-four pages of commentary, and sound indexes.

Waggoner, Hyatt H. *American Poets: From the Puritans to the Present.* New York: Houghton Mifflin, 1968. This volume is one of the most comprehensive and detailed histories of American poetry available. Waggoner is the established authority in the field. He gives Thoreau appropriate space and a sympathetic treatment. An appendix, detailed notes, an extensive bibliography, and a good index supplement the volume.

Richard J. Schneider;
bibliography updated by the editors

MELVIN B. TOLSON

Born: Moberly, Missouri; February 6, 1898
Died: Dallas, Texas; August 29, 1966

PRINCIPAL POETRY
A Gallery of Harlem Portraits, wr. 1932, pb. 1979
Rendezvous with America, 1944
Libretto for the Republic of Liberia, 1953
Harlem Gallery: Book I, The Curator, 1965
"Harlem Gallery" and Other Poems of Melvin B. Tolson, 1999

OTHER LITERARY FORMS
Melvin B. Tolson wrote three unpublished novels, "Beyond the Zaretto" (written in late 1920's), "The Lion and the Jackal" (written in late 1930's), and "All Aboard" (written in 1950's). In addition, he composed a number of full-length and one-act plays, including "The Moses of Beale Street," "Southern Front," "Bivouac on the Santa Fe," and "The House by the Side of the Tracks," all of which were unpublished. From 1937 to 1944, Tolson wrote a column titled "Caviar and Cabbage" for the *Washington Tribune*.

ACHIEVEMENTS
While Melvin B. Tolson earned little critical attention throughout most of his life, his work was not without recognition. In 1939 he won first place in the National Poetry Contest award sponsored by the American Negro Exposition in Chicago for "Dark Symphony." In 1945 he won the Omega Psi Phi Award for creative writing, while in 1951, he earned *Poetry* magazine's Bess Hokin Prize for "E. & O. E." He served as poet laureate of Liberia, Africa, in 1947, and was appointed permanent Bread Loaf Fellow in Poetry and Drama, 1954. The 1960's brought two additional distinctions, the District of Columbia Citation and Award for Cultural Achievement in Fine Arts in 1965 and the National Institute and American Academy of Arts and Letters Award in Literature in 1966. Tolson also earned fellowships from the Rockefeller Foundation and Omega Psi Phi and served as mayor of Langston, Oklahoma, from 1952 to 1958. Posthumously, Tolson won the

Ralph Ellison Award from the Oklahoma Center for the Book in 1998.

BIOGRAPHY

Melvin Beaunorus Tolson was born on February 6, 1898, to the Reverend Alonzo Tolson and Lera Tolson. Tolson's father was, as his grandfather had been, a minister in the Methodist Episcopal Church. His father, who was fond of discussing Western philosophy during fishing trips, expected Tolson to follow him into the ministry and was disappointed when his son chose a different vocation. Tolson's mother was part Cherokee Indian by heritage and her father had been killed for resisting enslavement. Along with a family friend, Mrs. George Markwell, a white woman who made her library available to the precocious youth, Tolson had the early benefit of knowledge and learning in his immediate surroundings. The family moved from Missouri to Oklahoma, and then to Iowa, but wherever he went Tolson was a popular classmate. In high school he captained the football team, participated in debating contests, and directed plays for the school's theater.

In 1919 Tolson entered Fisk University in Nashville, Tennessee. He later transferred to Lincoln University, the nation's oldest historically black college, in Oxford, Pennsylvania. In 1923, his senior year, he met the woman he would marry, Ruth Southall. After his graduation, they wed and moved to Marshall, Texas, where Tolson had secured his first teaching post, at Wiley College.

Although he continued writing plays, fiction, and poetry at Wiley, it was as the debating team coach that Tolson's name became well known throughout the Southwest. Putting his students through relentless drills, Tolson led his debate teams to nationwide championships for ten consecutive years. All the while Tolson was still writing poetry, producing a manuscript more than three hundred pages long, *A Gallery of Harlem Portraits*, in 1932, shortly after completing the course work for his master's degree at Columbia University. Though Tolson had modeled his poems on Edgar Lee Masters's popular *Spoon River Anthology* (1915), he could not find a publisher who believed in the marketability of the manuscript. These early poems would not be published in book form until 1979, thirteen years after Tolson's death.

In 1947 Tolson left Wiley College for Langston University, Langston, Oklahoma (just north of Oklahoma City), where he would remain until his retirement in 1964. Tolson was named Poet Laureate of Liberia and commissioned to write a poem celebrating the centennial of the country's birth. That led to *Libretto for the Republic of Liberia*, published as a book in 1953. This work showcases Tolson's shift from the free verse directness of *Rendezvous with America* to a more modernist, nonlinear style, characterized by obscure allusions, dramatic monologues, puns, and semischolarly footnotes.

Tolson had intended to revise his early manuscript, *A Gallery of Harlem Portraits* but felt dissatisfied with its populist lyricism. He had been studying the modernists—in particular, Ezra Pound, T. S. Eliot, and Hart Crane—and decided to revamp the project entirely. He planned to produce an epic, five-book history of the black man's journey in America that would, even more so than *Rendezvous with America*, demonstrate how well he had digested—and superseded—the modern poets. However, he managed to complete only the first volume, *Harlem Gallery*, before his death in 1966.

ANALYSIS

The precise meaning of the life and career of Melvin B. Tolson has vexed the literary establishment ever since his shift from the populist poetry of his first two books to the difficult, allusion-ridden poetry of his last work, *Harlem Gallery: Book I, The Curator*, published just before his death. Was Tolson so enthralled by the call to "make it new," articulated and demonstrated in the essays and poetry of Ezra Pound and T. S. Eliot, that he "sold out" the populist poetics of the Harlem Renaissance? Or did Tolson try to find a new poetics, navigating his poetic enterprise between the Scylla and Charybdis of Anglo-American modernism and African American populism?

Insofar as the debate around Tolson's work still rages, there is still no consensus within the African American literary community, much less the literary community at large, about the value of his poetry. Still, excepting Joy Flasch's book-length appreciation, *Melvin B. Tolson* (1972), it was not until the 1990's that critical commentators—Michael Bérubé, Hermine Dolerez,

Craig Werner, and Aldon Nielsen among them—started to reread and argue for the revolutionary, if incomplete, modernism of Tolson's poetic output.

In their introductory remarks to Tolson's second and third published books, *Libretto for the Republic of Liberia* and *Harlem Gallery*, both Allen Tate and Karl Shapiro focus on the extent to which Tolson's convoluted, experimental poems constitute black poetry. Both answer in the affirmative but for different reasons. For Tate, writing about *Libretto for the Republic of Liberia*, Tolson is "more" black than, for example, the Harlem Renaissance poets because, unlike them, he focuses on poetry as an art first and as an opportunity for the dissemination of political ideas second. Shapiro dismisses the issue of Tolson's relationship to high modernism. For him, Tolson "writes and thinks in Negro, which is to say, a possible American language." Both critics were taken to task by black and white commentators, Tate for his self-serving racism (Tolson is a poet because he writes like Eliot and Crane), Shapiro for his ignorance (Tolson's poetry could not be any less black). Tolson's work is, in toto, a contribution to this "debate," one that embraces the complications of what it means to be an artist in America even as it undermines presumptions about what it means to be a black artist in America.

A GALLERY OF HARLEM PORTRAITS

Although it was published posthumously in 1979, *A Gallery of Harlem Portraits* represents Tolson's earliest poetic style, largely influenced by the populism of Carl Sandburg and Langston Hughes. Simplicity of language and characterization is the prevailing attribute of this kind of poetry. The concept of the "portrait" was taken from Masters's *Spoon River Anthology*, itself a pedestrian version of Amy Lowell's—as opposed to Ezra Pound's—"Imagism," a poetics which deemphasizes duration and narrative in favor of the moment (a "snapshot" or "still life"). Like the politics of Sandburg and Hughes, Tolson's leftist politics influenced his poetic technique, which he viewed as another version of social realism.

RENDEZVOUS WITH AMERICA

If the structure of *A Gallery of Harlem Portraits* is, in part, the formal model for Tolson's last book, *Harlem Gallery*, then *Rendezvous with America* is its thematic link. Just as Tolson will claim all of world culture and learning as part of what it means to be a black artist in his last book, so in this book he claims all of America for all Americans:

> America is the Black Man's country,
> The Red Man's, the Yellow Man's,
> The Brown Man's, the White Man's.

The poems in this book, including "Dark Symphony," work to undermine the prevailing assumption of the early twentieth century that America could do without the contributions of "minorities." Here Tolson's revisionist history of America is meant to demystify and enlighten.

LIBRETTO FOR THE REPUBLIC OF LIBERIA

Commissioned by the cultural attache of Liberia, Tolson's third volume of poetry (the second to be published during his lifetime) is perhaps most significant because of its stylistic break from the traditional verse of *A Gallery of Harlem Portraits* (completed around 1932) and *Rendezvous with America* (1944). Although enjambment still dominates the poetic line, the poem is self-consciously organized by Tolson on the basis of the diatonic scale. Each section "represents" a musical note of the octave, from do, re, mi, and fa, to so, la, ti, and do. For Tolson, the rising musical scale becomes, as narrative structure, the evolutionary story of Liberia, as it grew from a haven from slavery into a utopian model for all Africa. This developmental schema is reinforced at the linguistic level by repetition, dialectical opposition, and the use of free verse and metrical verse stanza forms.

HARLEM GALLERY

As its title suggests, Tolson's last published book of poetry is structurally modeled on his first one, *A Gallery of Harlem Portraits*. Here, Tolson perfects the oblique invocations of classical learning and pedestrian colloquialisms that first appeared in the *Libretto for the Republic of Liberia*. Just as the *Libretto for the Republic of Liberia* is organized according to the Western diatonic musical scale, so *Harlem Gallery* is organized according to the Greek alphabet, proceeding from "Alpha" to "Omega."

Unlike the first book, which remained true to the spirit of Masters's *Spoon River Anthology*, *Harlem Gallery* philosophizes on the nature of African American art and the African American artist in relationship to his or her culture in general. Not surprisingly, Tolson endorses unqualified freedom for the artist. Still, he does not ignore the complex issue of the artist's responsibility to his or her community.

Situated as primarily a three-way debate between the curator, Dr. Okomo, and Hideho Heights, *Harlem Gallery* presents a broad spectrum of opinions on social, class, and racial issues. The issue, for his characters as for Tolson, revolves around the very nature of the black person. Is he or she primarily African or primarily American? What is "black culture"? Is the artist obligated to please a contemporary audience or to risk oblivion by creating art for an audience that may never exist?

Finally, one of the major unresolved tensions in the work is the way it savages the black middle class for aping as white middle class culture—the relevant text, cited several times, is sociologist E. F. Franklin Frazier's controversial *The Black Bourgeoisie* (1957)—while it also extols the black artist who mixes African and European artistic traditions in order to raise the level of black art. The difference in value Tolson assigns to black economic success and black artistic success is based on his cosmopolitanism, his belief in inclusion, in egalitarianism. For Tolson, a parochial art would be the cultural equivalent of capitalist self-interest. In a context where black urban populations found themselves trying to keep pace with their white counterparts, Tolson's rejection of individualistic self-interest on the economic front—and endorsement of apparent self-interest on the artistic front—placed him at odds with both the black bourgeoisie and black proletarian artists, like Langston Hughes, Haki Madhubuti, and Amiri Baraka.

Other major works

NONFICTION: *Caviar and Cabbage: Selected Columns by Melvin B. Tolson from the "Washington Tribune," 1937-1944*, 1982; *The Harlem Group of Negro Writers*, 2001.

Bibliography

Bérubé, Michael. "Masks, Margins, and African American Modernism: Melvin Tolson's *Harlem Gallery*." *Publications of the Modern Language Association of America* 105, no. 1 (January, 1990): 57-69. This article argues that Hideho Heights's infamous parable of the "sea-turtle and shark" in the "Phi" section of *Harlem Gallery* offers insight into Tolson's views on the African American artist's relationship to modernism in particular and African American culture's relationship to Anglo-American culture in general. Just as the sea-turtle, swallowed by a shark, can chew its way out safely through the stomach (as opposed to trying to escape through the mouth and risk being bitten), so too African Americans must "exit" Anglo-American culture from "within."

Flasch, Joy. *Melvin B. Tolson*. New York: Twayne, 1972. This is the first full-length biography of Tolson. Flasch summarizes Tolson's family and professional life and history in chronological order in the first chapter. The rest of the book consists of her chapter-by-chapter analyses of Tolson's published books of poetry.

Lenhart, Gary. "Caviar and Cabbage." *American Poetry Review* (March/April, 2000): 35-39. This article argues that Tolson's shift to a modernist poetics with the publication of *Libretto for the Republic of Liberia* was primarily influenced by Tolson's reading of Hart Crane's *The Bridge* (1930) rather than T. S. Eliot's *The Waste Land* (1922), that it was a way for Tolson to engage in—not escape—social and cultural issues. Thus Tolson's modernism was never at odds with his commitment to political activism.

Neilsen, Aldon L. "Melvin B. Tolson and the Deterritorialization of Modernism." *African American Review* 26, no. 2 (1992): 241-255. This article argues that Tolson's adaptation of modernist procedures in his later poetry was not a form of assimilation but, instead, an assertion of ownership. Insofar as modernism's roots are largely African and Asian, Tolson's later poetry reclaims modernism as an authentic, non-Western phenomenon.

Woodson, Jon. "Melvin B. Tolson and the Art of Being Difficult." In *Black American Poets Between Worlds, 1940-1960*, edited by R. Baxter. Knoxville: University of Tennessee Press, 1986. Woodson argues that the footnotes Tolson later added to *Libretto for the Republic of Liberia*, suggested by poet Karl Shapiro, were not only meant to align his work with that of the high modernists (in particular, Eliot and Crane) but also to blur the line between documentation and creation. Woodson argues that the footnotes became an additional stage of creativity for Tolson, insofar as they not only document sources but also recover modes of knowledge (African and Asian in particular) suppressed by Western history.

Tyrone Williams

CHARLES TOMLINSON

Born: Stoke-on-Trent, Staffordshire, England; January 8, 1927

PRINCIPAL POETRY

Relations and Contraries, 1951
The Necklace, 1955, revised edition 1966
Seeing Is Believing, 1958, 1960
A Peopled Landscape, 1963
American Scenes and Other Poems, 1966
The Way of a World, 1969
Renga: A Chain of Poems, 1971 (with Octavio Paz, Jacques Roubaud, and Edoardo Sanguineti)
Written on Water, 1972
The Way In and Other Poems, 1974
The Shaft, 1978
Selected Poems, 1951-1974, 1978
The Flood, 1981
Airborn = Hijos del Aire, 1981 (with Octavio Paz)
Notes from New York and Other Poems, 1984
Collected Poems, 1985, expanded 1987
The Return, 1987
Annunciations, 1989
The Door in the Wall, 1992
Jubilation, 1995
Selected Poems, 1955-1997, 1997
The Vineyard Above the Sea, 1999

OTHER LITERARY FORMS

Charles Tomlinson has published much work of translation, including *Versions from Fyodor Tyutchev, 1803-1873* (1960, with Henry Gifford), *Translations* (1983), and *Selected Poems* (1993; of Attilio Berto-

lucci's poetry). Among Tomlinson's many essays of commentary and criticism, the most significant are found in *The Poem as Initiation* (1967), *Some Americans: A Personal Record* (1981), *Poetry and Metamorphosis* (1983), and *American Essays· Making It New* (2001). As an editor, Tomlinson has introduced British readers to the work of poets previously little known in England. His editions include *Marianne Moore: A Collection of Critical Essays* (1969), *William Carlos Williams: A Critical Anthology* (1972), *Selected Poems* (1976, revised 1985; of William Carlos Williams's poetry), *Selected Poems* (1979; of Octavio Paz's poetry), and *Poems of George Oppen, 1908-1984* (1990). Tomlinson has also edited volumes of translations, *The Oxford Book of Verse in English Translation* (1980) and *Eros English'd: Classical Erotic Poetry in Translation from Golding to Hardy* (1992). Finally, Tomlinson has collaborated with other poets in writing experimental poetic sequences: the multilingual *Renga: A Chain of Poems* (1971; with Octavio Paz, Jacques Roubaud, and Edoardo Sanguineti) and the bilingual *Airborn = Hijos del Aire* (1981; with Paz).

ACHIEVEMENTS

Charles Tomlinson is generally recognized as a major English poet of the postmodern era. His work in traditional forms with conservative themes has set him apart from "apocalyptic" poets such as Dylan Thomas, as well as from the poets of "the Movement," such as Philip Larkin. Tomlinson, a successful painter, has achieved recognition for his style of precise vision in poetry, and he has been often noticed as a seminal force in bringing the work of William Carlos Williams and other American writers to the serious attention of British poets and critics.

His achievements in poetry (as well as in painting) have won Tomlinson many awards and honors, including the Bess Hokin Prize for Poetry in 1956, a traveling fellowship from the Institute of International Education in 1959-1960, the Levinson Prize for Poetry in 1960, the Frank O'Hara Prize in 1968, election as Fellow of the Royal Society of Literature in 1974, an honorary doctorate in literature from Colgate University in 1981, the Wilbur Award for Poetry in 1982, election as an Honorary Fellow of Royal Holloway and Bedford New

Charles Tomlinson

College (London University) in 1981, and the Bennett Award for achievement in literature in 1993.

BIOGRAPHY

Born in the English Midlands into a lower-class family, Charles Tomlinson was restless to escape the confinements of a mining community. The political conservatism of his father, Alfred Tomlinson, an estate agent's clerk, had a strong influence on the development of young Tomlinson's sensibility. Tomlinson attended Queen's College, University of Cambridge, from 1945 to 1948; while there he studied under Donald Davie, who became a lifelong friend and colleague. After receiving his degree, Tomlinson was married to Brenda Raybould. They moved to London, where Tomlinson taught in an elementary school and worked at his painting. In 1951 he published his first collection of poems.

In 1951-1952 he traveled in Italy, where he worked briefly as private secretary to Percy Lubbock. While in Italy he gradually abandoned his painting in favor of composing poems. Returning to London, he earned a master's degree from London University in 1954. In

1956 he took a position as lecturer in English poetry at the University of Bristol, where he later became a reader and then professor.

Tomlinson's next volume of poetry, *Seeing Is Believing*, attracted the attention of several American critics. In 1959 he fulfilled a long-held wish to meet William Carlos Williams, whom he visited in Rutherford, New Jersey. On the same trip to the United States, made possible by a fellowship, he also visited Yvor Winters in California. Before returning home, he visited Marianne Moore in Brooklyn, New York, and returned for a second visit with Williams in New Jersey.

With Henry Gifford he published the first of several joint projects of translation, *Versions from Fyodor Tyutchev, 1803-1873*, in 1960. Tomlinson was invited to serve as visiting professor at the University of New Mexico in 1962-1963. During this year he met two persons who would prove to be very important for his career, the Objectivist poets Louis Zukofsky and George Oppen. He was introduced to other young American writers, Robert Duncan and Robert Creeley, and he visited the painter Georgia O'Keeffe at her home in New Mexico.

His poems collected for *A Peopled Landscape* in 1963 showed how important William Carlos Williams had become for Tomlinson's style. After a reading tour of New York State for the Academy of American Poets, in 1967 he went back to Italy, where he met Ezra Pound and also Octavio Paz, who would become a valued friend.

Returning to the United States as Olive B. O'Connor Professor of Literature at Colgate University, Tomlinson delivered the Phi Beta Kappa lecture, which was published as *The Poem as Initiation*. He continued to travel in the United States and Europe, lecturing and working on his translations, from 1969 to 1971. Tomlinson's painting and poetry were brought together in *Words and Images* in 1972, and some of his poems were set to music by Stephen Strawley and recorded by Jane Manning in 1974. After another reading tour in the United States, his poetry and graphics were collected by the Arts Council of Great Britain as an exhibition at Hayward Gallery in 1978 in London and then toured Great Britain until 1981. Although Tomlinson did not cease his international traveling, his graphic work continued to bring him more recognition to match his reputation as a poet.

In 1982 he received the prestigious Wilbur Award for Poetry and delivered the Clark Lectures at Cambridge, titled "Poetry and Metamorphosis." Some of his poems were again set to music, in a song cycle that was performed in Belgium in 1985. The next year Keele University held an exhibit, "Charles Tomlinson: A Celebration," of his books, manuscripts, photographs, and graphics, and then established an archive of his poetry recorded for commercial issue on audio cassettes. Also in the 1980's Tomlinson published a selection of his poems in French and Italian, served as visiting professor at McMaster University, Canada, and delivered the Edmund Blunden Lecture in Hong Kong.

In 1992, he retired as professor of English from the University of Bristol. After his retirement, Tomlinson continued to travel, lecture, paint, and write poems. Bilingual selections of his poetry appeared in Spain, Germany, Italy, Portugal, and Mexico, and in 1997 his *Selected Poems, 1955-1997* was published in England and in the United States.

ANALYSIS

Throughout his career, Charles Tomlinson has used his arts of poetry and painting to challenge nature's objectivity with the shaping powers of human (subjective) imagination. He has spoken of the invitation to make meaning out of apparent meaninglessness, by discovering that "chance" rhymes with "dance," and that "chance" interrupts and enlivens the deadening effects of certitude. Therefore, in volume after volume Tomlinson tests the proposition expressed by the title of his third collection, *Seeing Is Believing*. At first, this seems to limit one's imaginative capacity (to believe) to the outlines of things in sight, to the exteriors of being. Gradually, however, it becomes clear that Tomlinson's aesthetic detachment is an illusion of objectivity, that his art warms with the energies of combating objects in natural settings, negotiating space for culture and ritual, and rescuing values from history to compensate for anger at what humankind threatens to waste through ignorance and brutality.

The only poem that Tomlinson chose to rescue from his first collection, *Relations and Contraries*, to include in his *Collected Poems* is one simply titled "Poem." Short though it is, "Poem" suggests a major interest of the early poetry: It describes a sequence of sounds heard by an "unstopped ear" from a winter scene of activity, including horses' hooves making "an arabesque on space/ A dotted line in sound." This containment of space with sound, to make "space vibrate," is an effort that Tomlinson's next volume, *The Necklace*, continues to make, as in "Aesthetic," where "reality is to be sought . . . in space made articulate." Imagination uses language to establish an order of things, set firmly in their own world, though subject to human play, as in "Nine Variations in a Chinese Winter Setting."

SEEING IS BELIEVING

This last poem takes its title from one by Wallace Stevens, the American poet whose work was an early important influence on Tomlinson. That influence continued to show in the third collection, *Seeing Is Believing*, which uses the painter's experience to capture an essential artistic attitude toward objects or acts in space. Thus "Object in a Setting" achieves the sense of being in a piece of glass that resists all efforts "to wish it a more human image," and "Paring the Apple" illustrates the beauty of art that forces "a recognition" of its charm even from those who look for a more "human" art in portraits. Still, the paring is an act of "human gesture," which compels its own recognition that art requires the human to be, and so all art is essentially a human endeavor. The poem, "A Meditation on John Constable," is art re-creating art: a poem about a painter making a painting. The title reinforces the very human essence of the artistic process: meditating about a human being who is an artist.

This is even more clear in those poems of *Seeing Is Believing* that occur as the consequence of visits to places. Although "At Holwell Farm" seeks to capture the "brightness" of air that is gathered "within the stone" of the farm's wall and buildings, it moves to a gentle observation that it is a "dwelling/ Rooted in more than earth," guarding an "Eden image." "On the Hall at Stowey" records a visit to a deserted house, allowed to fall into ruin while the fields about it continue to be fruitful and well attended. The poet is angry that five centuries of culture have fallen into decay here, where once pride of tradition was boldly beautiful. What humanity bestowed upon the objective space of nature, humanity has taken away through the objective distancing of time.

A PEOPLED LANDSCAPE

A Peopled Landscape takes the concerns of place and time more warmly into more poems, as in "Harvest Festival: At Ozleworth." The poet notices the ironic juxtaposition of remnants from both Roman and Christian history in the market scene of this country village: A harvest festival of pagan origins is conducted beneath the stone arch of a Christian church, to deepen the scene of space with the complexities of history. Working with juxtapositions of this kind, Tomlinson uses his return from a trip to the United States to observe differences between modern and traditional values in "Return to Hinton," where he lovingly catalogs the details of his home, whose "qualities/ are like the land/ —inherited." These are contrasted with life in a "rich and nervous land" where "locality's mere grist/ to build." This poem uses the three-layered verse form of Tomlinson's American model William Carlos Williams; the preference for the American style of poetry is a complication of the poem's theme, which admits its complicity in the process of modern detachment from traditional "farm-bred certainties." This same sense of separateness from tradition, along with a yearning to enjoy the pleasures of the past, is a strong element of "The Farmer's Wife" in the same volume.

AMERICAN SCENES AND OTHER POEMS

The impact and importance of American experience are dramatized by the title of Tomlinson's next volume, *American Scenes and Other Poems*, which nevertheless includes poems not immediately referring to American scenes or settings, such as "A Given Grace." This is one of Tomlinson's most discussed poems, partly because it continues to show the influence of Stevens as well as that of Williams and Moore. It does not use the three-layered form, but it establishes an Imagist posture associated with the Americans. The title, deliberately tautological, derives from the beauty of "two cups" set on a mahogany table; the "grace" given is a power of evocation from form to imagination, aptly recorded as the poem itself.

In "The Hill" a woman gives grace to the poet's perception. She climbs a hill, making it yield to her human pressure and take its shape of meaning from her presence. A more explicitly American scene is exploited in "The Cavern," which recounts a descent that begins as a tourist's jaunt but ends as a press toward "a deeper dark" where the self discovers its "unnameable and shaping home." The poem works with gentle irony as it works out the myth of Theseus exploring the labyrinth: It acquires additional force if the final discovery of the self in its "shaping home" also suggests that the self is the minotaur as well as, or instead of, the heroic Theseus. Yet there is further irony here, since the poem derives from Tomlinson's travels through the American Southwest, where he records a discovery about his deepest self (repeating the experience of his predecessor D. H. Lawrence). This self-discovery is repeated in other poems, such as "Idyll," which describes how the poet is drawn by the creative contrasts of quiet Washington Square in the heart of loud, bustling San Francisco. Here is not a desert cavern, but there is nevertheless a similar sense of self renewed by its identity in distance: A boy reading (beneath the lintel of a church upon which is carved a verse from Dante) draws the poet into a sympathetic identification as universal reader, for whom the message of the Square is a "poised quiescence, pause and possibility."

THE WAY OF A WORLD

One of Tomlinson's most acclaimed volumes is *The Way of a World*, which includes the lovely "Swimming Chenango Lake," a poem about establishing an artful relationship between human subjectivity and nature's objectivity. It sympathetically observes the poise of a swimmer, who has paused in a quiescent moment to study possibilities before leaping into an autumn lake. The swimmer is like an artist, measuring the "geometry of water" before attempting to master it with his skill, but the swimmer is also all humanity participating in the challenging processes of all nature. In this poem Tomlinson has brought together many of his career's themes: aesthetic observation through detachment, cold reflectiveness, and human calculation. Like the swimmer, human beings "draw back" from the cold mercilessness of nature, even as they force a kind of "mercy" from it, making nature sustain the human experience.

In this volume Tomlinson demonstrates more decisively his strong distaste for extremism of all kinds, whether political or artistic, even though he has himself explored the use of American experimental aesthetic practices. His poem "Prometheus" is a strong work of imagination in which the poet listens to a radio broadcast of music by the Russian composer Aleksandr Scriabin; since there is a storm outside his house at the time, the poet can juxtapose the two events, artistic and natural, to each other. Because Scriabin's *Prometheus* is a work intended to help further the apocalypse of revolution, his music is examined as an exercise in political irony. This is made possible by the mockery of "static" in the radio's transmission during an electrical storm; the static is a figurative vehicle for the poet's mockery of art in the service of political propaganda. Music is the source of inspiration for another poem of the volume, "Night Transfigured," which derives from a work by Arnold Schoenberg. This poem is a kind of conclusion to a three-poem sequence beginning with "Eden" and followed by "Adam," as the poet becomes a new Adam-artist transfiguring the night of modernism with his light of imagination.

Tomlinson includes in *The Way of a World* two interesting experiments of his art, "Skullshapes" and "To be Engraved on the Skull of a Cormorant." The former is one of the poet's several exercises in "prose poems," which escape rigid classification because they are not measured in verse but neither are they merely prose. "Skullshapes" is a meditation on the shapes of different kinds of skulls; these are shapes of nature that summon imagination to fill "recess and volume" and to trace the "lines of containment, lines of extension." This is what Tomlinson does with his short poem "To Be Engraved on the Skull of a Cormorant," in which he accepts nature's challenge to turn a space of death into a rhythm of living affirmation.

WRITTEN ON WATER

Tomlinson has said in interviews that he learned to be a poet by watching the water in canals running through his home village; the title of his collection *Written on Water* captures some of the feeling he has for that time of his childhood. Yet the title also carries other levels of meaning, including the interest a painter has in working with water (the source of life itself) and the chance an artist takes in any medium that his or her work will not last. From among the poems that focus on the

element of water, "Mackinnon's Boat" is an idyllic review of a day's work of fishing, sometimes presented from the view of a dog that lies in the bow of the boat, seemingly eager for return to land. This poem echoes the theme of "Swimming Chenango Lake," with its passage through and over a medium of nature as a mastery of its force. This same move of transcendence by human art, via imagination, occurs in "Hawks," which negotiates the element of air in its metaphors of achieving a right relationship between contraries.

THE WAY IN AND OTHER POEMS

Several of his poems in *The Way In and Other Poems* have brought Tomlinson much appreciative critical attention, particularly the sequence that begins with "Under the Moon's Reign." Other poems, however, continue the nostalgic review of the past that has often been a manner of his writing. There is a sharper edge to some of these poems, as the poet's sorrow turns more often into anger at what modern life has done to traditional values and ancient landscapes. "The Way In" ironically notices two old people, like an ancient Adam and Eve, puttering about in the waste regions of the city where the poet drives to work. He may regret what humans have done to the landscape and he may deplore the empty lives the old couple seem to live, but he feels himself contributing to the devastation as he depresses the accelerator of his automobile. "Gladstone Street" and "At Stoke" take him back to scenes of his youth, where there is no improvement of an industrial wasteland and where the changes are few; still, it brings evidence that whatever the poet has accomplished, he owes much to his origin in that place of "grey-black." These poems of return and observation often follow the shape of experience drawn from driving. In "Night Ride," the poet sees well by artificial lighting but deplores the loss of vision to see the stars. Progress may make "our lights seem more beautiful than our lives," but it can also blacken the optimistic planners of the past, such as Josiah Wedgewood's utopian schemes in "Etruria Vale." Tomlinson dates the beginning of a new era for Great Britain from the end of World War II, which is marked in "Dates: Penkhull New Road." He sees it as a place that expresses a time: "Something had bitten a gap/ Out of the stretch we lived in." This is a commentary on postwar Great Britain as much as it is an observation about the physical disruption of a street in an English village.

Space for imagination to work across landscapes of special places can be found in revisiting scenes of youth and childhood, but it can also be discovered without leaving a present scene. This is the tactic of the four-poem sequence beginning with "Under the Moon's Reign." Moonlight transfigures the landscape to create a new world, after the *Götterdämmerung* of twilight's apocalypse; this is the closest Tomlinson can come to acceptance of extremism, and he does so in a tone of quiet irony. It is in such a moonlit terrain that "Foxes' Moon" is set, to allow an interruption of England's "pastoral" existence by an alien, intruding presence: the foxes who "go/ In their ravenous quiet"—utterly different modes of being for humanity to contemplate. The third poem, "The Dream," takes the speaker into a wider world of contemplation, where new spaces are made of cities within cities; dreams are the proportioning of sleep that "replenishes/ To stand reading with opened eyes/ The intricacies of the imagined spaces." No amount of dreaming, however, nor any amount of artful creation, can relieve the anguish and pain of one who stands over the "little ash" of a loved one, in "After a Death." Articulating the space of words does not assuage the burden of vision that feels "the imageless unnaming upper blue" of "this burial place" straddling a green hill.

Perhaps ends of things, ends of lives, establish important terms of definition, as Tomlinson writes more often on this theme. As he puts it in his prose-poem of this volume, "The Insistence of Things," there is an "insistence of things" that "face us with our own death, for they are so completely what we are not." Thus moonlight shows, as does the grim determination of the foxes' barking between dreams, that death is a function of "the insistence of things."

THE SHAFT

The hard outlines of those insistences can be observed in history as well as across the spaces of the present. *The Shaft* collects poems that drive a shaft through time as well as into the dark depths of the earth. Extremist leaders of the French Revolution are presented in "Charlotte Corday," "Marat Dead," and "For Danton," to show the insufficiency of lives devoted to desperate

deeds. At the real center of being is a fecund darkness, as in the title poem, "The Shaft," which is a womblike cavity (reached through a "cervix of stone"); as one bends to enter, one feels "a vertigo that dropped through centuries." One cannot remain there for long; it is "a place of sacrifice," but it allows escape and rebirth, as there is a return to "the sun of an unfinished summer." One may draw upon the dark energies of being in one's quest for a way back into the realm of light, where work is to be done.

THE FLOOD AND THE RETURN

In both *The Flood* and *The Return* Tomlinson's poetry acquires more religious qualities, as he describes the renovating experience of fighting destruction from the very water that inspired his work as a poet and painter, and as he ritualizes his life to receive the gifts of loving human companions as well as coldly indifferent natural forces. "The Flood" describes how taken by surprise he was when the stream near his house broke its banks in a flood that swept through his stone wall and across the lower floor of his home; it shook his "trust in stone" and "awakened" his eyes to fresh perceptions of nature's force. That there is compensation from nature is celebrated in a poem that echoes William Wordsworth's "The Recompense," which follows the route of expectation of viewing a comet, being disappointed, and then discovering new energies from a moonrise to reward the efforts of unnourished hope. The same appreciation for compensations drives the imagination in "The Return," which prepares the poet for the return of his wife on a winter's journey after a time of separation from each other.

These volumes, *The Flood* and *The Return*, embody contrasting themes constant throughout Tomlinson's career as poet: the concern for values of historical culture that are threatened with annihilation and the opportunity for renewal that nature constantly offers to the human imagination. The poet refuses to be intimidated by apocalypses of nature or of history. Instead, he keeps his artist's eye alert for new objects to replenish his hunger for fresh experience to nourish his poetry and his painting.

ANNUNCIATIONS

The religious qualities that emerged in Tomlinson poetry during the 1980's become more explicit in *An-*

nunciations, a volume whose title suggests one of its chief themes: the "blessedness" of the physical world, a secular blessedness analogous to, yet profoundly different from, the divine blessedness announced by the Archangel Michael to the Virgin Mary. In "Annunciation," the volume's opening poem, a "flashing wing of sunlight" appears in an ordinary kitchen to announce an "unchaptered gospel." The sunlight comes not as a divine revelation but as a "domestic miracle" that will not "wait for the last day" to return. "[E]very day," the sunlight tells us, "is fortunate even when you catch/ my ray only as a gliding ghost." For Tomlinson, the momentary, accidental, yet recurrent visitation of sunlight, its play upon the surfaces of the world, is sufficient consolation, is miracle enough.

Many of the subsequent poems in *Annunciations* disclose similar "miracles," revealing a presence in the world that, in the words of critic Michael Edwards, "has preceded and will outlast us." This presence, says Edwards, is "ceaselessly entering local chance and circumstance" and "comes not from beyond but from within the world." Like the "flashing wing of sunlight" in "Annunciation," the presence revealed in other poems is naturalistic, not transcendent. Nevertheless, Tomlinson draws from it a sense of "religious" awe and comfort. The given world is revelation enough.

In several of the poems from *Annunciations*, the luminosity of the natural world takes the form of sunlight or moonlight. In "Variation," for example, a rising moon is "an unpausing visitant" that gradually illuminates the trees, one by one, "Setting each trunk alight, then hurrying on/ To shine back down over the entire wood." Near the end of this poem, Tomlinson shifts from the moon's illumination of a physical landscape to its illumination of human consciousness as it "pours/ Into the shadows and the watcher's mind." Similarly, in "Moonrise," the "watcher" of the moon is illuminated by "Its phosphor burning back our knowledge to/ The sense that we are here, that it is now." For Tomlinson, the mysterious presence of moonlight is an "annunciation" that, rather than take one out of the world, grounds one in it. Tomlinson suggests that the here and now is—or ought to be—sufficient.

THE DOOR IN THE WALL

Many poems in *The Door in the Wall*, like those in *Annunciations*, contemplate the world with a sense of "religious" awe, recording the passing of the seasons (geese "planing in" on "autumn gusts") or the strangeness of the natural world closely observed (mushrooms, gathered by moonlight, looking like "tiny moons," like "lunar fruits"). These two books also take readers to places less luminous and strange. While Tomlinson writes powerfully about the natural landscapes of the New Mexican desert and the Canadian wilderness, he also takes his readers to crowded, often troubled, urban centers like New York, San Francisco, and Tübingen. While he is not in any conventional sense a political poet, two pieces from *The Door in the Wall* explore leftist politics of the late 1960's: "Paris in Sixty-nine" and "Siena in Sixty-eight," the latter closing with a powerful image of the 1968 Soviet invasion of Czechoslovakia.

JUBILATION AND THE VINEYARD ABOVE THE SEA

Jubilation and *The Vineyard Above the Sea* include work written during the 1990's, the years following Tomlinson's retirement from academic life. The poems in these books remind readers that one of Tomlinson's great strengths as a poet is his capacity for precise, detailed description of the physical world. His "descriptions," however, are never mere renderings of the world's surfaces. Poems such as "The Cypresses," from *Jubilation*, and "On the Downs," from *The Vineyard Above the Sea*, are complex meditations on the world's "otherness." Such poems reveal in their "descriptions" a carefully established relation between observer and observed, a relation in which the world's otherness is given its due. In muting the claims of the perceiving self, Tomlinson enacts what he calls his "basic theme—that one does not need to go beyond sense experience to some mythic union, that the 'I' can be responsible only in relationship and not by dissolving itself away into ecstasy or the Over-soul."

These volumes also reconfirm Tomlinson as quintessentially a poet of landscape, of place. Like his earlier collections, *Jubilation* and *The Vineyard Above the Sea* contain a large number of poems, often sequences of poems, about the many places he has visited: Italy (a setting that appears repeatedly throughout his work), Greece, Portugal, and Japan, as well as his native England. All these locations—their physical contours, their languages, their cultures—enrich Tomlinson's poetry, making his work perhaps the least insular, least provincial, of any English poet writing since World War II.

While he remains an avid traveler, Tomlinson also acknowledges in these poems a competing urge: a homing instinct. "Against Travel," from *Jubilation*, celebrates the virtues of domesticity: "Those days are best when one goes nowhere,/ The house a reservoir of quiet change." At several points in *Jubilation*, the world out there gives way to a personal, domestic, closed-in world that Tomlinson has never before admitted so fully to his poetry. In "For a Granddaughter," a series of six "domestic poems," Tomlinson speaks in a self-revealing voice and from a private perspective rarely found in his earlier work. These poems and others suggest a sense of acceptance, a feeling of fulfillment, an easing into a new phase of life. Indeed, the book's title, *Jubilation*, puns on the word *jubilación*, Spanish for retirement, and in a poem called "Jubilación," Tomlinson celebrates his retirement in gently rhymed, easygoing, often humorous couplets addressed to a friend.

Tomlinson's has become an essentially domestic existence shared with his wife: "Books, music, and our garden occupy me./ All these pursuits I share (with whom you know)/ For Eden always was a place for two." Tomlinson's recent work shows clearly that his "pursuits," even in retirement, include writing poetry. The poems in *Jubilation* and *The Vineyard Above the Sea* confirm his status as an important poetic voice.

OTHER MAJOR WORKS

NONFICTION: *The Poem as Initiation*, 1967; *Some Americans: A Personal Record*, 1981; *Isaac Rosenberg of Bristol*, 1982; *Poetry and Metamorphosis*, 1983; *The Sense of the Past: Three Twentieth Century British Poets*, 1983; *The Letters of William Carlos Williams and Charles Tomlinson*, 1992; *William Carlos Williams and Charles Tomlinson: A Transatlantic Connection*, 1998; *American Essays: Making It New*, 2001.

TRANSLATIONS: *Versions from Fyodor Tyutchev, 1803-1873*, 1960 (with Henry Gifford); *Castilian Ilexes: Versions from Antonio Machado, 1875-1939*, 1963 (with Gifford); *Ten Versions from "Trilce" by César* *Vallejo*, 1970 (with Gifford); *Translations*, 1983; *Selected Poems*, 1993 (of Attilio Bertolucci)

EDITED TEXTS: *Marianne Moore: A Collection of Critical Essays*, 1969; *William Carlos Williams: A Critical Anthology*, 1972; *Selected Poems*, 1976, revised 1985 (of William Carlos Williams); *Selected Poems*, 1979 (of Octavio Paz); *The Oxford Book of Verse in English Translation*, 1980; *Poems of George Oppen, 1908-1984*, 1990; *Eros English'd: Classical Erotic Poetry in Translation from Golding to Hardy*, 1992.

MISCELLANEOUS: *Words and Images*, 1972; *In Black and White: The Graphics of Charles Tomlinson*, 1976; *Eden: Graphics and Poetry*, 1985.

BIBLIOGRAPHY

Bedient, Calvin. "Charles Tomlinson." In *Eight Contemporary Poets*. London: Oxford University Press, 1974. This study argues that Tomlinson has a narrow range but rich style. A review of his main theme, measuring relationships, is initiated through comparisons with Wordsworth, Williams, and Stevens. Bedient analyzes poems that drain images of ego and poems of intense and severe meditation. Bibliography and notes are included.

Clark, Timothy. *Charles Tomlinson*. Plymouth, England: Northcote House, 1999. Clark gives a brief but wide-ranging introduction to Tomlinson's career, covering not only his poetry but also his work as a translator, as a graphic artist, and as a collaborator in writing experimental, multilingual poetic sequences. The book features a detailed biographical outline, examples of Tomlinson's graphics, a bibliography, notes, and index.

John, Brian. *The World as Event: The Poetry of Charles Tomlinson*. Montreal: McGill-Queen's University Press, 1989. John says that Tomlinson's poetry creates a language of the senses, enlarges definitions, and pursues understanding of experience. His poems proceed as ceremonies of initiation toward an image of "Eden," explored in sometimes ironic ways while the poet aims to recover a bit of paradise after all. Included are a photograph, notes, a bibliography, and an index.

King, P. R. "Seeing and Believing: The Poetry of Charles Tomlinson." In *Nine Contemporary Poets: A Criti-*

cal *Introduction*. New York: Methuen, 1979. A substantial study, this essay presents Tomlinson's poetry as an independent endeavor in which the poet uses his painter's eye to search for a right relationship between people and places, time and history, to find delight in the act of seeing as the self adjusts to reality. There are notes, a bibliography, and an index.

Kirkham, Michael. *Passionate Intellect: The Poetry of Charles Tomlinson*. Liverpool: Liverpool University Press, 1999. This book provides a detailed critical reading of Tomlinson's poetry from the 1950's through the 1980's. Kirkham presents Tomlinson's work in an "unfolding sequence," focusing on the poet's "unified vision of the natural-human world." Includes a bibliography, notes, and index.

O'Gorman, Kathleen, ed. *Charles Tomlinson: Man and Artist*. Columbia: University of Missouri Press, 1988. Eleven essays, two interviews, a poem, a chronology, and a foreword by Donald Davie cover Tomlinson's career. Six essays present different perspectives on his poetry, and two provide overviews of his development. Three essays study interrelationships of his painting and poetry. Features illustrations, a bibliography, and an index.

Swigg, Richard. *Charles Tomlinson and the Objective Tradition*. Lewisburg, Pa.: Bucknell University Press, 1994. Swigg explores Tomlinson's place in an Anglo-American poetic tradition of "objectivity" that values the world's otherness, its existence apart from the ego of the poet. Much of the book focuses on the ways in which various writers within this tradition have influenced Tomlinson. A bibliography, notes, and index are included.

Weatherhead, A. Kingsley. "Charles Tomlinson." In *The British Dissonance: Essays on Ten Contemporary Poets*. Columbia: University of Missouri Press, 1983. This essay explores a question raised by Tomlinson, whether form is in objective reality or imposed by subjective perception. It also presents Tomlinson as a poet who bridges many of the divisions that separate contemporary poets and their themes. The volume includes notes, a bibliography, and an index.

Richard D. McGhee;
updated by Michael Hennessy

JEAN TOOMER

Born: Washington, D.C.; December 26, 1894
Died: Doylestown, Pennsylvania; March 30, 1967

PRINCIPAL POETRY

"Banking Coal," in *Crisis*, 1922
Cane, 1923 (prose and poetry)
"Blue Meridian," in *New American Caravan*, 1936
The Wayward and the Seeking, 1980 (prose and poetry; Darwin T. Turner, editor)
The Collected Poems of Jean Toomer, 1988

OTHER LITERARY FORMS

Most of Jean Toomer's work was in genres other than poetry. His one published volume of creative writing, *Cane*, contains only fifteen poems, mostly short, and fourteen pieces which appear to be in prose. Yet, they are all informed with the poet's rather than the novelist's sensibility, and some of them are poems in all but line breaks, while all of them use assorted poetic devices either throughout or sporadically.

Toomer published several pieces of fiction after *Cane*, generally quite experimental inasmuch as they lacked plot, often included philosophical meditations, and indeed often worked more like poetry, with impressionistic scenes and descriptions and an emphasis on developing a theme through juxtaposition of sections rather than an overall sequence of action. Among these are "Winter on Earth" (*The Second American Caravan*, 1929), "Mr. Costyve Duditch" (*The Dial*, 1928), and "York Beach" (*New American Caravan*, 1929). The first two were collected in the posthumous volume *The Wayward and the Seeking*, edited by Darwin T. Turner, along with a previously unpublished story from 1930, "Withered Skin of Berries," which is more in the style of *Cane*, though much longer than most of the pieces in that book.

Toomer published one short, fragmentary play during his lifetime, "Balo," in Alain Locke's collection *Plays of Negro Life* (1927), and two of several other plays which he wrote in *The Wayward and the Seeking*.

Nonfiction predominates in Toomer's work, indicating his concerns with philosophical and spiritual goals, as in "Race Problems and Modern Society" (1929), "The Flavor of Man" (1949), and *Essentials: Definitions and Aphorisms* (privately printed in 1931, some of its aphorisms having been printed earlier in *The Dial* and *Crisis*, with many appearing much later in *The Wayward and the Seeking*). These aphorisms are occasionally poetic and certainly worthy of contemplation, but they might be stronger if incorporated into actual poems. Portions of several versions of Toomer's autobiography appear in *The Wayward and the Seeking*. The rest of his many unpublished works, including many poems, remain in the Toomer Collection of the Fisk University Library.

ACHIEVEMENTS

Cane is one of the most memorable and appealing books in African American literature, conveying a vivid sense of the life of southern blacks around 1920 (though little changed since the time of slavery) and showing clearly the conflicts between the feelings of black people and the desensitizing and spirit-diminishing urban life they found in the North. Yet *Cane* is significant not merely for its content but for its innovative form and style as well. Its combination of prose and verse, stories and poems, produces a unified impression, with poems foreshadowing or commenting on adjacent stories and the stories and sketches exploring a multitude of perspectives on black life, rural and urban.

Jean Toomer's impressionistic style, his seductive but not mechanical rhythms, his brilliant imagery and figurative language, his manipulation of language to produce a wide range of emotional and literary effects, were refreshing to many black writers during and after the Harlem Renaissance of the 1920's. Instead of adhering strictly to traditional European models of form and meter (like that of his major black contemporaries Claude McKay and Countée Cullen) or the literary realism and straightforward narrative style of black fiction to that date, he joined the progression of revolutionary poets and fiction writers who were creating literary Modernism, from Walt Whitman on through James Joyce, D. H. Lawrence, Gertrude Stein, Sherwood Anderson, and T. S. Eliot, up to Toomer's friend and contemporary Hart Crane.

Very few of Toomer's other works come even close to the towering achievement of *Cane*, but its poems and poetic prose provided later writers a successful means of evoking the feel of the black experience. A reader can still sense echoes of its style in the evocative prose of novelist Toni Morrison.

BIOGRAPHY

Jean Toomer (born Eugene) spent most of his life resisting a specific racial label for himself. His childhood and youth were spent in white or racially mixed middle-class neighborhoods in Washington, and his parents were both light-skinned. Jean's father left shortly after his birth and his mother died after remarrying, so that the most potent adult influences on his life were his maternal grandparents, with whom he lived until his twenties. His grandfather, P.B.S. Pinchback, had been elected Lieutenant-Governor in Reconstruction Louisiana and served as Acting Governor in 1873. Toomer believed that his victory was helped by his announcement that he had black blood, although Toomer denied knowing whether it was true. One thing is clear: Pinchback had indeed served the Union cause in the "Corps d'Afrique."

Jean Toomer (Beineke Rare Book and Manuscript Library, Yale University)

Later in life Toomer denied that he was a Negro—an acceptable statement if one understands his definition of "Negro" as one who identifies solely with the black race, for he, with certainly a great deal of nonblack ancestry, saw himself as not white, either, but "American," a member of a new race which would unify the heretofore conflicting racial groups through a mixture of racial strains. The attainment of such an "American" race remained his goal throughout most of his life after *Cane*.

Toomer's education after high school was varied, from agriculture at the University of Wisconsin to the American College of Physical Training in Chicago. Rather than completing courses toward a formal degree, however, he pursued his own reading in literature and social issues while working at assorted jobs until he decided to devote all his efforts to writing.

The real nudge came in the form of a three-month stint as substitute principal of a school in a small Georgia town in the fall of 1921. He returned to Washington in November with material for a whole book. He published several poems and stories in assorted periodicals the following year and then gathered most of them and many new ones into a carefully structured book called *Cane*, published in 1923 by Boni and Liveright. The book caused a considerable stir among the influential white literati with whom he associated (such as Waldo Frank, Sherwood Anderson, and Hart Crane) and among black writers and intellectuals as well. Yet in its two printings (the second in 1927) it sold fewer than a thousand copies.

That same year, Toomer met the Russian mystic George Gurdjieff and embraced his philosophy of higher consciousness. After studying with him in France, Toomer returned to spread his teachings in America. A ten-month marriage to a white poet, Margery Latimer, ended with her death in childbirth in 1932. Two years later he married another white woman, Marjorie Content, and spent the rest of his life with her. This period in Toomer's life was largely devoted to self-improvement for himself and others, as he lectured and continued to write primarily philosophical and spiritually oriented work. He continued to publish some literary works until 1936, when his career came virtually to an end, despite attempts to have other works published. He became a Quaker and maintained no further identity with the black race, dying in 1967 largely forgotten.

ANALYSIS

Jean Toomer was the writer of one book; no matter how often the phrase is used to disparage him, it cannot be denied. Beyond *Cane*, his only other works of value are the long poem "Blue Meridian," a small amount of short fiction, and his autobiographical writings. His plays, most of his other poetry, and his nonfiction are negligible. Yet even had he written only *Cane*, he would always be remembered as a major African American author—and primarily as a poet.

CANE

Cane is an eccentric book, experimental and unclassifiable in its combination of poems and what is technically prose—pieces which are generally developed as short stories (somewhat like those of Anderson or Joyce) but are occasionally "mere" sketches, sometimes prose-poems without plot, encompassing no more than a few pages and conveying impressionistically the sense of a person's spirit. Some of the pieces approach drama, with conversation printed like dialogue, setting described as meticulously as for a stage designer, and action presented in the present tense.

Yet, whether prose, drama, or verse, all is imbued with a poet's sensibility: precise depiction of details using all the senses vividly, a rhythmic quality without slavish adherence to metrics, a sensitivity to words, phrasing, variations of theme, a fine ear for sound, and a polished sense of organic structure. Few books, whether prose or verse, have less of the prosaic than this one, which can put readers in an almost unabated state of intensity and exaltation, drawing them in by language, sound, rhythm, and form.

Toomer's purpose in this work is to embody what he sees as the dying folk spirit of the South by depicting the lives of its people and re-creating their feelings through language and rhythm. *Cane* achieves a vivid sense of the sensuality of its women, the alternating anguish and joy of life in the South, the toughness and beauty of the land of Georgia. These themes appear primarily in the first third of the book; the second third moves North into the city, where blacks from the South have difficulty fitting into the white-dominated social patterns while retaining roots in the South; in the final third, Ralph Kabnis, a Northern black man, comes South and the focus is on his conflict with the South, looking ahead to William

Faulkner's *Absalom, Absalom!* (1936) and Quentin Compson's climatic cry "I don't hate the South!" Throughout the book, Toomer shows both attraction to the South and a sense of holding back from it—on the part of a narrator in the first third, of Kabnis in the last third, and of assorted Northern-based characters in the middle third, who are losing touch with their black roots. The book, however, is hardly a glorification of the way of life of Southern blacks: Kabnis notes that things are not so bad as the North thinks; yet the South still hosts an occasional lynching, as Toomer several times reminds his readers. Still, Toomer appreciates a vitality in Southern blacks which disappears when they are removed from the land, a process that Toomer views as unfortunately inevitable in the modern world.

To create this sense of vitality and closeness to the land and the natural world, Toomer uses a vast array of references to nature—the pines, the cane fields, the sky at dusk, the red soil—as images themselves, as similes or metaphors in connection with his characters, or as recurring leitmotifs in the operatic development of his sketches. He uses rhythm and repetition to engage the reader in the immediacy of these sensory experiences. A close analysis of one of his pieces—"Karintha," the opening sketch in *Cane*—will illustrate Toomer's typical methods.

"Karintha"

Like other pieces in the book, "Karintha" opens with an epigraph, a song-like refrain of four lines which recurs throughout the sketch as a unifying device. The first of four paragraphs of varying lengths then introduces Karintha as a child, summing her up in the first sentence, which is poetically accretive rather than prosaically structured; the final adjective cluster echoes words from the epigraph's refrain. Two sentences in parallel construction follow, dealing with the actions the old men and the young men take with her, followed by two sentences in response to these, describing their respective feelings about her. The final sentence sums up the paragraph and "this interest of the male," with a metaphoric interpretation of it and a note of foreboding.

The second paragraph re-creates her girlhood in terms of concrete actions and images: visual (color, shape, light), auditory (sounds of feet, voice, silence),

kinetic (running, wind), tactile (stoning the cows, touching the earth). It sums up her sexual nature as well and ends with two sentences referring to the wishes of the old and young men from the first paragraph, regarding Karintha as she matures. Before Karintha is shown as a woman, the refrain of the epigraph is repeated, the first three lines each being cut by a few words. The new rhythm creates a pace appropriately faster than the wondering, more meditative earlier version.

The third paragraph makes assorted references to the subject matter and phrasing of earlier paragraphs. Repetitions of actual sentences and phrases and of sentence structure (in a series of short sentences showing what young men do for Karintha) evoke the sense of poetry, as does the second half of the paragraph, which, through indirection, reveals Karintha's murder of her infant. The birth is presented as a kind of emotionless miracle unconnected with Karintha herself, while the scene is given sensory richness. Juxtaposed, after ellipses, is the description of a nearby sawmill, its smoldering sawdust pile, and the heaviness of the smoke after Karintha's return. Ending this paragraph is a short song that someone makes up about smoke rising to "take my soul to Jesus," an unconsciously appropriate elegy for the unwanted baby.

The final paragraph begins as the third did—"Karintha is a woman"—and then echoes the last sentence of the first paragraph: "Men do not know that the soul of her was a growing thing ripened too soon." Toomer then suggests her unbreachable remoteness from men; the last sentence recalls the first in this sketch, describing her at twenty in the phrases used to describe her as a child. After a last repetition of her name, followed by ellipses, comes a repetition of the epigraph, followed by an ominous repetition of its last two words, "Goes down," and then more ellipses, hinting at the inevitable descent and defeat of this beautiful, vital creature, brought to maturity too soon through misuse by men.

Though printed as prose, this piece is essentially poetic; the outer details of Karintha's life are merely hinted, but Toomer's poetic prose gives a full sense of Karintha's person and appeal through the precise sensory details of the second paragraph, the recurring patterns of the old and young men's responses to her, and the use of songs as commentary. The echoes and repetitions of images and phrases act as leitmotifs, and Toomer's careful arrangement of them gives the piece a satisfying structure and a strong sense of Karintha's doom, trapped in an unchanging pattern.

FORM, STYLE, AND TONE

Such leitmotifs, along with vivid imagery and sentence patterns that are short, repeated, often fragmentary, are used throughout the prose pieces of *Cane* in place of rhyme and meter and line division to produce the quality of poetry. Indeed, many of these pieces (including "Rhobert," "Calling Jesus," "Seventh Street") must be read, like "Karintha," more as poetry than as fiction.

In the pieces clearly printed as poetry, Toomer is less experimental. Many of his poems use orthodox rhyme schemes and meters that a Henry Wadsworth Longfellow or James Russell Lowell would approve. Yet scarce as the poems in *Cane* are, they cover a variety of forms that few single books of poetry display. "Song of the Son," for example, is skillfully rhymed, beautifully evoking in five stanzas of flowing iambic pentameter the Southern music which the poet is trying to capture in literature—as he says in this poem, before it vanishes. There are poems of rhymed couplets and brief pieces such as the Imagists might produce. There is a "Cotton Song," such as the work songs that slaves or free but poor farmhands might sing. There is much free verse, notably in "Harvest Song." Toomer's choices are not arbitrary; they suit the moods and subjects of their respective poems, conveying the spectrum of feelings that the writer wishes to present, from joy and exaltation to bitterness and despair.

Toomer also varies style and tone, as well as form, to suit theme and mood. Grim and laconic irony flavors "Conversion," as the African succumbs to "a white-faced sardonic god." "Georgia Dusk" offers lush images both of Southern life and of the African past (a recurring motif throughout the book). "Portrait in Georgia," with its short free-verse lines, reads like a catalog of bodily parts, such as an auctioneer would have prepared. Each is described through images of Southern white violence: "lyncher's rope," "fagots," "scars," "blisters," "the ash of black flesh after flame." This poem makes no explicit statement, but the juxtaposition of human parts with these images, presented so simply and concisely, evokes a subtle sense of horror and sets up an appropriately ominous mood for the following story, "Blood-Burning Moon," which ends with an actual lynching. However attractive may be the Georgia of pines, red soil, sweet-smelling cane, and beauteous dusks, Toomer insists on reminding his reader of the dangers there as well, even without explicit condemnation of the bigoted whites or the oppressive social system. Toomer works by indirection, but without diminished effect.

"HARVEST SONG"

A similarly strong but quite different effect is achieved in "Harvest Song," which presents a field worker suffering at the end of a long day from chill, hunger, thirst, and fatigue. Each poetic "line" is made up of one or more sentences and takes up between one and five lines of print on the page. These sentences are generally short, simple statements that the speaker can barely utter, and they are often repeated, emphasizing his basic human needs, which remain unsatisfied. Toomer's words may not be those that the worker would actually use, but they mirror his thoughts closely, just as the prose pieces of *Cane* give a clear sense of their characters' minds and lives without using their actual language. The simple sentences and their repetition give an accurate sense of the worker's numbness. The poem's last long line (five sentences) is a more exalted outburst, though still despairing: The harvester beats his soft palms against the stubble in his field, causing himself pain that takes away his awareness of hunger, as the last sentence makes shockingly clear. "Harvest Song" indeed! The speaker hardly feels like singing with his throat parched from thirst; and what he harvests for himself means only more pain. Through the use of first-person narration and a simple style, Toomer evokes not pity for the poor worker, not an external look as in Edwin Markham's "The Man with the Hoe," but rather an empathy from within, allowing the reader to participate fully in the experience.

SPIRITUAL AND PHILOSOPHICAL BELIEFS

Too often, unfortunately, Toomer's later poetry drops the effective devices used in *Cane* and becomes didactic, explicitly philosophical, lacking *Cane*'s brilliantly realized images of concrete reality or its sharp, often startling metaphors. Toomer was mightily inspired by his few months in Georgia, and his sojourn even affected his interpretations of his own more familiar Washington and New York life; but after he had said what he had to say about the South, and the North in relation to the South, he seems to have exhausted his inspiration, except for his more "universal" themes, with only a little sense of poetry left, to be used in "Blue Meridian" and his stories "Winter on Earth" and "Withered Skin of Berries." The latter story returned Toomer to the lyrical style and poetic sense of structure of the *Cane* stories, but for the most part, Toomer preferred to ignore stylistic and literary matters and chose to express his spiritual and philosophical beliefs, largely influenced by George Gurdjieff's teachings, urging a regeneration of humanity that would eliminate the differences imposed by racial and other categories and bring people closer to God, one another, and the natural world.

"BLUE MERIDIAN"

This is the point that he makes explicitly in his last major work, the long poem "Blue Meridian," first published in full in *New American Caravan* (1936) after a selection from an earlier version had appeared in *Adelphi* and *Pagany*. A further revised version is printed in Langston Hughes and Arna Bontemps's anthology *The Poetry of the Negro, 1746-1949* (1949), which places more emphasis on God and more clearly reveals Toomer's notion of the transformed America. A few of the more minor revisions are for the better. This is the version published in *The Wayward and the Seeking*, with some incidental changes.

"Blue Meridian" follows a structure much like that of Whitman's longer poems, such as "Passage to India" or "Crossing Brooklyn Ferry," with recurring phrases or stanzas, often significantly altered. While it is not divided into individual sections, as Eliot's *The Waste Land* (1922) and Crane's *The Bridge* (1930) are—nor does it use the range of poetic forms of which Eliot and Crane availed themselves—it nevertheless follows those poems in being an examination and criticism of the twentieth century world, achieving a multifaceted view by varying tone and form.

Written largely in a hortatory, exalted style in an effort to invoke Toomer's higher spiritual goals for a better world an unified humankind, "Blue Meridian" explores the past and current conditions of America. The European, African, and "red" races are presented in appropriate images—even stereotypes—each being shown as incomplete. Toomer's goal, as in much of his prose, is to achieve a new race beyond individual racial identities, a "universal human being" to be called the "blue meridian," the highest stage of development beyond white and black, beyond divisions of East and West, of religion, race, class, sex, and occupational classification, and transcending the materialism of a commercial culture and the private concerns of individuals. The message is not so different from Whitman's, except for greater criticism of modern business and the insistence on the mingling of the races.

DETRACTIONS OF LATER WORK

Racial themes and the black experience are missing from Toomer's later poems—and even some of his earlier ones, such as "Banking Coal" (*Crisis*, 1922). He was living with a white wife, quite isolated from the African American literary world, or from any literary world at all. Certainly one should not say that a black writer (even one with so little black ancestry as Toomer) should write only on black themes, but any writer should write out of direct experience; too much of Toomer's poetry aside from *Cane* is vague and didactic, too intentionally "universal," too generally spiritualized, and essentially prosaic, like his aphorisms, which lack the bite of Ralph Waldo Emerson's.

Unfortunately, Toomer's vocabulary in this later poetry—including "Blue Meridian"—too often emulates that of Whitman at his most inflated moments, even when Toomer has a true poetic idea, as in "The Lost Dancer," which opens: "Spatial depths of being survive/ The birth to death recurrences. . . ." It is not so much the Latinate vocabulary, which Toomer's great contemporaries Crane and Stevens also used, but rather that, while they made much of the orotund, sensual sounds and suggestiveness of Latinate words, Toomer's word-choices are flat and vague, words made familiar through bombastic social-science jargon. Whereas the *Cane* poems stand out particularly for the vitality of their imagery, the apt metaphors and similes in "Face" and "Portrait in Georgia," the richness of language and sensory detail in "Song of the Son" and "Georgia Dusk," the harshness of the concrete nouns, verbs, and adjectives in "Harvest

Song," images in the later poetry are greatly minimized. Here Toomer abandons the exalted Romantic eloquence of "Song of the Son," the verbal and emotional starkness of "Harvest Song," in favor of making philosophical statements.

At his best, Toomer was a brilliant artist in words, a sensitive portrayer of the life he lived and observed, as well as a sincere and concerned member of the human race. *Cane* will forever keep his name alive and arouse an interest in his other work, however inferior most of it has turned out to be. The musical quality of his best poetry and prose will be admired, not for its mere beauty but for its aptness to its subjects: the beauty and appeal as well as the tragedy of the life of the South.

OTHER MAJOR WORKS

PLAY: "Balo," in Alain Locke's *Plays of Negro Life*, pb. 1927.

NONFICTION: "Winter on Earth," in *The Second American Caravan*, 1929; "Race Problems and Modern Society," 1929; *Essentials: Definitions and Aphorisms*, 1931; "The Flavor of Man," 1949.

BIBLIOGRAPHY

Benson, Joseph, and Mabel Mayle Dillard. *Jean Toomer.* Boston: Twayne, 1980. The first book-length study of Toomer, this volume is an excellent introduction to Toomer's life, work, and place in American literature. After a biographical chapter, the book examines Toomer's novel *Cane* and representative later works. The bibliography includes unpublished works by Toomer and an annotated list of secondary sources.

Byrd, Rudolph P. "Jean Toomer and the Writers of the Harlem Renaissance: Was He There with Them?" In *The Harlem Renaissance: Revaluations*, edited by Amritjit Singh, William S. Shiver, and Stanley Brodwin. New York: Garland, 1989. In this article, Byrd argues that Toomer should not be considered part of the Harlem Renaissance because he was not in Harlem for many of the Renaissance's most important years, he did not associate himself with other Harlem writers, and he refused to be labeled as a "Negro" writer.

Durham, Frank, ed. *The Merrill Studies in "Cane."* Columbus, Ohio: Charles E. Merrill, 1971. This volume is a collection of documents that reveal the history of Toomer's most important work, his novel *Cane.* Includes biographical essays, contemporary and more recent introductions to the novel, contemporary reviews, and critical essays.

Fabre, Geneviève, and Michel Feith, eds. *Jean Toomer and the Harlem Renaissance.* New Brunswick, N.J.: Rutgers University Press, 2001. A collection of essays by European and American scholars highlighting Toomer's bold experimentations, as well as his often ambiguous responses to the questions of his time.

Jones, Robert B. *Jean Toomer and the Prison-House of Thought: A Phenomenology of the Spirit.* Amherst: University of Massachusetts Press, 1993. A short study of the philosophical aspects of Toomer's work. Includes bibliographical references and index.

Kerman, Cynthia Earl, and Richard Eldridge. *The Lives of Jean Toomer: A Hunger for Wholeness.* Baton Rouge: Louisiana State University Press, 1987. One of the most comprehensive biographies of Toomer yet written, this volume traces in careful detail how the writer was influenced by his unstable childhood, his fascination with mysticism, and his brief career among the literary elite of the 1920's. Includes a chronology, nearly thirty illustrations, and an extensive bibliography.

Larson, Charles R. *Invisible Darkness: Jean Toomer and Nella Larsen.* Iowa City: University of Iowa Press, 1993. Arranged in four sections, each split between Larsen and Toomer. Treats each author's relation to the publishing practices of the Harlem Renaissance, offering critical-biographical readings of Toomer's *Cane* and stories, and examining both authors' formative years and their negotiation of their racial identity. Bibliography, index.

McKay, Nellie Y. *Jean Toomer, Artist: A Study of His Literary Life and Work, 1894-1936.* Chapel Hill: University of North Carolina Press, 1984. Primarily a literary analysis, this book examines Toomer's major published works, especially *Cane*, and places them in the contexts of American and African American literature. The relationship between Toomer's work and his life is also examined, drawing heavily on his autobiographical writings.

O'Daniel, Therman B., ed. *Jean Toomer: A Critical Evaluation.* Washington, D.C.: Howard University Press, 1988. This large volume contains forty-six essays and an extensive bibliography. The essays are arranged thematically, and cover Toomer's life; his work as novelist, short-story writer, poet, and playwright; his friendships with other writers; religious and male-female themes; and various interpretations of *Cane.* An excellent and accessible collection.

Scruggs, Charles, and Lee VanDemarr. *Jean Toomer and the Terrors of American History.* Philadelphia: University of Pennsylvania Press, 1998. Scruggs and VanDemarr examine sources such as Toomer's early writings on politics and race, his extensive correspondence with Waldo Frank, and unpublished portions of his autobiographies to illustrate the ways in which the cultural wars of the 1920's influenced Toomer's *Cane* and his later attempt to escape from the racial definitions of American society.

Scott Giantvalley;
bibliography updated by the editors

THOMAS TRAHERNE

Born: Herefordshire, England; c. 1637
Died: Teddington, England; October, 1674

PRINCIPAL POETRY

A Serious and Patheticall Contemplation of the Mercies of God, 1699 (better known as *Thanksgivings*)
The Poetical Works of Thomas Traherne, 1903
Traherne's Poems of Felicity, 1910

OTHER LITERARY FORMS

Thomas Traherne's reputation is based primarily on his religious works, both in poetry and prose. His treatises include *Roman Forgeries* (1673); *Christian Ethicks* (1675); and the meditation *Centuries of Meditations* (1908).

ACHIEVEMENTS

Thomas Traherne is usually categorized with the seventeenth century Metaphysical poets, although his poetry lacks the quality of wit that characterizes John Donne's and George Herbert's work. His poetry is religious and philosophical and bears closest comparison with that of Henry Vaughan, to whom it was attributed when first discovered in a London bookstall in 1896. Plato is the ultimate source of Traherne's thinking, both in verse and prose, and his works demonstrate his reading of many other writers in the Platonic tradition, including St. Augustine, St. Bonaventure, Marsilio Ficino, Pico della Mivandola, and the Cambridge Platonists. Scholars have generally judged Traherne to be more interested in philosophy than poetry. Perhaps as a consequence, his prose works have received more critical attention than his poetry, especially *Centuries of Meditations*, a devotional work in the Anglican tradition of Lancelot Andrewes and Donne. *Christian Ethicks*, published the year after Traherne's death, was the only systematic treatise intended for the educated English layman to appear in the thirty years following the Restoration. Because of the attention he paid to infant and childhood experiences and the importance he ascribed to them in the development of an understanding of divinity, Traherne has been suspected of the Pelagian heresy (which denies the doctrine of original sin). His name is frequently linked with such Romantic poets as William Blake and William Wordsworth, who also praised childhood innocence as the state in which humans are most closely in touch with the eternal.

BIOGRAPHY

The few bits of information known about Thomas Traherne's life come principally from John Aubrey's *Miscellanies* (1696), which reveals that Traherne was twice visited by apparitions, and from Anthony à Wood's *Athenae Oxoniensus* (1691-1692), where he is identified as a son of John Traherne, a shoemaker who was related to Philip Traherne, twice mayor of Hereford. Traherne also had a brother Philip, who revised and edited some of his poems. Traherne was educated at Brasenose College, Oxford, where he took his B.A. degree on October 13, 1656. He was ordained and, on December 30, 1657, was appointed to the Rectory at Credenhill, County Hereford. While at Credenhill, Traherne became spiritual adviser to Mrs. Susanna Hopton. She had become a Roman Catholic after the execution of Charles I but rejoined the Church of England after the Restoration and became the center of a religious society for which Traherne wrote *Centuries of Meditations*. Mrs. Hopton's niece married Traherne's brother Philip. Traherne returned to Oxford to take his M.A. on November 6, 1661, and his B.D. (Bachelor of Divinity) on December 11, 1669. In 1667, he became chaplain to Sir Orlando Bridgman, Keeper of the Seals in the Restoration. Traherne's death occurred three months after his patron's, and he was buried beneath the reading desk in the church at Teddington on October 10, 1674. *Roman Forgeries*, the equivalent of a modern B.D. thesis, was his only work published in his lifetime, although he was preparing *Christian Ethicks* for publication at the time of his death. There may yet be more works of Traherne to be discovered, for as recently as 1964 a manuscript called "Select Meditations," also organized by "centuries," came to light and was established as Traherne's.

ANALYSIS

Modern readers first encountered Thomas Traherne as a poet, and the publication of his poems fortuitously coincided with the renewed interest in the seventeenth century poets signaled by H. J. C. Grierson's 1912 edition of John Donne. Although Traherne was not included in Grierson's famous 1921 anthology of Metaphysical poetry, he has always been categorized with those poets, although in the second rank. Traherne might be surprised to find himself among the ranks of the poets at all, for his verse, at least as much of it as has been discovered, comprises only a portion of his known writings, and there is reason to believe that he placed more importance on two of his prose works, *Christian Ethicks* and *Centuries of Meditations*. Thematically, and even stylistically, his poetry is of a piece with his prose, which deserves some consideration here, both for the light it throws on his poetry and for its own sake.

Widely and deeply read, intellectually eclectic, and religiously heterodox, Traherne reminds one of John Milton, whom he preceded in death by less than a month.

Both were modernists, sharing in the new humanist emphasis of their era. Traherne, however, found a place in the established Church, something that the great Puritan poet would have found impossible. Traherne lacked the genius that made Milton an original, and readers of the younger poet are always conscious of his debts to thinkers and writers greater than he. He copied into his Commonplace Book from those whom he especially admired, many of whom are in the Platonic tradition, such as Hermes Trismegistus, whose *Divine Pymander* Traherne copied in its 1657 English translation, and Henry More, the Cambridge Platonist, from whose *Divine Dialogues* (1668) Traherne copied extracts. Another unpublished manuscript (British Museum Manuscript Burney 126) is known informally as the Ficino Notebook because it consists of extracts from Ficino's Latin epitomes and translations of Plato. It also contains a long Latin life of Socrates and an otherwise unidentified work titled "Stoicismus Christianus."

Traherne's writings are almost exclusively religious, and the influence of Plato, without whom Christianity would be a very different religion, is therefore unsurprising. What is surprising is Traherne's apparent acceptance of Platonic doctrines usually rejected by the Christian Fathers, such as the doctrine of the soul's preexistence, and his modification of other doctrines, such as the traditional Platonic opposition of the material and spiritual worlds, from their usual adaptation to Christian dogma. Hints of the soul's memory of an existence previous to the earthly one is one of the motifs in Traherne's poetry that reminds readers of the Romantic poets, especially Wordsworth of the "Ode: Intimations of Immortality from Recollections of Early Childhood." Were it not for the fact that Traherne's work was not discovered until nearly fifty years after Wordsworth's death, scholars would doubtless have searched for the Trahernian influence on him. In *Centuries of Meditations*, 3.2, Traherne marvels, "Is it not strange that an infant should be heir of the whole world, and see those mysteries which the books of the learned never unfold?" His exaltation of infancy and childhood in particular makes him seem a precursor of the Romantic movement. Like Wordsworth, Traherne values childhood innocence because the "Infant-Ey," as he says in a poem of that title, "Things doth see/ Ev'n like unto the Deity."

Attributing such power to the child requires, as he paradoxically says, "a learned and a Happy Ignorance" and is one of the indications that Traherne believed in the preexistence of the soul. Although he never expressly states such a belief, it can be inferred from his writings, particularly *Centuries of Meditations* and *Christian Ethicks*, where he discusses other aspects of Neoplatonic mysticism.

On the other hand, Traherne rejects the traditional Platonic preference for the ideal world over the real. In fact, as Carol Marks has noted in "Traherne and Cambridge Platonism" (1966), Traherne holds that the spiritual world is enhanced by its physical actualization. Another way in which Traherne departs from strict Platonism is in his conception of time and eternity. For Platonic philosophers, as Richard Jordan points out in *The Temple of Eternity* (1972), time is the earthly, mortal image of eternity, but for Traherne, this is part of eternity, just as the physical world is part of God's unified creation. Here again, Traherne is reacting against the medieval emphasis on the opposition between this world and the next, finding instead a reconciliation.

His reaction to the Aristotelian dichotomies of the Scholastic philosophers is one of the affinities between Traherne and the Cambridge Platonists. He also shared their distaste for the Calvinist preoccupation with original sin and, like them, focused on man's potential, through the exercise of reason, to achieve happiness. In fact, as more than one scholar has suggested, Traherne's theology may have been Pelagian; his heavy stress on the power of childhood innocence almost requires a denial of the doctrine of original sin. Patrick Grant asserts in The Transformation of Sin (1974) that Traherne's theology is indebted to St. Irenaeus, one of the pre-Nicene Fathers to whom the Cambridge Platonists also looked for a method whereby pagan philosophy could be incorporated into Christianity. Stanley Stewart in *The Expanded Voice* (1970) finds Traherne aligned with the Arminians at Oxford who struck a balance between Pelagian "secularism" and Calvinistic determinism. Traherne's emphasis on man's potential for creation, which man shares with God, and his slight attention to sin, certainly distinguish him from Donne and Herbert. Traherne's accommodation of less traditional religious views probably was one of the factors that earned for him the position as chaplain to Bridgman, who allied himself overtly with the Latitudinarian cause and, before Traherne, had employed a Latitudinarian divine.

SEARCH FOR RELIGIOUS TRUTH

Traherne's approach to theology was essentially exploratory, searching for truth rather than dogma. "Let it be your Care to dive to the Bottom of true Religion, and not suffer your Eyes to be Dazled with its Superficial Appearance," he wrote in *Christian Ethicks*. That attitude is evident in *Roman Forgeries*, a polemic with the ostensible purpose of indicting the Roman church for its flagrant forgeries of documents and falsification of historical facts. Stewart's book sets the work in the rhetorical context of the anti-Papist tracts of the late Tudor and Stuart dynasties, but goes on to argue the preeminent influence of a 1611 work by Dr. Thomas James lengthily titled *A Treatise of the Corruption of Scripture, Councels, and Fathers, by the Prelats, Pastors, and Pillars of the Church of Rome for Maintenance of Popery and Irreligion*. Like James, Traherne's purpose is less to vent anti-Catholic vitriol, although *Roman Forgeries* observes convention in that regard, than to reexamine, scientifically, texts condemned as false, with an eye toward religious certainty.

Renaissance Platonists, such as those at Cambridge and such as Traherne, asserted that man was the bond of the universe, the link between the spiritual and the material, between the Creation and the Creator; that belief probably accounts for the self-centered quality of much of Traherne's work, especially *Centuries of Meditations*. The notion of man as microcosm is found in many places, but a probable source for Traherne is Pico's *Oratio de hominis dignitate* (1486, *Oration on the Dignity of Man*), which he especially praised. For Pico and others, when man was created in the image of God, he was also made the quintessence of the universe. Thus, although Traherne's philosophy of life seems rather self-centered, as more than one critic has pointed out, it is possible that he was using himself as microcosmic man. Stewart finds that the *Centuries of Meditations* is a self-centered work and yet not egotistic; rather, Traherne indulges in "a process of perfect narcissism," for in self-love one finds the beginning of love of the universe, created by God.

CENTURIES OF MEDITATIONS

Despite Traherne's identification as a poet, scholarly attention has concentrated on *Centuries of Meditations*, particularly in the years since the publication of Louis Martz's two studies, *The Poetry of Meditation* (1954) and, especially, *The Paradise Within* (1964), in which Martz places *Centuries of Meditations* in the tradition of the Augustinian meditative exercise. Much of Traherne's writing, including his poetry, derives from that tradition, including *Meditations on the Six Days of the Creation* (1717) and an unpublished work, *The Church's Year-Book*. The century was an established subgenre of the Anglican manual of meditation. Earlier examples include Thomas Wilson's *Theological Rules* (1615), organized in four centuries, and Alexander Ross's *A Centurie of Divine Meditations* (1646). Traherne's work is divided into five centuries, all except the fifth containing one hundred short meditations. Since the fifth century ends with the tenth meditation followed by the numeral "11," scholars have felt obliged to ponder whether the work is unfinished or whether perhaps Traherne purposely ended abruptly so that the reader (or perhaps his patron, Susanna Hopton), having become adept at meditation through studying the first four centuries, could complete the fifth meditation for himself on the forty-eight blank pages remaining in the manuscript. Such a fanciful explanation, the ultimate in self-effacement in an otherwise self-centered work, seems unlikely. Martz feels "a sense of completion" after the tenth meditation in Century Five, and says, mystically, that "the conclusion lies in the eloquent silence of those blank pages." Indeed, Traherne was not unaware of the importance of silence for the mystic, as his poem "Silence" demonstrates. "A quiet Silent Person may possess/ All that is Great or High in Blessedness," the poem begins. This poem, however, is followed in the Dobell Folio by other poems, not blank pages.

The most influential discussion of the source of the *Centuries of Meditations* is by Louis Martz, who sees it as an Anglican adaptation of the Augustinian meditative mode, particularly as exemplified by St. Bonaventure's *Itinerarium Mentis in Deum* (1259, *Journey of the Mind to God*). Martz finds a basis for Traherne's optimism in Augustine's discussion of the power of the human mind in *De Trinitate* (397-401, *On the Trinity*), and he identifies the *Centuries of Meditations* as a "confessional" work, moving through the three stages of confession of sin, confession of praise, and confession of faith that Augustine's *Confessions* (397-401) moves through. Traherne's five-part division mirrors St. Bonaventure's *Itinerarium Mentis in Deum*. Bonaventure's journey opens with a Preparation, corresponding to Traherne's first century. Traherne prepares for the meditative exercise by meditating on the cross and by introducing one of his most important images, Adam in Paradise. The central sections of Bonaventure's work set forth the Threefold Way to God, which is accomplished by Traherne's three central centuries. Traherne begins his contemplative journey autobiographically, drawing in centuries Two and Three on personal experience in this world, taken as a mirror of the divine world. In the fourth century, he leaves personal experience behind and attempts to discuss the divine principles themselves. Bonaventure's *Itinerarium* closes with a Repose, which corresponds to Traherne's fifth century.

Most subsequent commentators on the *Centuries of Meditations* pay homage to Martz, even when they disagree with him. Isabel MacCaffrey suggests in an appreciative review of Martz's book that Traherne's plan was not simply Augustinian but Ignatian ("The Meditative Paradigm," 1965), an idea that gains support from the knowledge that Traherne used an English translation of a meditative work by a Spanish Jesuit in the composition of the *Thanksgivings* and especially in the *Meditations on the Six Days of the Creation* and in *The Church's Year-Book*. Gerard Cox, who calls the application of Bonaventure and Augustine to Traherne "highly questionable," argues instead that the *Centuries of Meditations* is organized according to Platonic principles derived from the Cambridge Platonists Theophilus Gale and Benjamin Whichcote ("Traherne's *Centuries*: A Platonic Devotion of 'Divine Philosophy,'" in *Modern Philology*, 1971). Cox, however, undercuts his own discussion by conceding that the Platonic organizing principle "is not sufficiently in control" so that the *Centuries of Meditations* has often seemed "a haphazard collection of meditations." Jordan argues for a three-part structure for the work, each part devoted, respectively, to the world, the individual soul, and God, and points out that in his promised discussion of the attributes of God,

Traherne never mentions love, which he had discussed in relation to the other two topics. Century Five, then, Jordan suggests, must have been intended as a meditation on God's love. Although his three-part division of a work divided by its author into five parts seems strained, his explanation for the incomplete state of the fifth century is reasonable. Stewart dismisses all attempts to find or impose an order on the work as symptomatic of modern unresponsiveness "to literary experiences not based on novelistic assumptions about beginning, middle, and end," and claims that the *Centuries of Meditations* proceeds by accretion.

CHRISTIAN ETHICKS

Stewart claims that basically the same principle underlies the organization of *Christian Ethicks*, a collection of Baconian essays on various virtues, theological and moral. While each chapter does proceed in the exploratory fashion of Francis Bacon's essays, and while each one is self-contained, so that there is no particular necessity to the organization of most of the book—indeed the discussion of the cardinal virtues justice and prudence is interrupted by the discussion of the theological virtues, faith, hope, charity, and (Traherne's addition) repentance—Traherne nevertheless sees the whole as governed by a general purpose, as his preface "To the Reader" makes clear. One tradition from which *Christian Ethicks* derives is the gentleman's handbook, which instructed Renaissance men in the attainment of the various virtues required of a gentleman. Traherne's handbook, however, will be different. He will not treat the virtues "in the ordinary way," he says, as that has already been done; rather, he seeks "to satisfie the Curious and Unbelieving Soul, concerning the reality, force, and efficacy of *Virtue*" as a means to felicity. As Carol Marks says in the general introduction to the 1968 edition of *Christian Ethicks*, the work is distinguished by "persuasive emotion, rather than intellectual originality." Rhetorically speaking, "persuasive emotion" is an aim ascribed by seventeenth century rhetoricians to poetry, and indeed the work may be compared with Edmund Spenser's *The Faerie Queene* (1590, 1596), whose end was also "to fashion a gentleman." Traherne echoes, as well, Milton's purpose in *Paradise Lost* (1667) when he says, "You may easily discern that my Design is to reconcile Men to GOD."

Edmund Spenser claimed that the virtues celebrated by his poem were such "as Aristotle hath devised," and Carol Marks asserts that ethical textbooks in seventeenth century England all derived from the *Nicomachean Ethics* (unknown). Traherne's organizational plan, however, as outlined in the preface, is not really Aristotelian. He divides human history into four parts, according to the "estates" of Innocence, Misery, Grace, and Glory, and assigns to each its appropriate virtues. He emphasizes in his preface his reluctance to speak of vice, claiming to be completely occupied with the discussion of virtues. The arduous *via negativa* through the circles of hell was not for him. Rather, as Anne Ridler says in the introduction to her edition of the poems, Traherne is a "master of the Affirmative Way."

TRAHERNE'S POEMS OF FELICITY

Traherne's Platonism and Neoplatonic mysticism and his interests in meditation and ethical instruction recur throughout his poetry, and, indeed, there are occasional poems scattered among the prose works already discussed. The only poems published before the twentieth century are those known as the *Thanksgivings*, nine psalm-like poems praising God's creation. Traherne's other lyrics are in two different manuscripts known as the Dobell Folio, named for the bookseller who first identified the author, and *Traherne's Poems of Felicity*, a group of poems selected and transcribed by Traherne's brother Philip, who also edited them very heavily, as duplicate poems from the Dobell Folio demonstrate. He smoothed out rhythms, mended defective rhymes, regularized stanza forms, and made the expression "plainer" by substituting the literal for the metaphorical. Two versions of a line from one of Traherne's best-known poems, "Wonder," demonstrate Philip's method. In the Dobell Folio version, the line is "The Streets were pav'd with golden Stones." In *Traherne's Poems of Felicity*, only one word is changed, but it is a significant one: "The Streets seem'd paved with Golden Stones." Philip has changed the metaphor into a simile, making the line safer, less bold. The Dobell Folio comprises thirty-seven poems. All but six are also in *Traherne's Poems of Felicity*. The latter manuscript is, however, the only source for thirty-eight of its sixty-one poems. Because of the extensiveness of Philip's emendations to the poems also contained in the Dobell Folio, the textual accuracy of the poems for which Philip's version is the only source is clearly unreliable.

The Dobell Folio is a holograph, so it is likely that the poems in it were arranged in their present order by the author. The general plan seems to be man's spiritual biography from infancy to maturity. The opening poem is appropriately titled "The Salutation," although it is not a greeting to the reader, but the child's greeting to life. Childhood innocence, especially as it resembles the state of Adam in Paradise, is the subject of the first four poems. The next six, from "The Preparative" to "The Approach," concern ways of coming to know God, chiefly through appreciation of his works, a theme which recurs throughout the poems and is frequently expressed by catalogs of God's works. Traherne's reading of philosophers and theologians is everywhere apparent, most obtrusively in a poem called "The Anticipation" employing technical terminology from the Aristotelian tradition to exploit the paradox that God is at once the end, the means, and the cause of natural law. The titles of the last eight poems in the sequence reveal Traherne's Christianized Platonism. There are four, titled, respectively, "Love," "Blisse," "Desire," and "Goodnesse," among which are interposed four poems, each titled "Thoughts." Love and desire, according to Platonic doctrine, are the forces that motivate man to seek bliss and goodness, and thoughts are the means, the "Engines of Felicitie," to use one of his rare Metaphysical conceits. Thoughts are the means to a mystical apprehension of God, as quotations from "Thoughts: III" and "Thoughts: IV" exemplify: "Thoughts are the Angels which we send abroad,/ To visit all the Parts of Gods Abode." They are "the Wings on which the Soul doth flie."

His emphasis on "thoughts" in these poems is another reminder of Traherne's familiarity with the meditative tradition; John Malcolm Wallace has argued in "Thomas Traherne and the Structure of Meditation" (1958) that the poems of the Dobell Folio constitute a five-part meditation in the Augustinian-Jesuit tradition, as described by Martz. Whether such a process was the poet's intention cannot be proved. More recently, A. L. Clements in *The Mystical Poetry of Thomas Traherne* (1969) has interpreted the Dobell Folio using a somewhat simpler three-part framework. He sees the poems moving from childlike innocence, through fallen adult experience, to blessed felicity, the traditional Christian life-pilgrimage. Scholars seem to agree, in any case, that the manuscript is a patterned work of art and not simply a random collection of poems.

The same cannot be said about *Traherne's Poems of Felicity*. There can be little doubt of Traherne's authorship of all the poems of the manuscript, for they express the same themes and exhibit the same stylistic features as those in the holograph manuscript. Nevertheless, it cannot be said with certainty that choice lines are not Philip's revisions.

CRITICAL RECEPTION

Stylistically, Traherne's poetry has never received much critical approbation, although some recent critics have argued that New Critical tenets have made it impossible for twentieth century readers to appreciate Traherne. Two primary characteristics of his poetic—his heavy reliance on abstractions and his frequent catalogs of, for example, God's creations do not make for vivid verse. Yet his relative avoidance of imagery is deliberate, as the well-known poem on his poetic, "The Author to the Critical Peruser," attests. Traherne specifically rejects "curling Metaphors" in favor of "naked Truth." It may be, as some sympathetic scholars have thought, that his style represents his attempt to transcend imagistic language in an effort to apprehend Platonic ideas, but he is a difficult poet to enjoy for readers who have learned to admire concrete diction and sensual imagery. Such imagery as he does use is often biblical and Christian—images of light, fire, water, mirrors, and, from the Neoplatonic tradition, the eye and the circle. Like other contemporary Christian poets, he makes frequent use of paradoxes, a figure fundamental to Christian theology. One particularly striking hyperbolic, oxymoronic example is "Heavenly Avarice," which he uses to describe "Desire" in the poem of that title. Paradoxes, like abstractions, are part of his effort to raise the mind to the level where apparent opposites are seen to be one.

In English literary history, Traherne is himself something of a paradox. He has achieved a reputation as a poet, and yet his best work was done in prose. As a thinker, he did not achieve anything new, and yet his work demonstrates more consistently than any of the other Metaphysical poets that he was a serious student of philosophy and religion. He was a sort of quiet rebel, remaining in the established church and yet fearlessly examining, and sometimes abandoning, its doctrines. Traherne was not unique; he was very much a man of the Renaissance and Reformation; yet, to study him is to achieve a new insight into the intellectual life of seventeenth century England.

OTHER MAJOR WORKS

NONFICTION: *Roman Forgeries*, 1673; *Christian Ethicks*, 1675; *Meditations on the Six Days of the Creation*, 1717; *Centuries of Meditations*, 1908.

BIBLIOGRAPHY

Clements, A. L. *The Mystical Poetry of Thomas Traherne.* Cambridge, Mass.: Harvard University Press, 1969. Clements reviews Traherne's criticism, discusses the Christian contemplative tradition that provided the content for his writing, outlines the literary criticism found in his poetry, and provides separate chapters on the threefold spiritual process of innocence, fall, and redemption. Contains extended analyses on the poems "My Spirit" and "The Preparative."

Day, Malcolm M. *Thomas Traherne.* Boston: Twayne, 1982. Day's study of Traherne's meditations and poems focuses on his use of abstraction, paradox, and repetition to evoke in his readers a sight of eternity unlike the childlike vision earlier critics described in his work. Day provides a biographical chapter, thoughtful analyses of Traherne's work, a chronology, and an annotated select bibliography.

De Neef, A. Leigh. *Traherne in Dialogue: Heidegger, Lacan, and Derrida.* Durham, N.C.: Duke University Press, 1988. De Neef's study investigates the applicability to Traherne's work of three popular theories, with their themes of being, psychic identity, desire, and "the discursive economy of supplementarity." May prove relatively inaccessible to nonspecialists, but provides an interesting discussion of current literary theory, especially the new historicism, although it contains few extended analyses of Traherne's literary work.

Grant, Patrick. *The Transformation of Sin: Studies in Donne, Herbert, Vaughan, and Traherne.* Montreal: McGill-Queen's University, 1974. Using Traherne's early *Roman Forgeries* to establish Traherne's interest in Saint Irenaeus, Grant uses Irenaean beliefs in human potential to be godlike to reconcile two disparate threads—the Augustinian theodicy of guilt and the optimism in the Cambridge Platonists and hermeticism—in Henry Vaughan's work and particularly his prose.

Hawkes, David. "Thomas Traherne: A Critique of Political Economy." *The Huntington Library Quarterly* 62, no. 3/4 (2001): 369-388. An examination of one isolated and idiosyncratic attempt by Traherne to question the most basic assumptions of political economy after the Restoration in England. Hawkes suggests that Traherne identifies a very local and specific cause of what he calls, in the poem of the same name, "Misapprehension," portraying it as the spiritual effect of the system of exchange-value on which the market economy is based.

Lane, Belden C. "Traherne and the Awakening of Want." *Anglican Theological Review* 81, no. 4 (Fall, 1999): 651-664. Lane examines Traherne's argument that want is the very essence of God's being. Wanting is more than just a metaphor of the universe's affinity to relationship; it says something about how one exists as an interdependent being.

Martz, Louis L. *The Paradise Within: Studies in Vaughan, Traherne, and Milton.* New Haven, Conn.: Yale University Press, 1964. In a lengthy essay, Martz uses the Augustinian meditative tradition, as reflected in St. Bonaventure's *Intinerarium* (journey), to analyze Traherne's *Centuries of Meditations.* According to Martz, Traherne believed that Adam's original creative power still exists in man and that man's duty is to restore the paradise that Christ's sacrifice made possible. In an appendix, Martz discusses the Osborn manuscript, an early draft of Traherne's "Select Meditations."

Stewart, Stanley. *The Expanded Voice: The Art of Thomas Traherne.* San Marino, Calif.: Huntington Library, 1970. Although the bulk of his book is devoted to Traherne's prose, Stewart does devote two chapters to the poetry, which is discussed in the context of a literary tradition. Contains two extensive readings of Traherne's poems, "The Preparative" and the lesser known "Shadows in the Water."

Wade, Gladys Irene. *Thomas Traherne*. Reprint. Princeton, N.J.: Princeton University Press, 1944. New York: Octagon Books, 1969. Wade's book is the first modern scholarly treatment of Traherne's life and work (her book is divided equally between the two). In addition to individual chapters devoted to Henry Vaughan's major literary publications, Wade discusses Traherne as a Christian, a Platonist, and a mystic, and provides a bibliography of Traherne's criticism.

John Thomson;
bibliography updated by the editors

GEORG TRAKL

Born: Salzburg, Austria; February 3, 1887
Died: Krakow, Poland; November 3, 1914

PRINCIPAL POETRY
Gedichte, 1913
Sebastian im Traum, 1914
Die Dichtungen, 1918
Aus goldenem Kelch, 1939
Decline: Twelve Poems, 1952
Twenty Poems of Georg Trakl, 1961
Selected Poems, 1968
Dichtungen und Briefe, 1969 (poetry and letters)
Poems, 1973
Georg Trakl: A Profile, 1983

OTHER LITERARY FORMS

Although Georg Trakl is remembered primarily for his poetry, he did compose two one-act plays (*Totentag*, performed 1906, and *Fata Morgana*, performed 1906), but he later destroyed the manuscripts. His letters can be found in his collected works.

ACHIEVEMENTS

Georg Trakl was one of the major poets of German literary Expressionism (with Georg Heym and Gottfried Benn). Today, he is ranked by many critics and readers as one of the outstanding poets of the early twentieth cen-

tury. Like Rainer Maria Rilke, Stefan George, and Hugo von Hofmannsthal, who were his contemporaries, Trakl developed the heritage of Romanticism and French Symbolism into a very personal poetic diction which, in spite of its individual and original tone, shares some significant stylistic and philosophical features with the work of Trakl's fellow expressionist writers and artists. Trakl's rank as a poet was recognized during his lifetime only by a few (among whom was Rilke). Because the National Socialist regime in Germany and Austria rejected expressionism, claiming it to be a form of degenerate art, Trakl's achievement was fully recognized only after the end of World War II. His work has been particularly influential in Germany, France, and the United States.

BIOGRAPHY

Georg Trakl was born in Salzburg, Austria, on February 3, 1887. During high school, he decided to become a pharmacist. After serving his pharmaceutical apprenticeship, he studied pharmacy for four semesters in Vienna and earned his degree in 1910. Trakl wrote two one-act plays (*Totentag* and *Fata Morgana*), both of which were performed in Salzburg. The failure of the latter prompted him to destroy the manuscripts of both plays.

Trakl's earliest poems were written during the last years of the first decade of the twentieth century. In 1910 and 1911, Trakl served in the military as a dispensing pharmacist. After several unsuccessful attempts at a career as a pharmacist, he fell into severe depression and sought refuge from a hostile reality in drugs, to which he had easy access. He would have been unable to cope had it not been for the friendship and patronage of Ludwig von Ficker, publisher of the Austrian journal *Der Brenner*. Ficker published in his journal almost all Trakl's poetry written between 1912 and 1914. He was one of the few who recognized Trakl's poetic genius during the poet's lifetime. Besides his friendship, Ficker offered Trakl shelter and financial help.

In late August of 1914, with the outbreak of World War I, Trakl, who was serving as a lieutenant in the medical corps, was sent into combat. After the battle of Grodek in Galicia, he was ordered to care for ninety seriously wounded fellow soldiers who were housed in a barn. Not having the medical training and expertise necessary to help the wounded, Trakl was overwhelmed by the gruesome experience and suffered a nervous break-down. Comrades prevented him from shooting himself. A few weeks later, he was sent to the garrison hospital at Krakow for observation and psychiatric care. There, he was confined to a cell with another officer who was suffering from delirium tremens. On the night of November 3, 1914, Trakl died from an overdose of cocaine. The question of whether his death was accidental has remained unanswered.

Georg Trakl

ANALYSIS

Georg Trakl's poetry can be divided into three phases which followed one another within the brief period of approximately eight years. During these years, Trakl's poetic diction underwent profound changes. His early poetry (that written prior to 1909) reflects his groping attempts to find his own "voice." In the early poems, Trakl is unable to free himself fully from the Romantic and neo-Romantic stereotypes of German poetry. His major themes are sorrow, loneliness, the past, and biblical and erotic scenes. His extensive use of the refrain and of four trochee sequences also betrays the influence of Romantic writers, particularly Friedrich Hölderlin and Novalis. Trakl admired the nineteenth century French poet Charles Baudelaire as well as Johann Wolfgang von Goethe, Friedrich Nietzsche, and Fyodor Dostoevski, all of whom left their mark upon his writings. A noteworthy feature of Trakl's early poems is the presence of the first-person singular, which in his later poems dissolves to a point beyond recognition. This "I" and its inner world of feelings is distinguishable from externally perceived reality, even though, as in Romantic poetry, the boundary between a mimetic presentation of objects discernible to the senses and a configuration of images expressing the vision of the poet's "inner eye" is often impossible to delineate.

During the years from 1909 to 1912, Trakl's style changed noticeably. Whereas the early poems frequently show hypotaxis, the poems of this middle phase are predominantly paratactical. The reflective element that is still present in Trakl's earlier poems disappears and gives way to a more "lyrical" or musical principle, and semantic and syntactical patterns are selected according to the interplay of emotional impulse and sound patterns. The emotional impulse translates itself into

language in the form of many emotionally charged verbs, such as "threaten," "shiver," "tremble," "be silent," and "hark." The same anthropomorphic tendency that informs Trakl's use of verbs can be observed in his adjectives, most of which do not increase the visibility of his images but convey a vague yet suggestive emotional aura: for example, "lonely," "quiet," "horrible," "sweet," and "wonderful." Regarding sound composition, Trakl's drafts show clearly that he often changed words and made other revisions for purely "musical" reasons. As mentioned earlier, the first person dissolves into a number of objectified protagonists. Whereas Trakl's early poems still reflect an unshaken belief in a divine order of the universe represented by the symbols of the Christian Church, this belief appears to be shattered in the second phase.

Another, more significant change, however, allows one to distinguish between Trakl's poetry of the early phase and that of the second phase. The mimetic relation of poetic expression and the real world as experienced through sensory perception gives way to a new "visionary" approach, an "inner landscape" that defies the laws of realistic and logical presentation and thus poses many hermeneutical problems.

The third and last phase of Trakl's poetry developed in late 1912. The most noticeable changes are evident in a free rhythmical structure (without rhyme) and in a return to hypotaxis. Even though this means a loss in the musical quality of Trakl's late poems, his new free verse makes assonance and alliteration more obvious. It also allows Trakl's images greater visibility, for they are no longer veiled by rhyme and by a regular metrical pattern. The contrasting themes of sinfulness and purity which permeate the poems of the second phase culminate in the third phase in the creation of the mythical figure of a surrogate god, Elis, who represents the ideal of ethical purity.

In spite of its visionary quality, Trakl's poetic "world" never completely emancipates itself from the "real" world. Rather, the reader observes a gradual dissociation from a realistic representation, a shift toward the imaginary. This is why Trakl can indeed be called an expressionist, since the expressionist artist does exactly what Trakl attempts in his poems: He turns away from a realistic or naturalistic approach to the representation of reality. He no longer copies, imitates, reproduces. He follows the emotional impulse of his inner vision and expresses it, whether this means deforming or distorting reality as it is known, changing its perceptual and logical structure at will, or shifting from a representational to an abstract creative mode.

"IN WINTER" AND "THE OCCIDENT I"

Compare the first stanza of the poem "Im Winter" ("In Winter"):

> The field shimmers white and cold.
> The sky is lonely and vast.
> Jackdaws circle over the pond
> And hunters descend from the forest.

with the first stanza of "Abenland" ("The Occident I"):

> Moon, as if something dead emerged
> From a blue cave,
> And many blossoms fall
> Across the rocky path.
> Someone sick weeps silver tears
> Near the evening pond;
> In a black boat
> Lovers drifted beyond toward death.

The text of "In Winter" is clearly mimetic. It can at least be taken as the realistic description of a winter landscape, even though the scene depicted might be an imaginary one.

The second example, however, no longer presents a view of reality as it is traditionally and normally perceived. The images joined together in the stanza from "The Occident I" can still be construed, with some effort on the part of the reader, as the evocation of a moonlit night in spring. Yet, who is "someone sick," and why are the lovers in their black boat moving toward death? This stanza seems to have originated in a dream.

ABSTRACT AND ABSOLUTE TECHNIQUES

Because the poetic images unfold an inner landscape, the reader can no longer be sure whether he is to take them at their face value. Trakl scholars have long claimed that many images in Trakl's mature poetry are "ciphers"—that they point to a meaning other than their own. As part of a code, they have to be "deciphered," since they are poetic signs which stand for a signified meaning. Trakl's poetry, however, defies reduction to a system of ciphers, the meanings of which can be revealed by comparing all the contexts of a given cipher in the poet's work. Often such a contextual comparison yields a variety of different meanings, some of which are contradictory. This is true particularly in the case of Trakl's use of colors. Almost none of his color adjectives or nouns can be given a fixed meaning. An exception is the color "blue." It frequently appears in the context of images referring to God, to biblical scenes, to childhood, or to animal life. The common semantic ingredient in all these images is the concept of innocence. The words "blue" and "blueness" also sometimes convey the idea of salvation. The cipher "blue" thus stands for a positive semantic content, one that is opposed to the notions of darkness, death, decay, or decline which are prevalent in Trakl's poetry.

Some scholars have maintained that in those cases in which a cipher cannot be assigned a constant meaning abstracted from contextual comparison, Trakl uses "absolute ciphers"—that is, ciphers which are part of a code that is beyond decoding, because its "connection" with any signified meaning has been disjoined. Because of this disjunction of word and denoted content, the poet's language withdraws to a certain degree from reality, forming its own hermetic network of ciphers with multiple semantic content. If no common-meaning denominator can be abstracted from a given number of contexts, the image has to be interpreted within the context of the individual poem.

With caution, one can compare Trakl's poetic strategies to certain similar techniques in the paintings and sculptures of the artists of German expressionism. The latter no longer use colors in a realistic fashion (Franz Marc, for example, paints blue horses). Color in expressionist paintings takes on a symbolic emotional quality which originates in the artist's creative intuition. It is the artist's inner creative "vision" that seeks out its equivalents from the realm of real things for the purpose of artistic expression (regardless of any "realistic" modes of representation). Therefore, it is not a given outer reality that calls for mimetic reproduction in the work of art. Just as Trakl's poetic images lose their realistic and mimetic content and become imbued with an elusive and highly subjective emotional content, expressionist paintings exhibit a tendency toward loss of detail and toward elementary, "essential" forms, a tendency which ultimately leads to nonrepresentational art. This loss of the mimetic mode can be compared to the configurations of images in Trakl's mature and late poetry, which are no longer transparent with a rationally definable meaning "behind" the poetic ciphers. The ensuing darkness and elusiveness of Trakl's poetry (in conjunction with its musical quality) accounts for the often-noted enchanting and captivating effect of his verse.

PHILOSOPHICAL PERSPECTIVE

In spite of all the melodic obscurities in Trakl's poems, it is possible to abstract from his texts a relatively comprehensive view of life. Although Trakl does not offer a full-fledged and systematic "philosophy," his poems are informed by a rather consistent and, at the same time, diversified philosophical perspective that is based on his rejection of many aspects of modern reality. Like most of the expressionists of his generation, Trakl experienced modern industrialized society with its metropolitan cities as a pain-inflicting alien world of which he wanted no part. In Trakl's case, this phobia concerning modern reality was almost paranoiac. The poet's patron, Ludwig von Ficker, reported that he once took

Trakl to a large bank in order to deposit a certain sum in Trakl's name. The sight of this institution made Trakl physically ill, and he left the building trembling and perspiring heavily.

If there is an underlying guiding principle in Trakl's thought and poetic style, it is his dread of life in a totally administered, technologically manipulated, and utterly commercialized world. His poetry becomes the expression of his unwillingness to cope with such a life. This is why poetry is the theater of his inner visionary world, which ignores the accepted rules and laws of normal reality. Literature functions as a sanctuary which, while it still reflects some of the evil of life, contains the features of a better antiworld. Trakl's poetic world is shaped not only by a modern version of Romantic escapism, with all its magical and morbid charm, but also by the harshness of industrial society.

For Trakl, the effects of such a society are manifold. Man feels forlorn, like a stranger in this world. He wanders through life without a goal. The big cities epitomize the plight of modern man, who turns into an anonymous being in a mass society. In an astonishingly prophetic vision, Trakl sees Europe's metropolitan cities destroyed by fire. The poet does not deplore his somber foreboding, since, in his view, man's quest for ethical purity and spiritual nobility is being severely undermined by the brutal, materialistic impact of modern city life.

Trakl seems unable to find any solace in Christianity. Nevertheless, his poems contain numerous biblical references, many of which are an integral part of descriptions of landscapes. It must remain an open question whether Trakl secularizes the religious content of certain biblical words and phrases or whether he imbues nature with a new religious quality. He frequently claims in his poetry that religion is no longer alive. Having degenerated into a lifeless ritual, it has ceased to be a guiding and sustaining power in the life of modern man. Where religion fails, the door to the realm of God can be reopened only through the use of drugs, as expressed in Trakl's poem "Traumerei am Abend" ("Daydreaming in the Evening").

Among the abstract concepts (which are not images and thus not ciphers) that recur in Trakl's poetry are decay, disintegration, disease, and, ultimately, death. These concepts all point to a facet of reality which elicits the poet's lament even though it cannot be regarded as the fruit of modernity. Trakl often links decay and disintegration with man's sinfulness and with an undefined sense of guilt from which man cannot be freed.

MELANCHOLY

The mood in many of Trakl's poems is one of melancholy, anxiety, and desperation. Subdued emotions such as melancholy, however, prevail over the harsher expressions of negative emotions. The poet frequently establishes a connection between expressions of negative emotions and the themes of decay and sinfulness, which are in turn interrelated.

Trakl's view of life and human destiny is a somber and often gloomy one. Having become alienated from his world, especially from the world of the big city, man finds no comfort in religion and thus blindly pursues a meaningless life, drifting in the stream of time. Because everything ends in decay or death, time can be equated with suffering. In such a view, reality is difficult to love or even to accept. Nevertheless, life offers beauty and peace to those who know how to look for them in a hostile world. In Trakl's poems, one indeed finds a peculiar fusion of threatening and attractive features. It is hard to decide whether the positive ingredients belong to the descriptive-mimetic dimension in Trakl's work—which is, after all, still present to some degree—or whether they are the product of his inner poetic intuition. Nonmimetic expression and mimetic rendering of perceived impressions are often hardly distinguishable in Trakl's texts.

STYLISTIC DEVICES

A closer look at Trakl's principles of poetic composition reveals that the expressionist style breaks down in many different ways the established, "normal" modes of perception and logical thinking. The new expressionist "perspective" that emerges as Trakl's poetry matures is one that disengages the reader from the customary and conventional manner in which he grasps phenomenal reality as it appears to him—to his senses and his mind.

Trakl's "arsenal" of images, protagonists (the sister, the boy, the dreamer, the lovers, the child, the hunters, the shepherd, the farmer, the monk, the lepers), and abstract concepts is surprisingly small. The immense variety of the real world has been drastically reduced to a small number of images and concepts which are presented in various guises and which appear in ever-new configurations. This reduction represents a subtle first step toward the expressionist, nonmimetic mode of poetic composition.

Another stylistic device derived from the same basic artistic premises might be called "defocusing." Trakl likes to use nouns derived from past participles or adjectives. In the first stanza of his poem "The Occident I," one finds expressions such as *ein Totes* (something dead) or *ein Krankes* (something sick). The image has been reduced to its essential core (being dead, sick, and so forth), but no further individualizing details are given. It is almost impossible for the reader to "picture" anything concrete when such blurred images are evoked.

A very effective as well as expressive technique, the nonmimetic thrust of which goes far beyond mere defocusing, is the tendency to present images which denote destruction, dismemberment, and dissolution. This is a stylistic device used by many expressionist writers and artists. Here is an example taken from one of Trakl's late poems: ". . . the black face,/ That breaks into heavy pieces/ Of dead and strange planets." This "destructionism" can be interpreted either as a symptom of the broken and fragmented quality of reality itself (Trakl wrote to his friend Ficker in November, 1913: "It is such a terrible thing when one's world breaks apart") or as the poet's attempt to destroy symbolically a world with which he can no longer identify.

Synesthesia and stylistic devices which run counter to the customary ways of perception constitute yet another (though certainly not new) technique which allows the creative intuition of the expressionist to deform the established structure of reality. Trakl likes to blend heterogeneous qualities and processes that defy the norms and the logic of the real world: Walls are "full of leprosy," and the laughter of a human being "sinks into the old well." Inanimate objects take on human qualities, and vice versa.

The poetic inversion of customary modes of perception extends also to the presentation of time in Trakl's poetry. There are passages of lyrical prose in which the present tense alternates in a completely unrealistic way with the past tense. Furthermore, the "unborn" as well as the "dead" appear and speak in Trakl's poems, and time is sometimes experienced as "standing still," its flow abruptly changed to a state of dreamlike timelessness.

Trakl's lyrical transmutation of reality also leads to the dissolution of the conventional structure of space. The notions of "above" and "below" or "near" and "far" lose their accepted meaning when the poet writes such lines as "A white shirt of stars burns the shoulders which wear it" or "The autumn moon dwells silently near your mouth."

As mentioned earlier, the first-person singular, so frequently found in Trakl's early poetry, disappears in the poems written after 1909. It undergoes various transformations which show a tendency toward objectivization. The "I" becomes part of (or fused with) the images of the poet's imaginary world. It can turn into a "you"; that is, the poet addresses himself in the second person. Parts of the human being who once referred to himself as "I" now represent the lost "whole": "a heart," "the soul," "the forehead," "a face," "a head." A further step toward this objectivist direction can be seen in Trakl's use of unindividuated, anonymous human protagonists (the "stranger," the "lonely one," the "beholder," the "wanderer"). Here it is no longer possible to verify with any degree of accuracy whether such protagonists are indeed projections of the poet's self.

Since the expressionist world of Trakl's poems is a world that does not obey the laws of reality, it is small wonder that one finds it populated with mythical figures such as fauns, nymphs, Tritons, Satyrs, and dryads. The appearance of demons and ghosts occasionally contributes to the dreamlike atmosphere which is so characteristic of many of Trakl's texts.

Not only is the world described by Trakl an imaginary and in many ways an unreal one, but also the beholding subject, whether intended to be identical with the poet or not, appears in Trakl's poems as one who has lost the ability to experience reality in a normal, conscious, and sober way. The beholder either is a dreamer or is described as under the influence of alcohol or drugs (an obvious autobiographical reference). Dreaming and intoxication derange the mind in its attempt to order the stimuli received from reality.

In Trakl's poetry, the derangement of the world as conventionally perceived allows the construction of a new visionary world. This "inner landscape" becomes a haven for the poet, who finds himself unable to cope with the harsh realities of modern industrialized society. Deforming and transmuting reality, however, need not be interpreted only as an escapist gesture. It is equally significant as a gesture of protest (an elegiac rather than a strident one) against the threatening aspects of modernity.

OTHER MAJOR WORKS
PLAYS: *Fata Morgana*, pr. 1906 (lost); *Totentag*, pr. 1906 (lost).
MISCELLANEOUS: *Gesammelte Werke*, 1949-1951 (3 volumes); *Dichtungen und Briefe*, 1969.

BIBLIOGRAPHY
Graziano, Frank, ed. *Georg Trakl: A Profile*. This biographical study of Trakl's work concentrates on the poet's family relations, drug addiction, poverty, and depression, as well as the influence of World War I.
Sharp, Francis Michael. *The Poet's Madness: A Reading of Georg Trakl*. Ithaca: Cornell University Press, 1981. Critical interpretation of selected poems by Trakl. Includes the text of poems in English and German.
Williams, Eric, ed. *The Dark Flutes of Fall: Critical Essays on Georg Trakl*. Columbia, S.C.: Camden House, 1991. A collection of essays on the works of Trakl. Includes bibliographical references and index.
_____. *The Mirror and the Word: Modernism, Literary Theory, and Georg Trakl*. Lincoln: University of Nebraska Press, 1993. A critical study of Trakl's works that focuses on his contributions to modernism in Austria. Includes bibliographical references and index.

Christoph Eykman;
bibliography updated by the editors

TOMAS TRANSTRÖMER

Born: Stockholm, Sweden; April 15, 1931

PRINCIPAL POETRY
17 Dikter, 1954
Hemligheter på vägen, 1958
Den halvfärdiga himlen, 1962 (*The Half-Finished Heaven*, 2001; Robert Bly, translator)

Klanger och spår, 1966

Kvartett, 1967

Mörkerseende, 1970 (*Night Vision*, 1971)

Twenty Poems of Tomas Tranströmer, 1970

Windows and Stones: Selected Poems, 1972 (May Swenson, translator)

Elegy: Some October Notes, 1973

Stigar, 1973 (original poems and translations of Robert Bly's and János Pilinszky's poetry)

Citoyens, 1974

Selected Poetry of Paavo Haavikko and Tomas Tranströmer, 1974

Östersjöar, 1974 (*Baltics*, 1975)

Friends, You Drank Some Darkness: Three Swedish Poets, 1975 (with Harry Martinson and Gunnar Ékelöf)

Sanningsbarriären, 1978 (*Truth Barriers: Poems by Tomas Tranströmer*, 1980)

Dikter, 1954-1978, 1979

How the Late Autumn Night Novel Begins, 1980

Det vilda torget, 1983 (*The Wild Marketplace*, 1985)

Tomas Tranströmer: Selected Poems, 1954-1986, 1987

The Blue House = Det blå huset, 1987

Collected Poems, 1987

För levende och döda, 1989

For the Living and the Dead: New Poems and a Memoir, 1995

Sorgegondolen, 1996 (*Sorrow Gondola*, 1997)

New Collected Poems, 1997

Samlade dikter, 1954-1996, 2001

Tomas Tranströmer (Swedish Information Service)

OTHER LITERARY FORMS

Tomas Tranströmer's reputation rests primarily on his poetry. *Minnena, ser mig* (1993; *Memories Look at Me: A Memoir*, in *For the Living and the Dead*, 1995), prepared for *Contemporary Authors: Autobiography Series*, offers the poet's own insights into his work. In 2001, a volume of correspondence between Tranströmer and Robert Bly was published as *Air Mail: Brev, 1964-1990*.

ACHIEVEMENTS

In part because he is essentially a poet of images—an aspect of poetry which can be conveyed virtually without loss from one language to another—Tomas Tranströmer is the most widely translated contemporary Scandinavian poet, and his work has been highly influential abroad as well as in his native Sweden. He has been honored with the Bellman Prize (1966), the International Poetry Forum's Swedish Award (1971), the Petrarch Prize (1981), and a lifetime subsidy from the Swedish government. In 1982, Tranströmer became a member of the Swedish Bible Commission to work on a translation of the Psalms. In 1983, he received the Bonnier Prize for Poetry; in 1988, the Pilot Prize; in 1990, the Nordic Council Prize as well as the prestigious Neustadt International Prize for Literature, seen as often a precursor to the Nobel Prize; in 1992, the Horst Bienek Prize; and in 1998, the Ján Smrek Prize.

BIOGRAPHY

Tomas Tranströmer was born on April 15, 1931, in Stockholm, Sweden. His grandfather and other, more distant ancestors were ship pilots, and his father was a journalist. When Tranströmer was a child, his parents were divorced; from that time onward, he had a very close relationship with his mother, whose death, many years later, affected him greatly. From 1960 to 1965, he served as a psychologist at Roxtuna, a prison for juvenile offenders; since 1967, he has lived in Västerås, where, until 1990, he worked with disabled persons. This position allowed him to devote more time to his wife and two daughters, to playing the piano, and especially to writing.

In his early sixties, Tranströmer published memoirs of his early and adolescent years. Here one learns of his formative and familial school experiences, his interests in entomology and natural history, the war, the extreme anxiety that pervaded his life for a brief period, and the influence that museums and libraries have exercised on him.

ANALYSIS

Tomas Tranströmer's development as a poet has been marked by an extraordinary clarity of purpose. His first slim volume, *17 Dikter* (seventeen poems), acknowledged in Sweden as the debut of a major talent, set the pattern for his career. By publishing a collection comprising a mere seventeen poems, none of which is long, Tranströmer made a contract with his readers, a contract that is still binding: He has continued to publish slim volumes in which each poem is invested with all the care and intensity he can bring to it. Few contemporary poets have demonstrated this unassuming but absolute confidence in themselves and in their medium. The sparsity of Tranströmer's output might suggest that he is a hermetic poet, a creator of perfect verbal artifacts. Nothing could be further from the truth. For Tranströmer, the poem is an instrument of vision and a means of communication:

> My poems are meeting-places. Their intent is to make a sudden connection between aspects of reality that conventional languages and outlooks ordinarily keep apart. Large and small details of the landscape meet, divided cultures and people flow together in a work of art, Nature meets Industry etc. What looks at first like a confrontation turns out to be a connection.

Tranströmer's own definition of his aims cannot be bettered. His poems are indeed "meeting-places" for different levels of reality, brought together in the striking images which are the hallmark of his art.

NATURE IMAGERY

A typical poem by Tranströmer is short, lyric, telegraphic, strongly imagistic, and autobiographical; his recurring themes include philosophical problems, music, dreams, awakenings, obstacles, frontiers, and especially nature. Yet, if his is a poetry informed by nature—by black-backed gulls and ants, forests and mountains, water and storms—the poet transcends his natural imagery in a flight of continual self-discovery. This is where he differs so radically from many of his Scandinavian predecessors: Tranströmer's descriptive imagery is often merely the key through which the speaker achieves understanding of his specific situation. In the poem "Agitated Meditation," Tranströmer depicts a storm's effects and a "grey shark's belly," which logically leads to the ocean floor; this is followed by an algae-encrusted crutch, but the poem concludes with metaphysical precision: "He who/ wanders to the sea returns petrified."

TRANSITIONALISM

Tranströmer frequently achieves such shifts in perspective by a method that might be termed "transitionalism." "Det öppna fönstret" ("The Open Window") begins with a matter-of-fact, first-person narrative: "I shaved one morning standing/ by the open window/ on the second story." This mundane, prosaic tone is sustained for several lines; the crucial transition occurs when the narrator's electric razor, which has begun to hum with a "heavier and heavier whirr," suddenly becomes a helicopter on which the narrator is a passenger. "Keep your eyes open!" the pilot shouts to him; "You're seeing this for the last time!" The speaker looks down on the things of the Earth, houses and beetles and all, asking: "The small things I love, what do they amount to?" As he looks, he feels an increasing sense of urgency, and the poem concludes with the manifest need to see everything:

> Fly low!
> I didn't know which way
> to turn my head—
> my sight was divided
> like a horse's.

"AN ARTIST IN THE NORTH"

This is Tranströmer's favored method: a description of a physical situation metamorphosed into aphoristic reflections on spiritual or psychological states—a method exemplified in one of his finest poems, "En konstnär i norr" ("An Artist in the North"). The poem is a monologue spoken by the composer Edvard Grieg while on retreat in a small mountain hut. In the first three stanzas, Grieg recalls his past activities, including his triumphs as a conductor; now his only companions are a piano, the mountains, and a "peculiar light [that] leaks in directly from the trolls." In this setting, Grieg admonishes himself to

> Simplify!
> And hammer blows in the mountain came
> came
> came
> came one spring night into our room
> disguised as heartbeats.

This is Tranströmer at his apex, echoing Grieg's music and concluding enigmatically,

> Battlegrounds within us
> Where we Bones of the Dead
> fight to come alive.

Struggle, influences, the act of composing at the piano—all these are contained in this final onslaught. There can be little doubt that the need to simplify and the internal struggle are equally applicable to the creation of Tranströmer's poetry.

BALTICS

Baltics represents an extreme departure from Tranströmer's usual concise lyric pieces. A lengthy, often prosaic poem in six parts, it deals with the poet, his ancestors, and their Baltic environment. Because Tranströmer has come to value literal truth more than mere literary criteria, he emphasizes actual events, with the result that the poem often sounds like untransformed historical narrative, complete with names, dates, and other facts. This content may alternate with various manifestations of nature, but, regardless of content, *Baltics* is a sparse poem: Ships or wind, forest, and sea are all limned simply, and imagistic language is infrequent. In fact, although these pieces have unequal line lengths, they read, for all practical purposes, like prose poems, and at times they are as constricted as journal entries. What is important is not form, rhythm, or heightened language, but rather what the reader actually learns: Tranströmer's grandfather was a ship's pilot, he kept an almanac, and the ship's engine room had a pungent aroma; there is a font in a Gotland church upon which the name of the twelfth century mason Hegwaldr is still inscribed.

When philosophical transitions do occur, as in the third part of *Baltics*, they are extremely esoteric, and it is difficult to connect the physical and the metaphysical realms. Occasionally, however, Tranströmer's true gift shines through, as when he draws a parallel between a jellyfish, which becomes formless when it is taken out of the water, and "an indescribable truth . . . lifted out of silence and formulated to an inert mass. . . ."

"MIDWINTER"

Tranströmer's later poems are similar to their ancestors: short, sometimes succinct, explorations of an obvious manifestation that leads to an unusual or striking revelation. "Midvinter" ("Midwinter," from *Sorrow Gondola*) is an excellent example of how Tranströmer continues to transform the mundane into something entirely unexpected:

> A blue sheen
> radiates from my clothes.
> Midwinter.
> Jangling tambourines of ice.
> I close my eyes.
> There is a soundless world
> there is a crack
> where dead people
> are smuggled across the border.

This is ambiguously deceptive: We do not know if the dead are leaving, which is depressing and malign, or if they are returning (metaphorically, spiritually), which is uplifting and psychologically beneficial. Tranströmer, like Stéphane Mallarmé (as one critic observes), wants to mystify his readers with conundrums. Whereas Mallarmé often remains inexplicable and annoying, however, Tranströmer's ambiguity is, paradoxically, comprehensible and palliating.

HAIKUS

Even more compact are a series of *haikudikter* (haikus) in four sections. Many poets have moved away from verbosity toward silence. Succinct, sparse, denuded poetic articulations reflect the mimalist aesthetic that view with the prolixity so typical of twentieth century fiction. Thus, Paul Celan, Robert Creeley, or Bob Arnold prefer to leave the interpretive work to the reader's imagination.

TRANSTRÖMER'S DEVELOPMENT

A precise development can be traced through many of Tranströmer's books. His *17 Dikter* consists primarily of brief lyrical pieces that depict local natural manifestations. Multiple and complex images, metaphors, and similes provide a strong poetic center. In his second and third volumes, *Hemligheter på vägen* (secrets on the road) and *The Half-Finished Heaven*, Tranströmer continues his lyric homage to nature but expands to an international perspective; here, one finds some narrative verse as well as pieces on music, dreams, and other themes. Telegraphic and imagistic, these are simple poems with complex messages. It is in *Klanger och spår* (resonance and tracks) and *Night Vision* that Tranströmer makes such excellent use of his transitional method. These two volumes contain fewer nature poems and concentrate more on personal revelations that presumably function as actual catharses. *Stigar*, which along with his own poems incudes Tranströmer's translations of Robert Bly and the Hungarian poet János Pilinszky, is an extension of his earlier concerns, including nature, creativity, and even subtle political themes, while *Baltics*, with its long lines, prosaic quality, and motifs drawn from the poet's family history, is something entirely new. *Truth Barriers* assimilates the lyric, the prose poem, and many of the poet's thematic interests that have remained fairly constant for thirty years—particularly the mystical, quasi-religious respect for truth and the cosmos that has always informed Tranströmer's verse. For half a century, Tranströmer has produced a steady stream of peoms that most critics applaud.

TRANSLATIONS

Tranströmer is interested in translation—of both his own work and that of a host of international poets. He views the original creation of a poem as a translation form what could be called the ur-poem written in an ur-language. "Thus even the original version is a translation," according to Tranströmer. His work has been translated into more than forty languages, including German, Dutch, Spanish, and Hungarian.

INFLUENCE

In Tranströmer's work, one finds a diversity of interests, forms, and methods. His poetry is often insightful, striking in its richness of image and metaphor, but it can also be plodding, prosaic, and uninteresting. In an age of excruciating prolixity, Tranströmer is distinguished by the concision of his verse, reminiscent of Salvatore Quasimodo's late lyrics. Only infrequently does this succinct quality result in obscurity, for Tranströmer's verse, though at times oblique, is never deliberately arcane. One of the finest poets of his generation, Tranströmer has continued to grow, his later work confirming the earlier assessments. Robert Bly observes that his "poetry of silence and depths" has influenced many American poets.

OTHER MAJOR WORKS

NONFICTION: *Minnena, ser mig*, 1993 (*Memories Look at Me: A Memoir*, in *For the Living and the Dead*, 1995); *Air Mail: Brev, 1964-1990*, 2001 (with Robert Bly).

TRANSLATION: *Tolkningar*, 1999 (of many poets including James Wright, Robert Bly, and Sandor Weores).

BIBLIOGRAPHY

Bankier, Joanna. "Breaking the Spell: Subversion in the Poetry of Tomas Tranströmer." *World Literature Today* 64, no. 4 (Autumn, 1990): 591. A disscussion of several of Tranströmer's poems that describe how socialization imposes a role and turns life into a set of ritualized performances that minimize stylized movement.

Bly, Robert. "Tomas Tranströmer and 'The Memory.'" *World Literature Today* 64, no. 4 (Autumn, 1990): 570-573. A useful biocritical overview.

Fulton, Robin. Introduction to *New Collected Poems*, by Tomas Tranströmer. Newcastle upon Tyne, England: Bloodaxe Books, 1997. An excellent if brief biographical and analytical overview.

Ivask, Ivar. "The Universality of Openness: The Understated Example of Tomas Tranströmer." *World Literature Today* 64, no. 4 (Autumn, 1990): 549. A profile of Tranströmer and the international recognition he has found through his poetry.

Kaplinski, Jaan. "Presentation to the Jury." *World Literature Today* 64, no. 4 (Autumn, 1990): 552. Kaplinski describes Tranströmer as one of the most outstanding poets of the present age and is a fitting recipient of the Neustadt International Prize for Literature. A listing of his works is offered.

Rossel, Sven H. Review of *Tolkningar* by Tomas Tranströmer. *World Literature Today* 74, no. 1 (Winter, 2000): 253. Rossel's review includes biographical information on Tranströmer's career and work.

Sjoberg, Leif. "The Architecture of a Poetic Victory: Tomas Tranströmer's Rise to International Preeminence." *Scandinavian Review* 78, no. 2 (Autumn, 1990): 87. Tranströmer has enjoyed sensational publicity and critical acclaim. Reasons for this unusual success are outlined. Two of Tranströmer's poems are included.

Soderberg, Lasse. "The Swedishness of Tomas Tranströmer." *World Literature Today* 64, no. 4 (Autumn, 1990): 573. The poetry of Tranströmer is examined, and ways in which his poetry can be described as being specifically Swedish are discussed.

Robert Hauptman, updated by Hauptman

MARINA TSVETAYEVA

Born: Moscow, Russia; October 9, 1892
Died: Yelabuga, Tatar Autonomous Soviet Republic, U.S.S.R.; August 31, 1941

PRINCIPAL POETRY

Vecherny albom, 1910
Volshebny fonar, 1912, 1979
Iz dvukh knig, 1913
Versty I, 1922
Stikhi k Bloku, 1922, 1978
Razluka, 1922
Psikheya, 1923
Remeslo, 1923
Posle Rossii, 1928 (*After Russia*, 1992)
Lebediny stan, 1957 (*The Demesne of the Swans*, 1980)

Selected Poems of Marina Tsvetayeva, 1971
Poem of the End: Selected Narrative and Lyrical Poetry, 1998

OTHER LITERARY FORMS

Marina Tsvetayeva wrote a number of plays, including *Konets Kazanovy* (pb. 1922; the end of Casanova), *Metel* (pb. 1923; the snowstorm), *Fortuna* (pb. 1923; fortune), *Priklyuchenie* (pb. 1923; an adventure), *Tezey* (pb. 1927; Theseus), and *Fedra* (pb. 1928; Phaedra). Several of these were later expanded or combined and reissued under different titles. Tsvetayeva's prose is extensive. Parts of her diaries and her many memoirs have appeared in journals and newspapers, mostly abroad. Some of these prose pieces, together with literary portraits, critical essays, and letters, were collected in *Proza* (1953). A prose collection in English, *A Captive Spirit: Selected Prose*, appeared in 1980. Tsvetayeva also translated poetry, prose, and drama into French, and from French into Russian. Some of her letters, notes, and individual poems remain unpublished and unlocated, but émigré publishers continue to search for material. A modest number of plays and prose pieces have been printed in Soviet journals.

ACHIEVEMENTS

Recognition came to Marina Tsvetayeva late in life, following decades of critical neglect, official Soviet ostracism, and émigré hostility. Her suicide during World War II, not known to the world for a long time, engendered critical fascination with the details of her life, eventually followed by publication, republication, and scholarly evaluation of her work. The creative variety and quality of Russian writing in the first quarter of the twentieth century created a situation in which many talented poets, among them Tsvetayeva, escaped public attention. Her adherence to the old orthography and to pre-Revolutionary values, cast into unconventional, awkward-seeming syntax, caused her work to appear disjointed. Only the subsequent careful study of her form and language has revealed the verbal and stylistic brilliance of a unique poetic voice. Political events forced Tsvetayeva to live in exile with artistically conservative Russians who did not understand her poetic experiments. She courageously developed her style,

Marina Tsvetayeva

despite exclusion from émigré publishing houses and Soviet rejection of new forms, proudly suffering the ensuing material deprivation. Many of her themes are so closely linked to events in her life that it is difficult to comprehend them without biographical information; the publication of several critical and biographical studies has made her verse more accessible. Translations into English are beginning to appear, and literary scholars now acknowledge her as a major Russian poet.

Biography

Marina Tsvetayeva's birth on October 9, 1892, into an educated, artistic family, augured well for her poetic future. Her mother, a talented amateur pianist, instilled in her an appreciation for the fine arts and insisted on rigorous musical training, while her father's respected position as a professor of art at Moscow University provided exposure to the creative community in Russia. Nicolas II himself, with his family, attended the opening of Professor Tsvetayeva's lifelong project, the Moscow Fine Arts Museum. This august event

impressed Tsvetayeva and is reflected in both her poetry and prose, possibly contributing to the unswerving loyalty she displayed toward the imperial family, even when the expression of such sympathies proved dangerous. At age six, Tsvetayeva performed at a public piano recital and tried her hand at versification. Her mother's illness in 1902 necessitated a four-year stay abroad, during which Tsvetayeva developed her interest in literature at Swiss and German boarding schools. After the death of her mother in 1906, she reluctantly entered the Moscow *gimnaziya*, where she treated her courses rather casually. No longer attracted to music, she drifted in and out of schools, devoting all her time to the writing of poetry. She barely managed to complete secondary education, lagging two years behind her graduating class. A collection of poems written in her teens, *Vecherny albom* (evening album), was privately published in 1910 in an edition of five hundred copies. Several critics generously noted artistic promise in the volume, and the poet-painter Max Voloshin introduced Tsvetayeva to Moscow's literary world.

Tsvetayeva's independent, sometimes provocative demeanor—she smoked, bobbed her hair, traveled alone abroad—coupled with a budding literary reputation, brought a measure of local fame. At Voloshin's Crimean house, which served as an artists' colony, she met and shortly thereafter, in 1912, married the eighteen-year-old Sergey Efron, member of a prominent Jewish publishing family. In the same year, she issued her second book of verse, *Volshebny fonar* (the magic lantern), dedicated to her new husband. Neither this collection nor her third, *Iz dvukh knig* (from two books), caused much of a critical stir, with public attention diverted by an abundance of other talented writers and the imminent war. When Tsvetayeva's daughter Ariadna was born in 1912, she immediately became a frequently mentioned star in her mother's verse. Tsvetayeva's writings during the next ten years, disseminated primarily through public readings and occasional journal printing, also failed to receive critical acclaim. These pieces saw publication only in 1922 under the title *Versty I* (milestones I).

The Bolshevik Revolution found the poet in Moscow, nursing her second daughter, Irina, while Efron fought with the White Army in the south. Tsvetayeva coped poorly with the hardships of the Civil War. Unwilling to waste time at nonliterary jobs, she lived on the edge of starvation, and Irina died of malnutrition in a government orphanage in 1920. These years, however, were poetically Tsvetayeva's most productive. Between 1917 and 1921, she completed work that was eventually assembled into "Versty II" (unpublished), *The Demesne of the Swans*, *Razluka* (separation), and *Remeslo* (craft), and she developed friendships with the foremost poets of the time, among them Aleksandr Blok, Vladimir Mayakovsky, Osip Mandelstam, and Boris Pasternak. By 1921, Efron had made his way to Prague, where Tsvetayeva joined him with their surviving daughter a year later. During the following years, much of her work was printed by émigré houses in Berlin, Paris, and Prague. In 1925, having expanded her range to epic poems and plays, and following the birth of her son Georgy, Tsvetayeva set up residence in Paris, where a large colony of anti-Communist Russians had gathered. While her contact with foreign writers remained limited, she corresponded regularly with Marcel Proust and Rainer Maria Rilke. The latter, deeply impressed by her talent, addressed a long elegy to her in 1926.

Tsvetayeva's poetic style developed in exile, heavily reflecting Futurist trends. Its experimental nature did not find favor with conservative émigré writers or the public, and her 1928 collection, *Posle Rossii* (after Russia), largely escaped notice. Reluctantly, Tsvetayeva turned to prose to support herself but never managed a comfortable existence. Her romantic involvements testify to a growing estrangement from Efron, who changed his political outlook in the 1930's and became a Soviet agent. This step had disastrous consequences for the poet. In 1937, her daughter, a confirmed Communist, returned to the U.S.S.R. Later that year, Efron was implicated in several political murders, but he escaped to the Soviet Union before he could be brought to trial. Tsvetayeva, now ostracized by fellow exiles and in desperate financial straits, decided to follow her family back to Russia in 1939. Before her departure, she wisely left her manuscripts in several safe places. This collection later facilitated a Tsvetayeva revival by Western researchers.

The poet returned home to a chilly reception. Tsvetayeva's émigré status and well-known pre-Revolutionary sympathies precluded publication of her work. Only one poem appeared in print after her return, and no record of subsequent work exists or has been made public. Instead, a series of tragic events—the aftermath of Stalin's purges—drove her to record thoughts of suicide in her diary. Within months of her arrival, Ariadna was sent to a labor camp, where Tsvetayeva's sister, Anastasia, also spent the last decade of Stalin's rule. Efron disappeared and was executed some time later. Fellow Russians, fearing political contamination, shunned Tsvetayeva. By 1941, wartime evacuation found her with her teenage son in the Tartar Autonomous Republic, east of Moscow. The village of Elabuga could offer the penniless poet only a job as kitchen maid. Proud and stubborn as always, she insisted on a more dignified occupation. When an appeal to establishment writers quartered nearby failed, she hanged herself. The villagers, unaware of her artistic credentials, buried her without ceremony in an unmarked grave. Her son Georgy joined the army and is presumed to have been killed in action. When the "Thaw" began after Stalin's death, Ariadna returned from prison and, with the aid of no-longer-silent poets, devoted herself to promoting her mother's literary heritage. In 1956, a Soviet edition of selected poems appeared, followed by public readings and further publication, always in moderate proportion, carefully chosen to avoid anti-Soviet allusions. In 1980, the Moscow Excursion Bureau instituted a tour of places associated with Marina Tsvetayeva, during which the guide recites generous excerpts of her poetry. This revival, accompanied by an intense interest in her remarkable life, has led to a Tsvetayeva cult in the Soviet Union and a lively black market in her work, finally giving her the recognition so long withheld.

ANALYSIS

Marina Tsvetayeva's poetry is notable for its stylistic innovations, peculiarity of language, political sympathies, and autobiographical intensity. She did not immediately achieve mastery of style. Her early work shows that she was searching for a voice of her own, re-creating the language of Moscow's high society in a rather stilted, overly elegant fashion, punctuated by allusions to childhood and romantic longings which do not always mesh with her aristocratic tone. By the time she composed the poems collected in *Versty I*, the ornate phrasing had developed into a simpler language, but one reflecting old, already archaic Russian usage, thus evoking the poetic diction of earlier centuries. At the same time, Tsvetayeva destroyed this historic illusion by incorporating deliberately incongruous colloquialisms and by placing sacred Church Slavonic phrases in coarse contexts. This stylistic violence is redeemed by the expressive, sometimes whimsical quality of her language, which became the trademark of her later work. She selects significant words, often creating new ones by building on familiar roots, which can evoke extended images or form connections to the next phrase without any grammatical links. One of her favorite devices is the verbless stanza: She achieves the necessary cohesion by clever juxtaposition of sharply delineated nouns, producing a brittle, succinct, almost formulaic precision of line. Her lexical and phonetic experiments, especially her neologisms, evoke the work of Mayakovsky and other Futurists, but she manages to maintain a voice peculiarly her own, which is partially the result of her skill in combining archaisms with colloquialisms to produce an incongruous but striking blend of tradition and novelty.

In much of her later work, she also shifts the stress within the poetic line, carefully selecting her vocabulary to accommodate such prosodic deformation. Depending on the desired effect, Tsvetayeva drops unstressed syllables, adds dashes to represent syllables, or adds syllables to words, occasionally generating such awkward sequences that she feels it necessary to give intonation or pronunciation information in footnotes. Intensely interested in language expansion, she delighted in pushing poetic devices beyond existing limits. When employing enjambment, she broke the very word in half, creating odd, internal rhymes. These metric innovations, combined with her highly unusual diction, were responsible in part for the relative neglect which Tsvetayeva's work suffered for some time.

Theoretically, Tsvetayeva favored lost causes and failures. The most prominent example is *The Demesne of the Swans*, a cycle of mourning for the defeated White Army. The same compassion appears in the 1930 cycle on Mayakovsky, following his suicide, and in the poems condemning the German invasion of Czechoslovakia. Her loyalty to and love for the past led her again and again to reinterpret motifs from classical literature, with a particular emphasis on Russia's old epics and folklore.

A knowledge of Tsvetayeva's life does not merely enhance an understanding of her work; it is vital to it. Her poetry is a kind of diary in verse, a chronological account of her experiences, often inaccessible without further elucidation. When preparing her work for safekeeping before returning to Russia, she recognized the hurdles facing the reader and provided explanatory footnotes for many pieces. Even so, her verse demands time and attention before it yields its richness, and she is generally considered to be a difficult poet. The phonetic and semantic interplay which characterizes much of her work poses formidable challenges to the translator. Her inability or unwillingness to exist harmoniously with her surroundings—she continually stressed her otherness—led to a crippling isolation long before political exigencies forced her to extremes. While this withdrawal from the general community nourished her talents, it also lost her publishers, readers, friends, and family. In a December 30, 1925, letter to A. Tesková, she confessed that she had no love for life as such, caring only for its transformation into art. When that was no longer possible, she chose to end her existence.

VECHERNY ALBOM

Tsvetayeva's first book of verse, *Vecherny albom*, already shows the talent and originality of the later perfectionist, although it is still dominated by the immature, conventionally romantic confessions of a young girl. The poems are grouped around two thematic centers: hero worship and childhood feelings. She admires those who achieve a measure of exaltation and personal glory despite handicaps and mundane origin, among them Napoleon, Sarah Bernhardt, and Huck Finn. A special series is devoted to the doomed nobles featured in Edmond Rostand's works. When Tsvetayeva treats her early family life, she is equally idealistic, expressing impatience with the ways of the world: "I thirst for miracles/ Now, this minute, this very morning." The nursery verses also contain a fairy-tale dimension, filled with endearing diminutives, storytelling, the figure of her mother, and her own fear of leaving this shelter for adulthood. The metrical line and strophe are still traditional, although occasionally enlivened by flashes of lexical innovation. The second collection, *Volshebny fonar*, dedicated to her bridegroom, does not differ significantly in theme and style. The desire to linger in the safe haven of childhood remains strong. She implores Efron to honor these sentiments: "Help me to remain/ A little girl, though your wife," so that the marriage will proceed "From one fairytale into another." Family, friends, and husband are celebrated in sad and joyful verses. While a few snatches of brisk dialogue point to her later telegraphic style, rhyme and meter are strictly conventional. Forty-one poems from these first two volumes were collected in *Iz dvukh knig*, concluding Tsvetayeva's idealistic, romantic period.

VERSTY I

Versty I (milestone I) represents the maturing of Tsvetayeva's poetry—hence the title. In this collection, she trims her lexical material to a minimum, focusing on sharply delineated images to produce an aphoristic style, and her rigid metrical design gives way to the more contemporary mixed meter, called *dolniki*, with which she had begun to experiment. The book serves as a poetic chronicle of the year 1916. Its unifying theme is the city of Moscow, to which she pays homage in every group of poems. She connects writers, friends, and family with various places in town, and employs diverse poetic personae (tavern queens and beggars) and a range of colorful, lower-class expressions. Among those poets singled out are Anna Akhmatova, Blok, and Mandelstam. In cycles dedicated to the first two, Tsvetayeva cleverly rephrases the artists' own poetic idiom and adapts their metrical peculiarities to her own compositions, giving the reader the strange impression of two simultaneous poetic voices. A brief infatuation with Mandelstam resulted in an exchange of dedications. Finally, there are personal poems, walks around the city with Ariadna, and the poet's first separation from her daughter. In one striking composition, she envisions her own grand funeral procession winding through the streets of Moscow, quite unlike the pauper's burial for which she was destined. The voice of alienation, of being out of place, so dominant in her later verse, already prevails in a number of poems in this volume.

THE DEMESNE OF THE SWANS

The Demesne of the Swans, Tsvetayeva's most controversial book, saw its first publication only in 1957, with a later edition in 1980 featuring English translations facing the original. The printings in the West evoked protest in the Soviet Union, where the work has never been published. Although Tsvetayeva's expressionistic technique and verbal brilliance are particularly evident in these cycles, the provocative theme of a noble, courageous White Army overrun by vile Bolshevik hordes dominates the book. Tsvetayeva's outrage at the destruction of venerated tradition by reincarnated Tartar hordes screams from almost every page. In chronicling the downfall of Czarism, starting with Nicolas II's abdication and ending with the Communist victory in 1920, the poet reaches into Russia's epic past for motifs. She compares the White Army to the doomed troops of Prince Igor's campaign, whose defeat at the hands of looting Asiatics foreshadowed Russia's long suffering under the Tartar yoke. Conversely, the Red Army is depicted as an unseemly mob, stampeding all that is sacred and precious into the dust. Tsvetayeva's anguish concerning the unknown fate of Efron is evident but is overshadowed by the national tragedy, which she describes in dramatic effusion: "White Guard, your path is destined to be high/ . . . Godlike and white is your task/ And white is your body that must lie in the sands." Even the more personal poems in the volume are saturated with her hatred of the new regime. The intensity attending Tsvetayeva's treatment of the Civil War is in marked contrast to the poet's customary nonpolitical, disinterested stance and continues to affect her standing in the Soviet Union.

The remainder of Tsvetayeva's lyric output continues the driving rhythm, the aphoristically compressed line, and the discordant sound patterns introduced in *Versty I*. Rejection of the environment and notes of despair appear ever more frequently in her verse. Following the Revolution, she also produced epic narratives, adding new dimensions to her style but still basing the narrative on private experience or reaching into Russian history to re-create its heroic legacy.

Tsvetayeva's verse is part of the general poetic flowering and experimentation of the early twentieth century. Her approaches reflect the innovations of Russian Futurists, but she manages to preserve a voice of her own. Despite isolation and hardship in exile, she continued to explore new means of poetic expression, maintaining an artistic link with developments in the Soviet Union. When her extensive output was finally collected and published, she began to emerge as a major Russian poet.

OTHER MAJOR WORKS

PLAYS: *Konets Kazanovy*, pb. 1922; *Fortuna*, pb. 1923; *Metel*, pb. 1923; *Priklyuchenie*, pb. 1923; *Tezey*, pb. 1927 (also known as *Ariadna*); *Fedra*, pb. 1928.

NONFICTION: *Proza*, 1953; *Izbrannaia Proza v Dvukh Tomakh: 1917-1937*, 1979; *A Captive Spirit: Selected Prose*, 1980; *Art in the Light of Conscience: Eight Essays on Poetry*, 1992.

MISCELLANEOUS: *Izbrannye proizvedeniya*, 1965 (selected works).

BIBLIOGRAPHY

Brodsky, Joseph. "A Poet and Prose." *Less Than One: Selected Essays*. New York: Farrar, Straus and Giroux, 1986. Brodsky, a Russian-born émigré who won the Nobel Prize for literature in 1987, discusses Tsvetayeva's prose as an extension of her poetry, employing poetic devices, such as assonance and enjambment, and following an organic rather than linear structure. Although Brodsky assumes the reader is familiar with literary terms, his writing is highly accessible.

Cixous, Helene. *Readings: The Poetics of Blanchot, Joyce, Kafka, Kleist, Lispector, and Tsvetayeva*. Translated by Verena Andermatt Conley. Minneapolis: University of Minnesota Press, 1991. A comparative analysis of a variety of innovative writers by a noted French feminist thinker, geared toward a scholarly audience. Focusing on the correspondence preserved in *Nine Letters*, Cixous places Tsvetayeva in the context of poet-as-pariah.

Feiler, Lilly. *Marina Tsvetayeva: The Double Beat of Heaven and Hell*. Chapel Hill: Duke University Press, 1994. This psychological biography draws on both classical and postmodernist psychoanalytic theory—Sigmund Freud's notion of pre-Oedipal narcissism and Julia Kristeva's concept of depression as "the hidden face of Narcissus"—to explain the contradictory impulses evident throughout Tsvetayeva's work.

Makin, Michael. *Marina Tsvetaeva: Poetics of Appropriation*. Oxford: Clarendon Press, 1993. Eschewing biographical interpretation, Makin stresses Tsvetayeva's reliance on literary antecedents. Her finest poetry, he claims, rewrites myth and folktale, producing "source-based" poetry that transcends its origins. The text is well documented, contains a comprehensive source list, and provides original translations of the poetry discussed.

Schweitzer, Viktoria. *Tsvetaeva*. Translated by Robert Chandler and H. T. Willetts. Farrar, Straus and Giroux: New York, 1992. This biography portrays Tsvetayeva as alienated from the world since early childhood by her poetic sensibilities. The author argues that a compulsive "need to be needed" kept Tsvetaeva grounded in events of the real world. Illustrated with bibliography, chronology, index, and biographical notes.

Margot K. Frank;
bibliography updated by K Edgington

FREDERICK GODDARD TUCKERMAN

Born: Boston, Massachusetts; February 4, 1821
Died: Greenfield, Massachusetts; May 9, 1873

PRINCIPAL POETRY

Poems, 1860, 1863
The Sonnets of Frederick Goddard Tuckerman, 1931 (Witter Bynner, editor)
The Complete Poems of Frederick Goddard Tuckerman, 1965 (N. Scott Momaday, editor)

OTHER LITERARY FORMS

Although Frederick Goddard Tuckerman, like Henry David Thoreau, was an accomplished naturalist who kept a journal, and although during his lifetime he published observations of astronomical and meteorological phenomena, he is recognized primarily for his poetry.

ACHIEVEMENTS

Following almost complete obscurity during the late 1800's, Frederick Goddard Tuckerman has received considerable acclaim from modern critics and writers. In 1931 Witter Bynner ranked his sonnets "with the noblest in the language." Yvor Winters, in 1965, placed him with Emily Dickinson and Jones Very as "the three most remarkable American poets of the nineteenth century." Galway Kinnell, at a 1981 reading in Kansas City, Missouri, called Tuckerman the equal of Walt Whitman, Stephen Crane, and Dickinson. These judgments have, to some extent, been validated by the inclusion of Tuckerman's verse in recent anthologies. Although Tuckerman published only one book of poems, in 1860, his current critical recognition—particularly for his sonnets—is high. Not only is he praised for the quality of his verse, but he is also seen as an important figure opposing the mainstream of nineteenth century American Romanticism.

BIOGRAPHY

Frederick Goddard Tuckerman was born on February 4, 1821, in Boston, the youngest son of Edward and Sophia (May) Tuckerman. The poet's father was a partner in the Boston firm of Tuckerman, Rogers and Cushing, Wholesalers and Importers; he died in 1842, leaving an ample inheritance. Frederick—named for F. W. Goddard (a kinsman whose accidental death in 1820 while crossing the Lake of Zurich was the subject of an elegy by his traveling companion, William Wordsworth)—prepared for college at the private school of Bishop John Henry Hopkins and at the Boston Latin School. He entered Harvard with the class of 1841, but eye trouble forced him to leave college for a time. Later, he entered the law school, was graduated in 1842, and, after reading law in the office of Edward D. Schier, was admitted to the Suffolk bar in 1844. In 1847, he moved from Boston to Greenfield, in western Massachusetts. On June 17, 1847, he married Hannah Lucinda Jones, daughter of David S. Jones of Greenfield. They had three children: Edward, Anna, and Frederick. At Greenfield, Tuckerman abandoned the practice of law and lived a life of relative seclusion and retirement. He studied botany and astronomy, and he wrote poetry. Twice he traveled abroad. On the first of these excursions, in

1851, he met Alfred, Lord Tennyson. During the second visit, in 1855, he was Tennyson's guest at Farringford, the Isle of Wight. The friendship between the two men appears to have been cordial. Tuckerman wrote to his brother Edward, "At parting Mr. Tennyson gave me the original ms. of 'Locksley Hall,' a favour of which I may be justly proud, as he says he has never done such a thing in his life before, for anybody."

Several of Tuckerman's poems first appeared in *The Living Age, Putnam's*, and *The Atlantic Monthly*. In 1854, he had prepared a manuscript version of a book of poems. It is possible that he carried this manuscript with him when he visited Tennyson in 1855. In 1857, within a week after the birth of their third child, Hannah Tuckerman died. His wife's death caused Tuckerman to become even more withdrawn from the public. It was not until 1860 that the poems in the 1854 manuscript were printed, privately, by Ticknor and Fields of Boston. The volume was reprinted twice in America, in 1864 and 1869; there was also an English edition in 1863. Tuckerman sent complimentary copies of the 1860 *Poems* to an impressive list of his contemporaries: In addition to William Gladstone, the list included Ralph Waldo Emerson, Nathaniel Hawthorne, Henry Wadsworth Longfellow, William Cullen Bryant, and Jones Very (who had been his tutor, briefly, at Harvard). Thereafter, although he continued to write (his last sonnet sequence was written in 1872), he apparently made no further effort to gain public recognition. Tuckerman died Friday, May 9, 1873, at his boarding place, the American House, in Greenfield, Massachusetts.

ANALYSIS

Frederick Goddard Tuckerman's career as a poet illustrates a typical pattern in American letters: Honored by some recognition during his lifetime, he received virtually no critical attention until 1931, when his poetry was rediscovered, reexamined, and placed back on the reading lists of American scholars. This critical revival—like that of the Metaphysical school of poetry or that of the poetry of Robert Browning—has been sustained primarily in the academic world. With this pattern in mind, it is difficult to arrive at an objective evaluation of Tuckerman's work. Contemporaries such as Ralph Waldo Emerson, Nathaniel Hawthorne, and Henry

Wadsworth Longfellow gave his poetry careful praise. Emerson was most enthusiastic, commenting favorably on Tuckerman's "love of native flowers, the skill to name them and delight in words that are melodies. . . ." Hawthorne judged the 1860 volume of poems to be "A remarkable one," but he cautioned:

> I question whether the poems will obtain a very early or wide acceptance from the public . . . because their merit does not lie upon the surface, but must be looked for with faith and sympathy, and a kind of insight as when you look into a carbuncle to discover its hidden fire.

Longfellow assured Tuckerman that he had a "very favorable" opinion of the poems, but, like Hawthorne, he warned that "external success with the world" might be something quite different from "internal success."

"RHOTRUDA"

Tuckerman's "Rhotruda," which Emerson singled out for praise, is a good example of the kind of narrative poetry that won Tuckerman the cautious approval of his contemporaries. The poem, set in the time of Charlemagne, is about two lovers, Rhotruda and Eginardus. Visiting Rhotruda after curfew one night, Eginardus is trapped by a snowstorm; he cannot return to his room across the courtyard because the snow would reveal his footsteps. Rhotruda carries him on her shoulders so that only her footsteps mark the snow. Charlemagne, however, has seen the act. The next morning, he confronts the lovers with the truth. Instead of sentencing Eginardus to death, however, he orders the two lovers to marry. The final image of the poem is vividly expressed:

> . . . Like a picture framed in battle-pikes
> And bristling swords, it hangs before our view—
> The palace court white with the fallen snow,
> The good king leaning out into the night,
> And Rhotruda bearing Eginard on her back.

It is Tuckerman's unconventional sonnets, however, rather than his more traditional Tennysonian narratives, that have won for him his current recognition. Witter Bynner, in his appreciative introduction to the sonnets, sounded the keynote in Tuckerman's revival by recognizing in his work a style "as modern as any twentieth century sonneteer." He defended Tuckerman's liberties with metrics and rhyme schemes, asserting: "He was as ten-

derly conscious of his form as was ever any maker of the sonnet. Instead of bungling or staling the sonnet-form, he renewed it and, moulding it to his emotion, made it inevitable." Bynner also praised the intellectual honesty that Tuckerman brought to his work: "Never did a man write poetry more straightly to himself—with nothing fictitious. He is isolated in an intense integrity toward nature, toward his own mind, and toward the unknown God."

SONNET X

Sonnet X, in the fourth series of sonnets (from *The Complete Poems of Frederick Goddard Tuckerman*), dated 1860-1872, illustrates the qualities of Tuckerman's poetry that Bynner most admired. The first eight lines are marked by uneven metrics; one line has thirteen syllables. The rhyme scheme begins as a traditional Italian sonnet but skews itself into a curiously distorted figure: *abba, cdeedc, fggf*. In substance, the sonnet seems to follow the traditional Italian form: question, followed by answer. The question, however, is multiple: The listener is asked whether he has seen "reversed the prophet's miracle" (the worm that takes on the appearance of a twig), or whether he has wondered at the "craft that makes/ The twirling spider at once invisible," or "heard the singing sand," or "ever plucked the little chick-wintergreen star/ And tasted the sour of its leaf?" The answer is both mysterious and promising:

> . . . Then come
> With me betimes, and I will show thee more
> Than these, of nature's secrecies the least:
> In the first morning, overcast and chill,
> And in the day's young sunshine, seeking still
> For earliest flowers and gathering to the east.

VIEW OF NATURE: "REFRIGERIUM"

N. Scott Momaday, in his introduction to *The Complete Poems of Frederick Goddard Tuckerman*, continued in the direction initiated by Bynner. Momaday called Tuckerman's view of nature "noticeably different than that which predominates in the literature of his time and place," noting: "Where Emerson found realized in nature the transcendent spirit of the universe, Tuckerman saw only a various and inscrutable mask." Momaday characterized Tuckerman as a poet who kept "the stage properties of contemporary Romantic literature" but defined the Romantic sense of isolation "in terms of intellectual honesty rather than self-reliance"; who celebrated "fact" rather than "sentiment"; who trained his attention "upon the surfaces rather than the symbols of his world." "Tuckerman," Momaday wrote, "was a man who made herbariums. . . . His poems are remarkable, point-blank descriptions of nature; they are filled with small, precise, and whole things: purring bees and vervain spikes, shives and amaryllis, wind flowers and stramony."

Even in the sentimental "Refrigerium," this gift for description is evident. The poem, in three stanzas of seven lines each, is a lament for a lost love, "lying/ In a slumber sweet and cold." The specific details—the natural objects and furnishings of earth's vast "refrigerium"—are, however, presented with a naturalist's objectivity and accuracy: "Let the slow rain come and bring/ Brake and stargrass, speedwell, harebell,/ All the fulness of the spring. . . ." In many ways, the specificity of details contributes to the sentiment. The speaker notes, for example, how graves have run together in "the blending earth," the stones even being linked together by spiderwebs.

"THE CRICKET"

Winters, in the foreword to *The Complete Poems of Frederick Goddard Tuckerman*, sees in Tuckerman a modern sensibility that rivals that of the French Symbolists with its structure of "controlled association." "The Cricket," not published until 1950, illustrates what Winters most admires about Tuckerman's verse: imagery, combined with abstract statement sufficient to support a theme "of some intellectual scope." The poem, in five sections, is an ode (in the tradition of the "great odes" of John Dryden, Thomas Gray, John Keats, and William Wordsworth). In the first section, the poet invokes as his muse "a little cooing cricket." In section two, the speaker describes, with concrete, vivid detail, the sleepy afternoon; by the end of the day, the cricket muse has multiplied: "From tingling tassle, blade, and sheath,/ Rising from nets of river vines,/ Winrows and ricks . . ./ Rising and falling like the sea,/ Acres of cricks!" In section three, the significance of the poet's choice of muse is made clear: The cricket is both celebrant of sunshine and "bringer of all things dark." In section four, the speaker recalls the classical role of the cricket as a singer of grief. In section five, the speaker brings together the

themes of the preceding sections: praise, change, life, death. The poem concludes with a stoical celebration of the limited possibilities that life offers: "Rejoice! rejoice! whilst yet the hours exist—/ Rejoice or mourn, and let the world swing on/ Unmoved by cricket song of thee or me."

CRITICAL RECEPTION

Tuckerman's present reputation seems to be based on two characteristics: the close observation of nature—of facts rather than symbols—that placed him in opposition to his contemporaries; and a concern with the metaphysical enigma of life that gives his poetry a peculiarly modern tension and pessimism. Some critics have seen this latter quality as "a kind of chronic melancholy which for the most part appears to be indulgence." Others, however—particularly Momaday—value Tuckerman's poetry for both its artistic and its intellectual opposition to the mainstream of American Romanticism.

BIBLIOGRAPHY

Donoghue, Denis. *Connoisseurs of Chaos: Ideas of Order in Modern American Poetry.* 2d ed. New York: Columbia University Press, 1984. This wide-ranging study devotes a valuable chapter to recurrent oppositional themes in Tuckerman's poetry: public and private, human and natural, physical and metaphysical, and truth and ambiguity. Also offers brief but insightful comparisons of Tuckerman to other modern poets such as Emily Dickinson, T. S. Eliot, William Empson, Wallace Stevens, and Walt Whitman.

England, Eugene. *Beyond Romanticism: Tuckerman's Life and Poetry.* Albany: State University of New York Press, 1991. A combined biography and critical study, and the best source for information about Tuckerman. Written by the foremost expert on the poet, the book examines how Tuckerman was molded by, and yet reacted against, Romanticism. Includes extensive readings of individual poems, an index, and an exhaustive bibliography.

_____. "Tuckerman and Tennyson: 'Two Friends . . . on Either Side the Atlantic.'" *New England Quarterly* 57 (June, 1984): 225-239. This important essay explores how Tuckerman's poetry was strongly influenced by his friendship with Alfred, Lord Tennyson. The first half examines letters between the two men, while the second half demonstrates how, through his close study of the English poet, Tuckerman moved beyond him as a model and established his own unique poetic identity.

Golden, Samuel. *Frederick Goddard Tuckerman*. New York: Twayne, 1966. This widely available book provides basic information about Tuckerman's life and several insightful readings of his poems. Some of Golden's biographical reconstructions, however, are based too fully on Tuckerman's sonnets and not fully enough on other kinds of historical materials. For a more accurate biography, students should consult Eugene England's *Beyond Romanticism: Tuckerman's Life and Poetry*.

Hudgins, Andrew. "'A Monument of Labor Lost': The Sonnets of Frederick Goddard Tuckerman." *Chicago Review* 37, no. 1 (Winter, 1990): 64-79. A critical study of Tuckerman's sonnets.

Momaday, N. Scott. "The Heretical Cricket." *The Southern Review* 3 (January, 1967): 43-50. This brief, well-written study focuses on "The Cricket," considered by many critics to be Tuckerman's most important poem. Arguing that this ode is essentially anti-Romantic, Momaday compares "The Cricket" to William Cullen Bryant's "Thanatopsis" and finds the former more modernistic because it accepts death intellectually without sublimating it as a longed-for communion with nature.

Seed, David. "Alone with God and Nature: The Poetry of Jones Very and Frederick Goddard Tuckerman." In *Nineteenth Century American Poetry*, edited by A. Robert Lee. Totowa, N.J.: Barnes and Noble, 1985. A comparative study of the poetry of Tuckerman and Jones Very.

Winters, Yvor. Foreword to *The Complete Poems of Frederick Goddard Tuckerman*. New York: Oxford University Press, 1965. Although it is overly polemical, this short essay argues intriguingly that Tuckerman should not be placed uncritically in the New England poetic tradition, but rather that he fits more understandably in the tradition of French Symbolism and is especially close to the sensibilities of the French poet Paul Verlaine.

Robert C. Jones;
bibliography updated by the editors

CHASE TWICHELL

Born: New Haven, Connecticut; August 20, 1950

PRINCIPAL POETRY
Northern Spy: Poems, 1981
The Odds, 1986
Perdido, 1991
The Ghost of Eden, 1995
The Snow Watcher, 1998

OTHER LITERARY FORMS

Along with Robin Behn, Twichell is editor of *The Practice of Poetry: Writing Exercises from Poets Who Teach* (1992), a popular collection of poets' exercises collected from a wide variety of practicing poets who also teach creative writing.

ACHIEVEMENTS

Twichell received fellowships from the National Endowment for the Arts in 1987 and 1993, and from the Artists Foundation in Boston, the New Jersey State Council on the Arts, and the John Simon Guggenheim Memorial Foundation in 1990. In 1994, she won the Literature Award of the American Academy of Arts and Letters.

BIOGRAPHY

Chase Twichell grew up in the midst of the stresses of her parents' disintegrating marriage. Her father taught Latin at a prestigious boys' school; her mother raised Twichell and her two sisters while working in a bookstore. The family spent the summers in the Adirondacks, providing Twichell with a sense of connection to the wilderness that has been important to her life both personally and as a writer.

After elementary school in New Haven, Twichell attended an extremely strict boarding school in Maryland. She suffered from attention deficit disorder and consequently did poorly in school, but she managed to discover her calling to poetry while she was there.

She received a bachelor of arts degree from Trinity College, Hartford, Connecticut, in 1973 after studying at a number of other schools, including Wesleyan, where she studied with poet Richard Wilbur and began to publish her own poems and investigate Buddhism. After graduation from Trinity, she attended the Writers' Workshop at the University of Iowa, receiving her master of fine arts degree from that institution in 1976. Also while she was at Iowa, Twichell studied graphic design and printing, thus gaining the skills that enabled her to fulfill a childhood ambition to work in printing. After graduation from Iowa, she worked for Pennyroyal Press in Massachusetts, perfecting her ability in the printer's craft. Her first two books of poems were published during these years.

In 1985 she joined the faculty of the master of fine arts program at the University of Alabama, where she taught for three years, spending her summers in the Adirondacks. It was at Alabama that she met novelist Russell Banks, whom she married in 1989.

Twichell and Banks lived for a time in Princeton, New Jersey, where they taught during the academic year, continuing to summer in the Adirondacks. During this time she published *The Practice of Poetry* and *The Ghost of Eden*, the latter a collection of poems recording her commitment to the importance and preservation of wilderness. She has voiced the fact that this commitment informs her main critical judgments in a 1993 essay for *Ploughshares*, where she indicated that she had come to believe that all good poetry was of necessity political and that poetry that makes no reference to the larger world outside the poet is merely self-absorbed. Similarly, she rejected decoration in poetry, calling it "prettification" and thus gratuitous.

In 1998, Twichell and Banks left Princeton to live in the Adirondacks full time. There Twichell began to teach in Goddard College's master of fine arts program, continued to study Zen Buddhism, and founded the Ausable Press.

ANALYSIS

Twichell's announcement of her poetics in *Ploughshares* is her effort to reconcile her belief that the relationship between human beings and nature has undergone a deep and fatal change in the last decades, a change that heralds the death of nature in any traditional sense, along with her desire to express that belief in poetry. Clearly, if such poetry is to have impact, it must

address the crisis directly, and so in *The Ghost of Eden* the poems repeat her concern directly and often: human beings are killing the planet. Typically, the message is tied to a narrative that exemplifies the issue in Twichell's own clear, direct language, her short lines and brief stanzas.

THE GHOST OF EDEN

In *The Ghost of Eden*, the pictures of the animal world are sharp and vivid; often they are pictures of animals suffering because of the actions of human beings. "Animal Graves" provides a good example. It begins when the speaker has hit a baby garter snake with the lawn mower. The snake is badly wounded but still alive, so she must hit it again and again with the mower. As she does, she recalls the graves she made for animals when she was a child. She buried house pets and wild animals alike and marked the animal graveyard with the skull of a deer she found in the forest.

Now the dying snake coils itself upward to hiss at the mower, an instinctive gesture, which Twichell calls "dancing in the roar/ and shadow of its death." She

Chase Twitchell (© Miriam Berkley)

imagines its grave in the same childhood pet cemetery where the deer skull was finally carried off by neighborhood dogs "to bury/ in the larger graveyard of the world." In that world everything will finally be buried; nevertheless, she implies, fortunate creatures will meet a worthier death than the little snake sacrificed to a tidy lawn.

In "The Devil I Don't Know" the vegetarian speaker pushes her cart through the grocery store, looking with revulsion at the contents of the meat case, where the packages "look like body parts to me/ since I stopped eating them." The slaughtered animals, the animals stuffed with steroids, the package of chops that looks "like a litter of stillborn puppies"—all this evidence of human beings' unnatural treatment of animals make the speaker desire to make an elegy, a prayer in their honor. She cannot do so, however, because the death of these creatures seems to her like the death of God; what has died is "the holy thing itself." She must turn away from the devil she knows, the devil that eats these animals. Popular wisdom says this devil is safer than the one that is unknown, but Twichell disagrees. She longs for a new object of worship, a devil she does not know, but she fears that with the death of nature all worship is dead, too. The poem ends with the image of a swordfish, "gutted, garnished, laid out on ice."

Much of the imagery of "The Aisle of Dogs" recalls that of "The Devil I Don't Know." In this poem the speaker has gone to an animal shelter for kittens; as she walks the aisles, she sees dozens of dogs that have been brutalized by human beings. The worst is a pit bull that still lives, although someone has skinned it. It is being kept alive as evidence for the courts; when the case is finished the dog will be put down. Twichell's sympathies often lie with predatory animals, as here, where she seems drawn to the pit bull and "its incurable hatred/ of my species."

Some critics have considered Twichell's tone of *The Ghost of Eden* to be unnecessarily shrill in poems like "The Aisle of Dogs" or "The Devil I Don't Know." "The Smell of Snow" demonstrates Twichell's strongest voice in addressing her themes of the holiness of nature without relying on human brutality as a backdrop.

The poem begins with a night hike through an early winter forest, a dangerous time because the hunting season is open. The speaker and her companion hike without flashlights, since "only in the dark does the spectral magic/ survive"; she names the fox, raccoon, bear, and deer they see.

Suddenly a fisher, a larger cousin of mink and ermine, appears before her, powerful and utterly wild. It smells like snow, a smell that, as a child, she associated with the smell of God because it seemed so foreign to all human smells, just as the eyes of the fisher seem to see only wilderness. As she gazes after it, she feels "a sudden carnal ache," a longing to be the fisher's victim, "the one he would tear open/ drag off in pieces to devour." Devoured by the fisher, and it in turn devoured by coyotes or other animals, she would live united with the god of the planet, "become/ the words the wind says/ to the birch tatters"; she would survive as "spirit free of any human/ vision of the afterlife," the innocent devoured by the innocent.

THE SNOW WATCHER

In *The Snow Watcher*, the reader can see how Twichell has grown in new directions without compromising the old ones. These poems often appear like those of the earlier volume, but these join Twichell's concern for the planet with her interest in Zen Buddhism and its practice—a practice that urges the practitioner to view herself as one being in the multitude of the beings in the universe. The result is that these poems that are shorter, sparer, more oblique and often less didactic than those of the earlier volume.

Many are based on the Japanese form called the *tanka*, a five-line poem of five, seven, five, seven, and five syllables. The first three lines are supposed to make a complete statement on which the last two lines comment. Two poems about horses seem to exemplify this form. In "Wild Mare," the mare staring at the speaker seems to suggest the implacable otherness of nature. "Horse" proposes something similar—that horse and rider might be like soul and body. The human being is the rider, Twichell says "but everyone looks at the horse."

Twichell's spiritual growth in Buddhism is the central subject of these poems, which make up a sort of journal of her experience in the exercise. Some describe her childhood, a source for her desire to experience the emptying of self that Buddhism offers. A number of the poems describe the seated meditation called *zazen*; in it the practitioner learns to still the mind's running voice. Other poems are designated *Dokusan*, the term for the student's private interview with a teacher; during it the student is to demonstrate his or her spiritual growth. These "Imaginary Dokusan" allow the reader into the interview while they pretend to address the teacher. Almost all of the poems draw on nature, a intimate part of Zen poet's view of the world.

The poems depicting the poet's childhood portray the effects of the parents' discord on the child. In "The Black Triangle," for example, the parents' quarrel at dinner sends the child's mind far away: "It stands behind itself and looks out," somewhat in the way meditation trains the mind to detach from the physical world. In "The Wars," Twichell pictures a child who waits for the voices of the adults to grow dull so that she can slip unnoticed in to dinner. This training in detachment seems good preparation for the discipline of Buddhism, but still more is demanded of the student.

In "Zazen, Wired & Tired," Twichell talks of her impatience with the exercise: "Sitting zazen is like trying to be a tree," but gradually she progresses. In "A Last Look Back," she notes how change can occur behind one's back or while one is not looking. She thinks of the snow-filled forest and of a deer's tracks there, empty in the snow. "Each change in me" she says, "is a stone step/ beneath the blur of snow." The step's edges will appear in the spring, when she will look back to see her "former selves,/ numerous as the trees."

Students of Zen Buddhism often note its playful quality; that quality seems to have freed Twichell to use quiet humor in this volume. In "Imaginary Dokusan: Rat," Twichell calls herself "Ms. Zen, taking secret notes for a poem,/ about to slouch back into all her bad habits." In "Walking Meditation," she begins by calling herself "the first tall animal/ to walk the trail today. Apologies to the spiders."

The end of Buddhist meditation—the release of the student from the demands of all desire—is necessarily at odds with the poet's urge to share the right words with a reader. The result is a paradox, which Twichell notes several times near the end of this volume, most directly in "To the Reader: If You Asked Me." Here she laments that having the reader with her ends her privacy, filling her silent rooms with talk even though she wants that reader's visit. At the same time she knows that language is not all; her discipline has taken her far beyond it. She concludes that her role in this volume has been that of a broom sweeping an empty factory, feeling neither hostility nor nostalgia—just doing the job that must be done.

OTHER MAJOR WORK

EDITED TEXT: *The Practice of Poetry: Writing Exercises from Poets Who Teach*, 1992 (with Robin Behn).

BIBLIOGRAPHY
Burt, Stephen. Review of *The Ghost of Eden. The Times Literary Supplement* (July 7, 1995): 14. Praises the stark meditations of the book, though noting the shrillness of some poems. Compares the best favorably with Louise Glück.

Daniel, David. "About Chase Twichell." *Ploughshares* 19 (Winter, 1993/1994): 214-217. Daniel includes some biographical material and describes Twichell's poetics at that stage of her career, emphasizing her commitment to the importance of preserving nature.

Hirshfield, Jane. "Editors' Shelf." *Ploughshares* 25 (Spring, 1999): 195. As part of a series of brief reviews, poet Hirshfield recommends *The Snow Watcher* for its use of Zen practice blended with American language.

Olsen, William. "Lyric Detachment: Two New Books of Poetry." *Chicago Review* 38 (Summer, 1991): 76-89. Olsen reviews *Perdido* (along with a volume by Jorie Graham) in detail, praising Twichell's concrete imagery, which creates a sort of journey into a psychic underworld.

Ann D. Garbett

TRISTAN TZARA

Sami Rosenstock
Born: Moinesti, Romania; April 4, 1896
Died: Paris, France; December 24, 1963

PRINCIPAL POETRY

La Première Aventure céleste de Monsieur Anti-pyrine, 1916

Vingt-cinq Poèmes, 1918

Cinéma calendrier du coeur abstrait, 1920

De nos oiseaux, 1923

Indicateur des chemins de coeur, 1928

L'Arbre des voyageurs, 1930

L'Homme approximatif, 1931 (*Approximate Man and Other Writings*, 1973)

Où boivent les loups, 1932

L'Antitête, 1933

Primele Poème, 1934 (English translation, 1976)

Grains et issues, 1935

La Deuxième Aventure céleste de Monsieur Anti-pyrine, 1938

Midis gagnés, 1939

Une Route seul soleil, 1944

Entre-temps, 1946

Le Signe de vie, 1946

Terre sur terre, 1946

Morceaux choisis, 1947

Sans coup férir, 1949

De mémoire d'homme, 1950

Parler seul, 1950

Le Poids du monde, 1951

La Face intérieure, 1953

À haute flamme, 1955

Miennes, 1955

Le Temps naissant, 1955

Le Fruit permis, 1956

Frère bois, 1957

La Rose et le chien, 1958

De la coupe aux lèvres, 1961

Juste présent, 1961

Selected Poems, 1975

OTHER LITERARY FORMS

Although the largest part of Tristan Tzara's work consists of a vast body of poetry—filling more than thirty volumes—he did experiment with drama, publishing three plays during his lifetime: *Le Coeur à gaz* (wr. 1921, pb. 1946; *The Gas Heart*, 1964), *Mouchoir de nuages* (1924; *Handkerchief of Clouds*, 1972), and *La Fuite* (1947; the flight). His important polemical writings appeared in two collections: *Sept Manifestes Dada* (1924; *Seven Dada Manifestos*, 1979) and *Le Surréalisme et l'après-guerre* (1947; Surrealism and the postwar period). Much of Tzara's critical and occasional writing, which is substantial in volume, remains unpublished, including book-length works on François Rabelais and François Villon, while the published portion includes *Lampisteries* (1963; English translation, 1977), *Picasso et la poésie* (1953; Picasso and poetry), *L'Art Océanien* (1951; the art of Oceania), and *L'Égypte face à face* (1954).

ACHIEVEMENTS

Tristan Tzara's importance as a literary figure of international reputation rests primarily upon his relationship to the Dada movement. Of all the avant-garde movements which challenged the traditional foundations of artistic value and judgment at the beginning of the present century, Dada was, by consensus, the most radical and disturbing. In retrospect, the Dada aesthetic, which was first formed and expressed in Zurich about 1916, seems to have been a fairly direct response to World War I; the Dadaists themselves suggest as much in many of their works during this period.

The harsh, confrontational nature of Dada is notorious, and Tzara was one of the most provocative of all the Dadaists. In his 1930 essay, "Memoirs of Dadaism," Tzara describes one of his own contributions to the first Dada soiree in Paris, on January 23, 1920, in which he read a newspaper while a bell rang. This attitude of deliberate confrontation with the conventional, rational expectations of the audience—to which the Dadaists juxtaposed their illogical, satirical productions—is defended by Tzara in his most famous polemical work, "Manifeste Dada 1918" ("Dada Manifesto 1918"), in which he asserts the meaninglessness of Dada and its refusal to offer a road to truth.

To escape the machinery of human rationality, the Dadaists substituted a faith in spontaneity, incorporating the incongruous and accidental into their works. Even the name by which the Dadaists called themselves was chosen rather arbitrarily. According to most accounts (although this report is subject to intense difference of opinion among Dadaists), it was Tzara himself who chose the word *dada*, in February of 1916, by opening a French dictionary to a randomly selected entry.

Tzara's achievements are not limited solely to his leadership in the Dada movement. Until recently, Tzara's later work—which is more optimistic in tone and more controlled in technique—has been overshadowed by his more violent and sensational work from the Dada period. It is now becoming apparent to many readers and critics that the Surrealist phase of Tzara's work, the little-known work of his post-Surrealist phase, and his early pre-Dada work in Romanian, are equally important in considering his contribution to modern literature. In the 1970's and 1980's, largely through the work of editors and translators such as Mary Ann Caws, Henrí Behar, and Sasa Panǎ, this work became more readily available.

BIOGRAPHY

Tristan Tzara, whose real name was Sami Rosenstock, was born on April 4, 1896, in Moinesti, a small town in the province of Bǎcǎu, in northeastern Romania. His parents were Jewish, his father a prosperous merchant. Tzara first attended school in Moinesti, where Romanian was spoken, but later, when he was sent to Bucharest for his secondary education, he attended schools where instruction was also given in French. In addition to languages, Tzara studied mathematics and music. Following his graduation in 1913, he attended the University of Bucharest for a year, taking courses in mathematics and philosophy.

It was during this adolescent period, between 1911 and 1915, that all Tzara's Romanian poems were written. His first published poems appeared in 1912 in *Simbolul*, a short-lived Symbolist review that he helped to edit. These first four poems were signed with the pseudonym "S. Samyro." The subsequent poems in Romanian that Tzara published during this period were often signed simply "Tristan" or "Tzara," and it was not until near the end of this period, in 1915, that the first Romanian poem signed "Tristan Tzara" appeared.

In the fall of 1915, Tzara went to Zurich, in neutral Switzerland, where he became involved with a group of writers and artists—including Hugo Ball, Richard Huelsenbeck, Marcel Janco, and Hans Arp—who were in the process of forming an artistic movement soon to be called "Dada." This period, between Tzara's arrival in Zurich in the fall of 1915 and February of 1916, was the germinating period of the Dada movement. The Dadaists' first public announcement of the birth of a new movement in the arts took place at the Cabaret Voltaire on the evening of February 5, 1916—the occasion of the first of many such Dada soirees. These entertainments included presentations such as "simultaneous poems," which confronted the audience with a chaotic barrage of words made incomprehensible by the din; recitations of "pure sound-poems," often made up of African-sounding nonsense syllables and recited by a chorus of masked dancers; satirical plays which accused and insulted the audience; and, always, the ceaseless manifestos promoting the Dada revolt against conformity. Tzara's work during this period was written almost entirely in French, and from this time on he used that language exclusively for his literary productions.

As the activities of the Zurich Dadaists gradually attracted notice in other countries, especially Germany and France, Tzara's own fame as an artist spread to an increasingly larger audience. The spread of Dada's fame from Zurich to other centers of avant-garde activity in Europe was aided by the journal *Dada*, edited by Tzara and featuring many of his most provocative works. Although this journal lasted only through five issues, it did draw the attention of Guillaume Apollinaire in Paris, and through him the devoted admiration of André Breton, who was later to be one of the leaders of the Surrealist movement. At Breton's urging, Tzara left Zurich shortly after the Armistice was declared, arriving in Paris in December of 1919.

For a short period between January of 1920, when the first public Dada performance in Paris was held, and May of 1921, when Breton broke his association with Tzara to assume the leadership of the developing Surrealist movement, Breton and Tzara organized an increasingly outrageous series of activities which frequently resulted in public spectacles. Following Breton's break with the Dada group, Tzara continued to stage public performances in Paris for a time, collaborating with those who remained loyal to the Dada revolt. By July of 1923, however, when the performance of his play *The Gas Heart* was disrupted by a Surrealist counter demonstration, even Tzara regretfully admitted that Dada was effectively dead, a victim of its own destructive impulses. Tzara gave up the Dada ideal reluctantly and continued to oppose the Surrealists until 1929, when he joined the Paris Surrealist group, accepting Breton's leadership. Tzara's resumption of activities with Breton's group was also accompanied by an increasing move toward political engagement.

The same year that he joined the Surrealists, Tzara visited the Soviet Union, and the following year, in 1930, the Surrealists indicated their dedication to the Communist International by changing the name of their own journal, *La Révolution surréaliste*, to *Le Surréalisme au service de la révolution*. For Tzara, this political commitment seemed to be a natural outgrowth of his initial revolt, for, as he wrote later in *Le Surréalisme et l'après-guerre:* "Dada was born . . . from the deep feeling that man . . . must affirm his supremacy over notions emptied of all human substance, over dead objects and ill-gotten gains."

In 1935, Tzara broke with the Surrealists in order to devote himself entirely to the work of the Communist Party, which he officially joined at this time. From 1935 to 1937, he was involved in assisting the Republican forces in the Spanish Civil War, salvaging art treasures and serving on the Committee for the Defense of Culture. This political engagement continued during World War II, with Tzara serving in the French Resistance, all the time continuing to publish his work, despite widespread censorship, under the pseudonym "T. Tristan." In 1946 and 1947, he delivered the lectures that make up *Le Surréalisme et l'après-guerre*, in which he made his controversial assessment of Surrealism's failure to influence Europe effectively between the wars. In 1955, Tzara published *À haute flamme* (at full flame), a long poetic reminiscence in which he reviewed the stages of his lifelong revolt and reaffirmed his revolutionary aesthetic. Tzara continued to affirm the authenticity of his position until his death in Paris at the age of sixty-seven, a victim of lung cancer.

ANALYSIS

Whatever else Tristan Tzara was—Dada instigator and polemicist, marginal Surrealist, Communist activist, or Romanian expatriate—his great skill as a poet is

abundantly apparent. At his death, Tzara left behind him a vast body of poems, extremely diverse in style, content, and tone. Important features of his work are his innovations in poetic technique and his development of a highly unified system of symbolic imagery. The first of these features includes the use of pure sound elements, descriptive ideophones, expressive typography, enjambment which creates complex syntactic ambiguities, and multiple viewpoints resulting in a confusing confluence of speaking voices. The second important feature includes such elements as Tzara's use of recurring verbal motifs and refrains, ironic juxtapositions, and recurring image clusters.

Tzara's earliest period extends from 1911 to 1915 and includes all the poetry he wrote in his native Romanian. Until recently, little attention has been given to Tzara's Romanian poetry. Several Romanian critics have noted the decisive but unacknowledged influence on Tzara of the Romanian poet Urmuz (1883-1923), virtually unknown in the West, who anticipated the strategies of Dada and Surrealism. Much of Tzara's early work, however, is relatively traditional in technique, although it must be remembered that this period represents his poetic apprenticeship and that the poems were written when he was between the ages of fifteen and nineteen. The poetry of this period often displays a curiously ambivalent tone, mixing a detached ironic perspective—which is sometimes gently sarcastic and at other times bitterly resentful—with an uncritically sentimental nostalgia for the past. In some of the poems, one of these two moods dominates, as in Tzara's bitterly ironic treatment of war's destructive effect on the innocence of youth in "The Storm and the Deserter's Song" and "Song of War," or the romantic lyricism of such highly sentimental idylls on nature as "Elegy for the Coming of Winter" and "Evening Comes."

PRIMELE POÈME

The most successful poems of this period—later collected as *Primele Poème*—are those which mix nostalgia with irony, encompassing both attitudes within a single poem. The best example of this type of poem is "Sunday," whose conventional images of leisurely activities that occupy the inhabitants of a town on the Sabbath are contrasted with the bitter reflections of the alienated poet-speaker who observes the scene. The scene seems idyllic enough at first, presenting images of domestic tranquillity. Then the reflecting consciousness of the alienated speaker intrudes, introducing images that contrast darkly with and shatter the apparently false impression he himself has just created. Into the scene of comfortable regularity, three new and disturbing elements appear: the inescapable presence of death in wartime, the helplessness of parents to protect their children from danger, and the futility of art stagnated by decadence.

VINGT-CINQ POÈMES

This successful mixture of sentimental lyricism with ironic detachment is developed to an even greater degree in Tzara's first collection of poems in French, *Vingt-cinq Poèmes* (twenty-five poems), a collection which, although published after he had already arrived in Zurich, still resembles in technique and content the early Romanian poems. In "Petite Ville en Sibérie" ("Little Town in Siberia") there are a number of new elements, the most important of which are Tzara's use of typography for expressive purposes, the complex syntactic ambiguity created by enjambment, the rich confluence of narrative voices, and the appearance of images employing illogical juxtapositions of objects and qualities:

a blue light which flattens us together on the ceiling
it's as always comrade
like a label of infernal doors pasted on a medicine bottle
it's the calm house tremble my friend

This disorienting confluence of voices is deliberate, and it evokes in the reader a futile desire to resolve the collage (based on the random conjunction of several separate discourses) into a meaningful and purposeful poetic statement.

DE NOS OISEAUX

In Tzara's second period—extending from 1916 until 1924—he produced the Dadaist works which brought him international fame. To the collage technique developed in *Vingt-cinq Poèmes*, the poems that make up *De nos oiseaux* (of our birds)—the major collection from this period—introduce several innovations, including pure sound elements such as African-sounding nonsense words, repeated phrases, descriptive ideophones, use of multiple typefaces, and catalogs of discrete, separable images piled one upon the other. Tzara's collage

technique has become more radical in these poems, for instead of simply using the juxtaposition of speaking voices for creating ironic detachment, in the Dada poems the narrative itself breaks down entirely into a chaotic barrage of discontinuous fragments which often seem to lack any discursive sense. These features are readily apparent in "La Mort de Guillaume Apollinaire" ("The Death of Guillaume Apollinaire") and "Les Saltimbanques" ("The Circus Performers"), two of the best poems from *De nos oiseaux*.

"THE DEATH OF GUILLAUME APOLLINAIRE"

In his Dadaist elegy for Apollinaire, Tzara begins with a series of propositions that not only establish the resigned mood of the speaker but also express the feeling of disorder created in the reader by the poem itself. A simple admission of man's inability to comprehend his situation in the world is followed by a series of images that seem designed to convey the disparity the speaker senses between a world which is unresponsive to human needs (the unfortunate death of Apollinaire at such an early age is no doubt one aspect of this) and a world in which he could feel comfortable (and presumably learn to accept the death of his beloved friend):

if snow fell upward
if the sun rose in our houses in the middle of the night
just to keep us warm
and the trees hung upsidedown with their crowns . . .
if birds came down to us to find reflections of
    themselves
in those peaceful lakes lying just above our heads
THEN WE MIGHT UNDERSTAND
that death could be a beautiful long voyage
and a permanent vacation from flesh from structures
    systems and skeletons

The images of this poem constitute a particularly good illustration of Tzara's developing symbolic system. Although the images of snow falling upward, the sun rising at night, trees hanging upside down, and birds coming to earth at first appear unrelated to one another, they are actually related in two ways. First, Tzara is describing processes within the totality of nature which give evidence that "nature is organized in its totality." Man's sorrow over the inescapable cycles of life and death, of joy and suffering, is caused by a failure to understand that he, too, is a part of this totality. Second, Tzara's images suggest that if one's perspective could only be reversed, one would see the reality of things properly. This method of presenting arguments in non-discursive, imagistic terms was one of Tzara's primary poetic accomplishments, and the uses to which he put it in this elegy for Apollinaire were later expanded and developed in the epic scope of his masterpiece, *Approximate Man and Other Writings*.

"THE CIRCUS PERFORMERS"

"The Circus Performers," also from this period, illustrates Tzara's increasing use of pure sound elements in his work. The images of this poem attempt to capture the exciting rhythms of the circus performance that Tzara is describing. In the opening vignette of the poem, in what seems at first an illogical sequence of statements, Tzara merges the expanding and contracting rhythm of the verses with his characteristic use of imagery to convey thought in analogical, nondiscursive terms. Describing a ventriloquist's act, Tzara uses an image that links "brains," "balloons," and "words." In this image, "brains" seems to be a metonymic substitution for ideas or thoughts—that which is expressed by "words." Yet here the brains themselves are inflating and deflating, as are the balloons. What is the unstated analogical relation between the two? These words are treated like the words and thoughts of comic-strip characters—where words are enclosed in the "balloons" that represent mental space in newspaper cartoons. To help the reader more easily identify the analogy, Tzara has included an explanatory aside, enclosed in parentheses. A second example of Tzara's use of sound in this poem is the presence of "ideophones"—words that imitate the sounds of the actions they describe. Pure sound images devoid of abstract meaning are scattered throughout the poem.

APPROXIMATE MAN AND OTHER WRITINGS

By all standards of judgment, *Approximate Man and Other Writings*, a long epic in nineteen sections, is Tzara's greatest poem. It was Tzara's most sustained effort, its composition and extensive revisions occupying the poet between 1925 and 1931, the year that the final version appeared. Another important characteristic of the work is its epic scope, for *Approximate Man and*

Other Writings was Tzara's attempt to discover the causes of modern man's spiritual malaise, drawing on all the technical resources he had developed up to the time of its composition. The most important feature of the poem, however, is its systematic presentation of Tzara's revolutionary ideology, which had begun to reflect, in a guarded form, the utopian vision of Surrealism.

Approximate Man and Other Writings is about the intrusion of disorder into modern life, and it focuses on the effects of this disorder upon the individual person. Throughout the poem, Tzara makes it clear that what he is describing is a general disorder or sickness, not a personal crisis. This is one of the key ideas that is constantly repeated in the form of a refrain: "approximate man like me like you reader and like the others/ heap of noisy flesh and echoes of conscience/ complete in the only element of choice your name." The most important aspect of the poem's theme is Tzara's diagnosis of the causes of this debilitating universal sickness, since this indicates in a striking way his newly found attitude of commitment.

The first cause of man's sickness is the very condition of being "approximate." Uncertain, changeable, or lacking commitment to any cause that might improve the world in which he lives, Approximate Man wanders aimlessly. For Tzara, the lost key for curing the sickness is commitment, as Tzara himself declared his commitment to the work of the Communist Party in 1935, shortly after the completion of this poem.

Man's sickness arises not only from his inauthentic relationship with other men but also from his exploitative attitude toward nature—an attitude encouraged by the development of modern technology. In Tzara's view, this modern belief in man's preeminent importance in the universe is a mistaken one, as is evident in "The Death of Guillaume Apollinaire," and such vanity contributes to the spiritual sickness of humankind.

Tzara finds a third cause of man's spiritual sickness in man's increasing reliance upon the products of his own alienated consciousness, especially reason and language. In *Approximate Man and Other Writings*, Tzara's efforts to describe this solipsistic entrapment of man by his own systems gives rise to many striking images, as in the following passages: "vapor on the cold glass you block your own image from your/ sight/ tall and insignificant among the glazed frost jewels/ of the landscape" and "I think of the warmth spun by the word/ around its center the dream called ourselves." These images argue that human reason is like a mirror in which the reflection is clouded by the observer's physical presence, and that man's language is like a silken cocoon which insulates him from the external world of reality. Both reason and language, originally created to assist man, have become debased, and in order to attain a more accurate picture of the world, man must learn to rely upon his instinct and his imagination. These three ideas, which find their fullest expression in *Approximate Man and Other Writings*, form the basis of Tzara's mature poetic vision and constitute the most sustained expression of his critique of the modern sensibility.

OTHER MAJOR WORKS

PLAYS: *Mouchoir de nuages*, 1924 (*Handkerchief of Clouds*, 1972); *Le Coeur à gaz*, wr. 1921, pb. 1946 (*The Gas Heart*, 1964); *La Fuite*, 1947.

NONFICTION: *Sept Manifestes Dada*, 1924 (*Seven Dada Manifestos*, 1979); *Le Surréalisme et l'après-guerre*, 1947; *L'Art Océanien*, 1951; *Picasso et la poésie*, 1953; *L'Égypte face à face*, 1954; *Lampisteries*, 1963 (English translation, 1977).

EDITED TEXT: *Œuvres completes*, 1975-1991 (6 volumes).

BIBLIOGRAPHY

Browning, Gordon Frederick. *Tristan Tzara: The Genesis of the Dada Poem or from Dada to Aa*. Stuttgart, Germany: Akademischer Verlag Heinz, 1979. A critical study of Tzara's Dada poems. Includes bibliographical references.

Caldwell, Ruth. "From Chemical Explosion to Simple Fruits: Nature in the Poetry of Tristan Tzara." *Perspectives on Contemporary Literature* 5 (1979): 18-23. A critical study of selected poems by Tzara containing references to nature.

Motherwell, Robert, and Jack D. Flam, eds. *The Dada Painters and Poets: An Anthology*. 2d ed. Cambridge, Mass.: Harvard University Press, 1989. A collection of Dada documents including journals, reviews, and manifestoes that hold valuable biographical and historical details of the life and work of Tzara.

Peterson, Elmer. *Tristan Tzara: Dada and Surrational Theorist*. New Brunswick, N.J.: Rutgers University Press, 1971. A study of Tzara's aesthetics. Includes bibliographical references.

Richter, Hans. *Dada: Art and Anti-Art*. New York: Thames and Hudson, 1997. Through selections from key manifestos and other documents of the time, Richter records Dada's history, from its beginnings in wartime Zurich to its collapse in the Paris of the 1920's.

Varisco, Robert A. "Anarchy and Resistance in Tristan Tzara's *The Gas Heart*." *Modern Drama* 40, no. 1 (Spring, 1997): 139-148. Varisco argues that *The Gas Heart* is a form of anarchy against art, and specifically against the theater.

Steven E. Colburn;
bibliography updated by the editors

U

MIGUEL DE UNAMUNO Y JUGO

Born: Bilbao, Spain; September 29, 1864
Died: Salamanca, Spain; December 31, 1936

PRINCIPAL POETRY

Poesías, 1907
Rosario de sonetos líricos, 1911
El Cristo de Velázquez, 1920 (*The Christ of Velázquez*, 1951)
Rimas de dentro, 1923
Teresa, 1924
Romancero del destierro, 1928
Poems, 1952
Cancionero, Diario poético, 1953 (*The Last Poems of Miguel de Unamuno*, 1974).

OTHER LITERARY FORMS

Miguel de Unamuno y Jugo wrote prolifically throughout his life and produced numerous novels, short stories, dramas, and essays, as well as volumes of poetry. A mediocre dramatist who, under the influence of Henrik Ibsen, created talky stage works with uninspired characters, Unamuno achieved his greatest success with fiction, poetry, and the essay. His outstanding works of fiction include *Niebla* (1914; *Mist: A Tragicomic Novel*, 1928); *Abel Sánchez: Una historia de pasión* (1917; English translation, 1947); and *San Manuel Bueno, mártir* (1931; *Saint Manuel Bueno, Martyr*, 1956). A philosophical author, Unamuno explored rich and complex ideas in all his works, regardless of genre. Particularly noteworthy are two long collections of essays, *Del sentimiento trágico de la vida en los hombres y en los pueblos* (1913; *The Tragic Sense of Life in Men and Peoples*, 1921) and *La agonía del Cristianismo*, 1925 (*The Agony of Christianity*, 1928, 1960; in French *L'Agonie du Christianisme*, 1931), regarded by many critics as his central works.

ACHIEVEMENTS

Miguel de Unamuno y Jugo embodied the Spanish spirit and temperament in profound ways not seen in any Spanish writer since the Golden Age of Miguel de Cervantes, Lope de Vega, and Pedro Calderón de la Barca. In an oddly ironic twist, Unamuno began his career by attempting to "Europeanize" what he believed to be a backward Spain. Believing—as did many young Spanish artists—that Spain had lagged far behind the other European countries in its literature, art, music, and philosophy, Unamuno hoped to be able to take what was best in recent European advances and, by planting those seeds, allow new cultural life to grow in Spain. Yet, by the end of his prolific and distinguished career, Unamuno had not opened the windows of Spain so that new European light might shine on his land; instead, through his writing, he had given his country its *own* unique literary character. As artist and philosopher, Unamuno was a distinctly Spanish figure—a figure whose works the rest of Europe was forced to contemplate, explore, and assimilate. Throughout his career, Unamuno thrust Spain and the Spanish character at the rest of Europe, from his glorification of the Spanish landscape in such great poems as "Salamanca" and "On Gredos" to his assertion of the Spanish temper and the Spanish soul as it was mirrored in his own poetry and personality—a personality which, in William Barrett's words, "insists upon coming at you head on."

Unamuno was passionate in his convictions and claimed to understand philosophy only as poetry and poetry only as philosophy. In seeking to blur the distinction between poetry and philosophy, he was deliberately attempting to change the nature of poetry in his time. He had no interest in the elegance, decorum, and refinement of the poetry of his day. Poetry was held captive, in Unamuno's vision, by a precious "literatism," and he sought to free it from its literary bonds by proclaiming poetry the proper sphere of philosophy. Poetry could once again become a field of turbulent emotions and passionate thought if its smooth sheen of polished craft and beautiful art were fired by suffering, fear, doubt, and death. Even his seemingly most traditional poetic work, *Teresa*, a collection of love poems by a supposedly "unknown poet" to his beloved in the manner of Dante, Petrarch, or Torquato Tasso, is given a typical and characteristic twist by Unamuno. The poems are written to the beloved after her death. The whole series is not an ordinary cycle of love poems, but rather a study of the "metaphysics of love" and the spiritual link between love and death.

Unamuno believed that the basis for all art must be religious, and he believed that much of the art of his time had become the mere eruption of petty egos. He had little regard for Charles Baudelaire, Paul Verlaine, or Stéphane Mallarmé, preferring the more ambitious, if less refined, work of A. C. Swinburne, Robert Browning, and Walt Whitman. In creating poetry more concerned with substance than with form and in forcing large philosophical ideas back into the closed and refined poetry of his day, Unamuno not only made his poetry the living testament of a struggling soul, but also brought Spanish poetry into the forefront of the play of ideas in Europe.

BIOGRAPHY

Miguel de Unamuno y Jugo was born in Bilbao, Spain, an industrial center of the Basque province, on

Miguel de Unamuno y Jugo (Library of Congress)

September 29, 1864. He remained in Bilbao until he was sixteen and then attended the University of Madrid, where he received a doctorate in 1884. Returning then to the Basque region of northern Spain, he began to work as a tutor and to write articles for the local newspapers, all the while preparing himself for a teaching career. During this time he also began work on his first novel, *Paz en la guerra* (1897; *Peace in War*, 1983) and devoted himself to the study of foreign languages. In 1891, he was appointed to the chair of Greek at the University of Salamanca. In that same year, he married Concepción Lizárraga (Concha), a woman who remained in the background when her husband became a public figure, but who gave him a refuge from the limelight, a happy home, and nine children. His devotion to her was absolute throughout his life.

In 1897, one of Unamuno's sons contracted meningitis, resulting in terminal hydrocephalus. As a result, Unamuno suffered a grave religious crisis and, after years of Catholic upbringing and devoted observance of the faith, lost his trust in Catholicism. His spiritual struggle lasted for the rest of his life and came to be the major subject of many of his works—the torment of a soul that feels itself a Christian and yet is besieged by doubt.

Named rector of the University of Salamanca in 1900, Unamuno wrote extensively during the next fourteen years in many different forms—producing fiction, poetry, essays, and travel books—and completed his seminal philosophical work, *The Tragic Sense of Life in Men and Peoples*. Dismissed from the rectorship in 1914, he continued to teach, to write prolifically, and to be an outspoken public figure. His forthright criticism of the dictatorship of Primo de Rivera resulted in the loss of his position at the university and his exile to Fuerteventura in the Canary Islands in 1924. Although he escaped to Paris, he was unhappy and longed to return to his native land. He moved to Hendaye, a border town which offered him a view of the Basque mountains and thus some contact with his land, his home, and his family.

Unamuno's exile came to an end in 1930 when Primo de Rivera was overthrown. Unamuno returned to Spain in triumph, and, after the establishment of the Republic in 1931, the University of Salamanca reappointed him as rector; he was also elected deputy for the city of

Salamanca to the Constituent Assembly. The same year his second great philosophical work, *The Agony of Christianity*, was published. Within two months in the spring and summer of 1934, Unamuno lost his wife and a daughter, Salomé, and that fall he retired as a professor and was named lifetime rector of the university. At the outbreak of the Civil War in July, 1936, Unamuno lent his support to General Francisco Franco but soon became disillusioned with the intolerance of the military leaders and openly denounced them in a speech delivered at the University of Salamanca on October 12, 1936. He was promptly dismissed from his post and was confined to his home, where he died of a heart attack on December 31, 1936.

ANALYSIS

In an essay titled "Mi religión" ("My Religion"), Miguel de Unamuno y Jugo states that he has expressed his religion in his "song," in the poetry to which he devoted so much of his literary career. His poems do not offer logical explanations or reasoned analyses of his faith; rather, they are the cries of his soul. Unamuno's poetry represents a great accomplishment in the field of religious verse, but perhaps more important, it records the spiritual journey of a tormented soul through all the avenues of hellish doubt and divine exultation, a brutally honest record of a human soul through all the vicissitudes of faith, doubt, love, despair, and hope. Only a handful of modern writers—among them August Strindberg, Fyodor Dostoevski, and John Berryman—have confronted religious questions and their effects on heart and mind with such honesty, energy, and passion.

Poetry became the natural place for Unamuno to set down his philosophical ideas. After his spiritual crisis of 1897, he broke with the faith of his childhood because he could no longer tolerate the certainties of a dogmatic faith, the notion that the existence of God and the principal mysteries of the Christian religion could be proven through human reason and then codified by a worldly institution. For Unamuno, doubt was the fuel of faith. He became the enemy of rational attempts to systematize religious faith and championed the antirational believer, one who strives toward knowledge and ultimately faith, but does so through the pain of doubt, suffering and despair.

MEDIUM FOR PHILOSOPHY

In Unamuno's view, man is defined by his yearning for immortality, but each man in his lifetime seeks that immortality and hence finds his faith by a unique path. Poetry, Unamuno believed, could offer a place for the individual voice to express its unique pain, its unique insights. In poetry, the sacred flame that had been extinguished by dogma could be rekindled. That process could only begin, however, through suffering. In Unamuno's philosophical work, *The Agony of Christianity*, "agony" is used in the Greek sense of *agon* or struggle, not in the narrower modern sense of the product of pain. The struggle of each questioning soul is unique, and can only be expressed in a form such as poetry or fiction, which makes no pretensions to scientific objectivity.

As these emphases suggest, Unamuno was an important figure in the development of existentialism, standing between Søren Kierkegaard, a writer he admired deeply, and later thinkers such as Martin Heidegger, Jean-Paul Sartre, and Albert Camus. William Barrett observes that Unamuno's vision helped bring questions of life and death back into the philosophical arena and thus spurred the development of modern existential thought.

Indeed, poetry offered Unamuno an ideal medium for his philosophy. Fiction and drama required the transformation of his voice into other voices, the transformation of his life into other lives. In poetry, his voice could speak directly of its suffering, its pain, its ecstasy. Poetry opened itself to the display of pure emotion and could be a vehicle of antirationalism. In Unamuno's verse, structure and form are often deliberately subordinated to idea and content; the criticism—that his poetry lacked discipline—he wore as a badge of honor.

If he often neglected structure, however, Unamuno was obsessed with the precision and the perfection of the word. Poetry and the poet, in depending on the importance of the word, in caring for the precise truth of the word and in creating new life and new thoughts through the word, might reach toward the ultimate Word, the Word that was made flesh. Unamuno constantly asserts the parallel between the word in poetry and the Divine Word, even in his earliest poems, published in 1907. For example, in "¡Id con Dios!" ("Farewell, Go with God!"), he speaks directly to his own verse:

Go with God, since with Him you came to take
in me the form of words: like living flesh.

The role of the poet becomes the role of the priest, the function of art a sacred function, for in the creation of poetry the poet makes the Word flesh.

EL CRISTO DE VELÁZQUEZ

Unamuno's greatest poetic achievement, *El Cristo de Velázquez*, is a long sequence of poems which meditate on Velázquez's famous painting of the figure of Christ on the Cross. The poet never moves his eyes from the vision of the Savior; instead, he explores each element of the painting, each detail of the crucified body and each response of his own mind and heart. The canvas unveils to Unamuno the pain, the mystery, and the hope of all Christian thought, and he creates songs of complex beauty that explore his own love and fear, despair and hope. The titles of the individual poems in this "liturgical epic" offer hints as to the individual sparks of inspiration for each poem: "Luna" ("Moon"), "Ecce Homo," "Dios-obscuridad" ("God-Darkness"), "Sangre" ("Blood"), "La vida es sueño" ("Life Is a Dream"), "Paz en la guerra" ("Peace in War"), "Alba" ("Dawn"), "Rosa" ("Rose"), and so on.

At first, all thought and the universe itself are embodied in the figure of the crucified man-God, as in the poem "Moon," where the whiteness of Christ's body against the enveloping darkness of the background offers the poet assurance of God's presence and light, just as the moon in the black night radiates the light of the invisible sun. As the poems proceed, however, Unamuno comes to focus solely on the body of Christ itself, examining each detail of his human form in poems titled, "Corona" ("Crown"), "Cabeza" ("Head"), "Pelo" ("Hair"), "Frente" ("Forehead"), "Ojos" ("Eyes"), "Orejas" ("Ears"), and so on. The body becomes the poems. Throughout all the poems, images hurtle wildly by, for the suffering figure contains the whole universe and becomes the link for wide-ranging thoughts.

Unamuno's ideas are presented antirationally and nonlogically, for thought resides in his response to Christ's Passion and all it suggests of life and death, man and God, time and eternity, and not in reason or analysis. The poems are sprinkled with references to and paraphrases from both Old and New Testaments, the sources of the quotations being duly noted in the margin. The sacred texts become natural elements of the individual poems as the poet deliberately blends his own voice with the Divine Word of the Almighty. Above all, Unamuno reproduces for the reader the promise of freedom from time and death that he feels as he views Velázquez's painting. The painter's art is re-created for the reader: Art becomes a source of hope.

CANCIONERO, DIARIO POÉTICO

Unamuno's last major work of verse, his *Cancionero, Diario poético* (book of songs), consists of more than fifteen hundred brief meditations and hymns. Published in 1953, many years after Unamuno's death, these compositions record the poet's thoughts from 1928 to 1936, constituting a kind of spiritual diary. Each of the poems was composed by Unamuno in the morning after he had read a chapter of the Bible. These meditations on biblical passages provided a measure of his spiritual state as he began to "resume . . . strife" for another day.

The poems of *Cancionero* reach the ideal form that Unamuno had long been seeking for his poetry; they do not pretend to be anything other than direct meditations and do not need any other subject than the Word of God and the mind and heart of the poet himself. They possess an intimacy and immediacy that go to the heart of Unamuno's philosophy. Moment by moment, the soul searches for the sacred, recording its quest with precision and reverence.

This immersion in and love for the details of life's reality follows from Unamuno's Christian beliefs. When God himself became man and descended to assume flesh, he invested earthly life with eternal importance. Thus, there is nothing odd in Unamuno's addressing poems to a dead dog, a wild reed, or the "Forefinger of the Right Hand" of the crucified Christ. All life, all matter provokes meditation. For Unamuno, poetry *is* meditation, a means to stretch the soul: "the deeper into yourself you go,/ the larger your boundaries, my soul."

LEGACY

Unamuno once wrote of Blaise Pascal that his *Pensées* (1670; English translation, 1688) do not invite the reader to study a philosophy, but rather to become acquainted with a man, to penetrate the sanctuary of a soul bared to the quick. Unamuno's poetry makes the same invitation, for though it is philosophical poetry, the soul of the poet in all his complexity animates the poems. A poetry of philosophy, contemplation, meditation, religious hope and the agony of doubt, Unamuno's verse is most memorable for the unique, unswervingly honest voice of the poet himself. Indeed, Unamuno's poetry is more dramatic than his dramas, for in his poetry he brings his own character to startling life. Unamuno's intensity of personal vision combines with the ambition and universality of his themes and the precise energy of his language to create a poetry of richness, range, and lasting importance.

OTHER MAJOR WORKS

LONG FICTION: *Paz en la guerra*, 1897 (*Peace in War*, 1983); *Amor y pedagogía*, 1902; *Niebla*, 1914 (*Mist: A Tragicomic Novel*, 1928); *Abel Sánchez: Una historia de pasión*, 1917 (*Abel Sánchez*, 1947); *Tres novelas ejemplares y un prólogo*, 1920 (*Three Exemplary Novels and a Prologue*, 1930); *La tía Tula*, 1921 (*Tía Tula*, 1976); *San Manuel Bueno, mártir*, 1931 (*Saint Manuel Bueno, Martyr*, 1956); *Dos novelas cortas*, 1961 (James Russell Stamm and Herbert Eugene Isar, eds.).

PLAYS: *La esfinge*, wr. 1898, pr. 1909; *La venda*, wr. 1899, pb. 1913; *La difunta*, pr. 1910; *El pasado que vuelve*, wr. 1910, pr. 1923; *Fedra*, wr. 1910, pr. 1918 (*Phaedra*, 1959); *La princesa doña Lambra*, pb. 1913; *Soledad*, wr. 1921, pr. 1953; *Raquel encadenada*, wr. 1921, pr. 1926; *El otro*, wr. 1926, pr., pb. 1932 (*The Other*, 1947); *Sombras de sueño*, pr., pb. 1930; *El hermano Juan: O, El mundo es teatro*, wr. 1927, pb. 1934; *Teatro completo*, pb. 1959, 1973.

NONFICTION: *De la enseñanza superior en España*, 1899; *Nicodemo el fariseo*, 1899; *Tres ensayos*, 1900; *En torno al casticismo*, 1902; *De mi país*, 1903; *Vida de Don Quijote y Sancho según Miguel de Cervantes Saavedra, explicada y comentada por Miguel de Unamuno*, 1905 (*The Life of Don Quixote and Sancho According to Miguel de Cervantes Saavedre Expounded with Comment by Miguel de Unamuno*, 1927); *Recuerdos de niñez y de mocedad*, 1908; *Mi religión y otros ensayos breves*, 1910; *Soliloquios y conversaciones*, 1911 (*Essays and Soliloquies*, 1925); *Contra esto y aquello*, 1912; *Del sentimiento trágico de la vida en los hombres y en los pueblos*, 1913 (*The Tragic Sense of Life in Men and in Peoples*, 1921); *La agonía del Cristianismo*, 1925 (*The Agony of Christianity*, 1928, 1960; in French *L'Agonie du Christianisme*, 1931); *Cómo se hace una novela*, 1927 (*How to Make a Novel*, 1976); *La ciudad de Henoc*, 1941; *Cuenca ibérica*, 1943; *Paisajes del alma*, 1944; *La enormidad de España*, 1945; *Visiones y commentarios*, 1949.

MISCELLANEOUS: *Obras completas*, 1959-1964 (16 volumes).

BIBLIOGRAPHY

Callahan, David. "The Early Reception of Miguel de Unamuno in England, 1907-1939." *Modern Language Review* 91, no. 2 (April, 1996): 382. In 1936, Miguel de Unamuno came to England to be awarded honorary degrees by the Universities of London, Oxford, and Cambridge. Although he was referred to by a wide variety of writers in different contexts, Unamuno never became of any deep significance in England.

Fox, Arturo A. *El Edipo en Unamuno y el espejo de Lacan*. Lewiston, N.Y.: Edwin Mellen Press, 2001. Fox delves into the writer's psyche through a psychoanalytic approach to representative works. Fox's analyses of several of Unamuno's works was inspired by Jacques Lacan. In Spanish.

Jurkevich, Gayana. *The Elusive Self: Archetypal Approaches to the Novels of Miguel de Unamuno*. Columbia: University of Missouri Press, 1991. A psychological study of selected works by Unamuno. Includes bibliographical references and index.

_____. "Unamuno's Intrahistoria and Jung's Collective Unconscious: Parallels, Convergences, and Common Sources." *Comparative Literature* 43, no. 1 (Winter, 1991): 43. Jung and Unamuno are compared to develop an understanding of the relationship between Unamuno's "Intrahistoria" and Jung's collective unconscious. Jurkevich argues that Unamuno anticipated some of the most fundamental teachings of depth psychology.

Nozick, Martin. *Miguel de Unamuno*. New York: Twayne, 1971. An introductory biographical study and critical analysis of selected works by Unamuno.

Ouimette, Victor. *Reason Aflame: Unamuno and the Heroic Will.* Yale Romantic Studies 2d ser., vol. 24. New Haven, Conn.: Yale University Press, 1974. Presents an inner logic in Unamuno's thought centered on his concept of heroic fulfillment as the goal of human existence.

Rubia Barcia, José, and M. A. Zeitlin, eds. *Unamuno: Creator and Creation.* Berkeley: University of California Press, 1967. A collection of transcripts of lectures from a program commemorating the centennial of the birth of Miguel de Unamuno. Contains valuable biographical material and critical studies. Includes bibliographical references.

David Allen White;
bibliography updated by Carole A. Champagne

GIUSEPPE UNGARETTI

Born: Alexandria, Egypt; February 8, 1888
Died: Milan, Italy; June 1, 1970

PRINCIPAL POETRY

Il porto sepolto, 1916
Allegria di naufragi, 1919
La guerre, 1919
L'allegria, 1931, 1942 (includes revisions from *Il porto sepolto* and *Allegria di naufragi*)
Sentimento del tempo, 1933
Il dolore, 1947
La terra promessa, 1950
Gridasti, soffoco . . . , 1951
Un grido e paesaggi, 1952
Life of a Man, 1958
Il taccuino del vecchio, 1960
Morte delle stagioni, 1967
Dialogo, 1968
Giuseppe Ungaretti: Selected Poems, 1969
Vita d'un uomo: Tutte le poesie, 1969
Selected Poems of Giuseppe Ungaretti, 1975
The Buried Harbour: Selected Poems of Giuseppe Ungaretti, 1990 (Kevin Hart, translator and editor)

A Major Selection of the Poetry of Giuseppe Ungaretti, 1997

OTHER LITERARY FORMS

Giuseppe Ungaretti published literary and critical essays as well as poetry. Perhaps as a consequence of the negative criticism his work drew at first, Ungaretti was concerned to show his connection with the greatest voices of the Italian literary tradition. In discussing the importance of Giacomo Leopardi, Petrarch, or the poets of the Baroque period, Ungaretti provided a framework that assists in the interpretation of his own work. These essays also contain autobiographical information and descriptions of travel and foreign places.

Ungaretti translated poetry by such diverse figures as William Shakespeare, William Blake, Luis de Góngora, Sergei Esenin, Jean Paulhan, Saint-John Perse, and Jean Baptiste Racine. Notable for the English reader is Ungaretti's essay on Shakespeare's sonnets, "Significato dei sonetti di Shakespeare," in *Vita d'un uomo: Saggi e interventi* (1974; life of a man: essays and interventions), and an essay accompanying his translations of Blake.

ACHIEVEMENTS

With Eugenio Montale and Salvatore Quasimodo, Giuseppe Ungaretti stands as a leader of contemporary Italian poetry. His is the first modern poetic idiom in Italian. He renewed interest in, and criticism of, the tradition of Italian poetry and is considered the father of the dominant school of poetry in Italy in the twentieth century, the hermetic school. Though he never won the Nobel Prize for Literature, he had a significant international reputation and influence. He won the most prestigious prizes in Italy; the earliest was the Gonfaloniere Prize in Venice in 1932, followed by the Premio Roma in 1949, the Premio Montefeltro from Urbino in 1960, and the Etna-Taormina International Poetry Prize in 1966. Outside Italy, his poetry was honored in 1956 when he shared the Knokke-le-Zoute Poetry Prize with Juan Ramón Jiménez and W. H. Auden; in 1970, he received the Books Abroad Award (now the Neustadt International Prize for Literature) at the University of Oklahoma.

Ungaretti was perhaps the major voice in establishing Leopardi as the most important traditional influence on Italian poetry of the first half of the twentieth century, for he found in Leopardi a bridge between his own poetics and the long Italian tradition that had begun with Petrarch. He also wrote significantly of Baroque poetry, of Shakespeare and Blake, and of several poets of the French tradition.

Difficult in its austere, understated beginnings, Ungaretti's poetry grew deeper and yet more complex as he became responsive to traditional metrics; indeed, he was often accused of purposeful obscurity. There was no doubt, however, that Ungaretti spoke to other poets, for when Francesco Flora called his poetry "hermetic" because of its subjective content, involuted forms, and French Symbolist influences, he was unwittingly acknowledging Ungaretti's leading position in Italian poetry. Ungaretti himself, however, did not remain within what came to be called the hermetic school. The hermetics, it might be claimed, developed mannerisms and an abstruse poetic idiom. Ungaretti, with a possible exception here and there, though writing a difficult poetry, always used that difficulty to intensify communication, and not merely for its own sake.

Giuseppe Ungaretti

Biography

Giuseppe Ungaretti was born on February 8, 1888, to Italian parents, Antonio and Maria Ungaretti, in Alexandria, Egypt. Ungaretti's parents had emigrated from an area near Lucca, Italy, to Egypt, where his father, who was employed for a short time at the Suez Canal site, contracted an illness that was to lead to his death in 1890. The Ungarettis had opened a bakery in the Arab quarter of the city, however, and Maria Ungaretti, after her husband's death, continued this business quite successfully.

Ungaretti's education was French, but he was familiar with the Italian intellectual scene in Alexandria. He knew the Italian writer Enrico Pea and frequented Pea's house, called the *baracca rossa*, a gathering place for anarchists. At this time, the period between 1906 and 1912, Ungaretti's interests included politics, for he wrote and published some political essays. More important, however, Ungaretti came to know several writers both from Alexandria and abroad. He corresponded with Giuseppe Prezzolini, editor of the important literary magazine *La voce*. It was through Prezzolini, in part, that Ungaretti met many of the most notable writers and artists of his day when he finally left Alexandria in 1912, at the age of twenty-four, to travel to Italy and then to Paris.

Paris was the place of Ungaretti's first self-awakening. There, he met with men such as artists Pablo Picasso, Georges Braque, Fernand Leger, Giorgio Di Chirico, writer Max Jacob, sculptor Amedeo Modigliani, the Italian Futurists, and others. In 1913, Ungaretti followed Henri Bergson's courses at the Collège de France; in the same year, Mohammed Sheab, Ungaretti's friend since childhood, unable to adjust to European life, committed suicide. Ungaretti remembered him in the poem "In Memoria" ("In Memoriam"): "And only I perhaps/ still know/ he lived," he wrote, foreshadowing, as Frederic C. Jones points out in *Giuseppe Ungaretti: Poet and Critic*, Ungaretti's conviction that immortality is gained only in the memory of others.

By 1914, Ungaretti was in Italy, where he wrote the first poems later collected in *L'allegria* (the joy). In 1915, he was inducted into the Italian army and was sent to the Austro-Italian Front. The poems of *Il porto sepolto* (the buried port) were written while Ungaretti was on active duty; these poems also became a part of *L'allegria*. Ungaretti did not want to print the poems written at the front, because he felt that such an act would break the solidarity he had with his countrymen, but a friend of his, Ettore Serra, took them and insisted on publishing them in 1916. In 1918, Ungaretti was in Paris again. (Guillaume Apollinaire, a friend of Ungaretti, died soon after he arrived.) He stayed in Paris until 1921, supporting himself by working for an Italian newspaper. While there, he met and married Jeanne Duprix. During this time, Ungaretti's reputation was growing, and he began lecturing in France and Belgium.

In 1921, Ungaretti returned to Rome, where he was to live until 1936. Here the Baroque art of the city had a great impact on him, and eventually this influence led to the writing of *Sentimento del tempo* (the feeling of time). He continued his lecturing and worked in the press division of the Foreign Ministry. In 1925, a daughter, Anna Maria, was born, and in 1930 a son, Antonietto. In 1931, *L'allegria* was given its definitive title and published; this collection included the poems from 1914 to 1919. In 1932, Ungaretti received the Venice Premio Gondoliere, and in 1933 *Sentimento del tempo* was published.

In 1936, Ungaretti accepted a teaching position in Italian literature at the University of São Paulo, Brazil. His stay in Brazil was a dark time, for in 1937 his older brother, Constantino, died, and in 1939 his son, Antonietto, died after a mistreated attack of appendicitis. The trials Italy faced during World War II compounded Ungaretti's sense of loss, and his writing from this period represents a hiatus in the unfolding of his poetic vision. *Il dolore* (the grief), which emerged from this time, was published in 1947.

When Ungaretti returned to Italy in 1942, he accepted a position at the University of Rome. After the war, his right to retain his teaching post was disputed, for many criticized his apparent acceptance of fascism. In spite of this controversy, he retained his position and was very productive during the period following the war. Most of his translations were published during this time, as were several commemorative editions of his works. In his seventieth year, his wife, Jeanne, died.

During his last years, Ungaretti traveled around the world. In 1964, he gave a series of lectures at Columbia University in New York City. On a visit to São Paulo in 1966, Ungaretti met a young Brazilian poetess named Bruna Bianco, with whom he pursued a platonic love affair. *Dialogo* is a poetic dialogue between them. In 1967, *Morte delle stagioni* (death of the seasons), which collected the poems of Ungaretti's old age, was published. Ungaretti was to have one more passionate relationship, with a young Croatian girl, Djuna. In 1970 he traveled again to the United States to receive the Books Abroad Award at the University of Oklahoma. While on this trip, he developed bronchitis. He died in Milan on the night of June 1, 1970.

ANALYSIS

Giuseppe Ungaretti believed that great poets write "seemly biographies," for "poetry is the discovery of the human condition in its essence." Friendship, love, death, and man's fate, the great lyric themes, are the subjects of Ungaretti's poetry. Though his poems show a contemporary concern for autobiographical material, they blend this material with the imagery of the poetic tradition. The form of this poetry is discontinuous, sensuous, and elusive. Metonymy, hyperbaton, ellipsis, surprising juxtapositions of images, and the cultivation of unusual language are all characteristic of Ungaretti's style.

As "seemly biography," Ungaretti's lifework developed with the movement of his experience. His first major collection, *L'allegria*, reflected his experience of World War I. *Sentimento del tempo*, written during his first extended stay in Rome, unfolded around a religious crisis. *Il dolore*, the book Ungaretti said he loved most, chronicled the poet's struggle to come to terms with the loss of his brother and son and the disaster Italy faced at the end of World War II. *La terra promessa* (the promised land) and the later works grew out of the realization that aging and its consequences, the fading of the senses and of feeling, offer a final challenge to the poet.

L'ALLEGRIA

Ungaretti's first major collection, *L'allegria*, includes revisions of two earlier collections, *Il porto sepolto* and *Allegria di naufragi*, which had been published separately, as well as a group of poems written in France just before World War I. *L'allegria* is a work of self-discovery. In his notes to *Il porto sepolto*, Ungaretti says that though his first awakenings came in Paris, it was not until the war that he fully came to know himself. The young Ungaretti was an atheist. There was for him no God, nor any Platonic ideals, somehow infiltrating time, to serve as a basis for life's meaning. The war and its desolate landscapes came to take on something of the significance of his youthful experience of the desert. The desert was a void—as such it represented the emptiness of blind existence—but the desert was also a space in which mirages could blossom. So, too, the war brought Ungaretti to the bones of existence, and there he discovered his courage. The self-discovery he spoke of was the courage to resist the sweep of objective, hence depersonalized, events that depress the human spirit and force it into a life of merely private pleasures and pains. Poetry was the courage to transform the worn images of everyday existence into the perfection of dreams, to find an eternal moment even in the face of desolation. Of all the poets of World War I, Ungaretti is arguably the most affirmative. He cries out in "Pellegrinaggio" ("The Pilgrimage"), "Ungaretti/ man of pain/ you need but an illusion/ to give you courage."

Also arising from Ungaretti's Alexandrian experience of the desert is his identification of himself as a Bedouin poet. This image emerges as central in *L'allegria* and recurs throughout his works in any number of transformations. Ungaretti implies in the use of this image that the poet cannot be submerged in the familiar. Movement and change nourish the quintessential condition of poetry, *disponibilità* (availability to things). The Bedouin nature of the poet is required by the solitary reality that the emptiness of blind existence imposes on him. In the poem "Agonia" ("Agony"), Ungaretti pulls these themes together:

> To die at the mirage
> like thirsty skylarks
> Or like the quail
> past the sea
> in the first thickets
> when it has lost
> the will to fly
> But not to live on lament
> like a blinded finch.

The migration of the Bedouin, like that of birds, is a kind of eternal return. Human individuals are not lost in time

if they allow the mirage (beauty, or the flash of poetic insight) to beckon them to the depths of experience. The Bedouin poet's courage is his recognition that thirst and the loss of the will to fly are circumstances, as death is a circumstance. Though he knows that these will overtake him, they do not diminish his passion for flight and song. The poet is always moving back, but with openness; the truth he finds can be held in an image, briefly, but it can never become fixed or permanent. Ungaretti's spirit persists in its capacity to evoke the dream in the midst of the wasteland.

Ungaretti's poetic vision shares a great deal with that of the French Symbolists, for whom the world is a kind of nullity until it is transformed by human subjectivity—hence Charles Baudelaire's celebrated notion that man knows the world through "forests of symbols." In Ungaretti's poem "Eterno" ("Eternal"), there is a whole poetics in epigrammatic form: "Between one flower gathered and the other given/ the inexpressible null. . . ." If the gathering and giving of the flower stand for poetry, then every poem results from a struggle with the inexpressible, what Ungaretti calls the void, or blind existence. As in the Platonic idea of recollection, the soul perfects itself only through repeated struggles with forgetfulness until it gains real knowledge; so too, in Ungaretti, a movement through repeated loss and gain is implied. In his work, however, this movement is one of renewing, or re-creating, in such a way that the poet, thereby humankind, is brought in touch with his deepest nature.

In *L'allegria*, Ungaretti abandoned the rhetorical devices that had become rife in nineteenth century Italian poetry. He conceived the poet's task to be an "excavation of the word" to release its latent power and music. In "Commiato" ("Leavetaking"), Ungaretti addresses his friend Ettore Serra, saying, "poetry/ is the world humanity/ one's own life/ flowering from the word," and concluding, "When I find/ in this my silence/ a word/ it is dug into my life/ like an abyss." The abyss of which he speaks here is not the nullity between the gathered and the given word; it is, rather, the depth of memory that carries back beyond the individual into a mythic past. The abyss is present not in the expressive content of the words but in their power. "To find a *parola* [word]," Ungaretti declared in a note to the poems in *L'allegria*, "means to penetrate into the dark abyss of the self without disturbing it and without succeeding in learning its secret."

The culmination of this vision in *L'allegria* is found in the poem "I fiumi" ("The Rivers"), which opens with a scene from the battlefront. It is evening, a world of moonlight; a crippled tree evokes the desolation of war. The poet recalls that in the morning, he had "stretched out/ in an urn of water/ and like a relic/ rested." This is a ritual act, a baptism, for the poem goes on to recount something of a rebirth. Each epoch of the poet's life is represented by a river—the Isonzo, the river of war; the Serchio, the river of his forefathers; the Nile, the river of his birth and unconsciousness; and the Seine, the river of awakening self-awareness: "These are the rivers/ counted in the Isonzo." In the ancient image of the river, Ungaretti captures the subjective moment in which all the branches of his existence blossom together. Such a moment is a consolation and a confirmation of a path but is at the same time evanescent. There is the tantalizing sense that while the outward rivers are in a moment of vision, harmonious with the flow of one's life, such moments do not last: "My torment/ is when/ I do not feel I am/ in harmony." Nevertheless, Ungaretti suggests that there is a power working through his experience which is not identifiable with himself: "hands/ that knead me/ give me/ rare/ felicity." In *Giuseppe Ungaretti*, Jones suggests that "hands" refers to the power of ancestors working through the poet and establishing a bond between him and his tradition. However one interprets this image, it is a statement of conviction that the poet has tapped the depths of his being. Unlike his friend Mohammed Sheab, who ". . . could not/ set free/ the song/ of his abandon," Ungaretti found his voice. The poem concludes: "Now my life seems to me/ a corolla/ of shadows."

SENTIMENTO DEL TEMPO

The poems of Ungaretti's second major collection, *Sentimento del tempo*, grew out of a confrontation with the spirit of Rome. Jones paraphrases Ungaretti's reaction to the art of Rome: ". . . [he] tells us that the greatest shock he received after his transfer to Rome was precisely the sight of a totally Baroque architecture, one which on the surface at least appeared to lack all sense

of cohesion and unity." After that initial shock, he came to feel that in the Baroque style, things are "blown into the air," and the resultant fragmentation opens the way for a new ordering of things.

For Ungaretti, the Baroque bespeaks the absence of God. In Baroque art, the sense of absence is covered by an elaboration of sensuous detail and by the use of *trompe l'oeil*. Although Ungaretti saw in this expression of God's absence another manifestation of the emptiness of blind existence, the rhetorical responses of the Baroque did not appeal to him. Poetry was an exploration of the real; he would not abandon the concentrated forms of his first poems. Nevertheless, Baroque poetry gave him access to traditional meters and harmonies, and these he did employ. As he said in a note to *Sentimento del tempo*, he intially wanted to recover "the naturalness and depth and rhythm in the significance of each individual word," but his new project was "to find an accord between our traditional metrics and the expressive needs of today."

The traditional metrics of which he speaks were the hendecasyllable (as in Geoffrey Chaucer's "Whan that Aprill with his shoures soote/ The droghte of March hath perced to the roote") and the seven-syllable line, or *settinario*. These metrics are not simply imposed on his poetry. They are filtered through his intuition, syncopated, and brought together with a poetic style which remains staccato. Moments of passion are drawn out by the music of the line, which Ungaretti understood to be the actual rhythm of man's deepest self. The fragmented modern vision is sustained by underlying harmonies. A surface coherence of images achieved through rhetorical devices would be simply linear in its structure; musical harmonies in their polyvalence and rich suggestiveness make possible a multidimensional and deeper union of self and work.

French philosopher Henri Bergson, with whom Ungaretti had studied in Paris, provided the poet with one of the central distinctions of his poetics. Bergson distinguished between two forms of memory: voluntary and involuntary. Voluntary memory is analogous to the sense of space which focuses on space as an aggregate of discrete parts. Life, however, is primarily temporal, not spatial, and this analogy between memory and space conveys the essentially superficial character of voluntary memory. In voluntary memory, man stands in an extrinsic relationship to his past; forgetfulness is the essence of such a relationship. Ungaretti saw in this idea the psychological symbol for the void. What Bergson called involuntary memory, however, was as a unified flow. In involuntary memory, everything is retained. One gains access to involuntary memory through free action, action in which the past flows into and enriches the present. Ungaretti saw in involuntary memory the concept that would unify his poetics: Poetry was a mode of free action. Blending autobiographical elements with the appropriate imagery and language of the tradition, Ungaretti felt that he had returned to the living reality of poetry: a momentary making conscious of the collective unconscious.

Sentimento del tempo is written in several sections. "Fine di Crono" ("The End of Chronos") is both the title of a poem and the name of an important section of the work. Ungaretti presupposes a knowledge of the underlying myth: the murder of Chronos by his son, Zeus, who in his action revolted against the dark world of the Titans and successfully established the world of justice, the Olympian world. For Ungaretti, this revolution reflects the discovery of the deeper, liberating flow of memory beneath the fragmented memory of blind existence. Ungaretti, however, radically alters the traditional association of the Olympians with light. He associates the deeper sense of memory with the inner, subjective world of man; hence, things must be drawn out of the daylight experience of life into the world of memory and imagination that he associates with night. As Jones points out, "the poet tends to employ an inversionary technique throughout *Sentimento del tempo*, upturning the respective values of life and death." Ungaretti carries this inversion as far as he can, making death the realm of perfection and day the realm of imperfection—imagery recalling Plato's dialogue *Phaedo* (fourth century B.C.E.) in which Socrates argues that philosophy is a preparation for death. True life is the life of the spirit, and what most people take as life, the life of enjoyment, is death. Such a view expresses an ultimate human desire to give even death, that unknown standing wholly outside experience, a meaning.

The central collection of *Sentimento del tempo* is "Inni" ("Hymns"), whose subject is a religious crisis.

Here Ungaretti introduces the idea of *pietà* (compassion, pity, or piety), which fuses the ancient notion of respect for ancestors with the Christian notion of love for all humankind. In these poems, Ungaretti's self-declared condition is that of alienation, and through *pietà* he seeks a sense of solidarity with his fellowman. This search adds a moral dimension to the ambitions of a poet whose earlier works might be taken as seeking purely aesthetic resolutions.

The poem in "Hymns" titled "La pietà" ("Pity") is the most important single poem in *Sentimento del tempo*. It opens with an echo of Ungaretti's earlier self-depiction as "a man of pain." "I am a wounded man," he declares dramatically, going on to describe himself as an exile. This sense of exile is the profoundest sense of being out of harmony with the depth of experience Ungaretti has yet expressed: "I have peopled the silence with names./ Have I torn heart and mind to shreds/ to fall into the slavery of words?/ I rule over phantoms." Ungaretti conjures up his previous work and throws its value into doubt. The absence of God confronts the poet with the possibility that he has built on sand. In this, he is like Michelangelo, whom he regarded as the greatest Baroque artist (and after a group of whose works this poem is titled).

The second section of "Pity" develops the inversion of death and life met within all the sections of *Sentimento del tempo*. "They [the dead] are the seed that bursts within our dreams," he says. If there is a road open to God, it must be by way of memorial reawakening and restoration of the past. This is the very path that has led Ungaretti to the possibility of despair, but just as the desert had the double significance of the void and the mirage, so also might Ungaretti's religious despair be the other face of hope.

In "Pity," Ungaretti achieved something akin to prayer, but there was no discovery of a way back to a poetry of the divine. The poem's fourth section is, therefore, a portrayal of human life without God. "Man, monotonous universe," it begins. Every human action, considered by itself, is a frustration: "Nothing issues endlessly but limits." When man tries to turn toward God, "He has but blasphemies." This final line echoes the earlier ". . . do those who implore you/ Only know you by name?" "Pity" ends, then, without resolution.

Ungaretti has moved away from the atheism of his early years—in fact, he embraced Roman Catholicism—but, in his poetry, the stance of this Bedouin poet is that of an agnostic who seeks to believe. There is no room for dogma here.

In *La Poesia di Ungaretti* (1976), Glauco Cambon suggests that the metaphysical connection among memory, consciousness of the void, and "the dream of becoming" is paralleled in Ungaretti's later work by a moral connection among innocence, sin, and conscience. What had been, in the earlier work, the condition of man lost in blind existence deepens in the later work, taking on the significance of the Fall. Indeed, the next section of *Sentimento del tempo*, titled "La morte meditata" ("Death Meditated"), takes place in the Garden of Eden, and Eve is its central figure. Ungaretti gives a particularly modern shading to Eve by introducing an element of sensuality; he does this in order to include the sensuous, poetry's medium, in an image of restored innocence. As the symbol of restored innocence, Eve carries the double significance of death as a realm of perfection and as the realm of the terrible loss of innocence. If death is another face of blind existence, then Eve emerges against the void of death as the mirage emerges upon the desert. Ungaretti's choice of a female symbol to express the restored innocence for which poetry strives is characteristically Italian, recalling Petrarch's Laura, Dante's Beatrice, and Leopardi's Silvia.

IL DOLORE

The poems of *Il dolore* grew out of Ungaretti's experience of profound loss. In a poem about his brother Constantino's death, he writes: "I have lost all of childhood—/ Never again can I/ Forget myself in a cry." This nihilistic chord underlies the "bitter accord" of the collection.

"Tu ti spezzisti" ("You Shattered") is the greatest poem of the collection. It opens with the alien Brazilian landscape—a landscape unnerving and threatening: "That swarm of scattered, huge, gray stones/ Still quivering in secret slings/ Of stifled flames of origin. . . ." The references to nonhuman creation call to mind the poetic task of inwardly re-creating the world, but this landscape is presented with a force and a strangeness that make such a task overwhelming, if not impossible.

Against this landscape, Antonietto, Ungaretti's son who died, is likened to a small bird: on the one hand, the recalcitrantly primitive and foreboding; on the other hand, the fragile but keenly alive. Disaster is inevitable. "How could you not have shattered/ In a blindness so inflexible/ You, simple breath and crystal." The oppressive powers that brought down this small life are focused by reference to the sun: "Too human dazzling for the ruthless,/ Savage, droning, tenacious/ Roar of naked sun."

The rest of *Il dolore* grows out of a preoccupation with the possible destruction of Italy. A notable aspect of these poems is the emergence of the figure of Christ. Like Michelangelo, who desired faith but from whom God hid himself, Ungaretti might be seen as an odd sort of agnostic. The Christ of Ungaretti's poems is modified by the poet's humanism.

LA TERRA PROMESSA

La terra promessa contains poems written in the early 1930's, although the volume was not published until 1950. If, as Ungaretti says, the dominant season of *Sentimento del tempo* is summer, then the dominant season of *La terra promessa* is autumn. In this season, as Jones comments, "detached as the aging mind becomes from the flesh, it begins to see the world as a sensational Pascalian abyss . . . , which neither the fancy nor the imagination can any longer bridge over." Blaise Pascal, however, took joy in the promised liberation from the senses, something that Ungaretti cannot do. There would be no way to the restoration of "innocence with memory" without the sensuous imagination. For Ungaretti, the separation of sense and mind—the dying of sense—which threatens to undermine the poet's immediate engagement with things can be overcome through memory. The poet returns to the memories of youth to restructure them out of the knowledge of a full life, breathing new life into them.

The "promised land" of which Ungaretti speaks is promised because it is the place of renewed innocence. This symbol repeats and transforms his attempt to resolve the problem which was central to his writing from the beginning: How, without absolutes, does one live a human life in time? The answer he gave should be seen against a guiding mythology. As he says in *Vita d'un uomo: Tutto le poesie:*

Once upon a time there was a pure universe, humanly speaking . . . an absurdity: an immaterial materiality. This purity became a material materiality as a result of some offence perpetrated against the Creator by who knows what event. But anyway, through some extraordinary happening of a cosmic order, this material became corrupt—thereby time originated, and history originated. This is my manner of feeling things, it is not the truth, but it is a way of feeling: I feel things in this way.

This note to the poems of *La terra promessa* makes clear Ungaretti's mythological cast of mind. The Golden Age cannot be restored, but its power can be evoked by a process of memory akin to the ritual. Poems are such evocations, and in this collection, the rites of poetry are reconstitutions of memories through the informing insight of maturity. If old age is characterized by the decline, even death, of the senses, this does not imply that there is no bridge between the sensuous visions of youth and the understanding of old age. A purification of memory is possible, and such a purification leads back through the "tunnel of time" to innocence.

The key figure in this collection is Aeneas, though he never takes the stage, and the *Aeneid* (29-19 B.C.E.) of Vergil is a source of much of its symbolic material. One of the most important poems of the collection is titled "Cori descrittivi di stati d'animo di Didone" ("Choruses Descriptive of Dido's States of Mind"). In this group of nineteen fragments, the passing of Dido's beauty is mourned. This image has obvious resonance with the image of Eve as a figure of lost innocence, but only to contrast Dido with Eve. Dido is ultimately lost. She is here, as she was for Vergil, the contrast to Aeneas's virtue. She has no inner spiritual world. If Dido negatively echoes Eve, Aeneas positively echoes the image of the Bedouin poet.

Ungaretti's lifework was to open a way to cultural origins by means of his adventure in language. For Ungaretti, whatever measure of salvation can be found is to be found only through history. Man is alone, but through *pietà* he can move beyond his alienation toward solidarity with his fellows. The poet's access to the cultural flow of memory is gained through language. The language of poetry, Ungaretti said, is always in crisis,

but this is a condition of its renewal. Through the purification of language, the poet hands on the tradition intact and creatively reworked. In doing so, he holds open the possibility of perpetual renewal.

OTHER MAJOR WORKS

NONFICTION: *Il povero nella citta*, 1949; *Il deserto e dopo*, 1961; *Innocence et memoire*, 1969; *Lettere a un fenomenologo*, 1972; *Vita d'un uomo: Saggi e interventi*, 1974.

TRANSLATIONS: *Traduzioni*, 1936 (various poems and authors); *Venti-due sonetti de Shakespeare: Scelti e tradotti da Giuseppe Ungaretti*, 1944; *Vita d'un uomo: Quaranta sonetti di Shakespeare tradotti*, 1946; *L'Après-midi et le monologue d'un faune di Mallarmé*, 1947; *Vita d'un uomo: Da Góngora e da Mallarmé*, 1948; *Vita d'un uomo: Fedra di Jean Racine*, 1950; *Finestra del caos*, 1961 (of Murilo Mendes); *Vita d'un uomo: Visioni di William Blake*, 1965.

BIBLIOGRAPHY

Godorecci, Maurizio. "The Poetics of the Word in Ungaretti." *Romance Languages Annual* 9 (1997): 197-201. A critical analysis of selected poems by Ungaretti.

Jones, Frederic J. *Giuseppe Ungaretti: Poet and Critic*. Edinburgh: Edinburgh University Press, 1977. An assessment of Ungaretti's life and career. Includes bibliographic references.

Moevs, Christian. "Ungaretti: A Reading of 'Alla noia.'" *Forum Italicum* 25, no. 2 (Fall, 1991): 211-227. A critical study of one of Ungaretti's poems.

O'Connor, Desmond. "The Poetry of a Patriot: Ungaretti and the First World War." *Journal of the Australasian Universities Language and Literature Association* 56 (November, 1981): 201-218. An analysis of Ungaretti's poetic treatment of the First World War.

Samson-Talleur, Linda. "Ungaretti, Leopardi, and the Shipwreck of the Soul." *Chimeres* 16, no. 1 (Autumn, 1982): 5-19. A comparative study of the works of two poets.

Robert Colucci;
bibliography updated by the editors

LOUIS UNTERMEYER

Born: New York, New York; October 1, 1885
Died: Newtown, Connecticut; December 18, 1977

PRINCIPAL POETRY

The Younger Quire, 1911
First Love, 1911
Challenge, 1914
. . . and Other Poets, 1916
These Times, 1917
Including Horace, 1919
The New Adam, 1920
Heavens, 1922
Roast Leviathan, 1923
Collected Parodies, 1926
Poems, 1927 (with Richard Untermeyer)
Burning Bush, 1928
Adirondack Cycle, 1929
Food and Drink, 1932
First Words Before Spring, 1933
Selected Poems and Parodies, 1935
Long Feud: Selected Poems, 1962

OTHER LITERARY FORMS

Louis Untermeyer's poetry represents only a fraction of his total work. He put his name on well over a hundred books, ranging from *The Kitten Who Barked* (1962, a children's story) to *A Treasury of Ribaldry* (1956), and from his historical novel *Moses* (1928) to *A Century of Candymaking, 1937-1947* (1947). Most of his effort, however, went into four areas: anthologies of poetry, criticism, biography, and children's literature. Some of the most important works that he edited were *Modern American Poetry* (1919), *Modern British Poetry* (1920), and *A Treasury of Great Poems* (1942, 1955). He broke new ground in criticism with *The New Era in American Poetry* (1919, 1970) and provided a useful literary reappraisal in the book he edited *American Poetry from the Beginning to Whitman* (1931). His early textbook *Poetry: Its Understanding and Enjoyment* (1934, with Carter Davidson) paved the way for Cleanth Brooks and Robert Penn Warren's *Understanding Poetry* (1938) and a host of others. Although Untermeyer published one massive analytical biography, *Heinrich Heine: Paradox and Poet* (1937), he was better known for the biographical essays in *Makers of the Modern World* (1955) and *Lives of the Poets* (1959). Untermeyer's contributions to children's literature include collections of poetry such as *This Singing World* (1923-1926) and *Stars to Steer By* (1941), as well as many stories and collections of stories—among them, *Chip: My Life and Times* (1933), *The Donkey of God* (winner of the 1932 Italian Enit Award for a book on Italy by a non-Italian), *The Last Pirate: Tales from the Gilbert and Sullivan Operas* (1934), and *The Golden Treasury of Children's Literature* (1959, with Byrna Untermeyer).

ACHIEVEMENTS

Louis Untermeyer exerted a shaping influence on modern American poetry. That influence, however, did not derive from his own voluminous verse. Indeed, Untermeyer has not been greatly honored as a poet. His verse has escaped the scrutiny of modern scholars and his work was never awarded a Pulitzer Prize, although he did serve as the United States Poet Laureate Consultant in Poetry from 1961 to 1963. Moreover, Untermeyer seemed to regret his poetic profligacy and lamented that "too many facile lines of praise and protest" had filled his volumes. In *Long Feud*, he trimmed the canon of poems he cared to preserve to a spartan 118 pages.

If Untermeyer's impact as a poet was limited, his impact as a critic, critical biographer, and anthologist was almost limitless. He has been described as Robert Frost's Boswell, but he really ought to be seen as a twentieth century version of James Boswell and Samuel Johnson combined. Through appreciative reviews, loving editorial labors, and reverent selections in his anthologies, Untermeyer was able to do more for Frost than Boswell ever did for Johnson. Moreover, Untermeyer's engaging *Lives of the Poets* is a worthy sequel to Johnson's biographical sketches and is massively supplemented by the scientific, political, and literary biographies in his *Makers of the Modern World*.

Although Untermeyer modestly understated his contribution to Frost's success, Frost himself was quick to acknowledge it, saying publicly, "Sometimes I think I am a figment of Louis' imagination." Indeed, in an article for the Chicago *Evening Post* on April 23, 1915,

Untermeyer became the first reviewer in America to praise Frost's *North of Boston* (1914). He was the second scholar to praise Frost's poetry in a book, *The New Era in American Poetry*, and he was among the first to include Frost in an anthology.

As the friendship between the two poets strengthened, Untermeyer's advocacy continued. Every new edition of *Modern American Poetry* included more poems by Frost, who wrote appreciatively to his friend in 1941, "I look on [the anthology] as having done more to spread my poetry than any one other thing." Untermeyer continued to write warm reviews of Frost's poetry; he became Frost's earliest biographer; and he published the first volume of Frost's letters and conversations. In 1943, Untermeyer made himself "somewhat unpleasant" with his fellow judges on the Pulitzer Poetry Jury by insisting in a minority report that the year's prize should be awarded to *A Witness Tree*, making Frost the only author ever to win four Pulitzer Prizes.

What Untermeyer did massively for Frost, he did less passionately but just as selflessly for many other poets. *The New Era in American Poetry* devoted whole chapters to Vachel Lindsay, Carl Sandburg, Edwin Arlington Robinson, Amy Lowell, Edgar Lee Masters, and Ezra Pound, while also giving prominence to Sara Teasdale, Hilda Doolittle, Stephen Vincent Benét, and William Rose Benét. His ten editions of *Modern American Poetry* and nine editions of *Modern British Poetry* helped to win recognition and popularity for three generations of young poets. His service for nearly a quarter century as chairman of the Pulitzer Poetry Jury allowed him to assist the careers of Mark Van Doren, both Benéts, Karl Shapiro, Robert Lowell, W. H. Auden, Peter Viereck, Gwendolyn Brooks, Carl Sandburg, Marianne Moore, Archibald MacLeish, Theodore Roethke, Wallace Stevens, Elizabeth Bishop, Richard Wilbur, Robert Penn Warren, Stanley Kunitz, W. D. Snodgrass, Phyllis McGinley, and William Carlos Williams. He served as Merrill Moore's literary adviser during Moore's life, and he was a faithful literary executor after Moore's death.

In brief, through poems, lectures, reviews, anthologies, and personal services, Untermeyer did more than any of his contemporaries to win a popular audience for modern poetry.

Louis Untermeyer (Hulton Archive)

BIOGRAPHY

Louis Untermeyer was born in 1885 into a well-to-do family of German-Jewish jewelers. His formal education ended at fifteen when he refused to return to high school and discovered that Columbia University would not admit him without passing marks in algebra and geometry. He then worked in the family jewelry business while establishing his career as a poet and literary jack-of-all-trades. His literary successes allowed him to devote less and less time to the jewelry business until he formally resigned at the age of thirty-seven.

Untermeyer eventually moved away from New York City and bought Stony Water, a 160-acre farm in the Adirondacks that became the setting for some of his finest lyrics. Although he continued to earn his living through writing and lecturing, he made a brief stab at commercial farming, raising Hampshire pigs and Jersey cows, tapping maples, harvesting apples, and marketing Stony Water preserves. In his autobiography *Bygones: The Recollections of Louis Untermeyer* (1965), Untermeyer compared his situation with that of the gentleman farmer who celebrated the first anniversary of his venture into dairy farming by proposing a toast: "Friends," he said, "you will notice that there are two shaped bottles on the table. One shape contains champagne; the other contains milk. Help yourself to them carefully; they cost the same per quart."

The outbreak of World War II brought Untermeyer back to the city. He joined the Office of War Information, where he worked with Howard Fast, Santha Rama Rau, and the film director John Houseman. Later, as editor of the Armed Services Editions, Untermeyer oversaw the republication of forty works of literature a month. By the end of the war, he had helped to deliver some 122,000,000 books into the hands of American's servicemen.

When the war ended, Untermeyer wished to remain in a salaried position for a variety of reasons, not the least of which was the expense associated with his growing contingent of ex-wives. He accepted a position with Decca Records directing their efforts to sell recordings of plays and poetry. In 1950, he became a celebrity as one of the original panelists on CBS-TV's *What's My Line?* McCarthyism was, however, frothing and unfettered in the early 1950's, and Untermeyer became its victim, not because of communist sympathies on his part, but because nearly forty years earlier he had published a book titled *Challenge* (criticized at the time for too lavish praise of democracy) and worked on a liberal magazine called *The Masses*. The baseless hostility of the self-appointed censors was sufficiently rabid that Untermeyer was forced from the show and even from public life.

He retreated to the Connecticut countryside where he soon became intimate with Arthur Miller, Van Wyck Brooks, Robert Penn Warren, Malcolm Cowley, and actress Margaret Sullavan. Untermeyer's complete repatriation did not come until 1961, when he was honored by being chosen Consultant in Poetry to the Library of Congress. During the next two years, he was twice asked by the State Department to serve as a literary ambassador, giving lectures in India and Japan. In 1963, Untermeyer returned to his home in Connecticut, where he wrote his memoirs, published books for children, and continued to update his anthologies until his death on December 18, 1977.

The love of poetry demonstrated in Untermeyer's anthologies was in large part a love of passion, and for him a life of emotion was not a vicarious ideal only. In life, particularly in married life, Untermeyer experienced every variation of happiness, heartache, and humorous complexity. In all, he was married six times and divorced five times by a total of four women. In 1907, he married his first wife, the respected poet Jean Starr; he divorced her sixteen years later in Mexico and remarried her shortly thereafter in New Jersey (*not* New York, since state law there held that he had always remained married to Jean). These complications led Louis to wonder "which state was the state of matrimony" and whether he "might be committing bigamy by illegally marrying the same wife twice." Virginia, his second wife, married Louis in Mexico in 1923, became pregnant in Switzerland, delivered a baby in London, and divorced Louis (who had returned to Jean) in Missouri— all within a period of two years. Esther, the third wife and a lawyer, helped Louis to obtain a second Mexican divorce from Jean—this time by mail. Esther then married Louis in 1933 in a ceremony performed, appropriately, by a professional comedian. Louis and Esther lived together in contentment for a number of years before they gradually drifted apart. At sixty-two, Untermeyer divorced Esther in Mexico to marry his fourth wife, Byrna. When Esther learned of the divorce, she sued, alleging that Louis's Mexican divorce from Jean had been valid, while his Mexican divorce from her was not. The somewhat bemused judge ruled that Untermeyer had never been married to Esther or Virginia, was not married to Byrna, and remained legally tied to Jean from whom he had been separated for more than twenty years. Untermeyer subsequently persuaded Jean to divorce him in Nevada (their third divorce) so that he could marry Byrna a second time and live legally with the woman he loved.

Despite his fondness for children, Untermeyer was generally too busy to take much part in rearing his own sons. Richard, his son by his first wife, hanged himself at the age of nineteen. His second son, John, was reared by Virginia, who rarely allowed Louis to see the child. His adopted sons, Lawrence and Joseph, were reared less by Untermeyer than by his caretakers at Stony Water.

ANALYSIS

The qualities of mind and temperament that made Louis Untermeyer such a superb anthologist kept him from attaining the same level of excellence in his poetry. He was too appreciative of the moods, approaches, and words of others—too prone to imitation and parody. He was rarely able to find his own voice; or rather, his *own* voice was often the mockingbird's, wryly reproducing the songs of others. Moreover, the virtues of his impressionistic criticism—directness and clarity—were poetic vices in a period of Empsonian ambiguity.

Untermeyer's poems fall into five broad categories: parodies; modern recreations of religious or mythological events; adaptations of another poet's spirit, tone, or verse form; idealistic exhortations concerning social consciousness; and a few entirely new creations. Thus, Untermeyer's poems range from the overtly imitative to the mildly innovative. They vary widely in subject and style, but are unified by romanticism undercut with irony. This romanticism was a fundamental part of Untermeyer's personality. It guided him as he exuberantly collected belongings, friends, experiences, passions, and poems.

The instincts of a romantic collector were evident throughout Untermeyer's life. His earliest memories were of the "colorful mélange" of assorted portraits, porcelains, and petit-point cushions that littered his parent's home. During reveries before a Dutch landscape or a jeweled bird, Untermeyer's mind turned to fantasy, while his taste was tutored by delight in the diversity of the family's collections. His love of fantasy led him to read, as he put it, "a hodge-podge of everything I could lay my mind on": *The Arabian Nights' Entertainments* (c. 1450), the Rover Boys, *The Three Musketeers* (1844), *The Rime of the Ancient Mariner* (1798), Jean de La Fontaine's *Fables* (1668, 1673-1679, 1694), Alfred, Lord Tennyson's *Idylls of the King* (1859-1885), Dante's *Inferno*, and so on. This eclectic but diverting reading in bed by night naturally reduced Untermeyer to mediocrity in school by day. He found the classroom too limiting and controlled in its approach to life and learning.

Thus, at the age of seventeen, Untermeyer entered the family jewelry business—the first in what was to become the startlingly diverse collection of his occupations. Yet, even the jewelry business was too mundane for Louis. He devoted long afternoons to the unfinished verses he kept concealed in his desk beneath production reports and packets of gemstones. In the evenings he wrote poems and reviews, for which he found a ready market. His earliest collection of poems, *First Love*, was a vanity press edition subsidized by his father, but its sales quickly offset the cost of publication. His next volume, *Challenge*, was picked up by the Century Company, and Untermeyer's germinating poetic career obtained a firm roothold.

The dual careers of poet and businessman were insufficient to quench Untermeyer's romantic thirst for experience. He used his contacts in the literary world to help him to his third career as a magazine editor. He first obtained a position as a contributing editor to *The Masses*, where he made friends of such prominent left-wing personalities as Max Eastman and John Reed. He then became one of the founding editors of *The Seven Arts*, a short-lived (1916-1917) literary magazine that published pieces by Sherwood Anderson, D. H. Lawrence, Carl Sandburg, Robert Frost, Eugene O'Neill, Vachel Lindsay, and John Dewey. From 1918 to 1924, he was a contributing editor to the *Liberator*, from 1934 to 1937 he was poetry editor of the *American Mercury*, and for many years he wrote a weekly column for the *Saturday Review* (until 1952, *The Saturday Review of Literature*).

In 1919, Untermeyer collected and revised a number of his impressionistic reviews and published them in *The New Era in American Poetry*. When Alfred Harcourt decided to bring out an anthology of modern American poetry, Untermeyer was the logical editor. *Modern American Poetry* was followed in the next year by *Modern British Poetry*. Thus, Untermeyer, who had already been a success as a jeweler, poet, and magazine editor, now assumed the role of anthologist. It was the right task for a man who, by his own confession, had "the mind of a magpie" and who collected stamps, flowers, pictures of actresses in cigarette packs, cats (both living and artificial), careers, and wives. This multiplicity of interests continued to shape Untermeyer's life. In subsequent years, he became a gentleman farmer, publisher, record producer, and television celebrity. Despite these varied careers, Untermeyer always felt most at home at his desk. There, he wrote, "I am doing what I am supposed to do: fulfilling my function whether I write in the role of biographer, storyteller, editor of anthologies, impressionistic critic, or, occasionally, poet." The order of those activities says much about Untermeyer's own priorities and poetic self-image.

WORKS OF PARODY

For a collector who wished to be a poet, parody was the natural literary mode. Indeed, Untermeyer's first booklet, *The Younger Quire*, was a parody of *The Younger Choir*, an anthology of youthful poets (including Untermeyer) that was introduced and lavishly praised by Edwin Markham. Untermeyer's parody came to exactly twenty-four pages (one quire) and included a series of "back-of-the-hand tributes" combining "simulated innocence and real malice." He continued to write burlesques throughout his long career, publishing them in *. . . and Other Poets*, *Including Horace*, *Collected Parodies*, and *Selected Poems and Parodies*.

RELIGIOUS THEMES

Parody is, however, parasitic, and Untermeyer was too thoughtful and creative to remain locked into such a limited style. In another large group of poems, the penchant for parody is reined in as Untermeyer re-creates a religious, mythological, or literary event from a modern perspective. In "Eve Speaks," for example, Eve asks God to pause before judging her. She argues that Eden was a place for child's play and angelic calm but not a place for Adam who, being neither child nor angel, was formed to struggle and create. Untermeyer implies that eating the fruit of the tree of knowledge was essential to human fulfillment and that God had been wrong to forbid it. Thus, the poem is a typical statement of Untermeyer's philosophy of life. He implies that the Judeo-Christian religions have distorted the old myths in an effort to impose order and morality. For Untermeyer, the romantic collector, life is only truly lived through struggle, passion, sexuality, creation, and experience. All of these were to be gained only through knowledge, the forbidden fruit.

Untermeyer's romantic sensuality led him to fill his poems with descriptions of almost Keatsian opulence and vividness. The terrors of Judgment Day, for example, are suggested by phenomena: "trampling winds," "stark and cowering skies," "the red flame" of God's anger licking up worlds, the stars falling "in a golden rain."

Here, the pathetic fallacy, which often mars other descriptions by Untermeyer, becomes an effective indication of God's fearful power; before his wrath, the elements, too, cringe and flee. By standing unterrified amid such fury, Eve immediately wins the reader's respect, just as her boldness in questioning God's judgment had piqued the reader's interest. As she begins to explain herself, her description of Paradise is traditional except for the contemptuousness of the occasional reference to its "drowsy luxury" and "glittering hours." Such descriptive phrases prepare the reader to see Eden as Eve saw it, a place where Man and Woman are treated like children, "swaddled with ease" and "lulled with . . . softest dreams." The circling night-bird "out beyond the wood," the "broadening stream," and the distant hills become symbols of freedom, symbols of the unknown. Eve learns that individuality can be obtained only through rebellion, that knowledge must be reached through uncertainty, and that creation grows out of struggle. She eats of the fruit of sensual knowledge, as Untermeyer would have all men and women do.

Untermeyer makes other particularly interesting attempts to modernize religious mythology in "Sic Semper," "God's Youth," and "Burning Bush." The first of these looks at the myth of the Fall from another perspective. In "Eve Speaks," Untermeyer had made no mention of Satan; Eve's revolt grew out of her understanding of Adam's human needs. In "Sic Semper," Untermeyer brilliantly and economically overturns the traditional view of Satan. The fallen angel becomes "the Light-Bringer, Fire-Scatterer"—man's benefactor and not his foe. Lucifer and Prometheus become one, bringing light to minds in darkness. Then, in a horrifying betrayal, man—knowing too well the future costs of truth, wisdom, and love—puts Lucifer in hell.

Similarly, "God's Youth" is a delightful reconception of deity. The God of the Old Testament is himself old—bored by the unchanging march of years and the "yawning seasons." During the Creation, Untermeyer insists, "God was young and blithe and whimsical," letting loose his desires and filling the earth with "fancies, wild and frank." During the Creation, then, the child-god lived as Untermeyer would have the man-child continue to live.

"Burning Bush" is by far the most sacrilegious of Untermeyer's biblical recreations. The poem's title is an allusion to Exodus 3:2 in which the angel of the Lord appears to Moses in the form of a burning bush. Through imagery that is intentionally indirect and metaphoric, Untermeyer transforms the burning bush into a sexual symbol. In the still of the night "runners of the flame" fill the "narrowest veins," and in "an agony of Love" bodies burn but are not consumed. The biblical voice of God becomes the ecstatic cries of the lovers that later give way to "the still, small voice" of contentment in the postcoital quiet. The sexual act, which is itself "knowledge," passion, creation, and experience, becomes a metaphor for the presence of God, who *still* speaks to man through the burning bush. Through this metaphor, the poem becomes a twelve-line exposition of Untermeyer's temperament and philosophy of life.

EMULATION OF ROMANTIC THEMES

The poems in the third category of Untermeyer's verse all involve emulation. Many of them reflect the spirit and sometimes the words of the favorite poets of Untermeyer's youth: Robert Herrick, Heinrich Heine, A. E. Housman, Thomas Hardy, and Horace. They tend to be witty, ironic, and sensuous. They frequently deal with the traditional subject matter of romantic poetry— love, spring, snow, dawn, sunset, birdsongs, the moon, and the stars—but Untermeyer is well aware that these poetic topics can often become substitutes for real passions. The romanticism of many of these poems is, therefore, undercut by irony; in others—"Georgian Anthology" and "Portrait of a Poet," for example—Untermeyer is openly scornful of formalized, passionless romanticism. For this reason, Untermeyer classified himself (along with John Crowe Ransom, Robert Lowell, and Richard Wilbur) as a romantic ironist, but given his devotion to passion, struggle, and creativity, one can question the sincerity of much of the irony. One feels that Untermeyer's scorn of the romantic posturing of others is itself a form of romantic posturing.

On the whole, these are Untermeyer's least successful poems. Untermeyer *was* a romantic and therefore became a romantic ironist only with difficulty. Moreover, most of the poems give one the impression of having been written before and better by others. A typical example is "Fairmount Cemetery," a poem in Housman's style. The speaker looks back on the cemetery, his first trysting spot, and remembers his extravagant claims that

"love is all that saves"; meanwhile, the dead men lie "Chuckling in their graves." The cemetery setting is too obviously a contrivance, the claims of the lover are overblown and unrealistic, and the concluding commentary of the dead injects a crude blatancy. The only part of Untermeyer's personality that shows up in "Fairmount Cemetery" is the collector's love of varied poetic styles.

INFLUENCE OF ROBERT FROST

A smaller, but far better, group of poems was written in imitation of Frost's understated style. As in Frost's best lyrics, an understanding of life's tragic possibilities emerges through the speaker's recollection of an occurrence in nature. "Nightmare by Day," for example, begins with a setting and even a verse form that are nearly identical to Frost's in "Dust of Snow." In search of peace, the speaker has walked alone far into the woods until there are no more tracks in the snow. Something in front of him, glimpsed but not yet recognized, makes his "pulses freeze," and, as he watches, a trail of blood begins to grow, spreading as it melts the snow. The mystery of this image of death in a place of peaceful isolation disturbs the speaker so that ever after he himself awaits the sudden blow and the red droplets on the snow.

The impact of this terrifying incident is augmented by the plain diction and the stark imagery. In the poem, 98 of the 110 words are monosyllables; the average sentence contains only 9 words; the only colors are white, black, and red; the only objects are the snow, the speaker, the trees, the trail of blood, and one "chuckling crow." Yet, upon reflection, the incident itself is both mysterious and premonitory, just as the simple, unforced verse reveals, upon reflection, the technical difficulty of densely rhymed iambic dimeter.

If the poem has a weakness, it is in the improbability of the events described. At its best, Frost's lyric poetry grows out of an ordinary occurrence. That is not the case in "Nightmare by Day." Here, the ultimate situation is extraordinary. The blood is very fresh, but there has been no sign of a bleeding animal or of a hunter, and no sound of gunfire. These are not insuperable difficulties, of course; hawks and owls, for example, hunt silently and leave no trail. Untermeyer is, however, less interested in the incident as a natural phenomenon than as a symbol of sudden, unpredictable violence and impending death. Hence, he makes no effort to explain the ominous scene. Nevertheless, the odd congruence of events, the dreamlike improbability, demands recognition, and Untermeyer *does* recognize it, calling the entire incident a "dream" in the final stanza. The poem's title, however, "Nightmare by Day," emphasizes that the events have been real, and the nightmarish reality of this waking dream contributes largely to its impact.

An equally good imitation of Frost's style is found in "The Scraping of the Scythe." The poem grows out of the contrasts between two sounds: the song of the bluebird and the screech of the sharpening scythe. The one is a song of leisure, the other a sound of labor; the one pleasurable, the other painful; the one of the call of summer, the other the call of fall. As the speaker notes, when the two fill the air at once, one need not hear the words, "To know what had transpired." The sharpening of the scythe is an omen of colder weather to come and a symbol of inevitable death. Thus, in order *not* to hear that sound, the speaker never allows his own fields to be cut, but the reader knows that nothing can postpone the fall—and the speaker does, too.

The success of these poems arises at least in part from the fact that they are compatible with Untermeyer's outlook on life. If death is unavoidable and unpredictable, then it makes all the more sense to live fully, freely, and passionately. As much as Untermeyer admired Frost and Frost's poetry, he could not wholly endorse the somber pessimism embodied in Frost's style or the conservatism of Frost's personality. For a more compatible political and emotional outlook, Untermeyer occasionally turned to William Blake, whose radical politics and unconventional piety were much closer to his own views. Hence, Untermeyer's religious recreations make many of the same points that Blake did in his poems objecting to those who would bind "with briars [his] joys and desires."

INFLUENCE OF WILLIAM BLAKE

Sometimes Blake's influence on Untermeyer gives rise to weak imitation, as in "Envy," a poem in the manner of Blake's "The Clod and the Pebble," which pits the rooted willow against the meandering brook in a debate about lifestyles; a poem such as "Glad Day (After a Color Print by Blake)," however, grows out of inspira-

tion more than out of imitation. This paean to daylight is pure Untermeyer—lover of generosity, confidence, sensuality, clarity, and joy. Like "Eve Speaks," this poem excels in its descriptions, particularly in the personification of day, which becomes a naked body, free, outgiving, and rejoicing. Hence, as before, the pathetic fallacy is made tolerable because it is a "given," a part of Blake's drawing that Untermeyer must accept and explain.

Thus, Untermeyer's parodies, re-creations, and imitations derive from, and play upon, his strengths as a collector and a romantic, appreciative reader. The two final groupings are more original. One group of poems is largely hortatory. They include some of Untermeyer's most widely known pieces—"Caliban in the Coal Mines," "Prayer," and "On the Birth of a Child." They are light verse suitable for communicating their overt moral and political messages, but too blatantly propagandizing to qualify as significant poems. The best that can be said is that in them Untermeyer remains true to himself. Particularly in "Prayer," he speaks from the heart as he asks to remain "ever insurgent," "more daring than devout," "filled with a buoyant doubt," and wide-eyed and sensual while cognizant of others' misery. His final prayer, that of a thoroughgoing romantic, is to remain at the end of life "still unsatisfied."

INFLUENCE OF WALT WHITMAN

If the last group of Untermeyer's poems is derivative at all, it owes its inspiration to Walt Whitman. In a style all his own, Untermeyer attempts to describe common aspects of the contemporary world, often striving to see mundane things with a childlike wonder and a romantic imagination. The poems' titles identify their unconventional subjects: "In the Subway," "To a Vine-Clad Telegraph Pole," "A Side Street," "Boy and Tadpoles," "Food and Drink," "Hairdressing," "Hands," "Portrait of a Child," "Portrait of a Dead Horse," "Portrait of a Machine," and so on. In these poems, Untermeyer eschews both the subject matter of romantic poetry and the introspective approach of most modern verse. The poem "Still Life" is both an example of Untermeyer's approach and an explanation of it. Like Untermeyer's poems, a still-life painting portrays things, "A bowl of fruit upon a piece of silk," but it also conveys emotions through the choice of color and form. The still life contains no direct autobiography, but the artist's "voice so full of vehement life" can still be "heard." In the same way, Untermeyer's poems about modern life convey his perspective without descending into private symbolism, autobiographical digressions, or Freudian associations.

"Coal Fire" is a good example of what can be achieved through such verse. The poem explains to a child why fire comes out of coal. In doing so, it uses poetic devices that particularly appeal to children, yet it uses those devices with a mastery that should delight adults. The actual content of the poem is, however, entirely mundane; coal is the remnant of ancient trees. To interest the child, Untermeyer personifies parts of these trees, putting them in situations with which a child could empathize. Like children, each leaf must be "taught the right/ Way to drink light." Each twig must "learn/ How to catch flame and yet not burn." Each branch must grow strong on this "diet of heat." Simultaneously, Untermeyer develops a series of delightful paradoxes. The dead black coal was once a living green net. Before there was any running thing to ensnare, this net snared the sun. Paradoxically, the leaves "drink light," catch flame without burning, and eat heat. Finally, the poem's heavy alliteration and frequent rhyme heighten the delight, especially since the alliteration and the rhyme so frequently emphasize key words: "these . . . were trees," "to learn . . . not burn," "branch and . . . bough began," "to eat . . . of heat," and so on. More important, however, this lucid examination of coal-fire subtly describes the burning coal as though the light within it were passion imprisoned. The intensity of the verse increases as the fire fingers the air, grows bolder, twists free, consumes the imprisoning coal, "leaps, is done,/ And goes back to the sun." There is nothing allegorical in the poem, but a reader would have to be curiously insensitive not to recognize in it Untermeyer's love of freedom, light, and passion.

"A DISPLACED ORPHEUS"

In 1955, when Untermeyer had already lived his biblically allotted three score years and ten, he was selected Phi Beta Kappa poet by Harvard University. For a man who had virtually ceased composing poetry twenty years earlier, it was a rare opportunity to pronounce dispassionate judgment upon his long and extraordinarily varied career. The poem he wrote, "A Displaced Or-

pheus," did just that. In it, Orpheus awakens after a long silence to discover that he has lost the knack of moving mountains and assuaging lions. He attends a series of universities to relearn the lost art and produces sterile stanzas in the manner of W. H. Auden, T. S. Eliot, and William Empson. Although Untermeyer intended these parodies to illustrate the deficiencies of much modern poetry, they also illustrate the limitations of his own imitative approach to composition. Thus, Orpheus's situation becomes Untermeyer's. Time has stripped him of his reputation, and his failures have cost him the woman he loves. All that remains is the desire to struggle, the urge to create. Only when he retrieves his "still unbroken lute" and sings for "that last listener, himself," does he rediscover his power. The birds and beasts gather about him, the trees bow down, and his woman looks upon him with "rediscovering eyes."

One could wish that Untermeyer had taken Orpheus's lesson more truly to heart and that he had sung for himself more often, but perhaps then the passionate collector would only have delighted himself with more parodies. Songs coming out of the soul often have a hard and bitter birth. All but a few are stillborn. In "Eve Speaks," "Nightmare by Day," "Coal Fire," "A Displaced Orpheus," and a handful of others, Untermeyer produced more healthy offspring than most poets do. Posterity should be grateful.

OTHER MAJOR WORKS

LONG FICTION: *Moses*, 1928; *The Wonderful Adventures of Paul Bunyan*, 1945.

NONFICTION: *The New Era in American Poetry*, 1919, 1970; *Poetry: Its Understanding and Enjoyment*, 1934 (with Carter Davidson); *Heinrich Heine: Paradox and Poet*, 1937; *From Another World*, 1939; *A Century of Candymaking, 1837-1947*, 1947; *Makers of the Modern World*, 1955; *Lives of the Poets*, 1959; *The Letters of Robert Frost to Louis Untermeyer*, 1963; *Bygones: The Recollections of Louis Untermeyer*, 1965.

CHILDREN'S LITERATURE: *This Singing World*, 1923-1926 (3 volumes); *The Donkey of God*, 1932; *Chip: My Life and Times*, 1933; *The Last Pirate: Tales from the Gilbert and Sullivan Operas*, 1934; *Stars to Steer By*, 1941; *The Golden Treasury of Children's*

Literature, 1959 (with Byrna Untermeyer); *The Kitten Who Barked*, 1962.

EDITED TEXTS: *Modern American Poetry*, 1919; *Modern British Poetry*, 1920; *American Poetry from the Beginning to Whitman*, 1931; *A Treasury of Great Poems*, 1942, 1955.

MISCELLANEOUS: *A Treasury of Ribaldry*, 1956.

BIBLIOGRAPHY

Frost, Robert, and Louis Untermeyer. *The Letters of Robert Frost to Louis Untermeyer*. New York: Holt, Rinehart and Winston, 1963. The most valuable collection of Frost's letters to Untermeyer in a correspondence that lasted almost fifty years. The letters are remarkably edited.

Harcourt, Brace. *Sixteen Authors: Brief Histories, Together with Lists of Their Respective Works*. New York: Author, 1926. Offers short histories of sixteen authors and their works, including Sinclair Lewis, Carl Sandburg, Virginia Woolf, and Untermeyer. The entry on Untermeyer provides a fine assessment of Untermeyer's poetry and poetic development. Contains illustrations and a bibliography.

Lowell, Amy. "A Poet of the Present." *Poetry* 11 (December, 1917): 157-164. This review of Untermeyer's early verse volume, *These Times*, turns out to be a lovely appreciation of the young poet.

Pound, Ezra. *EP to LU: Nine Letters Written to Louis Untermeyer by Ezra Pound*. Edited by J. A. Robbins. Bloomington: Indiana University Press, 1963. A fine collection of letters written by Pound to Untermeyer. Useful as a source of information on Pound's perception of Untermeyer.

Untermeyer, Louis. *Bygones: The Recollections of Louis Untermeyer*. New York: Harcourt, Brace & World, 1965. The second of Untermeyer's reminiscences in which the eighty-year-old looks back on his life. Where the earlier "autobiography" was about other people, this one is primarily, and self-consciously so, about the author. It is a very personal volume focusing on the highlights of Untermeyer's career, including excellent chapters on the McCarthy years, his tenure at the Library of Congress, and his travels.

_____. *From Another World: The Autobiography of Louis Untermeyer*. New York: Harcourt, Brace,

1939. Untermeyer's first attempt at autobiography is devoted to anecdotes and comments on the author's friends and acquaintances among the literary community. It is significant in that it sheds light on the American renaissance which began before World War I. Untermeyer passes judgements, comments on works and relationships, and tells stories and jokes. In general he deals only with the surfaces of events and encounters and does not explore any issue in great depth. His style and energy are as vivid as the range of his acquaintances is impressive.

Jeffrey D. Hoeper;
bibliography updated by the editors

JOHN UPDIKE

Born: Shillington, Pennsylvania; March 18, 1932

PRINCIPAL POETRY

The Carpentered Hen, and Other Tame Creatures, 1958
Telephone Poles and Other Poems, 1963
Verse, 1965
Dog's Death, 1965
The Angels, 1968
Bath After Sailing, 1968
Midpoint and Other Poems, 1969
Seventy Poems, 1972
Six Poems, 1973
Query, 1974
Cunts (Upon Receiving the Swingers Life Club Membership Solicitation), 1974
Tossing and Turning, 1977
Sixteen Sonnets, 1979
An Oddly Lovely Day Alone, 1979
Five Poems, 1980
Jester's Dozen, 1984
Facing Nature, 1985
Mites and Other Poems in Miniature, 1990
A Helpful Alphabet of Friendly Objects, 1995

OTHER LITERARY FORMS

A prolific writer in all genres, John Updike is known chiefly as a novelist. His major works have been bestsellers and have won significant critical acclaim both from reviewers for highbrow publications and from academics. Among his most noted novels are *The Centaur* (1963), *Couples* (1968), and the four novels depicting the life of Harry "Rabbit" Angstrom: *Rabbit, Run* (1960), *Rabbit Redux* (1971), *Rabbit Is Rich* (1981), and *Rabbit at Rest* (1990). He is also an accomplished and respected writer of short stories, of which he has published several volumes, and a first-rate critic and essayist.

ACHIEVEMENTS

John Updike has been the recipient of numerous honors during is illustrious career, including a Guggenheim Fellowship (1959), a Rosenthal Award (1960), a National Book Award (1964), an O. Henry Award (1966), France's Foreign Book Prize (1966), a New England Poetry Club Golden Rose (1979), a MacDowell Medal (1981), a Pulitzer Prize (1982, 1991), an American Book Award (1982), National Book Critics Circle Awards for both fiction (1982, 1991) and criticism (1982), the Union League Club's Abraham Lincoln Award (1982), a National Arts Club Medal of Honor (1984), a PEN/Faulkner Award (1988), a National Medal of the Arts (1989), a Harvard Arts Medal (1998), and a National Book Foundation Award for Lifetime Achievement (1998).

Updike has achieved his fame largely through his novels. These works, and his growing collection of prose essays and reviews, have earned for him a reputation as one of America's leading literary voices. His poetry, on the other hand, has brought only modest acclaim. Many critics consider him only a dilettante in this genre, a show-off who is clearly skilled in handling poetic forms both traditional and modern. Since much of his work is gentle satire and light verse, he is often accused of lacking substance. Updike's record of publication for individual poems, however, belies that judgment to some degree. His poems have appeared in such journals as *The New Yorker* and *The Atlantic*, and even in *Scientific American*. As with much of his prose, Updike has shown an ability to deal in verse with a wide variety of experiences, making both the commonplace and the abstruse immediately accessible to his readers.

BIOGRAPHY

Born March 18, 1932, John Hoyer Updike grew up during the Depression in Shillington, Pennsylvania, and in the farming country outside this northeastern town. His father was a mathematics teacher, his mother an intelligent, well-read woman who encouraged her son's reading. The Updikes lived with John's grandparents during the novelist's earliest years; many of the boy's memories of life in that household have found their way into his fiction and poetry. A good student in high school, Updike went to Harvard in 1950 on a full scholarship. There, while majoring in English, he edited the *Lampoon* and entertained visions of becoming a commercial cartoonist. While still a student at Harvard in 1953, Updike married Mary Pennington, an art student at Radcliffe. The following year, he was graduated summa cum laude.

Updike's own artistic talent was further fostered by a year's study at the Ruskin School of Drawing and Fine Art in Oxford, England, immediately following graduation. There, his first child, Elizabeth, was born. She was to be followed in the next six years by three others: David (1957), Michael (1959), and Miranda (1960).

Updike's desire to achieve fame through the visual arts was put aside in 1955, when he received an offer to

John Updike (© Davis Freeman)

join the staff of *The New Yorker*, to which he had sold his first story the year before. His full-time association with the magazine ended in 1957, however, when he took the daring step of becoming an independent writer, moving his family to Ipswich, Massachusetts, and establishing an office there. His first book, a collection of poems titled *The Carpentered Hen, and Other Tame Creatures*, appeared in 1958.

The publication of two novels, *The Poorhouse Fair* (1959) and *Rabbit, Run*, brought Updike both critical and popular acclaim. For *The Centaur*, he received the National Book Award in 1964 and in the same year was elected to the National Institute of Arts and Letters. These were but the first of many honors.

Though a resident of New England continuously after 1957, Updike frequently traveled abroad. His first important trip was in 1964-1965, when he visited the Soviet Union, Romania, Bulgaria, and Czechoslovakia as a member of the U.S.S.R.-United States Cultural Exchange Program. In 1973, he served as a Fulbright lecturer in Africa. From his experiences in these countries, Updike brought back a wealth of materials that allowed him to expand his repertoire of characters beyond New England and Pennsylvania to include two of his most memorable creations: the middle-aged Jewish novelist Henry Bech and the African ruler Hakim Ellelou.

Updike and his family remained residents of Ipswich until 1974, when John and Mary were divorced. Shortly after the breakup of his marriage, Updike moved to Boston, then to Georgetown, Massachusetts. In 1977, he married Martha Bernhard, a divorcée whom he had known when both lived in Ipswich. Even during this period of personal difficulty, Updike's volume of writings poured forth unabated, and he went on to display both skill and versatility in a variety of literary genres.

Updike continued his prolific output through the 1980's, 1990's, and into the new millennium, winning his second Pulitzer Prize in 1991 for *Rabbit at Rest* and producing new novels, criticism, and children's poetry such as *A Helpful Alphabet of Friendly Objects*.

ANALYSIS

An appropriate starting point for an analysis of John Updike's poetry is Charles T. Samuels's summary remark in his brief study of the writer: "In verse," Samuels

notes, Updike "frequently exploits the familiar," often simply "as an occasion to display his talent for comic rhyme." What strikes the reader immediately about Updike's poems is his heavy reliance on everyday experience, whether autobiographical or generic, and the way he manipulates language to achieve distinctive, often unusual and amusing, rhyming and rhythmical patterns. Reviewers of individual volumes of Updike's work have not always been convinced, however, that this kind of rhetorical gamesmanship has offered sufficient compensation for a body of works that are, in fact, intellectually lightweight when compared to the serious fiction that Updike has produced during the past two decades. As a result, the serious student of Updike's poetry is faced with examining the work in a critical vacuum, or in the constant context of his fiction.

One can see, though, that Updike's poetry demonstrates his ability to work deftly within a variety of forms, turning them to his own purposes. His published poems include sonnets, free verse modeled on that of Walt Whitman and contemporary figures, Spenserian stanzas, elegiac quatrains, extended commentary in heroic couplets, and works that follow (at times almost slavishly) other poetic conventions. More often than not, the forms are used in parody, as are the manifold rhyme schemes that remind one of the cantos of Lord Byron's *Don Juan* (1819-1824) in their variety and in their reliance on sight rhyme or colloquial pronunciation for effect. For example, in "Agatha Christie and Beatrix Potter," Updike closes his short, humorous comparison of these authors (whose works he sees as essentially similar) with a couplet of praise for having given readers "cozy scares and chases/ That end with innocence acquitted—/ Except for Cotton-tail, who did it." Similarly, in a light limerick poking fun at young Swedish scholars, he opens with the couplet: "There was a young student of Lund/ Whose -erstanding was not always und."

Updike's art, especially his poetry, is thus intentionally enigmatic, because it contains a discoverable but not self-evident truth. The surface finish, whether comic, ironic, or sexually explicit, is often simply the bait to lure readers into the world of the poem. Once there, Updike asks his readers to look closely at their own lives, often challenging them to be as introspective about themselves as he is about his own experiences. In that way, he hopes to help others make sense of a world that he believes is essentially good and in which good men can prosper.

MANIPULATION OF "LIGHT VERSE"

Like many contemporary poets, Updike also relies on the appearance of the poem on the page for effect. In poems such as "Typical Optical," he prints various lines in different type styles and sizes to make his point: As one gets older, one's vision (literally) changes, and what one could see at close range as a child becomes blurred to more mature eyes. As a result, when Updike says that the novels of Marcel Proust and the poetry of John Donne "Recede from my ken in/ Their eight-point Granjon," he emphasizes the problem by printing the phrase "eight-point Granjon" in the type face and size to which it refers. Then, in his closing remark that his "old eyeballs" can now "enfold/ No print any finer/ Than sans-serif bold," he prints the final phrase in sans-serif type and has the final word in bold print. Similarly, the lines of the poem "Pendulum" are printed beneath the title at angles resembling the swinging of a pendulum on a clock, and individual words in the poem "Letter Slot" are arranged on the page to suggest letters falling through a mail slot onto the floor.

The reader often laughs at such tricks, but the poetry cannot be judged first-rate simply for the author's ability to manipulate both the language and the conventions of the tradition in which he works. As a consequence, Updike is too often dismissed as a dilettante in this field. A close examination of his published volumes, however, reveals that the author himself is careful to distinguish between "poetry" and "light verse." Much of what Updike calls "light verse" is simply poetic exercise, intended to highlight the wonderful ability of language to evoke amusement and thought in both reader and writer. Often the impetus for such poetry comes from the world around Updike: newspaper accounts, books that are popular best-sellers, visits he has made to various places where the benign incongruities of life manifest themselves to him. Poems such as "V. B. Nimble, V. B. Quick" may not offer substantial food for thought: The genesis of the poem—an entry in the British Broadcasting Corporation's *Radio Times* that "V. B. Wigglesworth, F.R.S., Quick Professor of Biology" will

speak on an upcoming program—triggers in Updike's mind a humorous comparison with the hero of the nursery rhyme "Jack Be Nimble, Jack Be Quick," and the resultant verse about a frenetic scientist dashing off experiments and hurrying off to talk about them provides momentary pleasure to readers without trying to make a serious observation about the world of science. This poem, and many others like it in the Updike canon, are simply offered as tidbits to evoke humor and sympathy in an otherwise somber world.

QUESTIONS OF IMPORTANCE

Because Updike is so facile at handling the many demands facing the poet, it is easy to overlook the serious nature of much of his output. A substantial number of his poems are attempts to examine the significance of his own life's experiences and to explore questions of importance to contemporary society. As in his fiction, Updike is especially concerned with the place of religion in the modern world, and often, beneath the surface playfulness, one can see the poet grappling with complex moral and philosophical issues. He is also a careful student of the literary tradition he has inherited, and his attempts to examine the place of literature as an interpreter of experience often find their way into his poems.

"LOVE SONNET"

The way in which Updike combines the comic and the serious is illustrated quite well in his poem "Love Sonnet." Its title suggests its subject, but the content is at first glance enigmatic. The opening line, "In Love's rubber armor I come to you," is followed by a string of letters printed down the page, as if they were the endings of lines which have been omitted: "b/ oo/ b./ c,/ d/ c/ d:/ e/ f—/ e/ f./ g/ g." The form of the sonnet has thus been preserved (the "oo" sound of the third line rhyming with the "you" at the end of the first line), but the content is absent. Adding simultaneously to the confusion and to the humor is the overt sexual implication of the only full line: One cannot mistake the literal meaning of the proposition. Nevertheless, a closer look at the poem, especially in the light of the literary tradition which it seems to parody, suggests that there may in fact be serious purpose here. Traditionally, sonnets have been poems about love. While their content has varied, the form itself has usually suggested to readers the kind of interpretation the poet expects. One looks for the words in a sonnet to be metaphors describing the way in which a speaker feels about his beloved. In this poem, however, the process is reversed. The overt reference to physical love-making is the metaphor: "Love's rubber armor" is the sonnet form itself, an elastic medium in which the lover, working within conventions—and protected by them—is able to "come to" his beloved and display both his wit and his devotion. In this way, then, Updike is making a comment on the literary tradition: The sonnet form has both strengths and weaknesses; its conventions provide a way to ensure that meaning is conveyed, but limit the extent to which the writer may put the form to use without risking misinterpretation. Appearing at first to be a risqué comic piece about a subject much talked of and trivialized in Updike's own society, "Love Sonnet" emerges as a serious statement about the nature of poetry itself.

UPDIKE'S "POEMS"

The special strengths and weaknesses of Updike as a poet can be seen in those poems which he presents to the world as "poems" rather than verses. In these he is often franker in discussions of sex, and the explicit language may offend some readers. No subject seems sacred, yet it is precisely the concern Updike has for sacred things in human life that leads him to write graphically about human relationships. From his study of everyday occurrences, Updike tries to isolate that which is important for man, to show how man constructs meaning from the disparate events of his own life.

"MIDPOINT"

The most extended example of Updike's use of individual events to make statements about universals occurs in his long autobiographical poem "Midpoint." Published as the centerpiece of Updike's 1969 volume of poetry, *Midpoint and Other Poems*, "Midpoint" is a collage of text, drawings, and photographs that traces the poet's life from infancy to its midpoint, as Updike reaches age thirty-six. Though the poem has been dismissed by some critics as "quirky," Updike himself insists that in it he demonstrates what is for him an artistic credo, a search for "the reality behind the immediately apparent." In "Midpoint," Updike reveals himself to be a believer in "pointillism" as both technique and philosophy: "Praise Pointillism, Calculus and all/ That turn the

world infinitesimal." Like Whitman in *Leaves of Grass* (1855), Updike takes his own life as an example of the human condition, finding in it something of value to share with other men.

"Midpoint" consists of five cantos, four of which are modeled closely on writers of the past. Each is preceded by a short "argument" reminiscent of that provided by John Milton in *Paradise Lost* (1667), in which Updike provides the reader with clues to the action of the canto. In the first, in stanzas reminiscent of those in Dante's *The Divine Comedy* (c. 1320), Updike reviews his childhood and his growing awareness of himself as a discrete entity in the universe. An only child, he comes to see himself as the center of that universe, a point around which the world revolves. Though to sing of himself (an allusion to Whitman) is "all wrong," he has no choice since he has no other subject so appropriate or about which he knows so much. The second canto consists exclusively of photographs: Updike as baby and young child, his parents, himself as a teenager, himself and his wife, their first child. These are printed with varying degrees of sharpness: Some appear crisply defined, some are little more than a blur of dots on the page. This intentional shifting of focus carries out graphically the theme Updike expresses in the "argument" that he prints at the beginning of the canto: "Distance improves vision." In a sense, the action in this canto repeats that of the first, but from another perspective: The reader sees what he has just read about.

The third canto, composed in Spenserian stanzas, is titled "The Dance of the Solids." Based on Updike's readings in *Scientific American*, it presents in verse a view of the way the universe is constructed. The bonding of atomic particles into larger and larger structures eventually "yield[s],/ In Units growing visible, the World we wield!" It would be easy to lose sight of the poet's purpose in these most ingenious iambic pentameter lines. Updike uses the language of science, and even mathematical formulas, with exceptional precision to present his argument. For example, in explaining what happens when a solid is heated, he writes: "$T = 3Nk$ is much too neat." The stanzas are not simply virtuoso performances; in them, Updike provides an analogy for examining the human condition. Just as the visible world is composed of subatomic particles combined in meaningful ways, so are men's lives simply the ordered and meaningful arrangements of individual incidents. To understand the meaning, one must first isolate and describe the incident.

The fourth canto, "The Play of Memory," contains text, line drawings, and close-ups from the photographs that appear in canto 2. The text is modeled on Whitman's poetic technique of free verse. In this section of the poem, Updike explores his marriage and the role sex plays in shaping human lives. The final canto, written in couplets that suggest the method of Alexander Pope in *An Essay on Man* (1733-1734), is a review of the modern scene in which Updike the poet finds himself. In it, he offers advice, alternately serious and satiric, for living. In the fashion of Arthur Hugh Clough in "The Last Decalogue," a parody of the Ten Commandments, Updike admonishes his readers: "Don't kill; or if you must, while killing grieve"; "Doubt not; that is, until you can't believe"; "Don't covet Mrs. X; or if you do,/ Make sure, before you leap, she covets you." As in the third canto, readers may become so enraptured with the wise witticisms and the deft handling of poetic form that they lose the sense of the canto's place within the poem. In fact, the poem has prompted more than one reader to wonder, as did the reviewer for *Library Journal* in 1970, what Updike was "up to" in "Midpoint."

If, however, one accepts what Updike himself has said about "Midpoint," that in it he attempts to explain his own attitudes about his life and art, one can see the poem as a kind of poetic credo, a systematic statement about the poet's acceptance of his role as poet. The many references to other artists and the conscious use of recognizable forms associated with specific poets and poems suggest that Updike is using his own life to make a statement about the way art is created. In fact, in the closing lines of the fifth canto, he observes, "The time is gone, when *Pope* could ladle Wit/ In couplet droplets, and decanter it." No longer can *"Wordsworth's* sweet brooding" or *"Tennyson's* unease" be effective as vehicles for explaining the human condition. The world is now a sad and perhaps an absurd place, and art has followed suit by offering those who come to it only "blank explosions and a hostile smile." Updike, who has accepted the notion of the absurd from modern theologians who have pointed out that faith cannot be rational

even if it is essential, offers this poem as an ironic, sometimes comic, and sometimes highly personal and hence prejudicial view of the world. For Updike, autobiography has become metaphor, because only by viewing the world through others' eyes can individuals hope to understand something of the significance of their own predicament. Similarly, as he has used the events of his own life to make a statement about life itself, Updike uses the forms of his predecessors to make a statement about the efficacy of art in the modern world.

OTHER MAJOR WORKS

LONG FICTION: *The Poorhouse Fair*, 1959; *Rabbit, Run*, 1960; *The Centaur*, 1963; *Of the Farm*, 1965; *Couples*, 1968; *Bech: A Book*, 1970; *Rabbit Redux*, 1971; *A Month of Sundays*, 1975; *Marry Me: A Romance*, 1976; *The Coup*, 1978; *Rabbit Is Rich*, 1981; *The Witches of Eastwick*, 1984; *Roger's Version*, 1986; *S.*, 1988; *Rabbit at Rest*, 1990; *Memories of the Ford Administration*, 1992; *Brazil*, 1994; *In the Beauty of the Lilies*, 1996; *Toward the End of Time*, 1997; *Bech at Bay: A Quasi-Novel*, 1998; *Gertrude and Claudius*, 2000.

SHORT FICTION: *The Same Door*, 1959; *Pigeon Feathers*, 1962; *Olinger Stories: A Selection*, 1964; *The Music School*, 1966; *Museums and Women and Other Stories*, 1972; *Too Far to Go: The Maples Stories*, 1979; *Problems and Other Stories*, 1979; *Three Illuminations in the Life of an American Author*, 1979; *The Chaste Planet*, 1980; *The Beloved*, 1982; *Bech Is Back*, 1982; *Trust Me*, 1987; *Brother Grasshopper*, 1990 (limited edition); *The Afterlife and Other Stories*, 1994; *Licks of Love: Short Stories and a Sequel, "Rabbit Remembered,"* 2000; *The Complete Henry Bech: Twenty Stories*, 2001.

PLAYS: *Three Texts from Early Ipswich: A Pageant*, pb. 1968; *Buchanan Dying*, pb. 1974.

NONFICTION: *Assorted Prose*, 1965; *Picked-Up Pieces*, 1975; *Hugging the Shore: Essays and Criticism*, 1983; *Just Looking: Essays on Art*, 1989; *Self-Consciousness: Memoirs*, 1989; *Odd Jobs: Essays and Criticism*, 1991; *Golf Dreams: Writings on Golf*, 1996; *More Matter: Essays and Criticism*, 1999.

EDITED TEXT: *The Best American Short Stories of the Century*, 2000.

BIBLIOGRAPHY

Broer, Lawrence R., ed. *Rabbit Tales: Poetry and Politics in John Updike's Rabbit Novels*. Tuscaloosa: University of Alabama Press, 1998. Twelve essays that demonstrate that Updike's Rabbit novels are a carefully crafted fabric of changing hues and textures, of social realism and something of grandeur. Includes bibliographical references and index.

Detweiler, John. *John Updike*. Boston: Twayne, 1972. This study attempts to demonstrate the qualities of irony and self-consciousness inherent in Updike's work. Proceeding chronologically, the author omits specific study of the poems, but the background work on Updike is important for a thorough reading of his verse. Includes a brief chronology, notes and references, and a select bibliography.

Greiner, Donald J. *The Other Updike: Poems/Short Stories/Prose/Play*. Athens: Ohio University Press, 1981. This analysis shows a growing concern with mortality and loss in the works of Updike. The author proposes that as a poet, Updike is primarily concerned with shaping the power of language. He traces his development from light verse to "spiritual confusion." Particular attention is paid to the development of themes and techniques. This is the best study of Updike's poetic output. Supplemented by a detailed chronology.

MacNaughton, William R., ed. *Critical Essays on John Updike*. Boston: G. K. Hall, 1982. The introduction to this volume gives an extremely useful survey of Updike's scholarship in English—from bibliographies and biographies to criticism and scholarship—reviewed in clumps of years (1958-1966, 1967-1974, 1975-1980). Each section looks at Updike's output, then reviews books, general articles, and articles on specific works. The preface has exhaustive notes that include bibliographical references. The body of the volume contains sixteen reviews of Updike's work and sixteen critical essays, none, unfortunately, on the poetry.

Rao, G. Nageswara, ed. *The Laurel Bough: Essays Presented in Honour of Professor M. V. Rama Sarma*. Bombay: Blackie and Son, 1983. This collection contains an essay titled "The Novelist as Poet: John Updike" by S. P. Appasamy. A reading of the poems with extensive quotations gives an excellent, though brief, analysis of Updike's verse. The author deals with the roots of Updike's Christianity and sees the beginning of the artist that came to be.

Samuels, Charles T. *John Updike*. Minneapolis: University of Minnesota Press, 1969. This taut, forty-three page pamphlet is a critical study inspired by Samuels's 1968 *The Paris Review* interview with Updike. Samuels looks at the author's work thematically and makes some early references to the poetry. Contains a bibliography.

Schiff, James A. *John Updike Revisited*. New York: Twayne, 1998. Schiff offers a critical reexamination of most of Updike's works up to 1998. Includes bibliographical references and index.

Vargo, Edward P. *Rainstorms and Fire: Ritual in the Novels of John Updike*. Port Washington, N.Y.: Kennikat Press, 1973. This examination of the novels shows them to be a "powerful indictment of the spiritual shallowness of contemporary America." Vargo looks at Updike's use of ritual through pattern, myth, and celebration and offers a system through which a reader can approach Updike's verse. This study is heavily influenced by a Christian reading of Updike.

Laurence W. Mazzeno;
bibliography updated by the editors

V

PAUL VALÉRY

Born: Sète, France; October 30, 1871
Died: Paris, France; July 20, 1945

PRINCIPAL POETRY

La Jeune Parque, 1917 (*The Youngest of the Fates*,
    1947; also known as *The Young Fate*)
Album de vers anciens, 1920 (*Album of Early Verse*,
    1971)
Charmes, ou poèmes, 1922 (*Charms*, 1971)

OTHER LITERARY FORMS

Paul Valéry's diverse and copious writings include
plays, such as *Mon Faust* (pb. 1946; *My Faust*, 1960);
musical drama such as *Amphion* (pr., pb. 1931; English translation, 1960), *Sémiramis* (pr., pb. 1934; English translation, 1960), and *Cantate du Narcisse* (pr.
1939; *The Narcissus Cantata*, 1960); dialogues such
as *Eupalinos: Ou L'Architecte* (1921; *Eupalinos: Or,
The Architect*, 1932) and *L'Âme et la danse* (1925;
Dance and the Soul, 1951); the witty Monsieur Teste series; essays on a wide range of subjects; translations
(such as that of Vergil's *Eclogues*, 43-37 B.C.E.); numerous book prefaces, speeches, and university lectures;
and an extensive correspondence with many illustrious contemporaries, such as André Gide and Stéphane
Mallarmé. Dwarfing this work in terms of volume
alone are the nearly twenty-nine thousand pages of his
notebooks, which he kept from 1894 until his death
in 1945. They record his thoughts on such diverse
subjects as psychology, mathematics, culture, and literary theory, and are considered to contain some of
the most beautiful prose ever written in the French language. Virtually the only literary form which Valéry
did not attempt was the novel. He considered the
genre, with its contradictory demand to create a fictional
reality, to be alien to his sensibilities, once remarking

that he was incapable of composing a work which began
with a line such as "The Marquise went out at five
o'clock."

ACHIEVEMENTS

The honors bestowed upon Paul Valéry by the
French people attest the veneration in which he was held
by his fellow countrymen. His talents were also recognized by many outside France. Not only was he instrumental in acquainting the rest of the world with French
culture, but also he enjoyed an international reputation
as a literary figure and as a keen analyst of politics and
culture. For a number of years, he served on the Committee on Intellectual Cooperation of the League of Nations. In 1935, he became a member of the Academy
of Sciences of Lisbon. Highly respected by the British
and the Portuguese, he received honorary degrees from
the universities of Oxford (1931) and Coimbra (1937).
Valéry was the last member of a trio of poets with similar aesthetic ideals and compositional practices (the
other members were Charles Baudelaire and Stéphane
Mallarmé); he was the last major French poet to use the
strict rules of French versification. The Surrealist poets,
for example, although finding much to admire in his
work, preferred other methods of poetic composition,
such as automatic writing. Although Valéry left no literary disciples to practice his aesthetic ideals, his works
and literary philosophy interested and stimulated such
diverse literary figures as T. S. Eliot, Rainer Maria
Rilke, Jorge Luis Borges, and Jean-Paul Sartre. Tzvetan
Todorov and other structuralists share with Valéry an interest in the relationship between the component elements of a work, although Valéry focuses on the *process*
of composition rather than on the analysis of the resulting literary discourse. Todorov credits Valéry with rede-
fining the word "poetics" to emphasize literary language
rather than rules of rhyme and versification. Others,
such as New Novelist Jean Ricardou, find Valéry's aesthetic in accord with their rejection of the subjectivity,
the false sense of "psychology," the insistence upon
verisimilitude, and the lack of compositional rigor
which they find characteristic of the traditional novel.
Thus, Valéry still speaks to a wide range of writers and
readers, and the beauty of his poetry, the incisive observations and lucid prose of his notebooks, and the contin-

uing influence of his literary theories assure his continued importance in French literature.

BIOGRAPHY

Paul Valéry was born October 30, 1871, in the small French seaport of Sète. His childhood was bathed in the sunlight, blue sky and water, and salt air of this Mediterranean setting. The young Valéry disliked intensely the regimented nature of his schoolwork and spent much of his free time studying objects which greatly interested him: painting, architecture, and poetry, especially that of Baudelaire, Théophile Gautier, and Victor Hugo. Valéry's first poems were composed in 1884, at the age of thirteen.

In that same year, Valéry's family moved to Montpellier. The year 1887 was marked by his father's death; in 1888, he entered law school at the university in Montpellier. His first published poem, "Rêve," appeared in 1889 in a small literary review. During this period, Valéry spent many hours studying mathematics (an interest which he maintained all his life), physics, and music (he especially admired the music of Richard Wagner,

Paul Valéry (© Verlag Ullstein, Berlin)

which had a grandeur he judged both "visceral" and "structural").

In 1890, Valéry met Pierre Louÿs, a young Symbolist poet and editor. Louÿs was to have a great impact on Valéry's future; not only did he help to further Valéry's literary reputation, but also he introduced the young man to others who were to play significant roles in his life. An introduction to Louÿs's uncle, André Gide, sparked a lasting friendship and voluminous correspondence which was to span the next fifty years. Louÿs also introduced his friend to Mallarmé. For Valéry, Mallarmé's works exemplified such perfection of form and control of language that all other poetry seemed inferior by comparison. In their subsequent correspondence, Mallarmé praised the young poet's work, and, perhaps as a result of this encouragement, Valéry's literary output increased dramatically; several of his poems soon appeared in print in Louÿs's literary review, *La Conque*, and elsewhere.

Valéry's literary career had hardly begun, however, when he chose to turn away from poetry as his primary occupation in favor of a life of study and contemplation. His biographers have sought to explain this action by referring to a growing predilection for introspection among young French intellectuals, to their common dislike of the then-popular Naturalistic novel and of objective and descriptive Parnassian poetry, to Valéry's feelings of inferiority in the face of the poetic perfection of his master, Mallarmé, and to Valéry's unrequited (and undeclared) love for a married woman, which left him frightened of his inability to control his strong feelings. No doubt these factors affected Valéry, but his decision in 1892 to devote his life to the cultivation of his intellect can just as easily be seen as a natural consequence of his introspective nature. His decision was greatly influenced by the intellectual and poetic theories of Edgar Allan Poe, which portrayed poetry as creating certain calculated effects. Valéry believed that the techniques required to produce these effects suppressed rather than expanded the intellect; thus, although he had already written several hundred poems, he concluded that the best path toward intellectual growth and wisdom was that of the thinker rather than the artist.

Thus began the period in Valéry's life somewhat erroneously termed the "Great Silence." For the next twenty years or so, he occasionally wrote and published, and he carried on an active social life, often frequenting Mallarmé's Tuesday evening salons and attending concerts and plays. In 1900, he married Jeannie Gobillard, niece of the Impressionist painter Berthe Morisot; the couple had three children. His main occupation during the years from 1892 to 1912, however, was the systematic and dispassionate study of the human mind. Charles Whiting indicates the great extent to which Valéry's method resembled that of René Descartes, in its insistence on intellectual independence, a rigorous method, the founding of all knowledge and certainty within the self, and the "ambition for reducing the process of the mind to measurable quantities." Perhaps in emulation of Leonardo da Vinci, Valéry began keeping a series of notebooks, in which he inscribed mathematical equations, aphorisms, ideas and their developments, bits of verse, and so on. By the time of his death, he had filled almost twenty-nine thousand pages.

During this period, the workings of international politics did not escape Valéry's attention. A prophetic essay on the threat posed by modern Germany, first published in England in 1897, was reprinted in France in 1915, and stirred the public's curiosity about Valéry. He published other works as well, including the essay "L'Introduction à la méthode de Léonard da Vinci" ("Introduction to the Method of Leonardo da Vinci") in 1895 and the philosophical tale "La Soirée avec Monsieur Teste" ("An Evening with Monsieur Teste") in 1896; the protagonist of the latter, Monsieur Teste, in many ways embodies Valéry's ideals of pure intellect and creative genius.

Although Valéry's family connections permitted him the leisure to pursue his interests, in 1897, he assumed a somewhat tedious clerkship with the War Ministry, and in 1900, he became private secretary to Mr. Edouard Lebey of the Havas Press Association. Valéry found the job with Lebey most stimulating, and it left him with ample free time for his own intellectual pursuits.

In 1912, André Gide and the publisher Gaston Gallimard urged Valéry to prepare a collection of his poetry for publication. Reluctant at first, he finally began to edit and revise his early poems (eventually published in 1920 as the *Album of Early Verse*) and to compose a new poem, *The Young Fate*, which was published in 1917. The poem was astonishingly successful in spite of its extreme hermeticism; it secured Valéry's reputation as a

great poet, and it is still considered one of the finest French poems of the twentieth century.

His work on *The Young Fate*, originally intended by Valéry as his farewell to poetry, inspired him to write other poems. In 1920, "Le Cimetière marin" ("The Graveyard by the Sea") appeared, and 1922 saw the publication of *Charms*, a collection of poems written between 1917 and 1921 (a new edition of *Charms* was published in 1926). Although Valéry continued to compose poetry, these collections contain most of his best work.

The death of Edouard Lebey, in 1922, made Valéry resolve henceforth to earn his living as a freelance intellectual. Valéry's name was everywhere prominent: He became a noted lecturer; produced pamphlets, prefaces, dedications, and new editions of his poems; and wrote the texts of two verse-ballets and a cantata. He was a brilliant essayist whose topics embraced art, philosophy, literature, and social and political criticism. One of his best-known essays, "La Crise de l'esprit" ("The Crisis of the Mind"), published in France in 1919, eloquently warned that the modern world's self-destructive tendencies could condemn it to join the Babylons and Ninevehs of the past; it included one of Valéry's most oft-quoted phrases: "Nous autres, civilisations, nous savons maintenant que nous sommes mortelles" ("We other civilizations, we know now that we are mortal").

His reputation ever-growing, Valéry was elected to the Académie Française in 1925; he became a *chevalier* of the Legion of Honor in 1923 and was subsequently promoted to more prestigious ranks. In 1933, he was named administrator of the Centre Universitaire Méditerranéen, at Nice, and he was appointed to a Chair of Poetics at the Collège de France in 1937.

Although his opposition to the Vichy government in World War II and his courageous public eulogy for the French Jewish philosopher Henri Bergson exposed Valéry to harassment by the German authorities during the occupation of France, it was typical of his generous spirit to speak out after the war in defense of three accused collaborators.

By 1945, Valéry was suffering from cancer; although very ill, he managed to complete the poetry course he had taught every winter since 1937 at the Collège de France. He died on July 20, 1945, at the age of seventy-three. Honored with a state funeral as one of France's greatest men, he was buried in his native Sète, in the cemetery which was the setting for one of his best-known poems, "The Graveyard by the Sea."

ANALYSIS

Paul Valéry's youthful views about poetry, which were anti-Romanticist and somewhat cynical, led him to reject literature as his primary occupation and to lead instead a life of contemplation and study, which he hoped would enable him to understand better the relationships among the phenomena of the world. When he eventually realized that universal knowledge was unattainable and that individual facets of reality could not be frozen or studied in isolation, he began to write poetry again. Where he had earlier rejected the Romantic and Platonic notion of Muse-inspired poetry, he came to grant inspiration its place in the creative process. Perhaps he found in poetry that synthesis of world experience which he had hoped to find in his studies of scientific phenomena. In any case, the years devoted to such study had produced in Valéry a vigorous and finely honed mind, and he perceived in poetry not only a rewarding exercise of the intellect but also the nearest approach that human beings could make to expressing the ineffable.

Valéry's poetic theories grew out of his strong interest in the workings of human psychology. His model of mental functioning, reflecting the findings of the then relatively new science of psychiatry, portrayed a network of constantly changing interactions of words, feelings, motor impulses, sensations, stimuli, responses, and so on. He thus saw human identity as infinitely varied rather than possessed of an unchanging essence. In Valéry's psychological model, various functions are continually interacting, but only the intellect has a transcendent understanding of them, although it has no control over many of the organism's functions. Moreover, the intellect of a scientist is likely to interpret a given electrical stimulus differently from the way the intellect of a musician or a poet would interpret it. This recognition of the variety among human intellects and of the primal authority of instinctive responses led Valéry to relinquish his earlier faith in calculated technique, a faith which had been influenced in part by Poe's ideas about the ability of a technically skilled poet to manipulate the emotions of his readers and to produce specific predictable effects in all readers.

Valéry connected this model of psychological functioning to a theory of poetry by postulating that the intellect, when stimulated, tends to interpret and classify the information it receives as quickly as possible, in order to return to its habitual state of rest. In terms of this model, prose differs from poetry because the goal of prose is to transmit information; effective prose presents data in such a way that the information is easy to process, is easily extractable from its form, which is relatively unimportant except as a container, a vehicle. The goal of poetry, on the other hand, is to increase internal excitation and awareness and to resist the intellect's attempts to classify and return to a resting state. Valéry therefore sought to create a poetry with "subjects" so fragile and elusive that they would simultaneously charm and mystify the intellect, and that would be presented in forms so compelling to the intellect that they would themselves become part of the message. To summarize Valéry's psychopoetic theory, one could say that rhythm, sound, the use of metaphor and other tropes, and the emotive aspects of language in general serve to increase and sustain the involvement of the subconscious mind and the physical body in the reading process. The interplay of images, memories, ideas, melodies, and sensations prolongs the pleasurable state of internal excitement and delays closure by the intellect, which, captivated by the poem's form, returns to it repeatedly, seeking to prolong or renew its experience.

This view of aesthetic experience has its implications for the poet as well as for the reader. Valéry recognized that the genesis of his poems was usually to be found not in a conscious decision to compose a poem upon a particular subject but rather in those verses, couplets, sentence fragments, or insistent rhythmic or sound patterns which came to him as "gifts" from that modern Muse, the unconscious. At the same time, these "inspired" verses needed to be refined by the poet's technical and analytical skills, and integrated with other verses, fashioned more by skill than by inspiration, so as to form a seamless, aesthetic whole. To be successful, Valéry believed, a poem must present difficulties for the poet as well as for the reader; he preferred to work with traditional poetic forms with fixed rhyme schemes and other compositional requirements, because he found that his struggles with these obstacles often produced new and unexpectedly beautiful networks of meaning and sometimes altered the original thrust of the poem.

Valéry was concerned with aesthetic process more than with aesthetic results. In his view, the stimulation and prolongation of aesthetic pleasure which a poem provides is as important for the poet as for the reader. While he is engaged in the creative process, the poet experiences the intellectual growth, spiritual insight, and emotional release that poetic creation stimulates as it keeps the poet's intellect from returning to a state of equilibrium. Because he believed that it was the poetic process and not the end product that provided aesthetic stimulation, Valéry never considered his poems finished, and he was constantly revising his work. He claimed in his essay "Au sujet du *Cimetière marin*" ("On 'The Graveyard by the Sea,'" published in a bilingual edition of "The Graveyard by the Sea" by the University of Texas Press, 1971) that the published form of that poem merely represented its state on the day it was taken away from him by the editor of the *Nouvelle Revue française*.

Although he never felt that poetry could be a product of purely spontaneous composition, Valéry's youthful conception of poetry as a series of calculated effects controlled by the poet was tempered as he matured. He came to believe in the role of inspiration and mystery in the poetic process, as it operated on the intellect of both poet and reader; he believed that the aesthetic experience was so rich and complex that the intellect could never fully contain or understand it.

This aesthetic individualism colored Valéry's attitude toward his readers; he believed that, just as a poet's unique identity marks his poem, so will different readers' identities color their responses to it. He was therefore generous with his critics; although he may have been privately amused by some interpretations, he gave his official blessing to such endeavors, saying, "My poetry has the meaning that people give to it."

Valéry may have been troubled, however, by those critics who sought to reduce his poems to prose summaries. In his own writings, he often stated that a poem cannot be summarized any more than can a melody, that the beauty and power of poetry stem precisely from the fact that it cannot be put into prose without disintegrating. This problem in poetic theory is illustrated by what Valéry and two well-known critical interpreters have said about "The Graveyard by the Sea," a poem characteristic of Valéry's work in terms of its contemplative mood, its philosophical themes, its formal perfection, and its harmonious and evocative language.

"THE GRAVEYARD BY THE SEA"

Perhaps his best-known poem, "The Graveyard by the Sea" was written following Valéry's years of contemplation and study. First published in 1920, it portrays human consciousness becoming aware of itself in relation to time, death, and the expanse of the cosmos. The speaker in the poem ponders this interior vastness of consciousness in an ironic setting: a cemetry overlooking the sea, surrounded by tombstones, under the noon blaze of an apparently motionless sun.

"The Graveyard by the Sea" is composed of twenty-four stanzas of six decasyllabic lines each, with a rhyme scheme of *aabccb*. Valéry resurrected the decasyllabic line, which had been all but abandoned by French poets in favor of the more flowing Alexandrine. Although he welcomed the difficulties posed by the ten-syllable line, he did not consciously choose it. In his essay "On 'The Graveyard by the Sea,'" he states that the poem's genesis took the form of certain unintelligible decasyllabic "murmurings," and he became obsessed with the idea of arranging them into six-line stanzas connected by a network of correspondences and tonal contrasts. The intricate requirements of this form prompted him to seek his subject matter in familiar childhood memories, in the sea and sunlight of his Mediterranean birthplace, Sète. These elemental images led him directly to the contemplation of death.

The composition of "The Graveyard by the Sea" thus resembled the composition of a piece of music, in which the melodic motifs—the ideas—are often the *last* aspects of the composition to take shape. Valéry's essay on this poem stresses his belief that ideas simply do not play the same role in poetry that they do in prose; he conceives of "pure poetry" as a nonreferential network of infinite resonances that profoundly touch the reader's sensibility and cannot be summarized in prose. Elsewhere, however, he acknowledged that this ideal of pure poetry was an impossibility, that actual poems are always combinations of "fragments of pure poetry enclosed in the matter of a discourse," and that readers need some thematic or narrative material to guide them through a poem.

An oft-quoted explication of "The Graveyard by the Sea" which attempts to provide just such a guide is that of Sorbonne professor Gustave Cohen. His *Essai d'explication du "Cimetière marin"* (1933), is largely an elucidation of the poem's thematic development. It regards the poem as the recounting of a philosophical journey, a sort of classical tragedy in four acts, with three characters: Nonbeing, or Nothingness (symbolized by the seeming immobility of the noonday sun); human consciousness (represented by the sea), torn between its desire to unite with Nonbeing and its drive to change and create; and the speaker (whom Cohen calls the author), who is alternately a spectator and a participant in a drama which will irrevocably mark his life.

In Cohen's act 1 (stanzas 1-4), the speaker, transfixed by the sun's unwavering gaze, surveys the sailboats and the sea below him. Seen through the tree branches and tombstones, they resemble a roof covered with doves: "This tranquil roof where doves are walking." All *seems* motionless, and one feels the speaker's longing to be forever absorbed into the eternal.

The second act (stanzas 5-8) depicts the author's serene acceptance of his inevitable death. Stanza 5 exquisitely describes the loss of corporeal form and the separation of body and soul at death as the slow melting in the mouth of a piece of fruit which then releases a flood of fragrant juices: "As a fruit dissolves into a taste/ changing its absence to deliciousness/ within a palate where its shape must die." The speaker gradually realizes that despite the attraction of eternal changelessness, the essence of human existence is one of constant change. In the finale to this section, Cohen sees the speaker as aware of the vastness of his own consciousness as it exists in that moment of anticipatory emptiness before a poem is born: "Between the void and the pure event,/ I await the echo of my hidden depths."

In the third section (stanzas 9-18), Cohen sees the speaker rejecting the Christian promise of eternal life, and anticipating instead the permanent loss of individuality, sensuality, and awareness that is the fate of the dead, who have forever "melted into a dense absence." He now realizes that his very individuality is what defines him as alive.

Cohen's act 4 (stanzas 19-24) is titled "Triumph of the Momentary, of the Successive, of Change and of Po-

etic Creation." The speaker recognizes that he cannot deny life; the worm which relentlessly gnaws the living is the worm of consciousness, which will not let him rest: "He lives on life, it's me he never quits!" The speaker is troubled momentarily by Zeno's paradoxes, but a fresh breath of salty air prompts him to brush aside his incertitude. The once-calm sea's curling waves reveal the creative energy constantly boiling beneath its surface; it is likened to the Hydra which swallows its own tail, a symbol of infinity and renewal. The poet's mind also boils with creative fervor; the poem ends with the speaker's vigorous acceptance of life and with a call to the waves to shatter the tranquil sea/roof where the dove/sails had been pecking.

Interpretations such as Cohen's, helpful as they are in understanding the poem, were subsequently faulted for dealing too little with the language and structure of the poem and for providing no basis for an assessment of its aesthetic quality. One such critique of this thematic approach to Valéry was that of Bernard Weinberg, whose well-known study of "The Graveyard by the Sea" in *The Limits of Symbolism* (1966) focuses instead on the poem's structure. Weinberg demonstrates how its principal metaphor develops from an initial state of apparent equilibrium in which sea, cemetery, and spectator seem to be equivalent, through a middle ground in which this balance is threatened and then disrupted, to the end, where the idea of balance is foregone and movement and change are embraced. Paying close attention to the lexical aspects of the poem's language (although neglecting the phonic and rhythmic aspects), Weinberg shows how the repetition and interplay of polyvalent words and images result in a tightly woven unity born out of poetic rather than logical necessity. For example, in his discussion of Valéry's use of Zeno's paradox of infinitely dividing distance (stanza 21), Weinberg shows how Valéry's language simultaneously recalls the poem's opening image of a sun fixed in the sky at high noon and introduces an upcoming allusion to the disparity between substance and shadow. In a later observation, Weinberg demonstrates how the poem's ending is linked to its beginning: The panther skin surface of the sea, spotted with "thousands and thousands of idols of the sun," echoes the "thousand tiles" of the opening sea/ roof image; *idole* is a further instance of the recurring religious vocabulary which first appears early in the poem and continues throughout ("temple," *idolâtre*, and so on); the image of the Hydra swallowing its tail recalls the earlier mention of the "forever-recommencing sea" ("The sea, the sea perpetually renewed!").

Concentrating mainly on the poem's diction and the development of its principal metaphor, Weinberg postulates that the presence and placement of every word and image in the poem have a structural justification deriving from and contributing to the poem's unity. Thus, he is able to conclude that "The Graveyard by the Sea" is an excellent poem, because it presents itself to the reader as "a consistent, consecutive, and unified whole."

Several decades of critical distance allow one to see not only the complementarity and differences in the interpretations of Cohen and Weinberg, but also certain shared limitations inherent in their approaches. Analyses of "The Graveyard by the Sea" that emphasize resolution (Cohen's) or unity (Weinberg's) or progression (both authors') tend to exclude or de-emphasize references in the poem to circularity and repetition and to those enigmas of existence which forever resist integration into a unified whole.

In the course of this poem, the reader does indeed witness the evolution of the speaker's thought to a point of decision, but the poem's vocabulary and imagery reveal this progression to coexist with references to repetition and circularity. In the poem's twenty-four stanzas, there are twenty-three words containing the prefix "re-." The opening image shows the speaker in a moment of contemplative repose following a previous interval of thought/ action and contemplation. Cyclical resonances characterize the poem's major images: The sun suggests the alternation of day and night, the Earth's orbit around the sun, and also evokes the representation of time as circularity (another critic, Bernard Vannier, sees "The Graveyard by the Sea" as a clock, with its twenty-four hours/stanzas each divided into sixty minutes/feet); the massive solidity of the "forever recommencing sea" is counterbalanced by the oscillation of the waves and the ebb and flow of the tide ("The change of the murmuring shores"); death, too, is portrayed not only as an end but also as the beginning of a cycle ("All goes under the earth, and re-enters the game!").

The image of the Hydra biting its tail (stanza 23) symbolizes a circularity in which endings are contained within beginnings, and vice versa. This same sense of connection and continuity can be seen in the poem's opening and closing stanzas; one has an initial impression of absolute stasis eventually giving way to absolute motion, but each state is linked to and anticipates its opposite. The calm opening stanzas of the poem subtly suggest movement beneath the surface; the sea, seen as a "tranquil roof," "pulses" (*palpite*) in the sunlight, and peace "seems to conceive itself" in this moment of repose. Conversely, coloring the speaker's closing mood of affirmation are hints that he still struggles against the forces of inertia, hesitation, and doubt: "The wind rises! . . . One must attempt to live!/ The immense air opens and closes my book,/ The powdery waves dare to surge over the rocks!") Beginnings in endings also appear in the speaker's closing exhortation to the waves to "break the tranquil roof where the sails were pecking"— a reprise of the poem's opening image. The two notions of circularity and progression are thus fused; insofar as this poem represents the universal experience of every individual who confronts the infinite, the speaker's ultimate decision to embrace life is as much a re-solution (a solving again) as it is a resolution.

But what of those elements that resist resolution or integration into a system, those paradoxes that confound the human mind? The speaker in the poem longs for the oblivion of nonbeing. As long as he is alive and changing, he will never know this peace; finding peace in death, he will also lose it, for he will lose all awareness. The vastness of nonbeing is pure and yet impure; changeless and sufficient unto itself, it needs an imperfect, changing human consciousness ("The flaw in [its] great diamond") to recognize and reflect its perfection. The speaker longs to merge with the absolute but cannot in his present form cross the boundary which separates him from the infinite. The poem abounds in images juxtaposed without being merged: In the cemetery, the living visit the dead, but there is no contact; the sea meets the land but remains forever separate; any substance which reflects the light has a dark half always in shadow. It should be noted, too, that the poem's protagonist does not ever resolve Zeno's paradoxes; in the end he impetuously allows his vital life-instincts to override the obstacles created by thought and logic.

It seems inappropriate to seek total unity and complete resolution in a poem in which paradox enjoys the status of a theme. According to Zeno's paradoxes, motion cannot exist, and a moving object can never arrive at its destination—yet arrows have been known to pierce their targets. Faced with things beyond comprehension, the living man is afforded a glimpse of infinite vastness; he, like the noonday sun in the poem's opening, "rests above the abyss."

This state of suspension, "between the void and the pure event," brings to mind the similar state which Zen masters seek to produce in their disciples by means of the koan, an enigmatic question which has no answer but the contemplation of which can lead to spiritual enlightenment. In "The Graveyard by the Sea," it is the contemplation of evocative language and poetic enigma that produces a sense of vastness and mystery. Explications that place too great an emphasis on unity and resolution risk stifling other, more elusive echoes which are equally a part of the poem's seductive charms.

OTHER MAJOR WORKS

SHORT FICTION: "La Soirée avec Monsieur Teste," 1896 ("An Evening with Monsieur Teste," 1925).

PLAYS: *Amphion*, pr., pb. 1931 (musical drama; English translation, 1960); *Sémiramis*, pr., pb. 1934 (musical drama; English translation, 1960); *Cantate du Narcisse*, pr. 1939 (musical drama; *The Narcissus Cantata*, 1960); *Mon Faust*, pb. 1946 (*My Faust*, 1960).

NONFICTION: *Eupalinos; Ou, L'Architecte*, 1921 (dialogue; *Eupalinos: Or, The Architect*, 1932); *Variété*, 1924-1944 (5 vols.); *L'Âme et la danse*, 1925 (dialogue; *Dance and the Soul*, 1951); *Analecta*, 1926 (*Analects*, 1970); *Regards sur le monde actuel*, 1931 (*Reflections on the World Today*, 1948); *Degas, danse, dessin*, 1938 (*Degas, Dance, Drawing*, 1960); *Les Cahiers*, 1957-1961.

MISCELLANEOUS: *Selected Writings*, 1950; *The Collected Works of Paul Valéry*, 1956-1975 (15 volumes).

BIBLIOGRAPHY

Anderson, Kirsteen. *Paul Valéry and the Voice of Desire*. Oxford, England: Legenda, 2000. An exploration of the power of voice as image and theme throughout Valéry's writing. Anderson highlights the tension between a dominant "masculine" imaginary and the repressed "feminine" dimension which underpins Valéry's work.

Gifford, Paul, and Brian Stimpson, eds. *Reading Paul Valéry: Universe in Mind*. New York: Cambridge University Press, 1998. A collection of essays by internationally recognized scholars offering a comprehensive account of Valéry's work. Perspectives are offered on the immense range of Valéry's experimental and fragmentary writings.

Kluback, William. *Paul Valéry: Illusions of Civilization*. New York: Peter Lang, 1996. A discussion of the meaning of civilization, in particular, Western civilization, as it was investigated in the philosophical works of Valéry. An illuminating study for anyone interested in the infrastructure of Valéry's philosophy as it embraced the questions of civilization, history, evil, love, and mortality.

_____. *Paul Valéry: The Realms of the "Analecta."* New York: Peter Lang, 1998. A study of a particular aspect of Valéry's philosophical work, the *Analects*. This is the realm of the imagination, of the image and metaphor. Readers are presented with epigrams that are designed to confuse and challenge their thinking.

Putnam, Walter C. *Paul Valéry Revisited*. New York: Twayne, 1995. An introductory biography and critical study of selected works by Valéry. Includes bibliographical references and index.

Whiting, Charles G. *Paul Valéry*, 1973. A concise critical study of selected works by Valéry. Includes an index and a bibliography.

Janet L. Solberg;
bibliography updated by the editors

CÉSAR VALLEJO

Born: Santiago de Chuco, Peru; March 16, 1892
Died: Paris, France; April 15, 1938

PRINCIPAL POETRY

Los heraldos negros, 1918 (*The Black Heralds*, 1990)
Trilce, 1922 (English translation, 1973)
Poemas en prosa, 1939 (*Prose Poems*, 1978)
Poemas humanos, 1939 (*Human Poems*, 1968)
España, aparta de mí este cáliz, 1939 (*Spain, Take This Cup from Me*, 1974)
Obra poética completa, 1968
Poesía completa, 1978
The Complete Posthumous Poetry, 1978
Selected Poems, 1981

OTHER LITERARY FORMS

César Vallejo wrote fiction, plays, and essays, as well as lyric poetry, although his achievement as a poet far outstrips that in any other genre. His short stories—many of them extremely brief—may be found in *Escalas melografiadas* (1923; musical scales). A longer short story, "Fabla salvaje" (1923; primitive parlance), is a tragic idyll of two rustic lovers. *Hacia el reino de los Sciris* (1967; toward the kingdom of the Sciris), set in the time of the Incas, is usually described as a novel, de-

César Vallejo

spite its brevity. *El tungsteno* (1931; *Tungsten*, 1988), is a proletarian novel with an Andean setting that was written in 1931, the year Vallejo joined the Communist Party. Another story, *Paco Yunque* (1969), is about the mistreatment of a servant's son by a classmate who happens to be the master's son.

Vallejo became interested in the theater around 1930, but he destroyed his first play, "Mampar." Three others, *Moscú contra Moscú*—later changed to *Entre las dos orillas corre el río* (pb. 1979; the river flows between two banks); *Lock-Out* (pb. 1979), and *Colacho hermanos: O, presidentes de América* (pb. 1979; Colacho brothers), never published during the poet's lifetime, are now available in *Teatro completo* (pb. 1979; complete theatrical work). His long essay, *Rusia en 1931: Reflexiones al pie del Kremlin* (1931; reissued in 1965), was followed by *Rusia ante el segundo plan quinquenal* (1965); *Contra el secreto profesional* (1973); and *El arte y la revolución* (1973). His master's thesis, *El romanticismo en la poesía castellana*, was published in 1954.

ACHIEVEMENTS

Finding an authentic language in which to write has always represented a fundamental problem for Latin American writers, since it became evident that the language inherited from the Spanish conquerors could not match Latin American reality. The problem of finding such a language goes hand in hand with that of forging a separate cultural identity. An important attempt at renovating poetic language was made by the Spanish American *Modernistas* around the turn of the century, but their verse forms, imagery, and often exotic subject matter were also becoming obsolete by the time César Vallejo reached maturity. It was thus up to him and his contemporaries to find a language that could deal with contemporary concerns involving war, depression, isolation, and alienation. Although hardly recognized in his lifetime, Vallejo did more than perhaps any other poet of his generation to provide an idiom that would at once reflect the Spanish tradition, his own Peruvian heritage, and the contemporary world. Aware of his heritage from Spain's great writers of the past, he blended traditional poetic vocabulary and tropes with homely Peruvian idioms and even the language of children. Where the result was still inadequate, he made up new words, changed the function of old ones, and incorporated a lexicon never before seen in poetry, often savaging poetic convention.

Vallejo's gradual conversion to Marxism and Communism is of great interest to those attempting to understand how collectivist ideals may shape poetry. The evolution of his ideology continues to be studied intensively by many individuals committed to bettering the conditions of poverty and alienation about which Vallejo wrote so eloquently—conditions which still exist in Latin America and other parts of the world. His unflinchingly honest search for both linguistic and moral solutions to the existential anguish of modern man gives his poems universal validity, while their density and complexity challenge critics of the most antithetical modes.

BIOGRAPHY

César Abraham Vallejo was born in Santiago de Chuco, a primitive "city" of some fourteen thousand inhabitants in Peru's northern mountains that could only be reached by a rail trip and then several days ride on mule or horseback. Both of his grandfathers had been Spanish priests and both of his grandmothers native Peruvians of Chimu Indian stock. His parents were literate and of modest means; his father was a notary who became a subprefect in the district. Francisco de Paula Vallejo and María de los Santos Mendoza were an upright and religious pair whose marriage produced twelve offspring and who were already middle-aged when their youngest child, César, was born. In his writings, Vallejo was often to remember the security and warmth of his childhood home—games with three of his older siblings, and particularly with his mother, who might have been especially indulgent with her sensitive youngest child.

At age thirteen, Vallejo left Santiago de Chuco to attend high school in Huamachuco, another mountain village, where he received an introduction to literature and began scribbling verses. Economic difficulties prevented him from continuing the university studies that he had begun in the larger coastal cities of Trujillo and Lima in 1911. The young man first went to work in a nearby tungsten mine—an experience that he would later draw upon for his Socialist Realist novel *Tungsten*—and then on a coastal sugar plantation. While there, he observed the tightly structured hierarchy that kept workers in misery while the middle class, to which he himself belonged, served the needs of the elite. In 1913, he returned to the University of Trujillo and was graduated two years later, having written a master's thesis titled *El romanticismo en la poesía castellana*. For the next few years, he studied law in Trujillo, supporting himself by becoming a first-grade teacher. One of his pupils, Ciro Alegría, later to become an important novelist, described Vallejo in those days as lean, sallow, solemn, and dark-skinned, with abundant straight black hair worn somewhat long, brilliant dark eyes, a gentle manner, and an air of sadness.

During these years, Vallejo became familiar with the writings of Ralph Waldo Emerson, José Rodó, Friedrich Nietzsche, Miguel de Unamuno y Jugo, Walt Whitman, and the early Juan Ramón Jiménez. Vallejo also read the poems of two of the leading Spanish-American *Modernistas*, Rubén Darío and Julio Herrera y Reissig, as well as those of Peruvian poets of the day. Vallejo declaimed his own poems—mostly occasional verse—at various public ceremonies, and some of them appeared in Trujillo's newspapers. Critical reception of them ranged from the cool to the hostile, since they were considered to be exaggerated and strange in that highly traditional ambience. Vallejo fell in love with a young Trujillo girl, Zoila Rosa Cuadro, the subject of several poems included in *The Black Heralds*. The breakup of this relationship provided one motive for his departure, after he had obtained a law degree, for Lima in 1918. There he found a position teaching in one of the best elementary schools and began to put the finishing touches on his first volume of poems.

Vallejo was soon in love with the sister-in-law of one of his colleagues, a woman identified only as "Otilia." A number of the *Trilce* poems, which he was writing at the time, deal with this affair. It ended when the poet refused to marry the woman, resulting in the loss of his job. This crisis was compounded by the death of his mother, a symbol of stability whose loss made him feel like an orphan. For some time, Vallejo had thought of going to Paris, but he decided to return first to his childhood home in Santiago de Chuco. During a national holiday, he was falsely accused of having been the instigator of a civil disturbance and was later seized and imprisoned for 112 days despite the public protests of many Peruvian intellectuals. The experience affected him profoundly, and the poems that he wrote about it (later published in *Trilce*) testify to the feeling of solidarity with the oppressed that he voiced for the first time. While in prison, he also wrote a number of the sketches to appear in *Escalas melografiadas*. In 1923, he sailed for Europe, never again to return to Peru.

While Vallejo's days in Lima had often been marked by personal problems, in Paris he experienced actual penury, sometimes being forced to sleep in the subway. Eventually, he found employment in a press agency, but only after a serious illness. He began to contribute articles to Lima newspapers, made friends with a number of avant-garde artists, and journeyed several times to Spain, where he was awarded a grant for further study. Increasingly concerned with injustice in the world, he made his first trip to Russia in 1928 with the intention of staying. Instead, he returned within three weeks, living soon afterward with a Frenchwoman, Georgette de Philippart, who was later to become his wife. With some money that had come to her, the pair set out on a tour by train through Eastern Europe, spending two weeks in Moscow and returning by way of Rome. As Vallejo's enthusiasm for Marxism was apparent in his newspaper articles, he found them no longer welcome in Lima, and in 1930, he was ordered to leave France because of his political activity. Once again in Spain, he wrote several plays and the novel *El tungsteno* and published *Rusia en 1931*, the only one of his books to sell well. No publisher could be found for several other works. After a third and final visit to Russia as a delegate to the International Congress of Writers, he wrote *Rusia ante el segundo plan quinquenal* and officially joined the Communist Party.

In 1932, Vallejo was permitted to return to Paris, where he tried unsuccessfully to publish some new poems. In 1936, the Spanish Civil War broke out, and Vallejo became an active supporter of the Republic, traveling to Barcelona and Madrid to attend the Second International Congress for the Defense of Culture. He visited the battlefront and learned at first hand of the horrors suffered by the Spanish people in the war. Returning to Paris for the last time, he poured his feelings into his last work, *España, aparta de mí este cáliz*

(1939; *Spain, Take This Cup from Me*). In March, 1938, he became ill. Doctors were unable to diagnose his illness, and Vallejo died a month later on Good Friday, the day before the troops of Francisco Franco won a decisive victory in Spain.

ANALYSIS

One of the unique qualities of César Vallejo's poetry—one that makes his work almost impossible to confuse with that of any other poet in the Spanish language—is his ability to speak with the voice and sensibility of a child, whether as an individual orphaned by the breakup of a family or as a symbol of deprived and alienated human beings everywhere. Always, however, this child's voice, full of expectation and hope, is implicitly counterposed by the adult's ironic awareness of change and despair. Inseparable from these elements is the poet's forging of a language capable of reflecting the register and the peculiarly elliptical reasoning of a child and, at the same time, revealing the hermetic complexity of the adult intellectual's quest for security in the form of truth. The poetry that is Vallejo's own answer to these problems is some of the most poignant and original ever produced.

THE BLACK HERALDS

The lines of Vallejo's subsequent development are already evident in his first volume, *The Black Heralds*, a collection of sixty-nine poems grouped under various subtitles. As critics have observed, many of these poems reflect his involvement with Romantic and *Modernista* poetry. They are conspicuous in many cases for their descriptions of idyllic scenes in a manner that juxtaposes words of the Peruvian Sierra and the vocabulary of Symbolism, including religious and erotic elements. Vallejo did not emphasize rhyme and rhythm to the extent that some *Modernistas* did, but most of these early poems are framed in verse forms favored by the latter, such as the Alexandrine sonnet and the *silva*. While demonstrating his impressive mastery of styles already worked out by others, he was also finding his own voice.

This originality is perhaps most evident in the last group of poems in *The Black Heralds*, titled "Canciones de Hogar" ("Home Songs"), poems dealing with the beginning of Vallejo's sense of orphanhood. In "A mi hermano Miguel in memoriam" ("To My Brother

Miguel in Memoriam"), the poet relives a moment of the childhood game of hide-and-seek that he used to play with his "twin heart." Speaking to his brother, Vallejo announces his own presence in the part of the family home from which one of the two always ran away to hide from the other. He goes on to remind his playmate of one day on which the latter went away to hide, sad instead of laughing as he usually was, and could not be found again. The poem ends with a request to the brother to please come out so as not to worry "mama." It is remarkable in that past and present alternate from one line to the next. The language of childhood, as well as the poet's assumed presence at the site of the events, lends a dramatic immediacy to the scene. At the same time, the language used in the descriptive passages is clearly that of the adult who is now the poet. Yet in the last verse, the adult chooses to accept literally the explanation that the brother has remained in hiding and may finally respond and come out, which would presumably alleviate the mother's anxiety and make everything right once more. The knowledge that the poet is unable (or refuses) to face the permanent alteration of his past may elicit feelings of tragic pathos in the reader.

"Los pasos lejanos" ("The Distant Steps") recalls the poet's childhood home in which his parents, now aged, are alone—the father sleeping and the mother walking in the orchards. Here, the only bitterness is that of the poet himself, because he is now far away from them. He in turn is haunted by a vision of his parents as two old, white, and bent roads along which his heart walks. In "Enereida," he imagines that his father has died, leading to a regression in time so that the father can once again laugh at his small children, including the poet himself, who is again a schoolboy under the tutelage of the village priest.

Many of the poems in *The Black Heralds* deal with existential themes. While religious imagery is pervasive, it is apparent that the poet employs it to describe profane experiences. Jean Franco has shown that in speaking of "the soul's Christs" and "Marías who leave" and of Communions and Passions, Vallejo trivializes religious language rather than attempting to inflate the importance of his own experiences by describing them in religious terms. As well as having lost the security and plenitude of his childhood home, the poet has lost the childhood faith that enabled him to refer in words to the infinite.

In the title poem, "Los heraldos negros" ("The Black Heralds"), he laments life's hard blows, harder sometimes than man can stand. He concludes that these blows come from the hatred of God, that they may be the black heralds sent by Death. In "Los dados eternos" ("The Eternal Dice"), God is a gambler throwing dice and may as easily cast death as life. In fact, the Earth itself is his die. Now worn to roundness, it will come to rest only within the sepulchre. Profane love is all that is left; while the beloved may now be pure, she will not continue to be so if she yields to the poet's erotic impulses. Love thus becomes "a sinning Christ," because man's nature is irrevocably physical. Several poems allude to the poet's ideal of redeeming himself through brotherly love, a thematic constant in Vallejo's work, yet such redemption becomes difficult if not impossible if man is lonely and alienated. In "Agape," the poet speaks of being alone and forgotten and of having been unable therefore to "die" for his brother. "La cena miserable" ("The Wretched Supper") tells of the enigma of existence in which man is seen, as in "Agape," as waiting endlessly for spiritual nurture, or at least for some answer concerning the meaning of life. Here, God becomes no more than a "black spoon" full of bitter human essence, even less able than man to provide needed answers. Man's life is thus meaningless, since he is always separated from what he most desires—whether this be the fulness of the past, physical love, God's love, or brotherly love.

Even in the poems most laden with the trappings of *Modernismo*, Vallejo provides unusual images. In "El poeta a su amada" ("The Poet to His Beloved"), he suggests that his kiss is "two curved branches" on which his beloved has been "crucified." Religious imagery is used with such frequency that it sometimes verges on parody, and critics agree that in playing with language in this way Vallejo is seeking to highlight its essential ambiguity, something he continues to do in *Trilce* and *Human Poems*, even while totally abandoning the imagery of *Modernismo*. Such stripping away of excess baggage is already visible in *The Black Heralds*. Antitheses, oxymorons, and occasional neologisms are also to be noted. While the great majority of the poems are elegantly correct in terms of syntax—in marked contrast to what is to become the norm in *Trilce*—there are some instances of linguistic experimentation, as when nouns are used as adjectives. In "The Distant Steps," for example, the mother is described as being "so soft, so wing, so departure, so love." Another device favored by the poet in all his later poems—enumeration—is also present. Finally, traditional patterns of meter and rhyme are abandoned in "Home Songs," with the poetic emotion being allowed to determine the form.

TRILCE

In spite of these formal adumbrations and in spite of the fact that *The Black Heralds* is not a particularly transparent work, there is little in it to prepare the reader for the destruction of language in the hermetic density of *Trilce*, which came along only three years later. These were difficult years for the poet, in which he lost his mother, separated from Otilia, and spent what he was later to refer to as the gravest moments of his life in the Trujillo jail. All the anguish of these events was poured into the seventy-seven free-verse poems of his second major work. If he suffered existentially in *The Black Heralds* and expressed this suffering in writing, it was done with respect for traditional verse forms and sentence structure, which hinted at an order beyond the chaos of the poet's interior world. In *Trilce*, this order falls. Language, on which "logical assumptions" about the world are based, is used in such a way as to reveal its hollowness: It, too, is cut loose and orphaned. Abrupt shifts from one metaphorical sphere to another make the poems' internal logic often problematic.

A hint of what is to come is given in the title, a neologism usually taken to be a hybrid of *tres* (three) and *dulce* (sweet), an interpretation which is in accord with the poet's concern about the ideal number expressed in several poems. It is not known, however, what, if any, concrete meaning the poet had in mind when he coined the word; it has become a puzzle for readers and critics to solve. It is notable that in "interpreting" the *Trilce* poems, critics often work out explications that seem internally consistent but that turn out to be related to a system diametrically opposed to the explication and system of some other critic. It is possible, however, to say with certainty that these poems deal with a struggle to do something, bridge something, say something. Physical limits

such as the human body, time, space, and numbers often render the struggle futile.

Two of the thematic sets of *Trilce* for which it is easiest to establish concrete referents are those dealing with the poet-as-child and those dealing with his imprisonment. In Poem III, the poet once again speaks in the voice of a child left at home by the adults of the family. It is getting dark, and he asks when the grown-ups will be back, adding that "Mama said she wouldn't be gone long." In the third stanza, an ironic double vision of years full of agonizing memories intrudes. As in "To My Brother Miguel in Memoriam," the poet chooses to retain the child's faith, urging his brothers and sisters to be good and obey in letter and spirit the instructions left by the mother. In the end, it is seen that the "leaving" is without remedy, a function of time itself; it eventually results in the poet's complete solitude without even the comfort of his siblings. In Poem XXIII, the mother, the only symbol of total plenitude, is seen as the "warm oven" of the cookies described as "rich hosts of time." The nourishment provided by the mother was given freely and naturally, taken away from no one and given without the child's being obliged. Still, the process of nurturing leads to growing up and to individuation and alienation. Several poems mythicize the process of birth but shift so abruptly to demythicize human existence that the result is at first humorous. In Poem XLVII, a candle is lighted to protect the mother while she gives birth, along with another for the babe who, God willing, will grow up to be bishop, pope, saint, "or perhaps only a columnary headache." Later, in *Human Poems*, there is a Word Incarnate whose bones agree in number and gender as it sinks into the bathtub ("Lomo de las sagradas escrituras"/"Spine of the Scriptures").

In Poem XVIII, the poet surveys the four walls of the cell, implacably closed. He calls up a vision of the "loving keeper of innumerable keys," the mother, who would liberate him if she could. He imagines the two longer walls as mothers and the shorter ones as the children each of them is leading by the hand. The poet is alone with only his two hands, struggling to find a third to help him in his useless adulthood. In Poem LVIII, the solid walls of the cell seem to bend at the corners, suggesting that the poet is dozing as a series of jumbled thoughts produce scenes in his mind that follow no easy logical principle of association. The poet sees himself helping the naked and the ragged, then dismounting from a panting horse that he also attempts to help. The cell is now liquid, and he becomes aware of the companions who may be worse off than he. Guilt suddenly overwhelms him, and he is moved to promise to laugh no more when his mother arises early to pray for the sick, the poor, and the prisoners. He also promises to treat his little friends better at play, in both word and deed. The cell is now boundless gas, growing as it condenses. Ambiguously, at the end, he poses the question, "Who stumbles outside?" The openness of the poem is similar to that of many others in *Trilce*, and it is difficult to say what kind of threat to the poet's resolutions is posed by the figure outside. Again, the poetic voice has become that of a child seeking to make all that is wrong in the world right once more by promising to be "a good boy." Of course, he is not a child at all, as the figure outside may be intended to remind both him and the reader. The result is once again a remarkable note of pathos tinged with poignant irony.

Many of *Trilce*'s poems deal with physical love and even the sexual act itself. "Two" seems to be the ideal number, but "two" has "propensities of trinity." Clearly, the poet has no wish to bring a child into the world, and sex becomes merely an act of organs that provides no solution to anything. While the poet seems to appreciate the maternal acts performed by his lover, he fails to find any transcendental satisfaction in the physical relationship, even though he is sad when it is over.

An important theme that emerges in *Trilce* and is developed more fully in *Human Poems* and *Spain, Take This Cup from Me* is that of the body as text. In Poem LXV, the house to which the poet returns in Santiago seems to be his mother's body. Parts of the body—the back, face, shoulder, eyes, hands, lips, eyelashes, bones, feet, knees, fingers, heart, arms, breasts, soles of the feet, eyelids, ears, ribs—appear in poem after poem, reminding the reader of human and earthly functions and the limitations of man.

In many ways, *Trilce* resembles the poetry of such avant-garde movements as Surrealism, Ultraism, and Creationism in the boldness of its images, its unconventional vocabulary, and its experimentation with graphics. Vallejo did have very limited exposure to some of this poetry after he reached Lima; his critics, however, generally agree that *Trilce* was produced independently. While Vallejo may have been encouraged to experiment by his knowledge of European literary currents, his work coincides with them as an original contribution.

HUMAN POEMS

As far as is known, the poems after *Trilce* were written in Europe; with very few exceptions, none was published until 1939, a year after the poet's death, when they appeared under the title *Human Poems*. While Vallejo's life in Peru was far from affluent, it must have seemed easy in comparison with the years in Paris, where he often barely subsisted and suffered several illnesses. In addition, while he did see a new edition of *Trilce* published through the intervention of friends in 1931, and while his *Rusia en 1931* did go into three editions during his lifetime, he could never count on having his writings accepted for publication.

Human Poems, considered separately from *Spain, Take This Cup from Me*, is far from being a homogeneous volume, and its final configuration might have been different had it been Vallejo who prepared the final edition rather than his widow. Generally speaking, the poems that it includes deal with ontological anguish whose cause seems related to physical suffering, the passage of time, and the impossibility of believing that life has any meaning. In fact, *Human Poems* examines suffering and pain, with their corollaries, poverty, hunger, illness, and death, with a thoroughness that few other works can match. At times, the anguish seems to belong only to the poet, now not only the orphan of *Trilce* but alienated from his fellowman as well. In "Altura y pelos" ("Height and Hair"), the poet poses questions: "Who doesn't own a blue suit?/ Who doesn't eat lunch and board the streetcar . . . ?/ Who is not called Carlos or any other thing?/ Who to the kitty doesn't say kitty kitty?" The final answer given is "Aie? I who alone was solely born." At least two kinds of irony seem to be involved here. The activities mentioned are obviously trivial, but neither is it easy to be alone. In the well-known "Los nueve monstruos" ("The Nine Monsters"), the poet laments the abundance of pain in the world: "Never, human men/ was there so *much* pain in the chest, in the lapel, in the wallet/ in the glass, in the butcher-shop, in arithmetic!" and "never/ . . . did the migraine extract so much forehead from the forehead!" Pain drives people crazy "in the movies,/ nails us into the gramophones,/ denails us in bed . . ." The poem concludes that the "Secretary of Health" can do nothing because there is simply "too much to do."

"The Nine Monsters" is representative of several features of *Human Poems*. The language is extremely concrete, denoting things that are inseparable from everyday existence. Much of the poem consists of lists, continuing a device for which the poet had already shown a disposition in his first work. Finally, the logic of the systems represented by the items named is hard to pin down, so that it is somewhat reminiscent of child logic in its eccentricity. Again and again, Vallejo's remarkable sensibility is demonstrated beyond any preciosity or mere posturing.

One reason for the poet's alienation is that he sees men as engaged in trivial occupations and as being hardly more advanced on the evolutionary scale than pachyderms or kangaroos, whereas he himself aspires to rise above his limitations. In "Intensidad y altura" ("Intensity and Height"), he tells of his desire to write being stifled by his feeling "like a puma," so that he might as well go and eat grass. He concludes, "let's go, raven, and fecundate your rook." He thus sees himself condemned not to rise above the purely mundane. Religion offers no hope at all. In "Acaba de pasar el que vendrá . . ." ("He Has Just Passed By, the One Who Will Come . . ."), the poet suggests that "the one who will come"—presumably the Messiah—has already passed by but has changed nothing, being as vague and ineffectually human as anyone else.

While the majority of these posthumously published poems convey utter despair, not all of them do. Although the exact dates of their composition are generally unknown, it is natural to associate those that demonstrate growing concern for others with Vallejo's conversion to Marxist thought and eventually to Communism. In "Considerando en frío . . ." ("Considering Coldly . . ."), speaking as an attorney at a trial, the poetic voice first summarizes the problems and weaknesses of man's humanity (he "is sad, coughs and, nevertheless,/ takes pleasure in his reddened chest/ . . . he is a gloomy mammal and combs his hair . . .") Then, however, he announces his love for man. Denying it immediately, he

nevertheless concludes, "I signal him,/ he comes,/ I embrace him, moved./ So what! Moved . . . Moved. . . ." Compassion thus nullifies "objectivity." In "La rueda del hambriento" ("The Hungry Man's Wheel"), the poet speaks as a man so miserable that his own organs are pulled out of him through his mouth. He begs only for a stone on which to sit and a little bread. Apparently ignored, aware that he is being importunate, he continues to ask, disoriented and hardly able to recognize his own body. In "Traspié entre dos estrellas" ("Stumble Between Two Stars"), the poet expresses pity for the wretched but goes on to parody bitterly Christ's Sermon on the Mount ("Beloved be the one with bedbugs,/ the one who wears a torn shoe in the rain"), ending with a "beloved" for one thing and then for its opposite, as if calling special attention to the emptiness of mere words. It is possible to say that in these poems the orphan has finally recognized that he is not alone in his orphanhood.

SPAIN, TAKE THIS CUP FROM ME

Although first published as part of *Human Poems*, *Spain, Take This Cup from Me* actually forms a separate, unified work very different in tone from the majority of the other posthumous poems—a tone of hope, although, especially in the title poem, the poet seems to suspect that the cause he has believed in so passionately may be lost. In this poem, perhaps the last that Vallejo wrote, the orphan—now all human children—has found a mother. This mother is Spain, symbol of a new revolutionary order in which oppression may be ended. The children are urged not to let their mother die; nevertheless, even should this happen, they have a recourse: to continue struggling and to go out and find a new mother.

Another contrast is found in the odes to several heroes of the Civil War. Whereas, in *Human Poems*, man is captive of his body and hardly more intelligent than the lower animals, *Spain, Take This Cup from Me* finds him capable of true transcendence through solidarity with his brothers and the will to fight injustice. A number of poems commemorate the battles of the war: Talavera, Guernica, Málaga. Spain thus becomes a text—a book that sprouts from the bodies of an anonymous soldier. The poet insists again and again that he himself is nothing, that his stature is "tiny," and that his actions rather than his words constitute the real text. This may be seen to represent a greatly evolved negation of poetic authority, first seen in *The Black Heralds* with the repeated cry, "I don't know!"

Nevertheless, *Spain, Take This Cup from Me* rings with a biblical tone, and the poet sometimes sounds like a prophet. James Higgins has pointed out certain images that recall the Passion of Christ and the New Jerusalem, although religious terminology, as in all Vallejo's poetry, is applied to man rather than to divinity. While Vallejo continues to use techniques of enumeration, which are often chaotic, and while he uses concrete nouns (including many referring to the body), he also employs abstract terms—peace, hope, martyrdom, harmony, eternity, greatness. The sense of garments, utensils, and the body's organs stifling the soul is gone and is replaced by limitless space. In Vallejo's longest poem, "Himno a los voluntarios de la República" ("Hymn to the Volunteers for the Republic"), a panegyric note is struck.

One of Vallejo's most immediately accessible poems, "Masa" ("Mass"), tells almost a parable of a dead combatant who was asked by one man not to die, then by two, and finally by millions. The corpse kept dying until surrounded by all the inhabitants of the Earth. The corpse, moved, sat up and embraced the first man and then began to walk. The simplicity of the story and of its narration recalls the child's voice in *Trilce*, promising to cease tormenting his playmates in order to atone for the world's guilt. In this piece, as well as in all Vallejo's last group of poems, however, the irony is gone.

POETIC CYCLE

It is thus possible to see the completion of a cycle in the four works. Disillusionment grows in *The Black Heralds*, and then alienation works its way into the language itself in *Trilce*. *Human Poems* is somewhat less hermetic than *Trilce*, but life is an anguished nightmare in which the soul is constrained by the ever-present body that seems to be always wracked with pain. Only in *Spain, Take This Cup from Me*, with the realization that men are brothers who can end their common alienation and suffering by collective action, does the poet regain his lost faith and embark upon a positive course. The orphan relocates the lost mother, whom he now sees to be the mother of all, since all men are brothers. The true significance of Vallejo's poetry, however, surely lies in his honesty in questioning all established rules of poetic expression, as well as the tradition of poetic authority, in order to put poetry fully in touch with the existential prison-house of twentieth century man.

OTHER MAJOR WORKS

LONG FICTION: *Fábula salvaje*, 1923 (novella); *El tungsteno*, 1931 (*Tungsten*, 1988).

SHORT FICTION: *Escalas melografiadas*, 1923; *Hacia el reino de los Sciris*, 1967; *Paco Yunque*, 1969.

PLAYS: *La piedra cansada*, pb. 1979; *Colacho hermanos: O, presidentes de América*, pb. 1979; *Lock-Out*, pb. 1979; *Entre las dos orillas corre el río*, pb. 1979; *Teatro completo*, pb. 1979.

NONFICTION: *Rusia en 1931: Reflexiones al pie del Kremlin*, 1931, 1965; *El romanticismo en la poesía castellana*, 1954; *Rusia ante el segundo plan quinquenal*, 1965; *El arte y la revolución*, 1973; *Contra el secreto profesional*, 1973.

BIBLIOGRAPHY

Adamsom, Joseph. *Modern Poetry and Deconstruction*. New York: Garland, 1988. Focuses on Vallejo as a "thinking" poet whose work engages philosophy.

Flores, Ángel. *Aproximaciones a César Vallejo*. 2 vols. New York: Las Américas, 1971. Sections on Vallejo's biography, conflicting aspects (such as the contrast between Quechua indigenous and Spanish influences), poetic themes, and literary influences and techniques.

Franco, Jean. *César Vallejo. The Dialectics of Poetry and Silence*. Cambridge: Cambridge University Press, 1976. The first book-length study in English of Vallejo's poetry and still a classic. Biography is followed by careful analyses of four major books of poetry: *The Black Heralds*, *Trilce*, *Human Poems*, and *Spain, Take This Cup from Me*.

Hedrick, Tace Megan. "Mi andina y dulce Rita: Women, Indigenism, and the Avant-Garde in César Vallejo." In *Primitivism and Identity in Latin America: Essays on Art, Literature, and Culture*, edited by Erik Camayd-Freixas and José Eduardo González. Tucson: University of Arizona Press, 2000. Relates the indigenism of "Dead Idylls" from *The Black Heralds* to the "avant-garde concerns and practices" of *Trilce*, often considered Vallejo's most brilliant work.

Lambie, George. "Poetry and Politics: The Spanish Civil War Poetry of César Vallejo." *Bulletin of Hispanic Studies* 69, no. 2 (April, 1992): 153-170. Analyzes the presence of faith and Marxism in *Spain, Take This Cup from Me.*

Niebylski, Dianna C. *The Poem on the Edge of the Word: The Limits of Language and the Uses of Silence in the Poetry of Mallarmé, Rilke, and Vallejo.* New York: Peter Lang, 1993. In a context of the language "crisis" of modern poetry and the poet's dilemma in choosing language or silence, Niebylski examines the themes of time and death in Vallejo's *Human Poems.*

Sharman, Adam, ed. *The Poetry and Poetics of César Vallejo.* Lewiston, N.Y.: Edwin Mellen Press, 1997. Collection of essays examining Vallejo's work from the perspectives of Marxism, history, the theme of the absent mother, and post-colonial theory.

Lee Hunt Dowling;
bibliography updated by Linda Ledford-Miller

MARK VAN DOREN

Born: Hope, Illinois; June 13, 1894
Died: Torrington, Connecticut; December 10, 1972

PRINCIPAL POETRY

Spring Thunder and Other Poems, 1924
7 P.M. and Other Poems, 1926
Now the Sky and Other Poems, 1928
Jonathan Gentry, 1931
A Winter Diary and Other Poems, 1935
The Last Look and Other Poems, 1937
Collected Poems, 1922-1938, 1939
The Mayfield Deer, 1941
Our Lady Peace and Other War Poems, 1942
The Seven Sleepers and Other Poems, 1944
The Country Year, 1946
The Careless Clock: Poems About Children in the Family, 1947
New Poems, 1948
Humanity Unlimited: Twelve Sonnets, 1950

In That Far Land, 1951
Mortal Summer, 1953
Spring Birth and Other Poems, 1953
Selected Poems, 1954
Morning Worship and Other Poems, 1960
Collected and New Poems, 1924-1963, 1963
The Narrative Poems, 1964
That Shining Place: New Poems, 1969
Good Morning: Last Poems, 1973

OTHER LITERARY FORMS

In addition to poetry, Mark Van Doren also wrote drama, fiction, and various nonfiction works. Two of his plays, *The Last Days of Lincoln* (1959) and *Never, Never Ask His Name* (1966), were produced in 1961 and 1965, respectively. The latter was published in *Three Plays*, together with two unproduced plays, *A Little Night Music* and *The Weekend That Was*. His works of fiction include the novels *The Transients* (1935), *Windless Cabins* (1940), *Tilda* (1943), and *Home with Hazel* (1957), as well as several books of short stories that were eventually published in three volumes as *Collected Stories* (1962-1968). Van Doren also wrote three books of children's fiction.

Van Doren's nonfiction works include *The Autobiography of Mark Van Doren* (1958) and critical and biographical works on various authors. He also did a great deal of editorial work, including anthologies and critical editions of works of fiction and nonfiction. The authors with whom he dealt critically include John Dryden, Henry David Thoreau, William Shakespeare, and Nathaniel Hawthorne.

ACHIEVEMENTS

One of Mark Van Doren's most impressive achievements is the sheer volume of his work; he was the author of fifty-six books and the editor of twenty-three books. He was honored with the Pulitzer Prize in 1940 for his *Collected Poems 1922-1938*. His other awards include Columbia University's Alexander Hamilton Medal in 1959, the Hale Award in 1960, the Huntington Hartford Creative Award in 1962, and the Emerson-Thoreau Award in 1963. He also received many honorary degrees. In addition to formal awards, Van Doren's poetry won praise for its craftsmanship from other better-

Pulitzer Prize-winning poet Mark Van Doren, left, with his son Charles at Columbia University in 1957. (AP/Wide World Photos)

known poets, including Robert Frost, Allen Tate, and T. S. Eliot.

BIOGRAPHY

Mark Albert Van Doren, the son of Dr. Charles Lucius Van Doren and Dora Ann Butz, was born on his parents' farm near Hope, Illinois, and lived there for the first six years of his life. Then Van Doren's parents moved with him and his four brothers to the university town of Urbana, Illinois, where Dr. Van Doren had planned to retire but instead continued to practice medicine.

Van Doren attended the University of Illinois at Urbana, as his well-known older brother Carl had done. Both men were strongly influenced by Stuart Sherman, an English professor, and Mark was also taught by Leonard Bloomfield, the linguist, then a young instructor of German. Van Doren received his bachelor's degree in 1914 and entered the university's graduate program in English. A course with Sherman in nineteenth century prose writers introduced Van Doren to the writings of Thoreau, the subject of his master's thesis, which was published in 1916. He received his master's degree in 1915.

Mark Van Doren again followed his brother Carl's footsteps, going in 1915 to study at Columbia University, where Carl had studied and where, at the time, he was teaching English. Carl helped to guide his brother's doctoral studies and even suggested the topic of Mark's dissertation, Dryden's poetry. Van Doren's academic career was interrupted in 1917 by World War I. His army career, during which he never left the United States, consisted mainly of paperwork and ended with the armistice in 1918.

At the beginning of 1919 Van Doren returned to New York to continue work on his dissertation. He was awarded a fellowship to study abroad in 1920 and spent the year in London and Paris, finishing his dissertation in London and receiving his degree upon his return home. His dissertation, like his master's thesis, was published. He spent the summer of 1920 serving as literary editor of *The Nation*, replacing Carl, who wanted some free time to devote to other literary projects; he began teaching at Columbia in the fall of 1920. Planning to teach for only a short time, he in fact remained at Columbia until his retirement in 1959. He also lectured regularly at St. John's College in Annapolis, Maryland, from 1937 to 1957, and in 1963 he came out of retirement to accept a visiting professorship at Harvard University.

In 1922 Van Doren married Dorothy Graffe, with whom he had worked on *The Nation*. They had two sons, Charles and John, and lived in New York and on a farm in Cornwall, Connecticut.

In addition to his teaching and writing, Van Doren also resumed work on *The Nation*. He served as literary editor from 1924 to 1928 and as film critic from 1935 to 1938, as well as being a frequent contributor in the period between those two positions. As literary editor, he published the works of then unknown poets such as Robert Graves, Hart Crane, and Allen Tate. *The Nation* was virtually a Van Doren family publication, with Carl, his first wife Irita, and Mark and his wife all serving in various editorial positions.

Another of Van Doren's professional activities was his participation in a radio program called "Invitation to Learning" from 1940 to 1942. This weekly CBS program consisted of the discussion each week of a great literary work. For a year the panel members were Van Doren, his friend Allen Tate, and Huntington Cairns. Van Doren also spent seven weeks reading Nathaniel Hawthorne's *The Scarlet Letter* (1850) fifteen minutes a day, for a CBS radio broadcast.

In 1953 Van Doren was semiretired from Columbia. He spent most of his time writing and traveling with his wife, the author of numerous books, including a biography of her husband. Six years later, at the age of sixty-five, Van Doren retired completely from college teaching. He continued to write until his death in 1972.

ANALYSIS

Although Mark Van Doren wrote more than one thousand poems, critics have not responded commensurately. Very few critics have seriously treated Van Doren's poetry, although other poets have praised it and almost no one has made unfavorable comments about it. More than one critic has suggested that the volume of the work has discouraged criticism. Since Van Doren wrote many good poems but none which have been singled out for special merit, a comprehensive study of his work would be a lengthy task. Van Doren's subject matter and style also vary so widely that choosing "representative" poems for study is virtually impossible. Finally, and most significantly, his poems can generally be grasped at first reading by any reader; unlike some of his contemporaries, Van Doren did not write poems requiring extensive annotation in order to be understood by the average reader. His poetry is therefore much more accessible than the work of many other modern poets, making the critic's work as interpreter for the most part unnecessary.

Despite the variety of Van Doren's poetry, some common themes do emerge. He frequently wrote about family and friends, love, death, animals, and nature—familiar "poetic" topics treated in a traditional manner. His imagery may be effective but is not startling or brilliant; his diction is precise but not unusual. His love for New England in general and his Connecticut farm in particular has caused critics to compare him with Robert Frost. Van Doren has also been compared with various other poets, from John Dryden to Edwin Arlington Robinson, but, as Allen Tate observed, any traces of other poets are blended to create a unique body of poetry. Taken as a whole, Van Doren's poetry is like no one else's. It is highly personal in that it is centered around the events, people, concerns, and literature he knew well.

A complete study of Van Doren's poetry reveals no poetic innovations or surprises; it is the work of a competent poet and careful craftsman. Several critics have accurately applied the term "lucidity" to his work. Even his most complex poems are not obscure, although they were written at a time in which obscurity in poetry often seemed to be considered more of a virtue than a flaw.

The most admirable quality of Van Doren's poetry, says Richard Howard in his foreword to *Good Morning: Last Poems*, is his insistence that each poem be the first poem, as he says in "The First Poem." This insistence probably accounts for the breadth of his poetry, for he approached each new poem as if it possessed not only newness but also primacy, and he regarded the poetry of others in the same manner as he regarded his own. At the same time, he acknowledged his debt to the many English lyric poets who preceded him and whose tradition he helped to continue.

"A WINTER DIARY"

Some of Van Doren's poetry deals with typically American subjects. "A Winter Diary," one of his longest poems, is a fictitious verse diary of a winter spent on his Connecticut farm. The poem is written in heroic couplets, the form which Dryden popularized in his poetic dramas. At the beginning of the poem, the speaker explains the reason for its being written: After a "certain winter" had ended, he wanted to record his many memories of it because he felt they were already beginning to fade.

Those memories begin with the end of the summer, when the speaker and his family see their neighbors, who have spent the summer in the country, returning to town. In previous years the speaker has joined in this exodus, but this time he is staying in the country and looking forward to the solitude that fall will bring. The poem records the memories and thoughts of the speaker through the winter to the beginning of spring. The events described in the poem are commonplace—a snowfall, family meals, games—but they are magnified by the joy and the sense of newness that the speaker feels. The winter, with its country solitude, has brought peace to him, and for once the spring represents an unwelcome intrusion. The poem, with its personal, "homey" tone, had much popular appeal and was admired by critics as well.

"THE SAGE IN THE SIERRA"

Another of Van Doren's poems, "The Sage in the Sierra," is also rather typically American. Its subtitle is "Emerson: 1871" and the speaker in the poem is Ralph Waldo Emerson himself. By 1871, Emerson had already written everything he was to write; speaking in the poem, he says that "they," a pronoun which in this poem is neither given nor requires an antecedent, are disappointed; they pity him because he is no longer writing. They want him to write, and they assume that he would if he could. Emerson, however, does not want to be seen or to see himself merely as the hand that holds the pen; from the Sierra and a Concord brook he has learned the power and importance of silence and is for the time being content, like them, simply to exist. In his youth, he says, his mind was a forest and he felt the need to capture every bird in words. Now that he is older, his mind is still a forest but he is content with only watching the birds. Even storms, emotional as well as actual, pass over him with little effect.

He compares the "pure fire" of his present life to the "smoke" of his writing, which has obscured his experiences rather than making them clearer to him. In his writing, he says, he attempted to give the world truth and knowledge. He suggests that his youthful arrogance was greater than his own knowledge at the time, and that having since then experienced what he had previously written about, he no longer feels the need to serve as the world's teacher. The poem ends with the statement that he wishes to be left alone to live his life quietly, for he refuses to help others experience life at the expense of his own. The poem is sensitive in its portrayal of Emerson and imaginative in its argument: Emerson stopped writing by choice, not because of the decline of his abilities. Van Doren uses Emerson as a representative of all creative artists, whom he sees here as sacrificing their own lives for their art and for humankind.

"NOW THE SKY"

Van Doren uses a more traditional theme in "Now the Sky." This poem is echoed in a section of "A Winter Diary" that uses the same astronomical imagery. The speaker, gazing at the stars on a calm night, asks himself a rather trite question: For how many years have men done what I am doing now? The stars are often seen as a symbol of eternity, since they existed before man and have outlasted centuries of men who have looked at them. The speaker sees the constellations first in these historical terms, but he says that modern man has knowledge that the earlier stargazers did not possess. Man once saw the constellations, he says, as pictures drawn on the sky, but modern man "knows" that this view is incorrect. Man looked upon the stars as a sort of nightly drama, with the characters interacting and heralding the arrival of each new season. The speaker says that the sky was like a room to ancient man, which people entered and left in predictable fashion.

To modern man, however, the constellations hold neither drama nor mystery. Man has tamed the animals and forsaken the heroes of the constellations through his scientific knowledge. He still has a "game" to play, however—the game of pretending that "the board was never lost," that man has kept the civilizing influence of earlier, less scientific ages. In its theme, the poem is more "modern" than much of Van Doren's poetry.

SONNETS

Van Doren's thirty-two sonnets are traditional and Shakespearean in form and similar to Renaissance sonnet sequences in subject matter, particularly to Edmund Spenser's *Amoretti* (1595). The thoughts expressed in the sonnets are neither original nor remarkable, but Van Doren's diction, in its clarity and simplicity, never descends to triteness. Like "A Winter's Diary," these sonnets show Van Doren's interest in traditional poetic forms that other modern poets had largely abandoned.

OTHER MAJOR WORKS

LONG FICTION: *The Transients*, 1935; *Windless Cabins*, 1940; *Tilda*, 1943; *Home with Hazel*, 1957.

SHORT FICTION: *Collected Stories*, 1962-1968.

PLAYS: *The Last Days of Lincoln*, pb. 1959, pr. 1961; *Three Plays*, pb. 1966 (includes *Never, Never Ask His Name*, pr. 1965).

NONFICTION: *Henry David Thoreau*, 1916 (Master's thesis); *The Poetry of John Dryden*, 1920 (dissertation); *Shakespeare*, 1939; *Private Reader*, 1942;

Liberal Education, 1942; *Noble Voice*, 1946; *The Autobiography of Mark Van Doren*, 1958; *The Essays of Mark Van Doren*, 1980.

CHILDREN'S LITERATURE: *Dick and Tom: Tales of Two Ponies*, 1931; *Dick and Tom in Town*, 1932; *The Transparent Tree*, 1940.

BIBLIOGRAPHY

Claire, William, ed. *The Essays of Mark Van Doren, 1942-1972*. Westport, Conn.: Greenwood Press, 1980. Although the emphasis here is on Van Doren's work as a critic, the introduction by Claire provides useful information on Van Doren's poetry and prose, discussing his early influences and development as a writer. Notes that Van Doren's critical approach was consistent with his position as a poet, namely that a poet "made statements and gave opinions as a professional on the theory that a civilized audience existed to hear them."

Hendrick, George, ed. *The Selected Letters of Mark Van Doren*. Baton Rouge: Louisiana State University Press, 1987. These letters, arranged chronologically, give insight into the literary and cultural world in which Van Doren lived. The introduction, although brief, provides some useful details about his poetry, such as his early influences and what other writers and critics thought of him.

Ledbetter, J. T. *Mark Van Doren*. New York: Peter Lang, 1996. A study of Van Doren's literary life and an examination of the major themes found in his work, focusing particularly on his poetry. Includes bibliographical references and index.

Southworth, James G. *More Modern American Poets*. Freeport, N.Y.: Books for Libraries Press, 1954. An interesting, in-depth critique of Van Doren that is sympathetic to his earlier works—citing him as a poet of "keen perception and sensitivity"—but that says he falls short in his later works. Southworth says, simply, that Van Doren writes too much and recommends that the poet look beyond "structural form to that of significant form."

Wakefield, Dan. "Lion: A Memoir of Mark Van Doren." *Ploughshares* 17, no. 2/3 (Fall, 1991): 100. A former student recalls Van Doren in several anecdotes. Van Doren's most lasting lesson was that one must be true to one's deepest instincts, one's "noble voice," and never pander to the marketplace.

Young, Marguerite. "Mark Van Doren: A Poet in an Age of Defoliation." *Voyages* (Winter, 1970): 60-62. Young explores the shadow quality in Van Doren's poems, citing "Like Son" ("the people are intangible"), "Uncle Roger" (the poet tells of the *memory* of a train), and "Old Whitey" (a horse with noiseless hooves). Discusses Van Doren's use of imagery, particularly his ability to elevate images into a state of divinity. A thoughtful review, complex in its explanation of the deeper reaches of Van Doren's work.

Claire Clements Morton;
bibliography updated by the editors

MONA VAN DUYN

Born: Waterloo, Iowa; May 9, 1921

PRINCIPAL POETRY

Valentines to the Wide World, 1959
A Time of Bees, 1964
To See, to Take, 1970
Bedtime Stories, 1972
Merciful Disguises, 1973
Letters from a Father and Other Poems, 1982
Near Changes, 1990
If It Be Not I: Collected Poems, 1959-1982, 1993
Firefall: Poems, 1993
Selected Poems, 2002

OTHER LITERARY FORMS

Two short stories by Mona Van Duyn were published in *The Kenyon Review* in the 1940's. She has published reviews and criticism in *College English, American Prefaces*, and many literary magazines.

ACHIEVEMENTS

One of the few poets today who succeed in incorporating a contemporary sensibility within tight and traditional forms, Mona Van Duyn did not receive appropriate recognition until she won the Bollingen Prize in

1971 and her book *To See, To Take* received the National Book Award in 1971. She had, however, won several prizes previous to those—the Eunice Tietjens Award, the Harriet Monroe Award from *Poetry*, the Helen Bullis Award from *Poetry Northwest*, the Hart Crane Memorial Award from American Weave Press, and first prize in the Borestone Mountain Awards Volume of 1968. She was one of the first five American poets to be awarded a grant from the National Endowment for the Arts. In 1972-1973 she held a Guggenheim Fellowship. The Loines Prize from the National Institute of Arts and Letters was given to her in 1976, and in 1980 she received the ten-thousand-dollar Fellowship of the Academy of American Poets. Washington University, Cornell College, the University of Northern Iowa, the University of the South, George Washington University, and Georgetown University have awarded her honorary doctorates. She received the Shelley Memorial Award in 1987, the Pulitzer Prize in 1991 for *Near Changes*, and was named U.S. Poet Laureate for 1992-1993, the first woman to be accorded that honor.

Van Duyn has published steadily since the appearance of *Valentines to the Wide World* in 1959. Her work has been praised by fellow poets as diverse as Carolyn Kizer, Richard Howard, Maxine Kumin, James Dickey, Alfred Corn, and Howard Nemerov. Critic David Kalstone spoke of her work as manifesting "a whole life *grasped*, in the most urgent and rewarding sense of the word." She achieves her effects by hard work, revising each poem extensively. "What I try to do," she has stated, "is move readers' minds and feelings simultaneously with a structure which is intense and formal. If beauty means integrity, then a poem should be beautiful."

BIOGRAPHY

Born in Waterloo, Iowa, in 1921, Mona Van Duyn began her career by being class poet in the first grade in Eldora, Iowa, where her father ran a service station, a cigar store, and a soda fountain. She wrote poems throughout childhood and adolescence, then studied writing at Iowa State Teachers College and the State University of Iowa. She met her husband, Jarvis Thurston, now professor of English at Washington University, while they were students. They were married on August 31, 1943.

Mona Van Duyn (© Herb Weitman)

In 1947, they founded and became coeditors of the magazine *Perspective, a Quarterly of Literature*, in whose pages were introduced such poets as W. S. Merwin and W. D. Snodgrass and other writers of stature. Van Duyn was instructor in English at the State University of Iowa in 1945, and at the University of Louisville from 1946 to 1950. From 1950 to 1967 she was lecturer in English at Washington University, St. Louis, and has since taught at the Salzburg Seminar in American Studies, at Bread Loaf, and at various other writers' workshops throughout the United States. Her first collection, *Valentines to the Wide World*, came out in 1959 in a fine art edition from Cummington Press, illustrated with prints by Fred Becker. Her next collection, *A Time of Bees*, was published by the University of North Carolina in its paperback series in 1964. Atheneum published *To See, To Take* in 1970, *Merciful Disguises*—her collected poems although not designated as such—in 1973, and *Letters from a Father and Other Poems* in 1982. Since 1950 Van Duyn and her husband have lived in St. Louis, where they have been the center of a literary community which has included such poets and novelists as Donald Finkel,

Constance Urdang, Howard Nemerov, William Gass, and Stanley Elkin.

Analysis

In an epigraph to one of her poems, Mona Van Duyn cites Norman O. Brown: "Freud says that ideas are libidinal cathexes, that is to say, acts of love." For Van Duyn also, ideas are acts of love. Hers is a poetry shaped around the impact of ideas on one who is in love with them. To write poetry is, for her, to engage in an act of love. To write poetry is to make real the world which, although it exists externally, becomes known only when the mind's projections play over it. The life from which she writes is the life of the mind; there are few overtly dramatic events in her poetry. Her mind is excited by language—hence the frequent literary references in her poems—but it is also excited by what is not-mind, everyday accidental happenings, intense emotions, whatever is irrational, recalcitrant, and unyielding to intellectual analysis or explanation. Her poems burst out of the tension between these polarities, the poem itself—often self-reflexive—being the only method she can find to maintain truth and sanity.

"Valentines to the Wide World"

A kind of poetic manifesto appears in an early poem, the second "Valentines to the Wide World" in the volume of that title, in which Van Duyn describes her dislike of panoramic scenes because they are too abstract; the vast view of nature provides only a useless exhilaration. She finds "the poem" more useful because its pressure breaks through the surface of experience and because it is specific. "It starts with the creature/ and stays there." This "pressure of speech," even if it is painful or akin to madness, is still what makes her appreciate her life, feeling that to spend it "on such old premises is a privilege." In the third "valentine" she sees the beauty of the world as "merciless and intemperate," as a "rage" which one must temper with "love and art, which are compassionate."

Compassion is an outstanding characteristic of Van Duyn's poetry, both as motive and expression, and yet it is manifested through a wrestling with intellectual questions and an urge to apply her knowledge. Van Duyn's long lines are particularly suitable for expressing discursive thought. Love and beauty are traditional themes of

Romantic poets, but in Van Duyn they are united with an affinity for the forms and emphases of literary classicism reminiscent of the eighteenth century, with its bent toward philosophizing in poetry and its allegiance to strict and rhyming forms, especially the heroic couplet.

"From Yellow Lake: An Interval"

A classic philosophical problem therefore arises for Van Duyn in her early poems—the split between mind and body. In "From Yellow Lake: An Interval," she expresses discontent with her body as an impediment to overcoming the separateness she feels. The language of the poem has theological undertones: The beetles are "black as our disgrace," a reference to human sin and evil. Crows flying overhead become her dark thoughts, feeding upon "my mind, dear carrion." The poet sees each creature as an analogue of something human—the turtle is "flat as our fate" and the pike's "fierce faith" hooks him fatally on the fisherman's lure. Having a modern mind, the poet cannot find any theological answer to her questioning of the meaning of the creation that painfully yet beautifully surrounds her. The poem supplies the only resolution: Summer has warmed her but she must go back to "the wintry work of living," that is, the life of the mind of an ordinary human being, and "conspire in the nailing, brutal and indoors,/ that pounds to the poem's shape a summer's metaphors." The notion of original sin has here been given a new twist: The animal body is "innocent," a parable or metaphor, a natural "given," and the summer is the warmth of love, whereas the mind is that which creates separation, which construes evil and perversely invents the forms of pain. The mind, even if separated from the natural world, is still the only thing she has to work with. Only the poem—actually the process of making a work of art—can heal the split between mind and body, winter and summer, pain and love, by creating reality through metaphor.

"To My Godson, on His Christening"

In Part I of "To My Godson, on His Christening," Van Duyn continues in a mildly theological context to ponder her awareness of human imperfection (the classical definition of original sin) which not even the poet's artistic effort can completely escape. Here "metaphors" are in effect charitable deeds, "beautiful doors" out of the walled-up room of existence that is everyone's fated life. In Part II, a lexicon is the poet's gift to the baby, to help him learn words, since his world will not come into existence until he can name it—that is, use language, the way God made the world by speaking the Word, the *Logos*. This remnant of Christian thought fades into the background as, in Part III, the poet's mind concentrates on the uniqueness and transitoriness of each individual and of the species. This recognition nevertheless provides a "feast of awareness" and pleasure in the new life that is the positive aspect of the transitory; the reader is reminded that both dying and being born continue constantly. Being born means coming into a world of pain, but also into a circle of other people who, like the poet, will oversee the child and care for him. This caring, whether religiously motivated or not, reveals the charity and generosity that is Van Duyn's most characteristic and attractive attitude throughout her work.

A TIME OF BEES

Charity, of course, is a synonym for compassionate love, and love in Van Duyn is a reiterated word and theme. The word "love" appears in all but three of the poems in *A Time of Bees*, the collection that followed *Valentines to the Wide World*. She does not abandon the theme of poetry, but here unites it with the theme of love in the long poem, "An Essay on Criticism," a tour de force in couplets that echoes Alexander Pope's eighteenth century poem of the same title and also explores the aesthetics of its day, leavening this subject matter with contemporary sensibility, idiom, and wit.

In the frame of this poem, the poet, about to open and cook a package of dehydrated onion soup, is interrupted by the arrival of a friend, a young girl who has fallen in love and has discovered "how love is like a poem." In the dialogue that follows, many famous critical theories of poetry are cited and explored. The girl in love speaks first. She clutches the poet's arm "like the Mariner," an allusion to Samuel Taylor Coleridge's *The Rime of the Ancient Mariner* (1798) which the poet employs to join an intense, even obsessed, Romantic view of poetry in one embrace with the classic love of intellect and rationality.

After the girl leaves, the poet continues to talk to herself as if gripping "a theoretical Wedding Guest"—Coleridge again—and to grapple inwardly and intellectually with various aspects of the interaction between life and art. She takes the side of the poem, "for I believe in art's process of working through otherness to recognition/ and in its power that comes from acceptance, and not imposition." At this point she finds tears falling into her onion soup, but onions did not cause them; the thought of love did. The poem has to be completed in a human reader's heart. In the complex punning of the last line—tears as "essay" (attempt)—life is asserted to be victorious over art, but poem-making is plainly what maintains their intricate and fruitful balance.

TO SEE, TO TAKE

In Van Duyn's next volume, *To See, To Take*, published in 1970, she endeavored to step away from autobiographical reference and to elucidate her concerns by adopting the technique of the persona. In "Eros to Howard Nemerov," for example, she speaks through the traditional personification of love, the Greek god, who is addressing the representative modern American poet with a humorous eye turned on the posturings and vagaries of hippie love in the 1960's. Van Duyn's observant eye and sense of humor lead her directly to satire in "Billings and Cooings from 'The Berkeley Barb,'" a satire still *à propos* now that "personal" want ads have become institutionalized. Many Van Duyn poems begin with newspaper quotations as epigraphs, a method she uses to initiate subtle and accurate political and social commentary; by this device she avoids obvious or propagandistic rhetoric that often mars overtly "political" poetry.

Van Duyn cannot be said to be entirely apolitical, but her focus is always personal. Personal love, individual consciousness of passing time is what she stresses. The theme of the passage of time emerges particularly in this volume in two memorial poems, "The Creation" and "A Day in Late October." In "The Creation" Van Duyn mourns a friend's death; as art is a metaphor for life, she sees the friend's life as having been taken away as a pencil drawing is erased. "A Day in Late October," written after the death of Randall Jarrell, asserts the primacy of death, life's inseparable companion, over art—the art of poetry—by means of an extraordinary divagation for this poet: She breaks out of the poetic form altogether and falls back on prose, which is a kind of death of poetry, to express "what cannot be imagined: your death, my death." Death and the passing of time cannot fail to reinvoke a sense of the preciousness of love; the word "love" is repeated as often in this collection as in the previous one.

Despite her adoption of the persona to avoid excessive "personality," two fine poems in this volume spring from autobiography, a mode in which she has both sharpened her technical skills and widened her attitude of appreciation. "Postcards from Cape Split" show her gift for straightforward description of the natural world. The facts of the place where she is vacationing in Maine carry their own intrinsic symbolic weight, so simply stating them is enough. The central motif of "Postcards from Cape Split" is abundance—unearned richness exemplified by hillsides covered with heliotrope, the sea surrounding the house whose interior mirrors the sea, a plethora of villages and shops, generous neighbors, flourishing vegetable gardens. The poet is dazzled and appreciative: "The world blooms and we all bend and bring/ from ground and sea and mind its handsome harvests." The mind remains a primary locus, but the emphasis here is on contentment and gratitude; the world's unasked for generosity is indispensable.

The second autobiographical poem, "Remedies, Maladies, Reasons" strikes quite a different note, although its power also stems from a straightforward statement of facts—the facts of Van Duyn's childhood. It is a record of her mother's acts and speeches that imposed on the child a view of herself as weak, ill, and in danger of dying. The record is brutal and nauseating; it continues in the mother's letters describing her own symptoms simply quoted in her own words, so overwhelming a body-hatred and self-hatred that it is miraculous that the poet survived it. The word "remedies" in the title has a heavily ironic ring, but by the time the poem ends, it has taken another turn of meaning: Implicitly the act of making a poem from these horrors relieves them. It provides a remedy by evoking the sight of her mother as an attractive woman and as the mother the child wanted, who came in the night when called and defended the child against her felt enemy, sickness. The poem's last line—"Do you think I don't know how love hallucinates?"—constructs a complex balance, reasserting that love still exists but has maintained itself internally by a costly distortion of external fact. Without overtly referring to poetry as an aid, this poem is a re-markable testimony to the capacity of shaped language to restore a sane perspective and to enable one's mind to open to revision of memory, an act of love that is analogous to revision of the language of a poem.

If vision and revision are the loving acts that give rise to the making of a poem, the poem itself is the "merciful disguise of metaphor" which masks the horror and brutality of the world, making it possible for humans to live with its limitations. The most stringent and widespread personal limitation that love undertakes culturally is marriage. Marriage is to love what the heroic couplet is to poetry. Van Duyn has chosen—or has found herself unable to escape from—both rigors. In her first volume she explored marriage as "the politics of love" in the wryly witty, rather lighthearted poem "Toward a Definition of Marriage." At the end of her third book appears the tough-minded, occasionally viciously clear-eyed poem "Marriage, with Beasts" in which one feels that the imagery of animals in a zoo, Swiftian in its satiric accuracy, hardly qualifies as "merciful disguise." It is pitiless exposé.

Marital combat is elevated to a cosmic, mythic vision of antagonistic masculine and feminine principles in the previously unpublished poem "A View" in the last section of *Merciful Disguises*. The "you" and the "I" of the poem are driving through Colorado. The mountain with its "evergreen masculinity" is obliviously and continuously ascendant over the depleted "mined-out" female earth. The ending is covertly linked with marriage: The "you," the car's driver, male by cultural definition as well as presumably in fact, asks the "I" how she is, and she says that she is "admiring the scenery, and am O.K." The "view" of the title is a pun indicating "opinion" as well as landscape; it is the closest that Van Duyn's poetry—always centered on a woman's consciousness—comes to embodying a feminist perspective as it presents a seemingly unbridgeable gap between the man's state of well-being and the woman's unending state of struggle and exhaustion.

LETTERS FROM A FATHER

By the time of the publication of *Letters from a Father and Other Poems* in 1982, the poet is far better than merely self-deprecatingly "O.K." The complexity of her relationship with her parents resolved itself in the gentleness and forgiveness that came with their deaths in

1980 within three months of each other. The title poem, "Letters from a Father," is a foreshadowing of those deaths as well as a revival and revision of the poet's childhood memories. This poem's power comes from its almost verbatim quotation of her father's words, a technique that verifies the poet's loving ability to give herself and her art wholly to someone else. She thereby redeems both the sad intractable fact of death and also the self-entangled contemporary language of poetry, which badly needs a reminder that it must have reference to something outside itself.

In the poem "The Stream," about the death of her mother, the poet returns to her original and perennial concern, love, and, in an extended metaphor, sees love as a narrow stream running below ground, held down, unseen, but finally finding its way up until it is visible. This vision of the stream of love also suggests the stream of time flowing toward death, a flow echoed by the long flowing line whose form—the couplet with slant end-rhyme, Van Duyn's favorite—seems to constitute the same sort of facilitating obstacle that the rock and earth present to the underground stream of water. That water rises higher in a narrow tube is a physical fact; thus love rises under "the dense pressure of thwarted needs, the replay/ of old misreadings." Her mother's death has brought the stream of love to light, revealing to her "the welling water—to which I add these tears."

The tears and the poem, as in the earlier but different context of "An Essay on Criticism," join in felicitous confluence. The stringent form, when one gives in to it, is what produces genuine depth and maturation in life as well as in art. Van Duyn's development as a poet has been steady and straight-forward, even relentlessly undeviating, without sudden switches of style or experimental or uncertain phases. She has never gone back on her commitment to work with tight forms, to deal with the world's pain, and to remain in love with the world despite its worst. Her poem "Since You Asked Me . . ." answers the question which must have been put to her a number of times: Why do you use rhyme and measure, since these are so old-fashioned and out of date? She says that she uses rhyme "to say I love you to language" and to combat the current linguistic sloppiness of "y'know?" and "Wow!" She uses measure because it is "not just style but lifestyle."

NEAR CHANGES

In *Near Changes*, for which she won the Pulitzer Prize for poetry, Van Duyn continues an exploration of her own situation as survivor. The death of both parents, chronicled in *Letters from a Father*, is part of a series of losses. In "The Block" the large house she and her husband bought in 1950 "just in case" they might still have children gradually becomes part of a "middle-aged block" and then an elderly one, where widows now reside where once there were couples, and where Mr. and Mrs. Thurston watch other people's grandchildren. This—like other long poems in this volume, especially "Glad Heart at the Supermarket" and "Falling in Love at Sixty-five"—demonstrates the absurdity of pigeonholing Van Duyn as a "domestic" poet. While her matter may include Coleman lanterns, lawn care and snow-shoveling, bean curd and complex carbohydrates, her meanings are as profound as those of any other poet drawn to the connections between life and death, constancy and change. The collection provides new evidence of her technical virtuosity as well: "Memoir, for Harry Ford" is a sestina; "Condemned Site," a distinguished villanelle recounting the loss of five good friends, some of whose first names many readers will recognize as major twentieth century American poets.

FIREFALL

Firefall (along with *If It Not Be I*) was published on the occasion of Van Duyn's appointment as U.S. Poet Laureate. She continues to develop major themes of her lifework, among them love and marriage, friendship, work, travel, stewardship, and the luminous quality of the ordinary. Many of the poems are about the work of other poets and about poetry itself. The volume includes a number of what she calls "minimalist sonnets," poems that preserve the fourteen-line count and the conventional rhyme patterns of Italian and English sonnets, but reduce the number of syllables and otherwise "deconstruct" the venerable form. "Summer Virus" is an attractive example of what she can do with such minimalism, as her rising temperature brings both mind and body to a state of "incandescence."

The book takes its title from a phenomenon she describes in "Falls," a memoir in free verse that begins in the flatness of her native Iowa and then takes her to the mysterious "firefall" of Yosemite (which she explains in one of her rare notes) and the "thunderous boasts" of Niagara, to college, to books, and to a lifetime of writing poems—a waterfall of words. "Falls" ends in a formal quatrain, in which a poet toward the end of her career invokes the "kernel hints" of her that the future reader may find among the "husks," returning to the Iowa cornfields among which the memoir begins.

A POET OF IDEAS

In a lecture delivered at the Library of Congress in 1993, Van Duyn discusses the difficulty women poets have had in getting published and understood. As successful as she has been, she notes that,

Blinded by the assumption that women do not have thoughts, do not write about ideas, reviewers who are incredibly talented at understanding the most difficult and private poetry of their own sex announce blithely that a poem of mine about the need for form in life and art is about walking a dog, or an analysis of friendship is about shopping for groceries.

She wonders in fact whether such reviewers even consider the possibility of metaphor. As light as her touch and as familiar her subject matter can be, all but the most casual reader must recognize that Mona Van Duyn is indeed a poet of ideas, one of the most accomplished and distinguished poets of her time.

BIBLIOGRAPHY

Burns, Michael, ed. *Discovery and Reminiscence: Essays on the Poetry of Mona Van Duyn*. Fayetteville: University of Arkansas Press, 1998. Contains tributes by fellow poets, critical and interpretative essays, biographical notes, and "Matters of Poetry," the revised text of Van Duyn's 1993 lecture at the Library of Congress.

Grim, Jessica. Review of *Near Changes: Poems*, by Mona Van Duyn. *Library Journal* 115 (March 15, 1990): 94. Grim calls Van Duyn's collection "reflective in a refreshingly straightforward way." Grim affirms that Van Duyn continues to address domestic themes, from the deep love developed through a long marriage to a trip to the grocery store.

Hall, Judith. "Strangers May Run: The Nation's First Woman Poet Laureate." *The Antioch Review* 52, no. 1 (Winter, 1994): 141. Hall examines Van Duyn's work in an effort to discover why she was the first woman to be appointed poet laureate of the United States.

Jones, Daniel, and John D. Jorgenson, eds. "Mona Van Duyn." *Contemporary Authors*, New Revision Series, Vol. 60. Detroit: Gale Research, 1998. Contains a short résumé of Van Duyn's career, as well as the author's analysis of her own work.

Jane Augustine;
updated by William T. Hamilton

HENRY VAUGHAN

Born: Newton-on-Usk, Wales; April 17, 1622
Died: Llansantffraed, Wales; April 23, 1695

PRINCIPAL POETRY
Poems, 1646
Silex Scintillans, parts I and II, 1650, 1655
Olor Iscanus, 1651
Thalia Rediviva, 1678
The Secular Poems of Henry Vaughan, 1958 (E. L. Marilla, editor)
The Complete Poetry of Henry Vaughan, 1964 (French Fogle, editor)

OTHER LITERARY FORMS

Henry Vaughan, whose religious poetry reflects the influence of John Donne and George Herbert, published translations of several religious and medical treatises.

ACHIEVEMENTS

Henry Vaughan is usually grouped with the Metaphysical poets, anthologized particularly with John Donne, George Herbert, Richard Crashaw, and Andrew Marvell. While there is some justification for this association, in Vaughan's instance it has resulted in a somewhat too narrow estimation of his work and its historical context. In the Metaphysical collections, to be sure, Vaughan has been represented by some of his best poems, such as "Regeneration," "The World," or "Affliction," drawn from *Silex Scintillans*. These works, however, have often been grouped in contrast with the lyrics from Herbert's *The Temple* (1633). Invariably Vaughan has been admired only as a lesser foil to his great predecessor; while admittedly Vaughan had his great moments, he lacked the sustained intensity of Herbert. Moreover, Vaughan's gracious preface to the 1655 edition of *Silex Scintillans* shows much regard for the creator of *The Temple*. Given such authority, it is not surprising that Vaughan's modern reputation, emerging in the Metaphysical revival of the twentieth century, has been overshadowed by the accomplishments of George Herbert.

Fortunately, recent scholarship has begun to redress the imbalances concerning Vaughan with thorough study of his work and his milieu. By his own admission, Vaughan lived "when religious controversy had split the English people into factions: I lived among the furious conflicts of Church and State" ("Ad Posteros" in *Olor Iscanus*). His was the time that saw a people indict, condemn, and execute its monarch in the name of religious fervor and political expedience. His was the time that saw the final vestiges of ancient families' power supplanted by parliamentary prerogatives of a potent middle class. Vaughan defined his place outside the struggle in order to take part in it as conservator of the Anglican-Royalist cause, a defender of the British Church in poetry and prose tied closely to the attitudes and values of pagan and Christian pastoral literature. Moreover, in his own Welsh countryside and lineage, Vaughan found the touchstone for his conservatorship, an analogue of the self-imposed exiles of early church fathers who took refuge from the conflicts and hazards of the world.

BIOGRAPHY

Henry Vaughan was one of twins born to Thomas and Denise Vaughan in 1622, ten years after a union that brought the elder Vaughan into possession of house and lands at Trenewydd (Newton-on-Usk). The father of the poet apparently had no calling except that of a gentleman, and in later life he seems to have been fond of suing and being sued by his relatives. The Vaughan family had resided in the Brecknock region of Wales for generations and traced their line back to David ap Llwellen, known as "Davey Gam," who was knighted and slain at the Battle of Agincourt in 1415. The poet's twin, also named Thomas, obtained a greater measure of fame in his own lifetime than Henry did. He was a philosopher of the occult sciences who at one point engaged in a pamphlet war with the noted Cambridge Platonist writer, Henry More. He settled near Oxford and died in 1666. Contemporary scholars have suggested that the elaborate pastoral eclogue, *Daphnis*, appearing in *Thalia Rediviva*, was the poet's farewell to his twin.

As befit the heirs of a minor country gentleman, the twins began their formal studies about 1632 with the Rector of Llangatock, Matthew Herbert, continuing until 1638. The poet recalls that Herbert, "Though one man . . . gave me double treasure: learning and love." Following this tutelage, the twins were sent off to Jesus College, Oxford. They were seventeen; they had grown up steeped in Welsh language and culture. While the record of Thomas Vaughan's matriculation at Jesus College survives, no similar record exists for the poet. He apparently remained in Oxford until 1640, when he set forth to London with the intention of studying law. Shortly after his arrival, the king's favorite, the earl of Stafford, and Archbishop Laud were indicted. Stafford was executed by a reluctant monarch in the following May. Perhaps at this time Vaughan began translating Juvenal's tenth satire on the vanity of human wishes. While at London, Vaughan began his poetic "apprenticeship," steeping himself in the writings of Ben Jonson and his Cavalier followers such as Thomas Randolph. These efforts were published in the *Poems* of 1646. One imagines the young Henry Vaughan's brief tenure in London as preparation for a respectable civic life, perhaps dividing his time between the city and the Welsh countryside. It was not to be.

In the summer of 1642, the first civil war erupted; Henry Vaughan hastened to Wales. There he accepted the post of secretary to the Chief Justice of the Great Sessions, Sir Marmaduke Lloyd, probably retaining it until 1645. At the same time, Vaughan courted Catherine Wise, the daughter of a Warwickshire family. The "Amoret" poems in the 1646 volume were probably written and arranged in honor of his courtship and subsequent marriage to her. With the outbreak of the second civil war, Vaughan left the service of the law to join the Royalist army.

The appearance of the first part of *Silex Scintillans* in 1650, arguably the finest volume of poetry published by anyone in the years of the Interregnum, was unspectacular. Not until 1655, when he added several poems and a revealing preface, did Henry Vaughan provide posterity with the ill-conceived notion of his religious "conversion." Of all the facts concerning Henry Vaughan's life, no nonevent is as important as the "conversion." It was invented in the nineteenth century by the Reverend H. F. Lyte, who edited the first publication of Vaughan's work since the poet's lifetime. Lyte took remarks in the 1655 Preface concerning Vaughan's illness as a metaphor for a spiritual malaise cured by a heavy dose of Protestant piety. As a result of Lyte's homily, Vaughan's secular poetry suffered absolute neglect until the mid-twentieth century. *Silex Scintillans* was considered artistic proof of a conversion because it is Vaughan's best, most sustained work. A more accurate reading of what happened to Henry Vaughan was that he matured, as a man and as an artist. He found his unique voice in the urgency of the moment, in the defeat of his religious and political party, in the example of Herbert's poetry, in the pastoralism of passages in the Bible, in the whole tradition of finding the virtuous life in rural surroundings.

One senses, throughout his mature work, Vaughan's urgent defense of the values of simplicity and rural piety tempered from within by resolve. Vaughan included translations of Boethius and Casimir Sarbiewski in *Olor Iscanus*. They offer a pattern of stoic acceptance of this world's reversals by seeking virtue in retirement. Retirement, as Vaughan sees it, is not passive, however. It is a conscious choice. Thus, his allusions to illness in his Preface to *Silex Scintillans* must be regarded within the larger context of his discovery of Herbert's poems and his condemnation of trifling, uncommitted poetry. Vaughan was always an Anglican and a Royalist. He did not convert: He simply found his way to fight back. From the remove of the country, Vaughan discovered a role for himself in a strife-torn society more potent than that of soldier or solicitor: as a poetic defender of God and king.

No doubt other events contributed to Vaughan's recognition of his poetic mission, including the death of a younger brother, William, in 1648, and of his first wife Catherine five years later. He married her sister Elizabeth in 1655, the same year that a translation of Henry Nollius's *Hermetical Physick* appeared. By then Vaughan had elected medicine as a new career. That he continued to write verse is evidenced by the dates of poems in Vaughan's final collection, *Thalia Rediviva*. Thalia is the Muse of pastoral poetry. Vaughan continued to see himself in terms of the rural tradition of poetry because he found there a synthesis of images, metaphors, and implied or explicit values that harmonized with his religious and political beliefs. He continued to practice medicine, according to one contemporary account, as late as autumn, 1694. When he died the following spring, he was buried overlooking the countryside he so long celebrated, in the churchyard of the faith he so vehemently defended, his stone reciting his link to the Silures, the ancient Welsh tribe from which he took his epithet, "The Silurist," by which he was often known.

ANALYSIS

Henry Vaughan's first collection, *Poems*, is very derivative; in it can be found borrowings from Donne, Jonson, William Hobington, William Cartwright, and others. It contains only thirteen poems in addition to the translation of Juvenal. Seven poems are written to Amoret, believed to idealize the poet's courtship of Catherine Wise, ranging from standard situations of thwarted and indifferent love to this sanguine couplet in "To Amoret Weeping": "Yet whilst Content, and Love we joyntly vye,/ We have a blessing which no gold can buye." Perhaps in "Upon the Priorie Grove, His Usuall Retirement," Vaughan best captures the promise of love accepted and courtship rewarded even by eternal love:

> So there again, thou 'It see us move
> In our first Innocence, and Love:
> And in thy shades, as now, so then
> Wee'le kisse, and smile, and walke again.

The lines move with the easy assurance of one who has studied the verses of the urbane Tribe of Ben. That other favorite sport of the Tribe—after wooing—was drink, and in "*A Rhapsodie*, Occasionally written upon a meeting with some friends at the Globe Taverne, . . ." one sees the poet best known for his devout poems celebrating with youthful fervor all the pleasures of the grape and rendering a graphic slice of London street life. Though imitative, this little volume possesses its own charm. Perhaps it points to the urbane legal career that Vaughan might have pursued had not the conflicts of church and state driven him elsewhere.

OLOR ISCANUS

The poet of *Olor Iscanus* is a different man, one who has returned from the city to the country, one who has seen the face of war and defeat. Nowhere in his writing does Vaughan reject the materials of his poetic apprenticeship in London: He favors, even in his religious lyrics, smooth and graceful couplets where they are appropriate. This volume contains various occasional poems and elegies expressing Vaughan's disgust with the defeat of the Royalists by Cromwell's armies and the new order of Puritan piety. The leading poem, "To the River *Isca*," ends with a plea for freedom and safety, the river's banks "redeem'd from all disorders!" The real current pulling this river—underscoring the quality of *Olor Iscanus* which prompted its author to delay publication—is a growing resolve to sustain one's friends and one's sanity by choosing rural simplicity. The idea of this country fortitude is expressed in many ways. For example, the Cavalier invitation poem, "To my worthy friend, *Master T. Lewes*," opens with an evocation of nature "Opprest with snow," its rivers "All bound up in an *Icie Coat*." The speaker in the poem asks his friend to pass the harsh time away and, like nature itself, preserve the old pattern for reorder:

> Let us meet then! and while this world
> In wild *Excentricks* now is hurld,
> Keep wee, like nature, the same *Key*,
> And walk in our forefathers way.

In the elegy for Lady Elizabeth, daughter of the late Charles I, Vaughan offers this metaphor: "Thou seem'st a Rose-bud born in *Snow,*/ A flowre of purpose sprung to bow/ To headless tempests, and the rage/ Of an Incensed, stormie Age." Then, too, in *Olor Iscanus*, Vaughan includes his own translations from Boethius's *The Consolation of Philosophy* (523) and the Horatian Odes of the seventeenth century Polish writer Casimir Sarbiewski. In these, the "country shades" are the seat of refuge in an uncertain world, the residence of virtue, and the best route to blessedness. Moreover, affixed to the volume are three prose adaptations and translations by Vaughan: *Of the Benefit Wee may get by our Enemies*, after Plutarch; *Of the Diseases of the Mind and the Body*, after Maximum Tirius; and *The Praise and Happiness of the Countrie-Life*, after Antonio de Guevara. In this last, Vaughan renders one passage: "*Pietie and Religion* may be better Cherish'd and preserved in the Country than any where else."

The themes of humility, patience, and Christian stoicism abound in *Olor Iscanus* in many ways, frequently enveloped in singular works praising life in the country. The literary landscape of pastoral melds with Vaughan's Welsh countryside. For Vaughan the enforced move back to the country ultimately became a boon; his retirement from a "world gone mad" (his words) was no capitulation, but a pattern for endurance. It would especially preserve and sustain the Anglican faith that two civil wars had challenged. In Vaughan's greatest work, *Silex Scintillans*, the choices that Vaughan made for himself are expressed, defended, and celebrated in varied, often brilliant ways.

SILEX SCINTILLANS

New readers of *Silex Scintillans* ("The Flashing Flint") owe it to themselves and to Vaughan to consider it a "whole book" containing engaging individual lyrics; in this way its thematic, emotional, and Imagistic patterns and cross references will become apparent. The first part contains seventy-seven lyrics; it was entered in the Stationers' Register on March 28, 1650, and includes the anonymous engraving dramatizing the title. Fifty-seven lyrics were added for the 1655 edition, including a preface. The first part appears to be the more intense, many of the poems finding Vaughan reconstructing the moment of spiritual illumination. The second part finds Vaughan extending the implications of the first. Above all, though, the whole of *Silex Scintillans* promotes the active life of the spirit, the contemplative life of natural, rural solitude.

Some of the primary characteristics of Vaughan's poetry are prominently displayed in *Silex Scintillans*. First, there is the influence of the Welsh language and Welsh verse. Welsh is highly assonant; consider these lines from the opening poem, "Regeneration": "Yet *it* was frost w*ith*in/ And surly w*i*nds/ Blasted my *i*nfant buds, and s*i*nne/ L*i*ke clouds eccl*i*ps'd my m*i*nd." The *dyfalu*, or layering of comparison upon comparison, is a technique of Welsh verse which Vaughan brings to his English verse. A second characteristic is Vaughan's use of Scripture. For example, the idea of spiritual espousal which informs the Song of Solomon is brought forward to the poet's own time and place. "Hark! how his *winds* have chang'd their *note*,/ And with warm *whispers call* thee out" ("The Revival") recalls the Song of Solomon 2:11-12. In "The Dawning" Vaughan imagines the last day of humankind and incorporates the language of the biblical Last Judgment into the cycle of a natural day. Will man's judge come at night, asks the poet, or "shal these early, fragrant hours/ Unlock thy bowres? . . ./ That with thy glory doth best chime,/ All now are stirring, ev'ry field/ Ful hymns doth yield."

Vaughan adapts and extends scriptural symbols and situations to his own particular spiritual crisis and resolution less doctrinally than poetically. In this practice, Vaughan follows Herbert, surely another important influence, especially in *Silex Scintillans*. Nearly sixty poems use a word or phrase important to *The Temple*; some borrowings are direct responses, as in the concluding lines of "The Proffer," recalling Herbert's "The Size." Sometimes the response is direct; Vaughan's "The Match" responds to Herbert's "The Proffer." Herbert provided Vaughan with an example of what the best poetry does, both instructing the reader and communicating one's own particular vision. This is Vaughan's greatest debt to Herbert, and it prompts his praise for the author of *The Temple* in the Preface to *Silex Scintillans*. Further, Vaughan emulates Herbert's book of unified lyrics, but the overall structure of *The Temple*—governed by church architecture and by the church calendar—is transformed in Vaughan to The Temple of Nature, with its own rhythms and purposes.

The Temple of Nature, God's "second" book, is alive with divinity. The Welsh have traditionally imagined themselves to be in communication with the elements, with flora and fauna; in Vaughan the tradition is enhanced by Hermetic philosophy, which maintained that the sensible world was made by God to see God in it. The poet no doubt knew the work of his brother Thomas, one of the leading Hermetic voices of the time. Henry Vaughan adapts concepts from Hermet-

icism (as in the lyric based on Romans 8:19), and also borrows from its vocabulary: Beam, balsam, commerce, essence, exhalations, keys, ties, sympathies occur throughout *Silex Scintillans*, lending force to a poetic vision already imbued with natural energy. "Observe God in his works," Vaughan writes in "Rules and Lessons," noting that one cannot miss "his Praise; Each *tree, herb, flowre*/ Are shadows of his wisedome, and his *Pow'r*."

Vaughan is no pre-Romantic nature lover, however, as some early commentators have suggested. Rather, *Silex Scintillans* often relies on metaphors of active husbandry and rural contemplation drawn from the twin streams of pagan and biblical pastoral. Many of the lyrics mourn the loss of simplicity and primitive holiness; others confirm the validity of retirement; still others extend the notion of husbandry to cultivating a paradise within as a means of recovering the lost past. Drawing upon the Cavalier poets' technique of suggesting pastoral values and perspective by including certain details or references to pastoral poems, such as sheep, cots, or cells, Vaughan intensifies and varies these themes. Moreover, he crosses from secular traditions of rural poetry to sacred ones. "The Shepheards"—a nativity poem—is one fine example of Vaughan's ability to conflate biblical pastoralism asserting the birth of Christ with "literary" conventions regarding shepherds.

Several poems illuminating these important themes in *Silex Scintillans*, are "Religion," "The Brittish Church," "Issac's Marriage," and "The Retreate" (loss of simplicity associated with the primitive church); "Corruption," "Vanity of Spirit," "Misery," "Content," and "Jesus Weeping" (the validity of retirement); "The Resolve," "Love, and Discipline," "The Seed Growing Secretly," "Righteousness," and "Retirement" (cultivating one's own paradise within). These are, of course, not the only lyrics articulating these themes, nor are these themes "keys" to all of the poems of *Silex Scintillans*, but Vaughan's treatment of them suggests a reaffirmation of the self-sufficiency celebrated in his secular work and devotional prose. In his finest volume of poems, however, this strategy for prevailing against unfortunate turns of religion and politics rests upon a heartfelt knowledge that even the best human efforts must be tempered by divine love.

THALIA REDIVIVA

Vaughan's last collection of poems, *Thalia Rediviva*, was subtitled "The Pass-times and Diversions of a Countery-Muse," as if to reiterate his regional link with the Welsh countryside. The John Williams who wrote the dedicatory epistle for the collection was probably Prebendary of Saint David's, who within two years became Archdeacon of Cardigan. He was probably responsible for soliciting the commendatory poems printed at the front of the volume. That Vaughan gave his endorsement to this Restoration issue of new lyrics is borne out by the fact that he takes pains to mention it to his cousin John Aubrey, author of *Brief Lives* (1898) in an autobiographical letter written June 15, 1673. Moreover, when it finally appeared, the poet probably was already planning to republish *Olor Iscanus*. Thus, though his great volume of verse was public reading for more than two decades, Vaughan had not repudiated his other work.

Nor would he have much to apologize for, since many of the finest lyrics in this miscellany are religious, extending pastoral and retirement motifs from *Silex Scintillans:* "Retirement," "The Nativity," "The True Christmas," "The Bee," and "To the pious memorie of C.W. . . ." Moreover, *Thalia Rediviva* contains numerous topical poems and translations, many presumably written after *Silex Scintillans*. The most elaborate of these pieces is a formal pastoral eclogue, an elegy presumably written to honor the poet's twin, Thomas. It is Vaughan's most overt treatment of literary pastoral; it closes on a note that ties its matter to the diurnal rhythms of the world, but one can recognize in it the spirit of *Silex Scintillans:* "While feral birds send forth unpleasant notes,/ And night (the Nurse of thoughts,) sad thoughts promotes./ But Joy will yet come with the morninglight,/ Though sadly now we bid good night!" Though not moving in the dramatic fashion of *Silex Scintillans* through a reconstruction of the moment and impact of divine illumination, the poems of *Thalia Rediviva* nevertheless offer further confirmation of Henry Vaughan's self-appointed place in the literature of his age.

OTHER MAJOR WORKS

MEDICAL TRANSLATIONS: *Hermetical Physick*, 1655 (of Heinrich Nolle); *The Chymists Key to Open and to Shut*, 1657 (of Nolle).

MISCELLANEOUS: *The Works of Henry Vaughan*, 1914, 1957 (L. C. Martin, editor).

BIBLIOGRAPHY

Calhoun, Thomas O. *Henry Vaughan: The Achievement of "Silex Scintillans."* Newark: University of Delaware Press, 1981. Calhoun claims that *Silex Scintillans* is in the tradition of lyric sequences that originated with Petrarch's *Le Rime*. After outlining that tradition, Calhoun examines the revisions in *Silex Scintillans* in terms of biographical details, historical events, and stylistic concerns. Of particular interest is his discussion of the influence of Hermetic medicine. "Regeneration," and "Resurrection and Immortality" receive lengthy analysis.

Davies, Stevie. *Henry Vaughan*. Chester Springs, Pa.: Dufour Editions, 1995. Davies' experience as a biographer, having published works on Milton, John Donne, and the Brontë sisters, pays off in this concise historical narrative of the life and works of Henry Vaughan. Includes an index and a bibliography.

Durr, R. A. *On the Mystical Poetry of Henry Vaughan.* Cambridge, Mass.: Harvard University Press, 1962. After reviewing standard Vaughan topics—conversion, relationship to George Herbert, childhood motif—Durr identifies three major metaphors in Vaughan's work: the growth of the lily, the dark journey, and the spiritual espousal. Contains exhaustive readings of three poems, "Regeneration," "The Proffer," and "The Night," as well as appendices concerning the "divine spark," the Book of the Creation, and mysticism.

Friedenreich, Kenneth. *Henry Vaughan*. Boston: Twayne, 1978. Friedenreich discusses three characteristics of Vaughan's style—the Welsh language, the Bible, and Hermetic philosophy—and illustrates their impact on Vaughan's work. *Olor Iscanus, Silex Scintillans*, and the major prose receive the bulk of the attention. Includes lengthy analyses of individual poems, a chronology, and a select annotated bibliography.

Garner, Ross. *Henry Vaughan: Experience and the Tradition*. Chicago: University of Chicago Press, 1959. Garner devotes separate chapters to Vaughan's spiritual quest ("Ishmael" becomes Vaughan), Hermeticism, nature poetry (with references to William Wordsworth), and religious poetry. Of particular interest is Garner's discussion of Vaughan's poetry in terms of E. M. W. Tillyard's five characteristics of the Elizabethan Age. Garner's index unfortunately does not include individual poems by Vaughan.

Post, Jonathan F. S. *Henry Vaughan: The Unfolding Vision*. Princeton, N.J.: Princeton University Press, 1982. Post, who divides his emphasis between Vaughan's secular and religious poems, declares the heart of his study is *Silex Scintillans*. Although he covers many of Vaughan's poems, some—among them "The Night" and "Regeneration"—receive lengthy analysis. Contains a general index, as well as an index to Vaughan's poems.

Rudrum, Alan, ed. *Essential Articles for the Study of Henry Vaughan*. Hamden, Conn.: Archon Books, 1987. Rudrum has reprinted twenty-one articles, only two of which are excerpts from books on Vaughan. He provides readers with a ready access to major Vaughan scholars analyzing individual poems such as "The Night" and "Regeneration," as well as discussing Vaughan's subjects such as nature, infancy, Hermeticism, and mysticism.

Simmonds, James D. *Masques of God: Form and Theme in the Poetry of Henry Vaughan*. Pittsburgh: University of Pittsburgh Press, 1972. Simmonds, unlike most Vaughan critics, stresses Vaughan's secular poetry, which he relates to Ben Jonson's ideas about the well-ordered poem. Both the love poetry and the satires are discussed in depth, and the book concludes with an illuminating treatment of the "bed-grave" image in Vaughan's poetry. Contains a bibliography and appendices concerning Vaughan's illness, the identity of Amoret, and profane literature.

Young, R. V. *Doctrine and Devotion in Seventeenth-Century Poetry: Studies in Donne, Herbert, Crashaw, and Vaughan*. Rochester, N.Y.: D.S. Brewer, 2000. Critical interpretation of English early modern and Christian poetry. Includes bibliographical references and index.

Kenneth Friedenreich;
bibliography updated by the editors

LOPE DE VEGA CARPIO

Born: Madrid, Spain; November 25, 1562
Died: Madrid, Spain; August 27, 1635

PRINCIPAL POETRY
La Dragontea, 1598
El Isidro, 1599
La hermosura de Angélica, 1602
Rimas, 1602
El arte nuevo de hacer comedias en este tiempo, 1609 (*The New Art of Writing Plays*, 1914)
Jerusalén conquistada, 1609
Rimas sacras, 1614
La Circe, 1621
La filomena, 1621
Triunfos divinos, 1625
La corona trágica, 1627
Laurel de Apolo, 1630
Amarilis, 1633
La gatomaquia, 1634 (*Gatomachia*, 1843)
Rimas humanas y divinas del licenciado Tomé de Burguillos, 1634
Filis, 1635
La Vega del Parnaso, 1637

OTHER LITERARY FORMS
Lope de Vega Carpio, one of literature's most prolific writers, wrote several prose works, including *La Arcadia* (1598), a pastoral romance; *El peregrino en su patria* (1604; *The Pilgrim: Or, The Stranger in His Own Country*, 1621), a Byzantine romance; *Los pastores de Belén* (1612; the shepherds of Bethlehem), a pastoral romance; *Novelas a Marcia Leonarda* (1621; stories for Marcia Leonarda, four short novels dedicated to his last love, Marta de Nevares); and *La Dorotea* (1632), a highly autobiographical novel in dialogue. Both his prose and his poetic productions, however, are overshadowed by his plays. Lope de Vega himself claimed to have written about eighteen hundred plays, probably an exaggeration, but even the most conservative estimates place the total at about eight hundred. Some of the better known are *Peribáñez y el comendador de Ocaña* (wr. 1609-1612, pb. 1614; *Peribáñez*, 1936); *El villano en su*

rincón (wr. 1611, pb. 1617; *The King and the Farmer*, 1940); *La dama boba* (pb. 1617; *The Lady Nit-Wit*, 1958); *El perro del hortelano* (wr. 1613-1615, pb. 1618; *The Gardener's Dog*, 1903); *Fuenteovejuna* (wr. 1611-1618, pb. 1619; *The Sheep-Well*, 1936); *El mejor alcalde, el rey* (wr. 1620-1623, pb. 1635; *The King, the Greatest Alcalde*, 1918); and *El caballero de Olmedo* (wr. 1615-1626, pb. 1641; *The Knight from Olmedo*, 1961). He also wrote many *autos*, one-act Eucharist plays composed for religious celebrations.

ACHIEVEMENTS

Lope de Vega Carpio lived during the most productive period of Spain's literary history, known as the Golden Age, and shone as its brightest light. He cultivated every literary form—succeeding in each one of them—and quickly gained popularity. A turbulent and charismatic personality, Lope de Vega participated passionately in every aspect of social life, including several scandalous love affairs, all of which he poeticized in one form or another. Writing was so much a part of him that, as some critics have said, his life was literature. He lived for, in, and through literature and was able to afford his carefree lifestyle because of literature; his numerous compositions brought him a steady flow of money. According to his first biographer, Pérez de Montalbán, Lope de Vega composed poems before he even knew how to write, and the author himself claimed that he wrote his first play at twelve. It is known that Lope de Vega was recognized as a good poet and playwright in his early twenties because Cervantes praises him very highly in *La Galatea* (1585). Lope de Vega's first collection of lyric poetry appeared in 1602 and, with some alterations and additions was reprinted several times during his lifetime. New collections were published periodically, some of them incorporating long narrative poems which also appeared separately. In 1604, the first volume of his plays was published, and by the time of his death, twenty-two additional volumes (containing twelve dramas each) had appeared. With these plays, Lope de Vega created a new dramatic pattern which, although he felt a need to defend and justify it in *The New Art of Writing Plays*, was accepted and imitated by dramatists for more than a century. Lope de Vega influenced the theater to such an extent that he is considered the founder of the Spanish national drama. Because of this exuberant creativity, coupled with his outgoing personality, he was sought after to promote and to organize literary events when a celebration was in order. Thus, one sees him organizing poetic jousts for any event requiring celebration, from the birth of a prince to the canonization of a saint.

Lope de Vega's literary genius was recognized by all his contemporaries, although some of them resented his immense popularity. In a fitting tribute, Cervantes called him the king of playwrights, a prodigy of nature.

BIOGRAPHY

Lope Félix de Vega Carpio was the third child of Félix de Vega Carpio and Francisca Fernández Flores. Both parents were from Santander and moved first to Valladolid, where their first two children were born. Félix de Vega seems to have had the same passionate traits of character that his son would later show. Infatuated with another woman, Félix de Vega abandoned his family to follow her to Madrid, but Francisca followed

Lope de Vega Carpio (Library of Congress)

her husband and managed to reunite the family. Out of this reconciliation came Lope de Vega, who would later poeticize the event in "Belardo' a Amarilis: Epístola séptima," inserted in *La filomena*, as he did with every aspect of his life.

Lope de Vega was taught Latin and Castilian by Vicente Espinel, a wellknown poet and novelist, and soon was recognized as a child prodigy. After a few years at the Jesuit Imperial College—which emphasized the study of grammar and rhetoric—he entered the service of the Bishop of Ávila, Don Jerónimo Manrique. Under Manrique's guidance, Lope de Vega studied for the priesthood at the University of Alcalá from 1577 to 1582 but abandoned his studies because of a love affair. It is possible, also, that he studied in Salamanca the next year before enlisting in the expedition to the Azores Islands. Upon returning from this expedition, Lope de Vega fell in love with Elena Osorio, thus beginning one of the most turbulent episodes of his life. Following a pattern that soon became a norm, pouring every event of his life into literature, Lope de Vega expressed his love for Elena in passionate verses that told everyone about their love affair. These poetic indiscretions jeopardized the reputation of Elena, a married woman, forcing her to end the relationship. Jealous and hurt, Lope de Vega wrote some compositions highly offensive to Elena and her family and disseminated them throughout Madrid. Elena's family took the case to court, and Lope de Vega was imprisoned while the trial took place and was later sentenced to exile—from the court for eight years and from the kingdom for two.

The court's sentence, not to be broken under penalty of death, did not have a marked effect on Lope de Vega, for soon after, he returned to Madrid and seduced Isabel de Urbina, a young woman from a prominent family. Trying to avoid the scandal, Isabel's father consented to the marriage of the two, and the wedding was done by proxy. A few months later, the poet went to Lisbon to enlist with the Spanish Armada. He was one of the lucky survivors of that disastrous expedition against England, which marked the decline of Spain as a world superpower. After his return, still under banishment from Castile, Lope de Vega went to Valencia with his wife. There, he saw several of his plays staged and began to pursue seriously his career as a playwright. In 1590,

when his banishment from Castile was ended, Lope de Vega went to Toledo and entered the service of the Marqués de Malpica. Later that year, he moved to Alba de Tormes in the province of Salamanca to work for the famous Duke of Alba as one of his secretaries. There, the poet spent some of the most peaceful days of his life, alternating his duties with his literary activity and going frequently to Salamanca, whose university life he portrays so well in his plays. This restful existence ended in 1594 when Isabel died in childbirth, leaving the playwright in great grief.

In 1595, Lope de Vega returned to Madrid, where he was soon involved in another scandalous love affair, this time with a wealthy widow, Antonia Trillo de Armenta. Three years later, the poet married Doña Juana de Guardo, a daughter of a butcher/fishmonger, hoping to better his financial situation with her dowry. At the same time, however, he began another affair with Micaela de Luján, the beautiful wife of actor Diego Díaz de Castro. Lope de Vega spent the next several years sharing his time with the two women, establishing separate homes and families with each.

In 1605, Toledo entrusted him with the organization of a poetic joust to celebrate the birth of Prince Philip, later King Philip IV. Lope de Vega acted as the judge of this contest, contributed verses of his own, and even introduced a "Soneto de Lucinda Serrana" ("Sonnet by Lucinda Serrana"), the pet name of the illiterate Micaela. In 1607, Lope de Vega found yet another love: Jerónima de Burgos, with whom the poet would be involved intermittently for the next ten years. Greatly disappointed, Micaela went back to Madrid and quietly disappeared from his life. Three years later, the playwright returned to the capital, where for a time he led a quiet life dedicated to his family, his writing, and his garden.

Lope de Vega's marriage to Doña Juana marks the most productive period of his life. During that time he published most of his long poems (*La Dragontea, El Isidro, La hermosura de Angélica, Jerusalén conquistada, The New Art of Writing Plays*) and romances (*La Arcadia, The Pilgrim, Los pastores de Belén*), two large collections of *rimas*, and three volumes of his collected plays. It was during this period, also, that the poet became acquainted with the duke of Sessa, starting a long epistolary friendship. Doña Juana died in 1613, leaving

Lope de Vega in a state of spiritual crisis which he decided to resolve by becoming a priest. His motivation in taking this step is not completely clear, for the poet continued involving himself with women even when he was preparing for his ordination. Critic Juan Luis Alborg justifies Lope de Vega's actions by saying that he incarnated tragically both the most extreme passions and the most intense religious fervor, but one should not overlook the fact that Lope de Vega was going through financial difficulties and was possibly seeking a more comfortable situation; as a priest, it was easier to obtain some sort of permanent pension. Lope de Vega sought and obtained a chaplaincy in the Church of Saint Segundo in Ávila, with an annual income of 150 ducats.

The ecclesiastical habit did not take Lope de Vega away from women. He was involved with Lucia de Salcedo in 1616 and made a trip to Valencia simply to be with her. The poet soon ended this relationship, however, to attend exclusively to his last love, Marta de Nevares. In her, Lope de Vega found the ideal woman whom he had long been seeking. Marta was married, however, and her enraged husband, Roque Hernández, almost managed to have Lope de Vega killed. Marta began separation procedures, but Roque Hernández died in the midst of the litigation, leaving her free to live with Lope de Vega.

Marta entered Lope de Vega's life in his late years, and she rejuvenated him. She influenced his writing tremendously, and the poet enjoyed another period of intense productivity. In a few short years, he published several volumes of his plays and of his poems, wrote new ones, and, following Marta's encouragement, attempted new literary forms. His private life, however, might have annoyed some people, for he sought the position of royal chronicler but did not obtain it. On the other hand, his living arrangement was not an obstacle when it came to celebrating religious events, such as the 1620 and 1625 poetic contests organized by the city of Madrid to celebrate the beatification and canonization of Saint Isidro. For both occasions, Lope de Vega was in charge of the entire celebration.

The last years of the poet were full of misfortune and disaster. Marta lost her sight and her sanity, becoming extremely violent at times, until she finally died in 1632, leaving Lope de Vega in a state of deep depression. His son Lope drowned two years later while on a pearl-hunting expedition off the coast of the Island of Margarita. Finally, his beloved daughter Antonia Clara was abducted by Cristóbal Tenorio that same year, and Lope de Vega never saw her again. The playwright found himself accompanied only by his memories. Still, he kept poeticizing his emotions and the events of his life. Feeling that death was approaching, Lope de Vega repented daily for his sinful life and finally attained the office of priest. During this time he published *Rimas humanas y divinas del licenciado Tomé de Burguillos* (human and divine verses) under the pseudonym Tomé de Burguillos, as well as *Gatomachia*, a burlesque poem which ridicules the excesses of the Renaissance epic, and his autobiographical novel *La Dorotea*, considered by many as one of the author's best works and one of the most beautiful examples of Spanish prose fiction.

Lope de Vega died in 1635, enjoying the greatest popularity of any living author, and so many people attended his funeral that, as Pérez de Montalbán recounted in *Fama póstuma* (1636), it looked like the funeral of a king.

ANALYSIS

Lope de Vega Carpio reacted poetically to every event of his existence, always leading the true life of an artist. Everything became a poetic pretext for the author, from his passionate love for Elena Osorio to the bitter disappearance of his daughter, Antonia Clara, near the end of his life. As critic José F. Montesinos says, "Lope's biography constitutes the most attractive chapter of our literary history . . . because it shows the existence of the artist in every moment—converting real life facts into poetic creation."

Lope de Vega was conscious of this relationship between life and literature, and he left testimony of it in several of his works. The "Soneto a Lupercio Argensola" ("Sonnet to Lupercio Argensola"), published in the first edition of the *Rimas*, ends with these lines:

> You tell me not to write, or not to live?
> Make sure that my love will not feel,
> Then I will make my pen not to write.

In *La Dorotea*, one of his last works, he writes: "To love and to write verses is all one and the same."

Perhaps because of this intense vitalization of his poetry, Lope de Vega did not write great metaphysical poems, like Francisco de Quevedo y Villegas, nor did he adapt fully to the new poetic school headed by Luis de Góngora y Argote. He remained a poet of emotions, of feelings, of passions, of love. What is transparent in his poetry, says Dámaso Alonso, is "the life of a man in its turbulent plurality, day after day, in love and in hate, in his picaresque profile and in his periods of true repentance and sincere search for God." In this manner, continues the Spanish critic, Lope de Vega is profoundly original, anticipating the Romantics. Furthermore, these characteristics are not exclusive to his lyric poetry but are present in his objective compositions as well. As Karl Vossler has pointed out, Lope de Vega was able to write with the most lyric and intimate tones when he was poeticizing someone else's love. This does not mean, however, that Lope de Vega was only a poet of natural and simple spontaneity, a poet who cultivated exclusively the popular and traditional meters. He was also a poet full of curiosity who liked to experiment with new forms and poetic conventions. Together with the traditionalist, one finds in Lope de Vega a Petrarchist, a sophisticated poet able to produce very complicated compositions, perfectly assimilating Italian models; a Góngorist, trying to imitate his most vocal enemy in obscure linguistic games; and even a philosophical poet who, unable to imitate Góngora properly, adopts an austere style that is the polar opposite of Góngora's Baroque extravagance.

Lope de Vega published several books of poetry during his lifetime. Most of them were miscellaneous volumes containing short and long poems and, in some cases, prose works. Unlike Garcilaso de la Vega, Luis de León, and Góngora, Lope de Vega did not cultivate lyric poetry as an independent art. Many of his lyric poems were first incorporated in his plays or prose works, from which they were later taken so as to rescue them from oblivion.

LA DRAGONTEA AND EL ISIDRO

Lope de Vega's first publication was *La Dragontea* (Drake the pirate), an epic poem divided into ten cantos and written in royal octaves. As the title implies, this poetic composition narrates the forays of Sir Francis Drake to the Spanish possessions, concluding with his death in Portobelo at the hands of his own men. Full of patriotic fervor, the poem reveals the common sentiments of the Spaniards toward England in the years after the ill-fated Armada. *La Dragontea* has been criticized by some for its partiality, although it is important to mention that the events are narrated objectively. The poem is also distinguished by the vivid realism of its maritime descriptions, in which Lope de Vega shows his knowledge of nautical vocabulary.

A year later, the ten-thousand-line poem *El Isidro* appeared, written in the popular *quintilla* (five-line stanza) and divided into ten books. Of rather mediocre quality, this work was intended to popularize the figure of Saint Isidro the Ploughman, or the Farmer, as a plea for his canonization. A work of great simplicity, *El Isidro* is not an epic poem, but rather a familiar story poeticized with unusual naturalness. In spite of its poetic flaws, there were several editions published during the seventeenth century, certainly the result of the canonization of the saint, which occurred in 1622.

In 1602, the poet published a large volume containing *La hermosura de Angélica* (Angelica's beauty), *Rimas*, and *La Dragontea*. Lope de Vega started writing *La hermosura de Angélica* when he was at sea with the Armada. The poem was probably inspired by the success of Luis Barahona de Soto's *Primera parte de la Angélica* (1586; first part of Angélica), and it clearly shows Lope de Vega's intention of following the steps of Ludovico Ariosto's *Orlando Furioso* (1516, 1521, 1532; English translation, 1591). The poem, divided into twenty cantos and written in royal octaves, presents such a mixture of adventures and fantastic events that it ends up becoming a kind of Byzantine novel, wild and extravagant. The best parts of the poem are those that are based on Lope de Vega's personal experience, in which the passionate humanity of the poet reveals itself.

JERUSALÉN CONQUISTADA

Lope de Vega's next poetic effort, perhaps the greatest of all, was *Jerusalén conquistada* (Jerusalem regained), a rather long epic poem of six thousand stanzas divided into twenty cantos. He composed this work to emulate Torquato Tasso and also to correct Tasso's omission of the Spaniards in his *Gerusalemme liberata* (1581; *Jerusalem Delivered*, 1600). The poet incorporates here a legend which assumes that Alfonso VIII of Castile participated in the Third Crusade (1187-1192). Furthermore, Alfonso is presented in the foreground of the action after the fourth book, competing with and even overshadowing Richard the Lion-Hearted; thus, a disproportionate part of the poem is dedicated to someone who did not go to Palestine at all. Lope de Vega wrote this poem with unusual care, resulting in many beautiful passages. The author himself esteemed the work highly, as he told the duke of Sessa: ". . . it is something that I have written in my best age and with a different dedication from what I put into the writings of my youth, in which appetite prevailed over reason." In spite of this praise, Lope de Vega did not produce the great masterpiece he set forth to write. His intentions were to give Spain a national epic, doing for his country what Luís de Camões had done for Portugal with *Os Lusíadas* (1572; *The Lusíadas*, 1655). The poet, however, could not accommodate his genius to this enterprise, for, as Alborg says, "he was not able to sustain the solemnity and dignity of intonation that such a composition required." Instead, he assembled an amalgam of adventures, magicians, demons, and angels, much in the manner of a chivalric romance. In addition, he introduced material drawn from his personal life, portraying his mistress, Micaela de Luján, and their illegitimate children.

THE NEW ART OF WRITING PLAYS

In 1609, Lope de Vega published *The New Art of Writing Plays*, a didactic poem in which the playwright presents his formula for success in the theater. He had been writing plays for quite some time by then and had been involved in several controversies regarding his departure from the Aristotelian rules. A mature man of forty-seven, Lope de Vega expresses proudly what he considers to be the correct approach of his trade—that is, to please the common man. He advises playwrights to mix the tragic with the comic, as Nature does; to observe only the unity of action; to avoid an empty stage; to use a language appropriate to the speakers and to adjust the dialogue accordingly; to use different verse forms in accordance to the dramatic situation; to avoid obscure passages; to make the whole appear probable; and to use all the tricks of the trade.

Following the taste of the period, Lope de Vega also wrote several mythological poems, some of which appeared in 1621 with other short compositions. The nightingale in *La filomena* narrates the classical myth of Progne and Philomene in the first part, while the second part, written in *silvas*, portrays the poet, disguised as a nightingale, reciting a diatribe against the crow. "La Andrómeda" tells the fable of Andrómeda and Perseo, showing Gongoristic influences. In *La Circe*, Lope de Vega amplifies that episode of Homer's *Odyssey* (c. 800 B.C.E.) with the arrival of Ulysses at the island of Circe, his voyage to Hell, and the love between Polifemo and Galatea.

LA CORONA TRÁGICA AND LAUREL DE APOLO

In 1627, Lope de Vega published *La corona trágica* (the tragic crown), a five-thousand-line poem written in memory of Mary Stuart, Queen of Scots. Here once again, Lope de Vega reflects Spain's hatred for England and Queen Elizabeth, whom the poet addresses with repulsive and offensive names and likens to infamous women from the Bible and from mythology. On the other hand, Mary Stuart is presented as a pure martyr of the Catholic Church. It is a rather dull poem, but, as critic George Ticknor claims, "it savors throughout of its author's sympathy with the religious spirit of his age and country; a spirit, it should be remembered, which made the Inquisition what it was." Lope de Vega dedicated this poem to Pope Urban VIII, who, in turn, gave the poet a degree of doctor of divinity and the Cross of the Order of Saint John.

If his desire to emulate Tasso and Ariosto resulted in the composition of *Jerusalén conquistada* and *La hermosura de Angélica* respectively, the example of Cervantes' *Viaje del Parnaso* (1614) inspired Lope de Vega to write his *Laurel de Apolo*. A seven-thousand-line poem divided into ten *silvas, Laurel de Apolo* is a catalog of nearly three hundred Spanish poets, as well as some Portuguese, Italian, and French authors and nine Spanish painters. Lope de Vega praises them all very freely, without much artistic discrimination; although he apologizes for possible unintentional omissions, there are some noticeable absences, such as Juan de la Cueva, Saint Teresa de Ávila, and Saint John of the Cross. The poem also presents Lope de Vega's ideas about writing poetry, discussing metrics, Italian influence and innovations, and many other topics. Following his well-established custom, the poet introduces some autobiographical notes.

GATOMACHIA

Near the end of his life, Lope de Vega wrote what is probably his best poetic composition, *Gatomachia*, a burlesque poem divided into seven *silvas* or *cantos*, which he published in 1634 in a miscellaneous volume under the pseudonym of Tomé de Burguillos. The work is a marvelous parody of the pedantic Renaissance epic, a genre that Lope de Vega himself had cultivated. It narrates the love affair of two cats, Micifuf and Zapaquilda, and the pretensions of a third one, Marramaquiz, who tries to seduce Zapaquilda with the help of the magician Garfiñanto. Marramaquiz fails, but during the wedding of the lovers he kidnaps the bride and takes her to his castle. With the help of his friends, Micifuf captures the fortress, kills Zapaquilda's captor, and is reunited with his beloved; together, they live happily ever after. The tone of the poem is festive and light throughout, particularly the last two *silvas*, where Lope de Vega parodies both epic poets and traditional ballads, always with great success. Lope de Vega dedicated this work to his son, who would die before the book was published.

Lope de Vega used various verse forms in his poetic compositions, but he succeeded especially in two of them: the romance and the sonnet. The romances, or ballads, make up the first important group in Lope de Vega's poetic production. This traditional meter, derived from the epic, had become very popular during the poet's lifetime, as is attested by the publication of the anthology *Romancero general* in 1600 and 1604. Lope de Vega found the lightness of the romance very much in consonance with his vibrant poetic genius, and he used it to poeticize, for example, his love for Elena Osorio, his libels against her family, and his marriage to Isabel de Urbina. In the fashionable Moorish and pastoral romances, he found a vehicle to express his intimacy, and, disguising his identity under fictional Moorish lovers or shepherds, he wrote some of the best examples of the genre. When the poet suffered a spiritual crisis after the death of his wife Doña Juana de Guardo, he also expressed his most fervent religious sentiments in this poetic form. Lope de Vega's romances became very popular in his own time, a popularity that has endured, for they have a special freshness that makes them readable even today.

Lope de Vega was also a master of the sonnet. He used it frequently in his plays and even jokes about composing one in the well-known "Soneto a Violante" ("Sonnet to Violante"), included in *La niña de plata* (wr. 1607-1612, pb. 1617; the stunning beauty). Lope de Vega took many of these sonnets out of his plays and published them in different collections. The first such collection, *Rimas*, contained two hundred sonnets, the majority of which are dedicated to Micaela de Luján; in the refinements and subtleties of *Rimas*, one can clearly see the influence of Petrarch. Lope de Vega's humanity transcends the artificial structure of the form, however, giving these poems a genuine depth of feeling. As Montesinos says, these sonnets "combine literary motifs of two or three generations of poets with Lope's personal experience. In this sense, they are, perhaps, his most characteristic poetic collection." Lope de Vega cultivated the sonnet during his entire life, leaving other collections of different tones, such as those published in *Rimas sacras* (sacred verses), in which the poet fuses his most noble and spiritual feelings with a very refined poetic technique.

OTHER MAJOR WORKS

LONG FICTION: *La Arcadia*, 1598; *El peregrino en su patria*, 1604 (*The Pilgrim: Or, The Stranger in His Own Country*, 1621); *Los pastores de Belén*, 1612; *Novelas a Marcia Leonarda*, 1621; *La Dorotea*, 1632.

PLAYS: *Los comendadores de Córdoba*, wr. 1596-1598, pb. 1609; *El nuevo mundo descubierto por Cristóbal Colón*, wr. 1596-1603, pb. 1614 (*The Discovery of the New World by Christopher Columbus*, 1950); *El mayordomo de la duquesa de Amalfi*, wr. 1599-1606, pb. 1618 (*The Majordomo of the Duchess of Amalfi*, 1951); *El anzuelo de Fenisa*, wr. 1602-1608, pb. 1617; *La corona merecida*, wr. 1603, pb. 1620; *La noche toledana*, wr. 1605, pb. 1612; *Los melindres de Belisa*, wr. 1606-1608, pb. 1617; *El acero de Madrid*, wr. 1606-1612, pb. 1618 (*Madrid Steel*, 1935); *Castelvines y Monteses*, wr. 1606-1612, pb. 1647 (English translation, 1869); *La niña de plata*, wr. 1607-1612, pb. 1617; *Peribáñez y el comendador de Ocaña*, wr. 1609-1612, pb. 1614 (*Peribáñez*, 1936); *La buena guarda*, wr. 1610, pb. 1621; *Las flores de don Juan, y rico y pobre trocados*, wr. 1610-1615, pb. 1619; *El villano en su rincón*, wr. 1611, pb. 1617 (*The King and the Farmer*, 1940); *Fuenteovejuna*, wr. 1611-1618, pb. 1619 (*The Sheep-Well*, 1936); *Lo cierto por lo dudoso*, wr. 1612-1624, pb. 1625 (*A Certainty for a Doubt*, 1936); *El perro del hortelano*, wr. 1613-1615, pb. 1618 (*The Gardener's Dog*, 1903); *El caballero de Olmedo*, wr. 1615-1626, pb. 1641 (*The Knight from Olmedo*, 1961); *La dama boba*, pb. 1617 (*The Lady Nit-Wit*, 1958); *Amar sin saber a quién*, wr. 1620-1622, pb. 1630; *El mejor alcalde, el rey*, wr. 1620-1623, pb. 1635 (*The King, the Greatest Alcalde*, 1918); *Los Tellos de Meneses I*, wr. 1620-1628, pb. 1635; *El premio del bien hablar*, wr. 1624-1625, pb. 1636; *La moza de cántaro*, wr. 1625-1626, pb. 1646?; *El guante de doña Blanca*, wr. 1627-1635, pb. 1637; *El castigo sin venganza*, pb. 1635 (based on Matteo Bandello's novella; *Justice Without Revenge*, 1936); *Las bizarrías de Belisa*, pb. 1637; *Four Plays*, pb. 1936; *Five Plays*, pb. 1961.

BIBLIOGRAPHY

Brushatin, Israel. "Playing the Moor: Parody and Performance in Lope de Vega's El primer Fajardo." *Modern Language Association of America* 107, no. 3 (May, 1992): 566. Lope de Vega's play "El primer Fajardo" chronicles the making of a Castilian hero of the Christian conquest. The parallels between the play's motifs and Lope's official writing as secretary to the duque de Sessa are examined.

Hayes, Francis C. *Lope de Vega*. New York: Twayne, 1967. An introductory biographical study and critical analysis of selected works by Lope de Vega. Includes bibliographic references and an index.

Heiple, Daniel L. "Political Posturing on the Jewish Question by Lope de Vega and Faria e Sousa." *Hispanic Review* 62, no. 2 (Spring, 1994): 217. During the Spanish Inquisition, Lope de Vega wrote a poem celebrating the persecution of Jews. Manuel de Faria e Sousa, who shared Vega's anti-Semitic views, also wrote a sonnet in tribute to Vega. Their writings are examined.

Morrison, Robert R. *Lope de Vega and the Comedia de Santos*. New York: Peter Lang, 2000. A study of Lope's twenty-five *Comedias de Santos* which clarifies their cultural setting, and traces their ancestry.

Morrison encourages greater attention to the lyricism and techniques of these distinctive plays. The appendices include an annotated bibliography of the *Comedias de Santos*.

Parker, Jack M., and Arthur M. Fox, eds. *Lope de Vega Studies 1937-1962*. Toronto: University of Toronto Press, 1964. A critical survey of selected works by Lope de Vega and an annotated bibliography.

Rennert, Hugo A. *The Life of Lope de Vega*. New York: B. Blom, 1968. An exhaustive biographical study of the life and work of Lope de Vega. Includes bibliographic references.

Juan Fernández Jiménez;
bibliography updated by the editors

VERGIL

Publius Vergilius Maro

Born: Andes, near Mantua, Cisalpine Gaul (now in Italy); October 15, 70 B.C.E.

Died: Brundisium (now in Italy); September 21, 19 B.C.E.

PRINCIPAL POETRY

Eclogues, 43-37 B.C.E. (also known as *Bucolics* English translation, 1575)
Georgics, c. 37-29 B.C.E. (English translation, 1589);
Aeneid, c. 29-19 B.C.E. (English translation, 1553)

OTHER LITERARY FORMS

Vergil's greatness stems from his poetic works.

ACHIEVEMENTS

Vergil is considered by many to be the greatest poet of ancient Rome, and his influence reaches well into the modern era of Western poetry. Vergil mastered three types of poetry: pastoral (*Eclogues*), didactic (*Georgics*), and national epic (*Aeneid*). This mastery is reflected in the final words of his epitaph, "cecini pascua, rura, duces" ("I sang of shepherds, farmlands, and national leaders"). Vergil's fame was assured even in his own lifetime, as Tibullus, Sextus Propertius, and Horace praised and emulated him. His harshest critic was himself, and it was his dying wish that the unfinished *Aeneid* be destroyed. The Emperor Augustus himself intervened, however, and the poem was rescued and edited by Varius and Tucca in 17 B.C.E. The works of Vergil influenced Ovid and Manilius, and Vergil's epic craft established a tradition which was followed by Lucan, Statius, Silius Italicus, and Valerius Piaccus. Writers of satire, epigram, and history, such as Juvenal, Martial, Livy, and Tacitus, also show the influence of Vergil's thought, language, and prosody. The first critical edition of the *Aeneid*, the work of Probus, appeared in the time of Nero, and the Verona scholia also record interpretations based on editions by Cornutus, Velius Longus, and Asper in the late second century C.E. By this time, the poetry of Vergil had become a school manual, used for teaching grammar, rhetoric, and language.

In the fourth and fifth centuries C.E., Nonius and Macrobius discussed and quoted the works of Vergil. The tradition of *centos* soon arose, in which poets employed clever rearrangements of lines of Vergilian poetry to create poems with new meanings. The admiration of Vergil's works eventually approached a kind of worship, with the superstitious practice of consulting random lines of his poetry as one might consult an oracle.

Dante and John Milton both studied Vergil, and their great epics owe much to his works, especially the *Aeneid*. John Dryden called the *Georgics* "the best poems of the best poet"; Alfred, Lord Tennyson, described Vergil's hexameters as "the stateliest measures ever moulded by the lips of man."

Vergil's achievement is therefore enormous. He raised the dactylic hexameter to new levels of grandeur, he elevated the Latin language to new beauty, and he set new standards for three types of poetry. Perhaps his greatest achievement lies in the vision of the imperial grandeur of Rome depicted in the *Aeneid*.

BIOGRAPHY

Publius Vergilius Maro was born on October 15, 70 B.C.E., in Andes, an Italian town located near present-day Mantua. He was not born to Roman citizenship, but the franchise was later granted to his native province. His early education took place at Cremona and at Mediolanum, now called Milan. Like most promising young men of his era, Vergil eventually made his way to Rome, where he studied philosophy, rhetoric, medicine, and mathematics; he also completed preparation for the legal profession, although he spoke only once as an advocate. At this time, he also made the acquaintance of the poets who remained from Catullus's circle and absorbed from them the Alexandrian ideals of poetry. In 41 B.C.E., the farm belonging to Vergil's family was confiscated and given to the soldiers of Mark Anthony. According to tradition, this personal catastrophe, referred to in eclogues 1 and 9, was remedied by Octavian himself (after 23 B.C.E., the Emperor Augustus) in response to a personal appeal by Vergil, but many scholars believe the loss of the farm was permanent; the references in the *Eclogues* are subject to interpretation. It was during this period, from about 43 to 37 B.C.E., that Vergil wrote the ten *Eclogues*, working first in Northern Italy and later in Rome. The success of the *Eclogues* resulted in an introduction to Maecenas, Octavian's literary adviser, and this personal connection assured financial support for Vergil's literary activities

Vergil (Library of Congress)

and provided an entrée into the circle of Rome's best writers and poets.

In 38 or 37 B.C.E., Vergil met the great Roman poet Horace and arranged for Horace to meet Maecenas. It was at this time that the two poets and their colleagues, Varius and Tucca, participated in the famous journey to Brundisium described in Horace's *Satires* (35, 30 B.C.E.). From that point on, Vergil lived and wrote in Southern Italy, at a country house near Nola and at Naples. From 37 to 29 B.C.E., he worked slowly on the *Georgics*, a didactic poem in four books which instructs the reader in various aspects of agriculture and animal husbandry. Finally, in 29 B.C.E., Vergil began his greatest undertaking, the *Aeneid*, an epic poem which describes the journey of the hero, Aeneas, from the ruins of Troy to the west coast of Italy; in the poem, Aeneas's son Iulus is linked to the Julian clan from which the Emperor Augustus claimed descent. The writing of this poem also proceeded laboriously. In 19 B.C.E., Vergil embarked on a journey to Greece and the East, during which he hoped to polish and revise his epic. During his journey, he fell ill at Megara; shortly after reaching Brundisium, the port city on the east coast of Italy which serves as the gateway to Greece, he died. He was buried at Naples, and his dying request for the unrevised *Aeneid* to be destroyed was fortunately countermanded by the orders of Augustus.

Little is known of the character of Vergil, except that he was a shy and reclusive man who never married. He was also of weak physical constitution, often ill. The main source of information about Vergil's life and character is the biography by Aelius Donatus, from the fourth century.

ANALYSIS

In order to understand more fully the poetry of Vergil, his works should be considered in the light of two relationships: his literary connection with the Greek poetry on which his works are modeled, and his personal and ideological connection with the builders of the Roman Empire. Vergil, like most Roman artists, worked within genres invented by the Greeks, but he also left on his works a uniquely Roman imprint. It was his great genius that he was able to combine both Greek and Roman elements so effectively.

ECLOGUES

Vergil's earliest major work was a group of ten short poems called the *Eclogues*, or the *Bucolics*. The poems are set in an idealized Italian countryside and are populated by shepherds. Vergil has clearly modeled the poems on the thirty idylls of Theocritus, a Greek poet of about 310 to 250 B.C.E. who lived primarily in Sicily. The *Eclogues* are, in fact, the most highly imitative of Vergil's three works, although the Roman element asserts itself clearly. In the first eclogue, which is one of the most Roman, Vergil tells of two shepherds, Tityrus and Meliboeus. Tityrus has retained his farm in the face of confiscation, and he relaxes among his sheep while Meliboeus, ejected from his fields, drives his weary livestock to new pastures. Tityrus expresses his gratitude to the young Octavian, whom he depicts as a god. Here, Vergil uses the Theocritean framework, but the content of the poem reflects Vergil's own private and public Roman experience. Eclogue 2, by contrast, follows Theocritus in both form and substance. Here, the shepherd Corydon bemoans his failure to win Alexis, imitating Polyphemus's lament of the cruelty of Galatea in the *Idylls* (third century B.C.E.). Similarly, the capping contest between shepherds Menalcas and Damon in Eclogue 3 closely follows idylls 4 and 5.

Eclogue 4 is perhaps the most famous, as well as the most Roman. Here, the shepherd format has been abandoned. The poem honors the consulship of Vergil's early local patron, Asinius Pollio, during which the former governor helped negotiate the Treaty of Brundisium. Welcoming the hope of peace, Vergil predicts the coming of a new Golden Age. His ideas about the cycle of ages are based on a number of sources, including the Sybilline Books and the "ages of man" in Hesiod. Because the new era of peace is here connected with the birth of a child, scholars of the Middle Ages believed that the poem held a messianic message, predicting the birth of Christ. Present-day scholars disagree about the identity of the young child: Some argue that Vergil refers here to the children of Pollio, who were born around this time, while others believe that the poem expresses hope for the future offspring of Mark Anthony and Octavia, or perhaps of Octavian and his new wife, Scribonia. In any case, the language of the eclogue is sufficiently vague to preclude any clear identification.

Eclogue 5 returns once again to the Theocritean format: Two shepherds, Mopsus and Menalcas, engage in a contest of amoebaean verse (poetry written in the form of a dialogue between two speakers). They sing of the death and deification of Daphnis, also a shepherd, and in so doing they reprise the song of Idyll 1. Eclogue 6 maintains the pastoral theme: Two shepherds catch Silenus (a mythological woodland deity with horses' ears and tail) and induce him to sing of the world's creation and other legends. The preface to this poem, however, deals with more Roman matters: Vergil dedicates the poem to Varus, the man who succeeded Pollio as legate in the region of Vergil's birthplace. Apparently the new legate had urged the poet to write an epic; here the poet demurs. Eclogue 7, like eclogues 2, 3, and 5, adheres to the Theocritean model: Melliboeus tells of a contest between shepherds Thyrsis and Corydon.

Eclogue 8, like Eclogue 4, is dedicated to Pollio. Two shepherds sing an amoebaeic: Damon grieves over the faithlessness of Nisa, and Alphesiboeus sings of a young woman's attempts to secure the love of Daphnis by magic charms. The latter topic has as its model Idyll 2 of Theocritus, but the ethos is Roman. Eclogue 9 returns to the farm confiscations discussed in Eclogue 1. Shepherd Moeris has been ejected from his farm; shepherd Lycidas expresses surprise, since he had thought that the poetry of Menalcas (Vergil's persona) had secured the safety of all the farms of the region. The collection concludes with Eclogue 10, in which Gallus (a real-life Roman) grieves for the loss of an actress named Lycoris.

Critics agree that these poems, although very artificial, are exercises which show the power of a great poet early in his development. Eclogues 2, 3, 5, and 7, among the first written, follow the Theocritean model rather closely, working within the conventionalized framework of the pastoral genre. Other eclogues introduce matters closer to Vergil's life and times, such as the farm confiscations dealt with in eclogues 1 and 9 (and alluded to in 6) and the problems of Gallus in Eclogue 10. Eclogue 6 offers the promise of greater works to come, and this promise is redeemed first in the *Georgics* and later in the *Aeneid*.

GEORGICS

The *Georgics* comprise four books of dactylic hexameter verse on the subject of farming and animal husbandry. The basic Greek model is Hesiod's *Works and Days* (c. 700 B.C.E.); however, Vergil's sources for the *Georgics* also include the Alexandrian scientific poets and the Roman Epicurean poet, Lucretius. The *Georgics* are very Italian, and the Hesiodic model provides only a form and an outline: The poet distances himself from his model to a much greater degree than in the *Eclogues*. Vergil's own words suggest that Maecenas, the great Augustan literary patron, suggested the subject matter of this poem. Augustus's vision of the new order, the Pax Romana, had as its cornerstone a revival of "old Roman" virtues, religion, and the simple agrarian life. The *Georgics*, then, aimed to present the simplicity and beauty of Italian country life as an important element of Augustus's new empire. Once again, Vergil is working with a Greek model and Roman ideas, but in the *Georgics* the model is less intrusive and the Italian element predominates.

Book 1 of the *Georgics* deals with the farming of field crops and the relationship of weather and constellations to this pursuit. Vergil stresses the importance of Jupiter and of Ceres, the goddess of agriculture. Near the end of the book, the discussion of weather phenomena leads the poet to a description of the ominous cosmological omens that accompanied the assassination of Julius Caesar in 44 B.C.E.; Vergil closes the book by expressing his hope that Augustus will save Rome and by expressing his regret that years of civil war have prevented the people of Italy from peacefully farming their lands.

In book 2, Vergil treats the matter of vines and trees, especially the olive tree. He instructs the reader on the propagation, growth, planting, and tending of these plants. Technical discussions of soils, vines, and proper seasons are included, and here the Hesiodic and Alexandrian models are evident, although not predominant. Praise for the agriculture of Italy leads to praise of the country as a whole, and then of its chief, Augustus. The book concludes with a paean to the life of the farmer, especially as contrasted with the life of war. The themes of Augustus's new order find eloquent voice.

Book 3 of the *Georgics* takes up the subject of cattle and their deities. At the beginning of the book, Vergil tells the reader that Maecenas urged the writing of the *Georgics*, and Vergil also promises future works in praise of Augustus and Rome. Following these literary comments, the poet once again turns to technical matters: care of broodmares, calves, and racing foals; the force of love among animals; sheep and goats; and the production of wool, milk, and cheese. A discussion of disease in sheep leads into the very famous and poignant description of the plague, based on similar passages in Lucretius and Thucydides.

In book 4, Vergil turns to the subject of bees and beekeeping. He discusses the location of hives, the social organization of bees, the taking of honey, and the very ancient practice of obtaining a new stock of bees by using the carcass of a dead animal. The book closes with the stories of Aristaeus and Arethusa, and finally of Orpheus.

The matter of sources, then, is much more complex in the *Georgics* than in the *Eclogues*. The *Georgics* reveals a wide variety of sources and a poet who is more confident and thus more willing to depart from his models. Vergil's relationship to Maecenas, Augustus, and the new Roman order manifests itself both in the overall intent of the poem and in specific passages. The artificial landscape of the *Eclogues* yields to the reality and beauty of the Italian countryside.

AENEID

The final and most important work of Vergil's career was the twelve-book hexameter epic called the *Aeneid*. Vergil wished to pay homage to the great Greek epics of Homer (the *Iliad* and the *Odyssey*, both c. 800 B.C.E.) and Apollonius Rhodius (the *Argonautica*, third century B.C.E.), but Vergil also sought to create a work that would supplant the work of Ennius and glorify the Rome of his own day and its leader, Augustus. The solution lay in telling the mythological story of Aeneas, a Trojan hero who fought on the losing side in the great Trojan War. Homer mentions that Aeneas was purposefully rescued by the gods, and a firm post-Homeric tradition told of the hero's subsequent journey to Italy. Vergil, then, would tell the story of Aeneas's travels and of the founding of the Roman race, and in so doing would remain close to the Homeric era; at the same time, prophetic passages could look forward to the Rome of Vergil's lifetime, and the poem overall would stress Roman virtues and ideals. In the figure of Aeneas, Vergil had discovered the perfect transition from the Homeric world in which epic was rooted to the Augustan era of his own day.

The first six books tell of the wandering journey of Aeneas and his men from Troy to the western coast of Italy, a voyage which was impeded by false starts, the anger of the goddess Juno, and Aeneas's own fears, hesitations, and weaknesses. Vergil chose as his basic model for these books Homer's *Odyssey*, also a tale of wandering. Since books 6 through 12 of the *Aeneid* describe the battles between Aeneas and the Italic tribes which opposed him, the poet here emulated the *Iliad*, an epic of war. Indeed, the opening phrase of the *Aeneid*, "I sing of arms and of the man" ("Arma virumque cano"), sets forth this two-part plan very clearly.

Book 1 begins with an introduction in which Vergil states his aim: He will tell of the deeds and sufferings of Aeneas, a man driven by destiny, whose task is to found the city of Rome in the face of strong opposition from Juno, the queen of the gods, whose anger is rooted in past insults (the judgment of Paris, the rape of Ganymede) as well as future offenses (the defeat of Carthage by Rome) of which the gods have advance knowledge. The actual narrative begins not at Troy but in medias res. Aeneas and his Trojan remnant are off the coast of Sicily, about to sail to Italy, when Juno conspires with Aeolus to cause a storm at sea. When the hero finally appears for the first time, he is cold and frightened, wishing that he had died at Troy. It is at once obvious that Aeneas is no courageous Homeric hero, but a man who must learn through difficulty to understand obedience to destiny and dedication to duty—the very Roman quality of *pietas*, or piety. Indeed, the first six books of the epic demonstrate Aeneas's growing maturity and piety, which increase as he comes to understand fate's grand plan for the future of Rome.

Neptune soon intervenes, calming the wild seas; this act is described in terms of a unique simile—Neptune and the seas are compared to a statesman using words to calm a rebellious mob—which surely is a vague allusion to the great Augustus ushering in an era of peace on the heels of decades of civil war. Aeneas's party finds harbor in North Africa, and the scene quickly changes to Olympus, where Venus complains bitterly to Jupiter about the way her son is being treated. The king of the gods responds with a prophecy: He tells of Aeneas's Italian wars; of the founding of Alba Longa by Aeneas's son Iulus (also called Ascanius); of Romulus and Remus;

of the boundless future empire; of Julius Caesar; and, finally, of the new era of peace. Augustus is not explicitly named, but the final lines refer to his Pax Romana, the era of Roman peace. In the short term, Jupiter arranges for Aeneas to receive a warm welcome in Carthage in the person of Queen Dido. Dido's history is related, and it is remarkably similar to that of Aeneas: She, too, is the widowed leader of a group of refugees, from Tyre, and her people have found their new home, which they are building happily, like bees in summer. The leaders meet, and their mutual sympathy is soon deepened through the machinations of Venus and Cupid; Dido falls in love with Aeneas.

Dido arranges a welcoming banquet for her guests, and after dinner Aeneas agrees to tell the story of the fall of Troy, his escape, and his subsequent wanderings in the Mediterranean basin. Books 2 and 3, then, constitute a flashback, the device also used in the *Odyssey*. In these books Vergil adheres more clearly to his sources than elsewhere in the epic. Book 2, which relates the fall of Troy, relies on the epic cycle, of which only fragments have survived to modern times. Aeneas loses his wife, Creusa, but he escapes carrying his father, Anchises, on his shoulders, bearing the household gods, and holding his son, Ascanius, by the hand. The stories of Laocoön and Cassandra, the death of Priam, and the figure of Helen all derive from the Greek tradition, but Aeneas's ultimate acceptance of destiny and the picture of his devotion to father and son serve to underline ideals and values that are distinctly Roman. Book 3, the narrative of Aeneas's wanderings, contains many episodes based on the *Odyssey* and a few which come from Apollonius. The Trojans make several erroneous attempts to find their new homeland, but omens and progressively clearer prophecies keep them on the track of destiny. Aeneas is warned by Helenus to seek further prophetic information in Italy from the Cumaen Sibyl. The monsters of Greek epic appear, interspersed with more realistic episodes. The book concludes with the most painful incident of all, the death of Anchises. Thus, Aeneas concludes his recollection of the past, a narrative based on the Greek models but heavily laden with Roman ideas of destiny, perseverance, and devotion to duty.

Book 4, perhaps the most famous in the *Aeneid*, tells of the ill-fated love of Dido and Aeneas. Dido's frenzied emotion is pitted against Aeneas's growing *pietas*. Drawing on book 3 of Apollonius's *Argonautica*, Vergil tells the tragic tale. Fire and wound imagery convey Dido's passion in a subjective manner. Through the machinations of the goddesses, the two leaders find themselves driven by a rainstorm, which interrupts a formal hunt, to the same cave. Here they enjoy a sexual union which Vergil surrounds with perverted wedding imagery. Aeneas and Dido live together openly, but only Dido perceives the relationship as a marriage. Aeneas has made no lasting commitment, and, worse, the outside world is offended by their conduct. Iarbas, an earlier and unsuccessful suitor of Dido, prays to Jupiter for satisfaction; as a result, Mercury is dispatched to remind Aeneas of his duty. Aeneas at first tries to hide his impending departure, but this fails, and the confrontation which follows does not change the hero's mind. Obeying the call of destiny, Aeneas leaves Carthage. Dido has lost her self-respect and the respect of her people and their neighbors. She commits suicide on a pyre, abandoning her kingdom and her sister Anna. Roman virtue has defeated the passion of the foreign queen, and Aeneas has triumphed over his own weaknesses.

Book 5 describes the funeral games for Anchises and is clearly based on book 23 of the *Iliad*. Like Homer, Vergil uses the games to show his hero in the role of leader and judge. Later in the book, a mutiny of the women in Aeneas's party, incited by Juno, is put down, but most of the ships are burned. A portion of the party elects to remain in Sicily, and Aeneas's father appears in a night vision, urging him to come to the underworld. The book closes with the death of the helmsman Palinurus, which offers a fitting transition to book 6, the narrative of Aeneas's journey to the underworld.

Aeneas arrives at Cumae, meets the Sibyl, and hears a short-term prophecy of events in Italy: He will marry a new wife, but there will be more bloodshed, and Juno will continue to hinder Aeneas's progress. Before Aeneas can descend to the underworld, there are lengthy preliminaries, perhaps aimed at emphasizing the difficulty of a mortal's descent to Hades: Aeneas must obtain the golden bough, a sign of fortune's favor; he must perform the requisite sacrifices; and he must bury his dead comrade Misenus. Finally, Aeneas is permitted to descend to an underworld based largely on book 11 of the

Odyssey, as well as on folk tradition. After encountering the traditional creatures of the underworld, including the ferryman Charon, Aeneas meets a succession of three figures from his past, beginning with the most recent: First, there is Palinurus the helmsman; next, in the Fields of Mourning, Aeneas finds the silent Dido, who turns away from the hero to the comfort of her first husband, Sychaeus; and, finally, Deiphobus, a Trojan warrior, describes his own death amid the sack of Troy. Through these three encounters, Aeneas makes his peace with the past, an essential preparation for his greeting of the future later in the book. An interlude follows, during which the Sibyl describes Tartarus, the place where the guilty are punished; here again, Vergil relies on Homer and folk tradition.

Aeneas moves on to the Elysian fields and a tearful reunion with Anchises. This portion of the book has many different sources, among them Lucretius's Epicureanism, Pythagorean doctrines of the transmigration of souls, Platonism, and Orphism. Here, mythology yields to history and philosophy. Anchises explains the future to Aeneas, but this prophecy is more detailed than any thus far. Moreover, Anchises is able to illustrate his words by showing Aeneas the souls of the great future Romans as they line up for eventual ascent to the upper world. Here, in the exact center of the epic, a powerful passage reiterates the history of Rome as future prophecy. We meet the Alban kings and Romulus, and then the chronological order is interrupted for the highly emphatic introduction of Augustus himself: It is predicted that he will renew the Golden Age in Latium, and elaborate phrases describe the new boundaries of the Roman Empire under his rule. Aeneas is reminded that his own courage is needed if all this is to come about.

The history lesson now resumes with the early Roman kings who followed Romulus—Numa, Tullius, Ancus Marcius—and then the Tarquin kings from Etruria. The heroes of the early Republic, such as Brutus and Camillus, follow, and then the chronology is once again interrupted for the introduction of Caesar and Pompey and an admonishment against the evils of civil war. The list of Romans resumes with Mummius, Aemilius Paulus, and other great warriors; the emphasis here is on those whose victories expanded the Empire. Anchises closes with a generalized description of the fields of endeavor in which Romans will achieve greatness—sculpture, oratory, and astronomy—but he isolates leadership and government as the unique responsibility of Rome toward the world. One last shade remains to be named, and that is Marcellus, Augustus's nephew and heir, who showed great promise but died very young. Aeneas then departs from the underworld, through the gate of sleep, taking with him a new and more complete understanding of Roman destiny and his duty to fulfill that destiny; his growth as a man is complete, and in the remaining books he fights an enemy which is purely external.

Book 7 begins the "Iliadic" portion of the *Aeneid*, which describes the war in Latium; Vergil marks the new subject with a second invocation to the Muse and calls his new subject "a greater theme" and "a greater labor." Avoiding Circe's island, the Trojans sail the coast and enter the Tiber River. The mood is tranquil and calm as Vergil introduces the new cast of characters: King Latinus, an older man, who has one child; his daughter Lavinia, much sought after as a wife; Queen Amata; and Turnus, a Rutulian king and relative of Amata, and Amata's preferred choice among Lavinia's suitors. The omens, however, argue against Turnus and in favor of a heretofore unknown foreign prince. The Trojans, meanwhile, have disembarked on the banks of the Tiber, where a serendipitous omen makes clear that they have, at long last, found their future home. Aeneas and his men are received warmly by Latinus, who offers both alliance and the hand of Lavinia; the Latin king has some understanding of fate and of his own role in Rome's destiny.

The founding of Rome, however, is not so easy a task: Aeneas's relentless enemy, Juno, greets the happy welcome and the new alliance with rage. She searches out Allecto, a gruesome Fury, and sends her to kindle the anger of Amata, using a snake to stir up the queen's emotions. Amata passionately opposes the alliance, the marriage, and the slight to Turnus; she is compared to a top, a madly spinning child's toy, and she passes her fury on to the other matrons of Latium. Allecto moves on to infect Turnus with jealousy, hatred, and lust for war. Once again, Roman piety is opposed by *furor* (passion), here represented by Allecto, Amata, and Turnus; the main symbols of *furor* are snakes and fire—as used earlier in connection with Dido's passion. Still, Allecto's work is not yet complete: She virtually assures the coming of war by inducing Iulus, Aeneas's son, to wound a stag which is the favorite of a girl called Silvia. Silvia summons the men of the region, and the conflict bursts into armed struggle. Latinus withdraws into his palace, and Juno takes the final irrevocable step of forcing open the gates of the temple of Janus, nothing less than formal declaration of war. (Vergil's own times witnessed the closing of those gates, an event which Augustus saw as his greatest achievement.) The book concludes with a catalog of the Latin allies: the impious Mezentius and his son Lausus; Camilla, a female warrior patterned after Penthesilea, the Amazon fighter and Trojan ally described in the epic cycle; and Turnus himself, decked out for war. The catalog, a Homeric device, introduces the characters who will fight in the books that follow, thereby increasing interest in future events. Thus concludes the book which began so differently, on a tranquil note of sunrise, the Tiber, alliance, and betrothal.

Aeneas must also seek allies for the imminent battle, and to that end he sails up the Tiber to Etruria. This journey and the visit with King Evander provide the subject for book 8. En route to Etruria, the omen of the white sow marks for Aeneas the future site of Rome. When the Trojans arrive, they find Evander's people celebrating an ancient feast in honor of the victory of Hercules over the brigand Cacus. Vergil devotes many lines of verse to the retelling of this tale, partly because it conforms to the Augustan theme of civilization overcoming savagery, and partly because Aeneas must learn and assume the customs of Italy as he leaves his Trojan past behind him. Evander offers his guests a brief tour of the area, pointing to future Roman landmarks and discussing the history and lore of central Italy. The Etruscan also provides background information about Mezentius and agrees to an alliance with Aeneas, sending a contingent of warriors led by his own son, Pallas.

In the meantime, Aeneas's mother, Venus, has urged her husband, Vulcan, god of fire and metalworking, to create arms for Aeneas. Vergil follows Homer (in *Iliad*, book 18) in offering a lengthy description of his hero's shield, but whereas the Homeric shield depicted scenes of the human condition, universal in their implication, Aeneas's weapon offers a lesson in Roman history:

Ascanius is depicted with his offspring; the wolf suckles Romulus and Remus; the Romans carry off the Sabine women; Romulus and Tatius make peace; Horatius and Manlius perform their heroic exploits; and Rome's enemies are punished in Hades. In the center of the shield is depicted the raging battle of Actium, the naval conflict of 31 B.C.E. in which Augustus (then Octavian) defeated Mark Anthony while Antony's foreign wife, Cleopatra, fled; the gods of war surrounded the scene. Other panels show Augustus celebrating his triumph and consecrating temples that honor the far-flung boundaries of his empire. Aeneas does not understand everything on the shield, but he lifts it high, signaling his willingness to take on the responsibility of Rome's destiny.

Book 9 is contemporaneous with book 8, describing events in Latium during Aeneas's absence. Iris, Juno's messenger, inflames Turnus to begin the battle: They attack the Trojan fleet. At the urging of Cybele, the mother goddess, the ships are rescued and metamorphosed into sea nymphs. The frightened Rutulians withdraw, ending the day of battle. That night, Nisus and Euryalus, two Trojans bound by special friendship, volunteer to cross enemy lines in order to reach Aeneas. In a scene based on the *Iliad*, book 10, the night raid ends in catastrophe: Both are killed, although their mutual devotion prevails even in the face of death. Cruel Turnus beheads the two Trojans and impales the heads on pikes as prizes of battle, much to the despair of Euryalus's mother. As the battle continues, Ascanius prevails, killing the insolent Numanus; Turnus, too, enjoys a moment of glory, killing Pandarus, before he escapes by leaping into the Tiber. The book is very reminiscent of the *Iliad* in its gory battle descriptions, but Vergil adds his own imprint with a series of wild animal similes.

Book 10 opens with a council of the gods: Venus and Juno bicker, and Jupiter refuses to take sides. Back in Latium, the weary Trojans are cheered by the return of Aeneas, who brings with him Evander's men and a host of Etruscan allies. The battle resumes, led by Turnus, Mezentius, and Mezentius's son Lausus on the side of Latium, and Aeneas, Pallas, and Iulus on the side of Troy. Turnus kills Pallas and puts on his sword belt, spurring Aeneas to furious deeds of battle; Aeneas's rage at Turnus, however, is frustrated by Juno, who removes Turnus from the battle. In a confrontation with Mezentius, Aeneas kills Lausus and then the repentant Mezentius himself, promising first to bury his enemy. The material of the book is again very Iliadic, but the compassion of Aeneas for friend and foe alike and the emphasis on the father-and-son relationship are very Roman.

Book 11 begins with a truce, during which Evander poignantly receives the corpse of his son, and both sides mourn their dead. The Latins hold a council of war, and it is reported that Diomedes, a Greek hero now living in Italy, will not aid their cause: The years at Troy have made him weary of war, and he respects the renowned piety of Aeneas. A rancorous discussion between Turnus and the Latin Drances is interrupted by the news that Aeneas and his allies are on the march. The battle now resumes, with Turnus guarding the city while the warrior maiden Camilla advances against the cavalry. Camilla excels in battle but is mortally wounded by Arruns; Opis, a nymph attending Diana, avenges Camilla's death, killing Arruns.

In book 12, Turnus, now wounded, speaks with Latinus. He pleads for an opportunity to face Aeneas in single combat. Amata and Lavinia weep, and Latinus favors appeasement, but Turnus and Aeneas agree to a duel. Aeneas prays, divulging his plan for equality of Trojans and Latins and respect for Latin custom. But the compact for single combat is broken when Juturna, a nymph and sister of Turnus, incites the Rutulians and one of them hurls a javelin. Aeneas is wounded as he shouts for both sides to remain calm and respect the truce, but the battle erupts, and Aeneas, now a martyr to the cause of peace and respect for law, is healed by his mother and soon returns to the fray. When the battle reaches the walls, Amata, believing Turnus to be dead, kills herself. As the conflict approaches its climax, Jupiter and Juno reach an agreement: Juno will withdraw from the battle and cease her harassment of the Trojans, and the newly unified nation of Trojans and Latins will be called Latins, using Latin language and Latin dress. Juno will be worshiped and honored by the pious new nation. Juturna, too, withdraws from the conflict, and Aeneas confronts Turnus. The Rutulian is wounded and he surrenders all claim to Lavinia. Aeneas is moved by Turnus's words of acceptance, but a glance at Pallas's sword belt, now worn by Turnus, spurs him to deliver the mortal blow. The epic closes with the flight of Turnus's shade to the world of the dead.

Book 12 completes the portrait of Aeneas as the personification of Roman leadership: He is strong yet compassionate; he obeys and upholds the law; his victory promises to spare the conquered and honor their laws and customs. The confused Trojan fugitive of book 1 has made his peace with his Trojan past and has evolved into a pious, devoted, and progressive leader—a symbol of the glory of Augustan Rome. Turnus, too, commands respect in this book. He possesses all the natural vigor of primitive Italy, which, once harnessed by just government, provides an important component of Roman greatness.

The works of Vergil are thus characterized by a creative tension between deference to Greek models and allegiance to Roman history and values. In the *Eclogues*, Vergil was still striving to find the correct balance, but in the *Georgics* and in the *Aeneid* he skillfully infused the old Greek forms with the moods and themes of his own day. Augustus's new vision of peace and empire found eloquent expression in the timeless hexameters of Rome's greatest poet.

BIBLIOGRAPHY

Comparetti, Domenico. *Vergil in the Middle Ages.* Translated by E. F. M. Benecke. 1895. Reprint. Princeton, N.J.: Princeton University Press, 1997. A masterpiece of intellectual history, this work covers the poet's reception and identity from antiquity to late medieval times (through Dante). Comparetti looks not only at Vergil's critical reception but also at the popular Christian folklore surrounding him and at his impact upon Italian and European self-identity.

Jenkyns, Richard. *Virgil's Experience, Nature and History: Times, Names, and Places.* New York: Clarendon Press, 1998. This large-scale work concerns itself with examining Vergil's ideas of nature and historical experience as compared with similar ideas throughout the ancient Western world. Jenkyns also discusses the influence of Vergil's works on later thought, particularly regarding views of nature, the landscape, and the environment.

Martindale, Charles, ed. *The Cambridge Companion to Virgil.* New York: Cambridge University Press, 1997. This collection of twenty-one essays (including the editor's introduction) is divided into four sections covering the translation and reception of Vergil's works, his poetic career, historical contexts, and the content of his thought. A helpful dateline is included, as well as some illustrations and numerous bibliographies.

Otis, Brooks. *Virgil: A Study in Civilized Poetry.* Norman: University of Oklahoma Press, 1995. This classic work argues for Vergil as a sophisticated poet who presented mythic, well-known material in a new and meaningful style to his urban readers. Covers the *Aeneid,* the *Bucolics,* and the *Georgics.* A useful survey of Vergilian scholarship is included as a foreword in the 1995 edition.

Perkell, Christine, ed. *Reading Vergil's "Aeneid": An Interpretive Guide* Norman: University of Oklahoma Press, 1999. Contains several essays covering various aspects of the work on a book-by-book basis. The editor also provides an introduction discussing the work's historical background and themes. Several essays on such topics as influences and characters conclude this fine study.

Laura M. Stone;
bibliography updated by Craig Payne

ÉMILE VERHAEREN

Born: Saint-Amand, Belgium; May 21, 1855
Died: Rouen, France; November 27, 1916

PRINCIPAL POETRY
Les Flamandes, 1883
Les Moines, 1886
Les Soirs, 1887
Les Débâcles, 1888
Les Flambeaux noirs, 1890
Les Apparus dans mes chemins, 1891
Les Campagnes hallucinées, 1893

Les Villages illusoires, 1895
Les Villes tentaculaires, 1895
Les Heures claires, 1896 (*The Sunlit Hours,* 1916)
Les Visages de la vie, 1899
Petites Légendes, 1900
Les Forces tumultueuses, 1902
Toute la Flandre, 1904-1911 (includes *Les Tendresses premières,* 1904; *La Guirlande des dunes,* 1907; *Les Héros,* 1908; *Les Villes à Pignons,* 1910; *Les Plaines,* 1911)
Les Heures d'après-midi, 1905 (*Afternoon,* 1917)
La Multiple Splendeur, 1906
Les Rythmes souverains, 1910
Les Heures du soir, 1911 (*The Evening Hours,* 1918)
Les Blés mouvants, 1912
Poems of Émile Verhaeren, 1915
Les Ailes rouges de la guerre, 1916
The Love Poems of Émile Verhaeren, 1916

OTHER LITERARY FORMS

Émile Verhaeren wrote several plays, one of which, *Les Aubes* (1898; *The Dawn,* 1898), was immediately translated into English by Arthur Symons. In the early 1880's, Verhaeren's art criticism, which was published in journals, had a considerable impact, popularizing Impressionism in Belgium. Throughout his life, he continued to produce criticism, treating Low Country painters of the past as well as evaluating artists of his own day. In view of Verhaeren's deep interest in aesthetics and art history, it is no wonder that students of his poems have consistently viewed them in the light of painting and graphics.

ACHIEVEMENTS

Émile Verhaeren's literary reputation has suffered a steady decline since his death. Very popular and highly regarded in his lifetime, commanding both a large readership and respect from such demanding critics as Paul Valéry, he is virtually unread today. Nevertheless, Verhaeren is among Belgium's preeminent poets, and his works, though out of fashion, are of great historical value, reflecting diverse and even contradictory aesthetic trends of his time. A Naturalist, a Symbolist, a proto-Expressionist, Verhaeren was above all a poet with a passionate faith in humanity.

BIOGRAPHY

Émile Verhaeren was born on May 21, 1855, in Saint-Amand, in the vicinity of Antwerp. During his schooling at the Jesuit College of Sainte-Barbe in Gand (Ghent), he was to form friendships with three others who were destined to make their mark in Belgian literature: Georges Rodenbach, Maurice Maeterlinck, and Charles van Lerberghe. These men became aware of the Symbolist ferment that was going on in France and was beginning to filter across the borders to Belgium. Verhaeren, in his youth, had been influenced by the works of Alphonse de Lamartine, from whom he gained an appreciation for the purely musical possibilities of poetry, and of Victor Hugo, from whom he learned the skill of arranging poetic collections into architectonic wholes. A reluctant law student at the University of Louvain, Verhaeren gave himself over to a debauched life that was later to contribute crucial motifs to his first important poetic collection. It was also in Louvain that he began to publish poetry. Called to the bar in Brussels in 1881, he came into contact with a group of artists and writers known as "Young Belgium." In Brussels, he developed a deep enthusiasm for the visual arts as well as a new political awareness. Under the influence of the Young Belgium group, Verhaeren abandoned the practice of law and devoted himself to art criticism and to the creation of a highly visual style of poetry.

Always extremely sensitive, Verhaeren suffered a nervous breakdown in 1887. His mental illness inspired a series of highly personal poems based on psychological self-revelations. Part of his emotional trauma had stemmed from a confrontation with the urban squalor of *fin de siècle* London. He was soon to be reconciled, if only in part, to the inextricable combination of good and evil in the technological revolution that was transforming the cities and, by degrees, the European countryside. A series of travels on the Continent gave him a new breadth of vision as well as deepening his interest in social problems. It was during this time, in 1891, that Verhaeren became an active Socialist. He formed a close friendship with the leader of Belgium's Labor Party and gave lectures at the Université Libre at the party's newly established Maison du Peuple at Brussels. Besides actively working for voting and parliamentary reforms, he assisted in the publication of a radical journal, *La Société nouvelle.*

An internationalist in a time of divisive nationalism, Verhaeren formed close friendships with people all over Europe, including Romain Rolland, Jules Romain, Rainer Maria Rilke, and Stefan Zweig—indeed, the latter was to write an important critical biography of Verhaeren. Verhaeren met the not-so-brave new world of the twentieth century with a refreshing sense of optimism, an optimism that distinguished him from the late Symbolists with whom he is often associated. His happy marriage to Marthe Massin reinforced his positive vision and gave him a desperately needed stability.

Verhaeren's vision was not, as too many critics would have it, a naïve, otherworldly optimism. His was a hard-won hopefulness, tempered by the harsh realities of suffering and exploitation that had inspired his political convictions. Nevertheless, nothing in his experience had prepared him for the horrors of World War I, which destroyed his lifelong faith in humanity. Verhaeren and his wife took refuge in England and Wales, and the poet sought to aid his beleaguered country and exiled compatriots with a flood of verse and of prose, including *Les Ailes rouges de la guerre* (the red wings of war), *La Belgique sanglante* (1915; *Belgium's Agony,* 1915), and *Parmi les cendres* (1916; amid the ashes). During a return to France, he was killed in an accident at the Rouen train station.

ANALYSIS

Émile Verhaeren's first collection of poetry, *Les Flamandes* (the Flemish), was a propitious beginning. While it contained a considerable strain of Naturalism, derived from the French novelist Émile Zola and from the Belgian poet Camille Lemonnier, *Les Flamandes* was an unusually accomplished performance for a first work. The collection demonstrates Verhaeren's ability to convey a sense of both the vitality and the brutality of life by means of a harsh diction and a dynamic rhythm; it also reveals his painterly gift for visual imagery.

"THE PEASANTS"

Of this collection of poems, the introductory section to "Les Paysans" ("The Peasants") is the most often anthologized. The poem consists of an introduction followed by three sections, all four parts making a complete statement or picture in itself. Verhaeren's pictorial sense, as well as his interest in art history and its influence on his poetry, is apparent in the first line of "The Peasants," in which Jean-Baptiste Greuze, the eighteenth century genre painter, is mentioned. Greuze is known for his highly sentimentalized vision of the peasants; in the words of Verhaeren, "Ces hommes de labour, que Greuze affadissait/ Dans les molles couleurs de paysanneries" (These men of labor, which Greuze romanticized/ In pale colors of the rustic scene). Verhaeren goes on to describe how beautiful these paintings looked amid the rococo decor of a Louis-Quinze salon. With this devastating reference to the leading icon maker of the myth of the happy peasant, Verhaeren constructs in this work the very illusion he seeks to shatter. He concludes the opening lines of this poem with a scathing dismissal of this myth: "Les voici noirs, grossiers, bestiaux—ils sont tels" (They are dull, coarse, bestial—all that).

In the nineteenth century, the myth of the peasant as revolutionary, which was created in the eighteenth century by the events of the French Revolution, pervaded the political scene, despite the fact that the peasants repeatedly showed themselves to be the mainstay of conservative, even Royalist, governments. Verhaeren observes that ill-educated people are unable to formulate a larger view of history and the world. They know nothing beyond their village, fearing and cheating all strangers. Ironically, it is their sons who provide the soldiers for the nationalistic entities that are beyond their comprehension. The only political reality which can attract their dull sense is "le roi, l'homme en or, fait comme Charlemagne" (the king, the man in gold, looking like Charlemagne). A progressive republic is beyond their grasp; if given the vote, they use it to elect glorious anachronisms such as Louis Napoleon. Country people, according to Verhaeren, are completely unable to take up the revolutionary activities that begin in the cities of Europe:

Et s'ils ont entendu rugir, au loin, les villes,
Les révolutions les ont tant effrayés,
Que, dans la lutte humaine, ils restent les serviles,
De peur, s'ils se cabraient, d'être un jour les broyés.

(And if they hear the distant roar of urban
Revolutions they are so afraid

That, amid the human struggle, they remain servile
From fear that if they arose they would be brutally put
    down.)

The three sections of "The Peasants" present three tableaux of country life among the poor. First, a village is described with its row of thatched cottages. The poet says of the peasants who live there that they are victims of harsh labor and climate. Second, a kitchen is portrayed with the meticulous attention to detail that characterizes Dutch or Flemish still lifes. The third and longer section, bringing the work to a colorful close, is a series of descriptions of the peasants' *kermesses* (fairs), where brutal merrymaking prevails. The view of the peasants in the three sections follows the Naturalistic theory that peasants are only human beasts. The sections are three concrete pieces of Naturalistic documentation, supporting the generalizations of the introduction. The whole is saved from dullness by the rich allusions to paintings by Peter Brueghel and other Dutch masters and by the lively rhythm, which threatens to fracture the confines of the Alexandrine.

"THE MILL"

Verhaeren's mental breakdown resulted in a trilogy of collections: *Les Soirs* (the evenings), *Les Débâcles* (the collapses), and *Les Flambeaux noirs* (the black torches). These are personal psychological confessions of the poet. The poems are, as one might expect, dark and often morbid.

A representative and often excerpted poem from *Les Soirs* is "Le Moulin" ("The Mill"), a poem that again demonstrates Verhaeren's painterly instincts. "The Mill" evokes, in vivid color and sharply delineated details, a winter landscape dominated by a windmill. The purple sail of the mill stands out against the gray sky. A few huts are set before the reader in carefully chosen details such as the following: "Une lampe de cuivre éclaire leur plafond/ Et glisse une lueur aux coins de leur fenêtre" (A copper lamp illuminates their ceiling/ And slips a gleam to the corners of their windows).

"The Mill" also demonstrates, however, what John Ruskin called the "pathetic fallacy," projecting human emotions onto nature. While certainly evocative in its details, "The Mill" is by no means an exercise in purely objective description. The poet has projected his depressed state onto the scene; for example, the daylight is said to be "suffering" and "Les nuages sont las" (the clouds are tired). The manic-depressive oscillations of "The Mill" are typical of many of Verhaeren's mood pieces.

TWO TRILOGIES

During the period from 1890 to 1910, when Verhaeren's attentions turned to social issues, he produced two trilogies that are breathtaking in their all-encompassing scope. The first includes *Les Campagnes hallucinées* (the deluded countries), *Les Villages illusoires* (the illusory villages), and *Les Villes tentaculaires* (the tentacular cities); the second trilogy consists of *Les Visages de la vie* (the aspects of life), *Les Forces tumultueuses* (tumultuous forces), and *La Multiple Splendeur* (the multiple splendor). These works demonstrate a turning away from a subjective fixation on the self toward a new objectivity in dealing with the world. They are informed by a strong faith in human progress, but this optimism is not unmixed: Verhaeren never forgets the darker side of the new machine age.

Les Villages illusoires is one of Verhaeren's most popular works and one of his most carefully designed collections. The pieces that constitute it alternate between detailed realistic descriptions of various types of workmen going about their activities and quiet mood pieces that describe natural phenomena and that offer interludes between scenes of dynamic, often frenetic, activity.

"THE SNOW"

The most often anthologized poem of this collection is "La Neige" ("The Snow"), one of the atmospheric interludes. This lyric paints a melancholy winter scene not unlike that of "The Mill." The continuous snow is not merely described; its falling is compared in texture to the craft of weaving: "La neige tombe indiscontinûment/ Comme une lente et longue et pauvre laine" (The snow falls without pause/ Like slow and long and paltry wool). The monotony of the image is paralleled in the repetitive, almost droning, recurrence of *n*, *m*, and *l* sounds and the redundancy of three adjectives joined by the repeated *et* (and). Repetition, in fact, dominates the poem—lines two through four, for example, all rhyme (*laine*, *plaine*, and *haine*). Words such as *neige*, *tombe*, and *monotone* recur like verbal leitmotifs.

The phrase "la morne et longue et pauvre plaine" of the third line is repeated verbatim in the twenty-fifth line. Sometimes rhymes are replaced by a more evocative series of half rhymes or assonances (for example: *des âmes*, *et diaphane*, *sans flamme*, and *les cabanes*).

"The Snow," too easily dismissed as a formalistic virtuoso piece, must be viewed in the larger context of *Les Villages illusoires* if it is to be understood properly; conceived in sweeping designs and rendered with broad strokes, the collection is rather like a single panel from Peter Paul Rubens's great ceilings in the Banqueting House in London or the Jesuit Church in Antwerp. It is this sweeping, Whitmanesque vision that characterizes Verhaeren's verse at its best, rewarding readers who explore his neglected œuvre.

OTHER MAJOR WORKS

SHORT FICTION: *Five Tales*, 1924.

DRAMA: *Les Aubes*, pb. 1898 (*Dawn*, 1898); *The Plays of Émile Verhaeren*, pb. 1916.

NONFICTION: *La Belgique sanglante*, 1915 (*Belgium's Agony*, 1915); *Parmi les cendres*, 1916.

MISCELLANEOUS: *Œuvres d'Émile Verhaeren*, 1914 (includes all his poetry and prose).

BIBLIOGRAPHY

Jones, P. Mansell. *Verhaeren*. New Haven, Conn.: Yale University Press, 1957. A short biographical study of Verhaeren's life and work. Includes a bibliography.

Thum, Reinhard H. *The City: Baudelaire, Rimbaud, Verhaeren*. New York: P. Lang, 1994. A comparative critical study of the works of three authors. Includes bibliographical references and index.

Rodney Farnsworth;
bibliography updated by the editors

PAUL VERLAINE

Born: Metz, France; March 30, 1844
Died: Paris, France; January 8, 1896

PRINCIPAL POETRY

Poèmes saturniens, 1866

Fêtes galantes, 1869 (*Gallant Parties*, 1912)

La Bonne Chanson, 1870

Romances sans paroles, 1874 (*Romances Without Words*, 1921)

Sagesse, 1881

Jadis et naguère, 1884

Amour, 1888

Parallèlement, 1889, 1894

Femmes, 1891 (English translation, 1977)

Bonheur, 1891

Chansons pour elle, 1891

Liturgies intimes, 1892

Odes en son honneur, 1893

Élégies, 1893

Dans les limbes, 1894

Épigrammes, 1894

Chair, dernière poésies, 1896

Invectives, 1896

Hombres, 1903 (English translation, 1977)

Selected Poems, 1948

Femmes/Hombres, 1977 (includes English translation of *Femmes* and *Hombres*)

OTHER LITERARY FORMS

Most of Paul Verlaine's other published works are autobiographical writings and critical articles on contemporary poets. During his lifetime, he published two plays which were performed—*Les Uns et les autres* (pr. 1884; the ones and the others) and *Madame Aubin* (pr. 1886)—and one short story, *Louise Leclercq* (1886). A collection of seven other short stories, *Histories comme ça* (1903; stories like that), was published posthumously.

The most significant of his critical writings were published under the title *Poètes maudits* (1884; cursed poets), which includes articles on Tristan Corbière, Arthur Rimbaud, Stéphane Mallarmé, Villiers de L'Isle-Adam, and others. Verlaine's *Confessions* (*Confessions of a Poet*, 1950) was published in 1895. Many of his previously unedited writings were published posthumously in a 1903 edition of his works, which includes several autobiographical pieces as well as some original ink drawings. All his prose works were published in the 1972 Pléiade edition.

Paul Verlaine (Library of Congress)

ACHIEVEMENTS

Paul Verlaine is universally recognized as one of the great French poets of the nineteenth century. His name is associated with those of his contemporaries Charles Baudelaire, Rimbaud, and Mallarmé. His most famous and frequently anthologized poems, such as "Chanson d'automne" ("Song of Autumn"), "Mon rêve familier" ("My Familiar Dream"), "Clair de lune" ("Moonlight"), and "Il pleure dans mon coeur" ("It Is Crying in My Heart"), are readily recognized and often recited by persons with any knowledge of French poetry. Many of his poems, including those cited, have been set to music by serious composers.

Verlaine's admirers include both saints and sinners, for Verlaine is at once the author of one of the most beautiful collections of religious poetry ever published and the writer of some explicitly erotic poems. During his lifetime, Verlaine's poetic genius was recognized by only a handful of poets and friends. His penchant for antisocial and occasionally criminal behavior (he was jailed twice for potentially murderous attacks) undoubtedly contributed to his lack of commercial success or popular recognition during his lifetime. By the end of his life, he had gained a small measure of recognition and received some income from his royalties and lecture engagements.

BIOGRAPHY

Paul Marie Verlaine was born in Metz, France, on March 30, 1844, the only child of Captain Nicolas-Auguste Verlaine and Elisa Dehée Verlaine. The family moved often during Verlaine's first seven years, until Captain Verlaine retired from the army to settle in Paris. Verlaine attended the Lycée Bonaparte (now Condorcet) and received his *baccalauréat* in 1862.

Verlaine's adoring mother and equally adoring older cousin Elisa Moncomble, whose death in 1867 affected him profoundly, spoiled the sensitive child, encouraged his demanding capriciousness, and helped him to become a selfish, immature, unstable young man.

After his *baccalauréat*, he worked in an insurance office and then found a clerical job in municipal government, which he kept until 1870. In 1863, he published his first poem, "Monsieur Prudhomme." He met Catulle Mendès, an editor of the literary magazine *Le Parnasse contemporain*, in which Verlaine published eight poems. In 1866, he published his first volume of poetry, *Poèmes saturniens*, and in 1869 a second volume, *Gallant Parties*.

Alcoholism began to take its toll on his personal life. Twice in drunken rages he threatened to kill his mother. His family tried to marry him to a strong-willed cousin, a fate which he avoided by proposing to Mathilde Mauté, whom he married in 1870 and who inspired his third volume of poetry, *La Bonne Chanson*.

Having served as press officer to the Commune of Paris during the 1870 insurrection, Verlaine subsequently fled Paris and lost his government job. He helped to found a new journal, *La Renaissance*, in which he published many of the poems included in his 1874 volume, *Romances Without Words*.

Verlaine's drinking and his friendship with Arthur Rimbaud led to violent domestic scenes. Following several fights and reconciliations with Mathilde, Verlaine ran off to Brussels with Rimbaud in July, 1872. During the following year, the two poets lived together in Brussels and London and then returned to Brussels. On July 10, 1873, Verlaine, in a drunken rage, fired a revolver at Rimbaud, who had threatened to leave him. Verlaine was convicted of armed assault and sentenced to two years in prison.

In prison, Verlaine converted to a mystical form of Catholicism and began to write the poems for the volume *Sagesse*, published in 1880. After his release in 1875 and until 1879, he held teaching positions in England and France. He formed a sincere and probably chaste relationship with one of his students, Lucien Létinois. They attempted a joint farming venture which failed and then returned to Paris, where Verlaine tried to get back his old government job but was turned down because of his past record. This disappointment, coupled with the sudden death of Lucien in 1883, caused Verlaine to become profoundly discouraged.

After another ill-fated farming venture, Verlaine abandoned himself for a long period to drinking and sordid affairs. A drunken attack on his mother cost him a month in prison in 1885. During his last ten years, his economic distress was somewhat eased by his growing literary reputation. He continued writing and published several more significant volumes of verse.

From 1890 to his death in 1896, Verlaine moved in and out of several hospitals, suffering from a swollen, stiffened leg, the terminal effects of syphilis, diabetes, rheumatism, and heart disease. He lived alternately with two women who cared for him and exploited him. During his last years, he was invited to lecture in Holland, Belgium, and England.

ANALYSIS

In two articles on Baudelaire published in *L'Art* in 1865, Paul Verlaine affirms that the overriding concern of a poet should be the quest for beauty. Without denying the role of inspiration and emotion in the process of poetic creation, Verlaine stresses the need to master them by poetic craftsmanship. Sincerity is not a poetic virtue. Personal emotion must be expressed through the combinations of rhyme, sound, and image which best create a poetic universe in which nothing is the result of chance.

The most obvious result of Verlaine's craftsmanship is the musicality of his verse. Sounds flow together to create a sonorous harmony which repetitions organize and structure as in a musical composition. In his 1882 poem "L'Art poétique," Verlaine gives a poetic recipe which begins with the famous line, "Music above everything else." He goes on to counsel using odd-syllabled lines, imprecise vocabulary and imagery (as if veiled), and nuance rather than color. The poet should avoid wit, eloquence, and forced rhyme. Poetic verse should be light and fugitive, airborne and slightly aromatic. The poem ends with the somber warning, "Anything else is literature."

The subject matter of Verlaine's carefully crafted poetry is frequently his personal experience, certainly dramatic and emotionally charged material. The prologue to *Poèmes saturniens* reveals his consciousness of his miserable destiny. Throughout the rest of his poetry, he narrates the various permutations of his self-fulfilling expectation of unhappiness. "Moonlight," which serves as a prologue to his second volume of verse, presents gallant eighteenth century lovers "who don't appear to believe in their happiness." This skepticism clouds the fugitive moments of happiness throughout Verlaine's poetic pilgrimage. *La Bonne Chanson* is Verlaine's homage to marital bliss. Poem 17, filled with images of love and faithfulness, begins and ends with the question, "Isn't it so?" Poem 13 ends with a similar worry: "A vain hope . . . oh no, isn't it so, isn't it so?" In *Sagesse*, which proposes Catholic mysticism as the ultimate form of happiness, the fear of a return to his old ways haunts the poet's peaceful communion with God.

Because sex, love, God, and wine all fail to provide a safe haven from his saturnine destiny, Verlaine must seek another refuge. What he finds, perhaps not entirely consciously, is sleep. With surprising frequency the final images of Verlaine's poems are images of sleep; many of his musical pieces are thus lullabies whose delicate, soothing images—from which color, laughter, pompousness, loudness, and sharpness have been banished—lead the poet's battered psyche to the unthreatening harbor of sleep. Often, a maternal figure cradles the poet's sleep or stands watchfully by. In many poems in which the sleep motif is not explicit, the imagery subsides at the end of the poem, leaving an emptiness or absence analogous to the oblivion of sleep.

POÈMES SATURNIENS

Verlaine's first volume of poetry was published by Lemerre in November, 1866, at the author's expense. It

drew very little critical or popular attention. The title refers to the astrological contention, explained in the prologue, that those like Verlaine who are born under the sign of Saturn are doomed to unhappiness, are bilious, have sick, uneasy imaginations, and are destined to suffer.

The volume is the work of a very young poet, some of the poems having been written as early as 1861. They are consequently of uneven quality, but among them is the poem "My Familiar Dream," which is perhaps the most frequently anthologized of all Verlaine's poems and which, according to Verlaine's friend and admirer H. Suquet, the poet preferred to all his others. It is a haunting evocation of an imaginary woman who loves the poet, who understands him, and who is capable of soothing his anguish.

The central section of the volume, titled "Paysages tristes" ("Sad Landscapes"), contains the most "Verlainian" of the poems: vague, melancholy landscapes, inspired by his memories of the Artois region, whose fading colors, forms, and sounds reflect the poet's soul and whose ultimate disappearance translates as an innate desire for oblivion.

The first of these poems, "Soleils couchants" ("Setting Suns"), a musical poem of sixteen five-syllable lines, describes a rising sun so weakened that it casts a sunset-like melancholy over the fields, inspiring strange raddish ghosts in the poet's imagination. The short, odd-syllabled lines create a musical effect reinforced by alliteration and repetition—the phrase "setting suns," for example, is repeated four times in a poem about dawn!

"Promenade sentimentale" ("Sentimental Walk") presents a twilight scene through which the wounded poet passes. The vaguely lit water lilies that glow faintly through the fog in the evening light are swallowed up by the shroud-like darkness in the poem's final image.

"Nuit du Walpurgis classique" ("Classical Walpurgis Night") is full of allusions. Phantoms dance wildly throughout the night in a landscape designed by Johann Wolfgang von Goethe, Richard Wagner, Antoine Watteau, and André Le Nôtre. At dawn's approach, the Wagnerian music fades and the phantoms dissolve, leaving "absolutely" nothing except "a correct, ridiculous, charming Le Nôtre garden." Another noteworthy tone poem, "Chanson d'automne" ("Song of Autumn"), a melodic eighteen-line lyric composed of four- and three-syllable lines, combines *o*'s and nasal sounds to reproduce a melancholy autumn wind which carries off the mournful poet like a dead leaf.

Verlaine's first collection of verse reveals the influence of Baudelaire, Victor Hugo, Charles Leconte de Lisle, Théodore de Banville, and Théophile Gautier—and of Verlaine's young friends Louis de Ricard and Joseph Glatigny. It is a carefully crafted and original volume, demonstrating that at twenty-four Verlaine had already mastered the art of poetry and discovered most of the themes of his later works.

GALLANT PARTIES

The mid-nineteenth century's rediscovery of the paintings of Watteau is confirmed by several works dedicated to that artist and to his times, including one by the Goncourt brothers, *L'Art du 18ème siècle*, which undoubtedly had a strong influence on Verlaine's choice of this subject and his interpretation of it. During the composition of the poems of *Gallant Parties*, Verlaine undoubtedly consulted some of the published reproductions of Watteau's works as well as his one painting in the Louvre collection, *Embarkation for Cythère*, a vast work devoted to eighteenth century gallantry, its rites, costumes, myths, poetry, and fashionable devotees. These aristocratic gallants and the characters from *The Italian Comedy*, also painted by Watteau, come alive in Verlaine's second published volume of poetry.

The often-anthologized "Moonlight" opens the volume and sets the mood. This musical evocation of the songs and dances of the masked characters and the relationship between their costumes and their souls insist upon the underlying sadness of both. The gallant aristocrats are somewhat sad beneath their fantastic disguises because they do not really believe in the love and life of which they sing. Their dispersed song is absorbed by the moonlight.

These same characters sing, dance, walk, skate, and love through the rest of the volume, sometimes assuming stock character names from commedia del l'arte—Pierrot, Clitandre, Cassandre, Arlequin, Colombine, Scaramouche, and Pulcinella—and sometimes classical names—Tircis, Aminte, Chloris, Eglé, Atys, Damis.

The landscapes of *Gallant Parties* are very different physically and psychologically from those of the *Poèmes saturniens*. They are sculpted, landscaped, arranged, and peopled. Paths are lined by rows of pruned trees and mossy benches. Fountains and statues are harmoniously placed around well-kept lawns. The relationship between the characters and the landscape is no longer a natural sympathetic mirroring. Nature has been artificially subdued to reflect the characters' forced gaiety and becomes a mocking image of the vanity of their pursuits. One of the obvious formal characteristics of the volume is the presence of dialogue and monologue, couched in the artificial, erotic language of gallantry. There are many allusions to "former ecstasies," "infinite distress," and "mortal languors."

The volume's overriding pessimism is orchestrated by the arrangement of the poems. The latent sadness of the apparently carefree gallants in "Moonlight" becomes the dominant feeling in the second half of the work. While humorous love play and inconsequential erotic exchanges dominate the first half, several disturbing images—such as the statue of a snickering faun who anticipates eventual unhappiness and the sad spectacle of a statue of Cupid overturned by the wind—foreshadow the volume's disastrous conclusion, the poem "Colloque sentimentale" ("Sentimental Colloquium"), in which a ghostly "form" tries to recall a past sentimental adventure. The cold, solitary park, witness to the scarcely heard dialogue, swallows up the desperate efforts to recall a past love as well as the negations of those efforts. One of the lovers tries unsuccessfully to awaken memories of their past love, which the other negates repeatedly: "Do you remember our former ecstasy?" "Why do you want me to remember it?" "Does your heart still beat at the sound of my name?" "No."

ROMANCES WITHOUT WORDS

The Franco-Prussian War of 1870 and the Commune separated Verlaine from his Parnassian friends and led him toward new friendships and a new form of poetry, toward a modernistic vision which replaced the artificiality of Parnassian inspiration with an attempt to capture the essence of contemporary life. During 1872 and 1873, Verlaine wrote the poems of *Romances Without Words*, which was published in 1874. All the poems precede the episode with Rimbaud which resulted in Verlaine's imprisonment. The period was emotionally difficult for Verlaine. Torn between love for Mathilde and dependence on Rimbaud, Verlaine was tormented by his vacillations. *Romances Without Words* fuses his new poetic ideal with his personal struggle.

The sad, lilting songs which make up the first part of the volume, titled "Ariettes oubliées" ("Forgotten Melodies"), include one of the most frequently quoted of Verlaine's poems, "It Is Crying in My Heart," in which the gentle sound of the rain falling on the town echoes the fall of tears within his heart. A more interesting poem, however, is the musical twelve-line poem "Le Piano que baise une main frêle" ("The Piano Kissed by a Fragile Hand"), in which the light, discreet melody rising from the piano corresponds to the faintness in the fading evening light of the visual impression of slight hands on a barely discernible piano. A series of vague, fleeting adjectives seep out of the perfumed boudoir to disappear through a slightly opened window into a small garden. The hushed sonorities of the poem coincide with the diminished intensity of the images. One remarkable phrase in the tenth line embodies both the musical effects and the characteristic tone of Verlaine's verse: "fin refrain incertain" ("delicate, uncertain refrain").

While the influence of music on Verlaine's poetry is certain, the importance of painting is no less significant. *Gallant Parties* is to a great extent a tribute to the painting of Watteau. The "Paysages belges" ("Belgian Landscapes") which Verlaine paints into *Romances Without Words* are a tribute to the Impressionist school of painting, whose birth corresponds with the date of composition of the collection. Verlaine knew Édouard Manet and Ignace Henri Fantin-Latour and was certainly interested in their technique. The impressionistic Belgian landscapes which Verlaine has painted are carefree and gay, carrying no reflection of the shadow of Mathilde which haunts the rest of the volume. The first poem in the section, "Walcourt" (a small, industrial town in Belgium), reflects the gaiety of the two vagabond poets (Verlaine and Rimbaud) in a series of brightly colored images which flash by, without help of a verb, in lively four-syllabled lines: tiles and bricks, ivy-covered homes, and beer drinkers in outdoor bars.

The gaiety of the Belgian countryside is interrupted by a bitter poem, "Birds in the Night" (original title in English), which Verlaine had first titled "La Mauvaise Chanson" ("The Bad Song") as an ironic counterpart to his previous book of poems, *La Bonne Chanson*, devoted to marital bliss. "Birds in the Night" accuses Mathilde of a lack of patience and kindness, and of treachery. The suffering poet offers his forgiveness. The poem suggests a singular lack of understanding of the real causes of their marital discord.

The last section of *Romances Without Words* contains visions of Verlaine's London experience, but the image of Mathilde pierces through the local color with haunting persistence. All six of the poems have English titles. The most interesting is "Green," in which the poet presents to his mistress fruits, flowers, leaves, branches, and then his heart, which he commends to her care. The poem ends with the desire for a restful oblivion upon the woman's breast.

SAGESSE

Only seven of the poems in *Sagesse* were actually composed while Verlaine was in prison. The rest were written between the time of his release in 1875 and the spring of 1880. The volume was published at the end of that year. The title refers to Verlaine's intention to live virtuously according to the principles of his new faith and should perhaps be translated not as "wisdom" but as "good behavior." The volume is divided into three parts, the first of which dwells on the difficulty of converting to a virtuous life, the almost daily battles with overwhelming temptation. The second part narrates the poet's mystic confrontation with God, primarily through a cycle of ten sonnets. The last part describes the poet's return to the world and contains many of the themes and images of his earlier nature poetry. These poems are not overtly religious; the prologue to this part, "Désormais le sage, puni" ("Henceforth, the Virtuous, Punished"), explains the virtuous poet's return to a contemplative love of nature.

Poems 6 and 7 of the first part, both sonnets, are the most poetic of Verlaine's evocations of the contrast between his former and his present preoccupations. Poem 6 presents his former joys as a line of clumsy geese limping off into the distance on a dusty road. Their departure leaves the poet with a welcome emptiness, a peaceful sense of abandonment as his formerly proud heart now burns with divine love. Poem 7 warns of the prevailing appeal of the "false happy days" which have tempted his soul all day. They have glowed in his memory as "long hailstones of flame" which have symbolically ravaged his blue sky. The last line of the poem exhorts the poet's soul to pray against the storm to forestall "the old folly" which threatens to return.

Three of the most moving poems of the third part were written in prison, one on the very day of Verlaine's sentencing: "Un Grand Sommeil noir" ("A Great Black Sleep"). This poem, as well as "Le Ciel est, par-dessus le toit" ("The Sky Is, Beyond the Roof") and "Gaspard Hauser chante" ("The Song of Kaspar Hauser"), sings of the poet's despair, plaintively expressing his self-pity, his regrets, and his total sense of shock in the early days of his imprisonment. The third part of *Sagesse* also contains two of Verlaine's most finely crafted sonnets. "L'Espoir luit comme un brin de paille dans l'étable" ("Hope Glistens Like a Blade of Straw in a Stable") is perhaps his most Rimbaudian and most obscure poem. An unidentified protector speaks to the poet reassuringly as he rests in a country inn. The voice is maternal and encourages the poet to sleep, promising to cradle him. The voice shoos away a woman whose presence threatens the poet's rest. The poem opens and closes with a fragile image of glistening hope, which, in the final line, opens up into a hoped-for reflowering of the roses of September.

The sonnet "Le Son du cor" ("The Sound of the Hunting Horn") is perhaps the best example of Verlaine's poetic art. It was written before his imprisonment, probably in the spring of 1873. This very musical poem blends the sound of the hunting horn, the howling of the wind, and the cry of a wolf into a crescendo which subsides to a mere autumn sigh as the falling snow blots out the last colors of the setting sun. The painful notes of the opening stanza are completely obliterated as day gives way to a cradling, monotonous evening.

OTHER MAJOR WORKS

SHORT FICTION: *Louise Leclercq*, 1886; *Histoires comme ça*, 1903.

PLAYS: *Les Uns et les autres*, pr. 1884; *Madame Aubin*, pr. 1886.

NONFICTION: *Poètes maudits*, 1884; *Mes hôpitaux*, 1891; *Quinze jours en Hollande*, 1892; *Mes prisons*, 1893; *Confessions*, 1895 (*Confessions of a Poet*, 1950); *Les Mémoires d'un veuf*, 1896; *Charles Bau-*delaire, 1903; *Critiques et conférences*, 1903; *Souvenirs et promenades*, 1903; *Voyage en France par un français*, 1903.

BIBLIOGRAPHY

Blackmore, A. M., and E. H. Blackmore, eds. *Six French Poets of the Nineteenth Century: Lamartine, Hugo, Baudelaire, Verlaine, Rimabud, Mallarmé*. New York: Oxford University Press, 2000. This anthology of poetry is preceded by a strong introduction, notes on text and translations, a select bibliography, and a chronology.

Carter, A. E. *Verlaine*. New York: Twayne, 1971. Reprint. Detroit: Gale, 1985. An introductory biographical study and critical analysis of selected works by Verlaine. Includes a bibliography.

Frank, Bernhard. "Verlaine's Wooden Steeds." *The Explicator* 46, no. 2 (Winter, 1988): 29. The language of Paul Verlaine's poem "Wooden Steeds" ("Chevaux de Bois") is examined. Verlaine, via rhyme and the manipulation of syllables, subtly depicts the circularity and speed of the carousel, and also the seesaw motion of its steeds.

Ivry, Benjamin. *Arthur Rimbaud*. Bath, Somerset, England: Absolute Press, 1998. A biography of Rimbaud which details his two-year affair with Verlaine. Ivry delves deeply into the relationship, and especially its sexual aspects including possible dalliances with other men, misogynistic outbursts, and graphically sexual poems.

Lehmann, John. *Three Literary Friendships: Byron and Shelley, Rimbaud and Verlaine, Robert Frost and Edward Thomas*. New York: Henry Holt, 1984. An examination of the way these friendships influenced each poet's work. J. R. Combs, commenting for *Choice* magazine, notes, "[Lehmann] argues convincingly that after Verlaine and Rimbaud became friends and lovers, they became more productive literarily."

Lepelletier, Edmond Adolphe de Bouhelier. *Paul Verlaine: His Life, His Work*. Translated by E. M. Lang. New York: AMS Press, 1970. The only English translation of the hefty 1909 biography.

Nicolson, Harold George. *Paul Verlaine*. 1921. New York: AMS Press, 1997. This venerable biography remains useful and in print.

Richardson, Joanna. *Verlaine*. London: Weidenfeld and Nicolson, 1971. A short biographical study of the life and works of Verlaine. Includes bibliographic references.

Robb, Graham. "Rimbaud, Verlaine, and Their Season in Hell." *New England Review* 21, no. 4 (Fall, 2000): 7-20. An excerpt from *Rimbaud*, a biography of nineteenth century poet Arthur Rimbaud, by Graham Robb is presented. The selection features an altercation Rimbaud experienced with his friend and homosexual lover, poet Paul Verlaine, in which violence broke out after Rimbaud announced his intention to leave Verlaine and return to his wife and children.

Sorrell, Martin. Introduction to *Selected Poems*. New York: Oxford University Press, 1999. Sorrell's strong introduction is useful for beginning students in this bilingual edition of 170 newly translated poems by Verlaine.

Paul J. Schwartz

JONES VERY

Born: Salem, Massachusetts; August 28, 1813
Died: Salem, Massachusetts; May 8, 1880

PRINCIPAL POETRY

Essays and Poems, 1839
Poems by Jones Very with an Introductory Memoir by William P. Andrews, 1883
Poems and Essays by Jones Very: Complete and Revised Edition, 1886
Poems and Essays by Jones Very: James Freeman Clarke's Enlarged Collection of 1886 Re-edited with a Thematic and Topical Index, 1965
Jones Very: Selected Poems, 1966
Jones Very: The Complete Poems, 1993

OTHER LITERARY FORMS

Jones Very wrote a few critical essays, the best of which were originally collected, along with a selection of his poetry, in *Essays and Poems* (1839). Such essays

as "Epic Poetry," "Hamlet," and "Shakespeare" have been particularly rich resources for biographers and literary critics interested in understanding Very's poetic goals and practices. Also, about 117 sermons survive in manuscript form, the results of his service as a supply minister for nearly four decades.

ACHIEVEMENTS

Both during his life and after, Jones Very's significance as a poet has generally been understood in relationship to the American Transcendentalist movement. Of particular importance to biographers and critics has been Very's connection to Ralph Waldo Emerson, Transcendentalism's chief spokesperson and writer. Certainly, Emerson's sponsorship of Very resulted in the only book-length publication of Very's poems during Very's lifetime, in 1839, a volume which Emerson edited and for which he made the necessary contacts with a publisher. For a very short period, during the years 1838 and 1839, Jones Very seemed to Emerson and his associates to be the epitome of the American Transcendentalist poet linked to divinity, expressing intuitive insights and truths about the universe in pure and beautiful language.

Later biographers and literary critics have been able to observe that Very's connection to the Transcendentalists and Emerson was at best a mixed blessing. Although it resulted in early publication of his efforts, it also made it difficult to perceive that Very, at least for a short time, was a unique and powerfully mystical poet in his own right. Interestingly, many of the poems which Emerson chose not to include in his selection of poetry for Very's first publication are the ones which now seem most central and original. Since the majority of Very's poems are sonnets, he also has assumed importance as one of the most successful of America's writers of poetry in the sonnet form.

BIOGRAPHY

Jones Very was born in Salem, Massachusetts, in 1813 to a sea captain father and a strong-minded, highly independent, and somewhat atheistic mother. Very sailed with his father for nearly two years, beginning at age nine, but after his father's untimely death in 1824 Very attended school in Salem for three years, excelling as a scholar, until at age fourteen he left for employment in an auction room. He refused to give up his goal of enrolling at Harvard, however, and continued his self-education through extensive reading, eventually obtaining the help of a special tutor as well as securing employment as an assistant in a Latin school, preparing younger boys for entrance into college. During this time, his earliest, rather imitative poems began appearing in a local newspaper, the Salem *Observer.*

So advanced was Very in his scholarly ability that he was able to enter Harvard in February, 1834, as a second-term sophomore. His years at Harvard were crucial in Very's progress as a scholar, poet, and religious thinker. He distinguished himself as a student, eventually graduating second in his class in 1836 with particular expertise in Latin and Greek. He continued to write poetry, including the class songs for his sophomore and senior years, as well as poems imitative of William Wordsworth and William Cullen Bryant.

Most important, however, under the influence of some of his Unitarian teachers and classmates, he began to turn to religion in a serious way for the first time in his life, thus deviating radically from his mother's skepticism. Particularly in his senior year, he experienced what he called "a change of heart," becoming convinced "that all we have belongs to God and that we ought to have no *will* of our own." During the next two years, while staying on at Harvard as a tutor in Greek and a student at the Divinity School, he gave himself to the struggle of ridding himself of his own will and becoming perfectly conformed to the will of God working within him. His poetry writing more and more partook of this spiritual battle, centering on intense religious feelings and intuitions within the framework of the traditional Shakespearean sonnet form.

Very delivered a lyceum lecture on the subject of epic poetry in Salem in December of 1837. Elizabeth Palmer Peabody, a prominent Transcendentalist and reformer, attended this lecture and immediately recognized the uncommon promise of Very as a thinker. Knowing nothing of his poetry writing, she immediately set up a connection between Very and Ralph Waldo Emerson, which resulted in Very's lecturing at Concord in April of 1838. Very also began attending some of the so-called Transcendental Club meetings during the spring

and summer of 1838. Emerson was much taken with Very's depth of thought and his insights into William Shakespeare and encouraged him to continue his writing about poetry, but Emerson, like Peabody, seems to have been unaware of Very's own poetic productions during these months.

Very's spiritual journey reached some sort of a high point in the fall of 1838, when he evidently experienced what he thought was the total replacement of his own will by the will of God. This perhaps mystical experience immediately resulted in his proclaiming to students and friends that the end of the world and Christ's Second Coming were occurring, as evidenced in Very's own new relationship with divinity. He claimed that the Holy Spirit was speaking through him, and he urged those who listened to experience this Second Coming through a similar banishing of their own wills. Such statements were upsetting to some students and brought the displeasure of the Harvard authorities. Very was sent home to Salem, where his similar proclamations to ministers and leaders regarding their need of repentance and reformation led to his being removed to the McLean Asylum in Charlestown as one who was perhaps insane.

Although Very was released from the hospital after a month, his newfound spiritual intensity continued to challenge his new Transcendentalist friends and Salem society. It was during this period of heightened spiritual feeling that Very's poetry began to flow rapidly from his pen, with more than three hundred sonnets produced during just over one year of religious exaltation from September, 1838, to the latter part of 1839. Emerson became aware of Very's poetry during this time and undertook the job of selecting and editing the poems that were collected in the small volume *Poems and Essays.*

Interestingly, the publication of the poems seemed to coincide with the decline of Very's religious intensity and with his return to a more mundane, albeit dedicated, religious life. For the next forty years, he lived in Salem with his siblings, never marrying but serving as a supply minister to Unitarian churches in the New England area, presenting sermons in the absence of the regular ministers. He continued to produce poetry, but not at the rate nor with the intensity and originality of the poems authored in 1838 and 1839. He died in 1880 in relative obscurity.

ANALYSIS

During the course of his long poetic career, Jones Very authored some 870 separate poems, many of them published in newspapers and magazines of his day, but only 65 appearing in the thin volume edited by Emerson in 1839. It is common for biographers and literary critics to separate the poems written by Very during his period of growing religious excitement in the late 1830's from the largely imitative poems written before that period and the competent but not strikingly intense poems written in the four decades after that period. It is the poetry of the so-called ecstatic period which most interested and challenged the Transcendentalists and has continued to impress readers in the various generations since. Although repetitious in themes and format, the sonnets from the religiously intense phase of Very's experience carry a certain power and originality markedly lacking in the poetry written before and after this period.

POEMS OF SPIRITUAL INTENSITY

During the late 1830's, poems literally poured from Very's pen, sometimes, according to Elizabeth Peabody, at the rate of one or two a day. Very, convinced that his will had been totally replaced by the will of divinity, believed that these sonnets were in essence not authored by him but rather were the words of God or the Holy Spirit. Written rapidly, seemingly without revision (how could one revise the words of God?), with little attention to formalities such as spelling and punctuation, the poems of this phase have presented serious editorial issues to editors from Emerson to the present. Yet, the lack of formality and polish helps to bring immediacy to the poems, the best of which seem particularly forceful in their expression of religious passion.

"The New Birth," a sonnet that seemingly recalls Very's intense feelings of change as a result of the key mystical experience in the fall of 1838 when he became convinced of the subjugation of his own will, nicely illustrates the power of Very's poetry during this period. The poem begins with the announcement that "'Tis a new life," followed by a vivid figure of how "thoughts" no longer "move" as before, "With slow uncertain steps," but now "In thronging haste" like "the viewless wind" (a traditional biblical image for the Holy Spirit) enter "fast pressing" through "The portals." Such a change has resulted because human "pride" (the will)

has been "laid" in the "dust." The thoughts demand "utterance strong" (perhaps the writing of poetry as well as the face-to-face confrontation with teachers and friends), imaged as the sound of "Storm-lifted waves swift rushing to the shore" whose "thunders roar" "through the cave-worn rocks." The poem ends with the speaker in the poem ecstatically announcing as "a child of God" his new freedom, his awakening from "death's slumbers to eternity."

Most of the other sonnets written during this period of high religious feeling center on the traditional Christian themes of death, rebirth, the Second Coming, resurrection, and hope, often with figures and allusions highly dependent on biblical sources. Not all of them are successful, often being little more than paraphrases of Scripture.

However, some of them are very striking, perhaps the most interesting to modern readers being those poems in which the poet or the speaker in the poem assumes the voice of God or Christ, poems so stunningly transcendental in their linkage of humanity to divinity that they were not for the most part included by Emerson in the little volume published in 1839, perhaps because he feared the probable attacks of conservative Christians. For example, Christ seems to be the speaker in "I Am the Bread of Life," while God seems the central voice in "The Message." Even more complicated is a poem such as "Terror," which centers on the end of the world. The poem begins with the speaker as a seemingly human witness to last-time events: "Within the streets I hear no voices loud,/ They pass along with low, continuous cry." Yet by the end of the poem, the speaker has become God, who calls loudly to humans: "Repent! why do ye still uncertain stand,/ The kingdom of my son is nigh at hand!" Although this seemingly audacious commandeering of a divine voice is perfectly understandable, given Very's belief that his poems were indeed during this period the products of divine authorship, for the uninitiated reader such a mixture of the human and the divine is at minimum attention-getting as well as a challenge to ordinary religious thinking.

POEMS WRITTEN BEFORE AND AFTER THE PERIOD OF RELIGIOUS INTENSITY

The largely imitative poems written prior to the late 1830's show a poet progressing in competence and often center on themes and didactic approaches typical of the early Romantic movement in England and the United States. His poems about nature, for example, usually focus first on some observable aspect of his surroundings, followed by overt linkage, often somewhat sentimentally, to an appropriate lesson. "The Wind-Flower" begins with the personification of this early spring blossom as one that "lookest up with meek, confiding eye/ Upon the clouded smile of April's face" and then praises the "faith" of this frail flower, willing to bloom with the threat of winter still around, as being "More glorious" than that of "Israel's wisest king" (Solomon). Such innocent "trust" is, the poem suggests, something humans can learn from, as the last line of the poem underscores, "A lesson taught by Him, who loved all human kind." Other nature poems of the early period which illustrate this tying of the observation of natural phenomena to religious and moral lesson-giving include "The Robin" and "The Columbine."

Throughout the last four decades of his life, Very continued to write moralizing poems on nature as well as poems centering on the biblical themes characteristic of the sonnets composed during his ecstatic period of the late 1830's. He also turned to writing poems with links to the social and historical events of his time. Such poems show his poetic competence and his interest in current events, but usually do not achieve anything like lasting artistic merit. His abolitionist stance is mirrored in the poem "The Fugitive Slaves," for example, while his reaction to the Civil War and Reconstruction can be seen in such poems as "Faith in the Time of War" and "National Unity." Very also penned the lyrics to numerous hymns during this final phase of his poetic career, including such relatively well-known examples as "Father, Thy Wonders Do Not Singly Stand" and "We Go Not on a Pilgrimage."

BIBLIOGRAPHY

Barlett, William Irving. *Jones Very: Emerson's "Brave Saint."* Durham: Duke University Press, 1942. This first "modern" biographical and critical study of Jones Very presents a balanced analysis of his life and poetry, and, perhaps most important, publishes numerous poems heretofore uncollected, thus bringing to light some of the best poetry of Very written during his ecstatic period.

Clayton, Sarah Turner. *The Angelic Sins of Jones Very.* New York: Peter Lang, 1999. This full-length study of Jones Very centers on a "New Historicist" approach to how readers in various decades have received and understood Very's poetry, from the time of the Transcendentalists to the present age. The book is particularly effective at bringing together an abundance of scholarly and critical responses to Very's poetry while illuminating how certain lasting qualities of Very's writing continue to fascinate readers.

Deese, Helen R., ed. *Jones Very: The Complete Poems.* Athens: University of Georgia Press, 1993. Deese has provided an inestimable service for readers interested in Very's poetry by bringing together all the poems and editing them with an appropriate scholarly approach and apparatus. Of immense value, also, is her introduction to the volume, which covers Very as a person, thinker, and poet, perhaps the most concise and insightful review of the research on Very.

Gittleman, Edwin. *Jones Very: The Effective Years, 1833-1840.* New York: Columbia University Press, 1967. This work presents an exhaustive treatment of Very's life and writing during the years of his religious awakening. Gittleman approaches Very's biography from a psychological perspective and asserts that Very's religious mania had its roots in family relationships.

Lyons, Nathan, ed. *Jones Very: Selected Poems.* New Brunswick, N.J.: Rutgers University Press, 1966. Perhaps more important than the poems selected by Lyons are his considerations of Very's religious stance and his interpretations of key Very poems in the introduction to this work.

Delmer Davis

PETER VIERECK

Born: New York, New York; August 5, 1916

PRINCIPAL POETRY

Terror and Decorum: Poems, 1940-1948, 1948
Strike Through the Mask!, 1950

The First Morning, 1952

The Persimmon Tree, 1956

The Tree Witch: A Poem and a Play (First of All a Poem), 1961

New and Selected Poems, 1932-1967, 1967

Archer in the Marrow: The Applewood Cycles, 1967-1987, 1987

Tide and Continuities: Last and First Poems, 1995-1938, 1995

OTHER LITERARY FORMS

Metapolitics: From the Romantics to Hitler (1941) is a criticism of nineteenth century Romanticism, which Peter Viereck argues lies at the base of Nazism. Viereck has also written several volumes defending his variety of political conservatism, including *Conservatism Revisited: The Revolt Against Revolt, 1815-1949* (1949), *Shame and Glory of the Intellectuals* (1953), and *The Unadjusted Man* (1956).

ACHIEVEMENTS

Since the 1940's, Peter Viereck has won wide recognition for his poetry, which follows the style he calls Manhattan classicism. His poetry emphasizes form and rhyme and displays remarkably effective wordplay. He places great stress upon morality and uses his verse to defend the humanist values he professes. Critics sometimes accuse him of being overly didactic, but many consider him a major American poet. Viereck has received a Guggenheim Fellowship for his poetry and won the Pulitzer Prize for Poetry in 1949. He received the New England Poetry Club Prize in 1998 and the Anne Sexton Poetry Prize, awarded by *Agni* magazine, in 1999.

BIOGRAPHY

Peter Robert Edwin Viereck was born in New York City on August 5, 1916. He achieved remarkable scholastic success in his college years and was graduated from Harvard University summa cum laude in 1937. After attending the University of Oxford on a fellowship, he returned to Harvard, where he received his M.A. and Ph.D. in European history.

Parallel with Viereck's rise in the academic world, a more dramatic story was taking place. Viereck's father,

George Sylvester Viereck, was a noted journalist and author whose circle of friends included Sigmund Freud, H. L. Mencken, and Kaiser Wilhelm II. He had temporarily lost popularity during World War I, since his sympathy for Germany put him at odds with the policy of the United States. The decade of the 1920's, however, was characterized by disillusionment with American participation in the war, and Viereck was to a large extent restored to favor.

Adolf Hitler's rise to power in January, 1933, changed the picture once more. It soon became evident that Viereck was not prepared to abandon his sympathy for Germany. He became an apologist for Hitler (indeed a paid agent of the Reich), and almost all of his friends deserted him. During World War II, he was arrested and tried for sedition.

Peter Viereck broke with his father and has rarely mentioned him in his writing. Perhaps as a reaction against the senior Viereck, much of his activity as a historian has concentrated on analyzing the rise of the Nazis to power.

After completing his military service in World War II, Viereck taught at several universities. He soon settled permanently at Mount Holyoke College in Massachusetts. To Viereck, academic life is not a detached pursuit of knowledge but rather a way of coming to grips with current problems. He developed an unusual variety of conservatism and has written several books explaining and defending it. Although his books have been widely reviewed, few American conservatives count themselves as his followers.

Viereck's reputation rests principally on his work as a poet; collections of his poetry have won for him considerable attention and admiration. Although respected by most critics as a presence in American poetry, he has not had especial influence on other poets. After many years, Viereck retired as Professor Emeritus of Russian and Eurasian History from Mount Holyoke College, where he had been a scholar and teacher throughout most of his writing and teaching career. In 1997, Viereck was living at his home in South Hadley, Massachusetts. As of 2001, he had apparently stopped writing for publication except for an occasional letter to the editor of *The New York Times* or *The Mount Holyoke News*, in which he demonstrated his keen and ongoing interest in world affairs.

ANALYSIS

Peter Viereck has been remarkably consistent in adhering to certain principles throughout his career as a poet. Together, these principles make up the "Manhattan classicism" mentioned earlier; understanding them is crucial for anyone who wishes to read him.

Deeply affected by the rise of Nazism and Communism in the twentieth century, Viereck has asked one fundamental question throughout his career: How did these nefarious systems arise and maintain themselves? In part the answer lies in the particular historical circumstances of each case. In Viereck's opinion, a deeper and more general cause underlies the events that preoccupy most historians. Romanticism is the culprit; it is Viereck's principal aim in both his poetry and his prose to expose and combat this artistic movement.

His conclusion at once raises a further question: What does Viereck mean by Romanticism? He has chiefly in mind the uncontrolled display of emotion. Romantic artists such as Richard Wagner thought that their superiority to the ordinary run of men titled them to disregard moral restraint in their work. What counted was that artists express themselves fully, and they need answer to no one but themselves. This approach has had disastrous consequences when extended from art to politics. Viereck rejects the notion that what is true in art can be false in politics and holds that since the ignoring of moral restraint has been disastrous in politics, it must be halted at its artistic source.

Rather than be the expression of the artist's unbridled feelings, a poem should illustrate "humanist values." Viereck does not intend anything controversial by this phrase; he has in mind the ordinary moral virtues. Although interested in religion, he does not require poets to adhere to Christianity or any other creed; he himself is not a believer.

It may appear so far that much fuss has been made over very little. After all, few poets see themselves as Nietzschean immoralists. Yet Viereck does not think it sufficient for poets to accept morality in their lives or even to avoid contradicting its rules in their poetry. He maintains that poets have the duty to defend and explain moral principles in their work. His didactic notion of proper poetry has been rejected by most of his contemporaries, though some poets, most notably Yvor Winters, profess a similar view.

Viereck carried the point one step further. A writer should not only defend correct morality but must also assail those writers who set themselves against its unyielding requirements. To Viereck the main twentieth century example of the betrayal of artistic responsibility has been Ezra Pound. Pound's devotion to the Fascist regime of Benito Mussolini is in Viereck's opinion the logical outcome of his poetic principles. Pound's main work, the voluminous *The Cantos* (1970), advocates a repellent political and ethical position—and this suffices to discredit it as outstanding poetry. So great is Viereck's distaste for Pound that some mention of him surfaces in nearly everything Viereck writes.

The requirements of humanist values extend beyond content. Many twentieth century poets have curtailed or abandoned altogether the use of meter and rhyme. To Viereck this betokens the lack of discipline that is the core of Romanticism. His own poetry is almost always written in standard metrical form and displays to the full his talent for rhyme.

TERROR AND DECORUM

These principles were fully evident in Viereck's first published verse collection, *Terror and Decorum*. The first poem in the book, "Poem," exemplifies Viereck's artistic credo. In part influenced by Charles-Pierre Baudelaire and T. S. Eliot, Viereck views the poet as the guardian of language, with the responsibility to maintain a tight control over it; if this task is not attended to, "lush adverbs" and other uncontrolled parts of speech may get out of hand. True to his own principles, Viereck wrote "Poet" in strict iambic pentameter, his favorite poetic form.

"Poet" displays the tensions and paradoxes of Viereck's position. Although Romanticism is anathema, the exalted view of the poet he professes here is a key doctrine of the great Romantics. Like Percy Bysshe Shelley, to whom poets are the unacknowledged legislators of humankind, Viereck considers the poet to be a monarch. Through poets' control of language, they can dominate the politics of their time. Further, although "Poet" calls for restraint, it itself is characterized by elaborate metaphor and personification.

The reader might so far have the impression that Viereck is a grim Savonarola, incapable of humor. This is decidedly not the case; indeed, one of Viereck's chief weapons in his struggle against disorder is satire. He also indulges in ordinary wit; in one notable instance, he constructs a long poem from the World War II slogan "Kilroy was here."

Although "Kilroy" treats the slogan humorously, it soon becomes apparent that Viereck has a serious message to expound. The anonymous soldier who writes "Kilroy was here" wherever he goes symbolizes the adventurer, and Viereck compares him to Ulysses, Orestes, and, in the poem's climax, God. Kilroy displays the spirit of free individualism that Viereck holds to be the proper human attitude. Unsure of what, if anything, is the ultimate basis of the world and of values, the individual must make his or her own way.

"Kilroy," like "Poet," shows Viereck's love-hate relation with Romanticism. The adventurer is a stock figure of Romanticism, but the supposed anti-Romantic Viereck devotes the poem to praise and advocacy of him. The tension in Viereck's position extends to the poem's style. Viereck defends strict adherence to form, but "Kilroy" is an unusual mix of genres. It begins as a humorous poem but shifts to a serious expression of Viereck's ethics and metaphysics. It does not follow from the presence of dissonances in his work that Viereck is a bad poet. His efforts to maintain a system of belief against certain contrary tendencies in his personality add to his poems' interest.

THE FIRST MORNING

Like that of any other good poet, Viereck's work is not all of a piece. As his career developed, his verse tended to become more lyrical. A good example of his lyrical style is "Arethusa, the First Morning," which appeared in *The First Morning*. Arethusa was a sea nymph changed by Artemis into a spring. The poem pictures the former nymph wondering what has happened to her. Viereck uses her perplexity to introduce a meditation about the stages of life and the nature of consciousness. What, if anything, can one really know?

Viereck has no answer to this question. Rather, his response is that human beings cannot have any knowledge of what lies behind the world that appears to them. Specifically, there is no reason to think that life has any meaning beyond what individuals can give it. There is no life beyond death, and human beings do not fit into a cosmic scheme of things.

The annihilation of death fills Viereck with dread. This reaction is present in other works besides "Arethusa."

What ought one's response to be? When a doe steps into the spring, Arethusa feels a kinship with her and a sympathy for all nature. Viereck suggests that the experience of the unity of the world can help humankind deal with the fear of death, to the extent that anything can do so. The attitudes displayed in "Arethusa" are of great importance to Viereck; perhaps anxious that readers not forget them, he included another version of the poem, titled "River," in *New and Selected Poems*. The new version drops the mythological references but retains the message of the original.

As always, Viereck finds enemies of correct doctrine to combat; in *The First Morning*, it is New Criticism that is the target of his wrath. He assails this style of criticism in a section of the book called "Irreverences," which consists of a series of short rhyming verses, written in a mocking style; "1912-1952, Full Cycle" is probably the poem in this group that most effectively conveys his thought.

Viereck's mockery was motivated by much more than personal rivalry or the fact that the New Critics did not care for his verse and rarely if ever discussed it. He thought that their views were inimical to sound art. They contended that a poem was an artifact that ought to be studied apart from the intentions of the author, which at best were a matter of conjecture. The historical background of the poem was also irrelevant: History and criticism were separate disciplines that ought not to be mixed.

To Viereck these views were merely a variant of the Romantic artist's betrayal of moral responsibility. Adherence to them would prevent poets and critics from teaching the very lessons Viereck thought it most urgent to convey. If a poem was a self-contained entity, it could not at the same time be an instrument for teaching virtue. Small wonder that Viereck believed himself justified in using every literary weapon at his command against New Critics such as Allen Tate. Satire was his chosen instrument in "Irreverences," but to a large extent his project backfired. Many of the volume's reviewers failed to see the serious purpose behind his work, and the book was not very favorably received.

THE PERSIMMON TREE

"Nostalgia," a poem included in *The Persimmon Tree*, enables the reader to come to a fuller understanding of Viereck's ideas. The poem depicts God, who has absented himself from the world for eight thousand years, deciding to return to earth for a surprise visit. Instead of receiving a warm welcome from his creation, he is recognized by no one; he is no longer worshiped. The poem makes evident that for Viereck God, if he exists at all, has no benevolent intentions or even much interest in human beings. He is an arbitrary and capricious power, and people must make their way without him.

"Nostalgia" illustrates another tension in Viereck's position. Many people who lack religious belief think that morality can be built on nonreligious foundations. The questions "Does God exist?" and "What are the foundations of morality?" are to philosophers such as David Hume and John Stuart Mill distinct and independent. Viereck is not entirely in their camp. The reader senses that Viereck's absence of faith makes him doubt the basis of morals as well. When he insists on upholding the virtues and condemns poets who fail to do so, he is in part suppressing his fear that morality is in fact without basis.

THE TREE WITCH

Another part of Viereck's philosophy comes to expression in *The Tree Witch*. This is both a poem and a play, but only the former will be discussed here. The work has an unusual theme. An old tree has been cut down to make room for an eight-lane highway, and some "fifty-year old children" separate a dryad from the tree and chain it in a garage. The poem features alternating lines by the human beings and the dryad. (A dryad is a tree spirit; talking trees are featured in *Terror and Decorum* and are a trademark of Viereck's poetry.)

Viereck's sympathies are clearly on the dryad's side. The men who imprison her claim to be acting for her welfare, but they are enemies of nature. By taking her away from the tree, they (along with those who have cut down the tree) kill her.

Viereck uses this bizarre account to symbolize the struggle between nature and technology which he thinks characteristic of the twentieth century. Machines, once built, have a dynamic of their own that leads people to fall victim to these supposed tools. People increasingly subordinate themselves to machines; labor has become monotonous and overly rapid.

True value lies in harmony with nature, which must be respected for its own sake rather than viewed as raw material for the creation of tools. Technology out of control returns Viereck to a theme prominent early in his career. He views it as a central element to the rise of Nazism and Communism. The correct attitude toward nature is an essential part of the humanist values Viereck defends.

Here once more Viereck is led into paradox. The defense of nature against all-powerful machines is a mainstay of Romanticism. Many of the persons Viereck is most concerned to attack for their political follies are fervent proponents of this view. The philosopher Martin Heidegger, whom Viereck attacks as a Nazi in *Metapolitics*, made warnings about the imminent takeover of the world by technology a key theme of his teaching. For a professed anti-Romantic, Viereck adopts a large number of Romantic positions.

ARCHER IN THE MARROW: THE APPLEWOOD CYCLES, 1967-1987

Viereck issued his longest continuous work, *Archer in the Marrow*, in 1987. This is an epic poem composed in "cycles" on which Viereck worked for twenty years. The work depicts a three-way conversation between God, the man he has created, and contemporary humankind. The theme of the epic is whether human beings are "things" determined by outside forces or, on the contrary, have the power to control their own fate and surpass themselves.

Viereck presents God as anxious to keep human beings under his thumb. Human beings cannot withstand the divine power, but they have an ally who gives them a fighting chance in the struggle for autonomy. God is afraid of Eve or Aphrodite, whose feminine nature symbolizes attunement with nature. Eve rarely appears directly in the poem, and her views and characteristics must be pieced together from the lines of the other characters. In spite of her elusiveness, she is humankind's best chance for salvation. Viereck, apparently worried that readers might not get the message, includes in the book a commentary explaining his poem.

Throughout his career, Viereck has defended a clearly expressed set of values. He has braved the perils of nonconformity, since didactic poetry is out of fashion. Much more than a preacher in verse, Viereck is a gifted literary artist who has devoted his poetic talents to conveying a message he thinks of vital concern. The tensions in his views show that he has had to struggle against himself to keep his poetry under the firm control he thinks proper.

TIDES AND CONTINUITIES

In 1995 Viereck, at age seventy-nine and in deteriorating health, published what he expected to be his last collection of poetry. He told a reporter for the *Daily Hampshire Gazette* that he was retiring from writing life and that he intended to dedicate the proceeds from his last book to the Clio-Melpomene Prize, an award he had established for maverick students at Mount Holyoke College who were doing creative, original work in poetry or history. *Tide and Continuities: Last and First Poems 1995-1938* is by far the best collection of Viereck's poetry because it contains, in addition to his latest poetic works, poems he personally selected from past publications to represent him after his death. The poems in part 1, titled "Mostly Hospital and Old Age," are among Viereck's last works. They were, as Viereck states in his preface, "mostly begun in hospitals in my seventies." Their theme is "old age and its coming to terms with the archetypal trio: Persephone, Dionysus, Pluto (here the farmer's daughter, the traveling salesman, the basement janitor)."

Part 6 of *Tide and Continuities* is titled "Tide and Completions." This section consists of three long poems composed between 1992 and 1995 and intended to unify the poems of the past and the present. As Viereck says with characteristic humor, "The occasional repetition of certain leitmotif phrases is serving this unifying function. Often the 'I' in the newer poems is not me but a goofy dying Everyman, trying to ululate [i.e., howl, wail, lament] past doc and nurse." Viereck may have lost his health but not his quirky sense of humor or his zest for life. What is most impressive about his later poems is his courage in the face of pain and death. He uses his personal plight as an occasion for discussing the Promethean plight of mankind as a whole. He has remained remarkably consistent in his philosophic views throughout his long career and remarkably consistent in his rationale of poetic technique. He discusses technical aspects of poetry in the preface to his last book.

Tide and Continuities received deplorably scant notice by literary critics. An exception was the long review in *Humanitas* by Professor Michael A. Weinstein, who obviously considered Viereck one of the most important American poets of modern times. Weinstein compares Viereck to such formidable poets as Lucretius, Dante Alighieri, and Johann Wolfgang von Goethe, as well as to such distinguished philosophers as Irving Babbitt, José Ortega y Gasset, and George Santayana.

Another exception to the general silence that followed publication of the aged Viereck's last book was Peter Kirby, W. Guy McKenzie Professor of English at Florida State University, who reviewed *Tide and Continuities* thoughtfully, though not always reverently, for *Parnassus: Poetry in Review*. Kirby paid particular attention to Viereck's experiments with rhyme and meter, quoting extensively from several poems as illustrations. Although he did not like everything Viereck included in his last collection, he stated that poems from part 1, "Mostly Hospital and Old Age," are among the best of their kind. According to Kirby, Viereck extends the legacy of such classic satirists as Samuel Johnson, Jonathan Swift, and Alexander Pope.

"GATE TALK FOR BRODSKY"

Viereck published his long poem "Gate Talk for Brodsky" in *Humanitas* in 1997 at the age of eighty. This complex poem is the last of Viereck's "Persephone dialogues." According to Weinstein, it is an act of pulling together the diverse and often contradictory themes and theses Viereck developed in his prose and poetry over nearly sixty years. The poem is offered as a memorial to Joseph Brodsky, expatriate Soviet rebel poet and winner of the Nobel Prize in Literature in 1987, who died the year before the poem's publication.

OTHER MAJOR WORKS

NONFICTION: *Metapolitics: From the Romantics to Hitler*, 1941; *Conservatism Revisited: The Revolt Against Revolt, 1815-1949*, 1949; *Shame and Glory of the Intellectuals*, 1953; *The Unadjusted Man*, 1956.

BIBLIOGRAPHY

Brodsky, Joseph. Foreword to *Tide and Continuities: Last and First Poems, 1995-1938*, by Peter Vierek. Fayetteville: University of Arkansas Press, 1995, pp. xiii-xv. Prominent Russian-born poet Joseph Brodsky contributed a rhymed foreword to Viereck's last published book. This amusing but sincere tribute contains an edifying overview of Viereck's life and personality as well as a shrewd analysis of his contribution to literature.

Ciardi, John. "Peter Viereck: The Poet and the Form." *University of Kansas City Review* 15 (Summer, 1949): 297-302. This early article remains one of the best analyses of Viereck's work. Ciardi gives a carefully balanced treatment of Viereck's ideas and techniques. As a poet himself hostile to modernism, Ciardi sympathizes with Viereck's negative view of Pound.

Hénault, Marie. *Peter Viereck*. New York: Twayne, 1969. A rare book-length study of Viereck's work. It gives a relatively comprehensive account of Viereck's poetry and prose to the date of publication, although some of the poetry is not discussed. Hénault is very favorable to Viereck and defends him against negative reviewers.

Kirby, David. "Lasting Words." *Parnassus: Poetry in Review* 21 (1996): 113-130. Kirby, a professor of English at Florida State University, uses his review of Viereck's *Tide and Continuities* as a springboard to analyze the aging poet's life's work. He compares Viereck with another distinguished elderly poet Theodore Weiss. Kirby irreverently remarks that "each is the kind of old-boy writer your average performance poet or radical feminist would shove cheerfully into the wood chipper," and predicts that "sooner or later these two poets are going to be Dead White Males."

Rossiter, Clinton. *Conservatism in America*. New York: Vintage Books, 1962. Essential for understanding Viereck's political and ethical ideas. Rossiter notes the importance of moderation for Viereck. Undue expression of emotion is to be avoided, both in politics and in literature. Rossiter brings out the unity of Viereck's prose and poetry: All his works aim to convey his firmly held beliefs.

Viereck, Peter. "Gate Talk for Brodsky." In *Humanitas*, Vol. X, No. 2 (1997): 4-21. Written at the age of eighty, this is the last of Viereck's "Persephone dialogues," a meditation on death and dying. In "Gate Talk for Brodsky," Viereck continues to display his wit, his plucky existentialism, and his abiding inter-est in poetic technique. The poem contains a moving farewell to the dead Joseph Brodsky, his old friend and colleague.

_____. Preface to *Tide and Continuities: Last and First Poems, 1995-1938*. Fayetteville: University of Arkansas Press, 1995, pp. xvii-xix. Viereck explains the unconventional organization of his collection of old and new poems and defends his poetic rationale, including the adherence to rhyme and meter that has distinguished his classical modernism. He still considers what he calls the formless variety of free verse to be the main danger to American poetry, yet believes that what he calls the new formalism will provoke a reaction back to the most formless of free verse once again.

Weinstein, Michael A. "Dignity in Old Age: The Poetical Meditations of Peter Viereck." *Humanitas* 8, no. 2 (1995): 53-67. In this lengthy review of *Tide and Continuities*, Weinstein lauds Viereck as a formidable philosophical poet, a civilized humanist, and a civilized existentialist. Weinstein focuses his discussion on four poems which illuminate Viereck's mature vision of human existence: "Crass Times Redeemed by Dignity of Souls," "Rogue," "At My Hospital Window," and "Persephone and the Old Poet."

_____. "Peter Viereck: Reconciliation and Beyond." In *Humanitas*, Vol. X, No. 2 (1997): 22-40. Weinstein, a professor of political science at Purdue University, discusses Viereck's long poem "Gate Talk for Brodsky," published in the same issue of *Humanitas*, and then continues his article with a comprehensive and astute analysis of Viereck's long career as a political philosopher, a major American poet, and a poetry critic.

Bill Delaney, updated by Delaney

ALFRED DE VIGNY

Born: Loches, France; March 27, 1797
Died: Paris, France; September 17, 1863

VIGNY, ALFRED DE

Critical Survey of Poetry

PRINCIPAL POETRY
Poèmes, 1822
Eloa, 1824
Poèmes antiques et modernes, 1826, 1829, 1837
Les Destinées, 1864

OTHER LITERARY FORMS

Apart from the evidence of the poetry itself, nowhere is there more certain testimony that, as a literary artist, Alfred de Vigny considered himself, first and foremost, a poet than in the posthumously published *Le Journal d'un poète* (1867; a poet's diary). Given its well-chosen title by Vigny's friend and literary executor, Louis Ratisbonne, the journal is a kind of mixed personal and literary diary covering the years from 1823 to 1863. Along with entries on personal events and philosophical observations are extensive notes on Vigny's reading and on his literary projects. The latter, many of which are but germs of ideas for works which were never developed or completed, are predominantly concerned with poetry.

In the France of the early nineteenth century, however, it was drama, not poetry or fiction, which was considered the true proving ground of literary merit, and the establishment of the Romantic movement was largely accomplished "on the boards." Vigny played no small part in this task, two of his dramatic works being considered watersheds in the history of the Romantic theater. The first of these was the premiere of Vigny's translation of William Shakespeare's *Othello* (1604), *Le More de Venise* (1829; the Moor of Venice), which helped pave the way for the more sensational success of Victor Hugo's *Hernani* at the Comédie-Française in 1830. The second work was the three-act prose drama *Chatterton* (pr., pb. 1835), which developed the popular theme of the poet, the man of genius, persecuted by an uncomprehending, materialistic society. The sensational first performance of *Chatterton* was the greatest public triumph not only in Vigny's career, but also in that of the female lead, the celebrated actress Marie Dorval, who was Vigny's mistress. Vigny's two other works for the stage were composed as display pieces for Dorval: *La Maréchale d'Ancre* (pr. 1831) and the one-act *Quitte pour la peur* (pr. 1833).

Vigny produced one historical novel, *Cinq-Mars* (1826; *Cinq-Mars: Or, A Conspiracy Under Louis XIII*,

1847); an "experimental" novel, *Stello* (1832); two novel fragments, *L'Alméh* (1831), concerning Napoleon Bonaparte's invasion of Egypt, and *Daphné* (1912), an account of Julian the Apostate; and a work that some consider one of the masterpieces of nineteenth century French fiction, *Servitude et grandeurs militaires* (1835; *The Military Necessity*, 1919), a collection of three stories depicting the soldier's life and exploring the meaning of military experience.

ACHIEVEMENTS

Alfred de Vigny's literary output is remarkably small, particularly in comparison with that of most of his contemporaries. Moreover, his reputation in France (he is virtually unknown in the English-speaking world) rests almost exclusively on three works: the drama *Chatterton*, the collection of stories *The Military Necessity*, and the posthumous verse collection *Les Destinées*. Nevertheless, Vigny is ranked by general consensus as one of the four great poets of French Romanticism, along with Alphonse de Lamartine, Alfred de Musset, and Victor Hugo. Vigny consciously set himself apart from these contemporaries in order to find a distinct, individual style not bound to any literary "school," and the very inclusion of his name in this quartet extends one step further the already misty, indeterminate boundaries of the term "Romantic."

Vigny, by temperament and discipline, stood in dramatic contrast to his contemporaries. He was incapable of the lyric effusion of Lamartine, the confessional tones of Musset, the technical *brio* or the self-proclaimed "voice of the people" attitude of Hugo. Vigny's verse is predominantly sober, dry, and spare; he had no taste for the verbal display which characterized Hugo's collection *Les Orientales* (1829; *Eastern Lyrics*, 1879), and, although Vigny had a genius for scene setting, he was rarely sidetracked by the details of the purely picturesque.

Vigny's greatest contribution to the poetry of his time was the introduction of a measure of more profound and more consistent thought than that of any of his major contemporaries. His virtual innovation of the *poème philosophique* provided a new form in an age drunk with delight in the adaptation of forms from the past (such as the epic, and the lyric forms of the elegy and ode). Vigny was the "thinker" among the Romantics (which in no way implies that he was an original or significant philosopher), and it is perhaps not so much for his individual works as for the quality and content of his thinking as a whole that he is remembered. His ideas concerning the role of the man of genius in society, the relationship between man and God, and the significance of human effort and existence were the inheritance he bequeathed to the artists who followed him, Théophile Gautier, Charles Baudelaire, Leconte de Lisle, Stéphane Mallarmé, and Albert Camus among them. Vigny's output was slight, his works of genius even smaller in number, but without Vigny there would be a tremendous intellectual gap in the flow of modern French letters.

BIOGRAPHY

Alfred Victor de Vigny led an essentially quiet, uneventful life in an age noted for the turbulent, sometimes melodramatic lives of its political and artistic figures. He was largely a private man, with a personality of many seeming contradictions. Deeply religious, he subscribed to no single creed or system of belief throughout his adult life, yet on his deathbed he returned to the Catholicism of his upbringing. A man of great literary ambitions, he disdained to publish a single volume for the last twenty-six years of his life. Of a pessimistic and stoic disposition, he possessed an ultimately optimistic belief in the progress of the species.

Vigny's parents were of the old, pre-Revolution, provincial *noblesse.* They had somehow escaped both the guillotine and forced emigration but were required to live under constant government supervision. Of their four children, three died in infancy. The last, Alfred Victor, a rather sickly child, was to be the sole survivor and the family's ultimate scion. Throughout his life, Vigny attached great importance to his noble descent, but he tended to exaggerate the family's degree of nobility, eventually adopting the title of "Count" based on some spurious claims of his father. The family moved to Paris when Vigny was not quite two years old, and, not many years later, his mother undertook strict control of her son's education. This instruction was a curious combination of liberal, rationalist philosophy, absorbed by way of Jean-Jacques Rousseau, and an *ancien régime* adherence to the institutions of Church and monarchy. In a youth

passed during the turbulence of the Directorate, the Consulate, and the Empire, Vigny was taught to view the Revolution as a hideous reversal of the natural order, to judge Napoleon Bonaparte as a consummate charlatan, and to long for the restoration of the monarchy.

With the fall of Napoleon in 1814 and the restoration of Louis XVIII, opportunities resurfaced for Royalist nobility, and the seventeen-year-old Vigny was enrolled in the elite, ceremonial Gendarmes du Roi as a sublieutenant. Thus, he inaugurated a long and disillusioning military career. During those years, he was transferred from regiment to regiment, always serving honorably, but chafing, like so many young men of his time, at the lack of opportunity for significant advancement and for some chance at glory through action. There was little chance for either, however, in the years immediately succeeding the Napoleonic era; opportunity and stimulation would have to arise in other quarters.

In the early 1820's, when stationed outside Paris, Vigny was introduced into the literary circles of the capital, attending the salons of Madame d'Ancelot and Charles Nodier, where Vigny would eventually meet and befriend the young Victor Hugo. Vigny began to write seriously and, in 1822, published his first volume of poetry, *Poèmes*, followed in 1824 by a miniature epic poem, *Eloa*. In anticipation of war with Spain, his regiment was transferred to various posts in central and southern France, and it was in 1825 in one of these posts that he met and soon married Lydia Bunbury, the daughter of a wealthy and somewhat eccentric lord, Sir Hugh Bunbury. Both Vigny and his mother had cultivated and sealed this alliance, at least partly, in expectation of a sizable inheritance, but Lydia's father was not pleased with the marriage and cut the couple off with a small allowance. After Sir Hugh's death in 1838, Vigny became involved in a lawsuit aimed at claiming an inheritance, an effort which left him and his wife little better off than before. Early in the marriage, Lydia suffered three miscarriages which left her a lifelong invalid. Intellectually, she had little in common with her husband, but neither this nor her physical condition caused Vigny to abandon her, although he had a succession of mistresses throughout the marriage, several of whom could hardly have been unknown to his wife. The marriage held together, however, with Vigny assuming the household duties, managing the slender budget, and, in the end, devotedly attending Lydia in her final sickness.

After numerous successive leaves of absence from the army, Vigny was placed on permanent and honorable retirement in the spring of 1827. A period of great literary activity ensued, which saw the success of the historical novel *Cinq-Mars*, the republication of *Poèmes antiques et modernes*, and a generally successful series of works for the stage, culminating, in 1835, in the stunning reception of the three-act drama *Chatterton*. In 1831, Vigny had begun a relationship with Marie Dorval, the famous actress who was to play the female lead in *Chatterton*. This liaison, which would last until 1838, proved to be highly unstable, as a result of Dorval's increasingly frequent absences from Paris when on tour and Vigny's violent fits of jealousy. The years with Dorval also saw the publication of the novel *Stello* and a collection of three stories culled from Vigny's experience of army life, collectively titled *The Military Necessity*.

Upon his mother's death in 1837, Vigny inherited the country property of Maine-Giraud, where, in reserved retirement from public life, he and his wife would remain almost exclusively until their deaths. Vigny never published a full-length book after *The Military Necessity*, but he composed a good deal of poetry and puzzled over the ultimate disposition of a selection of poems for a final collection, which was not to be published until after his death by his friend and literary executor, Louis Ratisbonne. Of the eleven poems that constitute this final collection, *Les Destinées*, several were published individually during Vigny's lifetime in the literary review *Revue des deux mondes*, among them "La Mort du loup," "Le Mont des Oliviers," "La Maison du berger," and "La Bouteille à la mer."

In addition to this creative activity, Vigny made five unsuccessful attempts (from 1842 through 1845) to be admitted to the Académie Française and was finally elected in 1846. He also stood for election as a Royalist candidate to the National Legislative Assembly in 1848, but he was defeated by his Bonapartist opponent. Vigny's campaigning had been rather too patrician: His political opinions were printed for distribution, but he had disdained to circulate among the constituency he hoped to represent. In any case, the Revolution of 1848

had begun to erode Vigny's loyalties, and he began to question the actual accomplishments of the Bourbon regime. He never again seriously considered a career as an elected official.

In 1860, Vigny's wife began to fail, and for two years he attended and nursed her faithfully. When she died in December, 1862, Vigny was unable to attend the funeral because he was suffering from the painful stomach cancer that would eventually kill him. Before he died, after years of proudly refusing to submit to a religious creed, Vigny received the last rites and was reconciled with the Catholic Church. He died in Paris on September 17, 1863, and is buried in the cemetery of Montmartre.

ANALYSIS

Traditionally, discussions of Alfred de Vigny's poetry have been characterized by a focus on the ideas which inform individual poems as well as on the quasi-philosophical "system" which informs his œuvre as a whole. In Vigny studies, technical analysis of how such ideas are expressed (through prosody, form, and so on) has always taken second place to discussion of what is said. If this is so, it is largely a result of the emphasis the poet himself placed upon the concept of the poem as an artistic medium for the exploration of philosophical issues, the concept of the *poème philosophique*. It is certain, from numerous entries in the personal and literary diary *Le Journal d'un poète*, that Vigny conceived of all the technical aspects of poetry as being at the service of underlying philosophical concepts. Discussing poetry in one of his letters, he states: "All of humanity's great problems can be discussed in the form of verse."

Vigny's central themes are few; taken together, they lend one another a resonance which virtually endows them with the coherence of a philosophical system. Humanism is the unvarying foundation of that quasi system; human experience is examined repeatedly in terms of three fundamental relationships: the relationship of the individual man with God, with society, and, in ultimate solitude, with the self. These themes possess a natural kinship, and a Vigny poem may deal with any combination of the three simultaneously. The figure of Christ in the poem "Le Mont des Oliviers" (the Mount of Olives), for example, is seen in relation to God (*to* whom he prays), in relation to man (*for* whom he prays), and in relation to his own double identity as God and man. In "La Bouteille à la mer" (the bottle in the sea), man is seen as purveyor of his own individual knowledge and experience for the benefit of society, but the transmission of knowledge and experience from man to man is a precarious affair in the hands of Divine Will. Vigny's poetry is often obsessed with the special isolation of the poet, the man of genius and vision (a preoccupation finally symbolic of the condition of the species itself). The theme of the particular plight of the poet ran throughout his career, from the youthful "Moïse" (Moses) to the valedictory "L'Esprit pur" (the pure spirit). Religion (the traditional Judeo-Christian ethic, at least) offers little relief for *la condition humaine*, for Vigny conceives of it as the impossible dialogue between a confused creation and a deaf (or at any rate dumb) Creator. In spite of the dark pessimism of this vision, Vigny ultimately asserts the liberating capacity for human dignity in the face of limitations and sustains the idea of progress through human endeavor.

In the early stages of his career, Vigny seized upon the idea of a single, concrete symbol to serve as a dramatic metaphor in each individual poem. The symbol could be a simple object, such as a flute or a bottle cast into the sea; an animal, such as the wolf; or it might be in the form of a person (usually from the Bible), such as Jephthah's daughter, Samson, or Moses. Such symbols frequently attain a mythic dimension appropriate to the scope of the idea expressed, and all Vigny's technical efforts went into their animation.

"MOÏSE"

Some critics have argued that Vigny's most successful realization of the *poème philosophique* came, not in the poems of his maturity (collected in *Les Destinées*), but in a work of his youth (written at the age of twenty-five), the masterful "Moïse." Indeed, Moses—lawgiver, leader, prophet—serves as a perfect symbol for Vigny's concept of the poet-prophet, spiritually and intellectually isolated from his fellow man. Vigny himself stated that his Moses "is not the Moses of the Jews"; he is rather the man of genius in all times, laboring under the weight of the knowledge he attempts to impart to a society which shuns him.

The poem consists of 116 lines in the French heroic meter (Alexandrines in rhyming couplets), a prosodic scheme with an effect of great weight and deliberation. The Alexandrine is a rhetorical and dramatic line which reinforces seriousness of tone and helps create in this Moses a figure of immense and tragic proportions. The poem opens with a vividly descriptive segment (lines one through forty-four) in which the reader views, through the prophet's eyes, the sunlit tents of the Israelite encampment and, farther in the distance, the vast stretches of the Promised Land. Moses is ascending Mount Nebo to speak with the Lord, and his ascent underscores his dual relationship with the people, for he is both superior to them and increasingly excluded from their society. Upon reaching the summit, Moses is surrounded by a dark cloud, so that his interview with God is cloaked in deepest secrecy, to the confusion of those below. Moses begins his speech, a plaint, with lines which, with some variation, serve as a refrain throughout the course of the poem: "Je vivrai donc toujours puissant et solitaire?/ Laissez-moi m'endormir du sommeil de la terre" ("Must I, then, live always mighty and apart?/ Let me sleep the sleep of the earth").

Moses outlines his accomplishments as leader of his people: He has power over the seas and over nations; he has conducted the Israelites to the threshold of their salvation. The power he has gained and the control which he exercises, however, come from the knowledge he has acquired as the "elect of God" and which he, in turn, must impart to the uncomprehending masses. The price has been heavy. From the moment of his birth, he has been a stranger to his fellow men, whose "eyes lower before the fire of my eyes." He is literally wearied to death, for this virtual loss of his humanity has created a barrier of fear in his relations with his kind. In the final segment of his plaint, he begs with simple dignity for release from his fate as a man of vision. There is no divine response, at least in words, and, as the reader shifts perspective to the Israelite camp below (privileged to return to common humanity as Moses is not), the black cloud of mystery lifts from the mountaintop and the prophet is seen no more. The reaction of the people is simple and somewhat coolly observed: "Il fut pleuré" ("He was mourned"). The actions of Vigny's God are inscrutable and inexplicable. Moses is indeed relieved of his burden, but the reader never learns the answers to Moses's single question: "Why?" As the poem ends and the Israelites take up their journey once more, the mantle of leadership descends upon Joshua, who proceeds onward through the wasteland, "pensive and paling."

"LE MONT DES OLIVIERS"

There is something even more ominous about the silence and mystery surrounding God in the poem "Le Mont des Oliviers" from the collection *Les Destinées*, written many years after "Moïse." Drawing once again from Scripture, Vigny dramatizes the scene of Christ's agony in the Garden of Gethsemane prior to his betrayal, arrest, and Crucifixion. Vigny again achieves a heroic scale in his portrayal of Christ, but in the symbol there is an added poignancy, resulting from Christ's dual nature as both God and man. The mental and physical torment caused by Christ's philosophical dilemma is presented with a vividness never quite achieved in the portrayal of Moses.

The poem (149 lines, again in Alexandrine rhyming couplets) is divided into three unequal sections and a single-stanza postscript. In the first section, the reader becomes acquainted with Christ's peculiar circumstances as partaker in both human and divine natures, as Christ casts a "human thought" over the thirty-three years of his life among men. The second and longest section is spoken by Christ himself. Unlike Moses, he prays for permission to live and complete his task. In his ministry, he has brought the message of brotherhood, spirit over flesh, and substance for symbol, but he has not yet brought the certitude which alone will deliver humankind from the twin bonds of "Evil and Doubt." He realizes that after his death the message will be perverted, even by his followers, and he fears the uselessness of his sacrifice. He begs to serve as the instrument not only of God's forgiveness of man, but also of man's pardon of a God who can permit evil and doubt. Only certainty will reopen the paths of communication between Creator and created: "All will be revealed when man finally comprehends/ The place from which he came and that to which he travels." As Jesus finishes his prayer, he catches sight of the approaching torch of Judas through the trees. Is this one flash of light amid the surrounding obscurity the ironic answer to his request? The torchlight is the final image of the scene

proper, but the poem itself is formally concluded by a brief postscript, appended some twenty years after the original publication of the piece as a separate poem in *Revue des deux mondes*. It is a single stanza clearly cast in the form of a moral, and its title, "Le Silence," makes a double reference: "The righteous man will counter absence with disdain,/ Responding with only cold silence/ To the everlasting silence of the Divine."

The message (or the moral, at least) is clear: Man is forced to establish his own dignity, with or without God. Because this moral was appended, accusations that it is not fully integrated with the dramatic metaphor have some force. Taken as a whole, however, "Le Mont des Oliviers" is a fine example of the poet's habit (in later years) of turning spiritual or intellectual doubt into positive matter.

"LA MORT DU LOUP"

An even finer example, perhaps, of this tendency is found in "La Mort du loup" (the death of the wolf), again from *Les Destinées*. The inspiration for the poem was two lines in Lord Byron's *Childe Harold* (1818): "And the wolf dies in silence—not bestow'd/ In vain should such example be." Vigny's poem is praiseworthy from many perspectives: its unity of symbol and idea, its prosodic virtuosity, and its brilliant achievement of scene-setting. It is arranged in three sections of varying length, each of which is characterized by a different point of view. This shifting perspective gives tremendous dramatic scope and roundness; all the characters involved have their moments in the spotlight.

The first and longest section is seen from the hunters' perspective (signaled by the use of first-person plural pronouns). Passing through the murky, almost nightmarish atmosphere of a thick wood, they come upon the tracks of a family of roving wolves (*loups voyageurs*); soon they reach a clearing and are greeted by the flaming eyes of the father wolf. Two wolf cubs are at play, but in silence, for they understand that man, the enemy, is close at hand. The she-wolf, whose dignity is compared to that of the she-wolf who suckled Romulus and Remus, anxiously watches over the cubs. The wolf, realizing that he has been caught unaware, stands his ground. Between his iron jaws, he grabs one dog from the pack of hounds as the hunters open fire and plunge their knives into his body. The wolf calmly regains his former guarding position and dies, steadily watching the hunters, without uttering a cry.

The brief second section gives the viewpoint of a single hunter (signaled by the use of the first-person singular), the narrator of the tale. The wolf's dignity in the face of death unnerves him, and he is unable to pursue the escaping she-wolf and cubs. He realizes that the she-wolf has not abandoned her mate through fear, but to ensure the survival of her cubs. They must be taught resistance. They must avoid at all costs the compromising pact made between man and domesticated animals. They must learn not only the defiance but also the stoic wisdom of her mate, their father. The final section also begins in the voice of the narrator, but it ends with the words ascribed by the narrator to the wolf—that is, from the perspective of the dying wolf himself:

To lament, to weep, to pray, are all equally cowardly.
Actively accomplish your long and weary task
On the path which Fate has chosen for you.
Then, afterwards, like me, suffer and die without a
    word.

The nobility and optimism of Vigny's anthropomorphic wolf may be subtle, but they are clear. The philosophy promulgated in the wolf's dying words is more than mere stoic resignation. It is, rather, a constructive, ultimately hopeful stratagem for countering the limitations imposed by destiny: "Actively accomplish." The moral of "La Mort du loup" goes one step further than that of "Le Mont des Oliviers" (and is more organically incorporated), for in the former, action supplants restraint and silence. In both poems, the positive thread of Vigny's thought serves to balance the deep pessimism of the scenes depicted. It is this affirmation of human worth, through the symbols of Christ and the wolf, that develops into the faith in human progress which underlies one of the final poems of *Les Destinées*, "La Bouteille à la mer."

"La Bouteille à la mer" is divided into twenty-six (numbered) stanzas, each composed of seven Alexandrine lines. The first stanza serves as a brief prelude, urging the reader to forget the fate of the poets who have gone on before and were prevented by untimely death from completing their work. Indeed, the reader is urged to set aside the personality of the poet altogether and hearken only to the message of the poem. A fable follows, relating the story of the captain of a ship about to founder in perilous seas. He encloses the ship's log, with its scientific records and observations, in a bottle, and he casts the bottle overboard just before the ship goes down, entrusting it to Divine Will, praying that it might reach human hands again. The log is the message of experience, the "sublime testament for future voyagers," and, after it undergoes its own hazardous journey, it is eventually retrieved by a simple Breton fisherman. Incapable of reading, the fisherman brings the bottle to the nearest wise man, who recognizes the log as the "treasure of thought and experience" and rejoices in the unceasing, if precarious, triumph of human knowledge.

LES DESTINÉES

The poems collected in *Les Destinées* are undoubtedly Vigny's greatest poetic achievements, and they deserve to be better known in the English-speaking world. In spite of their quality, they have not gone without serious criticism. Vigny has been accused of not fully integrating form and concept, of creating moral messages which are detachable from his dramatic metaphors, of occasional laboriousness and excessive rhetoric, and of becoming enamored of scene-setting while losing the thread of the narrative. Others have vigorously supported his achievement and underscored the integrity of Vigny's self-effacing approach to the difficult task of expressing a personal philosophy in poetic form. As critic Michel Mourre has observed, Vigny, in contrast to the other Romantics, refused to "make a spectacle of himself." He was able to endow his work with his particular sensibility without slipping into solipsism. Moreover, if it is true that Vigny's great legacy to French poetry is the transmission of philsophical concepts, then it may be admitted, at the very least, that his ideas are vividly drawn and, for the most part, have survived any technical weakness.

OTHER MAJOR WORKS

LONG FICTION: *Cinq-Mars*, 1826 (*Cinq-Mars: Or, A Conspiracy Under Louis XIII*, 1847); *L'Alméh*, 1831; *Stello*, 1832; *Daphné*, 1912.

SHORT FICTION: *Servitude et grandeurs militaires*, 1835 (*The Military Necessity*, 1919).

PLAYS: *Le More de Venise*, pr. 1829 (translation of William Shakespeare's *Othello*); *La Maréchale d'Ancre*, pr. 1831; *Quitte pour la peur*, pr. 1833 (one-act); *Chatterton*, pr., pb. 1835.

NONFICTION: *Le Journal d'un poète*, 1867.

BIBLIOGRAPHY

Bowman, Frank Paul. "The Poetic Practices of Vigny's *Poèmes philosophiques*." *Modern Language Review* 60 (1965): 359-368. Vigny was justly famous for his use of Stoic philosophy in his poems. This essay examines Vigny's skill in persuading his readers to admire his characters, who maintain their dignity in the face of true suffering.

Doolittle, James. *Alfred de Vigny*. New York: Twayne, 1967. This short book is still the best introduction in English to Vigny's lyric poetry and to his more famous historical novels, including *Cinq-Mars* and *The Military Necessity*. It contains a lengthy annotated bibliography of studies on Vigny.

McGoldrick, Malcolm. "The Setting in Vigny's 'La Mort du loup.'" *The Language Quarterly* 29, nos. 1/2 (Winter/Spring 1991): 104-114. In one of Vigny's best-known poems, the speaker is a hunter who kills a wolf but finally comes to admire the dying wolf's courageous efforts to protect his family. Shows how the setting in a forest isolates the hunter from others and makes him reflect on the consequences of his actions.

McLeman-Carnie, Janette. "Monologue: A Dramatic Strategy in Alfred de Vigny's Rhetoric." *Nineteenth-Century French Studies* 23, nos. 3/4 (Spring/Summer, 1988): 253-265. Some of Vigny's most famous poems are dramatic monologues in which the speaker conveys his understanding of what he sees before him. Vigny was also a dramatist, and this essay examines his skill in making his readers identify with the internal struggles of his speakers.

Wren, Keith. *Vigny's "Les Destinées."* London: Grant & Cutler, 1985. A thoughtful study of Vigny's posthumously published book of poetry. This short book describes the artistry and philosophical depth of this work.

Theodore Baroody;
bibliography updated by Edmund J. Campion

JOSÉ GARCÍA VILLA

Born: Manila, Philippines; August 5, 1914
Died: New York, New York; February 7, 1997

PRINCIPAL POETRY

Many Voices, 1939
Poems by Doveglion, 1941
Have Come, Am Here, 1942
Volume Two, 1949
Selected Poems and New, 1958
Poems 55, 1962
Poems in Praise of Love, 1962
Appassionata: Poems in Praise of Love, 1979

OTHER LITERARY FORMS

In 1929, José García Villa edited the first comprehensive anthology of Filipino short stories in English, for the *Philippines Free Press*. The earliest published volume of his own work was also a collection of stories, *Footnote to Youth: Tales of the Philippines and Others*, released by Scribner's in 1933. Many of these tales had appeared earlier in *Clay*, the mimeographed literary magazine which he founded at the University of New Mexico and which first drew the attention of Edward O'Brien. *The Best American Short Stories of 1932*, in fact, was dedicated to Villa by O'Brien, whose introduction included Villa "among the half-dozen short story writers in America who count" and compared him with one of O'Brien's earlier discoveries, Sherwood Anderson. Even as O'Brien was prophesying a career for Villa as novelist, however, the young writer had already turned his attention exclusively to poetry. The stories, therefore, retain their interest chiefly as preliminaries to attitudes and techniques associated with Villa's poems.

A third of the twenty-one stories in *Footnote to Youth* are semiautobiographical portraits of a hermit protagonist suffering self-imposed isolation in the Philippines, New Mexico, and New York City. There is a repetitive pattern of rejected illegitimate children, either unwanted or inadequately cared for; of antagonism between fathers and grown sons; of the protagonist's alienation from those with whom he is, only temporarily, most intimate; of a love-hate identification with José Rizal, martyred hero of the 1896 Revolution, as a father-image whose own paternity is clouded; of rejection in courtship and marriage; of self-importance recovered through sentimentalized identification with the suffering Christ, the god mocked and misunderstood.

This sense of recoil from hurt was conveyed in Villa's stories principally through antinarrative devices. In some cases, the paragraphs are numbered and condensed, so that typographically they resemble stanzas in a poem. Nor is incident allowed to flow into incident. O'Brien wrote of Villa's combining "a native sensuousness of perception and impression" with the "traditionally Spanish expression of passionate feeling in classical reticence of form." More likely, however, the compartmentalization of the narrative indicates the aftermath of a series of unhappy encounters between a sensitive personality and an insensitive world unprepared to give him the recognition he deserves. The stories dazzle with color, their principal emotion being intensely lyrical.

ACHIEVEMENTS

As a self-exile from the Philippines for decades, José García Villa earned awards and a reputation in both the Western and Asian worlds. In the United States, he was the recipient of a Guggenheim Fellowship, an American Academy of Arts and Letters Award, a Bollingen Fellowship, and a Rockefeller grant. In Greenwich Village during the 1940's and 1950's he was considered a "regular," as a member of the New Directions avant-garde. In Great Britain his reputation also flourished, as a result of Edith Sitwell's high praise of his "great and perfectly original work." Gradually such distinction, coming from overseas, influenced his countrymen at home. Although there were complaints that he did not write about subjects identifiably Filipino, and that he did not write with the folk simplicity of Carlos Bulosan's *New Yorker* tales of sweet-sour satire, an entire generation of college-educated Filipinos began not only to envy his success but also to emulate his sophistication and inventiveness. The prominence given him by this growing cult assisted in securing for him a Pro Patria Award, in 1961, and a Cultural Heritage Award in 1962. In 1973, he became the first Filipino writer in English to be declared a National Artist, with a government pension for life.

BIOGRAPHY

José García Villa once insisted that "Biography I have none and shall have none. All my Pure shall beggar and defy biography." He was requiring that his identity be sought exclusively in his poems, his purer self. For most of his life he maintained just such distances, shunning intimacies.

Whenever he boasted that his physician-father was chief of staff for General Aguinaldo during the Revolution of 1896, he identified himself less with the healer, in that figure, than with the power of the prototypical rebel. In fact he strenuously resisted his father's attempt to make a doctor of him. At the University of the Philippines he turned instead to the study of law, whose logic and case-history specifics he also soon found too constraining. He was temporarily suspended from college in June, 1929, for having written "Man Songs," a poem too sexually explicit for the times and the authorities. In that same year, for his story "Mir-i-Nisa," a fable of native

José García Villa (Library of Congress)

courtship, he became the first recipient of an award in what was to become a distinguished annual contest in the *Philippines Free Press*. Because he felt unappreciated by his father and inadequately recognized by his fellow Filipinos, he spent the prize money taking himself into exile in the United States. He was determined to be answerable only to himself.

In 1932, he received a B.A. from the University of New Mexico, where his literary magazine *Clay* published the first work (a poem) by William Saroyan, the early writing of William March, David Cornel de Jong, and others, as well as many of his own short stories. These attracted the attention of Edward O'Brien, who dedicated *The Best American Short Stories of 1932* to Villa and placed eleven of his tales on that year's list of distinctive stories. Elated, Villa went to New York City, taking *Clay* with him, the magazine that O'Brien declared to be the prospective rival of Whit and Hallie Burnett's *Story* magazine. Although Villa had difficulty finding salaried work during the Great Depression and claimed that he was discriminated against because of his nationality, in 1933 Scribner's published his collection of stories, *Footnote to Youth*, dedicated to O'Brien, who wrote an introduction to the volume. In 1939 his first book of poems, *Many Voices*, appeared in Manila; in 1940 it won honorable mention in the Commonwealth Literary Contest. The following year, *Poems by Doveglion* was published in Manila and *Have Come, Am Here* in the United States in 1942. The latter was in close contention for the Pulitzer Prize. Befriended by Mark Van Doren, he pursued graduate studies at Columbia on a partial scholarship from that university and another from the Commonwealth of the Philippines. As an avocation, he painted geometric portraits in the cubist mode and hung them in his apartment next to several by E. E. Cummings.

By 1942 he was working for the Philippine embassy in Washington, D.C., clipping newspaper stories of the battles on Bataan and Corregidor. His mind, however, was less on his clerical duties than on his own writing. When he was refused a raise because he typed so slowly, Villa exclaimed, "What do you take me for, a mechanic?" He returned to New York at once and married Rosemarie Lamb, by whom he later had two sons. In 1949, he published *Volume Two*, the book which in-

troduced his experimental "comma poems." He became an associate editor with New Directions, as well as with the Harvard *Wake* for special issues on Marianne Moore and Cummings. His poems have consistently appeared in American and world anthologies since the 1940's. In 1958, a largely retrospective work, *Selected Poems and New*, was released. He taught poetry workshops at both the City College of New York and, from 1964 to 1973, the School for Social Research. In various ways he was also attached to the Philippine Mission to the United Nations until he was declared a National Artist in 1973. In the 1980's he served as editor of *Bravo: The Poet's Magazine*. Near the end of his life in 1997, his work had been out of the public eye for more than thirty years, and out of print for more than fifteen. Despite his withdrawal from the public literary scene, he continued to devote his critical powers to formulating a philosophy of poetics and teaching at New York colleges. He also conducted poetry workshops at his apartment. As a former student remembered, "Along with strong, extremely dry martinis, Villa served critiques of his students' poems. He tore apart narrative pieces, arguing that real poetry was lyrical, 'written with words, not ideas.' He even told pupils not to read fiction, to purge their work of any narrative element."

ANALYSIS

Both his admirers and his detractors agree on the essential inwardness of José García Villa's poetry. For the latter, this is a symptom of narcissism hardly useful to the urgent needs of a newly independent nation. For the former, it is a sign of a transcendent mysticism whose universality should be given priority over nationalism. The poet himself declared that he was not at all interested in externals, "nor in the contemporary scene, but in *essence*." His dominant concern was not description but metaphysics, a penetration of the inner maze of man's identity within the entire "mystery of creation."

The poems themselves, however, often suggest something less than such perfection and therefore something more exciting: purification-in-process, the sensual nature in man struggling to survive transfiguration. The body strains to avoid emasculation even as the spirit ascends. Consequently, the flesh seems glorified, although not in any ordinary spiritual manner which would diminish the splendor of the sense. Edith Sitwell, in her Preface to *The American Genius* (1951), refers to this paradox as an expression of "absolute sensation," mingling a "strange luminosity" with a "strange darkness." Villa himself best epitomized the blinding heat of this attempted fusion by repeatedly adopting the persona/pseudonym "Doveglion": a composite Dove-eagle-lion.

MANY VOICES AND POEMS BY DOVEGLION

Even the ordinary early poems, replete with piety and puppy love and first gathered in *Many Voices*, then in *Poems by Doveglion*, occasionally manage to move the imagination toward the outermost limits of language, a crafted inarticulateness conveying the inexpressible. When he was seventeen, Villa could compare the nipple on the coconut with a maiden's breast, and drink from each; but later lyrics match God and genius, both suffering "The ache of the unfound love" and, in their lonely perfection, left contending for primacy with each other. For Villa, these maturer poems were also the first attempts to create by wordplay, combining "brilliance and/ consecration." A romantic vocabulary emerges, repeated like a code or incantation: star, wind, birds, roses, tigers, dark parts, the sun, doves, the divine. More experimentally, he inverted phrases and therefore logic, in expectation of profound meaning beyond the rational. He wrote, "Tomorrow is very past/ As yesterday is so future" and "Your profundity is very light./ My lightness is very profound." Above all, he is trying to "announce me": "I am most of all, most." The defiant rebel who was his own cause begins to be apparent in these poems published in the Philippines.

HAVE COME, AM HERE

Even as *Many Voices* and *Poems by Doveglion* were going to press, however, his experiments had taken a quantum leap forward. When Sylvia Townsend Warner came to New York in 1939 as Britain's delegate to the Third Congress of American Writers, she was astounded by the verses being prepared for *Have Come, Am Here*, which included the best of Villa's previous work and much more. It was two years later that the book reached the hands of Sitwell, whose eyes fell on the poem "My most. My most. O my lost!," a brief litany of the protagonist's "terrible Accost" with God; she was moved by its "ineffable beauty." The volume is a mix-

ture of adoring love lyrics and joyous, combative rivalry with God. To convey their "strange luminosity," she felt compelled to make comparisons with the religious ecstasies of William Blake and Jakob Boehme, as well as with such other mystics as St. Catherine of Genoa and Meister Eckhart.

It was a matter of special pride for Villa to note that in six of his poems he introduced a wholly new method of rhyming which he called "reversed consonance." As he explained it, "a rhyme for *near* would be *run, green, reign*," with the initial *n-r* combination reversed in each instance. Such a rhyme, of course, is visible if the reader has been forewarned; but even then the ear can hardly notice the event. Still, the device is one more variation among Villa's many attempts, through decreation and reassemblage, to penetrate the energy fields of convention and release explosive forces from the very "depths of Being," as Sitwell puts it. Much more interesting, however, and more successful than reversed consonance in satisfying this quest for fire is the inexorable forward force of both his love lyrics and his "divine poems." Occasionally these poems are indistinguishable from one another because the protagonist addresses both his beloved and his God with the same possessive, mastering rhetoric: "Between God's eyelashes I look at you,/ Contend with the Lord to love you. . . ." At times in compulsive narcissism the protagonist even treats them as mirrors for himself, then briefly relents, guiltily considering himself to be Lucifer or Judas. Such interplays of ambiguity are made inevitable by the poems' brevity and density, the constant ellipses and startling juxtapositions: oranges and giraffes, pigeons and watermelons, yellow strawberries, "pink monks eating blue raisins," the crucified Christ as peacock, the wind shining and sun blowing.

Sometimes in these poems one can recognize the synaesthesia of the French symbolists, E. E. Cummings's curtailments of standard grammar, Blakean nature as divine emblems, or the equivalent of cubist/ surrealist transformations of reality. Mostly, however, Villa was an original. One senses in him a compelling inner necessity to prove that purity proceeds from the proper combination of what are normally considered impurities. His was the rebel's revenge against mediocrity, a Promethean ascent-in-force to regain godhead.

Fellow poet Rolando Tinio, in *Brown Heritage* (1967), says that Villa "speaks of God becoming Man and concludes that Man has become God." Villa's countrymen grudgingly accepted his preeminence abroad. Villa, however, always thought of himself as too exceptional to be a representative Filipino. He would not live in the shadow of his wealthy father in the Philippines; at best he could make a desperate living in New York during the Depression and World War II. Emotionally homeless, he fortified his exile by offering in his poetry a protagonist both essential and universal. For Villa that meant a rejection of common codes and orders, a rising above all local circumstances. *Have Come, Am Here* reflects this profound need for self-justification.

Resounding critical acclaim for the poems of *Have Come, Am Here* came instantly, from Sitwell, Richard Eberhart, Horace Gregory, Marianne Moore, and well over a dozen world anthologists. For them, Villa's poetry was as cryptic as a Zen *koan* and therefore as rewarding as any other religious meditation, the very dislocation of syntax soliciting a revelation. Still others, entranced by their initial experience of *Have Come, Am Here*, have reported that later readings showed a tendency in Villa toward formula that was too facile, as if, were any poem shaken hard enough, its words would finally form another, by the laws of chance and permutation. The poetic vocabulary is not only too romantic for pragmatic readers, but it is also rather impoverished because it is more repetitive than resonant. Similarly, these poems, whether sacred or profane, ultimately manifest the same basic love for a self more praised than explored. Readers accustomed to tangible substance and foreseeable consequences are troubled by an incandescence that, for them, blinds more than it illuminates.

VOLUME TWO

The same polarity of reaction occurred with the appearance of the "comma poems" in *Volume Two*. Between each word in these poems Villa placed an unspaced comma, "regulating the poem's density and time movement." His intent was to control the pace of each poem's progress with measured dignity. The effect resembles musical notation, although Villa preferred to compare the technique with Georges Seurat's pointillism. Unlike reversed consonance, this innovative device

does indeed add "visual distinction." It cannot, however, rescue such verses as Villa's "Caprices" or most of his aphorisms; it can only make them seem pretentious. Some of the new "divine poems," nevertheless, were among the author's best, their dynamics rising from the mystery of things seen in mid-metamorphosis: for example, "The, bright, Centipede" beginning its stampede from "What, celestial, province!" Villa's quarrels with his co-Creator ("My dark hero") also managed a magnificence which can pass beyond self-celebration. There is as much visionary quickening in the image of "God, dancing, on, phosphorescent, toes,/ Among, the, strawberries" as in the inscrutable Lion carrying "God, the, Dark, Corpse!" down Jacob's ladder. In poems as powerful as these, the commas seem like sacerdotal vestments woven from metallic mesh. In lesser poems, however, the commas serve merely as a façade to conceal or decorate an inner vacuousness. A few poems, in fact, were rescued from his earliest volumes and have merely been rehabilitated through use of this fresh overlay.

OVERRELIANCE ON ROMANTIC PHRASING

More serious questions than those raised by *Volume Two*'s unevenness have been directed toward Villa's perpetual reliance on a small cluster of romantic terms whose effect was reduced as their possible combinations approach exhaustion. Furthermore, the prolonged role of rebel led Villa to virtual self-imitation in the steady use of reversals, negatives, and reductives. The "not-face" and "un-ears" of his earlier lyrics became an established pattern later: "In, my, undream, of, death,/ I, unspoke, the, Word"; "the, Holy,/ Unghost—"; "Unnight,/ Me"; "In, not, getting, there, is, perfect, Arrival"; "The, clock, was, not, a, clock"; "May, spring, from, *Un*—,/ Light. . . ." By substitution, strange, suggestive equations can emerge ("Myself, as, Absence, discoverer,/ Myself, as, Presence, searcher"), but so can codes so manneristic that others can imitate them successfully ("Yesterday, I, awoke, today"; gold black-birds; blue-eyed trees). Two different kinds of innocence are offered: that of the true visionary breaking through the barriers of ordinary reality to a tranquillity beyond words and worry; and that of the mindless child playing at anagrams with alphabet blocks (as the poet himself much earlier playfully signed himself "O. Sevilla").

Much mirroring is bound to occur in a poet who is less God-driven, as Richard Eberhart claims Villa was, than obsessed with the trinity of his own godhead (Poet, Word, and Poem), as Tinio suggests. Within those confinements, intensity has to compensate for lack of variety; and critics of all persuasions admit that, at his best, Villa did brilliantly manage that irresistible tenacity, that sense of seizure, even if at the expense of the subject's being its sole object. Dismissing nakedness for the sake of translucent nudity, he came to sacrifice more and more the sensate body of other persons to exclamations on his own exultant sensibility. That habit limits the plausibility of comparisons which Villa offered between his own work and the paintings of Georges Seurat or Pablo Picasso. Seurat, understanding the optics of his day, provides in each canvas the subjective process of atomized vision and the objective configurations of person, place, and thing which that process projects. Picasso, similarly, even in a hundred portraits of the same model, admits and conveys the realization of plenitude, of multiple perspectives, as both perceiver and perceived undergo subtle alterations in time, angle of vision, psychological attitude, degree of rapport, and the like.

SELECTED POEMS AND NEW

That no such plenitude, no such endless surprise was available to Villa became clear with the publication of *Selected Poems and New*. There are several noteworthy new comma poems in this collection, though no startling innovations within that general usage. "Xalome," "And, if, Theseus—then, Minotaur," "Death and Dylan Thomas," and "The Anchored Angel" at least offer ponderous objects for contemplation which, unlike his aphorisms, his lighthearted cries over the blue-eyed bird in a tree, and "A Valentine for Edith Sitwell," appropriate with ease the pace provided by the commas. Such objects also warrant the invitation to meditation which Villa's associational techniques offered in the best of his poems.

By far the larger part of the previously unpublished section of this volume is devoted to forty-eight "adaptations," conversions of other people's prose into poems. His sources were Rainer Maria Rilke's letters, Simone Weil's notebooks, André Gide's journals, and book reviews and letters to the editors of *Time* and *Life*. No word of his own is interjected into the originals, although "to achieve the tightness of verse" he omitted occasional "connectives and extra adjectives." In several cases, borrowing from the visual arts, Villa offered what he calls collages: the original lines of a *Life* magazine caption, for example, rearranged in their sequence; or portions from two different sections of a book brought together. Many of these adaptations received critical praise, particularly as they showed a masterful control of musical phrasing, in a variety of tempos and turns that indicate once more the limitations of the comma as a single musical measure. The value of the adaptations naturally depends so heavily on the intrinsic merit of the originals—Franz Kafka, Henry Miller, William Carlos Williams—that one might have expected the application of this kind of craft to others' work as an early stage of apprenticeship. The adaptations lack, for example, the degree of participation-beyond-translation visible in Robert Lowell's volume of "collaborations," *Imitations* (1961); nor have they generated any insights or techniques, as did Ezra Pound's experience with free translations from Provençal poetry which allowed him, in his *Cantos*, to adapt documents from American history as well as selected phrases and ideograms from the Italian and the Chinese.

CULTURAL REIDENTIFICATION

After *Selected Poems and New*, Villa's effort was devoted less to improving his reputation than to maintaining it, particularly in the Philippines. A number of chapbooks appeared in Manila, in 1962, reprinting portions of his earlier writing, to reestablish himself in his native land. This latter-day identification with a culture which finds no specific presence in his poems and from which he remains geographically remote seemed rather anomalous, but there are Filipinos who think he performed better ambassadorial service than many foreign affairs officers. Villa's egocentric poetry is at the opposite extreme from the Filipinos' sense of togetherness (*bayanihan*) or the family extended through ritual kinship. His role as rebel was not incongruous, however, if viewed from his people's long history of oppression as a Spanish colony; the Philippine Revolution of 1896, which briefly established a republic whose rejection by the United States caused the Philippine-American War, 1899 to 1902; the Commonwealth years, during which Filipinos had to prove their superiority in order to be considered equals; the guerrilla years of World War II;

and the strains of political but not quite economic independence thereafter.

Whether he intended it or not, Villa reinforced the feeling of those Filipinos who demand that they be defined by their own mores and folkways; his "unsonment" poems can be taken as collective resentment of paternalism, however benevolent, preferred by former colonial powers. Even the seeming blasphemy of certain "divine poems" resembles the hybrid religious observances among Asia's only Christian people, once resentful of Spanish religious orders that served as arms of overseas administrations. The nationalists can understand in Villa their defiance and aspiration, the right to self-determination, the refusal to be humiliated by anyone. For these various reasons, Villa continued to be ranked highest among an increasing number of distinguished Filipino poets.

OTHER MAJOR WORKS

SHORT FICTION: *Footnote to Youth: Tales of the Philippines and Others*, 1933; *Selected Stories*, 1962.

EDITED TEXTS: *Philippine Short Stories*, 1929; *A Celebration for Edith Sitwell*, 1946; *The New Doveglion Book of Philippine Poetry*, 1993.

MISCELLANEOUS: *The Portable Villa*, 1962; *The Essential Villa*, 1965; *The Anchored Angel*, 1999.

BIBLIOGRAPHY

Abad, Gemino H. "The Self as Genius and God as Peacock: A Study of 'Mysticism' in José García Villa's Poetry." *University College Journal* 8 (1964): 172-185. After a thoughtful analysis of symbolism and theme, Abad concludes that Villa, despite external appearances, is not in the Metaphysical tradition of Western literature. Abad focuses on such important symbols as skull, rose, and fire, and such important themes as the Catholic dogma of hypostasis.

Casper, Leonard. *New Writing from the Philippines: A Critique and Anthology.* Syracuse, N.Y.: Syracuse University Press, 1966. The section on Villa in this book is indispensable, not only because it comes from the foremost critic of Philippine literature but also because it puts into proper perspective the achievement of a poet and short-story writer who was lauded too much and too soon.

Demetillo, Ricaredo. *The Authentic Voice of Poetry.* Diliman: University of the Philippines, Office of Research Coordination, 1962. The chapter on Villa not only establishes historical context but also does an excellent job of establishing his place in Philippine literature and of delineating his strengths and weaknesses, concluding that Villa is a second-rate poet.

Grow, L. M. "José García Villa: The Poetry of Calibration." *World Literature Written in English* 27 (Autumn, 1987): 326-344. This article contends that Villa is usually revered for the wrong reasons. He is hampered by moral earnestness and thus does not make the fullest use of his lyric gifts, which are visible in spectacular opening lines.

Meredith, William. "Second Verse, Same as the First." *Poetry* 75 (February, 1950): 290-295. This short study concentrates on the famous "comma poems." It is ideal for students because it cites and analyzes complete poems as examples. Meredith's verdict is that only the playful poems are successful experiments in punctuation and diction.

Santos, Bienvenido N. "José García Villa in Exile." In *Philippine Harvest: An Anthology of Filipino Writing in English*, edited by Maximo Ramos and Florentino B. Valeros. Manila: E. F. David, 1953. Although a bit more difficult to find than some other studies, this article is worth the effort needed to locate it. Written by one of the great Filipino authors, the article is an exceptionally close-up biographical sketch, which incidentally reveals Santos as much as it reveals Villa.

Tabios, Eileen, ed. *Anchored Angel: Selected Writings of José García Villa.* New York: Kaya, 1999. Brings together a collection of Villa's writings with critical essays by a number of leading Filipino and Filipino American scholars. Among the contributors of critical essays are E. San Juan, Jr., Luis Francia, Nick Carbo, Nick Joaquin, and Alfred Yuson.

Tinio, Rolando S. "Villa's Values: Or, The Poet You Cannot Always Make Out, or Succeed in Liking Once You Are Able To." In *Brown Heritage: Essays on Philippine Cultural Tradition and Literature*, edited by Antonio G. Manuud. Quezon City: Ateneo de Manila University Press, 1967. In spite of the rather unfortunate choice of title, Tinio has done sound scholarship here, up to the standard of the rest of the contents of this massive, but landmark, volume. A must for any student of Philippine life or letters. The title is self-explanatory.

Leonard R. Casper

FRANÇOIS VILLON

Born: Paris, France; 1431
Died: Unknown; 1463(?)

PRINCIPAL POETRY

Le Lais, 1489 (wr. 1456; *The Legacy*, 1878; also known as *Le Petit Testament, The Little Testament*)

Le Grand Testament, 1489 (wr. 1461; *The Great Testament*, 1878)

Ballades en jargon, 1489 (*Poems in Slang*, 1878)

Les Œuvres de Françoys Villon, 1533 (Clément Marot, editor)

The Poems of Master François Villon, 1878

Ballads Done into English from the French of François Villon, 1904

The Testaments of François Villon, 1924

The Complete Works of François Villon, 1928

The Poems of François Villon, 1954, 1977, 1982 (includes *The Legacy, The Great Testament*, and some shorter poems; Galway Kinnell, translator)

OTHER LITERARY FORMS

François Villon indicates in *The Great Testament* that he also wrote a romance titled "Le Rommant du pet au diable" (romance of the devil's fart). This work, apparently about an elaborate student prank, is not extant, and Villon's mention of it is the only evidence that it ever did exist.

ACHIEVEMENTS

Of all the poets of the Middle Ages, perhaps only Dante and Geoffrey Chaucer are better known and more admired than François Villon. He has been widely praised since his own time by voices as diverse as those

of Clément Marot in the sixteenth century and Nicolas Boileau in the seventeenth; by Robert Louis Stevenson (whose admiration for Villon's poetic genius was even stronger than his revulsion at the depravity of the poet's life) and Algernon Charles Swinburne; by Dante Gabriel Rossetti, Ezra Pound, and William Carlos Williams. Remarkably enough, Villon has found his way into popular culture as well. He has been the subject of motion pictures (*Beloved Rogue*, with John Barrymore, 1927), novels such as Francis Carco's *Le Roman de François Villon* (1926), and popular songs by George Brassens, Reggiani, and others.

The usual explanation for Villon's extraordinary popularity is exemplified by Pound's contention (in *ABC of Reading*, 1934) that Villon is the most "authentic" of poets and (in *The Spirit of Romance*, 1910) that he is the only poet without illusions. He is, in this view, notable for accepting and admitting his own failures and depravity and speaking of them forthrightly, frequently with regret but always without shame. It is the presumed presence of the poet in his poetry, the fact that when he says "I" he is referring to himself rather than to a disembodied allegorical voice, that readers have found refreshing and appealing. Nor is the world around the poet an abstract or idealized place. His poetry is more firmly rooted in his own historical and geographical context (Paris at the end of the Middle Ages, a place and time of social and intellectual turmoil) than is that of any other medieval poet. His city, its students and thieves and judges, its priests and prostitutes, are both his *dramatis personae* and his subject.

The personal element in Villon's poetry—his honesty, sincerity, and authenticity—is related, according to the usual view, to his apparent lack of poetic artifice. Pound insisted that "Villon is destitute of imagination; he is almost destitute of art." He is considered to be without affectation, personal or literary. It is presumably the voice of a fallible, ordinary man, and not the calculated utterance of a poet, that the reader hears. Such is the reaction of many students, casual readers, poets, and critics alike. Such an assessment must represent, however, something of a misreading if it is intended literally. The Villon to whom readers are drawn is clearly a persona which he has crafted with great care and subtlety, and while that persona has much in common with the historical Villon, one is nevertheless the creature of the other. Villon is far from "destitute of art": While a very great poet and a very bad one might *appear* to be destitute of art, only the former is likely to be remembered. Perhaps one should say instead that Villon is destitute of *obvious* art: The impression of artlessness is his most artful illusion.

Although many generations have read and admired Villon, they have seen entirely different things in him—hero or coward, criminal or degenerate or tortured soul. This multiplicity of readings suggests that Villon is a great and complex poet, whose themes have universal appeal and whose command of his poetic resources is equal to the demands that his vision places on them.

BIOGRAPHY

François Villon was born François de Montcorbier (or perhaps des Loges) and later took as his own the name of his benefactor, Guillaume de Villon. He was a native of Paris, born there the year Joan of Arc died, and presumably reared there. He received his baccalaureate in 1449 and became a Master of Arts three years later.

François Villon (Library of Congress)

Much of the fragmentary information which is available concerning Villon's life comes from legal documents dating back to 1455. In that year, he was involved in a brawl and killed a priest named Phillippe Chermoye or Sermoise, but he was later pardoned for justifiable homicide. The following Christmas season, he and others committed a burglary at the College of Navarre, after which he apparently fled Paris.

In 1461, Villon was in a dungeon at Meung. Incarcerated there for reasons unknown, he was (as he says in *The Great Testament*) cruelly mistreated by Bishop Thibault d'Aussigny, but along with other prisoners he was released when the newly crowned King Louis XI passed through the town. Evidently unable to stay out of trouble, Villon was before long imprisoned once again, this time at the Châtelet in Paris. He was soon released again, but he had been incriminated in the College of Navarre burglary by a talkative accomplice, Guy Tabary, and had to agree to repay his share of the loot. Very soon, Villon was arrested yet again, following a brawl. This time, he was sentenced to be hanged; the sentence was commuted, however, and he was exiled instead. At that point, the trail ends, and further references to him (in François Rabelais's works, for example) are probably pure fictions. He died during or after 1463.

At some time, perhaps after he first fled from Paris, Villon spent a while at Blois, at the court of Charles d'Orléans, and a poem is preserved (titled "Je meurs de seuf auprès de la fontaine"/ "I Am Dying of Thirst near the Fountain") which he composed for a poetry contest held by Charles. His first long poem, *The Legacy*, was composed shortly after the 1456 Christmas burglary, while *The Great Testament* was written following his release from the Meung prison.

ANALYSIS

François Villon's poetry offers a depiction of his narrator so vivid and effective that readers have traditionally inferred that the narrator is the poet himself, assuming that Villon is dispensing with poetic mediation in order to express directly the thoughts and fears of a fifteenth century Parisian. That readers find themselves fascinated with Villon the man, even to the point of ignoring his poetry, is a testimony to the mastery of Villon the artist. The methods by which he creates and presents his narrator thus provide one of the most accessible keys to an analysis of his poetry. Foremost among his methods is the thematic inconsistency and apparent formlessness that one would expect to characterize, not literary activity, but the thoughts of a complex human being.

Although Villon generally deals with sober and important themes (injustice and intolerance; disease, decrepitude, and death), the tone of his poetry is not always as heavy as these subjects would suggest. Villon can be lighthearted and playful one instant, sober and bitter the next. Throughout his work, he shows himself to be a master of irony. In many cases, that irony is directed at his enemies, whom he may characterize either as magnanimous friends or as needy and worthy citizens. (In a number of such cases, Villon's ironic intent was revealed to posterity only in the last century or the present one, when historical research permitted the identification of most of the people mentioned by the poet.) He also, however, directs his irony at himself; for example, he may present himself as love's martyr, the victim of an unhappy affair, when in fact it is clear that his "broken heart" is a thinly veiled reference to his criminal activity.

At times, Villon's irony and humor fall away, and he launches into a direct and abusive attack on his enemies. This invective, all the more striking because it brusquely interrupts a lighter tone and sometimes interrupts another thought, has convinced readers that this, at least, is the "real" Villon, yet such "outbursts" can also be regarded as carefully planned poetic effects designed to add realism to his persona. Similarly, Villon often suspends banter and invective alike to offer a simple, plaintive statement of regret or a plea for forgiveness—although he is likely to cancel such a statement in turn by a joke or another attack. His work is thus built on contrast and digression, on a systematic rejection of consistency. His poetry is carefully composed so as not to appear to have been carefully composed, and it is certainly as dynamic as any ever written.

THE LEGACY

Villon's first long poem, *The Legacy*, is a work of 320 octosyllabic lines arranged in eight-line stanzas. It was probably composed around the end of 1456, after the burglary at the College of Navarre, when Villon had

fled from Paris or was preparing to do so. Characteristically, Villon uses events from his own life, and the premise for *The Legacy* is the necessity that he leave the city. The work is thus a *congé* (leave-taking), a traditional genre describing one's reasons and preparations for a departure. Critics have sometimes interpreted *The Legacy* as an alibi intended to provide evidence that Villon was away from Paris when the Christmas robbery took place. It is more likely that his fictional absence was an "inside joke" for the benefit of his friends or accomplices who knew of his involvement in the burglary.

In any case, the robbery itself is not mentioned in the poem. Instead, the narrator tells us that he is leaving because a love affair has ended painfully. His discussion of the relationship and its end is replete with mock allegorical imagery drawn from the traditional vocabulary of courtly love. He thus speaks of the "prison of love," the "pain of love," and "sweet glances." He concludes that his only recourse is to flee, but his poetic intent quickly becomes clear when we note that the word he uses, *fouïr*, means not only to "flee" but also to "copulate," and his double meaning is obvious when he insists, for example, that he must "plant in other fields." Specifically, he announces that his destination is Angers, but, as David Kuhn has pointed out in *La Poétique de François Villon*, "going to Angers" was a slang reference to orgasm.

Following this introduction is a series of bequests, in which Villon, by antiphrasis, leaves to others fictitious possessions or exaggerated assets (his money, tents, and fame—the first two nonexistent, the third undesirable), makes obscene puns (his *branc*, which he bequeaths to Ythier Marchant, means either "sword" or "excrement"), and bestows otherwise ironic gifts (as when he leaves money to "three poor orphans"—who, research has revealed, were actually three rich merchants and usurers).

The third and final section of *The Legacy* offers a closure which is an elaborate parody of Scholastic language; typically, however, Villon's lines constitute not only an indictment of Scholasticism but also a system of sexual, specifically masturbatory, imagery. Thus, Villon closes the circle of his poem—although he does so in an unexpected way. He has told us that he is leaving a woman and that he is leaving Paris. He announces his destination (Angers), which indicates also his sexual intention, and that intention is enacted in the "Scholastic" section and achieved when, at the end, Villon's senses clear and, his "candle extinguished" and his "ink frozen," he is unable to continue writing. While some scholars have interpreted these details as realistic images of Villon's miserable existence, they are rather the burlesque conclusion of his sexual situation: He is spent. *The Legacy* thus relates travel, courtly and Scholastic thought, and poetic effort in a complex progression that ends in mock-pathetic autoerotic exhaustion.

THE GREAT TESTAMENT

The Great Testament, written five days after *The Legacy*, is longer (2,023 lines), generally less comical, and far more complex. It is considered to be a mature and serious recasting of *The Legacy*, and indeed many of the same persons and images recur in it. While this view can claim some justification, however, it would be unjust to the earlier poem to see in it nothing more than a prefiguration of Villon's mature work. *The Legacy* is a comic masterpiece in its own right; *The Great Testament* uses some of the same methods and materials to produce a masterpiece of an entirely different sort. Indeed, the two works have relatively little in common other than certain characters and the fact that each of them offers a series of ironic or burlesque bequests. Even the irony varies. That of *The Legacy* appears for the most part good-natured. In *The Great Testament*, the irony is most often bitterly vituperative, and at times Villon suspends his ironic detachment altogether, as when, at the very beginning of the poem, he launches into a vicious attack on Bishop Thibault, who mistreated Villon in prison.

The subject of *The Great Testament* is no longer the loss of Villon's love, but the loss of his youth and the impending loss of his life. He is, he suggests, an aging and weak man who regrets his wasted youth and must put his life in order. Yet, there is another side of him, a side that has no desire to waste even a precious hour of life preparing for death: He has too much to do, perhaps too many friends to see and pranks to play, but especially he has too many scores to settle and too many enemies to malign. Thus the poet presents, developed in sharp relief, the two sides of his character: the heart and the flesh, the conscience and the appetites, the contrite sinner preoccupied with the hereafter and the mortal des-

perately clinging to life, preoccupied with the present. Much of the artistic tension of the work derives from the conflict of these opposing impulses, intercutting each other ever more quickly and more frantically as the poem progresses.

The form of *The Great Testament* could be described with a fair degree of accuracy as a structure of digression. The pattern is set when Villon interrupts his very first sentence to launch into the lengthy attack on Thibault, then soon after to offer elaborate praise of King Louis XI, before finally returning to the ostensible subject of the work. Although the ultimate destination of the poem (the narrator's death) is clear from the beginning, the path to it is circuitous, as the poet digresses repeatedly to offer details of his past, his associates, his fears and regrets.

The work incorporates a number of lyric pieces (*ballades* and *rondeaux*) which represent in most cases the illustration or crystallization of a thematic development. These lyric poems are thought by some scholars to have been composed earlier and chosen for use in *The Great Testament* (a contention that has not been proved and that is of no great consequence in any case, because whether they were written early or late, their inclusion indicates that they satisfactorily served Villon's purposes). The best known of these pieces is the "Ballade des dames du temps jadis" ("Ballad of Dead Ladies"), which, along with two accompanying poems, the "Ballade des seigneurs du temps jadis" ("Ballad of Men from the Past") and the "Ballade en vieil langage françoys" ("Ballad in Old French"), develops the *ubi sunt* motif in regard to illustrious persons from the past. While the "Ballad of Dead Ladies" is justly praised, its meaning has been distorted in English by the traditional translation of its famous refrain as "Where are the snows of yesteryear?" *Antan*, the last word of the refrain, means simply "last year," and the correct rendering of the line, while robbing it of a rather romantic poignancy, restores its effectiveness in another way: Villon is, after all, contrasting the passing of a fragile and rather commonplace phenomenon with the loss of remarkable, famous, and (by implication) equally fragile women from history.

It is in fact typical of Villon *not* to reach for the extravagant image or the elaborate paraphrase; often his most effective passages are, as here, impressive for their directness and simplicity. He also has a tendency to move from the distant to the immediate, from the abstract to the concrete. Thus, for example, while these early ballads effectively suggest the loss of life and fame, that theme is far more strikingly developed when he later refers simply to "skulls stacked up in cemeteries" or when he presents the lament of Belle Hëaulmiere, an aging prostitute who recalls the firm, attractive body she once had and contrasts it with the shriveled and repulsive form it has now, to her horror, become. Her contemplation is followed by a *ballade* in which she urges a group of prostitutes to seize the day.

These lyric poems are inserted irregularly, but with increasing frequency toward the end. The subject matter, moreover, follows a general evolution toward the realistic, direct, and sometimes coarse. From the three *ballades* treating illustrious people from the past (and from another early one, a masterful prayer to Notre Dame intended to be offered by Villon's simple and naïve mother), he goes on to present Hëaulmiere and, later, la Grosse Margot (Fat Margot, a prostitute whose consort Villon is, and the subject of a poem by Robert Louis Stevenson, who describes her as "grimy" and as "gross and ghastly"). Villon's themes—misery, aging, and death—are hardly subjects to be developed abstractly in pretty ballads, and indeed the appeal of his poetry for many is precisely that he is willing to suspend obvious poetic musing and present death in all its ugliness and pain—and himself as a man whose flesh is weak and whose spirit is only sporadically willing.

Even though *The Great Testament* is bitter, vituperative, and often uncompromisingly realistic, and even though its predominant tone is sober, it is by no means devoid of comedy, although the humor of *The Great Testament* is humor with a sharp edge. The "three poor orphans" reappear here, as do a number of other characters from *The Legacy*; in this case, however, Villon's banter only thinly covers a venomous attitude. He jokes about his legatees, but the jokes are mostly intimations of sexual and other disorders on the part of his adversaries. Nor does he spare himself: He indicates (as he did in his earlier poem) that he is a martyr to love, but the specific details he offers in support of that suggestion have led some scholars to theorize that his martyrdom took the form of advanced syphilis.

Throughout the poem, we hear Villon's two voices (sinner and penitent) clearly, but the work is also structured around a variety of other voices, and in some cases other narrators appear as well. The interplay of voices in *The Great Testament* is in fact very complex, and toward the end, as the tempo quickens and the realism intensifies, these complexities multiply. In the fiction of the poem, Villon presents himself as aging, becoming increasingly infirm, and approaching death. Indeed, at the end, he composes his own epitaph, and his fiction even includes looking back from beyond the grave to describe his death. In this section, some passages are not only in the past but also in the third person, as though another narrator were taking over. At one point, Villon comments in the first person on his third-person character: "Et je croy bien que pas n'en ment" ("And *I* do not think *he* is lying"; emphasis added). This is the culmination of a movement that has developed throughout the work, whereby Villon creates two entities, a persona and a character, who periodically merge and separate and who are finally established as entirely distinct from each other. The interplay of voices confirms the poet as partially independent of the character he creates; the latter follows the fictional course set for him (lamenting his age, preparing his will, and dying), while the poet uses him and the text to indulge in an examination of, and commentary on, life, death, sexuality, the judicial system, his friends, enemies, and accomplices—and above all, Villon himself.

The Great Testament is thus a remarkable portrait of its narrator, of Paris, of the life led by a medieval "student, poet, and housebreaker" (according to Stevenson's characterization), but it is also a remarkable poem, a masterpiece of verbal wit, of structural complexity, of poetic voice and virtuosity. *The Legacy* is in many ways a remarkable work of undeniable merit, but it is lighter not only in tone but finally in literary weight. *The Great Testament* is the complex and mature masterpiece of a consummate poet.

POEMS IN SLANG

Whether *Poems in Slang* is also a masterpiece remains open to question: The poems included are virtually incomprehensible to modern readers. Many of the words and expressions, drawn from underworld slang, have been identified through documents that preserve them; the meaning of others can be deduced from their context. Still, enough mysteries remain to frustrate critical efforts. Pierre Guiraud, in *The Slang of Villon*, has offered one of the more elaborate and controversial attempts to deal with these poems, proposing three distinct levels of meaning and consequently three translations for each. The first level deals with criminal activity, the second with cheating at cards, the third with sodomy. Whether Guiraud has successfully deciphered Villon's system—and a good number of scholars remain unconvinced—the fact remains that the *Poems in Slang* are still largely inaccessible. Modern scholars cannot adequately assess the poetic value of the volume because their attention is still on its meaning, in the most basic sense: the definition of words. For the present, these poems must remain an enigma, a closed system constructed in a language that is largely foreign even to the best specialists in Villon's Middle French.

His remaining miscellaneous poems are extremely varied in subject matter, style, date of composition, and literary value, and the very authorship of some of them is disputed. Certain of them are no more than playthings or poetic pastimes. Others, however, are very interesting, and two deserve brief comment here. "L'Épitaphe Villon" ("Villon's Epitaph") offers a horrible portrait of corpses on the gallows—swinging in the breeze, flesh rotting, eyes pecked out by birds—and asks for compassion and absolution. "Le Débat du cuer et du corps de Villon" ("The Dialogue of Villon's Heart and Body") provides a confrontation of basic human impulses, as the personified heart attempts to persuade the body to abandon its dissolute ways. Both poems are reminiscent in certain ways of *The Great Testament*, the former in the realistic images of death, the latter in the dramatization of the fundamental conflicts within Villon and within all of us, and both of them in the impressive poetic sensibility that informs them.

For Algernon Charles Swinburne, Villon was "our sad bad glad mad brother." That is indeed what Villon has been for most readers. What is conspicuously absent from such assessments (except perhaps by implication) is precisely Villon's artistic status, his success in creating the persona which many readers mistake for the poet. When one looks directly at his poetry—stripping away the veneer of romantic imagery, bypassing Victo-

rian revulsion at his manners and character, going beyond popular distortions and fanciful interpretations—it becomes clear that Villon is, quite simply, the finest French poet of the Middle Ages and an enduring artist for any age.

BIBLIOGRAPHY

Anacker, Robert. *François Villon*. New York: Twayne, 1968. As Anacker's bibliography indicates, this is perhaps the first book-length study of Villon's poetry in English since 1928. Writing for the general reader, Anacker limits the scholarly apparatus to a dozen notes and references but gives an overview of Villon's world before analyzing *The Legacy/The Great Testament*, and miscellaneous poems, ending with an assessment of Villon's poetic achievement.

Brereton, Geoffrey. "Francois Villon." In *An Introduction to the French Poets: Villon to the Present Day*. 2d ed. London: Methuen, 1973. Brereton balances his commentary between Villon the poet and Villon's poetry, giving a general assessment of Villon's poetic technique and personality as it is reflected in the poetry.

Daniel, Robert R. *The Poetry of Villon and Baudelaire: Two Worlds, One Human Condition*. New York: Peter Lang, 1997. Daniel traces many themes that both of these poets shared, such as mortality and the *danse macabre*, or dance of death. The result is an illumination of the poetry of a modern and a medieval poet that highlights Villon's medieval and modern characteristics.

Fox, John. *The Poetry of Villon*. New York: Thomas Nelson and Sons, 1962. One of the more recent works that focuses on Villon's poetry rather than his personality, Fox's study takes a commonsensical approach to the text by allowing for multiple interpretations of it and looks closely in separate chapters at the sound and rhythm in Villon's poetry, at the word order and phrasing, and at theme, image, and symbol. Fox's analysis contains ample citations of Villon's poetry and concludes that Villon's major achievement is in his realistic style and vivid depiction of lived experience.

Omans, Glen. "The Villon Cult in England." *Comparative Literature* 18, no. 1 (Winter, 1966): 16-35. Glen

Omans traces the development of Villon's persona among English readers in Victorian England, which to a large extent determined how Villon has been perceived by American readers. A highly romanticized portrait of Villon as the vagabond poet led to fascination with the man at the expense of an appreciation of the poetry itself. Omans's study suggests that the appearance of several translations of Villon's poetry is a sign that modern critics and scholars wish to direct attention back to the poetry and to establish a more accurate portrait of Villon himself.

Peckham, Robert D. *François Villon: A Bibliography.* New York: Garland, 1990. This comprehensive text is the starting place for anyone wishing to understand Villon's poetry, his influence, and his times. Peckham lists all the manuscripts containing Villon's poetry and translations of it, and he includes the critical texts relating to the poetry, even works inspired by Villon's poetry, up to 1985.

Villon, François. *François Villon's "The Legacy" and "The Testament."* Translated by Louis Simpson. Ashland, Oreg.: Story Line, 2000. Simpson's preface provides a useful introduction to Villon's life and times, and the notes provide commentary on Villon's language and clarify the many obscure allusions that enrich Villon's poetry.

Norris J. Lacy;
bibliography updated by Bernard E. Morris

ELLEN BRYANT VOIGT

Born: Danville, Virginia; May 9, 1943

PRINCIPAL POETRY
Claiming Kin, 1976
The Forces of Plenty, 1983
The Lotus Flowers, 1987
Two Trees, 1992
Kyrie, 1995
Shadow of Heaven, 2002

OTHER LITERARY FORMS

Ellen Bryant Voigt is also known for her critical essays on poetry. She explores and defines lyric, narrative, style, structure, form, and other concepts of genre and versification: tone, image, diction, gender, tension, and voice. The central concern of her criticism and artistic practice is testing differentiation between the modes and impulses of lyric and narrative. Essays written over a period of fifteen years are collected in *The Flexible Lyric* (1999).

The title essay, the longest and most ambitious, develops definitions of lyric and narrative, form and structure, and texture and voice that reveal how the elements of each pair are set in tension in the best poetry. Quoting from Randall Jarrell, who regarded tension as "a struggle between opposites," Voigt considers unity in a poem to emerge from tension, and this emergence to be the necessary function of a poem. Lyric is "a moment lifted out of time but not static, movement that is centripetal and centrifugal rather than linear; an examination of self which discovers universal predicament; insight embodied in individuated particulars and at the same time overriding them." Voigt illustrates her point by briefly tracing the evolution of lyric poetry from the Renaissance through the late twentieth century in order to show that form does not limit the poet's freedom but rather impels the evolution of lyric poetry.

ACHIEVEMENTS

Voigt's awards for poetry include the Emily Clark Bach Award, the Haines Poetry Award, a Pushcart Prize, and grants from the Leila Wallace-*Reader's Digest* Fund, the National Endowment for the Arts, and the Guggenheim Foundation. Her book *Kyrie* was a finalist for a National Book Critics Circle Award.

BIOGRAPHY

Ellen Bryant was brought up in Chattam, Virginia, by Lloyd Gilmore Bryant, a farmer, and Missouri Yeats Bryant, an elementary school teacher. The experience of family, nature, and hard work comprises much of the subject matter of her poetry. Farm existence provided awareness of dependence on nature. Will and destiny, hard work and choice, natural order and persistence in the face of the unpredictable afforded by this kind of life, are at the heart of her artistic concerns.

She credits her early and long training in music as the central influence in her art. Not only was it formative in her "impulse for order," but also it contributed to her love of "solitude." Surrounded by many relatives, Voigt found her life "exceedingly claustrophobic." Playing piano was her time to herself:

> I can look back and see poem after poem that takes up the friction between that solitary individual and whatever that social unit is, be it small or large.

Music resounds in the body, eliciting sensory feeling. At the same time it provides a sense of control through form, both constraining and fluid. Relating this to her writing, Voight has said, "I make a musical decision before I make any other kind of decision. . . . If I can't hear it, it just never gets written."

Beginning piano lessons at the age of four along with her older sister, Voigt continued her music education through a degree in 1964 at Converse College in Spartanburg, South Carolina, where she discovered her dislike of performance, her love for music theory, and her passion for literature. While she was working a summer job playing lounge music at a resort, a friend introduced her to the poetry of Rainer Maria Rilke, E. E. Cummings, and William Butler Yeats. Having had no real poetry education until then, she says she was "starved" for it.

Voigt earned a master of fine arts degree from the University of Iowa in 1966, studying principally with Donald Justice. She settled with her husband in Cabot, Vermont, taught poetry, and began a family. Major concerns of her art are the family relationship, its disorders and orders, choice and fate, and opportunities for truth and moral reflection.

Publishing her early work in journals, Voigt did not complete her first book until 1976. Each of her books explores the nature of lyric and narrative and their interaction as she strives to keep narrative in the background while plumbing the depths of lyric. Her 1995 collection, *Kyrie*, disperses narrative through a long sequence of sonnets.

ANALYSIS

Ellen Bryant Voigt is known for finely wrought, compressed forms delivered with a passionate moral sensibility. Profoundly influenced by her extensive early musical training, Voigt's poetry employs and extends traditional versification as it explores struggles relating to work, family, and the vicissitudes of life. Her poems push the limits of lyric and narrative as she sets emotionally heightened moments out of time—singing—against the storied linearity of the past and tries to unite them.

"SONG AND STORY"

"Song and Story," the concluding poem of *Two Trees*, Ellen Bryant Voigt's fourth volume of poems, distills the chief concern of her artistic life. She gathers and articulates the two impulses that have driven her, that she sees driving human life. Music reaches from the atemporal realm into story with its softening, easing rhythms; the singer has emerged from pain and reaches back to another who is in the midst of pain. The impulse of lyric is thus hope, promise, choice to continue, and praise of the atemporal or cyclical against story's inevitable onward movement toward death of the individual. As Stephen Cramer has written, "Voigt's work as a whole recites the tale of one artist's 'will to change.'" With her own story she provides the story of human choice in the face of what is given by earth and society.

CLAIMING KIN

Voigt's vision matured over two decades of experimentation. The poems of her first book discover the music of the body, its breathings and varied motions in the midst of life, especially family life. The rhythms of family participants in small stories are set harmonically in tune and then against each other, as in the title poem, "Claiming Kin." Writing of her mother, the poet begins:

> Insistent as a whistle, her voice up
> the stairs pried open the blanket's
> tight lid and piped me
> down to the pressure cooker's steam and rattle.

Other household objects the mother wields make their insistent noises, while the poet as a small child is a "pale lump blinking at the light" of her mother's "shiny kingdom" of noisy "razzle-dazzle." The mother has another, a night rhythm apposite to the poet's self, a "Soft ghost, plush as a pillow," who "wove and fruited against the black hours."

In "The Feast of the Assumption of the Virgin," the Madonna "Mourns . . . as if reaching for fruit," and a priest's blessing of young girls joins music and fruit, joy and hurt:

> . . . when the bells release
> a shower of pollen,
> each mouth opens to rapture
> like a wound.

Pain is the price of joy. Composed of loose iambics and snatches of ballad rhythms, these poems' rhythms function to advance and constrain extremity let loose by often shocking images: the beheading of a hen, a jealous child wishing her older sister dead, a dream life of murdering, "stones/ with their mouths sewn shut." Music reaches into silence to seed it, but each person remains isolated; song is not much help to any but the poet herself.

THE FORCES OF PLENTY

Voigt's view of the shift from her first to her second collection, *The Forces of Plenty*, is that she "moved clarity up over resonance." Where before Voigt was most intent on making music, she began her shift toward narrative. Less concerned with capturing the intense emotion in a moment of time, she renders small vignettes with people now listening to the music the world offers. The music is quieter, calmed by interludes of stopping the daily round to listen. In "The Spire," a poem about the function of lyric and reminiscent of Marianne Moore's "The Steeple-Jack," a church on a mountain provides connection to the people in the town. Forms made by human hands and thought "can extend the flawed earth/ and embody us," giving a continuity of story to our lives. Yet the bells of the church ring over "the village/ houses . . . allied in a formal shape/ beside a stream, the streets concluding/ at the monument. Again the ravishing moment/ of the bell," at which the townspeople are pictured stopping each of their various businesses, each having its own ongoing rhythm, as the bell inserts sound into their time to call them momentarily out of linear time to lyric ecstasy.

Voigt has said the long poem "Taking the Fire Out" is a "watershed" poem pointing toward her next collection, *The Lotus Flowers*. Each of its six sections presents a small narrative scene rendered with lyric intensity and questioning. The repeated line "Nothing is learned by turning away" bespeaks the poet's honest effort to choose to know what is true.

THE LOTUS FLOWERS

Composed in the wake of her parents' deaths, *The Lotus Flowers* revisits the poet's Southern childhood and revises its terms and story. Most of the poems move from sharply and clearly delivered short narratives toward lyric conclusions. They resolve in moments of felt sense and understanding, shifting the vignettes into what she has called "back story." Even when story is out front, it is unreliable. Writing in "Short Story" of her grandfather killing a mule, she is not sure what the truth is, "The story varied/ in the telling." Each person has a version, each according to his experience. Lyric is individual expression of feeling what is universally felt, though the difficulty of reaching across the gulf of separation persists. "A Song" portrays an alienated singer who can find no comfort, no way out of pain.

In "The Lotus Flowers," a group of adolescent girls camping in the wilderness is connected like spokes in a wheel, each small self necessary to the bright whole as the lesser stars in the constellations they view overhead are essential to the shape of constellations and the stories told about them. In this poem, narrative delivers a clarity of vision that resolves on the timeless intensity that is lyric's signature.

TWO TREES

In *Two Trees*, Voigt arrives at her matured vision: The singer, who has gone through and emerged from grief, can now reach back in song to those still immersed in suffering. The poems move on classical and biblical myths of innocence and experience. The rhythms too are more classical, more certainly iambic, weaving in and out of pentameter. The rhythmic strategy holds tradition in its bosom as the men and women Voigt writes about hold the story of birth, life, death, and begetting in wisdom and sorrow. At the same time the lines move in and out of tradition, in desire of reaching "over the wall" of the line, as the "first man and woman" do in "Two Trees," desiring both the tree of knowledge and the tree of life that is "over the wall." The second tree, never tasted but yearned for, is beauty and perfection, which could not be known except for the first tree. Now both trees are in "the foreground": The formal problem is recognized as one of balance between story and song, but it is song that the poet aligns with hope, with the human will to strive for the beauty and felt fulfillment of oneness and connection, the theme that marks this volume.

KYRIE

Kyrie threads a narrative line across fifty-eight sonnets, each a moment of lyric expression in the voice of one of several recurring character-speakers from a small New England town during the winter of 1917-1918, as World War I was concluding and a deadly influenza epidemic raged. By giving voice to individuals immersed in loss, fear, and grief, Voigt reaches into the heart of lyric's capacity to express common bonds in the depths of shared feeling. The rhythmic strategy of moving from the sonnet's conventional iambic pentameter base reaffirms literature's shared tradition of lyric as reaffirming social contact. The volume recalls Edgar Lee Masters's *Spoon River Anthology* (1915), but instead of speaking honestly finally only from the dead as his characters do, Voigt's speak from life, drawing forth emotional energies to cope with the threat of death surrounding them on two fronts—influenza and war. The power of the combined voices singing rises over and against the plague and the war, "The sun still up everywhere in the kingdom." Unlike the constricted, mostly failed lives of Masters's characters, Voigt's continue to look forward with hope. Singing celebrates life, exceeds the time of destruction and its effects.

OTHER MAJOR WORKS

NONFICTION: *The Flexible Lyric*, 1999.

BIBLIOGRAPHY

Holden, Jonathan. "The Free Verse Line." In *The Line in Postmodern Poetry*, edited by Robert Joseph Frank and Henry M. Sayre. Urbana: University of Illinois Press, 1988. Holden uses Voigt's poetry to show how good free-verse music is made of rhythmic phrases that match the poet's attention.

Pope, Deborah. "A Litany in Time of Plague." *Southern Review* 32, no. 2 (Spring, 1996): 363-369. An extended review of *Kyrie,* examining the relative success of Voigt's formal, narrative, and thematic experiment.

Smith, Dave. "Speculations on a Southern Snipe." In *The Future of Southern Letters*, edited by Jefferson Humphries and John Lowe. New York: Oxford University Press, 1996. An examination of the Southern pastoral as a flight from home and a yearning to return and repair damage. Voigt is an example of the difficulty facing a poet who has inherited a Southern background and seeks to repair community.

Suarez, Ernest, Trey Stanford, and Amy Verner. "Ellen Bryant Voigt." In *Southbound: Interviews with Southern Poets*. Columbia: University of Missouri Press, 1999. Focuses on Voigt's Southern roots and influence, which Voigt seeks to minimize. Suggests her move away from the South and its immersion in story is a rejection of roots, except for her brief return to her childhood in *The Lotus Flowers*.

Voigt, Ellen Bryant. "Song and Story: An Interview with Ellen Bryant Voigt." Interview by Stephen Cramer. *The Atlantic* Online, November 24, 1999. This interview focuses on Voigt's creative concerns and evolution beginning with her childhood. Voigt speaks of her progressive development of form, style, and themes in her books.

Rosemary Winslow

MIHÁLY VÖRÖSMARTY

Born: Kápolnásnyék, Hungary; December 1, 1800
Died: Pest, Hungary; November 19, 1855

PRINCIPAL POETRY

Zalán futása, 1825
Minden munkái, 1864 (12 volumes)
Összes munkái, 1884-1885 (8 volumes)
Összes művei, 1960-1979 (18 volumes)

OTHER LITERARY FORMS

Although best known for his lyric and epic poetry, which comprises six of the eighteen volumes of the critical edition of his works published in 1979, Mihály Vörösmarty was also an important dramatist during the formative years of the Hungarian theater. His Romantic historical dramas are seldom performed today, but they still present enjoyable reading for students of the period. On the other hand, his *Csongor és Tünde* (pr. 1830; Csongor and Tünde), a fairy play having strong philosophical overtones and bearing the influence of William Shakespeare's *A Midsummer Night's Dream* (1595-1596), is regularly staged and has been translated into several languages. In order to nurture the fledgling Hungarian National Theater, Vörösmarty ably translated the classics: His Hungarian renderings of Shakespeare's *King Lear* (1605) in 1856 and *Julius Caesar* (1599-1600) in 1840 are unsurpassed to this day.

Through his theoretical and critical writings, Vörösmarty was influential in defining the aesthetic issues of his times and in encouraging the emerging trends of Romanticism and populism. As an editor or associate of several of the period's most important journals, he introduced and encouraged the talents of young artists, including the twenty-one-year-old Sándor Petőfi, thus greatly enriching the literature of Hungary. He also authored and compiled a number of dictionaries, grammars, and handbooks for the Hungarian Academy of Sciences. His extensive correspondence provides invaluable documentation of the period's political and cultural life.

ACHIEVEMENTS

Born into what is considered one of the most exciting and eventful periods in the political and cultural development of Hungary, Mihály Vörösmarty made a significant contribution to nearly every aspect of his nation's intellectual life. Vörösmarty began his literary career fully committed to classical ideals, and he never lost his admiration for the craftsmanship of the Greek and Latin poets, but he soon fell under the influence of the prevailing literary trend, Romanticism. Calls for national revival were sounding all over the Continent, and in Hungary such calls were perhaps louder and more impatient than elsewhere. Vörösmarty became one of the most enthusiastic and effective of the reformers, and he served their cause with his literary as well as his political activities.

Two specific characteristics of his œuvre distinguish him from his contemporaries: As a descendant of the nobility, he remained bewildered and somewhat repulsed by the idea of mass movements. This background made him a reluctant and pessimistic advocate of radical democratic transformation and somewhat colored the sincerity of his social proclamations. On the other hand, he was able to progress beyond the limitations of his

nationalistic contemporaries at a surprisingly young age, and by the 1830's, he was able to view the fate of Hungary in a more inclusive context. In his best philosophical poems (few of which have been translated into English), he speaks with total conviction and determination about the future of humankind. Vörösmarty's mature poetry is remarkably free of the feelings of inferiority and ethnocentricity which had often characterized the works of earlier Hungarian poets.

BIOGRAPHY

As the oldest of nine children in a noble but impoverished Roman Catholic family in western Hungary, Mihály Vörösmarty could obtain a higher education only with the help of wealthy patrons. After attending the gymnasium at Székesfehérvár and Pest, and losing his father when he was seventeen, he had to accept the post of private tutor with the aristocratic Perczel family. At the same time, he continued his studies toward a law degree. These years of servitude and the hopeless love he felt for his employer's daughter left marks of sensitivity, wariness, and pessimism on his character.

In 1823, Vörösmarty obtained a position as a law clerk while maintaining his post with the Perczel family. He had been writing poetry and drama since he was fifteen, and the lively company of his peers contributed to the further development of his talent, making him conscious of the importance of patriotic literature. During this time, he also made contact with the restless noblemen of the countryside who were conducting a determined campaign of resistance in the face of the absolutist Viennese government. Under their influence, Vörösmarty wrote the first of his anti-Habsburg poems and a number of expressive, complex historical dramas. The memory of unhappy love and the realization of limitations placed upon him by a rigidly structured society continued to haunt him, and in 1826, he left the Perczel household. His goal to "become an independent man and a writer" was instrumental in his decision to settle in Buda, which was emerging as the cultural center of Hungary. Faced with squalor and the indifference of the reading public, he was on the verge of giving up his literary activities and setting up a law practice, when he was offered the editorship of the *Tudományos Gyüjtemény*, one of the most prestigious journals in Hungary.

He edited this publication and its supplement, the *Koszorú*, from 1828 to 1832. While this provided him with a steady income, the drudgery of the work and disheartening political developments occurring at the time, made his voice somber and pessimistic.

During the early years of the 1830's, the Reform movement gained new momentum, and the cultural life of Hungary was also invigorated by the publication of *Aurora*, the first genuine literary monthly, edited by József Bajza, Ferenc Toldy, and Vörösmarty. The poet's financial situation had improved. His works were regularly published, he won several literary prizes, and in 1830, he became an elected (and paid) member of the Hungarian Academy of Sciences. He contributed significantly to the linguistic, orthographic, and lexicographic publications of the Academy, was instrumental in the democratization of its bylaws, and remained active in public life, largely through the journals *Athenaeum* and *Figyelmező*, which became the arbiters of Hungarian cultural and literary affairs. His cautious stand on political reforms notwithstanding, he attracted the suspicion of the Habsburg police.

When the first permanent Hungarian theatrical company became active in Buda in 1833, there was an urgent need for original Hungarian dramas. Vörösmarty enthusiastically supported this company and contributed five successful plays in as many years. His activities as a dramatist and critic were instrumental in the development of the Hungarian theater.

In 1836, Vörösmarty and a small circle of intellectuals founded the Kisfaludy Társaság, named after the recently deceased Károly Kisfaludy, the first professional writer-poet of Hungary, who had played a significant role in making the twin communities of Buda and Pest, the cultural center of the country.

The 1830's witnessed the full development of political lyricism in Vörösmarty's work. Among other writings, he produced more than 150 incisive epigrams which demonstrated his commitment to a course of sensible reforms and revealed his acute sensitivity to the public and aesthetic issues of the times.

The 1840's were the most eventful years in Vörösmarty's life. In 1842, to the consternation of his friends, he married the eighteen-year-old Laura Csajághy. Theirs was a successful and happy marriage, and they had four children. The livelier political atmosphere and the liberalizing tendencies of the decade encouraged and motivated him, while the impending specter of a revolution occasionally filled him with doubt and foreboding. Lajos Kossuth, Ferenc Deák, and Miklós Wesselényi, the leaders of the Hungarian independence struggle, were among his friends, and he was elected president of the National Circle, one of the centers of political activity. His participation in aesthetic debates was reduced somewhat, but his prestige and influence enabled him to help the younger generation of poets and writers to gain recognition; for example, he was first to publish the works of the young Sándor Petőfi, the foremost Hungarian lyric poet.

After the revolution of March 15, 1848, Vörösmarty took an active part in political activities, wholeheartedly supporting the policies of Lajos Kossuth. He obtained a seat in the Chamber of Deputies, and later, during the months of armed struggle, was appointed judge by the independent Hungarian government. Hungary's defeat in the War of Independence crushed Vörösmarty; after several months in hiding, he reported to the imperial authorities, who, after an investigation, cleared him in 1850. Disappointed and disillusioned, Vörösmarty concentrated on providing a livelihood for his family. Since he was only marginally successful as a landowner, he was often forced to accept the charity of his supporters. Finding himself unable to resume fully his literary activities, he produced only a few bitter, tragically prophetic laments and elegies and turned more and more to alcohol for consolation. In 1855, his deteriorating health forced him to move to Pest, where he died two days after his arrival. The Habsburg authorities took every measure to quell any popular outpouring of sympathy; in spite of this, Vörösmarty's funeral turned into the first mass demonstration against Austrian rule since 1849. His friends, through private correspondence, were able to collect a sizable amount to provide for the widow and children of the poet.

Analysis

Mihály Vörösmarty experimented with versification as a teenager, and he was amazed and overjoyed when he discovered that the Hungarian language was readily adaptable to the requirements of metrical poetry. Because the early decades of the nineteenth century were considered the golden age of literary classicism in Hungary, and because Vörösmarty's education at the gymnasium was also heavily classical, it is not surprising that he produced a great number of odes, epigrams, and other verse forms patterned after the poets of antiquity. The other important influence in his early youth was an all-pervasive patriotism, which obliged him to produce a number of historical epics. In these, he demonstrated a naïve view of Hungarian nobility and its relationship to the king, attributing any conflicts between the two to personal rivalries and the divisive intrigue of (usually foreign) courtiers.

ZALÁN FUTÁSA

The work that stands out among his early creations and that made him a nationally known poet was *Zalán futása* (the flight of Zalán), a heroic epic in ten cantos, completed in 1825. Vörösmarty successfully combined the treatment of a major Hungarian literary motif with the use of polished classical hexameters, while putting into practice his conviction that the depiction of epochal events from the nation's history was an excellent way to reawaken a national consciousness in nineteenth century Hungarians. He also revived the genre of the heroic epic in Hungarian literature, paralleling the activities of Miklós Zrínyi (1620-1664). Vörösmarty's work is a patriotic epic, notwithstanding its many interpolated lyrics, which relate episodes of love, fulfilled or unrequited—recounting how the chieftain Árpád and his Hungarians (Magyars) achieved victory in 896 over the Slavic settlers of the Danubian basin. Medieval chronicles discovered in the eighteenth century provided much of Vörösmarty's source material; he also drew on the Ossianic ballads and nationalistic literature of the time.

For nineteenth century Hungarians, *Zalán futása* derived its significance from an insistent tone that ran throughout its descriptions of battle scenes, war councils, and military preparations. Vörösmarty urged his generation of "indolent, soft, and lethargic" Hungarians to emulate Árpád and his heroic warriors. The epic is not, however, a call to arms, but rather a summons to patriotism. Indeed, what makes it enjoyable reading today is that its message, although outdated, is expressed not in strident, ethnocentric proclamations, but in a personal, elegiac voice, gently chiding rather than criticizing the weak descendants of mighty forefathers. Vörösmarty's deeply felt convictions are given full ex-

pression through the magic of language (a reformed and rejuvenated Hungarian) and style (a seductively personal blend of classical forms and pre-Romantic turns). Even in this, his best-known epic creation, Vörösmarty was essentially a lyric rather than an epic poet.

The classical influence always remained discernible in Vörösmarty's works: He continued to reject the effusive rhetoric of fashionable poetry, to defend pure sentiment from the inroads of mere sentimentality, and to seek an ultimate rationale behind man's existence and the course of human history. At the same time, he could not resist Romanticism, especially since it emphasized the role of the individual, the power of the supernatural, and the incomprehensible and erratic nature of human events—traits which made Romanticism especially attractive to Hungarians. Even in his early works, Vörösmarty had exhibited an exalted manner of expression and an unusual breadth of vision; these are elements of his natural pre-Romantic disposition. In *Zalán futása*, however, he reveals even more of his Romanticism, in the frequency of intimate episodes, the role of Titans and fairies, and the depiction of earthy love affairs, while in form, structure, and the presentation of his central characters, he strictly conforms to classical requirements.

USE OF FOLK TRADITIONS

Around the end of the 1820's, the liberal intelligentsia of Hungary began to turn toward the commoners in their search for allies against Habsburg oppression. The clearest thinkers among them also realized that the cultural regeneration of the country could not be accomplished without the adoption and utilization of folk traditions, especially folk literature. The wave of literary populism, so eloquently promoted by Johann G. Herder and the Grimm brothers in Germany, made rapid gains in Hungary. From the first decades of the nineteenth century, the poets made it one of their goals to be able to write in the manner of folk songs or, indeed, to write "folk songs." Vörösmarty's works in this genre resembled the genuine article more closely than did those of his contemporaries. He was intimately familiar with life in rural Hungary and was able to use the expressions of the villagers with ease. His folk songs include didactic lyrics placed in the mouths of his Populist heroes, as well as lyrical passages that express his own feelings. An excellent example of the latter is "Haj, száj, szem" ("Hair,

Lips, Eyes"), a flirty outpouring of infatuation that imaginatively mirrors the sentiments expressed in one of the popular songs of the time. In adapting the direct and unaffected voice of the Hungarian people to formal literature, Vörösmarty was the direct forerunner of the most brilliant Hungarian Populist poet, Sándor Petőfi.

CSONGOR ÉS TÜNDE

Csongor és Tünde, a fairy play in five acts, completed in 1830, profited greatly from Vörösmarty's use of Populist elements. It tells the story of two lovers who, after becoming separated, overcome a number of earthly and mythical temptations and obstacles in order to be reunited. Beyond this, however, the play is a dramatic tale with philosophical and allegorical overtones. Csongor seeks not only his own happiness but the fulfillment of humankind as well. The setting of his sojourn is the entire earth; the three wanderers whom he meets represent the worst of negative human traits, while the monologue of Night reveals the course of human history. The story has a moral: Greed, conquest, and the desire for abstract knowledge do not necessarily bring happiness; on the contrary, they can be destructive.

Vörösmarty based *Csongor és Tünde* on a sixteenth century epic, the *Story of Prince Argirus*, which had survived as cheap popular entertainment. Nevertheless, the play has remained enjoyable and worthy of the stage. This may be because it presents a romantic panorama of the world, with everyday figures, conspiracy, jealousy, evil, and the drunkenness of lust. It is presented in harmonic unity and speaks in a popular, expressive language. The formal elements of classicism are present: The humorous passages are set in rhymed or unrhymed trochaic tetrameters, while the words of wisdom are spoken in iambic pentameters and hexameters. At the same time, Vörösmarty made judicious use of folkloric elements by introducing witches, fairies, trees with golden apples, the realms of Dawn and Night, and even the sons of the Devil fighting over their inheritance. The two heroes have their earthly counterparts in their escorts, whose realism provides a sober counterpoint to the idealism of Csongor.

SOMBER OUTLOOK

Crises and disillusionments were not infrequent in Vörösmarty's life. For more than ten years, he carried the memory of a youthful love doomed to failure by the values of a society based on titles and wealth. The poet never became a revolutionary, but his belief in rational, deliberate progress under the leadership of his class, the liberal nobility, was severely shaken. Much of his pessimism and sense of inferiority resulted from this early failure. Although he later successfully courted and married a woman twenty-four years his junior, dark thoughts and doubts continued to surface in his poems. Vörösmarty was also sensitive to the events of public life, which are reflected in the violently alternating emotions of his poems. He glowed with energy and optimism when the dynamism of the political scene and the liberalization of public discussions seemed to justify his faith in progress. At other times, such as when the assembly of Hungarian noblemen had disbanded without solving the problems entrusted to their care or when the cause of Polish independence was dealt a serious blow by the Austrian-inspired Galician peasant rebellion, his outlook became somber, and he wrote dark poems about the hopelessness of the human condition. "Az emberek" ("Mankind") posits malevolent intellect and the misguided anger of the masses as the two greatest obstacles to the fulfillment of humanity's dreams.

"THE SUMMONS"

In 1836, Vörösmarty wrote his best-known political poem, "Szózat" ("The Summons"). It appeared at a time when the outcome of the sharpening struggle between Vienna and the Hungarian reformers was undecided and when the Habsburg counteroffensive against the Hungarian independence movement was discouraging many of the more cautious liberals. Vörösmarty wrote what could be considered an affirmation of faith in the future of Hungary, but his scope was no longer narrowly nationalistic. With an enlarged and refined historical consciousness, he placed the fate of his country in the context of world history. The best and most promising characters of Hungary's history are invoked and made part of the new Hungarian course of action, in which the possibility of compromise is not mentioned. This is not a call to the weak, shiftless descendants of long-dead heroes; in the meticulously rhymed lines of this Romantic ode, which became the second national anthem of Hungary, the historical consciousness of a small but unbroken nation is proclaimed before the world.

SOCIOPOLITICAL CONTENT

Throughout the 1830's, the voice of Vörösmarty's lyricism steadily grew stronger though at the expense of his epic output. In more than a hundred epigrams, he demonstrated that there was no aspect of national life which escaped his attention. After 1835, he turned to the women of Hungary, a hitherto largely ignored segment of the population, and encouraged them to become active participants in the nation's cultural life. In the 1840's, the course of political events accelerated, adding new depth to the social content of Vörösmarty's poems. Inexperienced Hungarian leaders were thwarted by indecisiveness and internal squabbles. Vörösmarty seldom participated in these destructive recriminations, but his poems reveal the acute struggle raging within him.

"Gutenberg Albumba" ("For the Gutenberg Album") greets the decade on an accusatory note; according to Vörösmarty, the world is not deserving of the great heritage of Johann Gutenberg, inventor of the printing press. In "Liszt Ferenchez" ("To Ferenc Liszt"), he continues to broaden his concept of progress, striking the tones of a proud citizen of the world. His 1843 poem "Honszeretet" ("Patriotism") proposes the elimination of noble privileges and the cultivation of a strong bourgeoisie, with special stress on the full political and social equality of the common people.

"Gondolatok a könyvtárban" ("Thoughts in the Library") recapitulates Vörösmarty's ideas and states his political creed. It may also be considered the greatest document of the struggle with conscience experienced by nearly all nineteenth century Hungarian liberals. The poem starts with a passionate accusation aimed at humanity, pointing to a "horrible lesson": While millions are born into misery, only a few thousand enjoy the good life. Vörösmarty asks: "Where is the happiness of the majority?" In answer, the poet advocates the universal solidarity of humankind and continuous striving for a better future.

POET OF NATIONAL TRAGEDY

The bloodless and relatively nonviolent revolution of 1848 filled Vörösmarty with hope for the future; he greeted the freedom of the press, the institution of an accountable national government, and the abolition of serfdom with joyous and inspiring poems. As the reactionary circles of Austria planned to take stern measures against the Hungarian reformers, the poet began to have forebodings of tragedy and advised against rash, immoderate action. The counsel of confident Hungarian radicals, however, prevailed; there was a desperate armed struggle between the imperial forces and the small army of independent Hungary. By the autumn of 1849, the Hungarians were defeated, with the help of sizable Russian forces, and the worst forebodings of Vörösmarty were realized.

Because he had actively supported the cause of "rebels," Vörösmarty was forced into hiding to avoid the vengeance of the imperial military authorities. By 1850, he thought it advisable to turn himself in to the authorities, who dismissed his case after a brief investigation. The man was free, but the poet was fatally wounded, not only by the military defeat and the subsequent humiliation of his nation, but also by the loss of his friends (some of whom died on the battlefield, some of whom were imprisoned, and some of whom chose exile) and by the shattering of his hopes and beliefs. In the sterile atmosphere of absolutist control, there was hardly a trace left of Hungarian cultural life: Publications ceased, institutions were disbanded, and even the reading public lost its disposition to support Hungarian literature. Vörösmarty encountered serious problems supporting his family, and his literary activities suffered.

Vörösmarty became "the poet of national tragedy," reduced to expressions of hopelessness and grief over the fate of a nation which was being destroyed in full view of an "uncaring, indifferent world." The obsessive power of this erstwhile lyric voice, however, reached new heights in "A vén cigány" ("The Old Gypsy"); completed about a year before the poet's death, it became one of Vörösmarty's most-recited poems. It was befitting that Vörösmarty chose the figure of an aged musician-entertainer to symbolize the fate of the Hungarian poet of the times. The poet looks toward the future of humankind even while examining its present predicament and arrives at a mood of faint hopefulness only after having traversed the whirlpools of despair. In the process, the language and the association of the images have become almost demented, and the poet expresses with near-biblical intensity his exaltation and pain. Hope is not dead; in his swan song, the fatally broken poet calls for a "cleansing storm" to bring a better world and a genuine occasion for universal rejoicing.

OTHER MAJOR WORKS

PLAYS: *Csongor és Tünde*, pr. 1830; *A kincske-resök*, pr. 1833; *Vérnász*, pb. 1833; *A fátyol titkai*, pr. 1834; *Arpád ébredése*, pr. 1837; *Marót Ban*, pb. 1838; *Julius Caesar*, pr. 1840 (translation of William Shakespeare's play); *Lear király*, pr. 1856 (translation of Shakespeare's play).

BIBLIOGRAPHY

Basa, Eniko Molnár, ed. *Hungarian Literature*. New York: Griffon House, 1993. A historical and critical analysis of Hungarian literature. Includes bibliographic references.

Jones, D. Mervyn. *Five Hungarian Writers*. Oxford, England: Clarendon Press, 1966. A critical study of Vörösmarty's works and those of four other Hungarian writers including Sándor Petofi, József Eötvös, Kelemen Mikes, and Miklós Zrínyi.

Klaniczay, Tibor, József Szauder, and Miklós Szabolcsi. *History of Hungarian Literature*. London: Collet's, 1964. Provides a historical background to the works of Vörösmarty. Includes bibliographic references.

Menczer, Béla. *A Commentary on Hungarian Literature*. Castrop-Rauxel, Germany: Amerikai Magyar Kiadó, 1956. A critical study of selected works of Hungarian literature. Includes bibliographic references.

Reményi, József. *Hungarian Writers and Literature*. New Brunswick, N.J.: Rutgers University Press, 1964. A critical and historical study of Hungarian novelists, critics, and poets.

András Boros-Kazai;
bibliography updated by the editors

ANDREI VOZNESENSKY

Born: Moscow, U.S.S.R.; May 12, 1933

PRINCIPAL POETRY

Mozaika, 1960
Parabola, 1960
Treugol'naya grusha, 1962
Antimiry, 1964 (*Antiworlds*, 1966)
Akhillesovo serdtse, 1966
Voznesensky: Selected Poems, 1966
Antiworlds and the Fifth Ace, expanded edition 1967
Stikhi, 1967
The Shadow of Sound, 1969
Dogalypse, 1972
Little Woods: Recent Poems by Andrei Voznesensky, 1972
Soblazn, 1978
Nostalgia for the Present, 1978
Stikhotvoreniia: Poemy, 1983
An Arrow in the Wall: Selected Poetry and Prose, 1987
Rov, 1987 (*The Ditch: A Spiritual Trial*, 1987)
On the Edge: Poems and Essays from Russia, 1991
Gadanie po knige, 1994

OTHER LITERARY FORMS

Andrei Voznesensky is known primarily for his lyric poetry; however, he has produced a body of experimental work that challenges the borders between literary forms. For example, his long work "Oza" (1964) is a literary montage alternating verse with prose passages and incorporating several points of view. *Avos* (1972; *Story Under Full Sail*, 1974), based on the life of the Russian diplomat and explorer Nikolai Petrovich Rezanov, is sometimes classified as poetry, sometimes as prose. Voznesensky's prose writings include a short memoir, "I Am Fourteen," which sheds light on his friendship with the famed Russian writer Boris Pasternak; "O" (about), which appears in *An Arrow in the Wall*, a critical commentary on art and literature; "Little Crosses," an essay on spirituality; and the introductory chapter to the monograph *Chagall Discovered: From Russian and Private Collections* (1988). In addition, he has written a play, *Save Your Faces* (1971), and has collaborated on musical and theatrical pieces such as the "rock opera" *Iunona i Avos* (Juno and Avos).

ACHIEVEMENTS

During the early 1960's Andrei Voznesensky, like his contemporary Yevgeny Yevtushenko, enjoyed enormous popularity in the Soviet Union. His books sold hundreds of thousands of copies as soon as they were

Andrei Voznesensky (© Arkady Hershman)

published, and fans flocked to public readings held in athletic stadiums to accommodate audiences of ten thousand and more.

His poetry, which is intellectually demanding, drew critical acclaim internationally as well as within the Soviet Union. His literary awards span three decades. *Antiworlds* was nominated for the Lenin Prize in literature in 1966, and "The Stained Glass Panel Master" won the State Literature Prize in 1978. He was awarded the International Award for Distinguished Achievement in Poetry in 1972, and his collection *An Arrow in the Wall*, edited by William Jay Smith and F. D. Reeve, received the *New York Times* Editor's Choice Award in 1987.

BIOGRAPHY

Born in Moscow in 1933 to a well-educated family, Andrei Andreyevich Voznesensky was exposed to art and literature at an early age. His mother, a teacher, read him poetry and inspired his interest in major Russian writers. His father, a professor of engineering, introduced him to the work of the Spanish artist Francisco de Goya, which would later inspire "I Am Goya," one of Voznesensky's best-known poems. While growing up, Voznesensky pursued interests in the arts, especially painting, but he did not focus on poetry until 1957, the year he completed a degree from the Moscow Institute of Architecture. Then, in a strange twist of fate, a fire at the institute destroyed his thesis project. For Voznesensky, this was a sign that his future lay not in architecture but in poetry.

In the same year, he met the famed Russian writer Boris Pasternak, with whom he had been corresponding. Pasternak served as a mentor for Voznesensky, but the younger poet quickly found his own voice. The similarities between the work of the two authors lie in their moral vision and their goals as writers to revive Russian literature after years of oppression under the dictatorship of Joseph Stalin. An essential difference is in their fates. In spite of an easing of government censorship following Stalin's death in 1953, Pasternak was expelled from the powerful Soviet Writers' Union for the 1957 publication of *Dr. Zhivago*. The novel's free-thinking protagonist criticizes Soviet Communism. However, in the changing literary-political climate of the time, Voznesensky quickly became one of the best-known poets in the Soviet Union. In 1960 his first collection, *Mozaika* (mosaic), appeared in print, and he published a number of collections in rapid succession, as audiences responded enthusiastically to the freshness of his work.

The success of Voznesensky, his contemporary Yevgeny Yevtushenko, and other "liberal" writers created a backlash within the Writers' Union. By 1963 Voznesensky had come under attack from the more orthodox literary establishment, the government-controlled press, and Soviet premier Nikita Khrushchev. Unlike Pasternak, who was censored for the content of his writing, Voznesensky was denounced for his innovative style, which critics claimed produced a decadent, superficial art, devoid of meaning. Charges of formalism and obscurantism resurfaced throughout the 1960's and into the following decade.

In response, Voznesensky addressed his critics directly in his poetry, and he began to produce verse on the subject of creative freedom and the nature of art. He defended the complexity and ambiguity of his work, asserting, "if the poems are complicated, why then, so is life." He also spoke out against government censorship. In 1967 he openly supported fellow writer Aleksandr Solzhenitsyn, who had been expelled from the Writers' Union and later exiled from the Soviet Union for his attack on Soviet censorship. In 1979 Voznesensky participated in the publication of an independent literary journal.

In spite of recurring conflicts with government and the conservative literary establishment, Voznesensky incurred only minor punishment. Throughout his career, he has been able to travel abroad, live comfortably, and publish regularly. He remained committed to innovative and experimental art forms, producing a body of work that challenges conventional classification. Married to the writer and critic Zoia Boguslavskaia, he had one son.

ANALYSIS

The American poet W. H. Auden remarked that Andrei Voznesensky is a writer who understands that "a poem is a verbal artifact which must be as skillfully and solidly constructed as a table or a motorcycle." Voznesensky is well known for his technical virtuosity and structural innovation. His metric and rhyme schemes vary, often determined by the aural and visual aspects of the work. He pays close attention to surface patterning and sound play—assonance, alliteration, shaped text, stepped lines, palindromes—and often startles the reader with shifts in perspective, incongruous juxtaposition of images, and unexpected rhyme created by inserting slang or colloquial language into a line. He confronts the reader with a staggering array of metaphor, historical reference, and cultural allusion. Evidence of his early training in painting and architecture abounds in his work, which has been described as cubist, surrealist, and futurist. Voznesensky acknowledged, "As a poet I have been more profitably influenced by ancient Russian churches and by the works of Le Corbusier than by other poets."

Voznesensky's concern with technique and experimentation relates directly to the content of his writing and his central concern with human destiny, which he views as dependent on interconnectedness. For him, without a sense of connection to one another, to culture and tradition, and to the planet, humanity may fall into a destructive spiral. In a mechanized, technological world, the potential for fragmentation and alienation is great. The responsibility of the artist is to expose relationships, to "peel the skin from the planet."

Voznesensky seeks to achieve his goal by breaking away from habitualized methods of seeing, from routines that limit and fragment vision. His wordplay, his seemingly bizarre selections of imagery, his multiple perspectives, and his blurring of genres are all designed to defamiliarize the world, allowing the reader to discover the spiritual ecosystem of existence. While Voznesensky's themes are universal, his innovativeness, particularly his sound play, makes his work difficult to translate. Effective English versions of his work are the Haywood/Blake 1967 edition *Antiworlds and the Fifth Ace* and the award-winning collection *An Arrow in the Wall*, edited by William Jay Smith and F. D. Reeve.

"I AM GOYA"

One of the earliest and best-known of his poems, "I Am Goya," (1959) exemplifies Voznesensky's skill in creating new forms to examine broad themes. He frames the poem by opening and closing with the same line, "I am Goya." In identifying with Goya, a nineteenth century Spanish painter known for his harsh depictions of war, Voznesensky establishes an immediate link across time, space, and artistic genres. He reinforces these links in each of the four stanzas with an eclectic range of images and allusions and by the repetition of the first line. The horrors of war belong to all ages, and the artist's role is to transcend the immediate and speak to the universal, "hammer[ing] stars into the unforgetting sky—like nails."

Voznesensky composed "I Am Goya" aloud rather than writing it on paper in order to develop fully the aural qualities of the verse. He described it as "picking the words, so that they would ring out" like the bells of an ancient monastery playing "the music of grief." To this end, Voznesensky combines repetition of sounds with an uninterrupted beat that tolls throughout the poem. The rhythms of the poem anticipate the powerful image "of a woman hanged whose body like a bell/ tolled over a blank square," then embed it in a synesthetic format.

"PARABOLIC BALLAD"

Voznesensky considered "Parabolic Ballad" (1960) one of his best poems. Citing the career of the French painter Paul Gauguin as a model, Voznesensky justifies the ambiguity and experimental nature of his own work and reasserts his aesthetics. Like Gauguin, who "To reach the royal Louvre,/ Set his course/ On a detour via Java and Sumatra," the poet must not take the direct route, choose the ready-made symbol, or speak in clichés. Rather, the artist must follow the trajectory of a rocket, a parabola, in order to escape "the earth's force of gravitation" and explore the far side of the universe.

"OZA"

Written in 1964, a year after Voznesensky was denounced for formalism and obscurity, "Oza" is a bold response to his critics. This complex narrative poem contemplates the fate of humanity in a technological society and continues to experiment with poetic structure. Sections of prose alternate with poetry, themes intersect, and point of view shifts. The work is rich in literary and historical allusion. One section parodies Edgar Allan Poe's poem "The Raven"; another satirizes former Soviet dictator Joseph Stalin.

Introduced as a diary found in a hotel in Dubna, the site of a Soviet nuclear research facility, "Oza" describes a world rearranged by technology. The protagonist, Zoia, is a well-meaning scientist transformed through her own arrogance and complacency into an automaton named Oza. Zoia means "life" in Russian, but in the rearrangement of letters of her name, the "I" has been lost, suggesting the loss of self in a rigidly mechanized culture. Like Zoia/Oza, the poet risks losing his identity. In a scene described sometimes comically from the perspective of a ceiling mirror, the poet is invisible, immune to the inversion of the reflecting surface, and alienated from his fellow beings. Although unseen, he makes himself heard, proclaiming "I am Andrei; not just anyone/ All progress is regression/ If the progress breaks man down."

THE DITCH: A SPIRITUAL TRIAL

This long narrative poem explores human greed. The actual ditch is the site of a massacre near Simferopol, a city on the Crimean Peninsula, where in 1941 twelve thousand Jews were executed by Nazis. In the 1980's, grave robbing occurred at the site. Although in 1985

several men were convicted and received prison sentences—and it is to this event that the "trial" of the subtitle alludes—the looting continued. On a visit to the site two years after the trial, Voznesensky observed skulls that had been excavated and smashed for the bits of gold in the teeth.

As in earlier works, Voznesensky employs contrasting imagery, shifts in perspective, and inversions. A prose "afterword" introduces the work, suggesting an inversion of values. The mixture of voices and genres and the range of references take the subject beyond the specific crime into an examination of human nature.

GADANIE PO KNIGE

Inspired by traditional Russian fortune-telling, *Gadanie po knige* (telling by the book) examines the interconnectedness of chance and design. In this collection, Voznesensky takes his word play to a new level, creating complex, multilingual meanings. Like a fortune-teller, he shuffles language and lays it out in patterns: circles, palindromes, anagrams. At times he mixes English words with Russian ones, switching between the Cyrillic and Roman alphabets as well; he fragments words from both languages and rearranges the syllables. What may initially appear random, pointless, or merely amusing surprisingly yields meaning, as when he exploits phonetically MMM, the name of a financial institution involved in a costly scandal. He connects MMM with the English word "money," the Russian word for "mania," and finally, the Russian slang for "nothing."

OTHER MAJOR WORKS

LONG FICTION: *Avos*, 1972 (*Story Under Full Sail*, 1974).

PLAYS: *Save Your Faces*, pr. 1971; *I Am Goya*, pr. 1982 (music by Nigel Osborne); *Iunona i Avos*, pr. 1983 (music by Alexei Rybnikov).

NONFICTION: *The Shadow of Sound*, 1969.

BIBLIOGRAPHY

Airaudi, Jesse T. "Hard to Be a God: The Political Antiworlds of Voznesensky, Sokilov, and the Brothers Strugatsky." In *Visions of the Fantastic: Selected Essays from the Fifteenth International Conference on the Fantastic in the Arts*, edited by Allienne R. Becker. London: Greenwood Press, 1996. Airaudi provides a sound rationale for Voznesensky's use of the fantastic to escape from the false, primary world imposed by governments and ruled by ideologies. Airaudi places Voznesensky in the tradition of the Russian writer Nikolai Gogol, yet suggests Western readers can best understand Voznesensky in terms of surrealism.

Brown, Deming. *Soviet Russian Literature Since Stalin.* London: Cambridge University Press, 1978. This well-documented literary history provides a good overview of the complex and ever-fluctuating relationship between literature and politics in the two decades following the death of dictator Joseph Stalin. Voznesensky is referred to throughout the book and is a key figure in the fifth chapter, "The Younger Generation of Poets."

Carlisle, Olga. *Poets on Street Corners: Portraits of Fifteen Russian Poets.* New York: Random House, 1968. In this collection of biographical sketches, Carlisle, the granddaughter of noted Russian writer Leonid Andreyev, has included poets who write about and for ordinary Russians living ordinary lives. Her chapter on Voznesensky features lengthy quotations from interviews with the poet between 1963 and 1967. Voznesensky's comments on the significance of poetry and the role of the poet are particularly illuminating.

Plimpton, George, ed. *Beat Writers at Work: The Paris Review.* New York: Random House, 1999. Conversations between Voznesensky and American poets Allen Ginsberg and Peter Orlovsky provide an entertaining, behind-the-scenes look at the writers as they discuss the poet's craft.

Porter, Robert, ed. *Seven Soviet Poets.* London: Gerald Duckworth, 2000. Porter's slender collection provides a thoughtful introduction, bibliographies, a historical reference guide, annotations, and biographical time lines for Voznesensky as well as other twentieth century Russian poets. These sections are in English, but the poetry is in Russian. For readers who are new to the language, the collection provides a good starting point with a supplemental vocabulary.

K Edgington

W

DAVID WAGONER

Born: Massillon, Ohio; June 5, 1926

PRINCIPAL POETRY

Dry Sun, Dry Wind, 1953
A Place to Stand, 1958
Poems, 1959
The Nesting Ground, 1963
Staying Alive, 1966
New and Selected Poems, 1969
Working Against Time, 1970
Riverbed, 1972
Sleeping in the Woods, 1974
A Guide to Dungeness Spit, 1975
Collected Poems, 1956-1976, 1976
Travelling Light, 1976
Who Shall Be the Sun?, 1978
In Broken Country, 1979
Landfall, 1981
First Light, 1983
*Through the Forest: New and Selected Poems, 1977-
    1987*, 1987
Walt Whitman Bathing: Poems, 1996
Traveling Light: Collected and New Poems, 1999
The House of Song, 2002

OTHER LITERARY FORMS

Best known as a poet and novelist, David Wagoner has also written plays—An Eye for an Eye for an Eye was produced in Seattle in 1973—as well as short fiction and essays. He edited and wrote the introduction to *Straw for the Fire: From the Notebooks of Theodore Roethke, 1943-1963* (1972).

ACHIEVEMENTS

It is possible that David Wagoner will be best remembered as one of the finest "nature" and "regional" poets of twentieth century America, and as one who has been instrumental in generating renewed interest in Native American lore. To categorize him so narrowly, however, does disservice to his versatility, and to the breadth of his talent and interests. Publishing steadily since the early 1950's, Wagoner has created a body of work that impresses not only for the number of volumes produced, but also for their quality. His novels have been praised for their energy and humor and in many cases for the immediacy of their Old West atmosphere. He received a Ford Fellowship for drama (1964), but it is as a poet that he has been most often honored: with a Guggenheim Fellowship (1956), a National Institute of Arts and Letters Grant (1967), a National Endowment for the Arts Grant (1969). *Poetry* has awarded him its Morton Dauwen Zabel Prize (1967), its Oscar Blumenthal Prize (1974), and its Eunice Tietjens Memorial Prize (1971). *Sleeping in the Woods* and *Collected Poems, 1956-1976* were nominated for National Book Awards, and *In Broken Country* for an American Book Award. Wagoner was elected a chancellor of the Academy of American Poets in 1978, succeeding Robert Lowell. In 1991, he was awarded the $25,000 Ruth Lilly Poetry Prize and in 1997 he was honored with the Ohioana Book Award for *Walt Whitman Bathing*.

BIOGRAPHY

David Russell Wagoner was born on June 5, 1926, in Massillon, Ohio, and was reared in Whiting, Indiana, the son of a steelworker. After receiving his B.A. degree from Pennsylvania State University in 1947, and his M.A. from Indiana University two years later, Wagoner began his teaching career at DePauw University, returning after a year to Pennsylvania State University. During this time, he was deeply influenced by Theodore Roethke, with whom he had studied as an undergraduate. In 1954, Roethke was instrumental in Wagoner's move to the University of Washington, where he is now Professor of English. X. J. Kennedy has speculated that perhaps "the most valuable service Roethke ever performed for Wagoner was to bring him to the Pacific Northwest and expose him to rain forests"—and to the culture of the Northwest Coast and Plateau Indians, one might add. Not only has Wagoner made use in his own poems of specific Native American myths and legends, but he has also absorbed the Indians' animistic spiritual-

David Wagoner (© Paul V. Thomas)

ism into his own philosophy. In the author's note to *Who Shall Be the Sun?*, he explains that Indians "did not place themselves above their organic and inorganic companions on earth but recognized with awe that they shared the planet as equals." Wagoner finds this equality "admirable and worthy of imitation," as much of his poetry indicates.

When not teaching, Wagoner has worked as a railroad section hand, a park policeman, and a short-order cook. He is a member of the Society of American Magicians. Since 1966 he has served as editor of *Poetry Northwest* and actively contributes poetry and commentary to a range of literary journals, including *Antioch Review*, *Atlantic*, *Harvard Review*, *New England Review*, *Poetry*, and *Prairie Schooner*.

ANALYSIS

Despite David Wagoner's accomplishments and honors, and despite the fact that his poems appear regularly in mass-circulation magazines such as *The New Yorker* and *The Atlantic Monthly*, as well as the literary quarterlies, he is generally conceded to be among the most under-appreciated of American poets. With the exception of "Staying Alive," few of his works are included in major poetry anthologies. There are several possible explanations for this. First, he lives in Seattle and has chosen as his primary subject matter the land and people of the Pacific Northwest—thus giving rise to the dismissive "regional" label. It is also possible that some of his own best qualities may work against him. His subject matter is anything but trendy; the reader searches his poems in vain for Vietnam, the Cold War, civil unrest, the sexual revolution, drugs, The Rolling Stones, or Watergate. The only explicit social comment one is likely to find is contained in a half dozen or so poems addressing the Weyerhaeuser Company, a logging firm, and its practice of clear-cutting three-mile swaths of virgin forest.

Perhaps the major problem, as X. J. Kennedy suggests, is Wagoner's very "readability." Much of his poetry seems, at least on first encounter, curiously unpoetic, even prosy. His unpretentious language and casual, conversational tone frequently combine with his sense of humor to create a deceptively simple surface for his complex and serious ideas. This simplicity does make the work accessible; on the other hand, it may actually encourage the casual or first-time reader to dismiss Wagoner's work as lightweight.

Even in his most alienated and melancholy early poems, Wagoner's wit continually asserts itself. He is fond of puns, palindromes, and other forms of wordplay, and makes frequent use of colloquialisms, folk sayings, clichés, non sequiturs, and other lunacies of ordinary speech, often twisting words or phrases in such a way that they take on startling new meanings. Still, it is not as a semantic magician that Wagoner should be remembered; there are not a great many "quotable" lines—in the sense of the exquisite image of dazzling insight to be isolated for admiration out of context—in his work. Wagoner is at least as much philosopher as poet, and his poems, effective as they are when looked at individually, together take on cumulative power and meaning. Outwardly dissimilar poems are often interrelated below the surface to a marked degree. The result is a coherent, explicitly delineated philosophy, a "way" of life based on acceptance, self-reliance, and a profound reverence for the natural world.

Those who insist on calling David Wagoner a regional or nature poet are certainly correct, to a point. From his earliest collection on, his work has amply indicated a sensitivity to the landscape around him. Later poems, in particular, have been praised for their descriptive qualities. The same can be said of many writers, but the use to which Wagoner has put his rain forests, mountains, rivers, and coastlines, is uniquely his own. His wilderness, with its unsentimental, uncompromising beauty, serves on one level as a conventional metaphor: the landscape, physical and spiritual, through which one travels on one's life journey. Rather than seeing rocks, trees, and animals, however, as separate entities to be reacted to—climbed over, caught and eaten, run from—Wagoner views the natural world as the medium through which humans can best learn to know themselves. Put another way, if one can accept one's place as a part of the ongoing natural processes of life, death, decay, and rebirth, one begins to "see things whole." It is this sense of wholeness, this appreciation for the interrelatedness of all the "organic and inorganic companions on earth" to which Wagoner invites his reader, as if to a feast.

The way to this ideal state involves an apparent paradox: In order to find oneself, one must first lose oneself, shedding the subject/object, mind/body, spirit/intellect dualities typical of "rational" Western thought. In "Staying Alive," a traveler lost in the woods is faced not only with problems of physical survival but also with "the problem of recognition," by anyone or anything external that might be looking for him, as well as recognition of his own true nature. Unable to make contact with others, the traveler is advised that "You should have a mirror/ With a tiny hole in the back . . ." that will reflect the sun and flash messages, that will reflect one's familiar physical image and that, because of the aperture, will also allow one to see through one's physical self to the wholeness of the surrounding natural world.

It is clear that, in Wagoner's view, modern industrial society has created too many wastelands and polluted waterways, and more than enough fragmented citizens such as "The Man from the Top of the Mind," with "the light bulb screwed into his head,/ The vacuum tube of his sex, the electric eye." This gleaming creature of pure intellect can "Bump through our mazes like a genius rat" but is incapable of any human emotion except destructive rage. On every level, it would appear, one has become estranged—from oneself, from others and from one's environment. In place of this fragmentation and alienation, Wagoner offers synthesis: the ability to see and experience things whole. In a remarkable series of poems, he not only extends the offer but also provides an explicit, step-by-step guide—a Scouts' handbook or survival manual for the reader to follow.

"HANDBOOK" POEMS

Although these "Handbook" poems span several volumes (from *Staying Alive* through *In Broken Country*), they are best read as a single group. All are similar in language and tone; all address an unnamed "you," offering advice for coping with problems that might arise on a wilderness trip. Should one find oneself lost, one need only remember that "Staying alive . . . is a matter of calming down." Further poems instruct one on what to do when "Breaking Camp," or "Meeting a Bear" ("try your meekest behavior,/ . . . eyes downcast"), even after "Being Shot" ("if you haven't fallen involuntarily, you may/ Volunteer now . . ."). In each case, "you," the reader, are put in touch—in most cases both literally and figuratively—with something that has previously seemed foreign or outside the realm of ordinary human experience. In other words, lack of sensitivity to natural processes results in estrangement and isolation. By becoming more receptive, and perhaps less "top of the mind" rational, one allows for the possibility of "rescue" in the form of new understanding.

Frequently, since they typically involve a stripping away of the ego, these new insights prove to be humbling. Traveling "From Here to There," one can see the destination easily, while the distance deceives and one is confused by mirages: "Water put out like fire, . . . flying islands,/ The unbalancing act of mountains upside down." The problem of recognition resurfaces; nothing is what it seems. There is nothing to do but keep slogging: "One Damn Thing After Another," until finally, having "shrugged off most illusions" you "find yourself" in a place "where nothing is the matter/ . . . asking one more lesson." Still harder to accept are the lessons that teach acquiescence in mortality; lessons that teach that even a violent death is as much a part of the life process as birth. In "Being Shot," one finds oneself helpless on the forest floor, "study[ing]/ At first hand . . . the symptoms of shock." With Wagoner's open and accepting life view, death is as natural and therefore as necessary as birth, and "To burrow deep, for a deep winter," as "Staying Alive" advises, will result, come spiring, in a renewal of some kind, if only because—should one not survive—one's decaying body will provide nutrients with which to feed other forms of life.

A series of poems in the final section of *In Broken Country* provide a guide to survival in the desert rather than the forest. Similar in tone and intent to the earlier "Handbook" poems, these divert from "The Right Direction" past "The Point of No Return," where ". . . from here on/ It will take more courage to turn than to keep going." The process is what matters.

DRY SUN, DRY WIND

The "you" in these poems is never identified. There is a strong sense that the reader is being addressed directly, as if he or she has enrolled in an Outward Bound course and is receiving a curious mix of practical and cryptic last-minute advice before setting out on a solo adventure. There is also a sense of the poet talking to himself, working his own way both from the industrialized northern Indiana of his youth to the rain forests of Washington, and, in a parallel journey, from a sense of alienation to one of harmony. In *Dry Sun, Dry Wind*, Wagoner's first collection, his affinity with nature is already apparent, but no real contact seems possible. The poet remains isolated, seeing about him images of destruction ("sun carries death to leaves"), decay and uncertainty ("last year's gully is this year's hill"). Time flies; memory is unable to delay it. The natural environment, blighted though it is, is "Too much to breathe, think, see" ("Warning"). In the early poems, the relationship between man and nature—or man and anything or anyone else—was generally one of conflict, an ongoing struggle for control resulting in disillusionment: a war, rather than a reconciliation, of opposites. "Progress" was often best achieved through violence to the land, and the stillness that in later works will open the way to enlightenment has precisely the opposite effect in early poems such as "Lull." Recognition, and, by extension, synthesis, are possible only when "the wind hums or wheels," creating movement, a kind of artificial life.

It is perhaps significant that none of the poems from this first volume has been included in any subsequent collection. The suggestion is that Wagoner quickly moved beyond these early efforts, struggling with his own problem of recognition as he searched for a true voice of his own. The major themes are there, often apparent only in their negative aspects, as, for example, the fragmentation and conflict that will yield in later poems to synthesis. In addition, there is at least one poem that deserves reading on its own merit.

"Sam the Aerialist" is "sick of walking." He wants to fly. Like the poet, like the trickster of Native American myth, like dreamers everywhere, he hungers for the impossible and yearns to exceed his natural bounds. In this, Sam is like most of the human race. His crime is not so much his desire to fly as it is his attitude, which is aggressive, self-serving, exploitative: Sam has a "lust for air" that is anything but properly reverent. The birds, therefore, instead of sharing their secrets with him, "have kept/ Far from his mind." "Birds are evil," Sam concludes,

> they fly
> Against the wind. How many have I pulled
> Apart . . .
> To learn the secret?

Sam learns by destroying. He lacks the empathy that could move him toward true understanding, and he remains isolated, cut off from his own nature as well as that around him.

Although he is never again referred to by name, there is a sense in which Sam the Aerialist's presence is felt throughout Wagoner's later poetry. He represents a kind of high-technology Everyman; his failings are the failings of society at large. He makes a stubborn but useful pupil. If such a one can absorb the early wisdom of "The Nesting Ground," that sometimes standing still will gain one more than flight; if he can follow where the "Handbook" poems lead and lose himself in the discovery that there is a bottom as well as a top to his mind, then perhaps all is not lost. Certainly, there is an aspect of Sam in the "you" to whom the "Handbook" poems speak.

Another step beyond specific survival lore in Wagoner's progress from alienation to harmony is represented by several groups of poems based on the mythology of the Northwest Coast and the Plateau Indians. Wagoner's interest in Native American culture is long-standing. "Talking to the Forest," included in *Staying Alive*, responds to a Skagit tribesman's statement: "When we can understand animals, we will know the change is halfway. When we can talk to the forest, we will know the change has come." In *Riverbed*, "Old Man, Old Man" teaches that "Every secret is as near as your fingers." It was in the 1974 collection *Sleeping in the Woods*, however, that the pivotal group, "Seven Songs for an Old Voice," first appeared. This Voice, still singing the ancient animistic wisdom as reverently as it did in the days before the Iron People (whites) arrived, offers hymns equally to Fire, which keeps enemies away, and to the Maker of Nightmares, who "eat[s] my sleep for . . . food." Other songs address death, the soul leaving the body and returning to it, and the First People, nonhumans who became rocks, animals, plants, and water when they learned of the coming of humankind. No matter what the subject, the tone is one of acceptance and awe. Death is part of life. Terrifying as they are, nightmares are not to be denied. The Voice promises to "drink what you bring me in my broken skull,/ The bitter water which once was sweet as morning."

WHO SHALL BE THE SUN?

These "Seven Songs" are included in *Who Shall Be the Sun?* along with other previously collected poems, new groups of "Songs for the Dream-Catchers," "Songs of Only-One," "Songs of He-Catches-Nothing," and two groups of Myths and Legends—one each from the Plateau and Northwest Coast Indian tribes. Wagoner explains in his Author's Note that the Myths and Legends are retellings of existing stories. The Songs are original works, but Wagoner stresses his debt to the Indians' spirit if not their words.

As Robert K. Cording points out, these Indian-lore poems allow Wagoner to blend several hitherto separate themes. For the native American, the interrelationship of man and nature has traditionally been a given, as has a belief in the power of various religious and quasi-religious rituals and practices that non-Indians might call magic. Magic, as a motif, appears fairly frequently in Wagoner's earlier work; in this collection, human beings "magically" converse with the spirits of the First People in the trees above them and the dust beneath their feet. It is not only the First People who are capable of such transformations. Animals can take on human shapes; humans too can put on different skins. In certain situations the dead can return to earth and the living can cross in safety to the land of the dead. Magic here is more than sleight-of-hand and an Indian's dreams are tools more powerful than the technology of Sam the Aerialist, as the title poem shows. "Who Shall Be the Sun?" the People ask, and despite his apparent lack of suitability for the job, Snake's ability to dream, coupled with his seemly modesty, allows him to succeed where the assertive, egocentric Raven, Hawk, and Coyote (who can merely think) have failed.

"Who Shall Be the Sun?" and other poems in the Myth and Legend sections are written in a language that closely echoes the cadences of English prose translations of Indian legends with which the reader may be familiar. The song groups are distinct from one another, the tone and rhythm consistent with each singer's personality and the subject addressed. It should be noted that although the pervading attitude is one of reverence and peace, not all of these poems present such a harmonious picture. Coyote and Raven, classic tricksters, are as likely to cause harm with their pranks as they are to improve the lot of those they purport to help, as the Indian culture, like any other, has always had its share of misfits, liars, and thieves. There is disease, madness, and death, of course, as well as someone called Only-One, who, half-blinded by the beak of an injured heron he had attempted to heal, sees only halves of things. Scarred by smallpox, neither truly dead nor truly alive, Only-One is an isolated soul. He dances with Dead Man, and the half-girl he takes for his bride turns out to be the bird that blinded him.

IN BROKEN COUNTRY

Following *Who Shall Be the Sun?*, Wagoner returned to a more characteristic range of subjects. *In Broken Country* mixes poems about love, childhood memories, parents, poets (including a lovely elegy to Roethke), bums, and prisoners (Wagoner himself included). A dozen desert "Handbook" poems are preceded by a series of self-parodying mock-"Handbook" entries. *Landfall* also covers a broad range, although a particularly strong unifying cord runs throughout. A number of the most moving poems are about making contact with one's past, not merely in the sense of looking back and remembering, but in trying for reconciliation with aspects of one's life that may have caused one pain. Over the years, Wagoner has written poems about his father—puttering around the house, building a wall—a pleasant-seeming man, drained by his job in the steel mill. A certain edgy ambivalence of tone in these poems has kept the elder Wagoner an insubstantial figure. "My Father's Garden" changes this, introducing the reader to a man who picked "flowers" for his family: "small gears and cogwheels/ With teeth like petals," found in the scrap-heap he passed on his way to work, work which "melted" his mind to the point that all he retained of an education in the classics was enough Latin and Greek for crossword puzzles. Paired with this is "My Father's Ghost," an extraordinary piece based on a Midwestern folk saying and reminiscent in tone of the Indian songs. Having performed the proper rituals, the poet should be able to see his father's spirit; but the charms do not work. The room stays empty. It is necessary to "imagine him," then; "and dream him/ Returning unarmed, unharmed. Words, words. I hold/ My father's ghost in my arms in his dark doorway."

The final section, "A Sea Change," describes a journey with no destination, in which the poet and his wife leave forest, desert, and marsh behind and head out to sea. This sea voyage is more explicitly psychological than the "Handbook" poems, but here, too, reconciliations take place. The travelers must come to terms with the unfamiliar element to which they have entrusted their lives; in doing so, they will discover that it is not so foreign as they thought. They must overcome their dread of the dimly seen monsters coiling in the depths. In doing so, they discover that the monsters never break through the "mirror" of the water's surface—suggesting, perhaps, that to accept one's demons as the Old Voice singer accepted nightmares and death is to rob them of much of their power. In contrast to Wagoner's explicitly instructive poems, the Sea Change group does not explain precisely by what means these primal fears are to be overcome or how other changes are to be brought about. At journey's end, "Landfall," the two travelers simply come "wallowing" ashore like their "hesitant helpless curious ancestors," having somehow been in touch with a past too dim for memory or rational understanding. On feet that "keep believing/ In the sea," they regain firm ground, asking, "Have we come home? Is this where we were born? . . . this place/ Where, again, we must learn to walk?"

Wagoner's own answer to this would be yes, over and over again, on all ground and in all weather, backward, on our hands, on water, and on air. Getting there means starting over; starting over means rebirth, renewal, a second chance to see things whole. In many ways, this is just what Wagoner has been doing throughout his career.

WALT WHITMAN BATHING

In *Walt Whitman Bathing*, Wagoner finds inspiration in American experience and landscape, translating it into stacked, searching clauses: "Above the river, over the broad hillside/ and down the slope in clusters and strewn throngs,/ cross-tangled and intermingled,/ wildflowers are blooming, seemingly all at once." Story and lyric take alternating turns at center stage, and his lines consistently find their breath—long and short, substantial and supple—as in "Mapmaking," from the compelling sequence on landscapes: "You fix your eyes on [landmarks], one at a time,/ And learn the hard way/ How hard it is to fabricate broken country."

The first half of the book consists of poems of nostalgic, personal reminiscence and public eulogies. He advises, in "In the Woods" that as "you" find "yourself" contemplating the trees,

> Now you may make yourself at home by doing without
> The pointless heroics of moving, by remaining
> Quiet, by holding still
> To take your place as they have taken theirs: by right
> Of discovery in this immanent domain,
> Simply by growing
> Accustomed to being here instead of nowhere.

The book's second half revisits many of Wagoner's familiar settings, themes, and stylistics: there is nature without trivial transcendence, flora and fauna, and verses heavy with pronouns, addressed to his ever-present and insistent "you." His insights run deep and are expressed with a soft-spoken directness intimately linked to his skepticism about humankind's role in the cosmos. Wagoner talks quietly with us—when not penned in the second-person singular, his poetry beckons us near—about the relativity of the self and about "Searching for more than you at the end of you."

Wagoner also presents moving poems about human affection, often set during his midwestern boyhood. "My Father Laughing in the Chicago Theater" memorably portrays "Two hundred and twenty horizontal pounds/ Of defensive lineman, of open-hearth melter" doubling over at the quips of vaudeville comics. Several poems also center on American Gothic-era memories (red-nosed cops, trained bears, boys who wear "nightgowns"), images kept from cliché by Wagoner's sure touch. Never folksy, the poems are plainspoken and display a formal virtuosity that allows Wagoner to penetrate beneath the surface, as when sketching his parents in three-stress lines: "They stand by the empty car,/ By the open driver's door,/ Waiting. The evening sun/ is glowing like pig-iron." The sum effect of the book is authoritative but detached, descriptive yet minimalistic.

TRAVELING LIGHT

Culling poems from forty-five years of published work, this generous retrospective calls on Wagoner's experiences of hiking and camping in mountain wilderness, comments on urban angst and paranoia based on his everyday urban existence, and provides a glimpse into his personal experience with literature, love, and death. His plain midwestern diction and even tone prevent him from moving into portentousness à la Sandburg, whom he meets and raises stakes on in such poems as "A Day in the City" and "The Apotheosis of the Garbageman." With a nod to Robert Penn Warren, he masters the poetic sequence ("Landscapes" or "Traveling Light"), and in a series on his late father, a steel-mill worker, he colloquially recalls his own sympathetic gestures:

> I shook the dying and dead
> Ashes down through the grate
> And, with firetongs, hauled out clinkers
> Like the vertebrae of monsters.

OTHER MAJOR WORKS

LONG FICTION: *The Man in the Middle*, 1954; *Money, Money, Money*, 1955; *Rock*, 1958; *The Escape Artist*, 1965; *Baby, Come On Inside*, 1968; *Where Is My Wandering Boy Tonight?*, 1970; *The*

Road to Many a Wonder, 1974; *Tracker*, 1975; *Whole Hog*, 1976; *The Hanging Garden*, 1980.

PLAY: *An Eye for an Eye for an Eye*, pr. 1973.

EDITED TEXT: *Straw for the Fire: From the Notebooks of Theodore Roethke, 1943-1963*, 1972.

BIBLIOGRAPHY

Boyers, Robert. "The Poetry of David Wagoner." *The Kenyon Review* 32 (Spring, 1970): 176-181. An appreciative review noting that *Staying Alive* marks a turning point in Wagoner's development. Boyers states that from now on, Wagoner could claim to be a major figure in contemporary American poetry.

Lieberman, Laurence. *Unassigned Frequencies: American Poetry in Review, 1964-1977*. Urbana: University of Illinois Press, 1977. The article on Wagoner, "David Wagoner: The Cold Speech of the Earth," looks at how this poet maps out a topography through his choice of words and images. Compares the later poems with the earlier ones and cites the same imagination but with greater depth of vision. Offers strong, in-depth criticism of *Collected Poems, 1956-1976* and places Wagoner in the company of Walt Whitman, Robert Frost, Edgar Lee Masters, and William Stafford.

McFarland, Ronald E. *The World of David Wagoner*. Moscow: University of Idaho Press, 1997. Presents literary criticism and interpretation of Wagoner's writings, and looks at the role of the American Midwest and Northwest in literature.

O'Connell, Nicholas. *At the Field's End: Interviews with Twenty Pacific Northwest Writers*. Seattle: Madrona, 1987. The interviewer explores with Wagoner the subjects of his poems and how he has recreated the Northwest landscape on paper. Examines the structure and sense of rhythm in his poems. Of particular note is a discussion of *Who Shall Be the Sun?*, a collection of poems that Wagoner read aloud to the Blackfeet tribe and for which he received much praise.

Pinsker, Sanford. *Three Pacific Northwest Poets: William Stafford, Richard Hugo, and David Wagoner*. Boston: Twayne, 1987. A useful and insightful introduction to Wagoner's poems, analyzing his choice of themes and techniques. Contains critical commentary on all of his major poems. Notes that among Wagoner's strengths is his "sense of the dramatic."

Waggoner, Hyatt H. *American Visionary Poetry*. Baton Rouge: Louisiana State University Press, 1982. Chapter 7, "Traveling Light," explores Wagoner's identity as a visionary poet through his nature poems. Examines Wagoner's portrayal of the wilderness and how he guards himself in his poems. A sympathetic critique that praises Wagoner's volume, *The Nesting Ground*.

Sara McAulay,
updated by Sarah Hilbert

DIANE WAKOSKI

Born: Whittier, California; August 3, 1937

PRINCIPAL POETRY

Coins and Coffins, 1962
Discrepancies and Apparitions, 1966
The George Washington Poems, 1967
Inside the Blood Factory, 1968
The Moon Has a Complicated Geography, 1969
The Magellanic Clouds, 1970
The Motorcycle Betrayal Poems, 1971
Smudging, 1972
Dancing on the Grave of a Son of a Bitch, 1973
Looking for the King of Spain, 1974
Virtuoso Literature for Two and Four Hands, 1975
Waiting for the King of Spain, 1974
The Man Who Shook Hands, 1978
Cap of Darkness, 1980
The Magician's Feastletters, 1982
The Collected Greed, Parts 1-13, 1984 (Part 1 pb. in 1968)
The Rings of Saturn, 1986
Emerald Ice: Selected Poems, 1962-1987, 1988
Medea the Sorceress, 1991
Jason the Sailor, 1993
The Emerald City of Las Vegas, 1995
The Butcher's Apron: New and Selected Poems, 2000

OTHER LITERARY FORMS

Diane Wakoski wrote three critical essays that were published by Black Sparrow Press: *Form Is an Extension of Content* (1972), *Creating a Personal Mythology* (1975), and *Variations on a Theme* (1976). These essays, with other essays that had originally appeared in *American Poetry Review*, where she was a regular columnist between 1972 and 1974, and in her books of poetry, were reprinted in *Towards a New Poetry* (1980).

ACHIEVEMENTS

More popular with poetry readers than with poetry critics, Diane Wakoski has nevertheless carved a niche for herself in American poetry. A prolific writer (she has published some fifty books of poetry) and indefatigable reader of her own poetry, she has gained a following of readers who appreciate her intensely personal subject matter, her personal mythology, her structural use of digression and repetition, and her long narrative forms. Throughout her work the subject is herself, and the themes of loss, betrayal, and identity recur as she probes her relationships with others, most often father figures and lovers. Though her poems are read sympathetically by feminists, she is herself not political and rejects the notion that she can be identified with a particular ideology or school of poetry. Her work has brought her several awards, among them the Bread Loaf Robert Frost Fellowship and the Cassandra Foundation Award, as well as grants from such sources as the Guggenheim Foundation and the National Endowment for the Arts. *Emerald Ice* won the Poetry Society of America's William Carlos Williams Award.

Her work, sometimes criticized for its perceived self-pity, actually uses loss or betrayal as the impetus for the speaker to work through different self-images and gender reversals to celebrate—usually with a trace of ironic self-awareness—beauty or the self, and, in effect, to solve the problem posed at the beginning of the poem.

BIOGRAPHY

Diane Wakoski was born in Whittier, California, in 1937 to parents who shaped not only her life but also her poetry. Shortly after her birth, her father, John Joseph Wakoski, reenlisted in the navy and made it his career. Her contact with the "Prince Charming" figure, as she describes him in an autobiographical account, was infrequent and unfulfilling, leaving her with a sense of loss she later explored in her poetry. Her relations with her mother were equally unsatisfying and stressful; by the time she left high school, Wakoski says, she found her mother, whom her father had divorced, a "burden." Speaking of her childhood, Wakoski claims that she was born into a "world of silence," that she was "surrounded by silent people." She was poor, emotionally isolated (she also had few friends), and—from her own point of view—physically unattractive. These factors surely relate to the fixation with male figures and subsequent betrayal in her poems and explain, to some extent, the compulsive need to analyze, to dissect, and to communicate at length in a prolific body of work.

The only positive reinforcement she received in high school was from sympathetic teachers who encouraged the development of her academic talents. She also discovered that she enjoyed performing for an audience. (This "exhibitionistic" tendency, as she has described it, is reflected in her poetry readings, which are very much "performances.") After graduation from high school,

Diane Wakoski (© Thomas Victor)

she passed up a scholarship to the University of California at Berkeley and attended Fullerton Junior College because she expected her high school sweetheart to enroll there as well. When he attended a different college and responded dutifully, not supportively, to the news of her pregnancy, she experienced a "betrayal," rejected his marriage proposal, and subsequently gave up her baby for adoption.

In the fall of 1956, after attending a poetry class at Whittier College, she enrolled at Berkeley, where she began writing poetry in earnest, publishing some of it in *Occident*, the campus literary magazine. Wakoski believes that her career was launched when her student poetry reading at the San Francisco Poetry Center resulted in another reading there, this time as a "real" poet. Before she left Berkeley she was pregnant again, this time by a fellow artist-musician with whom she later moved to New York; since marriage did not seem appropriate and both were career-minded, she again gave up her baby for adoption.

In New York, Wakoski continued to write poetry and give poetry readings, while she became acquainted with several established writers, one of whom, LeRoi Jones (later Amiri Baraka), published some of her poems in *Four Young Lady Poets* in 1962. *Coins and Coffins*, her first book of poems, was also published in 1962, but it was not until 1966, with the publication of *Discrepancies and Apparitions* by a major publishing house, Doubleday, that she became an established poet. In rapid succession she published two of her most important books, *The George Washington Poems* and *Inside the Blood Factory*, as well as the first four parts of *Greed*. During the late 1960's she also experienced a failed first marriage and a few failed romantic relationships, one of which produced the raw material for *The Motorcycle Betrayal Poems*, her most publicized collection of verse.

The 1970's were a productive decade for Wakoski, who averaged more than two books per year, maintained an almost frenetic pace with poetry readings, and gained at the University of Virginia the first of many academic posts as writer in residence. She also began a long-standing association with Black Sparrow Press, which has published many of her books. Of particular interest in this decade is the appearance of two collections of poetry concerning yet another mythological figure, the

King of Spain. During this period she turned her attention to criticism, writing a regular column for *American Poetry Review* and publishing a collection of her criticism in *Towards a New Poetry*.

Wakoski's personal life continued to provide content for her verse: Her second marriage ended in divorce in 1975. The following year, she began teaching at Michigan State University, where she would remain. In 1977, she renewed her friendship with poet Robert Turney and was married to him in 1982. The 1980's also saw the completion of *Greed*, which she had begun in 1968, and other books of poetry, though her productivity decreased. Other significant publications included *The Rings of Saturn* and *Medea the Sorceress*, two volumes that rework old themes and myths but also extend Wakoski's "universe," which is at once personal and all-inclusive. *Medea* became the first of four books that make up her series *The Archaeology of Movies and Books*, her major endeavor of the 1990's.

ANALYSIS

Since Diane Wakoski believes that "the poems in her published books give all the important information about her life," her life and her art are inextricably related. She states that the poem "must organically come out of the writer's life," that "all poems are letters," so personal in fact that she has been considered, though she rejects the term, a confessional poet. While most readers have been taught to distinguish between the author and the "speaker" of the poem, Wakoski is, and is not, author and speaker. She refers to real people and to real events in her life in detail that some critics find too personal as she works through a problem: "A poem is a way of solving a problem." For Wakoski, writing a poem is almost therapeutic; it is talking the problem out, not to a counselor or even to the reader, but to herself. She has said, "The purpose of the poem is to complete an act that can't be completed in real life"—a statement that does suggest that there are both reality and the poem, which is then the "completed" dream. As a pragmatist, she has learned to live with these two worlds.

Wakoski believes that once a poet has something to say, the content, he or she finds the appropriate form in which to express it. In her case, the narrative, rather than the lyric, mode is appropriate; free verse, digression,

repetition, and oral music are other aspects of that form. She carves out a territory narrowly confined to self and then uses the universe (the moon, the rings of Saturn, Magellanic clouds), history (George Washington, the King of Spain), personal experience (the motorcycle betrayal poems), and literary feuds to create, in the manner of William Butler Yeats, her personal mythology. The mythology is, in turn, used to develop her themes: loss and acceptance, ugliness and beauty, loss of identity and the development of self; that is, the themes are dualistic and, significantly, susceptible to the resolution she achieves in the poem. For her, poetry is healing, not fragmenting.

COINS AND COFFINS

Coins and Coffins, her first book of poetry, is dedicated to La Monte Young, the father of her second child and another in a series of lost loves. In this volume, she introduces the image of the lost lover, thereby creating her own personal mythology. "Justice Is Reason Enough" is a poem indebted to Yeats: "the great form and its beating wings" suggests "Leda and the Swan." The "form" in this poem, however, is that of her apocryphal twin brother, David, with whom she commits incest. She mourns her brother, "dead by his own hand," because of the justice that "balances the beauty in the world." Since beauty is mentioned in the last line of the poem, the final mood is one of acceptance and affirmation.

DISCREPANCIES AND APPARITIONS

The missing lover is also the central figure of *Discrepancies and Apparitions*, which contains "Follow That Stagecoach," a poem that Wakoski regards as one of her best and most representative. Though the setting is ostensibly the West, with the archetypal sheriff and Dry Gulch Hollow, the hollow quickly becomes a river, the speaker, a swimmer in a black rubber skin-diving suit, and the tough Western sheriff, a homosexual authority figure. The opening lines of the poem, "The sense of disguise is a/ rattlesnake," suggest the poses and masks, even the genders, she and the lover-sheriff put on and discard as he fails her: "oh yes you are putting on your skin-diving suit very fast running to the/ ocean and slipping away from this girl who carries a loaded gun." The roles are reversed as she assigns herself the potency he lacks: His gun "wanders into/ hand," while her phallic gun is constantly with her. The poem ends with characteristic confidence: "So I'll write you a love poem if I want to. I'm a Westerner and/ not afraid/ of my shadow." The cliché cleverly alludes to the "shadow" as the alter ego, her second, masculine self; the lover, it is implied, rejects his own wholeness.

THE GEORGE WASHINGTON POEMS

In *The George Washington Poems*, dedicated to her father and her husband, she continues to debunk the American hero, this time taking on "the father of my country" (a title that is given to one of the poems), the patriarchal political and militaristic establishment. In the twenty-three poems in the volume, "George Washington" appears in his historical roles as surveyor, tree chopper, general politician, and slave owner; however, he also anachronistically appears as the speaker's confidant, absentee father, and (sometimes absentee) lover. When the first poem, "George Washington and the Loss of His Teeth," begins with the image of "George's" (Wakoski refers irreverently to "George" throughout the poems) false teeth, Wakoski wittily and facetiously undercuts the historical image of male leadership in the United States.

In "The Father of My Country," Wakoski demonstrates both the extraordinary versatility of the "George Washington" figure and the way repetition, music, and digression provide structure. The first verse-paragraph develops the idea that "all fathers in Western civilization must have/ a military origin," that all authority figures have been the "general at one time or other," and concludes with Washington, "the rough military man," winning the hearts of his country. Often equating militancy and fatherhood and suggesting that it is the military that elicits American admiration, the speaker abruptly begins a digression about her father; yet the lengthy digression actually develops the father motif of the first verse-paragraph and examines the influence he has had on her life. Although his is a name she does not cherish because he early abandoned her, he has provided her with "military,/ militant" origins, made her a "maverick," and caused her failed relationships. Having thought her father handsome and having wondered why he left her, she is left with the idea of a Prince Charming at once desirable and unattainable. When she speaks of "Father who makes me know all men will leave me/ if I love them," she implies that all of her relationships are fated reenactments of childhood love betrayed.

At the end of the poem she declares that "George" has become her "father,/ in his 20th. century naval uniform" and concludes with a chant, with repetitions and parallels, that expresses both her happiness and her uncertainty: "And I say the name to chant it. To sing it. To lace it around/ me like weaving cloth. Like a happy child on that shining afternoon/ in the palmtree sunset her mother's trunk yielding treasures,/ I cry and/ cry,/ Father,/ Father,/ Father,/ have you really come home?"

INSIDE THE BLOOD FACTORY

Inside the Blood Factory, Wakoski's next major poetic work, also concerns George Washington and her absentee father, but in this volume her range of subject matter is much wider. There is Ludwig van Beethoven, who appears in later poems; a sequence concerning the Tarot deck; a man in a silver Ferrari; and images of Egypt—but pervading all is the sense of loss. In this volume the focus, as the title implies, is on physiological responses as these are expressed in visceral imagery. The speaker wants to think with the body, to accept and work with the dualities she finds in life and within herself.

Inside the Blood Factory also introduces another of Wakoski's recurring images, the moon, developed more extensively later in *The Moon Has a Complicated Geography* and *The Magellanic Clouds*. For Wakoski, the moon is the stereotypical image of the unfaithful woman, but it is also concrete woman breast-feeding her children, bathing, communicating with lovers, and menstruating. Wakoski insists on the physicality of the moon-woman who is related to the sun-lover, but who is also fiercely independent. She loves her lover but wants to be alone, desires intimacy ("wants to be in your wrist, a pulse") but does not want to be "in your house," a possession. (Possession becomes the focus for the ongoing thirteen parts of *Greed*.) When the question of infidelity arises, the speaker is more concerned with being faithful to herself than to her lover(s). In this poem ("3 of Swords—for dark men under the white moon" in the Tarot sequence) the moon-woman can be both submissive and independent, while the sun-lover both gives her love and indulges in his militaristic-phallic "sword play."

As is often the case in Wakoski's poetry, an image appears in one volume and then is developed in later volumes. Isis, a central figure in *The Magellanic Clouds*, is introduced in "The Ice Eagle" of *Inside the Blood Factory*. The Egyptian goddess-creator who is simultaneously mother and virgin, appears as the symbolic object of male fear: "the veiled woman, Isis mother, whom they fear to be greater than all else." Men prefer the surface, whether it be a woman's body or the eagle ice sculpture that melts in the punch bowl at a cocktail party; men fear what lies beneath the surface—the woman, the anima—in their nature.

THE MAGELLANIC CLOUDS

The Magellanic Clouds looks back at earlier volumes in its reworking of George Washington and the moon figures, but it also looks ahead to the motorcycle betrayal figure and the king of Spain. Of Wakoski's many volumes of poetry, *The Magellanic Clouds* is perhaps the most violent as the speaker plumbs the depth of her pain. Nowhere is the imaging more violent than in the "Poems from the Impossible," a series of prose poems that contain references to gouged-out eyes, bleeding hands, and cut lips.

Isis, the Queen of the Night speaker, figures prominently in *The Magellanic Clouds*. In "Reaching Out with the Hands of the Sun," the speaker first describes the creative power of the masculine sun, cataloging a cornucopia of sweetmeats that ironically create "fat thighs" and a "puffy face" in a woman. The catalog then switches to the speaker's physical liabilities, ones that render her unbeautiful and unloved; with the "mask of a falcon," she has roamed the earth and observed the universal effect that beauty has on men. At the end of the poem the speaker reaches out to touch the "men/ with fire/ direct from the solar disk," but they betray their gifts by "brooding" and rejecting the hands proffered them.

In "The Queen of Night Walks Her Thin Dog," the speaker uses poetry, the "singing" that recurs in Whitmanesque lines, to penetrate the various veils that would separate her from "houses," perhaps bodies, in the night. The poem itself may be the key in the locked door that is either an entrance or an exit—at the end of the poem, "Entrance./ Exit./ The lips" suggests a sexual and poetic act. In the third poem, "The Prince of Darkness Passing Through This House," the speaker refers to the "Queen of Night's running barking dog" and to "this house," but the Prince of Darkness and the Queen of

Night are merged like elemental fire and water. Like a Metaphysical poet, Wakoski suggests that the universe can be coalesced into their bodies ("our earlobes and eyelids") as they hold "live coals/ of commitment,/ of purpose,/ of love." This positive image, however, is undercut by the final image, "the power of fish/ living in strange waters," which implies that such a union may be possible only in a different world.

The last poem in the volume, "A Poem for My 32nd Birthday," provides a capsule summary of the speaker's images, themes, and relationships. In the course of the poem she associates a mechanic with a Doberman that bites, and then she becomes, in her anger, the Doberman as she seeks revenge on a lover who makes her happy while he destroys her with possessive eyes that penetrate the "fences" she has erected. After mentioning her father and her relatives, who have achieved "sound measure/ of love" ("sound measure" suggests substance but also a prosaic doling out of love), she turns to her mother, who threatens her with a long rifle that becomes a fishing pole with hooks that ensnare her. The speaker reverts to her "doberman" behavior, and, though she persists in maintaining "distance," she uses her poems and songs to achieve acceptance: "I felt alive./ I was glad for my jade memories."

THE MOTORCYCLE BETRAYAL POEMS

In *The Motorcycle Betrayal Poems*, betrayal, always a theme in Wakoski's poetry, becomes the central focus; the motorcycle mechanic represents all the men who have betrayed her. The tone is at times humorous, so much so that the poems may not be taken seriously enough, but there is also a sense of desperation. These poems explore the different roles and images available to define identity, and the roles are not gender-bound. The speaker, who expresses her condition in images of isolation and entrapment, is fascinated with aggressive male roles, embodied in the motorcyclist. While she wryly admits that she is the "pink dress," she at times would like to reverse the roles; she is also aware, however, that the male roles do not satisfy her needs, do not mesh with her sexual identity. In this collection her identity is again developed in terms of lunar imagery, this time with reference to Diana, associated with the moon and the huntress, here of the sexual variety, and with the desert: both are lifeless, and both reflect the sterility of her life. The speaker does suggest, through the water imagery that pervades her poems, that this condition is not permanent, that her life can be sustained, but only through a man's love. Ultimately, the speaker is plagued with another duality: She desires what has persistently destroyed her.

SMUDGING

The same contradictory feelings about men are reflected in the title poem of *Smudging*, a collection of verse that includes King of Spain poems, prose poems, two parts of *Greed*, and miscellaneous poems touching on recurrent themes, motifs, and myths. "Smudging," another of Wakoski's favorite poems, encapsulates many of the themes as it probes the divided self. There are two "parts" of the speaker, the part that searches "for the warmth of the smudge pot" and the "part of me that takes your hand confidently." That is, the speaker both believes that she has the warmth and fears that she lacks it. Like her mother, she must fear the "husband who left her alone for the salty ocean" (with associations of sterility and isolation); yet she, like the orange she metaphorically becomes, transcends this fear through "visions" and the roles she plays in her head—these make her "the golden orange every prince will fight/ to own."

With Wakoski, transcendence seems always transitory; each poem must solve a problem, often the same one, so that the speaker is often on a tightrope, performing a balancing act between fear and fulfillment. As the poem moves to its solution, the speaker continues to waver, as is the case in "Smudging." At the beginning of the poem, the speaker revels in warmth and luxuriance; she refers to amber, honey, music, and gold as she equates gold with "your house," perhaps also her lover's body, and affirms her love for him. Even before the change signaled by "but" occurs in the next line, she tempers the image: "the honeysuckle of an island" is not their world but "in my head," and the repetition of "your" rather than "our" suggests the nagging doubts that lead to memories of her childhood in Orange County, California. The fear of the laborers outside the house, the memory of the absentee father—she has left these behind as she finds love and warmth with her mechanic lover, whose warmth is suspect, however, because he "threw me out once/ for a

whole year." Mechanically expert, he does not understand or appreciate her "running parts" and remains, despite their reunion, "the voices in those dark nights" of her childhood. She, on the other hand, has become the "ot metal," "the golden orange" that exists independently of him.

DANCING ON THE GRAVE OF A SON OF A BITCH

Dancing on the Grave of a Son of a Bitch is a bit of a departure from Wakoski's earlier poetry, although it is consistent in mythology and themes with the rest of her work. The title poem, dedicated to her motorcycle betrayer, the mechanic of "Smudging," reiterates past injustices and betrayals, but the speaker is more assured than vengeful. Despite the opening curse, "God damn it," and her acknowledgment that his leaving made her "as miserable/ as an earthworm with no earth," she not only has "crawled out of the ground," resurrecting herself, but also has learned to "sing new songs," to write new poems. She denies that hers is an angry statement, affirming instead that it is joyful, and her tone at the end of the poem is playful as she evokes the country singer's "for every time/ you done me wrong."

There is similar progression in the "Astronomer Poems" of the volume. As in earlier poems, she uses the moon/sun dichotomy, but there is more acceptance, assurance, and assertiveness as she explores these myths. In "Sun Gods Have Sun Spots," she not only suggests male-sun blemishes but also affirms her own divinity in a clever role reversal: "I am/ also a ruler of the sun." While "the sun has an angry face," the speaker in "The Mirror of a Day Chiming Marigold" still yearns for the poet or astronomer to study "my moon." Wakoski thus at least tentatively resolves two earlier themes, but she continues to develop the King of Spain figure, to refer to the "rings of Saturn," to include some Buddha poems and some prose fables, and to use chants as a means of conveying meaning and music. In her introduction to the book, she explains that she wishes readers to read the poems aloud, being "cognizant" of the chanted parts. Since Wakoski is a performing poet, the notion of chants, developed by Jerome Rothenberg, was almost inevitable, considering her interest in the piano (another theme for future development) and music. In fact, Wakoski uses chants, as in "Chants/Chance," to allow for different speakers within the poem.

VIRTUOSO LITERATURE FOR TWO AND FOUR HANDS

Virtuoso Literature for Two and Four Hands, a relatively slender volume of poetry, not only alludes to Wakoski's fifteen years of piano study but also plays upon the keyboard-typewriter analogy to explore past relationships and her visionary life. Two of Wakoski's favorite poems, "The Story of Richard Maxfield" and "Driving Gloves," which are included in this volume, involve people she resembles, one a dead composer and artist and one a Greek scholar with a failed father, but the poems conclude with affirmations about the future. It is not Maxfield's suicide that disturbs the speaker; she is concerned with his "falling apart," the antithesis of his "well-organized" composing. The poem, despite the repetition of "fall apart," ends with her certainty "that just as I would never fall apart,/ I would also never jump out of a window." In the other poem, the speaker begins with familiar lamentations about her sad childhood and turns to genes and the idea of repeating a parent's failures. Noting that she, like her mother, wears driving gloves, she is terrified that she will be like her boring, unimaginative mother; Anne, like her unpublished novelist/ father, is a bad driver. Despite Anne's belief that "we're all like some parent/ or ancestor," the speaker tells Anne that "you learned to drive because you are not your father" and states that she wears gloves "because I like to wear them." Asserting that their lives are their own, she dismisses the past as "only something/ we have all lived/ through." This attitude seems a marked departure from earlier poems in which her life and behavior are attributed to her father's influence.

WAITING FOR THE KING OF SPAIN

While *Waiting for the King of Spain* features staple Wakoski figures (George Washington, the motorcycle mechanic, the King of Spain), lunar imagery (one section consists of fifteen poems about an unseen lunar eclipse, and one is titled "Daughter Moon"), and the use of chants and prose poems, it also includes a number of short poems—a startling departure for Wakoski, who has often stated a preference for long narrative poems. As a whole, the poems continue the affirmative mood of *Virtuoso Literature for Two and Four Hands*. The King of Spain, the idealized lover who loves her "as you do not./ And as no man ever has," appears and reappears,

the wearer of the "cap of darkness" (the title of a later collection), in stark contrast to the betrayers and the George Washington persona. Here, too, there is less emphasis on the masculine—sun imagery, though it appears, and more of a celebration of the moon imagery.

The two poems in the collection that Wakoski considers most illustrative of her critical principles are warm, accepting, flippant, and amusing. In "Ode to a Lebanese Crock of Olives" the speaker again refers to the body she regards as physically unattractive, but she accepts her "failed beach girl" status and stacks the deck metaphorically in favor of abundance ("the richness of burgundy,/ dark brown gravies") over the bland ("their tan fashionable body"). In fact, the "fashionable" (always a negative word for Wakoski) body provides the point of contrast to affirm Wakoski's own beauty: "Beauty is everywhere/ in contrasts and unities." This condemnation of thinness is extended to art and poetry in "To the Thin and Elegant Woman Who Resides Inside of Alix Nelson." For Wakoski, fullness is all: "Now is the time to love flesh." Renouncing the Weight Watchers and *Vogue* models of life and poetry, she argues for the unfettered fullness of "American drama" and the "substantial narrative." Wakoski declares, "My body is full of the juice of poetry," and concludes the poem with an amusing parody of the Lord's Prayer, ending with "Ah, men" (surely the source of the false doctrine of beauty).

THE MAN WHO SHOOK HANDS

The Man Who Shook Hands represents a point of departure for Wakoski, who seems in this volume to return to the anger, hostility, and bitterness of her earlier poems. The feelings of betrayal, here embodied in the figure of a man who merely shakes hands the morning after a one-night relationship, resurface as the speaker's quest for love is again unsuccessful. The speaker in "Running Men" is left with the "lesson" the departing lover "so gently taught in your kind final gesture,/ that stiff embrace." The sarcasm in "gently" and "kind" is not redeemed by her concluding statement that she lives "in her head" and that the only perfect bodies are in museums and in art. This realization prepares the reader for the last line of the volume: "How I hate my destiny."

GREED

Although the temporally complete *Greed*, all thirteen parts, was published in 1984, parts of it were printed as early as 1968, and Wakoski has often included the parts in other collections of her poetry. It is bound by a single theme, even if greed is defined in such general terms that it can encompass almost everything. It is the failure to choose, the unwillingness to "give up one thing/ for another." Because the early parts were often published with other poems, they tend to reflect the same themes—concerns with parents, lovers, poetry—and to be written in a similar style. Of particular interest, however, given Wakoski's preference for narrative, is part 12, "The Greed to Be Fulfilled," which tends to be dramatic in form. What begins as a conversation between the speaker and George becomes a masque, "The Moon Loses Her Shoes," in which the actors are the stock figures of Wakoski mythology. The resolution of the poem for the speaker is the movement from emotional concerns to intellectual ones, a movement reflected in the poetry-music analogy developed in part 13.

LATER POETRY

Wakoski's other later poetry suggests that she is reworking older themes while she incorporates new ones, which also relate to her own life. In *Cap of Darkness* and *The Magician's Feastletters* she explores the problem of aging in a culture that worships youth and consumption; this concern is consistent with the themes of *Virtuoso Literature for Two and Four Hands*.

The Rings of Saturn, with the symbolic piano and ring, and *Medea the Sorceress*, with its focus on mythology and woman as poet-visionary, reflect earlier poetry but also reflect the changing emphasis, the movement from emotion to intellect, while retaining the subjectivity, as well as the desire for fulfillment, beauty, and truth, that characterize the entire body of her work. The latter volume became the first part of a major Wakowski endeavor, at this point a tetrology, with the collective title *The Archaeology of Movies and Books. Jason the Sailor, The Emerald City of Las Vegas*, and *Argonaut Rose* are the other three parts.

The best introduction to Wakoski's art—her themes and methods—is *The Butcher's Apron: New and Selected Poems, Including "Greed: Part 14,"* published in 2000. In fashioning this collection, Wakoski decided to cut across a wide body of work by selecting those poems that concern food and drink. Moreover, as she writes in the intro-

duction, "All of the poems in this collection . . . focus on the on-going process of discovering beauty and claiming it for myself." At the same time, she has built a structure that outlines her personal mythology as it is revealed by or rooted in geographical and cultural landscapes. Part 1, "A California Girl," concerns her self-projection "as a daughter of the Golden State," while later parts elaborate and complicate Wakoski's shifting personae. Thus, her arrangement of older and newer poems is made in the service of a mythic map of her inner terrain.

Though often compared to Sylvia Plath, a comparison she destroys in part 9 of *Greed*, and often seen as squarely in the feminist mainstream, Diane Wakoski remains a unique and intensely personal voice in American poetry. She is constantly inventive, rarely predictable, and, in a way that somehow seems healthy and unthreatening, enormously ambitious.

OTHER MAJOR WORK

NONFICTION: *Creating a Personal Mythology*, 1975; *Towards a New Poetry*, 1980.

BIBLIOGRAPHY

Brown, David M. "Wakoski's 'The Fear of Fat Children.'" *The Explicator* 48, no. 4 (Summer, 1990): 292-294. Brown observes how the poem's common diction and grotesque imagery work to create a successful postmodern confessional in which the speaker expresses not only guilt but also the urge for self-reformation.

Gannon, Catherine, and Clayton Lein. "Diane Wakoski and the Language of Self." *San Jose Studies* 5 (Spring, 1979): 84-98. Focusing on *The Motorcycle Betrayal Poems*, Gannon and Lein discuss the betrayal motif in terms of the speaker's struggle for identity. The poems' speaker uses the moon image to consider possible alternative images for herself, and in the last poem of the book she achieves a "richer comprehension of her being."

Hughes, Gertrude Reif. "Readers Digest." *Women's Review of Books* 18, no. 7 (April, 2001): 14-16. Treats *The Butcher's Apron* along with collected works volumes by Carolyn Kizer and Kathleen Raine. Hughes is sometimes perplexed by Wakoski's line breaks and sentence structures. She feels that Wakoski's candor "disarms, but also unnerves." This qualified appreciation does give high praise to "Greed, Part 14," which is granted the status of a major long poem that redeems much else in the collection.

Lauter, Estella. *Women as Mythmakers: Poetry and Visual Art by Twentieth-Century Women*. Bloomington: Indiana University Press, 1984. Lauter devotes one chapter to Wakoski's handling of moon imagery in several of the poet's books. Though she sometimes uses conventional woman-moon and man-sun associations, Wakoski reverses the stereotypes as she explores male-female relationships. There is also a related discussion of Isis and Diana as aspects of the speaker's personality.

Martin, Taffy Wynne. "Diane Wakoski's Personal Mythology: Dionysian Music, Created Presence." *Boundary 2: A Journal of Postmodern Literature* 10 (Fall, 1982): 155-172. According to Martin, Wakoski's sense of absence and lost love prompts desire, which in turn animates the poetry, giving it life. Martin also discusses Wakoski's mythmaking, her use of digression as a structural device, and her use of musical repetition.

Newton, Robert. *Diane Wakoski: A Descriptive Bibliography*. Jefferson, N.C.: McFarland, 1987. Newton unravels Wakoski's career in print through its first quarter century.

Ostriker, Alicia Luskin. *Stealing the Language: The Emergence of Women's Poetry in America*. Boston: Beacon Press, 1986. An outstanding history of women's poetry, Ostriker's book includes extended readings of some of Wakoski's works, especially *The George Washington Poems*. For the most part, Ostriker focuses on the divided self (the all-nothing and the strong-weak) in Wakoski's poetry and discusses the ways in which the poet's masks and disguises become flesh. There is an extensive bibliography concerning women's poetry.

Wakoski, Diane. Interview by Taffy Wynne Martin. *Dalhousie Review* 61 (Autumn, 1981): 476-496. Martin elicits detailed answers from Wakoski about a wide range of topics: part 10 of *Greed*, her relationships with her parents, the literary influences on her poetry, and her responses to many New American poets. Of particular interest is Wakoski's discussion of how memory functions as narrative and how it can structure a poem.

_____. *Towards a New Poetry*. Ann Arbor: University of Michigan Press, 1980. The book includes not only Wakoski's criticism, much of which is commentary to her own poetry, but also five revealing interviews, only two of which had previously been published in major journals. In the introduction, Wakoski lists her "best" poems, the ones she believes illustrate her personal mythology, her use of image and digression, and the kind of music she thinks is important to contemporary poetry.

Thomas L. Erskine,
updated by Philip K. Jason

DEREK WALCOTT

Born: Castries, St. Lucia, West Indies; January 23, 1930

PRINCIPAL POETRY
Twenty-five Poems, 1948
Poems, 1951
In a Green Night: Poems, 1948-1960, 1962
Selected Poems, 1964
The Castaway and Other Poems, 1965
The Gulf and Other Poems, 1969
Another Life, 1973
Sea Grapes, 1976
The Star-Apple Kingdom, 1979
The Fortunate Traveller, 1981
Midsummer, 1984
Collected Poems, 1948-1984, 1986
The Arkansas Testament, 1987
Omeros, 1990
Poems, 1965-1980, 1992
The Bounty, 1997
Tiepolo's Hound, 2000

OTHER LITERARY FORMS
Derek Walcott has written many plays, published in *Dream on Monkey Mountain and Other Plays* (1970),

The Joker of Seville and O Babylon!: Two Plays (1978), *Remembrance and Pantomime: Two Plays* (1980), and *Three Plays* (1986), as well as *The Odyssey* (1993), *The Capeman*, a musical with music by Paul Simon (1998), and *The Haitian Trilogy* (2001). His nonfiction includes his Nobel lecture, *The Antilles: Fragments of Epic Memory* (1993); a collaboration with Joseph Brodsky and Seamus Heany, *Homage to Robert Frost* (1996); and a collection of essays, *What the Twilight Says* (1998).

Derek Walcott (Virginia Shendler)

ACHIEVEMENTS

Derek Walcott's work is infused with both a sacred sense of the writer's vocation and a passionate devotion to his island of birth, St. Lucia, and the entire Caribbean archipelago. A cultural dichotomy supplies the major tensions in his writing: He combines native French Creole and West Indian dialects with the formal, high structures of English poetry. His mystic sense of place and eruptive imagination are poised against a highly controlled metrical form. As a lyrical and epic poet he has managed to encompass history, culture, and autobiography with an intensely aesthetic and steadily ironic vision. Walcott is arguably a major poet in his ability to dramatize the myths of his social and personal life, to balance his urgent moral concerns with the ideal of a highly polished, powerfully dense art, and to cope with the cultural isolation to which his mixed blood sadly condemns him.

The Dream of Monkey Mountain, his most highly lauded play, won the 1971 Obie Award. His book *Another Life* received the Jock Campbell/New Statesman Prize in 1974. He received the *Los Angeles Times Book Review* poetry prize in 1986 for *Collected Poems*. In 1972, he received not only an honorary doctorate of letters from the University of the West Indies, but also an O.B.E. (Officer, Order of British Empire), and he was named honorary member of the American Academy and Institute of Arts and Letters in 1979. Other awards and fellowships include a Guggenheim fellowship in 1977, the American Poetry Review Award in 1979, the International Writer's Prize of the Welsh Arts Council in 1980, a John D. and Catherine T. MacArthur Foundation grant in 1981, the Queen Elizabeth II Gold Medal for Poetry in 1988, and the St. Lucia Cross in 1993. Walcott received the 1992 Nobel Prize for literature.

BIOGRAPHY

Derek Alton Walcott was born in Castries, the capital of St. Lucia, to a civil servant, Warwick, and Alix, the head of a Methodist grammar school. St. Lucia is a volcanic island of 238 square miles in the Lesser Antilles, halfway between French Martinique to the north and English St. Vincent to the southeast. It was discovered by Christopher Columbus in 1502, then contested for generations by the French and British, until the latter gained legal control in 1803, to yield their colonial hold only in 1959. Yet the Gallic influence remains, insofar as the population of about 100,000, largely of black African descent, speaks a Creole patois.

Since Walcott is descended from a white grandfather and black grandmother on both sides of his family, he has found himself ineluctably suspended between loyalties, resentments, fears, and fantasies. He has referred in essays to a schizophrenic boyhood, split between two lives: the interior pull toward poetry and the exterior push toward the world of action, as well as the raw spontaneity of his native argot opposed to the syntactical sinews of formal English. Inescapably, he has been both victim and victor of his divided culture, a kind of Caribbean Orestes who shuttles between the legends and folklore of his upbringing and the formal traditions of the cosmopolitan West. In his work Walcott has made much of the bridging geography of the West Indies, since they link Columbus and Crusoe, Africa and America, slavery and colonialism, exploitation and emancipation. Curiously, he even compartmentalizes his writing, stressing oral tales and folk language in his plays while suffusing most of his poems with an Elizabethan richness and Miltonic dignity of diction.

In *Another Life* Walcott has rendered an autobiographical narrative of his childhood and early career. This long narrative poem unfolds the evolution of a poet who will always consider himself "the divided child." At school he was taught European art, history, and literature, but his mother insisted on connecting him to the Africa-based culture of the black St. Lucian majority. A landscape painter and teacher, Harry Simmons, and a drawing and drinking friend, Dunstan St. Omer, sought to fashion him in their images. Walcott discovered, however, that "I lived in a different gift,/ its element metaphor" and abandoned the canvas for the printed page.

In part 3, "A Simple Flame," he falls in love with Anna, but her golden body cannot long compete with his passion for poetry,

> which hoped that their two bodies could be made
> one body of immortal metaphor.
> The hand she held already had betrayed
> them by its longing for describing her.

He mythicizes his Anna, dissolving her into all the literary Annas he has adored: Eugene O'Neill's Anna Christie, Leo Tolstoy's Anna Karenina, and the great modern Russian poet Anna Akhmatova. He leaves for study abroad.

In part 4, "The Estranging Sea," he returns home, "one life, one marriage later" (to Fay Moston, from 1954 to 1959). He encounters Dunstan, called "Gregorias," and finds him alcoholic, unable to hold a job, painting poorly, failing even at suicide. He learns that Harry Simmons *has* killed himself, with his body lying undiscovered for two days. Walcott then scathingly denounces ill-wishers who condemn their promising

artists to an early grave. He finds comfort and hope in the sea, wishes a peaceful rest to his friends and loves, and dedicates himself to literature, his fury spent:

> for what else is there
> but books, books and the sea,
> verandahs and the pages of the sea,
> to write of the wind and the memory of
>   wind-whipped hair
> in the sun, the colour of fire?

Walcott made his debut as a writer in 1948, with *Twenty-Five Poems*, privately printed at Barbados with a two-hundred-dollar loan from his mother and hawked by the author through the streets of Castries. In 1951 he released his second collection, *Poems*, while studying at the Mona campus of the University of the West Indies. During the 1950's he taught at secondary schools and colleges in St. Lucia, Grenada, and Jamaica. In 1958 he moved to Trinidad and there founded, in 1959, the Trinidad Theatre Workshop, with which he remained associated as both playwright and director until 1976, seeking to blend Shakespearean drama and calypso music, Bertolt Brecht's stage craft with West Indian folk legends. Crucial in his development as a dramatist were several months he spent in New York City in 1958, studying under José Quintero on a Rockefeller grant, learning how to incorporate songs and dances into a dramatic text.

For many years Walcott has divided his time between a home in Trinidad and teaching positions in the United States, including visiting professorships at Columbia and Harvard universities and lectureships at Yale and Rutgers universities. Since 1985 he has been a visiting professor at Boston University. His career has been both prolific and versatile, not only as poet and playwright but also as producer, set designer, painter, critic, and cultural commentator. He has been married three times, each marriage ending in divorce, and has one son from his first marriage and two daughters from his second.

ANALYSIS

Derek Walcott's first important volume of verse, *In a Green Night: Poems, 1948-1960*, was a landmark in the history of West Indian poetry, breaking with exotic native traditions of shallow romanticism and inflated rhetorical abstractions. In such entries as "A Far Cry from Africa," "Ruins of a Great House," and "Two Poems on the Passing of an Empire," he began to confront the complex personal fate that would dominate all of his work—his identity as a transplanted African in an English-organized society. In "A Far Cry from Africa" he concludes,

> I who am poisoned with the blood of both,
> Where shall I turn, divided to the vein?
> I who have cursed
> The drunken officer of British rule, how choose
> Between this Africa and the English tongue I love?
> Betray them both, or give back what they give?
> How can I face such slaughter and be cool?
> How can I turn from Africa and live?

Using the English tongue he loves does not preclude Walcott from feeling outrage at the degradation to which the British Empire has subjected his people, "the abuse/ of ignorance by Bible and by sword." He calls "Hawkins, Walter Raleigh, Drake,/ Ancestral murderers and poets." Yet this rage-filled poem ends on a note of compassion, as the speaker recalls that England was also once an exploited colony subject to "bitter faction." The heart dictates anger, but the intelligence controls and mellows feelings, perceiving the complexity of human experience.

IN A GREEN NIGHT

In the initial poem, "Prelude," the young poet looks down on his island and sees it beaten into proneness by indifferent tourists who regard it as insignificant. Yet he knows that his poetry is a means of transcending his land's triviality "in accurate iambics." He thus sets the stage and plot for his personal odyssey as an artist, which he would undertake over and over again in his career. With the duplicity of a guerrilla and the self-conscious stance of T. S. Eliot's J. Alfred Prufrock, he plans to "straighten my tie and fix important jaws,/ And note the living images/ Of flesh that saunter through the eye."

In the poem's concluding stanza, the speaker states that he is "in the middle of the journey through my life," as Dante was at the opening of his *Inferno* (c. 1320). He encounters the same animal as the Florentine poet—

a leopard, symbolizing self-indulgence. Walcott thus merges his identity as an islander with his mission as a poet, his private self becoming a public metaphor for art's affirmation.

In "Origins" he composes a creation myth of his native place, finding in the cosmogonic conditions of his landscape a protean identity as an individual and an epic consciousness of his culture, akin to that of Walt Whitman and Pablo Neruda. The sonic boom of the first two lines—"The flowering breaker detonates its surf./ White bees hiss in the coral skull"—is reminiscent of the acoustical flamboyance present in such Hart Crane poems as "Voyages" and "O Carib Isle." The warm Caribbean waters become an amniotic bath for the poet, who sees himself as "an infant Moses" envisioning "Paradise as columns of lilies and wheat-headed angels." In sections 3 and 4 of his long poem Walcott pays homage to his island's language, laying out undulating strings of images in the manner of Aimé Césaire, another West Indian poet and dramatist, with the roll of surrealistic phrases imitating the roll of the surf.

In a Green Night exhibits Walcott's remarkable formal virtuosities. He can compose rhyming quatrains of iambic tetrameter, as in the title poem, or a traditional sonnet sequence, such as in "Tales of the Islands," that combines subtle metrical music with exuberant energy. He can chant like Dylan Thomas ("A City's Death by Fire"), be as astringent as W. H. Auden ("A Country Club Romance"), or indulge in Creole language ("Parang"). Like Andrew Marvell, whose Metaphysical poetry was an influential model for the early Walcott, he is caught between the pull of passion and his awareness of its futility.

THE CASTAWAY AND OTHER POEMS

In *The Castaway and Other Poems* Walcott's focus on the artist's role becomes more overt, as he describes the poet as the archetypal artist-in-exile, thus a castaway, symbolizing also West Indians in general as historical discard from other cultures. He perceives the poet, paradoxically, as both the detached observer of society and its centrally located, living emblem. Walcott adopts the protean Robinson Crusoe image for this purpose, dramatizing him as Adam, Columbus, Daniel Defoe, even God, as the first inhabitant of a second Paradise, as discoverer and ruler of the world he has made. He insists on a complex relationship between the creative, exploring artist and a largely imperceptive community that tends to isolate and ignore him, yet that the poet nonetheless persists in representing. Sometimes he finds art inadequate in trying to order inchoate life, as in "Crusoe's Island":

> Art is profane and pagan,
> The most it has revealed
> Is what a crippled Vulcan
> Beat on Achilles' shield.

THE GULF AND OTHER POEMS

The next collection, *The Gulf and Other Poems*, deepens the theme of isolation, with the poet extending his sense of alienation to the world of the 1960's: John Kennedy's and Che Guevara's killings ("The Gulf" and "Che"), racial violence in the United States ("Blues"), the Vietnam War ("Postcards"), the civil war in Nigeria ("Negatives"). The gulf, then, is everywhere, with divisions mocking people's best efforts at unity, intimacy, order, harmony, happiness. Despite his disappointments, Walcott employs the gulf image ambivalently. To be sure, it encompasses the moral wasteland that the world has largely become; more optimistically, however, it stands for a healing awareness of separateness whereby the castaway, Crusoe-like artist understands his identity and place in the world. In the last analysis, Walcott insists, it is the poet's art that endures: "some mind must squat down howling in your dust,/ some hand must crawl and recollect your rubbish,/ someone must write your poems." The poet's apartness does not, then, result in his total alienation—he still commits his art to the world's experiences.

ANOTHER LIFE AND SEA GRAPES

In *Another Life*, Walcott avoids self-centered egotism as he mythologizes his island life, reimagining the *Iliad* (c. 800 B.C.E.) in the context of his own land and culture and using the odyssey motif to sustain this long poem. He even envisages his islanders as Homeric archetypes (Ajax, Cassandra, Helen, and others), engaged in an intense quest for their national identity. The poet's journey becomes a microcosm of the West Indian's, indeed the New World's, search for wholeness, acceptance, and fulfillment. As the young Derek Walcott is taught by Gregorias, the peasant-painter-pal, he devel-

ops his talent—though for letters rather than the visual arts—within the context of an artistic tradition that articulates the dreams and needs of his people. He ends the superbly sustained narrative by celebrating both the painter's and the poet's mission:

> Gregorias, listen, lit,
> we were the light of the world!
> We were blest with a virginal, unpainted world
> with Adam's task of giving things their names.

Sea Grapes is a quieter, more austere book than *Another Life*, a calm after the storm, with many of its poems elegiac, elegant, sparely constructed, sad. The prevailing mood of the volume is one of middle-aged acceptance, maturation, and resignation: "why does my gift already look over its shoulder/ for a shadow to fill the door/ and pass this very page into eclipse?" ("Preparing for Exile"). Again, Walcott rehearses the tensions of his divided heritage as a West Indian trying to accommodate his African instincts to the formalities and calculations of European modes. In the title poem he equates himself to the sea-wandering Odysseus, longing for Nausicaa while duty-bound for his home and family, torn between obsession and responsibility, and poignantly concludes, "The classics can console. But not enough." A five-part, long work, "Sainte Lucie," is a psalm to St. Lucia, mixing French Creole with English, vernacular speech with stately diction.

THE STAR-APPLE KINGDOM

The Star-Apple Kingdom is a lyrical celebration, studded with vivid images. Its most ambitious poem, "The Schooner Flight," features a seaman-poet, Shabine, a fleeing castaway from his island; Shabine is clearly a Walcott double, with "Dutch, nigger and English" in him so that "either I'm nobody, or I'm a nation." Shabine's ordeal is the allegory of Everyman. He loves his wife and children but also desires the beautiful Maria Concepcion. Like Odysseus, he encounters terrors and defeats them; unlike Odysseus, he often runs away from his duties rather than toward them. He does manage to escape a web of corruption and betrayal, however, and matures into a waterfront Isaiah whose vision embraces his people's history, learning to appreciate nature's simplicities, "satisfied/ if my hand gave voice to one people's grief."

The protagonist of "The Star-Apple Kingdom" is more sophisticated, satirical, and astute than Shabine, with his reflections more acerbic and cerebral. The poem begins as he peruses a photograph album dating from the Victorian era, featuring such subjects as "Herefords at Sunset in the Valley of the Wye." Then he ponders the miseries of blacks excluded from the joys of the plantation aristocracy, "their mouths in the locked jaw of a silent scream." A dream possesses him. In it he plunges into a nightmare procession of Caribbean injustices, both during and after the rule of colonialism. Awakening at dawn, he feels rejuvenated and serene. His eye falls on an elderly, black cleaning woman who now represents to him his people's strength and endurance, with a "creak of light" evoking the possibility of a better future for both her and them.

THE FORTUNATE TRAVELLER

In *The Fortunate Traveller* Walcott largely removes his pulsating sensibility from his home turf, focusing on New England, Manhattan, the American South, Chicago, London, Wales, and Greece. In "Old New England" he apprentices himself to the American vernacular, sounding somewhat like Robert Lowell in such statements as "Old Glories flail/ the crosses of green farm boys back from 'Nam." Yet no one can successfully assume a new idiom overnight, and Walcott's pentameters usually retain their British, Yeatsian cadences:

> The crest of our conviction grows as loud
> as the spring oaks, rooted and reassured
> that God is meek but keeps a whistling sword.

Some of Walcott's many virtues are evident in this collection: He is deeply intelligent, keeps enlarging his range of styles and reach of subjects, has a fertile imagination, and often commands precise, sonorous eloquence. In "Hurucan" he compellingly summons the god of hurricanes, "havoc, reminder, ancestor," who stands allegorically for the world's oppressors. In "The Hotel Normandie Pool," he masters both his social topic and personal memories. At the pool Walcott imagines a fellow exile, Ovid, banished from Rome to a Black Sea port, facing the rigors of a harsher climate yet continuing to compose his verses, epitomizing the predicament of an educated colonial poet writing in the language of an empire.

The book's best poem is its last, "The Season of Phantasmal Peace." It begins at twilight, as migrating birds lift up the net of the shadows of the earth, causing a "passage of phantasmal light/ that not the narrowest shadow dared to sever." These singers unify the earth's various dialects and feel "something brighter than pity" for creatures that remain below, wingless, in their dark holes and houses. The birds close the poem by undertaking an act of brief charity, lifting their net above betrayals, follies, and furies. The poem thereby lifts whatever darkness exists for an instant of peace, constituting a transcendent surge of song beyond the implied darkness of the world's wars and hatreds.

MIDSUMMER

Midsummer is a gathering of fifty-four poems, a number that corresponded to Walcott's age when the book was published. These lyric poems give the sense of their author noting his preoccupations during the course of a year. He equates midsummer with boredom, stasis, middle age, midcareer, and the harsh glare of self-examination, as he tries to fix the particular tone and texture of his inner life from one summer to the next. He turns ethnographer, chronicling hotel and motel life in Rome, Warwickshire, New York, Boston, and Chicago. Two-thirds of the sequence is set, however, in the tropics of Central America and his Caribbean islands.

As always, Walcott is nowhere comfortably at home. In the West Indies, he sees that "our houses are one step from the gutter," with "the doors themselves usually no wider than coffins." Once more, he plays Odysseus-in-exile: "And this is the lot of all wanderers, this is their fate,/ that the more they wander, the more the world grows wide." Writing to a friend in Rome, he contrasts its ancient heritage with the Caribbean area's sand-weighted corals, its catacombs with "silver legions of mackerel." In Boston, he mocks the stale air of cobble-stoned streets and Transcendentalist tradition, feeling self-consciously black amid New England's white spires, harbors, and filling stations, with pedestrians, moving like "pale fishes," staring at him as though he were a "black porpoise."

Unable to resolve his dilemma of perpetual uprooting, Walcott is graceful enough to parody his wanderings among cultures and his position as a prodigal son who cannot arrive at any home or rest. In "LI" he tells himself, half-mockingly, "You were distressed by your habitat, you shall not find peace/ till you and your origins reconcile; your jaw must droop/ and your knuckles scrape the ground of your native place."

In poem 27, Walcott sardonically describes the American impact on the West Indies, such as a chain-link fence separating a beach from a baseball field. "White, eager Cessnas" dot an airstrip in St. Thomas; fences separate villas and their beaches from illegal immigrants; "bulldozers jerk/ and gouge out a hill, but we all know that the dust/ is industrial and must be suffered." Even a pelican "coasts, with its engine off." No wonder that he feels "the fealty changing under my foot."

COLLECTED POEMS, 1948-1984

In 1986 Walcott's American publisher issued his *Collected Poems, 1948-1984*, a massive 516-page tome that included selections from all of his previous books and the entirety of *Another Life*. Critical reception was largely laudatory, particularly welcoming Walcott's lyrical gifts, the extraordinary variety of his styles and settings, the sensuous eloquence and freshness of his language, the intensity of his tone, and his talent for uniting power with delicacy. Some reviewers, however, complained of inflated rhetoric, a penchant for grandiose clichés, diction that is overly ornamental, and a tendency to propagandize at the expense of authentic feeling.

THE ARKANSAS TESTAMENT

Walcott resumes his doomed search for a homeland in *The Arkansas Testament*. In the work's first section, "Here," he again inspects the society of his native island but finds only incomplete connections, fragmented friendships. In the moving "The Light of the World," set in a minibus in St. Lucia, the speaker segues from social intimacy to abandonment. He leaves the vehicle, concluding, "They went on in their transport, they left me on earth./ . . . / There was nothing they wanted, nothing I could give them but this thing I have called 'The Light of the World.'" The "light" is Walcott's talent for writing—to which his fellow passengers are largely oblivious.

In the "Elsewhere" section, the poet searches for fulfillment in other countries, praying "that the City may be just/ and humankind be kind." In the title poem, consisting of twenty-four segments of sixteen lines each, the

speaker wanders from a motel in Fayetteville, Arkansas, to an all-night cafeteria, then returns to his motel, noting the exploitation of black Americans and calling the American flag "the stripes and the scars." His conclusion is, as usual with Walcott, bleak: "Bless . . . / these stains I cannot remove/ from the self-soiled heart."

Images of dislocation and disharmony pervade the book, inducing a melancholy mood. Walcott refers to the Sphinx, to sirens and satyrs—all of them half-human, half-animal. Doors are unhinged, telephone calls are unanswered, poetry goes unread; justice and mercy are usually unmet. *The Arkansas Testament* is a musical chant mourning the world's many woes.

OMEROS

Omeros is a colossal modern epic, Walcott's most ambitious achievement, which universalizes his persistent themes of displacement, isolation, exploitation, estrangement, exile, and self-division. He merges the island chain of his Caribbean with the Mediterranean island chain now called Greece, where the *Iliad* and *Odyssey* (c. 800 B.C.E.) are conventionally attributed to an Achaean bard, Homer, whose name is "Omeros" in modern Greek form. Omeros/ Homer makes several appearances in the poem, most frequently as Seven Seas, a poor, blind fisherman, but also as an African tribal singer and as a London bargeman, thus helping to internationalize this narrative of more than eight thousand lines.

The links between the ancient Greeks and modern Antilleans are plausible enough: Both societies were and are seafaring, and both inhabit islands rife with legends, ghosts, and natural spirits. Walcott takes an audacious gamble when he assumes that the Caribbean patois, with its linguistic uncertainties, is capable of occasionally declaiming in classically patterned verse; he uses three-line stanzas in a salute to Dante's *terza rima*. He safeguards his venture, however, by minimizing the Creole argot and having most of the action related by a patently autobiographical, polished narrator: a displaced poet living in Boston and Toronto, visiting the Great Plains and the sites of American Civil War battles and encountering Omeros in both London and St. Lucia.

Walcott likens his squabbling, scrounging fishermen to the ancient Greeks and Trojans, and projects Homeric counterparts in his modern Caribbean Helen, Achille, Hector, Circe, and Philoctete. Helen works as a housemaid in the home of Major and Mrs. Plunkett. As in Greek mythology, she is beautiful, proud, lazy, shallow, selfish, and magnetically irresistible to men. When she is fired by Mrs. Plunkett, she goes to work (occasionally) as a waitress, exciting the libidos of two fishermen friends, Hector and Achille. Walcott likens her to Judith and Susannah, Circe and Calypso, with her body creating a stirring drama out of every appearance.

Walcott's Hector differs drastically from Homer's, who had an ideal marriage to Andromache and was the Trojans' indispensable hero. This Hector abandons, at Helen's behest, his dignified but poorly paying work as a fisherman for the degrading but more lucrative job of taxiing tourists, hustling passengers at the wharf and airport. Paralleling Homer, Achille kills Hector in a fight over Helen, she settles down with him, and they will be parents to her expected child, sired by Hector.

The poem's focus expands further as it deals with Major Plunkett. At first he seems a stereotypical British colonial, with his "pensioned moustache" and Guinness-drinking taste. Walcott associates him, however, with not only the end of the Empire but also Montgomery's World War II victories in the Middle Eastern desert, and further with American Caucasian settlers displacing the Indians. Undertaking genealogical research, the major discovers an ancestor who took part in the victory of the British Navy's Admiral George Brydges Rodney over Admiral François-Joseph-Paul de Grasse's French fleet, acquiring St. Lucia as part of the British West Indies.

Then there is Philoctete, a fisherman disabled by a festering sore on his thigh. The link with the Greek myth is evident. Philoctetes, listed as one of the Greek Helen's many suitors, wanted to lead a flotilla of seven ships against Troy, but never reached it. Bitten on the foot by a snake on the island of Lemnos, he was ostracized by the other Achaean chieftains because the stench of his infected, rotting flesh nauseated them. Walcott's Philoctete is wounded by a rusty anchor and is also abandoned by his fellows while Achille undertakes a journey to Africa.

In the end, Philoctete is cured by a native healer and rejoins the island's fishing community. Yet the only cure Walcott offers is the palliative of his poem: "Like Philoctete's wound, this language carries its cure,/ its

radiant affliction." *Omeros* holds much woe and desolation in its complex web, but Derek Walcott's epic is a magnificent feat of cultural interweaving.

THE BOUNTY

Some critics have discerned in Walcott's post-Nobel poetry a slow coming to acceptance of his colonial and colonized identity. The poems of *The Bounty* reflect not only the bounty of nature, but also the ship, H.M.S. *Bounty*, which first brought breadfruit from the Pacific to the Caribbean islands. This fruit is a staple foodstuff, but the conjunction of a Pacific fruit and an African population only occurred as the result of European colonization and exploration. As always, abundance and oppression go ironically hand in hand. Perhaps as a result of winning the Nobel—certainly a the archetypal mark of international acceptance—Walcott's poems seem to show the poet more at peace with his colonial heritage. Being neither one thing nor another can create the permission to be anything and everything. The Carribean's "lack of history," which has so bedevilled Walcott at times, becomes a state of grace in which the evils of history can be overcome, or simply ignored.

TIEPOLO'S HOUND

Tiepolo's Hound marks Walcott's return to the autobiographical narrative poetic form. Walcott interweaves his own life with meditations on the life of Camille Pissarro, the Caribbean-born Sephardic Jew who emigrated to France and became a noted Impressionist painter. The poem revisits Walcott's long-standing interest in the visual arts and is illustrated with several of the poet's own paintings.

The poem is marked by shifts in direction and focus, although its uncertainties are justified by its underlying autobiographical core: Walcott's wrestling with his own problems of cultural identity, which gives a tension both to his meditations on Pissarro and to the quest, driven by the intensity of his memory of a brush stroke representing a hound's thigh in an eighteenth century Venetian painting—by Giovanni Battista Tiepolo, or possibly by Paulo Veronese; the uncertainty is one of the driving forces of the poem—seen long ago in a museum.

In a densely tangled passage late in the poem, the original vision of the hound, its revelation "so exact in its lucency" of art's power, is the event that has led Walcott in his own development as an artist and has brought him to a point where he is both a Theseus searching through labyrinths for the minotaur beast which is "history," and the beast itself, "a beast// that was my fear, my self, my craft,/ not the white elegant wolfhound at the feast." He continues:

> If recognition was the grace I needed
> to elevate my race from its foul lair
> by prayer, by poetry, by couplets repeated
> over its carcase, I was both slain and slayer.

Both recrimination and nostalgia threaten to surface in *Tiepolo's Hound* as he describes his journey to Venice—the museum Europe to which he had been introduced in childhood by his father's art books—to look for Veronese and Tiepolo, and struggles to reconcile his deep admiration for Pissarro with the feeling that Pissarro somehow betrayed his origins.

What resolves this emotional tangle, and makes the book finally a moving whole of which "Tiepolo's hound" can be the triumphant concluding image, is the combination of Walcott's homage to Pissarro's persistence as an artist in France through experiences of alienation and recurrent self-doubt, and Walcott's own poetic and painterly love of the Caribbean landscape which, in childhood, they shared. Walcott imagines Pissarro's discovery that the monumental works of European tradition that he finds in the Louvre are not where he can find himself, and imagines his discovery of his own vision outside the museum, in the streets of Paris and the modern, secular, myth-erasing art of the nineteenth century, with its new understanding of light. Walcott's account of Pissarro dwells especially on the years Pissarro spent in Pontoise, painting its landscapes and buildings again and again in changing lights and weathers, never getting it "right," suffering poverty and repeated rejection by the Academy, and always trying again.

The loose yet carefully structured poetic form he uses is a satisfying medium for a meditative art that in some respects is an equivalent of Pissarro's. Like Pissarro, he circles, comes back again and again to the same subjects, the same problems, the same images, though always with a difference. His fundamental verse form here is couplets, arranged so that the end sounds of one couplet rhyme, sometimes very loosely, with the end sounds of the next, a malleable *ab, ab* form which

lends itself to a discourse that makes distinctions, draws boundaries, only to let them blur again (as, for instance, with the similarities and differences between himself and Pissarro). The rhymes allow sharply pointed effects, linking "St. Thomas" and "Pontoise," for example, and "Pissarro" and "sorrow," but are usually less obtrusive. Walcott likens his couplets to Pissarro's brush strokes; he also gets a flowing and sliding effect with syntactical slips and with words whose meanings point in two directions (Pissarro, newly in Pontoise, is "an immigrant/ prodigal with confirmations," both the prodigal runaway from his native place and the artist prodigal with talent and discovery).

Loose forms and long, circling poems that evade tight narrative structure are liable to overinclusiveness, to long passages that lose poetic intensity, and *Tiepolo's Hound* does not avoid these failings. The intensity of the moment, the moment of artistic revelation, however, is the center of the poem and the justification, paradoxically, of its meanderings:

> . . . in the tints of Tiepolo's sky,
> in the yellowing linen of a still life by Chardin,
> in that stroke of light that catches a hound's thigh,
> the paint is all that counts, no guilt, no pardon,
> no history, but the sense of narrative time
> annihilated in the devotion of the acolyte,
> as undeniable as instinct, the brushstroke's rhyme
> and page and canvas know one empire only: light.

Light dominates Walcott's Caribbean landscapes, and Tiepolo's hound, metaphorically the inspiration for Walcott's fiction of Pissarro, finally points him back to the black Caribbean hound that is "the mongrel's heir," an abandoned puppy: "we set it down in the village to survive/ like all my ancestry. The hound was here." Coming near the end of the poem, this passage makes sense of the inconclusiveness of Walcott's search for the Venetian painting that has haunted his memory; his pilgrimage has a conclusion after all in his return home and the voyage into self that the poem has created. In its last lines, the poet looks to the constellations, reformed by his book: "the round// of the charted stars, the Archer, aiming his bow,/ the Bear, and the studded collar of Tiepolo's hound."

OTHER MAJOR WORKS

PLAYS: *Henri Christophe: A Chronicle*, pr., pb. 1950; *The Sea of Dauphin*, pr., pb. 1954; *The Wine of the Country*, pr. 1956; *Ione*, pr. 1957; *Drums and Colours*, pr. 1958; *Ti-Jean and His Brothers*, pr. 1958 (music by Andre Tanker); *Malcochon: Or, Six in the Rain*, pr. 1959; *Dream on Monkey Mountain*, pr. 1967; *Dream on Monkey Mountain and Other Plays*, pb. 1970; *In a Fine Castle*, pr. 1970; *The Joker of Seville*, pr. 1974 (adaptation of Tirso de Molina's *El burlador de Sevilla*; music by Galt MacDermot); *The Charlatan*, pr. 1974; *O Babylon!*, pr. 1976; *Remembrance*, pr. 1977; *The Joker of Seville and O Babylon!: Two Plays*, pb. 1978; *Pantomime*, pr. 1978; *Marie LaVeau*, pr. 1979; *Remembrance and Pantomime*, pb. 1980; *Beef, No Chicken*, pr. 1981; *The Last Carnival*, pr. 1982; *The Isle Is Full of Noises*, pr. 1982; *A Branch of the Blue Nile*, pr. 1983; *To Die for Grenada*, pr. 1986; *Three Plays*, pb. 1986; *Viva Detroit*, pr. 1990; *Steel*, pr. 1991 (music by MacDermot); *The Odyssey*, pr. 1992, pb. 1993; *The Capeman: A Musical*, pr. 1997, pb. 1998 (music by Paul Simon); *The Haitian Trilogy*, pb. 2001.

NONFICTION: "Meanings: From a Conversation with Derek Walcott," 1970 (in *Performing Arts*); *The Antilles: Fragments of Epic Memory*, 1993 (Walcott's Nobel lecture); *Homage to Robert Frost*, 1996 (with Joseph Brodsky and Seamus Heaney); *What the Twilight Says: Essays*, 1998.

BIBLIOGRAPHY

Balakian, Peter. "The Poetry of Derek Walcott." *Poetry* 148 (June, 1986): 169-177. This sensitive, eloquently written article surveys Walcott's work from his earliest text through *Collected Poems, 1948-1984*. Balakian firmly declares Walcott a major modern poet, ranking him with William Butler Yeats, Rainer Maria Rilke, and Pablo Neruda.

Bobb, June D. *Beating a Restless Drum: The Poetics of Kamau Brathwaite and Derek Walcott*. African World Press, 1998. Examines the influence of colonization and slavery on the Caribbean's most important anglophone poets, linking them to a specifically Caribbean tradition rooted in African mythologies and other influences. Bibliography, index.

Brown, Lloyd W. "The Personal Odyssey of Derek Walcott." In *West Indian Poetry*. Boston: Twayne, 1978. Brown studies the evolution of Walcott's career in four major collections: *In a Green Night, The Castaway and Other Poems, The Gulf and Other Poems*, and *Another Life*. A sensitive and learned analysis.

Burnett, Paula. *Derek Walcott: Politics and Poetics*. Gainesville: University Press of Florida, 2001. Sees the drama and poetry together designed to create a legacy for modern Caribbean society, incorporating myth, identity, and aesthetics. Notes, bibliography, index.

Davis, Gregson, ed. *The Poetics of Derek Walcott*. Durham, N.C.: Duke University Press, 1997. A collection of critical essays on the poetry. The cornerstone essay is one in which Walcott reflects on poetics, illuminating his masterpiece *Omeros*. Other contributors focus on central thematic concerns as well as modes of expression.

Dove, Rita. "Either I'm Nobody, Or I'm a Nation." *Parnassus: Poetry in Review* 14, no. 1 (1987): 49-76. Dove appraises Walcott's career from his earliest poems through *Collected Poems, 1948-1984*, with particularly illuminating interpretations of *Another Life* and *The Star-Apple Kingdom*. She concentrates on the poet's metrics and imagery, stressing his imaginative sea symbolism.

Hamner, Robert D. *Derek Walcott*. New York: Twayne, 1993. Hamner conducts a thorough exploration of Walcott's plays, poems, and critical articles, ending with *The Star-Apple Kingdom*. His approach is extremely cautious: He will usually cite another author's analysis rather than risking his own. The text is supplemented by a selected bibliography of both primary and secondary sources and an index. Hamner does not annotate his secondary references.

King, Bruce. *Derek Walcott: A Caribbean Life*. New York: Oxford University Press, 2000. The first literary biography, with reference to letters, diaries, uncollected and unpublished writings, and interviews in the Caribbean, North America, and Europe. Sees Walcott, born into a Protestant mulatto elite on St. Lucia, as driven by the need to justify his life and fulfill his talents but often considering himself to be an example of fallen humanity. Also addresses how his work as a painter influenced his vision.

Morris, Mervyn. "Derek Walcott." In *West Indian Literature*, edited by Bruce King. Hamden, Conn.: Archon Books, 1979. This incisive and succinctly worded chapter considers *Another Life, The Castaway and Other Poems, The Gulf and Other Poems*, and *Sea Grapes*. Morris makes a number of astute observations, but since he also deals with Walcott's early plays, considerations of space preclude extended analyses of the poetry collections.

Thieme, John. *Derek Walcott.* New York: St. Martin's Press, 1999. An introductory biography and critical interpretation of selected works. Includes bibliographical references and index.

Gerhard Brand,
updated by Anne Howells and Leslie Ellen Jones

ALICE WALKER

Born: Eatonton, Georgia; February 9, 1944

PRINCIPAL POETRY

Once: Poems, 1968

Five Poems, 1972

Revolutionary Petunias and Other Poems, 1973

Good Night, Willie Lee, I'll See You in the Morning: Poems, 1979

Horses Make a Landscape Look More Beautiful, 1984

Her Blue Body Everything We Know: Earthling Poems, 1965-1990 Complete, 1991

OTHER LITERARY FORMS

Although Alice Walker's poetry is cherished by her admirers, she is primarily known as a fiction writer. The novel *The Color Purple* (1982), generally regarded as her masterpiece, achieved both popular and critical success, winning the Pulitzer Prize and the National Book Award. The Steven Spielberg film of the same name, for which Walker acted as consultant, reached an immense international audience.

Other Walker fiction has received less attention. Her first novel, *The Third Life of Grange Copeland* (1970), depicts violence and family dysfunction among folks psychologically maimed by racism. *Meridian* (1976) mirrors the Civil Rights movement, of which the youthful Walker was actively a part. Later novels, *The Temple of My Familiar* (1989), *Possessing the Secret of Joy* (1992), and *By the Light of My Father's Smile* (1998) have employed narrative as little more than a vehicle for ideas on racial and sexual exploitation, abuse of animals and the earth, and New Age spirituality. *In Love and Trouble: Stories of Black Women* (1973) and *You Can't Keep a Good Woman Down* (1981) revealed Walker to be one of the finest of late twentieth century American short-story writers. There was also time for an occasional children's book (*To Hell with Dying*, 1988, is particularly notable) and several collections of essays (*In Search of Our Mothers' Gardens: Womanist Prose*, 1983, is the most lyrical) that present impassioned pleas for the causes Walker espoused.

ACHIEVEMENTS

At numerous colleges, as a teacher and writer in residence, Alice Walker established herself as a mentor, particularly to young African American women. Her crusades became international. To alert the world to the problem of female circumcision in Africa, she collaborated with an Anglo-Indian filmmaker on a book and film. She was a voice for artistic freedom, defending her own controversial writings and those of others, such as Salman Rushdie. In her writings and later open lifestyle, she affirmed lesbian and bisexual experience. Yet the accomplishment in which she took most pride was her resurrection of the reputation of Zora Neale Hurston, a germinal African American anthropologist and novelist, whose books had gone out of print.

Walker won the Rosenthal Award of the National Institute of Arts and Letters for *In Love and Trouble: Stories of Black Women* and received a Charles Merrill writing fellowship, a National Endowment for the Arts award, and a Guggenheim Fellowship. Her second book of poetry, *Revolutionary Petunias and Other Poems*, received the Lillian Smith Award and was nominated for a National Book Award. Her highest acclaim came with the novel *The Color Purple*, for

Alice Walker (Jeff Reinking/Picture Group)

which she won the American Book Award and the 1983 Pulitzer Prize.

BIOGRAPHY

Alice Walker was the youngest of eight children born to a Georgia sharecropper and his wife. Her father earned about three hundred dollars per year, while her mother, the stronger figure, supplemented the family income by working as a maid. Walker herself was a bright, confident child, until an accident at age eight blinded her in one eye and temporarily marred her beauty. At this time she established what was to become a lifelong pattern of savoring solitude and making the most of adversity. She started reading and writing poetry.

Because of her partial blindness and her outstanding high school record, Walker qualified for a special scholarship offered to disabled students by Spelman College, the prestigious black women's college in Atlanta. When she matriculated there in 1961, her neighbors raised the bus fare of seventy-five dollars to get her to Atlanta.

As a Spelman student, Walker was "moved to wakefulness" by the emerging Civil Rights movement. She took part in demonstrations downtown, which brought her into conflict with the conservative administration of the school. Finding the rules generally too restrictive, and refreshed with her new consciousness, she secured a scholarship at Sarah Lawrence College in Bronxville, New York. She then felt closer to the real action that was changing the country. At Sarah Lawrence College she came under the influence of the poet Muriel Rukeyser, who recognized her talent and arranged for her first publications. She also took a summer off for a trip to her "spiritual home," Africa. She returned depressed and pregnant, contemplated suicide for a time, but instead underwent an abortion and poured her emotions into poetry.

After graduation, Walker worked for a time in the New York City Welfare Department before returning to the South to write, teach, and promote voter registration. She married Melvyn Leventhal, a white Jew, and worked with him on desegregation legal cases and Head Start programs. Their child, Rebecca, was born during this highly productive period. By the time the marriage ended in 1976, Walker was already becoming recognized as a writer, though she did not become internationally famous until after the publication of *The Color Purple*.

Walker continued to write during the 1980's and 1990's, though never again achieving the acclaim or the notoriety that *The Color Purple* brought her. Critics complained of her stridency, the factual inaccuracies in her writings, and her tendency to turn her works of fiction into polemics. Many African Americans felt that her writings cast their society in a grim light. Walker moved to California and lived for several years with Robert Allen, the editor of *Black Scholar*. Times had changed; the motto was no longer "black and white together," marriages between Jews and African Americans were out, and black-black relationships were in.

As the millennium neared its close, Walker became more alert to the problems women of color faced throughout the world. Taking a female partner, she decided to devote her time and talents to celebrating women and rectifying wrongs committed against them.

ANALYSIS

Alice Walker writes free verse, employing concrete images. She resorts to few of the conceits, the extended metaphors, the latinate language, and other affectations often found in poetry. Readers frequently say that her verses hardly seem like poetry at all; they resemble the conversation of a highly articulate, observant woman. While her poetry often seems like prose, her fiction is highly poetic. The thoughts of Miss Celie, the first-person narrator of *The Color Purple*, would not have been out of place in a book of poetry. Boundaries between prose and poetry remain thin in the work of Walker. Her verse, like her prose, is always rhythmic; if she rhymes or alliterates, it seems only by accident. The poetry appears so effortless that its precision, its choice of exact image or word to convey the nuance the poet wishes, is not immediately evident. Only close scrutiny reveals the skill with which this highly lettered poet has assimilated her influences, chiefly E. E. Cummings, Emily Dickinson, Robert Graves, Japanese haiku poems, Li Bo, Ovid, Zen epigrams, and William Carlos Williams.

Walker's poetry is personal and generally didactic, generated by events in her life, causes she has advocated, and injustices over which she has agonized. The reader feels that it is the message that counts, before realizing that the medium is part of the message. Several of her poems echo traumatic events in her own life, such as her abortion. She remembers the words her mother uttered over the casket of her father, and makes a poem of them. Other poems recall ambivalent emotions of childhood: Sunday school lessons which, even then, were filled with discrepancies. Some poems deal with the creative process itself: She calls herself a medium through whom the Old Ones, formerly mute, find their voice at last.

Some readers are surprised to discover that Walker's poems are both mystical and socially revolutionary, one moment exuberant and the next reeking with despair. Her mysticism is tied to reverence for the earth, a sense of unity with all living creatures, a bond of sisterhood with women throughout the world, and a joyous celebration of the female principle in the divine. On the other hand, she may lament that injustice reigns in society: Poor black people toil so that white men may savor the jewels that adorn heads of state.

In 1991, Walker published a complete edition of her poems written between 1965 and 1990, titled *Her Blue Body Everything We Know: Earthling Poems, 1965-1990 Complete*. A few additional verses were added to those taken from her collections, along with a revealing commentary. While the entire body of Walker's poetic work is unified by a few constant themes, each of the major collections does have its own emphasis and focus.

ONCE: POEMS

Walker's first collection of poetry communicates her youthful impressions of Africa and her state of mind during her early travels there, as well as the melancholy she felt upon her return to a racist United States, when thoughts of death, particularly by suicide, tormented her. Perhaps the epigram from French philosopher Albert Camus, which prefaces the book, expresses its mood best: "Misery kept me from believing that all was well under the sun, and the sun taught me that history wasn't everything."

The title poem of the collection contains several loosely connected scenes of injustice in the American South, small black children run down by vans, because "they were in the way," Jewish Civil Rights workers who cannot be cremated according to their requests because their remains cannot be found, and finally a black child waving an American flag, but from "the very/ tips/ of her/ fingers," an image perhaps of irony or perhaps of hope.

There are meditations on white lovers—blond, Teutonic, golden—who dare kiss this poet who is "browner/ Than a jew." There are memories of black churches, where her mother shouts, her father snores, and she feels uncomfortable.

The most striking poem is certainly "African Images," an assortment of vignettes from the ancestral homeland: shy gazelles, the bluish peaks of Mount Kenya, the sound of elephants trumpeting, rain forests with red orchids. Yet even glimpsed in the idealism of youth, Africa is not total paradise. The leg of a slain elephant is fashioned into an umbrella holder in a shop; a rhinoceros is killed so that its horn may be fashioned into an aphrodisiac.

REVOLUTIONARY PETUNIAS AND OTHER POEMS

Walker's third collection of poems is divided into two parts. The first is titled "In These Dissenting Times . . . Surrounding Ground and Autobiography." She proposes to write "of the old men I knew/ And the young men/ I loved/ And of the gold toothed women/ Mighty of arm/ Who dragged us all/ To church." She writes also "To acknowledge our ancestors" with the awareness that "we did not make/ ourselves, that the line stretches/ all the way back, perhaps, to God; or/ to Gods." She recalls her baptism "dunked . . . in the creek," with "gooey . . . rotting leaves,/ a greenish mold floating." She was a slight figure, "All in white./ With God's mud ruining my snowy/ socks and his bullfrog spoors/ gluing up my face."

The last half of the collection, "Revolutionary Petunias . . . the Living Through," begins with yet another epigram from Camus, reminding the reader that there will come a time when revolutions, though not made by beauty, will discover the need for beauty. The poems, especially those referred to as "Crucifixions," become more anguished, more angered. Walker becomes skeptical of the doctrine of nonviolence, hinting that the time for more direct action may have come. The tone of the last poems in the collection may be expressed best by the opening lines to the verse Walker called "Rage." "In me, " she wrote, "there is a rage to defy/ the order of the stars/ despite their pretty patterns."

GOOD NIGHT, WILLIE LEE, I'LL SEE YOU IN THE MORNING

The fourth poetry collection expands on earlier themes and further exploits personal and family experiences for lessons in living. The title poem is perhaps the most moving and characteristic of the collection. Walker shared it again on May 22, 1995, in a commencement day speech delivered at Spelman College. As a lesson in forgiveness, she recalled the words her mother, who had much to endure and much to forgive, uttered above her father's casket. Her last words to the man with whom she had lived for so many years, beside whom she had labored in the fields, and with whom she had raised so many children were, "Good night, Willie Lee, I'll see you in the morning." This gentle instinctive act of her mother taught Walker the enduring lesson that "the healing of all our wounds is forgiveness/ that permits a promise/ of our return/ at the end."

HORSES MAKE A LANDSCAPE LOOK MORE BEAUTIFUL

The fifth major collection of poetry took its title from words of Lame Deer, an Indian seer who contemplated the gifts of the white man—chiefly whiskey and horses—and found the beauty of horses almost made her forget the whiskey. This thought establishes the tone of the collection. These are movement poems but, as always, they remain intensely personal and frequently elegiac. The poet seems herself to speak:

> I am the woman
> with the blessed
> dark skin
> I am the woman
> with teeth repaired
> I am the woman
> with the healing eye
> the ear that hears.

There is also lamentation for lost love:

> When I no longer have your heart
> I will not request your body
> your presence
> or even your polite conversation.
> I will go away to a far country
> separated from you by the sea
> —on which I cannot walk—
> and refrain even from sending
> letters
> describing my pain.

OTHER MAJOR WORKS

LONG FICTION: *The Third Life of Grange Copeland*, 1970; *Meridian*, 1976; *The Color Purple*, 1982; *The Temple of My Familiar*, 1989; *Possessing the Secret of Joy*, 1992; *By the Light of My Father's Smile*, 1998.

SHORT FICTION: *In Love and Trouble: Stories of Black Women*, 1973; *You Can't Keep a Good Woman Down*, 1981; *The Complete Stories*, 1994; *Alice Walker Banned*, 1996 (stories and commentary).

NONFICTION: *In Search of Our Mothers' Gardens: Womanist Prose*, 1983; *Living by the Word: Selected Writings, 1973-1987*, 1988; *Warrior Marks: Female Genital Mutilation and the Sexual Blinding of Women*, 1993 (with Pratibha Parmar); *Anything We Love Can Be Saved: A Writer's Activism*, 1997; *The Way Forward Is with a Broken Heart*, 2000; *Sent by Earth:*

A Message from the Grandmother Spirit After the Attacks on the World Trade Center and Pentagon, 2002.

CHILDREN'S LITERATURE: *Langston Hughes: American Poet,* 1974; *To Hell with Dying,* 1988; *Finding the Green Stone,* 1991.

BIBLIOGRAPHY

Bloom, Harold, ed. *Alice Walker.* New York: Chelsea House, 1999. A good introduction to Walker's work, with samples of critical responses from such publications as *Ms.* and *Artisan Review.*

Dieke, Ikenna, ed. *Critical Essays on Alice Walker.* Contributions in Afro-American and African Studies 189. New York: Greenwood Press, 1999. Especially well suited for use in college literature classrooms, this collection gives particular attention to Walker's poetry and her developing ecofeminism.

Lauret, Maria. *Alice Walker.* New York: St. Martin's Press, 2000. Provocative discussions of Walker's ideas on politics, race, feminism, and literary theory. Of special interest is the exploration of Walker's literary debt to Zora Neale Hurston, Virginia Woolf, and even Bessie Smith.

Walker, Melissa. *Down from the Mountaintop: Black Women's Novels in the Wake of the Civil Rights Movement, 1966-1989.* New Haven, Conn.: Yale University Press, 1991. Places Walker beside other African American women whose fiction mirrored the racial plight that called forth the Civil Rights movement.

Walker, Rebecca. *Black, White, and Jewish: Autobiography of a Shifting Self.* New York: Riverhead, 2001. A self-indulgent but nevertheless insightful memoir by Alice Walker's daughter. Rebecca Walker, who describes herself as "a movement child," grew up torn between two families, two races, and two traditions, always in the shadow of an increasingly famous and absorbed mother.

Winchell, Donna Haisty. *Alice Walker.* New York: Twayne, 1992. The Twayne volumes almost always present the best overview of their subjects. This one is no exception, though much has happened in Walker's career since its publication.

Allene Phy-Olsen

RONALD WALLACE

Born: Cedar Rapids, Iowa; February 18, 1945

PRINCIPAL POETRY

Plums, Stones, Kisses, and Hooks, 1981
Tunes for Bears to Dance To, 1983
People and Dog in the Sun, 1987
The Makings of Happiness, 1991
Time's Fancy, 1994
The Uses of Adversity, 1998

OTHER LITERARY FORMS

Ronald Wallace has published short fiction, books of literary criticism, and scholarly articles and reviews in a number of journals. In 1989 he edited a poetry anthology, *Vital Signs: Contemporary American Poetry from the University Presses.*

ACHIEVEMENTS

Wallace's writing has garnered many honors, including several poetry awards from the Council for Wisconsin Writers. A book of short stories won the Mid-List Press First Fiction Award. He has received a Creative Writing Fellowship and three Creative Writing Grants from the Wisconsin Arts Board. He also won a Distinguished Teaching Award from the University of Wisconsin in Madison.

BIOGRAPHY

Ronald William Wallace grew up in St. Louis, Missouri. A voracious reader in grade school, his interest in writing began in fifth grade, when he started to keep a diary. He became interested in poetry in ninth grade when a weary teacher attempted to entertain her class by giving students poems to read. Reading Emily Dickinson, Wallace says he was moved though he did not understand the poems, nor did he think his friends would appreciate his newfound interest. After reading Dickinson, he said, "I wrote poetry in secret, I read poetry in secret, and I dreamed of one day being a real poet and writer."

At the College of Wooster he enrolled in premedicine studies but found he liked only the English courses.

After a breakup with a girlfriend, Wallace dealt with the pain by writing poetry and ultimately decided that he would become a poet.

After earning his Ph.D. but feeling uncommitted to teaching, Wallace and his wife spent a year in Europe, where he wrote poems, some of which appeared in his first book, *Plums, Stones, Kisses, and Hooks*, a work rejected by ninety-nine publishers before being accepted. After that he published additional books of poetry, a number of chapbooks, works of literary criticism, and short stories. He once said that he was most interested in poets "who embrace the personal, the simple, the clear, the straightforward, the accessible. Many of these poets are exploring traditional forms and humor as a way of renewing poetry and possibly reaching a larger audience." The statement aptly describes Wallace's poetry as well.

Hired at the University of Wisconsin in Madison for a one-year position, Wallace established himself there, founding *The Madison Review* and building the creative writing program to six staff members and six fellows teaching in one of the few postgraduate fine arts programs in the United States. He became director of creative writing at Madison, director of the Wisconsin Institute for Creative Writing, and poetry editor for the University of Wisconsin Press.

ANALYSIS

Ronald Wallace writes with great clarity about common, everyday subjects: relationships with his family, including his memories of an ambivalent relationship with his father, who suffered from multiple sclerosis; nature and things bucolic, especially life on his farm and his observations of animals; food; and people he has known. The poems have a confessional quality to them. Reviewers have used the word "honest" to refer to his voice and "moving" to describe the effect of the poems, which are characterized by an openness and willingness to reflect on aspects of life that are not always pleasant. Linda Falkenstein points out that every one of Wallace's collections has contained a poem about worry; it is also the title of one of his chapbooks of fiction.

Contrasting himself with the so-called language poets, Wallace admires "clear accessible language, the sense that you're hearing what the poet really does think

and believe and has done or seen or experienced." Two additional characteristics of Wallace's work that reflect trends in contemporary American poetry are an interest in traditional forms and the use of humor.

Besides his books of poetry, Ronald Wallace has published more than five hundred poems in magazines and anthologies. His later work uses closed forms extensively. Having grown up believing free verse to be "the only form of poetry worth writing," Wallace says he never expected to be considered a New Formalist. Although closed-form poems appear in some of his earlier collections, *Time's Fancy* (1994) includes many more.

PLUMS, STONES, KISSES, AND HOOKS

Wallace's first book introduces the topics of family and nature, which are the mainstay for much of his work. Several poems focus on his father and children, and in some of the poems, Wallace writes from others' points of view, such as his father, his daughter, a bullhead, a cat, a hippopotamus, and a medicine man.

"Oranges" is characteristic of how Wallace develops metaphor. The poem begins with the eating of an orange. Then:

> I walk across the lake.
> Ice fishermen twitch their poles until
> perch flicker the surface, quick
> and bright as orange slices.
> The sun ripens in the sky.
> The wind turns thin and citrus,
> the day precise, fragile.

The orange in the poem acts as both tenor and vehicle. For the reader, the poem creates the impression of unified experience, with the various characteristics of an orange becoming a means of apprehending other things. Such description represents experience in a fresh way and "makes it new," in the words of Ezra Pound and the style of the Imagist poets.

In "Oranges" and in other poems, Wallace uses nature not so much as an end in itself but rather as a means to reflect on the human. In "Prayer for Flowers," the qualities that help plants thrive become goals for successful human life: "Show me the disguises of coral root/ that I may go unnoticed among enemies,/ the tenacity of columbine/ that I might thrive in the unlikely place."

While there is little rhyme or formal verse, the sound of the language, through assonance, consonance, and alliteration sometimes rises to music, as in these lines from "Cleaning House": "You feel this September enter your head/ to sweep up the clutter of summer:/ its tractors and grackles, its harvests and roots,/ its skies stuffed with sunshine and pollen."

TUNES FOR BEARS TO DANCE TO

In terms of his personal relationships, the poems are revealing and not always complimentary to Wallace himself. In "Picture of Two Bugs, Hugging" he describes the situation of a daughter believed to be disabled: "At six months, white, unlovely as a slug,/ the doctors clucking their tongues: *Microcephalic*." Later in the poem he describes his feelings: "How I wanted/ to swat you away, smash those cries/ against wall or ceiling, take you by your/ furry legs, and pin you, sprawling, down."

The passage above includes the characteristic extended-type metaphor. "Wild Strawberries," too, uses nature metaphorically to examine relationships as Wallace writes about picking strawberries with his wife. The poem reflects on the challenge of marriage and, along with others, points out the fragility of human relationships.

The poems are not all solemn, however; Wallace shows his sense of humor in a number of them, sometimes mocking himself. In "The Assistant Professor's Nightmare," Wallace the professor is impressed with his lecturing ability ("all the pencils nodding their heads/ in astonishment") until the shaking head of a teaching assistant rattles him: "Suddenly confidence/ slips out of my voice, sits down/ in the front row, snoring." "In a Pig's Eye" satirizes political correctness. "You Can't Write a Poem About McDonald's" proves the statement is not true. "The Facts of Life" describes parents explaining sex to their six-year-old. Like his earlier book, *Tunes for Bears to Dance To* uses much free verse, though it also contains sestinas and sonnets.

PEOPLE AND DOG IN THE SUN

Falkenstein writes, "Wallace sees the upside constantly balanced by the downside." Her statement describes well the poems in this book, which again are a mixture of open and closed forms and which include the familiar topics of Wallace's father and the farm. The poems about the farm celebrate nature and the simple grandeur of living things, but that tone is in contrast to the poems about Wallace's father. The opening poem refers to the American ideal of changing one's life by moving to the country, but clearly Wallace's old farm is no utopian world, "the pastures gone to boulders and weeds,/ a fury of dandelions and wild mustard." Indeed, in "The Cinematics of Loss," written in third person, the farm becomes an imagined place of loneliness and isolation.

In the background of many of these poems is an awareness of the passage of time and of loss. In "Assembling" Wallace struggles to assemble a piece of equipment, thinking, "And now, here at the flanged end/ of late middle age, I find myself/ rattled by the simplest instructions."

In the sestina "The Poet, Graveside" he reminds himself

> Soon enough, we'll all be nothing more
> than figures in some unforgotten poem
> (if we're lucky). *God, don't let us be
> cut off, incomplete, like a sestina, ending here.*

In "Poppies," a poem that combines the painting of Georgia O'Keeffe and the loss of his father, Wallace writes about the dissolution of the intensity of grief itself as a kind of loss. However, the awareness of time passed does not preclude a happier tone. "Matheny" and "Thirteen" portray affectionate memories of adolescence. "Softball," another sestina, shows Wallace wondering if he is too old to play the game but ends with him hitting the ball "over the fielders' heads and the field,/ smaller and smaller until it's nothing like a ball." In the title poem he muses on the situation of old couples, aware they are close to death, "their names written on water," but as in "The Poet, Graveside" there is hope that perhaps art may somehow mitigate life's losses.

THE MAKINGS OF HAPPINESS

The tension between hope and pessimism continues in Wallace's fourth book, published in 1991. It is most evident in the contrast between the second and third sections of the collection, titled "Breakdown" and "The Makings of Happiness," respectively. The first section of this book of mostly open forms includes poems about family and Wallace's memories of his youth: basketball, sexual experience, smoking, and summer Bible camp.

"Breakdown" focuses on personal and social struggle: parental fears, awareness of impending death, violence, and war. In "Headlines" a car accident raises a question about the possibility of keeping children "safe inside the formal garden you've prepared/ for them." Two poems reflect on being forty years old. In "At Forty" death looms in consciousness. In "Turning Forty" the theme of memory, important in the first part of the book, also emerges. Time "spirals, silent, circling/ back on itself, an old dog, settling/ on the same tired spot again." The poem's suggestion that time is not progression so much as cycle anticipates a theme in Wallace's subsequent book, *Time's Fancy*. "The Hell Mural," (panels 1 and 2, the first a sestina, the second a villanelle) reflects on Hiroshima, Japan, and artists' portrayals of human suffering.

The third section offers a hopeful perspective. "Building an Outhouse" creates an analogy between the builder and the poet, humorously overturning the notion of time-as-ravager: "let the nub of your plainspoken pencil prevail/ and it's up! Functional. Tight as a sonnet./ It will last forever (or at least for awhile)/ though the critics come sit on it, and sit on it. "Hope is not always easy, however, but sometimes hard won through tribulation. In "Apple Cider" the harvest is carried out against a backdrop of remembered deaths: "Memory squeezes us dry/ beyond sweetness, beyond weeping." Yet the poem ends by affirming life even as one is aware of the world's hostility. While the ties created by family bring with them pain or frustration, they also seem to provide the best solace, and Wallace celebrates kinship in "The Fat of the Land," about a family reunion.

TIME'S FANCY

This is a darker, more philosophical, and more abstract book than Wallace's others, and it uses more closed forms than the others as well, including Petrarchan and Shakespearean sonnets, canzones, ballades, and a pantoum. The title, from a passage by W. H. Auden, suggests time will have its way with us. "Quick Bright Things" is a somewhat-Keatsian reflection on the change of seasons and, ultimately, on change itself. Wallace describes the "tenuous" beauty of late summer and reflects on the relationship between ephemeral beauty and the desire to prevent change: "Against the permanence/ of darkness and silence, we'll spin out/ a tenuous deliquescence. We'll sing."

Paradoxically, there is affirmation in the knowledge of death itself, since it involves an appreciation of beauty. In fact, many other poems in this volume imply an interdependence between opposites or at least an attempt to understand the world as a cyclical interplay of dichotomies.

The theme receives humorous treatment in "Why I Am Not a Nudist," which explains how romantic love is nurtured by a glimpse rather than an open vista: "the still small pleasure/ of the withheld sweet familiar/ stays mysterious after all." Here pleasure, conventionally associated with possession, instead emerges from what is "withheld." In "Why God Permits Evil" Wallace states that without it, "who/ could know or choose the good?" While the poem is philosophical, it is not ponderous, because it is grounded in the humorous dilemma of a sixth-grader embarrassed by his lack of pubic hair.

Often, the poems' forms reinforce their themes and contain a "turn" or shift in tone or thought. This is a natural tendency in a form such as the sonnet but is used effectively in other poems as well.

THE USES OF ADVERSITY

Wallace explained the impetus for this collection of one hundred sonnets: "On May 31, 1994, it came to me that I should write a sonnet a day for a year." Writing in such a form allows him to "tap" into the "great energy" of the tradition, and it also serves the more practical function of encouraging composition. He stated, "formal verse helps *generate* poems. Technique is discovery." The poems, covering topics from childhood to adulthood, are variations on the sonnet, sometimes with a strict rhyme scheme, sometimes without, sometimes following the Petrarchan, sometimes the Shakespearean form, sometimes combining both. Jay Rogoff observes that the poems in the book reveal a deliberate progression to "a moving ritual defense against darkness."

OTHER MAJOR WORKS

SHORT FICTION: *Quick Bright Things: Stories*, 2000.

NONFICTION: *Henry James and the Comic Form*, 1975; *The Last Laugh: Form and Affirmation in the Contemporary American Comic Novel*, 1979; *God Be with the Clown: Humor in American Poetry*, 1984.

EDITED TEXT: *Vital Signs: Contemporary American Poetry from the University Presses*, 1989.

BIBLIOGRAPHY

Chappell, Fred. "Family Matters." *The Georgia Review* 45 (1991): 767-777. Reviews *The Makings of Happiness* in the context of other works about family.

Falkenstein, Linda. "The Hero of Ron Wallace's New Fiction Looks a Lot Like the Author Himself. Or Does He?" *Isthmus* (February 25, 1995). This article focuses mainly on *Quick Bright Things* but includes biographical information and Wallace's thoughts about writing in general.

Wallace, Ronald. "'He Is Mad Which Makes Two': A Sonnet Project." *AWP Chronicle* 30, no. 1 (1997). This article details the writing of *The Uses of Adversity*. In it, Wallace explains how he came to write the book, as well as his ideas about poetic form.

_____. "'To Tell One's Name': The Audience for Poetry." *Wisconsin Academy Review* (Summer, 1996): 9-13. This essay contains biographical information and an overview of trends in contemporary American poetry.

Steven R. Luebke

EDMUND WALLER

Born: Hertfordshire, England; March 3, 1606
Died: Hall Barn, England; October 21, 1687

PRINCIPAL POETRY

Poems, 1645, 1664, 1686, 1690, 1693
"A Panegyrick to My Lord Protector," 1655
"A Poem on St. James' Park as Lately Improved by His Majesty," 1661
"Instructions to a Painter," 1666
Divine Poems, 1685
The Second Part of Mr. Waller's Poems, 1690

OTHER LITERARY FORMS

In 1664, Edmund Waller collaborated with Charles Sackville, the Earl of Dorset, Sir Charles Sedley, and several other young wits in translating Pierre Corneille's play, *Pompée* (c. 1642). He also had a hand in a Restoration adaptation of Francis Beaumont and John Fletcher's play *The Maid's Tragedy* (1610-1611); the revisions were printed in the second 1690 edition of the *Poems*. Three of Waller's speeches before the Short and Long Parliaments are reprinted by Elijah Fenton in *The Works of Edmund Waller, Esq., in Verse and Prose* (1729); extracts from speeches made in the Restoration parliaments can be found in Anchitell Grey's ten-volume *Debates of the House of Commons, from the Year 1667 to the Year 1694* (1763). Waller's extensive correspondence, both personal and political, has not been collected in any one edition.

ACHIEVEMENTS

Although his poems were circulating in manuscript form from the late 1620's, Edmund Waller garnered little critical attention until nearly twenty years later. The discovery of his plot against Parliament in 1643 pushed him into the political limelight; the publication of his poems in 1645 in four separate editions is in part attributable to the desire of the booksellers to capitalize on his public notoriety. The innovations of Waller's poetry—his peculiar style of classical allusion and his perfection of the heroic couplet—were fully appreciated only with the Restoration. As Francis Atterbury remarked in his "Preface to the Second Part of Mr. Waller's *Poems*" (1690), Waller stands "first in the list of refiners" of verse and ushers in the "Augustan age" of English poetry. John Dryden's comment in the "Preface to Walsh's Dialogue concerning Women"—"Unless he had written, none of us could write"—pays full tribute to Waller's role in charting the public mode so essential to Restoration and eighteenth century poetry. The Augustans continued to laud Waller; as late as 1766, the *Biographica Britannica* described him as "the most celebrated Lyric Poet that ever England produced."

With the Romantic reaction against neoclassical taste, Waller's reputation plummeted. Critics condemned his poetry as vacuous and artificial; doubts about the probity of his actions during the civil war reinforced the aesthetic judgments. Elizabeth Barrett Browning's dismissal of Waller in *The Greek Christian Poets and the English Poets* (1863)—"He is feeble poetically, quite as surely as morally and politically"—exemplifies how biographical considerations distorted the critical picture. Edmund Gosse, the most important nineteenth century critic of

Edmund Waller (© Michael Nicholson/Corbis)

Waller, savaged his subject in *From Shakespeare to Pope* (1885). Although Gosse argued that Waller's role in the rise of neoclassicism was lamentable, he did at least recognize that Waller had played a crucial role in that movement.

Despite the resurgence of interest in seventeenth century poetry led by Sir Herbert Grierson and T. S. Eliot early in the twentieth century, Waller's reputation continued to languish until the 1960's. Since then, several book-length studies and articles have examined the precise character and extent of Waller's influence on Augustan verse. Although no "Waller Revival" seems to be in the offing, his position in the history of English poetry now appears fairly secure. Future studies will probably focus on Waller's relation to other Caroline writers, an aspect of his work that still remains for the most part neglected.

Waller was certainly not the inventor of the heroic couplet, but he played a critical part in gaining its acceptance as the preferred verse form for neoclassical poetry. His style of classical allusion, singular in the 1620's and 1630's, provided the model for English poets of the suc-

ceeding century. Waller's innovations, however, were more valuable for public, political poetry than for meditative or amatory verse; Gosse's complaint that his technique proved deadly to eighteenth century lyric is more than a little justified. Waller's glory and his bane lie in his position as one of the truly transitional figures in English literature. Because he straddles the Renaissance and the Restoration, critics have been hard put to decide where to place him. As recent studies suggest, however, this transitional position renders Waller's works all the more important. The current interest in periodization will continue to make Waller the focus of critical scrutiny.

BIOGRAPHY

Edmund Waller was born on March 3, 1606, into a wealthy landowning family. John Hampden, the future parliamentary leader, was a maternal first cousin; Oliver Cromwell was a more distant kinsman. The death of Robert Waller in 1616 left his ten-year-old son the heir to an estate worth £3,500 per annum. Anne Waller, the poet's mother, sent him to Eton, and from there he proceeded to Cambridge. In 1620, he was admitted a Fellow-Commoner of King's College, but appears to have left without taking a degree. Waller may have represented Agmondesham, Buckinghamshire, in the Parliament of 1621; it is certain that he sat for Ilchester in the Parliament of 1624 at the age of eighteen.

In July, 1631, Waller married Anne Bankes, the wealthy heiress of a London mercer, against the wishes of her guardians. The Court of Aldermen, which had jurisdiction over the wardship of Mistress Bankes, instituted proceedings against Waller in Star Chamber; only the personal intervention of King Charles I appeased the Aldermen and they dropped their suit upon payment of a fine by the young bridegroom. Anne Waller died in October, 1634, after bearing a son and a daughter.

Waller had begun writing verses at a young age. What is generally supposed to be his earliest poem, "On the danger of His Majesty (being Prince) escaped in the road at St. Andrews," was composed sometime during the late 1620's. A series of occasional poems on Charles I and Henrietta Maria constituted the bulk of Waller's literary production during the late 1620's and early 1630's. With his good friend George Morley, later Bishop of

Winchester, the poet joined the philosophic and literary circle that Lucius Carey, Viscount Falkland, gathered about him at Great Tew. During this period Waller also became an intimate of Algernon Percy, who succeeded to the Earldom of Northumberland in 1632, and his sisters Lucy Hay, the Countess of Carlisle, and Dorothy Sidney, Countess of Leicester. Sometime after the death of his wife, Waller commenced a prolonged poetic courtship of Lady Leicester's daughter Dorothy, whom he celebrated under the name of Sacharissa (from the Latin *sacharum*, "sugar"). Many, though by no means all, of Waller's best-known lyrics are addressed to Lady Dorothy. It is questionable whether the Sidneys ever took Waller seriously as a suitor; in any event, with the marriage in July, 1639, of Lady Dorothy to Lord Spencer of Wormleighton, later created Earl of Sunderland, the poet was disappointed in his hopes. Waller and Lady Sunderland were frequent correspondents for the remainder of their lives. An anecdote relates that the pair met at the house of Lady Woburn after both had attained old age. The widowed Lady Sunderland asked, presumably in jest, "When, Mr. Waller, I wonder, will you write such beautiful verses to me again?" "When, Madam," replied the poet, "your ladyship is as young and handsome again."

With the political upheavals of the early 1640's, Waller entered upon the most active phase of his public career. He sat in the Short Parliament of 1640 as the member for Agmondesham; he was returned to the Long Parliament, which convened in November, 1640, for St. Ives. Waller at first aligned himself with the constitutional moderates who resisted the abuses of the royal prerogative, but as the temper of Parliament grew more radical he increasingly took the side of the king. Waller played a prominent role in the attack on ship-money, of which his cousin Hampden was the most prominent opponent; his speech condemning what he considered an unlawful tax was immensely popular and reportedly sold twenty thousand copies in one day. On the other hand, Waller attacked the proposals to abolish the episcopacy, arguing that such tinkering with fundamental institutions would lead to the abolition of private property and undermine the bases of English society. With the outbreak of the civil war in August, 1642, Waller remained in the parliamentary stronghold of London, but soon became embroiled in a scheme to end the conflict by delivering the city to the king. "Waller's Plot" was discovered in May, 1643, and its leaders arrested. Waller confessed all, an action that alienated him from many royalists; his brother-in-law, an accomplice in the plot, was hanged on the basis of Waller's testimony. Waller himself escaped execution by paying a fine of ten thousand pounds and reportedly spending three times that amount in bribes. After a year and a half in prison, the poet was released and banished to the Continent.

Waller spent the next six years in France and Italy. During that period, he married his second wife, Mary Bracey, and his poems were published, purportedly without his permission, in England. In 1651, Waller received a pardon from Parliament and returned to England in January, 1652. He soon reached an accommodation with the Cromwell regime, and in 1665, published his famous "A Panegyrick to my Lord Protector." In the same year, he was appointed a Commissioner of Trade.

When the monarchy was later restored, Waller made the transition easily, he being among the first to greet the newly arrived Charles II with a poem titled "Upon his Majesty's Happy Return." When Charles complained that this panegyric was inferior to that composed for Cromwell five years earlier, Waller made the celebrated reply, "Poets, Sir, succeed better in fiction than in truth." Waller's wit ensured his retention of a firm position at court during the reign of Charles and during that of his brother James II. The poet also continued to serve in Parliament, steering a moderate course between the court and country parties and periodically reminding his colleagues of the importance of trade to England's greatness. He was a primary supporter of measures to extend religious toleration to Catholics and to Protestant dissenters.

Waller's second wife died in 1677, and soon afterward he retired to his home at Hall Barn, renowned for the woods and gardens that the poet had laid out himself. In his last years, Waller apparently underwent a religious conversion; rejecting his earlier works, he turned to composing hymns and meditations on spiritual themes. He died at Hall Barn on October 21, 1687, surrounded by his children and grandchildren, at the age of eighty-one.

ANALYSIS

Edmund Waller's poetic corpus is singular in its homogeneity. Although his career spanned more than half a century, it is difficult to trace any stylistic development; as Samuel Johnson remarks in his "Life of Waller," "His versification was, in his first essay, such as it appears in his last performance." What changes do appear in Waller's poetry are primarily thematic rather than technical and can be attributed to the demands of genre rather than to any maturation in style. An examination of several poems composed at different periods of Waller's life and for very different occasions demonstrates this uniformity and, at the same time, demonstrates the innovations that Waller brought to seventeenth century verse.

"OF HIS MAJESTY'S RECEIVING THE NEWS OF THE DUKE OF BUCKINGHAM'S DEATH"

Waller's earliest poems are mainly panegyrics composed on Charles I and Henrietta Maria. In "Of His Majesty's receiving the news of the Duke of Buckingham's death," one of the best of these pieces, Waller charts the program that English poets would follow for the next century in celebrating the virtues of the Stuart monarchs. The assassination of George Villiers, Duke of Buckingham, in 1628 constituted a major blow, both political and emotional, to the young king. According to the Earl of Clarendon, Charles publicly received the news with exemplary calm. When a messenger interrupted the monarch at prayers to blurt out the report of Buckingham's death, Charles continued to pray without the least change of expression; only when the service was completed and his attendants dismissed did he give way to "much passion" and "abundance of tears." In his panegyric, Waller celebrates the king's public response to the assassination and suppresses the unedifying private sequel. Charles's refusal to suspend his household's devotions is viewed as an act of heroic piety:

> So earnest with thy God! can no new care,
> No sense of danger, interrupt thy prayer?
> The sacred wrestler, till a blessing given,
> Quits not his hold, but halting conquers Heaven.

The conceit of the "sacred wrestler," which implicitly identifies Charles with the biblical patriarch Jacob, emphasizes that it is only through exertion that the king masters his natural impulses of grief and fear. His outward composure proceeds from a tenacious courage rather than from any lack of feeling. The direct address of the first line and the succession of present tense active verbs inject the description with dramatic urgency. Although threatened by personal harm and lamed ("halting") by the loss of his chief minister, Charles struggles and triumphs. By subordinating his personal grief to a faith in divine providence, the king "conquers" no mere earthly kingdom, but heaven itself.

Waller provides a context for Charles's heroism by comparing his response to Buckingham's death with the behavior of Achilles and of David in similar circumstances. While Achilles reacts to the death of Patroclus with "frantic gesture," Charles maintains a princely serenity; while David "cursed the mountains" for the death of Jonathan, Charles prays. The English king represents the ideal Christian hero, of which David and Achilles were but imperfect types: His absolute self-control and religious faith crown those virtues that he shares with the heroes of biblical and classical antiquity.

Charles's composure in the face of adversity constitutes both the justification and the outward manifestation of his kingship. Waller's contemplation of Charles Stuart's simultaneous humanity and divinity explodes in a final burst of compliment:

> Such huge extremes inhabit thy great mind,
> Godlike, unmoved, and yet, like woman, kind!
> Which of the ancient poets had not brought
> Our Charles's pedigree from Heaven, and taught
> How some bright dame, compressed by mighty Jove,
> Produced this mixed Divinity and Love?

The poet's initial sympathy with the king in his effort to master his grief and fear gradually shades into an awed recognition of his godhead: Dramatic struggle concludes in masquelike apotheosis.

Several aspects of Waller's technique in "Of His Majesty's receiving the news of the Duke of Buckingham's death" constitute innovations in Caroline verse. Although nearly every seventeenth century poet employed classical and biblical mythology in his work, Waller exploits this legacy in a new way; the detailed comparisons between Charles and Achilles and David anticipate the elaborate typological schemes used so effectively by poets such as John Dryden in *Absalom and Achitophel* (1681) or Alexander Pope in his Ethical Epistles. Accompanying this predilection for allusion is Waller's use of the extended simile and the Homeric epithet. All these devices derive from classical epic: By his own admission, Waller's early reading consisted mainly of Vergil, George Chapman's translation of Homer, and Edward Fairfax's translation of Torquato Tasso's *Gerusalemme Liberata* (1580-1581, *Jerusalem Delivered*).

More striking than the presence of sustained classical allusion, perhaps, is the regularity of Waller's verse. Of the nineteen couplets in the poem, all but one is closed; the individual lines are by and large end-stopped and the few instances of enjambment are not particularly dramatic. In short, Waller is using the heroic couplet with sophisticated ease in this poem of 1628-1629. Waller's sense of balance within individual lines is no less precise: Rhetorical devices such as zeugma and chiasmus lend the poem an unmistakable Augustan ring.

"OF THE LADY WHO CAN SLEEP WHEN SHE PLEASES"

The presence of these devices in panegyrics on the monarchs seems appropriate, but their translation to lyric is a surprising development. "Of the lady who can sleep when she pleases," for example, addresses the conventional amatory situation of the indifferent mistress and the love-harried suitor, but the classical frame of reference imparts an unwonted air of formality to the lover's plaint:

> No wonder sleep from careful lovers flies,
> To bathe himself in Sacharissa's eyes.
> As fair Astraea once from earth to heaven,
> By strife and loud impiety was driven;
> So with our plaints offended, and our tears,
> Wise Somnus to that paradise repairs.

In the remaining fourteen lines of the poem, Waller introduces yet another four deities and several more extended similes. Johnson notes with approval that Waller avoids Petrarchan and Metaphysical conceits and that his amorous verses "are less hyperbolical than those of some other poets. Waller is not always at the last gasp; he does not die of a frown, nor live upon a simile." Allusion, in fact, appears to fill the void left by Waller's

abandonment of more traditional amatory conceits. The epic style brings with it an almost epic detachment; even when treating the most emotionally charged situations or intimate passions, Waller maintains a tone of cool suavity. The seduction poem "To Phyllis," for example, opens dramatically—"Phyllis! why should we delay/ Pleasures shorter than the day?"—but the ensuing arguments are abstract, general, and lifeless. It is hard to imagine that a real woman or a real love is in question. After pointing out the insignificance of the past and the uncertainty of the future, Waller's speaker makes his climactic appeal: "For the joys we now may prove,/ Take advice of present love." It is instructive to compare the parallel plea made by the lover in Thomas Carew's nearly contemporary poem, "To A. L. Perswasions to love":

> Oh love me then, and now begin it,
> Let us not loose this present minute:
> For time and age will worke that wrack
> Which time or age shall ne're call backe.

Waller's poem is smooth and precise, but Carew's *suasoria* is more impassioned and psychologically sensitive. Carew here imparts an urgency to his request that Waller, for all his rhetorical skill, never quite musters.

"THE STORY OF PHOEBUS AND DAPHNE, APPLIED"

Waller himself suggests the rationale behind his detachment in one of his best-known poems, "The story of Phoebus and Daphne, applied." The opening lines establish the parallel between the classical myth and the speaker's own love affair:

> Thyrsis, a youth of the inspired train,
> Fair Sacharissa loved, but loved in vain.
> Like Phoebus sung the no less amorous boy;
> Like Daphne she, as lovely, and as coy!

Her suitor's poetic gifts notwithstanding, Sacharissa refuses to yield. After a long chase, Thyrsis achieves a wholly unexpected prize:

> All but the nymph that should redress his wrong,
> Attend his passion, and approve his song.
> Like Phoebus thus, acquiring unsought praise,
> He catched at love, and filled his arm with bays.

The theory that poetry springs from a sublimated passion is hardly new, but the equanimity with which the speaker accepts his fate surprises the reader. Apparently no regret accompanies the loss of Sacharissa; as Warren Chernaik observes in *The Poetry of Limitation* (1968), "It is clear that Waller is happier with the poems (and the praise) then he would have been with the girl." Despite its frigid conclusion, "The story of Phoebus and Daphne, applied" contains a valid psychological insight. Amatory poetry is grounded in aspiration rather than in fulfillment; the pursuit of Sacharissa brings its own reward, though not the one for which the speaker had hoped. In "When he was at sea," however, Waller denies even this relation between poetry and love:

> Whilst I was free I wrote with high conceit,
> And love and beauty raised above their height;
> Love that bereaves us both of brain and heart,
> Sorrow and silence doth at once impart.

"Passion" is denied even a catalytic role in the composition of poetry; Waller's antithesis not only distinguishes between, but also absolutely opposes, the two realms of experience. In insisting upon this separation, Waller denies amatory verse any effective role in courtship. The love poem becomes a mere literary exercise. Viewed in the light of "When he was at sea," Waller's response when Charles II questioned the inferiority of his panegyric on the Restoration to that on Cromwell—"Poets, Sir, succeed better in fiction than in truth"—seems less a politic evasion than an accurate statement of his artistic principles.

"GO, LOVELY ROSE"

Waller's avowed detachment from "passion," however, at times renders him an astute observer of amatory psychology. "Go, lovely rose," perhaps the most frequently anthologized of Waller's lyrics, revitalizes a traditional topos:

> Go, lovely Rose!
> Tell her that wastes her time and me
> That now she knows,
> When I resemble her to thee,
> How sweet and fair she seems to be.

The surprising yet apt zeugma of line 2 and the graceful intimation of mortality in the word "seems," which fore-

shadows the *carpe florem* admonition in the final stanza, exemplify the witty economy that the poet displays in his best work. In "To a fair lady, playing with a snake," Waller contemplates with bemused detachment the "innocence, and youth, which makes/ In Chloris' fancy such mistakes,/ To start at love, and play with snakes." A comic delicacy suffuses the treatment of the adolescent's simultaneous repulsion from and attraction to sexuality. "The fall" similarly integrates first love into the larger natural patterns of creation and decay. Waller's gentle eroticism and deft wit, sharpened by absolute rhetorical control, render his lyrics eminently memorable and eminently quotable.

"A PANEGYRICK TO MY LORD PROTECTOR"

With his return to England in 1655, Waller again resumed the public and political poetry that had been the object of his earliest work. In technique, "A Panegyrick to my Lord Protector" resembles the pieces written on Charles I in the 1620's and 1630's: the mixture of biblical and classical allusion, the typological mode, and the epic similes combine to heroize Cromwell and legitimate his government. Waller's central conceit is an extended comparison between England and ancient Rome. As the death of Julius Caesar initiated a period of civil strife that ceased only with the emergence of Augustus, so Cromwell triumphs over the factious Parliament that assumed control after the execution of Charles. Waller retains a certain sympathy for Charles, as the parallel with the great Caesar makes clear, but his major concern is with the new, imperialistic England that Cromwell strives to forge. "A Panegyrick to my Lord Protector" is a strong poem, but more a public performance than an investigation of the crisis in loyalties that Cromwell's rule provoked. It lacks the rich ambiguities in perspective that distinguish Andrew Marvell's poem on the same theme, "An Horatian Ode upon Cromwell's Return from Ireland."

Waller's willingness to pen panegyrics for both Cromwell and the Stuarts disgruntled royalists in his own day and gave him a reputation as a venal timeserver that has persisted into the twentieth century. It can be plausibly argued, however, that the poet's devotion is to England rather than to its rulers, and Waller was not alone in recognizing how Cromwell's capable rule quashed faction at home and raised the nation's prestige abroad. With the political chaos that succeeded Cromwell's death in 1658 and the emergence of Charles II as the one leader who could reunite Englishmen, Waller was quick to reassert his loyalties to the house of Stuart. The panegyrics that form the greatest part of Waller's Restoration poetry are, with a few exceptions, competent but undistinguished. "A Poem on St. James' Park as lately improved by His Majesty" is a panegyric *cum* topographical poem in the tradition of Sir John Denham's "Cooper's Hill." Drawing on the classical tradition of *concordia discors*, Waller presents the order of the park as a harmonious microcosm of the universal order. Structures in the landscape such as the Palace of Whitehall and Westminster Abbey assume a symbolic function, becoming reminders of the eternal values upon which England's greatness is based, whoever the ruler. The willingness to experiment with a new genre that Waller demonstrates in "A Poem on St. James' Park as lately improved by His Majesty" is also evinced by "Instructions to a Painter," a poem in which he "advises" an artist how to depict the British naval victory at Lowestoft in June, 1665. Waller's panegyric, which omits the less edifying details of the sea fight, elicited a series of satiric rejoinders that served to establish the "advice to a painter" trope as a standard motif in Restoration poetry.

"OF THE LAST VERSES IN THE BOOK"

The religious pieces of Waller's last years betray no flagging in poetic energy; as Atterbury remarks in his "Preface" to the 1690 *Poems*, "Were we to judge barely by the wording, we could not know what was wrote at twenty and what at fourscore." Perhaps the most moving passage of the religious poems is the final conceit in "Of the last verses in the book":

> The soul's dark cottage, battered and decayed,
> Lets in new light through chinks that time has made;
> Stronger by weakness, wiser men become,
> As they draw near to their eternal home.
> Leaving the old, both worlds at once they view,
> That stand upon the threshold of the new.

The fine image of the battered cottage in many ways sums up Waller's poetic career. Without forfeiting his basic values, Waller nevertheless learned to adjust to the shifting circumstances of seventeenth century England. Like "The Trimmer" popularized by George Savile,

Marquess of Halifax, Waller retained an allegiance to moderation and balance in an age in which strong loyalties and excessive partisanship were the political and literary norm. Although his individual poems rarely achieve greatness, they are consistently witty, perceptive, and stylistically distinguished. The homogeneity of Waller's achievement, in fact, may be said to be his greatest triumph inasmuch as it provided one of the few fixed standards of excellence in a period of radical change. Waller's emphasis on balance and harmony, coupled with a willingness to incorporate new genres into his repertory, rendered him a fitting figure to usher in the new Augustan age.

OTHER MAJOR WORKS

plays: *Pompey the Great*, pb. 1664 (translation of Pierre Corneille); *The Maid's Tragedy*, pb. 1690 (adaptation of Francis Beaumont and John Fletcher).

NONFICTION: *The Workes of Edmund Waller in This Parliament*, 1645; *Debates of the House of Commons from the Year 1667 to the Year 1694*, 1763 (10 vols.).

MISCELLANEOUS: *The Works of Edmund Waller, Esq., in Verse and Prose*, 1729 (Elijah Fenton, editor).

BIBLIOGRAPHY

Chernaik, Warren L. *The Poetry of Limitation: A Study of Edmund Waller*. New Haven, Conn.: Yale University Press, 1968. Chernaik's book vividly depicts the political, cultural, and literary context in which Waller wrote his Cavalier lyric poetry, formal occasional poems, and heroic satire, but there are few extended analyses of his works. Contains a chapter accounting for the rise and fall of Waller's literary reputation.

Gilbert, Jack G. *Edmund Waller*. Boston: Twayne, 1979. Gilbert explores the complex relationship between Waller's political career and poetry, devotes separate chapters (with extended analyses of some poems) to the lyric and the political poems, and concludes by defining his view of art and fixing his position in English literature. Supplemented by a helpful chronology and an annotated select bibliography.

Hillyer, Richard. "Edmund Waller's Sacred Poems." *Studies in English Literature, 1500-1900* 39, no. 1

(Winter, 1999): 155-169. At age 79, Waller published *Divine Poems*, the fruits of his late rebirth that crowned the final collected edition of his works printed during his lifetime. Waller's sacred poems are discussed.

Kaminski, Thomas. "Edmund Waller, English Precieux." *Philological Quarterly* 79, no. 1 (Winter, 2000): 19-43. Kaminski places Waller in an authentic seventeenth-century context that should enable the reader to grasp both what was new in his poetry and why it should have been praised so highly during his life and for nearly a century after his death. Waller attempted to bring English verse closer to a Continental standard of wit and sophistication, and so, Kaminski asserts, he was the first, and perhaps the only, English *précieux* poet.

Miner, Earl. *The Cavalier Mode from Jonson to Cotton.* Princeton, N.J.: Princeton University Press, 1971. Miner utilizes Waller to demonstrate past Ben Jonson Cavalier motifs and provides lengthy analyses of "At Penshurst" and "A Poem on St. James' Park as lately improved by His Majesty," two topographical poems that express the social order that characterizes Cavalier poetry.

Piper, William Bowman. *The Heroic Couplet.* Cleveland: Case Western Reserve University, 1969. Provides an overall assessment of Waller's use of the heroic couplet from the early imperfections to the mature style reflected in "On St. James' Park." For Piper, however, Waller was not among the great poets, and he is compared unfavorably to Ben Jonson with respect to the Penshurst poems.

Richmond, H. M. "The Fate of Edmund Waller." In *Seventeenth-Century English Poetry: Modern Essays in Criticism,* edited by William R. Keast. Rev. ed. London: Oxford University Press, 1971. Richmond attributes Waller's decline in popularity and in literary merit to his faults as a person (his feigned madness, bribery, and informing to save his life), rather than to his poetic talents and the lack of the thought/feeling tension associated with the metaphysical poets.

Williamson, George. *The Proper Wit of Poetry.* Chicago: University of Chicago Press, 1961. Williamson discusses Waller's Restoration and Augustan wit

in the poems "On a Girdle" and "The Story of Phoebus and Daphne, applied." For Williamson, Waller's use of myth as the chief source of his wit was unique among his contemporaries.

Michael P. Parker;
bibliography updated by the editors

WALTHER VON DER VOGELWEIDE

Born: Probably lower Austria; c. 1170
Died: Near Würzburg, Germany; c. 1230

PRINCIPAL POETRY
Songs and Sayings of Walther von der Vogelweide,
    1917
Poems, 1952
Die Gedichte, 1959

OTHER LITERARY FORMS
Walther von der Vogelweide was exclusively a lyric poet.

ACHIEVEMENTS
Walther von der Vogelweide is recognized as the single most important Middle High German lyric poet. According to Peter Wapnewski, he made two pioneering contributions to literary history. First, he moved German courtly love poetry from the sterile artificiality of conventional literature to a fresh personal expression, even inventing a corresponding lyric genre, the *Mädchenlieder* (songs to a common-class girl, sometimes also misleadingly called songs of "lower love"). Second, he gave a new nobility to didactic and political poetry. Kuno Francke goes so far as to see in Vogelweide's love songs "the struggle for the emancipation of the individual" which eventually led to the overthrow of "the whole system of medieval hierarchy" and "an anticipation of this great emancipation movement, a protest of the individual against the dictates of society." Peter Rühmkorf, in his *Walther von der Vogelweide, Klopstock und Ich,* deromanticizes the ultrapatriotic German image of Vogelweide and sees him primarily in individualistic

terms as a "self" struggling for personal identity and recognition in a time of social crisis.

This much is certain: Whether addressing an emperor, a pope, or a high nobleman or lady, Vogelweide speaks with courage, authority, and clarity; he is not intimidated by any class distinctions. In his love poetry, he is not satisfied with a one-sided platonic relationship or an adulation of mere external beauty or high social status; for him, love is a shared affection, a reciprocal meeting of hearts and minds, an inner attitude, an important ennobling force in the lives of men and women. The scope of Vogelweide's themes and the tone and manner of their treatment make it unmistakably clear that his office as a lyric poet went beyond courtly entertainment and included functions of political propaganda and ethical critique, functions which are performed today by the communications media. Yet Vogelweide, like other medieval lyric poets, composed and sang his own songs, and he was more highly praised by his contemporaries for his singing than for his lyrics.

BIOGRAPHY

Walther von der Vogelweide was born about 1170, possibly of the lower nobility. Because the term *Vogelweide* was a common word meaning bird-sanctuary, numerous places have claimed to be the poet's birthplace, most conspicuously Vogelweidhof, near Bozen, South Tyrol, where an impressive monument in his honor has been erected; since this region did not belong to Austria at the time and the Austrian dialect was not spoken there, however, scholars speculate that Vogelweide probably was born in lower Austria. Wherever his birthplace, the poet "learned to sing and recite in Austria," appearing at the court of Duke Frederick in Vienna about 1190 and probably learning his craft from Reinmar von Hagenau.

In 1198, Vogelweide's patron died; Vogelweide was forced to leave Vienna to begin the uncertain life of a wandering minstrel. The only extant historical document concerning him is a receipt showing that Wolfger, Bishop of Passau, had given "to the singer Walther de Vogelweide five solidi for a fur coat on Saint Martin's Day in the year 1203." Among his many other patrons was Count Hermann of Thuringia, at whose court he met Wolfram von Eschenbach, author of *Parzival* (1200-

1210), and other lyric poets. Vogelweide wrote songs for three emperors; after Philip of Swabia was murdered and his successor Otto IV allegedly did not pay the poet enough, Vogelweide shifted his allegiance to Friedrick II, who eventually rewarded him with a small property near Würzburg in about 1220. Presumably, Vogelweide did not participate in the Crusade of 1228 and died about 1230 near Würzburg, where his grave could still be seen in the cathedral garden half a century later. Another minstrel, Hugo von Trimberg, grieved over Vogelweide's death with the words, "Ah Sir Walther von der Vogelweide, I would feel sorry for whomever forgot you."

ANALYSIS

In only one generation, from 1180 to 1210, the great flowering of Middle High German courtly culture under the Hohenstaufen Dynasty produced—in addition to four great epic writers, Hartmann von Aue, Gottfried von

Walther von der Vogelweide (© Bettmann/Corbis)

Strassburg, Wolfram von Eschenbach, and the anonymous author of *The Nibelungenlied* (c. 1200)—numerous lyric poets, the most renowned of them being Walther von der Vogelweide. Even princes and emperors ranked among the courtly love poets. The roots of this German medieval poetry are multiple: Provençal and northern French courtly love poetry, indigenous songs and Goliardic verse such as that collected in *Carmina burana* (1847), and a variety of Latin secular and religious genres (eulogies, sequences), some dating back to antiquity. Medieval German poetry features a great variety of meters and melodies, since the minstrel was expected to compose a new meter and melody for each song.

Courtly love poetry (*Minnesäng*) was symptomatic of a new secular culture that rejected the "contempt of the world" preached for centuries by the monastic orders and that sought instead to harmonize eternal salvation with earthly happiness. The role of women in the courts and castles was to elevate and dignify life and to convey a certain *hoher muot* (joy of life) which was the crowning virtue in the knightly code. Although the love songs sometimes have a trace of the occasional in them—they often are addressed to a particular woman and reflect specific circumstances—such love poetry was not a stylized proposal for a literal love relationship, but an artistic achievement, a fictional, public musical presentation on the theme of love for the amusement and edification of the entire court (estimated as usually comprising between thirty and seventy persons). Since the idolized woman was supposed to be of high rank, married and virtuous, no erotic reciprocation was expected but, at most, a greeting or token of appreciation. Praise of the woman was not a means to an end but an ennobling activity in itself, for the lady represented the humane ideal of beauty and dignity for which this secular knightly society was striving. Her being not only was physically beautiful and charming but also encompassed a catalog of virtues such as honor, self-discipline, constancy, moderation, and loyalty—traits of a proud, aristocratic society.

MÄDCHENLIEDER

Walther von der Vogelweide regarded highly his function as a courtly love poet who could express for the men and women of his society the emotions of body and soul. Under Vogelweide's predecessor and teacher, Reinmar von Hagenau, *Minnelyrik* (love poetry) had de-

generated into a genre that was obsessed with the monotonous theme of the unrequited lover. Vogelweide broke with this tradition—and from von Hagenau—and introduced many new dimensions into the thematics of courtly love poetry. His *Mädchenlieder* scandalized society by directing love and the title *Frouwe* (noble lady) to a common-class girl. He also introduced into courtly poetry a mature, reciprocally fulfilled marital love, contrary to the tradition of unrequitedness. Late in life, he rejected the ribaldry and crudity that was brought into courtly love poetry under the influence of peasant dances by a new generation of minstrels, including Neidhart von Reuenthal. Finally, he turned away from "Lady World" and his "many errors" as a *Minnesänger* and addressed God Himself as "you sweet true Love." Underlying this broad span of the love concept in Vogelweide's poems is the medieval idea of "gradualism," which sees all reality as an ascending ladder of being, each rung different in degree but analogous to the ones above and below—from the various levels of earthly reality, through man who is both body and soul, to the heights of spirit in God.

Paul Stapf divides the love lyrics chronologically into six periods: early love songs, songs from 1198 to 1203, high courtly love, *Mädchenlieder*, new high courtly love, and late songs.

Vogelweide's early love songs, written before leaving the Viennese court in 1198, though still quite within the conventions of the genre, already display the sharp tension created by the ambiguity of traditional love poetry. On the one hand, it was supposed to represent an approved public relationship involving "conversation" with and "instruction" as well as "praise" of the woman by the poet, who was rewarded with a "greeting" or token of esteem, all strictly on a platonic level; on the other hand, by the very nature of love between man and woman, it sometimes involved an implicit erotic attraction which threatened to erupt into socially unacceptable amorous fulfillment. In these early poems, the poet's love is rejected; the woman is unapproachable and on the defensive; she has maintained her dignity as a woman and will hold him accountable for any violation of proper decorum. In some poems, she would like to grant his desire for a love affair, but social pressure prevents it; she has a duty to maintain her honor. With a touch of resignation, she submits to the dictates of society: "Mir tuot einer slahte wille" ("Can She Alone Be Happy When All Others Are Sad?"). Sometimes the concept of honor is deepened to a personal ethical code. She wants "to have a woman's proper qualities . . . since a beautiful body is worthless without understanding," that is, without moral responsibility.

Perhaps the very ambiguity and wide range of meaning of courtly love is what invites some poems to be highly rational and analytical: "Whoever says that love is a sin, should first reflect well, for love contains many a distinction which one can rightly enjoy, and its consequence is constancy and great happiness. . . . I am not speaking of false love, which would better be called non-love: I will always oppose it." Yet the same poem also speaks from living experience: "No one knows what true joy is who did not receive it from a woman." Vogelweide leaves no doubt as to the edifying and positive nature of love: "Love is the source of all good qualities; without love no heart can be truly happy."

CARMINA BURANA

Vogelweide's departure from the court at Vienna marks a sharp break in his life and poetry and begins a second stage of his creative activity, his early years as a wandering minstrel, from 1198 to 1203. His songs now show the direct influence of the vagabond poets of the *Carmina burana*. One single theme runs through them all: how summer follows winter and love chases away sadness. Their execution is smoother and the nature imagery is brighter, used economically like a kind of symbolic shorthand: In winter, the frost hurts the little birds so much that they no longer sing; in summer, the girls will be playing ball in the street again (a rare glimpse of medieval everyday life). The poet celebrates the great power of May over man and nature. Perhaps May is a magician, he suggests; wherever his delight goes, no one is old. The winter of 1198 must have been particularly severe; the poet believed he would "never again pick red flowers in the green meadows." His death, he muses, would have been "a loss to all good men who long for joy and who like to sing and dance."

HIGH COURTLY LOVE POEMS

The poet's third period, from 1203 to 1205, was characterized by poems of "high courtly love" which were traditional, rational, and sophisticated. Most of the poems of this period are united by a single theme: constancy and reciprocity. These are two sides of the same coin: The lady demands fidelity on the poet's part and rebukes him for praising other women; the poet replies that he cannot continue praising only her if she refuses to reciprocate his love.

A highly optimistic poem called "Ir Sult sprechen" ("Speak a Welcome") illustrates the poet's praise of other women: He has seen many countries, and German ways please him the best. German men are handsome, and German women are like angels; whoever scolds any of them is mistaken (probably an allusion to the Provençal poet Peire Vidal's castigations of German manners). Whoever seeks virtue and pure love should come to Germany. "From the Elbe to the Rhein and back again as far as Hungary live the best people I have ever known in the world. If I can judge good upbringing and beauty, by God, the women are nobler here than anywhere else." Now a harsh note is struck: His lady reproaches him for praising other women and thus being guilty of inconstancy. As if enraged at the lady's rebuke, he retaliates in the song "Staet ist ein Angest und ein Nôt" ("Constancy Is Fear and Torment"), harping ironically on constancy, naming it twelve times in two short stanzas, and finally exclaiming "Lady Constancy, set me free!"

Poem after poem reflects a period of strife, for example, "Saget mir ieman, waz ist Minne?" ("What Is Loving?"), "Daz ich dich sô selten grüeze" ("That I So Seldom Praise You Is No Misdeed of Mine"), and "Mîn Frowe ist ein ungenaedic Wîp" ("My Lady Is a Cruel Woman"). Finally, in "What Is Loving?," the poet hammers out the principle that will lead to the end of his relationship with this "lady" and to his abandonment of one-sided courtly love: "Love is the joy of two hearts. If they share equally, then love is there; if this is not so, then one heart cannot receive it." The poet, however, does not conceal a sour, unchivalric remark: "If I have grown old in her service, she's not gotten any younger either." Finally, he exhorts his young rival: "Avenge me and whip her old skin with fresh switches."

"LOWER LOVE" SONGS

The fourth group of songs (written after 1203 and therefore somewhat overlapping the previous group) overcomes this discord and enters a new phase of fulfillment with a woman of equal or lower rank. In

"Herzeliebez Frowelîn" ("Little Maid So Dear"), whatever joy the poet experienced in this world was caused "by her beauty, her goodness, and her red mouth that laughs so lovingly." He responds to those who criticize him for directing his love songs to a person of lower rank, claiming that "they don't have any idea what love is, they have never experienced true love, since they love only for wealth or external beauty. What kind of love is that?" He reiterates his reason for having changed from "high courtly love" to this more satisfying relationship: "A Lover's affection is nothing if it goes unrequited. One-sided love is worthless; it must be shared, permeating two hearts and none besides."

The most famous of Vogelweide's songs of "lower love" is "Unter der Linden" ("Under the Linden-Tree"), in which a naïve, common-class girl rejoices in her love experience under the linden tree, the crushed flowers still showing the place where the couple had lain. What he did with her no one will ever know except he and she and the little bird that sang the refrain "Tandaradei!" Equally masterful is the poem "Die welt was gelf, rôt unde blâ" ("The World in Red and Blue Was Gay"), also called the "vowel poem" since, in German, each stanza rhymes with one of the vowels *a, e, i, o,* and *u*; it is a highly graphic poem calling for the end of winter. One wryly humorous poem, "Wer kan nû ze danke singen" ("Who Can Please Everyone with His Song?"), lauds the poet's broad range of experience, which makes it possible for him to sing a wide variety of songs, but observes that people still are dissatisfied.

NEW HIGH LOVE

In his fifth period, that of "new high love" (from 1205 to about 1220), Vogelweide's songs show more depth, maturity, and formal perfection. The "lady" seems to be of very high social rank, and the relationship is a conventional one. There is sadness at court; the times are unsuited for song; true love has died; and the whole world is beset with troubles. Song is tempted to wait for better times, as in "Die zwîvelaere Sprechent" ("The Doubters"). The exuberance of youth is over, and the poet articulates a positive attitude even toward the unequal relationship represented by conventional courtly love, as long as there is some reciprocation: "He is certainly also fortunate who observes her virtues precisely so that it moves his heart. An understanding

woman should respond with affection." This kind of love can motivate poetry: "Just a loving look from a woman gives joy to the heart. . . . But what is like the happiness where a beloved heart is faithful, beautiful, chaste, and of good morals? The lucky man who has won this does nothing wrong to praise it before strangers." The importance of moderation is explained in "Ich hoere iu sô vil tugende jehen" ("I Hear You Speak of So Many Virtues") and "Allerwerde keit ein Füegerinne" ("Coordinator of All Values, Lady Moderation"). One of Vogelweide's very best poems and the crown jewel of this period is "Sô die Bluomen ûz dem Grase dringent" ("When the Flowers Spring Out of the Grass"), which compares a beautiful May day with a beautiful noblewoman in all her finery. If the poet had to choose between the two, the outcome would be: "Sir May, you would have to become March before I gave up my lady."

LATE SONGS

Three poems can adequately represent the late songs (from 1220 to 1230). "Ir reinen Wîp" ("Ye Women Pure") is a sort of literary testament: "For forty years or more I have sung of love and of how one should live" (note the educational function of the poet). In "Frô Welt" ("Lady World"), he renounces the world because, while her beauty is lovely to look at from the front, from behind she is so horridly shameful that he wishes to spurn her forever. In "Ein Meister las" ("A Wise Man"), he meditates on the transitory quality of life and says, "It is high time for penance, since I, a sick man, now fear grim death." The poem ends in a vein of religious repentance, an emphasis found in several poems, including the long *Leich.*

SPRUCH

About half of Vogelweide's poems belong to the broad genre of *Spruch* (political or didactic) poetry. Vogelweide's type of *Spruch* was formerly believed to have been a single-stanza spoken poem, but the melodies of some of them have been recovered, and it is now known that they were not recited but sung. Friedrich Maurer's "song-theory" brought together in a single poem stanzas of the same "tone" or melody that had been variously scattered in the manuscripts. In Maurer's view, each "tone" of a political song was invented in its own separate period, and thus stanzas belonging to one "tone" could be dated far apart in Vogelweide's time, although some of them were written over a period of a few years. "Each tone," Maurer asserts, "has its briefly extended time of origin, but especially its own theme and subject matter." Poems with different melodies, even though thematically similar, are not contemporaneous. The advantages of Maurer's theory are that it facilitates study of the gradual evolution of Vogelweide's stanzaic art; it enriches interpretation by retrieving the overarching meaning connecting the stanzas of one "tone"; and it elucidates stanza-internal meaning by contrast and comparison. Maurer's theory, however, has not been unanimously accepted by scholars. Paul Stapf, editor of a fine annotated edition and modern German translation of Vogelweide's poems, rejects Maurer's theory in favor of more accurate dating of the individual stanzas. Annette Georgi, in her study of the Latin and German *Preislied*, seems to follow Maurer.

The major controversy discussed in Vogelweide's political poems is the struggle between the Empire and the Papacy during the period of turmoil following the election of two pretenders to the imperial throne in 1198. After the death of Henry VI, son of Frederick Barbarossa, the Hohenstaufen faction elected Henry's brother, Philip of Swabia, to succeed him, while the opposing Guelphs elected Otto IV of Brunswick. When Philip was murdered, Otto succeeded him with the approval of Pope Innocent III, who later shifted his support to the Hohenstaufen Frederick II. During this time, the petty princes tried to stake their own areas of power at the expense of the Crown. In these controversies, Vogelweide supported first Philip, then Otto, and finally Frederick II, probably reflecting the successive allegiances of his princely patrons. In the poem "Diu Krône ist elter danne der Künec Philippes sî" ("The Crown Is Older than King Philip"), Vogelweide argues for Philip—his legitimacy based on the preestablished condition that the crown, which is older than he, fits him so well, a poetic allusion to the Hohenstaufen's possession of the real Imperial crown (while his opponent Otto IV was crowned in the proper place, Aachen, and by the right ecclesiastic, the Bishop of Cologne). Another poem in the "Philip tone" parallels, with some doctoring of historical facts, a procession of Philip at Magdeburg with the birth of Christ; Philip's wife Irene (later renamed Mary), daughter of the Byzantine Emperor, is compared with the Virgin Mary, "rose without thorn, dove without gall." Again the possession of the right insignia is stressed, but an even stronger title, the link with the great Hohenstaufen predecessors, is compared with the Trinity: "There walked an Emperor's brother and an Emperor's son in one garment, though the names are three" (Frederick, Henry, and Philip). To medieval man, accustomed to thinking in terms of the "analogy of being," the impact of this poem confirming divine appointment must have been great.

"I Was Sitting upon a Rock"

Written in the "imperial tone," the most famous of Vogelweide's poems, "Ich saz ûf eine Steine" ("I Was Sitting upon a Rock"), depicts Vogelweide in the pose in which he is illustrated in the *Manessische Handschrift*: sitting on a large rock with his legs crossed and his chin and one cheek supported by the palm of one hand. He was pondering very anxiously on "how one should live in the world." He could give no advice on "how one could acquire three things," so that none of the three would be ruined. The first two are honor and property, "which often are harmful to one another"; the third is God's grace, "which is worth more than the other two." The poet would like to have all three in one chest, but unfortunately it is impossible for property, worldly honor, and God's grace ever to dwell in one heart. "Paths and roads are blocked to them: Treachery lies in ambush, violence moves on the street; peace and justice are very sorely wounded. The three have no safe convoy, until these two recover." The subject of the stanza is how to order one's life correctly in this world.

The main components of the poem are seven abstract nouns; the main structuring device is a system of mathematical vectors which creates an ethical topography and conveys an impression of objective moral certainty. There are three goals that one should attempt to attain in life: honor (a), property (b), and God's favor (c), which is more valuable than property and honor and is also eternal. There are two instrumental goods: peace (d) and justice (e). Because a and b are incompatible and together endanger c, one cannot hope to attain them all. At this point, an extended metaphor is inserted: The streets are insecure for a, b, and c, since two negative abstractions, treachery (f) and violence (g), threaten. The two ancillary values d and e are sorely wounded. The solution to *a*, *b*, and *c*'s predicament would be an extension and reversal of the metaphor "unsafe roads." This solution cannot be achieved until the two ancillary values *d* and *e* have the "remedy" that corresponds to their "ailment." A secondary rhetorical figure occurs twice, an *apo koinu* (the relation of one grammatical component to two others, one before and one after it); the clause "I could give no advice" can relate to the "how" clause before and the "how" clause after it. Similarly, "unfortunately this cannot be" negates both "I wanted to put them in one chest" and the possibility that honor, property, and God's favor might come together in one heart.

"OTTO TONE"

Of the six poems in the "Otto tone," the first in Maurer's sequence welcomes Otto IV and announces the submission of the princes, specifically of Vogelweide's patron Dietrich von Meissen; the second alludes to the eagle and lion on Otto's coat of arms and calls upon him to establish peace in Germany with "generosity" and "power" and to direct his country's power against the pagans. The third, "Hêr Keiser" ("Sir Emperor"), calls even more emphatically for a crusade: "Sir Emperor, I am an official messenger and I bring you a message from God: you govern the earth, he governs the kingdom of heaven: he has ordered me to complain to you (you are his regent) that in his Son's land the Pagans are exulting to the disgrace of you both. You should protect His rights." The fourth Otto poem, "Hêr Bâbest" ("Sir Pope"), refers to the contradiction created when the Pope first endorsed Otto and then switched to support his opponent: "We heard you command Christendom as to which Emperor they were to obey. . . . You should not forget that you said: 'Whoever blesses you let him be blessed; whoever curses you, let him be cursed with a complete curse.' For God's sake, think that over, if the honor of the clergy means anything to you." The fifth Otto poem applies the same complaint to the clergy at large: "We laymen are puzzled by the clergy's instructions. What they taught us till a few short days ago, they now want to contradict. . . . One of the two instructions is false." The sixth Otto poem retells the story of Jesus with the coin, and the conclusion gains cogency because the Middle High German words for "Caesar" and "Emperor" are identical: "Render to the Emperor what is the Emperor's and to God what is God's."

ANTI-PAPAL POEMS

The thread of unity in Vogelweide's political stance is his advocacy of a strong, united Empire. This explains why in a good number of his poems he opposed the Papacy, blaming Papal interference in the affairs of the *Reich* for the widespread disorder in Germany. In the poem "Künc Constantin der gap sô vil" ("King Constantine Gave So Much"), an angel cries "Alas, alas, three times alas" because of Constantine's famous (forged) donation of temporal power to the Papacy, which poisoned all Christendom by striking at its civil head: "All princes now live in honor except that the highest one is weakened. . . . The clergy want to pervert secular law." From the first, Vogelweide had blamed the Pope for appointing two Germans to one throne "so that they would destroy and devastate the realm" and had identified cupidity as the motive: "Their German silver flows into my Italian coffers." Elsewhere Vogelweide minces no words about the negative influence of the clergy: "You bishops and noble clergy are misled. See how the Pope ties you with the devil's ropes. If you tell us he has St. Peter's keys, then tell us why he scrapes his words out of the Bible." He then accuses the clergy of simony and of being the devil's spokesmen. Certain lines most clearly identify the evil as seen by Vogelweide: "If [the Pope] is greedy, then all are greedy with him; if he lies, all lie with him; and if he deceives, they deceive with the same deception." Vogelweide's viewpoint is clear: Christendom is ailing because its highest religious authority, the Pope, undermines the chief secular authority, the Emperor; moreover, by the Pope's high authority, the evil at the top contaminates all the parts.

PATRONAGE POEMS

An astonishing number of Vogelweide's poems deal with complaints about inadequate financial support or a lack of respect from one patron or another, including the Emperor Otto, whose stinginess Vogelweide blames for his change of allegiance to Frederick. At first, the modern reader may be repelled by an impression of crass venality, but in time, he perceives the need of a poet struggling in a marginal, insecure existence for a basic livelihood and for minimal social acceptance in the feudal class system. Two poems treat of a misunderstanding with a noble patron because a subordinate official had failed to give Vogelweide the promised clothing.

Two others describe a lawsuit against a certain Gerhart Atze for shooting Vogelweide's horse on the grounds that its "relative" had bitten off Atze's finger. Apparently, Vogelweide's class status was at stake, but, whatever the outcome, Vogelweide avenged himself on Atze by poetic mockery. Other poems testify to the difficulties of being a dependent, wandering, unpropertied poet. One poem summarizes Vogelweide's weariness with the wanderer's life: "Tonight here and tomorrow there, what a juggler's life that is." The reader rejoices with Vogelweide when he finally receives from Frederick the small property that gives him a home of his own: "I have my fief, all the world, I have my fief! Now I do not fear the frost on my toes."

"ELEGIE"

One of the most poignant poems Vogelweide wrote is the famous "Elegie," consisting of three stanzas all beginning with "Alas." The second stanza deals with the sad state of the Empire and the "ungentle letters" from Rome (excommunicating Frederick II in 1227); the third is a call for a crusade, and contains a primitive but striking image of fallen earthly reality: "The world is beautiful on the outside, white, green and red, and within black in color, dark as death." In the first stanza, Vogelweide looks back on his life with elegiac poignancy like a reawakening Rip van Winkle: "Alas, where have all my years vanished? Did I dream my life, or is it true? Was all I dreamed existed really nothing? . . . My former playmates are tired and old. The meadow has been plowed, the forest has been cleared: If the river didn't flow as it once did, truly my sorrow would be great."

BIBLIOGRAPHY

Berleth, Richard J. *The Orphan Stone: The Minnesinger Dream of Reich.* New York: Greenwood Press, 1990. See index for Berleth's use of Vogelweide's lyrics in this study of the relationship of the German political scene and German lyric poetry. Mixes biographical, literary, and the broader political elements of Vogelweide's career and output.

Gibbs, Marion E., and Sidney Johnson. *Medieval German Literature: A Companion.* New York: Garland Press, 1997. See pages 267-279 for an overview of Vogelweide's life and works, with a few translated passages and bibliography.

Jones, George. *Walther Von der Vogelweide.* New York: Twayne, 1968. A brief but comprehensive study of Vogelweide's life and major works. The first monographic treatment in English.

Kaplowitt, Stephen J. *The Ennobling Power of Love in the Medieval German Lyric.* Chapel Hill: University of North Carolina Press, 1986. Studies the theme for twenty-one minnesingers in twenty-one short chapters, of which Vogelweide's is the longest at forty-five pages. Poems are discussed and described, but scantly quoted.

McFarland, Timothy, and Silvia Ranawake, eds. *Walther Von der Vogelweide: Twelve Studies.* Oxford: Meeuws, 1982. A collection of essays that covers a wide range of issues regarding influences on Vogelweide, his influences on the genre, and his works' forms and content.

Richey, Margaret F., ed. *Essays on the German Love Lyric.* Oxford: Basil Blackwell, 1943. Includes a short essay on Vogelweide and his work, along with seven poems in English translation.

Sayce, Olive. *The Medieval German Lyric, 1150-1230: The Development of Its Theme and Forms in Their European Context.* Oxford: Clarendon Press, 1982. A widely ranging and very readable study that places Vogelweide and his works in both the German and broader European streams of lyric development.

Werbow, Stanley, ed. *Formal Aspects of Medieval German Poetry.* Austin: University of Texas Press, 1969. Includes numerous references to Vogelweide's works.

Ziegler, Vickie. *The Leitword in Minnesang: Stylistic Analysis and Textual Criticism.* University Park: Pennsylvania State University Press, 1975. Includes close studies of Vogelweide's poems 42.21 and 52.23.

David J. Parent;
bibliography updated by Joseph P. Byrne

WANG WEI

Wang Youcheng
Born: Daiyuan Prefecture, Shanxi Province; 701
Died: Zhangan, China; 761

PRINCIPAL POETRY

Major poems, including "Written While Crossing the Yellow River to Qing-he," "To the Frontier," "For Vice-Magistrate Zhang," and "The Deer Enclosure," can be found in *Wang Wei: New Translations and Commentary*, 1980 (Pauline Yu, translator). Other poems are collected in *Laughing Lost in the Mountains: The Poems of Wang Wei*, 1991 (Willis Barnstone, Tony Barnstone, and Shu Haixin, translator).

OTHER LITERARY FORMS

Although known primarily for his poetry, Wang Wei was also the author of several important writings pertaining to various traditions in Tang Dynasty Buddhism, in particular his funeral inscription for the *stēlē* of the Sixth Chan (Zen) Patriarch, Hui-neng. In addition, Wang was an accomplished musician and painter, acquiring considerable renown for the latter talent after his death. No painting authentically attributable to him is extant, but numerous copies of several of his works were executed over a period of centuries. One of the best known of these is the long scroll depicting his country estate on the Wang River. From the Song Dynasty onward, when only copies of his works survived, he became glorified as the preeminent Chinese landscape painter, with his work honored as the prototype of *wen ren hua* (literati painting)—amateur rather than academic, intuitive and spontaneous rather than formalistic and literal.

ACHIEVEMENTS

Wang Wei is generally acknowledged to be one of the major poets of the Tang Dynasty (618-907), the most brilliant period in the long history of Chinese poetry; he was probably the most respected poet of his own time. In one of the many classificatory schemes of which traditional Chinese critics were particularly fond, he was labeled the "Poet Buddha," ranked with the two poets of the era who were to exceed him in fame, Li Bo (701-762), the "Poet Immortal," and Du Fu (712-770), the "Poet Sage." This appellation reflects Wang's association with Buddhism, which flourished in eighth century China, but it is important to note that very few of his poems are overtly doctrinal or identifiable solely with any one of the many traditions or lineages of Buddhism active during the Tang.

Like those of most men of letters of the time, Wang's life and works reflect a typically syncretic mentality, integrating yet exploring the conflicts among the goals and ideals of Confucian scholarship and commitment to public service, Daoist retreat and equanimity, and Buddhist devotion. Such issues, however, are not dealt with directly or at length in his works. His poetry relies on suggestion rather than direct statement, presenting apparently simple and precise visual imagery drawn from nature which proves elusive and evocative at the same time. He eschews definitive closure for open-endedness and irresolution, leaving the reader to attempt to resolve the unanswered questions of a poem. His best poems rarely include any direct expression of emotion and frequently suppress the poet's own subjective presence, yet this seeming impersonality has become the hallmark of a very personal style.

Because Wang's poems embody what Stephen Owen has called "the artifice of simplicity," they were frequently imitated, both by the coterie of court contemporaries at whose center he stood and by later poets, followers of the "Wang Wei school." Although many of the imitators were able to replicate the witty understatement, the stark imagery, and the enigmatic closure of Wang's work, none—by general critical agreement—succeeded in probing to the same extent depths of emotion and meaning beneath a deceptively artless surface.

BIOGRAPHY

Wang Wei (also known by his cognomen, Wang Mochi, and his courtesy name, Wang Youcheng) was the eldest child of a prominent family in Shanxi Province. He became known for his precocious poetic, musical, and artistic talents and was well received by aristocratic patrons of the arts in the two capital cities of the empire. After placing first in his provincial examinations at the age of nineteen, Wang went on to pass the most literary of the three main types of imperial civil-service examinations in 721, one of the thirty-eight successful candidates that year. (Typically, only one or two percent of the thousands of candidates recommended each year for this highly competitive examination would pass.) He received the *Jinshi* (presented scholar) degree and began his slow but steady rise through government ranks.

Like all Chinese scholar-bureaucrats, Wang moved from post to post and to various parts of the empire, most of which appear in his poetry. From his position as a court secretary of music in the western capital of Chang-an, he was sent to the east in Shandong (720's), back to the capital (734), to the northwest frontier (737), south to the Yangzi River area (740), and back to the capital (742). His career was interrupted at intervals by temporary losses of favor, factional intrigues, and various infractions, the most serious of which was his collaboration—though forced—in the puppet government of the rebel general An Lu-shan, whose armies overran the capitals and forced Emperor Su-tsung into exile from 755 to 757. Only the intercession of Wang's younger brother, Wang Jin, who had fought valorously with the loyalist forces, secured a pardon for the poet in 758. The next year, he attained the high-ranking sinecure of *shangshu youcheng* (undersecretary of state) and is thus frequently referred to as "Wang Yu-ch'eng." In this respect, his career differed markedly from that of his two most famous poet contemporaries, Li Bo and Du Fu, neither of whom passed the imperial examinations or enjoyed Wang's considerable family connections. Unlike them, Wang never suffered severe financial hardship (despite the posing of some of his poems), maintaining a relatively secure position in the social and cultural center of what was later to be perceived as the golden age of the Tang Dynasty itself, the reign of Emperor Xuanzong (713-755).

The date of Wang's marriage has not been recorded, nor the number and names of any children he may have had. His wife died around 730, however, and Wang remained celibate thereafter—somewhat unusual for the times and an index of his devotion to Buddhist principles. It was in fact around the time of his wife's death that he began a serious study of Buddhism. In addition to the several essays and inscriptions connected with issues and figures in Tang Buddhism that are included in Wang's collected works, the most illuminating evidence of his religious commitment is his choice of cognomen, Mochi. Combined with his given name, Wei, these syllables form the Chinese transliteration (Weimochi)

of one of the Buddha's best-known contemporaries, Vimalakīrti, said to have preached a sutra that became especially popular in China, not only for its doctrines but also because he himself remained a layman throughout his life. Vimalakīrti also espoused such central Confucian social ideals as filial piety and loyalty to the ruler and demonstrated to the Chinese that the good Buddhist did not necessarily have to leave his family and retreat to a monastery.

This example was an important one for Wang, for his religious beliefs never led him to abjure totally his political and social relationships. Popular legend has long held Wang to have been but a reluctant bureaucrat, and his poetry speaks frequently of a desire for reclusion. Wang did spend much of his time on retreat in various locations, particularly at his country estate at Lan-t'ien on the Wang River, which he acquired around 750 and where he eventually built a monastery. All the same, he remained officially in office until his death.

ANALYSIS

The poems of Wang Wei were first collected by his brother, Wang Chin, at imperial request and presented to the throne in 763. The number of poems that can be attributed definitively to him is small—371, compared with the thousand or more each of Li Po and Tu Fu. The official dynastic history records his brother as telling the Emperor that there were once ten times that many, the rest having been lost during the turmoil of the An Lu-shan Rebellion.

Whatever the case, the poems for which Wang is best remembered have fostered an image of him as a private, contemplative, self-effacing observer of the natural scene. In fact, however, despite references in several poems to his solitude behind his "closed gate" at home, many of his poems were inspired by social occasions—visits from or to friends, journeys of fellow bureaucrats to distant posts, his own departures to new offices—and by official occasions as well. Wang was a highly successful court poet, the master of a graceful, formally regulated style whose patterns had been perfected during the seventh century.

The ability to write poetry on any occasion was expected of all government officials and was in fact tested on the civil-service examination. Several of

Wang's poems bear witness by their titles to having been written "to imperial command" on some formal court occasion—an outing to the country, an important birthday, the construction of a new building, the presentation of some gift—and often "harmonize respectfully" with the rhymes of a model poem composed by the Emperor himself. Most of these poems were written in a heptasyllabic eight-line form with rigidly regulated rules of tone, parallelism, and rhyme. Poets in attendance would vie with one another to complete their poems first, and there was often some official evaluation of literary quality. Other poems in Wang's corpus arose out of less formally decorous contexts but reveal nevertheless the demands upon the Tang poet to be able to respond to the stimulus of an occasion in an apparently spontaneous and sincere, appropriate, economical, and witty manner.

"LADY XI"

A good example of Wang's mastery of the literary and contextual demands of the poem written on command is his early work "Xi furen" ("Lady Xi"). He is said to have composed this poem at the age of twenty (nineteen by Western reckoning), when he was preparing for the imperial examination and in residence at the court of the Emperor's half brother, Li Xian, Prince of Ning. It is one of several poems in Wang's collection for which was noted his supposed age at composition—unverifiable, but attesting the recognition of his early prowess. An anecdote recorded in a collection of stories attached to poems compiled in the ninth century provides the necessary explanation of the background of the poem. The Prince, it seems, had been attracted by the wife of a pastry vendor and had purchased her as his concubine. After a year had passed, he asked her if she still thought of her husband, but she did not reply. The Prince then summoned the vendor, and when his wife saw him, her eyes filled with tears. Ten or so people were present at the time, including Wang, and their patron commanded them to write a poem on the subject. Wang's quatrain was the first completed, and everyone else agreed that none better could be written. The Prince then returned the pastry vendor's wife to her husband.

In the poem itself, there are, surprisingly, no overt references to the couple in question. The first two lines express a simple and general denial—that loves of the past can be forgotten because of present affections. The

last two lines conclude with an allusion, but not to the pastry vendor and his wife; they refer to a text, a story in the Tso commentary on the "Spring and Autumn Annals" (722-481 B.C.E.) of the Chun Qiu (sixth to fifth century B.C.E.), one of the Confucian classics. There it is recorded that the king of Chu defeated the ruler of Xi and took the latter's wife as his own. Though she bore him children, Lady Xi never spoke to her new spouse, and when finally asked why, she is said to have answered: "I am but one woman, yet it has been my fate to serve two husbands. Although I have been unable to die, how should I dare to speak?"

This poem illustrates concisely Wang's typical "artifice of simplicity," his ability to charge the briefest of poems—twenty syllables in all—with a considerable burden. Typically, denials open and close the poem, revealing Wang's penchant for the open-ended quality of negation as opposed to assertion. What could have been a merely sentimental episode becomes dignified here through the link made to the moral dilemma of a historical ruler's wife and by the poet's choice not to mention the contemporary protagonists at all. Typically effective, also, is the poet's refusal to make any direct comment. Understatement and allusion work hand in hand here to make a point that is no less clear for not being stated explicitly.

THE WANG RIVER COLLECTION

These same methods of indirection and evocation, of using objects and events to suggest something lying beneath the surface, distinguish Wang's most famous poems, his limpid and apparently selfless depictions of natural scenes. These works are not, as a rule, devoid of people, and much of their impersonal quality derives simply from the general tendency of the classical Chinese language to avoid the use of subjective pronouns and to remain uninflected for person, tense, number, gender, and case. Wang does, however, exploit the inherent potential of the language to create indeterminate or multiple meanings more than do most other traditional poets. This is true, for example, of several poems in his well-known sequence, the Wang River collection. As Wang's preface explains, this group of twenty pentasyllabic quatrains, each of which names a site on Wang's country estate, was written in the company of one of his closest friends, a minor official named Pei Di (born 716). Pei wrote twenty poems to match those of his host, and these are also included in standard collections of Wang's poetry.

As Owen has noted in his history of poetry in the High Tang, Wang's quatrains as a whole probably represent his most significant contribution to generic development, particularly because of his substitution of enigmatic understatement for the epigrammatic closure more common at the time. The Wang River collection is informed by some of the key modes of consciousness of the poet's entire œuvre: an emphasis on perceptual and cognitive limitations, a transcendence of temporal and spatial distinctions, and a sense of the harmony of the individual and nature. This is especially true of the fifth and probably most famous poem in the sequence, "Lu zhai" ("Deer Park").

"DEER PARK"

This poem exemplifies typical quatrain form, narrowing its focus from the massiveness of a mountain to a ray of the setting sun entering a mossy grove. Each line presents a perception that is qualified or amplified by the next. What is given in the first line as an "empty mountain," where no people are seen, reverberates with echoes of human voices in the second line. Whether these echoes signify that other people are actually present on the mountain at some distance or are intended metaphorically, to suggest the poet's memories of friends in an altogether different location, however, remains unspecified. The third line places the plot in a specific place and time—toward sunset, when "returning" (*fan*) light sends a "reflected" (also *fan*) glow through an opening into a glade. The fourth line suggests that the poet has been in the grove that same morning, or perhaps all day, and thus knows that the light is shining on the blue-green moss "again."

More than a brief nature poem, "Deer Park" links keenly observed and deceptively simple perceptions with far-ranging Buddhist implications. In her study *Wang Wei*, Marsha L. Wagner has made some important observations about the title: that "Deer Park" was the name of the site near Benares where the Buddha preached his first sermon after becoming enlightened, that it was an alternate name for the monastery Wang built on his Wang River estate, and that the deer not caught in a trap was a conventional Buddhist symbol for the recluse. Within the poem itself, the crucial word is *kong* (empty), on which hinges more than the question about the unpopulated state of the mountain. *Kong* is also the translation of the Sanskrit word *śūnyatā*, which was a key term in the Buddhist traditions with which Wang was familiar, denoting the illusory or "empty" nature of all reality and the ultimate reality, therefore, of "emptiness." *Kong* is one of the most frequently recurring words in Wang's poetic vocabulary—translated sometimes as "empty," at other times meaning "merely" or "in vain," in each case with the same powerful resonance. Moreover, the vision of the light entering the grove, the counterpart of beams of moonlight in other poems, provides a concrete image of the experience of enlightenment itself. The poem as a whole, then, encapsulates key Buddhist notions about the nature of reality and human perception of it.

"Deer Park" provides a good example of how Wang suggests religious and philosophical doctrines and attitudes in an indirect manner. Even in poems that treat Buddhist subjects more directly, doctrinal elements are generally merely implicit. Many of his accounts of journeys to monasteries, for example, are by convention metaphorical from the outset: Since temples were frequently located high in the mountains, visiting them required an effort that represented the physical counterpart to the progress toward enlightenment. Several of Wang's poems on this topic emphasize the spiritual implications of the physical ascent, among which "Guo Xiangji si" ("Visiting the Temple of Gathered Fragrance") is particularly well known.

"VISITING THE TEMPLE OF GATHERED FRAGRANCE"

Wang opens "Visiting the Temple of Gathered Fragrance" with a profession of ignorance. He does not "know" the temple, and this at once suggests several possibilities: He does not know of its existence, of its location, or of its significance—or perhaps he has discarded a rational, cognitive kind of "knowing" for an intuitive, nondifferentiating awareness more conducive to true spiritual knowledge. In any event, this special kind of ignorance sets the tone for the description of the journey up the mountain, each stage of which contains images of extreme ambiguity and vagueness. The second line speaks of "entering cloudy peaks," but the verb can refer either to the action of the speaker or to the location of the monastery, thus deliberately blurring the distinction between the traveler and his destination, or subject and object. The obscurity of these cloudy peaks is frequently associated in Wang's poetry with temples and transcendent realms and suggests the inadequacy of merely sensuous perception on such a journey of the spirit.

The poem continues to reinforce this sense of linguistic and perceptual ambiguity. The phrase "paths without people" in the third line can also be read as "no paths for people," thus further suggesting the speaker's venture into unknown territory, untraveled by others; this experience must be undertaken in absolute solitude. This sense of mystery is evoked again in the question of the following line: "Where is the bell?" As in the opening couplet, Wang reveals here a distrust of visual perception and purely intellectual cognition. Presumably the sound of a bell from somewhere deep in the mountains confirms the existence of the monastery, at least, if not its precise location. Has he heard the bell himself, though? He does not say. Thus, he must continue his ascent without the comforting knowledge of where he is or where he is going.

In the third couplet, the images appear to be more concrete than those in the preceding lines, but they are in fact equally ambiguous. In each line of the third couplet, the verb can be read either actively or passively, suggesting that the processes occurring cannot be subjected to rational analysis; they can be apprehended only intuitively as one total experience in which subject and object are indistinguishable. Furthermore, Wang's diction also undermines the sensuous precision of the couplet. Rather than focusing on the concreteness of the nouns—"stream" and "sun"—he speaks of the former's "sound" and the latter's "color," so that in each case he is describing an abstraction rather than a concrete object.

The final couplet of the poem in no way diminishes the mysterious quality of the journey. Wang has reached a pond—perhaps at the monastery, though he does not say—whose bends and curves continue to recall the winding paths of other spiritual journeys. What does it mean for the pond to be "empty"? Is it dried up, deserted, illusory, or an image of ultimate reality? In the last line, Wang simply presents a process without speci-

fying the subject or the precise nature of the object. The "peaceful meditation" may be that of a monk from the temple or the poet himself, or it may not refer to an individual at all but rather to an intangible atmosphere of the place. The "poison dragons" tamed by the meditation are traditionally interpreted as passions or illusions which may stand in the way of enlightenment, and many possible sources in Buddhist texts have been suggested. They are controlled and not eliminated, present by virtue of their very mention, thus suggesting Wang's awareness, in this poem, at least, of the effort required to attain the tranquil and selfless union with the world that, in so many of his poems, he seems to possess.

This harmony is one that transcends boundaries between subject and object and those of language as well; hence Wang's reliance on understatement and what he does not say. One well-known poem, however, flirts briefly with the possibility that perhaps words are not inadequate after all. "Chou Chang shaofu" ("In Reponse to Vice-Magistrate Chang") opens quite discursively with an observation that occurs frequently in Wang's poetry on the contrast between past and present priorities. The profession that only age has enabled him wisely to reject worldly involvement is familiar also to readers of the poetry of Tao Qian (365-427), the poet of the past with whom Wang most strongly identified and in whose eighth century revival he played an instrumental role. Like Tao, who left office early on matters of principle, Wang claims also to be rejecting the "long-range plans" associated with governmental policy. He now "only" (or "emptily"–*kong* again) knows "to return to the old forest," and the word "return" recalls the importance of the same word for Tao, who employed it frequently for the implications it possessed in early Daoist literature of getting back to one's original nature, uncorrupted by civilization and its trappings.

The third couplet of "Visiting the Temple of Gathered Fragrance" provides images of Wang's newfound freedom. Pine winds blow loose the belt of his robe, and the moon provides congenial companionship as he plays the zither, the instrument traditionally associated with scholar-recluses. The penultimate line turns to a question posed by the addressee of the poem and suggests that Wang will finally put into words the wisdom he has gained, the "reasons for success and failure" or the "principles of universal change." His response in the last line, however, provides no easy answer, only an enigmatic image of a fisherman's song that can be read in a number of ways.

In the first place, the last line in the third couplet may be regarded as a nonanswer in the tradition of the Chan or Zen koan, by means of which a Buddhist master attempts to bring a student to enlightenment by answering a rational question with a *non sequitur*, thus jolting the latter out of conventional, logical, categorical modes of thinking, and liberating his mind to facilitate a sudden, intuitive realization of truth. Wang's answer, then, would deliberately bear no relationship to Chang's query, seeking instead to reject such cognitive concerns or indeed denying the validity of his question.

There is a second possibility. Because the fisherman, along with the woodcutter, was a favorite Daoist figure representing the rustic, unselfconscious life in harmony with nature, this final line may be read as a simple suggestion to change to follow the example of such recluses and escape from official life to the freedom and serenity of country living. This is a realm, moreover, where the vicissitudes of the world and such distinctions as failure and success will have no meaning.

Yet a third interpretation of the line hinges on a possible reference to a specific fisherman's song, the "Yufu" ("Fisherman"), included in the southern anthology, the *Songs of Ch'u*, compiled during the Han Dynasty. In the earlier poem, a wise fisherman converses with the fourth century B.C.E. poet Qu Yuan, who had been a loyal minister to the king of Chu and committed to the Confucian ideal of service but who was slandered by others at court and banished. He remained self-righteous about his inflexible moral purity and later chose suicide rather than compromise his principles. In this song, when Qu Yuan meets the fisherman, he explains the reasons behind his exile; the fisherman suggests that it might have been more circumspect to adapt to the circumstances, but Ch'ü Yüan insists that he would rather drown than do so. The fisherman departs with a gentle mocking reply, singing that if the waters are clean, he will wash his hat-strings in them, and if they are dirty, he will wash his feet. Unlike the self-righteous Ch'ü Yüan, the fisherman can adjust to the conditions he finds and paradoxically remains freer of their

influence. Ultimately, perhaps, he realizes that, when seen from a higher perspective, the waters are all the same.

If Wang's use of this allusion is to be granted, then he is certainly affirming the kind of unifying vision and transcendence of distinctions that underlies his poetry as a whole. Perhaps the more important point, however, is Wang's failure to allow a definitive resolution to the question at all. The conclusion to this poem, as to so many of his poems, is purposely inconclusive and open-ended, leaving the reader to puzzle out what answers there may be.

BIBLIOGRAPHY

Barnstone, Tony, Willis Barnstone, and Xu Haixin, trans. *Laughing Lost in the Mountains: Poems of Wang Wei*. Hanover, N.H.: University Press of New England, 1991. Excellent translation of 171 poems. The critical introduction, "The Ecstasy of Stillness," by the Barnstones provides insights into these poems.

Robinson, G. W., trans. *Poems of Wang Wei*. Harmondsworth, Middlesex, England: Penguin, 1973. With a lucid introduction about the poet's life and poetic achievements.

Wagner, Marsha L. *Wang Wei*. Boston: Twayne Publishers, 1981. An excellent study of Wang Wei's poems and his career, with elaborate notes and a useful bibliography. Covers his accomplishments as a nature poet, court poet, Zen Buddhist poet, and painter.

Walmsley, Lewis Calvin, and Dorothy Brush Walmsley. *Wang Wei: The Painter-Poet*. Rutland, Vt.: Tuttle, 1968. An examination of Wang Wei's poems in the context of the art of Chinese traditional painting. With helpful illustrations.

Weinberger, Eliot. *Nineteen Ways of Looking at Wang Wei*. Mount Kisco, N.Y.: Moyer Bell, 1987. This little book offers insights into the art of translating Chinese poems. With commentary by both Weinberger and Octavio Paz.

Young, David, trans. *Five T'ang Poets: Wang Wei, Li Po, Tu Fu, Li Ho, Li Shang-yin*. [S.l.]: Oberlin College Press, 1990. Provides an opportunity for appreciating Wang Wei along with contemporary poets during the Tang Dynasty.

Yu, Pauline. *The Poetry of Wang Wei: New Translations and Commentary*. Bloomington: Indiana University press, 1980. Excellent translations of 150 poems with insightful commentary. Also includes the Chinese texts of the poems.

Pauline Yu;
bibliography updated by Qingyun Wu

ROBERT PENN WARREN

Born: Guthrie, Kentucky; April 24, 1905
Died: West Wardsboro, near Stratton, Vermont; September 15, 1989

PRINCIPAL POETRY
Thirty-six Poems, 1935
Eleven Poems on the Same Theme, 1942
Selected Poems, 1923-1943, 1944
Brother to Dragons: A Tale in Verse and Voices, 1953
Promises: Poems, 1954-1956, 1957
You, Emperors, and Others: Poems, 1957-1960, 1960
Selected Poems: New and Old, 1923-1966, 1966
Incarnations: Poems, 1966-1968, 1968
Audubon: A Vision, 1969
Or Else—Poem/Poems, 1968-1974, 1974
Selected Poems, 1923-1975, 1976
Now and Then: Poems, 1976-1978, 1978
Being Here: Poetry, 1977-1980, 1980
Rumor Verified: Poems, 1979-1980, 1981
Chief Joseph of the Nez Percé, 1983
New and Selected Poems, 1923-1985, 1985

OTHER LITERARY FORMS
In an era when poets are often as renowned and influential as critics, Robert Penn Warren nevertheless stands out inasmuch as he achieved success on two creative fronts, having as great a critical reputation as a novelist as he has as a poet. This accomplishment is not limited to the production of one singular work or of a sporadic body of work; rather it is a sustained record of development and achievement spanning more than three decades. His fiction includes the novels *Night Rider* (1939), *At Heaven's Gate* (1943), *All the King's Men* (1946), *World Enough and Time: A Romantic Novel* (1950), *Band of Angels* (1955), *The Cave* (1959), *Wilderness: A Tale of the Civil War* (1961), and *Flood: A Romance of Our Time* (1964), and there is also a short-story collection, *The Circus in the Attic and Other Stories* (1947). There can be no doubt that *All the King's Men*, a highly fictionalized and richly wrought retelling of the rise and fall, by assassination, of the demagogic Louisiana governor Huey Long, has justifiably attained the status of an American classic; it is not only Warren's best novel but also his best-known work. The story of Willie Stark, the country-boy idealist who becomes far worse an exploiter of the public trust than the corrupt professional politicians he at first sets his heart and soul against, embodies many of Warren's most persistent themes, in particular the fumbling process self-definition becomes in a universe awry with irony and a world alive with betrayal and mendacity. Made into an Oscar-winning film, the novel was also very successfully adapted as a play by Warren in the 1950's.

Warren's considerable influence on the life of letters in twentieth century America was also exercised in a series of textbooks that he edited jointly with the noted critic Cleanth Brooks. The first, *An Approach to Literature* (1936), coedited as well by John Thibault Purser, was followed by *Understanding Poetry: An Anthology for College Students*, edited by Warren and Brooks, in 1938, and *Understanding Fiction*, also edited by Warren and Brooks, in 1943. These texts utilized the practices (just then being formulated) of New Criticism, which encouraged a close attention to the literary text as a self-contained, self-referring statement. It is certain that several generations of readers have had their entire attitude toward literature and literary interpretation determined by Warren and Brooks's effort, either directly or through the influence of teachers and critics whose values were shaped by these landmark works.

ACHIEVEMENTS
Robert Penn Warren was undoubtedly one of the most honored men of letters in American history. Among his numerous awards and honors were a 1936 Houghton-

Mifflin Literary Fellowship for his first novel, *Night Rider*; Guggenheim fellowships for 1939-1940 and 1947-1948; and Pulitzer Prize wins for his novel *All the King's Men* (1947) and the poetry volume *Now and Then* (1979). (He was the only person to have won a Pulitzer for both fiction and poetry.) He also won the National Book Award for poetry with the volume *Promises* in 1958, the National Medal for Literature (1970), and the Presidential Medal of Freedom (1980). He was one of the first recipients of a genius grant, a Prize Fellowship from the MacArthur Foundation, in 1981. In 1986 he was selected to be the first poet laureate of the United States, and he served in that distinguished capacity until age and ill health required him to resign the position in 1987.

BIOGRAPHY

Robert Penn Warren was born on April 24, 1905, amid the rolling hills of the tobacco country of south-

Robert Penn Warren (© Washington Post; courtesy of the D. C. Public Library)

western Kentucky, in the town of Guthrie; he was the son of Robert Franklin Warren, a businessman, and Anna Ruth (Penn) Warren. He spent his boyhood there, and summers on his grandparents' farm in nearby Trigg County. Both grandfathers were Confederate veterans of the Civil War, and he was often regaled with firsthand accounts of battles and skirmishes with Union forces. The young Warren grew up wanting to be a sea captain, and after completing his secondary education in neighboring Clarksville, Tennessee, he did obtain an appointment to the United States Naval Academy at Annapolis.

A serious eye injury prevented his attending, however, and in 1920 Warren matriculated instead at Vanderbilt University in Nashville, set on becoming an electrical engineer. In his freshman English class, Warren's interest took a fateful turn as the young professor John Crowe Ransom and another, advanced student, Allen Tate, introduced him to the world of poetry. The two were at the center of a campus literary group called the Fugitives, and Warren began attending their meetings and soon was contributing to their bimonthly magazine, *The Fugitive*, which he edited in his senior year. Under the tutelage of Tate and Ransom, he became an intense student not only of earlier English poets, particularly the Elizabethans and such seventeenth century Metaphysical poets as John Donne and Andrew Marvell, but also of the contemporary schools that were emerging from the writings of older poets such as A. E. Housman and Thomas Hardy, as well as from the work of William Butler Yeats and T. S. Eliot.

Warren was graduated summa cum laude from Vanderbilt in 1925, taking a B.A. degree, and he continued his graduate studies at the University of California at Berkeley, from which he obtained an M.A. in 1927. He then enrolled in another year of graduate courses at Yale University and went on to spend two years as a Rhodes Scholar at the University of Oxford in England, which awarded him a B.Litt. degree in 1931.

While at Oxford, Warren completed his first published book, *John Brown: The Making of a Martyr* (1929), which took a rather callow, Southerner's view of the legendary hero of the abolitionist cause. When Paul Rosenberg, one of the editors of the *American Caravan* annual, invited him to submit a story, Warren "stumbled on" fiction writing, as he later recounted the incident. The result, "Prime Leaf," a story about labor troubles among tobacco growers back in his native Kentucky, would later find fuller expression in his first published novel, *Night Rider*.

Back in the United States, Warren joined the Agrarian movement, an informal confederation of many of his old Fugitive colleagues who were now espousing a return to agrarian, regional ideals in a Depression-ravaged America that was rapidly becoming more and more industrialized, urbanized, and, at least inasmuch as the images generated by popular culture were concerned, homogenized.

After teaching for a year as an assistant professor of English at Southwestern College in Memphis, he became, in 1931, an acting assistant professor of English at Vanderbilt. He remained there until 1934, when he moved on to accept a position at Louisiana State University in Baton Rouge. After promotion to associate professor in 1936, Warren took a full professorship at the University of Minnesota in 1942.

In 1935, while at Louisiana State, Warren had cofounded *Southern Review*, an influential journal with which he would remain until it folded in 1942. From 1938 to 1961, meanwhile, Warren served on the advisory board of another prestigious quarterly, *Kenyon Review*.

In 1930 Warren had married Emma Brescia, whom he divorced in 1951, shortly after accepting a position as professor of playwriting at the School of Drama of Yale University. On December 7, 1952, Warren married the writer Eleanor Clark, by whom he would father his two children, Rosanna, born in 1953, and Gabriel, born in 1955. Warren left his position with the drama school in 1956, but in 1961 he returned to New Haven, Connecticut, to rejoin the Yale faculty as a professor of English. From that time onward he made his home in nearby Fairfield and summered in Stratton, Vermont.

Warren continued his distinguished career as a teacher, poet, novelist, critic, editor, and lecturer virtually to the end of his long life. In February, 1986, the Librarian of Congress named him the first official poet laureate of the United States, a position he held until 1987. On September 15, 1989, the poet died at his summer home in West Wardsboro, near Stratton. He was eighty-four years old.

ANALYSIS

Robert Penn Warren was blessed twice over. He was a son of and grew up in a region of the country renowned for its love of the land and devotion to earthy folk wisdom and the art of storytelling. There was also a love of language, particularly the fustian spirit of the orator and the preacher, based on a deep, dark respect for the Word, orotund and oracular.

Added to that, however, Warren spent his formative years in a world that was making the transition from the comparative bucolic and optimistic sensibilities of the late nineteenth century to the frenzied, fearful, frenetic pace of the post-World War I 1920's. Poetry was being called into service by young people everywhere to try to explain what had happened, or at least give it manageable shape. T. S. Eliot's *The Waste Land* (1922) set the tone. At Vanderbilt among his fellow Fugitives, Warren was quickly put in touch with the new poetry that was emerging.

It is this combination of effects and influences that made Warren's poetry and gave it its vision. From the first, he hovered between the old and new—the mannered style, the modern flip; the natural scene, the symbolic backdrop; the open gesture, the hidden motive; original sin, the religion of humankind. This peculiar vantage point scored his vision, for it allowed him to know at first hand what his age was surrendering at the same time that it allowed him to question the motives for the surrender and the terms of the victory, the name of the enemy—or, better yet, his face.

Warren can bring the personal into the most profound metaphysical musings without blinking an eye or losing a beat, because finally the source of all vision, at least for Warren, is the darkest of selves at the heart of one's being, the unknown brother who shares not only one's bed but also one's body and makes, or so it seems, one's decisions. Self-discovery is Warren's trail, and the reader who follows it discovers that while it begins in coming to grips with the painful processes of caring in an uncaring world, it concludes in accepting caring as a moral obligation rather than merely a state of mind or soul. Like most twentieth century poets, Warren was really trying to reinvigorate the heroic ideal.

EARLY POEMS

The early poem "To a Face in a Crowd" echoes the world-weary angst typical of the period, the 1920's, by rendering an urban apocalypse in the bleak, stark terms of lonely souls lost in vacant vistas, finding their meager consolations in passing strangers who may—or may not—be spiritual kindred with similar dreams and like despairs. It is night, and adjectives and nouns collide in a litany of pessimism and negativism: "lascivious," "lust," "bitter," "woe," "dolorous," "dim," "shroud." This vision is mitigated, however, by the markedly poetic tone of the language: "Brother, my brother, whither do you pass?/ Unto what hill at dawn, unto what glen. . . . ?" While there is hope, the speaker seems to be saying that the idyllic interlude is no longer a viable option; instead, "we must meet/ As weary nomads in this desert at last,/ Borne in the lost procession of these feet."

Among these early poems, "The Return: An Elegy" is by far the most successful effort, for in it Warren eschewed the derivative and imitative tone, mood, and theme of poems such as "To a Face in the Crowd" and found what time would prove to be the beginnings of his own voice and vision.

The setting is simple, though not at first easily discerned: in a Pullman as the train carries the speaker back home to the hills to attend his mother's funeral. Sentiment is kept at bay, almost with a vengeance, it might seem: "give me the nickels off your eyes/ . . . / then I could buy a pack of cigarettes." Only an occasional, italicized lapse into poeticized feeling—"*does my mother wake*"—among the details of the rugged mountain-country landscape that the speaker intersperses with his thoughts gives the sense that a profound emotional turmoil is seething beneath the modernist "flip": "Pines drip without motion/ The hairy boughs no longer shake/ Shaggy mist, crookbacked, ascends."

As the poem continues, however, the reader is gradually forced to realize that it is the tension between the speaker's grief and his desire not to sentimentalize his loss that gives the poetry its incredible and peculiarly modern motive power: "*the old fox is dead/* what have I said." Thus, the speaker earns the right to lapse into the unabashed sentiment, at poem's end, of "this dark and swollen orchid of my sorrow."

This rare ability to combine the most enduring verbal expressions of human feelings with the most fleeting of contemporary realities and attitudes in a poetry that magi-

cally maintains its precarious balance between traditional poetic tone and style and the most ragged-edged and flippant of modern sensibilities continued to give Warren's work its own shape and direction as he expanded his range in the 1930's and 1940's. In "Pursuit," for example, his vision of the urban landscape has hardly improved, but it is peopled with three-dimensional emblems of a faltering, seeking humanity—"the hunchback on the corner," "that girl the other guests shun," "the little old lady in black." "Original Sin: A Short Story," meanwhile, places the reader in Omaha and the Harvard Yard and speaks of as cosmopolitan an image as "the abstract Jew," yet it ends its commentary on humanity's fated failings with country images of "the backyard and . . . an old horse cold in pasture."

So much is in keeping, of course, with the social and literary ideals that the original Fugitives formulated when they coalesced into the Agrarian movement. Their notion was that American democracy was not an urban but a rural phenomenon, forged by a link between the people and the land. In this regard, regionalism—the countryman's sense of place and of a devotion to his people—was not a pernicious thing but involved the very health of the nation, a health that the increasing pressures toward homogeneity of people and culture in sprawling urban centers could not only threaten but perhaps even destroy. Poets such as Warren became spokespersons both for that lost agrarian ideal and for the simple country folk forced by economic necessity into the anonymity of large cities, where they lived at the edge of squalor and struggled to maintain their small-town dignities.

Warren combines all these themes and concerns in "The Ballad of Billie Potts." As the speaker recounts the story of Big Billie, his wife, and their son, Little Billie, he mixes in long, parenthetical sections in which he seems to be addressing himself rather than the readers, urging himself to return—as if he could—to the lifestyles of those hillbillies "in the section between the rivers," where they were poor by urban standards but rich in spirit, in faith in themselves, and in the power of familial love. In the lost idyll mode reminiscent of William Wordsworth's "The Ruined Cottage" and "Michael," the story of Little Billie's travails and his parents' despair when circumstances force the boy to leave "his

Pappy in Old Kaintuck/ And [head] West to try his luck"
is really a twentieth century throwback's yearnings for
what were simpler and certainly more communal times.
For him now there is only the endless urban tedium, the
vacant, lonely sameness, maddeningly monotonous and
vaguely threatening: "And the clock ticked all night long
in the furnished room/ And would not stop/ And the *El*-
train passed on the quarters with a whish like a terrible
broom/ And would not stop."

Warren never ceased to contrast the earthiness of
country values and country life with the mind-forged
manacles that constrain the individual within the modern industrial landscape. At the heart of his vision, however, is a sense of the sad wasting of time and of love
that mortality forces one constantly to consider. Clearly
the problem is not "out there"; it is within us. The increasing urbanization of America is not the enemy, then,
it is simply the latest battlefield—not the disease, but the
symptom. The disease is life, and the ageless enemy is
our insatiable need to try to make it make sense, to try to
make it hurt less.

For Warren, then, one can hope only to keep oneself
spiritually and emotionally—and painfully—alive in a
world that tends undeniably toward death and decay. His
villains become those who deny that life is hardship, as
much as those who visit hardships on others. Behind the
indictment, though, there is always the lance of forgiveness, aimed as much at the heart of the speaker who
dreads the pain of his feelings as at the iniquities that
arouse it.

As the poet himself became a father and middle-
aged, children rather than the lonely crowd figured more
and more as the best emblems of the tragic core of the
human condition, as well as of the human capacity to
endure and transcend. The poetry consequently finds its
locus more and more in personal experience, the day to
day providing sufficient grist for the poet's thinking and
feeling mill.

PROMISES

"The Child Next Door," from the prize-winning
volume *Promises: Poems, 1954-1956*, focuses not on
the child "who is defective because the mother," burdened with seven already, "took a pill," but on an older
sister, who is twelve and "beautiful like a saint," and
who takes care of "the monster all day":

I come, and her joy and triptych beauty and joy stir hate
—Is it hate?—in my heart. Fool, doesn't she know that
the process
Is not that joyous or simple, to bless, or unbless,
The malfeasance of nature or the filth of fate?

Warren's unstinting, almost embarrassing honesty as he
records his feelings and attitudes, an honesty exercised
in his poetry from as early as "The Return," gains him an
edge of intimate moral ambiguity in this more mature
poetry. The present poem concludes: "I think of your
goldness, of joy, how empires grind, stars are hurled,/ I
smile stiff, saying *ciao*, saying *ciao*, and think: this is the
world." Whether that is the expression of a bitter resignation or a casual dismissal or a measure of joyful acceptance, the speaker will give no clue: "this is the
world." Readers are left to measure the sizes of their
own hearts and thereby experience both the pain of observing life too closely and, if they wish, the expiation of
letting it go.

By now a cosmopolitan himself, Yale professor with
an Oxford degree and summer home in Vermont, the
boy who is father to the man did not forget the Kentucky
hill-country source of his vision. In reminiscences such
as "Country Burying (1919)," the autobiographical
rather than symbolical and metaphysical seems to prevail, but there is still a telling tale. The poem is a
requiem for all those lost "boy's afternoon[s]" when life
was so present, even there amid tokens of death, and the
mind more receptive, but the spirit would be somewhere
else: "Why doesn't that fly stop buzzing—stop buzzing
up there!" Apologies to Emily Dickinson aside, those
were a boy's thoughts in 1919: In the poem they are
some measure of the adult's remorse as he reached mid-
century. Now there is not only the pain of the present to
endure; there is the pain of the past, its loss, as well.

BROTHER TO DRAGONS

This sense of remorse was never absent from Warren's poetry, but now it is outspoken and unremitting, and
it becomes a major motivating factor in the later poetry.
Brother to Dragons, a historical novel in verse written in
the form of a play that the author calls a poem, is the apex
of all Warren's previous pessimism, displaying little of
his often-whimsical capacity to turn heel but not turn coat
on caring too much for the human condition. In the larg-

est sense, the poem is a severe indictment of the human animal. With some liberties but no real distortion of the facts, it recounts the tale of Lilburn Clarke, a Kentuckian who in the early nineteenth century brutally murdered a black slave over a trifling offense. Beyond the tragic scope of those facts, there was an even more tragic rub in Warren's view: Clarke was the nephew of Thomas Jefferson, himself a paradoxical figure who could pen the Declaration of Independence and still be a slaveholder, and who believed in the perfectibility of humankind.

Warren, who appears himself as a character in the poem by carrying on a pointed philosophical debate with Jefferson, used the bare bones of the story to call into question the worth, let alone the authenticity, of all human ideals. Still, in the lengthy monologue with which the poem concludes, he insists that despite this sorry record of human endeavor in the name of ideals that are always betrayed, "we must argue the necessity of virtue."

YOU, EMPEROR, AND OTHERS

By the time the 1950's ended, Warren had established a new métier as a social commentator with an equally self-accusatory eye. In *You, Emperor, and Others*, the public and the private, the man and the child, the father and the son all find expression. "Man in the Street," with its singsong rhythms and nursery-rhyme, chorus-like echoes, hits the gray flannel suits with their black knit ties and Brooks Brothers shirts not where they live but where they work, where each of them somehow makes accommodations with the vacuities of the corporate world. If it is a vision that virtually lends an air of nostalgic romance to an early poem such as "To a Face in the Crowd," "Mortmain" harks back to "The Return." It is the speaker's father who is dying now, but the irreverent flippancy of the earlier poem is not even there to be turned away from: "All things . . . // Were snatched from me, and I could not move,/ Naked in that black blast of his love." It is a poem in five parts, and in the last of those, "A Vision: Circa 1880," he imagines his father as a boy, "in patched britches and that idleness of boyhood/ Which asks nothing and is its own fulfillment." The poem ends with a turn to pure lyricism, without any reaching out to metaphysical solutions or conceits, merely the wholly verbal bounty of language giving life to dead time in images of a present, natural splendor.

POETRY THEMES

Warren published seven additional volumes of poetry from 1960 to 1980, and the lyrical mode itself intensified into the speculative tone that he apparently could not abandon. Still, as he reminds the reader in the 1968 volume, *Incarnations*, "You think I am speaking in riddles./ But I am not, for// The world means only itself" ("Riddle in the Garden"). In *Audubon*, meanwhile, he asks, "What is love," and reminds the reader that "one name for it is knowledge," as if attempting to justify his lifelong preoccupation with trying to understand human beings and their place on earth and in the universe.

As the poet grew older, mortality became even more of an obsessive theme, and the issues of time past and time present, the poet now having a wealth of experience to draw upon, found even more expression in this new admixture of a metaphysical lyricism. In "Paradox," for example, from the "Can I See Arcturus from Where I Stand?" section of *Selected Poems, 1923-1975*, stargazer man is brought down to earth, or at least to a sense of his limits, when he confronts a retelling of Zeno's paradox of the arrow and its unreachable goal. The natural simplicity and personal quality of the setting—a run on a beach that causes the speaker to recollect an earlier spirited chase—remove from the poem the bane of a *de profundis* that often intruded into Warren's most youthful metaphysical flights; the information is presented not as insight but as the sort of everyday truth any feeling, thinking person might draw from experience, should he or she care to. Indeed, the poem is finally a tender love lyric worthy, in its formal rhapsodic effect, of A. E. Housman:

> I saw, when your foot fulfilled its stride,
> How the sand, compressed, burst to silver light,
> But when I had reached that aureoled spot
> There was only another in further stride.

This bringing all vision down to earth is best exemplified in a late poem such as "Last Meeting." It is another hill-country recollection; the poet, now by all accounts elderly, recalls being back home once and meeting an elderly woman who had known him as a boy. Now she too is dead. "All's changed. The faces on the street/ Are changed. I'm rarely back. But once/ I tried to find her grave." He failed, he explains, but promises that he will yet succeed. Still, "It's nigh half a life-time I haven't managed,/ But there must be enough time left for that." People's failures are little things, he seems to be saying toward the end of his creative life, and because Warren has done such an incredible job of exploring them in every other permutation throughout his long career, the reader should pay heed to the conclusions he reaches. People's failures, no matter how great, are little things; it is the burden of remorse they carry for them that is great.

Like Thomas Hart Benton, who painted the great vistas of Western deserts in his later years, Warren turns to the overlooked and the insignificant to find beauty and, in it, significances he may have missed. In "Arizona Midnight," "dimly I do see/ Against that darkness, lifting in blunt agony,/ The single great cactus." He strains to see the cactus; "it has/ its own necessary beauty." One must see through the apparent agony into the heart of the thing and seek out the beauty there, rather than pausing too long to reflect only on the tragic surface—which one can see only dimly, in any event.

CHIEF JOSEPH OF THE NEZ PERCÉ

It is no wonder, then, that one of Warren's last completed volumes was *Chief Joseph of the Nez Percé*. Here he returns to the tragic record that is the past, to betrayal and injustice and the bitter agony of exile despite one's having "done the right thing." Yet this time, in Joseph's enduring the arrogance of office and the proud man's contumely, Warren finds an emblem of triumph despite apparent defeat. Now he can see history not as irony, filled with the tragic remorse that looking back can bring, but as process and "sometimes, under/ The scrutinizing prism of Time,/ Triumphant." It seems to be the declaration of a total peace, and one cannot help but hear, as Warren surely must have hoped one would, echoing behind those words Chief Joseph's own: "I will fight no more forever."

A victory that is won against no odds is a sham. A victory that is won against life's own bitter truths is poetry. It certainly is Robert Penn Warren's.

OTHER MAJOR WORKS

LONG FICTION: *Night Rider*, 1939; *At Heaven's Gate*, 1943; *All the King's Men*, 1946; *World Enough and Time: A Romantic Novel*, 1950; *Band of Angels*,

1955; *The Cave*, 1959; *Wilderness: A Tale of the Civil War*, 1961; *Flood: A Romance of Our Time*, 1964; *Meet Me in the Green Glen*, 1971; *A Place to Come To*, 1977.

SHORT FICTION: *Blackberry Winter*, 1946; *The Circus in the Attic and Other Stories*, 1947.

PLAYS: *Proud Flesh*, pr. 1947; *All the King's Men*, pr. 1958.

NONFICTION: *John Brown: The Making of a Martyr*, 1929; *Modern Rhetoric*, 1949 (with Cleanth Brooks); *Segregation: The Inner Conflict in the South*, 1956; *Selected Essays*, 1958; *The Legacy of the Civil War: Meditations on the Centennial*, 1961; *Who Speaks for the Negro?*, 1965; *Democracy and Poetry*, 1975; *Portrait of a Father*, 1988; *New and Selected Essays*, 1989.

EDITED TEXTS: *An Approach to Liberature*, 1936 (with Cleanth Brooks and John Thibault Purser); *Understanding Poetry: An Anthology for College Students*, 1938 (with Brooks); *Understanding Fiction*, 1943 (with Brooks); *Faulkner: A Collection of Critical Essays*, 1966; *Randall Jarrell, 1914-1965*, 1967 (with Robert Lowell and Peter Taylor); *American Literature: The Makers and the Making*, 1973 (compiled by Warren, Brooks, and R. W. B. Lewis).

BIBLIOGRAPHY

Bedient, Calvin. *In the Heart's Last Kingdom: Robert Penn Warren's Major Poetry*. Cambridge, Mass.: Harvard University Press, 1984. Bedient places Warren in the tradition of the poet-seeker who will know the truth at all costs.

Clark, William Bedford, ed. *Critical Essays on Robert Penn Warren*. Boston: G. K. Hall, 1981. The selection covers both the poetry and prose and includes twenty contemporary reviews, an interview, and eight in-depth articles. Among the authors are Malcolm Cowley, John Crowe Ransom, and Harold Bloom.

Grimshaw, James A. *Understanding Robert Penn Warren*. Columbia: University of South Carolina, 2001. A critical survey of selected works and an introductory biography. Includes bibliographical references and an index.

Justus, James H. *The Achievement of Robert Penn Warren*. Baton Rouge: Louisiana State University Press,

1981. A comprehensive and scholarly work, Justus sees Warren's major theme as a search for self-knowledge and examines the entire corpus, including the fiction and nonfiction prose as well as the poetry.

Madden, David, ed. *The Legacy of Robert Penn Warren.* Baton Rouge: Louisiana State University Press, 2000. A collection of critical and biographical essays on Warren's life and work. Includes bibliographical references and an index.

Walker, Michael. *Robert Penn Warren: A Vision Earned.* New York: Barnes & Noble, 1979. Walker's thesis is that Warren is best understood when he is examined as a regionalist, a Southern writer with outside interests. The book deals with the prose as well as the poetry.

Warren, Robert Penn. *Robert Penn Warren Talking: Interviews 1950-1978.* Edited by Floyd C. Watkins and John T. Hiers. New York: Random House, 1980. A collection of eighteen interviews conducted in a variety of modes and settings over a period of nearly thirty years, ranging from a session with students at Vanderbilt to a Bill Moyers transcript. Gives insights not only into Warren's thought and development during the period but also into the personality of the man as it emerges in the give-and-take of live discourse.

Russell Elliott Murphy;
bibliography updated by the editors

ISAAC WATTS

Born: Southampton, Hampshire, England; July 17, 1674
Died: London, England; November 25, 1748

PRINCIPAL POETRY

Horae Lyricae, 1706, enlarged 1709
Hymns and Spiritual Songs, 1707
Divine and Moral Songs for Children, 1715
The Psalms of David, 1719
Reliquiae Juveniles: Miscellaneous Thoughts in Prose and Verse, 1734

OTHER LITERARY FORMS

Isaac Watts's verse and prose is almost exclusively religious, although—as a practicing divine interested in the instruction of youth—he authored tracts that could be classified as pedagogical *and* theological. Foremost among these is a collection of prayers for little children titled *The First Catechism,* 1692. This collection was followed by *The Art of Reading and Writing English,* 1721; *The Christian Doctrine of the Trinity,* 1722; *Logick: Or, The Right Use of Reason,* 1725; *An Essay Towards the Encouragement of Charity Schools,* 1728; *A Caveat Against Infidelity,* 1729; and his last work, *Useful and Important Questions Concerning Jesus, the Son of God,* 1746. Watt's *Sermons on Various Subjects,* in three volumes, appeared between 1721 and 1727.

ACHIEVEMENTS

Isaac Watts, the Father of English hymnody, ranks as the highest among the Nonconformist writers of divine poetry during the eighteenth century. For more than a century he held the respect of those British and American Nonconformists who sought spiritual uplift from the worship services of their particular denominations. Although Watts established his literary reputation as a hymnodist, as a writer of divine odes for congregational worship, he saw himself as a poet, although one who later renounced poetry for the sake of edification. Among lower-class Christians, Watts sought to promote what he termed "pious entertainment," which, unfortunately, prevented him from achieving his potential as a pure literary artist. Indeed, on more than one occasion he felt the need to apologize for being so easily understood, for having written poetry that could be read without difficulty.

In addressing the simpler souls of the English-speaking world, Watts managed to fuse image with thought and emotion, attaining a level of intensity not often reached by his more learned Augustan colleagues. In so doing, he relieved the English hymn of considerable poetic excess—complex theology and imagery that, during the late seventeenth and early eighteenth centuries, were regarded as essential ingredients of divine poetry. Watts, however, recognized immediately the difference between the high aesthetic level of divine poetry and the practical regions in which congregational song had, out of necessity, to function. Thus, he set out to compose a body of verse representative of the vigorous human spirit. He aimed at poetry and song that applied the Gospels to the various experiences of life. He strived for clarity of language, simplicity of diction, and sympathy of understanding so that thousands of English worshipers, both within and without the religiosocial establishment, could lean upon his hymns as the natural expression of their own religious feelings.

Watts combined, in his hymnody, the soul of a poet and the conviction of a preacher. As a recognized cleric, he cast aside the theological mantle and reached down to the humblest of Christians, beckoning them to walk with God upon the high ground of Christian piety. Thus, he set a fashion and provided a model; for the last half of the eighteenth century, a whole school of hymnodists would continue his vitality and his directness. The key to Watts's legacy was the relationship of hymnody to literature. He stood as one of the few poets of the Augustan age who managed to preserve the spiritual enthusiasm of Protestant dissent and at the same time demonstrate that such enthusiasm could achieve some semblance of poetic expression. As both Independent divine and classical poet, he formed an obvious link between the zeal of the seventeenth century and the evangelical revival of George Whitefield and John and Charles Wesley. Most important, that link—that transition—was built upon Watts's conviction that poetic and religious inspiration could be harnessed and combined by a person such as himself: a learned man, competently able to draw from tradition ideas congenial to his own times and his own temperament.

Isaac Watts (Hulton Archive)

BIOGRAPHY

Isaac Watts was born at Southampton on July 17, 1674, the eldest of his father's nine children. Isaac Watts, senior, stood as a respected Nonconformist, one so serious about his essentially Puritan religious convictions that he served two prison terms rather than conform to the establishment. After his release he maintained a successful boarding school at Southampton.

Young Watts began his education under the direction of Reverend John Pinhorne, rector of All Saints Church and headmaster of the Southampton Grammar School, who taught him Greek, Latin, and Hebrew. The boy's talent for learning and his taste for verse prompted citizens of the city to offer him a university education for eventual ordination into the Church of England. Of course he refused, which meant that he drifted, in 1690, toward the Nonconformist academy at Stoke Newington, London, under the care of Thomas Rowe, pastor of the Independent congregation at Girdler's Hall. Watts joined that congregation three years later.

In 1694, at the age of twenty, Watts left Rowe's academy and returned to Southampton. During this period he wrote the majority of hymns that would appear in *Hymns and Spiritual Songs:* "Behold the glories of the Lamb" was supposedly the first, composed in an attempt to elevate the standards of praise and prayer. Others followed, principally the results of requests from friends: "There is a land of pure delight" came from an uplifting experience upon viewing the scene across Southampton Water. Watts, however, returned to the district of Stoke

Newington as tutor to the son of a prominent London Puritan, Sir John Hartropp. The tutor pursued his own investigations into theology and philosophy with the same intensity as his pupil, which may have been the principal reason for the eventual decline in his health.

In the meantime, Watts turned his attention from pedagogy to divinity. He preached his first sermon in 1698 and continued that activity for the next three years. Then, in 1702, he was ordained minister of the Independent congregation at Mark Lane, a pulpit that had been filled by such eminent Nonconformist orators as Joseph Caryl (1602-1673) and his successor, Dr. John Owen (1616-1683). Watts's congregation reflected the prominence and affluence of London Nonconformity, and the diminutive divine presided over it for the next ten years. In 1712, he became seriously ill with a fever, and his assistant, Samuel Price, assumed the role of copastor at the time when the congregation moved to another chapel just built in Bury Street. At that point, Sir Thomas Abney took the ailing Watts into his home, and he remained with the family until his death (Sir Thomas himself having died in 1722). Indeed, the *Divine and Moral Songs for Children* was written for and dedicated to Sir Thomas's daughters.

Because of his illness and general state of incapacity, there is really nothing to note concerning the last thirty-five years of Watts's life. He spent his days largely in study and in preparing his poetry and prose for publication. In 1728, Edinburgh University bestowed, unsolicited, the degree of Doctor of Divinity upon the poet, who died at Stoke Newington on November 25, 1748. He was buried at Bunhill Fields, the London resting place of Nonconformists, and a monument was erected to him in Westminster Abbey.

ANALYSIS

Criticism of Isaac Watts's poetry has ranged from what could be termed "kind" to that which is obviously and totally negative. In his *Life of Watts* (1781), Samuel Johnson set the critical tone by complaining of the irregularity of his measures, his blank verse, and his insufficiently correspondent rhymes. As was his method, however, Johnson did find merit in Watts's smooth and easy lines and religiously pure thoughts, combined with ample piety and innocence. Still, the London sage wished

for greater vigor in the hymnodist's verse. In the nineteenth century, critical commentators made sport of the sing-song patterns of Watts's children's hymns, while Lewis Carroll delighted in parodies of such pieces as "Let dogs delight to bark and bite," "'Tis the voice of the sluggard," and the "Busy bee." Such strokes secured for Watts the lasting reputation of an Independent minister who accomplished little, poetically, beyond penning stiff moral verses for little children in his spare moments.

Careful reading of the poet's prefaces to those collections intended for mature minds, however, reveals him to have been his own rather stern critic. As late as 1734, with his major poetry already published, Watts proclaimed (in *Reliquiae Juveniles*) that he had made no pretense to the name of poet, especially since the age and the nation had produced so many superior writers of verse. More than the mere conventional expression of humility, the statement leads directly to an examination of those "superior" souls steeped in classicism who helped Watts develop his poetic theories and practices. One, Mathias Casimir Sarbiewski (1594-1640)—although outside both Watts's age and his nation—demonstrated the advantages of a form, the ode, that he could easily adapt to congregational and private worship. The other, John Milton—like Watts a Nonconformist and a classicist—proved that blank verse could convey both meaning and elegance.

HORAE LYRICAE

Sarbiewski—the Polish Jesuit, classical reviser of the breviary hymns under Pope Urban VIII, and known generally as the Christian Horace—wrote Latin odes and biblical paraphrases that became popular shortly after their publication in England in 1625 and 1628. Watts translated certain of those odes in his *Horae Lyricae* (both 1706 and 1709 editions); many other poets, both earlier and later, also translated some of Sarbiewski's works: Among them were Henry Vaughan (in 1651), Sir Edward Sherburne (1651), the compilers of *Miscellany Poems and Translations by Oxford Hands* (1685), Thomas Browne (1707-1708), and John Hughes (1720). Even Samuel Taylor Coleridge translated Casimir's "Ad Lyram," but after the early nineteenth century little interest was expressed in the works of the Polish Jesuit. Watts probably discovered Casimir sometime between

1680 and 1690, when studying Latin at the Free School at Southampton under the tutelage of the Reverend John Pinhorne, rector of All Saints church. The earliest printed evidence of Casimir's influence appeared in Book II of *Horae Lyricae* in the form of an ode to Pinhorne, in which the young Watts thanked his schoolmaster for introducing him to the Latin poets, particularly Sarbiewski. The extravagant praise of Casimir and the translation of his poetry make it clear that Watts never really lost his schoolboy regard for that poet. In fact, in the Preface to the 1709 edition of *Horae Lyricae*, Watts admitted that he often added or deleted as many as ten or twenty lines in order to fit the original sense to his own design. Further, he apologized for not having been able to capture Casimir's force, exactness, and passion of expression.

Thirteen acknowledged translations and imitations of modern Latin appear throughout Watts's poems and hymns; ten of these come from Sarbiewski. The Casimir translations may be found in both the 1706 and 1709 editions of *Horae Lyricae*: "The fairest and only beloved," "Mutual love stronger than death," "Converse with Christ," "Forsaken yet helping," "Meditation in a Grove," "Come, Lord Jesus," "Love to Christ present or absent," and the long narrative that received considerable praise from Robert Southey, "The Dacian Battle." In *Reliquiae Juveniles*, a collection of earlier poetry and prose, Watts included translations of "To Dorio" and "The Hebrew Poet." In the first piece, Watts reacted to what he termed the softness and the beauty of two four-line stanzas describing a lyric poet's first attempts on the "harp" and his introduction to the lyric form. He complained, however, of the difficulties of translation. "The Hebrew Poet" is very long—thirty four-line stanzas. Again, Watts notes the difficulty of accurate translation from the Old Testament Psalms: How does the translator Christianize the piece, yet at the same time retain the "Hebrew glory" and the quality of the original Latin ode? Early in the poem, he mentions "The Bard that climb'd to Cooper's-Hill," referring to Sir John Denham, who succeeded as a poet concerned with meditative and speculative subjects but who failed as a translator of the Psalms of David.

Despite his misgivings, Watts managed to do justice to Sarbiewski's Latin poetry. His study of Casimir and the practical exercise of translating his odes taught the Nonconformist poet to think in terms of higher Nature while praising God. Thus, his hymns challenged the Augustans to regard natural objects closely and with a certain degree of enjoyment, a characteristic found lacking in the vast majority of Watts's less pious contemporaries—principally John Sheffield, William Wycherley, Bishop Thomas Sprat, William Walsh, Bernard Mandeville, and, foremost among them, Jonathan Swift.

In his upbringing and training, and in his conception of the poet's purpose, certain tantalizing parallels exist between the early careers of Watts and John Milton. Milton died the same year that Watts was born. Both emerged from Puritan homes, having been exposed to the dominant literary and cultural traditions of their times. After classical educations (although Milton's was longer and perhaps more formal), both returned to their homes for further study, meditation, and work. As students, they both wrote Latin verse dedicated to their tutors: Milton's "Ad Thomas Iunium, Praeceptorem Suum" (1627) when he was nineteen, Watts's corresponding "Ad Reverendum Virum Dom. Johannem Pinhorne" (1694) at the age of twenty. Finally and more significantly, the two poets proclaimed the merits of biblical poetry and paraphrase; both determined that the poet's work was a divine mission, inspired by the love of God.

In an essay titled "Of the Different Stops and Cadences in Blank Verse" (1734), Watts acknowledged his debt to Milton, a debt that may appear to counter the criticism of Dr. Johnson. He labeled Milton the esteemed parent and author of blank verse, of which *Paradise Lost* (1667) must stand as the noblest example. Milton, according to the Nonconformist hymnodist, assured his readers that true musical delight need not consist of rhyme, or even in the jingling sounds of like endings. Instead, that pleasure could easily be found in appropriate numbers, fit quantity of syllables, and the principal theme of the piece as it proceeds from one segment of a poem to another. Watts, however, must not be identified as an imitator of Milton or even as a follower; rather, his reliance upon Miltonic blank verse provided a sharp point of departure from the predominant form of the Augustan Age. He wrote blank verse when almost every other poet sped forward on the quick airs of the couplet.

His particular blank verse, however, was indeed distinct from anything previously written in the form. It was neither epic, as was Milton's, nor dramatic, as was the verse of William Shakespeare and his successors. Instead, Watts's lines were lyrical and meditative blank verse, in the manner which William Cowper and then William Wordsworth would develop so brilliantly.

Watts acknowledged the superiority of Milton's verse to his own; nevertheless, he formulated five specific rules whereby the legacy of the great Puritan epic poet could be maintained but improved. Watts's criticism of Milton's blank verse began in *Horae Lyricae*, in which he declared that Milton's lengthy periods and parentheses ran him out of breath, while certain of his numbers seemed too harsh and uneasy. Watts refused to believe that roughness and obscurity added anything to the grandeur of a poem—even to an epic. Furthermore, he could not understand how archaisms, exoticisms, and "quaint uncouthness of speech" could be affected by poets merely for the sake of being labeled "Miltonian." Thus, instead of imitating Milton, Watts chose to experiment with his meter, producing in *Horae Lyricae* a combination of religious and poetic earnestness with great vividness and intensity.

RELIQUIAE JUVENILES

Watts advanced his own theories of prosody, generally opposing the neoclassical traditions of the early eighteenth century—which may well be a major reason for his neglect today. In his *Reliquiae Juveniles*, Watts argued that a writer of verse should be attentive to the ear as well as to the eye. Challenging the dominance of the couplet, he complained that the form tended to end too abruptly and often without necessity. Such practice (he believed) produced poems that proceeded with excessive regularity; this uniformity, according to Watts, becomes tiresome and offensive to every sensitive ear. His criticism of the closed couplet, then, was tied to rhyme, punctuation, and general sentence sense, and he argued that poets often ended their couplets without being attentive to meaning.

In "Of the Different Stops and Cadences in Blank Verse," published in *Reliquiae Juveniles*, Watts set down five extremely exact rules (which he had followed in composing the majority of his congregational hymns) whereby the tiresome and offensive uniformity of the couplet could be avoided. First, he suggested that the poetic sentence be extended to between six and ten lines. Further, although he could identify at least ten places within a line where the sentence could end with the inclusion of a fixed stop, Watts cautioned against that stop occurring too early or too late. Third, he argued that two lines in succession ought not to appear in which the poet places a strong stop at the first or the ninth syllable. Most important to his argument was the rule that the final line in a poetic sentence or poetic paragraph should contain the sense of that passage, and that the next line should introduce a new scene, episode, or idea. Finally, Watts believed that every line should end with a short pause, which would provide respite, but not an end to the sense. In that fifth rule, the reader immediately sees Watts's concern for a poem in blank verse—a divine ode—that is to be written for or adapted to congregational worship.

Perhaps the most outstanding example of Watts's ability to apply his own rules to his own poetry is his most anthologized piece, "The Day of Judgment," from the 1706 edition of *Horae Lyricae*. In both content and form, those thirty-six lines have received more critical attention than any other Watts poem or hymn. Amy Reed, in relating "The Day of Judgment" to the various influences upon Thomas Gray's *An Elegy Written in a Country Churchyard* (1751), emphasizes Watts's skill in consistently offsetting the negative aspects of life: human vanity and the horrors of death and judgment. In their place, he introduced the thought of the saving power of Christ and the bliss of the righteous in heaven. Unfortunately, the lowest among the humble Christians who came into contact with Watts's poems relied only on their uncontrolled imaginations and saw only the gruesome elements of his Judgment Day: the fierce north wind, red lightning, bloody trumpets, and gaping waters quick to devour sinners. Another scholar, Enid Hammer, views the poem as a leap into the nineteenth century, believing it to be the link between the sapphics of Sir Philip Sidney and those of Robert Southey and Charles Lamb. Watts himself was so dedicated to the idea of the poem that he produced a prose version for the introduction to an essay, "Distant Thunder" (1734), another commentary on the theme of judgment.

Watts must be given credit for poetic and critical skills beyond a single poem on judgment or a single essay on the stops and cadences in blank verse. As a writer of religiously inspired odes and hymns for congregational worship, he stood almost alone, promoting the spiritual ardor of Protestant dissent. No doubt the eighteenth century reader and worshiper must have stood in awe at the wide range of that expression. Watts could, for example, strike fear into the hearts of children with his description of hell (as in "Heaven and Hell"); he could ascend to heights of extreme tenderness (as in the well-known cradle hymn, "Hush, my dear, lie still and slumber"); he could visualize eternity in the hand of the very God that made all men (as in his most noted hymn, "O God, our help in ages past").

Although he set out to Christianize the Old Testament Psalms and to make David speak as a Christian, Watts also needed to consider those eighteenth century Britons who would be his readers and his singers. Thus, in his hymns he saw clear parallels between Judea and Great Britain; historical events such as the gunpowder plot, the coming of William III and Mary to England, the end of the Stuarts and the accession of the Hanoverians, and the Jacobite uprisings, were occasions to set forth, poetically, clear lessons, sound political doctrine, and general thanksgiving. Watts had no real interest in limited or local occurrences; his primary focus was upon the larger issues that concerned, politically and intellectually, the citizens of a legitimate Christian nation. He limited his hymnody to the same three or four general areas: the weakness of man, the imperfections of society, the transience of human existence, and the hopes and fears of common creatures. Watts was nondenominational as long as he remained within those perimeters; he could rightfully claim that his hymns and psalm paraphrases held fast to the common denominators of universal Christianity.

Only relatively recently have scholars of hymnody, theology, and poetry been able to determine Watts's purpose as a hymnodist. In his three major hymn collections (*Horae Lyricae, Hymns and Spiritual Songs,* and the hymns for children) he developed a complete system of praise, a process by which persons at all stages of their lives could come together to express their feelings, experiences, and beliefs. Watts sought to make the di-

vine ode representative of the individual worshiper's response to the word of God. *The Psalms of David* and the *Hymns and Spiritual Songs* became the poetical guidebooks by which the diverse denominations of British and American Nonconformity achieved fullness and directness of religious and ethical thought, especially during the eighteenth and early nineteenth centuries when authority and direction were lacking.

Despite the reception of Watts's hymns and psalms in England and America during the eighteenth and nineteenth centuries, the present age seems unwilling or unable to determine the poet's rightful place in British literary history. Although evangelical churchmen continue to hold him in esteem, his literary position is less secure. Nevertheless, few will challenge Watts's capabilities as a poet or his skills in prosody; all will accept him as an experimenter, willing to challenge the popular poetic forms of his era. Watts was a wise and discriminating theorist who developed rules of prosody patterned after the brightest lights of the seventeenth century. Despite his credentials, however, literary historians have not willingly allowed him to represent both English hymnody *and* English poetry. That is most unfortunate. Watts wrote verse that consciously explicated the doctrines of religious nonconformity and applied them to almost every facet of human experience. For that reason, the poems have not always been easily separated from the hymns, thus detracting from a full understanding of his verse. Watts intended a fusion between the poem and the congregational hymn, and a careful reading of his prose and poetry reveals his total concept of literature: He held it to be a repository wherein poetry and hymnody could eventually meet. Unfortunately, such a concept never has found a large audience, and Watts remains an Augustan poet of the second rank.

OTHER MAJOR WORKS

NONFICTION: *The First Catechism*, 1692; *The Art of Reading and Writing English*, 1721; *Sermons on Various Subjects*, 1721-1727 (3 vols.); *The Christian Doctrine of the Trinity*, 1722; *Logick: Or, The Right Use of Reason*, 1725; *An Essay Towards the Encouragement of Charity Schools*, 1728; *A Caveat Against Infidelity*, 1729; *Useful and Important Questions Concerning Jesus, the Son of God*, 1746.

BIBLIOGRAPHY

Adey, Lioney. *Class and Idol in the English Hymn*. Vancouver: University of British Columbia Press, 1987. This history of English hymnody places Watts's remarkable career in theological and historical perspectives while explaining the role hymns occupied in the church life of eighteenth century England. Adey's particular contribution is his argument that Watts's stern Calvinist upbringing determined his portrait of a Father God in his psalms and hymns. Adey's bibliography is a gold mine of primary sources related to Watts and the hymnody of his era.

Argent, Alan. *Isaac Watts, Poet, Thinker, Pastor*. London: Congregational Memorial Hall Trust, 1999. A brief biographical study of Watts and his work.

Bailey, Albert Edward. *The Gospel in Hymns*. New York: Charles Scribner's Sons, 1950. A standard history of gospel hymnody places Watts at the center of the revolution in church music through his "rhymed theology." Bailey's extensive catalog of Watts's hymns, psalms, and poems is especially useful to researchers.

Benson, Louis Fitzgerald. *The English Hymn: Its Development and Use in Worship*. Richmond, Va.: John Knox Press, 1962. Benson presents a rather extensive analysis of Watts's religious poetry as he surveys English hymnody from its origins to the nineteenth century. Benson concludes that part of Watts's achievement consists of demonstrating the relationship between psalm paraphrase and actual poetry.

Escott, Harry. *Isaac Watts: Hymnographer*. London: Independent Press, 1962. In this biography, Escott uses biographical facts from Watts's life to underscore his critique of contemporary hymnology in his times and his body of poetic collections. Watts is seen here as a reformer and a precocious advocate of a new theology of music for a generation of Protestant Nonconformists.

Maclear, J. F. "Isaac Watts and the Idea of Public Religion." *Journal of the History of Ideas* 53, no. 1 (January, 1992): 25. Isaac Watts's ideas about public religion are discussed. Watts developed a comprehensive and detailed formulation of national religion over two decades before Jean-Jacques Rousseau.

Marshall, Madeleine F., and Janet Todd. *English Congregational Hymns in the Eighteenth Century*. Lexington: University Press of Kentucky, 1982. The authors find Watts's determination to redefine hymnography not only as setting Scripture to melody but also as the art of narrating the effect of Scripture on the life of individual Christians and his unique innovation to English church music. In a time of rationalistic Deism, Watts's poetry sought to bring God the Father closer to human life as it is lived.

Sizes, Sandra A. *Gospel Hymns and Social Religion*. Philadelphia: Temple University Press, 1978. Sizes argues that Watts's hymns served as rallying anthems for his Nonconformist theological perspective. Her delineation of the effects of religious poetry and psalmody on social change in pre-Victorian England is particularly useful in understanding Watts's place in the evangelical reformation of his times.

Tanke, Susan S. *Make a Joyful Noise unto the Lord*. Athens: Ohio University Press, 1979. Tanke's thesis posits Watts as the father of modern hymnography who not only wrote hymns but also forged a system and theory behind their construction. Provides particular insight into the methodology Watts used in crafting several of his best known hymns.

Samuel J. Rogal;
bibliography updated by the editors

ADAM WAŻYK

Born: Warsaw, Poland; November 17, 1905
Died: Warsaw, Poland; August 13, 1982

PRINCIPAL POETRY
Semafory, 1924
Oczy i usta, 1926
Wiersze zebrane, 1934
Serce granatu, 1943

OTHER LITERARY FORMS

A cursory glance at Adam Ważyk's output would suggest that he was a versatile writer who practiced all principal literary forms and pursued various interests. All his major works, however, refer in one way or another to his poetry, his poetic program, or his biography as a poet. Among his novels, for example, the most important one, *Epizod* (1961), is an autobiographical account of his participation in Polish avant-garde movements before World War II. His insightful essays, which cover a wide range of problems from Polish versification through the history of Romanticism to French Surrealism, seem to have one common denominator: They are various versions of Ważyk's continuous quest for his own poetic roots. His plays are a somewhat irrelevant part of his output. He attached greater importance to his numerous translations of poetry from French, Russian, and Latin into Polish, and indeed he ranks among the most outstanding Polish representatives of the art of translation. The broad scope of his interests in this field (at various times, he translated such disparate poets as Alexander Pushkin, Arthur Rimbaud, Aleksandr Blok, Guillaume Apollinaire, Max Jacob, Vladimir Mayakovsky, Paul Éluard, and Horace) reflects his constant search for a tradition and his changing conception of the role of poetry.

ACHIEVEMENTS

Adam Ważyk's literary career falls very distinctly into three phases, which stand in sharp contrast as far as both their specific character and their current appreciation are concerned. His first two collections were acclaimed and still are regarded as highly original contributions to Polish avant-garde poetry of the 1920's. After those promising beginnings, Ważyk lapsed into silence as a poet, to resurface only in the 1940's. His volume *Serce granatu* opened the second phase of his career, during which he appeared to be one of the staunchest promoters and supporters of Socialist Realism in poetry. This period, undoubtedly Ważyk's worst, came to an abrupt end in 1955 with the publication of his famous "Poemat dla dorosłych" ("Poem for Adults"), a harbinger of the antidogmatist renewal of Polish culture in the mid-1950's. "Poem for Adults" remains Ważyk's best-known work, although it has been artistically surpassed by his later work. It is the last phase of his development that seems to be most valuable from today's point of view. In his poems published in the 1960's and 1970's, Ważyk in a certain sense returned to his poetic beginnings, but he also enriched his cubist method with a new significance resulting from his reflection on twentieth century history. Today, his poetry can by no means be considered a relic of the past; on the contrary, its impact on contemporary Polish literature is increasingly appreciated.

Adam Ważyk

BIOGRAPHY

Adam Ważyk was born into a middle-class family of Jewish descent. After having been graduated from a Warsaw high school in 1924, he began to study mathematics at Warsaw University but soon found himself engrossed in the vigorous literary life of the 1920's. He made his literary debut very early by publishing a poem in the monthly *Skamander* in 1922. He entered into closer contact, however, not with the influential and popular poetic group called Skamander but with its opponents, who formed various avant-garde groups. Ważyk associated first with the Futurists (he was a coeditor of their publication, *Almanach Nowej Sztuki*) and later with the so-called Cracow Vanguard. His own position within those groups remained rather individual, however, and not fully consistent with their programs. In his two books of poems published in 1924 and 1926, he appeared as a Polish adherent to French cubism and Surrealism. In the 1930's, he stopped writing poetry altogether and shifted to fiction, the most interesting example of which was his autobiographical novel *Mity rodzinne* (1938).

The outbreak of World War II prompted a dramatic change both in Ważyk's life and in his art. In September, 1939, he arrived with other refugees at the city of Lvov, which soon fell prey to the Soviet invasion. Ważyk joined those Polish intellectuals who decided to collaborate with Soviet authorities. In the early 1940's, he lived in Saratov and Kuibyshev, where he was made an officer in the Polish Army formed under Soviet auspices. In this capacity, he was in charge of cultural activities of the army, controlling its theater's repertory and its radio programs as well as writing popular military songs. In 1944, he returned to Poland with the rank of captain, with the Soviet-controlled Kościuszko Division.

In Stalinist Poland, Ważyk was entrusted with various official functions: Among others, he served as secretary general of the Polish Writers' Union; worked as an editor of the chief organ of Socialist Realism, the weekly *Kuźnica*; and between 1950 and 1954 served as editor in chief of the monthly *Twórczość*. In 1953, he was awarded a State Literary Prize for his poetry and translations.

On August 19, 1955, the weekly *Nowa Kultura* published Ważyk's long "Poem for Adults," which immedi-

ately became the object of perhaps the fiercest political controversy in postwar Polish literature. Praised by advocates of the political and ideological "thaw," the poem provoked, on the other hand, violent accusations from the Communist Party hardliners and a number of officially sponsored public protests and condemnations; the editor in chief of *Nowa Kultura* lost his position in the wake of the Communist Party's outrage. The poem, however, gained enormous popularity; it was under its influence that the new wave of "settling accounts" with Stalinist ideology soon emerged to dominate Polish literary life for the next several years.

The last decades of the poet's life were spent mostly in Warsaw, where in the 1960's and 1970's Ważyk wrote and published numerous collections of poems, essays, and poetic translations as well as his only postwar novel, *Epizod*. His gradual withdrawal from public life was counterpoised by his growing recognition as a writer.

ANALYSIS

In Adam Ważyk's poetic career, there were two dramatic turnabouts, the first of which can be described as vehement acceptance of the doctrine of Socialist Realism and the other as its equally vehement rejection. Thus, the middle segment of his work forms a strictly demarcated enclave that does not seem to have anything in common either with Ważyk's avant-garde beginnings or with his last phase. There is an apparent discontinuity, then, and only a closer look allows the reader to discern a hidden logic in Ważyk's development.

As a young poet, Ważyk was obsessed with one of the central problems of twentieth century psychology: the problem of the discontinuity of perception. Under the influence of the art and poetry of the French cubists, he discovered that the overall perception of an object is, in fact, twofold: The final impression of a whole is preceded by the act of perceiving its separate elements. Accordingly, his early poetry focused on that first stage of the act of perception by showing the world as a mosaic of stray fragments of everyday reality, put together by the means of syntactic juxtaposition. Such a perception of reality as a discrete sequence of its elements was a major source of lyrical illumination.

It was, however, a source of growing doubt and increasing anxiety as well. Discontinuity meant also disorder, lack of hierarchy, and the absence of any system of values. It is deeply significant that the young Ważyk was not able to identify fully either with the Futurists (whose anarchism he repudiated) or with the Cracow Vanguard (whose program of constructivism he considered naïve and overly optimistic). The twentieth century seemed to have brought liberation from oppressive rationalism, but what in the 1920's had appeared as a refreshing sense of freedom was, in the 1930's, already acquiring a threatening suggestion of chaos. Therefore, in Ważyk's prewar poetry the technique of loose juxtapositions paradoxically coincides with an explicit craving for some undefined "order" that only the future might bring. In the 1930's, apparently unable to reconcile those two opposite tendencies, he discarded poetry altogether.

It was only Ważyk's acceptance of Communist ideology that, a decade later, allowed him to resume writing poetry. Communism offered him a new, seemingly consistent and comprehensive vision of his dreamed-of "order." He could not, however, return to his previous stylistic manner: The new belief could be expressed only by the means of utterly regular, classical forms. Such a marriage of Communism and classicism was, incidentally, not quite unprecedented in Polish poetry, to mention only the work of Lucjan Szenwald. Ważyk pushed that tendency to its extremes: He not only, to use the words of Mayakovsky, "stepped on the throat of his song," but also assumed, as it were, a totally new artistic identity. The former avant-garde experimenter changed into a classicist; the turbulent youth became a poet official and member of the Establishment; the cubist turned into a Socialist Realist. In the 1940's and early 1950's, Ważyk's painstaking efforts to create his own version of Stalinist classicism yielded, however, rather uneven results. A few of the poems written in that period achieve an uneasy marriage of stylistic allusions to Horace with propaganda slogans, but the majority of them appear today as embarrassing examples of downright didacticism and blatant whitewash, made even worse by Ważyk's propensity for using journalistic clichés and monotonous rhythms.

"POEM FOR ADULTS"

The literary audience of the 1950's, which knew Ważyk as an official poet of Stalinism and a relentless exterminator of "bourgeois" tendencies in Polish culture, was, therefore, completely astounded by the 1955 publication of his "Poem for Adults." In this long poetic manifesto, Ważyk not only returned to his prewar methods of discontinuous presentation, juxtaposition, and free verse, but also gave vent to his bitter political disillusionment and moral perplexity. Instead of prophesying the rosy future, he again—as in his early phase—focused his attention on particulars of everyday reality. This time, however, such a perspective led to more disquieting conclusions: The scrupulous, unflinching observation of reality was used not for its own sake but in order to confront the empty promises and hypocritical slogans of official ideology.

From today's point of view, "Poem for Adults" seems to be slightly naïve and content with half measures. Its speaker still sincerely believes in the mirages of Communist ideology; it is not ideology but reality that does not measure up to lofty principles. Accordingly, he resents not his own short-sightedness but some mysterious manipulators who duped him and his generation. The poem stopped halfway, then, but it nevertheless had a galvanizing impact on Polish literature. In Ważyk's own career, it also marked the beginning of his return to his previous artistic integrity.

RETURN TO CUBIST ROOTS

This return was particularly noticeable in the 1960's and 1970's, when Ważyk's poetry underwent a remarkable evolution while remaining faithful to his philosophical and psychological obsessions. The problem of discontinuity of perception acquired new significance, set against the background of twentieth century history and the poet's own experiences. Ważyk's most ambitious poems from that period can be interpreted as attempts to reconstruct the effort of human consciousness, memory, and logic, trying to set reality in order despite its apparently chaotic character. The long poem *Labirynt*, for example, is a paradoxical attempt to revive the old genre of the descriptive poem in order to prove its futility; seemingly a quasi-epic story taking place in a middle-class milieu in prewar Poland, it is actually a poem about the shortcomings of human memory, which can visualize the past only as a "labyrinth that leads no one knows where." In another long poem, *Wagon*, the speaker's observation post is a train compartment; his indiscriminate registration of juxtaposed objects, minute facts, and the travelers' insignificant behavior proves to be another fruitless effort of the human mind faced with the chaos of external reality.

In poems such as these, and particularly in his last, excellent volume, *Zdarzenia*, Ważyk's evident return to his cubist beginnings has, however, some new implications. The familiar method of juxtaposition of images serves more complex purposes. The world smashed into pieces is no longer a source of innocent illumination, nor is it a reason for yearning for some "order" imposed by history. On the contrary, the world's disarray appears to be an irreversible process started by the twentieth century disintegration of stable systems of values. Although Ważyk in his final phase was far from moralizing, his poetry can be read as an indirect comment on the immorality of the present epoch.

OTHER MAJOR WORKS

LONG FICTION: *Człowiek w burym ubraniu*, 1930; *Latarnie świeca w Karpowie*, 1933; *Mity rodzinne*, 1938; *Epizod*, 1961.

NONFICTION: *W stronę humanizmu*, 1949; *Mickiewicz i wersyfikacja narodowa*, 1951; *Przemiany Słowackiego*, 1955; *Esej o wierszu*, 1964; *Od Rimbauda do Éluarda*, 1964; *Kwestia gustu*, 1966; *Surrealizm*, 1973; *Gra i doświadczenie*, 1974; *Dziwna historia awangardy*, 1976; *Cudowny kantorek*, 1980.

BIBLIOGRAPHY

Eile, Stanisław and Ursula Phillips, eds. *New Perspectives in Twentieth-Century Polish Literature*. Basingstoke, Hampshire, England: Macmillan, 1992. A historical and critical analysis of Polish literature. Includes bibliographical references and an index.

Gillon, Adam, and Ludwik Krzyzanowski, eds. *Introduction to Modern Polish Literature*. Enlarged ed. New York: Hippocrene Books, 1982. An anthology of translations of Polish literature with some commentary.

Miłosz, Czesław. *The History of Polish Literature*. 2d ed. Berkeley, Calif.: University of California Press, 1983. A critical study of the history of Polish literature that provides a historical and cultural background to the works of Ważyk. Includes bibliographic references.

Stanisław Barańczak;
bibliography updated by the editors

BRUCE WEIGL

Born: Lorain, Ohio; January 27, 1949

PRINCIPAL POETRY

Executioner, 1976
A Sack Full of Old Quarrels, 1976
A Romance, 1979
The Monkey Wars, 1985
Song of Napalm, 1988
What Saves Us, 1992
Lies, Grace, and Redemption, 1995 (Harry Humes, editor)
Sweet Lorain, 1996
After the Others, 1999
Archeology of the Circle: New and Selected Poems, 1999
Not on the Map, 1996 (with Kevin Bowen; John Deane, editor)

OTHER LITERARY FORMS

Although Bruce Weigl has published primarily poetry, he also translated poetry from the Vietnamese— Poems from Captured Documents (1994; with Thanh Nguyen) and *Mountain River: Vietnamese Poetry from the Wars, 1945-1995* (1998; with Nguyen Ba Chung and Kevin Bowen)—and Romanian, *Angel Riding a Beast* (1998; with Liliana Ursu). Weigl's translations make available poems to which the common reader would not have access. Weigl has spoken of how pervasive poetry is in Southeast Asia; reading the Vietnamese perspective provides a fuller picture of the impact of the war. In addition, Weigl has written several volumes of criticism, including *The Giver of Morning: On Dave Smith* (1982), *The Imagination as Glory: The Poetry of James Dickey* (1984; with T. R. Hummer), and *Charles Simic: Essays on the Poetry* (1996).

ACHIEVEMENTS

Published internationally, Weigl's poetry has been translated into Vietnamese, Czech, Dutch, German, Spanish, Chinese, Slovenian, Bulgarian, and Romanian. He has received many national awards, including a Paterson Poetry Prize, the Pushcart Prize, a Yaddo Foundation Fellowship, and a National Endowment for the Arts Grant. In 1988 he was nominated for a Pulitzer Prize for *Song of Napalm*. His poems have appeared in *The Nation, American Poetry Review, Ploughshares, The New Yorker*, and *Paris Review*, as well as many other magazines and journals.

BIOGRAPHY

Bruce Weigl was born in Lorain, Ohio, on January 27, 1949, to Albert Louis Weigl and Zora Grasa Weigl. Oberlin College awarded him his B.A. in English in 1974. He received his M.A. from the University of New Hampshire in 1975 and his Ph.D. in 1979 from the University of Utah, mentored by poet Dave Smith.

He has had an extensive teaching career. He was an instructor at the Lorain County Community College and assistant professor of English at the University of Arkansas, Little Rock. At Old Dominion University in Norfolk, Virginia, as assistant professor, he was director of the Associated Writing Program. He has taught in the writing program at Pennsylvania State University and in the M.F.A. in writing program at Vermont College.

Weigl served in the U.S. Army in Vietnam, from 1967 until 1970, earning the Bronze Star. Emerging from a working-class background, he completed his higher education after the war. In his poetry, two themes emerge, seemingly at cross purposes. First is the horror of war, especially its effect on the psyches of young men who were ill prepared for what would come. The second is the primacy of love that at once underscores that horror and attempts to atone for it. The love poems undercut the rules of the society that would control the course of love, as war situations do.

ANALYSIS

Bruce Weigl describes the impetus for his work by saying that a writer must come to terms with his or her background, as it is the major source of one's subject matter. Weigl grew up in around industry, amid steel mills and the working class. Born in industrial and agricultural Middle America, Weigl's working-class background informs his poetry and shapes the way he perceives the Vietnam War. The speaker of these poems is often a young, fairly naïve man who gets caught up in an unpopular cause, who must find a way to transcend the limitation of mere survival. The poet, therefore, finds himself trying to bring his imaginative sensibilities to a hostile environment in an attempt to transform it and make it livable, with as little cost to his psyche as he can manage. Weigl's poetry clearly demonstrates the care that the poet takes to render a full account of the situations in which he finds himself, yet to do so with a high degree of craft. The artistic development of his style does not take a backseat to his important message, however.

Bruce Weigl's poetry serves to give voice to thousands of soldiers who saw action in the Vietnam War during late 1960's and early 1970's. While the sincerity of these poems provides a forum of discourse so that these experiences may benefit from national attention, their high literary quality merits the esteem in which they are held as literature.

"SONG OF NAPALM"

"Song of Napalm," from *The Monkey Wars*, begins with a bucolic description of horses that the speaker and his wife watch. The initial description of the poet and his wife lifts them beyond the concerns of this world into a holy realm. However, this domestic scene foreshadows a frightening darkness that the poet experiences: "Trees scraped their voices in the wind, branches/ Crisscrossed the sky like barbed wire/ But you said they were only branches."

The speaker pauses as if to catch his breath and take stock of himself, believing that the "old curses" have gone. However, visions from his war experiences intrude once again:

> Still I close my eyes and see the girl
> Running from her village, napalm
> Stuck to her dress like jelly,
> Her hands reaching for the no one
> Who waits in waves of heat before her.

These lines evoke the famous photograph of a young Vietnamese girl burned by napalm, running naked along a road toward the camera that immortalized her. The poet is alienated from both the domestic tranquillity that his wife represents and the haunting visions that his memory brings. Yet he forces a door to open between these two worlds.

The girl runs with wings of escape beating inside her, using a freedom that she does not possess. In fact, she is able to run only a few feet before her burns and wounds bring her down, as she dies in a fetal position: "Nothing/ Can change that, she is burned behind my eyes." The poet is forced to accept the world as something that his words alone cannot change. Not even the redemptive, healing love of his wife fades this vision. A persistent theme in Weigl's other poems is the poet's struggle to find solace in the love of family and friends in order to dispel the power that his war experience exerts.

"ON THE ANNIVERSARY OF HER GRACE"

In "On the Anniversary of Her Grace," from his 1988 collection *Song of Napalm*, the poet evokes his power to show how the war scarred his ability to love. The opening description of weather conditions foreshadows the desperate state of the poet's mind. Images of darkness, floods, and destruction presage the devastation that the war wreaks on the poet's spirit. Although the poet dreams of his beloved, these dreams are restive in spite of his recalling a kiss, because "Inside me the war had eaten a hole./ I could not touch anyone." The war robs the poet of his openness to love, central to his self-image.

Often the use of repetition induces a meditative, trancelike state. The poet uses that device, repeating "I could . . . I could," until finally he says, "I could not." The effect mesmerizes. Images of the war erode his sensibilities, ensuring that the poet cannot accept the forgiveness and healing which the woman offers. He fears his "body would catch fire," recalling the image of the napalm-burned children, joining them in their unwilling sacrifice.

Intense feelings of love remind the poet that he is a stranger in two worlds, with one foot planted firmly in each. Even when the poet is not ostensibly narrating his experiences of the war, even when the love poem focuses on the beloved, the war intrudes as if he cannot manage two disparate worlds.

"FIRST LETTER TO CALUMPANG"

In "First Letter to Calumpang," from *Sweet Lorain*, the poet expresses love to his wife by using images that reflect the war: "There is a blood from touching, and a fire;/ I've had them in my mouth." The poet's use of blood echoes both the blood rush of sexual excitement and the blood certainly present in war. Fire carries the dual connotation of sexual desire and the fire of war and napalm. With these images that are at once tender and fierce, the war is never far away.

ARCHEOLOGY OF THE CIRCLE

The poems in Weigl's 1999 collection represent both new works and selections from his previous volumes. In them, he continues to struggle with his feelings of love for others as well as self-acceptance. The war has taken its toll. In "Anniversary of Myself," the poet says:

> The fingers of my gloves had holes.
> I don't know what I was doing.
> There had been a war
> and my people
> had grown disenchanted.

Disillusionment comes from the poet's growing awareness of his numbness to his inner being, the core of himself, the part of himself that nurtures love relationships.

Consequently, the poet comes to relive the advice that he was given during the war, in "Our Independence Day," saying, "Let it go, boy,// let the green/ untangle from your body." These poems represent a letting go that empowers the speaker. These are not poems of surrender to a greater power; instead, the poet releases these poems into the community of discourse wherein they can become change agents in the lives of other men and women who know war.

INFLUENCE OF THE VIETNAM WAR

Except for the Civil War (1861-1865), no war in American history was as controversial or as divisive as the Vietnam War. The most striking outcome of this war emerged when soldiers did not come home to the welcoming crowds that filled World War II newsreels. Called "baby killers" and generally reviled, soldiers had few official support systems to help them return to a society that disowned them. Sometimes, families themselves embodied national divisions, with members for and against the war living under the same roof. Thus, Weigl's emotional incapacity in the presence of the lover reflects a common reality of personal and familial rupture.

Poems speaking about familial life stateside seem to present a conclusion to the struggle to relate. In some poems, when Weigl speaks with great tenderness about his wife and child, about chance encounters in a supermarket, about memories of work, a pervasive sadness still informs the poems. Yet an emotional salvation occurs for the poet when he is able to ground himself in those relationships which are stronger than his nightmares about the war. "The Happiness of Others," the poet says in the poem of that name, "is not like the music I hear/ after sex/ with my wife of the decades." He refers to her as "my wife my rope my bread." His wife is the rope that holds him firmly tethered to the present. Without her, war memories could overtake him.

Although his private world is forever marked by his war experiences, his familial attachments provide the safety net that allows him to retrieve those memories, yet not be overwhelmed by them. The great body of work results from the poet's willingness to go into a darkened landscape and emerge wholly creative.

OTHER MAJOR WORKS

TRANSLATIONS: *Poems from Captured Documents*, 1994 (with Thanh Nguyen); *Mountain River: Vietnamese Poetry from the Wars: 1945-1995*, 1998 (with Nguyen Ba Chung and Kevin Bowen); *Angel Riding a Beast*, 1998 (of Liliana Ursu; with the author).

NONFICTION: *The Giver of Morning: On Dave Smith*, 1982; *The Imagination as Glory: The Poetry of James Dickey*, 1984 (with T. R. Hummer); *Charles Simic: Essays on the Poetry*, 1996; *The Circle of Hanh: A Memoir*, 2000.

EDITED TEXT: *Writing Between the Lines: An Anthology on War and Its Social Consequences*, 1997 (with Kevin Bowen).

BIBLIOGRAPHY

Beidler, Philip. *American Literature and the Experience of Vietnam*. Athens: University of Georgia Press, 1982. Beidler discusses *A Romance*, noting that the war is being brought forth beyond private consciousness into the larger collective myth. Poems represent a spiritual quest toward wisdom. While imitative of the literary romance, the poems at times challenge that form. Many poems point away from the war toward common experiences of anxiety and fear.

_____. *Re-writing America: Vietnam Authors in Their Generation*. Athens: University of Georgia Press, 1991. Beidler notes the development of Weigl's career as a direct emergence from the evolution of his mythic consciousness as a result of the war. The book presents an examination of *A Romance* and *The Monkey Wars* within the tradition of a visionary quest.

Christopher, Renny. *The Viet Nam War: The American War*. Amherst: University of Massachusetts Press, 1995. This book discusses how Weigl's poetry moves beyond reportage into a realm of introspection, an internal dialogue in the context of external events. Uses "Him, on the Bicycle" to illustrate Weigl's use of perceived and experienced distance from self and other as an attempt to bridge cultures.

Gotera, Vincente F. "Bringing Vietnam Home: Bruce Weigl's *The Monkey Wars*." In *Search and Clear*, edited by William J. Searle. Bowling Green, Ohio: Bowling Green State University Popular Press, 1988. The author notes how Weigl never allows the reader to dismiss the inextricable link to American violence and pathos. War is an exaggeration of common forms of violence. Weigl's work breaks apart the myth that the United States regained national innocence by admitting that involvement in Vietnam was a mistake.

Jason, Philip K. *Acts and Shadows: The Vietnam War in American Culture*. Lanham, Md.: Rowman & Littlefield, 2000. Presents an examination of *Song of Napalm*. The author questions the source of love and cruelty and notes that the poems speak of the poet's awareness of violence deep within all people. A further examination of those images that confront, then upset, reader expectations.

Lomperis, Timothy J. "Reading the Wind." In *The Literature of the Vietnam War*. Durham, N.C.: Duke University Press, 1987. Speaks of the role of imagination in liberating the mind from cold facts and statistics in order to provide a context for emotional understanding. The author uses "Him, on the Bicycle," as one example.

Schroeder, Eric James. *Vietnam: We've All Been There*. Westport, Conn.: Praeger, 1992. In an interview, Weigl emphatically rejects the notion that writing was a form of therapy for him. He suggests, paradoxically, that the war both ruined his life and made him a writer. He speaks of his emergence as a poet and his affinity to Wilfred Owen's work. Weigl states that writing is the greatest act of affirmation life can accomplish.

Martha Modena Vertreace-Doody

PHILLIS WHEATLEY

Born: West Coast of Africa (possibly the Senegal-Gambia region); 1753(?)
Died: Boston, Massachusetts; December 5, 1784

PRINCIPAL POETRY

Poems on Various Subjects, Religious and Moral, 1773
The Poems of Phillis Wheatley, 1966, 1989 (Julian Mason, Jr., editor)

OTHER LITERARY FORMS

Phillis Wheatley's cultivation of the letter as a literary form is attested by her inclusion of the titles of several letters in each of her proposals for future volumes subsequent to the publication of her *Poems on Various Subjects, Religious and Moral* (1773). Regrettably, none of these proposals provoked enough response to secure publication of any new volumes. Scholars continue to discover both poems and letters that Wheatley names in these proposals. The letters mentioned in them are addressed to such noted persons as William Legge, second earl of Dartmouth; Selina Hastings, Countess of Huntingdon; Dr. Benjamin Rush; and George Washington. They display a graceful style and articulate some of Wheatley's strongest protestations in support of the cause of American independence and in condemnation of Christian hypocrisy regarding slavery.

ACHIEVEMENTS

From the time of her first published piece to the present day, controversy has surrounded the life and work of America's first black poet, and only its second published woman poet, after Anne Bradstreet. Few poets of any age have been so scornfully maligned, so passionately

defended, so fervently celebrated, and so patronizingly tolerated. Yet, during the years of her young adulthood, Phillis Wheatley was the toast of England and the colonies. For years before she attempted to find a Boston publisher for her poems, she had published numerous elegies celebrating the deaths of many of the city's most prominent citizens. In 1770, she wrote her most famous and most often-reprinted elegy, on the death of "the voice of the Great Awakening," George Whitefield, chaplain to the countess of Huntingdon, who was one of the leading benefactors of the Methodist evangelical movement in England and the Colonies.

Not finding Boston to be in sympathy with her 1772 proposal for a volume, Wheatley found substantial support the following year in the countess of Huntingdon, whose interest had been stirred by the young poet's noble tribute to her chaplain. Subsequently, Wheatley was sent to London, ostensibly for her health; this trip curiously accords, however, with the very weeks that her book was being printed. It is likely that she proofread the galleys herself. At any rate, she was much sought after among the intellectual, literary set of London, and Sir Brook Watson, who was to become Lord Mayor of London within a year, presented her with a copy of John Milton's *Paradise Lost* (1667) in folio. The earl of Dartmouth, who was at the time secretary of state for the colonies and president of the board of Trade and Foreign Plantations, gave her a copy of Tobias Smollett's translation of *Don Quixote* (1755). Benjamin Franklin, to whom she would later inscribe her second book of poetry (never published), has even recorded that, while in London briefly, he called on Wheatley to see whether "there were any service I could do her."

In the opening pages of her 1773 volume appears a letter of authentication of Wheatley's authorship which is signed by still another of the signatories of the Declaration of Independence, John Hancock. Added to the list of attesters are other outstanding Bostonians, including Thomas Hutchinson, then Governor of Massachusetts, and James Bowdoin, one of the founders of Bowdoin College. Later, during the early months of the Revolution, Wheatley wrote a poem in praise of General Washington titled "To His Excellency General Washington." As a result, she received an invitation to visit the general at his headquarters, and her poem was published by Tom

Paine in *The Pennsylvania Magazine*. John Paul Jones, who also appreciated Wheatley's celebration of freedom, even asked one of his officers to secure him a copy of her *Poems*.

Nevertheless, she did not continue to enjoy such fame. A country ravaged by war has little time, finally, for poetry, and Wheatley regrettably, perhaps tragically, faced the rejection of two more proposals for a volume of new poems. Thwarted by the vicissitudes of war and poverty, Wheatley died from complications resulting from childbirth. Even so, her poetry has survived and is now considered to be among the best of its period produced in America or in England. It is just beginning to be recognized that, contrary to the opinion of those who would dispose of Wheatley as a mere imitator, she produced sophisticated, original poems whose creative theories of the imagination and the sublime anticipate the Romantic movement.

BIOGRAPHY

The known details of Phillis Wheatley's life are few. According to her master, John Wheatley of Boston, she

Phillis Wheatley (Library of Congress)

"was brought from Africa to America in the Year 1761, between Seven and Eight Years of Age [sic]." Her parents were apparently sun-worshipers, for she is supposed to have recalled to her white captors that she remembered seeing her mother pouring out water to the sun every morning. If such be the case, it would help to explain why the sun is predominant as an image in her poetry.

Her life with the Wheatleys, John and Susanna and their two children, the twins Mary and Nathaniel, was probably not too demanding for one whose disposition toward asthma (brought on or no doubt exacerbated by the horrible "middle passage") greatly weakened her. The Wheatleys' son attended Harvard, so it is likely that Nathaniel served as the eager young girl's Latin tutor. At any rate, it is certain that Wheatley knew Latin well; her translation of the Niobe episode from Ovid's *Metamorphoses* (before 8 C.E.), Book VI, displays a learned knowledge and appreciation of the Latin original. Wheatley's classical learning is evident throughout her poetry, which is thick with allusions to ancient historical and mythological figures.

The turning point of Wheatley's career, not only as an author but also as a human being, came when her *Poems on Various Subjects, Religious and Moral* was published in London in 1773. After she returned from England, having been recalled because of Susanna Wheatley's growing illness, she was manumitted sometime during September, 1773. It is probable that Wheatley was freed because of the severe censure that some English reviewers of her *Poems* had directed at the owners of a learned author who "still remained a slave." At this very point, however, the poet's fortunes began a slow decline. In 1778, at the height of the war and after the deaths of both John and Susanna Wheatley, she married John Peters, a black man of some learning who failed to rescue the poet from poverty.

Wheatley died alone and unattended in a hovel somewhere in the back streets of the Boston slums in 1784, truly an ignominious end for one who had enjoyed such favor. She was preceded in death by two of her children, as well as by the third, to whom she had just given birth. She was at most only thirty-one years old. Given Wheatley's vision of the world "Oppress'd with woes, a painful endless train," it should not be surprising that her most frequently adopted poetic form is the elegy, in which she always celebrates death as the achievement of ultimate freedom—suggesting the thanatos-eros (desire for death) motif of Romanticism.

ANALYSIS

Beginning in the 1970's, Phillis Wheatley began to receive the attention she deserves. George McMichael and others, editors of the influential two-volume *Anthology of American Literature* (1974, 1980), observe that she and Philip Freneau were "the most important poets" of America's Revolutionary War era. To be sure, one of the major subjects of her poetry is the American struggle for independence. Temporal freedom is not her only subject, however; she is also much concerned with the quest for spiritual freedom. Consequently, the elegy, in which she celebrates the Christian rewards of eternal life and absolute freedom after death, is her favorite poetic form. In addition, she delights in describing God's creation of nature's splendors and sometimes appears to enjoy the beauties of nature for their own sake and not simply as acts of God's providence. It is in her poem "On Imagination," however, that Wheatley waxes most eloquent; in this poem, perhaps her most important single work, she articulates a theory of the imagination which strikingly anticipates that of Samuel Taylor Coleridge. Indeed, Wheatley's affinities with Romanticism, which run throughout her poetry, may come to be seen as her surest claim to a place in literary history.

Such an approach to this early American poet contradicts the widespread critical view that Wheatley was a highly derivative poet, inextricably mired in the neoclassical tradition. Her preference for the heroic couplet, one of the hallmarks of neoclassicism, has deceived many into immediately classifying her as neoclassical. One must recall, however, that Lord Byron also had a passion for the couplet. Surely, then, one must not be satisfied with a cursory glance at Wheatley's adoption of the heroic couplet; one must go on to explore the content of her poetry.

THE POLITICAL POEMS

Her political poems document major incidents of the American struggle for independence. In 1768, she wrote "To the King's Most Excellent Majesty on His Repealing the American Stamp Act." When it appeared, much revised, in *Poems on Various Subjects, Religious and Moral*, the poet diplomatically deleted the last two lines of the original, which read, "When wars came on [against George] the proudest rebel fled/ God thunder'd fury on their guilty head." By that time, the threat of the King's retaliation did not seem so forbidding nor the injustice of rebellion against him so grave.

"America," a poem probably written about the same time but published only recently, admonishes Britain to treat "americus," the British child, with more deference. According to the poem, the child, now a growing seat of "Liberty," is no mere adorer of an overwhelming "Majesty," but has acquired strength of his own: "Fearing his strength which she [Britain] undoubted knew/ She laid some taxes on her darling son." Recognizing her mistake, "great Britannia" promised to lift the burden, but the promise proved only "seeming Sympathy and Love." Now the Child "weeps afresh to feel this Iron chain." The urge to draw an analogy here between the poem's "Iron chain" and Wheatley's own predicament is irresistible; while America longs for its own independence, Wheatley no doubt yearns for hers.

The year 1770 marked the beginning of armed resistance against Britain. Wheatley chronicles such resistance in two poems, the second of which is now lost. The first, "On the Death of Mr. Snider Murder'd by Richardson," appeared initially along with "America." The poem tells how Ebenezer Richardson, an informer on American traders involved in circumventing British taxation, found his home surrounded on the evening of February 22, 1770, by an angry mob of colonial sympathizers. Much alarmed, Richardson emerged from his house armed with a musket and fired indiscriminately into the mob, killing the eleven- or twelve-year-old son of Snider, a poor German colonist. Wheatley calls young Christopher Snider, of whose death Richardson was later found guilty in a trial by jury, "the first martyr for the common good," rather than those men killed less than two weeks later in the Boston Massacre. The poem's fine closing couplet suggests that even those not in sympathy with the quest for freedom can grasp the nobility of that quest and are made indignant by its sacrifice: "With Secret rage fair freedom's foes beneath/ See in thy corse ev'n Majesty in Death."

Wheatley does not, however, ignore the Boston Massacre. In a proposal for a volume which was to have been published in Boston in 1772, she lists, among twenty-seven titles of poems (the 1773 volume had thirty-nine), "On the Affray in King Street, on the Evening of the 5th of March." This title, naming the time and place of the Massacre, suggests that the poet probably celebrated the martyrdom of Crispus Attucks, the first black to lose his life in the American struggle, along with the deaths of two whites. Regrettably, the poem has not yet been recovered. Even so, the title alone confirms Wheatley's continued recording of America's struggle for freedom. This concern shifted in tone from obedient praise for the British regime to supplicatory admonition and then to guarded defiance. Since she finally found a publisher not in Boston but in London, she prudently omitted "America" and the poems about Christopher Snider and the Boston Massacre from her 1773 volume.

She chose to include, however, a poem dedicated to the earl of Dartmouth, who was appointed Secretary of State for the Colonies in August, 1772. In this poem, "To the Right Honourable William, Earl of Dartmouth, His Majesty's Principal Secretary of State for North America," she gives the earl extravagant praise as one who will lay to rest "hatred faction." She knew of the earl's reputation as a humanitarian through the London contacts of her mistress, Susanna. When the earl proved to support oppressive British policies, the poet's expectations were not realized; within four years of the poem's date, America had declared its independence. Since her optimism was undaunted by foreknowledge, Wheatley wrote a poem which was even more laudatory than "To The King's Most Excellent Majesty on His Repealing the American Stamp Act." Perhaps she was not totally convinced, however; the poem contains some unusually bold passages for a colonist who is also both a woman and a slave.

For example, she remarks that, with Dartmouth's secretaryship, America need no longer "dread the iron chain,/ Which wanton *Tyranny* with lawless hand/ Had made, and with it meant t'enslave the land." Once again Wheatley uses the slave metaphor of the iron chain. Quite clearly she also accuses the Crown of "wanton *Tyranny*," which it had wielded illegally and with the basest of motives—to reduce the colonies to the inhu-

man condition of slave states. Here rebellious defiance, no longer guarded, is unmistakable; the tone matches that of the Declaration of Independence. It is a mystery how these lines could have gone unnoticed in the London reviews, all of them positive, of her 1773 volume. Perhaps the reviewers were too bedazzled by the "improbability" that a black woman could produce such a volume to take the content of her poetry seriously.

In this poem, Wheatley also presents a rare autobiographical portrait describing the manner in which she was taken from her native Africa. The manuscript version of this passage is more spontaneous and direct than the more formally correct one printed in the 1773 volume, and thus is closer to the poet's true feelings. It was "Seeming cruel fate" which snatched her "from Afric's fancy'd happy seat." Fate here is only apparently cruel, since her capture has enabled her to become a Christian; the young poet's piety resounds throughout her poetry and letters. Her days in her native land were, nevertheless, happy ones, and her abduction at the hands of ruthless slavers doubtless left behind inconsolable parents. Such a bitter memory of the circumstances of her abduction fully qualifies her to "deplore the day/ When Britons weep beneath Tyrannic sway"; the later version reads: "And can I then but pray/ Others may never feel tyrannic sway?" Besides toning down the diction, this passage alters her statement to a question and replaces "Britons" with the neutral "others." The question might suggest uncertainty, but it more probably reflects the author's polite deportment toward a London audience. Since, in the earlier version, she believed Dartmouth to be sympathetic with her cause, she had no reason to exercise deference toward him; she thought she could be frank. The shift from "Britons" to "others" provokes a more compelling explanation. In the fall of 1772, Wheatley could still think of herself as a British subject. Later, however, after rejoicing that the earl's administration had given way to restive disillusionment, perhaps the poet was less certain about her citizenship.

Three years after the publication of her 1773 volume, Wheatley unabashedly celebrated the opposition to the "tyrannic sway" of Britain in "To His Excellency General Washington," newly appointed Commander-in-Chief of the Continental Army; the war of ideas had become one of arms. In this piece, which is more a paean to freedom than a eulogy to Washington, she describes freedom as "divinely fair,/ Olive and laurel bind her golden hair"; yet "She flashes dreadful in refulgent arms." The poet accents this image of martial glory with an epic simile, comparing the American forces to the power of the fierce king of the winds:

> As when Eolus heaven's fair face deforms,
> Enwrapp'd in tempest and a night of storms;
> Astonish'd ocean feels the wild uproar,
> The refluent surges beat the sounding shore.

For the young poet, America is now "The land of freedom's heavendefended race!" While the eyes of the world's nations are fixed "on the scales,/ For in their hopes Columbia's arm prevails," the poet records Britain's regret over her loss: "Ah! cruel blindness to Columbia's state!/ Lament thy thirst of boundless power too late." The temper of this couplet is in keeping with Wheatley's earlier attitudes toward oppression. The piece closes as the poet urges Washington to pursue his objective with the knowledge that virtue is on his side. If he allows the fair goddess Freedom to be his guide, Washington will surely emerge not only as the leader of a victorious army but also as the head of the newly established state.

In Wheatley's last political poem, "freedom's heaven-defended race" has won its battle. Written in 1784 within a year after the Treaty of Paris, "Liberty and Peace" is a demonstrative celebration of American independence. British tyranny, the agent of American oppression, has now been taught to fear "americus" her child, "And new-born *Rome* shall give *Britannia* Law." Wheatley concludes this piece with two pleasing couplets in praise of America, whose future is assured by heaven's approval:

> Auspicious Heaven shall fill with favoring Gales,
> Where e'er *Columbia* spreads her swelling Sails:
> To every Realm shall *Peace* her Charms display,
> And Heavenly *Freedom* spread her golden Ray.

Personified as Peace and Freedom, Columbia (America) will act as a world emissary, an emanating force like the rays of the sun. In this last couplet, Wheatley has captured, perhaps for the first time in poetry, America's ideal mission to the rest of the world.

The fact that Wheatley so energetically proclaims America's success in the political arena certainly attests her sympathies—not with the neoclassic obsession never to challenge the established order nor to breach the rules of political and social decorum—but with the Romantic notion that a people who find themselves unable to accept a present, unsatisfactory government have the right to change that government, even if such a change can be accomplished only through armed revolt. The American Revolution against Britain was the first successful such revolt and was one of the sparks of the French Revolution. Wheatley's steadfast literary participation in the American Revolution clearly aligns her with such politically active English Romantic poets as Percy Bysshe Shelley and Lord Byron.

THE ELEGIES

In her elegies, on the other hand, Wheatley displays her devotion to spiritual freedom. As do her political poems, her elegies exalt specific occasions, the deaths of people usually known to her within the social and religious community of the poet's Old South Congregational Church of Boston. As do her poems on political events, however, her elegies exceed the boundaries of occasional verse. The early, but most famous of her elegies, "On the Death of the Rev. Mr. George Whitefield, 1770," both illustrates the general structure in which she cast all seventeen of her extant elegies and indicates her recurring ideological concerns.

Wheatley's elegies conform for the most part to the Puritan funeral elegy. They include two major divisions: First comes the portrait, in which the poet pictures the life of the subject; then follows the exhortation, encouraging the reader to seek the heavenly rewards gained by the subject in death. The portrait usually comprises three biographical steps: vocation or conversion; sanctification, or evidence of good works; and glorification, or joyous treatment of the deceased's reception into heaven. Wheatley's elegy on Whitefield surprisingly opens with the glorification of the Great Awakener, already in heaven and occupying his "immortal throne." She celebrates the minister's conversion or vocation in an alliterative line as "The greatest gift that ev'n a God can give." Of course, she writes many lines describing the good works of a man wholly devoted to the winning of souls during the seven visits which he made to

America during and after the period of the Great Awakening.

Whitefield died in Newburyport, Massachusetts, on September 30, 1770, having left Boston only a week or so before, where he had apparently lodged with the Wheatley family. Indeed, the young poet of sixteen or seventeen appears to recollect from personal experience when she observes that the minister "long'd to see *America* excel" and "charg'd its youth that ev'ry grace divine/ Should with full lustre in their conduct shine." She also seizes this opportunity to proclaim to the world Whitefield's assertion that even Africans would find Jesus of Nazareth an "*Impartial Saviour.*" The poem closes with a ten-line exhortation to the living to aspire toward Whitefield's example: "Let ev'ry heart to this bright vision rise."

As one can see, Wheatley's elegies are not sad affairs; quite to the contrary, they enact joyful occasions after which deceased believers may hope to unite, as she states in "On the Death of the Rev. Dr. Sewell, 1769," with "Great God, incomprehensible, unknown/ By sense." Although man's senses may limit his firsthand acquaintance with God, these same senses do enable him to learn *about* God, especially about God's works in nature. The poem in the extant Wheatley canon which most pointedly addresses God's works in nature is "Thoughts on the Works of Providence." This poem of 131 lines opens with a ten-line invocation to the "Celestial muse," resembling Milton's heavenly muse of *Paradise Lost*.

Identifying God as the force behind planetary movement, she writes, "Ador'd [is] the God that whirls surrounding spheres" which rotate ceaselessly about "the monarch of the earth and skies." From this sublime image she moves to yet another: "'Let there be light,' he said: from his profound/ Old chaos heard and trembled at the sound." It should not go unremarked that Wheatley could, indeed, find much in nature to foster her belief, but little in the mundane world of ordinary men to sustain her spiritually. The frequency of nature imagery but the relative lack of scenes drawn from human society (with the exception of her political poems, and even these are occasions for abstract departures into the investigation of political ideologies) probably reflects the poet's insecurity and uncertainty about

a world which first made her a slave and then gave her, at best, only second-class citizenship.

In "An Hymn to the Morning," one of her most lyrical poems, Wheatley interprets the morn (recall her mother's morning ritual of pouring out water to the rising sun) as the source of poetic afflatus or inspiration. The speaker of the poem, Wheatley herself, first perceives the light of the rising sun as a reflection in the eye of one of the "feather'd race." After she hears the song of the bird which welcomes the day, she turns to find the source of melody and sees the bird "Dart the bright eye, and shake the painted plume." Here the poet captures with great precision the bird's rapid eye movement. The bird, archetypal symbol of poetic song, has received the dawn's warm rays which stimulate him to sing. When the poet turns to discover the source of melody, however, what she sees first is not Aurora, the dawning sun, but Aurora the stimulus of song reflected within the "bright eye" of the bird.

In the next stanza the poet identifies the dawn as the ultimate source of poetic inspiration when she remarks that the sun has awakened Calliope, here the personification of inspiration, while her sisters, the other Muses, "fan the pleasing fire" of the stimulus to create. Hence both the song of the bird and the light reflected in its eye have instructed her to acknowledge the source of the bird's melody; for she aspires to sing with the same pleasing fire which animates the song of the bird. Like many of the Romantics who followed her, Wheatley perceives nature both as a means to know ultimate freedom and as an inspiration to create, to make art.

It is in her superlative poem, "On Imagination," however, that Wheatley most forcefully brings both aspirations, to know God and to create fine poetry, into clear focus. To the young black poet, the imagination was sufficiently important to demand from her pen a fifty-three-line poem. The piece opens with this four-line apostrophe:

Thy various works, imperial queen, we see,
How bright their forms! how deck'd with pomp by thee!
Thy wond'rous acts in beauteous order stand,
And all attest how potent is thine hand.

Clearly, Wheatley's imagination is a regal presence in full control of her poetic world, a world in which her "wond'rous acts" of creation stand in harmony, capturing a "beauteous order." These acts themselves testify to the queen's creative power. Following a four-line invocation to the Muse, however, the poet distinguishes the imagination from its subordinate fancy:

> Now, here, now there, the roving Fancy flies;
> Till some lov'd object strikes her wand'ring eyes,
> Whose silken fetters all the senses bind,
> And soft captivity involves the mind.

Unlike the controlled, harmonious imagination, the subordinate fancy flies about here and there, searching for some appropriate and desired object worthy of setting into motion the creative powers of her superior.

FANCY AND MEMORY

In "Thoughts on the Works of Providence," the poet describes the psychology of sleep in similar fashion. Having entered the world of dreams, the mind discovers a realm where "ideas range/ Licentious and unbounded o'er the plains/ Where Fancy's queen in giddy triumph reigns." Wheatley maintains that in sleep the imagination, once again "Fancy's queen," creates worlds which lack the "beauteous order" of the poet sitting before a writing desk; nevertheless, these dream worlds provoke memorable images. In "On Recollection" Wheatley describes the memory as the repository on which the mind draws to create its dreams. What may be "long-forgotten," the memory "calls from night" and "plays before the fancy's sight." By analogy, Wheatley maintains, the memory provides the poet "ample treasure" from her "secret stores" to create poetry: "in her pomp of images display'd,/ To the high-raptur'd poet gives her aid." "On Recollection" asserts a strong affinity between the poet's memory, analogous to the world of dreams, and the fancy, the associative faculty subordinate to the imagination. Recollection for Wheatley functions as the poet's storehouse of images, while the fancy channels the force of the imagination through its associative powers. Both the memory and the fancy, then, serve the imagination.

Wheatley's description of fancy and memory departs markedly from what eighteenth century aestheticians, including John Locke and Joseph Addison, generally understood as the imagination. The faculty of mind which they termed "imagination" Wheatley relegates to

recollection (memory) and fancy. Her description of recollection and fancy closely parallels Coleridge's in the famous thirteenth chapter of *Biographia Literaria* (1817), where he states that fancy "is indeed no other than a mode of Memory emancipated from the order of time and space." Wheatley's identification of the fancy as roving "Now here, now there" whose movement is analogous to the dream state, where "ideas range/ Licentious and unbounded," certainly frees it from the limits of time and space. Coleridge further limits the fancy to the capacity of choice. "But equally with the ordinary memory," he insists, "the Fancy must receive all its materials ready made from the law of association." Like Coleridge's, Wheatley's fancy exercises choice by association as it finally settles upon "some lov'd object."

If fancy and memory are the imagination's subordinates, then how does the imagination function in the poet's creative process? Following her description of fancy in "On Imagination," Wheatley details the role the imagination plays in her poetry. According to her, the power of the imagination enables her to soar "through air to find the bright abode,/ Th' empyreal palace of the thund'ring God." The central focus of her poetry remains contemplation of God. Foreshadowing William Wordsworth's "winds that will be howling at all hours," Wheatley exclaims that on the wings of the imagination she "can surpass the wind/ And leave the rolling universe behind." In the realm of the imagination, the poet can "with new worlds amaze th' unbounded soul."

Immediately following this arresting line, Wheatley illustrates in a ten-line stanza the power of the imagination to create new worlds. Even though winter and the "frozen deeps" prevail in the real world, the imagination can take one out of unpleasant reality and build a pleasant, mythic world of fragrant flowers and verdant groves where "Fair Flora" spreads "her fragrant reign," where Sylvanus crowns the forest with leaves, and where "Show'rs may descend, and dews their gems disclose,/ And nectar sparkle on the blooming rose." Such is the power of imagination to promote poetic creation and to release one from an unsatisfactory world. Unfortunately, like reality's painful intrusion upon the delicate, unsustainable song of John Keats's immortal bird, gelid winter and its severe "northern tempests damp the rising fire," cut short the indulgence of her poetic world, and lamentably force Wheatley to end her short-lived lyric: "Cease then, my song, cease the unequal lay." Her lyric must end because no poet can indefinitely sustain a mythic world.

In her use of the imagination to create "new worlds," Wheatley's departure from eighteenth century theories of this faculty is radical and once again points toward Coleridge. Although she does not distinguish between "primary" and "secondary" imagination as he does, Wheatley nevertheless constructs a theory which approaches his "secondary" imagination. According to Coleridge, the secondary imagination, which attends the creative faculty, intensifies the primary imagination common to all men. Coleridge describes how the secondary imagination operates in this well-known passage: "It dissolves, diffuses, dissipates, in order to recreate;/ or where this process is rendered impossible, yet still at all/ events it struggles to idealize and to unify." In spite of the fact that Wheatley's attempt to dissolve, diffuse, and dissipate is assuredly more modest than Coleridge's "swift half-intermitted burst" in "Kubla Khan," she does, nevertheless, like the apocalyptic Romantics, idealize, unify, and shape a mythopoeic world. Proceeding in a systematic fashion, she first constructs a theory of mental faculty which, when assisted by the associative fancy, builds, out of an act of the mind, a new world which does indeed stand in "beauteous order." This faculty, which she identifies as the imagination, she uses as a tool to achieve freedom, however momentary.

Wheatley was, then, an innovator who used the imagination as a means to transcend an unacceptable present and even to construct "new worlds [to] amaze the unbounded soul"; this practice, along with her celebration of death, her loyalty to the American struggle for political independence, and her consistent praise of nature, places her firmly in that flow of thought which culminated in nineteenth century Romanticism. Her diction may strike a modern audience as occasionally "got up" and stiff, and her reliance on the heroic couplet may appear outdated and worn, but the content of her poetry is innovative, refreshing, and even, for her times, revolutionary. She wrote during the pre-Revolutionary and Revolutionary War eras in America, when little poetry of great merit was produced. Phillis Wheatley, laboring under the disadvantages of being not only a black slave but also a woman, nevertheless did find the time to depict that political struggle for freedom and to trace her personal battle for release. If one looks beyond the limitations of her sincere if dogmatic piety and her frequent dependence on what Wordsworth called poetic diction, one is sure to discover in her works a fine mind engaged in creating some of the best early American poetry.

OTHER MAJOR WORKS

MISCELLANEOUS: *Memoir and Poems of Phillis Wheatley: A Native African and a Slave*, 1833; *The Collected Works of Phillis Wheatley*, 1988 (John Shields, editor).

BIBLIOGRAPHY

Barker-Benfield, G. J. and Catherine Clinton, comps. *Portraits of American Women: From Settlement to the Present*. New York: St. Martin's Press, 1991. A collection of essays that locate the histories of women and men together by period. Includes portraits of Phillis Wheatley and others designed to appeal to a wide range of readers. Includes bibliographical references.

Bassard, Katherine Clay. *Spiritual Interrogations: Culture, Gender, and Community in Early African American Women's Writing*. Princeton, N.J.: Princeton University Press, 1999. A historical analysis that includes a discussion of the works of Wheatley. Includes bibliographical references and index.

Jones, Jacqueline. "Anglo-American Racism and Phillis Wheatley's 'Sable Veil,' 'Length'ned Chain,' and 'Knitted Heart.'" In *Women in the Age of the American Revolution*, edited by Ronald Hoffman and Peter J. Albert. Charlottesville: University Press of Virginia, 1989. This sometimes difficult study includes fascinating biographical information and offers a close reading of dozens of poems. Jones delineates the importance of *Poems on Various Subjects, Religious and Moral* as an early commentary on slavery and on American female thought.

Richmond, Merle. *Phillis Wheatley*. American Women of Achievement series. New York: Chelsea House, 1988. Written for young adults, this biography is lively and informative. The dozens of illustrations include a portrait of Wheatley and a sample of her handwriting. Contains suggestions for further reading, a chronology, and an index.

Rinaldi, Ann. *Hang a Thousand Trees with Ribbons: The Story of Phillis Wheatley.* New York: Harcourt, 1996. This fictionalized biography is aimed at younger readers and is written in the style Wheatley might have used to write her own autobiography between young childhood and majority. In addition to relating the fateful events of her life, starting with her abduction from Senegal, she discusses writing and its significance. Rinaldi appends a note explaining issues of fact and fiction in her work.

Robinson, William H., ed. *Critical Essays on Phillis Wheatley.* Boston: G. K. Hall, 1982. This fascinating collection of sixty-five essays contains early comments and reviews, including several by Wheatley herself, important reprinted essays from 1834 to 1975, and five critical evaluations original to this book. An editor's introduction provides a biographical and critical overview. Supplemented by a chronology and an index.

_____. *Phillis Wheatley: A Bio-Bibliography.* Boston: G. K. Hall, 1981. After a brief biography and review of the critical reception, this volume presents an annotated list of representative writings about Wheatley from 1761 to 1979. Includes reprinted appendices commenting on two of the poems, and an extensive index.

_____. *Phillis Wheatley and Her Writings.* New York: Garland, 1984. This is by far the finest introduction to Wheatley by the preeminent Wheatley scholar. Presents a brief biography, the text of all the poems and surviving letters (several in facsimile) with an analysis, nine appendices providing background information, a bibliography, and an index.

John C. Shields;
bibliography updated by the editors

JOHN WHEELWRIGHT

Born: Milton, Massachusetts; September 9, 1897
Died: Boston, Massachusetts; September 15, 1940

PRINCIPAL POETRY

North Atlantic Passage, 1925
Rock and Shell: Poems, 1923-1933, 1933
Footsteps, 1934
Masque with Clowns, 1936
Mirrors of Venus: A Novel in Sonnets, 1914-1938, 1938
Political Self-Portrait, 1919-1939, 1940
John Wheelwright: Selected Poems, 1941
Collected Poems of John Wheelwright, 1972

OTHER LITERARY FORMS

Upon his death in 1940, an obituary in *Time* magazine described John Wheelwright as "one of the most famous unheard-of poets in the U.S." As well as being a poet, however, Wheelwright was a militant in the realm of socialist theory and practice who wrote numerous essays for periodicals such as the *Partisan Review* and *The New Republic*. He was also the author of speeches on contemporary political events and issues, which he delivered from soapboxes in public settings in and around Boston.

The themes Wheelwright explored in his prose writing included his views on poetry, architecture, and developments in socialist politics in the United States. The highly literate and cultured writer also saw the possibilities of radio as a powerful vehicle for poetry and made extensive use of the medium in broadcasts in the Boston area.

ACHIEVEMENTS

John Wheelwright is an uncommon case of a poet whose political activities, commitments, and ideals find coherent, organic, and fresh expression in verse. Wheelwright's complex, rich background combined a rebellious, iconoclastic streak inherited from his ancestor John Wheelwright (1592-1679), an antinomian who founded settlements in New England; and a classicist education based on the Bible and Latin and Greek philosophy and literature. This background, together with a vigorous reading and committed practice of socialist principles, makes for a poet whose work is often didactic. "The main point," wrote Wheelwright "is not what noise poetry makes, but how it makes you think and act—not what you make of it, but what it makes of you."

John Wheelwright

Wheelwright wrote "revolutionary poetry," which was a sophisticated expression of the spirit of euphoric optimism of the 1920's and the social upheaval that marked the 1930's. As a public figure, Wheelwright had an important impact on intellectuals and workers of his time and extended the New England freethinking tradition of such figures as Thomas Paine, Ralph Waldo Emerson, and Henry David Thoreau.

BIOGRAPHY

John Taylor Wheelwright was born in Milton, Massachusetts, on September 9, 1897, into a socially prominent family. His father, Edmund March (Ned) Wheelwright, a descendant of the eighteenth century minister and political figure John Wheelwright, was a creative architect and freethinker who designed some of Boston's most remarkable public buildings. John's mother, Elizabeth Boott (Bessie) Brooks, was a descendant of Peter Chardon Brooks (1767-1849), a prosperous merchant who at one time was called the richest man in New England. As Alan Wald remarked in his book *The Revolutionary Imagination* (1983), a "blended heritage of

saints, traders, political and military leaders, pioneers, and Brahmins profoundly shaped the mind and the art of the poet John Wheelwright."

From his father's side, Wheelwright acquired intellectual curiosity and a penchant for rebellion. His father's suicide, two years after a mental and emotional breakdown, created a spiritual crisis for the teenage John, who was provided guidance by his teachers at St. George's preparatory school in Rhode Island. Seeking solace in religious thought, Wheelwright at one point considered entering the priesthood and believed the role of the poet to be similar to that of the priest.

Wheelwright remained profoundly religious throughout his short life, rejecting his parents' Unitarianism for the Anglican Church. In the 1930's he adopted a socialism whose idealism paralleled, if it did not replace, Wheelwright's religious fervor. Socialism allowed the poet, a man of the word in every sense, to channel a deeply ingrained sense of justice into community action and become a man of word and deed.

From his mother, whose name, Brooks, he officially adopted at the age of fourteen, he acquired a sense of pride and authority. Bessie Brooks's public manner and awareness of social place and responsibility shaped Wheelwright's uncompromising bearing in the public sphere, to which he chose to devote his energies.

After a privileged childhood of private schools, during which he nurtured interests in poetry, drama, and ideas, Wheelwright, like his father, attended Harvard University. He was eventually expelled because of poor grades, which resulted not from lack of talent but from a lack of application; he frequently skipped classes and missed examinations. This did not prevent Wheelwright from participating fully in the activities and publications of the Harvard Poetry Society. He published poems in *Eight More Harvard Poets* in 1923.

During a stay with his mother in Florence, Italy, Wheelwright published his first important collection, *North Atlantic Passage*. This, like much of his other work, was privately printed. Wheelwright followed his father's example and sought training in architecture in the late 1920's at the Massachusetts Institute of Technology. Without obtaining a degree, he briefly set up a practice. At the time of his death, among the books he had in preparation was a history of Romantic architecture.

Although the early phase of Wheelwright's poetic career combined self-examination with an unorthodox interest in the Bible, the 1930's brought public involvement. He was a member of the New England Poetry Club, an organization that he discussed in his *A History of the New England Poetry Club, 1915-1931* (1932). He became a member of the Socialist Party of Massachusetts in 1932. He taught, edited publications, and prepared and delivered speeches for public assemblies. The poetry from this period incorporated and developed themes addressed in his public life. These were collected in *Political Self-Portrait, 1919-1939*, published in the last year of his life, which was suddenly ended when he was hit by a drunken driver while crossing the street. Wheelwright was forty-three.

ANALYSIS

"The story of John Wheelwright ends with a salutary synthesis of political commitment and literary achievement," wrote Wald. Although there was a quiet revival of interest in Wheelwright after the 1960's, the poet's work remains outside the cannon of great literature, and his work is still undergoing assessment. Public ignorance of Wheelwright's literary achievement has at times been attributed to an alleged obscurity in his work, but the political nature of his didacticism may also have played a part in his marginalization. Nonetheless, Wheelwright's oeuvre can be richly rewarding to explore. From the precociously individual work of his youth to the "more dissonant and more complex" statements of his maturity, noted Matthew Josephson in *The Southern Review* in 1971, emerges the voice of a man who "was forthright and had the strength and courage for life on his own terms."

ROCK AND SHELL

Wheelwright's first major collection, *Rock and Shell*, contained two remarkable long poems. The first, "North Atlantic Passage," originally published in pamphlet form in Florence, Italy, in 1923, makes use of the then-emerging Surrealist technique of associative logic and imagery, and the modernist feature of polyphonic voices to explore the theme of "the One and the Many." The second, "Forty Days," is a revision of the story of the apostle Thomas, which the poet based on a reading of the apocryphal Gospels. It presents Wheelwright's unorthodox ideas on religious material, exploring, as it does, the poet's own confrontation with doubt and faith. Wheelwright's budding social conscience resulted in such poems as "Come Over and Help Us," based on the 1920's murder case of Nicola Sacco and Bartolomeo Vanzetti. Notable among the shorter poems are elegies on his friend Harry Crosby and renowned poet Hart Crane.

POEMS FOR A DIME

Wheelwright's evolving political convictions, deeply ingrained sense of justice, and desire for involvement in public life found some satisfaction in his work on radio, in his correspondence course on rebel poetry for workers, and in his setting up a small magazine called *Poems for a Dime*. A notable contribution to the popular publication was Wheelwright's own "Footsteps," a verse drama in the tradition of English poets Percy Bysshe Shelley and George Gordon, Lord Byron, which deals with labor issues. It was also at this time that Wheelwright wrote poetry and criticism for *Arise!*, a monthly publication of the Socialist Party, and presented his weekly poetry readings and commentary on Boston radio stations WORL and WIXAL.

In "Verse + Radio = Poetry," a brief, unpublished commentary on the possibilities of radio, Wheelwright offered insights into his poetics, stressing orality and voice:

How poetry looks is as the smell of turpentine to a painter's pigment. Radio compels poetry to sound. . . . [A] printed poem is not a poem. Only a spoken poem is a poem. A poem must speak. . . . Inflection even more than vocabulary conveys thought. . . . If people speak out, they think out straight. If they think out straight, they take chances to better life about them.

MIRRORS OF VENUS

In *Mirrors of Venus*, a sonnet sequence that critic Austin Warren called "a modern *In Memoriam*" (referring to Alfred, Lord Tennyson's elegy), Wheelwright's experimentations with form move into the foreground. The poet's classicist education and reading make for poetry that is filled with allusions to Greek mythology, biblical archetypes, and other tropes derived from the history of Western civilization, but Wheelwright's phrasing and handling of form are strikingly unconventional.

One poem, "Spider," even recalls the brevity, tone, and phrase quality of Japanese verse:

While the spider Sun drops down her web of sky
viol phrases of the bridges are resounding . . .
Their staccato street lamp notes are pitched too high
to reach our ears with their crescendent sounding . . .

Why do we labor to make metaphors
Debussy, Whistler, and both of us are bores . . .
In your hair, also is a Hokusai!

The sonnet sequence is given the structure of a novel, with five chapters, through which a development of the themes of love, death, guilt, and redemption are developed. The speaker comes to terms with the experience of loss (of his father and his friend Ned Couch). In these poems Wheelwright progresses from self-examination and self-disgust to a renewed faith.

POLITICAL SELF-PORTRAIT, 1919-1939

The "renewed faith" involved what Wheelwright termed "social hope" and "eternal solidarity," which he found possible in his commitment to working for the betterment of the common lot with the Socialist Party. This marks the last and most productive phase of Wheelwright's life. The fusion of poetic talent, religious questioning, and social good deeds allowed the poet to attain his poetic ideals. The poetry in this collection is evidence of the "word made into deed," a central issue in Wheelwright's thinking. He addresses it explicitly in at least two poems in *Political Self-Portrait*: "The Word Is Deed" opens the collection with

John begins like *Genesis*:
In the Beginning was the Word;
Engles misread: *Was the Deed.*
But, before ever any Deed came
the sound of the last of the Deed, coming
came with the coming Word
(which answers everything with dancing).

In "Bread-Word Giver," a poem that invokes Wheelwright's like-minded ancestor and namesake, Wheelwright calls to "John, founder of towns,—dweller in none;/ Wheelwright, schismatic,—schismatic from schismatics" to "keep us alive with your ghostly disputation." Although the connecting thread is the split between word and deed, there is a broad range of thematic nu-

ance in *Political Self-Portrait*, expressed in lyrics and two dramatic poems that explore theory and practice, thought and action.

"DUSK TO DUSK"

At the time of his death, Wheelwright had several writing projects either completed or near completion. Among these was a group of poems titled "Dusk to Dusk," which were included in *Collected Poems of John Wheelwright*, edited by Alvin H. Rosenfeld and Austin Warren and published in 1972. Although "Dusk to Dusk" contains numerous lyrics of a personal nature, the dramatic poems are particularly powerful. "Masque with Clowns," which originally appeared in *Poems for a Dime*, describes a national election campaign and circumscribes the issues faced by farmers and workers during the 1930's. "Evening Mystery in Three Episodes" addresses class power struggles and the issue of race, making use, all the while, of allegorical figures such as Loyalty and Nihilism. "Morning: A Paraphrase" returns to the apostle Thomas's theme found in the earlier "Forty Days." Again, polyphonic voices are interwoven as the dramatic poems splice together language of poetic romanticism, classical allusions, billboards, slogans, and common speech. These late poems, like his first, reveal the truth in Austin Warren's observation that Wheelwright was "constitutionally incapable of imitating or being schooled, and he sounds like no one else."

OTHER MAJOR WORKS

NONFICTION: *A History of the New England Poetry Club, 1915-1931*, 1932.

BIBLIOGRAPHY

Ashbery, John. *Other Traditions.* Cambridge, Mass.: Harvard University Press, 2000. Wheelwright is considered alongside fellow writers John Clare, Thomas Lovell Beddoes, Raymond Roussel, Laura Riding, and David Schubert in this publication of a Charles Eliot Norton Lecture delivered by Ashbery at Harvard in 1989. Ashbery shares many similarities with Wheelwright, and he celebrates the poet's eccentricities and the richness of possible interpretations of his work.

Damon, S. Foster, and Alvin H. Rosenfeld. "John Wheelwright: New England's Colloquy with the

World." *Southern Review* 7 (April, 1972): 311-348. "Wheelwright's writing remains largely ignored. Both the man and his work clearly stand in need of being reintroduced," write the authors, who go on to show how Wheelwright is a poet of "intense imagination and strong critical intelligence." This essay provides an excellent critical overview of Wheelwright's activities as a writer, editor, and social activist and provides some glimpses into the family history and personal psychology of the poet.

Gregory, Horace, and Marya Zaturensak. *A History of American Poetry, 1900-1940*. New York: Harcourt, Brace, 1946. Written shortly after Wheelwright's death, this book contains a chapter on the 1920's, in the context of which Wheelwright's poetry is considered. Close attention is given to select quoted passages, and the authors place the poet in the context of both his historical antecedents and the issues of the poet's contemporaries, providing anecdotes and bits of biography along the way.

Josephson, Matthew. "Improper Bostonian: John Wheelwright and His Poetry." *Southern Review* 7 (Spring, 1971): 509-541. Josephson provides a personal but well-informed and responsibly researched account of Wheelwright's activities and his place in the history of American letters. Passages of poetry and prose are examined and discussed with the goal of providing insights into Wheelwright's personal and professional evolution.

Wald, Alan M. *The Revolutionary Imagination: The Poetry and Politics of John Wheelwright and Sherry Mangan*. Chapel Hill: University of North Carolina Press, 1983. An excellent, detailed study of Wheelwright and contemporary Sherry Mangan, both of whom were active in the political left in the 1930's United States. A highly defined picture of the poet emerges, with as much attention given to family history, psychological portrait-sketching, outlining of the currents of thought, and public events of the period, while bringing in the poetry to show how the life and work meshed.

Warren, Austin. *New England Saints*. Ann Arbor: University of Michigan Press, 1956. Warren identifies two strains in the New England character—the "Yankee trader" and the "Yankee saint"—and de-

votes his book to a study of the latter. Wheelwright's family, of course, contained both, but the poet himself was devoted in word and deed to the betterment of himself and others and earns, in Warren's estimation, the designation of "saint." The chapter on Wheelwright served as introduction to the *Collected Poems of John Wheelwright*, published in 1972. While considering Wheelwright's thought and actions, it focuses on praising the poet's literary gifts, claiming that although he was a "saint," Wheelwright was also "a poet whose books will one day take their rightful place in American poetry and scripture."

Paul Serralheiro

WALT WHITMAN

Born: West Hills, New York; May 31, 1819
Died: Camden, New Jersey; March 26, 1892

PRINCIPAL POETRY

Leaves of Grass, 1855, 1856, 1860, 1867, 1871, 1876, 1881-1882, 1889, 1891-1892
Drum-Taps, 1865
Sequel to Drum-Taps, 1865-1866
Passage to India, 1871
After All, Not to Create Only, 1871
As a Strong Bird on Pinions Free, 1872
Two Rivulets, 1876
November Boughs, 1888
Good-bye My Fancy, 1891
Complete Poetry and Selected Prose, 1959 (James E. Miller, editor)

OTHER LITERARY FORMS

Walt Whitman published several important essays and studies during his lifetime. *Democratic Vistas* (1871), *Memoranda During the War* (1875-1876), *Specimen Days and Collect* (1882-1883, autobiographical sketches), and the *Complete Prose Works* (1892) are the most significant. He also tried his hand at short fiction, collected in *The Half-Breed and Other Stories* (1927), and a novel, *Franklin Evans* (1842). Many of his letters and journals have appeared either in early editions or as parts of the New York University Press edition of *The Collected Writings of Walt Whitman* (1961-1984; 22 volumes).

ACHIEVEMENTS

Walt Whitman's stature rests largely on two major contributions to the literature of the United States. First, although detractors are numerous and the poet's organizing principle is sometimes blurred, *Leaves of Grass* stands as the most fully realized American epic poem. Written in the midst of natural grandeur and burgeoning materialism, Whitman's book traces the geographical, social, and spiritual contours of an expanding nation. It embraces the science and commercialism of industrial America while trying to direct these practical energies toward the "higher mind" of literature, culture, and the soul. In his Preface to the first edition of *Leaves of Grass*, Whitman referred to the United States itself as "essentially the greatest poem." He saw the self-esteem, sympathy, candor, and deathless attachment to freedom of the common people as "unrhymed poetry," which awaited the "gigantic and generous treatment worthy of it." *Leaves of Grass* was to be that treatment.

As James E. Miller points out in his edition of Whitman's *Complete Poetry and Selected Prose* (1959), the poet's second achievement was in language and poetic technique. Readers take for granted the modern American poet's emphasis on free verse and ordinary diction, forgetting Whitman's revolutionary impact. His free verse form departed from stanzaic patterns and regular lines, taking its power instead from individual, rolling, oratorical lines of cadenced speech. He subordinated traditional poetic techniques, such as alliteration, repetition, inversion, and conventional meter, to this expansive form. He also violated popular rules of poetic diction by extracting a rich vocabulary from foreign languages, science, opera, various trades, and the ordinary language of town and country. Finally, Whitman broke taboos with his extensive use of sexual imagery, incorporated not to titillate or

shock, but to portray life in its wholeness. He determined to be the poet of procreation, to celebrate the elemental and primal life force that permeates man and nature. Thus, "forbidden voices" are unveiled, clarified, and transfigured by the poet's vision of their place in an organic universe.

Whitman himself said he wrote but "one or two indicative words for the future." He expected the "main things" from poets, orators, singers, and musicians to come. They would prove and define a national culture, thus justifying his faith in American democracy. These apologetic words, along with the early tendency to read Whitman as "untranslatable," or barbaric and undisciplined, long delayed his acceptance as one of America's greatest poets. In fact, if judged by the poet's own test of greatness, he is a failure, for he said the "proof of a poet is that his country absorbs him as affectionately as he has absorbed it." Whitman has not been absorbed by the common people to whom he paid tribute in his poetry.

Walt Whitman (Library of Congress)

Today, however, with recognition from both the academic community and such twentieth century poets as Hart Crane, William Carlos Williams, Karl Shapiro, and Randall Jarrell, his *Leaves of Grass* has taken its place among the great masterworks of American literature.

BIOGRAPHY

Walt Whitman (christened Walter) was born in West Hills, Long Island on May 31, 1819. His mother, Louisa Van Velsor, was descended from a long line of New York Dutch farmers, and his father, Walter Whitman, was a Long Island farmer and carpenter. In 1823, the father moved his family to Brooklyn in search of work. One of nine children in an undistinguished family, Whitman received only a meager formal education between 1825 and 1830, when he turned to the printing trade for the next five years. At the age of seventeen he began teaching at various Long Island schools and continued to teach until he went to New York City to be a printer for the *New World* and a reporter for the *Democratic Review* in 1841. From then on, Whitman generally made a living at journalism. Besides reporting and freelance writing, he edited several Brooklyn newspapers, including the *Daily Eagle* (1846-1848), the *Freeman* (1848-1849), and the *Times* (1857-1859). Some of Whitman's experiences during this period influenced the poetry that seemed to burst into print in 1855. While in New York, Whitman frequented the opera and the public library, both of which furnished him with a sense of heritage, of connection with the bards and singers of the past. In 1848, Whitman met and was hired by a representative of the New Orleans *Crescent*. Although the job lasted only a few months, the journey by train, stagecoach, and steamboat through what Whitman always referred to as "inland America" certainly helped to stimulate his vision of the country's democratic future. Perhaps most obviously influential was Whitman's trade itself. His flair for action and vignette, as well as descriptive detail, surely was sharpened by his journalistic writing. The reporter's keen eye for the daily scene is everywhere evident in *Leaves of Grass*.

When the first edition of his poems appeared, Whitman received little money but some attention from reviewers. Included among the responses was a famous letter from Ralph Waldo Emerson, who praised Whit-

man for his brave thought and greeted him at the beginning of a great career. Whitman continued to write and edit, but was unemployed during the winter of 1859-1860, when he began to frequent Pfaff's bohemian restaurant. There he may have established the "manly love" relationships which inspired the "Calamus" poems of the 1860 edition of *Leaves of Grass*. Again, this third edition created a stir with readers, but the outbreak of the Civil War soon turned everyone's attention to more pressing matters. Whitman himself was too old for military service, but he did experience the war by caring for wounded soldiers in Washington, D.C., hospitals. While in Washington as a government clerk, Whitman witnessed Lincoln's second inauguration, mourned over the President's assassination in April, printed *Drum-Taps* in May, and later added to these Civil War lyrics a sequel, which contained "When Lilacs Last in the Dooryard Bloom'd."

The postwar years saw Whitman's reputation steadily increasing in England, thanks to William Rossetti's *Selections* in 1868, Algernon Swinburne's praise, and a long, admiring review of his work by Anne Gilchrist in 1870. In fact, Mrs. Gilchrist fell in love with the poet after reading *Leaves of Grass* and even moved to Philadelphia in 1876 to be near him, but her hopes of marrying Whitman died with her in 1885. Because of books by William D. O'Connor and John Burroughs, Whitman also became better known in the United States, but any satisfaction he may have derived from this recognition was tempered by two severe blows in 1873. He suffered a paralytic stroke in January, and his mother, to whom he was very devoted, died in May. Unable to work, Whitman returned to stay with his brother George at Camden, New Jersey, spending summers on a farm at Timber Creek.

Although Whitman recuperated sufficiently to take trips to New York or Boston, and even to Colorado and Canada in 1879-1880, he was never again to be the robust man he had so proudly described in early editions of *Leaves of Grass*. His declining years, however, gave him time to revise and establish the structure of his book. When the seventh edition of *Leaves of Grass* was published in Philadelphia in 1881, Whitman had achieved a total vision of his work. With the money from a Centennial edition (1876) and an occasional lecture on Lincoln, Whitman was able by 1884 to purchase a small house on Mickle Street in Camden, New Jersey. Although he was determined not to be "house-bound," a sunstroke in 1885 and a second paralytic stroke in 1888 made him increasingly dependent on friends. He found especially gratifying the friendship of his secretary and companion, Horace Traubel, who recorded the poet's life and opinions during these last years. Despite the care of Traubel and several doctors and nurses, Whitman died of complications from a stroke on March 26, 1892.

ANALYSIS

An approach to Walt Whitman's poetry profitably begins with the "Inscriptions" to *Leaves of Grass*, for these short, individual pieces introduce the main ideas and methods of Whitman's book. In general, they stake out the ground of what Miller has called the prototypical New World personality, a merging of the individual with the national and cosmic, or universal, selves. That democratic principles are at the root of Whitman's views becomes immediately clear in "One's-Self I Sing," the first poem in *Leaves of Grass*. Here, Whitman refers to the self as a "simple separate person," yet utters the "word Democratic, the word En-Masse." Citizens of America alternately assert their individuality—obey little, resist often—and yet see themselves as a brotherhood of the future, inextricably bound by the vision of a great new society of and for the masses. This encompassing vision requires a sense of "the Form complete," rejecting neither body nor soul, singing equally of the Female and Male, embracing both realistic, scientific, modern man and the infinite, eternal life of the spirit.

LEAVES OF GRASS

Whitman takes on various roles, or engages in what Raymond Cook calls "empathic identification" (*Walt Whitman Review*, 1964), to lead his readers to a fuller understanding of this democratic universal. In "Me Imperturbe," he is at ease as an element of nature, able to confront the accidents and rebuffs of life with the implacability of trees and animals. As he suggests in *Democratic Vistas*, the true idea of nature in all its power and glory must become fully restored and must furnish the "pervading atmosphere" to poems of American democracy. Whitman must also empathize with rational

things—with humanity at large and in particular—so he constructs what sometimes seem to be endless catalogs of Americans at work and play. This technique appears in "I Hear America Singing," which essentially lists the varied carols of carpenter, boatman, shoemaker, woodcutter, mother, and so on, all "singing what belongs to him or her and to none else" as they ply their trades. In longer poems, such as "Starting from Paumanok," Whitman extends his catalog to all the states of the Union. He intends to acknowledge contemporary lands, salute employments and cities large and small, and report heroism on land and sea from an American point of view. He marks down all of what constitutes unified life, including the body, sexual love, and comradeship, or "manly love." Finally, the poet must join the greatness of love and democracy to the greatness of religion. These programs expand to take up large parts of even longer poems, such as "Song of Myself" or to claim space of their own in sections of *Leaves of Grass*.

Whitman uses another technique to underscore the democratic principle of his art: He makes the reader a fellow poet, a "camerado" who joins hands with him to traverse the poetic landscape. In "To You," he sees the poet and reader as passing strangers who desire to speak to one another and urges that they do so. In "Song of the Open Road," Whitman travels the highways with his "delicious burdens" of men and women, calling them all to come forth and move forever forward, well armed to take their places in "the procession of souls along the grand roads of the universe." His view of the reader as fellow traveler and seer is especially clear in the closing lines of the poem:

Camerado, I give you my hand!
I give you my love more precious than money,
I give you myself before preaching or law;
Will you give me yourself? will you come travel with me?
Shall we stick by each other as long as we live?

Finally, this comradeship means willingness to set out on one's own, for Whitman says in "Song of Myself" that the reader most honors his style "who learns under it to destroy the teacher." The questions one asks are one's own to puzzle out. The poet's role is to lead his reader up on a knoll, wash the gum from his eyes, and then let him become habituated to the "dazzle of light" that is the natural world. In other words, Whitman intends to help his reader become a "poet" of insight and perception and then release him to travel the public roads of a democratic nation.

This democratic unification of multiplicity, empathic identification, and comradeship exists in most of Whitman's poems. They do not depend on his growth as poet or thinker. Yet, in preparing to analyze representative poems from *Leaves of Grass*, it is helpful to establish a general plan for the various sections of the book. Whitman revised and reordered his poems until the 1881 edition, which established a form that was to remain essentially unchanged through succeeding editions. He merely annexed materials to the 1881 order until just before his death in 1892, then authorized the 1892 version for all future printings. Works originally published apart from *Leaves of Grass*, such as *Drum-Taps* or *Passage to India*, were eventually incorporated in the parent volume. Thus, an analysis of the best poems in five important sections of this final *Leaves of Grass* will help delineate Whitman's movement toward integration of self and nation, within his prescribed portals of birth and death.

"SONG OF MYSELF"

"Song of Myself," Whitman's great lyric poem, exemplifies his democratic "programs" without diminishing the intense feeling that so startled his first readers. It successfully combines paeans to the individual, the nation, and life at large, including nature, sexuality, and death. Above all, "Song of Myself" is a poem of incessant motion, as though Whitman's energy is spontaneously bursting into lines. Even in the contemplative sections of the poem, when Whitman leans and loafs at his ease observing a spear of summer grass, his senses of hearing, taste, and sight are working at fever pitch. In the opening section he calls himself "nature without check with original energy." Having once begun to speak, he hopes "to cease not till death." Whitman says that although others may talk of the beginning and the end, he finds his subject in the now—in the "urge and urge and urge" of the procreant world.

One method by which Whitman's energy escapes boundaries is the poet's ability to "become" other people and things. He will not be measured by time and space, nor by physical form. Rather, he effuses his flesh in eddies and drifts it in lacy jags, taking on new identities with every line. His opening lines show that he is speaking not of himself alone but of all selves. What he assumes, the reader shall assume; every atom of him, and therefore of the world, belongs to the reader as well. In Section 24, he represents himself as a "Kosmos," which contains multitudes and reconciles apparent opposites. He speaks the password and sign of democracy and accepts nothing which all cannot share. To stress this egalitarian vision, Whitman employs the catalog with skill and variety. Many parts of "Song of Myself" list or name characters, places, occupations, or experiences, but Section 33 most clearly shows the two major techniques that give these lists vitality. First, Whitman composes long single-sentence movements of action and description, which attempt to unify nature and civilization. The poet is alternately weeding his onion patch, hoeing, prospecting, hauling his boat down a shallow river, scaling mountains, walking paths, and speeding through space. He then follows each set of actions with a series of place lines, beginning with "where," "over," "at," or "upon," which unite farmhouses, hearth furnaces, hot-air balloons, or steamships with plants and animals of land and sea. Second, Whitman interrupts these long listings with more detailed vignettes, which show the "large hearts of heroes"—a sea captain, a hounded slave, a fireman trapped and broken under debris, an artillerist. Sections 34-36 then extend the narrative to tales of the Alamo and an old-time sea fight, vividly brough forth with sounds and dialogue. In each case, the poet becomes the hero and is actually in the scene to suffer or succeed.

This unchecked energy and empathy carry over into Whitman's ebullient imagery to help capture the physical power of human bodies in procreant motion. At one point Whitman calls himself "hankering, gross, mystical, nude." He finds no sweeter flesh than that which sticks to his own bones, or to the bones of others. Sexual imagery, including vividly suggestive descriptions of the male and female body, is central to the poem. Although the soul must take its equal place with the body, neither abasing itself before the other, Whitman's mystical union of soul and body is a sexual experience as well. He loves the hum of the soul's "valved voice" and remembers how, on a transparent summer morning, the soul settled its head athwart his hips and turned over on him. It parted the shirt from the poet's "bosom-bone," plunged its tongue to his "bare-stript heart," and reached until it felt his beard and held his feet. From this experience came peace and the knowledge that love is fundamental to a unified, continuous creation. Poetic metaphor, which identifies and binds hidden likenesses in nature, is therefore emblematic of the organic world. For example, in answering a child's question, "What is the grass?" the poet offers a series of metaphors that join human, natural, and spiritual impulses:

I guess it must be the flag of my disposition, out
of hopeful green stuff woven.
Or I guess it is the handkerchief of the Lord,
A scented gift and remembrancer designedly dropt,
Bearing the owner's name someway in the corners,
    that we may see and remark, and say *Whose*?

The grass becomes hair from the breasts of young men, from the heads and beards of old people, or from offspring, and it "speaks" from under the faint red roofs of mouths. The smallest sprout shows that there is no death, for "nothing collapses," and to die is "luckier" than anyone had supposed. This excerpt from the well-known sixth section of "Song of Myself" illustrates how image-making signifies for Whitman a kind of triumph over death itself.

Because of its position near the beginning of *Leaves of Grass* and its encompassing of Whitman's major themes, "Song of Myself" is a foundation for the volume. The "self" in this poem is a replica of the nation as self, and its delineation in the cosmos is akin to the growth of the United States in the world. Without putting undue stress on this nationalistic interpretation, however, the reader can find many reasons to admire "Song of Myself." Its dynamic form, beauty of language, and psychological insights are sufficient to make Whitman a first-rate poet, even if he had written nothing else.

CELEBRATION OF SELF AND SEXUALITY

The passionate celebration of the self and of sexuality is Whitman's great revolutionary theme. In "Children of Adam" he is the procreative father of multitudes, a champion of heterosexual love and the "body electric."

In "From Pent-Up Aching Rivers," he sings of the need for superb children, brought forth by the "muscular urge" of "stalwart loins." In "I Sing the Body Electric," he celebrates the perfection of well-made male and female bodies. Sections 5 and 9 are explicit descriptions of sexual intercourse and physical "apparatus," respectively. Whitman does not shy away from the fierce attraction of the female form, or the ebb and flow of "limitless limpid jets of love hot and enormous" that undulate into the willing and yielding "gates of the body." Because he sees the body as sacred, as imbued with divine power, he considers these enumerations to be poems of the soul as much as of the body.

Indeed, "A Woman Waits for Me" specifically states that sex contains all—bodies and souls. Thus, the poet seeks warm-blooded and sufficient women to receive the pent-up rivers of himself, to start new sons and daughters fit for the great nation that will be these United States. The procreative urge operates on more than one level in "Children of Adam"—it is physical sex and birthing, the union of body and soul, and the metaphorical insemination of the poet's words and spirit into national life. In several ways, then, words are to become flesh. Try as some early Whitman apologists might to explain them away, raw sexual impulses are the driving force of these poems.

"CALAMUS" POEMS

Whitman's contemporaries were shocked by the explicit sexual content of "Children of Adam," but modern readers and critics have been much more intrigued by the apparent homosexuality of the "Calamus" poems from the 1860 edition of *Leaves of Grass*. Although it is ultimately impossible to say whether these poems reflect Whitman's homosexual associations in New York, it is obvious that comradeship extends here to both spiritual and physical contact between men. "In Paths Untrodden" states the poet's intention to sing of "manly attachment" or types of "athletic love," to celebrate the need of comrades. "Whoever You Are Holding Me Now in Hand" deepens the physical nature of this love, including the stealthy meeting of male friends in a wood, behind some rock in the open air, or on the beach of some quiet island. There the poet would permit the comrade's long-dwelling kiss upon the lips and a touch that would carry him eternally forth over land and sea.

"These I Singing in Spring" refers to "him that tenderly loves me" and pledges the hardiest spears of grass, the calamus-root, to those who love as the poet himself is capable of loving.

Finally, two of Whitman's best lyrics concern this robust but clandestine relationship. "I Saw in Louisiana a Live-Oak Growing" is a poignant contrast between the live oak's ability to "utter joyous leaves" while it stands in solitude, without companions, and the poet's inability to live without a friend or lover near. There is no mistaking the equally personal tone of "When I Heard at the Close of the Day," probably Whitman's finest "Calamus" poem. The plaudits of others are meaningless and unsatisfying, says Whitman, until he thinks of how his dear friend and lover is on his way to see him. When his friend arrives one evening, the hissing rustle of rolling waves becomes congratulatory and joyful. Once the one he loves most lies sleeping by him under the same cover, face inclined toward him in the autumn moonbeams and arm lightly lying around his breast, he is happy.

Other short poems in "Calamus," such as "For You O Democracy," "The Prairie Grass Dividing," or "A Promise to California," are less obviously personal. Rather, they extend passionate friendship between men to the larger ideal of democratic brotherhood. Just as procreative love has its metaphorical implications for the nation, so too does Whitman promise to make the continent indissoluble and cities inseparable, arms about each other's necks, with companionship and the "manly love of comrades." Still other poems move this comradeship into wider spans of space and time. "The Moment Yearning and Thoughtful" joins the poet with men of Europe and Asia in happy brotherhood, thus transcending national and continental boundaries. "The Base of All Metaphysics" extends this principle through historical time, for the Greek, Germanic, and Christian systems all suggest that the attraction of friend to friend is the basis of civilization. The last poem in the "Calamus" section, "Full of Life Now," completes Whitman's panoramic view by carrying friendship into the future. His words communicate the compact, visible to readers of a century or any number of centuries hence. Each seeking the other past time's invisible boundaries, poet and reader are united physically through Whitman's poetry.

"CROSSING BROOKLYN FERRY"

"Crossing Brooklyn Ferry" is the natural product of Whitman's idea that love and companionship will bind the world's peoples to one another. In a sense it gives the poet immortality through creation of a living artifact: the poem itself. Whitman stands motionless on a moving ferry, immersed in the stream of life and yet suspended in time through the existence of his words on the page. Consequently, he can say that neither time nor place nor distance matters, because he is with each reader and each fellow traveler in the future. He points out that hundreds of years hence others will enter the gates of the ferry and cross from shore to shore, will see the sun half an hour high and watch the seagulls floating in circles with motionless wings. Others will also watch the endless scallo-edged waves cresting and falling, as though they are experiencing the same moment as the poet, with the same mixture of joy and sorrow. Thus, Whitman confidently calls upon the "dumb ministers" of nature to keep up their ceaseless motion—to flow, fly, and frolic on—because they furnish their parts toward eternity and toward the soul.

Techniques match perfectly with these themes in "Crossing Brooklyn Ferry." Whitman's frequent repetition of the main images—sunrise and sunset, ebb and flow of the sea and river, seagulls oscillating in the sky—reinforces the belief in timeless, recurring human experience. Descriptions of schooners and steamers at work along the shore are among his most powerful evocations of color and sound. Finally, Whitman's employment of pronouns to mark a shift in the sharing of experiences also shows the poem's careful design. Whitman begins the poem with an "I" who looks at the scenes or crowds of people and calls to "you" who are among the crowds and readers of present and future. In Section 8, however, he reaches across generations to fuse himself and pour his meaning into the "you." At the end of this section, he and others have become "we," who understand and receive experience with free senses and love, united in the organic continuity of nature.

"SEA-DRIFT" POEMS

The short section of *Leaves of Grass* entitled "Sea-Drift" contains the first real signs of a more somber Whitman, who must come to terms with hardship, sorrow, and death. In one way, this resignation and accommodation follow the natural progression of the self from active, perhaps callow, youth to contemplative old age. They are also an outgrowth of Whitman's belief that life and death are a continuum, that life is a symphony of both sonatas and dirges, which the true poet of nature must capture fully on the page. Whereas in other poems the ocean often signifies birth and creation, with fish-shaped Paumanok (Manhattan) rising from the sea, in "Tears" it is the repository of sorrow. Its white shore lies in solitude, dark and desolate, holding a ghost or "shapeless lump" that cries streaming, sobbing tears. In "As I Ebb'd with the Ocean of Life," Whitman is distressed with himself for daring to "blab" so much without having the least idea who or what he really is. Nature darts upon the poet and stings him, because he has not understood anything and because no man ever can. He calls himself but a "trail of drift and debris," who has left his poems like "little wrecks" upon Paumanok's shores. Yet, he must continue to throw himself on the ocean of life, clinging to the breast of the land that is his father, and gathering from the moaning sea the "sobbing dirge of Nature." He believes the flow will return, but meanwhile he must wait and lie in drifts at his readers' feet.

"OUT OF THE CRADLE ENDLESSLY ROCKING"

"Out of the Cradle Endlessly Rocking" is a fuller, finally more optimistic, treatment of the poet's confrontation with loss. Commonly acknowledged as one of Whitman's finest works, this poem uses lyrical language and operatic structure to trace the origin of his poetic powers in the experience of death. Two "songs" unite with the whispering cry of the sea to communicate this experience to him. Central to the poem is Whitman's seaside reminiscence of a bird and his mate, who build and tend a nest of eggs. When the female fails to return one evening, never to appear again, the male becomes a solitary singer of his sorrows, whose notes are "translated" by the listening boy-poet. The bird's song is an aria of lonesome love, an outpouring carol of yearning, hope, and finally, death. As the boy absorbs the bird's song, his soul awakens in sympathy. From this moment forward, his destiny will be to perpetuate the bird's "cries of unsatisfied love." More important, though, Whitman must learn the truth that this phrase masks, must conquer "the word" that has caused the bird's cries:

Whereto answering, the sea,
Delaying not, hurrying not,
Whisper'd me through the night, and very plainly
    before daybreak,
Lisp'd to me the low and delicious word death,
And again death, death, death, death.

Whitman then fuses the bird's song and his own with death, which the sea, "like some old crone rocking the cradle," has whispered to him. This final image of the sea as an old crone soothing an infant underscores the central point of "Out of the Cradle Endlessly Rocking": Old age and death are part of a natural flux. Against the threat of darkness, one must live and sing.

DRUM-TAPS

Like the tone of "Sea-Drift," darker hues permeate Whitman's Civil War lyrics. His experiences as a hospital worker in Washington, D.C. are clearly behind the sometimes wrenching imagery of *Drum-Taps*. As a wound dresser he saw the destruction of healthy young bodies and minds at first hand. These spectacles were in part a test of Whitman's own courage and comradeship, but they were also a test of the nation's ability to survive and grow. As Whitman says in "Long, Too Long America," the country had long traveled roads "all even and peaceful," learning only from joys and prosperity, but now it must face "crises of anguish" without recoiling and show the world what its "children enmasse really are." Many of the *Drum-Taps* lyrics show Whitman facing this reality, but "The Wound Dresser" is representative. The poet's persona is an old man who is called upon years after the Civil War to "paint the mightiest armies of earth," to tell what experience of the war stays with him latest and deepest. Although he mentions the long marches, rushing charges, and toils of battle, he does not dwell on soldiers' perils or soldiers' joys. Rather, he vividly describes the wounded and dying at battlegrounds, hospital tents, or roofed hospitals, as he goes with "hinged knees and steady hand to dress wounds." He does not recoil or give out at the sight of crushed heads, shattered throats, amputated stumps of hands and arms, the gnawing and putrid gangrenous foot or shoulder. Yet, within him rests a burning flame, the memory of youths suffering or dead.

Confronted with these horrors, Whitman had to find a way to surmount them, and that way was love. If there could be a positive quality in war, Whitman found it in the comradeship of common soldiers, who risked all for their fellows. In "As Toilsome I Wander'd Virginia's Woods," for example, Whitman discovers the grave of a soldier buried beneath a tree. Hastily dug on a retreat from battle, the grave is nevertheless marked by a sign: "Bold, cautious, true, and my loving comrade." That inscription remains with the poet through many changeful seasons and scenes to follow, as evidence of this brotherly love. Similarly, "Vigil Strange I Kept on the Field One Night" tells of a soldier who sees his comrade struck down in battle and returns to find him cold with death. He watches by him through "immortal and mystic hours" until, just as dawn is breaking, he folds the young man in a blanket and buries him in a rude-dug grave where he fell. This tale of tearless mourning perfectly evokes the loss caused by war.

Eventually, Whitman finds some ritual significance in these deaths, as though they are atonement for those yet living. In "A Sight in Camp in the Daybreak Gray and Dim," he marks three covered forms on stretchers near a hospital tent. One by one he uncovers their faces. The first is an elderly man, gaunt and grim, but a comrade nevertheless. The second is a sweet boy "with cheeks yet blooming." When he exposes the third face, however, he finds it calm, of yellow-white ivory, and of indeterminable age. He sees in it the face of Christ himself, "dead and divine and brother of all." "Over the Carnage Rose Prophetic a Voice" suggests that these Christian sacrifices will finally lead to a united Columbia. Even though a thousand may have to "sternly immolate themselves for one," those who love one another shall become invincible, and "affection shall solve the problems of freedom." As in other sections of *Leaves of Grass*, Whitman believes the United States will be held together not by lawyers, paper agreements, or force of arms, but by the cohesive power of love and fellowship.

"WHEN LILACS LAST IN THE DOORYARD BLOOM'D"

"When Lilacs Last in the Dooryard Bloom'd," another of Whitman's acknowledged masterpieces, repeats the process underlying *Drum-Taps*. The poet must come to terms with the loss of one he loves—in this case, the slain President Lincoln. Death and mourning must eventually give way to consolation and hope for the future. Cast in the form of a traditional elegy, the poem traces the processional of Lincoln's coffin across country, past the poet himself, to the President's final resting place.

To objectify his emotional struggle between grief on the one hand and spiritual reconciliation with death on the other, Whitman employs several vivid symbols. The lilac blooming perennially, with its heart-shaped leaves, represents the poet's perpetual mourning and love. The "powerful fallen star," which now lies in a "harsh surrounding could" of black night, is Lincoln, fallen and shrouded in his coffin. The solitary hermit thrush that warbles "death's outlet song of life" from a secluded swamp is the soul or spiritual world. Initially, Whitman is held powerless by the death of his departing comrade. Although he can hear the bashful notes of the thrush and will come to understand them, he thinks only of showering the coffin with sprigs of lilac to commemorate his love for Lincoln. He must also warble his own song before he can absorb the bird's message of consolation. Eventually, as he sits amidst the teeming daily activities described in Section 14, he is struck by the "sacred knowledge of death," and the bird's carol thus becomes intelligible to him. Death is lovely, soothing, and delicate. It is a "strong deliveress" who comes to nestle the grateful body in her flood of bliss. Rapt with the charm of the bird's song, Whitman sees myriad battle corpses in a vision—the debris of all the slain soldiers of the war—yet realizes that they are fully at rest and unsuffering. The power of this realization gives him strength to loose the hand of his comrade. An ever-blooming lilac now signifies renewal, just as death takes its rightful place as the harbinger of new life, the life of the eternal soul.

MATTERS OF SPIRIT

Whitman's deepening concern with matters of the spirit permeates the last sections of *Leaves of Grass*. Having passed the test of the Civil War and having done his part to reunite the United States, Whitman turned his attention to America's place in the world and his own place in God's design. As he points out in "A Clear Midnight," he gives his last poems to the soul and its "free flight into the wordless," in order to ponder the themes he loves best: "Night, sleep, death and the stars." Such poems as "Chanting the Square Deific" and "A Noiseless Patient Spider" invoke either the general soul, the "Santa Spirita" that pervades all of created life, or the toils of individual souls, flinging out gossamer threads to connect themselves with this holy spirit.

"PASSAGE TO INDIA" AND "PRAYER OF COLUMBUS"

In *A Reader's Guide to Walt Whitman* (1970), Gay Wilson Allen finds this late Whitman too often pathetically didactic and unpoetic, but he points out that the poet was still able to produce fine lyrics in his old age. One of these successful poems, "Passage to India," announces Whitman's intention to join modern science to fables and dreams of old, to weld past and future, and to show that the United States is but a "bridge" in the "vast rondure" of the world. Just as the Suez Canal connected Europe and Asia, Whitman says, America's transcontinental railroad ties the Eastern to the Western sea, thus verifying Columbus's dream. Beyond these material thoughts of exploration, however, lies the poet's realm of love and spirit. The poet is a "true son of God," who will soothe the hearts of restlessly exploring, never-happy humanity. He will link all human affections, justify the "cold, impassive, voiceless earth," and absolutely fuse nature and man. This fusion takes place not in the material world but in the swelling of the soul toward God, who is a mighty "centre of the true, the good, the loving." Passage to these superior universes transcends time and space and death. It is a "passage to more than India," through the deep waters that no mariner has traveled, and for which the poet must "risk the ship, ourselves and all."

Whitman also uses a seagoing metaphor for spiritual passage in "Prayer of Columbus," which is almost a continuation of "Passage to India." In the latter, Whitman aggressively flings himself into the active voyage toward God, but in "Prayer of Columbus" he is a "batter'd, wreck'd old man," willing to yield his ships to God and wait for the unknown end of all. He recounts his heroic deeds of exploration and attributes their inspiration to a message from the heavens that sped him on. Like Columbus, Whitman is "old, poor, and paralyzed," yet capable of one more effort to speak of the steady interior light that God has granted him. Finally, the works of the past fall away from him, and some divine hand reveals a scene of countless ships sailing on distant seas, from which "anthems in new tongues" salute and comfort him. This implied divine sanction for his life's work was consolation to an old poet, who, at his death in 1892, remained largely unaccepted and unrecognized by contemporary critics and historians.

LEGACY

The grand design of *Leaves of Grass* appears to trace self and nation neatly through sensuous youth, crises of maturity, and soul-searching old age. Although this philosophical or psychological reading of Whitman's work is certainly encouraged by the poet's tinkering with its structure, many fine lyrics do not fit into neat patterns, or even under topical headings. Whitman's reputation rests more on the startling freshness of his language, images, and democratic treatment of the common American citizen than on his success as epic bard. Common to all his poetry, however, are certain major themes: reconciliation of body and soul, purity and unity of physical nature, death as the "mother of beauty," and above all, comradeship or love, which binds and transcends all else. In fact, Whitman encouraged a complex comradeship with his readers to bind his work to future generations. He expected reading to be a gymnastic struggle and the reader to be a re-creator of the poem through imaginative interaction with the poet. Perhaps that is why he said in "So Long" that *Leaves of Grass* was no book, for whoever touches his poetry "touches a man."

OTHER MAJOR WORKS

LONG FICTION: *Franklin Evans*, 1842.

SHORT FICTION: *The Half-Breed and Other Stories*, 1927.

NONFICTION: *Democratic Vistas*, 1871; *Memoranda During the War*, 1875-1876; *Specimen Days and Collect*, 1882-1883; *Complete Prose Works*, 1892; *Calamus*, 1897 (letters; Richard M. Bucke, editor); *The Wound Dresser*, 1898 (Richard M. Bucke, editor); *Letters Written by Walt Whitman to His Mother, 1866-1872*, 1902 (Thomas B. Harned, editor); *An American Primer*, 1904; *Walt Whitman's Diary in Canada*, 1904 (William S. Kennedy, editor); *The Letters of Anne Gilchrist and Walt Whitman*, 1918 (Thomas B. Harned, editor).

MISCELLANEOUS: *The Collected Writings of Walt Whitman*, 1961-1984 (22 volumes).

BIBLIOGRAPHY

Allen, Gay Wilson. *The Solitary Singer: A Critical Biography of Walt Whitman*. Rev. ed. New York: New York University Press, 1967. A careful, scholarly biography based on extensive archival sources—including manuscripts and letters—that attempts to treat Whitman's life in terms of the poet's work. A valuable study of his career, although superseded, in some respects, by the biographies of Justin Kaplan and Paul Zweig.

Asselineau, Roger. *The Evolution of Walt Whitman*. Expanded ed. Iowa City: University of Iowa Press, 1999. Asselineau writes with authority on a vast range of topics that define both Whitman the man and Whitman the mythical personage. Asselineau placed himself in the role of the observer, analyzing Whitman's development with a kind of scientific detachment.

Gold, Arthur, ed. *Walt Whitman: A Collection of Criticism*. New York: McGraw Hill, 1974. Concentrates on academic criticism, on the poet's creative process, his literary reputation, his revisions of *Leaves of Grass*, and his vision of America in *Democratic Vistas*. A detailed chronology and a select, annotated bibliography make this collection a useful volume.

Kaplan, Justin. *Walt Whitman: A Life*. New York: Simon & Schuster, 1980. An elegant, deeply imagined biography that focuses on both Whitman and his times. Kaplan provides the fullest, most sensitive account of the poet's career, taking a chronological approach but managing to pinpoint and to highlight the most important phases of his subject's life. Kaplan's scholarship is impeccable.

Miller, James E., Jr. *Walt Whitman*. Rev. ed. Boston: Twayne, 1990. Miller concentrates on the development and structure of *Leaves of Grass*, its democratic "poetics," the major poems within it, "recurring images," "language and wit," and the "bardic voice." The first chapter and chronology provide a factual and analytical discussion of Whitman's biography, and Miller assesses the new criticism of the poet that has appeared since the original publication of his book in 1962. Supplemented by an annotated and updated bibliography.

Pearce, Roy Harvey, ed. *Whitman: A Collection of Crit-ical Essays*. Englewood Cliffs, N.J.: Prentice-Hall, 1962. A comprehensive collection of criticism, including commentary by Ezra Pound and D. H. Lawrence, three articles on the structure of *Leaves of Grass*, and additional discussion of the poet's style and other works. Contains a chronology of important dates, an introductory overview of the critical literature on Whitman, and a useful, annotated bibliography.

Reynolds, David S., ed. *A Historical Guide to Walt Whitman*. New York: Oxford University Press, 2000. Combines contemporary cultural studies and historical scholarship to illuminate Whitman's diverse contexts. The essays explore dimensions of Whitman's dynamic relationship to working-class politics, race and slavery, sexual mores, the visual arts, and the idea of democracy.

Woodress, James, ed. *Critical Essays on Walt Whitman*. Boston: G. K. Hall, 1983. Divided into reviews and early reactions, essays and other forms of criticism, with an introduction surveying the history of Whitman criticism. This collection provides a good history of Whitman's place in American culture and an informative, if highly selective, view of scholarly treatments of his work. Contains an index.

Zweig, Paul. *Walt Whitman: The Making of a Poet*. New York: Basic Books, 1984. This volume is not a chronological biography but rather a biographical/ critical meditation on Whitman's development as a poet. Zweig is steeped in the literature on Whitman and brilliantly explores how the "drab" journalist of the 1840's transformed himself into a major poet.

Perry D. Luckett;
bibliography updated by the editors

REED WHITTEMORE

Born: New Haven, Connecticut; September 11, 1919

PRINCIPAL POETRY
Heroes and Heroines, 1946
An American Takes a Walk, 1956

The Self-Made Man and Other Poems, 1959
The Boy from Iowa, 1961 (poetry and essays)
The Fascination of the Abomination, 1963 (poetry, stories, and essays)
Poems, New and Selected, 1967
Fifty Poems Fifty, 1970
The Mother's Breast and the Father's House, 1974
The Feel of Rock: Poems of Three Decades, 1982
The Past, the Future, the Present: Poems Selected and New, 1990

OTHER LITERARY FORMS

Reed Whittemore has published many essays and reviews in magazines, most of them of a literary nature, but also essays on education, science, and television. *From Zero to Absolute* (1968) consists mainly of a series of lectures he gave on poetry at Beloit College in 1966. *The Poet as Journalist* (1976) is made up of the short pieces he wrote for *The New Republic* when he was the literary editor for that magazine. In his literary essays he often praises, with some qualifications, the early modern poets such as Ezra Pound and T. S. Eliot but is rather critical of most of his contemporaries, particularly the Beat poets, whom he has mocked in his satirical verse.

The publication of Whittemore's *William Carlos Williams: Poet from Jersey* (1975) was a surprising departure for this writer of short personal essays. The biography was criticized by some reviewers for being too casually written and for taking, at times, an irreverent attitude toward its subject, yet the book does give a clear and sympathetic portrait of Williams and, at the same time, punctures some of the more pretentious opinions of Williams and his disciples about free verse and other poetic matters.

Whittemore's biography of Williams has led him to write books about the nature of biography: *Pure Lives: The Early Biographers* (1988) and *Whole Lives: Shapers of Modern Biography* (1990). These wide-ranging, erudite, and lively works trace biographical art from its beginnings (Plutarch, Aelfric) all the way to late twentieth century literary biographers (Richard Ellmann and Leon Edel). As in the Williams biography, Whittemore manages to combine his scholarly matter with a casual manner in interesting ways.

ACHIEVEMENTS

The most striking characteristic of Reed Whittemore's verse is its comedy. As Howard Nemerov pointed out many years ago, Whittemore is not only witty (an admirable trait) but also funny (a suspect one). His most distinctive poems are those about serious subjects—the failure of belief, the difficulties of heroism, the search for the true self—that make intelligent statements while at the same time being very clever and humorous. Whittemore's emphasis on intelligence, moderation, and comedy makes him a rather unfashionable writer today, but these very qualities account for the success of his best poems.

BIOGRAPHY

Edward Reed Whittemore II was born in New Haven in 1919, being given the name of his physician father. He attended Yale, was graduated in 1941, went on to serve in the Army Air Force during World War II, and was discharged as a captain. He continued his education at Princeton after the war, although he never received an advanced degree. He married Helen Lundeen in 1952, and they had four children. He often depicts himself in his poetry as a middle-class figure, with middle-class burdens of family and job. Although his poetry is not of a confessional nature, a picture of Whittemore as an affectionate and concerned family man does emerge from his poetry.

Whittemore taught in the English Department at Carleton College in Minnesota for nearly twenty years beginning in 1947 and was for a part of that time chairman of the department. In 1964 he was consultant in poetry at the Library of Congress. In 1968 he moved to the University of Maryland, eventually becoming professor emeritus.

Whittemore is rightly well known and admired as a magazine editor. From 1939 to 1953, he was the editor of *Furioso*, one of the liveliest literary publications of the period. What distinguished this magazine from all of its competitors was its fondness for comic parody and satire. This tradition was carried on with nearly equal distinction when Whittemore edited *The Carleton Miscellany* from 1960 to 1964. His work as the literary editor of *The New Republic* from 1969 to 1974 added some zest to the pages of that venerable publication.

ANALYSIS

Reed Whittemore has published fewer poems than many of his contemporaries have done, and most of them have been written in an ironic vein. His targets are the pretentious—both romantic and bureaucratic, both individual and institutional—against which he sets his own balanced, moderate point of view. The poems imply that the realism at their center is all the modern world has to offer in the way of belief.

At times, Whittemore runs the risk of being merely a writer of light verse, a maker of clever rhymed jokes, but in his best work he combines the sensible note of comedy with a seriousness of theme. This combination, along with his subtle command of form and sound in verse, make him a poet of consequence.

HEROES AND HEROINES

Whittemore's first book, *Heroes and Heroines*, consists primarily of poems about literature and literary figures. It is an amusing book that explores, through a series of comic poems, the idea of heroism in portraits of Don Quixote, Lord Jim, Hester Prynne, Lady Ashley, Gulliver, and many other characters from books. The poems display Whittemore's fondness for traditional verse forms—particularly the sonnet—his wit, and his interest in the theme of heroism; yet it is a book of very limited range that only hints at his potential as a poet.

AN AMERICAN TAKES A WALK

In Whittemore's second book, *An American Takes a Walk*, that potential is clearly displayed as he develops the comic tone that becomes the trademark of his work. That tone can be seen in his often reprinted poem "Lines (Composed upon Reading an Announcement by Civil Defense Authorities Recommending that I Build a Bomb-shelter in My Backyard)." The poem begins with a description of the dugout that the speaker and his friends had built as children and that he identifies with some vague notion of heroic fantasy, "some brave kind of decay." Now he is being asked to dig another hole "under the new and terrible rules of romance." "But I'll not, no, not do it, not go back," the poem proclaims; he knows that this time, if he conforms to the government's wishes, he will not be able to return to "the grown-up's house" as he had done as a child. This time the seeming child's play is play in earnest, a deadly absurdity. As Howard Nemerov has pointed out, Whittemore's poetry

is filled with images of entrapment and burial, and this poem can be read as more than a satirical thrust at Civil Defense. It contains the poet's rejection of safety and security as a kind of living death and seems to long for some world where daring and risk have meaning.

The problem, however, Whittemore's work implies, is that a heroism that risks all often leads to nothing. One of his funniest poems, "A Day with the Foreign Legion," makes a number of tough statements about the failure of heroic action, or its meaninglessness. The poem is based on a *Beau Geste* version of the Foreign Legion as it appears in motion pictures, where, when everything seems darkest, the characters make speeches that "serve as the turning point":

> After which the Arabs seem doped and perfectly
> helpless,
> Water springs up from the ground, the horses
> come back,
> Plenty of food is discovered in some old cave,
> And reinforcements arrive led by the girl
> From Canada.

That is what usually happens, but in this instance it is too hot; there is no magical ending and the audience is bitterly disappointed. The poem asks who is to blame—the film, the projector, "the man in the booth, who hastened away, as soon as the feature was over"? The poem answers, in a series of purposely confusing repetitions, that none of them is to blame, or all of them are, or possibly the culture is to blame. "It was the time, the time and the place, and how could one blame them?" The poem seems to be saying that in this time (modern) and this place (America) the world of romance and happy endings is finished.

The title poem, "An American Takes a Walk," mocks the idea of a tragic or sacred vision existing in the United States or American literature. When the American of the poem comes across a wood reminiscent of Dante's world of hell, it is a pleasant wood, hell in a "motherly habit."

> How in that Arden could human
> Frailty be but glossed?
> How in that Eden could Adam
> Be really, wholly lost?

The emphasis on innocence and on success in America, according to Whittemore, leads the American writer to adopt the demands of his culture. In "The Line of an American Poet," the poet writes for the market, following the supply-and-demand economy. He produces works, "Uniform, safe and pure," becoming another American success story.

Whittemore once described poetry "as a thing of the mind," saying that he "tends to judge it . . . by the qualities of the mind it displays" (*Poets on Poetry*, Howard Nemerov, editor). This emphasis on the mind, on intelligence, is an unusual one for a contemporary American poet. In recent years, the instinctual and the irrational have usually been seen as the sources of poetry. Whittemore's attitude is what leads him to reject the theatrical and fantastic, to be a realist and ironist. At the same time, however, it can be argued that this dominating intelligence in his work limits Whittemore, giving his poetry a kind of self-consciousness, a too-ready irony. He has written many poems about writing poems ("A Week of Doodle," "After Some Day of Decision," and "Preface to an Unwritten Text," for example, in *An American Takes a Walk*), about the difficulties of writing poems, about the fact that he has not written any poems. These pieces are often funny, but still they seem to point to some problem with his very notion of being a poet, a kind of debilitating self-awareness. At times he seems burdened with the idea of being a poet, as if it were a pompous occupation, apologizing for not offering a world view of proper scope for one who would call himself a poet.

"THE SELF AND THE WEATHER"

In his next few volumes, Whittemore continues the style developed in *An American Takes a Walk*. His poems give an amusing picture of suburbia and the academic life, worlds where trivial things matter. Even the weather—as in "The Self and the Weather"—can depress one's mood. The poem begins by declaring that it is tiresome to talk about the weather and goes on to talk about it—very amusingly—at considerable length. The poet finds he cannot write on a rainy day, staring out the window "at wet leaves, wet grass, wet laundry and so on," but he feels that a better man, "any man of resolve, any man with a mission," would rise above the weather, rise to where it always was sunny, and write. Such a person, however, would write treatises, not poems, "for treatises seldom/ Traffic in weather as poems do." These treatises would be written in underground rooms where the outside world will be represented by "a picture by some gay cubist of what could not possibly/ Be wet leaves, wet grass, wet laundry, and so on."

SATIRIC POEMS

The only new element in Whittemore's work at this time is found in a number of long, satiric poems written in rhyming, loosely metrical couplets. The purposely forced comic rhymes seem to imitate both Lord Byron and Ogden Nash. The targets range from the Beat poets to rocket scientists, and, although almost all the poems have amusing passages, they go on at entirely too great a length for their satiric purposes.

POEMS, NEW AND SELECTED

Although there is no revolutionary change in Whittemore's poetry after *An American Takes a Walk*, his poems do wear a somewhat more experimental guise, opening up in language and form, in the new poems that appeared in *Poems, New and Selected* in 1967. In the six poems labeled "shaggy" (that is, "Flint Shaggy," "Geneva Shaggy," and so on), Whittemore slips into a blackfaced comedian's voice reminiscent of the comic language of John Berryman's *Dream Songs* (1964). In other poems, such as "The Bad Daddy," and from later volumes "Death," "The Mother's Breast and the Father's House," and "Marriage," he moves toward an irrational side of his psyche that his earlier work explicitly rejected. Whittemore presents marriage as pigs eating each other and death as the lord that lives in the marrow: "Holy illiterate . . . spider of bone." A kind of fierce bitterness overwhelms these poems at times, in a manner not seen in his previous poetry.

"CLAMMING"

In the poem "Clamming," Whittemore writes one of his most successful antiromantic poems in his more familiar, amusing style. The poem begins with the poet telling of how he often repeats a story about the time he was trapped on a sandbar while clamming as a little boy and faced the Long Island Sound as his possible fate. There is not much to the story, but he keeps telling it because "it serves my small lust/ To be thought of as someone who's lived." He cannot get away from his ego: "The self, what a brute it is. It wants, wants./ It will not let go of its even most fictional grandeur." Now he has a son, small and sickly, and he would like to protect him from the sea and other dangers, but a greater danger might be too much self-regard, as represented by the oft-told tale of clamming, and that he does not want to pass on to his son. Finally, his advice to his son is to be careful but not too careful: "Lest you care too much and brag of the caring/ And bore your best friends and inhibit your children and sicken/ At last into opera on somebody's sandbar. Son, when you clam,/ Clam." The plea for realism and modesty in the ending of "Clamming" sums up very nicely the attitudes and strengths of Whittemore's poetry.

THE FEEL OF ROCK AND
THE PAST, THE FUTURE, THE PRESENT

In 1982, in *The Feel of Rock*, and more extensively in 1990, in *The Past, the Future, the Present*, Whittemore again created volumes selected from his previous poetry, adding a few new poems on both occasions. The fact that the additions of new poems are small seems to show that Whittemore has been concentrating on the writing of prose in the 1980's rather than the writing of poetry.

A number of the new poems continue Whittemore's satiric expressions of dissatisfaction with modern American culture: "It's a terrible thing to come to despise one's country," he states in one of his poems, but he obviously thinks that the ideals of America have been lost in the current political and social scene. In "The Destruction of Washington" he imagines some future archaeologist exploring the destroyed capital. Whatever they discover, he hopes that at least their ignorance will be less than ours.

Whittemore also has begun exploring his childhood and the lives of his parents in a few poems in these two volumes. "Mother's Past" is about the inability of the mother to take good photos, always moving, or putting her finger in front of the lens. The photos are often of young people going off on automobile excursions, while the photographer—the mother—remains behind. The speaker is dissatisfied with the record of a life represented by the photos: "Ask how many were missed that it takes to make a good/ Past for a life or a book./ The answer is always more pictures than poor mother took."

In "The Feel of Rock" the early life of the speaker's home is portrayed in the ironies of the opening stanza:

My father went broke on a shaded street.
My mother drank there.
My brothers removed themselves; they were
     complete.
I kept to my room and slicked down my hair.

As the poem continues, the speaker realizes that he resembles the father in his loneliness and unhappiness. Then he goes on to think about his father's burial (the mother already dead); the feel of rocks becomes the gravestones of his family. On a later return to the cemetery, he loses himself amid the maze of stones and wonders where his father has gone and whether life is only the world of rocks.

In "The Feel of Rock" and "Mother's Past," Whittemore is risking a personal tone rarely seen before in his work. Although the poems have at times a tentative quality, they add a new element to the work of this always interesting writer.

OTHER MAJOR WORKS

NONFICTION: *The Boy from Iowa*, 1961 (poetry and essays); *From Zero to Absolute*, 1968; *William Carlos Williams: Poet from Jersey*, 1975; *The Poet as Journalist*, 1976; *Pure Lives: The Early Biographers*, 1988; *Whole Lives: Shapers of Modern Biography*, 1989; *Six Literary Lives: The Shared Impiety of Adams, London, Sinclair, Williams, Dos Passos, and Tate*, 1993.

MISCELLANEOUS: *The Fascination of the Abomination*, 1963 (poetry, stories, and essays).

BIBLIOGRAPHY

Dickey, James. *Babel to Byzantium*. New York: Farrar, Straus & Giroux, 1968. Dickey classifies Whittemore as essentially a satirist, but he modifies his praise of his work because of Whittemore's tendency not to go deeply and personally into his subjects.

La Salle, Peter. "An Encounter with *Furioso*." *Raritan* 12, no. 4 (Spring, 1993): 109. The defunct literary magazine *Furioso* is profiled. In its time, it was as important as *Sewanee* or *Partisan*. *Furioso* was founded in 1939 by James J. Angleton and Reed Whittemore and published poetry by such names as

Ezra Pound, William Carlos Williams and E. E. Cummings.

Lieberman, Laurence. "New Poetry in Review." *Yale Review* 58 (Winter, 1968): 267-268. Lieberman praises Whittemore's poetry as perfectly pitched and displaying a flawless ear. He believes, however, that his targets of satire have become too familiar and feels that the poet seems satisfied in becoming a kind of "highbrow Ogden Nash."

Nemerov, Howard. *Poetry and Fiction: Essays*. New Brunswick, N.J.: Rutgers University Press, 1963. This is the most complete and sympathetic overview of Whittemore's poetry. Nemerov emphasizes Whittemore's concentration on heroism in action and its absence in modern society. He points out the frequency of the images of being locked up, walled in, or buried in the poetry and speculates that these images represent the isolation of the human condition.

Rosenthal, M. L. "Plastic Possibilities." *Poetry* 119 (November, 1971): 102-103. Rosenthal points out that even though Whittemore's poems often begin in joking self-irony, they can quickly turn to serious purposes in their conclusions. Whittemore's rejection of all romantic posturings determines the quality and tone of his poetry.

Whittemore, Reed. "Poetry as Discovery." In *Poets on Poetry*, edited by Howard Nemerov. New York: Basic Books, 1966. This is both an illuminating and a modest essay on Whittemore's discussion of his own work. He calls poetry "a thing of the mind," and he says that he judges it by the quality of the mind displayed. He also analyzes the relationship of poetry to self-discovery and the often melancholy conclusion of that discovery.

Michael Paul Novak

JOHN GREENLEAF WHITTIER

Born: Haverhill, Massachusetts; December 17, 1807
Died: Hampton Falls, New Hampshire; September 7, 1892

PRINCIPAL POETRY

Legends of New-England, 1831
Moll Pitcher, 1832
Mogg Megone, 1836
Poems Written During the Progress of the Abolition Question in the United States, 1837
Poems, 1838
Lays of My Home and Other Poems, 1843
Voices of Freedom, 1846
Poems, 1849
Songs of Labor and Other Poems, 1850
The Chapel of the Hermits and Other Poems, 1853
The Panorama and Other Poems, 1856
The Sycamores, 1857
The Poetical Works of John Greenleaf Whittier, 1857, 1869, 1880, 1894
Home Ballads and Poems, 1860
In War Time, 1863
Snow-Bound: A Winter Idyl, 1866
The Tent on the Beach and Other Poems, 1867
Maud Muller, 1869
Among the Hills and Other Poems, 1869
Ballads of New England, 1869
Miriam and Other Poems, 1871
The Pennsylvania Pilgrim and Other Poems, 1872
Hazel-Blossoms, 1875
Mabel Martin, 1876
Favorite Poems, 1877
The Vision of Echard and Other Poems, 1878
The King's Missive and Other Poems, 1881
The Bay of Seven Islands and Other Poems, 1883
Saint Gregory's Guest and Recent Poems, 1886
At Sundown, 1890

OTHER LITERARY FORMS

Besides his extensive poetry, John Greenleaf Whittier wrote numerous antislavery tracts, compiled editions of New England legends, edited various newspapers, and was active in abolitionist politics. Whittier's *Legends of New-England*, his earliest collection, was followed by the antislavery arguments in *Justice and Expediency: or, Slavery Considered with a View to Its Rightful and Effectual Remedy, Abolition* (1833), and *The Supernaturalism of New England* (1847). Whittier's finest prose work is perhaps *Leaves from Margaret Smith's Journal*

John Greenleaf Whittier (Library of Congress)

(1849), a Quaker novel in journal form. *Old Portraits and Modern Sketches* (1850) and *Literary Recreations and Miscellanies* (1854) followed, and the *Prose Works of John Greenleaf Whittier* were collected in two volumes in 1866.

Whittier also edited *Child Life* (1872) and *Child Life in Prose* (1874), as well as *Songs of Three Centuries* (1876). He wrote a masterful introduction to his edition of *The Journal of John Woolman* (1871), another notable American Quaker writer.

A full collection of Whittier's prose can be found in *The Writings of John Greenleaf Whittier* (1888-1889).

ACHIEVEMENTS

John Greenleaf Whittier was a remarkably prolific writer and reformer. As poet, editor, abolitionist, and religious humanist, Whittier managed to produce more than forty volumes of poetry and prose during his lifetime, not counting his uncollected journalistic work.

Through his antislavery poems he spoke for the conscience of New England, and he later celebrated the virtues of village life for an age that looked back upon them with nostalgia. Although honored and venerated as a poet during his later years, he was curiously guarded about his literary reputation, remarking to his first biographer, "I am a *man*, not a mere verse-maker." His belief that morality was the basis of all literature may have made him finally more of a moralist than a poet; his Quaker conscience would not permit him to produce "art for art's sake."

Early in life he patterned his verse after Robert Burns, writing dialect imitations of the Scottish poet to the extent of being called "the American Burns." He further corrupted his muse by imitating the worst of the popular, sentimental, and genteel verse of his age and did not achieve a distinctive poetic voice until midcareer. Like many a self-educated poet, Whittier lacked a clear sense of critical taste and judgment, especially in regard to his own work. He wrote too much too quickly and could not distinguish between his best poems and his inferior work. Even his later work is often tainted by melodrama, moralizing, and sentimentality. Yet when the worst has been said, the abiding strength of his work transcends its weaknesses.

His most obvious poetic strength is accessibility. Whittier wrote popular poetry that did not make great intellectual demands upon his readers. Unlike the modernists, who wrote for a select, highly educated audience, Whittier tried to reach the ordinary reader. Instead of composing dense, ironic, highly allusive verse requiring careful explication, Whittier's narratives and ballads were written in a common idiom that could be readily understood. His poetical materials were regional legend and folklore, topical events, and the personal resources of his Quaker faith. Their moral perspective is clear and forthright, at times didactic or moralistic, and it lacks the ambiguity or tentativeness favored by the New Critics. George Arms argues persuasively that Whittier and the other schoolroom poets simply cannot be appreciated according to current standards of taste, and so have been too often simply dismissed instead of being understood. Their strengths are seen as liabilities and they are faulted for lacking qualities foreign to their age.

The purview of Whittier's work was "common, natural things"—the realm of ordinary life. He rarely dealt with the extremes of human experience, except in some of his abolitionist poems. He shared the optimism and piety of his age and held to a romantic view of nature and a belief in the moral progress of man. His sense of moral order and probity may seem merely quaint or old fashioned to the modern reader, but his poems reflect moral convictions sincerely held. He devoted thirty years to the struggle against slavery and committed the better part of his talents and energy to that issue. If he lost his sense of social justice later in life and failed to comprehend the problems of an industrial society, that might well be excused by his age. Few men are capable of devoting themselves to more than one cause in a lifetime.

The alleged deficiencies in Whittier's poetics should also be judged in terms of his commitment to a popular rather than an academic style. Whittier favored a light, relaxed approach to his verse. Perhaps he overused mechanical rhymes, ballad meter, apostrophe, and hyperbole, but in his "Proem" he is frank to confess his limitations. His muse was not given to exalted flights, but spoke plainly for freedom and democracy. Whittier's readership steadily grew during his later years so that his reputation once seemed secure, but like those of the other Fireside Poets, it has suffered a sharp decline since his death. He is now read, if at all, as the author of "Snow-Bound: A Winter Idyl" and other nostalgic portraits of New England village life rather than as one of the leading poets of his age. Though his reputation may now be eclipsed by Walt Whitman, Emily Dickinson, and Herman Melville, no American poet of the nineteenth century better deserves the title of "poet of the common man" than Whittier.

BIOGRAPHY

John Greenleaf Whittier was born in Haverhill, Massachusetts, on December 17, 1807, in an old family homestead built by a Quaker ancestor. He was the second of four children in the family of John and Abigail Whittier, of old Quaker stock. Besides John Greenleaf, the Whittier children included an older sister Mary, a younger brother Matthew Franklin, and a younger sister Elizabeth Hussey. Several other relatives lived with the family, including a paternal grandmother, a bachelor un-

cle, and a maiden aunt. The poet's father, John Whittier, was an honest, industrious farmer who tilled his hard, rocky land in the Merrimack Valley with only marginal success. Whittier's mother, Elizabeth, was a model of quiet strength and deep refinement. She was noted in the community for her domestic industry and "exquisite Quaker neatness." The entire family attended Friends' services at Amesbury, nine miles away, even in poor weather.

Whittier's childhood was one of hard farm work (that eventually weakened his health) and the occasional freedom of the outdoors—a life of frugality, harmony, and affection later idealized in "Snow-Bound" and "The Barefoot Boy." There were few books in the Whittier household besides the Bible and *The Pilgrim's Progress* (1678), and the family depended for entertainment on the tales of his uncle Moses and the stories brought by itinerant Yankee peddlers and gypsies. Whittier's education was meager, consisting of sporadic attendance at the district school and several terms at Haverhill Academy. One of the local teachers, Joshua Coffin, introduced him to the poetry of Robert Burns, and made such a lasting impression on young Whittier that he was later commemorated in "To My Old School Master." As a boy, Whittier showed a natural gift for rhymes and verse, and wrote simple ballads in imitation of Robert Burns and Sir Walter Scott. His sister Mary sent one of these to the local newspaper, the Newburyport *Free Press*. The editor there, William Lloyd Garrison, was so impressed that he paid a personal visit to the Whittiers to urge further education for their son. Whittier's father was said to have replied to Garrison, "Sir, poetry will not get him bread."

His father finally relented and Whittier was allowed to enter Haverhill Academy at the age of nineteen. To pay his expenses he learned the craft of shoemaking, a common winter vocation among New England country folk. Meanwhile, his poems continued to appear in the Haverhill *Gazette* and other publications. At Garrison's behest, Whittier entered the world of Boston journalism and at twenty-two became editor of the *American Manufacturer*, a Whig trade weekly. In the summer of 1829 he was called home by the illness and death of his father, which required him to manage the farm and provide for his family. Still unhappy with the drudgery of farm life,

Whittier gladly accepted an invitation from Hartford, Connecticut, in July, 1830, to edit the *Weekly Review*. Unfortunately his health failed and Whittier was forced to resign from this attractive position within eighteen months and return to Haverhill in 1832. He was now twenty-five years old, ambitious, but without purpose or direction. A letter from Garrison in the spring of 1833 restored Whittier's spirits when he was invited to apply his talents to the abolitionist movement. From 1833 to the end of the Civil War, the abolition of slavery became the abiding goal of Whittier's life.

Immersion in abolitionist politics made him a master of satire and invective, but at the expense of his literary gifts. Out of his new commitment came *Justice and Expediency*, and that same year he was elected to the National Anti-Slavery Convention in Philadelphia. Thus began a thirty-year career of antislavery advocacy and agitation. Several times he was exposed to the threat of mob violence and barely escaped personal injury. He later said that he was prouder of his abolitionist work than of all his authorship, but this comment must be taken in the perspective of his career.

As a young man, Whittier had struggled to reconcile his worldly literary ambitions with his Quaker reticence and piety. As a poor country boy he had aspired to Boston gentility but lacked the education or means to move in Brahmin circles. One third of his poetry was written before he was twenty-five, though much of it was sentimental and imitative. When he shrewdly realized that poetry would not bring him the fame he sought, he turned to politics and reformism instead. The abolitionist movement gave him a focus for his talents and energies. He became involved in Essex County politics and by 1835 was elected to the Massachusetts Legislature. The following year he sold the Haverhill farm and moved to a small house in Amesbury, where he briefly edited the Amesbury *Village Transcript*. The next twenty years saw him editing various antislavery newspapers and writing numerous abolitionist poems and articles. Much of this was obviously hackwork, but occasionally he would write a notable poem in the heat of indignation, such as "Massachusetts to Virginia," "Barbara Frietchie," or "Laus Deo." His reform efforts interfered with his lyric gifts as a poet, however, and his best work came later in life, in his fifties and sixties, especially

after the Civil War. The *War Between the States* presented a particular dilemma to Whittier in pitting his antislavery sentiments against his Quaker commitment to nonviolence. He saw the need for emancipation, but did not approve of secession or the drift toward armed conflict. Yet he remained a loyal unionist and wrote poems and broadsides in favor of the Union cause. Titles such as "Our Countrymen in Chains" and "The Sabbath Scene" are little more than propaganda, but Whittier was writing to appeal to the emotions and feelings of ordinary people, and these antislavery verses enjoyed great popular success. Next to Harriet Beecher Stowe, he was perhaps the most effective propagandist for the abolitionist cause.

In his personal life, Whittier remained a resolute bachelor, despite several romantic attractions to Quaker admirers. He lived with his mother, two sisters, and a brother in Amesbury, and cherished the company of his family. Their successive deaths in the 1850's and 1860's, however, particularly the loss of his beloved sister Elizabeth in 1864, left him increasingly isolated. The idyllic poem "Snow-Bound" was written partially in memory of his tight-knit family, and with its publication in 1866 Whittier enjoyed his first large commercial success, and thereafter was able to live comfortably on his literary earnings. Henceforth his volumes of poetry came out regularly and sold well, but he was plagued with persistently poor health and never felt fully comfortable with his new fame or with the many visitors to his Amesbury cottage. Occasionally he would venture into Boston to join Ralph Waldo Emerson, Henry Wadsworth Longfellow, and Oliver Holmes at the Saturday Club, but more often he preferred to enjoy the simple company of his niece and her family at their country estate in Danvers.

After the war, Whittier had gradually become institutionalized as one of the Fireside Poets, and with this increased popularity came other honors. He served as a Harvard overseer from 1858 onward and as a trustee of Brown University from 1869 to 1892. Harvard also awarded him an honorary LL.D., in 1886, although Whittier was prevented by illness from attending the ceremony in person. On his seventieth birthday, his friends held a formal dinner in his honor, on which occasion Mark Twain embarrassed the guests when his humor misfired, his intended tribute being taken by some as parody.

In his later years, Whittier increasingly assumed the role of New England patriarch, invoking in his poems a sentimental and nostalgic view of village life. He felt out of touch with the changes in the postwar America of the Gilded Age, and increasingly withdrew to the quiet meditation of his Quaker faith. On September 3, 1892, he suffered a paralytic stroke, which led to his death four days later, on September 7, at the age of 84. Oliver Wendell Holmes spoke at his funeral, after which Whittier was buried in the Friends' section of the Union Cemetery in Haverhill, next to his parents and sister.

ANALYSIS

In the collected edition of his work, John Greenleaf Whittier decided to arrange his poems by topic, in ten categories, rather than present them in chronological order. He also suppressed many of the early verses that had proved embarrassing to him so that the supposedly complete 1894 edition of *The Poetical Works of John Greenleaf Whittier* is not really definitive, though it reflects the poet's final intentions. This arrangement obscures Whittier's development as a poet, but it does tell something about his major concerns and about the poetic forms in which he felt most comfortable. These include antislavery poems, songs of labor and reform, ballads, narratives and legends, nature poems, personal poems, historical poems, occasional verses, hymns and religious lyrics, and genre poems and country idylls.

From Whittier's collected verse, perhaps a dozen or so titles are distinctive. These include "Ichabod," "Massachusetts to Virginia," "Barbara Frietchie," "Telling the Bees," "Laus Deo," "The Trailing Arbutus," "Skipper Ireson's Ride," "First-Day Thoughts," and of course "Snow-Bound." A few other selections should be mentioned—"In School-Days," "The Barefoot Boy," and "Dear Lord and Father of Mankind"—simply because they are part of America's popular culture.

THE ABOLITIONIST POEMS

Many of Whittier's abolitionist poems are little more than crude propaganda, but with "Ichabod" he produced a masterpiece of political satire and invective. Cast in terms of a prophetic rebuke, the poem is directed at Daniel Webster, whose "Seventh of March" speech in favor of the Fugitive Slave Law aroused the wrath and enmity of many Northern abolitionists, who accused him of selling out to slave interests. Whittier portrays Webster, in terms of bitter denunciation, as a leader who has betrayed his countrymen and extinguished the life of his soul. His audience would certainly have caught the disparaging reference to I Samuel 4:21, "And she named the child Ichabod, saying the glory is departed from Israel!" Webster, a contemporary "Ichabod" in his fall from glory, becomes the object of scorn and pity for his betrayal of the antislavery cause.

This same contentious tone is also evident in another antislavery poem, "Massachusetts to Virginia," which contrasts the free strength of the North with the moral decadence brought about by slavery in the South. The poem recalls that both Commonwealth States had stood united in the War for Independence, and appeals to that sense of common fellowship in freedom. Though some passages are marred by stock declamatory phrases and excessive use of formal diction and hyperbole, the poem ably makes its point and ends with a ringing slogan, "No fetters in the Bay State,—No slaves upon our Land!"

To a staunch abolitionist, the ratification of the Thirteenth Amendment on December 18, 1865, was reason enough for an occasional poem, but Whittier's "Laus Deo" (literally "Praise God") expresses his personal jubilation at seeing a lifetime's work brought to completion. The poem describes the ringing of bells and firing of guns in Amesbury that accompanied the announcement that slavery had officially been abolished throughout the Union. The ten stanzas of trochaic tetrameter create a hymn of celebration and gratitude in which the Lord sanctions the righteousness of the Union cause.

On a more personal note, Whittier wrote many memorable verses in tribute to his Quaker faith, the finest of these perhaps being "First-Day Thoughts," in which he evoked the quiet grace and deep spirituality of the Friends' service. He captures the essence of Christian worship in the soul's contemplation of its creator through "the still small voice" of silent meditation. This same note of profound spiritual depth and reverence for the inner life appears in his famous hymn, "Dear Lord and Father of Mankind," which was adapted from the last six stanzas of "The Brewing of Soma." This inner faith grew with age and led Rufus M. Jones to comment later that Whittier "grasped more steadily, felt more profoundly, and interpreted more adequately the essential aspects of the Quaker life and faith" than any other of his age.

COUNTRY IDYLLS AND GENRE POEMS

Whittier's most lasting accomplishment, however, rests with his country idylls and genre poems, those set pieces and descriptive verses in which he evokes a memory of his childhood or presents an idealized view of the pleasures of rural life. In "The Trailing Arbutus," for example, a glimpse of this early spring flower on an otherwise cold and bitter day becomes the occasion for a moment of natural rapture. A better poem, "Telling the Bees," uses the New England custom of draping bee hives after a family death as a way of foreshadowing the narrator's sorrow at the loss of his beloved Mary. This particular poem, occasioned by the death of the poet's mother, contains some of his finest descriptive passages. Another genre poem, "In School-Days," treats of bashful love and childhood regrets nostalgically remembered, while "The Barefoot Boy" presents a stilted and somewhat generalized picture of rural childhood: Only in the middle stanzas does the poem rise above platitudes to a realistic glimpse of the poet's actual boyhood. With "Skipper Ireson's Ride," Whittier turned a New England legend into the material for a memorable folk ballad, although at the expense of historical veracity. The poem's mock-heroic tone does not mask the cruelty of the incident, in which Old Floyd Ireson was "tarred and feathered and carried in a cart" by the women of Marblehead for allegedly failing to rescue the survivors of another sinking fishing vessel. However factually inaccurate, Whittier's version of the legend captures the essential qualities of mob behavior in what one critic has called the most effective nineteenth century American ballad.

"SNOW-BOUND"

"Snow-Bound," subtitled "A Winter Idyl," is probably Whittier's most lasting achievement. The founding of *The Atlantic Monthly* in 1857 had given him a steady market for his verse, and when the editor, James Russell Lowell, wrote to him in 1865 requesting a "Yankee pastoral," Whittier responded with "Snow-Bound," which was published in the February, 1866, issue. The epigrams from Agrippa von Nettesheim's *Occult Philosophy* (1533) and Ralph Waldo Emerson's "The Snow

Storm" establish the parameters of the poem in what John B. Pickard has called the protective circle of the family and hearth against the ominous power of the winter storm. Through an extended narrative in four-beat rhymed couplets, Whittier recalls the self-sufficiency of his family and recounts their close-knit circle of domestic affection as seen through a week of enforced winter isolation. This theme is enhanced through a series of contrasts between light and dark, warmth and cold, indoors and outdoors, fire and snow. After taking the reader through the round of barnyard chores, the poet shifts his perspective indoors to describe the sitting room of the Whittier homestead. Part II of the poem begins with Whittier's recollections of the tales and stories the family shared during their long evenings before the fire, with father, mother, uncle, aunt, schoolteacher, and another female guest each taking turns with the storytelling. The evening's entertainment finally ends as the fire burns low in the hearth and each family member retires from the pleasant circle of light and warmth. Part III of the poem gradually shifts from the past back to the present, as the poet's memories of "these Flemish pictures of old days" gradually fade; just as the fireplace logs had earlier faded to glowing embers covered with gray ash, so the poet will now gradually relinquish these recollections that have warmed "the hands of memory." His concluding lines express the hope that these memories will touch other readers and uplift their hearts, like the fresh odors of newly cut meadows, or pond lilies' fragrance on a summer breeze. The shift in season enforces the contrast between past and present, distancing Whittier from his family, most of whom had since died.

LEGACY

While he was not a major poet, Whittier learned early from Robert Burns the value of the commonplace, and his best poetry reflects an affectionate understanding of New England country life. If his muse flew no higher than popular and occasional verse, at least he wrote well of what he knew best—the customs and folkways of Yankee farming; the spiritual resources of his Quaker faith, which taught him to place spiritual concerns over material needs; and the history and legends of Essex County. His most accomplished poems look ahead to Edwin Arlington Robinson and Robert Frost, who would further probe the diminished world of the

New England farm and village. Whittier stands directly in this tradition. His reputation has held better than those of the other Fireside Poets, and he will continue to be read for his grasp of several essential truths: the value of family affections, the importance of firm moral character, and the simple attractions of country life.

OTHER MAJOR WORKS

LONG FICTION: *Narrative of James Williams: An American Slave*, 1838; *Leaves from Margaret Smith's Journal*, 1849.

NONFICTION: *Justice and Expediency: Or, Slavery Considered with a View to Its Rightful and Effectual Remedy, Abolition*, 1833; *The Supernaturalism of New England*, 1847; *Old Portraits and Modern Sketches*, 1850; *Literary Recreations and Miscellanies*, 1854; *Whittier on Writers and Writing: The Uncollected Critical Writings of John Greenleaf Whittier*, 1950 (Edwin H. Cady and Harry Hayden Clark, editors); *The Letters of John Greenleaf Whittier*, 1975 (John B. Pickard, editor).

EDITED TEXTS: *The Journal of John Woolman*, 1871; *Child Life*, 1872; *Child Life in Prose*, 1874; *Songs of Three Centuries*, 1876.

MISCELLANEOUS: *Prose Works of John Greenleaf Whittier*, 1866; *The Writings of John Greenleaf Whittier*, 1888-1889.

BIBLIOGRAPHY

Grant, David. "'The Unequal Sovereigns of a Slave-holding Land': The North as Subject in Whittier's 'The Panorama.'" *Criticism* 38, no. 4 (Fall, 1996): 521-549. Whittier's "The Panorama" discusses the interdependence of the two ideals exploited by the Republicans' Democrats and conservative opponents: sovereignty and Union. The poem places the slave system as the root of the threats to the North.

Hollander, John, ed. *American Poetry: The Nineteenth Century*. New York: Library of America, 1993. A two-volume anthology with over 1,000 poems by nearly 150 poets that reveals the remarkable beauty and astonishing diversity of the distinctly American tradition of poetry that arose in the nineteenth century. Contains a biographical sketch of Whittier and a year-by-year chronology of poets and poetry.

Kribbs, Jayne K., comp. *Critical Essays on John Greenleaf Whittier*. Boston: G. K. Hall, 1980. Part of the Critical Essays on American Literature series. Kribbs's extended introduction locates four periods of the poet's writing career and suggests in conclusion that the central question about Whittier is not how great, but how minor a figure he is in American literature. All the essays are written by respected scholars. Contains a bibliography and an index.

Leary, Lewis Gaston. *John Greenleaf Whittier*. Twayne's United States Authors series 6. New York: Twayne, 1961. Although this introductory study looks at Whittier's life and art, the poetry discussion is more useful than the biographical section, which contains some errors and no new information. Leary discusses the poet's limitations, especially as a critic, and gives his subject perspective with references to Nathaniel Hawthorne, Herman Melville, and Henry David Thoreau. Supplemented by a bibliography.

Miller, Lewis H. "The Supernaturalism of *Snow Bound*." *New England Quarterly* 53 (1980): 291-307. A good reading on how Whittier broke through his usually plain style to create an impressive rhythm, tone, and syntax in his striking creation of a bleak landscape and snow-bound universe.

Pickard, John B. *John Greenleaf Whittier: An Introduction and Interpretation*. New York: Barnes & Noble Books, 1961. The book begins with a biographical summary; the last seven chapters are a critical guide to his work. Pickard discusses Whittier's control of local-color detail, the moralism of his nature poems, and the authenticity of his religious poems. Some of the poems discussed are "Last Walk in Autumn," "The Barefoot Boy," "Snow-Bound," and "The Double-Headed Snake of Newbury."

Wagenknecht, Edward. *John Greenleaf Whittier: A Portrait in Paradox*. New York: Oxford University Press, 1967. Wagenknecht leaves the usual methods of biography behind by arranging his facts and anecdotes topically rather than chronologically. The result is a vibrant and energetic portrait of Whittier that displays the richness of his inner and outer life. The thesis of this book is that many facets of Whittier's life seem paradoxical to one another. Includes a bibliography.

Warren, Robert Penn. *John Greenleaf Whittier's Poetry: An Appraisal and a Selection.* Minneapolis: University of Minnesota Press, 1971. In a sixty-page essay, Warren discusses "Snow-Bound," "Telling the Bees," "Ichabod," "To My Old Schoolmaster," and other poems addressing themes of childhood and nostalgia, as well as a controversial Freudian view of the poet's development. Includes thirty-six poems by Whittier.

Woodwell, R. H. *John Greenleaf Whittier: A Biography.* Haverhill, Mass.: Trustees of the John Greenleaf Whittier Homestead, 1985. This is the fullest biography, based on years of research. It is encyclopedic, but has a very good index. Woodwell's 636 pages are not highly readable, but he does include a useful review of Whittier's criticism.

*Andrew J. Angyal;
bibliography updated by the editors*

RICHARD WILBUR

Born: New York, New York; March 1, 1921

PRINCIPAL POETRY

The Beautiful Changes and Other Poems, 1947
Ceremony and Other Poems, 1950
Things of This World, 1956
Poems, 1943-1956, 1957
Advice to a Prophet and Other Poems, 1961
Loudmouse, 1963 (juvenile)
The Poems of Richard Wilbur, 1963
Walking to Sleep: New Poems and Translations, 1969
Digging for China, 1970
Opposites, 1973 (juvenile)
The Mind-Reader: New Poems, 1976
Seven Poems, 1981
New and Collected Poems, 1988
More Opposites, 1991 (juvenile)
Runaway Opposites, 1995 (juvenile)
Mayflies: New Poems and Translations, 2000

OTHER LITERARY FORMS

In addition to his success as a poet, Richard Wilbur has won acclaim as a translator. Interspersed among his own poems are translations of Charles Baudelaire, Jorge Guillén, François Villon, and many others. His interest in drama is most notably shown in his translations of four Molière plays: *Le Misanthrope* (1955, *The Misanthrope*), *Tartuffe* (1963), *École des femmes* (1971, *The School for Wives*), and *Les Femmes savantes* (1978, *The Learned Ladies*). In 1957, Random House published *Candide: A Comic Operetta* with lyrics by Wilbur, book by Lillian Hellman, and score by Leonard Bernstein. Wilbur admits that he attempted to write a play in 1952, but he found its characters unconvincing and "all very wooden." He turned to translating Molière, thinking he "might learn something about poetic theater by translating *the master*."

Wilbur has edited several books, including *A Bestiary*, with Alexander Calder (1955), *Poe: Complete Poems* (1959), and *Shakespeare: Poems*, with coeditor Alfred Harbage (1966). In 1976, Wilbur published *Responses, Prose Pieces: 1953-1976*, a collection of essays which he describes as containing "some prose by-products of a poet's life." His essays and other prose pieces are collected in *The Catbird's Song: Prose Pieces, 1963-1995* (1997) Most of his manuscripts are in the Robert Frost Library at Amherst College. His early work is housed in the Lockwood Memorial Library at the State University of New York at Buffalo.

ACHIEVEMENTS

Honored with degrees from numerous colleges and universities, Richard Wilbur, who was awarded the Prix de Rome in 1954, has also received two Guggenheim Fellowships (1952-1953, 1963), a Ford Fellowship (1960-1961), and a Camargo Foundation Fellowship (1985). *Things of This World* in 1957 brought him a Pulitzer Prize, the National Book Award, and the Edna St. Vincent Millay Memorial Award. In 1964, he was corecipient of the Bollingen Prize for his translation of *Tartuffe*. In 1987, he was named Poet Laureate of the United States, an honor that was soon followed by the Aiken Taylor Award for Modern American Poetry. President Bill Clinton bestowed the National Medal of the Arts on Wilbur in 1994. In 1996, he received the Robert

Frost Medal of the Poetry Society of America. In the same year, he received the T. S. Eliot Award.

BIOGRAPHY

Born to Lawrence and Helen Purdy Wilbur, Richard Purdy Wilbur was reared in a family that was moderately interested in art and language. His father was an artist, and his mother was a daughter of an editor with the *Baltimore Sun*. His maternal great-grandfather was also an editor and a publisher who established newspapers supporting the Democratic platform. In 1923, the family moved to a farm in North Caldwell, New Jersey, and Wilbur and his brother enjoyed their childhoods investigating nature, an activity which remains a strong focal point in his poems. His father's painting and his mother's link with newspapers led him at times to think of becoming a cartoonist, an artist, or a journalist. His love of cartooning continues, for he illustrated *Opposites* with bold line drawings. His interests were many, however, and he was encouraged by his family to explore any talents he wished. After graduating from Montclair High School in 1938, he entered Amherst College, where he edited the newspaper and contributed to *Touchstone*, the campus humor magazine. He spent summers hoboing around the country.

After graduation in 1942, Wilbur married Charlotte Hayes Ward (with whom he had four children), joined the Enlisted Reserve Corps, and saw active duty in Europe with the 36th Infantry Division. At Cassino, Anzio, and the Siegfried line, he began writing poetry seriously, embarking on what he calls creation of "an experience" through a poem. He sent his work home where it remained until he returned from the war to pursue a master's degree in English at Harvard. The French poet André du Bouchet read the poems, pronounced Wilbur a poet, and sent the works to be published. They were released as *The Beautiful Changes and Other Poems* in 1947; in 1952, the same year Wilbur received his master of arts degree from Harvard, he was elected to the Society of Fellows.

His status as a poet established, Wilbur began his teaching career. From 1950 to 1954, he was an assistant professor of English at Harvard. Then, from 1954 to 1957, he served as an associate professor at Wellesley College; during that time his award-winning *Things of This World* was published. In 1957, he went to Wesleyan University as a professor of English. He stayed there until 1977, when he accepted the position of writer in residence at Smith College, where he remained until 1986. He divides his time between Key West, Florida, and the Berkshire Mountains near Cummington, Massachusetts, where he occupies himself doing things which he says are "non-verbal so that I can return to language with excitement and move toward language from kinds of strong awareness for which I haven't instantly found facile words. It is good for a writer to move into words out of the silence, as much as he can."

ANALYSIS

Eschewing any obvious poetic version or formal, personal set of guidelines, Richard Wilbur has come to be regarded as a master craftsman of modern poetry. Although he sees himself as an inheritor of the vast wealth of language and form used by poets before him, Wilbur has consistently striven to create and maintain his own artistic signature and control over his own work. Having begun his career immediately after World War II and having been exposed to what has been called the Beat generation, Wilbur creates his poetry from an intriguing blend of imaginative insights and strict adherence to the niceties of conventional poetics. His is not the poetry of confession or hatred readily exemplified by Sylvia Plath, nor is it hallucinatory or mystical, as is much of Allen Ginsberg's work.

Wilbur began to write poetry because the war prompted him to confront the fear and the physical and spiritual detachment brought about by a world in upheaval. He says that he "wrote poems to calm [his] nerves." It is this sense of imposed order on a disorderly world that has caused some readers to think of Wilbur's poetry as a distant investigation into human life addressed to a small, educated audience and delivered by a seemingly aloof but omniscient observer. Nearly all Wilbur's poems are metrical, and many of them employ rhyme. Perhaps if a feeling of detachment exists, it comes not from Wilbur the poet but from the very standards of poetic expression. Every persona established by a poet is, in Wilbur's words, "a contrived self." This voice is the intelligent recorder of experience and emotion. It is Wilbur's voice in the sense that, like the poet, the persona discovers relationships between ideas and events that are grounded in concrete reality but that lead to abstracted views of nature, love, endurance, and place. He uses concrete images—a fountain, a tree, a hole in the floor—to explore imagination. His flights into imagery are not sojourns into fantasy; they are deliberate attempts to be a witness to the disordered and altogether varied life around him.

Wilbur achieves brilliantly what he sees poetry doing best: compacting experience into language that excites the intellect and vivifies the imagination. His voice and the cautious pace at which he works are not to be taken as self-conscious gestures. They are, to use his word, matters demanding "carefulness." He finds "gaudiness annoying, richness not." Wilbur's poetry is rich; it is wealthy in imagery and plot and rhythmic movement. He seems to believe that language cannot be guarded unless it is used to carry as much meaning as it can possibly bear. This freedom with language is not prodigal but controlled. Betraying poetry's ancestry would be anarchy for Wilbur. At the heart of his canon is the verbal liberty he finds in formalism. Consequently, in each line he hopes that at least one word will disturb the reader, providing a freedom found only within the architectonics of poetry's conventions. His poems enjoy humor and quiet meditation, and they lend themselves easily to being read aloud. Because of the freedom the rules of poetry give to them, Wilbur's poems are energetic, and his persona, peripatetic.

A SENSE OF DECORUM

If readers were to limit their interest in Richard Wilbur's poetry to a discussion of imagery, they would be misunderstanding and distorting some of the basic premises upon which he builds his poetry. Just as he sees each of his poems as an independent unit free of any entanglement with other poems in a collection or with a superimposed, unifying theme, so he views the creation of a poem as an individual response to something noticed or deeply felt. Because all worthwhile poetry is a personal vision of the world, Wilbur heightens the tension and irony found in his poems by establishing a voice enchanted by what is happening in the poem but controlled so that the persona is nearly always a reasonable voice recording details and events in an entirely believable way. His sense of decorum, then, plays a major role in creating the relationship between reader and poet.

Readers often react to Wilbur's decorum in one of two ways: Either they laud the fictive persona as a trustworthy human being, lacking deceit, or they hear him speaking from a plateau that is at best inaccessible to the reader because it is too distant from the mundane. Wilbur's decorum actually creates a median between these two extremes. Like Robert Frost, Wilbur believes that poetry must present shared experiences in extraordinary ways. His persona is not directed toward readers solely as readers of poetry. Rather, the voice is aimed sharply at defining the experiences that both readers and poet hold in common. Wilbur never talks *at* the reader, but rather, he addresses himself to the human condition. Often his voice is much more vulnerable and humorous than readers admit. Many of his poems are reminiscent of soliloquies. A reader may come to the poems the way a person may discover a man talking out loud to himself about personal experiences, all the while using the most imaginative, sonorous language to describe them. At his best, Wilbur provides moments when readers can recognize the deep humanity that runs through his work.

Although he looks for no overriding idea or central metaphor when he organizes a collection, Wilbur does return to themes that are at the heart of human life: nature, love, a sense of goodness and contentment, the search for direction, the need to feel a part of a larger unknown, a wider life. All of these topics are spiritual concerns. Unlike Edgar Allan Poe, whom he considers a writer who ignores reality to construct a world colored by the fantastic, Wilbur grounds his spiritual wanderings in the world that readers know. In this respect, he is capturing what is abstract in the mesh of concrete imagery, a feat also successfully accomplished by Frost and Emily Dickinson.

"LAMARCK ELABORATED"

Perhaps nowhere else do Wilbur's major themes so intelligently and ironically coalesce as in "Lamarck Elaborated," a poem dealing not only with nature and love but also with the inner and outer worlds that humans inhabit. Mankind's place in these two worlds and his ability to balance them provide a common experience for both poet and reader. The inner world of man, represented by the senses and the intellect, perceives the outer world framed by nature which, in turn, has the power to shape man's ability to interpret what he senses to be the physical world. Chevalier de Lamarck, a French naturalist whose life straddles the seventeenth and eighteenth centuries, believed that the environment causes structural changes that can be passed on genetically. Although man may assign names to the animals, plants, and objects that surround him, he is unable to control the changes that may occur in nature and that may, in turn, change him. Man has adapted to nature. Paradoxically, humankind's attempts at analyzing the natural state of things leads him to "whirling worlds we could not know," and what he thinks is love is simply an overwhelming desire causing dizziness. The poem's voice records man's obsession with his place in a scheme he wishes to dominate but cannot. Literally and figuratively, the balance between the inner and outer worlds "rolls in seas of thought."

The balance implied in "Lamarck Elaborated" is also investigated in "Another Voice." Here Wilbur probes the soul's ability to do good when man's nature is often to do bad. How can the soul feel sympathy when evil has been committed? How can it transform violence into "dear concerns"? Can the "giddy ghost" do battle with malevolence? Wilbur seems to suggest that the soul's response should be one of endurance as it acknowledges evil without becoming evil. The soul may not be able to rid itself of its "Anxiety and hate," two powerful forces, but neither will it relinquish its quiet sympathy that serves as a witness for compassion.

STAGES OF LIFE

Although "Another Voice" may conjure up a spirit of resignation as the poet ponders the weaknesses of the human soul, Wilbur's poetry contains many examples of contentment, complete happiness, and mature acknowledgement of human limitations. Wilbur reminds his readers that human beings cannot be or do all that they might wish to become or accomplish. "Running," "Patriot's Day," and "Dodwells Road" form a thematic triptych in which Wilbur muses about the stages of life and the reactions human beings have to these stages. The first poem is an account of the persona's memories of his boyhood and the abandonment that running provided. In the second, the persona is an observer of the Boston Marathon and of "Our champion Kelley who would win again,/ Rocked in his will, at rest within his run." The third poem presents the persona as both participant and observer. Having taken up the sport of jogging, as if to reaffirm his physical well-being, the speaker runs out of the forest and is brought to a halt by "A good ache in my ribcage." He feels comfortable in the natural setting surrounding him, a "part of that great going." The shouts of two boys (possibly the persona's sons) and the barking of a dog break the quiet, and the speaker finds delight in their running and leaping. In a gesture as inevitable as it is moving, the speaker gives the "clean gift" of his own childhood, his own vigor, to the boys.

"A HOLE IN THE FLOOR"

The voice that Wilbur assumes in his poems is often that of a person discovering or attempting to discover something unknown or removed. Usually the epiphany that the persona undergoes is centered around ordinary conditions or experiences. Sometimes the enlightenment produces extraordinary insights into human nature, the fragility of life, or the inexorable passage of time. A poem that manages to evoke poignancy, humor, and fear is "A Hole in the Floor," in which the speaker stands directly above an opening a carpenter has made "In the parlor floor." The use of the word "parlor" brings to mind turn-of-the-century home-life, a certain quaintness and security. Now that this *sanctum sanctorum* has been defiled, the speaker stares into the hole to view an unexpected scene. He is poised on the brink of a discovery and compares himself with Heinrich Schliemann, the excavator of Troy and Mycenae. He sees in the hole the vestiges of the house's origins: sawdust, wood shavings "From the time when the floor was laid."

Wilbur heightens the mythological tone of the poem by comparing the shavings to the pared skins of the golden apples guarded by the Hesperides in the garden on the Isles of the Blest. Although in the dim light the curly lengths of shaved wood may seem "silvery-gold," they remain concrete reminders of the carpenter's trade and of the creation of the structure in which the speaker now stands. If he senses that something primordial has been uncovered, he cannot quite convey his feelings. The speaker, of course, has given in to his own curiosity and wishes to be the explorer of unknown territories, the uncoverer of what had been private and hidden, but, at the same time, close by. Reveling in his investigation of the joists and pipes, he finally wonders what it is he thought he would see. He brings his consciousness back to the steady, mundane world of the parlor and upbraids himself for his curiosity and romanticism. He asks himself if he expected to find a treasure or even the hidden gardens of the Hesperides. Perhaps, he ponders, he has come face-to-face with "The house's very soul."

Unlike Frost's figure who is content to kneel by a well, see his own reflection, and then catch a glimmer of something at the bottom, Wilbur's speaker understands that what he discovers or believes he has discovered is something beyond the orderly, formal restrictions imposed upon him by the parlor. Somehow, the hidden realm on which the house stands adds an importance to what can in fact be known. Paradoxically, what the persona knows is his inability to fathom the unknowable, that "buried strangeness/ which nourishes the known." The parlor suddenly becomes "dangerous" because its serenity rests on uncertainty, darkness, and private beginnings. The "buried strangeness" not only resides at the foundation of the house, but it is also found in any human construction, a building, a passion, a theory, or a poem.

BALANCING OPPOSITES

"A Hole in the Floor" is further representative of Wilbur's poetry because it balances two opposites, and these contraries work on several levels: curiosity and expectation, the known and the unknown, and reality and imagination. It is a complex and beautifully crafted poem. Other poems that also investigate the balance between opposites include "Another Voice," "Advice to a Prophet," "Gemini," "Someone Talking to Himself," and "The Writer." Wilbur's obvious pleasure in riddles is another example of this taut balance between the unknown and the known, the question and the answer, the pause and the reply. In addition, *Opposites*, charming and witty as it is, has this same tense equilibrium built into it.

The contrast between opposing ideas is probably most evident in what could be called Wilbur's "two-voice" poems, those in which he presents "two voices going against each other. One is a kind of lofty and angelic voice, the other is a slob voice, and these are two parts of myself quarreling in public." The poem "Two Voices in a Meadow," which begins *Advice to a Prophet and Other Poems*, juxtaposes a milkweed's flexibility with a stone's tenacity. The milkweed yields to the wind's power to carry its cherubic seeds to the soil, and the stone attributes the solid foundation of heaven to its immovable nature. In "The Aspen and the Stream," the tree and the brook carry on a dialogue in which the aspen's metaphysics are countered by the stream's no-nonsense, literal approach to its place in the universal scheme of life.

Sometimes Wilbur's interest in opposites takes the form of a study of reconciliation through religion. Such poems as "Water Walker" and "A Christmas Hymn" suggest his concern with religious doctrine and its influence on private action and public thought. At other times, the balance is jarred because the persona is duped into believing something false or is misled because of naïveté. A more gullible person than the one in "A Hole in the Floor," the character in "Digging for China" burrows into the earth thinking that he can reach China. The speaker digs and digs to no avail, of course, and becomes obsessed and then delirious, "blinking and staggering while the earth went round." Admitting his folly, he confesses that "Until I got my balance back again/ All that I saw was China, China, China." He returns to whatever balance he may have known before his futile attempt to reach the Orient, but he enjoys no enlightenment of the spirit.

The tense balance between knowledge and ignorance may appear in Wilbur's poems when the persona is confronted with an abstraction so amorphous and foreign that it cannot adequately be defined, as in "A Hole in the Floor." At other times, Wilbur allows his characters to confront ideas, events, or feelings which are much more readily and vividly recognized. In such cases, the emotions, although private, have a larger, perhaps a more cosmic significance added to them; these are shared emotions, easily identifiable because nearly all human beings have experienced them. Even if man stands on the edge or the margins of experience, he is from time to time thrust squarely into life's demands and responsibilities. Wilbur elucidates this idea in poems such as "Marginalia," in which "Things concentrate at the edges," and "Our riches are centrifugal."

"BOY AT THE WINDOW"

Two poems that combine both the experience of living life fully and the experience of participating at its edges are "Boy at the Window" and "The Pardon." Both have titles which would befit paintings, and, indeed, Wilbur presents concrete stories colored and framed by his language and the structure of the poems themselves. Each has as its main character a boy who is both witness and participant. "Boy at the Window" is reminiscent of a classic Italian sonnet in its form and meter, although Wilbur divides the two sections into equal parts of eight lines each. Looking out from a window toward a snowman he has built, the boy is confronted by the "god-forsaken stare" of the figure "with bitumen eyes." The structure of the poem reinforces the balanced stares given by the boy and the snowman. Safe and warm, the boy intuitively knows that the snowman is an "outcast" from the world that the boy, himself, enjoys. The boy, however, does not mourn for the snowman; rather, the snowman "melts enough to drop from one soft eye/ A trickle of the purest rain, a tear." Surrounded as he is by "light" and "love," the boy understands, perhaps for the first time, fear and dread. The poem provides a quiet moment when the boy in his silence recognizes something about sin and futility and innocence and contentment. With its blending of childhood trust and energy with a maturer reflection on humankind's fall from grace, it evokes much the same mood as Dylan Thomas's "Fern Hill."

"THE PARDON"

"The Pardon" has as its plot a boy's confrontation with the death of his dog. At first he refuses to accept the event and tries to mask the experience just as "the heavy honeysuckle-smell" masks the odor of the decaying body. Admitting fear and the inability to "forgive the sad or strange/ In beast or man," the child cannot bring himself to bury the dog he loved "while he kept alive." After the boy's father buries the dog, the child sleeps and dreams of the dog's coming toward him. The boy wants to "call his name" to ask "forgiveness of his tongueless head." His attempts are checked, however, and he feels betrayed by his horror and his guilt. The poem is told from the perspective of a grown man who is remembering his childhood. Knowing the gesture may be ludicrous or ineffective, he "begs death's pardon now." Whether redemption occurs or the guilt is lifted is not told, but the very act of confronting this long-ago event is in itself a mature gesture of reconciliation and re-

morse, covered, perhaps, with shame and embarrassment. The rhyme scheme of the poem also suggests the persona's growing control over the incident, a control made possible by the passing of years and the accumulation of experience. The boy lacked a perspective; the man he has become provides it. Like his father before him, the speaker hopes to have the strength and the will to bury the dog, if not literally, then at least symbolically. As the persona moves toward this strength, the rhyme scheme, chaotic at the poem's beginning, settles into an obvious, harmonious pattern which parallels the speaker's growing dominance over his sorrow.

"WALKING TO SLEEP"

Wilbur is known and admired for his short poems whose imagery and subjects are compacted by his mastery of language and poetic convention. As if to reaffirm his commitment to the richness of these standards, his later collections have included long, dramatic monologues that remind readers of the oral tradition in poetry. "Walking to Sleep" and "The Mind-Reader" are poems that invite Wilbur's audience to explore the frontier, the wilderness of conscious thought and subconscious ruminating. The poems are both accessible and cryptic. Nowhere else has Wilbur created such sustained narrations, such talkative, complex tellers of his tales. In fact, he has noted that "Walking to Sleep" requires eight minutes to read aloud. The narrators are both conjurers and straightforward friends. Readers wish to believe them, but, at the same time, their manipulative language and their careful choice of details and information suggest an artifice. Both poems deal with the equilibrium between what is private, sleep and thought, and what is public, consciousness and action. Readers are led through the poems by the narrators who help the audience balance its way as if on a tightrope. In addition, the poems seem to be inviting readers to lose themselves in their own minds, an activity calling for leisure, courage, and an eagerness to embrace the unknown and the uncontrollable.

On its surface, "Walking to Sleep" is a sensuous account of sleep, sweeping from scene to scene, mirroring the act of dreaming. It begins *in medias res*, and readers are asked to have the poise of a queen or a general as they give themselves over to sleep and, more important, to the devices of the poem itself. Wilbur explores in ways that are whimsical, horrifying, and provocative the images that appear to a sleeper and to a poet as well. The poem may well be an exploration into the origins of poetry, and the narrator-poet may be speaking to himself as much as he is to an audience. His only direct warning to himself and his readers is the speaker's suggestion that the imagination never be allowed to become too comfortable; it must remain "numb" with a "grudging circumspection." Readers can feel the rhythms of sleep and love, creativity, and balance in the poem just as vividly as they sense the rhythms of meter, imagery, humor, and resignation. The poem is a masterful work controlled by the limitless power of man's imagination.

"THE MIND-READER"

"The Mind-Reader" deals with a man who thinks other people's thoughts. The narrator describes himself as a person condemned to finding what is lost, remembering what is forgotten, or foreseeing what is unknown. He is able to manipulate his listeners and his followers because of their superstitious awe of his ability, which they are afraid to disprove. He confesses that he "sometimes cheats a little," admitting that he has no clear, easy answers to give to questions about love, careers, or doubts. He sees his duties as being those of a listener rather than those of a man capable to prescience, and he wonders if "selfish hopes/ And small anxieties" have replaced the "reputed rarities of the soul." The irony in the poem is underscored when the speaker turns to his readers and asks them a question of huge, religious proportions. Like his audience, he now longs for guidance, "some . . . affection" capable of discovering "In the worst rancor a deflected sweetness." Ironically, he dulls his mind with drink and satiates himself with "concupiscence." To the great question of whether a gentle, proper, and completely honest, cosmic mind-reader exists, he has no answer.

"THIS PLEASING ANXIOUS BEING"

In "This Pleasing Anxious Being," one of twenty-five new poems included in *Mayflies*, Wilbur looks back on a childhood scene, a somewhat formal dinner, presumably a holiday feast such as Thanksgiving. The family is gathered around the table. The servant, Roberta, brings yams and succotash after the mother has rung the little bell to summon her. The father carves at the sideboard. Wilbur refers to this scene as the one where

safety was. He speaks of the lambent table and of the family whose faces drink the candlelight, using language in singular ways. Then, dwelling as he often does upon opposites, he remembers that this recollected past was once a hurried present that was fretful and unsure. As the poem ends, the recollection is of a small boy, feet kicking beneath the table, eager to be off to his play. Again, Wilbur employs opposites effectively, as he juxtaposes the formality of the dining room scene to the freedom and informality of child's play. The poem also juxtaposes real time and events and recollected time and events, becoming imbued with a sense of how nostalgia colors perceptions.

"A BARRED OWL"

In the celebrated "A Barred Owl," Wilbur again uses opposites to demonstrate how a single event can have different meanings, depending upon how it is presented and how it is perceived by those who are exposed to it. In this case, what Wilbur, in the first six-line rhyming stanza, calls the "boom/ Of an owl's voice" frightens a child awakened in a dark room. Those who rush to comfort her, presumably her parents, explain to her that what she has heard is merely a question posed by a forest bird that asks twice, "Who cooks for you?"

In the second six-line stanza, Wilbur philosophizes about how language can soften such realities as the frightening call of an owl that captures small rodents in its claw and eats them raw, a brutal act from which words protect the child. Pacified by the explanation she receives, the child is calmed and now can go back to sleeping peacefully.

In twelve rhyming lines, Wilbur creates two worlds, one of fear and terror, the other of peace and security. He possesses a rare sense of when to use the exact word, as in the second stanza, where he writes that words can "domesticate a fear." The four-syllable word "domesticate" is surrounded by simple one-syllable words, making it stand out and evoking the reader's attention in precisely the manner that Wilbur wishes. This—the only unusual word in the entire poem, with its preponderance of one- and two-syllable words—fixes attention on the line as little else could.

"A SHORT HISTORY"

In this two-line poem, Wilbur achieves a prodigious act of compression. In essence, he reduces the history of humankind to fifteen words: "Corn planted us; tamed cattle made us tame:/ Thence hut and citadel and kingdom came." In these few words, the poet traces life as we know it back to humankind's progress from a nomadic society to an agrarian society, one that required permanent structures and governments. In this poem, the leap from hut (a humble dwelling) to citadel (a fortification) to kingdom (a governmental construct) speaks much more than the simple nouns that express this complex social progression. The first three words immediately demand attention. Wilbur might have written, "We planted corn," but to have done so would have been to rob the line of the very vitality that draws readers into it. Just as Emily Dickinson used brief, clipped lines and unique grammatical constructions to give her lines the vitality that good poems require, so does Wilbur capture succinctly the precise constructions that vivify his lines.

THEMES

In the past, Wilbur's craft has been narrowly defined as the poetry of a mind set apart from the everyday world that human beings inhabit. Although his interest in balance is evident, his keen insight into contraries and the inner and outer lives of his characters is equally important to an understanding of what he is attempting in his poems. His work focuses on the enlightenment of the human spirit, but it never denies the darker impulses or fears which are brought to bear when doubt, resignation, or apathy appear as challenges to the harmony that civilized man strives to achieve. His poems are not so much reaffirmations of the beauty of life as they are records of an attempt at order, an order certainly suggested by the conventions of poetry. These conventions govern a poetic talent whose use of subject, meter, rhyme, and imagery provokes the senses and provides an ordinary understanding of life in an extraordinary and uncompromising way.

OTHER MAJOR WORKS

PLAY: *Candide: A Comic Operetta*, pr. 1956 (lyrics; book by Lillian Hellman, music by Leonard Bernstein).

NONFICTION: *Responses, Prose Pieces: 1953-1976*, 1976; *On My Own Work*, 1983; *Conversations with Richard Wilbur*, 1990 (William Butts, editor): *The Catbird's Song: Prose Pieces, 1963-1995*, 1997.

TRANSLATIONS: *The Misanthrope*, 1955 (of Molière); *Tartuffe*, 1963 (of Molière); *The School for Wives*, 1971 (of Molière); *The Learned Ladies*, 1978 (of Molière); *Andromache*, 1982 (of Jean Racine); *Four Comedies*, 1982 (of Molière); *Phaedra*, 1986 (of Racine); *The School of Husbands*, 1991 (of Molière); *The Imaginary Cuckold: Or, Sgarnarelle*, 1993 (of Molière); *Amphitryon*, 1995 (of Molière).

EDITED TEXTS: *A Bestiary*, 1955 (with Alexander Calder); *Modern American and Modern British Poetry*, 1955 (with Louis Untermeyer and Karl Shapiro); *Poe: Complete Poems*, 1959; *Shakespeare: Poems*, (with Alfred Harbage) 1966; *The Narrative Poems and Poems of Doubtful Authenticity*, 1974.

BIBLIOGRAPHY

Cummins, Paul F. *Richard Wilbur: A Critical Essay*. Grand Rapids, Mich.: Wm. B. Eerdmans, 1971. Defends Wilbur's poetry against the charge of passionless elegance; argues that the poet uses rhyme and meter skillfully to enhance tone and meaning. A largely thematic study. Includes a primary and a secondary bibliography (both of which, naturally, are dated), but no index.

Edgecombe, Rodney Stenning. *A Reader's Guide to the Poetry of Richard Wilbur*. Tuscaloosa: University of Alabama Press, 1995. Edgecombe provides some worthwhile insights into Wilbur's poems up to those included in *New and Collected Poems* (1988). He provides a brief but penetrating introduction, as well as an extensive bibliography and a serviceable index.

Field, John P. *Richard Wilbur: A Bibliographical Checklist*. Serif series: Bibliographies and Checklists 16. Kent, Ohio: Kent State University Press, 1971. For the student wishing to make further forays into Wilbur's poetry and thinking, this volume provides a valuable detailed listing of the poetry collections and their contents, articles, stories, edited works, book reviews, interviews, and manuscripts. A list of secondary sources is also supplied.

Hill, Donald L. *Richard Wilbur*. New York: Twayne, 1967. The biographical chronology extends only through 1964. Devotes a chapter each to *The Beautiful Changes*, *Ceremony*, *Things of This World*, and

Advice to a Prophet, with both thematic and technical discussions. A final chapter looks at Wilbur's prose writings and evaluates his place among twentieth century poets. Notes, a bibliography, and an index are included.

Hougen, John B. *Ecstasy Within Discipline: The Poetry of Richard Wilbur*. Atlanta, Ga.: Scholar's Press, 1995. The author's chief concerns are theological. Hougen provides some useful insights into the formal aspects of Wilbur's writing.

Michelson, Bruce. *Wilbur's Poetry: Music in a Scattering Time*. Amherst: University of Massachusetts Press, 1991. In this first comprehensive study of Wilbur's poetry since that late 1960's, Michelson attempts to counter the widespread opinion that Wilbur is a bland poet. Michelson's close readings of the major poems contradict and dispel much that has been written critically about the poet.

Salinger, Wendy, ed. *Richard Wilbur's Creation*. Ann Arbor: University of Michigan Press, 1983. A rich collection featuring, in part 1, many previously published reviews of Wilbur's chief works through 1976; contributors include such luminaries as Louise Bogan, Randall Jarrell, Donald Hall, and John Ciardi. The second half presents more comprehensive critical essays on various aspects of the poet's themes and craft. Valuable for its scope and for the quality of its writing.

Wilbur, Richard. *Conversations with Richard Wilbur*. Edited by William Butts. Literary Conversations series. Jackson: University Press of Mississippi, 1990. The nineteenth interviews collected here span about thirty years (beginning in 1962) and thus shed light on both changing times and the development of an important poet. Wilbur here responds to the critics who have labeled him as overly good-natured, lacking in passion, and too controlled. The poet also discusses how he approaches the writing of a poem, his opinions of creative-writing programs, and many other topics. Indexed.

_____. *On My Own Work*. Aquila Essays 20. Portree, Isle of Skye, Scotland: Aquila, 1983. This small book, apparently printed on an old fashioned mimeograph, is hard to find. Yet it is worth the search for a student who wants to explore Wilbur's own concept of his poetry. Despite his demurrals—"the ideas of any poet, when reduced to prose statement, sound banal and mine are no exception"—he is unfailingly articulate and interesting.

Walter B. Freed, Jr.,
updated by R. Baird Shuman

OSCAR WILDE

Born: Dublin, Ireland; October 15, 1854
Died: Paris, France; November 30, 1900

PRINCIPAL POETRY
Ravenna, 1878
Poems, 1881
Poems in Prose, 1894
The Sphinx, 1894
The Ballad of Reading Gaol, 1898

OTHER LITERARY FORMS

Oscar Wilde wrote a number of plays produced successfully in his lifetime: *Lady Windermere's Fan* (1892), *A Woman of No Importance* (1893), *An Ideal Husband* (1895), and *The Importance of Being Earnest: A Trivial Comedy for Serious People* (1895). Banned in London, his play *Salomé* was produced in 1893 in Paris with Sarah Bernhardt. Two plays, *Vera: Or, The Nihilists* (1880) and *The Duchess of Padua* (1883), were produced in New York after publication in England. Finally, two plays, *A Florentine Tragedy* (1906) and *La Sainte Courtisane*, were published together in the collected edition of Wilde's works in 1908. Wilde published one novel, *The Picture of Dorian Gray* (1891), serially in *Lippincott's Magazine*. Commercially and artistically successful with a number of his plays and his one novel, Wilde reached his peak in the early 1890's when he wrote little poetry. Wilde also wrote short stories and a number of fairy tales. His last prose work is a long letter, *De Profundis*, an apologia for his life. Parts of it were published as early as 1905, but the full work was suppressed until 1950.

ACHIEVEMENTS

G. F. Maine states that the tragedy of Oscar Wilde is that he is remembered more as a criminal and a homosexual than as an artist. Readers still feel overwhelmed by Wilde's life just as his personality overwhelmed his contemporaries. His greatest achievement is in drama, and his only novel–*The Picture of Dorian Gray*—is still widely read. In comparison, his poetry is essentially derivative.

Wilde modeled himself on the poets of a tradition that was soon to end in English literature, and most of his poetry appears in the earlier part of his career. Within this Romantic tradition, Wilde had a wider range than might be expected; he could move from the limited impressions of the shorter poems to the philosophic ruminations of the longer poems. Yet behind each poem, the presence of an earlier giant lurks: John Keats, William Wordsworth, Algernon Charles Swinburne. Wilde's most original poem, *The Ballad of Reading Gaol*, is not derivative, and its starkness shows a side of

Oscar Wilde (Library of Congress)

Wilde not generally found in his other poems. Wilde's poetry is a coda, then, to the end of a tradition.

BIOGRAPHY

Oscar Fingal O'Flahertie Wills Wilde was born in Dublin, Ireland, on October 15, 1854. Flamboyance, so characteristic of the adult Wilde, was an obvious quality of both of his parents. His father was noted for physical dirtiness and love affairs, one of which led to a lawsuit and public scandal. Something of a social revolutionary, his mother published poetry and maintained a salon for intellectual discussion in her later years. Wilde grew up in this environment, showing both insolence and genius. He was an excellent student at all his schools. He attended Portora Royal School, Trinity College in Dublin, and then won a scholarship to Magdalen College, Oxford. At this time, John Ruskin was lecturing, and Wilde was influenced by Ruskin's ideas and style. More important, he heard and met Walter Pater, who had recently published his *Studies in the History of the Renaissance* (1873). It is Pater's influence that is most obvious in Wilde's development as a poet. While at Oxford, Wilde visited Italy and Greece, and this trip strengthened the love of classical culture so obvious in his poetry.

In the 1880's, as he developed as a writer, he also became a public personality. He toured the United States for about a year, and in both the United States and England he preached an aesthetic doctrine which had its origins in the Pre-Raphaelites and Pater. He married in 1883 and had two sons. Wilde serially published his only novel, *The Picture of Dorian Gray*, which immediately created a sensation with the public. Thereafter, he wrote a number of plays, most notably *Lady Windermere's Fan* and *The Importance of Being Earnest*.

Wilde's last decade involved the scandal over his homosexuality. His chief male lover was Lord Alfred Douglas, whose father, the Marquess of Queensberry, tried to end Wilde's liaison with his son and ruin Wilde socially. Consequently, Wilde sued the Marquess of Queensberry for libel but lost the case and also had his homosexuality revealed. Tried twice for homosexuality, he was found guilty and finally sentenced to two years at hard labor. From his prison experiences, Wilde wrote his most famous poem, *The Ballad of Reading Gaol*. Released from prison, he wandered over the Continent for three years, broken physically and ruined financially. He died in Paris at the age of forty-six.

ANALYSIS

Oscar Wilde's poetry derives from the rich tradition of nineteenth century poetry, for, as Richard Aldington shows, Wilde imitated what he loved so intensely in the great poets of his century. Drawing from John Keats, Dante Gabriel Rossetti, William Morris, and Algernon Charles Swinburne, Wilde demonstrated an aestheticism like theirs in his lush imagery and in his pursuit of the fleeting impression of the moment. His poetry tries to capture the beautiful, as the Victorian critic John Ruskin had urged a generation earlier, but generally lacks the moral tone that Ruskin advocated. Wilde's poetry best fulfills the aesthetic of Walter Pater, who, in his *Studies in the History of the Renaissance*, advocated impressionism and art for art's sake. Indeed, Wilde paraphrased Pater's famous line of burning with a "hard, gemlike flame" in several of his poems.

Wilde published many poems individually before 1881, but his *Poems* of 1881 included almost all of these poems and many new ones. With this collection, he published more than half of the poetry that he was to produce. The collection of 1881 is a good representation of his aestheticism and his tendency to derivativeness. Wilde avoided the overtly autobiographical and confessional mode in these poems, yet they mirror his attitudes and travels as impressions of his life. The forms he tried most often in the collection were the Italian sonnet and, for longer poems, a six-line stanza in pentameter with an *ababcc* rhyme scheme. The smaller poetic output which followed the 1881 collection consists of a number of shorter poems, two longer poems, and *Poems in Prose*. The short poems break no new ground, *The Sphinx* heralds a decadence and a celebration of pain unequaled in the nineteenth century except by Swinburne a generation earlier. *The Ballad of Reading Gaol*, however, builds on Wilde's earlier efforts. Again, he avoids the confessional mode that one would expect, considering the horrors of incarceration out of which the poem grew. The persona of the poem is no longer an urbane mind observing nature and society, but a common prisoner at

hard labor generalizing about the cruelties of humans and their treatment of those they love. In this poem, despite its shrillness and melodrama, Wilde struck a balance between his own suffering and art, a balance which the impressionism of his poetic talents made easier. He dealt, as an observer, with the modern and the sordid as he had dealt earlier with art and nature. *Poems in Prose* is Wilde's effort at the short parable, offering neither the impressionism nor the formal qualities of his other poems, but ironic parables which refute the pieties of his era. Here Wilde is at his wittiest.

RAVENNA

Ravenna was Wilde's first long poem to be published, and it won the Newdigate prize for poetry while he was still at Oxford. Written in couplets, the poem deals with many of the themes which he developed for the 1881 collection; thus, *Ravenna* is the starting point in a study of Wilde's poetry. Like the later long poems, *Ravenna* develops through contrasts: northern and southern European cultures, innocence and experience, past and present, classical and Christian. As a city, Ravenna evokes all of these contrasts to the youthful Wilde.

The opening imagery is of spring, with a tendency to lushness typical of Keats. The boyish awe that Wilde felt in Ravenna is tempered, however, by recollection, for in the poem he is recalling his visit a year later. It is through recollection that he understands the greatness of the city, for in his northern world he has no such symbol of the rich complexity of time. What he learns from the English landscape is the passage of seasons which will mark his aging. He is sure, though, that with his love for Ravenna he will have a youthful inspiration despite his aging and loss of poetic powers.

Most of the poem is a poetic recounting of Ravenna's history. Wilde discusses the classical past of the city with reference to Caesar, and when he refers to George Gordon, Lord Byron's stay in the city, by association with Byron's last days in Greece, he imagines the region peopled with mythological figures; but the evening convent bell returns him to a somber Christian world. Recounting the Renaissance history of the city, Wilde is most moved by Dante's shrine. He closes the poem with references to Dante and Byron.

Wilde published twenty-eight sonnets in the 1881 collection, *Poems*, all of them Italian in form. Like his mentor Keats, Wilde used the sonnet to develop themes which he expanded in his longer poems.

SONNETS

"Hélas," an early sonnet not published in the 1881 collection, is his artistic manifesto that sets the tone for all the poems that followed. "Hélas" finds Wilde rhetorically questioning whether he has bartered wisdom for the passion or impression of the moment. In the sonnets that follow, he clearly seems to have chosen such moments of vivid impression.

In several sonnets, Wilde alludes to the poets who molded his style and themes, including two sonnets about visiting the graves of Keats and Percy Bysshe Shelley in the Protestant cemetery in Rome. He identifies himself with Keats as he never identifies with Shelley, and rightly so, for Keats's style and themes echo throughout the 1881 collection. Wilde also refers directly to Keats in another sonnet, "Amor Intellectualis," and to other poets important to him: Robert Browning, Christopher Marlowe, and particularly Dante and John Milton. The sonnet "A Vision" is a tribute to Aeschylus, Sophocles, and Euripides. On a larger scale than the sonnets, the longer poem "The Garden of Eros" presents Wilde's pantheon of poets with his feelings about them.

Some of the sonnets have political themes; in a number of these, Wilde advocates freedom, occasionally sounding like a Victorian Shelley. He is concerned with the political chaos of nineteenth century Italy, a land important to him for its classical past; "Italia" is a sonnet about the political venality in Italy, but it stresses that God might punish the corrupt. In his own country, Wilde idealizes the era of the Puritans and Oliver Cromwell; the sonnet "To Milton" laments the loss of democracy in England and advocates a return to the ideals of the Puritan revolution. In "Quantum Mutata," he admires Cromwell for his threat to Rome, but the title shows how events have changed, for Victorian England stands only for imperialism. This attack on British imperialism informs the long poem "Ave Imperatrix," which is far more emotional in tone than the political sonnets.

A number of Wilde's sonnets express his preference for the classical or primitive world and his antipathy for the modern Christian world. These poems have a persona visiting Italy, as Wilde did in 1877, and commenting on the Christian elements of the culture; "Sonnet on Approaching Italy" shows the speaker longing to visit Italy, yet, in contemplating far-off Rome, he laments the tyranny of a second Peter. Three other sonnets set in Italy, "Ave Maria, Gratia Plena," "Sonnet Written in Holy Week in Genoa," and "Urbs Sacra Aeterna," have Wilde contrasting the grandeur and color of the classical world with the emptiness and greyness of the Christian world. It is in these poems that Wilde is most like Swinburne. In other sonnets, he deals with religious values, often comparing the Christian ideal with the corruption of the modern Church he sees in Italy, or Christ's message with the conduct of his sinful followers. In "Easter Day," Wilde depicts the glory of the Pope as he is borne above the shoulders of the bearers, comparing that scene with the picture of Christ's loneliness centuries before. In "E Tenebris," the speaker appeals for help to a Christ who is to appear in weary human form. In "Sonnet, On Hearing the Dies Irae Sung in the Sistine Chapel," Wilde criticizes the harsh picture of a fiery day of judgment and replaces it with a picture of a warm autumn harvest, in which man awaits reaping by and fulfillment in God.

Wilde's best religious sonnet, "Madonna Mia," avoids the polemicism of some of his other religious sonnets, showing instead an affinity with the Pre--Raphaelite painting and poetry of a generation earlier. This sonnet is Pateresque in its hard impression, and it fulfills the credo suggested by the sonnet "Hélas." The picture Wilde paints in words is detailed: braided hair, blue eyes, pale cheeks, red lips, and white throat with purple veins; Wilde's persona is a worshiper of Mary, as Dante was of Beatrice.

"THE BURDEN OF ITYS"

"The Burden of Itys" is one of several long philosophic poems about nature and God to be found in the 1881 collection. Each of these poems has the same stanza form, a six-line stanza with an *ababcc* rhyme scheme; the first five lines are iambic pentameter, and the sixth is iambic heptameter. The stanza form gives a lightness which does not perfectly fit the depth of the ideas the poems present; it seems a form better suited to witticism than to philosophy.

Set in England close to Oxford, "The Burden of Itys" is similar in imagery and setting to Matthew Arnold's poems "The Scholar Gypsy" and "Thrysis." Wilde piles image on image of the flora of the region to establish the beauty of the setting, suggesting that the beauty of the countryside (and thus of nature in general) is holier than the grandeur of Rome. Fish replace bishops and the wind becomes the organ for the persona's religious reverie. By stanza thirteen, Wilde shifts from his comparison between Rome and nature to a contrast between the English landscape and the Greek. Because England is more beautiful than Greece, he suggests that the Greek pantheon could fittingly be reborn in Victorian England. A bird singing to Wilde, much like the nightingale singing to Keats, is the link between the persona imagining a revival of classical gods and actually experiencing one in which he will wear the leopard skin of a follower of Bacchus. This spell breaks, though, with another contrast, for a pale Christ and the speaker's religion destroy the classical reverie.

Brought back then to the Victorian world, as Keats was brought back to his world at the end of "Ode to a Nightingale," Wilde philosophizes and fixes the meaning of his experience in a way Keats never would have done. He stresses that nature does not represent the lovely agony of Christ but warm fellowship both in and between the worlds of man and animal. Even Oxford and nature are linked to each other, Wilde implies, as the curfew bell from his college church calls him back.

PHILOSOPHICAL POEMS

"Panthea" also works through dissimilarity, this time between southern and northern Europe, passion and reason, and classical and Christian thought. Wilde's rejection of the Church in "The Burden of Itys" is gentle, but in "Panthea" it is blatant. The gods have simply grown sick of priests and prayer. Instead, man should live for the passion and pleasure of an hour, those moments being the only gift the gods have to give. The poem emphasizes that the Greek gods themselves dwell in nature, participating fully in all the pleasures there. Their natural landscape, though, is not the bleak landscape of northern Europe, but the warm rich landscape of southern Europe.

Wilde proceeds to the philosophical theme of the poem, that one great power or being composes nature, and Nature, thus, subsumes all lives and elements and recycles them into various forms. For man to be reborn as flower or thrush is to live again without the pain of mortal existence; yet, paradoxically, without human pain,

nature could not create beauty. Pain is the basis of beauty, for nature exists as a setting for human passion. Nature, in Wilde's words, has one "Kosmic Soul" linking all lives and elements. Wilde echoes lines of Keats and Pater, and, uncharacteristically, William Wordsworth; Wilde's affirmation proceeds with lines and images from Wordsworth's "Ode: Intimations of Immortality from Recollections of Early Childhood."

"Humanitad" is the longest of the philosophical poems in the 1881 collection, and it has much less in common with the other two philosophical poems than they have with each other. While spring is imminent, the speaker responds only to the winter elements still persisting. He emphasizes (paraphrasing Pater) that he has no fire to burn with a clear flame. The difference here is with the renewal of spring and spiritual exhaustion, and the speaker must look outside himself for some source of renewal. At one point, the poem turns topical by referring to ideals of simplicity and freedom: Switzerland, Wordsworth, and Giuseppe Mazzini. Wilde invokes the name of Milton as epitomizing the fight for freedom in the past; and, at the same time, he laments that there are no modern Miltons. Having no modern exemplar, Wilde also dismisses death and love as possible solutions for his moribund life. Turning to science, Wilde also rejects it. Wilde then has no recourse, and he faces a meaningless universe until he touches on mere causality after having rejected science.

Causality leads to God and creed, for causality is a chain connecting all elements. Nature, as in "Panthea," cannot help the speaker, for he has grown weary of mere sensation. Accordingly, he turns to the force behind nature (in this instance, God as Christ), although he rejects orthodoxy. He sees modern man's creed as being in process, for man is in the stage of crucifixion as he tries to discover the human in Christ and not the divine. The persona then sees his emptiness as the suffering leading to renewal. It is the full discovery of Christ's humanity which will make modern human beings masters of nature rather than tormented, alienated outcasts.

THE SPHINX

Just as Wilde drew from classical mythology for many of his poems and then contrasted the gray Christian world with the bright pagan world, he used Egyptian mythology in *The Sphinx* to picture a decadent sadistic sensuality as distinguished from a tortured Christian suffering. The situation in the poem is that a cat has crept into the speaker's room; to the speaker, the cat represents the Sphinx. Now, giving his imagination play, the speaker reveals his own sadistic eroticism, a subject that Wilde had not developed in other poems. The style also represents a departure for him; the stanzas consist of two lines of iambic octameter with no rhyme, resulting in a languorous slow rhythm in keeping with the speaker's ruminations about sensuality and sadism.

The cat as Sphinx represents the lush, decadent, yet appealing sensuality found in Egyptian mythology. In half of the poem, Wilde rhetorically questions the Sphinx about mythological figures of ancient Egypt, asking who her lovers were and at the same time cataloging the most famous myths of Egypt. Wilde settles on Ammon as the Sphinx's lover, but then he discusses how Ammon's statue has fallen to pieces, thus suggesting that the lover might be dead. Yet the Sphinx has the power to revive her lover; Ammon is not really dead. Having earlier referred to the holy family's exile in Egypt, Wilde now mentions that Christ is the only god who died, having let his side be pierced by a sword. Christ then is weaker than Ammon, and, in this way, Wilde suggests that pagan mythology is more vital than Christian mythology. The speaker's reflections on love become orthodox at the end; he feels he should contemplate the crucifix and not the Sphinx. He returns to a world of penitence where Christ watches and cries for every soul, but the speaker sees the tears as futile. The poem then raises the question of whether human beings can be redeemed from their fallen condition.

THE BALLAD OF READING GAOL

Wilde's most famous poem, *The Ballad of Reading Gaol*, is a departure from any of the poems he had published previously. Sometimes overdone emotionally, the poem uses the prison as a metaphor for life and its cruelties. Wilde is the observer rather than the subject; in this way, he distances himself from his own experiences. The poem raises the thematic question of why man is cruel to other men, so cruel that he always destroys what he loves. It is through cruelty that men kill or destroy the ones they love, just as the prisoner whom Wilde observes, and who is soon to hang, murdered his lover. The mystery of man's cruelty was the mystery of the Sphinx

in Wilde's previous poem, but here the issue is the agony of the mystery rather than the decadent glory of cruelty, as in *The Sphinx*.

Wilde exploits the Gothic elements of the situation, dwelling on the macabre details of the grave of quicklime which dissolves the murderer's body. He uses the dread and gloom of the prisoners' lives to heighten the tone, but he often becomes shrill and melodramatic by emphasizing details such as the bag that covers the head of the condemned, tears falling like molten lead from the other prisoners as they observe the condemned, terror personified as a ghost, and the greasy rope used for the hanging. Ironically, the surviving prisoners are bedeviled by terror and horror, while the condemned dies calmly and serenely. Wilde uses a simple six-line stanza for a forcefully direct effect. The short lines alternate three and four feet of iambic pentameter with masculine rhyming of the second, fourth, and sixth lines. The stanza form is not one which suggests a reflective tone but rather a direct, emotional one.

The concluding motif of the poem is religious. The prison is a place of shame, where brother mistreats brother. Christ could feel only shame at what he sees his children do to each other there; but he rescues sinful man when he is broken by suffering and death. Even though the body of the hanged had no prayers said over it before interment in the quicklime, Christ rescued his soul. The surviving prisoners, their hearts broken and contrite, also gain salvation from the effects of their suffering.

POEMS IN PROSE

Wilde's *Poems in Prose* was the last collection published of all his poems except *The Ballad of Reading Gaol*, and the reader hears a different voice from that of the other poems, satirical and paradoxical like William Blake's in *The Marriage of Heaven and Hell* (1790). In Wilde's hands, the prose poem is a debonair and provocative parable on religious subjects. More often than not in his six prose poems, Wilde is trying to shock the bourgeoisie out of complacency and religious orthodoxy.

"The Artist" sets the tone of the prose poems; in this piece, the artist forsakes the oppressive sorrow of Christianity for the pursuit of hedonism. It is this kind of ironic reversal which the other prose poems also develop. In "The Doer of Good," Christ returns to find sinners and lepers he has saved or cured delighting in the sin, no longer wrong, from which he saved them. The one person whom Christ saved from death wishes that Christ had left him dead. "The House of Judgment" ironically shows the sinner complaining that his earthly life was hellish, and, confronted now with Heaven, he has no conception of it after his life of suffering. The most moving of the six is "The Teacher of Wisdom," in which Wilde shows that the finest act of man is to teach the wisdom of God. A hermit, having attained the knowledge of God, refuses to part with it by giving it to the young sinner who is imploring him. Frustrated, the sinner returns to sin, but, in so doing, extracts the knowledge from the hermit, who hopes to turn the sinner away from more sin. Fearing that he has parted with his knowledge, the hermit is consoled by God, who now, for his sacrifice, grants him a true love of God. In this parable, Wilde has transcended the satiric wit of the other parables to teach through irony.

OTHER MAJOR WORKS

LONG FICTION: *The Picture of Dorian Gray*, 1890 (serial), 1891 (expanded).

SHORT FICTION: "The Canterville Ghost," 1887; *The Happy Prince and Other Tales*, 1888; *A House of Pomegranates*, 1891; *Lord Arthur Savile's Crime and Other Stories*, 1891.

PLAYS: *Vera: Or, The Nihilists*, pb. 1880; *The Duchess of Padua*, pb. 1883; *Lady Windermere's Fan*, pb. 1892; *Salomé*, pb. 1893 (in French. pb. 1894); *A Woman of No Importance*, pr. 1893; *An Ideal Husband*, pr. 1895; *The Importance of Being Earnest: A Trivial Comedy for Serious People*, pr. 1895; *A Florentine Tragedy*, pr. 1906 (one act; completed by T. Sturge More); *La Sainte Courtisane*, pb. 1908.

NONFICTION: *Intentions*, 1891; *De Profundis*, 1905; *Letters*, 1962 (Rupert Hart-Davies, editor).

MISCELLANEOUS: *Works*, 1908; *Complete Works of Oscar Wilde*, 1948 (Vyvyan Holland, editor); *Plays, Prose Writings, and Poems*, 1960.

BIBLIOGRAPHY

Beckson, Karl E. *The Oscar Wilde Encyclopedia*. New York: AMS Press, 1998. At nearly five hundred pages, a compendium of useful information on Wilde and his times.

Ellmann, Richard. *Oscar Wilde*. New York: Alfred A. Knopf, 1988. In this comprehensive six-hundred-page study of Wilde's life, Ellmann argues that Wilde was conducting an examination of society and a reconsideration of its ethics. Not only has his best writing not lost its relevance, Ellmann believes, but his findings were always right. Supplemented by notes, a select bibliography, two appendices, and a detailed forty-nine-page index.

Eriksen, Donald H. *Oscar Wilde*. Boston: Twayne, 1977. This small volume is a useful corrective to studies of Wilde that see him and his work as anomalies of literature and history. After a brief chapter on Wilde's life and times, Eriksen makes critical and analytical assessments of his poetry, fiction, essays, and drama. A chronology, notes and references, an annotated bibliography, and an index supplement the text.

Gagnier, Regenia A. *Idylls of the Marketplace: Oscar Wilde and the Victorian Public*. Palo Alto, Calif.: Stanford University Press, 1986. This erudite study attempts to reach an understanding of Wilde by focusing less on his life and work and more on the relation of his work to his audiences. Leaning heavily on contemporary critical theory, it connects Wilde, Friedrich Engels, and Fyodor Dostoevski in ways that some may find more confusing than illuminating, but Gagnier's readings of the works are generally insightful and persuasive. Supplemented with a bibliography and an index.

Kohl, Norbert. *Oscar Wilde: The Works of a Conformist Rebel*. Translated by David Henry Wilson. Cambridge, England: Cambridge University Press, 1989. Interprets Wilde's works mainly through textual analysis, although it includes discussions of the society in which Wilde lived and to which he responded. Kohl argues that Wilde was not the imitator he is often accused of being but a creative adapter of the literary traditions he inherited. Supplemented by detailed notes, a lengthy bibliography, and an index.

McCormack, Jerusha Hull. *The Man Who Was Dorian Gray*. New York: St. Martin's Press, 2000. John Gray, the supposed model for Wilde's most famous character, is profiled in this examination of the life of a decadent poet turned priest. Although not focused on the poetry, this work reveals much about early twentieth century literary society and the emerging gay culture.

Miller, Robert Keith. *Oscar Wilde*. New York: Frederick Ungar, 1982. This 152-page study is a useful introduction to Wilde and his work. The opening chapter reviews his biography, and subsequent chapters condense earlier critical analyses of *The Picture of Dorian Gray*, the plays, and the fairy tales. The sixth chapter discusses *The Ballad of Reading Gaol*, which Miller admires, and the last chapter contains an objective evaluation of Wilde as an aesthete and an artist. Includes a lengthy chronology, notes, a brief bibliography, and an index.

Pearce, Joseph. *The Unmasking of Oscar Wilde*. London: HarperCollins, 2000. Pearce avoids lingering on the actions that brought Wilde notoriety and instead explores Wilde's emotional and spiritual search. Along with a discussion of *The Ballad of Reading Gaol* and the posthumously published *De Profundis*, Pearce also traces Wilde's fascination with Catholicism.

Raby, Peter. *Oscar Wilde*. Cambridge, England: Cambridge University Press, 1988. One of a series of excellent introductory critical studies to English and Irish authors. Includes biographical information because, Raby argues, it is most useful to see Wilde as indivisible from his works. The 1881 collection of poems, he says, makes it clear that Wilde's artistic purpose was a life's work. Supplemented with a chronology, notes, a bibliography, and an index.

Shewan, Rodney. *Oscar Wilde: Art and Egotism*. New York: Barnes & Noble Books, 1977. In this illuminating study, Shewan sees Wilde's attitude toward art reflected in John Keats and Percy Bysshe Shelley: Wilde devoted his career to exploring the self and applied his life to self-expression and self-dramatization. Supplementary material consists of a chronology, a bibliography, and an index.

Varty, Anne. *A Preface to Oscar Wilde: Preface Books*. New York: Longman, 1998. An introduction to the life and works, particularly the period 1890-1895.

Some discussion of earlier work provides view of some of the motivating forces behind his output. Also offers a chapter on his circle. Index.

Wilde, Oscar. *The Complete Letters of Oscar Wilde*. Edited by Merlin Holland and Rupert Hart-Davis. New York: Henry Holt, 2000. A collection of correspondence including previously unpublished letters that unveil the full extent of Wilde's genius in an intimate exploration of his life and thoughts. Includes bibliographical references and indexes.

Dennis Goldsberry;
bibliography updated by the editors

C. K. WILLIAMS

Born: Newark, New Jersey; November 4, 1936

PRINCIPAL POETRY
A Day for Anne Frank, 1968
Lies, 1969
I Am the Bitter Name, 1972
The Sensuous President, 1972
With Ignorance, 1977
Tar, 1983
Flesh and Blood, 1987
Poems, 1963-1983, 1988
A Dream of Mind, 1992
Selected Poems, 1994
New and Selected Poems, 1995
The Vigil, 1997
Repair, 1999
Love About Love, 2001

OTHER LITERARY FORMS

In collaboration with classical scholars, C. K. Williams has written verse translations of two Greek tragedies: one, in 1978, of Sophocles' *Trachinai* (435-429 B.C.E.; *The Women of Trachis*), and the other, in 1985, of Euripides' *Bakchai* (405 B.C.E.; *The Bacchae*). The translations, as their notes indicate, are for the modern stage as well as for modern readers. Williams hopes for a flowering of the "kernel" of Sophocles' tragedy within the translator's historical moment, "a clearing away of some of the accumulations of reverence that confuse the work and the genius who made them." The translations are thus not staid or literal but do aim for thematic accuracy and life. Williams also translated poems from Issa under the title *The Lark, the Thrush, the Starling* (1983). He has also translated *Selected Poems of Francis Ponge* (1994) and *Canvas*, by Adam Zagajewski (1991, with Renata Gorczynski and Benjamin Ivry). Personal and critical essays are collected in *Poetry and Consciousness* (1998), and Williams has produced an award-winning memoir, *Misgivings: My Mother, My Father, Myself* (2000).

ACHIEVEMENTS

C. K. Williams has received many and various recognitions. These include a Guggenheim Fellowship, the Bernard F. Conner Prize for the long poem by *The Paris Review* in 1983, the Lila Wallace-Reader's Digest Award, the Berlin Prize, and the PEN/Voelcker Award. *Flesh and Blood* won the National Book Critics Circle Award, and *Repair* won both the Pulitzer Prize and the *Los Angeles Times* Award for Poetry. His memoir, *Misgivings*, won the PEN America Center 2001 Literary Award.

BIOGRAPHY

Born November 4, 1936, in Newark, New Jersey, the son of Paul B. and Dossie (né Kasdin) Williams, Charles Kenneth Williams was educated at Bucknell University and at the University of Pennsylvania, where he was graduated with a B.A. in 1959. In 1965, he married Sarah Jones, and they had one daughter, Jessica Anne, who figures in Williams's personal poems. At the Pennsylvania Hospital in Philadelphia, he founded a program of poetry therapy and was a group therapist for disturbed adolescents.

A Day for Anne Frank led to the publication of two volumes of poetry in 1969 and 1972 that established Williams as a protest poet of the Nixon era. In 1975, Williams married Catherine Mauger, a jeweler, and with her had one son. He was a visiting professor at Franklin and Marshall College in 1977 and at the University of California at Irvine in 1978 before becoming professor of English at George Mason University. After spending

C. K. Williams (© Jim Kallet)

many years at George Mason, he joined the creative writing faculty at Princeton in 1996. In addition, he has taught creative writing at various workshops and colleges, including Boston University and Columbia University.

ANALYSIS

C. K. Williams achieved early success in the era of cynicism and protest surrounding the Vietnam War. His early work sketches in a tough, cryptic style the nightmare visions of a godforsaken world. *I Am the Bitter Name* is a howl of protest against the various corruptions of the world, lacking even the tonal variety and scant hope of his earlier work. Though powerful, Williams's protest poetry was seen by critics as an artistic dead end.

During the five-year interim between the publication of *I Am the Bitter Name* and *With Ignorance*, Williams remade his style, writing in long lines which fold back from the margin of the page and tell stories with prose-like lucidity. The sense of human suffering and isolation common in the earlier poems remains, but the long-line poems narrate dramatic tales set in American cities:

scenes of family life, recollections of childhood, and views from the windows of urban apartments. Exact description and conventional punctuation replace the blurred grammar and dreamlike flow of the earlier verse. The later Williams poses in his poems as a sympathetic survivor who, seeing clearly the complexities and disillusionment of contemporary life, shares astonishing personal associations with the reader.

Stylistic originality distinguished C. K. Williams's earliest work, and he has continued to evolve as a poet. Consistent in all periods of his work has been a "metaphysical" roughness and avoidance of merely literary polish. Meanwhile, he has treated frightening realities which are not conventionally subjects of poetry. His experimental style began with dreamlike lyrics with short run-on lines, sporadic punctuation, and startling leaps of image and diction. Strident in tone, sometimes shocking, the early poems found quick acceptance in the Nixon years.

LIES

Lies includes the long poem *A Day for Anne Frank*, which was published in a limited edition a year before it. In *Lies*, Williams anatomizes the horrors of modern history and existential despair. The absence of divine order grounds a series of nightmare visions with titles such as "Don't," "The Long Naked Walk of the Dead," "Loss," "Trash," "Downward," "Our Grey," and "It Is This Way with Men," which allegorizes men as spikes driven into the ground, pounded each time they attempt to rise. Williams's universe is the indifferent or hostile one of classic American naturalism, but it takes much of its apocalyptic substance from the Holocaust and from the Vietnam War. In spite of the negativity of his lyric outcries against suffering and waste, Williams's early poems burn, not only with terror but also with a passion that things should be better. Optimism, authority, and poetic form are smashed like atoms. Williams's complaint is that of the child-man against the parent universe in which he finds himself an unloved stepson.

There is monotony, even callowness, in this stance, in improbable metaphors and scatological language flaunted for shock value—expressing a gnostic rejection of his prison-body in the inhospitable universe. Nevertheless, *Lies* was critically acclaimed for its fusion of moral seriousness and verbal ingenuity. It concludes

with the long poem about Anne Frank, the quintessential victim of history; to borrow a comparison from one of Williams's poems, she was like a little box turtle run over by a bus. "It's horrible," he says in that lyric. *A Day for Anne Frank* displays the horrible motto "God hates you!"

I AM THE BITTER NAME

I Am the Bitter Name takes the technique of *Lies* one step further toward the abolition of technique—one step too far, most critics have argued. More homogeneous than *Lies*, this collection appears to try for and achieve self-portraits of apocalyptic incoherence. The poet displays, piled like monstrous fish, the products of his vigorous dredging of his nightmare unconscious. Critic Jascha Kessler, in one of the more positive reviews of Williams's work, catalogs his strengths and failings: "the simplicity, clarity of diction, haste and jumbling of his thought by the unremitting stroboscopic, kaleidoscopic pulsing of a voice from thought to speech to image to unvoiced thought." Impressed that the source of Williams's expression is valid, calling the book "real poems," Kessler is nevertheless disoriented by it. Other critics were less positive, charging that Williams's passionate flailings missed their targets or even dismissing the poems as sentimental and blurred.

As the tonal consistency of *I Am the Bitter Name* suggests, and as his later work confirms, Williams is a deliberate experimental stylist. Purged of commas, capitals, and periods, the poems sprout unpredictable question marks, exclamation points, and quotations. The sense spills over the ends of the short, jagged lines, so that it becomes almost a rule in these poems that a line end does *not* signal a break in sense. The effect is one of breathlessness, of a mind that, insofar as it is conscious at all, barely understands what it is saying. The reader seems to be hearing the raw emotive material of poetry at the moment of creation. Williams's vocabulary, too, suggests breathless, regressive speech, almost childishly simple but scatological—especially in the political poems. The voice again suggests a righteous man-child, outraged to surreal protest by the extent to which the real God and the real governments betray his standards.

Sometimes the words in *I Am the Bitter Name* are explicitly political, as in "A Poem for the Governments." This poem offers itself as an onion to make governments cry for the family of the imprisoned Miguel Hernandes, whose family has nothing but onions to eat. Reminding "mr old men" how they have eaten Miguel and "everything good in the world," the poem becomes "one onion/ your history" and concludes self-referentially, "eat this." Such explicit ordering of metaphor, common in *Lies*, is not the rule in *I Am the Bitter Name*, where even poems on political subjects dissolve into cryptic collisions of word and image. "The Admiral Fan," for example, begins with a "lady from the city" removing her girdle and baring her "white backside" in a barnyard and dissolves into a vision of her dismemberment, apparently not only by farm animals but also by a Washington lobbyist in a long car. She is emptied of "dolls." Her breasts become "dawn amity peace exaltation" in a vegetable field identified—as the grammar blurs—with nothingness, and flashing stoplights. Like the poems of André Breton, these let go even of grammatical structure in submission to the uprush of image and emotion.

WITH IGNORANCE

Between 1972 and 1977, Williams was divorced, was remarried, and received grants and teaching appointments; during this time, he dramatically reinvented his poetic style. Except for its closing title poem, *With Ignorance* withdraws from the nightmare abyss and grounds its associations on human stories expressed in conventionally punctuated long lines with all the clarity of good prose. The change was presumably as much psychological as stylistic. The mature Williams, turned forty, tells his daughter that he has already had the bad dreams: "what comes now is calm and abstract." Later, in "Friends," he stands outside the terrors of his earlier poems to observe that "visions I had then were all death: they were hideous and absurd and had nothing to do with my life." The style of these self-possessed reflections is easy informal prose, the style of a personal letter refined in its very plainness, which sets the stage in the more effective poems for sudden outbreaks of metaphysical anguish or human pathos equal to the best of his earlier verse.

In "The Sanctity," Williams remembers going home with a married coworker from a construction site and seeing homicidal hostility between his friend's mother and wife, and the coworker's rage—a dark side of his character wholly masked by the ironic idyll of the work-

place. The construction site is the only place, apparently, where the workmen feel joy, where they feel in power. Printed sources prompt some of the incantatory stories: an SS officer spitting into a rabbi's mouth to help him defile the Torah, until they are kissing like lovers; a girl paralyzed by a stray police bullet. Williams draws, however, usually from his experience: a veteran met in a bar, a friend in a mental hospital, an old bum seen after a marital quarrel, a girl he "stabbed" with a piece of "broken-off car antenna" when he was eight. Here, in grotesque anecdotes, Williams again examines the irrational in human life, the inevitable discord and suffering, but with a sympathy for recognizable human faces and characters missing from most of his earlier work. Political concerns are implicit in the presence of veterans and police bullets, but there is no preaching. The one short poem not narrative is "Hog Heaven," which begins, "It stinks," and develops in biblical repetitions and variations an enveloping nausea for the flesh, a theme and method common in the protest poems but expanded here in limber, Whitmanesque lines.

TAR

Tar demonstrates greater mastery of the anecdotal long-line style, telling longer and more complex stories with more restraint and power and returning at times to openly political themes. The title poem recalls the day of the near-disaster at the Three Mile Island nuclear plant, which was also a day of roofing work on the narrator's apartment building. Without ceasing to be themselves, the workmen become both trolls from the underworld and representatives of vulnerable humanity, their black tar-pots associated with the nuclear threat to the north. Williams's old vision of the apocalypse is here, but the symbols are stronger because they move in a narrative with a persuasive surface of its own. Williams is reclaiming techniques many contemporary poets have abandoned to fiction. As he masters the long-line narrative style, the lines become less plain—not necessarily more ornate, but more susceptible to ornamentation without losing their naturalness and tone of the grotesque.

Some of the poems in *Tar* begin with nature imagery and are leavened by it, though the suffering face of the city still always shows. "From My Window," for example, begins with the first fragrances of spring, budding sycamore, crocus spikes, a pretty girl jogging—but this is only an overture to the movement outside the narrator's window of two alcoholic veterans, one of whom is in a wheelchair, and their tragicomic accident in the street, which reveals the unlovely, childlike nakedness of the crippled one. Like many of Williams's narratives, this one takes a sudden turn near the end, recalling the able-bodied veteran pacing wildly in a vacant lot in falling snow, struggling to leave his imprint while the buildings stare coldly down.

Tar is almost as much a book of short fictions as of poems; characters include a man falling in love with a black woman who walks her hideously ill dog outside his window, a boy awakening to night terrors in the city, a decaying luxury hotel taken over by drug users, mental patients, and old women. A pornographic tintype centers a fantasy on immigrant life; a welterweight fighter awakens memories of a German widow, a refugee following her husband's plot against Adolf Hitler, who encouraged her daughter's affair with the narrator—as if his Jewishness could expiate her guilt. Two of the most interesting poems, "Neglect" and "The Regulars," narrate no unusual events but are minimal narrative sketches of a bus layover in a faded coal town and old men in a neighborhood undergoing gentrification—short stories in their use of description and dialogue, but in the cadences of Williams's taut, long lines.

FLESH AND BLOOD

Some of the poems in *Tar* use quatrains, four long lines clustered and endstopped. In *Flesh and Blood*, Williams invents and writes a sequence of lines in a form comparable to the sonnet in length and rhetorical structure, eight lines of about twenty syllables each, usually shifting direction after the fifth line. Moving away from the extended stories of earlier works, Williams does not lose focus on the pathos and character of the urban world, but, necessarily, his tales shrink into the frame—either to vignettes or to terse summaries like a gossiping conversation. Williams portrays victims of stroke and Alzheimer's disease, a poetry-loving bum, an unhappy wife, a sobbing child, a girlfriend who hates her body, and, in one subsequence, readers in a variety of places and poses.

There is always clarity in these portrait poems, usually wisdom and complexity, but little of the frenzy that burned in the earlier work. *Flesh and Blood* includes poems that develop allegorical subjects in abstract language, despite earlier critical disapproval of this method—particularly in "One of the Muses," the only poem in *Tar* which critics judged a failure. It is Williams's way, however, to take chances. His characteristic strength is his restlessness and formal creativity—his refusal to remain confined within a style after he has mastered it.

THE VIGIL

In the 1990's, Williams continued to expand his range, refine his art, and please greater numbers of readers and critics. In *The Vigil*, Williams again employs, with little variety, the long, rolling, syntactically suspenseful line that is not a line at all—at least not a conventionally measured line. Though Williams gives the reader rich stretches of intellectual and philosophical rumination, critic Richard Howard is probably correct in asserting that this technique works best in narrative and descriptive passages, in which Williams excels. It also works well in the poem or passage that is based on inventorying or list-making. In this volume, the eight-part sequence titled "Symbols" succeeds as a fine, organic correlation of Williams's aesthetic medium and his subject and theme.

REPAIR

Repair represents the work of a mature poet not only polishing a technique that is comfortable while applying his formula to new subjects, but also an artist for whom new experiences dictate formal departures. Perhaps this combination of factors—a rich and distinctive thirty-year body of work and evidence of new directions—brought this volume the Pulitzer Prize. Many of the poems on *Repair* are only newly finished; Williams had worked on them for many years and they have a familiar feel to those who have learned to read his work. Other poems have a more conventional stanza pattern and shorter lines than much of Williams's earlier work. One poem that has to do with his experiences as a grandfather takes the poet and the reader into new territory. Some will feel that the physical smallness and the youth of the grandchild gave rise to the unexpected short line in "Owen: Seven Days." Williams has commented on simply hearing a new, more jagged music that required what for him is an uncharacteristic prosodic result. Many of the poems, like the magnificent "Invisible Mending," have to do with reconciliation and acceptance. These activities of the heart, which are among the key meanings of the book's title, indicate the inner place that Williams has reached in the arc of life reflected in his poems, an arc begun in protest and anger.

OTHER MAJOR WORKS

NONFICTION: *Poetry and Consciousness*, 1998; *Misgivings: My Mother, My Father, Myself*, 2000.

TRANSLATIONS: *Women of Trachis*, 1978 (of Sophocles' play *Trachinai*; with Gregory Dickerson); *The Lark, the Thrush, the Starling*, 1983 (of poems by Issa); *The Bacchae*, 1985 (of Euripides' play *Bakchai*; with H. Golder); *Canvas*, 1991 (of Adam Zagajewski's poems; with Renata Gorczynski and Benjamin Ivry); *Selected Poems of Francis Ponge*, 1994.

BIBLIOGRAPHY

Bawer, Bruce. Review of *Tar*, by C. K. Williams. *Poetry* 144 (September, 1984): 353-355. Praises *Tar* for its portraiture, citing "Waking Jed" and "The Color of Time" as the best of the collection. Compares Williams to Walt Whitman, but says the former has more warmth and intensity of feeling. Argues that *Tar* is a reminder not only of "what poetry is all about, but what life is all about." An appreciative review.

Coles, Robert. Review of *With Ignorance*, by C. K. Williams. *The American Poetry Review* 8 (July/August, 1979): 12-13. Likens Williams to Søren Kierkegaard because both stay in the world while "groping for inner truth." Coles says Williams has achieved in these poems a "humble intelligence" and considers the task in these poems as a journey fraught with challenges.

Howard, Richard. Review of *The Vigil*, by C. K. Williams. *Boston Review*, Summer, 1997. Although Howard has serious and well-expressed reservations about the formal imposition of an extremely long line, he allows himself to admire those poems and passages in which Williams's technique works effectively. Howard praises Williams's successes in rendering "immediacy of sensation."

Phillips, Brian. "Plainly, but with Flair." *New Republic*, September 18, 2000, 42-45. Phillips reviews both *Repair* and the memoir *Misgivings*. He objects to Williams's habit of moralizing and of glossing the beginning of a poem at the end. Williams forces the reader away from direct experience toward a preferred comprehension. This habit undermines his great descriptive powers. Phillips also notes the tension between Williams's colloquial diction and his erudite range of references.

Riding, Alan. "American Bard in Paris Stokes Poetic Home Fires." *The New York Times*, October 4, 2000, p. E4. This flavorful piece of biographical journalism treats Williams's relationship with Paris as well as the patterns of his writing and teaching careers.

Santos, Sherod. "A Solving Emptiness: C. K. Williams and Charles Wright." In his *A Poetry of Two Minds*. Athens: University of Georgia Press, 2000. In a comparison of mid-career poems by both poets, Santos examines parallel aesthetic experimentation and the determination to overcome despair through art.

William H. Green,
updated by Philip K. Jason

MILLER WILLIAMS

Born: Hoxie, Arkansas; April 8, 1930

PRINCIPAL POETRY

A Circle of Stone, 1964
Recital, 1964
So Long at the Fair, 1968
The Only World There Is, 1971
Halfway from Hoxie, 1977
Why God Permits Evil: New Poems, 1977
Distractions, 1981
The Boys on Their Bony Mules, 1983
Imperfect Love, 1986
Living on the Surface: New and Selected Poems, 1989
Adjusting to the Light, 1992

Points of Departure, 1995
The Ways We Touch, 1997
Some Jazz a While: Collected Poems, 1998

OTHER LITERARY FORMS

In addition to his works of poetry, Miller Williams's books include literary criticism, translations, works on prosody, and anthologies of poetry and fiction. The list includes a history of American railroads (with James A. McPherson), translations from the work of Nicanor Parra and Giuiseppe Belli, critical analyses on John Crowe Ransom and John Ciardi, and a standard reference on prosodics titled *Patterns of Poetry: An Encyclopedia of Forms* (1986). He has also edited anthologies of poetry and has published many of his own poems, stories, critical essays, and translations in journals in the United States and abroad.

ACHIEVEMENTS

Miller Williams has been awarded the Henry Bellaman Poetry Prize, the Amy Lowell Award in Poetry from Harvard University, the New York Arts Fund Award for Significant Contribution to American Letters, the Prix de Rome for Literature and the Academy Award for Literature, both from the American Academy of Arts and Letters, the Poets' Prize, the Charity Randall Citation for Contribution to Poetry as a Spoken Art from the International Poetry Forum, and the John William Corrington Award for Literary Excellence. He has also received honorary doctorates from Lander College and Hendrix College. In 1994 he was named Socio Benemerito dell'Associazione, Centro Romanesco Trilussa, Roma. He was the inaugural poet for the second inauguration of President Bill Clinton. In 1999 the multinational editorial board of *Voices International* named him one of the best twenty poets in the world writing in English. He was selected one of the five hundred most important poets of all languages in the twentieth century, for inclusion by Roth Publishing Company on the compact disc *Poetry of Our Time*.

BIOGRAPHY

Miller Williams was born on April 8, 1930, in Hoxie, Arkansas, the son of a Methodist minister. He received a B.S. in zoology from Arkansas State College and completed his M.S. at the University of Arkansas in Fayetteville, after which he became a science teacher. In 1961 he received a Bread Loaf Fellowship, and in 1962 he joined the English department of Louisiana State University.

In 1971 Williams moved to the University of Arkansas and joined the creative writing program, working with the graduate program in creative writing and in translation. His academic career has included serving as visiting professor of U.S. literature at the University of Chile and as Fulbright Professor of American Studies at the National University of Mexico. For seven years he was a member of the poetry faculty at the Bread Loaf Writers' Conference. In 1976 he was made a fellow of the American Academy in Rome.

He has represented the U.S. State Department on reading and lecturing tours throughout Latin America, Europe, and Asia. His stories, translations, poems, and critical essays have appeared in a variety of journals in English, and his poems have been translated into several languages.

He has served as president of the American Literary Translators Association, founding editor of the *New Orleans Review*, founding director of the University of Arkansas Press, and Latin American editor for the third edition of *Benet's Reader's Encyclopedia*. He was also named University Professor of English and Foreign Languages at the University of Arkansas.

ANALYSIS

Williams's poetry offers an insightful look at the preoccupations and concerns of his time, from the mundane to the metaphysical, presented with an emphasis on the ordinary and on conversational language. In addition, he so skillfully uses form, meter, and rhyme that the patterns of his poems do not announce themselves. In conversational, straightforward language, his poems include blank verse, sonnets, sestinas, villanelles, dramatic monologues, and other variations of the simple and the intricate. Williams's greatest strength as a poet may be how natural he makes the most intricate poetic forms sound on the page. As he says in "For All Our Great-Grandchildren": "If you can listen/ I'll try to make it not sound like a lesson." Williams takes as his task seeing the hidden behind the visible and turning it into art. In "Notes from the

Agent on Earth: How to Be Human," he provides a succinct summation of his work: "Life is change that finds a changing pattern;/ art is change we put a pattern to." While characterizing his wide body of poetry in overall terms proves impossible, several themes recur.

HUMOR

One of the first things one notices in Williams's work is the humor that plays out in humans' visions of themselves, in wordplay, and in worldview. Williams has said, "I think of most of my poems as having a touch of dark, hopefully ironic humor about them." Titles of individual poems exemplify this: "After You Die You Don't Give a Piddling Damn"; "Why God Permits Evil: For Answer to This Question of Interest to Many Write Bible Answers, Dept. E-7"; "Talking to Himself He Gets a Few Things Settled in His Mind"; "Note to God Concerning an Earlier Communication"; "In Your Own Words Without Lying Tell Something of Your Background with Particular Attention to Anything Relating to the Position for Which You Are Applying, Press Down."

Along with the humor provided by the narrators' and characters' views of themselves and their world, and what they misunderstand about it, Williams finds humor in wordplay. In "On a Trailways Bus a Man Who Holds His Head Strangely Speaks to the Seat Beside Him," the speaker tells those around him that "I thanked a woman twice and kissed her hand/ because she said I was a perfect stranger."

"Style" offers a humorous take on the fads of poetry, describing a man who made a series of circles on a page and decided to call it a poem, "Not wanting to waste the paper or the time" and "having a dean impressed with anything." The poem succeeds, is anthologized, and creates numerous requests "for explanations he never gives." The narrator tells us that some would call it poetry, "assuming of course that it was done sincerely."

Williams's humor, from the line level to the ironic vision of many poems, extends to himself as well. In "My Wife Reads the Paper at Breakfast on the Birthday of the Scottish Poet," after his wife mentions Robert Burns is to be honored, she says to the poet, "'They found you out.'"

WHAT IS LEFT UNSAID

Williams once said, "We live life as if it were what we wanted; we read a poem as if it got to the truth of our lives. It never does, but the poet fails only because we all

fail." Within the lines of his poetry, he comments on the inability of words to convey all that people intend and the attempts of poets to do so. In "On Hearing About the Death of Mitzi Mayfair," he says,

> There has never been a poem
> to explain anything.
> For that reason
> many people who would otherwise
> write poems do not.
> Praise such people.

Williams's poetry concerns the precise fact, concrete imagery, and visual detail, yet relies as well on what does not get said. In "For Rebecca, for Whom Nothing Has Been Written Page After Page" Williams writes, "What matters when all the words are written and read/ is what remains not said,/ which is what long silences are for." Williams also comments on how, and why, to write poetry. In "Let Me Tell You," he tells poets to "First notice everything," because "You cannot twist the fact you do not know," even though "Nothing is less important/ than a fact." He emphasizes conversational tone by including the following: "Be suspicious of any word you learned/ and were proud of learning./ It will go bad." The reader is told to "take notes" on the tragedies as well as the trivialities of life in order to write poetry. The potential power of that poetry becomes clear in "Form and Theory of Poetry," which compares it to the power of a hurricane.

COMMENTING ON HUMAN NATURE

Much of Williams's work deals with individual human beings and the moments of insight, tragedy, triumph, failure, and routine in their lives. In "The Associate Professor Delivers an Exhortation to His Failing Students," what binds humans together is their fears, which the professor asks his students to list, to "Make a catechism" of, for "These are the gravity that holds us together/ toward our common sun." He tells his students that if they are ever asked "the only thing that matters after all," they should say "failing is an act of love/ because/ like sin/ it is the commonality within."

In Williams's poems, the reader sees a man having a moment of great insight, about to be lost on a bus ("One of Those Rare Occurrences on a City Bus"); a man who stopped at an accident but failed to wait for the ambulance to arrive ("Accident: A Short Story"); a senator rationalizing his decisions ("A Senator Explains a Vote"); an actress asking "How would you like it, never being able/ to grow old all together, to have yourself/ from different times of your life running around?" ("The Aging Actress Sees Herself a Starlet on the Late Show"); a truck-stop waitress recounting her life ("Ruby Tells All"); and various interpretations of Judas' act ("Think of Judas That He Did Love Jesus"). All these characters, and many more, illustrate moments of doubt, anxiety, insight, or regret.

Williams said, "I like a poem to be a little short story." Nowhere is that more evident than his character sketches, where ordinary, believable human beings wrangle with love, hate, death, despair, faith, and disappointment. Whether offering an epiphany or an illusion, his characters illuminate human nature in both the abstract and the particular. Many characters also illustrate the subjective nature of living in one's own head, how individual human beings create the meaning around them. In "Believing in Symbols," the narrator ponders the blinking number eight on his broken calculator, "the figure all the figures are made from," and notes the importance of symbols: "Believing in symbols has led us into war,/ if sometimes into bed with interesting people." In "The True Story of What Happened," the narrator sees an airplane fly by and imagines, when it is out of sight, that it has therefore crashed: "Inside my head two hundred seventy people/ including a crew of eleven disappeared/ leaving no trace but only vacancies."

QUESTIONS OF RELIGION

Often, religion plays a part in the characters' caught moments. From the preacher "building the gospel work by believable word/ out of the wooden syllables of the South (from "And When in Scenes of Glory") to the preacher's admission that "What we call acts and scientists call events/ are equally beyond us" (from "During the Hymn before the Christmas Sermon the Mind of the Young Preacher Wanders Again"), questions of God and the devil, Heaven and Hell, faith and doubt recur. On one hand, "What do we know that matters that Aeschylus did not know?" (from "After the Revolution for Jesus a Secular Man Prepares His Final Remarks"). On the other hand, what people do not, and cannot, know remains both reassuring and terrifying. In "If Every Person There Is but One," the reader is told to "Think of whatever moves as God/ or if nothing moves/ think how still we stand."

OTHER MAJOR WORKS

NONFICTION: *The Poetry of John Crowe Ransom*, 1972; *How Does a Poem Mean?*, 1975 (with John Ciardi); *Patterns of Poetry: An Encyclopedia of Forms*, 1986.

TRANSLATIONS: *Poems and Antipoems*, 1967 (of Nicanor Parra); *Emergency Poems*, 1972 (of Parra); *Sonnets of Giuiseppe Belli*, 1981.

EDITED TEXTS: *Southern Writing in the Sixties: Fiction and Poetry*, 1966-1967 (2 volumes; with John William Corrington); *Chile: Contemporary Writing in the Longest Land*, 1967; *Chile: An Anthology of New Writing*, 1968; *Contemporary Poetry in America*, 1973; *Railroad: Trains and Train People in American Culture*, 1976 (with James A. McPherson); *A Roman Collection*, 1980; *Ozark, Ozark*, 1981.

MISCELLANEOUS: *The Achievement of John Ciardi*, 1969 (critical introduction by Williams).

BIBLIOGRAPHY

Baker, David. "To Advantage Dressed: Miller Williams Among the Naked Poets." *The Southern Review* 26, no. 4 (Autumn, 1990): 814. Discusses Williams's development of a "verbal style" that draws readers into his work.

Burns, Michael, ed. *Miller Williams and the Poetry of the Particular*. Columbia: University of Missouri Press, 1991. A collection of essays on Williams and his poetry, including entries by Howard Nemerov, Maxine Kumin, and X. J. Kennedy. It also includes an interview with Williams.

Cifelli, Edward M. "The Poems of Miller Williams: Poetry from Illinois." *Art & Letters: A Journal of Contemporary Culture*, Fall, 2000. A review of the collected poems by the University of Illinois Press.

Quinn, Judy. "Inauguration Day Will Be Miller Time." *Publishers Weekly* 244, no. 1 (January 6, 1997): 20. Williams discusses his poem for President Bill Clinton's inauguration and the collection *The Ways We Touch* (1997).

Caroline Carvill

WILLIAM CARLOS WILLIAMS

Born: Rutherford, New Jersey; September 17, 1883
Died: Rutherford, New Jersey; March 4, 1963

PRINCIPAL POETRY

Poems, 1909
The Tempers, 1913
Al Que Quiere!, 1917
Kora in Hell: Improvisations, 1920
Sour Grapes, 1921
Spring and All, 1923
Collected Poems, 1921-1931, 1934
An Early Martyr and Other Poems, 1935
Adam & Eve & The City, 1936
*The Complete Collected Poems of William Carlos
    Williams, 1906-1938*, 1938
The Broken Span, 1941
The Wedge, 1944
Paterson, 1946-1958
The Clouds, 1948
Selected Poems, 1949
Collected Later Poems, 1950, 1963
Collected Earlier Poems, 1951
The Desert Music and Other Poems, 1954
Journey to Love, 1955
Pictures from Brueghel, 1962
Selected Poems, 1985
*The Collected Poems of William Carlos Williams:
    Volume I, 1909-1939*, 1986
*The Collected Poems of William Carlos Williams:
    Volume II, 1939-1962*, 1988

OTHER LITERARY FORMS

William Carlos Williams is best known for his poetry, but he did not limit himself to that form. His short-story collections include *The Knife of the Times and Other Stories* (1932), *Life Along the Passaic River* (1938), *Make Light of It: Collected Stories* (1950), and *The Farmers' Daughters: The Collected Stories of William Carlos Williams* (1961). Among his novels are *The Great American Novel* (1923), *A Voyage to Pagany* (1928), and the Stecher trilogy, composed of *White Mule* (1937), *In the Money* (1940), and *The Build-up* (1952),

and his best-known collection of plays is *Many Loves and Other Plays* (1961). He also wrote criticism and an autobiography. His essay collections include *In the American Grain* (1925) and *Selected Essays of William Carlos Williams* (1954). In addition, he and his mother translated Philippe Soupault's *Last Nights of Paris* (1929) and Don Francisco de Quevedo's *A Dog and the Fever* (1954).

ACHIEVEMENTS

William Carlos Williams's recognition was late in coming, although he received the Dial Award for Services to American Literature in 1926 for the "Paterson" poem and the Guarantor's Prize from *Poetry* in 1931; Louis Zukofsky's Objectivist number of *Poetry* in 1931 featured Williams. The critics, other poets and writers, as well as the public, however, largely ignored his poetry until 1946, when *Paterson*, Book I appeared. From that time on, his recognition increased steadily. He was made a fellow of the Library of Congress, 1948-1949, and appointed consultant in poetry to the Library of Congress in 1952, even though he never served because of political opposition to his alleged left-wing principles. In 1948 he received the Russell Loines Award for *Paterson*, Book II, and in 1950 the National Book Award for *Selected Poems* and *Paterson*, Book III; in 1953 he shared with Archibald MacLeish the Bollingen Prize for excellence in contemporary verse. Finally, in May, 1963, he was awarded posthumously the Pulitzer Prize and Gold Medal for Poetry for *Pictures from Brueghel*.

BIOGRAPHY

William Carlos Williams was born in Rutherford, New Jersey, on September 17, 1883. His father (William George Williams) was an Englishman who never gave up his British citizenship, and his mother (Raquel Hélène Rose Hoheb, known as "Elena") was a Puerto Rican of Basque, Dutch, Spanish, and Jewish descent. His father was an Episcopalian who turned Unitarian and his mother was Roman Catholic. He was educated at schools in New York City and briefly in Europe and was graduated with a medical degree from the University of Pennsylvania in 1909. After an internship in New York City and graduate study in pediatrics in Leipzig, he returned to his native Rutherford, where he practiced medicine until he retired. In 1909 he proposed to Florence (Floss) Herman and in 1912 they were married. Their first son, William Eric Williams, was born in 1914 and their second, Paul Herman Williams, in 1916.

Williams, a melting pot in himself, had deep roots as a second-generation citizen of the United States. From early in his life he felt that America was his only home and that he must possess her in order to know himself. Possessing the America of the past and the present would enable him to renew himself continually and find his own humanity. Unlike many writers of his generation who went to Europe, such as his friend Ezra Pound, Williams committed himself to living in America because he believed he had to live in a place to be able to grasp it imaginatively.

Williams met Ezra Pound when they were both at the University of Pennsylvania; their friendship was fierce and uneven throughout their lives. While at the University, he also met Hilda Doolittle (H. D.) and the painter Charles Demuth. In his early poetry, he imitated Pound and the Imagists, accepting the Imagist credo as presented in *Poetry*. His natural inclination was to treat things directly with brevity of language and without conventional metrics. He was also influenced by his painter friends, particularly by the cubists and the expressionists. Modern painters filled their canvases with mechanisms, and Williams called a poem a "machine made of words." During 1915 and 1916, he attended literary gatherings with the *Others* group and met Alfred Kreymborg, Marianne Moore, and Wallace Stevens.

He began writing poetry in a poetic wasteland that did not want new or experimental poetry. The poets who had been popularly admired were the three-name poets so greatly influenced by the English tradition. Walt Whitman was not regarded highly and Emily Dickinson was unknown.

Although he devoted much of his time to being a full-time physician in Rutherford, Williams was a prolific writer—a poet, short-story writer, novelist, playwright, essayist, and translator. He was neglected both by the general public and by the literary establishment for most of his career, and often in his frustration he erupted against his critics and other practicing poets. With the publication of *Paterson*, Book I, in 1946, however, he began to receive the recognition he felt he deserved.

During most of the last fifteen years of his life, he continued to write even though he was not in good health. In 1948, when he was sixty-five years old, he suffered a heart attack, and in 1951 he had his first stroke, which was followed by another serious one a year later. The next year he was hospitalized because of severe depression. Finally, in 1961, two years before his death, he gave up writing after he suffered a series of strokes. On March 4, 1963, at the age of seventy-nine, he died in Rutherford, where he had been born and had lived all his life.

ANALYSIS

Like Walt Whitman, William Carlos Williams attempted to create an American voice for American poetry. Both Whitman and Williams wanted to record the unique American experience in a distinctively American idiom, a language freed from the constraints of traditional English prosody. Whitman, as Williams says in his autobiography, broke from the traditional iambic pentameter, but he had only begun the necessary revolu-

William Carlos Williams (Irving Wellcome, courtesy of New Directions)

tion. It was then up to Williams to use "the new dialect" to continue Whitman's work by constructing a prosody based on actual American speech.

Williams's search for a new language using the American idiom was intertwined with his search for a new poetic measure. Although he wanted to recover the relationship between poetry and the measured dance from which he believed it derived, his concept of measure is elusive. He believed that Whitman's free verse lacked structure. Williams sought a new foot that would be fairly stable, yet at the same time was variable, a foot that was not fixed but allowed for variation according to what the language called for. While the traditional poetic foot is based on the number of syllables in a line, Williams based his poetic foot on "a measure of the ear." The proper measure would allow him to present the American idiom as controlled by the rhythm of American speech.

When Williams wrote his early poems, he had not yet developed his own poetical theory; he first wrote conventionally and then according to the Imagist credo. He created some very good pictures of "things" and his poems achieved a reality of their own, but they did not go beyond the particulars to express universal truths—something that involves more than merely recreating data.

In "The Red Wheelbarrow," for example, all the reader is left with is the picture of the red wheelbarrow and the white chickens beside it standing in the rain. In "Poem" the cat climbs over the jamcloset into the empty flower pot; Williams conveys nothing more than this picture. Other examples of Williams's poems of this period include "The Locust Tree in Flower" (the locust tree in flower is sweet and white, and brings May again), "Between Walls" (behind the hospital in the cinders of the courtyard shine the pieces of a broken green bottle), and "This Is Just to Say" (the poet tells his wife he has eaten the plums she was saving in the icebox).

In "To a Poor Old Woman," Williams does not convey any meaning beyond the picture he evokes of an old woman munching on a plum that she has taken from a bag she is holding in her hand. He does, however, experiment with the way he places the words of the line "They taste good to her" on the page. He repeats the line three times. First, he puts all the words on one line without a

period at the end of the line; then he writes "They taste good/ to her. They taste/ good to her." He is searching for the correct form to use—the elusive measure needed.

PATERSON

In the epic poem *Paterson*, Williams sought to cover the landscape of contemporary American society and to discover himself as an American poet. His twenty-year journey in *Paterson* is similar to that of Hart Crane in *The Bridge* (1930), Ezra Pound in the *Cantos* (1925-1972), and T. S. Eliot in *The Waste Land* (1922) and *Four Quartets* (1943). Just as Whitman revised the poems of *Leaves of Grass* (1855) continuously and frequently moved them from section to section within the volume, so Williams identified *Paterson* with his own continuing life as a poet.

Paterson consists of five books and a projected sixth; each book is made up of three sections. In "The Delineaments of the Giants" (*Paterson*, Book I, 1946), Mr. Paterson, as he wanders through the city Paterson, describes details of the town and the area around it: the valley, the Passaic Falls, and Garret Mountain. Williams creates a history for the city as he describes past and present inhabitants and events concerning both them and the city. In "Sunday in the Park" (*Paterson*, Book II, 1948), the persona walks through Garret Mountain Park on a Sunday afternoon; there he views the workers of Paterson in their Sunday leisure activities. "The Library" (*Paterson*, Book III, 1949) takes place in the library, where the persona searches to discover how best to express the aspects of the city of Paterson that he has described in the first two books. "The Run to the Sea" (*Paterson*, Book IV, 1951) takes place in two locales—New York City and an entrance to the sea. The first section consists mostly of dialogues between Corydon and Phyllis, and Phyllis and Paterson. The section involves Madame Marie Curie's discovery of uranium and a digressive discussion of economics in America. The final section of the fourth book presents accounts of events, mostly violent, concerning the inhabitants of Paterson; it ends with the persona and a dog headed inland after they have emerged from the sea. *Paterson*, Book V, which does not have a title, takes place in The Cloisters, a museum on the Hudson River in New York City. This book is shorter than the others and some critics refer to it as a coda to *Paterson*, Books I-IV. Having grown old, the persona contemplates the meaning of a series of unicorn tapestries in the museum.

Paterson can be difficult reading. The persona of the poem does not remain constant; moreover, "Paterson" refers to both the city and the man. There are a number of other personas in *Paterson* who are sometimes ambiguously fused. Paterson the city becomes Paterson the man, who is also a woman, who becomes the poet writing *Paterson*, who is also William Carlos Williams, a poet and a man.

In addition, Williams shifts from verse to prose without transitional devices, and there are many such shifts within verse passages, from persona to persona, and from subject matter to subject matter. The prose passages, sometimes taken directly from an exterior source, range from newspaper clippings and quotations from various books to letters by Williams's fictional personas.

Paterson is Williams's attempt to delineate his culture and to define himself poetically. The two quests are interrelated. Williams can present details of the America that he sees and describe aspects of her culture. He wants, however, to convey the truths in what he describes and the universals concerning his vision. To be able to do so, he must work out his poetic theory and discover himself as a poet.

In *Paterson*, Williams relied importantly on local particulars. First, he chose a city that actually existed. In *The Autobiography of William Carlos Williams* he writes of taking the city Paterson and working it up as a case, just as he worked up cases as a doctor. According to Joel Conarroe in *William Carlos Williams' "Paterson"* (1970), Paterson was a city that was similar to Williams's native Rutherford, but one that better possessed the characteristics that Williams needed for his poem. Paterson had existed since the beginning of America and therefore had a history. It was a very American city with a diverse population, about a third of which was foreign-born. Located on the Passaic River with the Passaic Falls, Paterson was bounded on one side by Garret Mountain. Partially because of these natural resources, it was one of the first industrial cities in America. Furthermore, its industry grew steadily and it was often the scene of well-known strikes. Fortunately for the action of the poem, Paterson also suffered a major fire, flood, and tornado.

Williams peoples his poem with persons who actually existed and uses events that actually occurred. Often, in the prose passages, he gives the specifics about the inhabitants and events. In *Paterson*, Book I, Williams develops a history for the city of Paterson. He tells the reader the number of inhabitants of each nationality living in Paterson in 1870. He describes some of the inhabitants. David Hower, for example, is a poor shoemaker who in February, 1857, while eating mussels, finds substances that turn out to be pearls. A gentleman in the Revolutionary Army describes a monster in human form, Pieter Van Winkle. His description is followed by the account of a 126-pound monster fish taken by John Winters and other boys. Mrs. Sarah Cumming, the wife of Reverend Hopper Cumming for two months, mysteriously disappears into the falls just after her husband turns from the cataract to go home. When the bridge that Timothy B. Crane built is being put across the falls, Sam Patch jumps to retrieve a rolling pin and thus begins his career as a famous jumper, a career that ends when he attempts to jump the falls of the Genessee River in 1829. The reader learns exactly what Cornelius Doremus owned when he died at eighty-nine years of age and what each item was worth. At one time the men of Paterson ravage the river and kill almost all of its fish. Finally, the reader is told about Mr. Leonard Sandford, who discovers a human body near the falls.

In *Paterson*, Books II-V, Williams continues to present details about the geography, inhabitants, and events of Paterson; as the poem progresses, however, he relies less on prose from historical accounts in books and newspapers and more on letters, dialogues, and verse. The particulars also become more personally related to the fictional poet of the poem or to Bill (Dr. Williams). There are passages about the Indians who first lived in the area. Williams includes a tabular account of the specimens found when men were digging an artesian well at the Passaic Rolling Mill, Paterson, and an advertisement concerning borrowing money on the credit of the United States. Phyllis, an uneducated black woman, writes several letters to her father. Throughout the poem a woman poet (C. or Cress), another poet (A. G.), and Edward or E. D. (Edward Dahlberg) write letters to a person without a name, to Dr. Paterson, to Dr. Williams, and to Bill.

In addition to all of these particulars, Williams deals with aspects of American society. A major weakness of contemporary American culture is the inability of man to communicate with others and even with himself. In *Paterson*, Book I, Williams immediately introduces the problems with language faced by the inhabitants of Paterson. Industrialization is one of the sources of their difficulties; industrialization and materialism separate them from themselves and from each other. The people walk incommunicado; they do not know the words with which to communicate. It is as if they face an equation that cannot be solved, for language fails them. Although there is a torrent in their minds, they cannot unlock that torrent since they do not know themselves.

Sam Patch is an example of a man who dies incommunicado. Before he attempts to dive into the falls of the Genessee River, he makes a short speech. The words, however, are drained of meaning and they fail him. He disappears into the stream and is not seen until the following spring, when he is found frozen in ice, still locked in by his inability to communicate.

In the second part of *Paterson*, Book II, Williams describes Madame Curie's discovery of uranium, a discovery that he relates to the need in America for the discovery of a new credit system. This system would be like "the radiant gist" that Madame Curie discovered and would cure America's economic cancer, a condition contributing to man's inability to communicate. The lust for money and the industrialization of society cut man off from his roots and from other men.

Humanity's problems with language are reflected in the relationships between man and woman. The love of man and woman consummated in marriage should be a means of communication, but in contemporary society "divorce" is the common word: "The language/ is divorced from their minds." In *Paterson*, Book I, Williams tells of Mrs. Sarah Cumming, who after two months of marriage has everything to look forward to, but who mysteriously disappears into the falls after her husband turns his back on her. Marriage, then, is no answer to the problem of communication. The words locked in the "falls" of the human mind must be released. Immediately after the prose section about Mrs. Cumming comes the passage "A false language. A true. A false language pouring—a/ language (misunderstood) pouring (misin-

terpreted) without/ dignity, without minister, crashing upon a stone ear. At least/ it settled it for her."

In *Paterson*, Book II, as Paterson walks through Garret Mountain Park, the breakdown of language is reflected in the religious and sexual life of the Paterson workers as they spend their leisure time on a Sunday afternoon. A sermon by the itinerant evangelist Klaus Ehrens is a meaningless harangue; he does not communicate with those in the park. The relationship between man and woman is reduced to a sexual act of lust without meaning; it is not even an act that will produce children. Language and communication between male and female is exhausted. Ironically, B. is told in a letter by someone who has been caring for a dog that the dog *is* going to have puppies; animals, unlike humans, remain fertile.

The first section of *Paterson*, Book IV, is primarily a narrative consisting of dialogues between Corydon and Phyllis, and Phyllis and Paterson. In both relationships the participants fail to communicate successfully. Corydon is an old lesbian who is half-heartedly attempting to seduce Phyllis, a virgin. Paterson is also an unsuccessful lover of the young black nurse. Phyllis writes letters to her Pappy in uneducated English. In the last letter she tells him of a trip with Corydon to Anticosti—a name that sounds Italian but is French. The two women have a guide who speaks French with Corydon. Phyllis cannot understand what they are saying; she does not care, however, because she can speak her own language. The dialogues reveal relationships in which there is a potential for love and communication, but in which there is a failure to communicate.

Williams describes the predicament of Paterson, but he wants to convey the universals of American society and go beyond the "facts" to the "ideas." Being able to express the general through "things" is part of Williams's quest to define himself as a poet. *Paterson* is a search for the redeeming language needed to enable contemporary man to communicate; the quest itself, however, is valuable even if the redeeming language is not discovered.

In the preface to *Paterson*, Williams states that the poem is the quest to find the needed language ("beauty") that is locked in his mind. Soon after, in *Paterson*, Book I, Williams indicates that he is attempting to determine "what common language to unravel." Mr. Paterson, the persona, will go away to rest and write. Thus, Williams begins his quest for the redeeming language.

Paterson, Book I, ends with a quotation from *Studies of Greek Poets* (1873) by John Addington Symonds in which Symonds discusses Hipponax's attempt to use a meter appropriate for prose and common speech. Symonds also notes that the Greeks used the "deformed verse" of Hipponax for subjects dealing with humanity's perversions. Thus, the Greek poets devised a prosody suitable to their society, just as Williams seeks a measure to express American society.

Throughout *Paterson*, several letters by the woman poet C., or Cress, interrelate the theme of man's failure to communicate, especially through heterosexual love, and the poet's function to solve this problem of language. The longest of her letters, covering six-and-a-half pages, appears at the end of *Paterson*, Book II. In it she complains about woman's wretched position in society. She is particularly upset about her relationship, or lack of relationship, with Dr. P. She has tried to communicate intimately and has shared thoughts with him that she has not shared with anyone else. He has rejected her. She accuses him of having used her; he has encouraged her first letters only because he could turn them into literature and use them in his poem. As long as her letters were only literature—a literature divorced from life—their relationship was satisfactory, but when she attempted to use her letters to communicate on a personal level, he turned his back on her. When her writings became an expression of herself, their friendship failed. She thus expresses an idea that E. D. had stated earlier in the poem—that the literary work and its author cannot be separated. An artist derives a unity of being and a freedom to be himself when he achieves a successful relationship between the externals, such as the paint, clay, or language that he uses, and his shaping of these externals.

In *Paterson*, Book II, the persona goes to the library to try to learn how, as a poet, to express the details of the city described in the first two books. The library contains many acts of communication, but all of them are from the past and will not serve the poet in his quest for the redeeming language that will free man and himself. The poet in the poem, and Williams himself by implication, have failed to communicate, both as poets and as men.

Briefly at the beginning of *Paterson*, Book III, Williams suggests the need for an "invention" without which the old will return with deadly repetitiveness. Only invention will bring the new line that in turn brings the new word, a word that is required now that words have crumbled like chalk. Invention requires the poet to reject old forms and exhausted words in order to find the new-measured language. Throughout this book there is destruction and violence. The natural disasters that occurred in Paterson (the flood, the fire, and the tornado) and made it necessary for the inhabitants to rebuild sections of the city suggest the poet's search in which he finds it necessary to destroy in order to create. The poet does not find what he is searching for, because both the invention and words are lacking. Nevertheless, he continues his search for "the beautiful thing."

Near the end of *Paterson*, Book III, the poet experiments with form and language. On one page Williams places the lines almost at random. It is as if someone has taped various typed lines carelessly on the page without making sure that the lines are parallel or that they make sense when read. There are numbers and words in both English and French. The reader is invited to consider the meanings evoked by "funeral *designed*," "plants," and "wedding bouquets." On the following page there are four passages in which the words are abbreviations meant to be a phonological representation of the words of an illiterate person. Immediately after these passages appears the tabular account of the specimens found when a water well is being dug. Water brings life and rebirth. The poet wants to unlock the language of the falls that had filled his head earlier and to create the new-measured language. He concludes that "*American poetry is a very easy subject to discuss for the/ simple reason that it does not exist.*"

In *Paterson*, Book IV, Williams returns to Madame Curie's "radiant gist"; the poet hopes to make a similar discovery in his poetry so that he can heal those who suffer from an inadequate language. The poet reminds himself that his "virgin" purpose is the language and that he must forget the past. At the end of the book he emerges from the sea, which has been presented in terms of violence, and heads inland eating a plum and followed by a dog that has also been swimming in the sea. Williams concludes that "This is the blast/ the eternal close/ the spiral/ the final somersault/ the end." Williams suggests process in this end; the end is a spiral similar to a Möbius strip in which the end is always a return to the beginning.

Again Williams interrelates the poet's art and the process of love. Both are a means of communication between man and woman and a way for a person to discover himself; both, he explains in *Paterson*, Book V, involve a paradox. The virgin's maidenhead must be violently destroyed in the sexual act for her to realize her potential to create another human being. The poet must destroy past forms to discover the form appropriate for his time; Williams must reject the language and form of past poetry to create the new-measured language that will express contemporary American society and provide for communication among men.

Paterson, Book V, contains a question and answer section in which Williams discusses his theory of poetry. Poetry is made of words that have been organized rhythmically; a poem is a complete entity that has a separate existence. If the poem is any good, it expresses the life of the poet and tells the reader what the poet is. Anything can be the subject of poetry. The poet in America must use the American idiom, but the manner in which the words are presented is of the greatest importance. Sometimes a modern poet ignores the sense of words. In prose, words mean what they say, but in poetry words present two different things: what they actually mean and what their shape means. Williams cites Pieter Brueghel as an artist who saw from two sides. Brueghel painted authentically what he saw, yet at the same time served the imagination. The measured dance, life as it is presented in art by the imagination, is all that man can know. The answer to the poet's quest is that "We know nothing and can know nothing/ but/ the dance, to dance to a measure/ contrapuntally,/ Satyrically, the tragic foot." The poet presents life in a form appropriate to the time in which he lives; he presents the particulars of life that are a contrast or interplay of elements directed by his sexual desires and need for love, his humanity.

LATER POEMS

It is in the poems that Williams wrote during the last ten years of his life that he achieves greatness—the poems collected in *The Desert Music and Other Poems*, *Journey to Love*, and *Pictures from Brueghel*. In these, he uses the new-measured language he had sought in *Paterson*, Books I-V; but, more importantly, he goes beyond "things" to "ideas." The poems are more than pretty subjects; in them he discovers "the beautiful thing."

Some of the best poems of this period are "The Descent," from *Paterson*, Book II; "Paterson: Episode 17," in *Paterson*, Book III; "To Daphne and Virginia"; "The Sparrow (To My Father)"; "A Negro Woman"; "Self-Portrait"; "The Hunters in the Snow"; "The Wedding Dance in the Open Air"; "The Parable of the Blind"; "Children's Games"; "Song," beginning "Beauty is a shell"; "The Woodthrush"; and "Asphodel, That Greeny Flower."

When Williams was asked in 1961 to choose his favorite poem for an anthology called *Poet's Choice*, he selected "The Descent" from *Paterson*, Book II. He said that he had been using "the variable foot" for many years, but "The Descent" was the first in that form that completely satisfied him. "Asphodel, That Greeny Flower," from *Journey to Love*, is another poem in which Williams truly succeeds, and a discussion of that poem provides a good summary to a discussion of Williams's poetry.

"ASPHODEL, THAT GREENY FLOWER"

In "Asphodel, That Greeny Flower" Williams uses his new-measured language, containing "fresh" words (the American idiom) written in a measure appropriate to his times and controlled by the rhythm of American speech ("the variable foot" in the triadic stanza). He is also concerned with creating a poem that has its own existence and is a "thing" in itself. Williams draws from the particulars of American life and his own life to evoke images of America and American culture; now that he has discovered the new-measured language, however, he can express universal truths about America and her culture. The poem at the same times expresses Williams's life as a poet and points to what he is and believes.

Williams uses his new-measured language to capture the flow of American speech as well as to reinforce and emphasize the content and meaning of the poem. For example, in one passage the measure of the lines suggests the urgency of the present, then slows into memory and reminiscence and finally into silence. At another point,

Williams's measure gives the sense of the rolling sea. James Breslin in *William Carlos Williams: An American Artist* (1970) discusses in detail Williams's use of the American idiom presented in "the variable foot" and triadic stanza.

Williams uses natural details such as the asphodel, the honeysuckle, the bee, the lily, the hummingbird, apple blossoms, strawberries, the lily of the valley, and daisies. He uses particulars from his own life: a trip he took with his wife, a time he was separated from her, and their wedding day. He makes references to his own poetry; a young artist likes Williams's poem about the broken green bottle lying in the cinders in the hospital courtyard and says he has heard about, but not read, Williams's poem on gay wallpaper.

The new-measured language enables Williams to draw from the facts and details of the local to reach the realm of the imagination and convey truths about humanity. He begins the poem by addressing the asphodel, but immediately, his "song" becomes one addressed to his wife of many years, not to the flower. Throughout the poem there is constant shifting between the image of the asphodel and Floss, as well as a fusing of the two particulars. The flower at times becomes a symbol. As Breslin explains, the poem is a continuing process as the "things" expand to the "ideas" beyond them, and the truths expressed contract back into the particular images.

The poem is a realistic love song that conveys the nature of the man who is the poet creating the poem. He asks his wife to forgive him because too often medicine, poetry, and other women have been his prime concerns, not her and their life together. The asphodel becomes a symbol of his renewed love for her in his old age. He can ask for her forgiveness because he has come to realize that love has the power to undo what has been done. Love must often serve a function similar to that of the poet, for the poet also must undo what has been done by destroying past forms in order to create new ones.

In "Asphodel, That Greeny Flower" Williams regrets that he has reached a time when he can no longer put down the words that come to him out of the air and create poems. Through the details of his poetry, he has attempted to express the general truths of the imagination. With his old age, however, he has gained knowledge that makes him optimistic. "Are facts not flowers/ and flowers facts/ or poems flowers/ or all words of the imagination,/ interchangeable?" "Flowers" or "facts," "poems" and "words of the imagination" are interchangeable, for everything is a work of the imagination. What is important is that love is a force of the imagination that rules things, words, and poems; love is life's form for poetry. Through love and poetry, all men will be able to communicate. Both love and works of the imagination, be they artistic endeavors or otherwise, are creative powers that are men's means of escaping death. This is the universal truth, the "idea" that Williams has come to, through the particulars of his poetry and his life.

OTHER MAJOR WORKS

LONG FICTION: *The Great American Novel*, 1923; *A Voyage to Pagany*, 1928; *White Mule*, 1937; *In the Money*, 1940; *The Build-up*, 1952.

SHORT FICTION: *The Knife of the Times and Other Stories*, 1932; *Life Along the Passaic River*, 1938; *Make Light of It: Collected Stories*, 1950; *The Farmers' Daughters: The Collected Stories of William Carlos Williams*, 1961; *The Doctor Stories*, 1984.

PLAY: *Many Loves and Other Plays*, pb. 1961.

NONFICTION: *In the American Grain*, 1925; *A Novelette and Other Prose*, 1932; *The Autobiography of William Carlos Williams*, 1951; *Selected Essays of William Carlos Williams*, 1954; *The Selected Letters of William Carlos Williams*, 1957; *The Embodiment of Knowledge*, 1974; *A Recognizable Image*, 1978; *William Carlos Williams, John Sanford: A Correspondence*, 1984; *William Carlos Williams and James Laughlin: Selected Letters*, 1989; *Pound/Williams: Selected Letters of Ezra Pound and William Carlos Williams*, 1996 (Hugh Witemeyer, editor).

TRANSLATIONS: *Last Nights of Paris*, 1929 (of Philippe Soupault; with Raquel Hélène Williams); *A Dog and the Fever*, 1954 (of Francisco de Quevedo; with Raquel Hélène Williams).

BIBLIOGRAPHY

Bremen, Brian A. *William Carlos Williams and the Diagnostics of Culture*. New York: Oxford University

Press, 1993. An examination of the development of Williams's poetry, focused on his fascination with the effects of poetry and prose, and his friendship with Kenneth Burke. Using Burke's and Williams's theoretical writings and correspondence, and the works of contemporary cultural critics, Bremen looks at how the methodological empiricism in Williams's poetic strategy is tied to his medical practice.

Coles, Robert. *William Carlos Williams: The Knack of Survival in America*. New Brunswick, N.J.: Rutgers University Press, 1975. This examination of Williams's work aims at an understanding of Williams as a poet and writer who was fascinated with the meaning and values of America. Coles offers a study of both poems and stories. Includes a bibliography and an index.

Fisher-Wirth, Ann W. *William Carlos Williams and Autobiography: The Woods of His Own Nature*. University Park: Pennsylvania State University Press, 1989. In this work, the author considers certain works by Williams as autobiography. Although this book is not a comprehensive survey of Williams's writing, it does add new insight into Williams's conception of the self and its relationship to the world. Offers passing treatments of *Kora in Hell* and *Paterson*. Supplemented by thorough notes and an index.

Lenhart, Gary, ed. *The Teachers and Writers Guide to William Carlos Williams*. New York: Teachers & Writers Collaborative, 1998. Offers more than a dozen practical and innovative essays on using Williams's work to inspire writing by students and adults, including the use of both his classics and his neglected later poems.

Laughlin, James. *Remembering William Carlos Williams*. New Directions, 1995. The founder of the publishing firm New Directions excerpts his *Byways* verse memoir of the many poets he has published over the years, capturing both humorous and poignant memories of poet-physician Williams.

Levertov, Denise. *The Letters of Denise Levertov and William Carlos Williams*. Edited by Christopher MacGowan. New York: New Directions, 1998. An engaging and lively collection of correspondence providing testimony of their remarkable friendship and a seedbed of ideas about American poetry. Levertov introduced herself to Williams in 1951 with a fan letter and their correspondence continued until his death. The letters chronicle their search (individually and together) for a set of formal poetic principles.

Townley, Rod. *The Early Poetry of William Carlos Williams*. Ithaca, N.Y.: Cornell University Press, 1975. In this work, both the life and art of Williams are examined. The author gives critical attention to both Williams's emotional and spiritual crises and examines the imaginative world of his early poems. Contains bibliographical references and an index.

Whitaker, Thomas R. *William Carlos Williams*. Twayne's United States Authors series. Boston: Twayne, 1989. This work provides a useful key to Williams's writing. The primary focus of Whitaker's study is the works themselves and not Williams's biographical or literary history. One of Twayne's United States Authors series. Includes a chronology, a selected bibliography, and an index.

Williams, William Carlos. *Interviews with William Carlos Williams*. Edited by Linda Wagner-Martin. New York: New Directions, 1976. Contains an introduction by Linda Wagner-Martin. Williams speaks candidly about himself and his work. Includes bibliographical references and an index.

Sherry G. Southard;
bibliography updated by the editors

YVOR WINTERS

Born: Chicago, Illinois; October 17, 1900
Died: Palo Alto, California; January 25, 1968

PRINCIPAL POETRY
The Immobile Wind, 1921
The Magpie's Shadow, 1922
The Bare Hills, 1927
The Proof, 1930
The Journey and Other Poems, 1931
Before Disaster, 1934

Poems, 1940
The Giant Weapon, 1943
To the Holy Spirit, 1947
Collected Poems, 1952, revised 1960
The Early Poems of Yvor Winters, 1920-1928, 1966
The Poetry of Yvor Winters, 1978

OTHER LITERARY FORMS

Though Yvor Winters believed his poetry to be his principal work, he was, during his lifetime, better known as a critic. His criticism was virtually coextensive with his poetry, the first published essays appearing in 1922 and the last volume in 1967. Controversial because of its wide-ranging and detailed revaluations of both major and minor writers in American, British, and French literature, the criticism indirectly but indisputably illuminates his own work as poet: by suggesting explanations for the changes it underwent, for the main styles he attempted, and even for details in individual poems.

His single short story, "The Brink of Darkness" (1932; revised 1947), is autobiographical. Its setting (the southwestern United States) and subject matter (hypersensitivity in isolation, the advent of death, psychological obsession to the brink of madness, the recovery of identity) are those of many poems, especially early ones, in the Winters canon.

ACHIEVEMENTS

Among his contemporaries, Yvor Winters was something of an anomaly. Instead of moving from traditional to experimental forms, he seemed to many readers to reverse that process. Before 1928, his published work was largely what is loosely called free verse, influenced by such diverse sources as the Imagists and French Symbolists, possibly Emily Dickinson, and certainly translations of Japanese and American Indian poetry. After 1930, Winters's published work used traditional metric and rhyme patterns exclusively. He appeared to stand against all the main poetic currents of his time.

At no time, however, early or late, did his poetry ignore modern influences. Among the poets he continued most to admire and emulate were Charles Baudelaire, Paul Valéry, Thomas Hardy, Robert Bridges, and Wallace Stevens. His effort consistently was to make use of the most fruitful traditions among all at his disposal, not merely those in fashion. Thus, many of his later poems are written in the great plain style of the Renaissance. In his most distinctive work, Winters tried to combine the sensitivity of perception which the recent associative and experimental methods had made possible with the rational structures characteristic of the older methods. The result was something unique in modern poetry. Even before his death, his influence was beginning to be felt in such poets as Edgar Bowers, J. V. Cunningham, Catherine Davis, Thom Gunn, Janet Lewis, N. Scott Momaday, Alan Stephens, and others.

In his criticism also, Winters went his own way, challenging accepted opinions and making enemies in the process. Not only did he define what he believed were mistaken and possibly dangerous directions in the thinking and methods of many American poets, novelists, and prose writers, but also, in his final volume, *Forms of Discovery: Critical and Historical Essays on the Forms of the Short Poem in English* (1967), he offered new and for many readers unpopular perspectives on the history of the short poem, both in Great Britain and in the United States. His criticism, however, is not primarily destructive in bent. For one thing, he revised the reputations of many distinguished poets who had already begun to sink into oblivion, such as George Gascoigne, Fulke Greville, and Charles Churchill from the older periods; Bridges, T. Sturge Moore, and Frederick Goddard Tuckerman from more recent times. For another, he found forgotten poems and qualities of major writers that deserved attention—such poets as Ben Jonson, George Herbert, Henry Vaughan, Hardy, Stevens, and Edwin Arlington Robinson. Finally, he formulated coherent theories about poems, and in fact all literary forms, as works of art, theories to which his own work as a poet and his evaluations of the work of others consistently subscribe. To ignore or dismiss this copious and wide-ranging body of work is to overlook one of the clearest, most precisely analytical, and most disturbingly persuasive voices in American criticism.

Of all the honors he received during his lifetime, Winters said he was proudest of an issue of the Stanford undergraduates' magazines, *Sequoia*, which paid tribute to him in 1961. In 1960, he rieceived the Bollingen Award from Yale University for his poetry, and in 1961, the Harriet Monroe Poetry Award from the University of Chicago. Having served on the faculty of Stanford University since 1928, Winters was made full professor in 1949, and in 1962 he became the first holder of the Albert L. Guerard professorship in English. In 1961-1962, a Guggenheim grant enabled Winters to complete the work on his last volume of criticism. By the end of his life, he was beginning to receive the acclaim that is due him. In 1981, *The Southern Review* honored him with an entire issue devoted to studies of his life and work.

BIOGRAPHY

Born in the first year of the twentieth century, Arthur Yvor Winters spent his earliest years in Chicago and in Eagle Rock (an area of Los Angeles), California. The landscape of Southern California near Pasadena provides the setting for two major poems in heroic couplets, "The Slow Pacific Swell" and "On a View of Pasadena from the Hills." Later, he returned to Chicago, was graduated from high school, and for one year attended the University of Chicago, where, in 1917, he became a member of the Poetry Club, which, in his own words, "was a very intelligent group, worth more than most courses in literature." By then he had begun to study his contemporaries—Ezra Pound, William Carlos Williams, Stevens, William Butler Yeats—and the diverse poetic styles appearing in the little magazines.

In 1918, having contracted tuberculosis, he was forced to move to Santa Fe, New Mexico, confined to a sanatorium for three years. The debilitating fatigue and pain, the resultant hypersensitivity to sound and sight and touch, and the sense of death hovering were experiences indelibly etched in his poetry then and later. In 1921, Winters began teaching grade school—English, French, zoology, boxing, basketball—in a coal-mining camp called Madrid, and he taught high school the following year in Cerrillos. These five years in the southwestern United States were a slow period of recovery in isolation, a time when his own study of poetry continued and his correspondence with many contemporary poets was active. It was also the time of his earliest publications.

The landscape of New Mexico suffuses the poetry of his first four volumes.

In the summer of 1923, Winters began the academic study that would eventually bring him to Stanford for his doctorate, earning a B.A. and an M.A. in romance languages, with a minor in Latin from the University of Colorado. The skills he acquired enabled him to translate many poems from French and Spanish (including thirteenth century Galician) and, between 1925 and 1927, to teach French and Spanish at the University of Idaho at Moscow. During this period, he married Janet Lewis, later a distinguished novelist and poet, whom he had met in 1921 on a return visit to Chicago; their wedding was in 1926 in Santa Fe, where she, too, had gone to cure tuberculosis. Together now, they moved to Stanford in 1927, when Winters was twenty-six years old; then, under the tutelage of his admired mentor in Renaissance studies, William Dinsmore Briggs, he began the systematic study of poetry in English that occupied him for the rest of his life.

Winters's life in California as a teacher, husband, father, and involved citizen is reflected everywhere in his later poetry. He became a legend at Stanford. Depending on which students were reporting, he was dogmatic, shy, reasonable, surly, kind, hilarious, humorless, a petty tyrant, or an intellectual giant. His disciples and detractors felt intensely about him; few were indifferent. The marriage of Winters and Janet Lewis was a lasting and loving one, and it nurtured their independent careers as writers. His daughter Joanna was born in 1931 and his son Daniel in 1938. Hardly one to withdraw into an ivory tower, Winters liked to get his hands dirty. The raising and breeding of Airedale terriers was a lifelong activity. He kept goats and a garden. He became deeply involved with the trial of David Lamson, a friend unjustly accused of murdering his wife. During World War II, he served as a Citizens' Defense Corps zone warden for Los Altos. These experiences are the kinds of occasions he wrote about in his later work.

Before his retirement from Stanford in 1966, Winters had already endured the first of two operations for cancer, the disease that killed him in 1968. His final effort as a writer, amid acute pain, was to see his last book, *Forms of Discovery*, through to publication after the death of his publisher and old friend, Alan Swallow.

ANALYSIS

The change in poetic forms from experimental to traditional—from Imagistic free verse to formalist poetry using the traditional plain style or post-Symbolist imagery—which Yvor Winters's poetry exhibits after 1930 is so dramatic that it is easy to overlook the continuity of certain stylistic features and thematic preoccupations throughout his career. From the very beginning of his poetic life, he abhorred an indulgent rhetoric in excess of subject matter; always he attempted an exact adjustment of feeling to intellectual content. He paid strict attention to the value of each word as an amalgam of denotative, connotative, rhythmic, and aural properties; to the integrity of the poetic line and the perfect placing of each word within it; and to the clarity and economy of a style that avoids cliché. A poem was for him a means of contemplating human experience in such a way that the meaning of that experience and the feelings appropriate to the meaning are precisely rendered.

THE IMMOBILE WIND

Thematic continuity exists also. His first volume of poems, *The Immobile Wind*, whatever immaturities of style it may exhibit, contains themes that he worked and reworked in all of his poems thereafter. As a collection, it speaks of man alone in an empty universe whose end is death, whose choices are existence or creation. Man lives and observes. If this is all, life remains an unrealized potential, the experience of which may be beautiful or terror-ridden but will lack the possibility of meaning which the artist may be able to create. To do this, the artist must choose his reality, must will it; to create his own world, he must give over the things of this one, for this world is merely phenomenal, the raw material of vision, a means at best, not an end: "And all these things would take/ My life from me." The end for all is death, and, in addition for the artist, the possibility of awareness. Religion offers no solace. The subject of the book is the poet, his growth and mission and death. The images in *The Immobile Wind* are sharp and self-contained and their meanings elusive; as one reads through these poems, however, the subjects and images repeat themselves, interweaving, and patterns of meaning begin to emerge.

In its continual allusiveness to itself and to its own images and in its occasional obscurities, *The Immobile Wind* is an irritating book, but it is not impenetrable. More accessible is *The Magpie's Shadow*, which consists of a series of six-syllable poems (a few stretch to seven) grouped according to the season of the year. Each is intended to convey a sharp sense impression; each as an evocation of a season is evocative also of the passage of time and hence of change and death. "The Aspen's Song," from the summer section, is characteristic: "The summer holds me here." That is the poem. The aspen tree is celebrating its moment of being alive, a moment that creates an illusion of permanence and immobility, an illusion because the summer is transient and the motion of change is there in the tree at every moment. The motion/stasis paradox of this image—present also in the oxymoronic title *The Immobile Wind*—recurs through Winters's poetry. No doubt inspired by translations of American Indian and Japanese originals, it also may be seen as an early manifestation of what he later came to call the post-Symbolist method: the sharp sensory image of metaphysical import.

THE BARE HILLS

The Bare Hills is Winters's last and most successful book devoted entirely to experimental forms. It is divided into three sections. The first, called "Upper River Country: Rio Grande," consists of twelve poems, each describing a month of the year; together, they are emblematic of the poet's progress through life, the poet growing more sensitive to the beauty and brutality around him and more aware of the meaninglessness of life and the inevitability of death. The second, called "The Bare Hills," consists of seven groups of three, four, or five poems each; it tells of the poet surrounded by death and cruelty but trying to learn, feeling inadequate to his task of creation, lacking an audience: He has but "this cold eye for the fact; that keeps me/ quiet, walking toward a/ stinging end: I am alone. . . ." The third section, called "The Passing Night," consists of two prose poems describing a bleak landscape of endless cold, a minimal level of existence, almost void of hope; the poet waits and remembers and observes, and that is all.

In many of these poems, Winters is continuing to experiment with the evocative image. For example, here is the third of four stanzas from one of the finest poems in this collection, "The Upper Meadows":

Apricots
The clustered
Fur of bees
Above the gray rocks of the uplands.

Out of context, the images seem vivid, perhaps, but randomly juxtaposed; in context, which has been describing the dying leaves at the advent of autumn, the transience of these living beings—apricots and bees—is felt, reinforced by the final stanza, ending with this line: "But motion, aging." The landscape evoked in the poem is beautiful, vibrantly alive, and dying. In an early review of *The Bare Hills*, Agnes Lee Freer called it "a book inspiring in its absolute originality."

THE PROOF

The Proof exhibits the transition from experimental to traditional forms. The first half of the volume consists of poems in the Imagistic/free verse manner of his early work; the second half contains several sonnets and a few poems in various traditional stanzaic patterns. Winters himself has said, "It was becoming increasingly obvious to me that the poets whom I most admired were Baudelaire and Valéry, and Hardy, Bridges, and Stevens in a few poems each, and that I could never hope to approach the quality of their work by the method which I was using." He had come to believe that, in poems of firm metrical pattern, more precise and hence more expressive rhythmical and aural effects were possible, the result being the communication of greater complexity of feeling. To this belief he adhered for the rest of his life.

"The Fable," originally a blank-verse sonnet but reduced to ten lines in the *Collected Poems*, is illustrative. After describing the sea, which "Gathers and washes and is gone," he writes:

But the crossed rock braces the hills and makes
A steady quiet of the steady music,
Massive with peace
        And listen, now:
The foam receding down the sand silvers
Between the grains, thin, pure as virgin words,
Lending a sheen to Nothing, whispering.

The sea is the wilderness surrounding us, emblematic of the empty universe and, in its ceaseless motion and ominous quiet, the process of dying. In the first line of this passage, the reversed feet in the first and third positions

are metrical irregularities that, by contrast, emphasize the slow evenness of the next two lines, an evenness that recalls the quiet heaving of the sea itself. The sibilant sounds in the fourth line quoted are also descriptively accurate and metaphysically charged: The sound of the sea washing through the sand is the voice of the emptiness itself, of "Nothing, whispering."

THE JOURNEY AND OTHER POEMS

His next volume, *The Journey and Other Poems*, consists of eight poems in heroic couplets. The first, "The Critiad," his longest poem, is an attempt to create satirical portraits in the manner of Alexander Pope; Winters chose to preserve neither it nor the last poem, "December Eclogue," in his collected works. The other six poems, most of them longer than his usual efforts, are among his most original, for they put the heroic couplet to new uses. "The Journey" through Snake River Country, for example, describes in forty-four lines a train trip at night through Wyoming and arrival at a destination in the morning. On a descriptive level, the poem is detailed and exact. On a symbolic level, it depicts a journey through hell, at the end of which the poet emerges intact from his spiritual trial. The following lines describe the poet's sudden awareness of the brutal and meaningless wilderness, the landscape of despair:

Once when the train paused in an empty place,
I met the unmoved landscape face to face;
Smoothing abysses that no stream could slake,
Deep in its black gulch crept the heavy Snake,
The sound diffused, and so intently firm,
It seemed the silence, having change nor term.

The poet has been describing the violence and squalor of life in the towns the train has passed through, and now he contemplates the empty landscape that harbors those towns. Descriptively, the language is very exact: The abysses are "Smoothing"—that is, being smoothed and stretching for endless distances—because of the river's ceaseless motion; the river's sound is diffused but also there, inevitably, forever, having neither change nor termination. One finds again the motion/stasis paradox which here is also a sound/silence paradox. In this quiet scene, decay is alive and busy; the river is the Snake, evil, eternal, obliterating all "Deep in its black gulch."

Iambic pentameter couplets have not been used in this way before.

BEFORE DISASTER

The next volume, *Before Disaster*, is a miscellaneous collection of poems in traditional forms: quatrains of three, four, or five feet; some sonnets; a few poems in rhymed couplets of varying line lengths. The subject matter is equally various: personal, as in "To My Infant Daughter" and "For My Father's Grave"; mythological, as in "Midas," "Orpheus," and "Chiron"; occasional, as in "Elegy on a Young Airedale Bitch Lost Some Years Since in the Salt-Marsh," "The Anniversary," "On the Death of Senator Thomas J. Walsh," "Dedication for a Book of Criticism," and so on. Here is the final stanza from a poem in the plain style called "To a Young Writer":

> Write little; do it well.
> Your knowledge will be such,
> At last, as to dispel
> What moves you overmuch.

Nothing could be plainer or seem simpler, but what is conveyed is a weighty sense of classical restraint and control, the power of realized truth.

COLLECTED POEMS

All the collections that follow are republications of old work, supplemented with either some new work or old work never before published in a book. The 1960 revision of his *Collected Poems*, however, represents something more than merely a new grouping. Even though it is a selection, hence incomplete, it arranges in chronological order the poetry he wished to keep, beginning with four poems from *The Immobile Wind* and ending with his last poems, "At the San Francisco Airport" and "Two Old-Fashioned Songs." Thus, it is a record of Winters's poetic life. The poems it contains are meditations on a wide variety of subjects: on the greatness of historical heroes, such as Socrates, Herman Melville, John Sutter, and John Day; on the greatness of legendary heroes, such as Theseus, Sir Gawaine, and Hercules; on the evil that people do, as in the poems that deal with World War II; on the vast beauty of the world, in such things as an orchard, a dirigible, California wine, the ancient manzanita, a Renaissance portrait, "summer grasses brown with heat," the "soft voice of the nesting dove,"

and so on; and on the ever-encroaching wilderness and our proximity to death: "Ceaseless, the dead leaves gather, mound on mound." The book is a reflection of a great mind, one at every moment intellectually alive as well as hypersensitive to physical reality. To read it is to partake of the richness, the depths of Winters's inner life. Because the poems exhibit the three very different methods Winters perfected—free verse, traditional plain style, and post-Symbolist imagery—to read the book is to understand something of poetry as an art. If Winters's belief in the power of literature to alter one's being is true, it is to change for the better as well.

OTHER MAJOR WORKS

SHORT FICTION: "The Brink of Darkness," 1932, revised 1947.

NONFICTION: *Primitivism and Decadence: A Study of American Experimental Poetry*, 1937; *Maule's Curse: Seven Studies in the History of American Obscurantism*, 1938; *The Anatomy of Nonsense*, 1943; *Edwin Arlington Robinson*, 1946; *In Defense of Reason*, 1947; *The Function of Criticism: Problems and Exercises*, 1957; *Forms of Discovery: Critical and Historical Essays on the Forms of the Short Poem in English*, 1967; *The Uncollected Essays and Reviews of Yvor Winters*, 1973.

BIBLIOGRAPHY

Gelpi, Albert. "Yvor Winters and Robinson Jeffers." In *A Coherent Splendor*. Cambridge, England: Cambridge University Press, 1987. Gelpi notes that Winters's early poems belie his critical precepts. They display the strong influence of Ezra Pound and William Carlos Williams, despite Winters's furious anti-Romantic denigration of both poets in his criticism. Winters strongly identified with the California landscape, as can be seen in *The Magpie's Shadow*. Gelpi compares his attitude to the West with that of Robinson Jeffers.

Gunn, Thom. "On a Drying Hill." In *The Occasions of Poetry*. San Francisco: North Point Press, 1985. Gunn, himself a noted poet, was a student of Winters at Stanford University. He describes Winters's strong personality and his efforts to convert his students to his critical principles. Foremost among these was the rejection of Romantic poetry. Winters sometimes surprised his pupils by praising the vivid images of the Romantic era's Hart Crane. His poetry and criticism emphasize the portrayal of individual details.

Kaye, Howard. "The Post-symbolist Poetry of Yvor Winters," *The Southern Review* 7, no. 1 (Winter, 1971): 176-197. Winters's poetry strongly evokes landscape. His ability to portray the external world in a precise manner was remarkable. In Kaye's view, Winters counts as one of the great twentieth century poets. His stress upon rationality and control reflects a fear of being overwhelmed by death and strong emotion. Winters's struggle with his emotions is a leitmotif of his poetry. He attempted to extirpate his own Romantic tendencies.

Rexroth, Kenneth. *American Poetry in the Twentieth Century.* New York: Herder, 1971. Rexroth contends that Winters was the true exile of his generation of writers. Most of his friends went to Paris, but health problems forced Winters to live in a dry climate. His move to Northern California kept him isolated, and his criticism became cranky and cliquish. He was an important poet who created an original variant of neoclassicism.

Wellek, René. "Yvor Winters." In *A History of Modern Criticism: American Criticism, 1900-1950.* Vol. 6. New Haven, Conn.: Yale University Press, 1986. Wellek gives a characteristically careful summary of the principles that underlie Winters's poetry and criticism. A poem should express a moral judgment. The judgment, based on absolute moral values, is ideally incapable of being paraphrased. Winters deprecated the expression of emotion not under the strict dominance of reason. His own poems often show the sort of emotion that he, in theory, rejected. Although he held narrow views, he brought to attention the question of the truth of poetry.

Winters, Yvor. *The Selected Letters of Yvor Winters.* Edited by R. L. Barth. Athens: Ohio University Press, 2000. Selected correspondence offering insights into the life of a brilliant man, erudite writer, and lofty poet. Includes bibliographical references and indexes.

Joseph Maltby;
bibliography updated by the editors

DAVID WOJAHN

Born: St. Paul, Minnesota; August 22, 1953

PRINCIPAL POETRY
Icehouse Lights, 1982
Glassworks, 1987
Mystery Train, 1990
Late Empire, 1994
The Falling Hour, 1997

OTHER LITERARY FORMS
Although David Wojahn is primarily a poet, he edited *The Pushcart Prize XI: Best of the Small Presses* (1986), along with Bill Henderson and Philip Levine. He also edited, along with Jack Myers, a comprehensive anthology of contemporary poetry, *A Profile of Twentieth Century American Poetry* (1991). He is a contributor to *Everything Human: On the Poetry of W. D. Snodgrass* (1993), edited by Stephen Haven; he edited and wrote a foreword to *The Only World: Poems* (1995), a posthumous collection of poetry by his wife, Lynda Hull; and wrote *Strange Good Fortune: Essays on Contemporary Poetry* (2000).

ACHIEVEMENTS
David Wojahn's poetry has earned him several major fellowships, including awards from the National Endowment for the Arts and the Fine Arts Work Center in Provincetown, Massachusetts. Wojahn merited success early in his career. Richard Hugo selected Wojahn's first collection, *Icehouse Lights*, as a winner of the Yale Series of Younger Poets contest. This award is given to the best collection written by a poet under forty years of age. *Icehouse Lights* was also selected for the Poetry Society of America's William Carlos Williams Book Award. Wojann's second volume, *Glassworks*, was awarded the Society of Midland Authors award for the best collection of poetry published in 1987. *Poetry* magazine awarded Wojann the George Kent Memorial Prize. From 1987 to 1988, he was the Amy Lowell Poetry Travelling Scholar. His poems have appeared in *The Georgia Review*, *The New Yorker*, *American Poetry Review*, and *Antioch Review*, as well as many other magazines and journals.

BIOGRAPHY

David Charles Wojahn was born and raised in St. Paul, Minnesota. His father, R. C. Wojahn, was employed by the Great Northern Railroad, on the Fargo-Minot-Whitefish run. Virginia Wojahn, his mother, was a bookkeeper for General Tire and Northwest Bank. Wojahn earned his bachelor of arts degree at the University of Minnesota, Twin Cities, in 1977, and his master of fine arts degree at the University of Arizona in 1980.

Wojahn's distinguished poetic career also embodies teaching creative writing and literature. In addition to being the Lilly Professor of English at Indiana University, he has also taught in the master of fine arts writing program at Vermont College. He has also been the assistant professor of English at the University of New Orleans, assistant professor of English at the University of Arkansas at Little Rock, and visiting professor of English at the University of Houston.

ANALYSIS

David Wojahn's poetry intensely weaves personal biography with events that extend to the outside world. Consequently, his poetry is not a self-contained body of work that seeks its own reference. Rather, each poem finds itself within cultural patterns that confront the speaker. Often, these poems speak of loss and longing. What comfort the poet receives comes through his struggle with processing his feelings through writing. Several poems illustrate the healing that comes through the artist's search for meaning, for closure. His poems question ultimate meaning of such symbols in light of human tragedies, of war, madness, and death. The struggle to understand the inevitable outcome, and ultimately to make peace for himself, empowers these poems.

GLASSWORKS

Glassworks features poems about real people—the poet's friends and family—embedded in a gentle narrative line which does not overwhelm the poem; rather, its flow allows each character to come forth, very human, very alive. "Satin Doll" uses a reference to big band music to explore the world of an aunt whose marriage failed. Looking at her sepia photo taken six years before he was born, the poet recalls the events of her life, which seemed to drive out its passion. He compares her to a drowned woman, her eyes staring back at the crowd. The poet imagines his aunt growing stronger, taking control, a very tender moment. Such moments strengthen Wojahn's poetry, rendered without irony or apology.

The poet uses the stuff of his life as source material. "Starlings" is a lovely, sad poem about a mother who stays awake worrying about the safe return of her husband who may be drunk, and the son who stays awake worrying about her. The form imitates the movement of the starlings—"Outside, they're waking too,"—whose noise keeps his mother awake:

> . . . I want to be
> the book she reads, before the noise
> begins to deafen us, before
> she wakes and never sleeps again.

Wojahn crafts this final stanza, weaving the poignancy of the situation with the presence of these birds, without naïve sentimentality.

"Dark-House Spearing" illustrates the difficulties a father and son experience in relating to each other, finally working out safe ways of communicating. However, the father wants company, not words, because of the death of his brother in an alcoholic coma ten years earlier. The poet tries to re-create memories for them, memories which could potentially heal the rift between them. However, after he tells his father the created version, his father says that the details are wrong. Because the father cannot remember the last words he said to his brother, he begins to distrust words altogether.

The poet's grandfather comes forward in the "Third Language" as a ghostly presence who fled Germany to escape the kaiser's army. This poem considers the effect which different language systems have on the emotional ties which speakers maintain. Landing in Boston, his grandfather speaks only German, although he knows Morse Code, believing that such knowledge has a future. In fact, there is little future in its use, made obsolete by radio. Furthermore, his speaking German makes him an object of suspicion in the eyes of his neighbors.

Other poems illustrate the fragility of life and the permanence of art. "Glassworks at Saratoga" describes the death of James White. Beginning with the bizarre death of a millionaire who cut his throat when shaving aboard a train that unfortunately lurched, the poem takes a chilling turn at a glassworks, where the poet purchased White's book. Finding a glass fragment that reminds him of his having deliberately cut his wrist when a woman left him, the poet recognizes himself as someone who knows loss, then affirms his own desire to live. Whether that loss defines itself permanently, as death, or whether there exists some possibility for recovery, such as the loss of a significant relationship, these lines are poetry from the inside.

The pain of loss is central to the next two poems. "Lot's Wife" gives voice to that woman, who was turned into a pillar of salt because she looked back at the destruction of Sodom, a biblical rendering of the mythical Orpheus-Eurydice story. The poet allows the wife to discuss her relationship with Lot, who would have saved her. Wondering whom Lot has become, she realizes that she has lost her very self to a husband who can see only what he believes that God has saved. Consequently, both lose. The husband loses his wife; the wife ultimately loses her selfhood.

Likewise, "Steam" examines the nature of loss, but without the protective cover of myth. The poet addresses his lover, expounding on the tension between what he needs from her and what she can give. Dark poignancy of deep pain evolves in these lines, as the reader becomes an intruder listening to the private conversation of two people who have lost the ability to talk to each other. The speaker seeks mutual healing through a renewal of trust but feels helpless when she cries out someone else's name in her sleep, someone who has hurt her.

The way the poet handles very painful occurrences, whether his or someone else's experiences, brings the reader into that world. These poems do not vampirize pain; instead, they are the poet's attempts to make whatever sense is possible of such experiences.

MYSTERY TRAIN

A thirty-five-section sequence exploring rock and roll highlights this 1990 volume, presenting a cross-cultural experience of contemporary popular music. Wojahn puts the musicians in relationship to poetry and to news events, enhancing situations creatively while maintaining an emotional accuracy.

In Jim Elledge's *Sweet Nothings: An Anthology of Rock and Roll in American Poetry* (1994), Wojahn describes his attraction to this material, noting his avid listening and collecting. Most of the poems in this section are sonnets whose form the poet has artistically explored. One such poem is "W. C. W. Watching Presley's Second Appearance on the 'Ed Sullivan Show': Mercy Hospital, Newark, 1956." While the line breaks and stanzaic pattern are similar to a William Carlos Williams poem, the poem is a sonnet, using couplets:

> The tube,
>   like the sonnet,
>   is a fascist form.
> I read they refused
>   to show this kid's
>   wriggling bum.

Using the sonnet, Wojahn suggests the conservative culture which looked askance at rock and roll, from which the music liberated itself. Creative tension between that culture and the music itself is embodied in the liberties that Wojahn takes with the sonnet form, as if using a received form constituted an act of aesthetic rebellion as complex and concrete as the music of which he writes. These poems do not glamorize the destructive aspects of the lives of these musicians, nor do they take a one-sided view of the cultural assumptions against which the musicians struggled. While the poems celebrate the music, there is, however, an air of sadness that ultimately prevails within and between the lines.

Other poems return to the familiar topics that Wojahn explores. In "Armageddon: Private Gabriel Calvin Wojahn, 1900-18," the poet addresses a relative killed during World War I, buried in a paper shroud used during that time to conserve cloth and timber. The poet gives his relative ecstatic visions of his own death, raised among "God-mad zealots/ Who . . . kept all books but the Bible from your sight." Illiterate, the man dictated letters home to his commandant, then signed them with his thumbprint. The poem's conclusion disallows for the easy solace found in fanatic visions: "Above the mass grave, a chaplain muttered scripture./ What survives of you? Neither words nor paper." In the end, Wojahn's poems challenge the reader, and the poet himself, to engage fully in life's mystery in such a way that no answers come easy.

LATE EMPIRE

Perhaps the darkest of Wojahn's collections, *Late Empire* contains many ideas and concerns which he continues from earlier volumes. However, there is no attempt to mollify their effects, either on himself or on the reader. No mask protects the reader from the insights of these poems, which are raw in their emotional energy. They speak of the end of the world as the poet knows it, not of the physical world accessible to anyone, but the destruction which comes through psychic turmoil.

The sonnet series "Wartime Photos of My Father" considers the poet's father's need for electroshock treatments, with his subsequent need for Thorazine. The reader profoundly experiences the father's mind. Because of these invasive treatments, the reader is caught between the father's sense of reality and delusion; struggle is very real in these poems. Again, the sonnet emphasizes the regularity of stanzaic demands compared to the mental shattering which the poet's father, and the poet as well, experience:

> Words to describe him: stranger, cipher, father.
> The son invents a cruelty, a hurt
> From years before the son was born—a unit
> For measuring distance, the white noise that shimmers
> Between our stuttering conversations,
> Two men who cannot talk or touch.

At one point, for example, the father tells a story about the tormenting of a German prisoner of war, in order to explain the grisly humor of a photograph, only to say that the event never happened. The sonnet effectively contrasts the disruption of war and its lasting aftermath with the regularity of a form that usually speaks of love.

Several poems concentrate on circumstances external to the poet's family. "Tomis" recounts the disappearance of a woman's daughter in Latin America, who had become active in political demonstrations. Her body was later found, reduced to bones. Other poems recount the destruction of a religious cult, similar to Jonestown, formed around a charismatic but crazy woman. Other poems speak of the impending destruction of the earth through unnatural disaster, such as the 1986 nuclear accident at Chernobyl. Wojahn handles these situations by keeping the reader drawn into the poems, not allowing either his rhetoric or his narration to overcome the general experience.

THE FALLING HOUR

The creative intelligence that informs the poems in Wojahn's 1997 collection is characteristic of his style. While continuing to evoke familiar themes, Wojahn's work explores new territory as well. "Rajah in Babylon" begins with the description of a tiger who, anesthetized, will be a sperm donor. Noelle, the poet's wife, must get a good shot with the tranquilizer gun. Touching the sleeping tiger who is "one four-thousandth of the world's tigers," the poet realizes complexity of the ties between life and death, how easily sundered they are, how varied and strange:

> I touch the ribs, the whorled sleeping flank,
> stutter of heartbeat, . . .
>
> *and there we wailed as we/ remembered Zion.*
> And slowly the liquid pearls in the flask, churn.

With allusions to the book of Psalms, poet William Blake, and musician Jimmy Cliff, Wojahn continues to mingle different cultural references as commentary.

One of the most beautiful poems in this collection, "God of Journeys and Secret Tidings," is a sonnet that speaks of the death of Wojahn's first wife, Lynda Hull. The restraint that the sonnet as poetic form requires is juxtaposed against the emotional power of the circumstances:

> And how, indeed, could such beauty be borne,
> except by the shoulders of a god? Here on the dome
> of hell it rains, and you are six months' dead.
> The answering machine tonight spins down—
> . . . .
> . . . And on them is your voice.

The poet acknowledges the powerful effect that words can have. For Wojahn as poet, words seem possessed of mythic, holy qualities. He writes as if he were a word-shaman, able at will to summon those powers.

OTHER MAJOR WORKS

NONFICTION: *Strange Good Fortune: Essays on Contemporary Poetry*, 2000.

EDITED TEXTS: *The Pushcart Prize XI: Best of the Small Presses*, 1986 (with Bill Henderson and Philip Levine); *A Profile of Twentieth Century American Poetry*, 1991 (with Jack Myers); *The Only World: Poems*, 1995.

BIBLIOGRAPHY

Elledge, Jim. *Sweet Nothings: An Anthology of Rock and Roll in American Poetry*. Bloomington: Indiana University Press, 1994. This anthology presents a collection of poems that use rock and roll as source material. Elledge includes Wojahn's comments about the poems collected here. Included are "Buddy Holly" (*Icehouse Lights*), "Song of the Burning" (*Glassworks*), and "W. C. W. Watching Presley's Second Appearance on 'The Ed Sullivan Show': Mercy Hospital, Newark, 1956" (*Mystery Train*).

Jauss, David. "To Become Music or Break: Lynda Hull as an Undergraduate." *Crazyhorse* 55 (Winter, 1998). A poignant essay discussing the poetry of Lynda Hull, David Wojahn's late wife. Written by her third teacher, the essay discusses Wojahn's influence on her poetry. Both men were her instructors at the University of Arkansas at Little Rock.

Stein, Kevin. *Private Poets, Worldly Acts*. Athens: Ohio University Press, 1997. Includes the essay "Manipulating Cultural Assumptions: Transgressions and Obedience in David Wojahn's Rock 'n' Roll Sonnets." Very comprehensive, this essay presents a cogent analysis of Wojahn's use of this material, especially in its working through the cultural assumptions against which the poems work.

Wojahn, David. "An Interview with David Wojahn." Interview by Jonathan Veitch. *Contemporary Literature* 36, no. 3 (Fall, 1995): 393-411. Wojahn comments on the influences that have shaped his poems. He notes his love for poets such as James Wright and Richard Hugo and his interest in family history, especially the way the mind works to remember events and details.

Martha Modena Vertreace-Doody

WOLFRAM VON ESCHENBACH

Born: Germany(?); c. 1170
Died: Germany(?); c. 1217

PRINCIPAL POETRY

Lieder, c. 1200
Parzival, c. 1200-1210 (English translation, 1894)
Titurel, c. 1217 (*Schionatulander and Sigune*, 1960)
Willehalm, c. 1212-1217 (*Willehalm*, 1977)

OTHER LITERARY FORMS

All surviving manuscripts of works attributed to Wolfram von Eschenbach lead to the conclusion that he was exclusively a poet. His masterpiece, *Parzival*, is considered the father of the *Bildungsroman*, or novel of development. This paternity is extremely tenuous, however, resting on affinities of characterization rather than of genre; the first recognizable novel did not appear until some 450 years after *Parzival*.

ACHIEVEMENTS

Although Wolfram von Eschenbach was roundly criticized by his contemporary Gottfried von Strassburg as a "fabricator of wild tales," other poets and especially Wolfram's audience were more appreciative. The extraordinarily large number of extant manuscripts—eighty-four separate manuscripts or fragments of *Parzival* and seventy-six of *Willehalm*—attests his popularity. In comparison, other major works of the High Middle Ages would seem to have been in less demand; *The Nibelungenlied* (c. 1200) exists in thirty-four versions, Gottfried von Strassburg's *Tristan und Isolde* (c. 1210; *Tristan and Isolde*, 1899) in only twenty-three. Still, modern critics also proclaim Wolfram to have been a careless poet, unrefined and unlearned. Yet, Wolfram's works sparkle with his own vital personality in an era of subdued conventionality. In contrast to the sophisticated stylists Gottfried and Hartmann von Aue, Wolfram wrote with color, depicting exotic scenes and exciting adventures in vibrant tones. His language is uniquely robust, studded with heroic (rather than courtly) terminology, Franconian dialect, and French loanwords, as well as a number of neologisms. Often chosen for resonance and acoustical effect, his language lends additional energy to his rhetorically crafted tales. His style is serious and humorous, insightful and charmingly frivolous. In short, Wolfram was a thoroughly delightful storyteller who constantly manipulated his audience as well as his characters.

Wolfram has attained immortality, however, not as a result of his personality or style. Because of his inferior social status as a layman, Wolfram was able to view courtly society from both within and without, to question assumptions and conventions with unusual detachment, often with humor. He fused disparate sources and traditions to form new and challenging visions of man and society which remain viable to this day. In *Parzival*, for example, he created a poem monumental in size and scope which illuminates timeless concepts such as ignorance and wisdom, grief and courage, guilt and salvation. This tale of the Holy Grail, of King Arthur's Round Table and attendant knights and ladies, transcends the realm of the courtly romance; indeed, the Arthurian circle is shown to be less than the ideal so often propagated by lesser poets. Of greater import is the development of an individual who ultimately attains the highest position on earth, a worldly king who represents the highest of spiritual values as well—a noble goal for all humankind. Wolfram's works all exhibit this critical yet hopeful attitude. James Poag writes in his *Wolfram von Eschenbach:* "As a man and poet [Wolfram] was totally committed to probing the implications of the chivalric way of life. In *Parzival* and *Willehalm*, he transformed the knightly calling into a poetic symbol of man struggling toward spirituality." Wolfram invested his poetry with vitality, humor, mystery, and a lofty purpose. These same qualities engage the reader, now as then, and will continue to command thoughtful consideration.

BIOGRAPHY

To possess factual information pertaining to the life of *any* courtly poet is a rare occurrence; the poet as professional writer and public figure is, after all, a relatively recent phenomenon. In the case of Wolfram von Eschenbach, few documented details exist. Fortunately, Wolfram was a personable poet who could not refrain from injecting his experiences and opinions into his works. From his utterances, scholars have been able to reconstruct a plausible, if sketchy, vita.

Drawing on literary references, dialect evidence, and geographical speculation, scholars have concluded that Wolfram's home was probably in Eschenbach, a Franconian town southeast of Ansbach in present-day Bavaria. There is no record of his family, of his formative years, or of his schooling. In fact, Wolfram's innocent pronouncement in *Parzival*, "I don't know a single letter of the alphabet," has become enigmatic: Does he intend to admit his unlearned background, to boast of his literary accomplishment despite his inability to read and write, or to twit his educated principal critic, Gottfried? In any event, it is clear that he was not formally educated, for influences of classical Latin writers (a staple in the monastery schools) are absent in his poems. Significantly, Wolfram himself never mentioned having "read" from his literary sources; his frequent references to having "heard" information leads scholars to presume that source material was actually dictated to him by a succession of literate scribes. One assumes today that

Wolfram von Eschenbach depicted as a knight. (© Bettmann/Corbis)

Wolfram was an autodidact who learned those things necessary for the background of his tales; he was certainly familiar with French literature of the day and well acquainted with the works of contemporary German authors.

Despite his fame as a poet, Wolfram considered himself to be first and foremost a knight, though it is unlikely that he ever wielded a sword. As a layman and member of the petty nobility, he was unpropertied and poor his entire life, at the mercy of his patrons and audience. One of Wolfram's patrons, at least for a time, was the fabled Landgrave Herrmann of Thuringia; the legendary *Sängerkrieg*, or troubadours' competition, at Hermann's castle, however, appears to be only that: a legend.

A definitive chronology of Wolfram's works cannot be established. His lyric poetry, of which only nine songs still exist, consists primarily of *Tagelieder*, or morning songs—some of the finest in German poetry. Since there are so few, and they are of a conventional nature, most scholars presume that they were created prior to Wolfram's greater epic poems. From historical references included in the work, it appears that *Parzival* was begun about the beginning of the thirteenth century and, with interruption, finally completed approximately ten years later. *Willehalm* would appear to be the most mature of Wolfram's writings in style and content, while the other fragment, *Schionatulander and Sigune*, contains a historical note which suggests that it originated well after the completion of *Parzival*. How, when, or where Wolfram died remains a mystery, though one contemporary insists that he died while writing the manuscript of *Schionatulander and Sigune*.

ANALYSIS

The small corpus of nine songs that can be safely attributed to Wolfram von Eschenbach were presumably composed early in his literary career. More than half of these can be categorized as *Tagelieder*, or morning songs, a type of courtly poem which Wolfram refined for his German audience. The typical situation depicts daybreak and the call of the watchman, announcing the day's arrival to a pair of young lovers. Obviously, the man must leave, for if he were seen, his honor and the lady's reputation would be ruined. There is a tearful farewell, a last embrace, and the man departs. Wolfram's songs develop this theme artistically, allowing each of the three figures—watchman, man, and woman—to present in turn the episode from his (or her) individual point of view. Wolfram employed rhythmic crescendos to accentuate the dramatic moments of daybreak and farewell in a sensual atmosphere.

One noteworthy variation among Wolfram's lyrics is the antimorning song. Here, the poet speaks directly to the watchman, reprimanding him for warning the waking lovers. In praise of connubial bliss, the poet extols the security of matrimony, which requires no secrecy and no painful farewells at dawn. Although this song is not one of Wolfram's finer creations, it does highlight his witty and often mocking temperament, a trait which can be traced throughout his later works. The same parodistic tone is evident in the remaining songs. The common theme in these poems is courting the favor of a lady. Conventional and even second-rank in appearance, these works display qualities which parody the entire established tradition of courtly love poetry. By pirating famous lines from other poems and including trite love phrases, Wolfram created fanciful songs which attest the superficiality of courtly conventions.

PARZIVAL

Wolfram's greatest achievement is clearly *Parzival*. This epic romance is enormous in scope, portraying literally dozens of legendary characters who span Europe and Asia over an extended period of time. The number of questions surrounding its creation are enormous as well: Which source or sources inspired Wolfram? Is *Parzival* indebted to Chrêtien de Troyes and Robert de Boron, to a combination of various related tales, or to the mysterious "Kyot," as Wolfram insists? Was the work interrupted by war or by Wolfram's changing mood? Was it written under the auspices of one or more patrons? Was the work composed in the same chronological order in which it appears today? Were the first two books—that is, the prologue—written only after the completion of the entire manuscript and then added to the beginning of Parzival's story? These are a few of the nagging questions surrounding Wolfram's classic tale. It is certain only that *Parzival* was not written in one uninterrupted effort and that publication of separate episodes preceded the final edition of almost twenty-five thousand lines.

Though *Parzival* is an Arthurian romance, it is clearly differentiated from earlier versions by its non-Celtic preoccupation with Christianity and the Holy Grail. Artificially divided into sixteen books by the philologist Karl Lachmann, the work traces the life and development of Parzival and his Arthurian counterpart, Gawan. In a prologue, the audience learns that Parzival's father, Gahmuret, was an exemplary knight. Through a series of adventures, Gahmuret wins and marries first a heathen queen and then a Christian queen, finally to die in chivalric pursuit of further love and fame. Upon the birth of her son, Parzival, the Christian queen fears that he will end like his father; therefore, she rears the boy in complete ignorance of courtly society. One day, young Parzival encounters several knights and immediately decides that he, too, must partake of this splendid life. For his protection, his mother sends him off in fool's garb and gives misleading advice, hoping that he will soon return unharmed and chastened. After his departure, she dies of a broken heart, but young Parzival perseveres, soon joining King Arthur's knights at the Round Table. He then discovers the Grail Castle and its king, Anfortas, who suffers from a most painful affliction. Failing to "ask the question"—that is, to show compassion and inquire as to the origins of the wound and the condition of the king—Parzival is expelled from the castle for his uncharitable silence. Because of his ignorance, inexperience, and overwhelming desire to become a knight, he commits numerous sins of omission and commission. Guided only by his heart and the wise counsel of the hermit, Trevrezent, Parzival matures through years of lonely struggle, proving that he is worthy of his responsibilities as a knight and as a Christian.

As Parzival wanders off into the wilderness in search of himself, Wolfram introduces Gawan, a member in good standing of Arthur's Round Table. Gawan is the epitome of the medieval knight, at once adept in chivalric combat and skillful in the conventional graces required of all nobility. He is ever willing to fight on behalf of a worthy cause or a beautiful lady, and he fulfills his Christian duties with similar ease. During the course of the tale, Wolfram clearly distinguishes Gawan from Parzival on one crucial issue: Gawan's Christianity is the fulfillment of a chivalric vow, an obligation to which he is committed, while Parzival's spiritual quest derives from inner motivation. Whereas Gawan accepts his religion unquestioningly, Parzival must struggle with doubt, at one point even renouncing God for his apparent injustice. This difference is finally decisive; it is the reason that Parzival and not Gawan will ultimately become Grail King—that is, the personification of the highest values both in worldly society (as king) and in the spiritual realm (of the Grail). At the conclusion of the epic, Parzival is crowned King of the Grail, reunited with his wife and friends, and introduced to a stranger from India; this speckled man is his half brother, Feirefiz, the child of Gahmuret's heathen queen. Together, from Europe to India (that being the extent of the known world in Wolfram's day), the sons of Gahmuret will uphold courtly and Christian values, to the benefit of all humankind.

It is clear, then, that *Parzival* is not the shallow, disorganized composition described by Wolfram's critics. The epic can and should be considered on various levels: as a historical depiction of the encounter between East and West, evidenced by the Crusades and the Christian mission to baptize the heathen hordes; as an Arthurian romance in which the knight's achievements are judged by this exemplary courtly society; as a "double novel" concerning the separate exploits of both Parzival and Gawan; and, finally, as an account of the spiritual development of a worthy soul from simpleton to sage, from sin to redemption and the attainment of humility and purity.

SCHIONATULANDER AND SIGUNE

Schionatulander and Sigune, like *Willehalm*, is an epic fragment composed at the end of Wolfram's life. The 164 stanzas of the original were later expanded by an anonymous poet who added more than six thousand stanzas to form *Der jüngere Titurel* (c. 1272)—though this final version does not seem to correspond to Wolfram's intentions. In any event, most scholars believe that the work is nearly complete as it now stands. There are few possibilities for diversion; the inevitable conclusion (Schionatulander's death) clearly limits the narrative's chronological scope.

Though there is an indication that *Schionatulander and Sigune* was Wolfram's final work, most scholars would prefer to place *Willehalm* in that position, based primarily on sentimental reasons. The latter deals with major ethical and philosophical questions concerning world peace and interdenominational coexistence, while the former is a tale revolving around two minor characters from *Parzival*. The German title *Titurel* is, in fact, a misnomer, corrected in the English translation (according to medieval custom, the title was taken from the name of the first character to appear). Thus, in a prologue, old King Titurel reflects on his long and eventful life before surrendering his kingdom and the Holy Grail to his son. Years later, one of Titurel's grandchildren marries a knight, only to die in childbirth; her surviving offspring is Sigune. Already the attentive listener will recall from *Parzival* this fateful name; Sigune is shown mourning the death of her beloved Schionatulander, who died at the hand of Orilus. This fragment, then, accounts for the earlier years of their relationship and clarifies their tragic fate. In short, the two youths fall in love and must abide by courtly convention—that is, they must restrain their passion. While on a walk in the forest one day, they discover a dog wearing a jeweled collar; the collar itself is inscribed with the love story of a similar couple. Before Sigune can finish reading the story, the dog dashes off. She then declares that she will not grant her love to Schionatulander until he brings back the collar. Here the fragment ends. From episodes appearing in *Parzival*, the listener knows that this pure, youthful love can never be fulfilled and that Sigune will spend the rest of her days mourning her lost lover until they are reunited in Heaven.

The theme here is tragic, the atmosphere filled with the poet's realization that life's brief happiness must be purchased at a fearful price. Sigune does not criticize the courtly conventions by which she must act (although some critics note that her trivial demand leads to her lover's death); as mentioned above, several other couples in Wolfram's works suffer similar losses. Sigune must learn to live with her fate and accept the fact that she was destined to love Schionatulander chastely, in sublimation of their great passion for each other. Loyalty, constancy, and God's grace will ultimately purify their love.

WILLEHALM

It is generally agreed that even had Wolfram not written his *Parzival*, he would deserve lasting fame for his *Schionatulander and Sigune* and for *Willehalm*. While *Schionatulander and Sigune* depicts the beauties and sorrows of courtly love, *Willehalm* is strikingly innovative in its treatment of timeless values. Wolfram's primary source, *Bataille d'Aliscans* (late twelfth century), was provided by Landgrave Herrmann of Thuringia for a commission, though the epic Wolfram created went far beyond the original, in scope and significance. The historical Willehalm (Guillaume d'Orange) contributed to the defeat of invading Arabs with his valiant efforts in combat, yet scarcely ten years later he renounced worldly ambitions and entered a monastery. Although Wolfram does not specifically emphasize this aspect of Willehalm's spiritual development, it becomes obvious that his story is intended as a sort of *Legende*, or life of a saint.

As one would assume from the French source, war is a major theme in *Willehalm*. Willehalm, the son of Count Henry of Narbonne, is sent into the world to seek his fortune at the court of Charlemagne. After numerous adventures, Willehalm marries Gyburg, the daughter of a heathen king who then invades Willehalm's realm to reclaim his daughter. Willehalm gathers his army and engages in fierce battles with the enemy. In spite of his ferocity, Willehalm's heroic exploits are not to be misconstrued; his immediate desire is simply to protect his wife. The increasingly murderous battle scenes are twice interrupted by carefully placed interludes; in both instances, Willehalm is able to rejoin Gyburg, and the couple enjoy a brief respite from the war in each other's arms. Here, Wolfram presents conjugal love as an extension of God's love, as a means to offset the brutal reality of life and as a form of *unio mystica* through which God's grace can be anticipated. Gradually, Willehalm and Gyburg come to the realization that both heathen and Christian are children of God, that it is a great loss when so many must die. Wolfram's is the first depiction in German literature of a loving, merciful God who would protect all his children, regardless of their faith. Following the conclusive victory over the heathen army, Willehalm's newly gained tolerance is very much in evidence; he frees his prisoners, allowing the vanquished to collect their dead and transport them to their homeland, there to be honored and buried according to their own religious customs.

Knights of the Middle Ages were deeply imbued with an Augustinian worldview: Heathens were servants of the Devil, and it was the duty of all Christians to destroy the infidel, thereby achieving more quickly the Kingdom of God on Earth. If one killed a heathen, honor and fame were the reward; if one were killed fighting heathens, so much the better, for the knight was guaranteed eternal life in Heaven. The Crusades were conducted in this spirit. Willehalm, too, pronounces his support for this credo at the outset, but as the story progresses and the slaughter mounts on both sides, Willehalm undergoes a dramatic change of heart. His initial missionary zeal, reminiscent of the Crusades, is replaced by understanding and tolerance. Thus does Wolfram combine his two major themes of war and love in a strikingly innovative presentation that proved extremely popular with its audiences.

Wolfram depicts two contending armies, heathen and Christian, which nevertheless are governed by similar conventions: knights on both sides fighting on behalf of their ladies in courtly service. Though the heathens are influenced by an almost carnal love which is raised to a religious fervor, the Christians are motivated by courtly love and spiritual devotion to God. Wolfram's critical insight here is that both sides represent poles of one great love which originates in God. This sophisticated concept of love is Wolfram's contribution to eternal respect, love, and peace.

Willehalm could have concluded with a happy ending reminiscent of fairy tales, but the older Wolfram sought a more realistic solution, one which recognized that life's brief joys are often outweighed by horrendous tragedy and sadness. Despite obvious similarities, the significant differences between *Parzival* and *Willehalm* concern the appearance of this new reality, akin to the modern concept of existential angst. Poag sees these differences in terms of a contrast between the underlying values of two distinct literary forms: "The structure of the romance [*Parzival*] pointed to a reliable reassuring order, whereas the structure of the battle epic [*Willehalm*] tends to call attention to the openness and uncertainty of human existence." In *Willehalm*, Wolfram demonstrates that courtly convention is precisely that: a formality which does not protect the individual from the vicissitudes of life. Here it becomes evident how far Wolfram has strayed from the Augustinian attitude. His literary creation, Willehalm, is no missionary zealot, possessed with exterminating the heathens. He is a defender of Christian values as embodied in the Holy Roman Empire, though his martial duties are as painful to him as his enforced separation from his wife, Gyburg. Yet she, too, plays an important role in this new vision of Christian tolerance, for in this character Wolfram has created perhaps the most vivid portrait of a woman in all medieval literature. Though Gyburg, as a woman, has no recourse to such knightly philosophy, she represents in her person the admirable traits of humanity, piety, mercy, and love which are a reflection of God's grace. Like Willehalm, Gyburg is proclaimed a saint at the story's conclusion.

Out of a desire for symmetry or the aforementioned sentimentality, most scholars would find it especially fitting if *Willehalm*—this mature, noble, and modern work—were Wolfram's last testament. His *Parzival* will continue to inspire readers with its idealism, but it is *Willehalm* which offers the most hope to humankind through its thoughtful and realistic portrayal of tolerance and universal love as antidotes to the eternal curses of prejudice, hate, and aggression.

BIBLIOGRAPHY

Green, Dennis H. *The Art of Recognition in Wolfram's Parzival*. New York: Cambridge University Press, 1982. Studies narration in Wolfram's poem, focusing on moments when the audience is given seemingly accurate information. The juxtaposition of true and false information puts the audience into the same position as Parzival, caught between certainty and ignorance while seeking a larger truth.

Groos, Arthur. *Romancing the Grail: Genre, Science, and Quest in Wolfram's Parzival*. Ithaca, N.Y.: Cornell University Press, 1995. With roots in the critical theory of Russian scholar Mikhail Bahktin, this study examines the narrative discourse of one of Wolfram's major poems. Unfortunately, Groos is not especially successful in applying a critical theory which was designed to interpret modern novels to this major work of medieval poetry. Moreover, Groos does not pay enough attention to Wolfram's other major works.

Hasty, Will, ed. *A Companion to Wolfram's Parzival.* Columbia: Camden House, 1999. A valuable guide to those readers who are familiar with modern literary theory. An anthology of critical essays, this work presents a variety of scholarly perspectives on Wolfram von Eschenbach, his major and minor works, and his cultural milieu.

Hutchins, Eileen. *Parzival: An Introduction.* London: Temple Lodge, 1979. A fine introduction to general subjects of importance for the study of the poet and his works. These subjects include an overview of romances, Grail legends, and various treatments of Parzival in folklore and other literary works.

Poag, James F. *Wolfram von Eschenbach.* New York: Twayne, 1972. One of the best introductions to the medieval poet and his works. Like other books in the Twayne series, this work offers general information on the author and his works. Further, Poag studies the structure, sources, and significance of *Parzival.* In addition, the study presents a short summary of previous scholarship on Wolfram von Eschenbach.

Todd C. Hanlin;
bibliography updated by Michael R. Meyers

WILLIAM WORDSWORTH

Born: Cockermouth, England; April 7, 1770
Died: Rydal Mount, England; April 23, 1850

PRINCIPAL POETRY

An Evening Walk, 1793

Descriptive Sketches, 1793

Lyrical Ballads, 1798 (with Samuel Taylor Coleridge)

Lyrical Ballads, with Other Poems, 1800 (with Samuel Taylor Coleridge, includes preface)

Poems in Two Volumes, 1807

The Excursion, 1814

Poems, 1815

The White Doe of Rylstone, 1815

Peter Bell, 1819

The Waggoner, 1819

The River Duddon, 1820

Ecclesiastical Sketches, 1822

Poems Chiefly of Early and Late Years, 1842

The Prelude: Or, The Growth of a Poet's Mind, 1850

Poetical Works, 1940-1949 (5 volumes; Ernest de Selincourt and Helen Darbishire, editors)

OTHER LITERARY FORMS

In addition to his poetry, William Wordsworth's preface to the second edition of his *Lyrical Ballads* is the single most important manifesto of the Romantic position in English, defining his ideas of the primary laws of nature, the working of the imagination, the process of association of ideas, and the balance of passion and restraint in human conduct.

ACHIEVEMENTS

William Wordsworth was one of the leading English Romantic poets. Along with William Blake (1757-1827), Samuel Taylor Coleridge (1772-1834), Lord Byron (1788-1824), Percy Bysshe Shelley (1792-1822), and John Keats (1795-1821), Wordsworth created a major revolution in ideology and poetic style around 1800. The Romantic writers rebelled against the neoclassical position exemplified in the works of Alexander Pope (1688-1744) and Samuel Johnson (1709-1784). Although all such broad generalizations should be viewed with suspicion, it is generally said that the neoclassical writers valued restraint and discipline, whereas the Romantic poets favored individual genius and hoped to follow nature freely. Wordsworth's poetry praises the value of the simple individual, the child, the helpless, the working class, and the natural man. Such sentiments were explosive in the age of the French Revolution, when Wordsworth was young. He helped to define the attitudes which fostered the spread of democracy, of more humane treatment of the downtrodden, and of respect for nature.

BIOGRAPHY

The northwestern corner of England, which contains the counties of Northumberland and Westmorland, is both mountainous and inaccessible. The cliffs are not as high as those in Switzerland, but they are rugged and the

William Wordsworth (Library of Congress)

land is settled mainly by shepherds and by isolated farmers. The valleys have long, narrow, picturesque lakes, and so the region is called the English Lake District. William Wordsworth was born and lived much of his life among these lakes. Many of the English Romantic writers are sometimes called "lake poets" because of their association with this area. Wordsworth was born in 1770 in the small town of Cockermouth in Cumberland. Although he later wrote about the lower classes, his own family was middle class, and the poet never actually worked with his hands to make his living. His father was a lawyer who managed the affairs of the earl of Lonsdale. The poet had three brothers (Richard, John, and Christopher) and a sister (Dorothy). For the first nine years of his life, the family inhabited a comfortable house near the Derwent River. William attended Anne Birkett's school in the little town of Penrith, where Mary Hutchinson, whom he married in 1802, was also a student. His mother died when he was seven. The two brothers, William and Richard, then boarded at the house of Ann Tyson while attending grammar school in the village of Hawkshead.

Apparently this arrangement was a kindly one, and the boy spent much time happily roaming the nearby fields and hills. He also profited from the teaching of his schoolmaster William Taylor, who encouraged him to write poetry. In 1783 his father died and the family inheritance was tied up in litigation for some twenty years. Only after the death of the earl of Lonsdale in 1802 was Wordsworth able to profit from his father's estate. With the help of relatives, he matriculated at St. John's College, Cambridge University. Although he did not earn distinction as a student, those years were fertile times for learning.

While he was a student at St. John's, between 1787 and 1791, the French Revolution broke out across the English Channel. During his summer vacation of 1790, Wordsworth and his college friend, Robert Jones, went on a walking tour across France and Switzerland to Italy. The young students were much impressed by the popular revolution and the spirit of democracy in France at that time. Wordsworth took his degree at St. John's in January, 1791, but had no definite plans for his future. The following November he went again to revolution-torn France with the idea of learning the French language well enough to earn his living as a tutor. Passing through Paris, he settled at Blois in the Loire Valley. There he made friends with Captain Michael Beaupuy and became deeply involved in French Republican thought. There, too, he fell in love with Annette Vallon, who was some four years older than the young poet. Vallon and Wordsworth had an illegitimate daughter, Caroline, but Wordsworth returned to England alone in December, 1792, probably to try to arrange his financial affairs. In February, 1793, war broke out between France and England so that Wordsworth was not able to see his baby and her mother again until the Treaty of Amiens in 1802 made it possible for him to visit them. His daughter was then ten years old.

In 1793 Wordsworth must have been a very unhappy young man: His deepest sympathies were on the side of France and democracy, but his own country was at war against his French friends such as Captain Michael Beaupuy; he was separated from Annette and his baby, and his English family associates looked on his conduct as scandalous; the earl of Lonsdale refused to settle his father's financial claims, so the young man was without funds and had no way to earn a living, even though he held a bachelor's degree from a prestigious university. Under these conditions, he moved in politically radical circles, becoming friendly with William Godwin, Mary Wollstonecraft, and Tom Paine. In 1793 he published his first books of poetry, *An Evening Walk* and *Descriptive Sketches*.

Wordsworth and his younger sister, Dorothy, were close friends. In 1795 the poet benefitted from a small legacy to settle with her at Racedown Cottage in Dorset, where they were visited by Mary Hutchinson and Samuel Taylor Coleridge. In 1797 they moved to Alfoxden, near Nether Stowey in Somerset, to be near Coleridge's home. Here a period of intense creativity occurred: Dorothy began her journal in 1798 while Wordsworth and Coleridge collaborated on *Lyrical Ballads*. A walking trip with Dorothy along the Wye River resulted in 1798 in "Lines Composed a Few Miles Above Tintern Abbey." That fall, Coleridge, Dorothy, and Wordsworth went to study in Germany. Dorothy and the poet spent most of their time in Goslar, where apparently he began to write *The Prelude*, his major autobiographical work which he left unfinished at his death. Returning from Germany, he and Dorothy settled in Dove Cottage in the Lake District. In 1800 he completed "Michael" and saw the second edition of *Lyrical Ballads* published. With the end of hostilities in 1802, Wordsworth visited Vallon and their daughter in France, arranging to make an annual child-support payment. Upon his return to England, he married Mary Hutchinson. During that year he composed "Ode: Intimations of Immortality from Recollections of Early Childhood."

In 1805 his brother John was drowned at sea. Wordsworth often looked upon nature as a kindly force, but the death of his brother in a shipwreck may have been a powerful contribution to his darkening vision of nature as he grew older. In 1805 he had a completed draft of *The Prelude* ready for Coleridge to read, although he was never satisfied with the work as a whole and rewrote it extensively later. It is sometimes said that when Wordsworth was a "bad" man, fathering an illegitimate child, consorting with revolutionaries and drug addicts, and roaming the countryside with no useful occupation, he wrote "good" poetry. When he became a "good" man, respectably married and gainfully employed, he began

to write "bad" poetry. It is true that, although he wrote prolifically until his death, not much of his work after about 1807 is considered remarkable. In 1813 he accepted the position of Distributor of Stamps for Westmorland County, the kind of governmental support he probably would have scorned when he was younger. His fame as a writer, however, grew steadily. In 1842 when his last volume, *Poems Chiefly of Early and Late Years*, was published, he accepted a government pension of three hundred pounds sterling per annum, a considerable sum. The next year he succeeded Robert Southey as poet laureate of England. He died April 23, 1850, at Rydal Mount in his beloved Lake District.

ANALYSIS

When the volume of poetry called the *Lyrical Ballads* of 1798 was published in a second edition (1800), William Wordsworth wrote a prose preface for the book which is the single most important statement of Romantic ideology. It provides a useful introduction to his poetry.

THE PREFACE TO LYRICAL BALLADS

Wordsworth's preface displays the idea of primitivism as the basis of the Romantic position. Primitivism is the belief that there is some primary, intrinsically good "state of nature" from which adult, educated, civilized man has fallen into a false or wicked state of existence. When Jean Jacques Rousseau began *The Social Contract* (1762) with the assertion that "Man was born free, and yet we see him everywhere in chains," he concisely expressed the primitivist point of view. The American and French revolutions were both predicated on Romantic primitivism, the idea that man was once naturally free, but that corrupt kings, churches, and social customs held him enslaved. The Romantic typically sees rebellion and breaking free from false restraint to regain a state of nature as highly desirable; Wordsworth's preface shows him deeply committed to this revolutionary ideology. He says that he is going to take the subjects of his poems from "humble and rustic life" because in that condition man is "less under restraint" and the "elementary feelings" of life exist in a state of simplicity.

Many writers feel that serious literature can be written only about great and powerful men, such as kings and generals. Some writers apparently believe that wounding a king is tragic, while beating a slave is merely funny. Wordsworth's preface firmly rejects such ideas. He turns to simple, common, poor people as the topic of his poetry because they are nearer a "state of nature" than the powerful, educated, and sophisticated men who have been corrupted by false customs of society. Many writers feel that they must live in the centers of civilization, London or Paris, for example, in order to be conversant with new ideas and the latest fashions. Wordsworth turns away from the cities to the rural scene. He himself lived in the remote Lake District most of his life, and he wrote about simple shepherds, farmers, and villagers. He explains that he chooses for his topics

> humble and rustic life . . . because, in that condition, the essential passions of the heart find a better soil in which they can attain their maturity, are less under restraint, and speak a plainer and more emphatic language; because in that condition of life our elementary feelings coexist in a state of greater simplicity, and consequently may be more accurately contemplated.

He sees a correspondence between the unspoiled nature of man and the naturalness of his environment. Romantic ideology of this sort underlies much of the contemporary environmentalist movement: the feeling that man ought to be in harmony with his environment, that nature is beneficent, that man ought to live simply so that the essential part of his human nature may conform to the grand pattern of nature balanced in the whole universe.

The use of the words "passion" and "restraint" in Wordsworth's quotation above is significant. English neoclassical writers such as Alexander Pope tended to be suspicious of human passions, arguing that anger and lust lead man into error unless such passions are restraint by right reason. For Pope, it is necessary to exercise the restraint of reason over passion in order for man to be morally good. "Restraint" is good; "passion" bad. Wordsworth reverses this set of values. Man's natural primitive feelings are the source of goodness and morality; the false restraints of custom and education are what lead man astray from his natural goodness. In his preface, Wordsworth seems to be following the line of thought developed by Anthony Ashley Cooper, earl of Shaftesbury (1671-1713) in his *An Inquiry Concerning Virtue or Merit* (1709). Shaftesbury asks his readers to imagine a "creature who, wanting reason and being unable to reflect, has notwithstanding many good qualities and affections,—as love to his kind, courage, gratitude or pity." Shaftesbury probably is thinking of creatures such as a faithful dog, a child too young to reason well, or a kindly mental defective. In such cases one would have to say that the creature shows good qualities, even though he lacks reasoning power. For Shaftesbury, then, to reason means merely to recognize the already existing good impulses or feelings naturally arising in such a creature. Morality arises from natural feeling, evidently present in creatures with little reasoning power.

Wordsworth's preface is heavily influenced by Shaftesbury's argument. He turns to simple characters for his poems because they exhibit the natural, primary, unspoiled states of feeling that are the ultimate basis of morality. Wordsworth's characters are sentimental heroes, chosen because their feelings are unspoiled by restraints of education and reason: children, simple shepherds, and villagers, the old Cumberland Beggar, an idiot boy, Alice Fell, and so on. While William Shakespeare often puts a nobleman at the center of his plays and relegates the poor people to the role of rustic clowns, Wordsworth takes the feelings of the poor as the most precious subject of serious literature.

The preface displays two kinds of primitivism. Social primitivism is the belief that man's state of nature is good and that it is possible to imagine a social setting in which man's naturally good impulses will flourish. Social primitivism leads to the celebration of the "noble savage," perhaps an American Indian or a Black African tribesman, who is supposed to be morally superior to the sophisticated European who has been corrupted by the false restraints of his own society. Social primitivism was of course one of the driving forces behind the French Revolution. The lower classes rose up against the repression of politically powerful kings and destroyed laws and restraints so that their natural goodness could flourish. Unfortunately, the French Revolution did not produce a morally perfect new man once the corrupt restraints had been destroyed. Instead, the French Revolution produced the Reign of Terror, the rise of Napoleon to military dictatorship, and the French wars of aggression against relatively democratic states such as the Swiss Republic. With unspeakable shock, Wordsworth and the other Romantics saw the theory of social primitivism fail in France. The decline of Wordsworth's poetic power as he grew older is often explained in part as the result of his disillusionment with revolutionary France.

A second kind of primitivism in the preface is psychological. Psychological primitivism is the belief that there is some level in the mind which is primary, more certain than everyday consciousness. In the preface, Wordsworth says that humble life displays "the primary laws of our nature; chiefly, as far as the manner in which we associate ideas." Here Wordsworth refers to a very important Romantic idea, associational psychology, which developed from the tradition of British empirical philosophy—from John Locke's *Essay Concerning Human Understanding* (1690), David Hume's *Enquiry Concerning Human Understanding* (1748), and especially David Hartley's *Observations on Man* (1749).

When Wordsworth speaks in the preface to the *Lyrical Ballads* about tracing in his poems the "manner in which we associate ideas," he is endorsing the line of thought of the associational psychologists. Poems trace the process by which the mind works. They help people to understand the origins of their own feelings about what is good and bad by demonstrating the way impressions from nature strike the mind and by showing how the mind associates these simple experiences, forming complex attitudes about what proper conduct is, what fidelity and love are, what the good and the true are. In *The Prelude*, one of Wordsworth's main motives is to trace the history of the development of his own mind from its most elementary feelings through the process of association of ideas until his imagination constructs his complex, adult consciousness.

Wordsworth's preface to the second edition of *Lyrical Ballads* set out a series of ideas which are central to the revolutionary Romantic movement, including both social and psychological primitivism, the state of nature, the "noble savage," the sentimental hero, the power of the imagination, and the association of ideas. These concepts are basic to understanding his poetry.

"LINES COMPOSED A FEW MILES ABOVE TINTERN ABBEY"

Wordsworth's "Lines Composed a Few Miles Above Tintern Abbey" (hereafter called simply "Tintern Ab-

bey") was composed on July 13, 1798, and published that same year. It is one of the best-known works of the English Romantic movement. Its poetic form is blank verse, unrhymed iambic pentameter, in the tradition of John Milton's *Paradise Lost* (1667). In reading any poem, it is important to define its dramatic situation and to consider the text as if it were a scene from a play or drama and determine who is speaking, to whom, and under what circumstances. Wordsworth is very precise in telling the reader when and where these lines are spoken. Tintern Abbey exists, and the poet Wordsworth really visited it during a tour on July 13, 1798. Because the poem is set at a real point in history rather than once upon a time, and in a real place rather than in a kingdom far away, it is said to exhibit "topographic realism." The speaker of the poem reveals that this is his second visit to this spot; he had been there five years earlier. At line 23 he reveals that he has been away from this pleasant place for a long time and, at lines 50-56, that while he was away in the "fretful stir" of the world he was unhappy. When he was depressed, his thoughts turned to his memory of this natural scene and he felt comforted. Now, as the poem begins, he has come again to this beautiful site with his beloved younger sister, whom he names directly at line 121. The dramatic situation involves a speaker, or persona, who tells the reader his thoughts and feelings as if he were addressing his younger sister, who is "on stage" as his dramatic audience. Although the poem is autobiographical, so that the speaker resembles Wordsworth himself and the sister resembles Dorothy Wordsworth, it is better to think of the speaker and his listener as two invented characters in a little play. When William Shakespeare's Hamlet speaks to Ophelia in his play, the audience knows that Hamlet is not the same as Shakespeare, although he surely must express some of Shakespeare's feelings and ideas. So, too, the reader imagines that the speaker in "Tintern Abbey" speaks for Wordsworth, but is not exactly the same as the poet himself.

The poem displays many of the ideas stated in the preface to the *Lyrical Ballads*. It begins with a description of a remote rural scene, rather than speaking about the latest news from London. In this rustic setting, the poet discovers some essential truths about himself. The first twenty-two lines describe the natural scene: the cliffs, orchards, and farms. This is a romantic return to nature, the search for the beautiful and permanent forms which incorporate primitive human goodness. The speaker not only describes the scene, but also tells the reader how it generates feelings and sensations in him. In lines 23-56, the speaker says that his memory of this pure, natural place had been of comfort to him when he was far away. Lines 66-90 trace the speaker's memory of his process of growing up: When he first came among these hills as a boy, he was like a wild animal. He was filled with feelings of joy or fear by wild nature. As a boy, nature was to him "a feeling and a love" which required no thought on his part. That childish harmony with nature is now lost. His childish "aching joys" and "dizzy raptures" are "gone by." As he fell away from his unthinking harmony with nature, his power of thought developed. This power is "abundant recompense" for the childish joys of "thoughtless youth." Now he understands nature in a new way. He hears in nature "The still sad music of humanity." At line 95, he explains that his intellect grasps the purpose and direction of nature, whereas his childish experience was more intense and joyous but incomplete. Now, as an adult, he returns to this natural scene and understands what he had only felt as a child, that nature is the source of moral goodness, "the nurse, the guide, the guardian of my heart, and soul of all my moral being."

At line 110, he turns to his younger sister and sees in her wild eyes his own natural state of mind in childhood. He foresees that she will go through the same loss that he experienced. She too will grow up and lose her unthinking harmony with the natural and the wild. He takes comfort in the hope that nature will protect her, as it has helped him, and in the knowledge that the memory of this visit will be with her when she is far away in future years. Their experience of this pastoral landscape is therefore dear to the speaker for its own sake, and also because he has shared it with his sister. He has come back from the adult world and glimpsed primitive natural goodness both in the scene and in his sister.

The poem employs social and psychological primitivism. The rural scene is an imagined state of primitive nature where human goodness can exist in the child, like Adam in the garden of Eden before the fall of man. The poem shows how the primitive feelings of the boy are generated by the forms of nature and then form more and more complex ideas until his whole adult sense of good and bad, right and wrong, can be traced back to his elementary childish experiences of nature. Reason is not what makes beauty or goodness possible; natural feelings are the origin of the good and the beautiful. Reason merely recognizes what the child knows directly from his feelings.

Critics of Wordsworth point out that the "natural" scene described in the opening lines is, in fact, not at all "natural." Nature in this scene has been tamed by man into orchards, hedged fields, and cottage farms. What, critics ask, would Wordsworth have written if he had imagined nature as the struggling jungle in the Congo where individual plants and animals fight for survival in their environmental niche and whole species are brought to extinction by the force of nature "red in tooth and claw"? If Wordsworth's idea of nature is not true, then his idea of human nature will likewise be false. While he expects the French Revolution to lead to a state of nature in joy and harmony, in fact it led to the Reign of Terror and the bloodshed of the Napoleonic wars. Critics of Romantic ideology argue that when the Romantics imagine nature as a "kindly nurse," they unthinkingly accept a false anthropomorphism. Nature is not like a kindly human being; it is an indifferent or neutral force. They charge that Wordsworth projects his own feelings into the natural scene and thus his view of the human condition becomes dangerously confused.

"MICHAEL"

"Michael: A Pastoral Poem" was composed between October 11 and December 9, 1800, and published that same year. It is typical of Wordsworth's poetry about humble and rustic characters in which the sentiments or feelings of man in a state of nature are of central importance. The poem is written in blank verse, unrhymed iambic pentameter, again the meter employed in Milton's *Paradise Lost*. Milton's poem explores the biblical story of the fall of Adam from the Garden of Eden. Michael's destruction in Wordsworth's poem shows a general similarity to the tragedy of Adam in *Paradise Lost*. Both Michael and Adam begin in a natural paradise where they are happy and good. Evil creeps into each garden and, through the weakness of a beloved family member, both Adam and Michael fall from happiness to misery.

The poem "Michael" has two parts: the narrative frame and the tale of Michael. The frame occupies lines 1-39 and lines 475 to the end, the beginning and ending of the text. It relates the circumstances under which the story of Michael is told. The tale occupies lines 40-475, the central part of the text, and it tells the history of the shepherd Michael, his wife Isabel, and their son Luke. The frame of the poem occurs in the fictive present time, about 1800, whereas the tale occurs a generation earlier. The disintegration of Michael's family and the destruction of their cottage has already happened years before the poem begins. The frame establishes the poem is set in the English Lake District and introduces the reader to the "I-persona" or speaker of the poem. He tells the story of Michael, and knows the geography and history of the district. A "You-character" who does not know the region is the dramatic audience addressed by the "I-persona." In the frame, "I" tells "You" that there is a hidden valley up in the mountains. In that valley there is a pile of rocks, which would hardly be noticed by a stranger; but there is a story behind that heap of stones. "I" then tells "You" the story of the shepherd Michael.

Michael is one of the humble and rustic characters whose feelings are exemplary of the natural or primitive state of man. He has lived all his life in the mountains, in communion with nature, and his own nature has been shaped by his natural environment. He is a good and kindly man. He has a wife, Isabel, and a child of his old age named Luke. The family works from morning until far into the night, tending their sheep and spinning wool. They live in a cottage far up on the mountainside, and they have a lamp that burns late every evening as they sit at their work. They have become proverbial in the valley for their industry, so that their cottage has become known as the cottage of the evening star because its window glimmers steadily every night. These simple, hardworking people are "neither gay perhaps, nor cheerful, yet with objects and with hopes, living a life of eager industry." The boy is Michael's delight. From his birth, the old man had helped to tend the child and, as Luke grew, his father worked with him always at his side. He made him a perfect shepherd's staff and gave it to his son as a gift. Now the boy has reached his eighteenth year and the "old man's heart seemed born again" with hope and happiness in his son.

Unfortunately, Michael suffers a reversal of his good fortune, for news comes that a distant relative has suffered an unforeseen business failure, and Michael has to pay a grievous penalty "in surety for his brother's son." The old man is sorely troubled. He cannot bear to sell his land. He suggests that Luke should go from the family for a time to work in the city and earn enough to pay the forfeiture. Before his beloved son leaves, Michael takes him to a place on the farm where he has collected a heap of stones. He tells Luke that he plans to build a new sheepfold there and asks Luke to lay the cornerstone. This will be a covenant or solemn agreement between the father and son: The boy will work in the city and meanwhile the father will build a new barn so that it will be there for the boy's return. Weeping, the boy puts the first stone in place, and leaves the next day for his work far away. At first the old couple get a good report about his work, but after a time Luke "in the dissolute city gave himself to evil courses; ignominy and shame fell on him, so that he was driven at last to seek a hiding-place beyond the sea." After the loss of his son, Michael still goes to the dell where the pile of building stones lies, but he often simply sits the whole day merely staring at them, until he dies. Some three years later, his wife Isabel also dies and the land is sold to a stranger. The cottage of the evening star is torn down and nothing remains of the poor family's hopes except the straggling pile of stones which are the remains of the still unfinished sheepfold. This is the story that the "I-persona," who knows the district, tells to the "You-audience," who is unacquainted with the local history and geography.

The poem "Michael" embodies the ideas proposed in Wordsworth's preface to the *Lyrical Ballads*. He takes a family of simple, rural people as the main characters in a tragedy. Michael is a sentimental hero whose unspoiled contact with nature has refined his human nature and made him a good man. Nature has imprinted experiences on his mind that his imagination has built into more and more complex feelings about what is right and wrong. The dissolute city, on the other hand, is confusing, and there Luke goes astray. From the city and the world of banking and finance, the grievous forfeiture intrudes into the rural valley where Michael was living in a state of nature, like a noble savage or like Adam before his fall.

The poem argues that nature is not a neutral commodity to be bought and sold. It is man's home. It embodies values. The poem demands that the reader consider nature as a living force and demonstrates that once one knows the story of Luke, one never again can look on a pile of rocks in the mountains as worthless. That pile of rocks was a solemn promise of father and son. It signified a whole way of life, now lost. It was gathered for a human purpose, and one must regret that the covenant was broken and the sheepfold never completed. Likewise, all nature is a covenant, an environment, filled with human promise and capable of guiding human feelings in a pure, simple, dignified, and moral way. The function of poetry (like the "I-persona's" story of Michael) is to make the reader see that nature is not neutral. The "I-persona" attaches the history of Michael to what otherwise might be merely a pile of rocks and so makes the "You-audience" feel differently about that place. Likewise, the poem as a whole makes the reader feel differently about nature.

"Tintern Abbey" and "Michael" both explore the important question of how man's moral nature develops. What makes man good, virtuous, or proper? If, as the preface argues, man is morally best when most natural, uncorrupted by false custom and education, then the normal process of growing up in the modern world must be a kind of falling away from natural grace.

"ODE: INTIMATIONS OF IMMORTALITY FROM RECOLLECTIONS OF EARLY CHILDHOOD"

Wordsworth's "Ode: Intimations of Immortality from Recollections of Early Childhood" (hereafter called "Ode: Intimations of Immortality") is also concerned with the process of growing up and its ethical and emotional consequences. The poem is written in eleven stanzas of irregular length, composed of lines of varying length with line-end rhyme. The core of the poem is stanza V, beginning "Our birth is but a sleep and a forgetting." Here the poet discusses three stages of growth: the infant, the boy, and the man. The infant at birth comes from God, and at the moment when life begins the infant is still close to its divine origin. For this reason, the newborn infant is not utterly naked or forgetful, "but trailing clouds of glory do we come from God." The infant is near to divinity; "Heaven lies about us in our infancy," but each day leads it farther and farther

from its initial, completely natural state. As consciousness awakens, "Shades of the prison house begin to close upon the growing boy." In other words, the natural feelings of the infant begin to become constrained as man falls into consciousness. A boy is still near to nature, but each day he travels farther from the initial source of his natural joy and goodness. The youth is like a priest who travels away from his Eastern holy land, each day farther from the origin of his faith, but still carrying with him the memory of the holy places. When a man is fully grown, he senses that the natural joy of childish union with nature dies away, leaving him only the drab ordinary "light of common day" unilluminated by inspiration. This process of movement from the unthinking infant in communion with nature, through the stage of youth filled with joy and natural inspiration, to the drab adult is summarized in stanza VII, from the "child among his new-born blisses" as he or she grows up playing a series of roles "down to palsied Age."

The poem as a whole rehearses this progression from natural infant to adulthood. Stanzas I and II tell how the speaker as a child saw nature as glorious and exciting. "There was a time when meadow, grove, and stream . . . to me did seem apparelled in celestial light." Now the speaker is grown up and the heavenly light of the natural world has lost its glory. Even so, in stanza III, his sadness at his lost childhood joys is changed to joy when he sees springtime and thinks of shepherd boys. Springtime demonstrates the eternal rebirth of the world when everything is refreshed and begins to grow naturally again. The shepherd boys shouting in the springtime are doubly blessed, for they are rural characters, and, moreover, they are young, near the fountainhead of birth. In stanza IV the adult speaker can look on the springtime or on rural children and feel happy again because they signify the experience he has had of natural joy. Even though, as he says in stanza X, "nothing can bring back the hour of splendour in the grass, of glory in the flower," the adult can understand with his "philosophic mind" the overall design of the natural world and grasp that it is good.

THE PRELUDE

The Prelude is Wordsworth's longest and probably his most important work. It is an autobiographical portrait of the artist as a young man. He was never satisfied with the work and repeatedly rewrote and revised it, leaving it uncompleted at his death. He had a fairly refined draft in 1805-1806 for his friend Coleridge to read, and the version he left at his death in 1850 is, of course, the chronologically final version. In between the 1805 and 1850 versions, there are numerous drafts and sketches, some of them of the whole poem, while others are short passages or merely a few lines. When a reader speaks of Wordsworth's *The Prelude*, therefore, he is referring not so much to a single text as to a shifting, dynamic set of sometimes contradictory texts and fragments. The best edition of *The Prelude* is by Ernest de Selincourt, second edition revised by Helen Darbishire (Oxford University Press, 1959), which provides on facing pages the 1805-1806 text and the 1850 text. The reader can open the de Selincourt/Darbishire edition and see side by side the earliest and the latest version of every passage, while the editors' annotations indicate all significant intermediate steps.

The 1805 version is divided into thirteen books, while the 1850 version has fourteen. Book I, "Introduction, Childhood and Schooltime," rehearses how the poet undertook to write this work. He reviews the topics treated in famous epic poems, in Milton's *Paradise Lost*, Edmund Spenser's *The Faerie Queene* (1590, 1596), and other works. He concludes that the proper subject for his poem should be the process of his own development. He therefore begins at line 305 of the 1805 version to relate his earliest experiences, following the ideas explored above in "Tintern Abbey" and his "Ode: Intimations of Immortality." He traces the earliest impressions on his mind, which is like the tabula rasa of the associational psychologists. "Fair seed-time had my soul, and I grew up/ Foster'd alike by beauty and by fear." He tells of his childhood in the lakes and mountains, of stealing birds from other hunters' traps, of scaling cliffs, and especially a famous episode concerning a stolen boat. At line 372, he tells how he once stole a boat and rowed at night out onto a lake. As he rowed away from the shore facing the stern of the boat, it appeared that a dark mountain rose up in his line of vision as if in pursuit. He was struck with fear and returned with feelings of guilt to the shore. Experiences like this "trace/ How Nature by extrinsic passion first peopled my mind." In other words, impressions of nature, associated with pleasure and pain, provide the basic ideas which the imagination of the poet uses to create more and more complex attitudes until he arrives at his adult view of the world. The process described in the stolen boat episode is sometimes called the "discipline of fear."

Book II concerns "School-Time." It corresponds to the three stages of man outlined in "Ode: Intimations of Immortality": infant, youth, and adult. As in "Tintern Abbey," in *The Prelude*, Book II, Wordsworth explains that his early experiences of nature sustained him when he grew older and felt a falling off of the infant's joyful harmony with the created universe. Book III deals with his "Residence at Cambridge University," which is like a dream world to the youth from the rural lakes: "I was a Dreamer, they the dream; I roamed/ Delighted through the motley spectacle." He talks of his reading and his activities as a student at St. John's College, concluding that his story so far has been indeed a heroic argument, as important as the stories of the ancient epics, tracing the development of his mind up to an eminence, a high point of his experience.

Book IV recounts his summer vacation after his first year of college, as he returns to the mountains and lakes of his youth, a situation comparable to the return of the persona in "Tintern Abbey" to the rural scene he had previously known. He notes the "inner falling-off" or loss of joy and innocence which seems to accompany growing up. Yet at line 344 he tells of a vision of the sun rising as he walked homeward after a night of gaiety and mirth at a country dance, which caused him to consider himself a "dedicated spirit," someone who has a sacred duty to write poetry. Later in this book he recounts his meeting with a tattered soldier returned from military service in the tropics and how he helped him find shelter in a cottage nearby. Book V is titled simply "Books" and examines the role of literature in the poet's development. This book contains the famous passage, beginning at line 389, "There was a boy, ye knew him well, ye Cliffs/ And Islands of Winander." There was a youth among the cliffs of the Lake District who could whistle so that the owls would answer him. Once when he was calling to them the cliffs echoed so that he was struck with surprise and wonder. This boy died while he was yet a child and the poet has stood "Mute—looking at the grave in which he lies." Another recollection concerns the appearance of a drowned man's body from the lake.

Book VI, "Cambridge and the Alps," treats his second year at college and the following summer's walking tour of France and Switzerland. When the poet first arrived at Calais, it was the anniversary of the French Revolution's federal day. The young man finds the revolutionary spirit with "benevolence and blessedness/ spread like a fragrance everywhere, like Spring/ that leaves no corner of the land untouched." Frenchmen welcome the young Englishman as brothers in the struggle for freedom and liberty and they join in a common celebration. The Alps were a formidable barrier in the nineteenth century, seeming to separate the Germanic culture of Northern Europe from the Mediterranean. Crossing the Alps meant passing from one culture to a totally different one. Ironically, the poet records his errant climb, lost in the fog and mist, as he approached Italy, so that the English travelers cross the Alps without even knowing what they had done. Perhaps the crossing of the Alps unaware is like his observation of the French Revolution. The poet *sees* more than he *understands*. Book VII treats of the poet's residence in London. As one would expect, the city is unnatural and filled with all kinds of deformed and perverted customs, epitomized at the Bartholomew Fair, "a hell/ For eyes and ears! what anarchy and din/ Barbarian and infernal! t'is a dream/ Monstrous in colour, motion, shape, sight, sound."

Book VIII, "Retrospect—Love of Nature Leading to a Love of Mankind," is in contrast to Book VII. Opposed to the blank confusion of the city, Book VIII returns to the peaceful, decent rural scenes of the Lake District. It contrasts a wholesome country fair with the freak shows of London. Nature's primitive gift to the shepherds is beauty and harmony, which the poet first experienced there. Such "noble savages," primitive men educated by nature alone, are celebrated as truly heroic.

Book IX tells of the poet's second visit to France and residence in the Loire Valley. It suppresses, however, all of the real biographical details concerning Wordsworth's affair with Annette Vallon and his illegitimate daughter. As he passes through Paris the poet sees "the revolutionary power/ Toss like a ship at anchor, rock'd by storms." He arrives at his more permanent home in the Loire Valley and makes friends with a group of French military officers there. One day as he wanders with his new friends in the countryside, he comes across a hunger-bitten peasant girl, so downtrodden that she resembles the cattle she is tending. His French companion comments, "'Tis against *that* which we are fighting," against the brutalization of humankind by the monarchical system. In later versions, at the conclusion of this book, Wordsworth inserts the story of "Vaudracour and Julia." This love story seems to stand in place of Wordsworth's real-life encounter with Vallon. Book X continues his discussion of his visit to France, including a second visit to Paris while the Reign of Terror is in full cry and the denunciation of Maximilien Robespierre takes place. This book also traces his return to England and the declaration of war by England against France, which caused the young Wordsworth deep grief. The French Revolution was probably the most important political event in the poet's life. His initial hopes for the French cause were overshadowed by the outrages of the Reign of Terror. His beloved England, on the other hand, joined in armed opposition to the cause of liberty. In the numerous reworkings of this part of his autobiography, Wordsworth steadily became more conservative in his opinions as he grew older. Book X in the 1805 text is split into Books X and XI in the 1850 version. In this section he explains that at the beginning of the French Revolution, "Bliss was it in that dawn to be alive,/ But to be young was very heaven." Yet the course of the revolution, running first to despotic terror and ending with the rise of Napoleon, brought Wordsworth to a state of discouragement and desolation.

Book XI in the 1805 text (Book XII in the 1850 version) considers how one may rise from spiritual desolation: Having lost the innocent joy of primitive youth and having lost faith in the political aims of the French Revolution, where can the soul be restored? At line 74, the poet tells how "strangely he did war against himself," but nature has a powerful restorative force. At line 258, he enters the famous "Spots of time" argument, in which he maintains that there are remembered experiences which "with distinct preeminence retain/ A vivifying Virtue" so that they can nourish one's depleted spirits. Much as in "Tintern Abbey," a remembered experience of nature can excite the imagination to produce a fresh vitality. Book XII in the 1805 version (Book XIII in the 1850) begins with a summary of nature's power to shape man's imagination and taste:

From nature doth emotion come, and moods
of calmness equally are nature's gift,
This is her glory; these two attributes
Are sister horns that constitute her strength.

The concluding book tells of the poet's vision on Mount Snowdon in Wales. On the lonely mountain, under the full moon, a sea of mist shrouds all the countryside except the highest peaks. The wanderer looks over the scene and has a sense of the presence of divinity. Nature has such a sublime aspect "That men, least sensitive, see, hear, perceive,/ And cannot choose but feel" the intimation of divine power. In this way, Nature feeds the imagination, and a love of nature leads to a sense of man's place in the created universe and a love for all humankind. The poem ends with an address to the poet's friend Coleridge about their mutual struggle to keep faith as true prophets of nature.

It is often said that Wordsworth's *The Prelude*, written in Miltonic blank verse, is the Romantic epic comparable to *Paradise Lost* of Milton. Other critics point to a similarity between *The Prelude* and the *Bildungsroman*, or novel of development. *The Prelude* is subtitled the "Growth of a Poet's Mind" and bears considerable resemblance to such classic stories as Stendhal's *The Red and the Black* (1830), in which the author traces the development of the hero, Julien Sorel, as he grows up. Finally, most readers find an important pastoral element in *The Prelude*. The "pastoral" occurs whenever an author and an audience belonging to a privileged and sophisticated society imagine a more simple life and admire it. For example, sophisticated courtiers might imagine the life of simple shepherds and shepherdesses to be very attractive compared to their own round of courtly duties. They would then imagine a pastoral world in which shepherdesses with frilly bows on their shepherds' crooks and dainty fruits to eat would dally in the shade by fountains on some peaceful mountainside. Such a vision is termed pastoral because it contrasts unfavorably the life of the real author and audience with the imagined life of a shepherd. *The Prelude* makes such pastoral contrasts frequently: for example, in the depiction of rural shepherds in the Lake District compared with urban workers; in the comparison of the life of a simple child with that of the adult; and in the compari-

son of the working classes of France and England with their masters. The pastoral elements in *The Prelude* are a natural consequence of the primitivism in the poem's ideology.

Wordsworth is one of the recognized giants of English literature, whose importance is nearly equal to Milton's or Shakespeare's. Even so, his work has been the subject of sharp controversy from its first publication until the present. William Hazlitt in his *Lectures on the English Poets* (1818) argues that Wordsworth is afflicted with a false optimism and that his idea of nature is merely a reflection of the human observer's feelings. Aldous Huxley in "Wordsworth in the Tropics" in *Holy Face and Other Essays* (1929) attacks the unnaturalness of Wordsworth's view of nature. John Stuart Mill's *Autobiography* (1873), on the other hand, discusses the restorative power of Romantic poetry and the capacity of Wordsworth to relieve the sterility of a too "scientific" orientation. R. D. Havens's *The Mind of a Poet* (1941) provides a detailed study of *The Prelude*, and additional commentary can be found in Abbie Findlay Potts's *Wordsworth's Prelude* (1953) and Herbert Lindenberger's *On Wordsworth's Prelude* (1963).

The apparent decline of Wordsworth's poetic powers in his later years has occasioned much debate. Was he disillusioned with the course of the French Revolution so that he could no longer bear to praise man's primitive nature? Was he so filled with remorse over his affair with Annette Vallon that his inspiration failed? Was he a living demonstration of his own theory of the development of man from infant, to boyhood, to adult: that as man grows older he becomes more and more remote from the primitive feelings of the infant who comes into this world trailing clouds of glory, so that old men can never be effective poets? In any case, the young Wordsworth writing in the 1790's and the first decade of the nineteenth century was a voice calling out that life can be joyful and meaningful, that man's nature is good, and that man is not alone in an alien world, but in his proper home.

OTHER MAJOR WORKS

NONFICTION: *The Prose Works of William Wordsworth*, 1876; *Letters of William and Dorothy Wordsworth*, 1935-1939 (6 volumes; Ernest de Selincourt, editor).

Critical Survey of Poetry

Critical Survey of Poetry

BIBLIOGRAPHY

Bloom, Harold, ed. *William Wordsworth*. New York: Chelsea House, 1985. This collection of eleven previously published critical essays includes some of the most advanced and influential work on Wordsworth. Bloom's introduction is a lively and persuasive overview. Other important essays include Frederick A. Pottle's "The Eye and the Object in the Poetry of Wordsworth," Paul de Man's "Intentional Structure of the Romantic Image" (which presents an opposing view to that of Pottle), Geoffrey H. Hartman's "The Romance of Nature and the Negative Way," and M. H. Abrams's "Two Roads to Wordsworth," which examines different critical approaches.

Bromwich, David. *Disowned by Memory: Wordsworth's Poetry of the 1790's*. Chicago: University of Chicago Press, 1998. Bromwich connects the accidents of Wordsworth's life with the originality of his works, tracking the impulses that turned him to poetry after the death of his parents and during his years as an enthusiastic disciple of the French Revolution.

Gill, Stephen. *William Wordsworth: A Life*. New York: Oxford University Press, 1989. This first biography of Wordsworth since 1965 makes full use of all the information that has come to light since that time, including the 1977 discovery of Wordsworth's family letters, as well as recent research on Wordsworth's boyhood in Hawkshead and his radical period in London. Contains excellent discussions of the poetry, including that of Wordsworth's later years, as Gill explores the paradox that as the poetry became weaker Wordsworth's place in the national culture grew stronger.

Hartman, Geoffrey H. *Wordsworth's Poetry, 1787-1814*. 1964. Reprint. New Haven, Conn.: Yale University Press, 1971. Hartman, an influential critic, provides essential reading for anyone wishing to understand Wordsworthian criticism. Hartman identifies an unresolved conflict in Wordsworth between consciousness and nature and argues that Wordsworth could never bring himself fully to trust the power of the imagination, which was always tending to free itself from any reliance on the external world of the senses.

Jacobus, Mary. *Tradition and Experiment in Wordsworth's "Lyrical Ballads," 1798*. Oxford, England: Clarendon Press, 1976. One of the most important studies of *Lyrical Ballads*. Jacobus argues that Wordsworth's strength lay in his ability to assimilate the literary traditions of the past with his own radical innovations. She explores the eighteenth century philosophical and literary background, Wordsworth's relationship with Samuel Taylor Coleridge, and contemporary ballads and magazine verse. Excellent discussions of most of the poems in *Lyrical Ballads*, notably "Tintern Abbey," "The Idiot Boy," "The Thorn," and "Goody Blake, and Harry Gill."

Lindenberger, Herbert. *On Wordsworth's "Prelude."* Princeton, N.J.: Princeton University Press, 1963. One of the best and most accessible of the many books on Wordsworth's masterpiece. It consists of thirteen essays, each of which approaches the poem in a different way. The first three chapters deal with Wordsworth's language, and are notable, among other things, for Lindenberger's examination of Wordsworth's imagery. Chapters 4 to 6 cover the organization of the poem, including Wordsworth's "time-consciousness." Other chapters cover the social dimension of the poem and *The Prelude: Or, The Growth of a Poet's Mind* in literary history.

Liu, Yü. *Poetics and Politics: The Revolutions of Wordsworth*. New York: P. Lang, 1999. Liu focuses on the poetry of Wordsworth in the late 1790's and the early 1800's. In the context of Wordsworth's crisis of belief, this study shows how his poetic innovations constituted his daring revaluation of his political commitment.

Mahoney, John L. *William Wordsworth: A Poetic Life*. New York: Fordham University Press, 1997. A biographical study using key and representative writings of Wordsworth to examine his literary achievements as well as his life. Written for the college-level student of English literature. Includes bibliographical references and index.

Noyes, Russell. *William Wordsworth*. New York: Twayne, 1971. Several short introductory studies of Wordsworth exist and this is one of the best. Noyes possesses a deep understanding of Wordsworth, and his elegant prose gets to the heart of the poetry. The book is arranged chronologically to show Wordsworth's development, and Noyes smoothly integrates biographical information with literary analysis. Includes a chronology and an annotated bibliography.

Rader, Melvin R. *Wordsworth: A Philosophical Approach*. Oxford, England: Clarendon Press, 1967. Focusing on the poetry of Wordsworth's "great decade," Rader outlines five stages in the development of Wordsworth's thought. In doing so, he provides one of the clearest analyses of the transcendental aspects of Wordsworth's philosophical thought, derived from the tradition of Spinoza, Immanuel Kant, and Plato. As a consequence of this emphasis, Rader minimizes the impact on Wordsworth of the associationism of David Hartley.

Todd K. Bender;
bibliography updated by the editors

BARON WORMSER

Born: Baltimore, Maryland; February 4, 1948

PRINCIPAL POETRY

The White Words, 1983
Good Trembling, 1985
Atoms, Soul Music, and Other Poems, 1989
When, 1997
Mulroney and Others: Poems, 2000

OTHER LITERARY FORMS

Baron Wormser has written essays and book reviews for various literary magazines. Two important book reviews, extensive analyses of the works of Polish poets Adam Zagajewski and Czesław Miłosz, reveal Wormser's extraordinary knowledge of Western poetry, history, and culture. He has published essays concerning William Blake, the spirit of poetry in a democracy, and the necessity of religious poetry in our time. In 2000 he melded his vast wisdom about poetry with his love of teaching into a book, written with David Cappella, titled *Teaching the Art of Poetry: The Moves*.

ACHIEVEMENTS

Baron Wormser started gaining critical stature in the 1980's and 1990's, as evident in the honors he accrued during these decades. In 1982 he won the Frederick Bock Prize from *Poetry*. In 1996 he won the Kathryn A. Morton Prize in Poetry and in 2000 he was appointed Maine's poet laureate. He also received fellowships from the National Endowment for the Arts and the John Guggenheim Memorial Foundation. His poems, reviews, and essays have appeared widely in such literary magazines such as *The Paris Review, Swanee Review, Harper's, New Republic*, and *Poetry*.

BIOGRAPHY

Born and reared in Baltimore, Baron Wormser grew up enjoying the city's rich ethnic diversity. He attended Baltimore City College, then a citywide public boys' school located near Memorial Stadium. In 1970, he was graduated from The Johns Hopkins University. He was married in 1969 in Brookline, Massachusetts. Toward the end of 1970, he and his wife chose up-country living, homesteading on a one-hundred-acre parcel at the end of an old logging road in Mercer, Maine. There they reared a daughter and a son. In 1972, Wormser began work as the librarian of School Administrative District 54 in Madison, Maine, a mill town approximately twenty-five miles from his home. The Wormsers's unconventional lifestyle in a house with no electricity and no indoor plumbing reflects not only their deep commitment to the natural world but also their serious endeavor to live as much of a life of the spirit as is possible in contemporary America.

While maintaining an active writing life and working as a high school librarian, he began to teach creative writing to high school students and discovered his gift for teaching. After the late 1980's, Wormser was busy teaching the writing of poetry at the University of Maine at Farmington, serving as a visiting professor at the University of South Dakota, and conducting workshops and seminars at the Frost Place in Franconia, New Hampshire.

ANALYSIS

Baron Wormser's poetry offers a deeply sympathetic look at what it means to be human. His distinctive voice, intelligent observations of the particulars of existence, and sense of humor blend with superior technical skill to reveal the strange complexities that underlie people's actions. Addressing a broad range of topics in his poetry, Wormser brings a heightened awareness of life's predicaments by tackling its large truths, revealing what humans share as they live.

Wormser's poetry seems to represent a departure for American poetry. His intellectualism clearly reveals a multifaceted vision of the world. Yet, for him, intellect is not distant and cool; it is a passion, a way to glimpse reality. His technical skill formalizes these glimpses of humanity. Wormser is an American poet with a sensibility that elevates his subject matter into a larger context. His imagination blends an eye for the obvious with intellectual perceptions about culture and civilization to create extraordinary insights into why people are the way they are. In this sense, Wormser's sensibility is quite distinguishable from that of his contemporaries and more akin to that of the poets of Eastern Europe.

Considered as a whole, Wormser's work is a type of bestowal, enriching the spirit. It is a poetry of exuberance, alive with the wonder of being, and filled with a deep knowledge of the world. Beauty manifests itself in the daily drama enacted by the individual, contending with obvious experience and natural emotion. This celebration of the commonality of life's vicissitudes reveals the essentially religious nature of Wormser's poetry. It is poetry that teaches the reader about human existence by articulating its source—the soul.

THE WHITE WORDS

In *The White Words*, the tension and irony created as the sublime rubs constantly against the everyday demonstrate the supreme beauty of life. It is people that act out this drama. The poem "Passing Significance," taking place in the sitting room of an inn, brings travelers together, each involved in his own interior world. Some read, some write, the innkeeper's wife worries about who is going to pay, a baby cries, a woman quietly sings, and a clerk rustles a newspaper. Even a dog sighs. The chief assessor, however, barges into the room, stamping snow off his boots, and decides immediately that there is "no one of importance here." Such is not the case. The poem informs the reader that each of these people in the sitting room is significant, and that a special state of mind must inhere within an individual in order for him or her to understand this simple yet complex fact of life. Fittingly, the poem ends with an epigrammatic lesson: "To study other people/ You must be free and easy and remember nothing."

Wormser's poetry is a poetry of nuance; it sees through the obviousness of how people live. This quality is well exemplified in the poem "Of Small Towns." Here the poet describes the mundane lives of the citizens of a small town, elevating them by revealing the nature of their humanity. In doing so, he dignifies not only the purpose of their lives but also the purpose of their town, showing how it ennobles the lives of its people. Ultimately, the town is its people, and vice versa.

What is distinctive about Wormser's poetry is this ability to exalt human experience, employing both the

Baron Wormser (© John Suiter)

intellect and the imagination. While the heart and soul of New England gently seep into almost every one of Wormser's poems, his insights transcend place. For example, in "Cord of Birch," a typically New England problem becomes a quest. After cutting some birch, the narrator decides to ask around the neighborhood about how well birch burns. After seeking out and listening to various contradictory opinions, he wanders home, pouting and disgruntled about his pile of wood. Eventually, it is winter that frees him of his worries. He burns the birch because he has no choice: Need lends him wisdom. Wormser accomplishes this progression from the exterior to the interior, from summer to winter, through the use of tightly controlled rhyming couplets.

In "Letter from New England," an odd moment during a midwinter funeral and a comment by the narrator's daughter inspire a realization of what an image can conjure, of what it means for an individual even to be aware of an image. "Beech Trees," a meditation on human nature, not only addresses the fact that stingy beech leaves refuse to fall even in the dead of winter but also uses the image of their dangling on a sapling in January to initiate a rumination about the lingering as well as the ending of things—a rumination that concludes with the revelatory notion that people and leaves are not all that different.

Wormser's poetry is more than a regional type. Throughout *The White Words* his wide-ranging intellect is brought to bear on political, social, philosophical, historical, and literary themes. Such themes emerge from specific contexts. In "Some Recollections Concerning the Exiled Revolutionary, Leon Trotsky," the poet sees Trotsky and even imagines his voice. Through the man's thinking, he elaborates on the essence of politics, providing a glimpse of what it means to be exiled and to be a revolutionary.

A poem such as "Report on the Victorians" displays Wormser's extensive knowledge of history and social mores. In a sharp narrative flow, anchored by a well-choreographed rhyme scheme, Wormser investigates the sensibility of Victorianism. For him, what is essential is how Victorians saw, felt, and responded to their times. Their manners, their prejudices, and their hopes and dreams interest him. In their customs and intellectual sensibilities, Wormser perceives an inherent archetype

within humanity that is composed of a duality, in this case fiendishness and hope, each element of which is found within the other. This archetype is an indelible part of human nature that connects all eras.

Wormser also tackles the philosophical. His formal and intellectual approach to a subject, which is very European, separates him from most of his contemporaries. The finely woven sonnet titled "Hegel and Co." is an example of Wormser's gift for shaping substantive material and filtering it through his imaginative lens so that the reader freshly perceives G. W. F. Hegel's awareness of his intellectual climate. Wormser seeks to re-create within the reader's mind the internal workings of the philosopher. Similarly, the poem "Henry James," using a formal stanza, ponders the novelist's milieu.

Wormser is very much a poet of the human environment. Setting and circumstance provide him with particular images that in turn allow him to probe the emotional domain. "Piano Lessons" is the quintessential example of how Wormser uses quotidian human activity to elicit a profound sympathy for and a deep understanding of the human predicament. Here the pathos of a young boy who cannot play the piano and of his teacher who cannot escape her lonely situation manifests itself in the last couplet, when, as the boy recalls, teacher and student "walked into the room where the piano stood/ For all that we wanted to do yet never would."

GOOD TREMBLING

With his second volume, *Good Trembling*, Wormser extends this sympathy for being human by fusing it with a larger cultural relevance. His brief statement "Words to the Reader" implicitly conveys a deepening concern for human conduct. His poems become paradigms of sharing, and they reveal the meaning in our lives by allowing us to sympathize with one another. Poetry functions to lead its readers to understanding about being human.

The narrow settings of place and time within each poem of this volume widen into the larger realm of history and culture. Wormser uses the concrete in order to contemplate these broad forces that continually sweep over individuals' lives. This type of sensibility, the ability to see the universal in the particular, reveals Wormser's brilliant capacity to capture the essence of human existence. Again, such a sensibility seems more

European than American. Thus the poem "Shards," for example, moves beyond a description of the remnants of an old homestead to become a reflection on what drives people to act the way they do.

Wormser envisions the sweep of history as a landscape shaped by the conduct of individuals. "By--Products," taking place in a stale, eerily lit Legion Hall, exposes the outcome of United States foreign policy through a legless Vietnam veteran's words and behavior. When Stan vocalizes his feelings, the force of history becomes a personal drama, not an abstraction.

In such poems as "Tutorial on the Metaphysics of Foreign Policy," "Europe," and "The Fall of the Human Empire" Wormser turns his intellectual and philosophic gaze toward the circumstances of being American. These circumstances are viewed from various perspectives that range from musing on U.S. government policies to delineating how the remnant sensibility of Europe resides in a small New England town to using a run-over dog to symbolize how people, as individuals, fit into the scheme of civilization.

One particular poem of this volume skillfully addresses the abstract nature of history and civilization alongside the concrete nature of life at the moment when they meet head-on. "I Try to Explain to My Children a Newspaper Article Which Says That According to a Computer a Nuclear War Is Likely to Occur in the Next Twenty Years" uses the common, all-too-real situation of a parent explaining the idea of death (with a wonderful use of personification) to his children as a means to stress the higher concern of how humankind has surrendered the natural world to the vastly indifferent world of politics.

ATOMS, SOUL MUSIC, AND OTHER POEMS

Atoms, Soul Music, and Other Poems, Wormser's third collection, represents the poet at his most ambitious and most visionary. As he deftly observes contemporary dilemmas, he explores the large ideas of history and civilization in terms of humankind's spiritual capacity. For him, the quality of being human in the present age can be measured by the depth of one's connection to this spirituality. Merely the titles of a group of poems in the first section of the book—"Kitchen, 1952," "1967," "1968," "1969," "Dropping Acid at Aunt Bea's and Uncle Harry's 40th Wedding Anniversary Celebration,"

and "Embracing a Cloud: Rural Commune, 1971"— suggest Wormser's sense of history as he contemplates life in twentieth century America. His chronicling of Americans' spiritual state extends across a range of modern experiences, including an Otis Redding and Aretha Franklin concert and an anniversary celebration at which one celebrant has taken a psychedelic drug. Nothing is trivialized in these portraits of modern life. Wormser's explorations probe the heart of Americans' daily rites. A fine example of this process is the poem "Married Sex." Here the poet unmasks the psyche of our sexual selves through a nimble portrait of passion in marriage—the web of familiarity that steals spontaneity even while it creates a ritualized joy in a couple's sexual encounters.

The long poem "Atoms" constitutes the second and final section of Wormser's third volume. Using the voices of several characters, Wormser ponders the trajectory of American culture by exploring the darker side of the covenant (an unspoken one) that every culture makes with death. "Atoms" exposes how nations are really at war with themselves and thus with their own people. Through the poem's characters, Wormser demonstrates how foolish it is to think that having a nuclear arsenal has prevented nuclear war. As he discusses politics in a postnuclear age, Wormser delves into the manner in which a culture conceives of evil. According to Wormser, American society has colluded with evil and has thus made death an unnatural danger. This collusion conceals itself in the political and social orthodoxy of the present—an orthodoxy that, although couched cunningly in rationalism as well as sincerity, inevitably results in war, death, and subjugation.

The central characters of "Atoms" give flesh to this crisis of modernity. They are pilgrims on a journey, and they contain the fire of atoms. Airman Hawkins wonders about the world he inhabits, a stranger in a strange landscape. John Lennon rocks and rolls for peace, his own messy soul a sad prophecy. The clergyman grounds his protests in a faith smothered by an indifferent, purgatorial world. The bureaucrat Keats, "an underdeputy for Nuclear Security Policy," and his superior, Horace, exemplify the granite officiousness of government policy. Wormser's description and juxtaposition of the characters' inner lives evoke the turbulence of contemporary America's spiritual state.

"Atoms" transcends its political observations to become an examination of spiritual worthiness. Only through a significant repentance of the internal, volitional kind, along with the nurturing of conscience, will Americans rescue themselves, Wormser seems to say. Atonement and humility become the means that allow people to accomplish the noblest of tasks—finding and speaking the truth. Thus, "Atoms" is one of America's few truly religious poems.

The cumulative power of "Atoms," derived from the poet's ability to modulate gnomic utterances, is built up through an incantatory rhythm that gives it the structure of an extended prayer. By using tight lines of uncommon clarity, Wormser keeps this rhythm pulsing through the varied depictions of each pilgrim character. Sharp images of human activity (at times ridiculously trite and indifferent) are continually contrasted with images of the innate, organic energy of life within all people. This multilayered texture of "Atoms" serves to illuminate the general theme of how the salvation of any civilization is, finally, determined by the spiritual actions of its members.

WHEN

In *When*, whether in Las Vegas, Sun City, or driving a Ford in 1978 on "The Nuclear Bullet Tour," Wormser beholds the myth of America: a myth of contradictions, covenants, and prayers for the unruly middle class—but a myth "[y]ou'd be a fool to refuse." The collection is a mix of autobiography and storytelling that never forgets a basic writerly tenet: locality is the only universality. Alice Fulton, who selected this volume for the Kathryn A. Morton Prize in 1996, commented that Wormser does not succumb to "the emotional gush and self-dramatization that characterize much contemporary poetry," a sentiment that testifies to his primary focus on the lives of others. Wormser hones in on specific details of his characters' actions, whether the subject is Beethoven's maid hearing strange sounds, a deli waiter bemoaning his work, or Wormser as a boy walking through Pikesville, Maryland, and imagining it to be Charles Baudelaire's Paris. The insights the characters achieve, however, and the emotions they feel are universal: A trucker who "skidded the better part of a quarter-mile/ toward a stopped school bus/ . . . and he said he saw himself as a boy." There are also a handful of extremely sensitive portraits and testimonials that again focus on other lives: a young man dead of AIDS, a Jew imagining that Dachau will be peaceful countryside. Taken together, the poems of *When* present a menagerie of wonderfully familiar strangers.

MULRONEY AND OTHERS

Mulroney and Others revisits Wormser's unique perspective on the world around him and again calls forth a universality of experience. The collection provides glimpses of Wormser's childhood, adolescence, and adulthood, as well as accounts of Vietnam veterans, draft dodgers, socialites, and outcasts. In the poem "Fatality," there is the finality of ending, not just in poetic structure but also with the thought woven into the fabric of the poem: the suddenness of death, followed by the quiet aftermath when life picks up and continues. Wormser's invitation to engage ourselves in seeing is irresistible, especially as he models the process with such impassioned interest. His poems tempt us to trade the obscurity of facile assumption for the powerful illumination of wonder. In Wormser's words, the universe is irrefutably personal.

OTHER MAJOR WORKS

NONFICTION: *Teaching the Art of Poetry: The Moves*, 2000 (with David Cappella).

BIBLIOGRAPHY

Birkerts, Sven. *The Electric Life: Essays on Modern Poetry*. New York: William Morrow, 1989. This wide-ranging book includes a condensed discussion of Wormser, connecting the poet's sense of place and occasion with his ability to enlarge upon the particular. A solid overview of the poet that hints at his larger, spiritual themes and the complex subtleties of his thinking process.

Boruch, Marianne. "Comment: The Feel of a Century." *American Poetry Review* 19 (July/August, 1990): 18-19. Included in this lengthy review of several poets is a discussion of Wormser's *Atoms, Soul Music, and Other Poems*. Despite the brief treatment of the book, two major points are made about his long poem "Atoms": that it tackles American culture and that it exemplifies the poet's attempt to capture the private and specific in a public manner.

Briggs, Edwin. "Poet Shapes an Image That's Fresh and True." *The Boston Globe*, May 29, 1983, p. D3. This review of *The White Words* gives a succinct account of Wormser's attitude toward language and of his use of tone and images to control the subject matter. It is an insightful glimpse into the poet's stance.

Mesic, Penelope. *Poetry* 144 (February, 1984): 302-303. In a balanced look at the poet's first book, this terse yet praiseworthy review of *The White Words* commends the poet's wit, technical skill, and use of details.

David Cappella,
updated by Sarah Hilbert

CHARLES WRIGHT

Born: Pickwick Dam, Tennessee; August 25, 1935

PRINCIPAL POETRY

The Dream Animal, 1968
The Grave of the Right Hand, 1970
The Venice Notebook, 1971
Hard Freight, 1973
Bloodlines, 1975
China Trace, 1977
The Southern Cross, 1981
Country Music: Selected Early Poems, 1982, 2d ed. 1991
The Other Side of the River, 1984
A Journal of the Year of the Ox, 1988
Zone Journals, 1988
The World of the Ten Thousand Things: Poems, 1980-1990, 1990
Chickamauga, 1995
Black Zodiac, 1997
Appalachia, 1998
Negative Blue: Selected Later Poems, 2000
A Short History of the Shadow, 2002

OTHER LITERARY FORMS

Halflife: Improvisations and Interviews, 1977-1987 (1988) is a collection of writings about poetry, Charles Wright's own and others, in the form of passages from his notebooks, essays, and interviews. *Quarter Notes* (1995) is a similar volume. Wright has translated Eugenio Montale's *The Storm and Other Poems* (1978) and Dino Campana's *Orphic Songs* (1984).

ACHIEVEMENTS

A major figure in American poetry, Charles Wright has received extensive critical recognition. Among his many awards are a Guggenheim Fellowship, the Edgar Allan Poe Award of the Academy of American Poets, an Institute Grant from the American Academy and Institute of Arts and Letters, the 1979 PEN Translation Prize, and the 1983 National Book Award in Poetry. Wright was honored with the Ruth Lilly Poetry Prize in 1993. *Chickamauga* won the Lenore Marshall Prize in 1996, and *Black Zodiac* was awarded both the Pulitzer Prize and the National Book Critics Circle Award in 1998.

BIOGRAPHY

Charles Wright was born in Hardin County, Tennessee, in 1935. After World War II, his family moved to Kingsport, Tennessee, where he was reared. During his final two years of high school, he attended Christ School, an Episcopal preparatory school in Arden, North Carolina. This experience, and his upbringing in the Episcopal church, has contributed profoundly to the religious quality of his poetry, what he has called its "spiritual anxieties." After being graduated from Davidson College, Wright served four years (1957-1961) in the United States Army. For three years he was stationed in Italy, an experience of extreme importance; while living in Verona, he acquired a copy of *The Selected Poems of Ezra Pound* (1928), and reading these poems in their Italian settings moved him to begin writing poetry himself in 1959. Pound has remained Wright's major poetic influence.

After military service Wright attended the University of Iowa Writers' Workshop, from 1961 to 1963. He spent the next two years as a Fulbright student at the University of Rome, translating Montale's poetry, and then returned to the Iowa Writers' Workshop in 1965-1966. He taught at the University of California at Irvine for seventeen years before returning to the South in 1983 as writer in residence and professor at the University of Virginia. He and his wife, the photographer Holly Wright, settled in Charlottesville, Virginia. They have one son, Luke.

ANALYSIS

Charles Wright's poetry, characterized by high ambition and profound seriousness, is suffused with spiritual yearning, seeking to discover a transcendent realm beyond the reality of the everyday physical world. His poems exploit memory and metaphysical speculation, moving freely between his past, his present, and his future death and dispersal. Intensely compressed and allusive, Wright's poetry can often be difficult to access. Basically lyrical and imagistic, the poems accrete layers of imagery, metaphor, and (in the later poems) anecdote, developing by association rather than by narrative.

This disjointed style is a chief innovation, characterized by what Wright has called the "submerged narrative" that runs beneath the poem, only occasionally breaking the surface. His insistence upon the primacy of the line, rather than the sentence or the stanza, is partly responsible for the disconnected style. The line, which in books following *China Trace* becomes unusually long and image-filled, is the basic structural unit. In early work, Wright tended to use the iambic line; although after *The Grave of the Right Hand* he rejected it, he retains the iambic ground in his carefully crafted free verse.

For Wright, poetry is a conduit to God. He believes that its purest purpose is contemplation of the mysteries of the divine. Wright admits that for him poetry is a substitute for religion. If so, it is a limited religion, one that only concedes the possibility of God and that merely savors the concept of redemption. "All my poems seem to be an ongoing argument with myself about the unlikelihood of salvation," he has said. Wright seeks to penetrate commonplace surfaces to explore ultimate reality, and the image is paramount in this endeavor. Because the tangible world is all the human being can experience directly, through the senses, Wright must seek the infinite through the concrete image. Replacing religious faith with belief in the numinous image, he resigns himself to an acceptance of language and metaphor as a simulacrum of the divine, thus the importance of the landscape in his poems, which are centered geographically in Italy and in eastern Tennessee and North Carolina.

These two regions are the most vital for Wright. He associates Italy with the life of the mind, with the wonder of intellectual and artistic awakening, while Tennessee and North Carolina evoke his childhood. Landscape has transcendent qualities in Wright's poetry, and the listing of place names is a kind of incantation. Because memory and his personal past play a central role, Wright's poems tend to be autobiographical. This autobiography is rather impersonal, however, since it is subsumed in his main subject, the search for God.

THE GRAVE OF THE RIGHT HAND

The Grave of the Right Hand collects apprentice work. Most of the poems are in regular stanza patterns, especially tercets, and in basically iambic short lines. They look traditional, unlike the poems in *China Trace*, the pivotal book in Wright's career, and succeeding volumes. Though most of Wright's stylistic innovation came later, *The Grave of the Right Hand* exhibits certain preoccupations that remain constant in his work: the emphasis on the image rather than rhetoric and a native obliqueness. From the start, Wright sought to communicate by suggestion instead of disclosure. He presents an imagistic gestalt that coheres, for the diligent reader, into

Charles Wright (© Nancy Crampton)

transcendent moments that reveal fleeting glimpses of abstract meaning. The characteristic images are already present: light, stars, blood, flowers, fog, clouds. Also evident are the landscape (one section is titled "American Landscape"), the elegiac quality and melancholy atmosphere, and the concern with absence, the negation of death.

"Self-Portrait" is the first of many poems with this title or some variation of it. This poem has a surreal flavor, with images that seem to have been selected from Giorgio De Chirico's paintings: "There is a street which runs/ Slanting into a square/ There is a marble hand." This street is eerily deserted. The poet, whose self-portrait the poem evidently paints, is notably absent. The final image, a pair of gloves nailed to a door, suggests both crucifixion and death, a parody of Christ's death and the poet's dread of his own mortality. There is no promise of salvation in the symbol, merely the intimation of redemption coupled with the certainty of death: The gloves, empty of human hands, remain behind like shed skins. This speculation about death and the dim possibility of transcendence is central to Wright's poetry.

HARD FREIGHT

Hard Freight, *Bloodlines*, and *China Trace* constitute a trilogy. Containing poems about place, childhood, family, adulthood, and spiritual longings, the books make up a sort of sketchy autobiography. The sequence is not chronological, since the first volume, *Hard Freight*, deals with the poet's present, while the second volume, *Bloodlines*, deals with his childhood, and *China Trace* with a speculative spiritual future.

Hard Freight is made up of individual lyrics that tend to be abstract and cryptic. It concerns Wright's adolescence and adulthood, including his life as a poet; thus it begins with several poems in homage to writers who have influenced him or who otherwise have been important to him. "Homage to Ezra Pound" appears to absolve Pound of his bad politics (he broadcast fascist propaganda during World War II and was arrested for treason following the American occupation of Italy) and to acknowledge Wright's debt of influence, characteristically using liturgical diction: "Here is your garment,/ Coldblooded father of light—/ Rise and be whole again."

Many of the poems ponder death, a constant theme for Wright. "Definitions" begins, typically, as a description of the flora in an unspecified setting. The images are threatening:

> The blades of the dwarf palm,
> Honing themselves in the wind;
> The ice plant, blistering red along
> Its green, immaculate skin.

Wright finds no consolation or hope in nature; instead, the organic world is unsettling, because it foreshadows his eventual death. The palm, ice plant, moon, and dark waters (presumably the Pacific Ocean near his Laguna Beach home) become dreadful omens, "something to listen for—/ A scar, fat worm, which feeds at the lungs;/ A cough, the blood in the handkerchief."

Hard Freight is autobiographical in an abstract way: It chronicles the evolution of a mind. Only a handful of poems narrate specific events or situations in the poet's life, and these generally center on a place from Wright's childhood or youth. He revisits the site as an adult, or via memory, generating from the emotions associated with it new and more complex feelings. So much referential detail has been abstracted from the poems that Wright usually depends upon the title to identify the locale and situation. Without the tag "*Bible Camp, 1949*" at the end of "Northhanger Ridge," the reader would not know the specific setting, which is crucial to the poem's meaning. Wright struggles with his religious upbringing, belittling organized religion, the "Bow-wow and arf" of "Father Dog" (God). Praying children "talk to the nothingness." Finally, Wright rejects the Christian belief in corporeal resurrection: salvation "sleeps like a skull in the hard ground,/ . . . as it's always slept, without/ Shadow, waiting for nothing." Northhanger Ridge is aptly described as "half-bridge over nothingness," for Wright's Christian training has degenerated into disbelief; nevertheless, the yearning for redemption abides, a "half-bridge" jutting into the void of his inevitable demise.

BLOODLINES

This wistful need to believe in an impossible salvation dominates the books from *China Trace* onward. According to Wright, *Bloodlines* and *Hard Freight* both deal with his childhood conflict with the Episcopal church. Most of the poems in *Bloodlines* depend upon memories of Wright's childhood and are thus more clearly autobiographical than those of the previous volume. With *Bloodlines* he established his practice of writing whole books of poetry rather than collecting disparate poems. The individual poems are linked by subject and form, and the structural heart of the volume is formed of two long complementary sequences, "Tattoos" and "Skins."

The two long poems were conceived as counterparts: "Tattoos" is composed of actual situations, whereas "Skins" is conceptual, its sections pertaining to abstractions such as truth and beauty. The twenty autobiographical sections of "Tattoos" describe momentous incidents in Wright's life, what he has called "psychic tattoos"—hence the title. Setting and narrative frame have been abstracted so that the poet can get to the pith of each experience, making the sequence an impressionistic collage. The lack of reference necessitates the notes that identify the place and situation of each section. Wright put the notes at the end of the sequence, to maintain its structural integrity. Most of the incidents are drawn from his childhood: the death of his father, a snake-handling religious service he witnessed in Tennessee, fainting at the altar as an acolyte, handwriting class.

The first poem begins with the image of fallen camellia blossoms outside his home in Laguna Beach, California; the red and white petals remind him of the red and white rose symbolism of Mother's Day. The wind of remembrance takes him back thirty years to his days as an acolyte at Saint Paul's Episcopal Church in Kingsport, Tennessee. The disagreeableness of his religious background is suggested by the image of memory as "the wind . . . bad breath/ Of thirty-odd years, and catching up." The roots of the camellia bush represent Wright's childhood, and the metaphorical description of petals as "scales of blood" suggests the pain and loss suffered in life. "Where would you have me return?/ What songs would I sing," asks the poet of the camellia bush, and answers his own questions in the succeeding poems. This initial section clearly introduces the motifs and concerns developed in the sequence, all characteristic of Wright's poetry: memory, death, religious skepticism, visionary longing for Heaven, Italy, and the importance of art to his life.

Wright conceived of "Skins" as a continuation of "Tattoos," but as an abstract, conceptual counterpart to the autobiographical specificity of the first poem. Thus "Skins," despite its corporal title, chronicles his intellectual evolution. Each section is built upon a particular abstract reference. The poem is structured as a stepladder, with ten sections ascending and ten descending, ending at the point of departure.

The subjects, as identified by Wright, are lofty: (1) Situation, Point A; (2) Beauty; (3) Truth; (4) Eventual Destruction of the Universe; (5) Organized Religion; (6) Metamorphosis; (7) Water; (8) Water/Earth; (9) Earth/Fire; (10) Aether, the fifth element; (11) Primitive Magic; (12) Necromancy; (13) Black Magic; (14) Alchemy; (15) Allegory; (16) Fire; (17) Air; (18) Water; (19) Earth; (20) Situation, Point A. The purpose is to organize and concretize Wright's attitudes toward elemental things. In effect, he is trying to understand the metaphysical nature of human life and his own position in the universe. The individual poems center on the four elements—earth, air, water, fire—all that human beings can know empirically about creation. These the poet accepts; he rejects false systems of transcendence—magic, necromancy, alchemy, and allegory.

CHINA TRACE

Wright intended "Skins," rather than the last three poems in *Bloodlines*, to be the launching point for *China Trace*, the final volume in the trilogy. Both books are suffused with spiritual yearning. *China Trace*, in fact, is an imaginative exploration of the poet's spiritual future. The book begins with a poem in which the speaker bids farewell to childhood, irrevocably ended by the death of his parents. Growing up entails many losses, especially of people, and their loss presages the poet's own: The poem says good-bye to "the names/ Falling into the darkness, face/ After face, like beads from a broken rosary." The last line fades into a symbol of lost faith.

The spiritual future Wright explores is his eventual death and his wish, in the face of skepticism, that he might be resurrected. Since he finds it impossible to believe any longer in the Christian Heaven, the closest he can come to salvation is decomposition and admixture with nature. This conviction is evident in many of the poems, particularly "Self-Portrait in 2035," in which the poet envisions himself after death as dirt and wood-rot:

"The root becomes him, the road ruts/ That are sift and grain in the powderlight/ Recast him."

Hard Freight and *Bloodlines* both concern Wright's past, while *China Trace* deals with his present. That is, the triggering situations of the poems are grounded in his present, but only to provide a launching point for speculation about his afterimage. "Snow," for example, appears to have begun as a meditation on the physical presence of snow. The evanescence of snow and its cycle of transmogrification from water to snow and back to water elicit the notion of the human body's inevitable reabsorption in nature, and the liturgical echo of "dust to dust": "If we, as we are, are dust, and dust, as it will, rises,/ Then we will rise, and recongregate/ In the wind, in the cloud, and be their issue." The book is paradoxical in that though all the poems express in some way Wright's wish to survive in a realm beyond death they disavow such salvation.

The poems in *China Trace* are short, none longer than twelve lines. Wright decided on this arbitrary limit in an attempt to write the most compressed poetry practicable. This compression contributes to the poems' difficulty and to their gnomic quality, which reveals the influence of Emily Dickinson. The condensation, as well as the title, also indicates the influence of Chinese poetry. Wright has said that he has an affinity for T'ang Dynasty poets, who focused on the landscape. Whether their interest in landscape kindled Wright's own or merely reflects it, the fact remains that he uses natural imagery in the same way the T'ang poets did. Like them, Wright imbues landscape with personal emotion and psychic drama. A preternatural dimension, if it could exist, would be perceptible only through the senses, so the infinite can be glimpsed only as an "undershine" of the finite, imaginary perhaps but still to be desired.

The fifty poems of the book, though discrete, are intended to make a whole. They are unified in one way by the speaker, who remains the same in every poem even though he is referred to in various poems as "I," "you," and "he." This character, whom one must assume to be different aspects of Wright's personality, advances from his parting with childhood in the first poem to a qualified revival as a constellation in the final poem, "Him." The title is a pun on "hymn," and the poem operates as a

hymn or prayer, expressing Wright's longing for transcendence. The character's transfiguration into a constellation in the Pacific sky is a metaphor for Wright's curious position—trapped between skepticism and the need to believe. The character's relinquishment of childhood is essentially a liberation from religion, since Wright associates the two. Yet this emancipation begets a dilemma, for only through the Christian faith can he gain salvation. His abortive ascension leaves him stranded in what Wright has called "the Heaven of the Fixed Stars (in the Dantescan cosmology)." This literary allusion suggests Wright's poetry. The act of writing a poem is a religious act, but it is ultimately dissatisfying, because while Wright may achieve some sense of transcendence through identifying with nature, he cannot get beyond the finite physical world. Thus his poetry is a heaven of his own making, but a very meager one.

Wright's line in *China Trace*, though tending to lengthen, remains relatively short, and his forms have retained the strictness of those in the earlier books. *China Trace*, however, marks the emergence of Wright's mature voice. In succeeding books, he opens up his forms and lengthens his line. The poems also become more imagistic and anecdotal; the subterranean narrative runs nearer to the surface.

THE SOUTHERN CROSS

The Southern Cross, a spiritual journey, continues the conceptual design of *China Trace*. The dead, a favorite subject of Wright, dominate *The Southern Cross*. The dedication, "For H. W. Wilkinson," actually refers to Wright's past and family history. Wilkinson's name happened to be stenciled on a metal locker Wright bought and in which he stored family relics, old letters, and the like. By dedicating the book to Wilkinson, Wright really was honoring his familial dead, about whom so many of the poems revolve. His unwillingness to ignore his extinct forebears is, perhaps, a reflection of his dread of oblivion. By writing about his dead, manifold and anonymous though they may be, he is saving them from the void. The ancestral dead in "Homage to Paul Cézanne" echo La Pia in Dante's *Purgatorio* (c. 1320): "Remember me, speak my name." The title notwithstanding, the poem is not about Cézanne but is intended to acknowledge Wright's long-standing interest in Cézanne's work and that painter's influence on Wright's technique.

Wright has said that he tried to adapt Cézanne's painting style to poetry by employing lines and stanzas in a way that approximates the painter's use of color and form. Wright's nonlinear stanzas, which never form an integral narrative, are roughly equivalent to the blocks of color that are not in themselves representational but add up to a coherent whole in Cézanne's paintings.

The second section arranges five self-portraits and four rebirth poems in alternation. The two types complement each other. The self-portraits typically picture Wright's eventual death and dispersal and reunification with the natural world, while the rebirth poems simulate belief in reincarnation, or at least in death as a portal to some other form of existence: "the future we occupied, and will wake to again . . ./ Pushing the cauly hoods back, ready to walk out/ Into the same night and the meadow grass, in step and on time" ("Mount Caribou at Night"). This is a kind of psychic play for Wright, seeming to console him in the manner of the wish-fulfillment dream.

The poems in section 3 resulted from a writer's game that Wright played with himself, setting himself a different challenge for each poem. "California Spring," for example, has a verb in each line, while "Dog Yoga" contains no verbs at all. Among other technical problems posed were to write a pair of poems using images from Dante, to write a verbal watercolor, and to write a poem from a photograph. In "Bar Giamaica, 1959-60," Wright fashioned a photograph he wished he had taken but did not. The poem was inspired by Italian photographer Ugo Mulas's picture of a Verona bar that Wright had frequented while living in Italy. Wright replaces the patrons of Mulas's bar with friends Wright had drunk with six years later. The poem is more than mere technical play; it is an attempt to defy time, to stanch the flow of losses. Such an effort, however, is futile. The congenial warmth of the remembered scene dissipates in an image of loss and emptiness, the outdoor table abandoned to the cold: "the snow falls and no one comes back/ Ever again, all of them gone through the star filter of memory,/ With its small gravel and metal tables and passers-by."

The long, abstract title poem makes up the final section. "The Southern Cross" alludes to Wright's Southern roots and the attendant burdens of history and religion.

His Christian upbringing compels his constant search for transcendence through language and landscape. Wright has said that memory and transfiguration are the subjects that most interest him. While these inform all of his work, they are the axes around which "The Southern Cross" rotates: "All day I've remembered a lake and a sudsy shoreline,/ Gauze curtains blowing in and out of open windows all over the South."

THE OTHER SIDE OF THE RIVER

Wright sees *The Other Side of the River* as an extension of *The Southern Cross*. Like the previous book, *The Other Side of the River* involves memory and transfiguration, and both are journal-like in their chronological arrangement and attention to quotidian matters. (In this, they anticipate *Zone Journals*.) *The Other Side of the River* is more anecdotal than its predecessor. Although the poems are not narratives, they incorporate fragmentary stories and anecdotes, rather than the autobiographical snippets of earlier poems, into their nonlinear structures. The titles establish the narrative, with the disjunctive anecdotes relating to the title. In the poems of the first section, Wright returns to the Tennessee of his upbringing for the narrative elements, while the poems of the second section are derived from his Italian experience. These are the two most psychically energized landscapes in Wright's world.

Memory works as a means of catharsis and shrift in "Lost Bodies" and "Lost Souls." The first juxtaposes emblems of the sublime to images of the lost world of Wright's childhood, that portion of his life already given over to death. The initial recollection of Torri del Benaco in Italy brings to mind the transcendent image of "almond trees in blossom,/ its cypresses clothed in their dark fire," and his mind instantly leaps to an image charged with lamentation for the lost faith of his boyhood:

And the words carved on that concrete cross

I passed each day of my life
In Kingsport going to town
    GET RIGHT WITH GOD/ JESUS IS COMING
    SOON

All that remains of that time is the cross and the absent Christ, whose moral precepts still affect Wright though he is apostate. The poem ends in acceptance of eternal oblivion, the knowledge that "this is as far as it goes," and on a note of sorrow for the lost body of Jesus, whose promise of salvation Wright can no longer believe in: "diesel rigs/ Carry out deaths all night through the endless rain." In the companion piece "Lost Souls," Wright seeks to expiate his survival guilt over the deaths of his parents, the "lost souls" of the title. The poem also emphasizes the importance of memory. After presenting two anecdotes from his young adulthood, Wright declares, "And nobody needs to remember any of that,/ but I do." He needs to remember his past to make sense of his life and, perhaps more important, to enlarge it: the moment is evanescent, and, lamentably, the past contains the bulk of his life.

ZONE JOURNALS

Zone Journals, according to the poet, speaks of the interrelationship of landscape and language and the way that landscape communicates metaphysical truths. Wright has treated this theme in all of his work. What he says has not changed, but the way he says it has. He takes his diaristic tendency to its ultimate state, writing poems as journal entries that concern daily matters and an underlying metaphysics, in a form that is looser, more conversational, and more spacious than any before. The inclusiveness of the poems necessitates the expansive form. Composed as irregular journal entries, the poems sprawl all over the page, packed with sensory impressions, reflection, autobiographical details, cultural and literary allusions, biographical facts about writers and artists, didactic intimations, and the like. These journal poems are essentially meditations. By contemplating the material world, Wright seeks to know God. The title suggests the vastness of his reach: "zone" refers to space and "journals" to time. The zones of the poems are sacred places. For Wright, some places possess a numinous force. Foremost among these are eastern Tennessee, the cradle of his spiritual sensibility, and Italy, the source of his creative energies. His enumeration of place-names has an incantatory intention. They are, in his own words, "Zen Koans."

"A Journal of the Year of the Ox" is the central poem of the book. Forty-eight pages long, it chronicles Wright's fiftieth year, running from January to December, 1985. The main hallowed places of the poem are Long Island in the Holston River, near Wright's birthplace of Kingsport, Tennessee, and the Veneto region of northern Italy. Long Island was the sacred ceremonial ground of the Cherokee nation and is thus a doubly significant place. Northern Italy was the site of Wright's intellectual transfiguration, where he discovered the importance of language and culture. His sojourn in Italy altered his worldview and redirected his ambitions. The effect, according to Wright, was that of a religious conversion: The scales dropped from his eyes, revealing the world of poetry, painting, and literature, which he has inhabited ever since.

In "A Journal of the Year of the Ox," Wright sets out on a mental pilgrimage to these two sacred places. One of his intentions apparently is "salvation," to rescue a portion of his past through memory. "Each year I remember less," he writes, and immediately recollects the Long Island of the Holston. Its historical and spiritual significance were unknown to him during his youth but existed despite his ignorance, just as the sublime, despite his inability to perceive it, exists as an "underimage" of the physical world. The unseen world is Wright's real concern; the invisible is more important to him than the visible: "what's outside/ the picture is more important than what's in." In the first journal entry, Wright is troubled and depressed by his current inability to believe this, as he did as a young soldier in Italy: today, he says, "the sky . . . hides no meanings." This is one of his dark moments, but darkness gives way to light, a major symbol in Wright's work. The heart of the poem is a rhapsodic depiction of a room of the Palazzo Schifanoia in Ferrara, and the Renaissance frescoes that cover its walls: "Up there in the third realm, light . . . / Washes and folds and breaks in small waves." The frescoes' scenes of peasant life, allegory, and classical divinities portray, Wright has said, "the tripartite levels of existence—everyday life, allegorical life, and ideal life." He finds this layering of worlds fascinating, for it approximates his assumption that a spectral dimension underlies the natural world. The final entry begins with a metaphor that implies Wright's hope of transfiguration: "I am poured out like water."

THE WORLD OF TEN THOUSAND THINGS

The World of Ten Thousand Things, Wright's second volume of selected poems, compiles the preceding three books, *The Southern Cross*, *The Other Side of the River*, and *Zone Journals*, along with a section of new poems titled "Xionia." Like *Country Music*—which collected the trilogy of *Hard Freight*, *Bloodlines*, and *China Trace*—this book is actually an ensemble composed of three book-length sections. Wright seems to conceive of his individual books as units within a tripartite whole. The new poems are labeled journals—for example, "Silent Journal"—but lack the dates and quotidiana of *Zone Journals*. Absent also is the anecdotal material, the ghost-narrative. Short poems alternate with longer ones. In their abstractness and brevity, these poems resemble those of *China Trace*. Wright seems to have circled back to a stylistic position he occupied earlier in his career, when his mature voice first emerged from its chrysalis.

NEGATIVE BLUE

The trilogy structure continues, and perhaps ends, with Wright's work of the 1990's. *Chickamauga*, *Black Zodiac*, and *Appalachia* are recombined into *Negative Blue*, a sequence that traces Wright's journey into middle age. The style remains consistent through these volumes, as does the overall outlook, though each unit has its characteristic tone, mood, and energy. However, in incorporating the parts of his latest trilogy into a single volume, Wright has avoided simply reprinting the individual component titles. Rather, he has dropped a handful of poems and added a new sequence, "North American Bear," comprised of seven new poems. Thus the subtitle, "Selected Later Poems," is in some conflict with the notion of a coherent, planned trilogy. Wright has created something of a publishing paradox.

However, paradox is nothing knew to Wright. It is the experiential medium through which his personas swims from decade to decade, at once denying the sufficiency of language and applauding its exclusive territory of truth-making. In between the seeing and the contemplating is the stuff of Wright's poetry, a body of utterance that is constantly in the service of contradiction and acceptance. As he tells us in "Broken English," "All speech pulls toward privacy / and the zones of the infinite," and "Without a syntax, there is no immortality." Wright has found the syntax.

OTHER MAJOR WORKS

NONFICTION: *Halflife: Improvisations and Interviews, 1977-1987*, 1988; *Quarter Notes*, 1995.

TRANSLATIONS: *The Storm and Other Poems*, 1978 (of Eugenio Montale); *Orphic Songs*, 1984 (of Dino Campana).

BIBLIOGRAPHY

Andrews, Tom, ed. *The Point Where All Things Meet: Essays on Charles Wright*. Oberlin: Field Editions, 1995. These twenty-seven essays make clear that Wright is one of a handful of poets around whom American poetry has been centered in the last quarter of the twentieth century. Contributors include David Kalstone, Helen Vendler, Calvin Bedient, David Walker, J. D. McClatchy, and Bonnie Costello.

Bedient, Calvin. "Tracing Charles Wright." *Parnassus: Poetry in Review* 10, no. 1 (1982): 55-74. Written in an oblique and lyrical style that is somewhat difficult to access, this article is perceptive and comprehensive. It treats Wright's career from *Hard Freight* to *The Southern Cross*, paying close attention to major themes and particularly to the liturgical elements of the books. Bedient does not examine the individual books but ranges randomly through them, drawing examples to exemplify his interpretations.

McClatchy, J. D. *White Paper: On Contemporary American Poetry*. New York: Columbia University Press, 1989. McClatchy draws upon his interview with Wright (see Wright's "The Art of Poetry XLI," below) to explicate Wright's major poem "The Southern Cross." He prepares for this explication with an informative overview of Wright's development as a poet and the primary characteristics of his style. McClatchy writes intelligibly and with discernment, covering a lot of ground in seventeen pages.

McCorkle, James. "Things That Lock Our Wrists to the Past: Self-Portraiture and Autobiography in Charles Wright's Poetry." In *The Still Performance: Writing, Self, and Interconnection in Five Postmodern American Poets*. Charlottesville: University Press of Virginia, 1989. This long, dense essay examines the relationship between self-portraiture and language in Wright's poetry. It analyzes the books through *The Other Side of the River*. McCorkle draws upon the theories of the deconstructionists for some of his methodology, so readers with some knowledge of deconstruction will find the essay more readily accessible.

Santos, Sherod. "A Solving Emptiness: C. K. Williams and Charles Wright." In his *A Poetry of Two Minds*. Athens: University of Georgia Press, 2000. In a comparison of mid-career poems by both poets, Santos examines parallel aesthetic experimentation and the shared determination to overcome despair through art.

Stitt, Peter. "Charles Wright: Resurrecting the Baroque." In his *Uncertainty and Plenitude: Five Contemporary Poets*. Iowa City: University of Iowa Press, 1997. Stitt demonstrates an affinity between Wright's style and concerns and those of the British Metaphysical poets of the early seventeenth century. Wright's poems, despite narrative elements, are meditative and circular. Stitt gives "Lost Bodies" a close reading. He also notes Wright's avoidance of politics and contemporary events.

Upton, Lee. *The Muse of Abandonment: Origin, Identity, Mastery, in Five American Poets*. London: Associated University Presses, 1998. A critical study of five poets, including Wright, dealing with sociologigal issues in their work. Includes bibliographical references and an index.

Wright, Charles. "The Art of Poetry XLI: Charles Wright." Interview by J. D. McClatchy. *The Paris Review* 31 (Winter, 1989): 185-221. This excellent interview provides important information about Wright's family history and its significance to his poetry. Wright discusses *Zone Journals* and *The Southern Cross*, among others, and the evolution of his style from his first book through *China Trace*. He also defines his poetics.

_____. *Halflife: Improvisations and Interviews, 1977-1987*. Ann Arbor: University of Michigan Press, 1988. The first half of this book contains selections from Wright's notebook, explications of several of his poems, and a few brief pieces about his own poetry and that of others. The second half of the book is composed of interviews that span Wright's career. The first, conducted at Oberlin College in 1977, provides a wealth of biographical information, as well as Wright's comments about many of his poems and books.

Rick Lott,
updated by Philip K. Jason

JAMES WRIGHT

Born: Martins Ferry, Ohio; December 13, 1927
Died: New York, New York; March 25, 1980

PRINCIPAL POETRY

The Green Wall, 1957
Saint Judas, 1959
The Branch Will Not Break, 1963
Shall We Gather at the River, 1968
Collected Poems, 1971
Two Citizens, 1973
Moments of the Italian Summer, 1976
To a Blossoming Pear Tree, 1977
This Journey, 1982
Above the River: The Complete Poems, 1990

OTHER LITERARY FORMS

Although his fame rests almost exclusively with his original poetry, James Wright made a valuable contribution in one other area of literary modernism—the translation. Ezra Pound insisted that translation was in itself an art of the highest creative order, and Wright (especially while he was collaborating with Robert Bly) brought the works of many distinguished European and Latin American authors to readers of English. Wright's translations for Bly's Sixties Press included poems by Georg Trakl, César Vallejo, and Pablo Neruda. Wright also translated Hermann Hesse's *Poems*, and, in collaboration with his son Franz Paul Wright, Hesse's *Wandering* (1972). In addition, he translated Theodor Storm's *The Rider on the White Horse and Selected Stories* (1964), as well as individual poems of several Latin American poets of the twentieth century.

ACHIEVEMENTS

Before his graduation from Kenyon College in 1952, Wright had won the Robert Frost Poetry Prize. A second major influence followed immediately. Wright received a Fulbright scholarship to the University of Vienna, Austria, where he studied the fiction of Theodor Storm. In his experiments with the deep image, Wright explored alternatives to the strict rhetoric by which Robert Lowell and his followers created one version of the confessional mode of postmodern poetry. His work with this style led James Dickey to call him "one of the few authentic visionary poets writing today." He was widely honored in literary and academic circles, and his *Collected Poems* won the Pulitzer Prize in 1972.

BIOGRAPHY

As he proclaims in many of his poems, James Arlington Wright was born in Martins Ferry, Ohio. Although he spent much of his adult life in New York City, Wright returned again and again in memory to the Ohio Valley he loved and despised with equal and intense passion for inspiration as well as material for his poems. His imagination was fired by the loneliness and emptiness of the lives of the Ohioans of his youth, and by the occasional flashes of kindness, charity, and decency they showed. At the same time, Wright's preoccupation with steel mills and strip mines confirms a profound concern for the beauty of nature that human beings so indifferently trample upon in the name of economic gain.

Wright left Ohio during World War II and served with the American Occupation Forces in Japan. Upon his discharge, he enrolled at Kenyon College, where he studied literature under John Crowe Ransom. Wright has since acknowledged that this association was a turning point for him, and the traditional structures of his first book, *The Green Wall*, reflect Ransom's influence. Wright's second volume, *Saint Judas*, was published in the same year as Robert Lowell's *Life Studies*, the book that more than any other marked the end of literary modernism in poetry. Lowell and Wright were working independently in the same direction, toward freedom from the insistence on objectivity that had characterized such great modern poets as T. S. Eliot, Ezra Pound, and Wallace Stevens. Like Lowell, Wright sought a more direct exploration of the self as poetic subject and embraced the open subjectivity that Lowell had pioneered. He would abandon the ornate rhetoric that Lowell was never willing to leave behind and would move well beyond Lowell in his experimentation with organic form.

Wright's chief influence on postmodern poetry may be his exploration of nondiscursive imagery and careful superimposition as a poetic method. His poems aim at a point of discovery, in which the images of the poem combine to produce a sudden realization of the secrets

James Wright (© Nancy Crampton)

of the inner, unconscious being. Although he repeatedly disavowed any interest in surrealism as an aesthetic credo, critics have regularly associated Wright and Bly with surrealism, and have called their work neo-Imagist or Jungian. The term "emotive imagination" was coined in an effort to define the process by which the poems evoke nondiscursive feelings in the mind of the reader. Perhaps the most appropriate term is Robert Kelly's "deep image," a concept enthusiastically promoted by Bly during the period of his and Wright's closest association. The Deep Image describes the effort to discover a specific object that has powerful emotional and prerational associations for the poet and can be controlled through surprise to evoke a similar set of associations in the consciousness of the reader. The effects of the deep image depend on careful juxtapositions, superimpositions, sudden leaps in tone or logic, timing, and muted shock.

While in Austria on his Fulbright scholarship, Wright became interested in the poems of Georg Trakl and later translated many of Trakl's and Storm's works, as well as those of several European and Latin American poets. These translations were valuable experiences for Wright, for they taught him alternatives to the traditional methods of English prosody, and he incorporated several of these elements into his own art.

Wright continued his education at the University of Washington, from which he took his M.A. degree in 1954 and his Ph.D. in 1959. At Washington, he studied with Theodore Roethke, whose impact on Wright was formative. Wright has acknowledged his personal reverence for Roethke; the extent of Roethke's poetic influence will be debated by scholars in the years to come.

Like many of his contemporaries, Wright pursued the profession of a teacher and the career of a poet. He taught English at the University of Minnesota for seven years, at Macalester College for two, and at Hunter College in New York from 1966 until his death in 1980. Unlike many of his contemporaries, however, Wright chose not to teach creative writing; he preferred to teach literature. He told a class at the University of Illinois in 1973: "I'm a teacher by profession, not a writer. . . . In fact, I don't even teach poetry."

During the final two decades of his life, James Wright emerged as one of the foremost voices in postmodern American poetry. Although he did not systematize his artistic views in essays, as many poets of both the modern and postmodern periods have done, Wright exerted a quiet but vigorous influence by his example. His constant experimentation with form offered younger poets an alternative to the studied objectivity and complex rhetoric of the modern period. By the 1970's, Wright had achieved recognition as a superb reader of his own poems and was in regular demand on the lecture circuit. His second marriage, to Anne Runk, brought new inspiration to his art, and the Wrights' travels in Europe, especially Italy, brought a new tenderness to his poems and particularly to his attitude toward Ohio. He died on March 25, 1980 in New York.

ANALYSIS

Readers who come to James Wright's poetry from a traditional or even a modernist orientation are likely to be struck by a distinctive blend of despair, compassion, and self-revelation. Even in a century characterized by anxiety in poetry, a century in which the most influential single poem would be called *The Waste Land* (1922), Wright's vision seems unusually bleak. The pessimism

is, however, balanced by a profound compassion for all mortal beings, which is at the heart of Wright's work. Whereas such great modernists as Eliot, Pound, Stevens, and Robert Frost sought objectivity through wit, irony, and rhetorical discontinuity, Wright has written directly of his anguished compassion for his fellow creatures.

"LYING IN A HAMMOCK AT WILLIAM DUFFY'S FARM IN PINE ISLAND, MINNESOTA"

The tone of many of his memorable poems borders on the depressive side. The famous "Lying in a Hammock at William Duffy's Farm in Pine Island, Minnesota" exemplifies the quality and intention of Wright's poetry of despair. At first, the charming and lengthy title, reminiscent of the chapter titles of the nineteenth century novels Wright loved so much, invites the reader to expect a witty poem celebrating the beauty of nature. Indeed, the poem is carefully built of a series of images that the viewer in such a hammock would be likely to perceive, and all of these images initially fulfill the pastoral expectation created by the title. A bronze butterfly gently blows in the wind and the sound of cowbells evokes a rustic placidity. Even horse droppings are invested with elegance, as they "Blaze up into golden stones," and a chicken hawk floats on the air above. The final line is a shocking reversal: "I have wasted my life." Critics are divided on the effect of this line. Some find it too sudden, and the turn to desolation unearned or contrived. Others hold that the line has a periodic effect and that its devastating contrast leads the reader to examine the images again for a principle of structure. To reexamine these contrasts is to discover that there is a carefully crafted intention at work. The images of the poem become progressively ominous, and the attitude they express has that ambiguous quality that Wright appreciated in Frost's poems. Upon this review, one notices that the butterfly is asleep, so its motion is in fact under the control of an outside force, the wind. The pastoral, auditory richness of the cowbells is balanced by a "movement into the distances of the afternoon." The pivotal image, the horse droppings, now carries a new ominous quality, for their transformation into golden stones is after all a matter of individual human perception. The hawk is not merely floating; it is "looking for home." The pessimism of the poem is not, therefore, arbitrary. Things in nature that appear to be, or can become under human perception, beautiful are in fact part of a process of decay and alienation. Nature speaks to human beings, but the message of nature can be a shocking or a depressing revelation.

LOVE POEMS

Not all of Wright's poems move readers to despair; a few can even be called poems of joy. Several are love poems, and "A Sequence of Love Poems" forms the center of *Saint Judas*. Love poems also are a very important component of *Two Citizens* and *This Journey*. These poems speak of the necessity as well as the rewards of human love, yet they are not simple, for they evoke a sense of separateness that not even love can transcend. In the elegant "Vision Between Waking and Sleeping in the Mountains," Wright's speaker discovers that even lovers must have secrets that cannot be shared. His beloved's secret separates them, as does a memory he cannot share even with his wife. He transforms this unpleasant thought into a genuine celebration of the very separateness of the lovers: "I love your secret. By God I will never violate the wings/ Of snow you found rising in the wind." The compounding of the contemporary curse with the traditional oath ("By God") emphasizes the determination of the poet to respect the secret of the beloved as an expression of the love he feels. All of the love poems deal with and ultimately rejoice in the final individuality of lovers. His poems in *Two Citizens* are "an expression of my patriotism, of my love and discovery of my native place. I never knew or loved my America so well, and I began the book as a savage attack upon it. Then I discovered it." The poet did not sentimentalize America, but his critical and judgmental stance came into balance with an appreciation of natural beauty, human kindness, and the blessings of human love. The pessimism of his most influential poetry would be balanced by an awareness of human and natural beauty.

IMAGES OF NATURE

Several of the works other than love poems can be considered celebrations, but the celebration is usually mixed with an awareness of the potential for despair. "Depressed by a Book of Bad Poetry, I Walk Toward an Unused Pasture and Invite the Insects to Join Me" treats the capability of art, or at least of inferior art, to produce depressing effects, but it celebrates the healing power of nature in the manner of William Wordsworth. A cricket's song effectively cancels out the resonance of the bad poems. Wright's deliberate quest for joy and the consolation of nature is most succinctly exemplified by "Today I Was So Happy, So I Made This Poem," a work that should be read in conjunction with "Lying in a Hammock at William Duffy's Farm in Pine Island, Minnesota." In this poem, images from nature combine to grant the poet a temporary release from the pressure of mortality. Observing a plump squirrel and the shining moon leads the poet momentarily beyond his mortality, and he discovers that "Each moment of time is a mountain." The joy is completed by the vision of an eagle rejoicing in the "oak trees of heaven," and the cry of the eagle becomes the cry of the poet: *"This is what I wanted."* The statement has both ethical and aesthetic implications. The celebration of a momentary escape from mortality and the ability to express that joy are desires of the highest order of artistic aspiration and of a recognition of the possibility of being at peace with the created world.

THE GREEN WALL

In an extraordinarily prophetic introduction to Wright's first volume, *The Green Wall*, W. H. Auden noted a tension that would, in the process of its resolution, lead to the development of Wright's distinctive poetic style. Auden saw in Wright's choice of material a particularly modern sensibility at work and observed that the persons with whom Wright chose to deal included lunatics, murderers, lesbians, and prostitutes. Even at the inception of Wright's poetic career, Auden saw the alienation that would characterize his mature works. Wright's characters "play no part in ruling the City nor is its history made by them, nor, even, are they romantic rebels against its injustices . . . they are the City's passive victims." This interest in the outcast created a dynamic tension, because Wright's early poems have the traditional formal orthodoxy of his acknowledged masters, Frost, Edwin Arlington Robinson, and Ransom. The force of Robinson's and Ransom's influence is especially apparent in the tension created by the use of traditional forms and meters to write about society's misfits and outcasts.

TENSION IN POETRY

In his first two volumes, Wright responded to this tension by aiming at a firm control through traditional prosody. Although he briefly gave up the writing of poems after the publication of *Saint Judas* because he felt he had reached a dead end, some critics have expressed preference for the control in these works over the expressive quality of his mature works. Paul Lacey praises "the power of sensitive spirit disciplined by a firm intellect and a craftsman's skill."

"TO A DEFEATED SAVIOR"

"To a Defeated Savior" handles the subjects of guilt and failure with the formal objectivity that characterizes the early poems. All four stanzas employ the traditional ballad form, alternately rhymed iambic tetrameter with end-stops reserved for the even-numbered lines. The poem addresses the guilt of a youth (Wright has said that an event that happened to his brother Paul inspired this work) who was unable to save a drowning swimmer. The poet's real interest is in the lasting consequences of the failure; the point of the poem is that all men are defeated saviors. Unable in his daily pursuits to forget completely his moment of heroic action, the youth is haunted by the vision of the drowning swimmer. The speaker discovers that the ultimate failure is fear: "You would have raised him, flesh and soul,/ Had you been strong enough to dare. . . ." The guilt derives from an intention on which the savior was unable to act because he could not control his fear.

The critical point is the universality of the savior's failure. This youth had a dramatic chance to reach out, to risk life for the love of his fellow human being. His failure is a synecdoche for the failure of all people at all times to risk enough for others: "The circling tow, the shadowy pool/ Shift underneath us everywhere." The undertow that drowned the swimmer is a synecdoche for the forces that threaten all humanity, so the savior's defeat, the inability to summon courage and strength adequate to the occasion, is universal. The voice of the poem is compassionate toward the savior, for all human beings must share his guilt. Still, the poem does not excuse this failure. It demands that the savior as well as the speaker come to terms with what might have been and by extension with the responsibility all human beings have to one another.

SAINT JUDAS

In *Saint Judas*, Wright continues to explore the tension between form and subject, and it is from this volume that the greatest number of Wright's poems have been anthologized. The influence of Robinson and Frost is still apparent, but the voice of the poems becomes more directly personal, and Wright himself emerges as the subject of most of the lyrics. The author preferred this over any of his other collections, in part because it was a chronicle of his coming to terms with his own pain. By the logic of the synecdoche that informs all of Wright's poems, this coming to terms with personal pain represents the struggle of humanity to come to terms with its existential anguish. "Saint Judas" is a sonnet, the form that has traditionally implied coherence in English poetry. Here the voice, in a book that has struggled toward direct lyrical expression, is that of Judas. Wright has admitted a primarily technical interest as the genesis of the poem. Moved by Robinson's "How Annandale Went Out," he set out to discover whether he too could write a genuine Petrarchan sonnet that would still be a dramatic monologue.

The traditional octave-sestet pattern of the Petrarchan sonnet offers Wright a form he can use for remarkable effects. The octave dramatizes Judas's despair as he goes to take his own life. His chance encounter with the brutal treatment of another man causes Judas to forget for a moment the reprehensible crimes of his own immediate past. A human instinct takes over and he rescues the victim. The sestet celebrates Judas's sainthood as the instinctive charity of a man who is already damned and on his way to commit the unpardonable sin, yet who automatically comes to the aid of his fellow man. The final lines may be among the most moving in contemporary poetry: "Flayed without hope,/ I held the man for nothing in my arms." Judas has nothing to gain from his act of charity, and for this reason the moment is profoundly moving.

Critics cannot agree on the discursive meaning of the phrase "for nothing." Some, like John Ditsky, associate the term with "bootless action" and therefore see Judas's role as one of whose "personal pointlessness he alone is aware. . . ." Ralph J. Mills, Jr., focusing on the ambiguity of human behavior, believes that the poem means that if a man can be at one moment treacherous and in despair, at another brave and heroic, then people should all be more merciful to their fellow man. Paul Lacey sees Judas not as a study in ethics or philosophy, but as the "supreme riddle, the man who will do evil for pay and good for nothing." The diversity of these views indicates the richness of the poem. Surely Wright wants his readers to reconsider human nature, for even the worst of men in the worst of times is capable of ethical action in and for itself, without an eye for reward in this world or the next.

"AN OFFERING FOR MR. BLUEHART"

"An Offering for Mr. Bluehart," like "To a Defeated Savior," employs the ballad form. It is a retrospective meditation on one of the poet's own childhood pranks, stealing apples from the orchard of a neighborhood grouch. Wright makes ironic use of the Tom Sawyer tone his situation might imply and transforms that tone into an elegy that is at the same time an effort to deal with personal guilt. Each of the three stanzas moves to a periodic reminder of the mutability of all things. In the first, the recollection of the boys' prank contrasts with sparrows that "Denounced us from the broken bough." The mention of the broken bough marks a shift in point of view, and the elegiac tone intensifies as the sparrows "limp along the wind and die./ The apples are all eaten now."

In the second stanza, the contrast between the laughing boys and Bluehart, the "lean satanic owner" who lay in wait for the pranksters, emphasizes the connotations of Eden inherent in the idyllic setting, and that set of contrasts is heightened by the poet's retrospective awareness of both the seriousness of their trespass ("We stole his riches all away") and the brutal futility of the old man's response: "He damned us to the laughing bone,/ And fired his gun across the gray/ Autumn where his life is done." With a sudden twist of his images, Wright moves from a merely crotchety old man to one whose rage provoked an attempt to kill his tormentors, and with a careful superimposition the old man's act of violence blends with his own mortality.

The final stanza is Wright's "offering" for Bluehart, a note of personal mourning such as characterizes many of his poems. The poet now mourns his old adversary by resisting the temptation to pick apples and he prays, "Now may my abstinence restore/ Peace to the orchard and the dead." This is at best an empty penance, and Wright knows that. His reversion to colloquial diction in the final line, "We shall not nag them anymore," indicates his awareness of the inadequacy of such a gesture.

There is at best the effort to make personal retribution for the sins of the past. In its compelling exploration of a trivial human guilt, this poem speaks to the need for all human beings to be aware of the consequences of their actions, for those actions will return in memory.

Identification with society's enemies and the dramatic effects this produces on the structure of the poem form the nucleus of the two most powerful poems of *Saint Judas*, "At the Executed Murderer's Grave" and "Saint Judas." The former may appear to express an almost perverse identification with George Doty, murderer, rapist, and thief, who had also been the subject of "A Poem about George Doty in the Death House," in *The Green Wall*.

"AT THE EXECUTED MURDERER'S GRAVE"

In its total impact, "At the Executed Murderer's Grave" is a profound study of the community of human guilt. The real subject of the poem is not Doty, but the killer's inescapable impact on the speaker. This speaker is aggressively Wright himself, for the poem begins with a startling effort at self-definition: "My name is James A. Wright, and I was born/ Twenty-five miles from this infected grave,/ In Martins Ferry, Ohio. . . ." This assertion of the self by name as well as origin launches the poet on a tortured review of his own relationship with Doty.

They share an origin, but one became a murderer and the other a poet. One element in the abiding effect of the poem is Wright's honest questioning of how far apart the two really are. Perhaps, Wright speculates, his own departure from Ohio allowed him to differ from Doty, because "Dying's the best/ Of all the arts men learn in a dead place." Yet the geographical distance between poet and murderer is in important ways an illusion. Doty remains at the center of the poet's consciousness, a ghost to be exorcised at the terrible cost of coming to terms with his own humanity. He declares, in a deliberate echo of the biblical Pharisees, "Doty, if I confess I do not love you,/ Will you let me alone?" To propose such a limit on human compassion is, of course, to evade the issue, for Wright knows that the real challenge is not to escape from or excuse the actions of the killer, but to wrestle with the dread of recognizing that both are part of the human condition, and to discover a viable relationship between the self and the political entity that electrocuted

Doty for his crimes. Doty's actions were clearly reprehensible to Wright, yet he ponders the implications of the "eye for an eye" system that condemned the killer: "And yet, nobody had to kill him either."

Even the obvious distinction, the choices the two men made, does not satisfy Wright. It could be argued that the choice to be a murderer and a rapist is to represent the worst in humanity, whereas to be a poet is to represent the best. Such a notion would be consoling, but Wright rejects the cliché of the heroism of artistic commitment. He says, "I croon my tears at fifty cents per line," a cruel indictment of the professionalism of the poet who transforms his grief into words and receives literal as well as metaphorical compensation. The verb "croon" connotes popular music and therefore an evasion of reality. This censure is reinforced when both the drunks and the police "Can do without my widely printed sighing/ Over their pains with paid sincerity." It is not enough, then, to invoke choice as a substantive difference between the self of the poet and the antithetical force, the murderer Doty.

Something about the killer will not let the poet forget their bond as men. He seems to reject uncritical compassion for humanity when he says of the bums and drunks of Ohio, "Christ may restore them whole, for all of me," but ambiguity is at work here. There is an abdication of responsibility to God, yet the modifying clause "for all of me" implies that the poet's own wholeness depends on Christ's restoration of society's outcasts. Doty is, however, not like the drunks. He is censured with Wright's typical ambiguity: "Idiot, he demanded love from girls,/ And murdered one." His action, brutal as it was, perverted an attempt to find love in a loveless world. In this, the worst of men, there is the same aspiration that animates Wright to be a poet, the need to discover an alternative to the passive acceptance of lovelessness.

This shared humanity cannot be escaped: "This grave's gash festers." It is a reminder of the emptiness of a world for which Ohio has become a synecdoche, and of the vindictiveness of human justice. The poem speculates on the distinctions among Doty, the poet, and all human beings at the Last Judgment. Like the killer, "we dead stand undefended everywhere" and those transgressions which had been hidden successfully will stand before "God's unpitying stars." This possibility forces Wright to one of the most painful realizations in all of his poems: "Staring politely, they will not mark my face/ From any murderer's, buried in this place./ Why should they? We are nothing but a man." At issue here is what in the eyes of God will distinguish those human beings who have not been guilty of crimes from those who have, and the discovery is that one cannot presume to know. Perhaps on the Day of Judgment all human beings will have to acknowledge their shared humanity before God and affirm the human community in his presence.

Wright is finally able to resign himself to his community with Doty as "killer, imbecile and thief:/ Dirt of my flesh, defeated, underground." Awareness of the evil of Doty's actions blends with recognition of the bonds that unite poet and killer as part of human nature. "At the Executed Murderer's Grave," then, is not simply a poem about compassion for one of society's enemies. Wright never excuses Doty and he resists, in the dramatic tension created by the poem, the influence of the killer until he must resign himself to it after having considered the Last Judgment. This is a poem of sterner stuff, of coming to terms with the nature all people share with the very worst of their species.

"DEAR JUDAS"

That acceptance takes the form of a very different theme in "Saint Judas." Like Robinson Jeffers thirty years before in "Dear Judas," Wright has the daring to choose as the hero of his poem the archetypal betrayer and the figure associated in the collective mind of a Christian culture with the most contemptible crime in human history. Technically, the poem is the most interesting in Saint Judas, for Wright chafed against the limits of traditional form in "At the Executed Murderer's Grave," and broke rather sharply with that orthodoxy in the succeeding books.

"TWO HANGOVERS"

From these poems on, Wright proceeded to discover a voice that was distinctively his own, exploring the implications of selfhood with increasing self-revelation, virtually abandoning traditional rhyme and metrical schemes, and expanding on the potential of the deep image, which works through surprise to capture a moment in the unconscious life of both reader and poet.

Paul Zweig has proposed that *The Branch Will Not Break* is one of the key books of the 1960's because Wright's articulation of a visionary style has appealed to younger poets as an alternative to the more formal and elaborate rhetoric of Robert Lowell and Richard Wilbur, the pathfinders of the previous decade.

The title of the volume comes from "Two Hangovers," a pair of poems that offer two opposing variations on the traditional motif of the morning hymn. In the first variation, all of the images from nature are transformed, as a result of the poet's condition, to disgust. The "old women beyond my window/ Are hunching toward the graveyard," so there is a reminder of mortality. The life-giving sun has a "big stupid face" and offers no consolation as it "staggers in" upon the poet's distorted consciousness. Even a sparrow's song reminds Wright of the Hanna Coal Company, a frequent symbol in the Ohio poems for human rapacity and exploitation of nature. This morning produces disgust: "Ah, turn it off." In the other variation, "I Try to Waken and Greet the World Once Again," a single image leads to joy, just as the several images of the first led to despair. A blue jay moves up and down on a slender branch outside the window, and human and natural delight are fused in an exquisite synthesis: "I laugh, as I see him abandon himself/ To entire delight, for he knows as well as I do/ That the branch will not break." This symbol expresses both an aesthetic and an ethical position. The world is filled with uncertainty, with occasions for delight and despair, all suggested by the vertical motion of the branch. What gives man the courage to continue and the joy to make that continuation worthwhile is the faith that progress through life, though perilous, is sustained by a connection with nature, a branch that will not break. The proper reaction to this faith is joy, and the best human reaction to the perils of life is delight in the process itself. The image has aesthetic implications, for the randomness of the bird's motion is like the freedoms Wright will claim for his art; but there remains that sense of the connectedness of things, the branch with the tree and the poem with a new kind of organic formal control.

Joy is a note that is rare in Wright's mature poems. Although faith in the ultimate harmony of man and nature persists, the distinctive poems explore through superimposition of images the inadequacy of individual or institutional reactions to this harmony.

"AUTUMN BEGINS IN MARTINS FERRY, OHIO"

"Autumn Begins in Martins Ferry, Ohio" returns to the detached speaker of the early poems, but the superimposition of images builds a subtle cause-effect relationship. The poet, in a high school football stadium, thinks about three separate but related character types. He associates, without commentary, "Polacks nursing long beers," the "gray faces of Negroes in the blast furnace" of a steel mill, and the "ruptured night watchman" at yet another mill. Frustration is what the characters have in common, for all of them are "Dreaming of heroes." These specific images are then generalized to represent "All the proud fathers" who, if proud, are also "ashamed to go home." The disparity between the ordinariness of their daily lives and the aspiration of their dreams makes them afraid of their families and even sexually impotent, for their wives are "Dying for love." The element of mortality surfaces again here, but the dominant effect is that the women, and by extension the entire families, are victims of the emptiness the husbands feel.

This extension is fully realized in the causal connection of the final stanza. "Therefore" is reserved to a line by itself to emphasize the causal sequence, and the poem concludes with a devastating indictment of the brutality and beauty of modern institutional life. "Their sons grow suicidally beautiful" because the sons are under pressure to live out the frustrated, proud fathers' dreams of heroism, so each autumn they "gallop terribly against each others' bodies." The pointlessness and disorder of the athletic contest are powerfully felt in this line. Although there is something insane and suicidal about this institutionalization of violence in which the sons are victims of their fathers' aspirations, there is a terrible beauty in the athletic training, and even the sacrifice, of the youths themselves.

"EISENHOWER'S VISIT TO FRANCO, 1959"

The censure of institutions as antithetical to the harmony of man and nature becomes overtly political in "Eisenhower's Visit to Franco, 1959," a parallel set of contrasts between light and darkness and between those who rule and those who are ruled. The American president and the Spanish dictator, caught in a ceremonious handshake, are illuminated by the glare of flashbulbs, the searchlights of "Clean new bombers from America," and Franco's polished escort of police. Franco's promise that "all dark things/ Will be hunted down" and the lights of the American airplanes imply cooperation between the two nations to seek out the dark things in Spain.

The contrasting stanza identifies the poet Antonio Machado, a "cave of silent children," and old men as the inhabitants of darkness. The epigraph from Miguel de Unamuno, "We die of cold, and not of darkness," becomes critical here, because there is a cold, sterile quality about the scene at the airfield, whereas the darkness features a creative man who walks by moonlight and children, the hope of the future. Wine, with both Dionysian and Eucharistic implications, "darkens in stone jars" and "sleeps in the mouths of old men." As wine darkens, it becomes richer. The political implication is that the life of the community rests with its ordinary citizens and creative outcasts, not in the leaders who conspire against them.

Franco has promised to "hunt down" the dark things, and America supplies the technology to implement that promise. The first two lines now become a terrifying thesis: "The American hero must triumph over/ The forces of darkness." The American hero may learn from the dictator how to turn the harsh light of authority on the lifeblood of the community, the private citizens.

"THE MINNEAPOLIS POEM"

The relation between the individual and the institutions that may challenge the integrity of the self is at the center of Wright's most technically remarkable work, "The Minneapolis Poem." In a series of stark images Wright empathizes with the poor, the outcasts, and the hopeless of the city. Readers are reminded of Auden's prophetic judgment, in the preface to *The Green Wall*, that Wright's characters are "the City's passive victims." Now, however, Wright is no longer an advocate for the victims; he has identified himself completely with them. As the poem moves from one seemingly random portrait of outcasts to another, it becomes clear that Wright's identification with the victims is also a profound questioning of the sociological and institutional ties that bind human beings into a community. The very fragmentary and seemingly random nature of "The Minneapolis Poem" expresses the central theme, the terror, violence,

and indifference at the heart of the modern City. Wright laments the nameless and even numberless old men who committed suicide in the winter and wonders, "How does the city keep lists of its fathers/ Who have no names?" Their anonymity and the indifference of the City leaves them with only the community of death, and Wright, despite his wish to console them, can only "wish my brothers good luck/ And a warm grave" in contrast to the bad luck and cold winters they knew in Minneapolis.

The second section of "The Minneapolis Poem" is a tour de force. Four groups are mentioned, but there is no possibility of their ever getting together to reshape the fragmented City. Even within these groups either fear or some sinister purpose dominates. "The Chippewa young men/ Stab one another shrieking/ Jesus Christ." America's first citizens are outcasts in the heart of America, and they invoke the name of the conqueror's god as a curse. Even their bond is violent; they take out their wrath and frustration on one another. In Wright's depiction of another group with a common purpose, the "Split-lipped homosexuals limp in terror of assault." Their common purpose is to avoid persecution by the heterosexual majority, but their injuries show how unsuccessful their subgroup has been. The middle class is represented when "High school backfields search under benches/ Near the Post Office." For what do they search? The very lack of specificity implies a sinister purpose, and a harsh description reinforces this possibility: "Their faces are the rich/ Raw bacon without eyes." The elite are here, too: "The Walker Art Center crowd stare/ At the Guthrie Theater." Unlike the other groups, this one expresses no purpose, merely anonymous unity. Their response to one of America's cultural landmarks is apathetic and pointless. It is clear that no organization of these groups into a single social unit is possible, and there is no creative force in any of them.

The poem notes other of the City's outcasts and enemies, the "legless beggars" who are gone and the black prostitutes from Chicago who know the policeman who poses as a patron to entrap them. The only things at home in Minneapolis are automobiles, products of modern technology that "consent with a mutter of high good humor/ To take their two naps a day." These autos, described by a felicity that ought to describe human behavior, speak to the impersonality and terror of modern urban life.

The terror turns inward as Wright, not identified with the poor and the nameless, claims that "There are men in this city who labor dawn after dawn/ To sell me my death." Just who these men are is not made explicit, and the uncertain identification fits well with the attitudes of uncertainty, alienation, and dread that the poem has created. Like the beggars, Chippewas, and prostitutes, the dealers in death are nameless. Who they are is less important than what they are: the logical consequences of the human community, the City, gone wrong.

Dread leads Wright logically to a contemplation of death, something close to his mind since the introduction of the suicides in the first stanza. Now death is personal, individual, and related directly to life in the City. He chooses not "To allow my poor brother my body to die/ In Minneapolis" and prays that he not be buried there. At first glance this may seem to be a morbid sentiment, but Wright intends to dramatize his rejection of the City in the tormented and fragmented form it has taken. He strategically invokes the patron of American poets: "The old man Walt Whitman our countryman/ Is now in America our country/ Dead." This sudden movement is a reminder of the death of the great bard of American democracy, the spokesman of brotherhood who is now one with the suicides and legless beggars of this poem. A closer look at the syntax reveals that the America Whitman knew, loved, and created is also dead.

"The Minneapolis Poem" concludes with Wright's wish not to be buried in the city, but "stored with the secrets of the wheat and the mysterious lives/ Of the unnamed poor." It is a jaded version of the return to nature of the Romantics. A community is asserted, and the image of the wheat suggests vitality in America among its citizens. As an alternative to the failed life of the city, the conclusion of "The Minneapolis Poem" is not intellectually satisfying, but as an expression of pain at the failure of a basic human institution to respond to human needs, the ending has a powerful emotional impact.

"Hook"

It is worth noting that "Hook," one of the most memorable poems in *To a Blossoming Pear Tree*, records a moment of unexpected human warmth in this same above city. A mutilated Sioux Indian gave a despairing

Wright cab fare to go home, and the memory leads Wright to one of his understated moments of appreciation for the decency of his fellow man. The money the Sioux gave him symbolizes the capacity of society's outcasts to care for one another.

"A Blessing"

Despite his preoccupation with death, despair, alienation, and anxiety, Wright sought to record moments of joy in his love for people and his reverence for nature. His "A Blessing," a simple account of the delight caused by the greeting of the poet and a nameless friend by two ponies, reaches toward mysticism and shows that this poet, so aware of the pain of modern life, could occasionally articulate moments of rapture.

"A Reply to Matthew Arnold of My Fifth Day in Fano"

In his final volume, *This Journey*, Wright articulates in a prose poem called "A Reply to Matthew Arnold of My Fifth Day in Fano" the artistic and thematic credo to which his poems form a lasting moment: "Briefly in harmony with nature before I die, I welcome the old curse." The curse is the many human failings and moral terrors his poems have documented. The attitude is vigorous welcome for man and his companion, nature, a defiant celebration of the very fact of mortality.

Other major works

NONFICTION: *Collected Prose*, 1983.

TRANSLATIONS: *Twenty Poems of George Trakl*, 1961 (with Robert Bly); *Twenty Poems*, 1962 (of César Vallejo; with Bly and John Knoepfle); *The Rider on the White Horse and Selected Stories*, 1964 (of Theodor Storm); *Twenty Poems of Pablo Neruda*, 1967 (with Bly); *Poems*, 1970 (of Hermann Hesse); *Wandering*, 1972 (of Hesse; with Franz Paul Wright).

Bibliography

Dougherty, David. *James Wright*. Boston: Twayne, 1987. This essential book provides the reader with a historical study of Wright's development as a craftsman, thereby allowing the individual to judge the poet's historical importance. In addition, the book suggests—and examines—the intended unity in each of Wright's books and provides readers with insightful readings of key Wright texts.

_____. *The Poetry of James Wright*. Tuscaloosa: University of Alabama Press, 1991. Critical interpretation of selected works by Wright. Includes bibliographical references and index.

Roberson, William. *James Wright: An Annotated Bibliography*. Lanham, Md.: Scarecrow Press, 1995. Good resource for locating articles and other publications by and about Wright.

Smith, Dave. *The Pure Clear Word: Essays on the Poetry of James Wright*. Urbana: University of Illinois Press, 1982. Attempts to determine the degree to which Wright confessed the truth and to which he fabricated reality in his work. The essays include W. H. Auden's foreword to "The Green War," Robert Bly's "The Work of James Wright," and a host of others that cover a variety of topics from Wright's personal life to his poetry. Supplemented by a select bibliography.

Stein, Kevin. *James Wright: The Poetry of a Grown Man*. Athens: Ohio University Press, 1989. An academic study that traces the growth of the entire body of Wright's work. The poems are examined to show that his stylistic changes are frequently more apparent than actual, that he experienced an ongoing personal and artistic evolution, and that the transition of his themes from despair to hope is the result of his gradual acceptance of the natural world.

David C. Dougherty;
bibliography updated by the editors

JAY WRIGHT

Born: Albuquerque, New Mexico; May 25, 1935

PRINCIPAL POETRY

Death as History, 1967
The Homecoming Singer, 1971
Soothsayers and Omens, 1976
Dimensions of History, 1976
The Double Invention of Komo, 1980
Explications/Interpretations, 1984
Selected Poems of Jay Wright, 1987
Elaine's Book, 1988
Boleros, 1991
Transfigurations: Collected Poems, 2000

OTHER LITERARY FORMS

Jay Wright has published several plays in *Hambone*, *Callaloo*, and *The Southern Review*. He has also written essays on African American poetry and poetics, the most important of which is "Desire's Design, Vision's Resonance: Black Poetry's Ritual and Historical Voice," which appeared in *Callaloo* (volume 10, number 1, 1987).

ACHIEVEMENTS

Jay Wright's poetic vision is unique in its cross-cultural approach to African American spiritual and intellectual history. He has been called one of the most original and powerful voices in contemporary American poetry. Though critical acclaim of his work has been slow in coming, he has received a number of prestigious awards: an Ingram Merrill Foundation Award and a Guggenheim Fellowship in 1974; an American Academy and Institute of Arts and Letters Literature Award in 1981; an Oscar Williams and Gene Derwood Writing Award in 1985; a MacArthur Fellowship that spanned the years 1986-1991; and the Academy of American Poets Fellowship in 1996.

BIOGRAPHY

Jay Wright was born in 1935 in Albuquerque, New Mexico, to Leona Dailey, a Virginian of black and Native American ancestry. His father, George Murphy, a light-complexioned African American construction worker, jitney driver, and handyman who later adopted the name of Mercer Murphy Wright, claimed both Cherokee and Irish descent. Wright remained with his mother until the age of three, when Leona gave the boy to the cook Frankie Faucett and his wife Daisy, a black Albuquerque couple known for taking in children. Daisy Faucett was as religious as her husband was proud and generous. Wright's early, intense exposure to the African American church was attributable to her. Mercer Wright, in the meantime, had relocated to California. It was not until his son was in his early teens that he went to live with his father, and later his stepmother Billie, in San Pedro. During his high school years in San Pedro,

Wright began to play baseball. In the early 1950's, he worked as a minor-league catcher for the San Diego Padres, the Fresno Cardinals, and the Aguilars of Mexicali. He also learned to play the bass in those days. In 1954 he joined the Army, and he served in the medical corps until 1957. He was stationed in Germany for most of that time, which gave him the opportunity to travel throughout Europe.

A year after his return to the United States, Wright enrolled in the University of California at Berkeley under the G.I. Bill. At Berkeley, he devised his own major in comparative literature and was graduated after only three years. Before deciding to continue his literary studies, Wright considered studying theology and spent a semester at Union Theological Seminary in New York on a Rockefeller grant. He left Union for Rutgers University in 1962. In 1964, Wright interrupted his graduate studies to spend a year teaching English and medieval history at the Butler Institute in Guadalajara, Mexico. He returned to Rutgers in 1965. During the next three years, Wright completed all the requirements for his doctoral degree except the dissertation. While at Rutgers, Wright lived and worked part-time in Harlem, where he came into contact with a number of other young African American writers, among them Henry Dumas, Larry Neal, and LeRoi Jones (who later changed his name to Amiri Baraka).

In 1968, Wright married Lois Silber, who joined him during his second and longest sojourn in Mexico. The couple lived briefly in Guadalajara and then moved to Jalapa, where they maintained a residence until the autumn of 1971. Many of Wright's poems recall these and other Mexican settings. Wright returned to the United States from time to time, spending brief periods as a writer in residence at Tougaloo and Talladega colleges and at Texas Southern University, as well as several months as a Hodder Fellow at Princeton University. In early 1971, the Wrights departed for Scotland. During Wright's two-year tenure as Joseph Compton Creative Writing Fellow at Dundee University, they lived in Penicuik, outside Edinburgh. Upon their return to the United States in 1973, the Wrights moved first to Warren and then to Piermont, New Hampshire.

Wright has traveled extensively throughout Europe, the United States, Central and South America, and Can-ada. In 1988, he was part of a group of writers who visited the People's Republic of China under the auspices of the University of California at Los Angeles. Since 1975, he has taught at Yale University, at the universities of Utah, Kentucky, and North Carolina at Chapel Hill, and at Dartmouth College.

ANALYSIS

The most distinctive feature of Jay Wright's poetry is what he himself calls "a passion for what is hidden." This passion for sounding the depths of varied histories and mythologies—Western European, African, Caribbean, North and South American, and Asian—takes the poetic shape of a spiritual quest that is at once intensely personal and compellingly collective. The object of Wright's quest is to restore to African American literature a sense of the breadth, the complexity, and the coherence of its cultural, historical, social, artistic, intellectual, and emotional resources. Writing poetry is his way of uncovering and reinventing eclipsed linkages between cultural traditions often believed to be separate. "For me, multicultural is the fundamental process of human history," he explained in a 1983 interview in *Callaloo*.

Wright's work exemplifies what Guyanese novelist Wilson Harris, whom Wright acknowledges as a major source of inspiration, has termed a poetics of the cross-cultural imagination. Wright's autobiographical persona embarks on poetic journeys into uncharted territories where familiar temporal, political, and linguistic boundaries blur and dissolve. Fragmented voices from many different historical periods and cultural traditions emerge as the poet's (and the reader's) guides through a veritable maze of historical and mythological references and allusions that ultimately come together in a rather unorthodox vision of African American or black culture. It is unorthodox within a United States context because of Wright's sensitivity to and insistence on continuities across, not just within, cultures. No African American, Wright insists, "can have escaped grounding in other cultures."

Though his poetic vision is firmly grounded in African American historical experience and expressive culture, Wright's sense of what it means to be a black poet is distinctly different from that of most African

American poets of his generation. Even if Wright's quest for creativity time and again leads him to specific African religions and folklore, mainly Akan, Nuer, Dogon, and Bambara, that quest is not predicated on a rejection of "Western" traditions. In that respect, Wright's poetics and cultural politics are more akin to those of Robert Hayden and even Melvin Tolson than to the work of Amiri Baraka and others who embraced black cultural nationalism in the late 1960's and early 1970's.

Wright's poetry is remarkable in its erudite and consistently innovative engagement with a wide variety of literary and cultural traditions. The scope of his vision and the depth of his perception can largely be attributed to Wright's extensive research in medieval and Renaissance literatures, music, anthropology, the history of religions, and the history of science. The notes appended to *Explications/Interpretations*, *Dimensions of History*, and especially *The Double Invention of Komo* point to some of the principal holdings of Wright's scholarly archives. The most important texts behind his poems are *The Akan Doctrine of God* (1944), by Ghanaian politician and philosopher J. B. Danquah, and the studies of Dogon and Bambara traditional societies conducted in the 1920's and 1930's by a team of French anthropologists under the direction of Marcel Griaule. Most consciously, Wright's poetry takes recourse to Griaule's *Conversations with Ogotemmêli: An Introduction to Dogon Religious Ideas* (1948) and his later collaboration with Germaine Dieterlen, *The Pale Fox* (1965). Yet annotations are atypical for Wright, who, though he yielded to the demands of his publishers in these instances, is usually adamant in his refusal to explicate his poetry to those who find it inaccessible. What lies behind this refusal is not arrogance or obscuration, as some critics have assumed, but what Wright sees as an abiding respect for the complexity and difficulty of the social, cultural, and historical processes his poetry tries to represent. An assimilation of a vast body of knowledge, his poetry demands rigorous intellectual and imaginative engagement from each reader.

The formal experiments in which he engages are as extravagant as the texture of his poetry is dense. A mixture of Italian, German, and Spanish interspersed with Dogon and Bambara ideograms, Wright's language is at times so unfamiliar that to describe it as "English" seems inadequate. Musical forms such as the blues and jazz, as well as a host of Caribbean and Latin American song and dance forms, are as integral to his poetic endeavors as are attempts at making English verse responsive to the "grammars" and metrics of other languages.

THE HOMECOMING SINGER

Semantic density and formal extravagance are particularly characteristic of the book-length poems that have followed Wright's first collection, *The Homecoming Singer*, which was preceded in 1967 by a chapbook, *Death as History*. These early poems, most of which are reprinted in *Selected Poems of Jay Wright*, tend to be more manageable from both a thematic and a linguistic point of view. *The Homecoming Singer* is important to Wright's canon not only as a record of his early artistic, spiritual, and intellectual development but also because it contains all the seeds of his later writing. The two opening poems, "Wednesday Night Prayer Meeting" and "The Baptism," inspired by the religious zeal of Daisy Faucett, lament the failure of institutionalized African American religions to provide spiritual resources for what Wright, with Wilson Harris, calls "the redefinition of the person." The tragic lack of "myths to scale your life upon" results in "the senseless, weightless,/ timedenying feeling of not being there" with which the poet is left at the end of "Reflections Before the Charity Hospital." Yet rather than leading to the despair and violence of LeRoi Jones's "A Poem for Willie Best," a text on which Wright brilliantly meditates in "The Player at the Crossroads" and "Variations on a Theme by LeRoi Jones," this alienation and dispossession heighten the poet's awareness, as in "First Principles," of "the tongues of the exiled dead/ who live in the tongues of the living." In "Destination: Accomplished," this new awareness grows into an abiding emotional and intellectual desire for "something to put in place." It is the death-challenging search for "new categories for the soul/ of those I want to keep" that finally directs Wright toward traditional African societies, their rituals and mythologies, in "A Nuer Sacrifice" and "Death As History."

Like all of Wright's poetry, though more explicitly so, *The Homecoming Singer* draws on autobiographical experience as a catalyst for the persona's introspective inquiries into the possible nature of an African American cultural and literary tradition. Memories of his two fathers, in "A Non-Birthday Poem for My Father," "Origins," "First Principles," and "The Hunting-Trip Cook," become occasions for acknowledging and examining the responsibilities the dead confer upon the living. This is what connects these presences from Wright's personal past, which also include his alcoholic stepmother in "Billie's Blues," to "the intense communal daring" of Crispus Attucks and W. E. B. Du Bois.

The Homecoming Singer also acquaints the reader with geographies to which Wright returns throughout his poetic career. In "An Invitation to Madison County," one of the best poems in this collection, the black American South offers unexpected memories and visions of community to the displaced poet, whose journey in this instance follows that of so many other African American writers in search of their cultural origins. The Southwest, which, along with California, provides the setting for Wright's family remembrances, is another place of origin; its history also connects the persona with the Mexico of "Morning, Leaving Calle Gigantes," "Chapultepec Castle," "Jalapeña Gypsies," and "Bosques de Chapultepec." "A Month in the Country" offers a fleeting glimpse of the "New England reticence" of New Hampshire, to which the persona escapes after "The End of an Ethnic Dream" to soothe his "blistered" brain. In later poems, all these places evolve into full-fledged symbolic geographies. "Sketch for an Aesthetic Project" and "Beginning Again," the two poems that close *The Homecoming Singer*, are the initial attempts of the "aching prodigal" at weaving his memories and his discontent into a poetic design that transcends individual experience. These poems are preludes to *Soothsayers and Omens*, the first volume of a poetic cycle that continues with *Explications/Interpretations*, *Dimensions of History*, and *The Double Invention of Komo*. Each of these book-length poems is part of a carefully constructed pattern or dramatic movement, and this is the order in which Wright places them.

SOOTHSAYERS AND OMENS

The poem that opens the first of *Soothsayers and Omens* four parts is significantly titled "The Charge." Reminiscent of Wright's homages to paternal figures in *The Homecoming Singer*, this poem focuses on fathers and sons "gathered in the miracle/ of our own memories." With "The Appearance of a Lost Goddess" and the rise of a female principle to complement and balance the male presences, the poet identifies himself as an initiate who has accepted the charge to reconstruct neglected and severed ties. This reconstruction takes the initial shape of six short poems titled "Sources" with which Wright inaugurates his systematic exploration of African cosmologies. "Sources" draws heavily on West African pre-Columbian mythologies, both of which become part of a collective memory. The two longer poems that follow and change the pace of the first part, "Benjamin Banneker Helps to Build a City" and "Benjamin Banneker Sends His 'Almanac' to Thomas Jefferson," weave elements of Dogon theology around quotations from the letters of the African American astronomer, an "uneasy" stranger in his own land who bemoans "the lost harmony" and the injustices of slavery.

Dogon ritual becomes even more significant in Part IV, whose title, "Second Conversations with Ogotemmêl," refers directly to Griaule's anthropological exploits. These are poems of apprenticeship that invoke different components and stages of the creation of the universe, represented by the water spirit Nommo, creator of the First Word (that is, language) and his twin Amma, Lébé, guardian of the dead, and the Pale Fox, agent of chaos. Wright's "Conversations" are characterized by exchanges and relationships very different from those that prevail between anthropologist and informer. For Wright's persona, Ogotemmêli is a spiritual guide or "nani" who "will lead me into the darkness" and whose silences promise the speech of redemption with which to mend "the crack in the universe." The terms and trajectory of Wright's journey into darkness, a sort of Middle Passage in reverse that leads back to Africa, are also indebted to Dante's search, even if the spiritual map (the "God") Wright's initiate "designs" is different. It is no coincidence, then, that "Homecoming," the poem that announces "a plan of transformations," is laced with quotations from *La divina commedia* (c. 1320; *The Divine Comedy*).

At the same time that *Soothsayers and Omens* initiates the reader into African mythologies, it also revisits Mexico and New Mexico, geographies already implicit in the pre-Columbian references of the opening poems. The most remarkable of the transitional poems in Parts II and III is "The Albuquerque Graveyard," a place to which Wright's persona returns to worry the dead, the "small heroes," with a quest for patterns that is as "uneasy" as Benjamin Banneker's. The poet's announcement that

> I am going back
> to the Black limbo,
> an unwritten history
> of our own tensions,

is a precise summary of his desire and purpose throughout *Soothsayers and Omens*: both to articulate a history that has not been written and to un-write a history that has neglected, even forgotten—the participation of Africans and African Americans in founding what is deceptively called "Western" civilization.

If *Soothsayers and Omens* is the "first design," the first step toward the articulation of a spiritual order, *Explications/Interpretations* marks the next logical stage in what Wright calls his "African-Hellenic-Judaic discourse." Dedicated to poet Robert Hayden and critic Harold Bloom, this volume generates somewhat different patterns and principles of order and also introduces a set of new players on a new stage in "MacIntyre, The Captain, and the Saints." This central dramatic poem enacts Wright's personal and intellectual ties with Scotland. MacIntyre, the Irish-Scottish clan to which the names Murphy and Wright can be traced, is Wright's autobiographical persona who, instead of conversing with Ogotemmêli, now turns to astronomer David Hume, poet Hugh MacDiarmid, and anthropologist Robert Sutherland Rattray. A new element in this poem is the use of ideograms, a strategy indebted to Ezra Pound's works, which Wright explores more fully in *Dimensions of History* and *The Double Invention of Komo*. Yet dramatic poetry, a form for which Wright has an undoubted preference, is not the only important formal aspect of this volume. *Explications/Interpretations* is also energized by the vital rhythms of African American music. The poem is divided into three parts, "Polarity's Trio," "Harmony's Trio," and "Love's Dozen," titles that already indicate Wright's concern with music and number. "Tensions and Resolutions" introduces dualism or twinning and balance as concepts that inform the poem's thematic and structural organization: "Each act caresses/ the moment it remembers,/ and the moment it desires." This double "act" is of course the act of writing, which makes Wright's poem a "field of action" along the lines of Charles Olson's "projective verse."

EXPLICATIONS/INTERPRETATIONS

That the rhythms of writing and speaking are formal articulations of the poet's being is crucial to understanding the dynamics of *Explications/Interpretations* and indeed of all of Wright's poems. The arrangement of the poems in groups of three, six, and twelve (plus one) already creates a sense of rhythm, which is rendered most explicit in "The Twenty-Two Tremblings of the Postulant," subtitled "Improvisations Surrounding the Body." This poem is a good example of Wright's kind of blues poetry, in which the compositional principle is derived not from the call-and-response structure of the blues lyrics, as is the case, for instance, in the poetry of Langston Hughes and Sterling Brown, but from the arrangement of the twenty-two short poems across a sequence of chords. Each poem corresponds not only to a different part of the human body but also to a musical bar that belongs to a specific chord, I, IV, or V. The last two bars, we are told at the end of the poem, are "tacit," which makes for a total of twenty-four bars, whose musical equivalent is a (doubled) blues line. *Explications/Interpretations* as a whole is a poetic improvisation on this basic blues line, one of the most distinctive rhythms of African American culture. These are the sounds of flesh and bone that constitute the poem's and the poet's "grammar of being." For Wright, who insists on poetry's social and historical responsibilities, these schemes, "the god's elemental bones," are "a launch-pad/ into the actual" ("Inscrutability").

Wright's emphasis in *Explications/Interpretations* on the body as a site of knowledge and action is indicative of his rejection of dualisms. The spiritual does not exist in separation from the material any more than male exists without female. They are what Wright conceives of as "twins," and the desired relationship between them is one of balance. This is most clearly articulated in "The Continuing City: Spirit and Body" and "The Body," two poems that lay out aesthetic and philosophical principles indebted to Danquah's *The Akan Doctrine* of *God*. In his notes, Wright identifies *Explications/Interpretations* as an attempt "to claim this knowledge as part of the continuing creative life of the America"; the Americas are what comes into full view in *Dimensions of History*.

DIMENSIONS OF HISTORY

Though *Dimensions of History* is dedicated to the late Francis Ferguson, with whom Wright studied at Rutgers, the book owes perhaps its most significant debt to Wilson Harris's notion of "vision as historical dimension." This third volume of Wright's poetic cycle maintains the tripartite structure of *Explications/Interpretations*, a scheme now more explicitly associated with the three stages of an initiation ritual: separation, transition, (re)incorporation. Part One, "The Second Eye of the World. The Dimension of Rites and Acts," announces this link not only by being itself divided into three poems but also by offering the reader a Dogon ideogram that, according to Griaule and Dieterlen, represents the separation of the twins, male and female, at the moment of circumcision. The historical dimension of separation within an African American context is (enforced) exile. This historical condition becomes the "special kinship" the poet's persona shares with his other selves, the dead to whose realm he descends and whose claims he seeks to understand in a spiritually barren land from which the god has retreated. Among them are once again Du Bois and Crispus Attucks, who are joined by the voices of and allusions to Frederick Douglass, St. Augustine, Toussaint L'Ouverture and many others who congregate in a text brimming with references to Aztec, Mayan, Incaic, Egyptian, Arabic, Christian, Yoruba, Akan, and, of course, Dogon and Bambara mythologies. Ogotemmêli's return in the figure of the blind sage at the beginning of the second poem commences the process of healing: "Anocheçí enfermo amanecí bueno" (I went to bed sick, I woke up well) are the words that open the third poem, at the end of which the persona names himself "a dark and dutiful dyēli,/ searching for the understanding of his deeds."

Part Two, titled "Modulations. The Aesthetic Dimension," consists of an assortment of poetic forms, many of them linked to Caribbean and Latin American musical forms and instruments such as the Cuban *son*, the *areito*, and the *bandola*, a fifteen-string Colombian

guitar. The shorter poems in "Rhythms, Charts, and Changes," "The Body Adorned and Bare," a section reminiscent of the meditations on the body in *Explications/Interpretations*, and "Retablos" (votive paintings) lead up to Wright's "Log Book of Judgments," a series of ethical and aesthetic formulations distilled from the persona's historical and ritualistic experiences. They culminate in the following lines from "Meta-A and the A of Absolutes": "I am good when I know the darkness of all light,/ and accept the darkness, not as a sing, but as my body."

Dimensions of History closes with "Landscapes. The Physical Dimension." whose themes and poetic architecture return to the history of the conquest of the Americas and to Náhua (Aztec) mythology and poetry. The most notable formal aspects of this final part are the encyclopedic monoliths, block passages that list the vital statistics of five American nations: Venezuela, Colombia, Panama, Mexico, and the United States. The spaces between these building blocks or "stones" are filled with Wright's own enchanted mortar, a possible translation of the Náhuatl-infused Spanish idiom *cal y canto* (literally, mortar and song) that joins Wright's compositional principles with his cross-cultural concerns. This syncretic idiom, which also conjures up such Latin American poets as Pablo Neruda and José María Arguedas, is a miniature representation of the rhizomes Wright's poem uncovers. It is one of his "emblems of the ecstatic connection." His poet's Middle Passages temporarily end with an image of the Great Gate of the ancient Mayan city Labná, a sole triumphal arc in a city without fortifications that is both "a gateway to the beautiful" and "the image of our lives among ourselves."

THE DOUBLE INVENTION OF KOMO

The Double Invention of Komo, which is dedicated to the memory of Marcel Griaule, may well be called the most African of Wright's poems. Wright's most sustained and ambitious effort in the genre of dramatic poetry, *The Double Invention of Komo* is a poetic reenactment of the initiation ceremonies performed by the all-male Komo society among the Bambara. The object of these highly formalized ceremonies is to maintain the Bambara's traditional intellectual, religious, and social values. *The Double Invention of Komo* "risks ritual's arrogance" to the extent that the logic and the specifics of this ritualistic process inform the poem's conceptual and formal structures. Of special importance to Wright are the 266 great signs, a system of ideograms that organizes Bambara cosmology. Each sign inscribes a different "name" or aspect of the god and binds him to the material objects and substances associated with Komo's altars, as in "*Dyibi*—obscurity—gold." As is evident from "The Initiate Takes His First Six Signs, the Design of His Name," such naming is an exceedingly complex process. What Wright is after is the sacred "grammar" of names that, ultimately, evolve into a secular "alphabet" of creation. *The Double Invention of Komo* is quite explicitly and self-consciously a poem about the metaphysics of writing, and this accounts for much of its difficulty.

The central preoccupation of *The Double Invention of Komo* is how to achieve self-knowledge through writing, how to fashion a language that would redress loss and dispossession. Writing, for Wright, is a process of simultaneous dismemberment and reassembly of meaning and community: It is both "scalpel" and "suture," both excision and circumcision. Like the ritual scars on the body of the initiate, poetic writing confers not only knowledge of traditional values but also kinship. It is as if the poet's pen were a ritual knife "cutting" the initiates (and the readers) into kinship, marking them as members of a special community. As the persona's status changes from that of an initiate to that of a "delegate," the statements made in *Dimensions of History*'s "Meta-A and the A of Absolutes" are reformulated: "What is true is the incision./ What is true is the desire for the incision,/ and the signs' flaming in the wound." It is in this sense that the Middle Passage, which all of the persona's journeys reenact, becomes a rite of passage that compensates for the violent psychic dismemberment and the geographical dispersal of the members of Africa's traditional cultures. Wright's key metaphor, the limbo, refers to Wilson Harris, who regards this dance, created on the crowded slave ships, as a form of silent collective resistance. Harris's sense of the limbo as a "structure of freedom" has been an inspiration for Wright since "the Albuquerque Graveyard." It also encapsulates the main concerns that have motivated Wright's explorations of the poetic potential of music and dance.

ELAINE'S BOOK

Given the usually all-male composition of Wright's imaginary communities and especially the emphasis on male initiation rituals in *The Double Invention of Komo*, the foregrounding of female voices in *Elaine's Book* is almost startling. While women are never entirely absent from his poetry, which frequently identifies creativity as a female principle, this is the first book in which they assume historical, rather than exclusively mythological, stature. They are an integral part of the poetic geographies Wright's persona traverses in his fascinating explorations of female otherness. The female voices in *Elaine's Book* assume many different identities: that of Yemanjá, the Yoruba/Afro-Cuban goddess of the waters; that of Hathor or Aphrodite; that of the Virgin of Guadalupe, whom Wright connects with the Aztec goddess Tonantzin; that of the African American poetess Phillis Wheatley; and those of many others who take their places right next to Octavio Paz, Paul Celan, and Friedrich Hölderlin, who now merely provide epigraphs.

Wright's poetic language is as rich as his symbolic geography is varied and extensive. His journey into the night, which begins with the sunset of "Veil, I," not only leads the reader to pre-Columbian Mexico, Spain, Scotland, and back to the United States, but also guides the reader across an ever-changing linguistic surface in which even historical documents, such as letters by Phillis Wheatley, the former slave Judith Cocks, Louisa Alexander, and the Harvard astronomer Cecilia Payne Yaposchkin take on poetic qualities of their own. *Elaine's Book* can be said to achieve resonance as well as consonance: Each fragment sounds new depths as it becomes part of a "nation," which, like the "city," is also a figure for the poem itself.

That a poet who lives in uncertain multiplicities, who knows neither his actual birth date nor his real name, should be fascinated by names and dates is hardly surprising.

BOLEROS

In *Boleros*, a book dedicated to his wife Lois, Wright's preoccupation is with imagining the fictions that, like his own father's stories, lead to names—in this case, names of Greek muses, of saint's days adorned with "graces and the seasons," and of places. "All names," he writes, "are invocations, or curses." Reinventing these stories and histories of origins is the poetic project of *Boleros* and the point of departure for further journeys across far-flung geographies of the spirit. As in *Elaine's Book*, the poet's guides are mostly female: Erato, Calliope, Euterpe, Thalia, Polyhymnia, Clio, Terpsichore, Urania. Yet the familiar Greek identities of these muses are complicated by the association of each of their personalities with concepts taken from another of Wright's favorite archives, *The Egyptian Book of the Dead* (first published in English in 1894). The resulting Africanization of the muses recalls Martin Bernal's compelling speculations in *Black Athena: The Afro-Asiatic Roots of Classical Civilization* (1987).

Many of the sites the poet's persona revisits in *Boleros* are familiar ones: Edinburgh, Guadalajara, Jalapa, New Hampshire, and always West Africa. The poet also takes up a number of new residences, however, most significant among them the city of Benares in Uttar Pradesh, one of the intellectual and cultural centers of traditional India. "Black spirits such as mine will always come/ to a crossroads such as this," the persona explains at the shores of the Ganges. As always, these geographic journeys become explorations of poetic form. Most striking in this regard are the six poems in "Sources and Roots" and "Coda," which are the title's most concrete reference points. The relatively brief poems in these final sections, many of which open with lines from popular Latin American songs, are daring in their use of Spanish meter and rhyme in an English-language environment. The results of such unexpected contact are wondrous formal hybrids, whose breaks with English accentuation are infused with Wright's wit and humor:

> Esta tierra da de todo.
> Oh, perhaps, you will see no sloe
> plum, or no white-tailed, ginger doe,
> break-dancing at sunset when snow
> shows us its blackberry wine skin.

Poems such as this are testimony to the transformations of vision and language at the many crossroads to which Wright's ceaseless poetic journeys lead. These transformations truly are Wright's "gift," for few poets have dared to bridge the troubled waters of cultural difference. Even fewer have succeeded so splendidly.

TRANSFIGURATIONS

Transfigurations: Collected Poems collects Wright's work produced over the course of more than twenty-five years of poetic exploration. The volume is hefty, providing more than six hundred pages of densely textured verse, including sixty pages of new poetry. Detailed references to West African, Haitian, Mexican, and European and American Christian religious rituals abound, as well as to the various political and poetic genealogies in which Wright situates himself. Geographic journeys expose the earth itself to the questioning soul of the poet. In a single poem, Wright travels from North Africa to Jamaica to Boston and then on to Spain, dropping historical allusions at every step. The esoteric network of obscure signs and allusions he uses serves to trace his own development in which, for nearly three decades, he has determinedly initiated himself into the mysteries of language, history, and sense.

Transformation and transfiguration act as the axes of this collection. A bulk of the poems in the volume speak to initiation, the human ceremonial act that marks transformation: the Mexican boy to whom a god says, "You must prepare for my eruption/ and the guarded way I have of guarding you," or the West African Dogon boy who undergoes the trials and tribulations of coming into adulthood, "If I were the light's sacred buffoon,/ I could read this meaning and mount/ my own awakening" in the spectacular poem "The Double Invention of Komo." A transfiguration, similarly, is a change of appearance, one that is accompanied with a sense of revelation. A refinement of vision, put to the service of metamorphosis, is one of Wright's most potent forces. For example, in "The Abstract of Knowledge/the First Test," Wright transfigures the scene of the Dogon boy encountering the first phase of his initiation, in which he must undergo an hallucinatory vision of the universe in the light of the knowledge that he will obtain from his vision. That vision changes knowledge, transfiguring it and transforming it. In these lines, a number of the features of Wright's poetry are apparent: the tightly rhythmical free verse—which lacks enjambment for the most part, the voice of the dramatic persona, the physical details, and a cosmological reach.

BIBLIOGRAPHY

Callaloo 6 (Fall, 1983). This special issue includes an excellent interview in which Wright outlines the theories behind his poetry. It also contains a general introduction to Wright's poetry by Robert B. Stepto, a rather superficial assessment of his early poetry by Gerald Barrax, and detailed commentary on the Benjamin Banneker poems by Vera M. Kutzinski.

Clifford, James. *The Predicament of Culture: Twentieth-Century Ethnography, Literature, and Art*. Cambridge, Mass.: Harvard University Press, 1988. This critical look at the rise of modern anthropology and its entwinement with literature is useful background reading for some of Wright's main sources, notably Marcel Griaule and his team. Equally relevant are Clifford's comments on the West's representation of other cultures and the negotiation of cultural differences.

Harris, Wilson. *The Womb of Space: The Cross-Cultural Imagination*. Westport, Conn.: Greenwood Press, 1983. While this study includes a brief discussion of *The Double Invention of Komo*, it is valuable primarily for its conceptualization of the literary dynamics of "the cross-cultural imagination." Though Wright's debt is to Harris's earlier writings, this book summarizes the main concepts and ideas that have guided Harris's thinking since the beginning of his career.

Kutzinski, Vera M. *Against the American Grain: Myth and History in William Carlos Williams, Jay Wright, and Nicolás Guillén*. Baltimore: The Johns Hopkins University Press, 1987. The second part of this book, "The Black Limbo: Jay Wright's Mythology of Writing," provides the fullest available commentary on Wright's poetry. Focusing on *Dimension of History* and its historical and theoretical sources, it places Wright's cross-cultural poetics within the context of the diverse cultural and literary histories of the Americas. Has detailed notes and a useful index.

Okpewho, Isidore. "Prodigal's Progress: Jay Wright's Focal Center." *MELUS* 23, no. 3 (Fall, 1998): 187-209. Wright's search for a satisfactory cultural identity through the successive volumes of his poetry is examined. Wright's movement from the autobiographical to the scholarly to a poetic self-creation through ritual and religion is traced.

Stepto, Robert B. "After Modernism, After Hibernation: Michael Harper, Robert Hayden, and Jay Wright." In *Chant of Saints: A Gathering of Afro-American Literature, Arts, and Scholarship*, edited by Michael S. Harper and Robert B. Stepto. Urbana: University of Illinois Press, 1979. This article concentrates on portions of *Dimensions of History*. It is useful for situating Wright's poetry within the "call-and-response" structures of an African American literary tradition whose central concern, according to Stepto, is with "freedom and literacy."

Welburn, Ron. "Jay Wright's Poetics: An Appreciation." *MELUS* 18, no. 3 (Fall, 1993): 51. The historical and metaphysical codes that add energy to Wright's poetry are examined. In spite of his relative obscurity, Wright deserves appreciation for his creative intellect.

Vera M. Kutzinski,
updated by Sarah Hilbert

SIR THOMAS WYATT

Born: Allington, England; 1503
Died: Sherborne, England; October, 1542

PRINCIPAL POETRY

The Courte of Venus, c. 1539 (includes three to ten Wyatt poems)
Certayne Psalmes Chosen Out of the Psalter of David, 1549
Songs and Sonettes, 1557 (known as *Tottel's Miscellany*, Richard Tottel, editor includes ninety to ninety-seven Wyatt poems)
Collected Poems of Sir Thomas Wyatt, 1949 (Kenneth Muir, editor)
Sir Thomas Wyatt and His Circle: Unpublished Poems, 1961 (Kenneth Muir, editor)
Collected Poems, 1975 (Joost Daalder, editor)

OTHER LITERARY FORMS

Sir Thomas Wyatt's *Plutarckes Boke of the Quyete of Mynde*, a prose translation of Plutarch's essay *Quiet of*

Mind, which he read in Guillaume Budé's Latin version, was made at the request of Queen Katherine of Aragon and published in 1528—his only notable work published in his lifetime. His original prose works are interesting in their own right. The state papers contain several fine examples of his correspondence. His most polished prose works are the defense he prepared for his trial in 1541 and his two letters of moral advice to his son. These letters make explicit the moral stance which underlies his poems, especially extolling honesty, which comprises "wisdome, gentlenes, sobrenes, disire to do good, frendlines to get the love of many, and trougth above all the rest." Wyatt's prose is distinguished by its clarity and directness, its easy, colloquial use of language, its lively intelligence, and its wit. Often in the diplomatic letters he makes his style more immediate by using direct discourse to report conversations.

ACHIEVEMENTS

The best of the court poets who wrote under Henry VIII, Sir Thomas Wyatt stands at a crossroads in English poetry, looking both backward and forward. His fluent native lyrics, perhaps written for musical accompaniment, show direct continuity with medieval popular song and with Chaucerian love imagery. At the same time, he opened the door to the Renaissance in English poetry, importing Italian and French forms and naturalizing them. His most influential innovation was the sonnet. Experimenting with translations from Petrarch's sonnets, he invented both the Italian and the English or "Shakespearean" sonnet forms. His successors—among them the earl of Surrey, Sir Philip Sidney, Samuel Daniel, Michael Drayton, and William Shakespeare—adopted and refined the sonnet form for their own famous sequences of love poems.

Wyatt introduced virtually every new stanza form that appeared in the sixteenth century. As the first English satirist, he experimented with terza rima, and in his epigrams with ottava rima. He also wrote several rondeaux after French models. His verse translations from the Psalms are the finest in the language, written at a time when English versions of biblical literature were few.

Comments by his contemporaries and the high degree of preservation of his works—he is, for example, by far the largest contributor to *Tottel's Miscellany*—testify to his high reputation in his own day. When Wyatt wrote, there were no formal standards of prosody in English. Soon after his death, metrical regularity, which he had helped to establish, prevailed. Unfortunately, Tottel's editors blurred some of his most powerful effects by regularizing his meter, and his younger and smoother contemporary, Surrey, came to be regarded as a better poet. To critics of the eighteenth and nineteenth centuries, Wyatt's poems, read in the light of their successors, appeared rough and jarring. The last century, with its interest in "organic" rhythm as opposed to fixed rules of meter, and in dramatic compression and conversational immediacy as opposed to formal diction, has reevaluated Wyatt and granted him precedence as the greatest poet of his age, not only as an innovator in form but as an original explorer of the effect on the individual mind of the insecurities and tensions inherent in love and politics.

BIOGRAPHY

Sir Thomas Wyatt was born into a family already in favor with the court. His father had served and prospered

Sir Thomas Wyatt (Hulton Archive)

under Henry VII and Henry VIII, holding a series of important offices, and purchasing as his principal residence Allington Castle in Kent, where the poet was born. Young Wyatt made his first court appearance in 1516, and probably entered St. John's College, Cambridge, the same year. He was suitably married in 1520 to Elizabeth Brooke, the daughter of Lord Cobham, with whom he had a son; but in 1526, they separated because of her infidelity. He was sent on important diplomatic missions, in 1526 to France and in 1527 to Italy, where he traveled extensively.

It is plausibly conjectured that Wyatt was a lover of Anne Boleyn before her marriage to Henry VIII. Some of his poems were probably written to or about her, and his imprisonment in 1536 seems to have been connected with her downfall. He was quickly released to his father's custody, however, and continued to enjoy the king's favor. Knighted, he was sent as ambassador to Spain to improve relations between Henry VIII and the Emperor Charles V and to prevent an alliance of the latter with France. On later embassies to France and Flanders, he continued this mission. In 1540, because of a shift in policy, his patron, Thomas Cromwell, was arrested and executed. Slanderous accusations found among Cromwell's papers led to Wyatt's imprisonment in 1541 and his subsequent preparations to reply to the charges. He was soon released, however, on condition that he leave his mistress, Elizabeth Darrell, who had borne him a son, and return to his wife. He continued to occupy important offices, serving as member of Parliament for Kent and vice admiral of the fleet. At about age thirty-nine he died of a sudden fever contracted on a diplomatic mission to meet the Spanish envoy at Falmouth.

ANALYSIS

Sir Thomas Wyatt was esteemed in his time for all the best qualities associated with the Renaissance courtier: military prowess, grace in art, skill in language, intelligence in council, and loyalty to his sovereign. The court of Henry VIII, himself a poet and musician, was receptive to the literary talents of such a man and capable of nourishing his worldly gifts, but the ways of politics and love were fraught with risks, as Wyatt's own career shows. It is against the background of this court,

with its political and amorous intrigues, the insecurities of favor both in love and in worldly ambitions, that Wyatt's poetry can best be considered.

Wyatt is known primarily as a poet of love. The conventions of courtly love, deriving from twelfth century Provençal poetry, are the usual basis of his imagery. This tradition concerns the relationship between the great lady and her courtier "servant." Love is treated variously as sickness, servitude, worship, and war. The lover is in agony, the lady disdainful, her beauties idealized by comparisons with nature. The tradition reached Wyatt through two main sources, Geoffrey Chaucer and Francesco Petrarch, the Italian strain developing more fully the spiritual aspect of courtly love.

Wyatt's treatment of the tradition he inherited adapts to it the conditions of his own insecure times. He uses the love convention to speak not only of his lack of satisfaction in love but about his unhappiness at other aspects of ill fortune. Since a direct judgment on contemporary events could have been dangerous to his political career, even to his life, it is likely that Wyatt used the guise of a disappointed lover to interpret the sense of betrayal, the melancholy, and the insecurity inherent in his career. Life and death lay at the king's whim. Friendship was risky and tenuous, since the adherents of those who fell in favor were in danger themselves. Although Wyatt's own career was generally successful, he suffered two severe setbacks. From his prison cell he may have watched Anne Boleyn and her former lovers, his friends and acquaintances—persons once high in fortune and favor—go to the block. Later, his life was endangered by friendship with Thomas Cromwell. Such experiences fostered a deep sense of insecurity, which he expresses in several ways: by use of love conventions, in which he explores and comes to terms with the feeling of betrayal; by satire, in which he can compare the dangers and deceptions of court life with the peace of the country; and by seeking God's support, in his translations of the Psalms. In all of his works, even in translations, it is clear that he is doing far more than merely following established forms. He is bringing stanzaic and rhythmic patterns, compression and directness of language, as well as the motif of disappointed love, to bear on the problems of expressing the strong and deep emotions of a sensitive individual, the complexities of a divided mind.

Looking at Wyatt's translations, one can see what kinds of changes he made to naturalize and individualize what he derived from his Italian models. It is impossible to determine an exact chronology for his poems, but it seems likely that those sonnet translations which are closest to their originals are earlier than those he adapts more fully to his own form and expression.

There was no equivalent in English of the sonnet form; Wyatt had to discover and invent it. For Petrarch's hendecasyllabic line, Wyatt devised a normally decasyllabic substitute, probably developed from Chaucerian models. Iambic pentameter was not, as it later was, a prescribed form, and Wyatt's lines must not be read as incompetent iambics. There are manuscript examples of his revisions away from metrical regularity, showing that the irregularity often criticized as "roughness" was intentional. Wyatt's line is open to variable stress which allows for dominance of speech rhythms and expression of nuances of feeling. While Petrarch's rhyme scheme divided the sonnet between octave in braced rhyme and sestet in alternative rhyme, Wyatt's three quatrains in braced rhyme allow for his rational progression of thoughts and images. The series of braced rhymes gives him several couplets with which to work as the poem progresses, to reinforce his contrasts and hammer home his feelings. He introduces a concluding couplet which he employs with great flexibility and variety of effect—unlike William Shakespeare, who too often used it lamely as a detached tag.

In several of the courtly love sonnets that Wyatt translates, he sharpens Petrarch's images and makes their expression more vivid while carefully pursuing an elaborate conceit. "The long love that in my thought doth harbor" explores love as war; Wyatt, who had participated in chivalric tournaments, conveys a vigorous, dramatic atmosphere of action in the field by use of energetic words and rhythmic pressure. "My galley charged with forgetfulness" pursues the conventional conceit of love as a ship in dangerous seas. Again, Wyatt achieves a feeling of energy, of rushing forward, opening with two run-on lines and blurring the Italian's sharp distinction between octave and sestet. This poem does not actually mention love, allowing wider application to the dangers of political life.

Another probably early translation shows how Wyatt uses courtly love conventions to focus attention more on the sufferer's state of mind than on the love situation. The original Petrarchan version of the sonnet "I find no peace, and all my war is done" appealed to Wyatt for its antithetical construction, portraying a divided mind; Wyatt's version shows how intricately he uses form to convey the sense of internal division. An essential aspect of much of his poetry is the "broken-backed" line, deriving from Anglo-Saxon through medieval lyric and still prevalent before metrical regularity became the norm. This line is divided sharply into two segments by a pronounced caesura. Each of the two resulting half-lines, containing two or three stresses, has an integrity related more to speech rhythm than to syllable counts. The divided lines point and balance the antitheses of the lover's internal division, but his balance is conveyed more intricately than in the original by the weaving together of phrases throughout the octave. The first three half-lines are parallel in structure: "I find," "I fear," "I fly." The first and last lines of the first quatrain are united by parallel sounds and structure: "and all my war is done," "and all the world I season"; a similar effect parallels the third line of the first quatrain and the second line of the second quatrain: "yet can I not arise," "yet can I scape no-wise." The imagery is traditional in the courtly love convention, but the structure dramatizes the tension in a mind whose suffering, itself, rather than the cause of his suffering, is the poem's focus.

Wyatt uses the conventions of the suffering lover but turns them around in "Was I never yet of your love grieved." Petrarch's lover, worn out with sighing, longs for death as a release and plans a beautiful sepulchre with his lady's name engraved on it; yet if she will be satisfied with his faithful love, he may survive. Wyatt says that he is *not* prepared to die and have a tomb with an inscription naming the lady as the cause of his demise. Such a tomb, in any case, far from being a monument to her, would be an indictment of her cruelty. Wyatt discards Petrarch's physical description of the tomb to focus on the lover's mood. That mood is one of independent cynicism: The lady may choose to accept his love and faith, but if she chooses instead to continue acting out her disdain, she will not succeed, and that will be her own fault. There is no Petrarchan veneration of the lady here. The lover, having exhausted himself trying, has reached the conclusion that the prize is really not worth the chase. Using the couplets formed by the braced rhyme of the quatrains, he produces a powerful stress on "past" in the third line, and increases the tension between the courtly love expectation and his own rebellion against it through the rhyme of "wearied" and "buried"—an association belied by the unexpected "not."

"WHOSO LIST TO HUNT"

A sonnet of similar subject and tone, whose subtlety and smoothness show Wyatt's confidence in having made the form his own, is "Whoso list to hunt." The Petrarchan sonnet on which this is based has a visionary, dream-like quality, picturing the lady as a white hind in a beautiful spring landscape disappearing from the poet's ken because Caesar (presumably God) has set her free (presumably by death). The tone of Wyatt's version is quite different. The mention of the hind is developed into an extended hunting metaphor. Instead of the solitary lover, he becomes a member of a crowd of hunters (suitors). He has thus introduced a dramatic situation, plunging into it abruptly and colloquially with direct address. The natural description of the original is replaced by the immediate, realistic atmosphere of the hunt, into which Petrarch's mention of the mind has led him: the pressing rivals, the net, the hot pursuit. His use of rhythm conveys this physical experience, as heavy stresses on the alliterated "Fainting I follow" suggest limping or labored breath, with the poet's abrupt about-face, the "turn" in the poem, coming in the middle of the sharply divided line. Wyatt attacks the artificiality of the courtly love tradition, remarking that to pursue this lady is "in vain," as in the preceding sonnet—a waste of effort. Unlike Petrarch's modest Laura, this lady is wild and spirited. She is inaccessible not because she is called by God but because she has already been claimed by his social superior (it is usually assumed that "Caesar" is Henry VIII, the hind Anne Boleyn). He further strains the convention by seeking reciprocity of affection, as opposed to one-sided worship of an ideal; to the Petrarchan lover, the pursuit, the service, is its own reward.

The structural pattern portrays the stages of the poet's argument: the first quatrain defining his plight; the second focusing more sharply on his feelings, from which he abruptly breaks; the third explaining why the case is hopeless; and the couplet giving the explanation an epigrammatic and ironic punch. With the awareness that pursuit of a highborn lady was often an essential stepping-stone to court favor, it is not straining interpretation to see in this particular love pursuit—in which idealized description of the lady has yielded to focus on the lover's feelings—a more general pursuit of fortune and success with the frustrations encountered in that struggle.

Some of Wyatt's lyrics seem to bear particular relation to his work on foreign models, such as the *strambotti* of the Italian poet Serafino de Ciminelli. Light in tone, the *strambotto* is an eight-line poem with six alternate rhymes and a concluding couplet. Examples in Wyatt's work are "Who hath heard of such cruelty before" and "Alas, madame! for stealing of a kiss?" Two of his finest lyrics which relate closely in mood to his sonnets and in form to his *strambotti* are "They flee from me that sometime did me seek" and "It may be good, like it who list." Both use three seven-line stanzas to portray intellectual or emotional development: A problem stated in the first stanza is reexamined in the third in the light of the second. Both have the rhyme scheme *ababbcc*.

"THEY FLEE FROM ME, THAT SOMETIME DID ME SEEK"

In Wyatt's most famous poem, "They flee from me, that sometime did me seek," the description of a specific experience may in part function as a figure to express general feelings about good fortune and its loss. This is especially likely if—as is often assumed—the poem refers to Anne Boleyn. Although the situation is a conventional one of courtly love, the setting and experience are real and immediate, the diction that of everyday speech. The dominant image, like that of "Whoso list to hunt," is of animals, but it is uncertain what animal the poet has in mind: deer, birds, or simply women. The wild and bestial is contrasted with the tame, courtly, and civilized quality suggested by the words "gentle" and "gentleness." The main rhetorical device is a simple contrast of past with present tense, past joys with present loss. The use of "they" in the first line may point to a sense of desertion by all the speaker's friends, similar to that expressed in the epigram, "Lux, my fair falcon," in which an animal image is used in more complex fashion, as an ironic contrast between loyal animals and disloyal men. The men are ultimately seen as even lower on the animal scale than the falcons, as the men are compared to lice leaving a dead body.

The first stanza of "They flee from me; that sometime did me seek" establishes the focal point of the speaker's mood, his sense of desertion. The remarkable second stanza recalls in minute detail and tingling immediacy a specific experience, in the light of which a new mood, irony, emerges in the third stanza. This final stanza begins with the rhythmic subtlety of abrupt conversational rhythm, the jolting caesura, and the insistence of many stressed monosyllables. In this line, the dream-vision of Petrarchan convention and the erotic dream of Chaucerian romance are banished. Once again the poet's insistence on reciprocity in affection has been violated, yet he reacts not with vengefulness or even rebellion, but with ironic detachment. He, with his humanity, his gentleness, has kept his part of the bargain. She, however, who once appeared "gentle, tame and meek," has now reverted to her wild animal nature. "Kindly" may be taken both in the sense of "according to nature" and ironically in its modern sense. The suggestion that *he* should be served better recalls ironically the courtly love tradition of the man's service to his lady on her pedestal, and thus Wyatt drives home again his insistence on reciprocity: Should service be given if not deserved? His conclusion is not, as in the courtly love tradition, and as the poem's opening suggests, one of sentimental agony, but musing, perhaps even amused understatement. One is left with a question: What does one deserve who repays loyalty with disloyalty? Yet there remains some sense of the reality and intensity of loss from the vividness of the scene described in the second stanza. Wyatt's ideal of a reciprocal and permanent love is more of this world than Petrarch's one-sided idealization, and its existence belies a charge against him of cynicism.

"IT MAY BE GOOD, LIKE IT WHO LIST"

"It may be good, like it who list" opens with a striking colloquial tone in mid-conversation. The debate symbolized by this dramatic situation is an internal one: The poet is uncertain whether to believe signs of friendship or affection in words and looks. He would like to, but having seen so many changes in human favor, fears

to commit himself. The form perfectly conveys the thought-movement, with its seesawing rhythm, produced by the broken-backed line, used with effect similar to that in "I find no peace, and all my war is done." Stanza one begins with half-lines strongly set off against each other by caesuras, on either side of which are stressed syllables, so that the movement seems to be first a pressing toward a decision, then a receding from it, a depiction in sound of the mind swinging back and forth between the desire to believe and the impulse to doubt— opposites that the poet cannot reconcile—with a question to reinforce his uncertainty. The second stanza states the doctrine of contrarieties more objectively, yet four lines of it maintain structurally and rhythmically the sensation of vacillation. The final stanza resolves the argument into another question, directed to the imaginary interlocutor, and the poet seems firmly to resolve the argument in the spondaic "Nay sir." The next line opening, "And yet," sets off the whole argument again, however, to leave it seesawing still in the concluding broken-backed line—"For dread to fall I stand not fast"—which has served as a refrain in the two preceding stanzas. The paradox is stressed in union by alliteration of opposite-meaning words, "fall" and "fast," which occupy corresponding positions in their respective half-lines.

The use of a refrain connects this poem with the other main lyrical form for which Wyatt is famous, sometimes called the "ballette." This form had its origin in popular song, toward which the musical impetus of Henry VIII's court drew the courtly minds of the time. Wyatt's ballettes probably had a social function: They may have been composed for musical accompaniment to be sung in company and were certainly circulated privately. They have short stanzas and simple meters, with short lines and often a refrain. Wyatt's tendency to compression is here at its finest, as he expresses strong and deep emotion in a simple manner and brief compass.

"SUCH HAP AS I AM HAPPED IN"

Wyatt's use of the refrain is exquisitely subtle and varied. He may, as in "Such hap as I am happed in," retain for the final line of each stanza the same rhythm and line length but alter the words of the refrain, then echo it at the beginning of the next stanza. By this means the intensity of feeling and the details of the mind's torture are progressively built up, until the poem comes to rest in its opening words, with the tortured mind drawn taut and caught in a circular trap, with no hope of escape. The poem's circularity depicts the speaker's plight.

He may repeat the same or similar words at the end of each stanza, letting them accumulate meaning and force in each recurrence from the stanza they follow, and progressively from all the preceding stanzas. "My lute awake" explores, with the subtle variations of its refrain, the relationship between the sufferer and his instrument. The first and final stanzas, almost identical, frame the poem, their minor variations exhibiting the effect of the mental progression through the intervening six. The second, third, and fourth stanzas explore the lover's plight, hinting at the possibility of retribution. The fifth, sixth, and seventh turn the tables and imagine the once-disdainful lady old and deserted, longing but daring not to express her desires (as he, ironically, is able to express his in the present poem). In the second two revenge stanzas, the poet discards the lute altogether and speaks for himself: "I have done" (finished) caring for you; you will suffer "as I have done." The sense of the opening refrain, "My lute be still, for I have done," is that the lover is finished with life. When he returns to echo it at the end, the accumulation of meanings makes it plain that he is finished with the lady. Though the last stanza echoes the first verbally, its sounds are brisker. The word "waste" now carries the full sense of time wasted in the love pursuit (similar to "As well as I may spend his time in vain" in "Whoso list to hunt"). The poet has moved from a pathetic opening through an emotional progression to a detached conclusion, a progress like that exhibited in "They flee from me; that sometime did me seek." The poem has served to delineate the lover's hurt feelings and, in a way, to cure them.

Wyatt's satires and psalms explore in their own way his basic problem of insecurity in public and private life. The satires were probably written in a period directly following one of his imprisonments, when he was relegated or had temporarily retired to his home in Kent. There he examines at length, in epistolary form addressed to his closest friends, the contrasts between courtly and country virtues, comparing the simple honesty of the country to the practiced dissimulation of the court.

SATIRES

His own imprisonment and the death of Anne and her lovers had introduced a somber gloom, which he explored in shorter poems such as "Who list his wealth and ease retain," in which he urges sequestration and anonymity as a means of holding onto life and safety. In the satires, he moves forward from this position, working through his disillusion to a contentment derived from interior strengths and virtues. This process is similar to that of the love poems, in which he works from a mood of despair or grief to one of detachment.

The satires are based on the models of Luigi Alamanni, a contemporary Italian poet, whose terza rima Wyatt imitates, and on the satiric moods and techniques of Horace and Juvenal. The first satire especially ("Mine own John Poyntz") and the other two less overtly employ Wyatt's favorite antithetical manner, using it not to portray a divided mind but to contrast two lifestyles, public and private. Despite the difficulty of the verse form (there are far fewer available rhymes in English than in Italian), the opening of this poem based on Alamanni's tenth satire is smooth, colloquial, and ruminative. As Wyatt catalogs the courtly vices, what stings him most, as in the love poetry, is the deceit which leads to a betrayal of friendship, of "gentleness": "The friendly foe with his double face/ [I cannot] Say he is gentle, and courteous there-withal." Two series of catalogs, the first of courtly "arts" that he cannot affect—five tercets beginning "I cannot"—and the second of foreign countries where he might be ("I am not . . . Nor am I") are joyously resolved both rhetorically and metrically in the regular iambic line, "But here I am in Kent and Christendom," where he invites Poyntz to visit him and share his attractive life of independence, hunting in good weather, reading in bad.

"MY MOTHER'S MAIDS, WHEN THEY DID SEW AND SPIN"

The second, and perhaps most attractive of the three satires, "My mother's maids, when they did sew and spin," again addressed to Poyntz, is the most effective, for instead of the catalog of vices paraded in the other two at some risk of monotony, it uses the Horatian fable of the town mouse and the country mouse to expound a moral. The language is appealingly homely, the approach intimate, and the poem's directness is assisted—

like that of some of the love poems—by direct discourse: "Peep,' quod the other, 'sister I am here.'/ 'Peace,' quod the towny mouse, 'why speakest thou so loud?'" The moral is that man should content himself with and use well the lot assigned him and, instead of outward reward, seek inward peace. A religious note is introduced here as Wyatt asks of God a punishment for seekers after worldly gain—a punishment which resembles what he imagines for the lady in "My lute awake": that they shall behold virtue and regret their loss.

Wyatt's versions of seven psalms were probably written, like his satires, during or after one of his imprisonments. The narrative prologues that introduce them and the conception of them as expressions of penitence are derived from Pietro Aretino's prose translations into Italian. This framework probably appealed to Wyatt because it places the psalms in the context of David's love for Bathsheba and the resultant sickness of heart and soul which he strives to cure with the aid of his harp. The verse is powerful and fluid; the rhyme scheme, as in the satires, is terza rima. An examination of Psalm 38 ("O Lord, as I thee have both prayed and pray") shows how the psalms develop and continue the preoccupations expressed in the love poems and satires. As in the love poems, the focus of attention, the diction, rhetorical devices, and movement of the verse, is on depicting internal conflict, the movement of the suffering and divided mind: "O Lord, thou knowst the inward contemplation/ Of my desire, thou knowst my sighs and plaints,/ Thou knowst the tears of my lamentation." This might be part of a love lament. So might the following description of agony, where meter and imagery unite to depict a profound emotional crisis: "My heart panteth, my force I feel it quail,/ My sight, mine eyes, my look decays and faints." Broken-backed lines divided in two reinforce the poet's desperation as the second half-lines rhythmically duplicate each other. There follows a detailed description of the evils and dangers of courtly life: Friendship is betrayed, "kin unkind" desert him, slander assails him, he is in danger of his life. Like the lover, he fears rejection and seeks—this time with God—the succor of a reciprocal relationship.

The poet of individual consciousness has tested his strength against the courtly love tradition which, in its lack of reciprocity, fails him and against court manners which, in their lack of honesty and loyalty, appall him. He thus seeks reciprocity, trust, and affection by turning his "inward contemplation" to God.

OTHER MAJOR WORKS

TRANSLATION: *Plutarckes Boke of the Quyete of Mynde*, 1528 (of Plutarch).

BIBLIOGRAPHY

Estrin, Barbara L. *Laura: Uncovering Gender and Genre in Wyatt, Donne, and Marvell*. Durham, N.C.: Duke University Press, 1994. A study acknowledging the tyranny to women that most Petrarchan poems impose. Includes bibliographical references and index.

Foley, Stephen Merriam. *Sir Thomas Wyatt*. Boston: Twayne, 1990. This major work examines the meaning of Wyatt's poetry and, more importantly, how he came to write in such pioneering forms in Tudor England. Foley creates a perceptive and highly original study of Wyatt, of early sixteenth century English poetry, and of methods that may be used to understand better Wyatt's work.

Harrier, Richard. *The Canon of Sir Thomas Wyatt's Poetry*. Cambridge, Mass.: Harvard University Press, 1975. This careful study attempts to establish the canon of Wyatt's poetry. Harrier analyzes the history and physical characteristics of Wyatt's manuscripts and scrutinizes them in the context of the poet's complete output of work. Problematic manuscripts such as Devonshire MS 17492 are studied, as are Wyatt's minor manuscripts.

Heale, Elizabeth. *Wyatt, Surrey, and Early Tudor Poetry*. New York: Longman, 1998. An indispensable resource containing critical interpretation of the works of two early English sonneteers. Includes bibliographical references and index.

Jentoft, Clyde W. *Sir Thomas Wyatt and Henry Howard, Earl of Surrey: A Reference Guide*. Boston: G. K. Hall, 1980. An invaluable book for the student of Wyatt. Contains annotated information from books, magazines, studies, and monographs, as well as introductions and commentaries from important editions of Wyatt's work, and sections about him that appeared in other scholarly works.

Ross, Diane M. *Self-Revelation and Self-Protection in Wyatt's Lyric Poetry.* New York: Garland, 1988. This book examines how Wyatt's attempts to express his themes relate to the lyric genre. Ross accomplishes this primarily by contrasting Wyatt's work to other Renaissance lyric poetry.

Thomson, Patricia, ed. *Wyatt: The Critical Heritage.* Boston: Routledge & Kegan Paul, 1975. The critical tradition of Wyatt's poetry is presented in sixteen commentaries on his work ranging from an unsigned 1527 preface to *Plutarckes Boke of the Quyete of Mynde,* to C. S. Lewis's comments written in 1954. Includes an informative introduction to this material and reflects on the contribution these essays have on contemporary readers' understanding and appreciation of Wyatt's poetry.

Arthur Kincaid;
bibliography updated by the editors

X

XIE LINGYUN

Hsieh Lin-yün

Born: Guiji, China; 385
Died: Canton, China; June 26, 433

PRINCIPAL POETRY

Xie Lingyun's extant collected works include nineteen tetrameter-line and pentameter verses on traditional *yuefu* (music bureau) themes (that is, new lyrics to old tunes and titles); seventy-three pentameter-line *shi* lyric poems, including several congratulatory odes in tetrameter; anagram verse (*lihe*, literally "parting and meeting"); and a set of eight poems imitating the styles of the "Seven Masters of the Chien-an Era" (196-220) in one folio. Complete translations of Xie Lingyun's poetic works may be found in J. D. Frodsham's *The Murmuring Stream: The Life and Works of Hsieh Ling-yün* (1967; 2 volumes).

OTHER LITERARY FORMS

Xie Lingyun's official biography, compiled during the early sixth century, records his collected works in twenty folios and notes that Xie compiled a history of the Jin Dynasty, elements of which still survive. Also extant are fourteen *fu* rhyme-prose compositions (that is, prose poetry, with rhythm and occasional rhyme) and twenty-eight items of official prose, letters, prefaces, eulogies, *in memoriams*, and Buddhist essays totaling four folios.

ACHIEVEMENTS

Important critics from the sixth century to the eighteenth century have been unanimous in attributing to Xie Lingyun both the founding of the *shan-shui* (literally "mountains and waters") or "nature" poetry, popular in his own day, and its highest development. His travels in mountain retreats, for which he invented special climbing boots with reversible studs, and which inspired his tumultuous landscape descriptions, further brought him into contact with newly introduced Buddhist ideals, and his profound philosophical speculations added dimensions to the religious debates of his time and to the evolution of Buddhist sectarian thought. A member of the most aristocratic of the Southern Dynasties' families, his great intellectual abilities and skill as a calligrapher and painter attracted the notice of emperors of two regimes, and he was involved—fatally, as it was to transpire—in the most serious matters of state. Locations in his native Kiangsu and Chekiang provinces are still named after him.

BIOGRAPHY

Following the flight of the Chin aristocracy in 317, south across the Yangtze River to escape the invading Topa tribes from central Asia, the Xie clan came to prominence among the handful of cultured land barons who dominated the ensuing Southern Dynasties era (317-589). Their eminence stemmed from successive generations of extraordinary political and intellectual brilliance. Xie Lingyun's own direct forebears included the distinguished poet Xie Kun (280-322) and the statesman Xie An (320-385). On Xie's mother's side, he was descended from the great calligraphers Wang Xizhi (321-379) and his son Wang Xianzchi (344-388).

The young Xie Lingyun was intellectually precocious, and, presuming upon his wealthy estate as a duke of the realm (the Duke of Kangluo), became notorious for his personal excesses and extravagances (even for the times) and for his sharp, critical wit. These tendencies, and his later consort with rebellious peasantry and ruffians, eventually brought about his downfall.

Near-contemporaneous records mention that as a child, Xie Lingyun was sent for safety to live with the Du family, esoteric Daoists associated with fine calligraphy, in Hangzhou (hence his sobriquet "Little Guest Xie"). These philosophical and artistic influences were ever to remain with Xie. Then, in 399-400, when Xie was fifteen, an uprising brought the Daoist-inspired rebel Sun En into Xie territories in Zheking and Kiangsu, and many of their clan, and the related Wang, were killed, including Xie Lingyun's father. The boy was transferred to the capital at Jiankang (modern Nanking) and lodged with his uncle, Xie Hun (who was married into the Sima royal family). Here, he acquired his first official appointment, in the service of a Sima prince, but in 406, with great political consequences, Xie was transferred into the entourage of a rival faction of the ascendant Liu clan.

At that time, Xie Lingyun's new patron, Liu Yi, headed the dominant clique at court, and he enjoyed the backing of the powerful Xie. By 410, however, the general Liu Yu had outmaneuvered supporters and contenders alike, so that Liu Yi, with Xie Lingyun in tow, found himself rusticated to a posting in Hubei. This chance circumstance brought about Xie Lingyun's first contact with the great Buddhist institution at Mount Lu, founded by the epoch-creating cleric Huiyuan (334-416). Here emerged the White Lotus sect of Buddhism, which, appealing as it did to the educated aristocratic laity, quickly attracted a coterie of extraordinary minds. The combination of religious intellectualism, the breathtaking mountain scenery, and release from court intrigue and official drudgery exerted incalculable affect upon Xie Lingyun's literary endeavors.

The idyll, however, did not last long. In the provinces, Liu Yi attempted a coup but was suppressed by Liu Yu's forces. Xie Lingyun was captured; Liu Yi hanged himself. Luckily, Liu Yu appreciated Xie Lingyun's talents, bringing him back to the capital and installing him in an administrative post. For the next half-decade, Xie Lingyun was in and out of trouble, including a charge of murder; larger events, however, were to shape his future: In January, 419, Liu Yu strangled the idiot Emperor An and replaced him with Sima Dewen. In the spring of 420, Dewen was deposed and later assassinated. Liu Yu then ascended to the throne as the first emperor of the LiuSong regime (420-479).

The Xie clan found favor with the new emperor, but in the intrigues over the succession, Xie Lingyun was again caught on the wrong side. Liu Yu died on June 26, 422, and Xie Lingyun's clique was exiled to Yongjia (modern Zhekiang Province). The way was long and perilous, and Xie Lingyun had become ill from tuberculosis and leg ulcers. He made a detour via the family estates at Shining and finally arrived in Yongjia in October that year. He remained bedridden for the winter months, contemplating Daoist and Buddhist thought; during this time, he produced a major contribution to the Buddhist tradition in China ("Discussion of Essentials"). Well enough by the spring of 423 to resume his duties, he nevertheless neglected official affairs and passed his time wandering in the hills until 424, when he resigned altogether, departed from Yongjia, and retired to an anchorite life at Shining. He devoted himself to costly repairs of the estate, damaged during the Sun En incursions; his monumental rhyme-prose "Dwelling in the Mountains" describes his labors and the wondrous beauties of the wilderness scene. His understanding of Buddhism, too, deepened at Shining, as witnessed by the four dozen or so poems he wrote there.

Another political upheaval occurred in August, 424, with the assassination of the emperor and the accession of Emperor Wen (reigned 424-453). Xie Lingyun was moved to write of his sorrows, and again he fell ill, but soon he was recalled to "illumine" an undistinguished court. He declined twice on account of problems with his legs but eventually accepted. His was the classic dilemma facing a Chinese bureaucrat: His duty was to serve, but he was disillusioned by the frustrations of public life. A scion of the highest aristocracy, he was yet denied consummate power by the upstart Sima and Liu monarchs and their minions. Nevertheless, he was assigned a congenial occupation—the compilation of an official history of the preceding Jin Dynasty, and an imperial bibliography. His verse and calligraphy had earned the royal epithet "twin gems," but his erratic behavior and unauthorized absences brought impeachment and disgrace. On April 1, 428, he found himself packed off once more to Shining, ostensibly on sick leave.

There, Xie Lingyun found his beloved cousin, the poet Xie Huilian, also in disgrace, and their mutual inspiration produced some of the most celebrated verse in the Chinese literary heritage. Dismissed from all offices in November of 428, he retired to his Daoist and Buddhist preoccupations, improvements to his estate, mountain-climbing, and the assembling of a vast library. Some eighteen months later, Xie Huilian was pardoned; his departure for the capital occasioned yet more perennially admired verse.

Xie Lingyun's intellectual and literary brilliance and his high-born status and wealth had thus far protected him from greater harm than mere rustication, but his arrogance and lack of political acumen had provoked serious enmities. Slander, deriving from friction over the mutual encroachments of public and private lands at Shining, intensified, and to defend himself, Xie Lingyun presented an eloquent appeal at the imperial court. Meanwhile, the emperor's forces returned from a disastrous defeat in the North, in 431, and a bitter controversy over Buddhist doctrine was resolved in Xie Lingyun's favor. Xie Lingyun was found innocent of the charges against him, but was granted office-in-exile in distant Kiangsi, where, still contemptuous of his duties, he was arrested by local officials. Driven to the limits of his uncertain patience, he seized the arresting officers and declared an uprising for the restoration of the Jin. His unpremeditated coup was easily put down, but even then, the emperor overlooked his indiscretions, and instead of being sentenced to death, Xie Lingyun was merely reduced to the status of a commoner and was banished to the malarial southlands of Canton. There, his influence gone, and the Sima loyalists dangerously active, he was again accused of sedition. Although unconvinced by the weak evidence, the emperor ordered Xie Lingyun's execution.

ANALYSIS

Early literary critics in China, particularly Zhong Hong (died 518) and Liu Xie (465-522), concerned themselves with the evolution of literary styles and forms. Their evaluations of Xie Lingyun's work therefore were concerned chiefly with placing him in the stream of literary history. According to Zhong Hong, Xie Lingyun's "talents were lofty and his diction flourishing, rich in charm and difficult to emulate," so that as "the master of the Yüan-chia period (424-453)" he transcended the literary giants who preceded him. Placing Xie Lingyun in the top rank of three categories of poets, Zhong Hong remarked that Xie Lingyun's poetry was derived from that of the politically minded Cao Zhi (192-232) and interspersed with elements of the florid Zhang Xie (flourished 295).

EARLY INFLUENCES

By the seventeenth or eighteenth century, in spite of evidence to the contrary, Xie Lingyun was firmly ensconced in Chinese literary history as the founder of *shan-shui* ("nature" or "landscape") verse. J. D. Frod-

sham demonstrates that landscape and nature themes were prominent from the earliest beginnings of Chinese poetry. In particular, Frodsham points out, Xie Lingyun's early landscape verse appears to have been molded by the instruction of his uncle Xie Hun. In the end, however, it matters less that Xie Lingyun was the inventor of the genre than that he was its most qualified exponent.

Among the various influences that enhanced Xie Lingyun's native literary genius were his childhood Daoist studies and his later association with the most advanced Buddhist intellectuals of his day; his personal involvement in the perilous political life of his times; and his travels in the course of official postings, exiles, and banishments in the forested mountains and rivers of South China—in the fifth century, still mostly virgin territory.

Unlike his predecessor Ruan Ji (210-263), for example, Xie Lingyun wrote very little poetry satirizing political evils. Occasionally he quotes from the Confucian canon, saying that when government is in decay it is proper to retire. Otherwise, he criticizes his own disinterest in mundane administration, apologizing to his liege-lord and eulogizing him rather than remonstrating with him. He admits that he is idle and stupid, his administration far from ideal, quite unworthy of the honors bestowed upon him. The emperor, on the other hand, is perfectly sincere and excels in the Way. Such was the accepted rhetoric of the time, and no great political or satirical construction should be placed on these worn lines.

Daoist anchorite escapism abounds in the poetry of Xie Lingyun, usually expressed in admiration for the sages of ancient tradition. Within the space of a few lines in a single poem, one reads both of his ambivalence toward an official career ("Throughout my life I'd have preferred distant solitude") and of the seductive appeal of a steady government salary. Free at last—inforced retirement—in bucolic tranquillity, he shakes off the dust of the world of affairs and chooses the simple life, strolling about his tumbleweed dwelling. After all, not for him the fret and frustration of mortal renown. No doubt he was sincere enough, but one always bears in mind that his immense wealth and nobility afforded him the easy choices of a glamorous life at the metropolitan court or gentlemanly retirement to his vast and lavish estates.

BUDDHIST THEMES

Overt expression of Buddhist affiliation also appears frequently in Xie Lingyun's verse, although it is in his prose works that his important dissertations on controversial doctrine lie. In his poetry, Buddhist themes such as the ephemeral and insubstantial nature of the world are generally introduced into larger concerns of scene and circumstance. The brevity and lyricism of the references in their contexts preclude theological exposition, but even so, one catches glimpses of the essence of Xie Lingyun's arguments: "Seeing all this, mortal thoughts vanish, In an instant of enlightenment, one attains to abandonment." Xie Lingyun's proposition that transcendental wisdom derived from sudden enlightenment, eventually vindicated by new textual evidence arriving from the troubled North, clashed with prevailing views in the South and earned for him the enmity of court favorites who subscribed to the current ritualistic and pedantic practices of gradual accumulation of Buddha-merit by which enlightenment was thought to be attained. (It is interesting, however, that religious persecution did not exist per se in Xie Lingyun's society; while religious conflicts may have exacerbated tensions, his rivals brought only civil charges against him.)

GROWING OLD

Anguish over political uncertainties seems to have troubled Xie Lingyun less than his enforced partings from friends and dear relatives, his peregrinations and illnesses, and his awareness of approaching old age. "Mindful of old friends, I was loath to depart," he writes. "A wanderer come upon the eventide, I cherish old [friends]." He describes how his hair has begun to show streaks of gray in the mirror and how his girdle hangs loosely about his shrunken girth. Pursuit of pay as a bureaucrat has brought him to his sickbed in exile, and he misses his friends as time and the seasons whirl by. The most celebrated expression of these concerns occurs in the set of five stanzas he wrote in matching reply to his cousin Xie Huilian, with whom he shared some eighteen months of banishment on the family estate at Shining. Prosodically, they feature an unusually developed anadiplosis in the last line of one stanza and the first line of the next.

LANDSCAPE THEMES

While these elements certainly feature conspicuously in Xie Lingyun's verse, it is overwhelmingly his *shan-shui* content, the treatment of landscape themes, for which he is renowned. Buddho-Daoist ideas, and his own sensitive humanity and love of the wild countryside, ubiquitously inform the tumultuous scenes he observes with a more profound contemplation of man in his universe. Nevertheless, it is the torrential cascade of crags and crevices, ranges and ridges that block out half the sky, peaks and precipices winding circuitously to bewilder the traveler's sense of direction, torrid summer forests, sunset birds in the trees of a riverbank, flying mists in abysmal ravines, the hooked moon among the autumn stars, pale willows murmuring in a breeze, crystal eddies in a bouldered stream—these things and more—that enrapture and awe the reader. Man—the traveler—may delight in the myriad creations and transformations of scene and season, but man is a traveler in time, too. He passes on, politician and poet, sorrowed by partings, wearied, sickened, and aged by the vexations of his path.

Xie Lingyun sees in grand nature the permanence of renewal and never tires of encountering these transformations. Thrusting up and growing, new bamboo is clad in spring-green shoots; tender reeds wear their purple blossoms. Each miracle further endears his world to the poet, ever responsive as he is to the beauties he sees all about him. The grandeur of the rugged mountains of his domain, traditionally the abode of divinities and sages, was a reminder to him of the insignificance and transience of social goals. Their neutrality and silence reinforced Xie Lingyun's Buddhist and Daoist notions of relativity and quiescence. If saddened and disappointed in his political fortunes, he was able to identify his own mortality in the passing seasons and ever-changing scene and with composure await his end.

BIBLIOGRAPHY

Chang, Kang-I Sun. *Six Dynasties Poetry*. Princeton, N.J.: Princeton University Press, 1986. The second chapter provides a scholarly discussion of Xie Lingyun's life and poems.

Frodsham, J. D. *The Murmuring Stream: The Life and Works of the Chinese Nature Poet Hsieh Ling-yün*. 2 vols. Kuala Lumpur: University of Malaya Press, 1967. A revision of the author's thesis at the Australian National University, Canberra, this insightful study includes plates, maps, and bibliography.

Hargett, James M. "The Poetry of Xie Lingyun." In *Great Literature of the Eastern World*, edited by Ian P. McGreal. New York: HarperCollins, 1996. Guide to the themes and style of Xie Lingyun's poems. Includes both biographical and bibliographical information.

Liu, Tien-chüeh, Ch'en Fang-cheng, and Ho Chih-hua, eds. *Hsieh Ling-yün chi chu tzu so yin*. Hsiang-kang: Chung wen ta hsüeh ch'u pan she, 1999. One in the series of concordances to works of writers of Wei-Jin and the Northern and Southern Dynasties. In Chinese.

Liu, Wu-chi, and Irving Yucheng Lo, eds. *Sunflower Splendor: Three Thousand Years of Chinese Poetry*. New York: Doubleday, 1975. Includes a good translation of Xie Lingyun's poems.

Nather, Richard B. "The Landscape Buddhism of the Fifth Century Poet Hsieh Ling-yun." *Journal of Asian Studies* 18 (1958/1959): 67-79. A critical examination of the correlation between nature and Buddhism in Xie Lingyun's poetry.

Sheridan, Selinda Ann. *Vocabulary and Style in Six Dynasties Poetry: A Frequency Study of Hsieh Ling-Yun and Hsieh T'iao*. Dissertation. Ithaca, N.Y.: Cornell University, 1982. Photocopy. Ann Arbor, Mich.: UMI Dissertation Information Service, 1988.

Westbrook, Francis A. "Landscape Transformation in the Poetry of Hsieh Ling-yün." *Journal of the American Oriental Society* 3, no. 3 (July-October, 1980): 237-254.

John Marney;
bibliography updated by Qingyun Wu

Y

MITSUYE YAMADA

Born: Fukuoka, Kyushu, Japan; July 5, 1923

PRINCIPAL POETRY

Camp Notes and Other Poems, 1976
Desert Run: Poems and Stories, 1988
Camp Notes and Other Writings, 1998

OTHER LITERARY FORMS

Mitsuye Yamada published two short stories in *Desert Run: Poems and Stories* and, in addition to producing her own work, has collaborated with others in editing poetry collections. Her essays on literature, personal history, and human rights have appeared in anthologies and periodicals, and she compiled a teachers' guide for Amnesty International. In 1981 PBS broadcast a documentary, *Mitsuye and Nellie: Two Asian-American Poets*, featuring Yamada and Chinese American writer Nellie Wong.

ACHIEVEMENTS

Mitsuye Yamada is one of the first writers to publish a personal account of the United States' internment of citizens of Japanese descent. Publication of the "camp notes" poems also marked an important event in the resurgence of feminist literature in the 1970's. Yamada has served on the national board of Amnesty International on the organization's Committee on International Development. She has received numerous awards for her writing, teaching, and human rights work.

BIOGRAPHY

Mitsuye May Yamada was born in Fukuoka, Kyushu, Japan, the third child and only daughter of Hide and Jack Yasutake. She was brought to the United States at age three and lived with her parents and three brothers in Seattle until she was nineteen, except for eighteen months in Japan with her father's family at the age of nine. Her high school education was curtailed in 1941 when her father, a translator for the United States Immigration Service, was imprisoned as an enemy alien. Mitsuye, her mother, and her brothers were later removed to internment camps in Puyallup, Washington, and Minidoka, Idaho. She spent eighteen months in the camps, finally leaving to work and study at the University of Cincinnati. She completed her bachelor's degree at New York University and a master of arts degree in English literature at the University of Chicago.

She was able to become a naturalized American citizen following passage of the McCarran-Walter Immigration Act and received citizenship in 1955. In 1950 she married chemist Yoshikazu Yamada. They lived in New York, where their four children were born, until the early 1960's, when the family moved to Southern California. In 1966 she began teaching in community colleges and was professor of English at Cypress Community College from 1968 until her retirement in 1989. Following publication of *Camp Notes and Other Poems* (1976), she held many university appointments as visiting professor, artist in residence, and consultant.

A lifelong commitment to human rights emerged as Yamada's response to her incarceration, and she has related her sense of urgency on the subject to years of living with a diagnosis of incurable emphysema when her children were very young. She was an early member of Amnesty International and has served on the executive board and national committees in that organization. Her two poetry collections were published by feminist presses; she organized a multicultural women writers group; she has participated in numerous projects addressed to concerns of women, ethnic groups, and environmental awareness. Following retirement she began to work with her older brother, Reverend Michael Yasutake, on prisoners' rights.

ANALYSIS

CAMP NOTES AND OTHER POEMS

Originally published by Shameless Hussy, a struggling feminist press, *Camp Notes and Other Poems* is a personal volume involving family participation. The cover illustration, by the author's older daughter, Jeni Yamada, is a line drawing of a female figure in three stages: a shy little girl, an older girl walking forward, and a striding woman carrying either a briefcase or suitcase. The ambiguity of the last figure can refer to the camp experience, where internees were able to bring only what they could carry, or to the author's professional life as writer, teacher, and activist. The author's husband contributed the book's calligraphy, and the volume is dedicated to Mitsuye Yamada's parents, husband, two daughters, and two sons. The actual "camp notes" poems center the volume and are bracketed by an opening section on the author's parents and a closing series of poems looking to the present and future.

The seven poems in the section titled "My Issei Parents, Twice Pioneers, Now I Hear Them" were written after the central "camp notes" set, and they look back to parents, grandparents, and great-grandparents. The section opens with a folk saying: "What your Mother tells you now/ in time/ you will come to know." The text appears first in brush-stroke ideograms, then in transliterated Japanese, and finally in the author's translation. The theme permeates the author's work, which engages with the ways that origins—"the mother"—shape a person, through both acceptance and resistance.

The next poem offers a portrait of "Great Grandma" figured in her orderly collection of ordinary objects: "colored stones," "parched persimmons," "powdery green tea." Great Grandma's static world and calm acceptance of fate stand in contrast to the turmoil, pain, and conflict documented in much of Yamada's work.

Two poems, "Marriage Was a Foreign Country" and "Homecoming," are narrated in the voice of the persona's mother; they tell stories of pain and difficulty of life as a Japanese immigrant woman in a country both alien and hostile. Following these poems are two poems relating to the speaker's father. Contrasting the mother's monologues, these dialogues comment on traditional Japanese wisdom that the father is attempting to impart.

The section titled "Camp Notes" highlights poems composed while Yamada was imprisoned with her mother and brothers in the Minidoka camp. Thirty years later the poems were culled from their early inscription in a large writing tablet, one of the few possessions the author could take with her to the camp. The section opens with another line drawing by Jeni Yamada, picturing a small child clutching a stuffed animal and seated amid piles of luggage. The first poems tally the upheaval of the removal experience with titles such as "Evacua-

tion," "Curfew," and "On the Bus." The title of "Harmony at the Fair Grounds" reflects the irony in many of these brief, acrid poems: The "grounds" on which the Japanese Americans were imprisoned were anything but "fair." The last lines offer a stark picture of concentration camp life: "Lines formed for food/ lines for showers/ lines for the john/ lines for shots."

A secondary subheading, "Relocation," designates poems about life in the Minidoka camp. The author continues to document the grim, degrading aspects of prison life, where monotony and uncertainty intensified the physical stresses of primitive, cramped quarters and the denial of amenities such as radios and cameras. Even more demoralizing are the irrationality, stupidity, and lies of the bureaucratic internment system. As the family huddles under bedclothes to survive a "Desert Storm" the speaker observes

> This was not
> im
> prison
> ment.
> This was
> re
> location.

Likewise, the opening of "Block 4 Barrack 4 'Apt' C" demolishes the excuse that relocation benefitted the imprisoned, noting that barbed wire protected the inmates from "wildly twisted/ sagebrush." In two poems the persona notes the paradox of guards locked inside their watchtowers. Hedi Yamada, the author's younger daughter, illustrated "The Watchtower" with a silhouette drawing of an adult holding a child's hand and gazing at such a tower; it is impossible to tell whether they are looking out of or into the prison area. The double bind of *Nisei* (second-generation Japanese American) citizens emerges in the protest to the "Recruiting Team":

> Why should I volunteer!
> I'm an American
> I have a right to be
> drafted.

As the persona notes in "The Trick Was," notwithstanding propaganda or disinformation, "the mind was not fooled."

Several poems return with poignancy to the theme of family. The author translates two *senryu* poems (three-line unrhymed Japanese poems) written by her father, at that time incarcerated at a camp in New Mexico. "The Night Before Good-Bye" pictures the mother performing the intimately caring task of mending her daughter's clothes. "Cincinnati," written after the actual camp experience, comes to terms with a racist assault, in which the speaker loses a lace handkerchief given her by her mother.

The remaining poems in this volume reflect the author's life from the end of the war through the 1950's and 1960's and introduce themes of personal challenge, illness, raising children, education, and activism. The section opens with another drawing by Jeni Yamada, suggesting a serene Japanese village scene of a cove surrounded by woods and mountains with small boats at anchor and a line of houses on the beach. The past is still important: The author recollects, in the twinned poems "Here" and "There," being taunted as an "outsider" by classmates in both Japan and the United States. "Freedom in Manhattan" opens particularly feminist concerns, depicting police officers' indifference to attempted rape.

DESERT RUN

The professional production of Yamada's second collection, published by Kitchen Table: Women of Color Press, testifies to recognition of the author and establishment of ethnic and women's cultural institutions in the twelve years after the appearance of *Camp Notes*. The later volume is professionally typeset, pages are numbered, and a single thematic illustration—a calligraphy of the author's name—appears on the cover, section divisions, and end of each poem. The author's husband again contributed the calligraphy, and the book is dedicated to her three brothers.

The poems in *Desert Run* extend themes introduced in *Camp Notes and Other Poems*, now developed in more discursive, meditative modes. The initial set, headed "Where I Stay," is a sequence completed after a camping trip in the Southern California desert. The experience was unique: Part of an experimental college course co-taught with a biologist to connect creative writing and natural science, it marked for the author a reexamination of the "desert" experience of internment.

The title poem, "Desert Run," meditates on the fragility, power, and beauty of the desert ecology, the author's contrast of her present interest in the desert with the earlier rancor and hatred of the apparently barren landscape, and her continuing sense of the irreparable injustice of arbitrary imprisonment. The address of this poem—the author's longest—embodies the speaker's difficult ruminations, as she speaks sometimes as a meditative "I" and at other times addresses a "you" that appears in other poems and that implies the "other," the "dominant" or "mainstream" or "official" American perspective. In this section, "Lichens" and "Desert Under Glass" are also notable close observations of nature.

Titles of the three remaining sections of this volume—"Returning," "Resisting," and "Connecting"—express the author's continuing project of synthesizing the disparate elements of her life. The poems and short story in "Returning" revisit experience and heritage in Japan. The grandmother's ambivalent pride and resentment over the emigration of the author's father emerges in "American Son," which with "Obon: Festival of the Dead" recollects the months Yamada spent as a child being tutored in Japanese language and culture.

A thread of women's stories and women's plight runs through the "Resisting" section. Two poems are framed in the personas of other women. "Jeni's Complaint," presented as in the voice of the author's daughter, captures the chaos of a multigeneration, multicultural family celebration. "I Learned to Sew" tells, in the Japanese Hawaiian cadence of the author's mother-in-law, a story of immigration, hardship, endurance, and survival; this poem contains a brief retelling of the Japanese folktale of Urashima Taro. The short story "Mrs. Higashi Is Dead" elaborates the anecdote briefly referred to in the poem "Homecoming" in *Camp Notes and Other Poems*.

The "Connecting" section of *Desert Run* contains half the poems in the volume and recapitulates the major themes: nature, human dignity, family, and roots. Several poems in this section are voiced by "fictional" personas, notably "The Club," a woman's narration of her husband's abuse. "Connecting" also refers to the links between the author's personal experience of injustice with those of others: a Holocaust survivor, a battered wife, even animals sacrificed for fur.

CAMP NOTES AND OTHER WRITINGS

This collection continues a canonization process. The volume reprints both *Camp Notes and Other Poems* and *Desert Run*. Although it contains no previously unpublished work, the poems and dedication of *Camp Notes and Other Writings* have been professionally typeset; also, the order of the poems has been substantially altered and the illustrations eliminated. One important addition is the cover illustration. A photograph taken around 1908 of the author's mother as a child, it commemorates a grade-school dramatization of the legend of Urashima Taro with Yamada's mother in the title role of the young man who married a water princess and lived under the sea for many years. A historical and documentary return to the author's origins, complementing anecdotal and personal connections, the photograph also serves as a return and gloss to the translation of the mother's folk saying that opens *Camp Notes and Other Writings*.

OTHER MAJOR WORKS

EDITED TEXTS: *The Webs We Weave*, 1986 (with John Brander); *Sowing Ti Leaves*, 1990 (with Sane Sachie Hylkema).

BIBLIOGRAPHY

Cheng, Scarlet. "Foreign All Your Life." *Belles Lettres* 4, no. 2 (Winter, 1989). A review of *Desert Run* and Hisaye Yamamoto DeSoto's short fiction collection *Seventeen Syllables*. The reviewer finds Yamada's poetry nostalgic and filled with lyricism but notes the way in which poems consistently confront pain and alienation.

Patterson, Anita Haya. "Resistance to Images of the Internment: Mitsuye Yamada's Camp Notes." *MELUS* 23, no. 3 (Fall, 1998). Examines poems in *Camp Notes and Other Writings* in light of the concept of "obligation" and the problematic issue of the seeming nonresistance by Americans of Japanese ancestry to unconstitutional imprisonment in concentration camps. The essay contains photographs from newspapers and other sources to illustrate images of Japanese Americans as visualized in American popular culture during and after World War II.

Schweik, Susan. "A Needle with Mama's Voice: Mitsuye Yamada's *Camp Notes* and the American Canon of War Poetry." In *Arms and the Woman: War, Gender, and Literary Representation*, edited by Helen M. Cooper, Adrienne Auslande Munich, and Susan Merrill Squier. Chapel Hill: University of North Carolina Press, 1989. Examination of Yamada's poems in the context of "war poetry" by women. The author considers the silencing of Yamada's voice between the writing of the "camp notes" poems and their publication thirty years later and maintains that such silence was brought about by the unique situation of Japanese American women—especially Issei women—who were considered "enemy aliens." The discussion compares mother-daughter and father-daughter expressions in the difference between retelling of transmitted oral tales versus translation of the father's poems.

Woolley, Lisa. "Racial and Ethnic Semiosis in Mitsuye Yamada's 'Mrs. Higashi Is Dead.'" *MELUS* 24, no. 4 (Winter, 1999). Using poems from *Camp Notes and Other Poems*, the author analyzes Yamada's short story "Mrs. Higashi Is Dead" according to a theory called "ethnic semiosis." The theory postulates that Americans realize "ethnicity" through performance in instances of contact between individuals from different ethnic backgrounds; these relational moments both define and contest characteristics considered as belonging to particular ethnicities. The analysis of Yamada's story examines how it reflects "ethnic semiosis" in the different ways that a mother and daughter interpret a request from a woman of a different ethnicity.

Yamada, Mitsuye. "A *MELUS* Interview: Mitsuye Yamada." Interview by Helen Jaskoski. *MELUS* 15, no. 1 (Spring, 1988). An interview that touches a wide range of topics. The poet reflects on family influences in her writing (her father founded a society devoted to the Japanese *senryu* poem) and the impact of the concentration camp experience on her life and work. Also mentioned are women's writing, human rights activism, political persecution of poets, and formal aspects of poetry.

Helen Jaskoski

WILLIAM BUTLER YEATS

Born: Sandymount, near Dublin, Ireland; June 13, 1865
Died: Cap Martin, France; January 28, 1939

PRINCIPAL POETRY

Mosada: A Dramatic Poem, 1886
Crossways, 1889
The Wanderings of Oisin and Other Poems, 1889
The Countess Kathleen and Various Legends and Lyrics, 1892
The Rose, 1893
The Wind Among the Reeds, 1899
In the Seven Woods, 1903
The Poetical Works of William B. Yeats, 1906, 1907 (2 volumes)
The Green Helmet and Other Poems, 1910
Responsibilities, 1914
Responsibilities and Other Poems, 1916
The Wild Swans at Coole, 1917, 1919
Michael Robartes and the Dancer, 1920
The Tower, 1928
Words for Music Perhaps and Other Poems, 1932
The Winding Stair and Other Poems, 1933
The Collected Poems of W. B. Yeats, 1933, 1950
The King of the Great Clock Tower, 1934
A Full Moon in March, 1935
Last Poems and Plays, 1940
The Poems of W. B. Yeats, 1949 (2 volumes)
The Collected Poems of W. B. Yeats, 1956
The Variorum Edition of the Poems of W. B. Yeats, 1957 (P. Allt and R. K. Alspach, editors)
The Poems, 1983
The Poems: A New Edition, 1984

OTHER LITERARY FORMS

William Butler Yeats was a playwright as well as a poet. During certain periods in his career he devoted more time and energy to the composition, publication, and production of plays in verse or prose than to the writing of nondramatic poetry. These plays, excluding several early closet dramas, were republished singly or in various collections from 1892 through the year of his death. *The Collected Plays of W. B. Yeats* was published in 1934, and a "new edition with five additional plays" appeared in 1952 (London) and 1953 (New York), the former being the "basic text." The genuinely definitive publication, however, is the admirably edited *Variorum Edition of the Plays of W. B. Yeats* (1966).

In addition to poems and plays, Yeats published prolifically during the course of his life in almost every imaginable genre except the novel. In fact, the record of such publications is so complex that little more than the merest outline can be given here. Numerous prose tales, book reviews, nationalistic articles, letters to editors, and so on far exceeded poems and plays in volume in the early stages of Yeats's career. In 1908, *The Collected Works in Verse and Prose of William Butler Yeats*—including lyrics, narrative poems, stories, plays, essays, prefaces, and notes—filled eight volumes, of which only the first contained predominantly nondramatic poetry. Previously, stories and sketches, many of them based wholly or in part upon Irish folk tales, had been collected in *The Celtic Twilight* (1893) and *The Secret Rose* (1897). Rewritten versions of those tales from *The Secret Rose* that featured a roving folk poet invented by Yeats were later published as *Stories of Red Hanrahan* (1904). Similarly, relatively formal critical and philosophical essays were collected and published as *Ideas of Good and Evil* (1903), *The Cutting of an Agate* (1912), and *Essays, 1931-1936* (1937).

A slender doctrinal book, *Per Amica Silentia Lunae* (1918), is generally regarded as something of a precursor to *A Vision* (1925). The first edition of *A Vision* itself, an exposition of Yeats's mystical philosophy, appeared in 1925. A considerably revised edition first published in 1937 has revealed to scholars that while the book unquestionably owes much to Mrs. Yeats's "automatic writing," as avowed, more than a little of its content is generally based upon Yeats's or his and his wife's earlier occult interests and contacts. In 1926, Yeats published a volume titled *Autobiographies*. In 1938, an American edition titled *The Autobiography of William Butler Yeats* was released, with the addition of several sections or units which had been published separately or in groups in the interim. Then, in 1955 a final British issue appeared with the original title and one sub-unit not included in the American edition. A posthumous supple-

William Butler Yeats, Nobel laureate in literature for 1923.
(© The Nobel Foundation)

ment to *Autobiographies* is *Memoirs* (1972), combining the draft of an earlier unpublished autobiography with a complete transcription of the private journal from which Yeats had used only selected portions in the post-1926 versions of his original book. A large and carefully edited collection of Yeats's correspondence, *The Letters of W. B. Yeats*, was published in 1954, and various smaller collections of correspondence with certain people have been published from time to time since the poet's death.

Most of Yeats's major prose, other than *A Vision*, *Autobiographies*, and his editor's introduction to *The Oxford Book of Modern Verse* (1936), has been collected and republished in three volumes printed simultaneously in London and New York. *Mythologies* (1959) includes *The Celtic Twilight*, *The Secret Rose*, *Stories of Red Hanrahan*, the three so-called Rosa Alchemica stories from 1897 (which involve Yeats's fictional personae Michael Robartes and Owen Aherne), and *Per Amica Silentia Lunae*. *Essays and Introductions* (1961) incorporates *Ideas of Good and Evil*, most of *The Cutting of an Agate*, *Essays, 1931-1936*, and three introductions written in 1937 for portions of a projected edition of Yeats's works which never materialized. *Explorations* (1962)

brings together a number of miscellaneous items, most of them previously not readily accessible. There are three introductions to books of legend and folklore by Lady Augusta Gregory, introductions to some of Yeats's own plays, a sizeable body of his early dramatic criticism, the essay "If I Were Four-and-Twenty," *Pages from a Diary Written in Nineteen Hundred and Thirty*, (1944), and most of the author's last prose piece *On the Boiler*, a potpourri including late political philosophy.

As to fiction not already mentioned, two stories from 1891—a long tale and a short novel—have been republished in a critical edition, *John Sherman and Dhoya* (1969), and a fine scholarly edition of Yeats's early unfinished novel, *The Speckled Bird* (published in a limited edition in Dublin in 1974), was printed in 1976 as an item in the short-lived *Yeats Studies* series. In another highly competent piece of scholarship, almost all of the previously mentioned early book reviews, nationalist articles, and so on, as well as some later essays, have been edited and republished in *Uncollected Prose by W. B. Yeats*, Volume 1 in 1970 and Volume II in 1976. Finally, the bewildering mass of Yeats's unpublished materials—thousands of pages of working drafts, notebooks, proof sheets, personal and family letters and papers, occult documents, automatic scripts, and the like—were made available on microfilm by the poet's son, Senator Michael Yeats, in 1975. Two sets of these films are housed, one each, at the National Library of Ireland and the State University of New York at Stony Brook. With the generous permission of Yeats's daughter and son, Anna and Michael, scholars are currently studying, transcribing, and editing many of these materials. Several books that employ or reproduce portions of them have been published. Several volumes of Yeats's letters, *The Collected Letters of W. B. Yeats,* trace his life and poetic influences between the years 1865 and 1904. Most of the letters included are from Yeats's twenties, when he was passionately involved with furthering two causes: his own career and Irish literature as a whole.

ACHIEVEMENTS

William Butler Yeats is generally regarded as one of the major English-speaking poets of the "modern" era (approximately 1890 to 1950). Some authorities go even further, designating him the most important twentieth century poet in any language. Although in his late career and for some time thereafter he was overshadowed by the poetic and critical stature of T. S. Eliot, in the years since Eliot's death, Yeats's reputation has continued to grow whereas Eliot's has declined. Like most modern poets, writing in a period labeled the age of the novel, Yeats has been relatively obscure and inaccessible to the general reader, but among academicians his eminence has flourished, and, even more significant, his influence upon other poets has been both broad and deep.

Even though he was never very robust, suffering from chronic respiratory problems and extremely poor eyesight throughout much of his adult life, Yeats lived a long, productive, and remarkably multifaceted life. How one person could have been as completely immersed in as many different kinds of activity as he was is difficult to conceive. Throughout his life he was involved in occult pursuits and interests of one kind or another, a preoccupation that has long been considered by many authorities (especially early ones) as more an impediment than a contribution to his literary career. Of more "legitimate" significance, he was, with a handful of associates, a leading figure in the initiation of the related movements that have come to be known as the Irish Renaissance and the Irish Literary Revival. Especially as a cofounder and codirector of the Irish National Theatre—later the famous Abbey Theatre—he was at the center of the literary movement, even aside from his prolific publication of poems, plays, essays, and reviews and the editorship of his sisters' artistically oriented Cuala Press. Moreover, between 1903 and 1932, Yeats conducted or participated in a series of five theater or lecture tours in America, thereby enhancing his renown in English-speaking countries on both sides of the Atlantic.

Major expressions of national and international recognition for such endeavors and achievements were forthcoming in the last decades of Yeats's life in such forms as honorary degrees from Queen's University (Belfast) and Trinity College (Dublin) in 1922, Oxford University in 1931, and Cambridge University in 1933; appointment as senator for the newly established Irish Free State in 1922; and, most gratifying of all, the Nobel Prize for literature in 1923. Furthermore, in 1935 Yeats was designated editor of the *Oxford Book of Modern Verse*, having declined previously an offer of knighthood

in 1915 and an invitation to lecture in Japan in 1919. From young manhood, Yeats had lived and played out the role of the poet in society, gesturing, posing, and dressing for the part. In middle years and old age, he experienced genuine fulfillment of his dream and enjoyed self-realization as "the great man" of Anglo-Irish literature within his own lifetime.

Yeats's greatest accomplishment, however, was the achievement, in both his life and his work, of an astonishing singleness or oneness in the midst of myriad activities. Driven by an obsessive precept which he labeled "Unity of Being," he strove unceasingly to "hammer" his thoughts into "unity." Though never a masterful thinker in terms of logic or ratiocination, Yeats possessed unequivocal genius of the kind recognized by today's psychologists as imaginative or creative, if not visionary. In addition to an almost infallible gift for the precisely right word or phrase, he had a mind awesomely capacious in its ability to conceive and sustain complexly interwoven structures of symbolic suggestion, mythic significance, and allusive associations. He used these abilities to link poem, poems to plays, and oeuvre to a self-consciously dramatic life, which was itself hardly other than a supremely sculpted *objet d'art*. By the time of his death at the age of seventy-three, Yeats had so completely interfused national interests, philosophical convictions, theories of symbolic art, and mythopoeic techniques of literary composition that he had indeed fulfilled his lifelong quest to master experience by wresting unity from multiplicity, achieving an intricately wrought identity of life and work in the midst of almost unimaginably manifold diversity.

BIOGRAPHY

The eldest son of an eldest son of an eldest son, William Butler Yeats was born on June 13, 1865, in Sandymount, Ireland, a small community on the outskirts of Dublin which has since been absorbed by that sprawling metropolis. His father, paternal grandfather, and great-grandfather Yeats were all graduates of Trinity College, Dublin, but only his father, John Butler Yeats, had begun his post-collegiate career in the city where he had studied. Both the great-grandfather and the grandfather had been clergymen of the Protestant Church of Ireland, the latter in County Down, near Northern Ireland, and the former at Drumcliff, near the west-Irish port town of Sligo, with which the poet is so thoroughly identified.

The reason for the identification with Sligo is that John Butler Yeats married the sister of his closest collegiate schoolmate, George Pollexfen, whose family lived in Sligo. Dissatisfied with the courts as a fledgling barrister, J. B. Yeats abandoned law and Dublin to follow in London his inclinations as a graphic artist in sketches and oils. The combination of limited finances and his wife's dislike of urban life resulted in numerous extended visits by her and the growing family of children back to Sligo at the home of the poet's maternal grandfather, a sea captain and partner in a shipping firm. Thus, Yeats's ancestral line doubled back upon itself in a sense. In the Sligo area he became acquainted with Yeats descendants of the Drumcliff rector, and in memory and imagination the west-Irish valley between the mountains Ben Bulben and Knocknarea was always his spiritual home.

Yeats's formal education was irregular, at best. His earliest training was in London at the hand of his father, who read to him from English authors such as Sir Walter Scott and William Shakespeare. He did not distinguish himself at his first school in London or at Erasmus High School when the family returned to Dublin in 1880. Declining to matriculate at Trinity in the tradition of his forebears, he took up studies instead at the Metropolitan School of Art, where he met George Russell (later Æ), who was to become a lifelong close acquaintance. Yeats soon found that his interests inclined more toward the verbal arts than toward the visual, however, and by 1885 he had discontinued his studies in painting and had published some poems. At this same relatively early time, he had also become involved in occult interests, being among the founders of the Dublin Hermetic Society.

In 1887, the family returned to London, where Yeats was briefly involved with the famous Madame Blavatsky's Theosophical Society. The years 1889 to 1892 were some of the most important in this crucially formative period of his life. He was active in the many diverse areas of interest that were to shape and color the remainder of his career. In rapid succession he became a founding member of the Rhymers Club (a young group of Pateresque *fin de siècle* aesthetes) and of the Irish Literary Society of London and the Irish Literary Society of Dublin (both devoted to reviving interest in native Irish

writers and writing). He also joined the newly established Hermetic Order of the Golden Dawn, a Rosicrucian secret society in which he became an active leader for a number of years and of which he remained a member for more than two decades. In 1889 Yeats published *The Wanderings of Oisin and Other Poems* and became coeditor of an edition of William Blake's work, an experience that was to influence greatly much of his subsequent thought and writing. No event in this period, however, had a more dramatic and permanent effect upon the rest of his life than his introduction in the same year to Maud Gonne, that "great beauty" of Ireland with whom Yeats fell immediately and hopelessly in love. The love was largely unrequited, although Maud allowed the one-sided relationship to continue for a painfully long time throughout much of the poet's early adult life—in fact, even after her marriage and widowhood.

From this point on, Yeats's life was a whirlwind of literary, nationalistic, and occult activity. In 1896, he met Lady Augusta Gregory and John Synge, with both of whom he was later to be associated in the leadership of the Abbey Theatre, as well as in investigation of the folklore and ethos of west-Irish peasants. The purpose of the Abbey Theatre, as far as these three were concerned, was to produce plays that combined Irish interests with artistic literary merit. The acquaintance with Lady Gregory also initiated a long series of summer visits at her estate in Coole Park, Galway, where his aristocratic inclinations, as well as his frequently frail physical being, were nurtured. During parts of 1895 and 1896, Yeats shared lodgings in London briefly with Arthur Symons, of the Rhymers Club, who, as author of *The Symbolist Movement in Literature* (1899), helped to acquaint him further with the French symbolist mode. Actually, however, through his intimate relationships with Hermetic lore and the English Romantics—especially Blake and Percy Bysshe Shelley—Yeats was already writing poetry in a manner much like that of his continental contemporaries. Later in 1896, Yeats moved in to 18 Woburn Buildings, Dublin, which came to be his permanent residence, except for rather frequent travels abroad, for an extended period.

At about the turn of the century and just after, Yeats abandoned his Pre-Raphaelite aestheticism and adopted a more "manful" style. Not wholly unrelated to this was his more outgoing involvement in the daily affairs of the nationalist theater movement. The fact should be remembered—for it is easy to forget—that at this time Yeats was in his late thirties, already moving into a somewhat premature middle age. In 1909 he met Ezra Pound, the only other major figure in the modernist movement with whom he was ever to develop an acquaintance to the point of literary interaction and influence. The relationship reached its apex in the years from 1912 to 1915, during which Pound criticized Yeats's romantic tendencies and, perhaps more important, encouraged the older poet's interest in the highly stylized and ritualistic Nō drama of Japan.

In the same years, another important aspect of Yeats's life and interests had been developing in new directions as well. Beginning about 1908-1909, his esoteric pursuits shifted from active involvement in the Order of the Golden Dawn to investigations in spiritism, séances, and "psychical research." This preoccupation continued until 1915 or 1916, at which point some biographers seem to indicate that it ended. Yet, in one sense, spiritism as an obsessive concern simply redoubled itself about this time upon the occasion of Yeats's late-life marriage, for his wife turned out to be the "mystic" *par excellence*, through whose mediumship came the ultimate flowering of his lifelong prepossession with occult aspects of human—and superhuman—experience.

After Maud Gonne MacBride's husband was executed for his participation in Dublin's 1916 Easter uprising, Yeats visited Maud in Paris and proposed to her, only to be rejected as upon previous occasions years before. He then became attracted to her daughter Iseult and proposed to her in turn. Once again rejected, he decided to marry an English woman whom he had known in occult circles for some years and who was a close friend of mutual acquaintances—Georgie Hyde-Less. On their honeymoon in 1917, Georgie began to experience the first of what came to be a voluminous and almost literally fantastic collection of "automatic writings," the basis of Yeats's famous mystic system, as elaborated in his book *A Vision*.

The various honors that Yeats received in the 1920's and 1930's have been outlined already under "Achievements." Ironically, from these same years, not earlier ones, came most of the poems and collections by which his importance as a major modern literary figure is to be measured. Two interrelated experiences were very likely the chief contributors to the newfound vigor, imagery, and stylistic devices characteristic of these late works—his marriage and the completion of his mystic system in *A Vision*. The nature and degree of indebtedness to the latter of these influences, however, has often been both misunderstood and overestimated. The connection can probably never be assessed with complete accuracy, whereas various other possible factors, such as his renewed interest in the writings of John Donne and Jonathan Swift, should not be ignored or minimized.

In 1926 and 1927, Yeats's health became a genuinely serious problem, and at times in the last dozen years of his life, to live seemed to him to be almost more difficult than to die. There can be little question that such prolonged confrontation with that ultimate of all human experiences is responsible for some of the combined profundity, choler, and—paradoxically—wit of his last poems and plays. During this period, winters were usually spent in various Mediterranean locales for climatic reasons. Death eventually came in the south of France in January, 1939. With characteristic doggedness, Yeats continued working to the very end; he wrote his last poem only a week before his death and dictated to his wife some revisions of a late poem and his last play after the onset of his final illness, only two days before he died. Because of transportation difficulties at the beginning of World War II, Yeats was initially buried at Roquebrune, France. His body was exhumed in 1948, however, and transported aboard an Irish corvette for reburial at Drumcliff Churchyard, as he had specified at the end of his valedictory poem, "Under Ben Bulben." As his friend and fellow author Frank O'Connor said upon the occasion, that event brought to its appropriate and symbolic conclusion a life which was itself a work of art long planned.

ANALYSIS

The complexity and fullness of William Butler Yeats's life was more than matched by the complexity and fullness of his imaginative thought. There are few poets writing in English whose works are more difficult to understand or explain. The basic problems lie in the multiplicity and intricacies of Yeats's own preoccupations and poetic techniques, and all too often the reader has been hindered more than helped by the vagaries of criticism and exegesis.

A coincidence of literary history is partly responsible for the latter problem. The culmination and conclusion of Yeats's career coincided with the advent of the "New Criticism." Thus, in the decades following his death, some of his most important poems became exercise pieces for "explication" by commentators whose theories insisted upon a minimum of attention to the author's cultural background, philosophical views, personal interests, or even thematic *intentions* (hence their odd-sounding term "intentional fallacy"). The consequence has been critical chaos. There simply are no generally accepted readings for some of Yeats's major poems. Instead, there have been ingenious exegeses, charges of misapprehension, countercharges, alternative analyses, then the whole cycle starting over again—in short, interpretational warfare.

Fortunately, in more recent years, simultaneously with decline of the New Critical movement, there has been increasing access to Yeats's unpublished materials—letters, diaries, and especially the manuscript drafts of poems and plays—and more scholarly attention has been paid to the relationships between such materials and the probable themes or meanings in the completed works. Even so, critical difficulties of no small magnitude remain because of continuing widespread disagreement among even the most highly regarded authorities about the basic metaphysical vision from which Yeats's poetic utterances spring, variously interpreted as atheism, pagan theism, quasi-Christian theism, Theosophy, sheer aestheticism, Platonic dualism, modern humanist monism, and existentialism.

SHIFTING PHILOSOPHIES

Added to the problems created by such a critical reception are those deriving from Yeats's qualities as an imaginative writer. Probably the most obvious source of difficulty is the highly allusive and subtly symbolic mode in which Yeats so often expressed himself. Clearly another is his lifelong practice of infusing many of his poems and plays with elements of doctrine, belief, or supposed belief from the various occult sources with which he was so thoroughly imbued. Futhermore, as to doctrine or belief, Yeats was constantly either apparently

or actually shifting his ground (more apparently than actually). Two of his better-known poems, for example, are appropriately titled "Vacillation" and "A Dialogue of Self and Soul." In these and numerous others, he develops and sustains a running debate between two sides of an issue or between two sides of his own truth-seeking psyche, often with no clear-cut solution or final stance made unequivocally apparent.

Related to this—but not simply the same—is the fact that Yeats tended to change philosophical or metaphysical views throughout a long career, again either actually or apparently, and, also again, sometimes more apparently than actually. One disquieting and obfuscating consequence of such mental habits is that one poem will sometimes seem flatly to contradict another, or, in some cases even aside from the dialogue poems, one part of a given poem may appear to contradict a different part of the same poem. Adjacent passages in the major piece "The Tower," involving apparent rejection of Plato and Plotinus alongside apparent acceptance of Platonic or Neoplatonic reincarnation and "translunar paradise," constitute a case in point.

To quibble at much length about Yeats's prevailing metaphysical vision is to indulge in delusive sophistry, however, if his more than moderate pronouncements on such matters in prose are taken at anything approaching face value. What emerges from the prose is the virtually unequivocal proposition that—having rejected orthodox Christianity—the poet developed his own theistic "religion." His ontology and cosmology are made from many pieces and parts of that almost unimaginably multiplex body of lore—exoteric and esoteric—sometimes referred to as the *philosophia perennis*: Platonism, Neoplatonism, Hermetic symbolism, spiritual alchemy, Rosicrucianism, and certain elements of cabalism. Moreover, as Yeats stated in several essays, he found still further parallel and supporting materials at almost every turn—in Jakob Boehme, Emanuel Swedenborg, and William Blake; in the folklore of the Irish peasantry; in classical mythology, Irish legends, and the seasonal rituals examined by Sir James Frazer; and in Asian and Oriental religions, among other places. In two different senses Yeats found in all these materials convincing bases for the perpetuation of his obsession with extracting unity from multiplicity. For one thing, all the similarities and parallels in theme and motif from the many diverse sources constituted in themselves a kind of unity within multiplicity. Furthermore, the "philosophies" involved were largely oriented toward oneness—Plato's Idea of the good, alchemy's distillation of the immutable *lapis* from the world of flux, Hermetism's theory of symbolic correspondences (as above, so below), Hinduism's Brahma, and so on.

In both thought and work, however, the unresolved opposites sometimes seem to loom as large as—or even larger than—the union itself. From this context came the so-called doctrine of the mask or anti-self (though not actually wholly original with Yeats). From that in turn, or alongside it, came the concept of the daimon, "guardian genius," or minor deity for each human being, a concept fundamental to a number of the traditional sources already cited. The greatest of all possible unions, of course, was the ultimate one of man with God, natural with supernatural, or temporal with eternal. Because of the *scintilla* principle, however, also inherent in parts of the tradition (the universe's permeation with tiny fragments of the godhead), the union of man and daimon became virtually equivalent to the ultimate divine union. This concept helps to explain a handful of otherwise misleading passages where Yeats occasionally seemed to be rejecting his usually dominant dualism for a momentary monism: For example, in "The Tower" man creates everything in the universe from his own soul, and in "Two Songs from a Play" whatever illuminates the darkness is from man's own heart. Such human wholeness and power, however, are not possible, Yeats would probably say, without communion with daimon.

In spirit, doctrine, or belief, then, Yeats remained preponderantly a romantic and a nineteenth century spiritualist as he lived on into the increasingly positivistic and empirically oriented twentieth century. It was in form, not content, that he gradually allowed himself to develop in keeping with his times, although he abjured *vers libre* and never wholly relinquished his attachment to various traditional poetic modes. In the direction of modernism, he adopted or employed at various times irregular rhythms (writing by ear, declaring his ignorance of the technicalities of conventional metrics), approximate rhymes, colloquial diction, some Donnean or "metaphysical" qualities, and, most important of all,

symbolic techniques much like those of the French movement, though not from its influence alone. The inimitable Yeatsian hallmark, however, remained a certain romantic rhetorical quality (despite his own fulminations against rhetoric), what he called passionate syntax, that remarkable gift for just the right turn of phrase to express ecstatic emotional intensity or to describe impassioned heroic action.

To suggest that Yeats consistently achieved great poetry through various combinations of these thematic elements and stylistic devices, however, would be less than forthright. Sometimes doctrinal materials are indeed impediments. Sometimes other aspects of content are unduly personal or sentimental. At times the technical components seem to be ill-chosen or fail to function as might have been expected, individually or conjointly. Thoroughly capable of writing bad poetry, Yeats has by no means been without his detractors. The poems for which he is famous, however—even those which present difficulties of understanding—are masterpieces, alchemical transformations of the raw material of his art.

"THE LAKE ISLE OF INNISFREE"

Probably the most famous of all Yeats's poems, especially from his early period and with popular audiences, is "The Lake Isle of Innisfree." A modern, middle-income Dublin housewife, chosen at random, has said upon mention of Yeats's name: "Oh, yes; I like his 'Lake Isle of Innisfree'; yes, I always did like 'The Lake Isle of Innisfree.'" Such popularity, as well as its representative quality among Yeats's early poems, makes the piece a natural choice for initial consideration here.

On the surface, there seems to be little that is symbolic or difficult about this brief lyric, first published in 1890. The wavering rhythms, syntactical inversions, and colorful but sometimes hazy images are characteristic of much of Yeats's youthful verse. So too are the Romantic tone and setting, and the underlying "escape motif," a thematic element or pattern that pervades much of Yeats's early work, as he himself realized and acknowledged in a letter to a friend.

The island of the title—real, not imaginary—is located in Lough Gill near the Sligo of Yeats's youth. More than once he mentioned in prose a boyish dream of living on the wooded isle much as Henry David Thoreau lived at Walden Pond, seeking wisdom in solitude. In other passages he indicates that while homesick in London he heard the sound of a small fountain in the window of a shop. The experience recalled Lough Gill's lapping waters, he says, and inspired him to write the poem. The most important factor for Yeats's emerging poetic vision, however, was his longstanding fascination with a legend about a supernatural tree that once grew on the island with berries that were food for the Irish fairy folk. Thus in the poet's imaginative thought, if not explicitly in the poem itself, esoteric or occult forces were at play, and in a figurative sense, at least, the escape involved was, in the words of the letter to his friend, "to fairyland," or a place much like it.

One of the most notable sources of praise for "The Lake Isle of Innisfree" was a letter from Robert Louis Stevenson in distant Samoa. Stevenson wrote that only two other passages of literature had ever captivated him as Yeats's poem did. Yeats himself said later that it was the earliest of his non-narrative poems whose rhythms significantly manifested his own music. He ultimately developed negative feelings, however, about his autobiographical sentimentality and about instances of what he came to consider unduly artificial syntax. Yet in late life when he was invited to recite some of his own poems for radio programs, he more than once chose to include "The Lake Isle of Innisfree." Evidently he wished to offer to that audience what he felt it probably wanted to hear. Evidently he realized that the average Irish housewife or ordinary working man, then as later, would say in response to the name Yeats: "Oh, yes, I like his 'Lake Isle of Innisfree.'"

"LEDA AND THE SWAN"

Technically, "Leda and the Swan" (1923) is a sonnet, one of only a few that Yeats ever composed. The spaces between quatrains in the octave and between the octave and the sestet—not to mention the break in line eleven—are evidently Yeats's innovations, characteristic of his inclination toward experimentation within traditional frameworks in the period of the poem's composition. The story from Greek mythology upon which the poem is based is well-known and much treated in the Western tradition. In the tale from antiquity, a Spartan queen, Leda, was so beautiful that Zeus, ruler of the gods, decided that he must have her. Since the immortals usually did not present themselves to humankind in their divine forms, Zeus changed himself into a great swan and in that shape ravished the helpless girl. The story has often been portrayed pictorially as well as verbally; Yeats himself possessed a copy of a copy of Michelangelo's lost painting on the subject. There has been considerable critical discussion of the degree of interrelationship between the picture or other graphic depictions and Yeats's poem, but to no very certain conclusion, except that Leda seems much less terrified in Michelangelo's visual version—where perhaps she might even seem to be somewhat receptive—than in Yeats's verbal one.

The poem has been one of Yeats's most widely praised pieces from the time of early critical commentaries in the first decade after his death. Virtually all commentators dwell upon the power, economy, and impact of the poem's language and imagery, especially in the opening sections, which seem to be concerned predominantly, if not exclusively, with mere depiction of the scene and events themselves. The poem's apparent simplicity, especially by Yeatsian standards, however, is decidedly deceptive. The greatest problem in interpretation is with the sestet's images of Troy in flames and with Agamemnon's death.

To understand the importance of these allusions to Greek history—and the deeper meanings of the poem—the reader must realize that Yeats intended the poem to represent the annunciation of a new era of civilization in his cyclic vision of history, the two-thousand-year-period of pagan polytheism that preceded the present age of Christian monotheism. As emphasized in Giorgio Melchiori's book *The Whole Mystery of Art* (1961), the poet later imaginatively balanced a second poem against "Leda and the Swan": "The Mother of God," in which another woman, Mary, is visited by another deity, the Holy Ghost, in the form of another bird, the divine dove, to initiate another period of history, the Christian era. The conscious intention of such a parallel between the two poems is attested by Yeats's having printed "Leda and the Swan" at the head of the chapter in *A Vision* titled "Dove or Swan," with a sentence on the next page stating explicitly that he thought of the annunciation which began Grecian culture as having been made to Leda. Equally unequivocal evidences are Melchiori's citation of a letter in which Yeats called the poem a classic annunciation, Yeats's note for the poem that speaks of a violent annunciation, and the fact that the poem's first submission to a publisher was under the title "Annunciation."

This last-mentioned fact relates to another point of critical disagreement. In a note, Yeats says that the poem was written in response to a request from the editor of a political review. As he worked, though, the girl and the swan took over the scene, he says, and all politics fell away. Some commentators have accepted or reaffirmed this assertion, failing to realize that Yeats—intentionally or unintentionally—overstated the case. Bird and woman did indeed so dominate the poet's imagination in the first eight lines that one critical consequence has been undue attention to the language and imagery of the surface there. When one recalls, however, that the pre-Christian era in Yeats's system was governmentally monarchical or totalitarian while the present era was imagined (however erroneously) as predominantly democratic, the perception dawns that the affairs of Leda's progeny, especially Helen as a causal factor in the Trojan war and Clytemnestra as a figure involved in its aftermath, constitute, in truth, "politics" enough. Otherwise, the allusions to the burning city and deceased king would be gratuitous deadwood in the poem, unaccountable anomalies, which is just exactly what they remain in those analyses that disregard them or minimize their importance.

Even recognition and acceptance of the themes of annunciation and history do not reveal the poem's full complexity, however, as the average reader himself may well sense upon perusal of the final interrogative sentence. This concluding question seems to constitute a third unit in the piece, as well as the basis of some third level of significance. The traditional octave-sestet relationship of the Italian sonnet created for Yeats a division into two parts with two different but related emphases. It is his unconventional break in line eleven, however, which achieves a tripartite structure at the same time that it introduces the thematic bases for an amalgamating—if not resolving—unity for all three parts of the poem and for all their interrelated levels of symbolic implication.

If the octave can be said to focus predominantly upon the "surface" level of "Leda and the Swan," with the allusions to antiquity adumbrating a historical level, then the final question—a real one rather than the rhetorical sort with which Yeats sometimes concluded poems—can be seen as the introduction of a philosophi-cal or metaphysical level. Given the possibility of such consort or interaction between the human and the divine, what supernatural effects—if any—are consequent for the mortal party? This issue, so relevant to the rest of this poem, is raised not only here or a few times in related pieces like "The Mother of God," but rather over and over again throughout the entirety of Yeats's canon. More than that, it is frequently voiced in those other places in surprisingly similar terms.

SEEKING A TRANSCENDENT UNION

The possibility of union between humankind and God, between natural and supernatural, is probably the most persistent and pervasive theme in all of Yeats's oeuvre. It is the strongest of those threads woven throughout the fabric of his work which create the unity within multiplicity previously considered. It was also unquestionably the motivating factor in his relentlessly moving from one occult preoccupation to the other. Moreover, the conviction that artistic inspiration was one of the more readily observable manifestations of such divine visitation upon the human sensibility was what made Yeats philosophically a confessed Romantic for life, regardless of what modernist elements of style or technique he may have allowed to emerge in the poetry of his later years.

A major emblem for such miraculous converse, elsewhere in Yeats just as in "Leda and the Swan," is sexual union. In several prose passages, for example, he draws explicit parallels between human interaction with the daimon or semidivine guardian spirit and a man's relationship with his sweetheart or lover. In another place, he conjectures that the "mystic way" and physical love are comparable, which is not surprising in light of the fact that most of his occult sources employed the same analogy and frequently spoke of the moment of union—mortal with immortal—as the "mystic marriage." Yeats's utilization of this particular sexual symbology is apparent in pieces such as "Solomon and the Witch," "A Last Confession," "Chosen," and *The Player Queen*, among others. Equally relevant is the fact that Yeats repeatedly used birds as symbols of discarnate spirits or deities. Finally, the two motifs—sexual union as an analogue for supernatural union and avian symbolism for the divine—occur together in at least two works by Yeats other than "Leda and the Swan": the plays *At the*

Hawk's Well (1916) and *The Herne's Egg* (1938), in the latter of which copulation between a woman and a great white bird is similarly fundamental to the piece's philosophical implications.

In Yeats's imaginative thought, such moments of transcendent union leave behind in the physical world some vestige of the divine condescension—the art object's "immortality" in the case of inspiration, for example. In more portentous instances, however, such as those imaged in "Leda and the Swan" and "The Mother of God"—with clear metaphorical interplay between the phenomena of creation and procreation, even if not voiced in so many words—the remnant is the conception of some demigod or incarnate divinity such as Helen or Christ, whose beauty, perfection, or power is so great that its presence on earth inaugurates a whole new cultural dispensation.

What one ultimately finds in "Leda and the Swan," then, is Yeats hammering out, in the midst of manifold antinomy, two kinds of unity at a single stroke. The three somewhat separate parts of the poem are joined in unity with one another, and, simultaneously, the poem as a unified whole is united to some of the most important themes that recur throughout his canon. This unity within multiplicity is achieved through Yeats's ingeniously imaginative manipulation of a single famous myth chosen from many that involve—either or both—godhead manifested in avian form and divine visitation upon humankind cast in the image of sexual conjugation.

"THE SECOND COMING"

Almost as synonymous with Yeats's name as "The Lake Isle of Innisfree" is the unusual and foreboding poem "The Second Coming," which was composed in January, 1919, and first published in 1920. It is one of Yeats's few unrhymed poems, written in very irregular blank verse whose rhythms perhaps contribute to the ominous effect created by the diction and imagery. The piece has had a strange critical reception, deriving in part from the paradox that it is one of Yeats's works most directly related to the system of history in *A Vision*, but at the same time appears to offer reasonably accessible meanings of a significant kind to the average reader of poetry in English.

The more obvious "meanings," generally agreed upon, are implications of disorder, especially in the first section where the falcon has lost touch with the falconer, and impressions of horror, especially in the second section with its vision of the pitiless rough beast slouching through the desert. In light of the date of composition, the validity of such thematic elements for both Yeats and his audience is immediately evident. World War I had just ended, leaving the Western world in that continuing mood of despondency voiced also in T. S. Eliot's *The Waste Land* (1922) (which shares with Yeats's poem the desert image) and in Gertrude Stein's—and Ernest Hemingway's—epithet of "a lost generation." In other words, despite the author's considerable further concerns, the piece on this level "caught a wave," as it were, so that it quickly came to be regarded by commentators and the author alike as prophetic—an attitude enhanced, of course, by the richly allusive title.

HISTORY AS SPIRAL

On a deeper level, "The Second Coming" is directly related to the cyclical conception of history which Yeats delineated in *A Vision*. As seen in the discussion of "Leda and the Swan," Yeats envisioned history in terms of two-thousand-year eras, each of which was ushered in by a portentous annunciation of some sort. If Zeus's descent upon Leda initiated the period from about 2000 B.C.E. to the year zero, and if the Holy Ghost's descent to Mary initiated the subsequent period from the year zero to approximately 2000 C.E., then in 1919 the poet could speculate that the next such annunciation might occur either just barely within his lifetime or else not very long thereafter. These two-thousand-year periods of culture were characterized, like so many other things in Yeats's imaginative thought, by opposition to each other, with the main oppositions in *A Vision* designated as *antithetical* (or "subjective") and *primary* (or "objective"). These labels, or *tinctures* as Yeats called them, are not always easy to define, but from reading his book one begins to sense their nature. In general, the *antithetical* is individualistic (self-centered), heroic, aristocratic, emotional, and aesthetic. It is concerned predominantly with inner being and is symbolized by a full moon. The *primary*, by contrast, is anti-individualistic (mass-oriented), saintly or sagelike, democratic, rational, and moral. It is associated mainly with external existence and is symbolized by either the sun or the dark of the moon. Yeats identified himself with the *antithetical* and associated many things that he disliked (such as democracy and "fact-finding" science) with the *primary*. Thus he favored the polytheistic era of Homeric and classical Greece (*antithetical*), whereas he rejected or spurned the moral and anti-individualistic monotheism (*primary*) which began with the birth of Christ.

Borrowing from Swedenborg and other esoteric sources, Yeats conceptualized the growth of these historical movements in terms of gyres or spirals, a feature of the system rather difficult to discuss without reference to diagrams. (One may see *A Vision* for diagrams in great sufficiency.) For the sake of convenience in depiction, the spirals (widening from vertex in larger and larger circles) are imaged as the outer "shells" surrounding them—that is, as cones. Furthermore, for purposes of two-dimensional representation on a book's page, each cone is usually regarded simply in terms of its profile—that is, as a triangle. However, since the entire system of *A Vision* is based on the proposition that the universe consists of numberless pairs of antinomies or contraries, no cone or triangle exists in isolation; instead, everyone is in locked interpenetration with an opposing cone or triangle, each with its vertex or narrowest point at the center of the other's widest expansion or base. Thus, Yeats conceived of the present two-thousand-year era not simply as one set of interlocked cones, but rather as *two* sets of one thousand years each, as is made quite explicit in the chapter that reviews history under the title "Dove or Swan." Thus, instead of the Christian gyre or cone sweeping outward toward its widest expansion at the year 2000 C.E., as most commentators seem to have assumed, the widest expansion of the triangle representing that *primary* religious dispensation occurred at about the year 1000 C.E., completely in keeping with the medieval Church's domination of virtually all aspects of life at that time. For the period following 1000 C.E., that religion's *declining* movement is represented by a *contracting* gyre, its base set against the base of its predecessor, forming, in two-dimensional terms, a figure that Yeats speaks of as shaped like an ace of diamonds. The Christian dispensation, then, is at the present time dwindling to its cone's or triangle's narrowest point, at the center of the opposing gyre's widest expansion, completely in keeping with the post-Darwinian upheaval in Victorian England about

science's undermining the foundations of the Church, subsequent notions of the "death of God," and so on.

What, then, *is* spiraling outward to its widest expansion in the twentieth century, the falcon's gyring flight having swept so far from the falconer that "the centre cannot hold"? The answer to this question lies in recognition of a point that appears rather clearly at various places in *A Vision*. In Yeats's system of history, every cone representing a *religious* dispensation has as its interlocking counterpart a cone that represents the *secular* culture of the same period. Thus, the two movements, religious and secular, live each other's death and die each other's life, to use an expression from Heraclitus that Yeats repeated time and again, in creative pieces as well as in his discursive prose. The birth of Christ came, then, as Yeats indicates with unequivocal clarity, at the time of an *antithetical* secular or political phenomenon at the very height of its development, at the widest expansion of its cone—the Roman Empire. As the gyre representing the *primary* Christian religious movement revolved outward toward its widest expansion in the Middle Ages, the power of the Roman Empire gradually declined until it vanished at about 1000 C.E. (Yeats uses the year 1050 in "Dove or Swan"). Then *both* movements reversed directions, with *primary* Christianity beginning to dwindle at the same time that a new secular life of *antithetical* nature started and gyred outward up to the present day. This—the widest expansion of an *antithetical* secular or political gyre in the twentieth century—is almost certainly what Yeats identified with Fascism, not the new annunciation to come. Such a collapsing and reexpansion of the *antithetical* spirals in the two-thousand-year period since the birth of Christ—two one-thousand-year cones tip to tip—created what Yeats called an hourglass figure superimposed upon (or, more accurately, interlocked with) the diamond shape of Christianity's *primary* religious dispensation.

TINCTURES: PRIMARY VS. ANTITHETICAL

The crucial point in interpreting "The Second Coming" is that the annunciation of every new religious dispensation involves what Yeats calls an *interchange of the tinctures*. In other words, at 2000 B.C.E., at the year zero, and at 2000 C.E., religion changes from *primary* to *antithetical* in quality, or vice versa, while secular life and politics change *tinctures* just oppositely. (Yeats was explicit about identification of the secular with politics.) No such interchange occurs, however, at the initiation of new secular gyres, as at 1000 B.C.E. or 1000 C.E. At those points the expanding or collapsing gyres of both aspects of life—religious and secular—simply reverse directions without their *tinctures* changing from *primary* to *antithetical* or the other way around. The importance of this feature of the system for meanings in "The Second Coming" can hardly be overstated. The interchange is sudden and cataclysmic, causing such strife in human history as the Trojan War soon after the annunciation to Leda from Zeus or the widespread battles of the Roman Empire soon after the annunciation from the Holy Ghost to the Virgin Mary. The abrupt change near the end of the twentieth century, of the *antithetical tincture* from secular life's widely expanded cone to religion's extremely narrowed one (and, vice versa, of the *primary tincture* almost instantaneously from the nearly extinguished religious gyre to the widest expansion of the counterpoised secular or political gyre), could in and of itself be catastrophic enough to warrant most of the portentous imagery and diction in Yeats's poem. Fearful concerns even more specifically related to the system than that, however, were involved in the piece's genesis and evolution. The annunciation of a new religious dispensation, *antithetical* in nature, would not have been anticipated by Yeats with foreboding, for he simultaneously favored the *antithetical tincture* and held in low regard the existing *primary* religious movement which was to be displaced. The only disappointing thing for Yeats about the forthcoming *antithetical* religion was that it would have no more than its merest beginnings within his lifetime or shortly thereafter, reaching its fullest expansion as a historical gyre not until the year 3000 C.E. The sudden imposition upon the world of a *primary* political system, on the other hand, at its widest expansion from the very outset, was quite another matter.

What might constitute such an ultra-*primary* or super-"democratic" political phenomenon for the aristocratic-minded Yeats as he looked about the European world in 1919? Other than the last stages of World War I, one particular violent upheaval had just occurred: the Bolshevik Revolution. Communism was for Yeats the horrifying rough beast slouching through the postwar wasteland to be born, its politically *primary* hour come round exactly as predicted by the gyres and cycles of history available to him from the "automatic scripts" which his wife had begun to write out more than a year before the poem's composition.

While this interpretational conclusion can be reached through a careful reading of *A Vision*'s sections on history, its validity has been made virtually unequivocal by Jon Stallworthy's publication of the poem's manuscript drafts (originally in his book *Between the Lines: Yeats's Poetry in the Making*, 1963, and again with fuller transcription of some partially illegible passages in the journal *Agenda*, 1971/1972). Along with several other convincing clues in these drafts occurs one line that leaves little to the imagination: "The Germany of Marx has led to Russian Com." Working with these same unpublished drafts as well as other materials, Donald Torchiana has made a persuasive case for the proposition that what upset Yeats most of all was the possibility that Ireland's civil strife in this same period made his country a highly vulnerable tinderbox for the spread of Marxist factions or Communistic forces (*W. B. Yeats and Georgian Ireland*, 1966). A letter by Yeats written later in 1919 makes this thesis virtually incontrovertible. In it the poet states that his main concern was for Ireland to be saved from Marxist values, because he felt that their fundamental materialism could only lead to murder. Then he quotes a catch-phrase that seems to echo lines from "The Second Coming": "Can the bourgeois be innocent?"

The manuscripts reveal much else as well. They show, for example, that from its earliest inception— a brief prose draft of the opening portion—"The Second Coming" was a decidedly political poem, not one concerned with some *antithetical* religious annunciation. Even the highly effective—though intentionally ironical—religious allusions to Bethlehem and Christ's return emerged relatively late in the poem's development. Moreover, the politics of concern are plainly of the *primary tincture*; the word "mob" appears repeatedly. When the expression "surely" occurred for the first time, it was followed by "the great falcon must come." Yeats, however, having said in a much-quoted passage elsewhere that he often used large noble birds to represent the subjective or *antithetical* and beasts that run upon the ground to symbolize the objective or *primary*, realized his momentary drift toward depiction of the birth of an *antithetical* religious entity and struck the line. Then later came the famous beast, with its blank solar (*primary*) gaze.

Although it might shock some readers to think that Yeats would identify Christ with a beast, and with a political ideology such as Marxism, the point that should not be overlooked is that while Christ may be alternately sacred or secular in Yeats's imaginative thought, he is always unalterably *primary*. *A Vision* is quite explicit in several places about Christ's being *primary*. The poem is therefore, about his second coming, although in a frighteningly unfamiliar secular guise: a mass-oriented and anti-individualistic political materialism that paradoxically corresponds to but simultaneously contravenes his previous mass-oriented and anti-individualistic spiritual teachings. After twenty centuries of religious equality urged by Christ the Lamb, a cataclysmic and leveling social anarchy is about to be loosed upon the world by Christ the Lion.

"AMONG SCHOOL CHILDREN"

Composed in 1926 and published in 1927, "Among School Children" is another of Yeats's most widely acclaimed and extensively studied poems. The two most "famous" interpretative readings are by Cleanth Brooks in *The Well Wrought Urn: Studies in the Structure of Poetry* (1947) and John Wain in *Interpretations: Essays on Twelve English Poems* (1955). Although both essays are almost belligerently "New Critical," each sees as the overall theme the relationships between natural and supernatural, or between matter and spirit, and the ravages wrought upon humankind by the passage of time. Most other analyses tend to accept this same general meaning for the poem as a whole, although almost inevitably there have been some who see the subject as the triumph of art, or something of that sort. With this poem, the problems and difficulties of interpretation have been not so much with larger suggestions of significance as with individual lines or passages in their relationships— or supposed relationships—to the poem's broadest meanings. Such tendencies toward agreement about the piece's general thematic implications are fortunate since they are in keeping with Yeats's own comments in notes and letters: that physical or temporal existence will waste the youthful students and that the poem is one of his not infrequent condemnations of old age.

The inspirational matrix for the poem was literal enough—a visit by Yeats in his role as senator in the newly established Irish Free State to a quite progressive school administered by a Catholic convent. Given this information, the reader will have no problems with stanza I. (Any analysis, incidentally, which suggests that Yeats felt that the children depicted were being taught the wrong kinds of things is open to question, for Yeats subsequently spoke to the Senate about the convent school in highly laudatory terms.) The next three stanzas, however, although they are generally thought to be less problematical than the last part of the poem, are somewhat more opaque than the casual-toned and low-keyed opening. In stanza II, the sight of the schoolchildren suddenly brings to the poet-senator's memory (with little transition for the reader) a scene in which a beautiful woman had told him of some childhood chastisement, probably by a schoolteacher. That memory, in turn, evokes for him a vision of what she must have looked like at such an age, perhaps not too much unlike the girls standing before him in the convent's hall.

There can be little doubt that the beautiful woman in question is the one by whom Yeats's aching "heart" was "driven wild" for a large part of his adult life—Maud Gonne. Time and time again throughout his canon, Yeats compares that special woman's almost divine or superhuman beauty to the beauty of Helen of Troy, who, in Greek mythology, was born to Leda after her visitation by Zeus. This information, then, helps to clarify such characteristically allusive terms in stanzas II through IV as "Ledaean body," "daughters of the swan," "every paddler's heritage," "Ledaean kind," and "pretty plumage." The alteration of Plato's parable (in the *Symposium*, probably one of the middle dialogues, where the basis of love is explained as the desire in divinely separated humankind for reunion in a sphere) to union in the white and yellow of a single *egg*, rather than the myth's division, also fits into this pattern of Ledaean imagery, at the same time that it looks forward to images and suggestions of generation or birth in subsequent stanzas.

Then, in stanza IV, with still another shift, the beautiful woman's *present* visage drifts before the poet's eyes. Surprisingly, despite the rather heavily connotative language of lines three and four, along with Yeats's comparison in the second quatrain of his own youth with his present old age (not to mention similar thematic implications in the entire poem), there has been some controversy about line one. The issue is whether Yeats meant to convey a vision of the woman still young and beautiful or, instead, ravaged by time and decrepitude. The word "Quattrocento," denoting fifteenth century Italian art and artists, might be taken to substantiate either side of such a debate, depending upon how it itself is construed; but along with virtually everything else in the stanza, the concluding—and later recurring—scarecrow image would seem to lend support to the suggestion of deterioration and decay.

If lines two through four of stanza V were removed, the stanza would not only be completely intelligible, but it would also be a rather concise statement of one of the poem's two main themes—the effects upon humankind of time's passage. Since lines two through four were included, however, along with other characteristically Yeatsian elements akin to them in subsequent stanzas, the poem's real difficulties begin to manifest themselves in its second half. In a note to the poem, Yeats indicates that the honey of generation is an image that he borrowed from Porphyry's essay "The Cave of the Nymphs," almost certainly with an intended symbolic suggestion, on one level, of the pleasures of sexual union. The same note, however, also indicates explicitly that the recollection mentioned is the soul's memory—à la William Wordsworth's "Ode: Intimations of Immortality"—of a prenatal condition higher and freer than earthly incarnation. At this point, Yeats's occult and esoteric beliefs that so many critics have found difficult to accept enter the poem. Brooks's reaction, for example, is virtual incredulity. To make interpretational matters even worse, Yeats evidently employed the honey image ambiguously to relate also to "the drug," presumably physically procreated or temporal existence, which allows or causes the prenatal memory to fade. Both the note and the draft versions of the poem (reproduced in Thomas Parkinson's *W.B. Yeats: The Later Poetry*, 1964) suggest the likelihood of such intentional or semi-intentional ambiguity. All this, along with what is probably the poem's least felicitous line—"sleep, shriek, struggle . . ."—has led to considerable exegetical dispute about who or what was betrayed—mother or shape? The ambiguity seems less intentional in this particular case, however, and the drafts, along with a certain amount of common sense, tend to indicate the child, a soul entrapped in flesh by the mother's generatively honeyed act.

Stanza VI is perhaps not too difficult once the reader realizes that the final line is, in effect, appositionally related to the main nouns in the other seven lines. In other words, the generally accepted thrust of meaning is that even the greatest and presumably wisest of men come to be, in time, like elderly poet-senators and everyone else, dilapidated old scarecrows. There is, however, a bit more wit and symbolism at work—or at play— in the stanza. For one thing, Yeats has chosen men who were teachers or students or—in two cases—both in turn: Plato, Aristotle, Alexander the Great, and Pythagoras. Furthermore, three of these four men spent their lives contemplating and theorizing about the same crucial and fundamental aspects of human experience which are the subjects of the poem—the relationships between spirit and matter and between being and becoming.

The second half of stanza VII is the most problematical unit in the poem. The first quatrain, however, gives little trouble. With a pun on the word "images," Yeats refers both to pictures in the maternal mind's eye and to religious icons or statuary. The "Presences" of line five are what create interpretational difficulties, again because here Yeats's occult views become involved, views which too few exegetes have been willing to address even as accepted by the poet himself. Yeats's use of a capital *P* and the expression "self-born" (compare "self-sown," "self-begotten," and "miracle-bred" on the very next page of *The Collected Poems of W.B. Yeats*) should be clues that some kind of divinity is being apostrophized in this stanza about worship. That, in turn, can lead to recognition of a third level of meaning for the punword "images." The mask, the antiself, and especially the daimon (not synonymous terms, but kindred ones in Yeats's esoteric thought and vocabulary) were sometimes referred to as the image, for they are, like a mirror image, simultaneously like and yet exactly opposite to the human individual. Furthermore, with the daimon, that special semidivine guiding or misguiding spirit, each man or woman is involved in an exasperating attraction-repulsion relationship which explains the poet's emphasis upon heartbreak and mockery. Fleetingly known—in actuality or by analogy—through such heightened experiences as the earlier stanzas' sexual love (passion), religious love (piety), or maternal love (affection), these hatefully loving guardian geniuses draw man onward from the flesh toward spiritual glory at the same time that they do all they can to frustrate every inch of his progress or enterprise along the way.

The first half of the closing stanza would be much more readily comprehensible if Yeats had retained his draft's version of the opening line, which began with the word "all" instead of "labor." That would have agreed with a draft line relating to the dancer, "all so smoothly runs," and would justify the status *usually* attributed to the concluding quatrain: perhaps the most successful of Yeats's famous passages whose antinomy-resolving symbols or images lift poet, poem, and reader above the strife of physical existence to a condition of triumphant affirmation or realm of artistically perfected unity. Dance and dancer are indivisibly—almost divinely—one. The tree—and the poem—are supremely organic wholes, greater than the sums of their parts. This seems to be Romantic lyricism at its transcendent best.

Such a conclusion, however, is too hasty. When its initial word was "all," the first quatrain of the final stanza rather plainly meant something like, "Life in this world is best when and where humankind achieves a balance between body and soul, between spirit and flesh." Yeats's eventual substitution of the word "labor," however, could well have been intended to add, among other things, the idea that such a balance is never easily come by nor readily sustained in this life. That would echo in one sense the feminine persona in "Adam's Curse," who says that women have to labor to become beautiful, as well as her interlocutor's rejoinder that subsequent to Adam's fall nothing very fine can be achieved or created without a great deal of labor. How, then, did the poet move so suddenly from the broken hearts and mockery of stanza VII to some rhapsodically evoked unity or triumph in the last four lines of stanza VIII? Perhaps the poem was never meant to suggest such a leap. There is, after all, no journey in this poem from one realm to another, as there is in "Sailing to Byzantium." The tree and the dancer are still very much in the sensuous physical realm. Perhaps the supposed transition has been only through some strange magic as unsavory to common sense as Yeats's occult inclinations were to the critics who have perpe-

trated this illusory transmutation. Perhaps, ironically, the un-Romantic critics have made Yeats much more Romantic in this particular poem than he ever *intended* to be. In all fairness, the point must be acknowledged, however, that Brooks and Wain themselves read the final stanza in much more neutral or negative terms than many of the commentators who have written subsequently. Almost unquestionably the chief influence upon numerous analyses of the final stanza in terms of transcendence and artistic unity has been Frank Kermode's book *Romantic Image* (1957), which takes the passage as a virtual epitome of the opposition-resolving powers of the symbolic mode, as the *image* of the Image.

"Among School Children" has a rather high incidence of puns and intentional ambiguities in addition to the ones already noted. The two most obvious further instances involve the words "labor" and "play," which have been commented upon both separately and together. Perhaps insufficient attention has been given, however, to possibilities of multiple meanings in that salient feature, the title. Yeats, an inveterate reviser, was well capable of changing a title if it no longer best suited the interests of his poem. Why would he have retained the title here if it did not fit the finished piece—the whole work as well as the opening portions? Some continuing concern with the symbolic implications of students and teachers has already been observed in stanza VI. Why would not or could not the same kind of thing be appropriate for that very important portion of the poem, its conclusion? Suppose, in contrast to prevalent interpretations of the last quatrain, that the questions asked there are real questions, such as schoolchildren ask, rather than rhetorical ones implying some transcendence or triumph over the rest of the poem's concerns. Like a staring schoolchild, man might well ask—in fact, for centuries he has asked—where the material world ends and the spiritual world begins, and how, in this temporal realm, he can separate the one from the other. The great rooted blossomer, then, may be more an emblem of the puzzles and problems studied in life's schoolroom than of some artistically achieved solution to them. Is man the newborn infant, the adolescent pupil, the youthful procreator, or the white-haired elder statesman—or none of these or all of these or more than all of these? In the face of such conundrums, all men are "among school children," seeking and inquiring, frequently without finding or being given reassuring answers.

"SAILING TO BYZANTIUM" AND "BYZANTIUM"

No work in Yeats's canon has won more renown or elicited more controversy than the so-called Byzantium poems, "Sailing to Byzantium" (1927) and "Byzantium" (1930). Critical opinion as to which is poetically superior has been almost, if not quite, equally divided. There is almost universal agreement, however, that the earlier and more frequently reprinted piece, "Sailing to Byzantium," is the easier to understand.

Several authorities, in fact, have gone so far as to say that "Sailing to Byzantium" explains itself or needs no extensive clarification; but if such were actually the case, the amount of commentary that it has generated would clearly constitute an anomaly. If nothing else, the general reader ought to have some answer to the almost inevitable question, "Why Byzantium?" Though it does not provide every possible relevant response to such a query, a much-quoted passage from *A Vision* indicates some of the more important reasons why and how Yeats came to let that great Near Eastern city of medieval times represent in his imagination a cultural, artistic, and spiritual ideal. He believes, he says, that one might have found there "some philosophical worker in mosaic" with "the supernatural descending nearer to him than to Plotinus even," that in "early Byzantium" perhaps more than at any other time in history "religious, aesthetic and practical life were one." Artists of all kinds expressed "the vision of a whole people," "the work of many that seemed the work of one" and was the "proclamation of their invisible master."

While there is no question whatever that "Sailing to Byzantium" is a richly symbolic poem, its genesis apparently involved a more or less literal level which, even though it has not been ignored, may not have been stressed in all its particulars as much as might be warranted. Yeats was first exposed to Byzantine art during a Mediterranean tour in 1907 which included Ravenna, where he saw mosaics and a frieze in the Church of San Apollinare Nuovo which is generally regarded as the chief basis of imagery in stanza III of "Sailing to Byzantium." Years later, however, two factors coincided to renew his interest, one of them involving a voyage in

certain respects interestingly akin to that in the poem. In the first half of the 1920's, Yeats had read rather widely about Byzantium in connection with his work on the historical "Dove or Swan" section of *A Vision*. Then in 1924, nearing sixty years of age, he became somewhat ill and suffered high blood pressure and difficulty in breathing. He was advised to stop work and was taken by his wife on another Mediterranean tour, this time seeking out other Byzantine mosaics, and similar craftsmanship that sharply contrasted art with nature, at places such as Monreale and Palermo, Sicily. As at least one commentator has pointed out, Yeats had no great regrets about leaving home at this time because of dissatisfaction with the political situation and depression about his health. The first legible words in the drafts of "Sailing to Byzantium" are "Farewell friends," and subsequent early portions make unequivocal the fact that "That country" in the finished poem is (or at least originally was) Ireland. Thus, the imaginative and poetic voyage of a sick old man leaving one locale for a more desirable one very probably had at least some of its antecedents in a rather similar actual journey a few years earlier.

Two symbolic interpretations of "Sailing to Byzantium" have been predominant by a considerable margin: Either the poem is about the state of the poet's spirit or soul shortly before and after death, or it is about the creative process and artistic achievement. A choice between the two might be said to pivot upon response to the question, "How ideal is the ideal?" In other words, does Byzantium represent this-worldly perfection on the aesthetic level or perfection of an even greater kind in a transcendent realm of existence? A not insignificant amount of the massive critical commentary on the poem (as well as on its sequel "Byzantium") has been in the way of a war of words about the "proper" reply to such a question, with surprisingly inflexible positions being taken by some of the combatants. Fortunately, however, a number of authorities have realized that there is no reason at all why both levels of meaning cannot obtain simultaneously and that, as a matter of fact, the poem becomes much more characteristically Yeatsian in its symbolic complexity and wealth of import if such a reading is accepted.

RETURN TO PHYSICALITY, SEXUALITY

About 1926 or 1927 and thereafter, an apparent major change—with emphasis upon apparent—seems to have taken place in Yeats's attitude toward life. On the surface, "Sailing to Byzantium" may look and sound like the culmination of a long line of "escape" poems, while many poems or passages written after it (for example, "A Dialogue of Self and Soul") seem to stress instead a plunge into the physicality of this world, even a celebration of earthly existence. Even though Yeats continued to write poems very much concerned with transcendence, supernaturalism, and otherworldliness, he developed in his late career a "new" kind of poem. These poems were often short, were frequently presented in series or sequences, and were frequently—but not always—concerned with a particularly physical aspect of worldly existence, sex.

These poems also share other attributes, a number of them related to Yeats's revived interest at the time in the ballad form. One group is titled, for example, *Words for Music Perhaps and Other Poems*, indicating their song-like qualities. In addition to the poems themselves being brief, the lines and stanza patterns are also short, the lines sometimes having as few as two stresses. Diction, syntax, and idiom are—again as in the ballad or folk song—colloquial and uncomplicated. Imagery, too, is earthy, sometimes stark or blunt. At times sound patterns other than rhyme contribute to the songlike effects, and some pieces, although not all, make effective use of the refrain as a device. In these verses Yeats has come a long way from the amorphous Pre-Raphaelitism of his early lyrics. In them, in fact, he achieves some of the most identifiably "modern" effects in his entire canon.

Related to that modernity is the fact that these late-life songs are anything but simple in content and meaning. Their deceptiveness in this regard has led some early critics to label them—especially the scatological ones—as tasteless and crude. More recent and perceptive analysts, however, have found them to be, in the words of one commentator, more nearly eschatological. What Yeats is doing thematically in such pieces, in fact, is by no means new to him. As in "Solomon and the Witch," "Leda and the Swan," and some other earlier pieces, he is using the sexual metaphor to explore some of the metaphysical mysteries of human existence. One significant difference, however, is that now the sexual experience itself sometimes seems to be regarded as something of a mystery in its own right.

CRAZY JANE POEMS

Almost as well-known as Yeats himself is his fictive persona "Crazy Jane," evidently based compositely on two old Irish women from the poet's experience, one early, one late. Like Shakespeare's—and Yeats's—fools, however, Jane is usually "crazy like a fox." In her series of poems, in the "Three Bushes" sequence, and in poems such as "Chosen," "A Last Confession," "Her Anxiety," "Consolation," and "The Wild Old Wicked Man," Yeats considers or deals with sexuality and sexual imagery in some six or seven different, though frequently interrelated, ways. At times, the poet seems to vacillate or contradict himself from one poem to another, a habit that at first makes understanding these pieces rather difficult. After a while, however, the phenomenon can be recognized for what it is: Yeats's characteristic technique of shifting ground or altering angle of vision in order to explore his subject the more completely.

One basic use of the sexual image has already been seen: The union of man and woman is parallel to or representative of the union of natural with supernatural, human with divine, or man with daimon. In some of these poems, however, the union seems to be so overwhelming that it almost ceases to be mere symbol and becomes the thing in itself, as in the last stanza of "Chosen" or in an unpublished poem where even the gyres are laid to rest in the bed of love. On the other hand (and at the other extreme) are poems that suggest that sex just does not accomplish very much at all, as in "The Chambermaid's Second Song" (last in the "Three Bushes" sequence), where after mere physical pleasure man's spirit remains "blind as a worm." A poem of this kind echoes a reported statement by Yeats that the most unfortunate thing about coitus is the continuing "virginity of the soul." In between the two extremes are poems that see sex as little better than a *pis aller*—"Consolation," for example, or "The Wild Old Wicked Man," whose protagonist chooses "the second-best" upon "a woman's breast." Then there are poems that contemplate the pleasures or problems of sexuality in this life in the light of a Swedenborgian intercourse of the angels ("A Last Confession" and "Crazy Jane on the Day of Judgment") or the Hermetic paradigm—as above, so below ("Ribh Denounces Patrick," though this piece is not in the ballad tradition). Still other poems in the collection, instead of comparing bodies in this world with spirits in the other world, use sexual symbolism to ponder the conundrums of the body-soul relationship here on earth, a theme reminiscent of "Among School Children." The Lady's three songs in the "Three Bushes" series fall into this category. Finally, Yeats sometimes uses the transience of sexual experience to parallel the ephemeral nature of all human experience, especially such heightened moments as mystic vision or artistic inspiration. Such an ironic self-consuming quality inherent in the sex act is touched upon in the first stanza of "Crazy Jane and Jack the Journeyman" and in "Her Anxiety," among other places.

"UNDER BEN BULBEN"

As indicated earlier in the biographical section, Yeats continued to work on poems and plays right down to the last day but one before his death. Although "Under Ben Bulben" was not his last poem, it was written quite consciously as a valedictory or testamentary piece in the summer and fall of 1938 when Yeats knew that death was not far away. While such a status for the poem has been widely recognized by authorities from a very early date, surprisingly little has been written about it until relatively recently.

Ben Bulben is the impressive west-Irish headland "under" whose shadow Yeats specified that his body be buried in the churchyard at Drumcliff where his great-grandfather had been rector a century earlier. In draft versions, "Under Ben Bulben" had two previous titles: "His Convictions" and "Creed." Furthermore, the opening lines that read "Swear by" in the finished poem originally read "I believe." Here, then, presumably, if anywhere, one should be able to find Yeats's final views on life and the human condition. Because the poem goes on, however, to indicate quite candid belief in the existence of supernatural spirits and, further still, in reincarnation or transmigration of the soul, modern critics who do not accept such quasireligious views have evidently declined to take the piece very seriously. One apparent consequence has been that they have had little adequate basis for understanding or glossing the epitaph with which the poem concludes.

Ironically, the epitaph has been very often quoted: "Cast a cold eye/ On life, on death./ Horseman, pass by!" Exegetical commentary on these three lines, however, has been almost as rare as that on the larger poem. Explication has been so minimal and inconclusive, in

fact, that as late as 1974 one spokesman, Edward Malins, asserted that determination of the epitaph's meaning and its intended audience "is anybody's guess." In terms of the framing poem's thesis of transmigration, however, along with evidence from other sources, the horseman can be identified as Yeats himself, a cosmic journeyer engaged in a vast round of cyclical deaths and rebirths, as outlined in *A Vision*. A cold eye is cast on both life and death because the point of possible release from the wheel of reincarnation to some ultimate beatific state such as that imaged in "Sailing to Byzantium" is at such great distance that the grave is little more than a way station on the cosmic odyssey. Thus, there is time or place for little more than a passing nod or glance toward either life or death. In the words of a passage from *A Vision* that is virtually a prose counterpart of the epitaph's verse, man's spirit can know nothing more than transitory happiness either between birth and death or between death and rebirth; its goal is to "pass rapidly round its circle" and to "find freedom from that circle."

The means of passing rapidly around *A Vision*'s great wheel is to live each incarnation properly "in phase." Failure in this endeavor can cause rebirth again into the same phase, thus slowing progress toward "freedom" or release. From his youthful days as a disciple of Walter Pater, Yeats had long regarded the living of life itself as an art. With the coming of *A Vision*, teleological impetus was added to this aesthetic conviction. In a note on "Sailing to Byzantium" from a radio script and in several poems, Yeats exclaims that he must "make his soul." In the terms of *A Vision*, then, once he knew the prescribed qualities of his current incarnation or phase on the wheel, he must shape and sculpt his very life until it becomes a concrete manifestation of that phase, a mythopoeic *objet d'art*.

In *Autobiographies*, on the other hand, Yeats states that when great artists were at their most creative the rest was not simply a work of art, but rather the "re-creation of the man through that art." Similarly, in a scrap of verse he said that whenever he remade a poem the real importance of the act was that, in the event, he actually remade himself. Thus emerged the ultimate unity. Yeats's life and his work became two sides of the one coin. The phenomena were mutually interdependent, the processes mutually interactive. As he forged his poems, Yeats also created his self. That created self, a living myth, was in turn the image reflected in his poetry, the center of vision embodied in the verbal constructs of his art.

OTHER MAJOR WORKS

SHORT FICTION: *John Sherman and Dhoya*, 1891, 1969; *The Celtic Twilight*, 1893; *The Secret Rose*, 1897; *The Tables of Law; The Adoration of the Magi*, 1897; *Stories of Red Hanrahan*, 1904; *Mythologies*, 1959.

PLAYS: *The Countess Cathleen*, pb. 1892; *The Land of Heart's Desire*, pr., pb. 1894; *Cathleen ni Houlihan*, pr., pb. 1902; *The Pot of Broth*, pr. 1902 (with Lady Gregory); *The Hour-Glass*, pr. 1903, pr. 1912 (revised); *The King's Threshold*, pr., pb. 1903 (with Lady Gregory); *On Baile's Strand*, pr. 1904; *Deirdre*, pr. 1906 (with Lady Gregory); *The Shadowy Waters*, pr. 1906; *The Unicorn from the Stars*, pr. 1907 (with Lady Gregory); *The Golden Helmet*, pr., pb. 1908; *The Green Helmet*, pr., pb. 1910; *At the Hawk's Well*, pr. 1916; *The Player Queen*, pr. 1919; *The Only Jealousy of Emer*, pb. 1919; *The Dreaming of the Bones*, pb. 1919; *Calvary*, pb. 1921; *Four Plays for Dancers*, pb. 1921 (includes *Calvary, At the Hawk's Well, The Dreaming of the Bones, The Only Jealousy of Emer*); *The Cat and the Moon*, pb. 1924; *The Resurrection*, pb. 1927; *The Words upon the Window-Pane*, pr. 1930; *The Collected Plays of W. B. Yeats*, pb. 1934, 1952; *The King of the Great Clock Tower*, pr., pb. 1934; *A Full Moon in March*, pr. 1934; *The Herne's Egg*, pb. 1938; *Purgatory*, pr. 1938; *The Death of Cuchulain*, pb. 1939; *Variorum Edition of the Plays of W. B. Yeats*, pb. 1966 (Russell K. Alspach, editor).

NONFICTION: *Ideas of Good and Evil*, 1903; *The Cutting of an Agate*, 1912; *Per Amica Silentia Lunae*, 1918; *Essays*, 1924; *A Vision*, 1925, 1937; *Autobiographies*, 1926, 1955; *A Packet for Ezra Pound*, 1929; *Essays, 1931-1936*, 1937; *The Autobiography of William Butler Yeats*, 1938; *On the Boiler*, 1939; *If I Were Four and Twenty*, 1940; *Pages from a Diary Written in Nineteen Hundred and Thirty*, 1944; *The Letters of W. B. Yeats*, 1954; *The Senate Speeches of W. B. Yeats*, 1960 (Donald R. Pearce, editor); *Essays and Introductions*, 1961; *Explorations*, 1962; *Ah, Sweet Dancer: W. B. Yeats, Margot Ruddock—A Correspondence*, 1970 (Roger McHugh, editor); *Uncollected Prose by W. B. Yeats*, 1970, 1976 (2 volumes); *Memoirs*, 1972; *The Collected Letters of W. B. Yeats*: 1986-1997 (3 volumes).

MISCELLANEOUS: *The Collected Works in Verse and Prose of William Butler Yeats*, 1908.

BIBLIOGRAPHY

Brown, Terence. *The Life of W.B. Yeats: A Critical Biography*. Malden, Mass.: Blackwell, 1999. Brown's book is very much a critical biography, attending more to Yeats's art than to his life with relatively little frolicking around in the poet's boudoir. Still, Brown conveys the texture of Yeats's life, selecting just the right details from what is now a copious historical record.

Ellmann, Richard. *Yeats: The Man and the Masks*. New York: Macmillan, 1948. Reprint. New York: W. W. Norton, 1978. Written by one of the most important literary biographers of the twentieth century, this study retains its appeal. Detailed, informative, and quite accessible, it presents comprehensive explanations of the life and writings. The index is thorough.

Henn, T. R. *The Lonely Tower: Studies in the Poetry of W. B. Yeats*. Rev. ed. London: Methuen, 1965. This study examines Yeats's writings in terms of certain recurrent themes. It provides an excellent account of the background of Yeats's ideas, showing how occultism, folklore, philosophy, and history interact throughout the work. Contains a complete bibliography.

Hough, Graham. *The Last Romantics*. London: Duckworth, 1947. Reprint. London: Methuen, 1961. New York: Barnes & Noble Books, 1961. Although much of this book is not directly about Yeats, it is indispensable for the study of his work in two ways. It is the most complete account of his intellectual context that has yet been done. The chapters on Yeats remain unsurpassed as a sensitive and sympathetic introduction to his poetry. Documented and indexed, but lacks a bibliography.

Jeffares, A. N. *W. B. Yeats, Man and Poet*. New York: Humanities Press, 1971. This small introduction by one of the foremost Yeats scholars and biographers offers a concise survey of his life and provides a basic commentary on the major poems. Includes an appendix, suggestions for further reading, and a bibliography.

Malins, Edward. *A Preface to Yeats*. New York: Charles Scribner's Sons, 1974. Malins includes everything a good introduction should have: a chronology, a summary of the biography, and insightful comments on the writings. Supplemented by an index and suggestions for further study.

O'Donnell, William H. *The Poetry of W. B. Yeats: An Introduction*. New York: Frederick Ungar, 1986. This attractive introduction is particularly informative in covering historical and cultural background. It summarizes the life and provides entries to reading the major poems; other writings, however, are not covered. The bibliography and index are reliable.

Raine, Kathleen. *W.B. Yeats and the Learning of the Imagination*. Ipswich, Mass.: Golgonooza Press, 1999. Raine argues that by his "learning of the Imagination" Yeats was not only a great poet but also a great imaginative mind. His work marks a cultural watershed in that whereas English poetry up to and including Eliot drew upon European civilisation, Yeats additionally drew upon world culture: Irish mythology, Arabic, Japanese, Indian wisdom and much besides.

Unterecker, John. *A Reader's Guide to William Butler Yeats*. New York: Farrar, Straus & Giroux, 1971. Unterecker's approach makes this handbook especially useful for beginning readers. He summarizes the major themes in an introductory section, then proceeds to present comments on selected poems. Complemented by a separate index, suggestions for further readings, and a chronology.

James Lovic Allen;
bibliography updated by the editors

YEVGENY YEVTUSHENKO

Born: Stantsiya Zima, U.S.S.R.; July 18, 1933

PRINCIPAL POETRY
Razvedchicki gryadushchego, 1952
Tretii sneg, 1955

Stantsiya Zima, 1956 (*Zima Junction*, 1962)
Shossye entuziastov, 1956
Obeshchaniy, 1957
Luk i lira, 1959
Stikhi raznykh let, 1959
Yabloko, 1960
Vzmakh ruki, 1962
Selected Poetry, 1963
Nezhnost, 1962
Bratskaya GES, 1965 (*Bratsk Station and Other New Poems*, 1966)
The Poetry of Yevgeny Yevtushenko, 1953-1965, 1965
Kachka, 1966
Yevtushenko: Poems, 1966
Poems Chosen by the Author, 1967
Idut belye snegi, 1969
Stolen Apples, 1971
Doroga Nomer Odin, 1972
Poyushchaya dambra, 1972
Otsovskiy slukh, 1975
From Desire to Desire, 1976
Ivanovskiye sitsi, 1976
V Polniy Rost, 1977
Golub' v Sant'iago, 1978 (novel in verse; *A Dove in Santiago*, 1983)
Tyazholive zemli, 1978
The Face Behind the Face, 1979
Ivan the Terrible and Ivan the Fool, 1979
Invisible Threads, 1981 (poems and photographs)
Ty na planete ne odin, 1981
The Poetry of Yevgeny Yevtushenko, 1981
Grazhdane, poslushaite menia, 1989
Early Poems, 1989
Stikhotvoreniya i poemy, 1990
The Collected Poems, 1952-1990, 1991
Pre-Morning: A New Book of Poetry in English and Russian, 1995

OTHER LITERARY FORMS
Yevgeny Yevtushenko's works in prose include *A Precocious Autobiography* (1963), first published in the Paris periodical *L'Express*; *Talant est' chudo nesluchainoie: Kniga statei* (1980; talent is not an accidental wonder), a collection of essays that are mainly on poetry, but

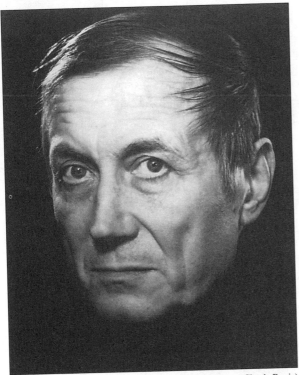

Yevgeny Yevtushenko (Jean-Claude Bouis)

also on music, film, and prose; *Yagodniye mesta* (1981; *Wild Berries*, 1984), a novel; and *Pod kozhey statuey sbobody* (1972; under the skin of the Statue of Liberty), a poetic drama.

ACHIEVEMENTS

Yevgeny Yevtushenko's appeal to a popular audience began with his first verses, which appeared in a sports magazine, *Sovjetskiy sport*, in 1949. His early publications, full of autobiographical revelations, charmed his audiences by their freshness and sincerity. After Joseph Stalin's death in 1953, Yevtushenko began to address deeper social and political issues and became known as a dissident voice in Soviet literature. During the period of liberalization under Nikita Krushchev in the late 1950's and early 1960's, Yevtushenko's personal and political poetry appeared in numerous Soviet journals and newspapers, including Sovjetskiy sport, *Yunost*, where he was on the editorial board, *Komsomolskaya pravda*, *Molodaya gvardiya*, *Literaturnaya gazeta*, *Pravda*, *Znamya*, *Ogonyok*, *Rossiya*, *Novy mir*, and *Oktyabr*. When *Stikhi raznykh let* (poems of various

years) appeared in 1959, twenty thousand copies were sold immediately. The 1962 collection *Vzmakh ruki* (a wave of the hand) enjoyed a sale of one hundred thousand copies.

Not all Yevtushenko's poetry, however, was so widely appreciated. When the controversial "Babii Yar" was published in *Literaturnaya gazeta* in 1961, many hostile articles appeared in the Soviet press, such as that of D. Starikov in *Literatura i zhizn*. It was during this same period that Yevtushenko wrote the script for Dmitri Shostakovich's controversial *Thirteenth Symphony* (1962), a work that uses the Babii Yar incident as its principal motif. Shortly thereafter, Yevtushenko began to travel abroad, to France, England, and the United States during the 1960's. This exposure made him one of the most popular Soviet poets. Articles about him as well as his poems appeared in *Paris-Match*, *London Observer*, *Der Spiegel*, *Time*, *Saturday Review*, *Holiday*, *Life*, *Harper's Magazine*, and many others. Known as a dynamic reciter of poetry, Yevtushenko has given many poetry readings both in the Soviet Union and abroad in a vibrant, declamatory style. He claims to have given 250 in 1961 alone.

Yevtushenko has been recognized throughout his career for both his literary and political achievements. He was given the U.S.S.R. Commission for the Defense of Peace award in 1965, the U.S.S.R. state prize in 1984, an Order of Red Banner of Labor, and his novel *Wild Berries* was a finalist for the Ritz Paris Hemingway award for best novel published in English in 1985. He has traveled widely and incorporated his observations and reactions into poetry, photography (*Invisible Threads*, 1981), film, drama, essays, and fiction.

BIOGRAPHY

Yevgeny Alexandrovich Yevtushenko was born in Stantsiya Zima, Siberia, in the Soviet Union, on July 18, 1933, of mixed Ukrainian, Russian, and Tartar blood. In his famous poem "Stantsia Zima" ("Zima Junction"), he describes in detail this remote Siberian town on the Trans-Siberian Railway about two hundred miles from Irkutsk and not far from Lake Baikal. Both his grandfathers were victims of Stalinist purges, a fact which helps to explain Yevtushenko's attitude toward Stalin. Yevtushenko's father was a geologist, and between the ages of fifteen and seventeen, young "Zhenya," as he was familiarly called, accompanied his father on geological expeditions to Kazakhstan and the Altai. His mother, of modest peasant stock, worked as a singer in Moscow during and after the war.

As a young boy in Moscow, Yevtushenko began to read Russian and foreign classics, familiarizing himself not only with the works of Leo Tolstoy and Anton Chekhov, but also those of Alexander Dumas, Gustave Flaubert, Friedrich Schiller, Honoré de Balzac, Dante, and many other foreign authors. In 1941, he was evacuated to Zima Junction, where he developed his love for the Siberian taiga and his horror of war. When his parents were separated in 1944, he returned to Moscow with his mother. His education from 1944 to 1948 was very desultory, and when he was expelled from school at fifteen, he ran off to join his father in Siberia for two years.

Among Yevtushenko's many interests was sports, and it was not accidental that his first verses were published in a sports magazine. He met the editors Tarasov and Barlas, who became his first mentors, although his continued interest in reading led him to other models, especially Ernest Hemingway, Aleksandr Blok, Sergei Esenin, and Vladimir Mayakovsky. Yevtushenko wrote in the style of the times, paying lip service to Stalin until the latter's death in 1953.

The year 1953 was a turning point in Yevtushenko's life, for along with many others he experienced disillusionment with the Stalinist regime. With the coming of the "Thaw" in 1956, he began to write poetry against the former rulers and, gradually, for freedom. In 1954, he married Bella Akhmakulina, whom he himself describes as Russia's greatest living woman poet, although the marriage was doomed to failure. Yevtushenko's meeting with Boris Pasternak in 1957 brought him into contact with his greatest mentor.

In 1962, Yevtushenko began to travel abroad. His great success and popularity was temporarily interrupted by the publication in Paris of *Primechaniya k avtobiografii* (1963; *A Precocious Autobiography*, 1963) without the permission of the Soviet authorities, for which infraction his travel was curtailed. He subsequently made trips abroad, however, including one to the United States in 1966, where he gave many poetry readings and charmed audiences with his warm and dynamic personality. He also visited Cuba, which he admired greatly as exemplary of the revolutionary ideal. Later travels to Rome, Vietnam, Africa, Japan, Alaska, California, and Florida also inspired poems. He lists sixty-four countries that he visited up to 1981. His second marriage, to Galina Semyonovna, and the birth of a son greatly inspired his life and work.

Since the 1970's he has been active in many fields of culture, writing novels, engaging in acting, film directing, and photography. His first novel, *Wild Berries*, was a finalist for the Ritz Paris Hemingway prize in 1985, and his first feature film, *The Kindergarten*, played in the Soviet Union, England, and the United States. He was appointed honorary member of American Academy of Arts and Sciences in 1987. He continued to be politically outspoken during this period as well, supporting author Aleksandr Solzhenitsyn when the Nobel Prize Winner was arrested and exiled.

With the advent of *glasnost* (a term used to refer to the gradual opening of Soviet culture and politics) in the late 1980's, Yevtushenko became a leading activist in the struggle to reform Soviet society. In 1989 Yevtushenko became a member of the Congress of People's Deputies and was appointed vice president of Russian PEN in 1991. In 1993 he received a medal as "Defender of Free Russia," which was given to those who took part in resisting the hard-line Communist coup in August 1991. In 1996, Yevtushenko joined the faculty at Queens College, New York. Although critical and popular reception of Yevtushenko's work has mostly hinged on the Soviet political climate, critics have generally praised the multicultural quality of his writings and regard Yevtushenko as Russia's premier but unofficial cultural emissary to the world.

ANALYSIS

Although not the most original poet of the post-Stalinist era in the Soviet Union, Yevgeny Yevtushenko has shown himself to be one of the most significant. This is essentially because he has been able to put his finger on the pulse of the times. He became the spokesman for a new generation, not only in his native land but also all over the world. Unflinchingly honest and sincere, he has spoken with clarity and courage on issues that threaten freedom. He is best known for his poems of protest, such as "Babii Yar" and "Stalin's Heirs." In the tradition of Russian poetry, he sees himself invested with a mission and a message, and he proclaims it fearlessly. He directs his criticism not only against the cult of personality, anti-Semitism, and oppression in his own land, but he speaks out against the same abuses in other countries, especially in the United States. Images of Martin Luther King, John and Robert Kennedy, and Allison Krause of Kent State University appeared in his work in the 1970's; the perils of television and advertising, war in Northern Ireland, and the threat of nuclear weapons in poems of the late 1970's. "Freedom to Kill," "Flowers and Bullets," and "Safari in Ulster," among others, explore these themes.

Yevtushenko knows how to combine the social with the personal and how to move effortlessly from one to the other. His poetry is extremely autobiographical and one can read his life by exploring his verse. He tells whimsically of his Siberian childhood in Zima Junction, in the poem by the same name; of his youth in Moscow; of his travels and disappointment in love; and of his family and child. He reflects on the idealism of youth and the fears of impending old age. He is especially sensitive to childhood, and can frequently combine his own experiences, a universal theme of childhood, and social observation. A typical poem is "Weddings," which recounts his folk dancing at ill-fated wartime weddings in Siberia.

A child of the North, Yevtushenko speaks best of nature when evoking the taiga, the lakes, and the rivers of Siberia, the smell of fresh berries or the blue glow of fresh snow in "Zima Junction," "Monologue of the Fox," and "The Hut." He is close to the sea, and often associates it with love ("The Sea"), with women ("Glasha, Bride of the Sea"), and with contemporary problems, as in "Kachka" ("Pitching and Rolling"). Nature, however, is not the most common source of images for this contemporary poet, who prefers the city with its neon lights, the sound of jazz, and the smell of smog. He is especially fond of New York and records his impressions in many poems such as "New York Elegy," "Smog," and *Pod kozhey statuey sbobody* (pr. 1972).

People, more than nature, dominate Yevtushenko's poetry. In the tradition of Fyodor Dostoevski, Anton Chekhov, and Maxim Gorky, the lowly and the downtrodden occupy an important place. Socialist Realism places an emphasis on the "people." Yevtushenko adopts this atti-

tude, but he goes even further, showing genuine sympathy for the worker and the peasant, especially evident in *Bratsk Station and Other New Poems*, in which he also speaks of the unmarried mother ("Nushka"). While extolling the humble and the poor he manifests hatred for the cruel overseer, the bully, or the compromiser. Such characters appear in "Babii Yar," "Zima Junction," and "Song of the Overseers" and in *Bratsk Station and Other New Poems*. He detests hypocrisy and slavery in any form and denounces it loudly in the Soviet Union, the United States, South Africa, and anywhere else in the world.

Women occupy an important place in Yevtushenko's verse. In keeping with his sympathy for the peasant and workers, he dedicates many poems to the hardworking Russian woman, as in "The Hut." Old women in particular are among his favorites, such as the one who brings the red flowers of the taiga to the workers of Bratsk Station. The young innocent girl in love, such as "Masha," the mothers who work for their young children and are never appreciated, the dancer, the singer: All these are living people who impart to Yevtushenko's works a strong dramatic quality.

The narrative, along with the lyric, is an important feature of Yevtushenko's poetry. He prefers the epic style, and "Zima Junction," *Bratsk Station and Other New Poems*, and *Ivan the Terrible and Ivan the Fool* illustrate this tendency, although he often falls short of his goals. All his verse is dynamic rather than static. Many of his shorter works have a balladlike quality; among these are "Glasha, Bride of the Sea," "Rhythms of Rome," and "Nushka" in *Bratsk Station and Other New Poems*. Dialogue occurs frequently and enhances the dramatic effect of his verse. *Pod kozhey statuey sbobody*, partially prose and partially verse, was staged in Moscow as a play in 1972; it satirized Russia as well as the United States.

Yevtushenko claims as his masters Hemingway (to whom he had dedicated one of his finest poems, "Encounter"), Esenin, Mayakovsky, and Pasternak, whom he knew personally and who offered friendly criticism of his early verse. The influence of Esenin and Mayakovsky is not always evident in his style, although at first glance he seems to be an avid disciple of Mayakovsky. Yevtushenko uses the "step lines" of Mayakovsky, but the verbal brilliance, bold speech, and innovation of the older poet are rarely evident.

Yevtushenko employs a colloquial style, with many words borrowed from foreign languages. His poetry is filled with vivid twentieth century speech, with frequent sound effects, internal rhymes, and wordplay not always evident in English translations. He uses a wide variety of rhymes and rhythms, as well as free verse. His earlier poems tend to be freer than the poems of the late 1970's and early 1980's, which make use of regular meters and indulge in much less verbal experimentation. At all times he seems to write with ease and facility, although his poems frequently give the impression of too great haste. He is a prolific, spontaneous poet who writes without looking back and sometimes produces profound and startling insights.

Yevtushenko is a poet who wishes to be accessible to as many people as possible. He refuses poetic isolation and an elitist concept of art. In fact, he has chosen photography as a medium because its meaning is immediately obvious and it does not lose in translation. Above all, he is an apostle of human brotherhood. He believes in kindness and mutual understanding. *Invisible Threads* captures this theme dramatically. He is satirical, disarmingly frank, yet idealistic and trusting. Images of Christ, the sea, African jungles, and neon lights all serve to highlight his essential optimism and hope for the future.

Yevtushenko's poetry falls into distinct periods. The first, from 1952 to 1960, contains poems of youthful enthusiasm and is extremely autobiographical, as in "Zima Junction," "The Visit," and "Weddings." Memories of war and the child's inability to grasp its impact appear in "Weddings," "Party Card," and "A Companion." Since Yevtushenko had not begun his travels at this time, his inspiration was limited to Russia, centering especially on Moscow, Siberia, and Georgia. Although Yevtushenko was born long after the Revolution and did not know it at first hand, he manifests amazing conviction and enthusiasm for its ideals. "Lies" and "Knights" are among the many typical examples. Lyricism, love, and, above all, human sympathy characterize this early period.

"ZIMA JUNCTION"

Perhaps the best and most important poem of this period is "Zima Junction," first published in the journal *Oktyabr* in 1956. It refers to a visit to his native village in 1953, after the death of Stalin, the Doctors' Plot, and the deposition of Lavrenti Beria. Relatives and friends in far-off Siberia are anxious to learn all the news at first hand from this Moscow visitor, who, they expect, has all the information and has known Stalin personally. He accepts their naïveté with humor and respect for their simple lives, while at the same time noticing how both he and they have changed, and how they too have anxieties beneath the apparent simplicity of their ways.

The return to Zima Junction is the occasion for a retrospective glance at his own past and the past of his ancestors, as he recalls his great-grandfather's trip to Siberia from his peasant village in the Ukraine, and his grandfather's revolutionary idealism. Yevtushenko returns to the place where he was born not only for the past, but also for the future, to seek "strength and courage." He realizes that he, like the people of the village, has changed, and that it is difficult to decide wisely on a course of action. He personifies Zima Junction, which speaks to him through the forest and the wheat, in some of his best nature images. The section "Berry-Picking" has frequently been reprinted separately.

Throughout the poem, local color abounds, and Yevtushenko's narrative quality emerges through images of such people as the barefoot berry picker, the garrulous fisherman, or the disappointed wife in the hayloft who complains of her ungrateful and inattentive husband. Yevtushenko's family such as Uncle Volodya and Uncle Andrei, simple laborers, contrast with Pankratov, "the ponderous didactic president." The wheat and the village speak to young Zhenya, who is on the uncertain threshold of manhood, urging him to explore the world over and to love people.

Although the poem consists of many isolated incidents, they are obviously linked by the village and its message of courage and hope. The style is simple and colloquial, interspersed with local Siberian and Ukrainian expressions. The dialogue is suited to the speaker, and the nature imagery is among Yevtushenko's best. Belief in revolutionary ideals is evident, and party ideology, although present, is sincere and unaffected. Yevtushenko began to acquire fame after publishing this poem, where the personal note becomes universal.

INFLUENCES OF TRAVEL

Yevheny's second distinct period—the poems of the 1970's—shows a broader scope and is mainly influenced by travel. Yevtushenko writes especially of the

United States, Latin America, Cuba, Alaska, Hawaii, and Rome. He speaks out more freely against hypocrisy and loss of freedom, and addresses social and political abuses, of which "Babii Yar" is the most significant example. At the same time, he professes strong patriotism, as evidenced in the lengthy *Bratsk Station and Other New Poems*. The North, especially Siberia, is an inspiration for his work, especially *Kachka*. The personal and autobiographical theme returns in poems about love and loss of love. A more serious note is expressed in images of guilt, suffering, and repentance. Poems such as "Twist on Nails" and "Torments of Conscience" (published in English in *Stolen Apples*) express these themes through religious and dramatic imagery, of which one of the most striking examples is that of the pierced hands of the crucified Christ. These are poems of maturity and considerable depth and sensitivity in both the personal and the social order.

"BABII YAR"

"Babii Yar" was first published in the *Literaturnaya gazeta* in 1961. It is a poetic meditation on the tragic fate of the Jews in Eastern Europe, thirty-three thousand of whom were killed by the Germans in 1941 at Babii Yar, a ravine near the city of Kiev. As an attack on Soviet anti-Semitism, the poem stimulated controversy in the Soviet press and provoked counterattacks from leading journalists, but Yevtushenko continued to publish. In the poem, Yevtushenko deplores the absence of a monument at Babii Yar. One has subsequently been erected, without reference to the specific massacre of 1941.

The poem is not confined to Soviet anti-Semitism; it attacks prejudice against all peoples, but especially against Jews everywhere. In the poem, Yevtushenko, who is not Jewish himself, identifies with all the Jews of the past: those in ancient Egypt, Christ on the Cross, Alfred Dreyfus, Anne Frank. Amid the harsh indictment of those who killed the Jews, Yevtushenko inserts delicate poetry: "transparent as a branch in April." He emphasizes the need for all people to look at one another and to recognize their responsibility and their brotherhood. By poetic transfer, Yevtushenko sees in himself each of these murderers and accepts responsibility for the terrible massacre. With characteristic optimism, he expresses trust in Russia's international soul, which will shine forth when anti-Semitism is dead.

BRATSK STATION

Bratsk Station was first published in the April, 1965, issue of *Yunost*. It is a long discursive poem of epic proportions: five thousand lines divided into thirty-five unequal and loosely connected parts. The main idea, as expressed by Yevtushenko himself, is a "controversy between two themes: the theme of disbelief expressed in the monologue of the Pyramid and the theme of faith, expressed by Bratsk Station." The Bratsk project was launched in 1958. It is a gigantic hydroelectric station, and it also contains lumber mills and plants for pulp, cardboard, wood by-products, and aluminum. Located in central Siberia along the Angara River, it is one of the largest hydroelectric plants in the Soviet Union. Yevtushenko sees it as a monument to free labor and considers the manpower that constructed it and keeps it in operation as a symbol of brotherhood, expressed in the word "bratsk," which means "brotherly."

The essential conflict is expressed in the recurring dialogue between the Egyptian Pyramid and Bratsk Station. Yevtushenko sees the Pyramid as a construction of slaves, and therefore it has no faith in itself. Moreover, it maintains that all men will ultimately turn to slavery and that freedom is only an illusory dream. This naïve interpretation of Egyptian history has provoked much criticism, notably from Andrei Sinyavsky in "In Defense of the Pyramid," where he maintains that Yevtushenko does not understand the significance of Egyptian society. The Bratsk Station, on the other hand, extols the free labor that built it, for it is the daughter of Russia who has attained freedom through centuries of suffering.

To illustrate the quest for freedom in the Russian soul, Yevtushenko evokes a number of events and heroes from Russian history, especially Stenka Razin, the Decembrists, and the followers of Mikhail Petrashevsky. To these he adds Russia's greatest writers; Alexander Pushkin, Tolstoy, Dostoevski, and the modern writers he so admires; Esenin and Mayakovsky, with a poem in the style of the latter. Finally, there are the unsung heroes of the people: Issy Kramer, the Light Controller, who still suffers from anti-Semitism; Sonka and Petka, the concrete pourers, and Nushka, the unwed mother. Yevtushenko relates that when he read his poem to the workers of Bratsk Station, mothers like Nushka held their children up to him, recognizing themselves in his poem.

Themes of socialism and patriotism abound in the poem, frequently exaggerated. Despite its loosely connected parts, the poem moves quickly, with dramatic and lively style and balladlike quality. There are echoes of "Babii Yar" in the Light Controller and of "Zima Junction" in the images of the taiga and the Simbirsk Fair, and the work is autobiographical as well as political and social. It begins and ends with poetry. In the "Prayer Before the Poem," Yevtushenko invokes Pushkin, Mikhail Lermontov, Nikolai Nekrasov, Blok, Pasternak, Esenin, and Mayakovsky and asks for their gifts (mutually exclusive, claims Sinyavsky). The final section, "The Night of Poetry," evokes the Siberian custom of improvising poetry and delivering it to musical accompaniment. In the moment of recitation, Yevtushenko sees before him the great Russian heroes and writers of the past and experiences with them the glory of freedom symbolized by Bratsk Station.

THE 1970'S

The years from 1970 to 1981 show both a return to basic structures in theme and composition and a broadening of scope into various genres: photography, the theater, novel, and essay. As the father of a child, Yevtushenko again writes about childhood, as in "Father and Son," "Walk with My Son," and "A Father's Ear." Now approaching middle age, he writes more of death ("A Child's Grave," "Come to My Tomb") and speaks of his desire to live in all lands and be all types of people possible, but to be buried in Russia. The travel theme is still uppermost, with an emphasis on the Far East, where Vietnam becomes an important social and political question. Yevtushenko, always against war, continues to make an appeal to human brotherhood in Northern Ireland, South Africa, and between the United States and Russia.

IVANOVSKIYE SITSI

Still drawn to the epic theme, Yevtushenko published *Ivanovskiye sitsi* in the journal *Avrora* in 1976. The title means literally "calico from Ivanovo," and refers to Ivanovo-Voznesensk, a large textile center important for the labor movement. In 1905, there was a strike there which led to the establishment of one of the first Soviets of Workers' Deputies. Yevtushenko is always fond of

wordplay, and thus uses "Ivan" in several contexts. There is Ivan the Terrible, czar of Russia from 1533 to 1584, the symbol of autocracy in constant conflict with the people. Ivan the Fool is an important but composite character from folk epic and represents the growing popular consciousness. The poem glorifies the Revolution and the proletariat and expresses faith in the consciousness of the working class, bearers of the Russian soul. Yevtushenko maintains, however, that the Revolution extols heroes of all nations: Joan of Arc, John Brown, and Anne Frank, and aims for human brotherhood and a real International.

INVISIBLE THREADS

Invisible Threads, published in the United States and composed of poetry and photography, takes its inspiration from Edward Steichen's *Family of Man* exhibit and emphasizes the same theme. It contains poems from the late 1970's and addresses contemporary themes such as the threat of atomic warfare, the conflict in Northern Ireland, and the universal themes of birth and death, the former inspired by the birth of Yevtushenko's son in London. In the poem "Life and Death," a balladlike lyric, Life and Death exchange places. Death realizes that she is respected, if only because of fear, whereas Life is not. Yevtushenko pleads again for human dignity. Religious images are more evident than in the past, although Yevtushenko sees salvation among human beings on earth. He wishes to echo every voice in the world and "dance his Russian dance on the invisible threads that stretch between the hearts of men."

THE COLLECTED POEMS, 1952-1990

The Collected Poems, 1952-1990 reflects Yevtushenko's poetic career in microcosm: vast and ever astonishing in its variety. The title is somewhat misleading, since the volume offers only a selection from Yevtushenko's extensive career, and in addition, several long poems are represented in excerpts only. The translations by twenty-five translators vary in quality: A few are revisions of earlier versions and because most of Yevtushenko's poems use slant rhyme relying heavily on assonance, few attempts were made to retain this feature in the English translations, or indeed to use rhyme at all.

Yevtushenko's characteristic political criticisms and commentary find a dominant place in this collection.

He praises Chile's Salvador Allende and Cuba's Che Guevara, condemns the Vietnam War, and deplores the situation in Northern Ireland. He also warns against Soviet political abuses, castigating militarists and dishonest bureaucrats. These critical poems range from "Stalin's Heirs" and "Babii Yar" from the early 1960's, to later poems, including "Momma and the Neutron Bomb" and poems about the dissident Andrei Sakharov and the Afghanistan war in the 1980's. When one considers that, due to censorship, many of Yevtushenko's poems were not published when they were written in the 1960's, his cynical critique of Soviet politics is understandable. Included in this collection are a number of his censored poems. Among them are verses to fellow Russian poets, "Russian Tanks in Prague," and "The Ballad of the Big," a bawdy tale about castration for the good of the party.

Another thread running through Yevtushenko's work is the importance of poetry and the responsibility of the poet to mankind. He constantly questions his own talent and mission, thus continuing the Russian tradition of meta-poetry. Likewise very Russian is the dialogue between writers living and dead that Yevtushenko carries on, in poems addressed to or evoking Boris Pasternak, Pablo Neruda, and Jack London, along with numerous others. He also blasts modern writers in "The Incomprehensible Poets," in which he admits: "My guilt is my simplicity./ My crime is my clarity." In "I Would Like," he notes: "I would like to belong to all times,/ shock all history so much/ that it would be amazed/ what a smart aleck I was."

Finally, personal accounts, like "On a Bicycle" and "Flowers for Grandmother" fill several pages in the collection. "Blue Fox" combines his concern for animals with an allegory of the collective state; "Monologue of an Actress" is a witty complaint by an aging actress that no worthwhile roles are left to play. His own experiences are represented here as well, contributing to his range of personal stories. His poetry is a kind of diary which details his extensive travels and especially his many love affairs. Remarkable love poems follow the poet from first love, to the birth of his sons, to the sadness of falling out of love again. The poems contain a rich fabric of quarrels, memories, farewells, even a conversation with his dog, who shares the poet's grief that his woman has gone. The human breadth that he captures is perhaps the strongest aspect of this collection.

OTHER MAJOR WORKS

LONG FICTION: *Yagodnye mesta*, 1981 (*Wild Berries*, 1984); *Don't Die Before You're Dead*, 1995.

PLAY: *Pod kozhey statuey sbobody*, pr. 1972.

NONFICTION: *Primechaniya k avtobiografii*, 1963 (*A Precocious Autobiography*, 1963); *Talant est' chudo nesluchainoe: Kniga statei*, 1980.

BIBLIOGRAPHY

Brown, Deming. *The Last Years of Soviet Russian Literature: Prose Fiction, 1975-1991*. New York: Cambridge University Press, 1993. History and criticism of late soviet era Russian literature. Includes bibliographical references and index.

_____. *Soviet Russian Literature Since Stalin*. New York: Cambridge University Press, 1978. A historical and critical study of Russian literature. Includes bibliographic references and an index.

Brown, Edward J. *Russian Literature Since the Revolution*. Rev. ed. Cambridge, Mass.: Harvard University Press, 1982. A survey and critical analysis of Soviet literature. Includes bibliographic references.

The Economist. "Past, Implacable." 306, no. 7535 (January 30, 1988): 75-76. Draws parallels between Yevtushenko's poetic themes and *glasnost*, concentrating on "Bukharin's Widow" and "Monuments Not Yet Erected."

Hingley, Ronald. *Russian Writers and Soviet Society, 1917-1978*. New York: Random House, 1979. A history of Russian literature of the Soviet era. Includes a bibliography and index.

Slonim, Mark. *Soviet Russian Literature*. 2d ed. New York: Oxford University Press, 1977. A historical and critical study of Russian literature.

Vanden Heuvel, Katrina. "Yevtushenko Feels a Fresh Wind Blowing." *Progressive* 24 (April, 1987): 24-31. Addresses Yevtushenko's views on Russian politics, poetry's public service, *glasnost*, and relations with the West.

Irma M. Kashuba,
updated by Sarah Hilbert

YOSANO AKIKO

Born: Sakai, Japan; December 7, 1878
Died: Tokyo, Japan; May 29, 1942

PRINCIPAL POETRY

Midaregami, 1901 (*Tangled Hair*, 1935, 1971)
Dokusō, 1901
Koōgi, 1904
Koi goromo, 1905
Mai hime, 1906
Yume-no-hana, 1906
Hakkō, 1908
Tokonatsu, 1908
Sabo hime, 1911
Shundeishū, 1911
Seikainami, 1912
Pari yori, 1913
Sakura Sō, 1915
Maigoromo, 1916
Shubashū, 1916
Myōjōshū, 1918
Wakakiotome, 1918
Hinotori, 1919
Tabi-no-uta, 1921
Taiyō-to-bara, 1921
Kusa-no-yume, 1922
Nagareboshi-no-michi, 1924
Ningen ōrai, 1925
Ruriko, 1925
Kokoro no enkei, 1928
Yosano Akiko kashu, 1938
Shiro zakura, 1942
The Poetry of Yosano Akiko, 1957
Tangled Hair: Selected Tanka from "Midaregami,"
    1971
Akiko shukasen, 1996
River of Stars: Selected Poems of Yosano Akiko, 1996

OTHER LITERARY FORMS

Although Yosano Akiko's married name was Yosano (placed before her personal name, in the normal Japanese order), she is commonly called "Akiko," which is her "elegant name." Among her many translations and modernizations, the most enduringly popular is her modern Japanese version of the greatest Japanese novel, *Genji monogatari* (early eleventh century; *The Tale of Genji*, 1881), written by Murasaki Shikibu. Akiko's version was published in 1912 and 1939. This monumental work revived general interest in Murasaki and other classical authors; it is included with Akiko's autobiography, novels, fairy tales, children's stories, essays, and original and translated poetry in the standard Japanese edition of her works, *Yosano Akiko zenshū* (1972).

ACHIEVEMENTS

Yosano Akiko is generally admired as the greatest female poet and *tanka* poet of modern Japan, as an influential critic and educator and as the grand embodiment of Romanticism, feminism, pacifism, and social reform in the first three decades of the twentieth century. She has been called a princess, queen, and goddess of poetry. In fact, Japanese Romanticism in the early twentieth century has been called the "Age of Akiko." She also influenced feminist writers internationally. She infused erotic and imaginative passion into the traditional *tanka* form (a poem of five lines containing five, seven, five, seven, and seven syllables respectively) at a time when it had grown lifelessly conventional, having lost the personal vitality of ancient times; in the same way, she revived certain classical qualities of the mid-eighth century *Manyōshū* (English translation, 1940) and other ancient collections, while introducing stunning innovations of style. Projecting her own life and spirit into the form, she insisted that every word be charged with emotion. Such intensity is rarely transmitted through English translations, but Kenneth Rexroth's are fine poems in their own right as well as the most expressive renditions of Akiko's strong but subtle art.

Akiko's first book, *Tangled Hair*, was an immediate success and remains her most popular collection. It contains 399 *tanka* about her tempestuous love for the man who became her husband, Yosano Hiroshi (known as "Tekkan"). Her sequence of poems dramatically reveals the agonizing and sometimes ecstatic interactions among Akiko, Tekkan, his second wife, whom he was divorcing, and another woman, Yamakawa Tomiko. Tomiko, a beautiful poet beloved by both Tekkan and Akiko, was the leader of *Shinshisa* (the new poetry society) and edited its journal, *Myōjō* (the morning star), the chief organ of Japanese Romanticism.

Altogether, Akiko published seventy-five books, of which more than twenty are collections of original poetry. She wrote approximately seventeen thousand *tanka* as well as five hundred poems in free verse, which she devoted primarily to social issues such as pacifism and feminism. One of her outstanding poems of this kind, "Kimi shinitamō koto nakare" ("Never Let Them Kill You, Brother!"), was addressed to her own brother, who participated in the attack on Port Arthur in 1904 during the Russo-Japanese War; Akiko disliked war, observing that it brought nothing but suffering and death. Her rhetorical question—How can the emperor, who does not fight, allow his subjects to die like beasts?—was so outrageously subversive at the time that people stoned her house. It was, in fact, the first criticism of the emperor, aside from political prose, that had been published. She was defended by Mori Ōgai and other writers, and this most famous of all Japanese antiwar poems has been revived periodically by antimilitarists. Akiko also courageously defended radicals who were executed in 1912.

Another often-quoted poem in free verse, "Yama no ugoku hi kitaru" ("The Day When Mountains Move"), was one of twelve of her poems to appear in *Seitō* (bluestocking) when that feminist journal was founded in 1916, establishing Akiko as the leading poet of women's consciousness in Japan. In 1921, with Tekkan, Akiko founded the Bunka Gakuin (culture school) for girls, where she worked as a teacher and dean, while also advancing the cause of women's education and social emancipation in essays in *Taiyō* and other journals. Between 1925 and 1931, with Tekkan and a third editor, she edited and published an authoritative fifty-volume set of Japanese classics, a work that helped to democratize the study of literature and gave her and her husband financial security. In 1937, she became an editor of a new edition of the *Manyōshō*. Her literary and financial success never interfered with her struggle for justice, which in her view was inseparable from literature. In "Kogan no shi" ("Death of Rosy-Cheeked Youth"), for example, she mourned the slaughter of Chinese boy-soldiers by the Japanese in Shanghai.

Some conservative critics ruthlessly denounced both Akiko and Tekkan for their scandalous lives and writings, which violated so many conventions, both literary and social. Undeterred by such attacks, Akiko struggled ceaselessly against prejudice and abuse to attain a high place among major Japanese poets of all eras.

BIOGRAPHY

Yosano Akiko was born in Sakai, Japan, December 7, 1878. Her father, Hō Sōshichi, owned a confectionery shop in Sakai, a suburb of Osaka. Both Akiko's father and her mother imposed traditional constraints on her, but she soon developed precocious literary enthusiasms and talents, thanks to the libraries of her great-grandparents; her great-grandfather was called the "master's master" of the town because of his knowledge of Chinese literature and his skilled composition of *haiku*. Akiko read all the literature that she could find from France and England, as well as from ancient and modern Japan—especially such classics as the *Manyōshū*, Sei Shōnagon's *Makura-no-sōshi* (early eleventh century; *Pillow Book*, 1928), and Shikibu's *The Tale of Genji* (which Akiko eventually translated from the archaic style into modern Japanese).

At age nineteen, she published her first poem in a local journal, and within three years she became prominent in Kansai-area literary activities. In 1900, Tekkan, the poet-leader of the new Romanticism, discovered Akiko's genius, began teaching her literature, brought her into his *Shinshisa* in Tokyo, and had her work published in the journal *Myōjō*; Akiko helped to edit the journal from 1901 until its demise in 1908, and again during its revival from 1921 to 1927. In 1901, Tekkan also edited and arranged publication for Akiko's first book, *Tangled Hair*. Her immediate success ensured her impact as a feminist and a pacifist, as well as the popularity of her many other books of poetry and prose, the royalties from which helped to finance Tekkan's three-year trip to France. Akiko was able to join him for six months in 1912, also visiting Germany, Holland, England, and Manchuria. She was inspired by European writers and artists, especially Auguste Rodin. She was also intrigued by the relative freedom of European women, and her tour strengthened her determination to change Japanese life through the power of the creative word. In addition to her vigorous cultural activities, she gave birth to thirteen children, rearing eleven of them to adulthood.

ANALYSIS

Not even the finest translations can fully convey the subtle nuances of tone, the delicacy of imagery, the great suggestiveness and complex allusiveness of Yosano Akiko's poetry—or indeed of most Japanese literature; English simply does not have the "feel" of Japanese, in sound, diction, grammar, or prosody. For example, there are no English equivalents for poignant sighs at the ends of many poems, or exclamations such as *ya!* and *kana!*

Fortunately, Kenneth Rexroth's masterful renditions reveal Akiko's sensibility, passion, and imagination in English poems that are themselves enduring works of art. In the selections from her work included in his *One Hundred More Poems from the Japanese* of 1974— in which the *romaji* text is given after each English version—Rexroth captures the erotic intensity which shocked Akiko's first readers. Other poems in this selection poignantly foreshadow separation—as a man fondles his lover in the autumn, as lovers gaze at each other without speaking or thinking of the future, or as a woman smells her lover's clothes in the darkness as he says goodbye. In others, the poet remembers writing a poem with her lover before separating from him; looks back on her passion like a blind man unafraid of the dark; contemplates sorrow as if it were hail or feathers falling; and watches cherry blossoms fall as stars go out in a false dawn. Such poems suggest the intricate, heartbreaking love story that comes alive, as in a novel, in hundreds of Akiko's original poems, many of them arranged to be read in a kind of narrative sequence. Most of them, however, are still unavailable in English.

Akiko also wrote many poems that calmly contemplate nature—poems in which, for example, snow and stars shine on her disheveled hair; an old boat reflects the autumn sky; ginkgo leaves scatter in the sunset; the nightingale sleeps with doubled-up jeweled claws; a white bird flying over the breakers becomes an obsessive dream; and cranes fly crying across Waka Bay to the other shore (an image traditionally suggesting Nirvana).

In his 1977 anthology, *The Burning Heart: Women Poets of Japan*, Rexroth included additional translations of Akiko's poetry. This collection illustrates how Akiko's influence has enabled women poets to speak out in a country whose literary tradition has been dominated by men. Some of Akiko's *tanka* included in the volume concern the love triangle in which Tomiko—Akiko's friend and her husband's lover—appears as a lily or queen in summer fields; Akiko's heart is envisioned as the sun drowned in darkness and rain. One of Akiko's poems in free verse, "Labor Pains," is also included; in it, the birth of her baby in likened to truth pushing outward from inwardness.

Rexroth usually renders Akiko's *tanka* in five lines, and he often approximates the normal syllable count without distorting sound or sense; his cadences, as well as his melodies and imagery, evoke the tone of the Japanese much more reliably than does H. H. Honda's rhymed quatrains, which seem more akin to A. E. Housman's verse than to Akiko's. Honda's book is useful, however, for readers with even an elementary knowledge of Japanese, for the original poem is given, in *kanji* and *kana* as well as *romaji*, under each translation; Honda's selections from nineteen of Akiko's books are arranged so the reader can follow the overall development of the poet's work and her growing consciousness of aging, of her children, and of her place in society and in the universe. Although he bypasses the explicitly erotic passages that attracted Rexroth, Honda does convey something of Akiko's sensuousness in poems that show her cherishing her five-foot-long hair after a bath or rain, gazing at herself in a mirror for an hour, caressing herself, and floating like a serene lily in a pond. Some of Honda's best renditions are "The Cherries and the Moon," a snow scene in Kyoto; "Upon the Bridge of Shijo," where twilight hail falls on the brow of a dancer; "Down in the Ocean of My Mind," where fish wave jewel-colored fins; "Like Open-eyed Fish," in which the fish are compared to the poet, who is unable to sleep; "There Side by Side," about being a slave to love; and the satirical poems "O That I Could," a defiance of Japanese conventionality, and "Naught Knowing the Blissful Touch," in which Akiko teases a youthful Buddhist monk.

Akiko's poetry is characterized by lyric, rhetorical, dramatic, and narrative strength. Each poem expresses an intense feeling of a particular moment in the poet's life, a feeling that is often too subtle, complex, or ambiguous to be fully comprehended by Westerners unfamiliar with the nuances of Japanese sensibility. The rhetorical thrust of many of Akiko's poems can readily be understood, however, especially in those poems concerned with dramatic conflicts between lovers, with the plight of women generally, and with protests against social conventions. The drama of Akiko's stormy life, concentrated in the *tanka*, reveals the intricate story of her romance, marriage, and literary career; thus, a study of her collections as unified works is usually more fruitful than formal analysis of individual poems. The narrative dimension of her work does not unfold chronologically, as a rule, but evolves cyclically from poem to poem, as she returns periodically to the dominant images and themes of her life. Indeed, the details of her life are inseparable from her poems, which require far more biographical knowledge on the part of the reader than is usually required for Western poetry. Such themes as love, jealousy, fear, loneliness, rebellion against oppression, and death are, however, universal, and may be directly and deeply appreciated by any reader.

TANGLED HAIR

The best English translations of Akiko's work, besides Rexroth's, are those by Sanford Goldstein and Shinoda Seishi. Their translation of *Tangled Hair* (which includes 165 of the 399 *tanka* in the collection, along with the Japanese originals) is supplemented by an excellent biographical introduction and useful notes based in part on the pioneering commentaries by Satake Kazuhiko. Goldstein and Shinoda's free-verse translations (usually in five lines, but without the conventional syllable count) are sensitive, vivid, and faithful to the meaning and feeling of the original, though not as intense. In "Yawahada no" ("You Have Yet to Touch"), the translators convey Akiko's seductive, sarcastic, teasing tone, as she asks an "Expounder of the Way" if he is not lonely for her blood and flesh. Satake's commentary on this poem identifies the "Expounder" as Tekkan; in Satake's reading, the poem reflects Akiko's impatience with Tekkan before he divorced his second wife and married her. Satake disagreed with Akiko's own interpretation of the poem as a generalized polemic against society, but its attack on hypocritical moralizing is surely as universal as it is personal. Akiko's rival Tomiko also figures in many poems in *Tangled Hair*. In "Sono namida" ("Tears in Your Eyes"), Akiko turns away unsympathetically from Tomiko's tears and gazes at the waning moon (always an image of sadness) reflected in a lake. The poignancy is heightened by knowledge that Akiko has just discovered that Tekkan still loves Tomiko, although he intends to marry Akiko.

Other poems evolve from customs such as the Dolls' Day celebration in "Hitotsu hako ni" ("Laying"), in which Akiko, in adolescence, sighs with some strange sexual awareness after putting the emperor and empress dolls together in a box; in an amazing image, she is afraid of her sigh being heard by peach blossoms. Sometimes Akiko identifies herself with women in ancient times, such as courtesans. In "Nakade isoge" ("Complain Not"), she tells a man to hurry on his way to other women who will undress him. Buddhism enters many of her poems in original ways. In "Wakaki ko no" ("Only the Sculptor's Fame"), she writes that she was attracted to the artist (probably Tekkan) because of his reputation when he was young, but now she is drawn to the face of the Buddha that he has carved (perhaps Tekkan's Buddha nature).

Sakanishi Shio's *Tangled Hair* includes translations not only from Akiko's first book but from eleven others as well, along with an informative introduction and a sketch of Akiko that might be compared to the photograph in Honda's volume. Sakanishi's versions are much more aesthetically subtle than Honda's and deserve close attention for their suggestively vivid imagery, natural speech rhythms, and artfully controlled syntax, all of which help to convey Akiko's tone. The sensuous and psychological implications of her hair are spun out in a variety of startling images. Her hair, for example, sweeps the strings of her koto, and its breaking strands recall the sound of the koto's strings; elsewhere, nightingales sing in a nest made from her fallen hair. Her discontent with traditional religions is manifest in her turning from the gods toward natural beauties, from the sutras to her own song, to the attractive flesh of a young monk, or to her loving husband. At other times, she prays to bodhisattvas while cherry blossoms fall on them and returns to sutras in bewilderment and despair, or sees the Buddha in the rising sun—a traditional image of Shingon Buddhism. Many of Akiko's poems included in Sakanishi's selection explicitly detail her life with Tekkan—her ambivalence about their original romance, resentful memories, ecstasies, the sadness of separation during his years in France, reunions, the agony of childbirth as three hearts beat in her body and one twin dies there, despair, children burning in volcanic eruptions, and renewed joy in rearing her children, to whom she gives her great-grandmother's prayer beads.

Thus, while the nuances of Akiko's verse remain resistant to translation, much of her artistry is accessible to English-speaking readers, who are now able to appreciate her significant contribution to the development of modern poetry in Japan.

OTHER MAJOR WORKS

LONG FICTION: *Genji monogatari*, 1912, 1939 (modern version); *Akarumi e*, 1913.

NONFICTION: *Nyonin sōzō*, 1920 (essays); *Yusho-sha to nare*, 1934; *Uta no tsukuriyō*, 1948; *Gekido no naka o yuku*, 1991; *Ai resei oyobi yuki*, 1993.

CHILDREN'S LITERATURE: *Watakushi no oitachi*, 1915.

MISCELLANEOUS: *Yosano Akiko zenshū*, 1972.

BIBLIOGRAPHY

Atsumi, Ikuko, and Graeme Wilson. "The Poetry of Yosano Akiko," *Japan Quarterly* 21, no. 2 (April-June, 1974). A short critical study of Akiko's poetic works.

Honda, H. H. Introduction to *The Poetry of Yosano Akiko*. Tokyo: Hokuseido Press, 1957. Honda's introduction offers some biographical details of Akiko's life.

Rowley, Gillian Gaye. *Yosano Akiko and "The Tale of Genji."* Ann Arbor: University of Michigan, 2000. A critical analysis of Akiko's modern Japanese version of *The Tale of Genji*. Includes bibliographical references and index.

Shinoda, Seishi, and Sanford Goldstein. Introduction to *Tangled Hair*. Rutland, Vt.: C.E. Tuttle, 1987. Shinoda and Goldstein offer some biographical and historical information as well as notes on the translations.

Morgan Gibson and Keiko Matsui Gibson

AL YOUNG

Born: Ocean Springs, Mississippi; May 31, 1939

PRINCIPAL POETRY

Dancing, 1969
The Song Turning Back into Itself, 1971
Geography of the Near Past, 1976
The Blues Don't Change: New and Selected Poems, 1982
Heaven: Collected Poems, 1958-1988, 1988
The Sound of Dreams Remembered: Poems, 1990-2000, 2001

OTHER LITERARY FORMS

Al Young is known primarily as a poet and novelist; his novels include *Snakes* (1970), *Who Is Angelina?* (1975), *Sitting Pretty* (1976), and *Ask Me Now* (1980). He has also published short stories in *Changes, Chicago Review, Encore, Essence, The Evergreen Review, Journal of Black Poetry, The Massachusetts Review, Place,* and *Rolling Stone.* He wrote the introduction to *Yardbird Lives!* (1978), a collection of writings that he and Ishmael Reed compiled from the biennial *Yardbird Reader.* He has written several screenplays, including "Nigger" (unpublished) based on Dick Gregory's autobiography, a film script for his novel *Sitting Pretty,* and the script for *A Piece of the Action* (in collaboration with Bill Cosby and Sidney Poitier).

Young has also written a series of autobiographical anecdotes, in *Bodies and Soul: Musical Memoirs* (1981), each of which is organized around his response to a specific song or musical performance. The title piece, for example, begins with his meditation on Coleman Hawkins's 1939 performance of "Body and Soul." *Bodies and Soul* was followed by other "musical memoirs," including *Kinds of Blue: Musical Memoirs* (1984), *Mingus/Mingus: Two Memoirs* (with Janet Coleman), and *Drowning in a Sea of Love: Musical Memoirs* (1995).

ACHIEVEMENTS

For his first collection, *Dancing,* Al Young won the National Arts Council Award for poetry. In 1968, Young received a National Arts Council Award for editing. In 1969, he received a Joseph Henry Jackson Award from the San Francisco Foundation for *Dancing.* The next year, his first novel, *Snakes,* appeared and was praised for its authentic portrayal of a young man, addicted to jazz, growing up in urban America.

Young received a Guggenheim Fellowship in 1974 and a National Endowment for the Arts Fellowship in 1975. His considerable work on small literary magazines includes founding and editing *Loveletter* (an avant-garde review of the 1960's), editing *Changes* (for the West Coast), and coediting, with Ishmael Reed, *Yardbird Reader*. He cofounded the Yardbird Publishing Corporation and continues to work actively in small-press publishing.

In the 1980's, Young turned increasingly to writing nonfiction, often having to do with music and film. He earned an Outstanding Book of the Year citation from *The New York Times* in 1980 for *Ask Me Now*, a Pushcart Prize in 1980, an American Book Award from the Before Columbus Foundation in 1982 for *Bodies and Soul*, and a Fulbright Fellowship in 1984.

BIOGRAPHY

Albert Young was born in Ocean Springs, Mississippi, near Biloxi, on the Gulf of Mexico. His childhood, which he characterizes as happy, was divided between rural Mississippi and urban Detroit. Though he moved

Al Young (© Miriam Berkley)

through several communities and schools, he values the flexibility that he gained by adapting to different subcultures. His father was an auto worker (in part, the model for Durwood Knight's father in *Ask Me Now*), and also a professional musician, like his son. For five years, Young sang and played the flute and guitar professionally, at first while attending the University of Michigan, then while working as a disc jockey at radio station KJAZ-FM, Alameda, California. The character MC in *Snakes* reflects some of Young's aspirations as a young jazz musician, and the poem "A Little More Traveling Music" reflects his divided roots in rural and urban music. American blues and jazz and their origins in African music have influenced the themes and the formal structures of Young's fiction and poetry.

Young has credited his interest in writing narratives to his early exposure to the art of Southern storytelling, and his fictional and poetic use of regional and ethnic vernacular draws upon his memories of Southern speech as well as his wide reading in American literature (especially the works of Zora Neale Hurston, Mark Twain, Langston Hughes, and Jesse Stuart) and British and European literature. Young married a freelance artist in 1963 with whom he would have a son. In 1966-1967, Young was a fellow in Advanced Fiction Writing at Stanford University; in 1969, he received his bachelor of arts degree in Spanish at the University of California, Berkeley; from 1969 to 1973 he held a lectureship in creative writing at Stanford. He has worked as a writing instructor for youth groups in San Francisco, Oakland, and Berkeley.

Young also spent many years in the 1970's and 1980's working as a film screenwriter for various Los Angeles-area studios. He was a writer in residence at the University of Washington in Seattle from 1981 to 1982, and served as the vice president of Yardbird Publishing Cooperative. He became a familiar face on the lecture circuit at universities throughout the United States. In the 1990's, he continued writing, contributing to anthologies and creating "musical memoirs." Though he has traveled widely—in Spain, France, Mexico, and the United States—he has made his home in Northern California. Many of his poems and novels record his sensitive observations on the diverse cultural lives of people in the San Francisco Bay area.

ANALYSIS

Al Young's poetry originates in visual and aural memories and in musical forms which are then developed through suitable language and prosody. The music that inspires his poetry includes rhythm and blues and jazz, and he makes effective use of various American dialects. The metaphor of dancing unites the visual images and musical forms, and suggests both the formality and the spontaneity of design in his poetry.

Young also writes about family relationships and does so with insight, humor, and affection. His fictional characters and poetic personas often center their identities in their family life, which enables them, somehow, to cope with the meanness and injustice of contemporary urban American society. The family relationships are hardly idyllic, and characters habitually annoy and occasionally hurt one another; nevertheless, the love they feel for one another transforms their lives. Although his work offers no simplistic ideological solutions, his poems and novels clearly reflect his belief in the writer's function: to change society by expanding the reader's perception of reality.

DANCING

Dancing, Young's first collection, explores many forms of dance, including "A Dance for Militant Dilettantes," "Dancing Day to Day," "The John Coltrane Dance," "Reading Nijinsky's Diary," "Dancing Pierrot," "A Little More Traveling Music," and "Dancing." Young's rejection of "monocultural values, of whatever hue," is reflected in the diverse cultural backgrounds of the poems in *Dancing*.

At the beginning of his collection, Young places an uncharacteristic poem, perhaps written after the manuscript of *Snakes* had been refused by a series of publishers interested only in black voices that were violently angry and bitter. "A Dance for Militant Dilettantes" implicitly rejects the advice of a friend who urges him to play the stereotypic role of a honky-hating African American activist, writing about bloodying "those fabled wine & urine-/ stained hallways." While modifying the Homeric cliché of wine-dark seas, Young's brilliant epithet exposes the contemporary racism of the publisher who wants to market "a furious nigrah" and of the militant dilettantes willing to sell out.

The poet in "Dancing Day to Day" lives in and writes about a multicultural world, in which people are fearful of violence and yet live, fairly contentedly, one day at a time. In the first four lines of this poem, Young echoes T. S. Eliot, in the "come and go" of his monotonous, trivial, habitual Prufrockian world, but, significantly, without Eliot's contempt:

> In my street
> the people mostly go.
> Very few come
> to what I'd call home.

The walking iambic meter of lines two and four alternates with the emphatic trochees of lines one and three, and his quatrain establishes the dominant metric pattern of the verse paragraphs that follow. This open design, built on no regular line length, perfectly expresses the speaker's relaxed attitude toward his neighbors, as well as the freedom of their daily natural movements.

"The John Coltrane Dance," a tribute to the music of John Coltrane, uses repetition, subtle assonance, and alliteration to suggest the emotional power of Coltrane's musical compositions and performances. The word "sound" occurs seven times, is echoed in "astound" and "surround," and introduces a pattern of sibilants. The line, "Mr Love Trane," occurs only twice (lines two and twenty-four), but its distinctive concluding spondee, lengthened by the long vowels, sets a metrical pattern that also occurs in lines eight ("tree dance"), fourteen ("smoothed stones"), sixteen ("hurt songs"), and eighteen ("sound cures"). Against the implied hesitation of this duple meter, Young syncopates rapidly moving feet of triple meter, such as the dactyl ("hovering," line six), the anapest ("where that sound," line fourteen) and the tribrach, or three unaccented syllables ("& cleansed the," line fifteen, and "on all the," line twenty-three). Traditional prosody offers these terms to describe lines of verse, but readers familiar with open forms in American poetry and listeners familiar with Coltrane's extended and complex rhythmic patterns may not need this abstract analysis to hear the musical phrases of Young's poem. The poem first invokes Coltrane as muse ("Fly on into my poem"), imitating both the sounds and the impact of one of his solo performances, then places his music within the social and political history of Black America (the migrations from Alabama, the confrontation over segregated schools in Little Rock, Arkansas, and the urban ghettos in the city of brotherly love, Philadelphia, Pennsylvania). Citing the function of the blues, expressing pain to soothe and heal it, Young identifies Coltrane's music as creating and keeping alive both collective and individual history. In a temporal metaphor moving from day to night, Young suggests that Coltrane's music also forecasts the future, as the "sunrise" of line nine is transformed into the "stars" of the final line. It is an optimistic poem, celebrating the growth of the spirit, through a history and an artistic form that recall dark nights of the soul.

In the playful "Dancing Pierrot," the speaking poet claims to have known the moons of China, Egypt, Mexico, Tokyo, Bahia, San Francisco, Tanzania, and the Moors; further, he claims to have known not merely fat and skinny moons (the lunar phases), but moons that shone "lifetimes ago." Clearly, he claims the international and timeless realm of the poet who speaks to all cultures, to all races, and to all ages. Like Jules Laforgue, whose Pierrot of *L'Imitation de Notre-Dame la Lune* (1886; "Imitation of Our Lady the Moon") appears in the title, Young imagines the poet as a kind of noble lunatic, drunk on moonlight. His dancing seems that of the marionette, jerkily bobbing at the end of his strings, an image reinforced by several short two- and three-syllable lines, and by the many one-syllable words; the lyrical fifth stanza, however, echoing "Drink to me only with thine eyes," breaks the confining strings and creates the feeling of freedom. The poet's function appears in the third of the poem's five stanzas, as he observes the effects of moonlight (imagination) on ordinary working people, whose aspirations the poet powerfully images as "armed to the eyes/ with star guns" (lines twenty-eight and twenty-nine). The workers, who might seem imprisoned by repetitive movements, have a vision of self-liberating power, which is articulated by the poet.

"Reading Nijinsky's Diary" also considers the madness of the artist, whose dance plays between the extremes of confinement ("bodily concern/ vinetangled nerve") and freedom ("—cut loose, freed/ to know ever for all"). The visual images that Young employs suggest the surviving photographs of Waslaw Nijinsky in costume for his roles as the faun in *Afternoon of a Faun* and as the rose in *Specter of the Rose*. The identification of the dancer with the dance, like that of the poet with the poem, carries the threat of insanity. For Young, unlike Nijinsky, the descent into madness is only temporary, and he is released by the incantation: "'My madness is my love/ for mankind.'"

"A Little More Traveling Music" is the autobiographical sketch of a poet and singer born in Mississippi, reared on the "Colored music, rhythmic & electrifying" broadcast over the radio, and on the music of a mother's recited family history. His move "up north" introduced him to the external, daily sounds of urban traffic and the internal music of moonlit dreams, and educated him in the sounds of written poetry. The third stanza narrates the return to "motherly music" and the poet's synthesis of that oral tradition with his formal education. The cycle of personal history culminates in his choice of vocation: "I turned to poetry & to singing." Performing and creating are made possible by listening to his "own background music."

The long poem "Dancing," which gives its title to the collection, responds personally and politically to the crises that Americans endured in the late 1960's. Admonitory rhetoric and judgmental images establish the poet as a cultural historian. The four sections of "Dancing," however, do not trace a chronology, since the work begins and ends in the night before a dawn, with the poet in the dark about his life, but hopeful. There are none of the theological issues that T. S. Eliot explores in *The Waste Land* (1922), and yet Young claims the same correlation between personal and cultural crises and records a spiritual descent followed by a mystical elevation. Writing in the oracular tradition of Walt Whitman, Allen Ginsberg, Amiri Baraka, and the Old Testament prophets, Young envisions a decade of personal experience in the context of his jeremiad on contemporary American culture. "Dancing" begins as the writer, struggling with his muse in the early evening, thinks of the world outside and of the roads he might have taken (heroin dealer, drunken bum, drifter).

Sobered by his thought that he "is capable of being assassinated/ at any moment" (as were Martin Luther King and Robert Kennedy in 1968), and saddened that people continue to live trivial, habitual lives, that the younger generation seeks violent solutions, and that America's commercialism assigns little value to his grandfather's work on a farm, the poet laments the corruption of "Ahhhhhmerica!/ you old happy whore." Sections one and two present the poet's confusion and the decline of America, culminating in a descent "to these dark places/ to these waters"—but, significantly, the drowning is only apparent. The moon is associated with the heart pumping blood, "washing the way clear for new origins," and the blood that is ritually spattered is, symbolically, that of fish.

At the end of section two, the speaker recognizes that attempting to bring "the promiseland" to a chosen few by violent means has only polluted his mind: "the knife doubles back." After this self-inflicted death, section three offers a new beginning: "Be the mystic/ & wage ultimate revolution." All stereotypic revolutionary roles are rejected, and the short homily concludes with the admonition to "Be yourself." Section four makes the connection between the speaker's own past dreams and his projected life. The steps to this new life he learns from a stranger met in April (in Young's calendar, not the cruellest month, but the time of resurrection). The poem concludes where it began, at the writer's desk in early evening, but with a new optimism. As he works, he envisions a people newly energized by the night, he hopes for the dawn, and he pronounces a blessing of peace. The final hortatory line—"Let the revolutions proceed!"—rejects the tyranny of any one ideological movement and advocates the proliferation of individual struggles.

THE SONG TURNING BACK INTO ITSELF

The Song Turning Back into Itself, a collection taking its name from a long poem in seven parts, includes forty-four poems grouped under the five headings "Loneliness," "The Song Turning Back into Itself," "The Prestidigitator," "Everywhere," and "The Move Continuing." In an interview published in *New Orleans Review*, Young explained that *The Song Turning Back into Itself* has three levels of meaning: that history moves in cycles; that American popular music is returning to its roots in folk, African, and other ethnic music; and that the individual, going through changes, nevertheless returns to an original, unique self.

These three returns are all explored in "The Old Fashioned Cincinnati Blues," which appears in the first group of poems. Dedicated to Jesse "Lone Cat" Fuller, and taking its form and its train-ride setting from the

blues, the poem is a nostalgic return to the poet's past—to a trip made by rail from Cincinnati, Ohio, to Meridian, Mississippi, by two young brothers, for a summer visit with grandparents and relatives left behind in the south. Vivid sensual images are fixed in his memory: "RC Cola coolers" and "tin tub baths" and "swapping ghost stories." The adult sees himself as essentially the same as the boy he was in 1949. The poet experiences his journey not just as a personal reminiscence, but as part of the American tradition, for the voice of Walt Whitman can be heard in Young's lines: "O Americana!/ United Statesiana!"

The seven numbered poems titled "The Song Turning Back into Itself" are a spiritual autobiography of the poet, from the baby's first breath through the adult shouting joyfully: "SING/ one sweet long song to undo/ all sickness & suffering." This persona draws on many sources for inspiration, including Billie Holiday (who sings "variations on the theme/ of human love &/ its shadow/ loneliness") and Rainer Maria Rilke (whose eighteenth "Sonnet to Orpheus" may be heard in "Feel today/ vibrating/ in the throat"). Singing the blues becomes, in these poems, an exploration of the singer's identity and roots. Images from his personal memories merge with historical events to suggest recurring cycles, as in the speculation: "Consider Nazis & crackers/ on the same stage/ splitting the bill."

GEOGRAPHY OF THE NEAR PAST

Images correlating personal and cultural history are also charted in *Geography of the Near Past*, a volume comprising five groups of poems: "The Sad Hour of Your Peace," "American Glamour," "Geography of the Near Past," "Some Recent Fiction," and "Boogie with O. O. Gabugah." The first group takes its title from a poem set on a beach at Santa Cruz, and the speaker's sadness at finding a crowded, noisy, banal scene where he had longed for some peace, dissolves in gentle irony as he realizes his nostalgia for a lonely beach where a kid once walked is not a real memory, but "a movie that was never even shot." Most of the poems in this group are occasional, alluding to specific events or observations in an ordinary life: hearing his unborn child move in his wife's womb, eating hot Mexican food with his pregnant wife, a father joyfully recognizing his son's separate life, thoughts while visiting a prison inmate, a meditation while visiting a musician dying of a drug overdose, the memory of writing in a rented room above a cabaret three nights before the building burned down. The endings and beginnings recorded in these poems intertwine.

The poems of "American Glamour" criticize the self-indulgence and spiritual emptiness found in contemporary culture. "Moss" reflects on the trendiness of The Rolling Stones' drug habit, treated by the media as part of their heroic glamour; counterweighting that story, the poet cites the suffering and deaths of the heroin addicts Charlie Parker, Billie Holiday, and Bela Lugosi, performers of an earlier era. Drug dependency is only one symptom of an exhausted society; the young couple in "Making Love After Hours" exemplify the emptiness of repeated transgressions. The poet's condemnation of their lifeless, loveless, casual intercourse is given in several correlative images: the TV movies flickering without sound, the "Yawning display in a budget-store window," and the stumbling drunks on the street. In "Ho" (whore) the poet adopts the voice and speech of a young but streetwise boy, who regretfully observes the trap of prostitution teaching a young woman that "heaven aint the only H in the dictionary." The success of this poem depends on the voice, which is convincing. The syntax is not standard English, but it perfectly conforms to a different set of rules. "I use to know her family" and "She just a skinny little sister" express his compassion and his sense of being connected with her tragedy.

The eleven poems grouped under the heading "Geography of the Near Past" are a traveling author's impressions of Manhattan, Boston, Providence, New Orleans, Detroit, Denver, Mexico City, any inner city, and an ugly stretch of suburban highway, which, together, compose a spiritual map of America. Here Young's verses have more regular line lengths and a loose iambic meter dominates. "Fun City Samba" and "Inner City Blues" conspicuously imitate the musical forms of their titles, and the music of speech heard in the inner city streets mixes easily with the author's more formal language. The final poem of this group is "Geography of the Near Past," and, unlike the others, it appears with each line centered on the page, creating an urn-shaped visual image. Written in the symbolist tradition,

"Geography of the Near Past" presents the perceptive individual's movement through life (or, in context, the author's journey across America) in the developing symbol of swimming: in the first stanza, swimming against the current but with the light; in the second stanza, swimming blindly through foam or fog; and, in the final stanza, seeing through the water-filmed eyes of fish surfacing. Rather than the absolute "beauty is truth, truth beauty," Young's poem assumes the relative and mystical truth of "each universe" seen through the imagination and experience of fellow swimmers. Young, in a later poem ("What Is the Blues?" from *The Blues Don't Change*), links this mystical symbol of swimming with a rediscovery of cultural roots, suggesting that the poet, in exploring and charting a personal geography, also unfolds a map of American social history.

"Some Recent Fiction" groups six poems, including a delightfully dry "Teaching," a dramatic prose poem titled "Cherokees," and a three-part aural dream narrative portraying the black revolutionary lover of a light-skinned woman named Zara, titled "Some Recent Fiction." The poem reveals the revolutionary's egotistic need to express contempt for others ("gentle reader/ creep who buys my hustle") and to dominate Zara (he speaks to her in imperatives, and she remembers the phrase "'I love you, Hitler'" from her experiences at "Bootlick State"). As in the dramatic monologues of Robert Browning, the speaker in this poem exposes his own shallowness to ridicule.

Young creates another dramatic persona in O. O. Gabugah, for whom he writes a mock literary introduction, giving his place of birth as "125th and Lenox in Harlem" and his real name as "Franklin Delano Watson" (he was born in 1945). Rejecting his parents' choice of a white hero's name, he has adopted the name Our Own Gabugah. "Brother Gabugah" is praised by this fatuous critic as "one of our strongest young Black revolutionary voices," and his character embodies the stereotype first defined in Young's "A Dance for Militant Dilettantes." After listing Gabugah's publications and his "Vanderbilt Fellowship to conduct research on Richard Wright," the editor notes that Gabugah does not write, but dictates his poems. The four examples that follow are less parodies of actual poems than imitations of the black activist literature that an American public expects: strident, preachy, and meandering expressions of rage. Each of O. O. Gabugah's poems adopts a different form: "The Old O. O. Blues" appears not in any recognizable blues form, but in a western European ballad stanza rhymed *abab*; "Black Queen for More Than a Day" is a delightfully bad free-verse poem, with mixed metaphors and silly similes and relentless alliteration; "What You Seize Is What You Get" approximates the typographic playfulness of E. E. Cummings and painfully spells out each one of its puns; and "A Poem for Players," listing the few occupations open to blacks in America, is written mostly in quatrains of irregular line length and irregular end rhyme, with the refrain "They'll let you play." O. O. Gabugah's simplistic political analysis assumes that an international conspiracy has assassinated blacks involved in political change, but in the final repetition of the refrain, Young's advocacy of individual self-discovery may be heard: "They'll let you play anybody but you." O. O. Gabugah is playing a profitable role, "funky Baaaaaad-ass/ Afro-headed," but it remains as stereotyped as Sambo.

THE BLUES DON'T CHANGE

Young's unique blending of whimsy and social satire also appears in one of the twenty-seven new poems published in *The Blues Don't Change*. It is a poem written in memory of two men who died on the same day in 1973: "W. H. Auden and Mantan Moreland." Not only does Young violate snobbish propriety by considering a poet of high culture, W. H. Auden, in the same text with a popular comic motion-picture actor, Mantan Moreland, but he also overturns his readers' expectations about their speech patterns. The poem consists of a dialogue between these two, in paradise, with Moreland praising Auden's *The Age of Anxiety* (1947) for "doubtless" engaging "our/ innermost emotions & informed imagination," and Auden responding, "No shit!" One can imagine the curiosity of a fellow poet as Young arranges for Moreland to ask Auden why he cut the line "We must all love one another or die" from his poem "September 1, 1939." The line was superfluous, as Auden's reply declares, "We gon die anyway no matter/ how much we love." Having justified Auden's technique, Young also defends Moreland, whose role-playing was harshly judged by militant activists. Auden praises Moreland's technique, "the way you buck them eyes/ & make out

like you running sked all the time." That fear, Auden notes, is the essence of "the black/ experience where you be in charge of the scene." Moreland did stop "shufflin'," and Young's poem reclaims with pride this actor's achievements.

Several of the poems in *The Blues Don't Change* are tributes to Black American musicians; most notable are "Billie," "The James Cotton Band at Keystone," "My Spanish Heart," and "Lester Leaps In." Each poem recreates the impact of their performances on a rapt listener. Listening to Billie Holiday while drinking, he seems to take in her song through his mouth. The sexuality that Holiday projected in her singing is expressed metaphorically in the listener's fantasy of swallowing her delightful body. The song and his drink intoxicate, "whirling/ me through her throaty world and higher." The listener recognizes the seductress that Holiday enacted in his tribute to her "Cleopatric breath." In contrast to the dreamily slow movement of lines in "Billie," "The James Cotton Band at Keystone" plays with a livelier rhythm, demonstrating "Believe me, the blues can be volatile too,/ but the blues don't bruise; they only renew."

The return to cultural roots revitalizes both the individual and society. In "The Blues Don't Change," his apostrophe to the relentless rhythm and brilliant images of the blues, Young again pays tribute to the uniquely American expression of life's pain and sadness, and to the performers whose artistry lifts the spirit. Working within American forms of speech and music, this poet soars, defining his own voice and enriching America's cultural heritage.

THE SOUND OF DREAMS REMEMBERED

More than a decade passed between Young's 1988 collection titled *Heaven: Collected Poems, 1956-1990* and his 2001 volume *The Sound of Dreams Remembered: Poems, 1990-2000*. *Heaven* filled nearly three hundred pages, displayed an abundant affection for the ordinary world, and showcased several influences (noted in the collection's introduction) that included Amiri Baraka (LeRoi Jones), Vladimir Mayakovsky, and Federico García Lorca.

The work of Langston Hughes and Charles Bukowski makes its influential mark on *The Sound of Dreams Remembered*. Disjointed thoughts, full of mystique and sentiment, like those of Bukowski, are apparent here.

The collection is a readable and topical history of the decade, providing meditations on love, travel, politics, and misbehavior. Casual blank verse gives way to fluid, rhyming iambic pentameter in poems like "The Old Country":

> What is it want,
> or need to haul or lug like Motorolas
> of the blood? Beep! The mileage we squander
> on these jumps from mayonnaise Minnesotas
> to curry Calcuttas, from Tokyos you could wander.

OTHER MAJOR WORKS

LONG FICTION: *Snakes*, 1970; *Who Is Angelina?*, 1975; *Sitting Pretty*, 1976; *Ask Me Now*, 1980; *Seduction by Light*, 1988.

NONFICTION: *Bodies and Soul: Musical Memoirs*, 1981; *Kinds of Blue: Musical Memoirs*, 1984; *Mingus/Mingus: Two Memoirs*, 1989 (with Janet Coleman); *Drowning in a Sea of Love: Musical Memoirs*, 1995.

EDITED TEXTS: *Yardbird Lives!*, 1978 (with Ishmael Reed); *Calafia: The California Poetry*, 1978; *Changing All Those Changes*, 1976 (with James P. Girard); *Zeppelin Coming Down*, 1976 (with William Lawson); *Quilt*, 1981 (with Reed); *Quilt 2*, 1982 (with Reed); *Quilt 4*, 1984 (with Reed); *Quilt 5*, 1986 (with Reed); *African American Literature: A Brief Introduction and Anthology*, 1996.

BIBLIOGRAPHY

Broughton, Irv. *The Writer's Mind: Interviews with American Authors*. Vol. 3. Fayetteville: University of Arkansas Press, 1990. Contains a rare and enlightening interview with Young in which he explains his poetic philosophy. This source is widely available and is useful to undergraduate as well as graduate students. A good overview.

Coleman, Janet, and Al Young. *Mingus/Mingus: Two Memoirs*. Berkeley, Calif.: Creative Arts, 1989. Not much has been written about Young, therefore, Young's own memoir becomes essential for understanding his life and work.

Lee, Don. "About Al Young." *Ploughshares* 19, no. 1 (Spring, 1993): 219. A short profile of Young's life as poet and screenwriter.

Nixon, Will. "Better Times for Black Writers?" *Publishers Weekly* 235 (February 17, 1989): 35-40. Young and several other African American writers and editors speak out regarding their reception in the publishing world.

Ross, Michael E. "Hollywood's Civil Servants." *The New York Times Book Review*, February 5, 1989, 12. Ross profiles Young and some other African American writers working in Hollywood, a town that is traditionally tough on its artists. A lively and interesting article for all students.

Schultz, Elizabeth. "Search for 'Soul Space': A Study of Al Young's *Who Is Angelina?* and the Dimensions of Freedom." In *The Afro-American Novel Since 1960*, edited by Peter Bruck and Wolfgang Karrer. Amsterdam: Gruner, 1982. Young's novel was written in 1975, a time when few fiction works by African Americans were being published. Schultz analyzes his work in terms of the quest for expression, especially when the speaker is out of the mainstream.

Judith L. Johnston,
updated by Sarah Hilbert

EDWARD YOUNG

Born: Upham, England; July 3, 1683 (baptized)
Died: Welwyn, England; April 5, 1765

PRINCIPAL POETRY

An Epistle to the Right Honourable the Lord Landsdowne, 1713

A Poem on the Last Day, 1713

The Force of Religion: Or, Vanquished Love, a Poem, in Two Books, 1714

On the Late Queen's Death, and His Majesty's Accession to the Throne, 1714

A Paraphrase on Part of the Book of Job, 1719

A Letter to Mr. Tickell Occasioned by the Death of Joseph Addison, 1719

The Instalment to the Right Honourable Sir Robert Walpole, Knight of the Most Noble Order of the Garter, 1726

Cynthio, 1727

Love of Fame, the Universal Passion: In Seven Characteristical Satires, 1728

Ocean: An Ode Occasion'd by His Majesty's Late Royal Encouragement of the Sea-Service, 1728

Two Epistles to Mr. Pope, Concerning the Authors of the Age, 1730

Imperium Pelagi: A Naval Lyrick, Written in Imitation of Pindar's Spirit, 1730

The Foreign Address: Or, The Best Argument for Peace, 1735

The Poetical Works of the Reverend Edward Young, 1741

The Complaint: Or, Night-Thoughts on Life, Death, and Immortality, 1742-1746 (commonly known as *Night-Thoughts*)

Resignation: In Two Parts, and a Postscript, 1762

OTHER LITERARY FORMS

Although Edward Young is known primarily for his poetry, he was also a successful playwright, theologian, and literary theorist. In 1719, Young's first play, *Busiris, King of Egypt* (pb. 1719) had a successful run at the

Edward Young (© Michael Nicholson/Corbis)

Theatre Royal in Drury Lane. His second play, *The Revenge: A Tragedy* (pb. 1721) was less successful in its initial production but more enduring. Declared by the great actor David Garrick to be "the best modern play," *The Revenge* was frequently revived throughout the eighteenth and nineteenth centuries. In 1753, Garrick produced Young's final tragedy, *The Brothers: A Tragedy* (wr. 1724, pr., pb. 1753).

In several prose works, Young addressed the religious controversies of his age. Anticipating the themes of his later poetry, *A Vindication of Providence: Or, A True Estimate of Human Life* (1728) examines the effect of passion on human happiness. *The Centaur Not Fabulous* (1755) uses satire to defend Christianity from the assaults of deism and licentiousness.

In 1728, Young completed his first work of literary theory, "A Discourse on Ode," which was published with *Ocean*. In 1759, at the age of seventy-six, Young published *Conjectures on Original Composition* (1759), a work that anticipates many ideas associated with Romanticism.

ACHIEVEMENTS

During his lifetime, Edward Young established connections with some of the leading authors of his time, including Joseph Addison, Alexander Pope, Jonathan Swift, Joseph Warton, and Samuel Richardson. Because of his achievements both as a member of the clergy and as a poet, Young was well respected by his contemporaries, and his poems were successful.

Unlike other poets of his age, Young rejected many of the principles of neoclassicism. Whereas poets like Alexander Pope sought to imitate classical authors and replicate the order they found in nature, Young believed poetry should explore the experiences of the individual, especially those experiences that remain inexplicably mysterious. As he wrote in *Night-Thoughts*, "Nothing can satisfy, but what confounds;/ Nothing, but what astonishes, is true." Recognizing the unique quality of his work, Joseph Warton described Young as a "sublime and original genius." Samuel Johnson remained more guarded, concluding, "with all his defects, he was a man of genius and a poet."

Young's work had considerable influence on later poets, especially those associated with British Romanticism (notably William Blake and Samuel Taylor Coleridge) and with the Sturm und Drang movement in Germany (Friedrich Gottlieb Klopstock and Johann Wolfgang von Goethe).

BIOGRAPHY

Edward Young was born in July, 1683, the son of a prominent clergyman and godson of Princess Anne. At age eleven, he enrolled in Winchester College. In 1702, Young was admitted to New College, Oxford, but left without a degree after his father's death in 1705. He eventually completed both the bachelor of laws degree in 1714 and the doctor of laws degree in 1719 at All Souls College, Oxford. While working on his degrees, Young established himself as a poet and sought to secure financial support from a patron. In 1713, he published his first poem, *An Epistle to the Right Honorable the Lord Lansdowne*. During that same year, Young completed *A Poem on the Last Day*, which was dedicated to Queen Anne, whose illness and subsequent death provided the occasions for Young's next poems in 1714: *The Force of Religion: Or, Vanquished Love, a Poem, in Two Books* and *On the Late Queen's Death, and His Majesty's Accession to the Throne*.

Young continued his search for patronage, eventually receiving an annuity from the duke of Wharton. In 1719, Young published *A Paraphrase of the Book of Job*, which shows his continued interest in the religious sublime, and *A Letter to Mr. Tickell Occasioned by the Death of Joseph Addison*, a loving tribute to Young's friend Joseph Addison, who died in 1719. Over the next several years, Young completed three plays and took deacon's orders in the Anglican Church. Turning his attention toward satire, Young completed several works that were collectively published in 1728 under the title *Love of Fame, the Universal Passion*. These satires helped Young secure a royal pension of two hundred pounds per year. He became a royal chaplain to the king in 1728 and published a patriotic poem, *Ocean*. In 1730, Young became rector at Welwyn, Hertfordshire. He continued writing both satire (*Two Epistles to Mr. Pope*) and occasional verse (*Imperium Pelagi*), hoping to receive more substantial preferment.

In 1731, Young married Lady Elizabeth Lee, a widow with three children and the granddaughter of Charles II. Young's son Frederick was born in 1732. After suffering the loss of his stepdaughter, his friend Henry Temple, and his wife, Young began writing his most famous poetry, *The Complaint: Or, Night-Thoughts on Life, Death, and Immortality*, which was published between 1742 and 1746 and collected in a single edition in 1750. During this time, Young established friendships with the duchess of Portland, who campaigned in vain for his advancement, and the novelist Samuel Richardson, who contributed to *The Centaur Not Fabulous* and *Conjectures on Original Composition*. In 1762, at the age of seventy-nine, Young published his last poem, *Resignation*. Following a long illness, Young died on April 5, 1765.

ANALYSIS

Focusing attention exclusively on his most distinctive work, *Night-Thoughts*, modern readers frequently overlook much of Edward Young's achievement. By the time he began writing *Night-Thoughts* in the 1740's, Young had been a successful poet for almost thirty years. Although there are common thematic concerns present in many of Young's works, his poetry is most notable for its diversity.

A POEM ON THE LAST DAY

One of Young's first published works, *A Poem on the Last Day* celebrates the Peace of Utrecht (1713), which ended the War of the Spanish Succession. Rather than offering a simple patriotic poem, Young uses the occasion of peace to explore the impermanence of all worldly things. The three-book poem, written with epic tone and in heroic couplets, begins with a survey of the natural world. Although nature seems to assert God's continual presence—"How great, how firm, how sacred, all appears!"—the world remains mutable and full of sin. Individuals, Young argues, should never forget the judgment of the last day. Recognizing that true greatness cannot be achieved during life, Young instructs his reader to tread on "virtues path" and to inherit divine knowledge and eternal salvation after death: "Thou, minor, canst not guess thy vast estate,/ What stores, on foreign coasts, thy landing wait."

THE FORCE OF RELIGION

A narrative poem written in heroic couplets, *The Force of Religion* recalls Lady Jane Grey's final hours before being executed by Mary Tudor. Celebrating the spiritual triumph of Protestantism over Catholicism, the poem addresses England's fear of Jacobitism during the final days of Queen Anne's reign. Young's purpose, however, exceeds the immediate political crises of his time. *The Force of Religion*, like *A Poem on the Last Day* and much of Young's later poetry, ultimately explores the conflict between the earthly and the eternal.

LOVE OF FAME, THE UNIVERSAL PASSION

Satire, the most characteristic form of eighteenth century literature, can be divided into two forms: Horatian and Juvenalian. In the preface to *Love of Fame, the Universal Passion*, Young places his work within the good-natured Horatian tradition:

> . . . laughing satire bids the fairest for success. . . . This kind of satire only has any delicacy in it. . . . Horace is the best master: he appears in good humour while he censures.

In contrast to harsh, vituperative Juvenalian satirists like Jonathan Swift, Young assumes that human folly can be corrected through humor. Like Joseph Addison and Richard Steele, who also wrote Horatian satire, Young structures his work around fictional characters that exemplify the specific follies. Although Young's use of character is unique in verse satire, he follows the traditions of his age by writing in heroic couplets and including elements of the mock epic.

For modern readers, the most interesting—and perhaps infuriating—satires are those that address women. Like other eighteenth century writers, Young calls for women to accept a subordinate role and warns them against worldly and intellectual ambition. For Young, "Women were made to give our [male] eyes delight," and they should "Beware the fever of the mind!" At times Young's satire loses its Horatian tone and becomes distinctly Juvenalian as he oscillates between celebrating feminine virtue and ridiculing feminine vice.

Young's satire ends with an acknowledgment that the love of fame is, if rightly applied, a divine gift that can lead individuals, such as George II, Queen Caroline, and Robert Walpole, to great and benevolent accomplishments.

THE COMPLAINT: OR, NIGHT-THOUGHTS ON LIFE, DEATH, AND IMMORTALITY

Critics have argued that *Night-Thoughts* originated as a response to Alexander Pope's *An Essay on Man* (1733-1734), which urges the reader to focus attention on the earthly and knowable. Hoping to show his reader the significance of the mysterious and sublime, Young reverses Pope's earthbound approach and sings of "immortal man." Through a series of nine meditative poems, an older speaker, sometimes assumed to be Young himself, councils Lorenzo, a younger man of pleasure who is inclined toward both atheism and deism.

Like other eighteenth century writers, Young initially argues for God's presence and human immortality from empirical evidence. Proclaiming that devotion is the "daughter of astronomy," Young suggests that the divine can be discovered through science. This argument, however, cannot persuade Lorenzo, who, as David B. Morris states, "will not be *argued* into faith." The speaker then explores the mysterious world of the night. In so doing, he does not reject reason but asserts that it must be aided by passion and feeling: "to feel, is to be fir'd;/ And to believe, Lorenzo! is to feel."

Although Young's poetry explores mortality and grief, his night is not a gloomy, melancholy place. Unlike the graveyard poets, such as Robert Blair and Thomas Parnell, who were fascinated by the physical and psychological horror of death, Young finds reconciliation and spiritual resurrection in the night. Near the end of the poem, the speaker proclaims, "Of darkness, now, no more:/ Joy breaks; shines; triumphs; 'tis eternal day." Having experienced the night in an emotional and deeply personal way, the speaker ends the poem with a hopefulness that sees beyond mortality.

OTHER MAJOR WORKS

PLAYS: *Busiris, King of Egypt*, pb. 1719; *The Revenge: A Tragedy*, pb. 1721; *The Brothers: A Tragedy*, wr. 1724, pr., pb. 1753.

NONFICTION: *A Vindication of Providence: Or, A True Estimate of Human Life*, 1728; *An Apology for Princes: Or, The Reverence Due to Government*, 1729; *The Centaur Not Fabulous*, 1755; *An Argument Drawn from the Circumstances of Christ's Death, for the Truth of His Religion*, 1758; *Conjectures on*

Original Composition in a Letter to the Author of Sir Charles Grandison, 1759 (better known as *Conjectures on Original Composition*).

MISCELLANEOUS: *The Complete Works, Poetry and Prose, of the Rev. Edward Young*, 1854

BIBLIOGRAPHY

Forester, Harold. *Edward Young: The Poet of "The Night Thoughts," 1683-1765*. New York: Erskin, 1986. Containing a wealth of information, this biography exceeds the earlier biographical works of Walter Thomas (*Le Poète Edward Young*, 1901) and Henry C. Shelley (*The Life and Letters of Edward Young*, 1914). Forester provides a thorough investigation of Young's career and his position within eighteenth century British culture.

Morris, David B. *The Religious Sublime: Christian Poetry and Critical Tradition in Eighteenth Century England*. Lexington: University Press of Kentucky, 1972. Morris's study provides a particularly useful reading of *Night-Thoughts* and positions Young's work within the context of eighteenth century religious controversies. Morris's discussion of the sublime, especially as it relates to the speaker's subjective, emotional responses, is particularly valuable, as is his discussion of Young's rhetorical strategy.

Nussbaum, Felicity. *The Brink of All We Hate: English Satires on Women, 1660-1750*. Lexington: University Press of Kentucky, 1984. Nussbaum provides a cogent discussion of Young's frequently overlooked satire, *Love of Fame, the Universal Passion*. Focusing exclusively on those parts of the work that concern women, Nussbaum reveals the very limited role that Young assigned to women. Equally important, Nussbaum finds in Young's work a shift, albeit an incomplete one, from the harsh ridicule of feminine weakness in the early eighteenth century to the lavish praise of feminine virtue in the later eighteenth century.

Patey, Douglas Lane. "Art and Integrity: Concepts of Self in Alexander Pope and Edward Young." *Modern Philology* 83, no. 4 (1986): 364-378. Patey's essay examines the relationship between Alexander Pope's *An Essay on Man* and *Night-Thoughts*. The two poems, Patey argues, present different understandings of the self and spirituality. For Pope identity and spirituality are social constructions. For Young identity is private and subjective. Through Young's poetry, "the soul is deliberately led to look inward, in order to disentangle itself from all merely worldly (and hence false) roles, and so to uncover its true self."

St. John Bliss, Isabel. *Edward Young*. New York: Twayne, 1969. This older study still provides an excellent starting point for readers of Young's poetry. Offering a chronologically based discussion of Young's major and minor works, the study is especially useful in correcting some of the misunderstandings about Young's works that have survived from the nineteenth century.

Wanko, Cheryl L. "The Making of a Minor Poet: Edward Young and Literary Taxonomy." *English Studies* 72, no. 4 (1991): 355-367. Wanko argues convincingly that Young's reputation suffered throughout the twentieth century because of "our system of literary taxonomy." Wanko demonstrates how eighteenth and nineteenth century appraisals of Young's work made him appear to be a literary anomaly.

Christopher D. Johnson

Z

ADAM ZAGAJEWSKI

Born: Lwów, Poland (now in Ukraine); April 21, 1945

PRINCIPAL POETRY

Komunikat, 1972
Sklepy mi(ęogon)sne, 1975
List, 1978
Oda do wielości, 1983 (with *List*)
Jechai do Lwówa, 1985
Tremor: Selected Poems in English, 1985
Płótno, 1990 (*Canvas*, 1991)
Dzikie czereśnie: Wybór wierszy, 1992
Ziemia Ognista, 1994
Trzej Aniołowie, Three Angels, 1997 (bilingual selection)
Mysticism for Beginners, 1997 (selection)
Pó ne Święta, 1998 (selection)
Pragnienie, 1999
Without End: New and Selected Poems, 2002

OTHER LITERARY FORMS

Although poetry constitutes the most important part of Adam Zagajewski's oeuvre, he also has written three novels: *Ciepło zimno* (1975; it's cold, it's warm), *Das absolute Gehör* (1982; absolute pitch), and *Cienka kreska* (1983; thin line). Zagajewski's fiction, patterned on the traditional *Bildungsroman*, is an ironic reworking of this nineteenth century genre.

Zagajewski also published a number of important essays and essay collections. His *Świat nie przedstawiony* (1974; the world not represented), coauthored by Julian Kornhauser, played a seminal role in shaping the literary consciousness of the decade. *Drugi Oddech* (1978; second wind) and *Solidarność i samotność* (1986; *Solidarity, Solitude: Essays*, 1990), continue probing the question of literature's ethical and social responsibility.

Dwa miasta (1991; *Two Cities: On Exile, History, and the Imagination*, 1995) and *W cudzym pięknie* (1998; *Another Beauty*, 2000) explore the richness and variety of Europe, as found in the author's memories, readings, and travels. Zagajewski is also the author of *Polen: Staat im Schatten der Sowjetunion* (1981; Poland: a state in the shackles of the Soviet Union), an analysis of the Polish state under Soviet rule.

ACHIEVEMENTS

The literary debut of Adam Zagajewski took place in a country oppressed by Soviet domination. This historical circumstance led the poet and other writers of his generation (known as the Generation 68, or the New Wave) to take upon themselves the duty of opposing both political oppression and the conformist attitudes found among Polish intellectuals, thus turning around the Communist slogan, "Writers are the conscience of the nation." Although in his later writings Zagajewski abandoned the earlier political agenda, his poetry never ceased to defend the human right to individual perception and sensitivity. Zagajewski's poems have been translated into English, French, German, Greek, Hebrew, Italian, and Swedish.

Zagajewski received a number of prestigious fellowships and awards, including the Jurzykowski Foundation Award, a fellowship from the Berliner Kunstlerprogram, the Guggenheim Fellowship, the Prix de la Liberté, the International Vilenica Award, the Kurt Tucholsky Prize, and the Tranströmer Prize.

BIOGRAPHY

Adam Zagajewski was born in Lwów to a family of Polish intelligentsia. When he was four months old, his family was forced to abandon the city of his birth and to move westward, reflecting the newly reshuffled Polish borders. The Zagajewskis settled in the Silesian town of Gliwice, where Adam spent his childhood and adolescence. Throughout these early years, his family kept alive the memory of their hometown: ". . . I spent my childhood in an ugly industrial city; I was brought there when I was barely four months old, and then for many years afterward I was told about an extraordinarily beautiful city that my family had to leave." Nevertheless, Zagajewski's sensitivity allowed him to find enchantment even in the unattractive town of his youth.

At the age of eighteen, Zagajewski left Gliwice to pursue a university education in the historic town of Cracow. After receiving degrees in philosophy and psychology at the Jagiellonian University, he worked as an assistant professor at the Akademia Górniczo-Hutnicza (University of Mining and Metallurgy). It was during this period that he became the cofounder of the poetic group Teraz (Now) as well as the coauthor of its literary program. The poets of Teraz emphasized the social importance of poetry and its role in reclaiming a language devalued by the rhetorical manipulations of a bureaucratic, totalitarian state. In 1972 Zagajewski became one of the editors of *Student*. He was also involved in editorial work at such prestigious literary journals as *Odra* and *Znak*. After signing a letter of protest concerning amendments to the Polish constitution in 1976, Zagajewski suffered the fate of many Polish writers of the time: The government placed a ban on his publications, effectively ending the official circulation of his works.

In 1979 Zagajewski won a scholarship from the Berlin Kunstlerprogram and went to Berlin. After a brief return to Poland, he emigrated to Paris in 1982. Unlike many Polish artists, Zagajewski chose to leave his homeland for personal, not political, reasons. In Paris he became involved in editing *Zeszyty Literackie* (literary review), a seminal émigré literary journal. In 1989 Zagajewski began teaching creative writing at the University of Houston, Texas, spending four months there out of each year.

Having moved from Lwów to Gliwice to Cracow to Berlin to Paris to Houston, in the course of his life Zagajewski became a wanderer and a citizen of the world. The poet described his own cosmopolitan status:

> I am now like a passenger of a small submarine, which has not one, but four periscopes. The first, and major, one points to my native tradition. The second opens up toward the literature of Germany, its poetry, its—onetime—desire of the infinite. The third—toward the landscape of French culture, with its penetrating intelligence and Jansenist morality. The fourth—toward [William] Shakespeare, [John] Keats and Robert Lowell, the literature of the concrete, of passion and conversation.

ANALYSIS

Critics frequently divide the poetry of Adam Zagajewski into two major periods: one "political," focused on the problems of the human community, the other "philosophical," concerned with the individual. The poet's first three collections, published during the 1970's, followed the poetic program of the Generation 68, with its emphasis on the social responsibilities of the artist in a totalitarian state. Beginning with the fourth collection, *Oda do wielości* (ode to plurality), published after his emigration to Paris, Zagajewski turned to a poetry of philosophical reflection, rich in complex metaphors and sophisticated symbolism. A number of his contemporaries had commented on the poet's passage from one period to the other. However, it is also important to emphasize the continuity of themes and methods in Zagajewski's work. Even in the most political poems, he deals with the oppression of the individual. Even the most private lyrical reflections are situated within the broader context of European, or world, culture.

KOMUNIKAT, SKLEPY MIĘSNE, AND LIST

When Zagajewski and other poets of his generation, such as Stanisław Barańczak, Julian Kornhauser, Ryszard Krynicki, Ewa Lipska, and others, set out to wage poetic war on the Communist state, they focused their efforts on laying bare the "falsified language" of state propaganda and bureaucracy. The newspeak favored by the government and disseminated by the mass media had become, according to the young poets, a tool of totalitarian oppression. Rather than representing reality, such language falsified it. In contrast, the poetry of the Generation 68 was to be plain, clear, and direct. It aimed at a sincere realism, a reclamation of the concrete. This goal is illustrated in Zagajewski's poem "Sklepy Mięsne" (meat shops). The poem describes the change from the older, straightforward term "butcher," to the new, sanitized "meat shop," a name that conceals rather than reveals the true nature of the establishment.

Another feature of Generation 68 poetry is an interest in the problems of its time, adequately reflected in the name of the poetic group Teraz (Now), of which Zagajewski was a co-creator. His early poetry collections, *Komunikat* (communiqué), *Sklepy Mięsne*, and, to a lesser extent, *List* (a letter), realized the ideals of contemporaneity and simplicity. These poems spoke of

Communist Poland in a language verging on the prosaic. They were characterized by a frequent use of the present tense (conveying a sense of immediacy), a scarcity of conjunctions and adverbs, and a disciplined syntax. Syntactic simplicity is particularly apparent in the first collection and gives way to slightly more sophisticated structures, such as inversion, in the later volumes. This simple, almost conversational form revealed a deep distrust of inflated or manipulative language. The goal of Zagajewski's early poetry was to defend the individual against the obscure manipulations, linguistic and otherwise, of the regime. Like other members of his generation, Zagajewski strongly believed in the ethical dimension of a poetic calling.

ODA DO WIELOŚCI

The title poem of Zagajewski's fourth collection, *Oda do wielości* (ode to plurality), introduced a theme that would become central to the poet's subsequent writing: a fascinated affirmation of the world's multiplicity and richness:

> I don't understand it all and I am
> even glad that the world like a restless
> ocean exceeds my ability
> to understand . . .
> You, singular soul, stand before
> This abundance. Two eyes, two hands,
> Ten inventive fingers, and
> Only one ego, the wedge of an orange,
> the youngest of sisters. . . .

While a number of poems in this 1982 collection still address painful political issues, such as "Petit," "Zwycięstwo" (victory), and "Ogień" (fire), others point in a new direction. Tadeusz Nyczek, in 1988, described this ideological shift in Zagajewski's writing as a turn from "no" to "yes," from negation (negating the totalitarian state) to affirmation (affirming the world, its richness, and its sensual existence). With the expansion of themes came an expansion of form: The syntax became more intricate; the metaphors became increasingly sophisticated and abundant. Zagajewski's later poetry is characterized by complex metaphorical structures of great intensity and beauty. Czesław Miłosz in 1985 described the artistic development of his fellow Pole and poet: "His poems have been acquiring a more and more sumptuous texture, and now he appears to me as a skillful weaver whose work is not unlike Gobelin tapestries where trees, flowers, and human figures coexist in the same pattern."

JECHAI DO LWOWA, CANVAS, AND ZIEMIA OGNISTA

Jechai do Lwowa (to go to Lwów), *Canvas*, and *Ziemia Ognista* (Tierra del Fuego), the collections published from the mid-1980's to the mid-1990's, offer sophisticated meditations on the nature of memory, history, art, culture, and the spiritual quest of humankind at the end of the twentieth century.

The poem "Jechai do Lwowa" ("To Go to Lwów") is an imaginary journey to the place of the poet's birth, conjuring up both the magic of the "lost" city, with its "white napkins and a bucket/ full of raspberries standing on the floor" and the ruthless political "scissors" which brought about destruction and exile. The poem "W obcych miastach" (in strange cities, from *Canvas*) captures the delight of journeys to unknown places: "In strange cities, there's an unexpected joy/ the cool pleasure of a new regard." Cities, visited in person or in the imagination, become an important theme in Zagajewski's poetry. "Widok Krakowa" (the view of Cracow, from *Jechai do Lwówa*) is a tender and eclectic portrait of the former Polish capital. "Widok Delf" (the view of Delf) from the same collection honors both the place and its painter.

These are poems deeply embedded in the European cultural tradition. Zagajewski pays poetic homage not only to Europe's metropolises but also to its artists and thinkers. The poet invokes the composers Franz Schubert and Wolfgang Amadeus Mozart, the painters Jan Vermeer and Rembrandt, the poet C. K. Norwid, the philosopher Friedrich Nietzsche, and many others.

While delighting in the richness of art and culture, Zagajewski remains aware of the reverse side of civilization—wars, genocide, cruelty. His poems present a world in a state of paradox. An acute awareness of the paradoxical nature of reality is expressed in the poem "Lawa" (lava) from *Canvas*:

> And what if Heraclitus and Parmenides
> are both right
> and two worlds exist side by side,

one serene, the other insane; one arrow
thoughtlessly hurtles, another, indulgent,
looks on; the selfsame wave moves and stands still. . . .

The proper response to a paradoxical reality is perhaps a stance of permanent inquiry, constant alertness and distrust. Such a mindset has always been part of Zagajewski's poetics. One of his preferred characters is the wanderer—homeless, always journeying toward a yet unknown goal. The collection *Ziemia Ognista* is dominated by traveling and homelessness, as in the poem "Szukaj" (search):

> I returned to the town
> where I was a child
> and a teenager and an old man of thirty.
> The town greeted me indifferently . . .
> Find another place.
> Search for it.
> Search for your true homeland.

Zagajewski's mature poetry has become a poetry of spiritual inquiry. Agnostic and mystical, it seeks the "nameless, unseen, silent." In "Gotyk" ("The Gothic," from *Jechai do Lwówa*), the speaker asks: "Who am I here in this cool cathedral and who/ is speaking to me so obscurely?" Another poem from the same collection brings the lament: "So many errors, with an incorporeal/ ruler governing a tangible reality." The title poem of the later volume *Ziemia Ognista* ends with the prayer: "Nameless, unseen, silent,/ save me from anesthesia,/ take me to Tierra del Fuego. . . ."

The contrast between the "anesthetized" late twentieth century with its bored, sate conformity, and the desire for a genuine spiritual experience is the theme of Zagajewski's next collection.

PRAGNIENIE

The *fin de siècle* collection *Pragnienie* (desire) opens with childhood memories and ends with a self-portrait of a mature artist, "between the computer, a pencil, and a typewriter, " living in "strange cities," listening to "Bach, Mahler, Chopin, Shostakovich," reading "poets, living and dead." This artist is no longer young and knows it. His voice has grown quiet, reflective. At this stage of his life, he has many dead to mourn. The collection contains a number of elegies dedicated to other poets (Joseph Brodsky, Zbigniew Herbert) and artists (Krzysztof Kieślowski, Józef Czapski). The theme of death and loss pervades this nostalgic volume.

Pragnienie is both a very private reflection on the poet's life, and, as Zagajewski's former translator Renata Gorczyńska has it, a report on the conditions of the human community at the end of the twentieth century. Zagajewski portrays a Western culture devoid of genuine spiritual values, atrophied, sedated, paralyzed with boredom. Always sensitive to the ethical role of literature, the poet has diagnosed a new threat to the human spirit: Like a totalitarian regime, mass culture blunts sensitivity and chokes metaphysical inquiry. Can poetry kindle a new flame? Awaken a new desire? These are the questions Zagajewski poses at the end of a troubled century.

OTHER MAJOR WORKS

LONG FICTION: *Ciełpo zimno*, 1975; *Das absolute Gehör*, 1982; *Cienka kreska*, 1983.

NONFICTION: *Świat nie przedstawiony*, 1974 (with Julian Kornhauser); *Drugi Oddech*, 1978; *Polen: Staat im Schatten der Sowjetunion*, 1981; *Solidarność i samotność*, 1986 (*Solidarity, Solitude: Essays*, 1990); *Dwa miasta*, 1991 (*Two Cities: On Exile, History, and the Imagination*, 1995); *W cudzym pięknie*, 1998 (*Another Beauty*, 2000).

TRANSLATIONS: *Świat i uczestnik*, 1981 (of Raymond Aron); *Religia, literatura i komunizm: Dziennik emigranta*, 1990 (of Mircea Eliade).

BIBLIOGRAPHY

Bieńkowski, Zbigniew. "The New Wave: A Non-Objective View." In *The Mature Laurel: Essays on Modern Polish Poetry*, edited by Adam Czerniawski. Chester Springs, Pa.: Seren Books, Dufour, 1991. A sensitive and balanced overview of New Wave poetry in the context of several earlier postwar poetic generations. Includes translations of poems by Zagajewski, Ewa Lipska, Julian Kornhauser, Stanisław Barańczak, and others.

Nyczek, Tadeusz. "Kot w mokrym ogrodzie." In *Emigranci*. London: Anex, 1988. A compelling account of Zagajewski's poetic transformation in the early 1980's, rendered in a friendly, conversational tone by a friend of the poet. In Polish.

Karpowicz, Tymoteusz. "Naked Poetry: A Discourse About the Newest Polish Poetry." *Polish Review* 1/2 (1976): 59-70. An insightful report on the state of Polish poetry, from the time Zagajewski was publishing his first collections. Written by a well-known Polish poet.

Shallcross, Bożena. "The Divining Moment: Adam Zagajewski's Aesthetic Epiphany." *Slavic and East European Journal* 44, no. 2 (2000): 234-252. An analysis of epiphany and its importance to the artistic sensitivity of Zagajewski; looks at Zagajewski's responses to works of art, such as Jan Vermeer's painting *Girl Interrupted in Her Music* and Carlos Saura's film *Flamenco*.

Witkowski, Tadeusz. "The Poets of the New Wave in Exile." *Slavic and East European Journal* 33, no. 2 (1989): 204-216. An account of the émigré works by poets once belonging to the New Wave; addresses the problem of poetry's ethical responsibility and presents the poetic and ideological debate between Zagajewski and another poet of his generation, Ryszard Krynicki.

Magdalena Mączyńska

PAUL ZIMMER

Born: Canton, Ohio; September 18, 1934

PRINCIPAL POETRY

A Seed on the Wind: Poems, 1960
The Ribs of Death, 1967
The Republic of Many Voices, 1969
The Zimmer Poems, 1976
With Wanda: Town and Country Poems, 1980
The Ancient Wars, 1981
Earthbound Zimmer, 1983
Family Reunion: Selected and New Poems, 1983
The American Zimmer, 1984
Live With Animals, 1987
The Great Bird of Love: Poems, 1989
Big Blue Train: Poems, 1993
Crossing to Sunlight: Selected Poems, 1996

OTHER LITERARY FORMS

Paul Zimmer has written a number of other works, including critical essays and personal memoirs, such as "The Importance of Being Zimmer" in *American Poets in 1976* (1976) and "In the Palm of My Hand" in *The Atlanta Journal and Constitution Magazine* (1980). Miscellaneous pieces by Paul Zimmer include "Zimmer's Old-Fashioned Summer Day Mud Cakes," a recipe, in *John Keats's Porridge: Favorite Recipes of American Poets* (1975), and "The Atomic Bomb," "Robert Frost," "Teaching Poetry," and "Strip Mining," radio commentaries written for recitation on *From the Press* between 1977 and 1978.

ACHIEVEMENTS

Paul Zimmer has received major awards such as the Borestone Mountain Award (1971), the *Yankee* Poetry Prize (1972), the Helen Bullis Award, *Poetry Northwest* (1975), two Pushcart Prizes (1977, 1981), an American Academy and Institute of Arts and Letters Award (1985), two National Endowment for the Arts Grants (1975, 1982), and a National Poetry Series selection (1988).

BIOGRAPHY

Paul Jerome Zimmer was born in Canton, Ohio, on September 18, 1934, to Jerome F. and Louise Surmont Zimmer. He enrolled in Kent State University in 1952 but had a tumultuous college career interrupted first by military service (1954-1955) then by academic ineptitude: He failed freshman English three times. During Zimmer's stint in the U.S. Army, which provided the young man with much free time and little to do, he discovered that he liked poetry. During those years, he voraciously read and tentatively wrote poetry. After his military service, he returned to college to continue studying poetry with an eye toward writing and publishing. After receiving his bachelor's degree in 1958, Zimmer wrote, "I had this complex that I was not terribly important, so . . . I made poems about other people and spoke through their bodies, their beings." The creator of the archetypical "Zimmer" persona would later find that his creativity abounded in the recollection of his own being.

After college, Zimmer held a number of jobs related to books: manager of the book department at Macy's department store in San Francisco (1961-1963), manager of the San Francisco News Company (1963-1964), and manager of the University of California, Los Angeles, bookstore (1964-1966). In 1967 he found an outlet for his poetic talents as assistant director of the University of Pittsburgh Press and editor of the Pitt Poetry Series (1967-1978). He directed the University of Georgia Press (1978-1984), then the University of Iowa Press (1984-1998). The author of "Sonnet: Zimmer Imagines Being Poet-in-Residence," he was twice named a university poet in residence, first at Chico State College (now California State University, Chico) in 1970 and then at Hollins University in 2001, where he was named Louis D. Rubin, Jr., writer in residence.

ANALYSIS

Although Paul Zimmer's poetry frequently features a character named Zimmer (particularly in the later books of verse), it would be reductive to claim that Zimmer writes solely from an autobiographical perspective. Certainly Zimmer represents a crucial part of the poet's psyche, but so too do his other characters, including Imbellis, Barney, and even Wanda. Rather than being viewed strictly as autobiographical writings, Zimmer's poems should be considered as a number of lenses through which the internal poetic self can be examined. Instead of speaking with autobiographical directness, Zimmer's poems often confront the self through a series of masks. Working through his own concerns with the traditions of English-language poetry, Zimmer's poems explore both the value of that tradition and the burdens it places on him as a poet. The self developed in Zimmer's poems often creates a kind of Whitmanesque tone of broad embrace, yet Zimmer's persona is more involved with doubt and anger than that of Whitman. This voice constantly questions the significance of American life, rather than more clearly celebrating it.

A SEED ON THE WIND

In many interviews, Zimmer identified his first book of poetry as *The Ribs of Death*. That volume, however, is the first book of his poetry to be published by a major press. His actual first book of verse, a privately printed limited edition of two hundred copies, was *A Seed on the Wind*. This slim volume, a selection of poems on a variety of natural topics such as animals, birds, and flowers,

demonstrates the genesis of Zimmer's themes. Nineteen poems laud the beauty and simplicity of the natural world in comparison to the dissolution and complexity of the human world. "A Hunting Song" demonstrates this contrast in fifteen terse, unrhymed lines. The human world, as represented by a foxhunting party, is frantic and murderous, breaking the silence of the deep wood with the loud barking of its hunting dogs. The natural world, as represented by the foxglove, although more delicate than the fox and hunting party, is shown to be more permanent and ever-living:

> Bruised by insect wings and
> Crushed perfumeless by
> Stumbling feet, they will
> Yet survive alone, defying
> The probings of our greenest thumbs.

Nature, as opposed to humanity, is eternal—it preceded and will follow humankind's encroachment, just as the foxglove remains long after the hunting party, having collected its bloody prize, has left the wood.

EARTHBOUND ZIMMER

Earthbound Zimmer, a book-length poem, consists of eleven separate movements, each of which describes a memory and its philosophical consequences. The verses, unrhymed quatrains, expand upon and delineate more carefully the preceding prose passages. So the rhythm of the book alternates between expansion and contraction as it moves from prose to verse. The language of verse is such that it explores symbols and archetypes, while the book as a whole develops into a meditation on the greater truths of life.

Even the theme inherent in the volume as a whole is cyclic in its rhythms. As writer Rod Jellerma commented, the poems pursue love through earth, air, fire, and water and also through the four seasons. Initial failure leads inevitably to love, to the birth of two children, and then to a final dissolution of all things in an almost medieval description of the cycle of life. For example, in "Mrs. Scheffley," Zimmer compares images of love and fire in verse, triggered by his memory, in prose, of an old lady in his neighborhood who burned to death in her own backyard trash fire:

> Fire was my beginning, begetter
>   of the wound I was born in, my parents

broken and smoking, hot darkness, enemies,
  the abrasive tongue of the bear.

Elsewhere, Zimmer describes nature arising to the warmth of spring out of the long, cold sleep of winter. These images of spring have been triggered by his memory of losing a fistfight started by his protest against the killing of baby mice in the spring—another example of his character Zimmer drawn into violence over internal guilt and compassion for living things:

Mountains poke circles in stars,
  fish poke circles in lakes;
I ascend through circumferences
  into the hills of spring,

earth smelling of decisions
  slow division of cells, sudden
boilings of minnows, seeds, cocoons,
  authority of grass once again.

These two verses, like those in the other nine sections of the poem, show Zimmer's careful blending of incidents in his life and stirrings of symbols from the collective unconscious, the deeper level within all humans that inspires myth and fable.

THE GREAT BIRD OF LOVE

This volume of verse, selected by poet William Stafford as one of the five volumes published in 1989 in the National Poetry Series, is, like *Earthbound Zimmer*, a selection of verses crafted by a master poet, celebrating the beauty of language, driven by images of mythological importance. In the title poem, the speaker is transformed into a phenomenal force, signified by a "the" before "Zimmer."

Other poems in the collection also display intense, allegorical imagery. Zimmer's images compel the reader to identify with each situation as the persona of The Zimmer comes of age. The book is a series of verses, each poem an episode of an overall story, filled with the joys and sorrows of life. It celebrates the commonplace in life, such as love and beer, bemoans the aging of one's father, and laments the selling of a childhood home. The poems are full of variety and the humorous voice of an experienced guide to life.

CROSSING TO SUNLIGHT

A collection of more than one hundred poems rang-

ing across thirty-five years, *Crossing to Sunlight* offers both a retrospective and a fresh look at the work of Zimmer. The volume begins with Zimmer's early, more structured and traditional writing, moves through the autobiographical poems of his middle years and the creation of his buoyant persona, Zimmer, and concludes with a generous selection of his mature work with its emphasis on durable basic themes.

A typical poem in this volume describes Zimmer in a moment of metaphoric insight, recalled long after the actual occurrence of the triggering incident: "Grouse" describes a rural neighbor's present of a dead bird. When taken apart as recommended, the gift provides Zimmer with "A ball of delicate meat the size/ Of a small, green apple." He is suffused with compassion for the dead bird at the same time that he is repulsed by its death.

The poems in *Crossing to Sunlight* range from parodic to amatory to self-effacing, with humor running throughout. "Zimmer Loathing the Gentry" ends with the comment that the wealthy and the powerful "sign their names and something happens./ While, Zimmer, I can write, Zimmer,/ All day, and nothing happens."

Crossing to Sunlight shows the Zimmer persona matured in surety and grace from the earliest poems but without having changed his basic function as a speaker of the key truths of life. Although the poet may have flunked freshman English in college and the character (as noted in *Earthbound Zimmer*) "is no native genius," Zimmer's Zimmer has an almost prophetic view of the way the world works. What the Zimmer persona observes and tries to shape into poetic words is often a world riddled with terror and disturbance. However, even such a terror-ridden world is also immensely rewarding. Like the self-portraits of the character Zimmer, the world is a place grown to fatness with its love of pleasure and beauty.

OTHER MAJOR WORKS

NONFICTION: *After the Fire: A Writer Finds His Place*, 2002.

BIBLIOGRAPHY

Aldan, Daisy. "The Words of the Tribe." *Poetry* 118, no. 1 (April, 1971): 35. Aldan suggests that there is a universal language inherent in Zimmer's poetry—that the incidents and emotions Zimmer describes are common to all of humanity. She sees Zimmer as giving a voice and a language to human experience.

Ingersoll, Earl. "The Holy Words: A Conversation with Paul Zimmer." In *The Post-Confessionals*, edited by Earl G. Ingersoll, Judith Kitchen, and Stan Sanvel Rubin. Cranbury, N.J.: Associated University Presses, 1989. This essay came out of an interview with Zimmer and has been published a number of times in slightly different forms. The interviewer seeks to elicit from the poet his self-perceived place in the history of American poetry: a "postconfessional" who, having developed his themes from the confessional poetry of Elizabeth Bishop and Anne Sexton, chooses to find the interior meanings of painful experience rather than simply express pain.

Morgenthaler, Eric. "Buses Prove to Be the Perfect Vehicle for a Poet's Work." *Wall Street Journal*, October 17, 1975. Morgenthaler details the everyday nature of Zimmer's writing. Zimmer's poems are universal in their appeal and accessibility, so it is telling to discover that Zimmer tended to write his poetry, or at least develop his ideas, in the midst of everyday life.

Wallace, Ronald. *God Be with the Clown: Humor in American Poetry.* Columbia: University of Missouri Press, 1984. Wallace's volume, although it deals with humorous verse in American poetry in general, sees Zimmer's poetry as infused with the gentle, self-effacing humor that is common among American poets but at the same time takes the expression of laughter to even more creative heights. Wallace is convincing when he describes humor as the keystone to understanding American poetry.

Julia M. Meyers

LOUIS ZUKOFSKY

Born: New York, New York; January 23, 1904
Died: Port Jefferson, New York; May 12, 1978

PRINCIPAL POETRY
Fifty-five Poems, 1941
Anew, 1946

Barely and Widely, 1958
I's (Pronounced "Eyes"), 1963
After I's, 1964
All: The Collected Short Poems, 1923-1958, 1965
All: The Collected Short Poems, 1956-1964, 1965
Catullus, 1969 (translation of Gaius Valerius Catullus; with Celia Zukofsky)
Little, 1970
All: The Collected Short Poems, 1923-1964, 1971
"A," 1978, 1993
Eighty Flowers, 1978
Complete Short Poetry, 1991

OTHER LITERARY FORMS
Louis Zukofsky was as much respected for his criticism as he was for his poetry. His volumes of criticism include *Le Style Apollinaire* (1934), *A Test of Poetry* (1948), *Prepositions: The Collected Critical Essays of Louis Zukofsky* (1968, 1981), and *Bottom: On Shakespeare* (1963). In 1932, he edited *An "Objectivists" Anthology.* A play, *Arise, Arise*, was published in 1962; a novel, *Ferdinand, Including "It Was"* in 1968.

ACHIEVEMENTS
Louis Zukofsky was, in many ways, a poet's poet, who won the admiration of such contemporaries as Ezra Pound and William Carlos Williams for his innovative use of language, for his stretching of the boundaries of poetic form, and for his perceptive readings of their works. With George Oppen and Charles Reznikoff, he became known as an Objectivist, a term he chose to distinguish these poets from Amy Lowell's Imagists and the French Symbolists. Objectivists were concerned with the precise use of language; with honesty and sincerity in their communication with their audience; and with the creation of a poem which in itself would be an object, part of the reader's reality.

Zukofsky's voice was that of an urban American Jew, tied to the Yiddish tradition of his immigrant parents, yet Americanized into twentieth century New York. He was conscious of living in what he called the "age of gears," where machines and technology dominated everyday life, and he was sensitive to social problems and movements—socialism, communism, Marxism, the Depression, urban unrest. His epic *"A"* provides an idiosyncratic autobiography of one poet's life from 1922 to 1976.

Throughout his life, Zukofsky taught at universities and colleges and, with reluctance, read his poetry in public. He was awarded the Lola Ridge Memorial Award of the Poetry Society of America in 1949; the Longview Foundation Award, 1961; the Union League Civic and Arts Foundation Prize of *Poetry* magazine, 1964; the Oscar Blumenthal/Charles Leviton Prize from *Poetry*, 1966; the National Endowment of the Arts and American Literary Anthology awards, 1967 and 1968; and was nominated for a National Book Award in poetry in 1968.

BIOGRAPHY

Louis Zukofsky was the son of Russian-Jewish immigrants and was reared on the lower east side of New York City. His father, a religious and deeply sensitive man, was a presser in a clothing factory; his mother was a gaunt, quiet, introspective woman. Zukofsky's first introduction to literature was through the Yiddish poems and stories read in his home, together with the plays produced at the renowned Thalia theater. In particular, he was attracted to the work of Solomon Bloomgarten, who wrote under the pen name Yehoash (an acronym of the initials of his Hebrew name) and earned much admiration for both his own poetry and for his Yiddish translations of major English and American poems. Zukofsky first read untranslated English literature in the public schools of New York. He began to write poetry in high school, then at Columbia University, where he was encouraged to continue by his professor, Mark Van Doren. Zukofsky received an M.A. degree from Columbia in 1924.

Zukofsky's first submission to *Poetry* was a translation of Yehoash, which was not published. His own work ("Of Dying Beauty") first appeared in the journal in January, 1924, and he published *Poem Beginning "The"* in *Exile*, a journal edited by Ezra Pound, who saw in the young poet a literary heir. Pound dedicated his own *Guide to Kulchur* to Zukofsky (along with the English poet Basil Bunting), promoted his work in *Exile*, and persuaded Harriet Monroe to turn over an issue of *Poetry* to him as guest editor. It was this issue, appearing in February, 1931, which made Zukofsky's work

visible to his contemporaries and established several poets—George Oppen, Charles Reznikoff, Basil Bunting, and Zukofsky himself—as Objectivists, a term conceived by Zukofsky but apparently approved by all. The Objectivists established their own press, To Publishers, a short-lived venture.

Zukofsky found only a small audience for his work, supporting his wife Celia (a composer, whom he married in 1939) and his son Paul (who became a virtuoso violinist) by teaching technical writing and literature at Brooklyn Polytechnic Institute between 1947 and 1966. He also taught English and comparative literature at the University of Wisconsin, 1930-1931; Shakespeare and Renaissance Literature at Colgate University in 1947; creative writing at Queens College, 1947-1948; and in the summer of 1958 was poet in residence at San Francisco State College.

Zukofsky preferred to write at night, never going to bed before one or two in the morning, and he revised continually. His epic poem *"A"* was the product of several decades of work, though sections were published at intervals. As his reputation waned, some friends believed he became bitter toward readers who would not take the time and effort to understand him, and the inaccessibility of his later poems seems to reflect his antagonism toward his audience. The 1960's, however, brought renewed interest in the Objectivists, and Zukofsky has been warmly praised by such critics as Hugh Kenner and Guy Davenport.

"A" was going to press and Zukofsky was working on *Eighty Flowers* when, in 1978, he died prematurely at the age of seventy-four.

ANALYSIS

Under pressure from Harriet Monroe to declare himself part of a new "movement" in poetry, Louis Zukofsky coined the term "Objectivist." Later, he admitted that the term was unfortunate; at the very least, it has been confusing to readers and critics who interpret objectivity as an indication that reality will be rendered undistorted by the poet's personality. Zukofsky did aim at such objective honesty or "care for the detail," as he put it, but he emphasized that being an Objectivist meant that the poet created a poem as an object, in much the same way that a builder constructs a house or a carpenter, a cabinet. These two aims—an objective rendering of reality and the creation of the poem as object—give Zukofsky's poetry its distinction.

The prevailing metaphor throughout Zukofsky's work is the correspondence between the ego and the sense of sight: *I* equals *eye* in his poetry and the terms are often playfully interchanged, as in the poems "I's (pronounced *eyes*)" or "After I's." Similarly, "see" becomes "sea" or even the letter *c* and "sight" is transformed into "cite." Like Benedictus de Spinoza (who figures in his works along with Ludwig Wittgenstein and Aristotle), Zukofsky was a lens-grinder; but Zukofsky's lenses were organic and his method of sharpening them was an ever closer examination of objects. Just as the objective lens of a microscope is the one in closest proximity to the object being studied, so Zukofsky as Objectivist attempted to apprehend objects directly and report on his findings.

Zukofsky believed that an object must be examined for its "qualities," and once these qualities are recognized, the observer can go no further in his understanding of the object. The object exists in itself and is not dependent on the observer for its existence. It is not the observer's function to postulate theories about the object, to explain, embellish, or comment upon it. He merely bears witness to its reality. Only by placing the object in the context of the poem can the poet use the object to communicate something of his own reality. In a poem, juxtapositions imply connections, transitions, and relationships between objects. The poet does not editorialize. "Writing presents the finished matter, *it does not comment*," Zukofsky wrote in *A Test of Poetry*.

In his concern for precise language to express visual perception and to render faithfully the qualities of an object, Zukofsky follows Ezra Pound's statements about Imagism: "Direct treatment of the 'thing'" using "no word that does not contribute to the presentation" (*Poetry*, 1912). Zukofsky, however, shared William Carlos Williams's concern that imagism, in the years since Pound first promoted the movement, had deteriorated into impressionistic "free verse," lacking form. "The Objectivist theory was this," Williams explained in his *The Autobiography of William Carlos Williams* (1951), "We had had 'Imagism' . . . which ran quickly out. That,

though it had been useful in ridding the field of verbiage, had no formal necessity implicit in it." The poem, he went on, "is an object, an object that in itself formally presents its case and its meaning by the very form it assumes."

Zukofsky also believed that the poem's form was one with its meaning. The objects, or elements, of the composition should take their meaning from their placement in the structure. The poet should not intrude his personality into the poem with what Zukofsky called "predatory intent": the use of decorative adjectives or adverbs, and especially the use of transitional passages or devices which might explain a poem's interior logic. In *Poem Beginning "The,"* for example, each line is numbered, but the numbers do not imply sequence. "Poetry convinces not by argument," Zukofsky wrote, "but by the *form* it creates to carry its content."

"HI, KUH"

Reporting about an object, Zukofsky's initial perception undergoes transformation into poetry. "Hi, Kuh" was Zukofsky's response to the billboard advertisement for Elsie, the Borden dairy company's cow. The advertisement showed "gold'n bees" which appeared to the eyes of the poet as eyes, and then when the astigmatic and myopic Zukofsky removed his glasses, they appeared as the shimmering windows of a skyscraper. "Hi, Kuh" also reminds the reader that the poet's "I" was moved to think of a haiku poem, with the last unexpected word elevating the meaning of the poem beyond that of a bystander commenting on a billboard. Zukofsky does not explain the thought process which led from Elsie the cow to the towering emblem of the city; he presents, flatly, objects which are assembled to reveal his meaning.

"MANTIS"

"Mantis" gives a more elaborate example of Zukofsky's method. The poem begins with a vivid description of a praying mantis encountered in a subway car. Gradually, the incongruity of the object in its surroundings, and its obvious helplessness, leads the poet to thoughts of a similar incongruity: the poor, who are helpless, alone, segregated from society, and as terrified as the mantis of an environment over which they have no control. "Mantis" was written as a sestina, a form Zukofsky rarely used, and one he knew was considered obsolete and archaic by many of his contemporaries. To defend his use of that form, he followed the piece by "'Mantis,' An Interpretation," written, he said, "as an argument against people who are dogmatic" about the use of old metered forms for modern poems.

Zukofsky maintained that both the form and language he used were suited to the experience of finding a mantis lost in the subway, so frightened that it flew against the poet's chest as if to communicate its despair. That experience was "only an incident," Zukofsky said, *compelling any writing.*" The mantis was the object which proved seminal for the poet's analysis of his own reality: "The mantis *can start/* History," Zukofsky wrote; and he was moved to think not only of the urban poor but also of Provençal and Melanesian myths, all alluded to in the poem. He was not interested in explaining how the incident led him to think of other things but tried to build a poem which, in its structure, echoed the experience. The poem's ungainliness reflects the lanky body of the insect; "'the lines' winding around themselves" reflect the contorted emotions of the poet as he experienced the encounter with the mantis; "the repeated end words" show his obsessive return to the same themes.

Zukofsky emphasized in his interpretation that the mantis experience engendered thoughts that were felt immediately, spontaneously, and apparently simultaneously. They were not, as William Wordsworth would have had it, recollected in tranquillity. The poet had no time for analysis or reflection. In the poem, then, Zukofsky tried to create what Gertrude Stein called the "continuous present," an ahistorical interval of time which is not caused by the past and which does not affect the future. By omitting transitions and relying, instead, on juxtaposition, Zukofsky forces the reader to experience an encounter with an object, in this case a mantis, with the same immediacy felt by the poet.

POEM BEGINNING "THE"

Much more complex, but with the same underlying intentions, is Zukofsky's *Poem Beginning "The,"* which he wrote in 1926. The poem begins with a brief preface acknowledging its sources. These include Johann Sebastian Bach, Ludwig van Beethoven, Yehoash, T. S. Eliot, Benito Mussolini, and Ezra Pound. Zukofsky had, of course, read Pound's *Hugh Selwyn Mauberley* (1920)

and Eliot's *The Waste Land* (1922) which allude to literary sources, and intended, like Pound and Eliot, to challenge the reader to work in order to understand the poem.

The structure is deceptively straightforward: six "movements" (anticipating the sections of *"A,"* the poem which seems to have grown directly from "The") and 330 lines, each numbered to remind the reader to stop before going on to the next line. "The," being a definite article, suggests that the poem might be less amorphous than *"A,"* but it is not easily accessible in its entirety. The first movement, titled "And out of olde bokes, in good feith," asks a series of questions about the meaning of some well-known literary works—among them, James Joyce's *A Portrait of the Artist as a Young Man* (1916), and *Ulysses* (1922), Eliot's *The Waste Land,* E. E. Cummings's *Is Five* (1926), and Virginia Woolf's *Mrs. Dalloway* (1925). Allusions to these works follow one another in a disjointed monologue until, at lines 52 and 53, the poet admits that his "dream" is over and he is awake. After a pause, he decides that men have not lived "by art" or "by letters," though it is never clear why the poet remains unsatisfied by the literary works about which he, apparently, dreamt.

The second movement, "International Episode," deals, for the most part, with a deeply personal incident: the suicide of Richard Chambers, the younger brother of Zukofsky's college friend Whittaker Chambers. This "Ricky" section sensitively portrays the sadness of a young man's death for the poet who grieves. Following the elegy, Zukofsky translates lines from Yehoash which encapsulate the theme of the elegy and transform it to myth. In the Yehoash section, a young Bedouin can only reign in his kingdom at night because he is threatened by the sun, and the "Desert-Night" takes on magical, ethereal qualities; Ricky, in the realm of the dead, also reigns in shadow and darkness "with the stars."

The "Ricky" section is a quiet, reflective core of a movement otherwise raucous and irreverent. The poet is walking on Broadway with an oddly named companion, "Peter Out," whose name suggests sexual puns. While they are trying to decide which show to see, the poet, in a kind of reverie, thinks of Ricky. Suddenly, however, Peter breaks in and the two engage in a vaudevillian dialogue with their exchanges placed in quotation marks as if they were titles of plays.

The fifth movement, "Autobiography," returns to some of the themes already set forth by Zukofsky. There is another translation from Yehoash, a neo-folk song with again, as in the "Ricky" section, lifts the themes of the movement to a mythical level. Here, Zukofsky deals with the immigration of Russian Jews to a place where there are "gastanks, ruts,/ cemetery-tenements" and where their children will be assimilated and will take as their culture Bach, William Shakespeare, Samuel Taylor Coleridge, and John Donne. The poet promises not to forget his heritage, carrying that theme further in "Finale, and After," the final movement, which begins with a Jewish folk song that may well have been sung to him as a child. He ends with a last translation from Yehoash, its inclusion itself a demonstration that his parents' heritage has not been lost; the lines celebrate the ability of the poet to "sing" and endure under any hardship—even that of coming to artistic maturity in a country where few poets are lauded.

In *Poem Beginning "The,"* Zukofsky omits all transitions which would help the reader understand the connection between Ricky and Yehoash, for example, or between Christopher Marlowe and Virginia Woolf. Because the poem is relatively short, however, with some accessible sections, it is not as difficult as the poem it most resembles, the epic *"A."*

"A"

"A" begins at a performance of Bach's St. Matthew's Passion in Carnegie Hall on Thursday evening, April 5, 1928, during Passover. As in "Mantis," this incident starts the poet's thoughts spiraling, this time on history, economics, art, Jews, physics, music, his family, Karl Marx, Henry Adams, Mickey Mouse, Hamlet, Walt Whitman, and Wittgenstein. The concert also indicates the poem's form, which consists of long "musical" movements and ideas which develop and interweave as fugues.

"A" is the autobiography of a poet in twentieth century America and may be approached as if it were an archaeological site. From an accumulation of objects, the reader might piece together the reality which existed at the site, but Zukofsky is careful to reveal the objects in precise juxtaposition. The cumulative effect of the ob-

jects, then, is more than the sum of the parts. Zukofsky likened a poem to beads on an Egyptian necklace: Each bead might be an interesting artifact, but only when strung in precise order do they form a distinct artistic object.

Each section of *"A"* reveals Zukofsky's care for detail and his effort to structure those details. In *"A"*-12, for example, the themes of the poet's heritage and his relationship to American culture which were presented in the final sections of *Poem Beginning "The"* are expanded and developed, with Zukofsky's father, Pinchos (anglicized as Paul), and his son, Paul, appearing throughout. The culture which Pinchos brought from Russia is depicted in several vignettes, and Paul's childhood is evoked by the boy's remarks, including even a reproduction of one of his valentines to his father. By interweaving details, Zukofsky reveals the transition from Paul, who fled the czar with his mournful songs, to Paul who has two balloons named Plato and Aristotle and is quickly becoming a prodigy on the violin, playing not his grandfather's Russian melodies but Bach.

"All who achieve constructions apart from themselves, move in effect toward poetry," Zukofsky wrote in *Prepositions*. *"A"* is Zukofsky's most elaborate structure, a report of a witness to modern reality who did not care to comment, only to build.

OTHER MAJOR WORKS

LONG FICTION: *Ferdinand, Including "It Was,"* 1968; *Little, for Careenagers*, 1970; *Collected Fiction*, 1990.

PLAY: *Arise, Arise*, pb. 1962 (magazine), pr. 1965.

NONFICTION: *Le Style Apollinaire*, 1934 (with René Taupin); *A Test of Poetry*, 1948; *Five Statements for Poetry*, 1958; *Bottom: On Shakespeare*, 1963; *Prepositions: The Collected Critical Essays of Louis Zukofsky*, 1968, expanded 1981; *Autobiography*, 1970 (text, with poems set to music by Celia Zukofsky); *Pound/Zukofsky: Selected Letters of Ezra Pound and Louis Zukofsky*, 1987 (Barry Ahearn, editor).

EDITED TEXT: *An "Objectivists" Anthology*, 1932.

BIBLIOGRAPHY

Ahearn, Barry. *Zukofsky's "A": An Introduction*. Berkeley: University of California Press, 1983. Zukofsky once said that a poet writes only one poem for his whole life. He began the eight-hundred-page poem "*A*" in 1928, when he was twenty-four years old, and did not finish it until 1974, when he was seventy. Ahearn gives the student a framework to understand this magnum opus. Includes bibliographical references and indexes.

Leggott, Michele J. *Reading Zukofsky's "Eighty Flowers."* Baltimore: The Johns Hopkins University Press, 1989. Leggott attempts to explain Zukofsky's rare work, written the last four years of his life. Zukofsky wanted to condense the sense of his lifetime of poetry into a last book. Leggott offers a plausible interpretation for *Eighty Flowers*, and thus explains the entire philosophy of Zukofsky's writing.

Penberthy, Jenny Lynn. "Lorine Niedecker and Louis Zukofsky: Her Poems and Letters." *Dissertation Abstracts International* 47 (October, 1986): 1326A. Zukofsky corresponded with Objectivist poet Lorine Niedecker for forty years, and his ideas substantially influenced her work. She even wrote some collage poems incorporating quotations from his letters to her.

Pound, Ezra. *Pound/Zukofsky: Selected Letters of Ezra Pound and Louis Zukofsky.* Edited by Barry Ahearn. New York: New Directions, 1987. Zukofsky considered Pound to be the greatest twentieth century poet writing in English. Therefore, he wrote to Pound more than he wrote to anyone else, in part to glean some words of literary wisdom. The two men met only three times, yet Zukofsky considered Pound to be his literary father.

Stanley, Sandra Kumamoto. *Louis Zukofsky and the Transformation of a Modern American Poetics.* Berkeley: University of California Press, 1994. Stanley argues that Zukofky's works serve as a crucial link between American modernism and postmodernism. Stanley explains how Zukofsky emphasized the materiality of language and describes his legacy to contemporary poets.

Terrell, Carroll Franklin. *Louis Zukofsky: Man and Poet.* Orono: National Poetry Foundation, University of Maine at Orono, 1979. Zukofsky essentially lived the history of twentieth century American poetry. This is the essential Zukofsky biography. It was written shortly after the poet's death in 1978, at the age of seventy-four. Contains a bibliography and an index.

Linda Simon;
bibliography updated by the editors

STEFAN ZWEIG

Born: Vienna, Austria; November 28, 1881
Died: Petropolis, Brazil; February 22, 1942

PRINCIPAL POETRY
Silberne Saiten, 1901
Die frühen Kränze, 1906
Die gesammelten Gedichte, 1924
Ausgewählte Gedichte, 1932
Silberne Saiten: Gedichte und Nachdichtungen, 1966

OTHER LITERARY FORMS

Stefan Zweig, one of the most prolific and, in his time, most widely read authors of the twentieth century, began his literary career as a poet, but his lyric poetry is not among his most important or most enduring achievements. His reputation rests largely on his short fiction, his biographies, his essays, and one of his plays. Zweig the storyteller is noted for his vivid, virtuosic style and his skillful psychological penetration of his characters. His work in the novella form ranges from *Die Liebe der Erika Ewald* (1904; Erika Ewald's love) to his last completed work, *Schachnovelle* (1942; *The Royal Game*, 1944), which poignantly foreshadows a time of increasing specialization, mechanization, and dehumanization in which men of mind are doomed to be checkmated by brutish technocrats. The collection *Erstes Erlebnis* (1911; first experience) contains sensitive stories of childhood and adolescence; the stories in *Verwirrung der Gefühle* (1927; *Conflicts*, 1927) and *Amok* (1922; English translation, 1931) deal with adult passions and problems. Zweig's only completed novel, *Ungeduld des Herzens* (1938; *Beware of Pity*, 1939), is a haunting portrayal of a crippled girl and her love. Recently discovered and published in 1982, *Rausch der Verwandlung* (intoxication of transformation) is a fragmentary novel about a lowly Austrian post-office clerk whose penurious life is transformed when she gets a taste of opulent living and again when she is drawn into the vortex of big-city crime.

Another literary form in which Zweig achieved great success and an international readership in more than thirty languages was the *vie romancée* (biographical novel). As a biographer, Zweig favored the cyclical form, attempting to present a "typology of the spirit." *Drei Meister* (1920; *Three Masters*, 1930) contains biographical studies of Honoré de Balzac, Charles Dickens, and Fyodor Dostoevski; *Der Kampf mit dem Dämon* (1925; *The Struggle with the Demon*, 1929) examines Friedrich Hölderlin, Heinrich von Kleist, and Friedrich Nietzsche, poets and thinkers who went insane or committed suicide; and *Drei Dichter ihres Lebens* (1928; *Adepts in Self-Portraiture*, 1928) presents the great autobiographers Casanova, Stendhal, and Leo Tolstoy. In 1935, these biographical studies appeared in one volume as *Baumeister der Welt*, appearing in English translation in 1939 as *Master Builders*. Another biographical trilogy, *Die Heilung durch den Geist* (1931; *Mental Healers*, 1932), explores the lives and influences of Franz Anton Mesmer, Mary Baker Eddy (who is debunked), and Sigmund Freud (to whom Zweig felt close intellectually and personally). Other biographical volumes include *Joseph Fouché* (1929; English translation, 1930), *Marie Antoinette* (1932; English translation, 1933), *Maria Stuart* (1935; *Mary, Queen of Scotland and the Isles*, 1935), *Magellan* (1938; *Magellan, Pioneer of the Pacific*, 1938), and *Balzac* (1946; English translation, 1946). *Triumph und Tragik des Erasmus von Rotterdam* (1934; *Erasmus of Rotterdam*, 1934) is a very personal book, for Zweig regarded the Dutch Humanist, who disdained political action in a turbulent age, as his spiritual ancestor and mentor. Zweig's collaboration with Richard Strauss on the comic opera *Die schweigsame Frau* (the silent woman), based on a work by Ben Jonson, became a *cause célèbre* in 1935 because of the composer's refusal to renounce his Jewish collaborator in Nazi Germany. Most notable among Zweig's several dramas is the powerful pacifist play *Jeremias* (1917; *Jeremiah*, 1922), which premiered in Switzerland. In his universally admired autobiography, *Die Welt von Gestern* (1944; *The World of Yesterday*, 1943), Zweig self-effacingly keeps his own life and work in the background as he presents a brilliant, poignant panorama of European life, thought, and culture in the first half of the twentieth century.

ACHIEVEMENTS

In both his life and his work, Stefan Zweig was a cultural mediator. All his life, he was a translator in an elevated sense, attempting to inform, to educate, to inspire, and to arouse appreciation and enthusiasm across literary, cultural, national, and personal boundaries. He once wrote that it was his aim

to understand even what is most alien to us, always to evaluate peoples and periods, figures and works only in their positive and creative sense, and to let this desire to understand and convey this understanding to others serve humbly and faithfully our indestructible ideal: humane communication among individuals, mentalities, cultures, and nations.

Stefan Zweig (Hulton Archive)

For fifteen years, Zweig's impressive home on the picturesque Kapuzinerberg in Salzburg was a shrine to his central idea, the intellectual unification of Europe, and the mecca of a cultural elite, many of whom Zweig numbered among his friends. His world travels as well as his bibliophilic pursuits, particularly his legendary collection of literary and musical holograph manuscripts, nurtured his art and aided his wide-ranging cultural and humanitarian activities. Zweig's correspondence with Martin Buber during World War I as well as other documents indicates that he prized the Diaspora and interpreted his Jewishness rather willfully as offering him an opportunity to be a citizen of the world: "Perhaps it is the purpose of Judaism to show over the centuries that community is possible without country, only through blood and intellect, only through the word and faith."

At an early age, Zweig became aware of the crisis facing his era, and for many years he was bedeviled by the growing antinomy between a bourgeois humanism whose position had become undermined by the failure of its adherents to commit themselves to positive action and the ever-rising current of political and social activism which was compelling individuals to commit themselves to some form of action. While Zweig's knowledge of history and the typology of human motivations and personalities could not have left him blind to the need for change, he consciously adopted and maintained an eminently apolitical stance.

Displaying a becoming awareness of the dignity and spiritual superiority of the dispossessed and the vanquished, Zweig repeatedly and movingly portrayed apolitical individuals (such as that "bibliosaurus," the transplanted Eastern European Jew Jakob Mendel, called "Book Mendel") caught up in the impersonal, unfeeling machinery of world politics and conflicts. Zweig's biographical study of Joseph Fouché, Napoleon's minister of police, is a great moral condemnation of *homo politicus*; teaching an object lesson in unprincipled behavior, the author warned the peoples of Europe against falling for politicians of that stripe. In an essay written in 1922, "Ist die Geschichte gerecht?" (Is there justice in history?), Zweig tried to supply a humanistic antidote and alternative to the cult of power, warning the masses against glorifying their oppressors and worship-

ing their chains. He pointed out that, all too often, history has been rewritten in favor of those who have prevailed by virtue of brute strength and that there is a tendency to create myths about the strong and the heroic, while the infinitely worthier heroes of everyday life remain unsung. Might and morality must be clearly sundered; it behooves man not to be bedazzled by the seductive glamour of success and to reexamine history from a humanistic point of view.

In *The World of Yesterday*, Zweig said about himself that as an Austrian, a Jew, a writer, a humanist, and a pacifist, he had always stood at the exact point where the global clashes and cataclysms of the century were at their most violent. His response to these blows of fate was an excessive objectivity and feckless neutrality, a reluctance to become involved in political action, and an increasing contempt for merely political adjustments. Zweig's frequently naïve stance is reminiscent of the inaction and near-paralysis of Viennese intellectuals at the turn of the century; he came to regard Europe as his "sacred homeland," and his Europeanism ultimately led him to view the tragedy of the Jews as only part of the larger and presumably more important tragedy of Europe.

While Zweig was a physician who could not heal himself, his undogmatic and nonideological humanism is eminently relevant to the present age. While his brand of liberalism is old-fashioned, his contribution to pan-European thought must be regarded as an enduring one. His was one of the first voices to call for a cosmopolitan community of the youth of Europe, and he proposed the establishment of an international university that would function interchangeably in several capital cities. In a lecture delivered in 1932, "Die moralische Entgiftung Europas" (the moral decontamination of Europe), Zweig called for well-organized student exchanges to reduce political tensions and collective animosities. He felt that the history of culture and of the human spirit rather than military or political history should be taught in the schools of the world. Some causes for which Zweig worked tirelessly and that seemed Utopian during his lifetime, such as Franco-German understanding, are actualities today. Zweig's apotheosis of Brazil, his last refuge, shows that his interest was not limited to Europe and that he was alive to both the problems and the potentialities of what is now called the Third World. "Our greatest debt of gratitude," wrote Zweig in his unfinished last work, a study of Michel de Montaigne, "is to those who in these inhuman times confirm the human in us, who encourage us not to abandon our unique and imperishable possession: our innermost self." These words also sum up Stefan Zweig's quest and his achievement.

BIOGRAPHY

The second son of a wealthy industrialist, Stefan Zweig had an early and auspicious start in literature in what he later described as a "world of security," taking "flight into the intellectual" from his father's stultifying business mentality and his mother's overbearing snobbishness. Having an essay accepted by Theodor Herzl, the influential editor of the prestigious Vienna daily *Neue Freie Presse*, was an important boost to the career of the fledgling writer, who soon became an outstanding member of the literary group *Jung Wien* (Young Vienna). His first book was published when he was still in his teens.

In 1904, Zweig earned a doctorate from the University of Vienna with a dissertation on Hippolyte Taine. Early trips to Germany, France, Belgium, Holland, England, Italy, Spain, India, and North America served to broaden the horizon of the young man, but what most decisively shaped Zweig's evolution from an aesthetically oriented man of letters to a "great European" was his encounter with the Flemish poet Émile Verhaeren. Zweig regarded Verhaeren's intense, vibrantly contemporary, and life-affirming poetry as a lyrical encyclopedia of his age. Zweig tirelessly served Verhaeren as a translator, biographer, and publicist. Zweig's European education was continued through his friendship with the French writer Romain Rolland, whose exemplary pacifist and humanist activities in wartime were a great inspiration to Zweig. While working at the Austrian War Archives in Vienna, Zweig was able to write his pacifist drama *Jeremiah*. He went to Zurich to join a group of intellectuals who, like himself, rejected nationalism and worked toward the restoration of the community of European men of mind.

In 1919, Zweig moved to Salzburg and was soon able to solemnize his union with the writer Friderike Maria Burger von Winternitz. The years in Salzburg,

where he lived with his wife and two stepdaughters, were his most productive ones. In addition to having his works published by the prestigious Insel Verlag of Leipzig, he became a trusted adviser to that publishing house, ever ready to help other writers and artists by introducing and championing their work. His readings and lectures took him all over the world. One of the most notable of these journeys was his trip to Russia in 1928 on the occasion of the Tolstoy centennial.

After 1933, the centrally located Salzburg became an inhospitable and dangerously exposed place, and an almost paranoid uneasiness took hold of the apolitical Zweig. His move to England in 1934 marked the beginning of years of insecurity, restless globe-trotting, and mounting despair. The breakup of his marriage was but one of many symptomatic events and situations that bedeviled the man who had acquired the coveted British citizenship and was materially far better off than most emigrants. Profoundly depressed by the fate of his spiritual homeland, Europe, and fearing that the humanist spirit was crushed forever, Zweig committed suicide in 1942 in a country which he had celebrated in a book as "a land of the future." He was joined in death by his second wife, Elisabeth Charlotte Altmann, whom he had married at Bath in 1939.

ANALYSIS

The poetry which Stefan Zweig began writing at an early age, published in *Die Gesellschaft*, *Die Zukunft*, *Die Welt*, *Deutsche Dichtung*, and other newspapers, periodicals, and almanacs, was informed by the *Zeitgeist* of *fin de siècle* Vienna. The last decades of the moribund Habsburg empire, governed by a six-hundred-year-old dynasty, were characterized by a latter-day *Weltschmerz*, by overrefinement and an aesthetic cult of beauty expressive of an aloofness from the world's pursuits, and by surface smiles masking a world-weary abandonment of political solutions. Zweig himself described these early efforts, impressionistic poems marked by preciosity, as "verses of vague premonition and instinctive feeling, not created out of my own experience, but rather born of a passion for language." The same may be said of the astonishingly precocious poems of Hugo von Hofmannsthal, who published his verse as a schoolboy under the pseudonym "Loris" and for whom Zweig always had admiration and affection, though it turned out to be a case of unrequited love. While Zweig's early poems, however, are eminently lyrical and display great musicality as well as a certain mastery of form, they lack the psychological penetration, the poetic intuition, and the linguistic magic of Hofmannsthal's poetry.

In 1900, Zweig wrote in a letter to Karl Emil Franzos: "I have published to date 150 or 200 poems, written double that number, and now have put together a volume under the title *Silberne Saiten* which contains 50, that is, a most stringent selection." That volume appeared in February of 1901 with a dedication "to my dear parents." It was well received, even by such established poets as Detlev von Liliencron, Richard Dehmel, and Rainer Maria Rilke. The *Revue allemande* noted that "a quiet, solemn beauty pervades the lines of this Young Vienna poet, a translucence rarely to be found in first works . . . Zweig is a virtuoso in technique; each single poem gives us fresh opportunity to enjoy the fineness of his diction, of immeasurable harmony and wealth of imagery." A severe judgment, however, was rendered by Erich Mühsam, who rejected "a book that, with its obtrusive sickly sweetness and insipid exaggeration, would hardly be worth mentioning were it not typical of the pretentious manner which is spreading ever more widely through the Young Vienna movement and which seeks to impress by mere playing with form." Even though Zweig had the satisfaction of seeing the eminent composer Max Reger set two of the poems from *Silberne Saiten*, "Neue Fülle" and "Ein Drängen ist in meinem Herzen," he soon disowned this early poetry and refused to have it reprinted in later collections.

DIE FRÜHEN KRÄNZE

Some of the young Zweig's characteristic feelings, themes, and stances (dreaming, longing, youthful ardor aiming at interpersonal relationships, evanescence, delicate autumnal and nocturnal moods, subtle transitions) are also in evidence in the poetry written in the early years of the twentieth century and published in Zweig's second collection, *Die frühen Kränze* (the early wreaths), issued in 1906. This volume is notable, among other reasons, for marking Zweig's first collaboration with the celebrated Insel Verlag. Here, Zweig presented his more mature, though still rather unoriginal poetry, with its

cyclical form adumbrating the later grouping of a number of his prose works. Thus, the series "Fahrten" (journeys) includes poetic evocations of a sunrise in Venice ("Sonnenaufgang in Venedig"), nights on Lake Como ("Nächte am Comersee"), and the city of Constance ("Stadt am See"). The sequence "Lieder des Abends" (songs of evening) contains the euphoric "Lied des Einsiedels" (hermit's song); the cycle "Frauen" (women) includes "Das fremde Lächeln" (a female stranger's smile), "Die Zärtlichkeiten" (the caresses), and "Terzinen an ein Mädchen" (terze rima for a girl); and the cycle "Bilder" (images, or portraits) includes one of Zweig's longest poems, "Der Verführer" (the seducer).

DIE GESAMMELTEN GEDICHTE

Many of these and other groupings are included in the more ambitious collection of his poems which Zweig published in 1924. Its first section, "Musik der Jugend" (music of youth), presents a selection from the early poems. The cycle "Die Herren des Lebens" (the masters of life), placed toward the end of the volume, gathers eleven of what may be described as lyric statues. Notable among these is the only poem (or work of any kind) of which Zweig is known to have made a recording: "Der Bildner" (the sculptor). This poem memorializes Zweig's visit to Maison Rodin at Meudon in 1913. He depicts the aged sculptor surrounded by his timeless and changeless works, those "frozen crystals of infinity," and describes his astonishment in the petrified forest of his studio as he prayerfully comes to realize what his true mission is: to represent, shape, and complete something more permanent than he is, to create life beyond his own life. "Der Kaiser" is a poetic evocation of Emperor Franz Joseph, and "Der Dirigent" (the conductor) was written in memory of Gustav Mahler.

Two of the most powerful poems in this collection were born of Zweig's vibrant pacifism. "Der Krüppel" (the cripple) is a sensitive poetic depiction of a war-injured man on crutches, and "Polyphem" evokes the mythical monster Polyphemus, the cannibalistic giant who comes under attack as the demon or bringer of war. The long "Ballade von einem Traum" (ballad of a dream), written after World War I, which concludes the *Die gesammelten Gedichte*, may be read as a highly personal allegory. In a nightmare, the poet feels that his vaunted private sphere has been invaded and his most secret self exposed. He reads the fiery handwriting on the wall: "Du bist erkannt!" (You are known!). Tormented by this revealing refrain, he finally awakes, grateful that his innermost thoughts have not, in fact, been betrayed and that his deepest self remains inviolate.

TRANSLATIONS

Zweig's activities as a cultural mediator, and in particular as a translator of poetry, significantly shaped his own creativity as a poet. His first great idol was Verhaeren, and Zweig's initial lack of self-sufficiency may have made him respond all the more strongly to certain antithetical traits which he found in the Belgian poet: a hymnal spirit, a prodigious strength, universal love, enthusiasm, and a feeling of exaltation. What others regarded as a barren field for poetry—the machines, the big cities, the industrial life, the masses of people, the entire ferment of modern civilization—Verhaeren considered eminently fertile material for poetic expression. His example purged Zweig's own poetry of the last vestiges of *fin de siècle* decadence. After the decisive caesura of World War I, however, Zweig did not attempt to emulate Verhaeren's poetic style. The three-volume edition of Verhaeren's writings that Zweig translated and edited for the Insel Verlag in 1910 included a volume containing his translations (from the French) of fifty-one of Verhaeren's poems; another volume had preceded it in 1904. Other French poets for whom Zweig served as a sensitive translator and commentator are Paul Verlaine, Charles Baudelaire, and Marceline Desbordes-Valmore. His translations from Verhaeren, Baudelaire, and Verlaine are rightly reprinted in the edition of Zweig's collected poetry issued in 1966.

"DER SECHZIGJÄHRIGE DANKT"

After the appearance of *Die gesammelten Gedichte* in the mid-1920's, Zweig concentrated on his fiction and biographies, writing poetry only occasionally. Particular poignance attaches to his last poem, "Der Sechzigjährige dankt" (the sixty-year-old gives thanks), which Zweig sent a few months before his death to close friends who had congratulated him on his birthday. This widely admired poem has been set to music by Henry Jolles and by Felix Wolfes. It bespeaks serenity despite the poet's presentiment of death, expresses calm detachment and resignation as "farewell's blazing gloss" opens

up new vistas, and says that what remains of life can be enjoyed *sub specie aeternitatis*, for the approach of old age frees one from the constraints, burdens, and goads of desire, ambition, and self-recrimination.

OTHER MAJOR WORKS

LONG FICTION: *Die Liebe der Erika Ewald*, 1904 (novella); *Der Zwang*, 1920; *Angst*, 1920; *Ungeduld des Herzens*, 1938 (*Beware of Pity*, 1939); *Schachnovelle*, 1942 (novella; *The Royal Game*, 1944); *Rausch der Verwandlung*, 1982.

SHORT FICTION: *Erstes Erlebnis*, 1911; *Amok*, 1922 (English translation, 1931); *Verwirrung der Gefühle*, 1927 (*Conflicts*, 1927).

PLAYS: *Tersites*, pb. 1907; *Der Haus am Meer*, pr., pb. 1912; *Jeremias*, pb. 1917 (*Jeremiah*, 1922); *Volpone*, pr., pb. 1926 (adaptation of Ben Jonson's play); *Das Lamm des Armen*, pb. 1929; *Die schweigsame Frau*, pb. 1935 (libretto).

NONFICTION: *Émile Verhaeren*, 1910 (English translation, 1914); *Das Herz Europas*, 1918; *Drei Meister*, 1920 (*Three Masters*, 1930); *Der Kampf mit dem Dämon*, 1925 (*The Struggle with the Demon*, 1929); *Sternstunden der Menschheit*, 1927 (*The Tide of Fortune*, 1940); *Drei Dichter ihres Lebens*, 1928 (*Adepts in Self-Portraiture*, 1928); *Joseph Fouché*, 1929 (English translation, 1930); *Die Heilung durch den Geist*, 1931 (*Mental Healers*, 1932); *Marie Antoinette*, 1932 (English translation, 1933); *Triumph und Tragik des Erasmus von Rotterdam*, 1934 (*Erasmus of Rotterdam*, 1934); *Baumeister der Welt*, 1935 (*Master Builders*, 1939); *Maria Stuart*, 1935 (*Mary, Queen of Scotland and the Isles*, 1935); *Castellio gegen Calvin*, 1936 (*The Right to Heresy*, 1936); *Magellan*, 1938 (*Magellan, Pioneer of the Pacific*, 1938); *Brasilien, ein Land der Zukunft*, 1941 (*Brazil: A Land of the Future*, 1941); *Die Welt von Gestern*, wr. 1941, 1944 (*The World of Yesterday*, 1943); *Balzac*, 1946 (English translation, 1946); *Briefwechsel, 1912-1942: Stefan Zweig, Friederike Zweig*, 1951 (*Stefan and Friderike Maria Zweig: Their Correspondence*, 1954); *Briefwechsel: Richard Strauss und Stefan Zweig*, 1957 (*A Confidential Matter: The Letters of Richard Strauss and Stefan Zweig, 1931-1935*, 1977).

BIBLIOGRAPHY

Arens, Hanns, ed. *Stefan Zweig: A Tribute to His Life and Work*. Translated by Christobel Fowler. London: W. H. Allen, 1951. A short biographical and critical study of Zweig's oeuvre.

Klawiter, Randolph J. *Stefan Zweig: An International Bibliography*. Riverside, Calif.: Ariadne Press, 1999. A valuable reference catalog of publications by and about Zweig.

Spitzer, Leo. *Lives in Between: The Experience of Marginality in a Century of Emancipation*. New York: Hill and Wang, 1999. A study of three broadly different yet compellingly similar human stories that range from the late nineteenth century to the mid-twentieth century. This important work focuses on three marginal groups—Jews in Austria, mulattoes in Brazil, and freed slaves in Sierra Leone—and their tragic quest for assimilation. Within the study of the experiences of Jews in Austria, Spitzer examines the historical, sociological, and psychological aspects of Stefan Zewig's life.

Zweig, Stefan. *Stefan Zweig, Joseph Gregor: Correspondence, 1921-1938*. Edited by Kenneth Birkin. Dunedin, New Zealand: University of Otago, 1992. A collection of letters that provides invaluable insight into Zewig's life and work. Includes bibliographical references and indexes.

Harry Zohn;
bibliography updated by the editors